WILLIAM STOUGHTON.

THE

NEW-ENGLAND

HISTORICAL AND GENEALOGICAL

REGISTER

1896

Volume L.

BOSTON
PUBLISHED BY THE SOCIETY
1896

Committee on Publication

Publishing Committee

ALBERT HARRISON HOYT, A. M.,   C. B. TILLINGHAST,
FRANK ELIOT BRADISH, A. B.,   GARDNER A. CHURCHILL,
JOHN WARD DEAN, A. M.

Editor
JOHN WARD DEAN, A. M.,

Facsimile Reprint
Published 1998

HERITAGE BOOKS, INC.
1540E Pointer Ridge Place
Bowie, Maryland 20716
1-800-398-7709

ISBN 0-7884-0865-8

INDEX OF SUBJECTS.

INDEX TO
GENEALOGIES AND PEDIGREES

IN THE REGISTERS,

VOLS. 1 TO 50.

By the Hon. WILLIAM W. WIGHT, of Milwaukee, Wisconsin.

Compiled from the Indexes of Subjects in the several volumes.

The heavy figures stand for volumes, the other figures for pages.

NEW-ENGLAND
HISTORICAL AND GENEALOGICAL
REGISTER.

JANUARY, 1896.

WILLIAM STOUGHTON,

LIEUTENANT-GOVERNOR OF MASSACHUSETTS.

By the Editor.

Two sketches of the life of Lieutenant-Governor Stoughton, whose portrait accompanies this article, have already appeared in the Register—one by Henry H. Edes, Esq., in the twenty-third volume, pages 25 to 27 ; and the other by the late William Thaddeus Harris, A. M., in the third volume, pages 117 to 118. But it seems proper to present an outline of his life to accompany his portrait.

William Stoughton[*] was the second son of Capt. Israel Stoughton of Dorchester, Mass., who returned to England, and served in the Parliamentary army.[†] Israel had at least two brothers—Rev. John Stoughton, D.D., rector of St. Mary's Church, Aldermanbury, London, and Thomas of Dorchester, Mass., and Windsor, Conn. Rev. Dr. Stoughton was the step-father of Rev. Ralph Cudsworth, the author of the "True Intellectual System of the Universe," and of Capt. James Cudworth of Scituate, New England.[‡]

The subject of this sketch was born in 1631 or 1632, probably in England, though his birth is sometimes given as at Dorchester, Mass. He was educated at Harvard College, where he was graduated in 1650. He remained here about a year after graduating. His father, who died in 1645, bequeathed to him one half of his library (Register iv., 51), and to his two other sons one quarter each. He studied theology in this country, and is said to have been invited to become the colleague of Rev. Richard Mather at Dorchester, as the successor of Rev. John Wilson, Jr., who had resigned his office in Dorchester, and had been settled in 1651 at Medfield.

---

[*] See a pedigree of Stoughton, probably of a family related to the New England Stoughtons, in Register, vol. v., p. 350.

[†] See an account of him in the Dorchester Antiquarian Society's History of Dorchester, Mass., pp. 83–6. His will is in the Register, vol. iv., p. 51, and his inventory in vol. vii., p. 333.

[‡] See Register, vol. iv., pp. 101–4; and vol. xxi., pp. 249–50.

Soon after this he went to England and was incorporated A.B. of Oxford University, April 28, 1652, became a fellow of New College, and was made Master of Arts June 30, 1653.* He preached awhile in the County of Sussex. He lost his fellowship after the restoration of Charles II. in 1660.

In 1662 he returned to Massachusetts and was made a freeman of the Colony May 3, 1665. The December following he was again asked to settle in the ministry at Dorchester. This invitation was several times repeated, but he could not be induced to accept the invitation. In 1666, after the death of Rev. Jonathan Mitchell, he received an invitation from the Church at Cambridge to become its pastor. He preached the Election Sermon at the annual General Court, April 29, 1668. He received the thanks of the Court, with a request to prepare it for the press. A sentence in this sermon has been oftener quoted than any other in early New England literature.†

In 1671 he was chosen an assistant, and was annually rechosen till 1677. He was elected to the same office in 1680, and held it till 1686. He was a commissioner for the United Colonies from 1674 to 1676, and from 1680 to 1686. In May, 1674, the General Court appointed him to keep the County Courts in Norfolk, and May, 1676, a similar order was passed to keep the County Courts at Portsmouth or Dover, and also at Wells in York County.

In 1676 Stoughton and Peter Bulkeley, speaker of the House of Deputies, were appointed, in compliance with the requisition of Charles II., agents to represent the colony before the king, to answer various complaints against the Massachusetts government. They left Boston October 31, 1676, and arrived in England December 20, following.‡ They discharged their duties with ability and discretion, though many of the colonists were not satisfied. He returned to New England July 24, 1679. He refused a second appointment to the same agency in 1680.

Stoughton and Joseph Dudley made, February 18, 1681–2, a "report of their transactions in the purchase of the Nipmuck territory, and as 'an acknowledgement of' their 'great care and pajnes,' the General Court granted to each of them one thousand acres of land in that country. It was laid out at a place called Marichonge, and the 'platt' was accepted by the Legislature 4 June, 1685." §

The charter of Massachusetts was declared vacant in 1685. On the 15th of May, 1686, a commission from King James II., dated September 27, 1685, was received in New England for organizing a new government, to consist of a president, a deputy president, and sixteen counsellors. The Council organized May 25. Joseph Dudley was named in the commission as president, and Stoughton was made deputy president. Their authority extended over Massachusetts,

---

* Foster's Alumni Oxonienses (1500–1714), vol. iv., p. 1432.
† See this number, page 71.
‡ Tuttle's Capt. John Mason (Prince Society), page 103.
§ Sibley's Harvard Graduates, vol. l., p. 198.

New Hampshire, Maine, and the King's Province. On the 26th of July, Stoughton was placed at the head of the courts.

On the 20th of December, 1686, Sir Edmund Andros arrived at Boston with a commission making him governor of New England. On the 3d of March, 1687, the courts were reorganized. Joseph Dudley was appointed Chief Justice, and Stoughton was made Judge Assistant.

Under the charter of William and Mary, he was Lieutenant-Governor of Massachusetts, and held the office from May, 1692, till his death, July, 1701. From November 17, 1694, to May 26, 1699, and from July, 1700, to his death, he was acting governor of the province. He was appointed June 2, 1692, by Governor Phips, Chief Justice of a special tribunal to try the witchcraft cases. The history of the doings of this court are familiar to the readers of New England history.* On the reorganization of the courts he was appointed Chief Justice December 22, 1692. This commission was renewed in 1695, and he held the office till within a short time of his death.

Stoughton's course on the witchcraft trials, over which he presided, finds few approvers. Judge Emory Washburn says : "He was sincere in his endeavour to ferret out the guilty causes of so widespread an evil, and pursued the victims with untiring assiduity, although, in so doing, he sacrificed all the better feelings of his nature, and prostituted the forms of justice to consummate a series of judicial murders that have no parallel in our history." † Mr. Sibley says : "Notwithstanding the excitement of the time, there can be no doubt that, if Stoughton had been as zealous to procure the acquittal as he was to bring about the conviction of the accused, this black page in the history of New England and humanity could never have been written." ‡

His popularity did not suffer by his course in this matter, and he never expressed regret for it. He died before the reaction against the delusion had gained much strength. His course as the chief executive of the colony met with general approval, and he died highly honored and respected. His death occurred at his residence in Dorchester, July 7, 1701. His epitaph, written by Rev. Increase Mather, is printed in the fourth volume of the REGISTER, page 275-6.

He was a liberal benefactor to Harvard College. "His benefactions to the institution," says Sibley, "exceeded those of any other person during the century. At a cost of over £1000 he erected the brick edifice called, in honor of him, Stoughton Hall. It was situated at a right angle with the present Massachusetts Hall, a little back of its northeast corner and facing to the west. The founda-

---

* See The Witchcraft Delusion of 1692, by Gov. Thomas Hutchinson, edited by Dr. William F. Poole, in the REGISTER, vol. xxiv., pp. 381-414.
† Judicial History of Massachusetts, p. 245.
‡ Harvard Graduates, vol. i., p. 200.

tion was laid 9 May, 1696, and the building was completed in 1699. It was one hundred feet long and twenty broad, and 'contained sixteen chambers for students, but no public apartments.'" He left the college, by will, other valuable property.

Stoughton Hall grew weak by age, and was injured, it is said, by the earthquake of 1755, so that in 1780 it was taken down. In 1804–1805 a new edifice was erected and called Stoughton Hall. This building is still standing to keep in remembrance the generous benefactor of Harvard College.

NOTE.—For other details see the two biographical sketches in previous volumes of the REGISTER, iii., 117–118; xxiii., 25–27; and those in Sibley's Harvard Graduates, vol. i., pp. 194–208; American Quarterly Register, by John Farmer, vol. viii., pp. 333–340, and Washburn's Judicial History of Massachusetts, pp. 242–247.

LETTER OF ALEXANDER McDOUGALL, 1779.

Com. by the late JOHN S. H. FOGG, M.D., of South Boston.

Head Quarters Peeks-Kill
15 Feby: 1779.

Sir,

Your favor of the 12, came to Hand, with the Prisoners. I have long known Ackerly was up, and his Business, but did not think his present Situation, of sufficient importance, of having him taken by K———. Mr: Plat will inform you, how I intend to Supply you with Bayonets,—He reached you I suppose, yesterday Evening. I intend to send down the Remains of Col⁰. Poors Regᵗ. for a few Days, to cover a Forage, making by Mr: Hayes near Mamarinack, and shall send by them Public Arms with Bayonets, to be exchanged for yours which want them. No good Officer or Man, now below, with you, must be Relieved 'till farther orders. Give the Officers of Poors all the advice and assistance you can. The Money taken from Ketor, will be divided among the Officers and Men, in such manner as you think proper. I shall send them down, Six for one, when I can raise Cash. Greaton's is at Pine Bridge, Nixon moves in two Days, to support Putnam. The Stated Express is on this side Croton, at his own House, his Name is John Cross, a Refugee from New York.— Give me the earliest advice, of any appearance of a Movement of the Enemy, on the River. Mrs: Pollock was detained with the last bad weather, two nights. She left this at 8 this morning.

I am Sir
Your Humble Servant,
ALEX. McDOUGALL.

Lieut Col⁰. Burr.

Superscription:

Public Service
Lieut: Coll Burr
Commanding on
the American
Alex. McDougall   Lines

DISTRICT OF PEPPERRELLBOROUGH, MAINE.

MARRIAGE INTENTIONS AND MARRIAGES.

[Copied for the REGISTER by FRANCIS E. BLAKE, Esq., of Boston.]

THIS district was incorporated in June, 1762, and the name was retained until 1805, when *Saco* was substituted.

The following items are recorded on a few stray leaves, which are now in such a bad condition as to render it impossible to decipher all of the entries. The records are attested by Tristam Jordan, District Clerk.

INTENTIONS.

Samuel Richards of Scarboro' and Eleanor Hanscom of Pepperellboro'.
April 30, 1768.
Isaiah Brooks and Sarah Burnam, both of Narragansett No. 1.
June 22, 1769.
Ezra Davis, Jr., and Susannah Hanscom, both of Pepperellboro'.
July 2, 1769.
William Clark and Rebecca Rumery, both of Pepperellboro'.
July 2, 1769.
Seth Mitchell and Mary Scammans, both of Pepperellboro'.
Feb. 24, 1770.
John Owen and Sarah Bradbury.   March 17, 1770.
Simon Phillbrook of Grenland, N. H., and Mary McClellan.
March 17, 1770.
Samuel Rice of Scarboro' and Jane Libby of Pepperellboro'.
March 21, 1770.
Abiathar Wood, Jr. [Record torn off.]
James Foss of Pepperellboro' and ——— of Scarboro'.   August [   ].
Douglass Robinson aud Sarah [   ]azleton of Buxton.   Sept. 19, 1772.
Joseph Fletcher and Sarah Edgcomb.   Sept. 8, 1772.
George Parcher, Jr., of Pepperellboro' and Mary Chamberlain of Scar-
boro'.   Sept. 10, 1772.
John Berry and Eunice [Kearl?].   Sept. 19, 1772.
John Chamberlain of Scarboro' and Lydia Foss.   Aug., 1773.
Thomas Dearring and Lucretia Townsend.   Sept. 11, [   ].
[Record torn off.   ] Elizabeth Jordan.   March 30, [   ].
Jordan Fairfield of Pepperellboro and Polly Tappan of [———osta?].
April 19, 1772.
Nathan Elder and Elizabeth Roberts, both of Narragansett No. 1.
April 18, 1772.
Freeman Scammans of Pepperellboro and Elizabeth Kimbal of Wells.
[No date.]
Ebenezer Wentworth and Jane Morrill, both of Narragansett No. 1.
April 25, 1772.
Jabez Lane and Sarah Woodman, both of Narragansett No. 1.
April 25, 1772.

James Weems (?) Nevins and Mary Mitchell, both of Pepperellboro'.
April 25, 1772.
Matthias Ridler, Jr., of Boston and Elizabeth Field of Pepperellboro'.
August 10, 1772.
Thomas [Record gone] and Anne Gor[   ] of Pepperellboro'.
[   ] 13, [   ].
Samuel Lowel and Charity Berry, both of Pepperellboro'.
April 13, 1771.
James Norton and Mary Davis.   May 11, 1771.
John Hammond and Lucy Foss, both of Pepperellboro'. May 12, 1771.
Wil[liam] [   ] Adeowando and Sarah Rumery of a place called Little
Falls.   March, 1775.
John [Bemis?] of Pepperellboro' and Hannah Fletcher of Biddeford.
March, 1775.
Peter Foss of Pepperellboro' and Mary Foss of Scarboro'.
March, 1775.
William Marry of Pepperellboro' and Margaret Haley of Biddeford.
April 2, 1755 (Sic.)

MARRIAGES.

George Jileson of a place called Mass Camps and Elizabeth Wadlin of
Little Falls.   Married Oct. 12, 1773.
Enoch Parker and Mary Rumery, both of Little Falls.
Married Dec. 26, 1774.
Daniel Hibbard of Sanford and Sarah Wadlin of Little Falls.
Married Feb. 16, 1775.
William Deering of Adeowando and Sarah Rumery of Little Falls.
April 3, 1775.
All by Pelatiah Tingley, Itinerant.
Joseph Elwell and Mehitable Black, both of Pepperellboro'.
Married August 21, 1768, by Samuel Jordan, Esq., of Biddeford.

LETTER OF MAJOR JOHN SHAPLEIGH, 1781.

Communicated by the late JOHN S. H. FOGG, M.D., of South Boston.

Sir

a Greable to orders from Col Ichabod Goodwin and He orders me to Detach twenty four men from our town to go to west Point and there to Du Duty for three months, and the Proporsion for your Company is five, which you are to Detach and to mak Your Return to me on the twenty six Day of this July, and when the Militia are Drafted there is a fine of ten Pound to be Paid in twenty four hour. the Detach ment is from the Band only and Every man is to Equip him self as the Law Dericts, and I send you a Resolve of the general Cort. Pray Dont Delay the time. This from your friend and humble servant

JOHN SHAPLEIGH Major

Kittery July 17 1781
To Capt Thomas Hammons.

JAMES BARRETT'S RETURNS OF MEN MUSTERED INTO SERVICE, 1778.

Copied for the REGISTER by FRANCIS E. BLAKE, Esq., of Boston.

THE following returns are all superscribed, "To John Avery, Esq., Deputy Secretary;" lists A and B at Watertown ; C, D, E at Boston.

A

June ye 22 ! 1778

To the Honor[b] Council for the State of the Massachusetts bay I have mustered the nine months men, and there names are as follows

Concord men.
Joseph Plomer
Jason Bemis
Oliver Buttrick
Cesar Kittle
William Diggs
David White
Benj. Perkins
Benj. Gould
Jeremiah Hunt, junr.

Townshand men.
William Scott
William Blain
Jonathan Patt, junr.
Jonathan Conck
Josiah Richardson

Hopkinton men.
Daniel Bowker
Levi Smith
Simeon Eames
John White
Joseph Welch
Isaac Woolson
Daniel Wheton

Ashby men.
Abel Richardson
Samuel Hincks
Samuel Davis

Woburn men.
Benj. Peirce
Jonathan Thompson
Job Miller
Josiah Porter
John Trask

Josiah Belknap
Josiah Brown
Daniel Green Brown
Samuel Tidd
Uriah Goodwin
Kemor Blackman
Eleaser Flagg Pool

Sherburn men.
Elias Grout
Benjamin Hawse
Benj. Ware
Caleb Gleason
Hopestill Fairbanks

Littelton men.
Abel Prator
David Baker
Peter Wright
Nathaniel Reed
Lemuel Dol

Stonham men.
John Hill
John Hill

Chelmsford men.
Joseph Cambers
Josiah Fletcher
Timothy Adams
John Crosby
Levi Proctor
Robert Pearce, jr.
William Gilson

Tewksbury men.
John Chamberlin
Thos. Hoadley

Jesse Holt
Joseph Frost
John Stearns
Roger Dutton

Acton men.
Joseph Reed
Ruben Lane
David Chaffin
Nathan Darby
Josiah Davis

Holiston men.
Joshua Kindall
Ichabod Seaver
Benj. Spear
moses Darling
Cuffe Cosons
Richard King

Lincoln men.
Joseph mason, jr.
William Thoming
Jonas Bond
Elijah mason
Abijah munroe

Chalston men.
John Penny
Robert Millet
William Dickson
Ephraim Aullet
Amos Winship

Billerica men.
Increase Wyman
Samuel Spring
Josiah Blanchard

Jonathan Baily
Benj. Baldwin
Stephen Bennet
Edward Pollard, jr.
Timothy Crosby
Solomon Willson

Newton men.
Thomas Fay
William Boyle
Caleb Jackson
Thomas Bileston
John Paark
Jonas Blandin
Peter Clark
Abner Davenport
Nehemiah Wilson

Bedford men.
Gideon Sanderson.
Waldner Stone
John Stevens

Sherly men.
Thomas Peabody
Simeon Harrington

Sudbury men.
Isaac Smith
Samuel Curtis
Ebeneser Staples, jr.

Elijah Aracis
Isaac Woodward
Abel Brigham
Abel Willis
Silas mosman
William maynard
Daniel maynard
John Sanders
Thomas Ames
Elijah Harrington
Samuel Sherman

Framingham men.
Joshua Hemenway
Timothy Pike
Caleb Staess
Aaron Hill

Dracut men.
John Diper
Jacob Hebberd
William Clough
Daniel Clough
Benjamin Bennem
Uriah Abbot

Cambridge men.
Silas Sargant
Joseph Burns
Silas Hobinson
Josiah Reed

Daniel Thornton
Chistofor Pain
Jesse Blackinton
Israel Blackinton
Abijah Brown
Christofor Decker

Groton men.
Josiah Stevens
Nathan Cory
Joseph Page
Simeon Foster
John Sheple, jr.
Shattuck Blood, jr.
Jonathan Colburn
Isaac Warren
Joseph Frost
Isaac Doge
Ebenezer Farnsworth
John Peirce
Francis White
Eleazer Green, jr.
Henry Davis

Stow men.
Maick ma Clerg
William Jewall
Charles Brown
Isaac Conant
Jonathan Jewet
Daniel Brown

JAMES BARRETT
Muster Master

B

June ye 23! 1778

To the Honor[b] Council for the State of the Massachusetts bay I have mustered the nine months men and there names are as follows

Wesford men.
Thomas Colburn
Ephraim Chamberlin
Jonas Wright
Jonas Blodget
Peter Hildreth
Aaron Blood

Westown men.
Daniel Davis
Joseph mastick
Peter Caris
James Beames
Samuel Baley
Cain Robinson
Jedathan Bemies

Natick men.
Benjamin Butcher
Jacob Speer
Lemons mareas

Wilmington men.
James Pearson, jr.
moses Devoson
Nathan Beard, jr.
Samuel Eames
oliver Adams

Dunstabel men.
Enock Spalding
Asa Emerson
Benjamin Dilson

Josiah Rholf
John mcNeihl

Waltham men.
John Kidder
John Baptist
Uena Hareet
Henry Barrin
Habakkuk Starns

Marlborough men.
Timothy Rand
Josiah Prest
Nathan Baker
Silas Baker
James Whitney

Rubin Preist

Pepperell men.
Nathan Loving
Dennis organ
William Green
Josiah mosher
Thomas Webbor
John Scot

Lexington men.
James Robinson
Asa Robinson
Ezra meriam

Watertown men.
Peter Lecop

Peter Asadet
John Leather
John Fulford
Samuel Sanger
Josiah Bright

Medford men.
Nathaniel Peirce
Isaac Green
Jonathan Anthony
Prince Hall
Whenham Cory
Prince Freeman

Malden men.
Antoney Rouehang

Peter Geowan
Joel Whittemore
Obad Jenkins
Andrew Farley
moses Bordman

Reding men.
John Worthebe
John Andrewson
Asa Hart
Edmond Flint
Samuel Ebenwood
Jacob Brown
Jonas Parker
Amos Briant
Nathan Felch

JAMES BARRETT
Muster Master

C

July ye 28! 1778

To the Honor[b] Council for the State of the Massachusetts bay   I have mustered the men Inlested into the Roughiland Servis agreabele to a resolve of the General Court of this State to Serve till the First Day of Jenary next

Lincoln men.
Thomas Smith
James Adams
Jonathan Abel

Acton men.
Samuel Hosma
John Faulkner
Soloman Piper
Amasa Piper

Lexington men.
Jonathan Lorany
Walter Russell
Thomas Adams
Isaac Durant
Daniel mason
Christopher man

Chelmsford men.
Hesekiah Shardrick
Robert Spaulding
Isaac marshall
David Putnam
Jacob Reed
Artemus Spaulding

Watertown men.
Newton Baxter
Ebenezer Curtis
Thomas Sarmer
Jedediah Larnard

Hopkinton men.
John Wesson
Amos Stimson
Solomon Walker
Jonathan Starnes
Archabell Wear
Thomas Low

Wesford men.
Thomas Robbins
Isaae Chandler
Levi Bixby
Silas Howard
Peter Prescott
Josiah Fletcher
Amsiah Hilddeth

Dunstable men.
Levi Butterfield
Ebenezer French

Eleazer Farale
Humphry Feagis

Pepperrall men.
Jonathan Steavens
Eleazer Nutting
William Lawrance

Sherburn men.
Simeon Lealand
Ebenezer Badcock
moses morse
oliver Learland
Asa Fairbanks

Westown men.
Solomon Parmenter
Abel Peirce
Phinas Stimson
Jonas Parmenter
David Livermore
John Roberts

Ashby men.
Caleb Nure
David Achbell

Dreacut men.
David Sawser
Timothy Kelley
Benjamen
John mears
Daniel Jaques

Towanshand men.
Thaddeas Spaulding
James Cutt
Peter Adams
Ebenezer Giles

Littelton men.
Jonathan Weatherbee
Samuel White
Peter Wheeler
John Dumpson

Billerica men.
Jason Kemp
William Leestone
Samuel Starnes
John Duren
William Frull
Timothy Duren

Bedford man.
Joshua Holt
John Abbott
Cambridg mores

Waltham men.
Jacob Bemis

Natick men.
John Badger
Joseph washburn

Framingham men.
David Brewer
Thaddeaus Hemingway
Silas Winch
Amos Underwood
moses Edget
Jacob Parmenter
Hannover Dickerson
Baraelius Wate

Tewksbury men.
William Browon
Jed Shed
Joseph French
Timothy Hunt
William Kedney

Holliston men.
moses Greenwood
Abner morse
Nathan Fisk
Joseph Foristall
John Foristall
Isaac Jenney

Cambridge men.
James Jones
Edmond Frost
William Bodman
Richard Hay
John Stone

Concord men.
John Estabrook
Paul Lamson

Groton men.
Samuel Kemp jr
Lemuel Parker jr
Lemuel Parker
John Trowbridge

Medford men.
Benjamin Pike
William Smith
Benjamin Stickney
Joseph Willson

Newton men.
Francis Parker
Peter Durell
Nathaniel Seger
Stephen Hastings

Wilmington men.
Paul Upton
Nathaniel Toy
Jonathan Kider
Samuel Buck

Woburn men.
John Russell
Jonathan Tyler
Ezra Wyman

Reading men.
Benjamin Flint
Daniel Graves
Thomas Sawyer
Jeremiah Eatton

JAMES BARRETT
Muster Master

D

September ye 19! 1778

To the Honor[b] Council for the State of the Massachusetts bay I have musterd the men Whose names are Heareafter menshond Sence my Last Returne viz—for the Rougdiland Servis to Serve till the first Day of Jeneary

for Sudbury men.

Peter Smith
Timothy moore
Ebenezer Parmenter

Stephen Bent
Jacob Johnson
Abel Tower

Samuel Cutting
Asahel Tower
Nathan Dudley

JAMES BARRETT
Muster Master

E

November ye 3^{q} 1778
To the Honor^{b} Council for the State of the massachusetts Bay I have musterd the men Whose names are Hereafter mensond Sence my Last Returne in the Roughdiland Service to Serve till the first of Jenuary next

Marlborough men.	Thomas Baker	James Bowers
Jason Harrington	Alexander Watson	Silas Gates jr
Phinehas Brigham	Phinehas moor	Solomon Rice
Abraham Stow	Job Goodell	Joseph Hale

JAMES BARRETT
Muster Master

LETTER OF PATRICK HENRY, 1776.

Com. by the late JOHN S. H. FOGG, M.D., of South Boston.

Sir.

In Pursuance of a Resolution of the Legislature, I am to appoint a fit Person in every County to collect from the Inhabitants of this Commonwealth all the BLANKETS and RUGS they are willing to spare for the use of the soldiery. I have to beg of you, Sir, to accept of that Appointment for your County, and to draw upon me for the Amount of the Purchase. When it is considered that those who are defending our Country are in the extremest want of Blankets, and that our Army cannot take the Field without a supply of that Article, I have Hopes that our worthy Countrymen will spare from their Beds a Part of that Covering which the exposed situation of the soldier teaches him to expect from the Humanity of those for whom he is to fight. From your Zeal for the publick service, I have the Pleasure to hope for your Exertion to forward this important Business, and send what Blankets you get to me.

I am, Sir,
Your most obedient humble Servant.

Dec. 19th 1776. P. HENRY.

Endorsed in handwriting of Thos. Jefferson :
"rec^{d} Jany : 28. 1777"

DORCHESTER, MASS., INTENTIONS OF MARRIAGES.

Copied by FRANCIS E. BLAKE, Esq., of Boston.

THESE records were taken from a note-book of James Blake, Town Clerk, the names not appearing in list of marriages published by Record Commissioners.

1744

April 28, Isaac How, Jr. of Dorchester & Sarah Tucker of Milton.
July 14, John Palmer and Mary How of Dorchester.
Aug. 25, Thomas Boucher (Bowker) of Boston & Mrs. Ann Tileston of Dorchester.

Nov. 30,　Edward White & Elinor Jones both of Dorchester.
Nov. 30,　John Lowder of Dorchester & Mary Chandler of Roxbury.

1745
April 15,　George Merifield of Dorchester & Abigail Mills of Needham.
April 19,　Abijah Neal of Bridgewater & Lydia Spear of Dorchester.
　　　　　("Married without a certificate by Mr. Nile as informed")
June　6,　Thomas Harris of Dorchester & Lucy Pierce of Watertown.
Aug. 20,　William King & Elizabeth Powel both of Dorchester.

1756
Oct. 11,　James Michaels of Dorchester & Rebecca Pender of Roxbury.

1747
June　2,　Samuel Bird of Dorchester & Mrs. Mable Jenner of Charlestown.
Oct. 31,　Ebenezer Hayden of Dorchester & Mary Chaplin of Roxbury.
Nov. 21,　Ebenezer Nightingale of Dorchester & Mary Dickerman of Stoughton.
Dec. 19,　Jacobus Derkinderen of Boston & Mary Fowler of Dorchester.

1748
July 27,　Ebenezer Wiswell, Jr. of Dorchester & Irene Lane of Hingham.

LETTER OF GEN. ARTEMAS WARD, 1775.

Com. by the late JOHN S. H. FOGG, M.D., of South Boston.

Headquarters June 12. 1775.

Gent^le

I have received yours of to day. With regard to the houses filled by the Inhabitants of Camb: after Enquiry, I cannot find that they occupy any more Room than is necessary for the accomodation of their Families, & I know of no other method of remedying the inconvenience of having the troops crowded than furnishing them with Tents as soon as possible.— The Chest of Arms should be glad might be delivered to Maj^r. Barber who is appointed store keeper, but in order that they may be repaired, it will be necessary that proper Supplies should be sent to the Armorers, who at present are destitute of materials, as I am informed. I directed that all the Horses should be sent you, agreeable to your desire. I am now informed my directions were complyed with, excepting such which it is said were stole.

I am Gent^l
Your hbl. Servt
ARTEMAS WARD.

Superscription:
　To
The Gent^n of the Committee
of Supplies
at
Watertown.

LETTERS OF ELBRIDGE GERRY.

Contributed by WORTHINGTON CHAUNCEY FORD, Esq., of Washington, D. C.

[Concluded from vol. xlix., page 441.]

Gerry to Jefferson.

Cambridge 20th Jany 1801

My dear Sir

 I now propose to finish my letter of the 15th, which was hastily concluded, to prevent inconvenience to my friend Lincoln.

 In revising your political faith, I am not clear, that we perfectly agree in regard to a navy. I wish sincerely, with yourself, to avoid the evils pointed out, as the result of a powerful navy. the expense & extensive operation of an immense naval establishment, if our resources would admit of it, might make us more haughty & enterprising than wise, an object of the envy, jealousy & hatred of some or of all the maritime powers, &, finally, the victim of our own "autocracy": & every one is left to judge from his own observations, whether this is not the natural tendency of an overgrown navy. but at the same time it appears to me expedient, if not necessary, to extend our views to such a naval establishment as will furnish convoys to our valuable commerce, & place us, at least, above the depredations & insults of small maritime powers. with this qualification, I readily confirm the avowal of your political faith as my own.

 Indulge me with some observations on the war party's adroitness, to take the credit to themselves of events, which they have labored abundantly to prevent, & to ascribe these, when popular, to means which they had adopted to promote a contrary effect. the martial attitude of the U. S., which is said to have prevented a war, & which I have before stated was not known in France at the time of the official declaration made to me, "that my departure from France would bring on an immediate rupture," did not then exist, as will appear by attending to facts. On the 18th of March, 1798, the French minister, in his letter to the Envoys of that date, signified the determination of the directory not to treat with two of them, & their readiness to open a negotiation with me. on the 23d of March Mr. Pickering enclosed to the envoys the President's instructions directing them, under certain circumstances, to put an end to the negotiation, & to demand their passports; & those instructions were delivered to me on the 12th of May. it must therefore be evident, that at the period of my resolution to remain in France, the martial attitude, so much boasted of, could not have been known there; because it did not then exist in the U. States. indeed if it had existed, it could not possibly have appalled France, in the zenith of her power; altho', as an evidence of her contempt, it might have prompted her to a declaration of War. but it is very curious, that when the Congretional declaimers wish'd, to make the war party popular, they held up the martial attitude, as the chef d'œuvre which prevented war; & when the principals wish'd to point the indignation of that party against the person whom they suppos'd to have merited it, they then asserted that he committed the unpardonable crime, & thus prevented the U. S. from rising to the highest pitch of national glory, by joining the coalition against France. this I am informed is stated in a late pamphlet issued from a prostituted press of that party at New York. peace with France was a measure of the last importance, in my mind, to the U. States; a war, wantonly provoked with her, would have made her vindictive & implacable, to the last degree, against this country; would have divided, & thus have weakened the nation; would have been immediately followed by a treaty, offensive & defensive, with G. Britain; would have made us compleately dependent on her; would on her part have promoted an hauteur & insolence proportionate to that dependence; & would finally have left us the alternative only, of being reunited to her government or of being left by a separate treaty of peace between her & France, victims to the vengeance of that exasperated & powerful republick. it is evident then, that if in efforts for preventing war there has been any merit, the war party are so far from a claim to it, as to be justly chargeable with having made every exertion to promote that fatal event.

The delicate situation in which I was placed, by the rejection of the other envoys, & by the declaration of the directory in regard to my departure, induced me to consider in every point of View, the effect of every measure which suggested itself; & that which was adopted, a proposition that the French government should come forward with the project of a treaty, & by the joint efforts of their minister & myself should acommodate it to the views & interests of the two nations; & that a French minister should be sent to our government to complete the business, will appear, I think, to have been the best, & would in a short time have been carried into effect, had not the Sophia arrived, or other measures intervened to defeat the proposition. but what, at that time, would have been the fate of the French minister & his project, even if the latter had contained provisions, exceeding the most sanguine expectations of the U. States ? or in what manner would similar provisions, presented by myself to the government in any form of a treaty, been received, at a time when revenge for real or supposed injuries took place of a principle of accommodation, & when, with many, not to be mad, was to be a traitor? it was indeed fortunate, all circumstances considered, that measures were not so matured, as to have been presented in any form to our government, either by a French minister or by myself, as their rejection must have increased the irritation on both sides, & have rendered more difficult a reconciliation; & it was not less fortunate, that my communications had a tendency to, & with the operation of other causes really did, produce the effect you predicted.

That in the first place I was abused, in some measure by republicans, was to me evident; for I had seen at paris, in the American newspapers severe strictures on my first conference with Mr. Talleyrand: but I agree with you, that they did not proceed far in their censures, & that the war party were malignant to excess. the "report" of Mr. Pickering I saw, "his letters & conversation," I knew nothing of, or even the President's last instructions, until published; but the former produced such an indignation & ineffable contempt for the man, as determined me at once to expose his partiality, malignity, & injustice; & disagreeable as it always is to the publick, to see ministers of the same ambassy contending with each other, I nevertheless determined to enter the lists with either or both of the other envoys, if they had come forward as Pickering's coadjutors. decency & propriety required, that after the request of the President, stated in my last, I should wait till his return, & till he could have an opportunity to explain matters. this he did without reserve, & communicated the breach, between himself & Pickering, produced in the first instance by the rejection of the most virulent parts of his report on my communications, & evidenced by the President's nomination of new Envoys to France. this information changed the complection of affairs, & as the plan of the war faction, of which Mr. Pickering was prime agent, was to bring on me the whole of Mr. Adams' as well as their own adherence, it was incumbent on me to defeat its purpose. I therefore communicated my remarks & strictures on Pickering's report to the President, & confided in him to do me justice. At that time the President had probably determined to dismiss Pickering, and whether he (the President) tho't that the disgrace of itself, altho' the result of intrigues against himself, was full satisfaction for the intrigues against me, or whether he tho't that a direct vindication of me would be trampling on a fallen foe, & perhaps implicate himself in some degree for having passed the report, no publick notice has been taken of the injustice sustained by me. indeed there was one consideration, in regard to a publick discussion of the affairs of the mission, which, independent of the disgrace generally attending public disputes & attaching itself to all parties, had great weight in my mind. immediately after the publication of my communications, & the nomination of new envoys, such a calm took place of the tempest which had before agitated the publick mind, as to promise a change of publick opinion; & the promise has been fulfilled to an extraordinary degree; in so much, as the war faction, who by means of the presses & their general arrangements, had in most of the states, & in this in particular the controul of the public opinion, at that time, are now generally execrated, if that happy state of tranquility, at the moment of it's return had been again interrupted by a discussion, which must inevitably have engaged the warmest passions of all parties, it was impossible to ascertain whether it could be again restored: & the greater the flame which might have been produced, the more would it have served the purposes of the war party: for their success depended on influencing the passions, & the republicans' success influencing the reason, of the people at large. but before a war should have been declared, & thereby our independence have been placed, as it inevitably must have been, on a precarious footing, I would have stated minutely every circumstance of the embassy, without regard to or consideration of delicacy, or of the feelings of any man. this I would have done, at the risk of personal destruction, for whilst the war party, faithfully rewarded the other envoys for declaring explicitly in favor of war, & " beamed " as you well express it, " meridian splendor " on them; not a solitary line was drawn in my favor: whilst " homage " was paid to a molten calf, whilst the continent was alive as the other envoys passed to their homes, the land ransacked for dainties to enrich the tables every where spread for them, & the imagination racked to invent toasts & publish eulogies in their praise, for having pursued measures, ruinous as we conceived, to their country : the most profound silence in every respect was observed by the real federalists & true republicans towards me, altho' at every hazard of my property life & reputation, & even of the welfare of my family, I had stood in the gap, on a forlorn hope, to repel a desperate enemy. indeed, a few days after my arrival, the branch faction at Boston, signified, that they wished to take publick notice of me, & only waited for me to come out in the papers, as the other envoys had done, in favor of a war. My answer which undoubtedly exasperated them, was that I did not consider myself as the minister of any one state, county or town, much less of a few individuals of the latter; that I was accountable to the governmt. only of the U. States; that I had rendered to it a statement of my whole conduct, & the government may make what use it pleased of my communications; but that I should take no other measures, & wanted not any notice, as it was called, taken of me, on that or any occasion. indeed the ridiculous folly of the Epicurean clubs and their toasts, reflected in my mind dishonor on the persons, who to attain such eclat could submit to be managed & played off as political puppets : & to sell their birthrights, for a mess of pottage. that I was " secretly condemned to oblivion," by that party, that they wished to have had me " guillotined, sent to Cayenne," or the temple, to be sunk in the sea, or been sacrificed by a mob, that they stood ready to write me down, as they expressed it, to attack me by all the vile & vulgar means of ribaldry, carricatures & effigies I had no doubt; & on my arrival had certain information that the mine was charged & train layed : yet the apprehension of this, disagreeable as it must be to any one, did not deter me from discharging my duty to the public. but when the friends of the revolution & independence of this country appeared by their silence to be overawed on this occasion, how could they expect that I would "come forward," take, as you pleased to term it, "the high ground of my own character, disregard calumny" & depending on the meer presumption of being " borne above it, on the shoulders of my grateful countrymen," take a step, which in regard to its effect, was at least problematical, & if unsuccessful would have been condemned probably by the republicans as rash & impolitic, & most assuredly by the war party, as vindictive & inflammatory. this party long before my mission to France gave unequivocal proof that they wished to place & keep me in the background that " I was never to be honored or trusted by them, & that they waited to crush me forever, only, till they could do it without danger to themselves ;" but this gave me no concern, I was above their favors, not being in quest of public office, or disposed to receive it at their hands, & above their frowns, viewing with indifference their impotent malice, whilst the country was free from the system of thralldom they were plotting against it. to prevent this I shall be ever ready to encounter any danger.

I recollect to have seen the expression you allude to of a member of Congress, unknown to me, that " to have acted such a part, I must have been a fool or madman." if his conduct on that occasion did not, in the public opinion, prove him to be both, it must have been for this reason only, that he was below public consideration & contempt.

I have been prolix, & could not avoid it, because you desired me to be explicit. my mind revolted at the idea of burning your 2d & 3d leaves, but rather than have exposed my friend, I would, after answering your letter, have promptly complied with your wish. the danger being now passed, I shalt defer it, untill I have the pleasure of again hearing from you.

I will now, my dear Sir, bid you adieu for the present, with an assurance of the highest respect & sincerest attachment, & that I remain your affectionate friend.

_____

Gerry to Jefferson.

My dear Sir   Cambridge 24th Feby. 1801.

At nine o'clock last evening, Mr. Lee, a warm friend of yours & mine, came up from Boston to inform me of your election.

The precarious state, in which by the wiles of party, the federal executive was suspended, the irritation which would have resulted from your non-election, even if Mr. Burr had obtained the vote, the great danger of a collision of parties, whose *habits* of animosity, established by their duration, would have made them equally violent in their support of & opposition to a President pro tempore, the triumph which such a disgraceful event would have given to the enemies of our revolution & republican government, & the disrepute it would have entailed on free governments in general, whose principles it would have been urged, however clearly delineated, will be always defeated by the factions which they naturally generate, all conspired to produce in my mind an extreme anxiety for the issue, with which it has pleased the supreme disposer of events to favor the U. States.

Under existing circumstances, your office is not enviable; your task is arduous. wisdom, moderation, & firmness, are indispensable, so to administer the government, as to temper the resentment of the injured, to enlighten & quiet the deluded & prejudiced, to confirm the wavering & by separating the chaff from the wheat, as far as filtration is necessary, to prevent in future a political fermentation. that you may be duly supported & be able to attain these important objects, & their natural concomitants the welfare of the nation, is my ardent wish, hope, & prayer.

By Judge Lincoln I wrote you two fugitive letters, which a want of leisure prevented me from correcting, digesting, or compressing. if they indicated too much feeling, it was naturally roused by the wanton, & the unprovoked aggressions of the feudal oligarchy.

I have mentioned Mr. Lee, as our mutual friend, but this is a consideration which has no weight in regard to my subsequent observations relative to him. My first acquaintance with him was at Paris, where his character was well established, both with Americans & Frenchmen, as a man of integrity, honor, morality, social virtue & pleasing manners, & of good information in the line of his commercial profession. that this was the opinion of all the envoys, was evident, from the honorable mention which they made of him to the President, & their letter of recommendation of him, for the office of Consul. he unfortunately arrived here, at the critical period of the federal mania, & being charged in the federal papers with being the bearer of private letters to yourself, Mr. Monroe & others, he was in great danger, for this unpardonable crime, of being the victim of popular resentment. from that time to this, he has been considered by the oligarchists, as a Jacobin : a reproachful term, without a definite meaning, but uniformly applied to brand with infamy, every man who has refused to abandon his rights & reason, & to become the tool of an unprincipled party. the unmerited attacks on his character, engaged in his behalf a number of respectable moderate men, & produced to the President additional recommendations of him for the office mentioned. if the President should make any such nomination, I think it probable that his name will be on the list; but as the former event is problematical, or if it should take place, it may be defeated in the Senate as it is now composed, I feel an obligation of Justice to present to your view, this upright, honest republican, who has been persecuted, because he was suspected of fidelity to his honorable engagements. perhaps it may be said, he is not a native of the U. States but his parents were, his father was imprisoned at halifax during the revolutionary war for advocating their cause; he has more relations in this state than any candidate for office, & was himself educated in it, & has made it his constant residence. he married moreover a daughter of Colo. Palfrey's, who was paymaster General of the Americas, & this lady, who is amiable & accomplished, has none but American connections. indeed the assurances which Mr. Lee has received from Government has led him to wait the event of the pending negotiation, & to refuse several lucrative offers of business, notwithstanding the indispensable calls of his amiable & increasing family; a circumstance which perhaps merits attention. either of the consulates of Bourdeaux, Marseilles, Havre, & Rouen, Cape Francois, or the great consulate of Guadaloupe, would answer his purpose. although in regard to yourself I think it unnecessary to bring into view that upright man & true American Mr. [Fulwar] Skipwith, yet the persecution he has suffered, because a republican, has interested my feelings in his behalf, & prompts me to express them.

And now, my dear Sir, permit me with the most sincere, respectful & affectionate attachments, to bid you adieu & to assure you that I remain your real friend & obedient servant.

Gerry to Jefferson.

Cambridge 29th April 1801
put into the office this day

My dear Sir

On the 22nd instant, I received your friendly letter of the 29th of March, twenty-three days after it was put into the post office. the seal is enclosed, having no impression ; but the appearance of having been wet, for the purpose of opening the letter. you can determine whether this was the case, or whether there is a probability of it : be this as it may, the seals of the letters which I have received for a number of years have been so often & so manifestly violated as to have destroyed my confidence in such institutions ; which in most if not in all countries, are mere political traps. among such a number of officers, as are in the department of a post office, it would be an extraordinary case, if every one was proof against the cor- rupt arts of faction ; & one prostituted officer on each line, is sufficient to betray all the secrets of the chief magistrate ; conveyed thro' this channel. indeed it will be no difficult thing to make arrangements for discovering the culprits ; but these must be constantly operative before they can cure the evil. I have tho't it necessary to be thus explicit to yourself, as I was to your predecessor ; because the success of an administration, perfectly just, mild, & honorable, as I am sure yours will be, in its views & measures, depends much on its preserving an impenetrable cabinet. the discovery of the political opinions of a private individual, can be of no great consequence, altho' directed to the supreme executive ; because before they can be adopted by the latter, they must be well examined, modified & digested, & in a crude state can only expose him to the calumnies & malice of party ; but those of the prime agent of politicks, if even expressed with caution & precision, have a tendency in many cases, in the present state of society, to excite jealousies & apprehensions in honest minds of a different persuasion, & are always abused by mal-contents, & even tortured, as your religious opinions have been, for the purposes of slander & vengeance. but you will think, as well as myself eno' has been said on this subject.

The Gazettes, ere this, have announced the disappointment of your ex- pectations in regard to my election. it has terminated as I supposed it would ; for those who were disaffected to our revolution & are now pining for monarchy, conceived, that a compleat overthrow of their antirepublican projects, would be the result of my administration, & have made the most incredible exertions to prevent it. their insolence has kept pace with their triumph, altho' it is well known that the office was not the object of my wishes. indeed the emolument is not above two-thirds of the sum, which, in addition to present expenses, I must have furnished, to have appeared decent : so that the office would have operated as a tax. as to titles, annual, or perennial, they are in my mind meer baubles ; for I am well convinced that

" Honor and shame from no condition rise ;
Act well your part, there all the honor lies "

but I could not have withdrawn myself from the nomination, without an injury, which I shall also endeavour to avoid, to the cause of republicanism, altho' the office was manifestly at variance with the greatest of all blessings, domestic happiness.

The principles which you have adopted, cannot fail, as I conceive, to render your administration successful. Official Gifts & bereavements, always have had, & always will have their effects; but it is not probable that the public will be so lost to its own interest, as to oppose its own government, for having removed from office, such as it conceived had malconducted, or for not appointing every expectant. it may nevertheless be expedient, to be guarded at all points; because great injury may result from the want of caution, none from the adoption of it.

Your inaugural speech, was in my mind, the best I have ever met with. no reasonable mind, however, could have supposed that you was pledged by it, to a disgraceful inattention to demerit; & yet by the *friends of order*, you are not allowed to judge of this, although obliged to do it, by the obligations of law, of an oath, & of honor. does this manifest a love of order, or of disorganization.

The change of political principles amongst the people, has principally arisen from the engrossment of the press. porcupine urged this very justly, as a sure mean of *governing* the public opinion : & his patrons rendered thereby, the term *republicanism*, for awhile, odious & disgraceful. but the Whigs, in nearly all the states, have rallied under republican presses, which, are continually multiplying, & must eradicate feudalism.

I propose soon to accompany Mrs. Gerry, & my eldest daughter to New York, & to write you from thence. they present their best respects to you, & be assured my dear Sir, that I remain with the most sincere & respectful attachment, your constant friend.

Gerry to Jefferson.

My dear Sir   Cambridge 4th May, 1801
           By my friend Mr. Lee, I have an opportunity of writing more freely, than by the post.

The folly of the mal-contents, in expecting by their siren arts to induce you to exchange the impregnable barriers of virtue & patriotism, for the defenceless trenches of intrigue & corruption, can only be equalled by their desperation & madness. relinquishing your friends, to depend on your enemies, you must have added to the list of those political martyrs, who becoming the victims of their own credulity, have, from the highest elevation, been hurled by their betrayers to the deepest pit of ignominy & oblivion. rely on it, you have nothing to hope from your opponents : in this quarter they have had a meeting & determined to oppose "the present order of things with their lives & fortunes;" this is unquestionable : & we accordingly see their slanderous batteries, in New York Boston, Philadelphia, are opened against yourself, republican leaders, republican states, & republicans in general; by printers so utterly devoted to their corrupt service, as not to admit in their gazettes, an answer to the most infamous & groundless calumnies. indeed, before your election, I was informed from undoubted, from high authority, that such an event "would put the constitution to the test." it is therefore incumbent on you, Sir, as expeditiously as circumstances will permit, to clear the augean stable of its obnoxious occupants; for so intimately connected are they, as in a common cause, to consider an attack on one, an attack on the whole. these observations I mean only to extend to the inveterate enemies & persecutors of republicanism & republicans; for whilst I hold in veneration an honest antirepublican,

& detestation a dishonest republican, yet, there is no apology in my mind, for a man, who, holding an office under a republican constitution, & bound by his oath & honor to support it, is aiming nevertheless, by the prostitution of his office, & the basest perfidy, to annul & subvert it. I think your attention ought not to be confined to the securing political agents, in whom you can place implicit confidence, in every important office; but that it should extend to the security of fortresses, magazines & arsenals, by placing them under the protection of faithful officers & corps, & preventing by proper defences their seizure or destruction. this precaution seems necessary, even if the country was not infested by a desperate faction; for we have foreign enemies, who are incessant in their endeavours to destroy us. & so far as pickets & trenches are adequate, the expense will be trifling, as the labour may be performed by the military corps. indeed, from the termination of the revolutionary war to this day, I have tho't that our military stores have been in too defenceless a state; such as is unparalleled in any other country. the loss of them, may be fatal, & therefore the risk of them, should, as I conceive, be prevented as much as possible. it may be necessary to observe precautions in conducting this matter, if deemed eligible; in order to defeat the arts which will be used to prevent it.

Too much attention cannot be paid in all the states to the organizing, arming & discipling the militia. the more extensive the plan, the better it will be. had the plan succeeded of a pampered federal militia, it would have destroyed the military spirit which ought to, & in some of the states does pervade all ranks of the people; & under an arbitrary federal Government would have subjected them to a small & contemptible corps of military fools. as to the necessity or great advantage of having a small proportion of our numerous militia, in compleat order, to the neglect & disparagement of the rest, to have provisional armies, or establish troops under any denomination for the defence of the country, the pretext has been proved by experience to be ridiculous: for if such establishments were not nurseries of vice, immorality & effeminacy, if after the troops have been embodied, clothed, fed, paid & disciplined twelve months, they would not be inferior to an equal number of our hardy yeomanry, taken from the field & disciplined a few weeks; still have we not seen lately a history of such military feats as were never before recorded, performed by conscripts, forced into the service, & after a few weeks discipline opposed to the best veteran troops in the world? your influence with the republican senators & representatives, may be extended to the states, & be productive of very salutary effect in this particular.

You are extremely fortunate in your choice of your principal officers; they are men whose counsel you can rely on, & whose wisdom, application, & firmness render them formidable to our common enemies. Mr. [Albert] Gallatin & General [Henry] Dearborn will it is hoped, find "clews" to unfold the misteries of office burning. twenty-five years, eight of which were occupied in a virulent revolution any war had revolved & the public papers were preserved, without the *wise* precaution of fire proof offices: but at the critical period of the change of an all wise, pious, patriotic, pure, & federal government, for that of an impious, philosophical, weak, selfish, & republican administration, two such offices or rather, their most important papers have been accidentally burnt, without the imputation of blame to any one. this is a curious termination to the history of federalism. I have still too good an opinion of your predecessor, to suppose that he was in the secret; but republicans must have an uncommon gulp, to swallow this as a contingency.

No one conceived that you would confirm the appointments made at the close of Mr. Adams' administration, except such as were perfectly agreeable to you. & it is generally expected, that amongst the first acts of the next Congress, will be a repeal of the extraordinary judiciary bill: the design of which was too palpable to elude common observation. in short, my dear Sir, unless the talents & opportunity which you have are wisely improved to establish republicanism on a solid basis, a parricidal end will be its fate. at least this is my apprehension.

Mr. Adams' conduct at your inauguration has wounded his real, & been severely censured by his pretended friends. excuse me from any remarks on the subject: your silen❦e shews you do not expect them. I must however acknowledge, that his conduct whilst in France, & since my return, towards myself, has by no means been satisfactory.

The last act of feudal desperation, is an attempt to sever the New England from the other states. this is as weak, as it is wicked. their own party, notwithstanding "the ægis of government & the temples of religion & justice" may all be "prostituted" to the purpose, would revolt at the measure. The federal constitution as amended, altho' not perfect, is under a republican administration, & in co-operation with the state systems, an excellent one, & shall ever have my support. the parts which require amendment, I hope will meet the propositions of the next Congress for this purpose.

The multiplying republican presses, is a measure of the utmost importance : I hope it will be attended to in the N. England states.

Thus have I expressed in haste, & without reserve, my ideas of the important political objects, which ought to be attained by republicans. if the suggestions are not well founded, the only loss will be of your time in reading them; my time is at my own disposal. but if the hints are just, it will be necessary to regard, in carrying them into effect, the important object which you mention, "harmony & social love among the citizens," the suaviter in modo, & the fortiter in re.

The object of Mr. Lee is to ascertain whether he is to expect a confirmation of his appointment; he is an honest republican, & worthy man, & I sincerely wish him success.

This letter supercedes the necessity of writing as I had proposed from N. York, & I have only to assure you, my dear Sir, of my sincere & most respectful attachment.

Gerry to Jefferson.

Dear Sir   Cambridge 27th October, 1803.

The message, which you did me the honor to transmit, I have read with great pleasure. it exhibits to my mind, respectful, friendly, firm, & vigilant conduct towards foreign powers—acquisitions of territory by purchase & cession, inestimable; as they respect the wealth, security, & happiness of our western sister states, the fiscal resources of the nation, & the excision of a fertile source of foreign & domestic war & discord—great wisdom & œconomy in the management of our finances—pleasing prospects of the extinguishment of the national debt—easy, judicious, & unexpected arrangements, for paying, without additional taxes, the Louisiana purchase —just, generous, & politic propositions, for attaching to us the inhabitants of that territory—effectual measures for preventing foreign territorial disputes—& in general, pacific, salutary & profound principles of policy, for the promotion of national peace, power, & prosperity.

This is, in a disinterested view of the subject, a just tribute; free from those servile practices, which are equally disgraceful to the addressor & addressed.

Three of the eastern states are still antirepublican. they had great merit in establishing their independance but owe the preservation of it to the southern states.

Pursue Sir your just system of politics, it must be sanctioned by the Sovereign of the Universe & infallibly raise the U. S. to the acme of national wealth, security & honor. this is my candid opinion & with few exceptions, I believe the opinion of the impartial part of the community.

Congress I hope will make effectual provision for preventing those elective contentions, which had nearly involved us in a civil conflict. I have the honor to remain, dear Sir, with unfeigned esteem & respect yours sincerely.

Gerry to Jefferson.

Dear Sir   Cambridge 15th March 1804

I am this day honored by your letter of the 3rd, & " as the unbounded calumnies of the federal party have obliged you to throw yourself on the verdict of your country, for trial," the United States are under infinite obligations to them, for this their conduct; as it will secure to the republican cause, the only candidate, in whom the public could cordially unite; & in regard to yourself, will have an effect the reverse of what they intended; by adding to the high lustre of your character.—your services therefore, as they have been, must continue to be all important to your country; & the with-holding them at this time, might have proved its ruin.

Our cases are widely different. You will march, Sir, in triumph to public life, for your ease; I must be active in it, for the benefit of a numerous & charming young family. . . .

The elevation to which you have raised your country, & which is almost inconceivable will, I sincerely hope, flash conviction in the faces of your political adversaries, & oblige them to acknowledge their errors.

Accept, dear Sir, my unfeigned attachment & wishes for your happiness, & my highest esteem & respect.

RADCLIFFE PEDIGREE.

The following pedigree of Radcliffe is interesting as showing the ancestry of Lady Mowlson, who was Anne, daughter of Anthony Radcliffe, an Alderman of London. It is taken from "Pedigrees of Hertfordshire Families. Collected by William Berry." Lithographed (not printed), London (no date), pp. 109–110.

The first and third volumes of the Publications of The Colonial Society of Massachusetts contain much interesting matter concerning Lady Mowlson's family and her gift to Harvard College; and a paper by Mr. Andrew McFarland Davis on Lady Mowlson's husband, Sir Thomas Mowlson, accompanied by a view of the Chapel built by him at Hargrave in Cheshire.   Henry H. Edes.

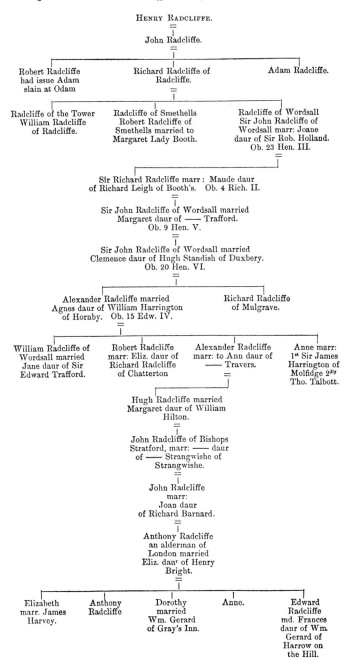

HENRY RADCLIFFE.
=
John Radcliffe.
=

Robert Radcliffe
had issue Adam
slain at Odam

Richard Radcliffe of
Radcliffe.
=

Adam Radcliffe.

Radcliffe of the Tower
William Radcliffe
of Radcliffe.

Radcliffe of Smethells
Robert Radcliffe of
Smethells married to
Margaret Lady Booth.

Radcliffe of Wordsall
Sir John Radcliffe of
Wordsall marr: Joane
daur of Sir Rob. Holland.
Ob. 23 Hen. III.
=

Sir Richard Radcliffe marr : Maude daur
of Richard Leigh of Booth's. Ob. 4 Rich. II.
=
Sir John Radcliffe of Wordsall married
Margaret daur of —— Trafford.
Ob. 9 Hen. V.
=
Sir John Radcliffe of Wordsall married
Clemence daur of Hugh Standish of Duxbery.
Ob. 20 Hen. VI.
=

Alexander Radcliffe married
Agnes daur of William Harrington
of Hornby. Ob. 15 Edw. IV.
=

Richard Radcliffe
of Mulgrave.

William Radcliffe of
Wordsall married
Jane daur of Sir
Edward Trafford.

Robert Radcliffe
marr: Eliz. daur of
Richard Radcliffe
of Chatterton

Alexander Radcliffe
marr: to Ann daur of
—— Travers.
=

Anne marr:
1st Sir James
Harrington of
Molfidge 2dly
Tho. Talbott.

Hugh Radcliffe married
Margaret daur of William
Hilton.
=
John Radcliffe of Bishops
Stratford, marr: —— daur
of —— Strangwishe of
Strangwishe.
=
John Radcliffe
marr:
Joan daur
of Richard Barnard.
=
Anthony Radcliffe
an alderman of
London married
Eliz. daur of Henry
Bright.
=

Elizabeth
marr. James
Harvey.

Anthony
Radcliffe

Dorothy
married
Wm. Gerard
of Gray's Inn.

Anne.

Edward
Radcliffe
md. Frances
daur of Wm.
Gerard of
Harrow on
the Hill.

BARNSTABLE GORHAMS.

THE OLD HOUSE IN WHICH THEY LIVED, AND THEIR SERVICES IN THE COLONIAL WARS.

By FRANK W. SPRAGUE, ESQ., of Cambridge.

IN the eastern part of the town, on the north side of the road, and several houses west of the Yarmouth line, stands an old house, formerly owned by the Gorhams, now owned by Mr. Gilmore. Lt. Col. John Gorham, in his will dated 1716, says : "I give to Shubael the house in which he now lives, and the lands called Stony Cove lands."* Col. Shubael and his sons, Col. John and Lt. Col. Joseph Gorham, took part in the siege of Louisburg. † Among those who have lived in the old house were Col. David Gorham, brother of Col. John, and Dr. John Davis ; also his son, Job C. Davis, Esq., for many years Register of Deeds.‡ "It is," says Gustavus A. Hinckley Esq., "one of the most interesting relics of old times, that vandalism, under cover of improvement, has permitted to remain, interesting from its family associations and the style of the domestic architecture and interior finish." It is the oldest of four houses now standing which were built by the Gorhams in early times, all of them upon the farm once owned by Capt. John Gorham, who settled in Barnstable in 1652.

The Gorhams took a very important part in the Colonial wars. In volume 67, Massachusetts Archives, there is a letter § from Capt. John Gorham, written to Governor Winslow, in 1675. Capt. Gorham's son John was in his company of soldiers during the war with king Philip and his tribe. In volume 30, page 500, Massachusetts Archives, may be found the following letter :

"Barnstable, April Ye, 8, 1697.

"To Major Walley, Commissioner for war, these may certify that to my certain knowledge, one John Manassos, an Indian servant to Mr. Tho. Smith of Eastham, went out Eastward ye last Expedition with Major Church, and served under Capt. Jothro, an Indian until now returned to Boston again.

JᵒN. GORHAM. ‖

Lieut. Governor Stoughton, in his instructions to Major Church, Aug. 12, 1696, says : "You are to advise as you can have occasion with Capt. John Gorham, who accompanies you in this expedition and is to take your command in case of your death." Lt. Col. John Gorham was second in command in the fourth and fifth expeditions against the French and Indians. His monument is near the

---

* Barnstable Records and Otis's Barnstable Families.
† Nova Scotia Archives.
‡ Barnstable Records, Otis's Barnstable Families.
§ I have given photographs of this letter to the N. E. H. G. Society and Mass. His. Society.
‖ Mass. Archives. vol. 30, page 500. This letter had not been indexed or published before.

Barnstable April ye 8th 1697

To major Walley Consistory for Warr those may Certifie that to my Certain knowledg one John manasses an Indian Jsrbant to mr Tho Smith of Eastham went out Easterward ye last Expodision with major Church & Jsrbon vndor Capt Jsthewo an Indian wille not Returned to Boston Againe

Jno Gorham

LETTER WRITTEN TO MAJOR JOHN WALLEY.

Unitarian meeting house in Barnstable. June 1, 1744, a joint committee of war was called with William Pepperrell of Kittery, President of the Council, at its head, five hundred men were impressed, two hundred were dispatched to reinforce Annapolis, which was understood to be threatened by the Indians.

Nov. 9, 1744, Governor Shirley reported to the Duke of Bedford that the French officer DuVivier had retreated from before Annapolis, upon Capt. Gorham's arrival with his company of Indian rangers from New England, and that Gorham had so used his command that the garrison was now entirely free from alarm.[*]

In 1745 Capt. Gorham was sent from Annapolis to Boston to raise troops. While there he was induced to join the expedition then fitting out against Cape Breton. He was appointed Lt. Col. of the 7th Massachusetts regiment, commanded by his father, Col. Shubael Gorham, and on the death of his father at Louisburg was promoted by Pepperrell to be a full colonel. After the capture of Louisburg he returned to Annapolis and was placed by Governor Shirley in command of the Boston troops sent to Minas with Col. Noble.[†] In July, 1749, he was a member of the Governor's Council in Nova Scotia. His brother Joseph was a lieutenant of rangers under Governor Cornwallis in 1749, and later held the rank of Lieut. Colonel in the regular army.

In 1749 Col. John Gorham was sent to England to explain the state of military affairs in the colonies. Governor Shirley, in a letter written to the Duke of Bedford, Oct. 13, 1749, says: " Capt. Gorham's activity and usefulness in his Majesty's service I cannot too much commend to your grace." Colonel Gorham and his wife, Elizabeth Allen, were presented at court. She was one of the most accomplished women of her day.

The following letter copied from the Massachusetts Historical Society, is one of several written by him to Sir William Pepperrell :

"In the Camp, May 7, 1745.

" Hon. Sir:—I beg the party from the grand Battery may be as private as possible in getting their boats ready and cannot be willing to proceed without Shaw, to be my pilot. If he is not come by land should choose to send a boat for him immediately and also the city may have as warm a fire as we can give them in different places, until one o'clock or two and then a cessation until they hear us engaged. Hope to have all ready, pray send Shaw.

" Sir, your most obedient, humble servant,
"JOHN GORHAM." [‡]

Miss Louisa Low of Stamford, Connecticut, daughter of the late John Gorham Low of Gloucester, owns a portrait, painted by

---

[*] This Col. John Gorham was son of Shubael and grandson of Lt. Col. John, of Church's expeditions, 1696.
[†] See Year Book for 1895. Society of Colonial Wars.
[‡] Dr. Samuel Abbott Green gave me permission to copy and to publish this letter.

Copley in 1762,* of Elizabeth Gorham Rogers, daughter of Col.
John Gorham and his wife Elizabeth Allan. The subject of this
portrait was born in 1739 in the old Gorham house, still standing
in Barnstable. This portrait was on exhibition in the " Loan Collection " at Copley Hall.

In Minister Chandler's diary of the First Church in Gloucester,
(Babson's History), are the following notes :

" Jan. 20, 1754, I drank tea at Capt. John Stevens, his new wife came
on Tuesday, she was the widow of Col. John Gorham of Barnstable."

Minister Chandler also says :

" The widow of Col. John Gorham brought with her to Gloucester,
besides three beautiful daughters, one son, Solomon Gorham."   " Nov. 6,
1759, I visited Eastern point, further end; married Daniel Rogers and
Elizabeth Gorham." †

The Gorhams were descended from four of the pilgrims on the
Mayflower, namely : John Tilley and his wife, Bridget Van De
Velde.

John Howland and his wife Elizabeth Tilley. The first John
Gorham married Desire Howland, one of the first born in Plymouth.

I have some encouragement that the " Old Gorham House " in
Barnstable will be marked by the " Old Colony Commission."

☞ This article has been gleaned from Massachusetts Historical Society,
Nova Scotia Archives, Palfrey's History of New England, Otis's Barnstable Families,
Gustavus A. Hinckley, Esq., of Barnstable, Major Nelson Gorham, of Fulton, New
York, Babson's History of Gloucester, Minister Chandler's Diary, 1754 and 1759,
Gorham Rogers, Esq., of Boston.

AN ACCOUNT OF PART OF THE FAMILY OF ABRAHAM
PERKINS OF HAMPTON, N. H., WHO LIVED
IN PLYMOUTH COUNTY, MASS.

By Hon. JOSEPH W. PORTER, of Bangor, Maine.

ABRAHAM PERKINS was one of the first settlers in Hampton, N. H.
He was made a Freeman May 13, 1640. He was a man of good education, an excellent penman, and much employed in town business. He died
August 31, 1683, aged about 72. His widow, Mary, died May 29, 1706,
aged 88. His will of August 22, 1683, was proved September 18, 1683.
In it he names wife and sons Jonathan, Humphrey, James, Luke and
David; to the last two he gave five shillings each, " as they have already
their share," daughters Abigail and Sarah ; granddaughter Mary Fifield "now
dwelling with me," and grandson John (probably son of Luke[2]). Children,
perhaps not in order:

* The portrait hung in one house in Gloucester for 90 years. Gorham Rogers, Esq.
of Boston, gave to me valuable assistance in looking up the history of this portrait.
† Minister Chandler's Diary.

In the Camps may 7th 1745 —

Hon L

I beg the party from the Grand
Gathery may be as private as
possible In Getting their boats Ready
and Cannot be Willing to proceed
Without thaw to be my pitot If
he is not Come by Land Should Chuse to
Send a boat for him Imeaditly and
also the Citty May have as Warme
a Fire as We Can Give them In
Different places Untill one Clock or too
and then a Cessation Untill they hear
Us Engaged Hope to have all Ready
pray send Shaw   For Your most obedient
                    Humble Sert Ino Gorham

LETTER WRITTEN TO SIR WILLIAM PEPPERRELL.

i. MARY,[2] b. Sept. 2, 1639; m. Giles Fifield, of Charlestown, 7 June, 1652. He probably lived in Hampton for several years and then returned to Charlestown. He m. 2d, Judith, widow of Samuel Convers, and daughter of Rev. Thomas Carter of Woburn, May 2, 1672; b. Oct. 14, 1660; d. 1676. Children, all bap. at Charlestown, June 19, 1670, except the first Richard :

1. *Mary*[3] *Fifield*, b. in Hampton, Nov. 28, 1659.
2. *Abraham Fifield*, d. in Woburn, Sept. 11, 1711, aged 57.
3. *Giles Fifield Jr.* He lived in Boston. Died and was buried Feb. 19, 1695. His widow Eliza d. June 16, 1743, aged 84.*
4. *Richard Fifield*, b. in Charlestown, Dec. 20, 1663. Died soon.
5. *Richard Fifield*, b. in Charlestown, Nov. 6, 1665, of Boston. Judge Sewall in his Diary under date of August 6, 1688, says : " Giles Fifield and wife Eliza at the wedding in our chamber of Richard Fifield and Mary Thurston." Their only daughter Mary Fifield was b. May 7–8, 1694, and m. Samuel Adams of Boston, April 21, 1713; their son Samuel Adams Jr. was b. Sept. 22, 1722. Patriot and Governor.
6. *John Fifield*.
7. *Mary Fifield*.
8. *Deborah Fifield*, by second wife, b. July 6, 1673, m. John Jackson of Cambridge.
9. *Thomas Fifield*, by second wife, b. Jan. 9, 1676.

ii. ABRAHAM, b. Sept. 2, 1639; of Hampton, N. H.
2. iii. LUKE, b. 1640–1; of Charlestown.
iv. HUMPHREY, b. Jan. 22, 1642; d. young.
v. JAMES, b. April 11, 1644; d. young.
vi. TIMOTHY, b. Oct. 5, 1646; d. young.
vii. JAMES, b. Oct. 5, 1647; of Hampton, N. H. · ———
viii. JONATHAN, b. May 30, 1650(?); of Hampton, N. H.
3. ix. DAVID, b. Feb. 28, 1653; of Bridgewater.
x. ABIGAIL, b. April 2, 1655; m. John Folsom, of Exeter, N. H., 1675.
xi. TIMOTHY, b. July 26, 1657; d. in a few months.
xii. SARAH, b. July 26, 1659. Living in 1683.
xiii. HUMPHREY, b. May 17, 1661; of Hampton, N. H.

2. LUKE[2] PERKINS (*Abraham*[1]) of Charlestown, born about 1641. An Indenture dated 4th mo. 3[d] day 1654, says that Luke Perkins, aged about " fortene " with the consent of his parents puts himself apprentice to Samuel Carter, shoemaker, both of Charlestown. John Green the elder, Giles Fifield and Thomas Jones signed the papers. He married Hannah, widow of Henry Cookery, and daughter of Robert Long, senior, March 9, 1663. She was admitted to to the First Church March 29, 1668. He died March 20, 1709–10. The son, Luke Perkins of Ipswich, was appointed administrator of estate March 12, 1712–13. Inventory : House £62, personal property £17. In the account of administration, widow Hannah was named, also son Luke, grandchild Elisabeth daughter of Jeremiah Wright, and Sarah daughter of William Emery. The widow died November 16, 1715, and the same year Luke[3] Perkins, of Plympton, as administrator of the estates of his father and mother sold the old homestead in Charlestown. Children :

i. HENRY,[3] b. 13th 11[mo] 166–.
ii. JOHN, b. May 10, 1664; d. April 16, 1667.
iii. LUKE, b. March 14, 1665; d. young.
iv. LUKE, b. March 18, 1667; of Ipswich and Plympton.

* Copp's Hill Epitaphs.

v. ELISABETH, b. April 15, 1670; m. Nicholas Lobdell, of Charlestown, Aug. 18, 1687. He d. 1698. Children:
   1. *Nicholas*, b. April 16, 1688; d. 1689.
   2. *Elizabeth*, b. Sept. 4, 1689; m. Jeremiah Wright, of Boston.
vi. JOHN, b. April 15, 1670.
vii. ABRAHAM, bap. 28th 5mo 1672.
viii. HANNAH, b. Dec. 9, 1673; m. Richard Way, of Charlestown.
   Their dau. *Sarah*[4] m. William Emery.
x. MARY, b. April 5, 1676.

3. DAVID[2] PERKINS (*Abraham*[1]), was born in Hampton, N. H., February 28, 1653. He married Elisabeth, daughter of Francis Brown
of Beverly, 1675–6. She was born October 17, 1654. He settled in Beverly about 1675. His wife was admitted to the Church
there 29th 5 mo 1683. Judge Mitchell, in his history of Bridgewater, gives him, his son David Jr.'s wife and children, and the
whole account is badly mixed. He was a blacksmith. He bought
lands in Beverly in 1677 and 1680, one parcel of which was an
orchard, bought of John Sampson, bounded on land of Mr. Hale,
and " Cow Lane," south and west by land formerly Richard Haines,
being eight rods below the "Great Rock." He was a juryman at
Salem, 1688, and had sold the most of his lands in Beverly prior
to that time. He moved to Bridgewater (South) in 1688, and
bought lands of the sons of Solomon Leonard. In 1694 he built
the mill in Bridgewater (South). This mill was situated where
Lazell, Perkins & Company's mill was in 1840. He was a man
of great influence and high character, and in his time the most
noted man of the town. He was the first Representative from
Bridgewater to the General Court of Massachusetts, after the
union of the two Colonies, 1692, 1694, and from 1704 to 1707
inclusive. His wife Elisabeth was dismissed from the church in
Beverly to Bridgewater church, 22d, 4m 1690. She died July 14,
1735, aged 80 (g. s.). He died October 1, 1736, aged 83 (g. s.).
In his will of June 17, 1736, he names sons David,[3] Abraham,[3]
Thomas[3] sole executor, and Nathan[3] deceased; grandsons David[4]
and Jonathan,[4] Nathan,[4] Timothy,[4] James[4] and Solomon,[4] and
granddaughters Martha[4] and Silence.[4]   Children:

i. MARY,[3] b. in Beverly.
ii. DAVID, b. in Beverly. Judge Mitchell in his history of Bridgewater does not give David[2] any son David[3] and gives the father,
   the son's wife and children. David[3] Perkins Jr. m. Martha,
   dau. of John and Sarah Howard, Feb. 1, 1699. He probably
   died 1737. In the settlement of his estate mention is made
   of his right in his father's estate and to the last clause of his
   father's will. Children.
   1. *John*,[4] b. Sept. 21, 1700.
   2. *Mary*, b. Dec. 10, 1702; m. Gideon Washburn.
   3. *Martha*, b. Nov. 30, 1704; m. 1st, Dr. Joseph Byram, 1724, and
      2d, Matthew Gannett, 1750. She d. 1779.
   4. *Elisabeth*, b. March 29, 1707.
   5. *Susannah*, b. Feb. 22, 1709; m. Samuel Allen, Aug. 5, 1733.
   6. *David*, b. Aug. 12, 1711; m. Alice Leach, 1738.
   7. *Jonathan*, b. March 16, 1714; m. 1st, Bethiah Hayward, Feb. 2,
      1738, and 2d, Priscilla Bourne.
   8. *Abraham*, b. July 16, 1716; m. Sarah Carver, 1743.
   9. *Sarah*,(?) Mitchell says, m. Jabez Carver, 1742, but Joshua E.
      Crane doubts if she was the dau. of David[3].

iii. NATHAN, bap. in Beverly, Sept. 13, 1685, of Bridgewater, m.
Martha, probably dau. of Solomon Leonard, Nov. 9, 1710. He
d. in 1723. (She m. 2d, Isaac Hayward, 1725). Children:

1. *Nathan*, b. Aug. 24, 1710; m. widow Sarah Pratt, of Solomon,
April 2, 1752. Six children.
2. *Solomon*, b. June 30, 1712, m. Lydia, dau. of Jonathan Sprague,
Dec. 31, 1753. He d. 1742-3. I find five children.
3. *Timothy*, b. Jan. 16, 1715; m. Susannah Washburn, March 18,
1736.
4. *Martha*, b. Dec. 10, 1717; m. Samuel Edson Jr. Sept. 26, 1738.
He d. Feb. 25, 1801, aged 87. She d. April 15, 1803, aged 86.
Ten children.
5. *James*, b. March 5, 1720; m. Bethiah Dunham, May 5, 1742.
He d. April 11, 1795.
6. *Silence*, b. 1723. Living in 1736.

iv. ABRAHAM, bap. in Beverly, 13th 11mo 1683-4. He settled in South
Kingston, R. I. Blacksmith. He m. 1st, Tabitha, dau. of
Nathaniel Niles and sister of Rev. Samuel Niles, May 23, 1708.
She d. Dec. 28, 1717. He was m. 2d, to Margaret Cross, June
29, 1718, by Rowse Helm, Justice. He sold negro Rose to
Capt. Nathaniel Niles, July 19, 1718. He was much employed
in town business. He d. 1746. Four children.

v. THOMAS, b. in Bridgewater, May 8, 1688. Lived on the old homestead. He m. Mary, dau. of James and Mary (Bowden) Washburn, Feb. 20, 1717. She was b. 1694, and d. April 23, 1750.
He d. June 5, 1761, aged 74 (g.s.). Children:

1. *Mary*,[4] b. Jan. 10, 1718, m. Joseph Hayward, 1742.
2. *Hepsibah*,[4] b. Feb. 15, 1720; m. 1st, Eleazer Carver Jr., April 3,
1746. He d. May 15, 1755. She m. 2d, Ebenezer Keith, Nov.
6, 1759; his second wife. He died of small pox April 12,
1778, aged 62 (g.s.). She d. April 12, 1810, aged 81 (g.s.).
Several children:
3. *Thomas*,[4] b. June 25, 1722; m. Mary, dau. of Solomon Pratt,
April 5, 1748. He d. Sept. 29, 1773. She d. 1778. Eight
children.
4. *Charles*,[4] b. Jan. 11, 1724; d. Oct. 1, 1726.
5. *Ebenezer*,[4] b. April 20, 1727; m. Experience Holmes, Feb. 28,
1751. He d. May 31, 1770, aged 45 (g.s.) Trinity Church.
Six children.
6. *Francis*,[4] b. Sept. 28, 1729; m. 1st, Susannah, dau. of Dea.
Robert Waterman of Halifax, published Nov. 27, 1762. She
was b. Feb. 6, 1742; d. July 21, 1771. He m. 2d, Philli-
bert, dau. of Ephraim Keith, March 2, 1775. He d. March 20,
1783, aged 54 (g.s.). The widow d. Sept. 29, 1814 (g.s.)
Trinity Church. I find eight children.

4. LUKE[3] PERKINS (*Luke,*[2] *Abraham*[1]) born March 18, 1667. Blacksmith. He married Martha, daughter of Lot and Elisabeth
(Walton*) Conant, May 31, 1688; marriage recorded in Salem
and Topsfield. He was famous for his records. He lived in
Marblehead, Beverly, Wenham, Ipswich (1704), and Plympton,
and in all these places recorded on the town records his marriage
and the dates of birth of his children! His wife was born in
Beverly, Aug. 15, 1664. She "took hold of God's Covenant
there for herself, and her children 30th day, 6th mo 1691." November 24, 1704, Luke and Martha (Conant) Perkins, formerly
of Beverly, now of Ipswich, sold John Filmore a house and barn
and about two acres of land on the road from Wenham to Bev.
erly near Wenham Pond in Beverly, which was formerly Lot

---

* Daughter of Rev. William Walton of Marblehead.

Conant's. The family went to Plympton about November, 1714.
William Churchill, Samuel Bradford and Isaac Cushman deeded
a lot of land of eighteen acres at Rocky Run. It is said that
this was given him as inducement to settle in Plympton as a
blacksmith. His uncle David⁷ Perkins,* of Bridgewater, in consideration for love and good will for his well beloved cousin
(nephew), gave him all his lands in Abington, viz.: One third
of the Solomon Leonard Purchase, and two thirds of the John
Robbins Purchase. He died in Plympton, Dec. 27, 1748, aged
82. His widow died Jan. 2, 1754, in her 90ᵗʰ year. Children:

 5. i. JOHN⁴, b. at Marblehead, April 5, 1689; of Plympton.
  ii. MARTHA, b. Sept. 19, 1691; d. young.
  iii. HANNAH, b. March 12, 1693.
 6. iv. LUKE, b. Sept. 17, 1695; of Plympton and ———.
 7. v. MARK, bap. in Beverly, April 30, 1699; of Bridgewater.

5. JOHN⁴ PERKINS (*Luke,*³ *Luke,*² *Abraham*¹) born at Marblehead,
 April 5, 1689. Lived in Plympton. Married Mary or Mercy
 Jackson there, April 18, 1721. He died 1728. In 1729 an
 allowance out of his estate was made to widow Mary and four
 children, viz: John,⁵ Mercy,⁵ Eleazer,⁵ Elisabeth.⁵

  i. JOHN.⁵
  ii. MERCY.
  iii. ELEAZER.
  iv. ELISABETH.

6. LUKE⁴ PERKINS (*Luke,*³ *Luke,*² *Abraham*¹) b. Sept. 17, 1695. He
 married Ruth, daughter of Robert Cushman of Kingston, Jan.
 28, 1716–17. She was born March 25, 1700. The Cushman
 Genealogy, page 131, says his father lived in Kingston and
 that the family went to Bridgewater; but query? I find a man
 of this name in Wrentham in 1755. Luke Perkins of Wrentham, blacksmith, mortgaged to Thomas Arnold of Smithfield,
 R. I., May 27, 1755, for £14, 11ˢ, a tract of land in Wrentham,
 bounded on land of Doctor John Druce, westerly and southerly
 by land of Capt. Jona. Whiting, easterly by a way leading to the
 Grist Mill northwards. Also a blacksmith shop and tools. I
 have made search for more of this man, but without avail. Children, according to Plympton Records:

  i. IGNATIUS,⁵ b. July 15, 1720. Lived in Wrentham and Freetown.
  ii. HANNAH, b. May 2, 1723; m. Capt. Nathaniel Shaw, of Carver,
   May 10, 1739. She d. May 2, 1802. He d. Aug. 25, 1800, aged 83.
  iii. MARY, b. June 28, 1726.

7. MARK⁴ PERKINS (*Luke,*³ *Luke,*² *Abraham*¹) baptized in Beverly,
 April 30, 1699. Blacksmith. He married Dorothy, daughter of
 Matthew Whipple Jr., of Ipswich (published as both of Ipswich),
 June 4, 1721. He owned the Covenant at the Third Church of Ipswich (Hamilton), Feb. 25, 1722. She was admitted to Wenham
 Church, Dec. 13, 1730; dismissed to the church in Ipswich, Jan. 2,
 1732, and admitted to the church in Bridgewater (North) 1741. He
 probably moved to Bridgewater (North) about 1740–41. His
 house was a short distance northeasterly from the depot in Brockton and was standing within the memory of the writer. He died

* Plymouth Records, Vol. ii., page 193.

Dec. 20, 1756. Widow m. 2d, Solomon Packard of Bridgewater, Oct. 5, 1760. She died May 1, 1782. The children of
Mark and Dorothy Perkins were:

   i. DOROTHY,[5] b. Feb. 4, 1722; bap. in Third Church, Ipswich, Feb.
      21, 1722. She m. Jacob Packard, of Bridgewater, Nov. 24,
      1742. He d. Feb. 2, 1777, aged 57. She d. Oct. 27, 1801.
  ii. MATTHEW,[5] b. June 25, 1723. A gravestone in Plympton says:
      "Matthew, son of Mark and Dorothy Perkins, his wife, died
      Mar. 10, 1724, aged 8 mos and 15 days," which shows that the
      family may have lived in Plympton for a time.
 iii. SARAH,[5] b. Ipswich June 25, 1725; m. Ebenezer Packard Feb.
      25, 1746.
 iv. JOSIAH,[5] b. Jan. 4, 1727; m. Abigail Edson, Aug. 17, 1755.
  v. JONATHAN,[5] b. Jan. 5, 1729; m. Abigail Packard, 1752.
 vi. ISAAC,[5] b. April 27, 1731.
vii. MARTHA,[5] b. Dec. 30, 1733; m. 1st, Nathan Packard, 1763; m.
      2d, Thomas Packard, Jan. 18, 1779–80.
viii. EBENEZER,[5] b. May 7, 1736; d. Nov. 9.
 ix. JOANNA,[5] b. Feb. 7, 1738; m. Levi Keith Nov. 8, 1759.
  x. MARY,[5] b. Feb. 16, 1739; m. Simeon Packard 1761.
 xi. JESSE,[5] b. Dec. 6, 1742. Soldier in French War and the Revo-
      lutionary War. Married 1st, Susannah Field, June 5, 1769;
      she d. June 30, 1789. Married 2d, Bliss Phinney, Nov. 12,
      1789; she d. March 8, 1808. Married 3d, Sally Silvester,
      Aug. 17, 1808. He d. Jan. 27, 1826, aged 84.

Ensign LUKE[5] PERKINS.

    Judge Mitchell, in his History of Bridgewater, says that he came
from Ipswich to North Bridgewater and was a nephew of Mark[4];
if so, he must have been a son of Luke[4] or John[4] of Plympton,
who were all the brothers Mark[4] had. He worked on the new
meeting house in North Bridgewater in 1749. He bought a pew
in the Front Gallery, Jan. 4, 1762, for £26, 13s, 4d. He was a
blacksmith, and a man of great ingenuity. The History of
North Bridgewater says that James and Luke Perkins manufactured muskets, small anchors, scythes, shovels and plow points.
He was a member of the Church and Parish. He was married
to Rebecca, daughter of James Packard, Aug. 24, 1749, by Rev.
John Porter. She was born July 1, 1732. He moved to East
Stoughton near the North Bridgewater line in 1759. Mr. Newton Talbot says, he bought lands in 1758 and 1759, and was taxed
in Stoughton, 1759, for two polls but no personal estate. He
was taxed as an "Ensign" in 1770. In April of 1776 he moved
back into North Bridgewater. He died April 23, 1776, aged 51
years (g. s.). His widow died in Maine, Nov. 14, 1796. His
children, all baptized at North Bridgewater Church except the
two oldest, and whose descendants are a multitude in Massachusetts and Maine, were:

   i. ANNA,[6] b. May 12, 1750 (Bridgewater Records). She m. 1st,
      Jonas Reynolds. He d. Aug. 5, 1795, aged 53. She m. 2d,
      Elijah Snell, 1798. Seven children.
  ii. JEMIMA,[6] b. April 10, 1753 (Brid. Records). She m. Joseph Rey-
      nolds, Sept. 17, 1772. Eleven children.
 iii. MARY,[6] b. Dec. 13, 1754 (Brid. Records); bap. in North Bridge-
      water Jan. 26, 1755; m. Capt. William French, of Stoughton,
      July 8, 1773. Six children I find.
 iv. JAMES,[6] b. June 9, 1757 (Brid. Records); bap. Sept. 1, 1757. He
      m. Betsey, dau. of Josiah Packard Jr., Sept. 23, 1783. He

moved to Minot, Me., about the time he was married. He d.
in 1844; his wife d. in 1839 at the age of 74. I find eleven
children; all but one had families.

v. KEZIAH,[6] b. June 25, 1759, in Stoughton; bap. in North Bridgewater, July 29, 1759; m. Matthew Packard, April 17, 1781. He
was b. April 10, 1756; d. 1795? Four children, all of whom
went to Maine.

vi. SUSANNAH,[6] b. April 17, 1761, in Stoughton; bap. May 24, 1761;
m. Simeon Brett Jr., Dec. 25, 1777. He was b. Oct. 12, 1753.
Three children.

vii. REBECCA,[6] b. March 7, 1763; bap. March 20, 1763; m. 1st, Josiah
Packard Oct. 10, 1782. She m. 2d, Charles Snell Jr., March
26, 1807. Four Children.

viii. MARTHA,[6] b. in Stoughton; bap. July 7, 1765; m. Gideon Lincoln, Aug. 13, 1781. Twelve children, some of whom went
to Maine.

ix. PHEBE,[6] b. in Stoughton; bap. Aug. 16, 1767; m. Asaph Howard, Esq., 1789. He moved to Minot, Me. Ten children—five
born in North Bridgewater, and five in Minot.

x. LUKE,[6] b. in Stoughton; bap. Sept. 1, 1771; m. Mary, dau. of
Nathan Snell, Nov. 14, 1797. Luke Perkins and Isaac Porter
owned a house together in 1798. Removed to Winthrop, Me.,
1804-5. Deacon of the Baptist Church, 1824-5. Probably d.
there Sept. 7, 1841, at the age of 71. I find only one child.

NOTE.—I am indebted to Geo. A. Perkins, M.D., of Salem, Mass., Hon. Newton Talbot
of Boston, and Joshua E. Crane Esq., of Bridgewater.

WILL OF WILLIAM LARRABEE OF MALDEN, MASS.,

FEBRUARY 12, 1691-2,

WITH THE INVENTORY OF HIS ESTATE.

Copied from the original at East Cambridge, by WILLIAM BLAKE TRASK, A. M., of Dorchester, Mass.

I william Leraby* doe Inioy a comfortabl mesuer of health undarstand-
ing And memory doe make and ordain my Last will and testement In order
and form as foloweth   first I commit my sole Into the marcyfull Hands
of my greacious god and my body after death unto the earth To be decently
buried: and for such Esteat as god hath giuen me I doe Thus dispose of It:

* William Larrabee, as the name is usually written, was made freeman 22d March, 1689-
90, in company with forty others, of his Malden townsmen, whose names are given in the
list furnished by our venerated friend and associate member, the Rev. Lucius R. Paige,
D.D., of Cambridge.
These Malden freemen are entered in the first of three volumes in the Massachusetts
Archives, at the State House, entitled, "Intercharter," arranged and thus named by the
late Rev. Joseph B. Felt.
Dr. Paige contributed to the REGISTER—vol. iii., pages 90-96, 187-194, 239-246, 345-352
—an entire list of freemen in the Massachusetts colony, as entered on the Records. If we
have numbered them correctly, there are 3738 from the Colony Records, and 918 from the
three "Intercharter" volumes; total, 4656, from the 18th of May, 1631, to 18th April, 1691,
there being an interim of four years during the usurpation of Andros, when the practice of
admitting freemen was discontinued, but resumed, "with some modifications," "after the
Revolution."

1 First I will that all my Just debts and funerall charges be discharged.
Item I give unto my Louing Kinsmen and Kinswoman* as foloweth
1 first to steuen Lareby I doe giue fiue pounds mooueble Esteat
2 Secondly to william Lareby I do giue fiue pounds mooueble Esteat
3 Thirdly to Isaac Lareby I doe giue fiue pounds mooueble Esteat
4 fourthly to Thomas Lareby I doe giue fiue pounds moouebl Esteat
5 fifthly to samuell Lareby I doe giue fiue pounds moouebl Esteat
6 sixthly to Beniamin Lareby I doe giue fiue pounds moouebl Esteat
7 seuenthly to Jane Lareby I doe giue fiue pounds mouebl Esteat
8 aightly to Janes daughter hanah I do giue fifty shilings moouebl
esteat   All and euery of Thes Legacys are to be truly and faithfuly payd
by my executor nathaniell Nichols† : after the diceas of my wiff Elizabeth
and the Legitees shall haue their proportions yeerly begining with the
Eldist to the last.

In Cas my Louing Kinsman John Lareby Coms from beyond Sea Before the abouesaid Legacys are payd then my Executor Is to pay Or what
may be then to pay to him In time and manor abouesaid And the abouesaid Legates are to rest satisfied with his loue ‡   Farther I doe settle all
this my Esteat both lands and mouebls upon my true and trusty executor Nathaniell Nicholes and to alow my wife a comfortable Liuing according to
the produce of such an esteat   And the aforsaid Elizabeth Is not to make
any conuayenc of aney part of the afforsaid Estate but to seeke the benifit
of the Esteat as shee is able and In case Elizabeth my wife sees It good to
goe of from the Estate either by marrig or other wise then The aforesaid
executor shall alow her forty shilings a year.

And If their be Just causs for my wife to liue a priuate Life by Leauing
my hous and Land and Estate : Then I doe will and Riquier my Only execu-

* It has heretofore been a question with others, as well as the writer of this note, as to
the meaning of " kinsmen and kinswoman," in its application to William Larrabee of Malden. Light has been thrown on this subject, however, in the discovery of an old petition
bearing date March 6, 1732-3, found by the late William M. Sargent, of Portland, the substance of which is printed in the REGISTER, vol. xxxviii., page 82, in which it is agreed by
the Committee and Proprietors that Stephen, William, John, Thomas, Samuel, Isaac, Benjamin, Ephraim and Jean Ashfield, children of Stephen, of North Yarmouth, should have a
ten-acre lot laid out and granted them," &c. ; but " John went to sea and dyed abrode and
Ephraim was killed by the Indians at North Yarmouth and there was no lot laid out either
for John or Ephraim." It seems quite plausible, therefore, to put this construction on the
matter : that William and Stephen may have been brothers, and the " kinsmen and kinswoman " nephews and niece of William. See " Saco Valley Settlements and Families,"
page 789. Ephraim may have been killed previous to February 12, 1691-2. He is not
mentioned in the will. The name of John occurs later in the instrument. It would seem
that William Larrabee, of Malden, was a soldier in King Philip's war, for Rev. Mr. Bodge,
in his work entitled "Soldiers in King Philip's War," under date of June 24, 1676, finds
among those "Credited under Capt. John Cutler," " William Lareby, 00.09.04." Again
the same year, " August 24, 1676, Maulden—Town Cr. By Sundrys accpt⁵ viz 49. 11. 03."
" William Laraby, 00. 09. 04." See REGISTER, vol. xlii., page 299 ; also, vol. xliii., p. 278.
    In a letter from Samuel Winthrop to John Winthrop, Jr., published in Massachusetts
Historical Collections, fifth series, vol. viii., page 243, the former writes : " Honored
Brother,—Yoʳˢ I receiued 30ᵗʰ Decembʳ, 1655, wᶜʰ mentions a former by Mʳ Laraby, & one
by Mʳ Jones, wᶜʰ neuer came to hand, nor euen heard of yᵉ ship or Thom. Harris."
    † Mr. Savage says that James Nichols, of Malden, married, April, 1660, Mary, daughter
of George Felt, and had, among other children, Nathaniel, born 1666.
    As William Larrabee, the testator, according to the same authority, married Elizabeth,
perhaps daughter, also, of George Felt (in November, 1655, see REGISTER, vol. x., p. 162),
it would seem that Nathaniel Nichols, the above-named executor, was a nephew to the
wife of William Larrabee.
    ‡ As this John Larrabee, according to the afore-mentioned petition, "went to See and
dyed abrode," he is doubtless the one referred to in the " Genealogical Gleanings in England," by Mr. Waters, as printed in the REGISTER, vol. xxxviii., p. 321.
    " John Larabee, of New England (evidently a mariner), appoints Elizabeth Crawford,
of London, his attorney, &c., 30 April, 1694. Proved 19 June, 1694," two years and more
after the making of the will of William Larrabee.

tor to let my wife Elizabath haue all her waring Cloaths wollen and linnen and my bed and furniture sutible And a return of the bed and furniture again at her deseas to my executor and further upon and during her Liuing a priuat Life my Executor shall pay or cause to be payd to my wiffe Elizabeth yearly and euery yeare fiue pounds per yeare: during her naturell single Life: This is to be payd In prouisions and cloathing such as Is produced upon the place at a price as Is betwixt man and man

Item. my will Is that my executor payes all my legecys to my Louing Kinsmen before named not In money nor as money but In moueball goods Chattils as they shall bee prized by men mutually Chosen betwixt and by my executor and The Legateys and this beeing don: he and they to Rest satisfied Their one and euery one giuing the executor a full discharg: And in case eney of the Legetes Rest not satisfied In this my will and testament that parson or parsons shall be depriued of eney benifet by this my will.

Item: further my will Is that In case my Louing Kinsman: nathaniell nicholes dyes without Issue Lawfuly begotten of His body, Then my will Is that my louing Kinsman william Lereby shall succeed upon the Estat and stand Ingaged To pay all the fore mentioned Legecyes to the Legetes aforsaid And to answer and make good all the within obligation mentioned to my Louing wife Elizabeth In wittnes to this my will I haue heereunto set my hand and seall this tweluether of feburary one thousand six hundred and ninty one two:

Further my will Is to request my louing naightbours John Green: and John Greenland to be the ouerseers of this my will:—further my will Is that Steuen leareby my Cursen Steuen Lerebys Eldest son shall haue my mare and colt

Signed   senr

WILLIAM ✕ LEAREBY

Signed sealed In
the presents of
Jacob Parker
Isaac Green*
John Greenland

October 24: 1692. Charlestowne
This Last Will & Testament of William
Leraby Deced prsented by ye Executor for
Probate

Jacob Parker Isaac Green John Greenland prsonally appearing before James Russell Esqr Commissionated to be Judge of Probate of Wills and Granting Administration within ye County of Middx Made oath that they were prsonally prsent and saw the Deced Subscriber William Lereby senr sign and seal and heard him own or Declare this to be his last Will and Testament and yt then When he So did he was of a disposing minde

Exad   JA: RUSSELL
  pr Samll Phipps Regr

---

* The original will may have been in the hand-writing of Isaac Green. A capital letter is generally used at the beginning of each line.

See Genealogy of the Larrabee Family (pages 787-873) in " Saco Valley Settlements and Families" (before referred to), by G. T. Ridlon, Sr., Portland, Me., 1895, published by the author; The Libby Family in America, page 41 (by Charles T. Libby). Mr. Libby says that William Larrabee, of Malden, a verbatim copy of whose will is given in the present article, "married, Nov. 1655, in Malden, Mass., Elizabeth, dau. of George and Elizabeth (Wilkinson) Felt. George Felt was the most prominent of the early settlers of North Yarmouth, Me., and thither his son-in-law Larrabee removed. He bought land of an Indian named Warromby. It was probably during Philip's war that he returned to Malden, where he died."

An Inuentary of ye estate of william Lerebe deseased The 28 of September 1692

Taken ye 4 of agust 1693

In money	03	0	0
one hous one barn 20 accrs of land	90	"	"
neat cattell	06	"	"
Twelue sheep	03	"	"
Two swine	01	"	"
one bed and furniture In ye lower rome	08	"	"
other beding and waring Cloaths ⎫			
And Iron ware : puter Chests ⎬	09	4	"
Cubberds : Chairs and other mouebls ⎭			

tot 120   4   0

William Green
John Greenland

Charlestowne : Aug^{st} 7th 1693. By ye Honourable James Russell Esqr Nathaniell Nickells Admitted Executo^r & allowed Adm͞con p^rsonally appearing made oath that this Containes a true Inuentory of ye Estate of William Lerreby late of Malden dec͞ed as far as Comes to his Knowledge & when more appears he will Cause it to be added

Sam^{ll} Phipps Reg^r   Jurat^r Coram   Ja : Russell

Endorsed :   William Lerebys Inventory 1693 Entered—p^d

INSCRIBED POWDER–HORNS.

By Hon. SAMUEL A. GREEN, M.D., of Boston.

THE Groton Historical Society has lately received two old powder-horns which have some interesting associations connected with soldiers of the town. One of them has been cut off at the bottom since it was originally made, and bears an inscription as follows :—

[SA]MVEL PARCE OF GROT^{ON}
HIS—HORN—174^7

The tradition in the family of the former owner is that the base of the horn was shot through by a bullet in one of the battles of the Revolution, after which the horn was somewhat shortened and again used for holding powder. Its appearance seems to confirm this account, as there are unmistakable traces of an injury on the edge of the base, which might have been made in that way. The horn is about thirteen inches long, and has upon it the rude drawings of two deer, and a part of a third one, of which the remainder was on the missing portion of the bottom.

The other horn is also about thirteen inches long, and has the following inscription :—

JOSIAH LAWRANCE 1747

and another hand has subsequently cut the name SAMUEL under that of JOSIAH. It has also the drawings of two deer, a moose (?), a horse, a child, and a gun.

On both these horns there is an attempt at some crude ornamentation around the names, resembling this : 〰〰〰〰〰. In both instances, probably, the carving was done with a jack-knife, and perhaps in camp when time hung heavy.

Mr. John Gilson, of Groton, owns another powder-horn found many years ago in his grandfather's house, which bears the following inscription :—

NO. 4: JVNE y^e. 19. 1746. WE. HAD. A.
FIGHT. JVNE y^e. 24. WE. HAD. A. FIG
HT. Att COLSPRING. &. AUGUST. y^e.
3. WE. HAD. A. FIGT. Att. No. 4

The horn is about fifteen inches long, and near the smaller end are the initials "I H.," that stand probably for the name of some member of the Hobart or Hubbard family, which surnames were often used indiscriminately. The ornamentation around the writing and between the lines somewhat resembles this :—ΛΛΛΛΛΛΛΛΛΛΛ. "Number 4" is the old name of Charlestown, New Hampshire. In early times, before they received their present names, the four southerly townships, lying on the east bank of the Connecticut River, immediately north of the Massachusetts line, were numbered in geographical order, and designated by their numbers alone. At the present day these towns are known as follows : Township No. 1, as Chesterfield ; No. 2, as Westmoreland ; No. 3, as Walpole ; and No. 4, as Charlestown.

The *Boston Daily Advertiser*, March 10, 1893, on its fourth page has a column headed "Hither and Yon," in which the writer mentions four powder-horns for sale at that time in New York. He says : "The third [horn] comes from Massachusetts. It bears the name, in large characters, of 'Jonathan Clark Lewis, made by J. G., Feb. the 27, 1773,' and the motto :—

> I, powder, with my brother ball,
> Most hero like doth conquer all.

It is curiously engraved with moose, fox, eagle, and a man snaring a deer."

In the issue of the same newspaper, March 13, the following communication appeared :—

To the Editor of The Advertiser :—In the "Hither and Yon" column of yesterday's *Advertiser* there is an allusion to an engraved powder-horn bearing the inscription : "Jonathan Clark Lewis, made by J. G., Feb. the 27, 1773," which is offered for sale by a dealer in New York. It may interest some of your readers to know that Mr. Lewis was a trader at Groton, where he lived, and died on April 7, 1781, "in the 37th year of his age." He was English by birth, and his tombstone in the Groton burying-ground is one of the very few that have armorial bearings cut on them. There can be no doubt as to the identity of the man, as before the Revolution middle names were very uncommon.   G.

Within the past twelve or thirteen years the subject of powder-horn inscriptions has been developed to an interesting degree by Mr. Rufus A. Grider, of Canajoharie, New York, who has made careful drawings of more than four hundred inscribed horns. His collection of such representations is both unique and artistic, and should be published for the benefit of scholars, as it contains many hints and suggestions of an historical character, not found elsewhere. Mr. Grider has made original researches along this line of study, which are worthy of high commendation. His pioneer labors in this direction justly entitle him to be regarded as the founder of a new antiquarian art.

CONTRIBUTION TO WYMAN GENEALOGY.

By MORRILL WYMAN, Jr., Esq., of Cambridge, Mass.

DURING a visit to England, in the autumn of 1895, I ascertained the following facts concerning the family of Francis and John Wyman who settled in Woburn, Massachusetts, in 1640.*

From the register of baptisms, deaths and marriages, in the church at West Mill, near Buntingford, Hertfordshire :—

1617	May 2ᵈ,	Francis Wyman married Elizabeth Richardson.
1618	April 5ᵗʰ,	Thomas ye son of Francis Wyman, baptized.
1619	Feb. 24ᵗʰ,	Francis, " " " " "
1621	Feb. 3ᵈ,	John, " " " " "
1623	March 14ᵗʰ,	Richard, " " " " "
1628	August 31ˢᵗ,	William, " " " "
1630	June 22ᵈ,	Elizabeth, the wife of Francis Wyman, buried.
1630	July —,	William, ye son of Francis Wyman, buried.

1656   July 12ᵗʰ, the wife of Francis Wyman of West Mill Green was buried.

1658   September 19ᵗʰ, Francis Wyman of West Mill Green was buried.

---

* An abstract of the will of Francis Wyman, of Westmill, in the county of Hertford, father of Francis and John, the Woburn immigrants, is printed in Waters's Gleanings for April, 1889, in the REGISTER, vol. 43, p. 156. A genealogy of the Wyman Family by the late Thomas B. Wyman was printed in the REGISTER, vol. 3, pp. 33–8, and reprinted in pamphlet form. A copy of this pamphlet, corrected and much extended, in manuscript, by the author, is preserved in the Library of the New-England Historic Genealogical Society.—EDITOR.

From the "Tithing Book" at West Mill:—

1617. Francis Wyman of "Reyners Croft" (?) paid tiths.
1618. Francis Wyman at Brook End paid tiths.

(Then follow many entries of the same kind.)
From the register of Baptisms, Deaths and Marriages, at Braughing:—

1653 March 5th, Thomas Wyman married Ann Godfrey.

Brook End is about one mile to the west of the West Mill church, and West Mill Green is about one half mile to the west of Brook End. Braughing is about two miles south east of West Mill.

It was stated to me that in the records of the church at Buntingford* there is recorded a marriage of Richard Wyman, about 1560. I was unable to examine the book to verify this statement.

The Wymans may be descended from the Wymond family. The crests of the Wyman and Wymond coat of arms are the same, and in the earliest records which I have found the name Wyman is very often written with a final "t," Wymant.

I am greatly indebted to Mr. James J. Shain, landlord of the George Hotel, Buntingford, for his aid in examining the records.

BALTHAZAR WILLIX.

By Frank W. Hackett, A.M., of New Castle, N. H.

For a surname "Willix" is odd enough. It scarcely can be English. Put "Balthazar" in front, and you get as curious a name as any one of those that for some peculiarity or other arrest attention in our early New England records.

Balthazar Willix was an early settler at Exeter, New Hampshire. One of the smaller shares of the lands was allotted him in the beginning of 1640, and his name, according to the accomplished historian of that town, appears at a later date frequently in the records, "in his own bold and handsome chirography."† He was one of the signers of the Exeter Petition of 1643 to the General Court of Massachusetts, to be taken under their government.‡

His wife, Hannah (or Annah) Willix, met with a terrible fate. In May, or June, 1648, as we learn from Bell, she was on her way from Dover to Exeter, when she was waylaid, robbed and most

---

* Buntingford is a small place in the county of Hertford, twelve miles n. n. e. from the county seat, and thirty-one miles north of London. The village consists of a single street on the shores of the river Rib. The trade there is principally in leather and malt. Braughing is in the same county, three miles south of Buntingford.—Editor.
† Bell's History of Exeter, page 40.
‡ N. H. Prov. Papers, vol. i. p. 171, where his name is misprinted—*Willis.*

brutally murdered, and her body flung into the river. "Whether
the perpetrator of the outrage was ever brought to justice is not
known." * Governor Winthrop notes this tragic occurrence with a
particularity of detail that, however characteristic of the Puritan
records of that day, rather shocks our modern ideas of the duty of
the chronicler.†

Not long after this dreadful event Willix, it seems, removed to
Salisbury, where, in 1650, he is found taxed four shillings in the
rate list.‡ He was subsequently married to Mary, the widow of
Thomas Hauxton. It was a brief union, for he died at Salisbury,
23 March, 1655. His widow died in July, 1675.§

So far as we are aware there is nothing remarkable about this
man, except his name ; and in this respect a daughter, "Haselphena," fairly competes with her father. It is likely that the family
has now become extinct in the male line. But we have lately come
across certain depositions relating to his children that are perhaps
worth printing, referring, as they do, to one or two names that may
interest somebody. In the library of the Portsmouth (N. H.)
Athenæum is a MS. record book of original entries made by nota-
ries public at Great Island (New Castle) and at Portsmouth, the
first entry being of date 24 October, 1692.‖ From this book we
extract three depositions, as follows : —

I.

The deposition of Francis Jones aged 57 or thereabouts, Testifieth &
sayeth that he very well knew Haselphena Willix, Annah Willix and
Susannah Willex all three the reputed Daughters of Belshazer Willex
sometime of Exeter in New England and Annah his wife of whom the
afore mentioned three sisters were borne & owned to be the children of sᵈ
Belshaser & Annah his wife The Deponent farther Testifieth that he
very well knew Robᵗ Rosco who married Annah Willex one of the three
sisters above named, wʰᵒ afterwarᵈ went to Roan Oke, or North Carolina,
and as I the sᵈ Deponent understood sᵈ Roscoe there died sᵈ Annah became
wife to one blunt & after his decease to one Southwell and last of all the
wife of one Collᵒ Leare in Virginia & farther sayth not

the mark of X FRANCIS JONES

This was sworn to before Nathˡˡ Fryer, Esq., President of the
Province, 15 April, 1696 ; acknowledged before Wm. Redford,
18 April, 1696 ; entered and recorded Nov. 11, 1696.

Francis Jones was of Portsmouth. On the opposite page of the

* Bell's History of Exeter, page 40.
† Winthrop's Journal, volume ii., page 326, where the unfortunate victim is spoken of as
"the wife of one Willip of Exeter."
‡ 3 REGISTER, 17.
§ 8 REGISTER, 223.
‖ It is a protest of Captain John Pickering attorney to Mʳ John Micoe of Boston merchant and compa' against Captain John Votear (comandr on board yᵉ Maj's ship of warr
called yᵉ Samuel and Mary) for forcibly bringing the shipp Dove on 1 October, 1692, from
the Isle of Sholes into yᵉ River Piscattaqua, and taking out of her fourteen barrels of gunpowder and one large Anchor.

book, he and his wife Susannah appear of record as ratifying, by deed, the acts of "our beloved kinsman, Thomas Pickering," done under a letter of attorney to him of 13th May, 1695. John Pickering and James Lovett are witnesses to the present instrument, which is acknowledged 18 April, 1696.

II.

The Deposition of Robert Smith aged about eighty-three years & John Smith aged about eighty (?) six years who sayth that wee know, the three daughter of Belshazer Willix sometime at Exeter in New England both when they were children and when they were grown to womans estate and they allways owned themselves to be sisters and were allwayes soe accounted and their names were Hasselphena Willix: Annah Willix and Susannah Willix, and Thomas Nudd aged about sixty six yeares allsoe Sayeth, that I lived a servant many years wth Mr Timothy Dalton at Hampton, and Anna Willix lived there a serv^t att the same times and Susannah Willix Lived a servant very near us, and thay allwayes Owned one another to be sisters and were allwayes soe accounted.

Robt Smith John Smith Thomas Nudd above came and apeared this 8th of May 1695 and made oath to the truth of all above written before me

Hen Dow Just. P. in New Hampshire

Recorded as a true copie of originall November 11th

WM REDFORD N. P.

Henry Dow was of Hampton, where it appears the deponents lived. The Reverend Timothy Dalton, minister of that town, died there 28 December, 1661. Ruth, his widow, died at Hampton, 12 May, 1666. As they were without children, the widow constituted Nathaniel Batchelder her heir; and one feature of the instrument for this purpose, executed 22 March, 1663, was that Batchelder was to pay £5 to Hannah Willix.*

III.

The Deposition of Wm ffifefield aged ab^t eighty years and Mary Fiefefield aged about seventy six years who sayth that thay very well knew Belshazer Willix and his wife sum times of Exeter in the province of New Hampsh^r in New England, and allsoe their three Daughters Haselphena Willix, Annah Willix and Susannah Willix wch were own Sisters the reputed children of the s^d Willix all borne to s^d Belshazer Willix of one woman & farther sayth not

W^m ffifeild & Mary his wife apeared this second day of May 1696, and made oath to the truth of all above written before me

HENRY DOW Justice P^c in New England.

William Fifield was of Hampton (*Dow's History of Hampton*, volume ii., page 707), where it may be that the date (November 9, 1683) given as that of the death of his wife Mary needs to be corrected.

There is nothing further found of record on the subject in this MS. volume. The purpose for which the depositions were taken is left wholly to conjecture.

* 27 REGISTER, 364.

INSCRIPTIONS AT SANTA CRUZ, CALIFORNIA, 1891.

Copied by B. FRANK LEEDS, Esq.

THE following inscriptions are from tombstones in the Old Cemetery (not the oldest, which is Roman Catholic) at Santa Cruz, Cal., being copied in September, 1891.* This cemetery is still used, though most of the burials are now made in the Odd Fellows Cemetery, nearly opposite and on the east side of the river San Lorenzo, which has been in existence from twenty-two to twenty-five years. The Old Cemetery, established some forty or more years before these epitaphs were copied, is an attractive bit of inclined ground on the flank of a plateau covered with native trees, mostly redwoods and horse-chestnuts, and a few exotics like the Italian cypress, etc.

Lot 1.†

Reuben H. Sawin, died May 2, 1884, aged 82 years.
Sarah S. Sawin, died July 17, 1889, aged 76 years.
Their children died in Massachusetts:
Hamilton, died June 28, 1842, aged 6 years.
Maria, died June 28, 1842, aged 3 years.
All natives of Mass.

Lot 2.

Levi R. Stoell, died May 13, 1880. A native of South Dedham, Mass.

Lot 3.

Hugh Leo, died July 29, 1878, ag^d 2 y. 1 m. 9 d.
Helen Newell, died Oct. 29, 1878, ag^d 4 mos. 22 d.
Children of C. E. and L. A. Russell.

Lot 4.

George Ellis, native of Scotland, died Oct. 19, 1877, aged 66 years.
Anne, wife of above, native of England, died Sep. 6, 1882, aged 76 years.
Another grave in this lot without a stone.

Lot 5.

Francis M. Kittredge, M.D., Littleton, Mass.
Oct. 10, 1810. Feb. 13, 1879.
Almira M. Kittredge, Lanesboro, Mass.
Nov. 12, 1817. July 8, 1885.
Ruel Kittredge, Sep. 12, 1839. Feb. 28, 1863.

Lot 6.

Mary Edith Beasley, born July 12, 1849, d. Oct. 5, 1872.
A marble cross.

---

* Mr. Leeds, who copied these inscriptions, was a resident of Santa Cruz in 1882, 1883 and 1884, but was a visitor in 1891 when they were copied.
† The lots are doubtless numbered—but the numbers here given are my own and are not likely to correspond with those used by the Cemetery Association.

Lot 7.

Alice C. Boston, died Dec. 4, 1882, aged 84 years.
J. B. (Boston), died Oct. 17, 1874.

Lot 8.

Nancy Ann, wife of David Ghasky, b. Apr. 20, 1818, d. Jan. 23, 1868.
David Ghasky, b. Portsmouth, Ohio, Jan. 9, 1806, died Aug. 16, 1877.

Lot 9.

Josephine Sharp, wife of Samuel Sharp, died Jan. 25, 1872, aged 33 y.
11 m. 12 days.
Three other small graves and two large graves, unmarked, in this lot.

Lot 10.

John Ford, native of New Jersey, died May 26, 1863, aged 43 years.
Four tallish Italian cypresses at corners of this lot.

Lot 11.

William H. Moore, b. Feb. 15, 1836, died Oct. 13, 1871.
Lizzie Nichols, wife of W. H. Moore, born July 4, 1833, died May 9,
1870.
Ida, daughter of W. H. and L. Moore, b. Mch. 17, 1855, d. Feb. 17,
1863.
(No name).   Roses lent, not given, to bud on earth and bloom in heaven.

Lot 12.

Catalina Maria, infant daugh^r of G. B. V. and E. A. DeLamater, died
Jan. 30, 1867,
Mary E. Cope, born Apr. 9, 1855, died Jan. 4, 1878.

Lot 13.
[blank.]

Lot 14.

Jane Heath, wife of Lucien Heath, born at Dayton, Ohio, Sep. 16, 1825.
Lucien Heath, born at Buffalo, N. York, May 10, 1819, died Dec. 19,
1888, ag^d 69 y. 7 m. 9 d.
Alice C. Heath, born at King's Valley, Oregon, Jan. 15, 1855, died July
18, 1876, aged 21 y. 6 m. 3 d.
An above ground tomb; of granite and limestone.

Lot 15.

Matilda A., dau^r of Addison and Sarah Newell and wife of R. K. Vestal,
d. Jan, 9, 1876, ag^d 35 years, 9 mos.   A native of Maine.
Emily F. Clark, wife of R. K. Vestal, died Mch. 3, 1883, aged 39 years,
5 months.   A native of New Hampshire.

Lot 16.

Eli Moore, a native of Gilford, N. C., b. Apr. 12, 1806, d. June 6, 1859.
Rachel B. Moore, wife of R. K. Vestal, b. Nov. 1, 1828, d. Jan. 4, 1851.
Elizabeth Palmer, wife of Eli Moore, b. Nov. 24, 1804, d. Dec. 7, 1883.
A native of Tennessee.
Elizabeth Moore, wife of E. Bender, b. Jan. 18, 1845, d. Jan. 7, 1874.

Lot 17.

A. P. Jordan, born in Brunswick, Maine, died Nov. 14, 1866, aged 40 years, 1 mo.

Little May.

Our Baby.

A fourth grave apparently with broken painted stake.

Lot 18.

J. B. Perry, died Oct. 23, 1871, aged 58 years.

Charles Green, died Mch. 31, 1871, aged 17 years.

S. R. Hillman, born Feb. 14, 1813, died July 4, 1884.

Lot 19.

Paul Emilio, born July 14, 1864, died Nov. 28, 1870.

On base of this stone in large letters the name Pioda.

Lot 20.

Charles W. Williams, b. Aug. 7, 1825, d. Mch. 12, 1872.

Lewis B. Williams, d. Jan. 5, 1869, ag^d. 11 mo. 28 d., son of C. W. and A. E. Williams.

Wood.

Anna Narcissa Williams, dau^r. of Chas W. and Anna Williams, died June 10, 1864, aged 11 mos. 20 days.

Wood.

Delcy V. Williams, died Jan. 15, 1869, ag^d 3 years, 1 mo. 11 d., dau^r. of C. W. and A. E. Williams.

Wood.

Lot 21.

Helen Mary Boston, died Aug. 5, 1852.

Lot 22.

George W. Wood, died Oct 28, 1885, aged 59 years.

Charity, wife of F. N. Stuart, d. June 26, 1883, aged 54 years.

Job and Mary Blanchard Stuart enjoyed life together 65 years.

Job born 1796, died 1884.

Mary born 1797, died 1885.

Natives of Vermont.

[To be continued.]

LETTER OF RICHARD O BRYEN TO ABIJAH CRANE, 1790.

Communicated by John C. Clapp, Esq., of Boston.

The Abijah Crane to whom the following letter was sent was an elder brother of Col. John Crane of Revolutionary fame. It was the latter who set out the Paddock elms near the old "Granary" burying ground in Boston. Both the brothers were members

of the Boston " tea party" in 1773. There does not appear to be
any record which shows that they had a sister or other relative by
the name of Rebecca, as named in the letter : —

City of Algiers January the 5th, 1790.

Mr Abijah Crane

Sir

I am the unfortunate Master of the ship Dauphin that Be-
longed to Mr Mathew and thomas Irvins of the City of Philadelphia. I
was Captured the 30th of J— [torn] fifty Leagues to the Westward of
Lisbon by and Algerine corsaire of 34 guns, and on the 16th of August,
brought to algiers where I and my crew were condemned to Slavery.

Sir I am the son of Rebecca Crane of Boston whom married William
O Bryen about the yeare 1757, and after a few years William O Bryen
his wife and 4 children moved to Ireland in hopes of Recovering a considerable Estate, which he was the Lawful Heire to. But unfortunately my
father Died shortly after his arrival in Ireland. My mother and her foure
young children was left, in a strange country, but was much assisted by the
worthy Relations of My father, the family of the Aldworths.

A few years after my mother married the Reverand Laurence Arundel,
now Dead, in the yeare of 1774, or 1772. I was bound apprentice to a sea
Capt in order that I should have and [an] oppertunity from my Line of Life
to Vissit my mother's Relations and friends. But the Vessel I was apprentice on board of used to trade to the Southern provinces, the American
war commenceing I sailed out of Philadelphia, But Never had the oppertunity of Going to Boston to see you and your Brother and the Rest of
My Mothers Relations.

There is allso in Algiers a Captain Stephens of Boston, whom commanded a schooner Belonging to Mr William Foster of Boston But unfortunately was captured the 25th of July 1785, & he & his Crew made
Slaves of.

It is Certainly Exceeding strange that 15 unfortunate americans should
be kept in slavery these 4½ years without Receiving any assurances of
Reliefe. Notwithstanding the sundry Petitions we have wrote, and that
the constitution is Ratified full 1 yeare and that American affairs wears a
favourable appearance.

Six of my crew has Died with the pest, and there is at present 15 unfortunate Americans in Captivity, & I Believe it will cost our country 30
thousand Dollars to extricate us from our present unfortunate situation.
It is several years since I seen My Mother but since I have been in captivity I have Received sundry Letters from my aged parent. I have often
heard her talk of you and your Brother and her other friends and Relations the McClanighans & Winslows of Falmouth and Cascobay & Kene-
beck & Dr. [torn] present unfortunate situation of your kinsman. I hope
through youre Influence and Seconded by my Friends in Philadelphia that
Congress will take our situation Into Consideration & Empower the American Ambassadors in Europe to finally Extricate & [the ?] unfortunate
Remnant of their countrymen from slavery.

Dr Sir you will excuse the Liberty I have taken in writeing you but as
I consider you to be the Relations of My mother, I sollicit youre Endea-
vours to Befriend Me & My Brother Sufferers in our present state of
Bondage & adversity. Should I Be Mistaken in supposeing you the Bro-

ther or Relation of My Mother, I trust I shall not gain your Displeasure, But that as youre Countryman & fellow citizen your Humanity towards the unfortunate will induce you to Leave no stone unturned to serve me. I shall Esteem it as a singular favoure in youre writeing me a few Lines please to Direct for me under cover to Monsr D^e Kerzey the french Consul in algiers or to the care of the Spanish cons^l Monsr D^e Las Uaris or to Charles Logie Esqr the British consul, or under cover to William Carmichael Esqr the American Ambassador at Madrid, this Gentleman Deserves my sincere thanks for many favours Rendered Me and my Brother sufferers in times of Impending Danger. America May obtain a peace with Algiers for the sum of 65 thous^d pounds ster & our Redemption Included, that is if the Negotiation is well managed, but america knows but Little of Barbary affairs.

Dr Sir

Your most Obedient

most Humble Servant

RICH^d O BRYEN

Superscribed:

Mr. | Abijah Crane | South End | Boston | North America

THE DE LOTBINIERES.

A BIT OF CANADIAN ROMANCE AND HISTORY.

By I. J. GREENWOOD, A.M., of New York City.

THE evening carillon was trembling on the summer air, and Stockbridge street was all aglow with slanting sunbeams, when I was aroused from musing by my host* of the Red Lion Inn placing in my hand a small roll of time-stained manuscript. " A bundle of old French letters, containing an autograph of Montcalm," he remarked, knowing our congenial tastes, and I, delighted at the prospect of an evening's agreeable occupation, was soon at work over the treasure-trove. How well the trouble of straightening out and arranging the crumpled papers was repaid, the following notes, somewhat extended from memoranda jotted down at the time, may give an idea.

There were in all fourteen letters, evidently part of the family archives of the De Lotbinières, a race which had reached Canada, about 1646, in the person of Louis-Théandre Chartier de Lotbinière, who became " Lieutenant Général Civil et Criminel de la Prévoté de Québec," in which city he was buried Sept. 11, 1690, aged 78. To his earliest progenitor, born about 1320, as we learn from Tanguay, his line of descent ran back through nine preceding generations, as follows: René-Pierre,[9] Alain,[8] Pierre,[7] Alain,[6] Clement,[5] César,[4] Alain,[3] Philippe,[2] and Joseph,[1] of Dijon. Pierre, a son of Clement, born about 1490, and a Councillor to the Parliament of Paris, was the first to adopt the suffix of De Lotbinière, which became the family name in the eighth generation.

Louis-Théandre,[10] who had married at Paris, Aug. 16, 1641, Marie-

* Mr. C. H. Plumb.

Elizabeth d'Amours de Clignancourt, had two children : René- Louis, born 1642, and Marie-Françoise, who was five years younger. The latter married, Oct. 17, 1672, Pierre de Joybert, Seigneur de Marçon et de Soulanges, Commandant en Acadie, and their daughter Louise-Elizabeth, b. Aug. 18, 1673, at the River St. John, Acadie, bapt. in Quebec, June 15, 1675, became the wife, Nov. 21, 1690, of Philippe de Rigaud, Chev. de Vaudreuil, Gov. of Montreal. De Rigaud, subsequently the Marquis de Vaudreuil, was, in 1703, Gov. of New France, and died in 1725, aged 82.

Réne-Louis Chartier de Lotbinière,[11] b. 1642 ; King's Councillor 1674, and, like his father, Lieut.-Gén. Civil et Criminel ; as lieutenant of a militia company of Quebec, he was present, Oct. 17, 1666, when the Sieur de Bois took possession of Andaraque and other posts of the Iroquois ; and as Col. of the Quebec Regt., he was at Fort Frontenac in the summer of 1684, in the rear-guard of the French expedition against the Senecas. He married Jan. 24, 1678, at Quebec, Marie-Madeleine Lambert, and was buried June 4, 1709. Of his sons : Eustache Chartier[12], bapt. Dec. 15, 1688, m. April 14, 1711, Marie-Françoise Renaud, who d. April 25, 1723, aged 30. He had been an Ensign in the troops, been recommended May 6, 1719, by his kinsman, the Governor, to fill a vacancy in the Superior Council, and continued to hold that office until his decease. The vacancy had been caused by the recent death of Claude de Berman, the aged Sieur de la Martinière, Judge, Counsellor, and Lieut.-Gén. Civil et Crim. This latter distinction, held by the Sieur de Lotbinière's family through two generations, had been bestowed by the King upon Martin, Sieur du Lino, against which choice Eustache made bold to protest and apply for the position himself. The reply, being No. 1 of the documents I had the pleasure of examining, is dated Paris, Sept. 1, 1719, and was written by Victor Marie, Duc d'Estrées, Maréchal de France. The services of Lotbinière's father and grandfather, in behalf of their King and the Colony, are acknowledged, but the applicant is admonished not to regard certain offices as family heir-looms ; to endeavor, rather, to render himself worthy of preferment, &c., &c.

After his wife's death, in 1723, the young man turned his mind to more serious occupation ; was ordained a priest, April 14, 1726 ; became Archdeacon and Dean of the Quebec Cathedral, and was there buried Feb. 14, 1749. His youngest child was :

Michel-Alain[13], Chartier de Lotbinière, bapt. April 12, 1723 ; cadet (marine), 1736 ; ensign, 1742 ; made the campaign of Acadie 1746 ; and was Captain 1757. The Gov.-Gen., the Marquis de La Galissonière (the same who afterwards defeated Admiral Byng, before Minorca), writing from Quebec, Oct. 20, 1748, to the Minister of Marine, states that he has employed the Sieur de Lotbinière as assistant engineer. Letters Nos. 2 and 3 were from Galissonière to Lotbinière ; the first, dated Paris, Monday, Sept. 24, 1752, stating that the writer is about sending 1200 livres for the benefit of M. de Lotbinière, M. des Essarts, and M. de Lusignan, and counts upon their standing by each other like good comrades. The other, addressed to M. de L., Royal Engineer at Quebec, is from Paris, Feb. 19, 1754 ; a long, friendly, interesting letter of six pages, touching principally on military matters and the fortifications at Quebec and Louisbourg. The writer also observes that " the mounting for the electrical globe, which you left me, is not sent, because, as you remarked on the paper in which it was wrapped, it was necessary to send, at the same time, a pneumatic machine (air pump), and, as you know, they never have what you want, I thought best to send you instruments which might be of use."

Meanwhile the young engineer had married, and Col. Franquet, who had been at Louisbourg since the summer of 1750, writes him (No. 4) from that point, Jan. 4, 1755, confirming his (Franquet's) recent appointment as Director of Fortifications in North America, and presents his respects to Madam de Lotbinière.

No. 5 is a letter from the Marquis de Vaudreuil, Gov.-Gen. of New France, dated Montreal, Sept. 15, 1756, to " M. de l'otbiniere, ingénieur a Carillon," better known to us as Fort Ticonderoga. The writer assures his kinsman (they were second cousins) that he alone has the principal direction of the works at Carillon, and urges him to press them forward at his best and to the satisfaction of M. le Marquis de Montcalm; that Madam⋅ de Vaudreuil thanks him for his kind remembrance, &c.   Portion of a seal impression in red wax is attached to the letter, being a lion rampant on a plain shield, with a lightly draped winged figure to the left as a supporter, while, pendant from the shield, hangs a military order, consisting of eight cannons joined together as a star.   The writer, Pierre-François, Marquis de Vaudreuil-Cavagnal, b. 1698, was the third son of the former Governor General, to which position he himself attained in 1755; the last to hold that position under the French.

Nov. 2, 1756, Lotbinière applied to the Minister of Marine for the position of Engineer-in-Chief of the Colony, as held by his late father-in-law De Lévy, and some two years later, writing to Marshal de Belle Isle, he says, " I flatter myself, my Lord, that you will be pleased to have the Cross of St. Louis conferred upon me. 'Tis a favor, I dare say, I have merited by the zeal I have evinced on all occasions."   The Marshal's comments upon him as an officer can be seen in the New York Col. MSS., vol. x. 889.

No. 6, from the Marquis de Montcalm, is in answer to a demand for sixty carpenters.   From Portage Camp, August 19, 1757, the Marquis states that he sends what he can from the various regiments, &c.

In No. 7 we have the most interesting manuscript of the series, being the " Continuation of a journal from July, 1758, to M. de Lotbinière's return, Jan. 10, 1761, to Paris," according to the heading.   Unfortunately the twenty-four pages preserved terminate with the 22d of May, 1759.   He had left Carillon, July 15, 1758, he writes, suffering from inflammation of the lungs, brought on by his exertions; but a few months' rest at Quebec, and a milk diet, had about restored him to health.   Rumors were continually reaching them as to the designs of the English for gaining possession of Canada; Louisbourg, &c., are already in the hands of the enemy. Feb. 7th he sets out for Montreal, where he arrives five days later, and, with De Vaudreuil, discusses plans for the approaching campaign; he also learns from the Governor the defensive plan of Lieut.-Col. M. de Pont-le-roy, Engineer-in-Chief for Quebec, a plan which embraces the district from the Falls of Montmorency to the river St. Charles, "not dreaming," says the writer, "of occupying the heights before Quebec, and totally neglecting that portion comprised between Sillery and Les Anses des Mers, deeming it impregnable;" whereas, he informs the Governor, this point should not be overlooked, since he remembers how, as a school-boy, he had scaled these heights rapidly and with no great difficulty.   He then proceeds to unfold his own plan of defence.   Having returned to Quebec, he notes that from the 20th to the 21st of May it froze to the thickness of two crowns. Here he finds the defensive works progressing on all sides, without any special duty having been assigned to himself, according to promise.   The chief engineer " told me, with quite an embarrassed air, that he was much obliged to me, but that he could dispense with causing me any fatigue, three engineers having come to him from France," and yet, a few days later, he sees that work had been given out to several officers of the line, for which they were evidently unfitted; " this proceeding, on the part of M. de pont Leroy, does not surprise me, having seen, from the moment of his arrival in Canada, that he regarded me with jealousy, &c." That a state of ill feeling existed between the parties is further confirmed by Pontleroy's own letters to the Minister of Marine, referred to in the report on Canadian Archives for 1887 (pp. 216 and 271) ; April 24, 1758, he makes complaints against M. de Lotbinière, who evidently thought himself better fitted than M. de Lévy for post of chief engineer. Towards the close of July he finds fault with Lotbinière's work in the construction of Carillon, and, later on, hints at his too lavish expenditure; and, December 1, writes that " M. de Vaudreuil desired to secure the appointment of his relative, M. de Lotbinière, as chief engineer, and he, Pontleroy, when he arrived, was looked upon as an intruder, and difficulties were put in his way. He asks that M. de Vaudreuil and the Intendant be instructed to give him their support in the discharge of his duty."

This friction, to call it by no worse name, continued in the department of Royal Engineers till the enemy cast anchor before their city ; all errors and oversights, so apparent to some, and to which others continued perversely blind, remained uncorrected ; the very heights which had been ignored were scaled, the decisive battle was fought, and five days later, on Sept. 18, 1759, Quebec surrendered, and the English became masters of Canada. The two leaders, Wolf and Montcalm, had both fallen, the one departing victorious and in honor, the other in the bitterness of chagrin and defeat; both sacrifices to a monarch's glory. " Heureux le général, s'il n'eût pas méprisé encore sous les murs de Québec les sages instructions qui lui donna Vaudreuil, il y a un mémoire détaillé des opérations par une officier du génie qui donne droit au Marquis," writes Bibaud, Jeune, in his " Pantheon Canadien," alluding, may we presume, to the missing portion of De Lotbinière's diary.

Returning to France, the Governor was thrown into the Bastille, and, though exonerated from all blame and finally released, died long after, burthened with poverty and years. No. 8 is a letter from his nephew, Le Chev. de Vaudreuil at Rochefort, April 27, 1762, to " M. de Lotbinière, officier du Canada, rue des bons enfans, chez M^{de} Audry, pres de la porte du palais Royal, à Paris." It discusses some money matters; then states that Canadians are arrested daily, as the testimony of all who have returned from that country is wanted; " happy are those who have not been mixed up in any affair of government. I am quite impatient to hear the end of this matter, persuaded that it cannot terminate otherwise than advantageously for my uncle."

Two years later, Feb. 28, 1764, the same party writes from " Paris, rue garnière," to " Mons. de Lotbinière, chez M. M. guinaud négociants, à Londres." This letter, No. 9, states that the Chevalier's brother would return from St. Domingo about June; other matter, of a private nature, is referred to, and M. de L.'s son is mentioned. A small seal in black wax is attached; device same as noted in No. 5, save that the supporters are differently arranged, and that the shield is surmounted with a jewelled coronet of three strawberry leaves, and that the military order is omitted. The brother alluded to was undoubtedly Joseph Hyc. Rigaud de Vaudreuil, Governor of St. Domingo.

As early as 1764 Lotbinière made application to the Lords Commissioners for Trade and Plantations desiring confirmation, in his favor, of two concessions of land, and in 1772 he was in England pressing his claims. One tract, called Alainville, granted him in 1758, by Governor Vaudreuil, lying partly on Lake George, partly on Crown Point River, with a frontage of over four leagues, and a depth of about five; the other tract of similar extent, lay opposite Crown Point, and was purchased in 1763 from the grantee, M. Champagne de Hocquart. These lands at the head of Lake Champlain had been annexed to the Province of New York, soon after the conquest of Canada, and set off to reduced officers of the British army. It is, perhaps, just here that No. 10 of the series comes in connection. It is written from Portmansquare (London), Feb. 6, 1774, by the Count de Belgivioso, who regrets being out when M. de L. called, and invites him to chocolate, next Monday, after 10½ A.M., as a conversation is desirable previous to an interview with the Minister, Lord Rochford.

Finally, Feb. 13, 1776, the Lords of Trade sent their opinion of the subject to the Committee of Privy Council, advising that, by way of compensation, a tract of 115,000 acres be granted the applicant in the Province of Quebec, otherwise he to pursue his claims by due course of law. That the land was accepted, the writer is not certain; his Letters Patent state that, having made a reclamation on the British government, he obtained a pension of 400 guineas, which, at the outbreak of the American Revolution, he gave up and offered his services to France, a step which debarred his ever returning to Canada as an English subject; and that he was, in 1776, sent to Boston on a mission, "which he fulfilled with that zeal which had ever characterized his operations."

Having reached the French colony of St. Pierre de Miquelon, off the coast of Newfoundland, he sailed thence in a schooner, with two domestics and a post-chaise, and arrived, early in November, 1776, at Chatham, on Cape Cod. Proceeding to Boston, he endeavoured to open correspondence with Dr. Franklin, who had sailed for France, and with the President of Congress. He says, "At the time I left France, the commission I accepted of could not be granted without a reserve of disowning me in case things did not succeed in the manner expected," and speaks of himself as "under the double risk of being disowned by your Congress, or by the Court which has secretly employed me, as one who may, and they know can be, of the greatest service to you by his knowledge of war and politics, as well as with the local of this Continent." That he might not be regarded as a presumptious pretender, he continues : "The whole system of defence in that country (Canada), after the defeat of Baron Dieskau, until the close of 1758, was solely my own, and that it ceased to be pursued only in the campaign of 1759, in which the Sieur Pont le Roy, a much older engineer than I, and who arrived in the summer of 1758, determined absolutely, in his mode of defence, to pursue the reverse of all that I had planned, &c." He writes also to his son, then a prisoner-of-war; chides him for espousing the side of England, and would like to take his place, temporarily, and send him to Canada for his mother and sister; adding "all my letters from France give me the title of Marquis. You run no risk in conforming to it."*

He returned to Paris, and No. 11 is a note from M. de Pont le Roy (so signed), about 1779, who writes that M. le Chev. de Lévis doubts not but that M. de L. is certain as to the height of the ramparts of Quebec, and so desires me to ask for him the height of that part &c.

* Force's Am. Archives, 5 S. III., 642–6, 1079–80.

About this time, again in quest of the Cross of St. Louis, M. de Lotbinière wrote to M. de Sartine, Minister of the Marine. In a letter (No. 12) from Versailles, Jan. 21, 1779, the Chev. de Lévis (afterwards Duke and Marshal) informs him that he is likely to get only a polite reply; that he should make out a memoir and sign it, stating his services in detail, and that he (Lévis) will present it to the minister and urge the suit. As Lotbinière favors "the qualification of Marquis, he had better so style himself in his memoir, that the reply sent him may be so addressed. Not to ask for more than one favor at a time, 'twere well to make no mention of the rank of Colonel, and frankly he would never get it, since he had never been employed on any expedition, and I do not see that they are disposed to do anything for Canada."

The next year brings a new minister, in the person of the Marquis de Castries, who, in No. 13, writes M. de Lotbinière, from Versailles, Nov. 14, 1780, thanking him for the complimentary letter on his recent appointment. The minister would like to do something for him, but the times are so unfavorable that it is something more to be wished than hoped for. Perseverance, however, met with its reward at last, and, in recognition of his services and those of his predecessors, Michel-Alaine Chartier de Lotbinière was made a Knight of St. Louis, and raised to the rank of Marquis, by the King of France, June 25, 1784, Letters Patent being filed in Paris, April 21st following; the only case of a native Canadian who attained that title. He died in New York, from yellow fever, in 1799, aged 76.

His wife, whom he married in Quebec, in 1747, was Louise-Madelaine, daughter of Gaspard Chaussegros de Lévy (or De Léry), Engineer of the Marine, and Knight of St. Louis. De Lévy, who died in March, 1756, had a son, Gaspard-Joseph, also an engineer, who, at the age of 32, in September, 1753, married Louise-Martel de Brouage, some seventeen years his junior; this, the first Canadian couple presented at the English Court, drew from his Royal Majesty the complimentary remark that if all Canadian ladies resembled Mme de Lévy, he had indeed made "une belle conquête."

The Marquis's son, who inherited the title upon his father's decease, was Michel-Eustache-Gaspard-Alain Chartier de Lotbinière, born Aug. 31, 1748, who now held the Seigneury and Chateau of Vaudreuil, with the Seigneuries of Rigaud and Beauharnois. He was at first a cadet in the 2d company of artillery, Capt. Azemard de Lusignan, in Canada, and, at the outbreak of the American Revolution, served as a captain at the Blockhouse of St. John: as a prisoner-of-war he had an allowance from Congress of two dollars per week from Nov. 2, 1775.* The last letter of the collection (No. 14) is addressed to him by Gov. Tryon, dated New York, Feb. 28, 1777, 9 A. M.; the Governor presenting his compliments and inviting Capt. Lotbinière to an interview in half an hour: "D'jeuner est pret.— Note Le Governeur sorte de sa maison á dix heure." In July, 1788, Capt. L. was placed by Lord Dorchester on a list of those worthy of recompense for their services, his award being 700 acres in the parish of L'Assomption. During the last war with England he was colonel of the militia of Vaudreuil. He was prominent as a Canadian statesman; was elected to the Chamber of Assembly, and unanimously named speaker in 1793; four years later he was called to the Legislative Council, and it was through his efforts that the French language was retained in the Legislature, and a larger share in the

* The Rev. M. Louis Lotbinière was appointed by Gen. Arnold, in Jan., 1776, as Chaplain to Col. James Livingston's Regt., and, after the retreat from Canada, was continued a Chaplain in the pay of the U. S.

administration of affairs secured to the French Canadians. Dying in 1821, at the age of 73, the male line of the race became extinct. His youngest daughter Julie Christine, b. June, 1810, m. Gaspard-Peirre-Gustave Joly, one of whose sons, M. de Lotbinière Joly, was killed at the assault of Delhi in September, 1857. The family name is still retained in that of a county of 735 square miles, and its seat of justice; Lotbinière having been represented, in 1861, in the Canadian Assembly, by Henry Gustave Joly, b. Dec. 5, 1829, the Premier of 1878, afterwards leader of the opposition, and recently knighted.

The Chateau Vaudreuil, purchased by the first Marquis de Lotbinière in 1767, from his kinsmen (the family of the original founder), became subsequently the College de St. Raphaèl. Destroyed in later years by fire, there was found under the foundation-stone, at the southeast angle, a leaden plate stamped with three fleurs de lys, and bearing this inscription, " Cette pierre a été posée par Dame Louise Elyzabeth de Joybert, femme de Haut et Puissant Seigneur Philippe de Rigaud, Chevalier, Marquis de Vaudreuil, Grand Croix de l'Ordre Militaire de St. Louis, Gouveneur et Lieutenant-Géneral pour le Roi de toute la Nouvelle-France Septentrionale, en 1723, ce 15 Mar." *.

EBEN PARSONS AND FATHERLAND FARM.

By Mrs. Susan E. P. Forbes, of Springfield, Mass.

The following sketch of an old-time Boston merchant and his country home was read before the Historical Society of Old Newbury, at their field-day meeting on Fatherland Farm, August 1st, 1895, and is contributed by the writer to the columns of the Regis-TER, prefaced with a slight description of its locality, and reference to the historical associations which have made it notable in the annals of New England's early days.

Fatherland Farm is situated in the parish of Byfield, Newbury, Essex County, Massachusetts. It contains one hundred and fifty acres, and is about equally divided between tillage and pasturage. The soil is exceedingly rich and fertile, and is entirely free from rocks and stones, which abound in adjacent acres. This farm is a part of the tract of land granted by the General Court of the Colony in 1635, to Richard Dummer and John Spencer, for the pasturage of "net cattel," brought over in Dutch ships by them, to the settlement then being formed in this locality, which bore the Indian name of Quascucunquin, meaning the waterfall. This term was doubtless applied to the territory hereabout on account of there being a natural barricade of rock across the bed of a small river that forms the northern boundary of the farm, over which the fresh water of this stream flows before entering the head of the Parker, a tide-river that winds its way

---

* In the roll of papers were two printed articles; one, a notice of services on Monday, March 19, 1784, at 4 p.m., in the Church of the R. R. P. P. Théatirs, for the benefit of the Enfans-Trouvés; Sermon by the Abbé Rousseau; about to be sent to Dowager Duchess de Cossé-Brissac; the other an Enlistment-Blank, 179 (*), for a private in the Infantry of the United States, during "the existing differences" with the French Republic; to be sworn to before a Justice of the Peace.

in a series of ox-bows through extensive marshes to Plum Island river and the ocean. Between this fall of fresh water and where it flows into the deep basin of the Parker—a few hundred yards from the old farm mansion —a road crosses the river over a wooden bridge, and just here is the little hamlet of Newbury Falls, of which the blanket mill, now owned by Mr. Samuel Williams of Boston, forms the nucleus.

It should be stated that during the same session of court at which the grant was made to Messrs. Dummer and Spencer, the name of Quascucunquin was—by petition of the inhabitants—changed to Newbury, and the little settlement at the junction of the rivers then took the name of Newbury Falls. The structure owned by Mr. Williams occupies the site of the first woolen mill started in America, portions of the machinery of which were made by Schofield Brothers, who came over from Yorkshire, England, in 1793. The carding machines were first put together by them in the stable of "Lord" Timothy Dexter in Newburyport, after which they were set up in the new factory at the Falls, which went into operation in the year 1795.

One of the earliest saw-mills in the country and a grain-mill were built here by Messrs. Dummer and Spencer in 1636, and the first machines for making nails in America was invented and set up at the Falls by Mr. Jacob Perkins. Many other small industries were started during the following century by Paul Pillsbury, a resident of the parish, whose remarkable ingenuity vented itself in the manufacture of improved machinery and shuttles for the mill: a bark-grinder which is said to have been "the prototype of all the bark, corn, coffee and spice mills in use to the present time"; a corn-sheller, a seed-sower, window-fastener and a rotary engine, beside many other implements which have proved of great use to mankind.

But aside from the fact that Newbury Falls was the American Nestor of small mechanical arts, it has a wider fame as the birth-place of the ancestors of Henry W. Longfellow, whose grandfather went forth from the paternal roof in early manhood to found a home in a neighboring state. The old premises are still held by relatives of the late poet bearing his name, but the huge granite horse-block for mounting to saddle and pinion—beneath an ancient and fast decaying elm—is the only visible monument left of those that were in days long gone by.

Newbury Falls is also noted for having been the early home of Judge Samuel Sewell, "the typical Massachusetts Puritan" whose illustrious descendants have graced the pulpit, bench and bar of our beloved Commonwealth through successive generations to the present time. A fragrant souvenir of the old Judge still thrives along the highways and hedges of his boyhood's home, in the wild sweetbrier—transplanted by himself from his native heath in Bishop-Stoke, England, to his farm at Newbury Falls.

Still another association, though of entirely different nature—according to a statement of the late John G. Whittier's to the writer—is attached to this locality, namely, that tradition asserts it to have been at Newbury Falls that the old-time witches were baptized by Satan and took the oath of allegiance to his sable majesty. Whether or not the influence of this legendary act affected the lives of the inhabitants for evil is not known, but since no tragedies have occurred among them, and generations of residents have pursued "the even tenor of their ways," maintaining good reputation, it may be believed that any evil power absorbed by air and water during the transaction was swiftly borne by wind and tide to sea, while that which might have clung to surrounding soil was speedily annulled by the influence of godly men and women who have gone forth from here to become a power for good in the world, and whose memory is an everlasting benediction upon the place of their nativity and earlier life.

Eben Parsons, the founder of Fatherland Farm, was the second son of Rev. Moses Parsons, who was ordained pastor of the Congregational Church in Byfield, Newbury, June 20th, 1745, and who during that summer removed his family from Gloucester to the old parsonage in this parish now occupied by the family of the late Hon. Isaac Wheelwright, in which mansion Eben was born, Feb. 27th, 1746. As a boy he attended the town school until the opening of Dummer Academy in 1763, when he became a pupil of that institution in charge of the famous Master Moody.

It is said of him that after leaving Dummer school he preferred business to the college education which was offered him by his father; and that accordingly he took his clothing in a bundle, and, with his shoes under his arm, started off on foot for Gloucester, declaring that when he had earned money enough to do so he should come back and buy the Dummer farm at Newbury Falls. In Gloucester, Eben Parsons engaged in fishing off the coast of Cape Ann, but soon extended the business, acquiring several vessels of his own, by which he obtained the means to engage largely in commercial pursuits, later on sending his ships to all foreign ports then open to trade. He finally became one of the largest importers in the country, and had the reputation of being in old time parlance,—"a princely merchant."

In May of 1767 Mr. Parsons was married to Mary, daughter of Col. John Gorham of Barnstable, and a few years later he removed to Boston, where he had purchased a large and valuable estate as a home for himself and family. The house was situated on Summer Street, its garden and grounds occupying all the space between what are now Otis and Winthrop places, while his cow pastured over the way on what was called Church Green on account of its being occupied by the edifice of the Unitarian Society which bore that name—"Church Green Society." The narrow passage way just below Devonshire on Summer street was the path to Mr. Parsons' barn, and is the only landmark now remaining of his home there.

In the year 1801, the subject of our sketch being then 55 years of age, carried out his declared intention of returning to his native town and buying the Dummer place. Deeds recorded in Salem court house attest to the fact that the first piece of land purchased by him in connection with this farm, was bought from Richard Dummer and wife under date of Sept. 10th of that year. The next parcels of land were bought from Shubael Dummer and wife and Simeon Danforth and wife, under dates of June 3d and 4th, 1803. Other deeds of land purchased by him are recorded in the same place. The present mansion was built by Mr. Parsons in 1802, as evidenced by the discovery, during late repairs, of coins of that date beneath hearth-stones of the main house and cottage adjoining, which latter was built for a seed house. having originally many small rooms divided into compartments for the storage of farm products in that line.

A humorous description of the raising of the mansion is given by Miss Sarah Ann Emery in her "Reminiscences of a Nonogenarian," which has been substantiated by several aged residents of Newbury, who were present at the memorable scene, some of whom were among those so unceremoniously precipitated into the cellar at the beginning of the musical exercises of the occasion, and who were afterward rewarded by Mr. Parsons for injury to clothing by the gift of silk dress patterns and material for new coats.

The house and other buildings being completed, the owner set about improving the premises by the building of solid walls of hewn stone which was brought in vessels from Cape Ann quarries to Newburyport, and thence transported by gundalows over Parker River to the farm. These walls were built seven feet in height and three feet wide, with a foundation of proportionate strength beneath the surface. Gate-posts of hammered granite were set deep into the earth at all openings in the massive walls, these, and the many-barred wooden gates which swung between, being furnished with wrought iron hinges, latches and staples of gigantic size, secured by mammoth padlocks, the keys to which were each attached to a large slip of brass or wood on which was inscribed the name of the particular gate to which it belonged. These keys were kept in a portable mahogany closet made for the purpose, and which is now in the possession of the writer, as also some of the ancient, ponderous keys, though the gates to which they were the open sesame—like the strong hands that operated them—have long since crumbled to decay. Well-curbs and troughs were constructed from the same staunch material as the walls and gate posts, these being fastened into shape by huge bolts of copper soldered into openings drilled in the stone for the purpose.

Meanwhile improvements on the land were going on, and during the years of 1808 and 1809 a marshy tract on the northern side of the farm was reclaimed, or manufactured into a fertile field by means of a very stout wall, impervious to water, being constructed along the margin of the Falls River at this point, and the entire space of bog filled in with stones and gravel, topped with loam, all of which ingredients were respectively drawn from neighboring premises by ox-team, and spread into level space by hand labor. The name of this new-made portion of the farm was Sewall's Point, as given in old letters of Mr. Parsons to his foreman, Jeremiah Allen, under whose supervision the work was carried on. The owner was then residing in his Boston home, which was not given up until after the death of his wife, Sept. 10th, 1810. But frequent visits were made by himself and family to this country place, which, out of regard for his father's memory and love for his native town he had named Fatherland Farm.

The journeys to Byfield were sometimes made by stage over the old turnpike, but more frequently in his own family coach, with driver and footman in the old-time livery. These arrivals created not a little sensation among the inhabitants of this rural district, as aged citizens of Newbury have enjoyed recalling and describing to the writer; and marvellous tales they tell of boxes and bags of silver coin brought over the road by oxen, with which to recompence the army of artizans of various kinds employed upon the premises.

However this may have been we have reason to believe that vast sums of money were expended by the owners to bring this goodly heritage into the high state of cultivation and beauty in which it was left for the occupancy of the next tenant and heir. The record for 1814 shows that the farm taxes of Eben Parsons were $744.20, his real estate being valued at $16,400, and his personal property at $80,000. At this period Mr. Parsons was a resident of Byfield, having removed hither soon after the decease of his wife. He was deeply interested in agriculture, and was a large contributor in many ways to the advancement of that science, using his commercial facilities in aid of this by the importation of fine breeds of cattle, sheep and swine, for the improvement of American stock, and by bringing from other countries various kinds of seeds, grain and grasses, as well as scions from foreign fruit and ornamental trees and shrubs.

He was fond of experiment in matters relating to farming, and while his efforts in this way might not all have been satisfactory to himself, they were in many instances highly successful, results being such as to encourage repetition.

Mr. Parsons was a man with ideas far ahead of the time in which he lived, and his opinions upon subjects connected with the pursuits in which he was engaged were often sought by men of the highest standing in commercial and agricultural affairs. Though not so renowned as his younger brother, the eminent jurist and chief justice of the commonwealth, yet he was possessed of great ability, and was probably as useful to the community in other ways as Theophilus was on the bench.

Eben Parsons died in his country home Nov. 2, 1819, at the age of 74 years. His remains, with those of other members of the family, rest in a tomb in the old Byfield cemetery, which was erected a year later by his son Gorham, agreeably to his father's intention.

Of thirteen children born to Mr. and Mrs. Eben Parsons, this son was the only one who survived the years of childhood. Gorham Parsons was born in Gloucester, July 27, 1768. His early years were spent in that town and in Boston, excepting the time he was a pupil at Dummer Academy. In April of 1790 he was married to Sarah, daughter of Capt. Thomas Parsons of Newburyport. After residing a few years in Boston he purchased a large and valuable estate in Brighton and made his home there, embellishing the place with lavish hand. Having inherited his father's fondness for agriculture he spared no pains in the cultivation of his farm, and in the production of choice fruits. He also continued the importation of fine cattle, sheep and swine. After the death of his father he kept up the Byfield farm in addition to the Brighton estate, but continued to reside at the latter place until after the death of Mrs. Parsons who preferred the home there to Fatherland Farm. She passed away on the 8th of December, 1837, soon after which event that property was sold and Mr. Gorham Parsons came to Byfield to reside. Being afflicted with the gout in the last years of his life, he was unable to carry out many of his plans for improvements on the farm, but his interest in all matters pertaining to agriculture flagged not until the end. That he was a valued member of the Massachusetts Agricultural Society, many letters and documents from its officials attest, while numerous and valuable prizes awarded for fine specimens of live stock and various agricultural products affirm the success of his efforts in that direction.

Neither father nor son aspired to the holding of state or town office, though a document exists bearing the seal of the Commonwealth and signed by His Excellency John Brooks, under date of Feb. 23, 1819, appointing Ebenezer Parsons to be a Justice of the Peace in the County of Essex.

Gorham Parsons died in the Byfield home in the month of September, 1844, at the age of 76 years. As the union of himself and wife was not blessed with living offspring, Fatherland Farm was given by will of the owner, in 1842, to a grand-nephew of his wife, who was also his own namesake, Gorham Parsons Sargent, then a minor, and the son of Hon. Winthrop Sargent of Philadelphia, Pa., who had, a few years previously, removed his family from that city to the farm, in order to care for Mr. Parsons in his declining days.

The place was appreciatively occupied by the Sargents until the spring of 1862, when it passed into the hands of Benjamin F. Brown of Waltham, who, in July following, sold it by public auction to his nephew, Benjamin

B. Poole of Newbury, under whose fifteen years of occupancy the premises suffered deterioration to a lamentable degree. From this condition of things the next owner, Jacob B. Stevens of Peabody, who came into possession of the place, by purchase, in the autumn of 1877, sought earnestly to retrieve the old estate, but his ability not being equal to the desire in this direction, he decided to part with the property, and thus, in October of 1881, Fatherland Farm came into the possession of one of the same blood, if not of the same name as its original founder; one to whom the old place is doubly dear from the association of visits made to it in earlier years, when, to her childish fancy, it seemed a very Paradise on earth, and from the fact that, in later years, it was a love gift to her from the one nearest and dearest to her in life.

NOTE.—Mrs. Alexander B. Forbes, the present owner of Fatherland Farm, is a direct descendant of Rev. Moses Parsons, through his daughter Snsanna. Mr. Forbes is a native of Brechin, Scotland, and came to this country in 1857 to take a position in the store of George Turnbull & Co. in Boston, where he remained until the spring of 1866, when, with a brother clerk, also a Scotchman, he went into business for himself in Springfield, under the firm name of Forbes & Smith, but which was in a few years changed to Forbes & Wallace. This firm was one of the founders of the Syndicate Trading Company of New York City, which has established agencies in the leading cities in Europe, and whose members are prominent dry-goods merchants in the principal cities of this country.

Mr. Forbes has expended a great amount of money in the efforts to restore the old farm to its pristine state of elegance, though his tastes have led him to embellish the place with a stud of beautiful equine specimens, rather than the cattle, sheep and swine which Mr. Parsons delighted in raising. He has also built extensive greenhouses for the cultivation of favorite flowers, while still keeping up the old-time garden terraces of bloom "lying sunward," as described by T. Buchanan Read in a local poem. But the principal attraction of the place lies in the old-time mansion itself, with its setting of extensive green lawn on all sides, shaded with lofty elms, maples, accasia and evergreen trees, which impart an atmosphere of rest and enjoyment, such as no modern structure in never so elegant surroundings can afford.

REMEMBRANCE MADE BY SIR NATHANIEL BACON.

Communicated by Capt. CHARLES HERVEY TOWNSHEND, of New Haven, Ct.

THE following abstract was made by me in pencil from the original at Henden, Midsx, Eng., April 8th, 1886, at the house of Wm. Ansel Day, Esq., Solicitor for the Marquis Townshend, and as the original was in Sir Nathaniel Bacon's handwriting and the name *Whiting* appearing, it occurred to me that I had read somewhere how the Rev. Samuel Whiting of Lynn, Mass., had been *wronged by a forged Deed* before his coming to New England, and so made this abstract for future reference.

"Remembrance made by Sir Nathaniel Bacon of Stifkey Norfolk Knt." No date.*

* He was buried at Stifkey, Norfolk, Nov. 7th, 1622.—c. h. t.

" Petition from Thomas Acheson against John Johnson, Guardian for *John Dean* against whom the Petition to the King was drawn." All in Sir N. B.'s hand as follows.   C. H. T.

" A remembrance of things that passed at Saxthorp Norf. at the meeting of Sir Charles Hayden, Sir Nathaniel Bacon Kts. and others."

It seems that Thomas Acheson and his brother Robert Acheson [Query, is the name Atkinson?] disposed of a messeauge and 25 acres of land in Hauworth of which Thomas Acheson was Lesee; *to one Whiting* by means of a Deed forged by Parson Flegg (minister), Robert Acheson having no interest in the house whatsoever. An attempt to make Whiting produce the Deed in court for inspection was made. Whiting assigned the house to John Dean, who was committed for contempt for refusing to produce the Deed in court for such a use.

[The names Henry Whiting and Water or Walter Whiting appear, but the papers show they were not the Whiting mentioned. There were several ministers mentioned in the original remembrance.*   C. H. T.]

EZEKIEL ROGERS, ROGER WILLIAMS AND JANE WHALLEY.

George Alan Lowndes, Esq., M.A., of Barrington Hall, Hatfield, Broad Oak, Essex, England, contributed in 1878-9 to the Transactions of the Essex Archæological Society, an article entitled " The History of the Barrington Family." The article appeared in the New Series of the Transactions, vol. i., pp. 251-273, and vol. ii., pp. 3-64.

Joan, the wife of Sir Francis Barrington, the first baronet of the name, was the daughter of Sir Henry Cromwell and aunt of the Protector Cromwell. Much information about the prominent Puritan families, found in Mr. Lowndes's articles will interest New England readers. We copy the following :—

Lady Barrington's sister Elizabeth married Mr. Hampden of Hampden, and was the mother of the celebrated John Hampden. A few of her letters to her sister are preserved, and one from her son to Sir Thomas Barrington, dated June 9th, 1643, nine days before he received the wound, of which he died.

Lady Barrington had much correspondence with Clergymen of the Puritan party, and the way in which they wrote to her pressing their opinions upon her, inquiring into the state of her soul, asking her to probe her conscience, admonishing, chiding, and sometimes encouraging her, is very striking.

One of these gentlemen, Mr. Ezekiel Rogers, to whom Sir Francis Barrington had presented the living of Rowley in Yorkshire, was cited by the Archbishop of York, for some ecclesiastical fault, and had to give up his

---

*Among the names in other Bacon and Townshend papers, Scottow, Coke, Newgate, Symonds, Man, Buttolph, Goodwin, Cobbet, King, Dean, Firman, Doughty, Mason, Phillips, Yates, Whiting, Whitfield, Ramsey, Palphry, Goddard, Burwell.

living, and he soon afterwards went to New England.   He had been Chaplain to Sir Francis's family at Hatfield, and after he was settled at Rowley, he frequently wrote to Lady Barrington, and after a short time stated his fears, that she did not attend, as diligently as she ought to do, to the state of her soul.   He drew up and pressed upon her, some rules for self examination, and pointed out to her also, how, and for what she ought to pray. He further insinuated, that since he had left Hatfield, he feared she did not confine herself, as she was bound to do, if really wishing to be one of God's elect, to the company and conversation of those who were God's known servants.   And, he must say, that he had observed, when paying a visit at Hatfield, that she was much wanting to herself in the choice of neighbours to associate with, and of acquaintances with whom she found intimacies. Many being persons who could not help her to find the Lord, or who, by experience could tell her what God had done to them for the salvation of their souls.   That she ought to discard such acquaintances who would never be profitable to her either by precept or example.

When Mr. Rogers left Rowley, he wrote to Sir Thomas Barrington, requesting that he might name the person to succeed him in the living, and that if Sir Thomas would do so, he knew a way by which a bargain might be made, keeping clear of the law against simony, that he, Rogers, might enjoy the greater parts of the emoluments of the living for his life.   To this Sir Thomas would not accede, and then Mr. Rogers accused him of declining to do so, merely that he might provide for a young man, a Mr. White, who had been tutor in Sir Thomas's family, and who, Rogers added, " was litale worthy of any such preferment," and who had not half the claims upon Sir Thomas that he himself had.

After his arrival in America, in his letters to Sir Thomas Barrington, he accused him of withholding from him the sum of £200, which he stated had been promised to him when he left Rowley, not for giving up the living, but for repayment of money he said he had laid out on alterations to the parsonage house there.   On Sir Thomas demurring to make this payment, Rogers pressed most strongly for it, declaring that it was his right, as it had been positively promised to him.   And that he was ready to make oath of the fact, adding however that he had not any witness to corroborate him, as the promise was made in a private conversation, and saying he wondered how that a man of quality would deny what was due, concluding thus—

Ah Sir, you are now about censuring the Hierarchy for persecuting of us : and shall I suffer in this way by my frend, and doe you think this faire towards (I say not a frend of 33 years standing) but an Exile for Jesus Christ ? if you that are Reformers, be not exact in yor walking with God in holiness and Righteousnes, my feares for you will be increased, Sir, my God hath kept me in all my dayes to my gray haires, & I beleeve I shall not want, but take you heed, you give me not cause to complane to God of you, for I beleeve he will heare.

He continued this strain of violent accusations even after Sir Thomas Barrington's death, in letters to Mr. Kendall, the steward at Hatfield, and appealed to him as to the justice of his claim; this claim, however Mr. Kendall never allowed to be due.   The whole of this correspondence is interlarded with religious sentences and quotations from the Bible.

Another Clergyman, Roger Williams, chaplain to Sir William Masham, paid his addresses to a neice of Lady Barrington's, and wrote to her Ladyship on the subject.   She objected to the marriage, and Mr. Williams soon after addressed to her one of the most extraordinary letters in the whole collection.   Some extracts from it are here given.

Mr. Lowndes gives extracts from this letter, but as the whole of it and the other letter referred to have been printed in the REGISTER, we omit it. They were furnished by Mr. Lowndes in 1889, and were printed in the number for July of that year, pages 316-320. We did not know of this article then or we should have referred to it.

This gentleman's zeal (sharpened probably by his disappointment) seems entirely to have overmastered his discretion, and Lady Barrington (as might be expected) was so greatly offended by this letter, that it was a long time before she would see or have any intercourse with Mr. Williams, although both Sir William and Lady Masham wrote to her on the subject trying to excuse him, and stating that it was only his ardent love of religion that made him address her as he had done. The two gentlemen above named are the most remarkable of Lady Barrington's clerical correspondents. There are many letters from other divines written in a most earnest, zealous and true Christian spirit.

Mr. Lowndes gives letters from her brother-in-law, Richard Whalley, father of Maj.-Gen. Edward Whalley, a member of the High Court of Justice and a signer of the death warrant of Charles I. The wife of Richard Whalley was Frances Cromwell, a sister of Lady Barrington. "Mrs. Whalley, at her death," says Mr. Lowndes, "left a large family, the eldest of which was [her] daughter Mary who was brought up under the care of her aunt, and afterwards married Sir Thomas Eliot. A younger sister, Jane, lived with Lady Barrington, and married a clergyman by the name of [William] Hook, who had the living of Upper Clatford in Hampshire. She often wrote to Lady Barrington, her letters are curious and amusing." One of these is as follows :—

To the hon^ble and my much
    esteemed Lady, the Lady
    Johan Barrington
    at Hatfield Broad
    Oake this be   d^d
Good Madam,
        It doth much rejoyce my harte to heare that it hath pleased God to recouever your Lady Ship of your great could for the which I desire as my duty bindes me unto you to give God most humble and harty thankes. Madam I would not have been thus long ere I had retourned a leter of true thankfullnes had I not been preuented by weaknes and sicknes, for when good man King was gone to hatfield at that time, Mr. Hook and I were scared in the night (as we thought by theues) that Mr. Hook lost his voyce that I thought would never com againe, and myselfe toke such a frite that I was fane to keepe my bed two dayes together—but now it has pleased God to reueale unto us the author of our frite which was our maide in letting in young fellowes into the house at unseasonable howers to riot with them both with our beare and bread; indede we did little suspect her because she came up to help us to call out theues. I thank God that she is gon for I have since her departure saued a peck of meale a weeke besides other tinges.

good madam, I give unto your Ladi Ship my most humble and hearty thankes for so much linnin received from you by William King, i did little thinke to have received such a larg extent of your Ladishipes loue. I confes that I have com short of deserving any thing, good madam I beseech you pray for me for I am brout very low through the hand of God, my ague dos yet contingu and begins to renew its strength, oh that it may please God to renew my inward graces of his holy Spirit in me which is more worth than x thousand worldes. I must be fane to cut of before I am willing, becase I am troubled with a grevious pane in my back. I am exceeding glad to hear of your Ladi ships health, I pray God of his mercy to contingu it my pore prayers shall alluaie be for the same.

I remaine

Your pore unworthy servant

JANE HOOK.

Mrs. Jane Hooke and her husband came to New England. He was the first pastor of the church at Taunton, in Plymouth colony. He left there about 1644 and became a colleague of Rev. John Davenport at New Haven. Mrs. Hooke returned to England in 1654, and her husband followed in 1656, and became chaplain to Cromwell. Two of his sermons are reprinted in Emery's Ministry of Taunton. There is good reason for thinking that Jane Whalley was the neice of Lady Barrington, whose hand was sought by Roger Williams. [See REGISTER, vol. xlv., pages 70-81.]

Mrs. Hooke's brother, Maj.-Gen. Edward Whalley, and his son-in-law, Col. William Goffe, both regicides, found a refuge in New England, a few years after she left these shores. Their story is well known.

DORCHESTER, MASS., WARNINGS FROM THE TOWN, FROM ORIGINAL PAPERS.

Copied by FRANCIS E. BLAKE, Esq., of Boston.

1725

May   8,   Clark Frisell at house of Edward Wiat.
July 27,   Sarah Lobkin at "ye Ministerial House."
           Sarah Knop (Knapp?) widow "often at house of Joseph Maudsley."

1726

April 11, Peter Warren, house of Ralph Pope. (late of Milton)
May 16,   Francis Negro & Ziporah his wife, house of Benjamin Everenden.
May 16,   John Stebbins and wife, house of Capt. Isaac Royal.
May 16,   Sarah Green wife of Joseph Green "a souldier at Castle William" house of Capt. Oliver Wiswell.
           Elizabeth Anderson, house of Jonathan Chandler.
           George Parterick, house of John Cox Senior.

Aug. 31,   Solomon Hewes notified Selectmen that Jonathan Chadock of
           Lyme " is come into Mr. Bats his house with his famly a wife
           and four small children they have not so much as a bed to ly
           on or pot or kettle or anything."—" They belong to Dorches-
           ter! that house was not set of to Wrentham."

Oct. 25   Constable was ordered to carry Jonathan Chadock
           with his family out of the town and deliver them to the Con-
           stable of the next town " in the way toward the town whence
           they Properly belong."

Sept. 8, Thomas Mitchel " on the 5th of August last " went to live with
           George Payson. Certified by Payson.

1727
Jan. 26,   Philip Gray & wife Hannah, house of Jonathan Chandler.
Feb. 16,   Thomas Wood, house of Jonathan Capen.
Feb. 20,   Elizabeth Wheelwright, house of Samuel Capen, Jr.
Feb. 20,   Ebenezer Dunton, house of Jacob Royal.
July 8,   Peter Warren, house of Samuel Robinson.
July 8,   John Miller and wife Margaret, house of John Stiles.
July 18,   David Rice, house of Samuel Robinson.
Oct. 4,   Lydia Maccume, house of Francis Price.
Dec. 30,   William Coyle and wife Elizabeth, house of James Barber.

1730
Nov. 20,   John Jackson and wife, house of John Beighton.

1731
May 6,   Elizabeth Chamberlain, house of William Weeks.

1733
Mch. 19,   Elizabeth Ward wife of William Ward and her family, house of
           John Bird.
Mch. 19,   John Stroaheen and family, house of John Stiles.
Mch. 16,   Mercy Shaw and daughter Mercy, widow of Joseph, house of
           Edward Capen.

1735
Mch. 29,   John Perry, house of Hezekiah Meroth.
Mch. 29,   Sarah Marshall, house of Nicholas Williams.

1736
April 6,   Roger Wilson, house of Enoch Wiswell.

1737
June 21,   Stephen Choate and family, house of John Cox.
Dec. 20,   John Mackfadden and wife.

1738
Jan. 19,   Thomas Trott, Jr. wife and family.
Jan. 22,   Joseph Parsons and wife.
June 26,   Elizabeth Cock.
Oct. 27,   Alice Knight.
Oct. 27,   Archibald Mumcrief wife and family. May 8, 1739 " constable
           ordered to take them to Rox. where they belong."

1739
Feb. 25,   John Glover, Jr.

1740

Jan. 19, John Evans, house of Benjamin Merifield. (Feb. 24 the constable could not find him.)

Jan. 19, Jane Jucee, house of Zechariah Trescott.

Nov. 24, Joseph Parsons, house of Robert Field. Mch. 28, 1741 he refused to depart and constable was ordered to convey him to Roxbury and thence to Boston where he belonged.

Nov. 24, Katherine Roke and children, house of Benjamin Everenden.

Nov. 24, Mary Marks, house of John White.

1741

Jan. 3, Benjamin Jordan, Jr., house of Samuel How.

Sept. 25, Mary Clark wife of Samuel Clark and children, house of Sarah Bishop.

1742

Jan. 7, Gurnel Price wife and family, house of Mary Plymton.

Jan. 7, Mary Jones, house of Joshua Sever.

April 28, Mary Perkins, house of Samuel Sever.

June 14, Stillbole alias Lucum Minot, house John Beighton.

1743

April 5, Mary Jones of Boston, house of Ebenezer Withington.

July 6, Rebecca Whitemore of Charlestown, house of Ebenezer Maudsley.

1745

Dec. 7, Elisabeth Baset of Boston, house of John Bradley, Jr.

NOTES AND QUERIES.

NOTES.

Hon. JAMES WALKER AUSTIN.—The *Boston Evening Transcript* of October 30, 1895, the day after the funeral of Judge Austin—whose necrology will be found in this number, pages 82–83—contains the following tribute to him:—

"After religious services at his late residence yesterday [Oct. 29] the mortal part of our dear friend, James Walker Austin, was laid to rest in the cemetery at Forest Hills. We shall behold his face no more, nor be welcomed by his cordial smile, but the memory of his virtues and of his useful life will ever be sweet and precious.

In every relation of his long and active life he was an example to be imitated and followed. Sincerity, truthfulness and frankness spoke in every accent of his voice, in the pressure of his hand, in his manly and gentle spirit. His affections, when once placed, were deep and lasting. His charity of thought and feeling and act seemed instinctive, but it rested on solid and enduring principles.

No one who knew him intimately in public or in social life could ever doubt that he was a man of positive opinions, or that he had any hesitancy, when occasion required, in expressing them; but he never unduly pressed his own views, and was eminently tolerant of the opinions, and even the prejudices, of his associates. While no man loathed selfishness, deceit, or treachery more than he, he condemned the act and pitied the offender. He avoided controversy, and strove to be a peacemaker.

After more than twenty years of acquaintanceship—for many years seeing him almost daily—the writer of these lines does not recall an instance of hearing Judge Austin utter a censorious remark upon any man or woman. And it is said that this temper and manner characterized him through his entire career—in his boyhood days, at the university, at the bar, on the bench, and in all the various associations of his life,—public, social and domestic.

But who can adequately express in words the prompt and unfailing sympathy he manifested for every form of woe and suffering? To many hearts surcharged with sorrow his ready and tender ministries have been a source of hope and courage, of comfort and of strength.

In his biographical sketch of his father, Hon. William Austin, prefixed to a volume of 'Literary Papers' of the last named, published in 1890, he says: 'My father died in my boyhood, and now, after fifty years, his pleasant smile, his kind heart, and the light of his countenance are still living memories.' Truly, the father was reproduced in the son.

He was, indeed, a rare man, and the world is poorer now that he has left us.

ALBERT H. HOYT."

GOD SIFTED A WHOLE NATION.—William Stoughton, in his Election Sermon, April 29, 1668, entitled "New England's True Interest," printed at Cambridge in 1670, uses this striking figure of speech, " *God sifted a whole Nation that he might send choice Grain over into this Wilderness.*" It has often been quoted. But when and by whom was attention first drawn to it? It may interest our readers to see the whole of the paragraph in which it occurs. We quote from pages 16 of the first edition and 19 of the second; it is as follows:

" And then in the last place, As to *New-Englands first wayes;* what glorious things might here be spoken, unto the praise of free-grace, and to justifie the Lords Expectations upon this ground? Surely God hath often spoke concerning His Churches here, and in *Jer.* 2. 2. *I remember the kindness of thy youth, &c.* O what were the open Professions on the Lords people that first entred this Wilderness? How did our Fathers entertain the Gospel, and all the pure institutions thereof, and those Liberties which they brought over? What was their Communion and Fellowship in the Administrations of the Kingdome of Jesus Christ? What was the pitch of their Brotherly love of their Zeal for God and his Wayes, and against wayes destructive of Truth and Holiness? What was their Humility, their Mortification, and their Exemplariness? How much of Holiness to the Lord was written upon all their wayes and transactions? God sifted a whole Nation that he might send choice Grain over into this Wilderness."

NICHOLAS BROWN.—In volume II. of the manuscripts of the Rhode Island Historical Society are several papers relating to Captain Thomas Cheney's company, raised in Massachusetts for the expedition against Canada. The paper, numbered 364, is entitled: " A State of the Pay of the Non-Commission Officers & Private Men of Capt Thomas Cheney's Company in the Regiment of Foot of wch the Honble Brig^r Genl Dwight is Colonel, rais'd in the Province of the Massachusetts Bay for His Majesty's Service for an Expedition against Canada in 1746, & dismissed from said service 31 Octo^r 1747," which precedes a list of the names of the soldiers, the number of days' service and each man's full pay. The names are as follows:—

George Watkins, Saml Scott, Andrew Stephens, William Chub, sergeants; Nath. Williams, Samuel Loomis, Aaron Ashley, Philip Bacon, corporals; George Harris, Cotton Fletcher, drum^{rs}; John Allen, Joseph Altenson, Samuel Bryan, Nicholas Brown, William Bancroft, Jonathan Ballard, Nathaniel Bacon, Abraham Bass, David Bishop, John Church, Isaac Corbin, Jonathan Church, Jabez Corbin, Stephen Coller, Stephen Corbin, Eliphalet Carpenter, Abel Drake, Samuel Dewey, Samuel Davison, Nathan Davis, Benjn Dike, Josiah Davis, William Edmonds, Azariah Ferry, John Franklin, Joshua Gary, Ebenezer Gale, Jonathan Gleason, Ebenezer Holden, William Hodges, Armour Hamilton, Simeon Hitchcock, William Halley, Thomas Higgins, Joseph Hall, Elisha Hatch, Samuel Hains, Benajah Hall, John Hallowell, Benjamin Harris, Benjamin Howes, Benjamin Hide, Nathan^l Harrington, Samuel Jackson, Daniel Jackson, Ebenezer Jaques, Robert Keyes, William Loomis, Aaron Loomis, John Lafelen, John McDaniel, John McLain, Peter Marshall, James Maceright, William Man, William Mullin, William Negro, Cuffe Negro, Samuel Negro, Jonathan Olds, John Perkins, Christopher Perkinson, Gideon Pratt, Samuel Pegan, John Polley, John Rolfe, Paul Rich, Ephraim Rice, John Richardson, Benj[a] Robertson, Elisha Spencer, Benoni Sacket, Ephraim Stiles, Ephraim Smith, Joseph Sweatman, Samuel Stevens, Benj[a] Sacket, Thomas Stevens, Junr., Ebenezer Sayward, John Stacey, Steven Stringer, Benj[a] Scott, John Turner, Elijah Town, John Vene, Thomas Webster, Samuel Warfield, William Wakefield, John Woodberry, Joseph Wait.

Can any one inform me who is the Nicholas Brown in the above list? The name is the same as that of my paternal great-grandfather, born in Providence in 1729. He lived there all his life, and I can find no mention of his military service, but think it possible that in view of the great interest felt throughout the colonies in the war against the French he may have joined a Massachusetts company. I shall be very grateful to any one who can offer me any suggestions or aid me in establishing the identity of this Nicholas Brown.

Providence, R. I. JOHN NICHOLAS BROWN.

YALE.—Savage says that the widow Yale, who married Gov. Theopolis Eaton, was a daughter of Bishop Moreton of Chester. Said bishop died at the age of 93 without children, and was never married. Yale married daughter of Bishop Lloyd of Chester; his widow married Governor Eaton.

33 West 32d Street, New York. BYAM K. STEVENS.

INGALLS ANCESTRY.—In the opening pages of the History of Lynn, Mass., by Alonzo Lewis and James R. Newhall, appears the following: "The first white men known to have been inhabitants of Lynn were *Edmund Ingalls* and his brother *Francis Ingalls.*" "A record preserved in the family of the former says, 'Mr. Edmund Ingalls came from Lincolnshire, in England, to Lynn, in 1629.'" As this Edmund Ingalls was one of my ancestors, I have been desirous of learning something more concerning HIS ancestry than is conveyed in the above. When in England this last summer, I spent a month in genealogical research, and obtained a considerable amount of information concerning a number of New England families from whom I am descended; information that has not been published in any records that I have seen, and which I conclude is not generally known. I went to Lincoln, and in searching through the old wills in the probate court attached to Lincoln Cathedral, I came upon the will of *Robert* Ingalls of Skirbeck, undoubtedly the father of the above Edmund and Francis. I consider this to have been a fortunate find, as it conclusively certifies that they came from Lincolnshire, as stated in the History of Lynn, but also gives the continued line in England, and the place from whence they came. The will is as follows :—

"In ye name of God, Amen. I, Robert Ingolls of Skirbeck, quarter of Skirbeck, in the County of Lincoln, yeoman, being sick of body but of good and perfect memorie, &c., &c. I give and bequeath unto Elizabeth my wife during her natural life, &c. After her decease to Edmund my eldest sonne who was lawfully begotten. And for want of issue after Edmund's death to Robert, my second sonne, & for want of issue after his death to ffrancis my youngest sonne & failing issue to the natural heirs of me Robert Ingolls for ever. I give Robert Ingolls £20, and I give ffrancis Ingolls £30, both one year after my decease. I give my maid servant Anne Cleasbie £5, and to all of Henry Cleasbie's children one ewe lamb. To every one of Cousin Henry's children one ewe lamb. I give to my brother Henry a black fleeced cowe. I give to the poor of Skirbeck 10 shillings. I give one half of the balance to Elizabeth my wife during her natural life & then all to Edmund to whom I leave one half at once." Wife Elizabeth & sonne Edmund are appointed Executors. Wm. Shinfold & Robt. Harrison are appointed Supervisors of the Will and he gives them 2s. 6d. each for their pains. The will is dated 12th of July 1617, and is signed Robert Ingolls his mark. The above is only partially an exact copy, avoiding needless repetition and such matter that was of little interest.

The children of Edmund were: 1st, Robert (named after his grandfather, whose will is above); 2d, Elizabeth; 3d, Faith; 4th, John; 5th, Sarah; 6th, Henry (named after his great uncle, named in his grandfather's will); 7th, Samuel; 8th, Mary; 9th, Joseph. I am descended through Henry, the 6th child, and Mary Osgood; then through Capt. Samuel Ingalls and Mary Watts; then through John Haseltine of Chester, N. H., and Mary Ingalls; then James Haseltine of Haverhill, Mass., and Abigail Mooers (sister of Gen. Mooers of Revolutionary fame); and then John Haseltine of Philadelphia and Haverhill, and Elizabeth Stanley Shinn. Can any one give me any information concerning the ancestry of Mary Watts, who married Capt. Samuel Ingalls? Another will which I should have included in this article is that of *Henry Ingall*, dated June 1st, 1555. In it he gives to his wife Johan. He also wills that his youngest children shall have every one £10, which was left to them (probably in the will of an earlier ancestor, which as yet I have not been able to find). If any die before coming of lawful age that share to be divided amongst the rest. Gives to the maintenance of the high altar, 12d. The balance of his effects to be divided amongst his six children. Joan, wife, executrix. Names a sonne James, and brother-in-law Thos. Wytton.

1416 Chestnut Street, Philadelphia. CHARLES F. HASELTINE.

QUERIES.

ATWELL—MAINE.—I am anxious to obtain information of John Atwell and John Maine, settlers at Casco Bay between 1630 and 1640. I wish the maiden name of wife and names of children of John Atwell Sr. of Casco Bay, 1640; and of John Maine of Casco Bay, 1640. I wish also the name of husband of widow Hatwell, or Atwell, Casco Bay, 1657, who later married Richard Martine.

15 East 49th Street, New York City. FRANCIS H. MARKOE, M.D.

THOMAS WHITE admitted to the church at Charlestown, March 22, 1668; married Nov. 17, 1663, Mary the daughter of William Frothingham who came from Yorkshire, Eng., in 1630; died Sept. 30, 1716, in 80th yr. g. s., so he was born about 1636. Children: *Thomas*, b. Oct. 15, 1664; m. Sarah Rand. *William*, b. Sept. 12, 1667; m. Mercy ———. *Samuel*, b. Oct. 24, 1669; m. Anne ———. *Elizabeth*, b. Feb. 28, 1671; m. Joseph Sweetser. Any information relating to him previous to his appearance in Charlestown would be greatly appreciated.

A. H.

PERRY IRISH.—Information of the ancestry of Perry Irish, who was a soldier in the War of 1812. Enlisted at Rensselaerville, N. Y., Aug. 24, 1812. Was married to Amanda Farwell at Murray, N. Y., in 1817. He died at Murray, N. Y., Jan. 17, 1841. When was he born? Who were his parents? M. C. C.

WINN.—Information wanted of the ancestry of John Winn, birth unknown, died Jan. 8, 1827, near Newburgh, N. Y. Where was he born? Who were his parents? He had two sons,—perhaps others—Isaac and Steven. Isaac was born April 4, 1791. Where was he born? He died near Satten, N. Y. Isaac married Elizabeth Smith of Montgomery, N. Y. She died at the house of her daughter Mrs. Louis Rhodes, at Milton, N. Y., Jan. 8, 1835. Who were Elizabeth Smith's parents? M. C. C.

ALLEN.—Information wanted of the ancestors of Benjamin Allen of Charlestown, No. 4. He married Peggy Spofford (or Spafford) daughter of Capt. John Spofford, one of the earliest settlers of Charlestown. The children of Benjamin and Peggy (Spofford) Allen were: *Eunice*, born Aug. 4, 1753; married ——— Rogers of Orford. *Olive*, b. Jan. 5, 1755; m. Simon Church. *Lucy*, b. March 28, 1758; m. Walter Geer. *Asa Spofford*, b. Nov. 22, 1762; m. Polly Furgurson. *Nathan*, b. May 4, 1768; m. Deborah Farwell. *Prudence*, b. May 14, 1769; m. Isaac Farwell. *Benjamin*, b. June 1, 1770; m. Beulah Temple. *Abigail*, b. Feb. 8, 1774; m. Jesse Farwell. *Caleb*, b. April 11, 1776; soldier in War of 1812. *Fanny*, b. May 3, 1779; m. Joseph Burt of Windsor, Vt., died in New York State at the age of 90. M. C. C.

Address, M. C. C., care *N. E. Hist. Gen. Soc., 18 Somerset St., Boston.*

DUDLEY.—Wanted, the ancestry of Abigail Dudley, daughter of William and Mary (Roe) Dudley, who was born at Saybrook, Conn., May 24, 1667; married John Kent of Suffield, May 9, 1680, and died at Suffield October 26, 17—(?).

Xenia, O. (Miss) EMMA C. KING.

LEONARD, WASHBURN, AMES, &C:—1. Who was Elizabeth Leonard, wife of James Washburn, 1720?

2. Who were the parents of Michael, Benjamin and Cheney Ames, brothers, born about 1750 to 1760?

3. Also of Sarah Ames, who married Stephen Ives of New Haven, 1769? She was born 1751.

4. Who was Esther Benedict, married Joseph Ives of Wallingford, 1697?
Waterbury, Conn.   K. A. PRICHARD.

THOMAS MERRITT was a resident of Rye, N. Y., in 1673. Constable 1684; commissioner of Indian purchases 1694; vestryman 1694; on committee to select a minister 1697; on committee to obtain a charter for Rye 1697; deputy to the General Court at Hartford 1699; on committee to settle the White Plains line in 1702, and the line between Rye and Greenwich 1707; on grand jury 1713–16. Sold land to Samuel Merritt in 1720. His second wife, married in 1688, was Abigail daughter of Robert Francis of Wethersfield. He had four sons—Thomas, Joseph, Ephraim and Samuel—living in 1699. I should like to know the names of his parents and his first wife; also the dates of his birth and death and the births of his sons.   DOUGLAS MERRITT.
Leacote, Rhinebeck, N. Y.

HUBBARD QUERIES.—1. In 1719 Daniel and Josiah Blodgett, brothers, went from Woburn, Mass., to Stafford, Conn., were among the first settlers of that place. Can any one give their descendants?

2. Among the untraced Hubbards in the new Hubbard history appear the following: Old South Church records—Lazarus Hubbard to Jane Vodin, Oct. 9, 1702, by Cotton Mather; Lazarus Hubbard to Mary Harron, March 7, 1744. I would like to know the connection, if there is any, between these and the Lazarus Hubbard of Methuen, who had wife Abigail and children: Thomas, b. 1770; Isaac, b. 1772; Joanna, b. 1775; and Jacob, b. 1777. Would also like Abigail's name and ancestry.   MRS. CHAS. L. HARMON.
312 Pratt Street, Manchester, N. H.

HUNTINGTON.—Wanted, the ancestry of Hannah Huntington, who married Nathan Fitch of Lebanon, Conn., June 19, 1725, and died February 1, 1738.
Xenia, O.   (Miss) EMMA C. KING.

REPLIES.

GEORGE'S ISLAND.—In the REGISTER, 1879, vol. 33, p. 442, *Notes and Queries,* I find this Query by Hon. Joseph W. Porter: "George's Island.—How early was this island called by its present name, and how did it derive its name? May it not have been Gorges?"

Mr. Porter probably means the group of islands called "St. George's islands" at the mouth of the St. George's river. No particular island in this group is called "George's Island." When Capt. George Waymouth in 1605 established his "Penticost Harbor" *between* these islands, he gave a name to but one, where he wooded and watered and set up his first cross, this he called *Insula sancti cruce,* "Because here we set up our first cross." Champlain passed it five days after Waymouth left, and named it "La Neff," stating that it was *ten leagues* from the mouth of the Kennebec. In the year 1607 the ship "Mary and John" of the Popham expedition commanded by Capt. Gilbert (having separated at the Azores from her companion ship the "Gift of God," Capt. Popham) came to anchor under this island where he found Waymouth's cross, and called it "St. George" in honor of its first discoverer George Waymouth, and the name has since been given to the whole group collectively, as well as to the river near by, that Waymouth explored. Capt. Waymouth gave the name "St. George" to the island lying far out to sea, Monhegan. Waymouth's christening of this island did not survive, it still retains its Indian name "Monhegan." The island that Waymouth called *sancti cruce* is supposed to be either the present "Allen's" island, or "Burnt" island.   GEO. PRINCE.
Boston, Mass.

MAVERICK.—Let me correct an error in my note in the October (1895) number of the REGISTER, upon Rev. John Maverick. Instead of living at Okehampton, as I carelessly stated, Maverick was rector of Beaworthy, a parish about eight miles to the northwest of Okehampton. The present rector of Beaworthy, the Rev. F. A. Willis, LL.D., writes me, Sept. 25, 1895 : " After searching the registers of this parish I have failed to find the name of Maverick in any of them, but this is hardly to be wondered at, as the date of his incumbency is so long ago as 1615."

" Edmandus Arscotte " should read " Edmundus."

Through the continued kindness of the historian of Plymouth (R. N. Worth) I am enabled to announce the discovery of the place and time of the marriage of the Rev. John Maverick, and the name of his wife. The Ilsington register contains the entry of John Maverick's marriage to Mary Gye, October 28, 1600. " Guy," says Mr. Worth, " is not a name current in the locality, and her presence in Ilsington is only reasonably explained by her marriage."

New Castle, N. H.   FRANK W. HACKETT.

THATCHER.—Whilst recently scanning the parish registers of Hawkesbury, Gloucestershire, I met with the following baptism : Anne, daughter of Peter Thatcher, aged about 13, baptized 2 February, 1680. Possibly this Peter Thatcher may have been a collateral of Mr. Peter Thatcher, whose portrait appeared in the REGISTER for January, 1883, and therefore it may be worth while to record this extract here.   W. P. W. PHILLIMORE.
124 Chancery Lane, London, Eng.

HISTORICAL INTELLIGENCE.

OLD FAMILIES OF AMESBURY AND SALISBURY.—David W. Hoyt, author of the Hoyt Family Genealogy and other genealogical papers, has collected much material for a genealogy of all the early settlers of Salisbury and Amesbury, with a few related families of Newbury and Haverhill. A complete genealogy covering this ground would include about one hundred and seventy-five different surnames. Very few of these have had any adequate genealogy published, and some of those few contain statements and dates which should be corrected. Mr. Hoyt has written out already the earlier generations of Challis, Chase, Clement, Colby, Currier, Davis, Fowler, Huntington, Martin, Morrill, Sargent, Wells, Williams, Worthen, and many others, including additions and corrections of some already printed. If sufficient encouragement is given, the book will be published. Subscriptions may be sent to David W. Hoyt, Providence, R. I., or to W. H. B. Currier, Amesbury, Mass. Price, $5.

HISTORY OF DANBURY, CT.—Mrs. Susan Benedict Hill has in preparation a history of this town, which will be published this winter or early in the spring. The work was begun by James M. Bailey (the Danbury News Man), but was left unfinished at his death in 1894. We feel confident that Mrs. Hill will make a careful and interesting book that will do honor to Danbury. It will be a volume of about 600 pages, with 150 illustrations.

GRAVES FAMILY GENEALOGY.—The first volume, containing a sketch of the family in England for 800 years, and genealogy of the family of Thomas Graves of Hartford, Conn., 1645, and of Hatfield, Mass., 1661, will be issued about the middle of January, 1896. It will be profusely illustrated with pictures of distinguished men of the English and American family, coat-of-arms and crest, views of location of first settlers at Hatfield and Sunderland, Mass., and objects of interest.

This work is being compiled by John C. Graves, member of the Buffalo Historical Society, and can be obtained from him. His address is No. 32 Board of Trade Building, Buffalo, N. Y. Subscription price, $12 for the three volumes, or $5 for each volume if ordered separately.

TITLES OF HONOR.—Under this title Hon. William Everett, LL.D., contributes to the *New England Magazine* for September last an article which we would advise all our readers to study. "No child of New England," says Dr. Everett, "can extend his reading or his observation to the history of Old England, without encountering titles and titled personages," and he proceeds in a clear and interesting manner to explain the various titles used which will prevent the use of them in an improper way. Many intelligent people often use titles of honor in a wrong sense. This article shows a thorough knowledge of a perplexing subject, and contains much curious and interesting information.

SOLDIERS OF KING PHILIP'S WAR. *By the Rev. George M. Bodge, A.M.*—The first edition of this invaluable book was exhausted soon after its publication, and copies have been sold at more than double its original price. Yielding to a growing demand, shown by applications from Libraries, Historical Societies, and especially Genealogists and those interested in the "Society of Colonial Wars" and kindred organizations, the author has decided to issue a new and enlarged edition, for subscribers. Much new material has been accumulated since the first edition was issued; and with great pains and difficult research, full lists of the grantees of the "Narragansett Townships" have been collected and will be published in this edition. These lists contain some sixteen hundred names and afford positive evidence of participation in the campaign against the Narraganset Indians, in which their great "Swamp Fort" was taken, December 19, 1675. Important additional evidence is afforded in the fact that, in nearly all cases, the names of the heirs or assigns of the grantees are given, with their place of residence at the time of the granting of the townships, from 1733 to 1736. Only a small edition will be printed. Terms &c. Price per volume, strongly bound in cloth, $5.00; half morocco, $6.00. Sent to subscribers, as soon as published, on receipt of price. Address Geo. M. Bodge, Leominster, Mass.

GENEALOGIES IN PREPARATION.—Persons of the several names are advised to furnish the compilers of these genealogies with records of their own families and other information which they think may be useful. We would suggest that all facts of interest illustrating family history or character be communicated, especially service under the U. S. Government, the holding of other offices, graduation from college or professional schools, occupation, with places and dates of birth, marriage, residence and death. When there are more than one christian name they should all be given in full if possible. No initials should be used when the full names are known.

Allen.—Frank Allen Hutchinson, Esq., 187 Nesmith Street, Lowell, Mass., has in preparation Genealogical Sketches of the Allen Family of Dedham and Medfield. The book will make about 100 pages and the price will be $3.00 in cloth.

Beecher.—Mrs. Helen Beecher McGraw, 456 Russell Avenue, Cleveland, Ohio, is preparing a genealogy of the Beecher Family and will be pleased to hear from any one interested in the subject.

Dickerman and Dickman.—A genealogy of the family descended from Thomas Dickerman of Dorchester, through his sons, Thomas of Malden, Abraham of New Haven, and Isaac of Boston, is now nearly ready for publication. Communications may be sent to E. D. Dickerman, 15 Lake Place, New Haven, Conn., who invites correspondence from all persons interested in the work.

Fisk and Fiske.—Fred C. Pierce, 161 Dearborn Street, Chicago, is compiling the genealogy of the descendants of the early residents of New England by the name of Fisk-Fiske. He has succeeded in tracing the family back to 1300 and has connected all the early emigrants in this country in one family. Persons by this name will confer a favor and assist him in his work by sending their names and addresses and such information as they may have of the family to him as above.

Nevens.—William Nevens, Esq., of Falmouth, Maine, has now nearly ready for publication a Genealogical Record of the Nevens or Nevins Families of New England, including those of Palmer and Gloucester, Mass., and of Pelham and Hollis, N. H. Price, $4.50.

NECROLOGY OF THE NEW-ENGLAND HISTORIC GENEALOGICAL SOCIETY.

Prepared by the Historiographer, Rev. Ezra Hoyt Byington, D.D., of Newton, Mass.

The sketches of deceased members prepared for the Register are of necessity brief, because the space that can be appropriated is quite limited. All the materials for more extended memoirs which can be gathered are preserved in the archives of the Society, and they will be available for use in preparing the "Memorial Biographies," of which five volumes have been issued and a sixth volume is in preparation. The income from the Towne Memorial Fund is devoted to the publication of these volumes.

Hon. Henry Oscar Houghton, A.M., of Cambridge, a life member of this Society for the last ten years, was born in Sutton, a fine farming town in Caledonia County, Vermont, April 30, 1823, and died quite suddenly in North Andover, Mass., August 25, 1895.

He was a descendant of the seventh generation, from John Houghton, who was born in Lancaster, England, who came to New England in the early years of the settlement of Massachusetts, and who died in 1684. The ancestral line was: John[1], born in England; John[2], Jr., born in Massachusetts in 1650; Jacob[3], born 1674; Jacob[4], Jr., born 1696; Abraham[5], born 1725; William[6], born in Bolton, Mass., March 23, 1774, who was the father of Henry Oscar.

When he was ten years of age his parents moved to Bradford, Vt., where there was an excellent academy. His older brother had entered the University of Vermont, at Burlington, and his example furnished a stimulus to Henry to gain a liberal education. He attended the academy a few terms, and at the age of thirteen determined to go to Burlington, the college town, and learn the trade of a printer. He used to describe to his friends the setting out on this journey across the State by stage, to gain his first knowledge of the greater world beyond his rural home. He became an apprentice in the office of the *Burlington Free Press* (now a prosperous daily), and learned to set type. With the assistance of his brother, the apprentice boy was prepared for college. He saved from his earnings eighty dollars, with which he proposed to begin his course in college. The failure of his employer, just as he was ready to enter college, led to the loss of his small capital, and he entered the Freshman Class, at the age of nineteen, with only a shilling in his pocket. He went back to the printing office, and used every hour he could spare from his studies in earning his living. He was graduated in 1846, one of the best scholars in his class. He was at that time three hundred dollars in debt. His first effort was to earn money to pay this debt. Not succeeding in obtaining a position as a teacher he went to Boston and entered a printing office again. His first work there, it is believed, was to assist in reading the proofs of Professor Torrey's translation of Neander's Church History, which was then publishing by Crocker & Brewster. His classical knowledge fitted him to correct the Latin and Greek quotations. He made an engagement in the office of the *Boston Evening Traveler*, where he was employed in setting type, reading proof, and reporting public speeches. Three years later he was able to purchase the interest of one of the partners in the firm of Freeman & Bolles, at that time engaged in printing in Cambridge. After three years more the other partner retired, and the firm of H. O. Houghton & Company was formed. They occupied an old building, which had been erected for an almshouse, on the banks of the Charles River, as their printing house. That was the starting point of the Riverside Press. Mr. Houghton determined to do better printing than had been done in this country. He imported his inks from England, and selected the better grades of paper, and did the proof reading himself. In these ways he obtained the best work of the best publishers. Ticknor & Fields gave him a share of their printing. He printed the first number of the *Atlantic Monthly*, which was issued in 1857,—a magazine which he afterwards owned.

In 1864 he determined to add to his business as a printer that of a publisher. He formed a partnership with Mr. Hurd of New York, under the name of Hurd & Houghton. They brought out fine editions of Dickens, Bacon, Carlyle, Macaulay and others, and soon gained a high rank among publishers. The next step in his prosperity was secured by the union of his firm with that of J. R. Osgood & Company, in 1878, under the firm name of Houghton, Osgood and Company. Two years later Mr. Osgood retired, and the new firm of Houghton, Mifflin & Company was formed, which has continued to this day. These firms have published the books of the foremost authors of New England: Longfellow, Whittier, Holmes, Emerson, Lowell, Thoreau, Hawthorne, and the others. This house has maintained the leading place among the publishers of New England. Mr. Houghton was from the first the leading spirit, his effort being to make books which should satisfy the literary and artistic sense of the best class of readers.

The relations of Mr. Houghton with authors were very intimate. His office on Park Street became a gathering place for literary men. Dr. Holmes, Mr. Lowell, Mr. Aldrich, and some of the others were often seen there. It has been his custom to celebrate the seventieth birthday of the leading contributors to the *Atlantic Monthly* by a breakfast or a dinner, or a garden party, at which he gathered large numbers of his literary friends. Many will remember the Whittier dinner party, the Holmes breakfast, and the Stowe garden party. A few years since he gave a brilliant reception to the author of Tom Brown at Rugby, at which were present, Emerson, Holmes, Longfellow, John Fiske, James T. Fields, E. P. Whipple, T. B. Aldrich, Howells, Dr. Peabody, Josiah Quincy, C. F. Adams, Dr. Hale, and a number of other men of distinction.

On his fiftieth birthday his co-partners and his employés presented to him a costly fountain, erected in front of the Riverside Press. On his seventieth birthday his employés presented him with a silver loving cup, with a beautiful inscription.

His interest was not limited to his business. He was a good citizen, and gave much time to the interests of the public. He was elected a member of the Common Council in Cambridge in 1868, and of the Board of Aldermen in 1869. His services were so acceptable that in 1872 he was chosen Mayor of Cambridge. He was one of the leaders in securing our present international copyright. For many years he was president of the Vermont Association in Boston. He cultivated the acquaintance of those who had come from the State of his nativity. Some of the most delightful addresses he ever made were at the meetings of this Association. A year or two ago the Vermonters residing in Boston gave him a public dinner, at which he gave an interesting narrative of his early life in Vermont, and of his struggles with poverty while he was gaining his education.

He was a leading member of the Harvard Street Methodist Episcopal Church, in Cambridge, and for almost thirty years superintendent of its Sunday School. He was known as a man of profound religious convictions, and of simple faith and trust.

The great sorrow of his life was the death of his wife, April 13, 1891. Soon after her death he made an extended foreign tour, visiting not only the countries of Europe, but Egypt and the Holy Land.

He loved his business, and preferred it to any other. Ten years ago he said to a friend, that he would not change his place to become President of the United States. He had realized the ambition of his life in becoming a leading publisher of the best class of books. It was a special satisfaction to him that he had been able to carry the art of book-making to such perfection in this country. His success was due to his admirable taste and unwearied diligence.

He was a corresponding member of the Vermont Historical Society, and he delivered an address at its annual meeting a year ago. He was also a member and an officer of the Massachusetts Society of the Colonial Wars. He has been a generous contributor to the funds of our own Society, and watched its growth with an intelligent interest.

Mr. Houghton was married September 12, 1854, to Nancy Hyer Manning. He left one son, H. O. Houghton, Jr., who is a member of the firm, and three daughters.

WILLIAM WETMORE STORY, A.M., LL.B., D.C.L., of Rome, Italy, an honorary member of this Society, was born in Salem, Massachusetts, February 12, 1819, and died in Vallambrosa, Italy, October 6, 1895.

His father was Joseph Story, who was born in Marblehead, Mass., September 18, 1779. He was a Judge of the Supreme Court of the United States, and is accounted one of the greatest of American jurists. His grandfather, Dr. Elisha Story, was one of the famous "Boston Tea Party," and later was a valuable surgeon in the army of Washington. His great grandfather, William Story, was Register in the Court of Admiralty at the time of the Revolution, and for years before. Of his earlier ancestors, Mr. Savage states that he has "not been able to find progenitors before Elisha, of the third generation preceding, who probably came from England in the last year of William III."

Mr. W. W. Story was graduated at Harvard in the famous class of 1838, and from the Law School, where he pursued his studies under the direction of his father, and of Professor Greenleaf, in 1841. For five years he devoted himself to his profession as a lawyer, and gave promise of a career as great as that of his father. He published, 1842-7, three volumes of reports of cases in the Circuit Court of the United States for the First Circuit, and in 1844 a treatise on the law of contracts, and in 1847 a treatise on the law of sales of personal property. His health was broken by his intellectual work, and he went abroad to study art, and from that time devoted himself to sculpture and to literature. He is one of the small number of men who have been eminent in three departments of intellectual activity—the law, literature and art.

His publications are too numerous to be named in this notice. In 1844 he delivered, at Harvard, a poem on Nature and Art, before the Phi Beta Kappa. In 1851 he published the Life and Writings of his father, in two volumes; a volume of poems in 1856; Roba di Roma, in 1862; Graffiti d' Italia, 1869; Tragedy of Nero, 1875; Excursions in art and letters, 1891; and a number of others, at various times between 1847 and 1891.

He was a painter of no small merit; but his reputation in art depends chiefly upon his work as a sculptor. He received from the friends of Mr. Justice Story at the bar a commission to execute a statue of him as a memorial. He studied the works of the great artists at Rome as a preparation for this service. His statue, which is now in the chapel at Mount Auburn, represents his father, in his judicial robes, with a book in his hand. The likeness is said to be good, but there is little vigor in the work.

Mr. Story resided in the old palace of the Barberini in Rome, and many of the members of this Society have been welcomed to his studio. He was an American in his tastes and sympathies, although his reputation as an artist is perhaps higher in England than in this country. He served as Commissioner of the United States, on the fine arts, at the World's Fair at Paris, in 1879. He kept up his acquaintance with his own country by frequent visits, although his home was in Italy. In 1877-8 he delivered courses of lectures on Art in Boston and New York. Among his best known works are the statue of Edward Everett, that of George Peabody, and that of Josiah Quincy. His most famous work is his Cleopatra, now in the Metropolitan Museum of Art in New York. He held for some years a professorship in Rome. He received the degree of D. C. L. from Oxford.

His wife, to whom he was married in Boston in 1843, was a member of the Eldridge family. They celebrated their golden wedding two years ago. They have left three children—Waldo, who is a sculptor, Julian, and a daughter who married Sig. Peruzzi, a descendant of a famous family of Florence.

WALDO HIGGINSON, A. M., of Boston, was born in Boston, May 1, 1814, and died in Boston, May 4, 1894. He was a descendant of the Rev. Francis Higginson, who was educated at the University at Cambridge, England, and received the degree of B. A. in 1609, and of M. A. in 1613. He was born in 1587, and came to New England in 1629. He was the first minister of Salem; a man of learning and piety.

Mr. Higginson was the son of Stephen and Louisa (Storrow) Higginson. His maternal ancestors included the first of the three Governors Wentworth of Portsmouth, N. H. He was prepared for college in a private school in Cambridge, of which William Wells was the teacher. He was also, for a time, under the instruction of R. W. Emerson, and was also at the celebrated school

taught by George Bancroft and J. G. Cogswell, at Round Hill, Northampton.
He was graduated from Harvard in 1833, having a part at Commencement, and
being a member of the Phi Beta Kappa. He was for many years the secretary
of the class. The records of his class, which he had kept with great care, were
destroyed in the Boston fire of 1872. He was at much pains to restore these
records in subsequent years, and he caused them to be printed in a volume, at
his own expense. Among his classmates were Professors Francis Bowen,
Joseph Lovering, H. D. Torrey, Morrill Wyman, Jeffries Wyman and G. E.
Ellis.

He spent the first year after his graduation in Alexandria, Va., chiefly in the
family of his brother-in-law, Rev. Reuel Keith, D.D. Returning to Boston he
studied law for a time in the office of Judge Jackson. Without completing his
studies he decided to become a civil engineer, and spent the summer of 1837 in
Georgia, on the State railroad across the Alleghanies. Later he was assistant
engineer, under Col. J. M. Fessenden, in building the Eastern Railroad, afterwards establishing himself as a civil engineer in Boston. Between 1845 and
1853 he was agent and engineer for the Boston & Lowell Railroad Corporation,
resigning this employment because of a stroke of paralysis, produced by over-
work. In 1856 he became president of the New-England Mutual Insurance
Company. After some years he advised the discontinuance of this company, as
he had become satisfied that the principle of mutual insurance was not adapted
to railroad people. The affairs of the company were wound up without loss to
those insured.

He was for a long time president of the Arkwright Insurance Company for
manufacturing establishments. On his resignation in 1891 a vote was passed
by the directors of the company, which set forth in the warmest terms the
respect and affection which they cherished for their associate and friend. They
bore witness to the value of his services and the wisdom of his counsels; to
his " profound and beneficent influence in smoothing away the difficulties which
have sometimes arisen in the course of the work," his " judicial friendliness,"
" the even balance to which all deferred," his " sincerity and tact in removing
slight causes of friction." This tribute from his associates in business gives
us a very clear impression of the strength and practical wisdom of our late
associate.

He was elected a resident member of this society September 3, 1845, resigned
on account of business engagements in 1853, and was re-elected thirty years
later. He was one of the overseers of Harvard University, from 1869 to 1873,
and was a prominent member of the committee which raised the means for erecting Memorial Hall. He served for a long time as Chairman of the Committee
of Overseers to visit the Theological School, which his father, Stephen Higginson, while steward of the college, had enlarged and strengthened. Our associate also founded, in the University, the George D. Sohier prize for scholarship
in modern languages, giving to this prize the name of a brother-in-law.

He married, December, 1854, Mary Davies, daughter of William Davies So-
heir of Boston, but they had no children.

Hon. JAMES ROBINSON NEWHALL of Lynn, a resident member of this Society,
elected January 3, 1883, was born in Lynn, December 25, 1809, and died in Lynn,
October 24, 1893.

He was a descendant of Thomas Newhall, who came from England in 1630,
and settled in Lynn a year or two after the town was begun. His second son,
Thomas, born in 1631, was the first white child born in Lynn, and was baptized
by Mr. Bachiler, the first minister of Lynn, the first Sunday after his arrival,
June 8, 1632. He was a man of integrity, a farmer, whose name appears frequently in the early records of the town. His third son, Joseph, was born September 22, 1658. He is said to have perished in a great snow storm. His
seventh son, Benjamin, was born April 5, 1698. He had fourteen children.
His second son, James, born July 11, 1731, was a magistrate, and was known
as " 'Squire Jim." He was the father of Benjamin, born Jan. 19, 1774, who
was the father of Judge Newhall, the historian of Lynn, of whom we are writing. The family of Newhall is very numerous in Lynn. At one period there
were eight men there who bore the name of James Newhall, not one of whom
had a middle name. They were distinguished as 'Squire Jim, Phthisicy Jim,
Silver Jim, Bully Jim, Increase Jim, President Jim, Nathan's Jim, and Doctor
Jim.

Judge Newhall was a self-made man. His father had a large family to provide for, and his mother died when he was a child. He left home, to make his way in the world, at the age of eleven. He attended the public schools as much as he was able; but, in his fifteenth year, he entered the office of the *Salem Gazette*, to learn printing. Before he was twenty-one he was employed as foreman in one of the principal book offices in Boston. In 1829 he was employed in the *Confidence* office in New York. At the age of twenty-two he returned to Lynn, and was employed in the office of the *Mirror*. He afterward purchased the office and was for some years engaged in the printing and newspaper business. In 1844 he began the study of the law, and was admitted to the bar in 1847. He opened an office in Lynn, and secured a good business as a lawyer. In 1869 he was commissioned as Judge of the Lynn Police Court, an office which he held for ten years. In 1882 he took an extended tour abroad, visiting the most important cities in Europe.

Mr. Newhall was not much in public life, excepting as Judge of the Police Court. He was, however, at one time, Chairman of the School Board, and President of the Common Council. He devoted a large part of his time, in his late years, to historical studies. He published "Liñ; or, Jewels of the Third Plantation," a book which George W. Curtis compared to the Sketch Book by Washington Irving. The History of Lynn, published in 1865, bears on its title page the names of Alonzo Lewis and James R. Newhall. A large part of this work is from the pen of Judge Newhall. He also published Centennial Addresses in 1876, and "Lynn—Her First Two Hundred and Fifty Years," by invitation of the city authorities, at the anniversary in 1879. He contributed to the History of Essex County, and to that of Worcester County. His Annals of Lynn, published in 1883, brought the history of the city to that date. He was for several years president of the Lynn Press Association.

He was twice married. In October, 1837, he married Dorcas B. Brown of Salem. His second wife was Elizabeth Campbell, daughter of the late Josiah Newhall, who survives him.

ELISHA CLARK LEONARD, of New Bedford, Mass., was born in Rochester, Mass., September 3, 1819, and died in New Bedford, September 7, 1894.

The Leonards of Massachusetts are descended from an ancient English family. It is said that the Leonards of England were interested in the iron works at Bilston, Stafford County, The three brothers who came to this country about the middle of the seventeenth century were sons of Thomas Leonard, who seems to have lived at Pontypool, Monmouth County, Wales. Henry Leonard, son of Thomas, was at Lynn in 1642, and it is supposed he was engaged in the iron works in that town at that date. In 1652 the town of Taunton voted that Henry Leonard and his brother James have free consent "to set up a bloomery work on the Two-Mile River." This was the first iron manufactory in the old colony. The Leonards were interested in iron works in various places, so that it used to be said that " where you can find iron works, there you will find a Leonard."

The ancestral line of our late associate in this Society runs thus: Thomas,[1] James[2] (who married in Lynn, and was made a freeman in that town in 1668), Benjamin,[3] Joseph[4] (born January 22, 1692), Philip[5], George[6], Nehemiah[7] (who married Hannah Tinkham [Clark]), and Elisha Clark.[8]

Mr. Leonard was a successful business man, a genealogist, and an antiquarian. He was educated in the Friends Academy in New Bedford, and the Peirce Academy in Middleboro', under Professor J. W. P. Jenks.

In his early manhood he was engaged in the oil business with his father in New Bedford. In 1850 he engaged in the same business in Springfield, with Mr. Francis Rodman. In 1856 he engaged in the carpet business in New Bedford. In 1857 he was a member of the City Council. In 1871-2 he was United States assistant assessor, and in 1873-76 he was deputy collector of internal revenue. Since that time he has not been in active business.

He wrote a number of valuable papers for the Old Colony Historical Society, of which he was for many years a director. Among his historical papers were: Reminiscences of the Ancient Iron Works and Leonard Mansions of Taunton; and King Philip's Gift to James Leonard. He left a fine collection of family records, and much valuable material concerning ancient boundaries and landmarks.

He was also a prominent member of the Masonic fraternity, and occupied a number of honorable positions in that order.

Hon. William W. Crapo, of New Bedford, spoke of Mr. Leonard, at a memorial meeting held in Historical Hall in that city, as the most gifted historical student in the community : "He loved the old colony, its history, its traditions, its men. No incident of the early times was too minute for his patient investigation. Give him a clew and he would hunt and delve until he found the answer."

Mr. Leonard married, November 24, 1842, Elizabeth Bourne Ellis, daughter of Thomas and Rosetta Howland Ellis. A son and two daughters survive him.

JAMES CARNAHAN WETMORE, Esq., of Columbus, Ohio, was born in Whitestown, N. Y., May 1, 1813, and died in Elizabethtown, N. J., August 13, 1895. He was descended from Thomas Wetmore, who was born in the west of England in 1615 and came to New England in 1635, and settled, it is supposed in Weathersfield, Conn., though he removed subsequently to Hartford. He was made a freeman in Middletown in 1652, and he seems to have been among the earliest settlers of that town. In 1670 his property was assessed at £125 10s. The ancestral line is as follows: Thomas[1]; Izrahiah,[2] born in Middletown March 8, 1656–7; Judge Seth,[3] born in Middletown November 18, 1700. He married, as his third wife, Hannah, daughter of Rev. Timothy Edwards of East Windsor, who was the father of President Edwards. Dea. Oliver,[4] born at Staddle Hill, near Middletown, May, 1752. He married Sarah, daughter of Elisha Brewster, a descendant of Elder Brewster. Rev. Oliver,[5] born at Staddle Hill, December 15, 1774, who was ordained in 1807, and served as a home missionary many years, and died in Utica, N. Y., January 1, 1852. James Carnahan.[6]

The subject of this sketch was thus one of the lineal descendants of Elder Brewster, so distinguished in the history of the Pilgrims at Plymouth, and was also descended from the father of President Edwards. He was educated in the common schools in Oneida County, N. Y., and at an academy near his early home. His life was for the most part devoted to business. At the age of fifteen he was employed in a store in Utica, where he spent two years. He had a better situation for the next two years, though he did not like the business. In 1832 he went to New York, where he secured a situation with a jobber of cotton goods. He was four years in New York, and then removed to Mississippi, and, after some years, to New Orleans. While there, the Mexican war broke out, and he accompanied General Taylor to Mexico, and was engaged in the battle of Buena Vista. After the war he went to San Lois Potosi, and was the first American to bring goods by that route to that city, Later he removed to the city of New York, became a member of the Stock Exchange, and opened an office in Wall street. In 1847 he removed to Ohio. During the civil war he was the military agent for Ohio, at Washington.

In 1861 he published "The Wetmore Family," a very thorough genealogical, biographical and historical work, of six hundred and seventy pages. He devoted two years and a half to the preparation of this work. It is one of the best of the family books, full of historical information, which the author had collected from ancient records and letters, as well as from books. The student of the early history of New England will find this work a mine of curious information concerning the life of the people in the earlier generations of our history.

He married, May 29, 1851, Catharine Mary De Hart, daughter of the Hon. William and Mary (Barber) Chetwood of Elizabethtown, N. J. They had one son, John Chetwood Wetmore, born August 22, 1856.

Mr. Wetmore was a life member of the Young Men's Christian Association.

He was elected a corresponding member of this Society September 4, 1861, soon after the publication of the Wetmore genealogy and biography.

Hon. JAMES WALKER AUSTIN, A.M., LL.B., of Boston, was born in Charlestown, Mass., January 8, 1829, and died in Southampton, England, October 15, 1895. He was the son of William Austin, who was born in Lunenburg, Mass., March 2, 1778, and was graduated at Harvard College in 1798, and was a member of the Suffolk Bar. A volume of his writings, with the title of The Literary Papers of William Austin, with a biographical sketch by his son, James Walker Austin, was published by Little and Brown in 1890. His mother was Lucy Jones of Charlestown.

The family was descended from Richard Austin of Bishopstock, England, who came to Charlestown, Mass., in May, 1638.   The succession of generations was as follows: Richard[1]; Richard[2] second, born in England 1632, died August 15, 1703; Ebenezer[3], died January 16, 1723; Ebenezer[4] second; Nathaniel[5], died December 25, 1862; William[6], born March 2, 1778; James Walker[7].

He was prepared for college in the schools of Charlestown, and at the Chauncy-Hall School, Boston, and was graduated from Harvard College in 1849, and from the Law School two years later, and was admitted to the Suffolk bar in 1851.   He went in 1851 to California, and thence to the Sandwich Islands. He was attracted by the beauty and fertility of the islands, and he determined to settle there.   He was admitted to the bar in that country, and in 1852 was appointed District Attorney.   He was elected to the Hawaian parliament, and re-elected for three sessions.   He was Speaker of the House one session.   In 1868 he was appointed Judge of the Supreme Court, by a special act of the legislature, and he was chosen to revise the criminal code of the islands, in connection with two other judges of the Supreme Court.   He had been a member of the commission to revise the civil code two years before.   These codes are modeled on those of the State of Massachusetts.   He was the guardian, a number of years, of Lunalilo, the heir to the throne.

He returned to the United States in 1872 for the education of his children, after a residence at the Sandwich Islands of twenty-one years.   He became a member of the Suffolk bar, and continued to practice law until a few years ago.

Judge Austin was a man of strong character, and of many accomplishments. His integrity was unimpeachable.   He had a large circle of friends at the Islands, where he had much to do in building up a vigorous and well ordered community.

He married July 18, 1857, Ariana Elizabeth, daughter of John S. Sleeper, ex-mayor of Roxbury.   He went to Europe September 15, of this year, with his wife and daughter, and they were with him at the time of his death.   One of his sons graduated at Harvard in 1887, and is now a member of the Suffolk bar. Another son is a member of the firm of Austin & Doton, merchants in Boston.

Judge Austin was elected a resident member of this Society in 1874, and became a life member in 1878.   He served as one of the directors of the Society twelve years, from 1877 to 1889, and contributed very much to its growth.

Ex-Governor OLIVER AMES, of North Easton, Mass., a life member of this Society, since 1883, and a very liberal contributor to its funds, was born in North Easton, February 4, 1831, and died there October 22, 1895.

His father was the celebrated financier and Congressman, Oakes Ames,[4] born January 10, 1804, who married Eveline O. Gilmore.   His grandfather was Oliver,[3] who was the son of John,[2] who was the son of Thomas.[1]

Governor Ames was educated in the public schools of his native town, and in the academies at Attleboro, Leicester and Easton.   He served an apprenticeship of five years in his father's manufacturing establishment, mastering the business in its most minute details.   After his apprenticeship he entered upon a special course at Brown University.   His favorite studies were history, geology and political economy.   In 1863 he became a member of the firm, and for several years superintended the mechanical business of the establishment.   At his father's death, in 1873, he became directly connected with various corporations, banks and other institutions, in which his father had been interested.   He paid the indebtedness of his father's estate, amounting to eight millions of dollars, and legacies amounting to a million more.   He was concerned in erecting the Oliver Ames Library Building and the Memorial Hall at North Easton, both splendid structures, which he and his relatives presented to the town.

In 1880 Mr. Ames was elected a member of the State Senate, and re-elected in 1881.   In 1882 he was elected Lieutenant Governor of Massachusetts, as a Republican, although the candidate for Governor on the same ticket was defeated.   He was re-elected to the same office in 1883, 1884 and 1885.   In 1886 he was elected Governor.   His rare abilities as a business man were of great service to Massachusetts, and his administration was a very useful one.   He was re-elected in 1887.   It was Governor Ames who recommended the enlargement of the State House, which is now in progress.   He laid the corner stone of the new building, December 21, 1890.   It was one of the last of his public acts. He has been an invalid for several years, and has not been much in public life.

Governor Ames was a man of literary taste and culture.   Architecture was with him a special study, and he had a fine appreciation of music and painting.

He owned a choice collection of paintings and statuary. His house on Commonwealth Avenue is a monument of his architectural taste. He was a hospitable man, faithful in his friendships, and generous in his benefactions. He was very popular with the workingmen in his factories. His estate was a very large one.

On the 14th of March, 1860, he married Miss Anna C. Ray of Nantucket. His family consists of two sons and four daughters.

BENJAMIN CUSHING, A.B., M.D., of Dorchester, who was elected a resident member of this Society, April 6, 1887, was born in Hingham, Mass., May 9, 1822, and died in Dorchester, October 16, 1895. His father was Jerom Cushing, who was born in Hingham in 1780, and died there in 1824. His mother was Mary Thaxter, who was born in Hingham in 1784, and died in Dorchester in 1867. He was descended in the seventh generation from Matthew Cushing and Margaret Pitcher, who came from Hingham, England, in 1638, and settled in Hingham, Mass. On the Thaxter side, his great grandfather was Major Samuel Thaxter, who, at the capture of Fort William Henry by the French and Indians, was taken prisoner and tied to a tree. Seeing some French officers going by he appealed to them, asking if they allowed a commissioned officer to be so treated. One of the French officers cut his bonds, saying, " Quick, walk." The major made his way home to Hingham, to be greeted, on riding into town, by the remark, " Why, Major, we've buried you." His funeral sermon had, indeed, been preached, as another survivor of the massacre had reached home and reported the major lost.

After the death of Jerom Cushing, his widow, with her children, came to live in Dorchester with her unmarried brother, Dr. Robert Thaxter.

Dr. Benjamin Cushing was prepared for college at Derby Academy, in Hingham, and was graduated from Harvard University in 1842. During his college course he spent a winter in Cuba, for the benefit of his health. He went to Calcutta, on a sailing vessel, after he was graduated. In 1846 he was graduated from the Harvard Medical School, and went to Paris for a year's further study of his profession. The discovery of the surgical use of ether was made while he was in Paris, and he saw the first two operations in which it was used.

He began the practice of medicine in Dorchester, on his return from Paris, in 1847, being associated at first with his uncle, Dr. Thaxter. All his professional life has been in Dorchester. During the civil war he volunteered to act as surgeon, and was sent to Fortress Monroe. After the close of the war he made a second trip to Europe, in 1866, and a third in 1875.

Dr. Cushing was a faithful and very skilful physician. His heart was always open to the calls of suffering. He was a true friend, full of public spirit, wise in counsel and generous in his gifts. He was a member of the Massachusetts Medical Society, and was Chairman of the Visiting Board of the Danvers Hospital for the Insane. He was also one of the consulting physicians of the City Hospital. He was much interested in certain proposed reforms in the treatment of dipsomaniacs. He served for a long time on the School Board of Dorchester. During the past few years Dr. Cushing has had a very interesting correspondence with Mr. H. J. Moule of Dorchester, England, and many pictures, books, and other mementoes have passed between the old town and its American namesake.

He married, in 1848, Anna Quincy Thaxter of Hingham.

LEONARD BOLLES ELLIS, Esq., of New Bedford, was born in New Bedford, March 11, 1838, and died in the same city March 13, 1895.

His father was Caleb L. Ellis, a prosperous man of business in New Bedford. The family line reaches back several generations in this country, and the descendants are very numerous.

Mr. Ellis was educated in the public schools. He completed a three years' course of study in the High School, which was of very great service to him in the work of his life. In 1859 he entered into business in company with his father. The civil war interrupted the business for some years, and he turned his attention to the manufacture of picture frames. In 1866 he bought the picture business of Mr. Orlando T. Marvin, and opened a store for the sale of works of art. He had the nature of an artist, and his store was for many years a very attractive place for those who loved art. It became a social centre for persons of culture in the city. Many famous paintings were brought to New

Bedford by his enterprise, and he had much to do in developing a taste for art. In later years the changes in business interrupted the sale of many things in his line, but he was to the last interested in paintings and engravings. He remained in this business twenty-five years.

His artistic temperament gave him a special interest in music. He was for many years the president of the Choral Association of New Bedford. He published a series of articles on the history of music in that city. He was for many years a trustee of the Free Public Library, and a faithful public servant in that capacity.

Mr. Ellis's tastes led him into historical studies, and he has left two valuable books : a History of the Fire Department of New Bedford, which was first published in successive numbers of the *Evening Standard* of that city, and a History of New Bedford, which is said by some good authorities to be the best ever written. Both of these works show the patient industry of their author, and his skill in weaving great masses of facts into interesting and truth-telling narratives. He was also the author of a number of detached historical articles, the latest being his History of Methodism in New Bedford.

Mr. Ellis was a man devoted to the best ideals of life, and had, to an unusual degree, the respect and confidence of all who knew him. An insidious and fatal disease hung over his life for many years, but he continued his work to the last. He was a prominent member of the Masonic fraternity for many years. He was long a member of the Methodist church, and for some years was superintendent of its Sunday School.

He was elected a resident member of this Society January 2, 1895.

JOHN WILKINS CARTER, Esq., of West Newton, a resident member of this Society, elected June 3, 1891, was born in Boston June 30, 1843, and died at Harwich, Mass., July 5, 1895. He was the son of Richard Bridge Carter, who was born in Lancaster, Mass., August 30, 1808. His mother, Lucy Lazelle Hobart, was born in Abington, Mass., October 4, 1817.

Mr. Carter was descended, on his father's side, from Rev. Thomas Carter, who came from England about 1630. He traced his descent from Rev. Thomas,[1] Rev. Samuel,[2] Samuel,[3] Ephraim,[4] Oliver,[5] Richard Bridge,[6] to John Wilkins.[7] On his mother's side he was descended from Edmund Hobart,[1] who came from England to Charlestown in 1633, Thomas,[2] Aaron,[3] Isaac,[4] Colonel Aaron,[5] Benjamin,[6] to Lucy Lazelle.[7]

He attended private and grammar schools up to his 12th year, when he was sent to Mr. Hunt's Crystal Lake Seminary for two years. He was prepared for college in the Boston Latin School, and entered Harvard College in 1861. After his Freshman year at Harvard he enlisted in the 45th regiment, Massachusetts Volunteers, from which he re-enlisted into the 17th infantry regiment of the regular army. He received a commission and participated in all the severe campaigns of the army of Virginia, until December, 1864, when he resigned, because his health had been seriously impaired.

After leaving the army he spent two or three years with Dunbar, Hobart & Whidden, in Abington, Mass. He returned to Boston in 1867 and entered the firm of Carter Brothers, manufacturers of paper and ink. After the Boston fire of 1872 he sold his interest in the manufacture of paper, and took charge of the manufacture of inks, under the firm name of Carter, Dinsmore & Co., in which business he continued until his death.

He married January 21, 1874, Helen Burrage, daughter of Johnson Carter Burrage, by whom he had four children, two sons and two daughters.

Some time after his return from the army his college degree was given to him out of course. He served a number of years as a member of the Board of Aldermen in Newton. He devoted a great deal of time to the study of sewerage, and was chairman of the committee on sewerage. He crossed the sea to gain fresh information, and on his return he made a report which was full of information in regard to modern methods of sewerage, and many of his ideas were incorporated in the system finally adopted in the Garden city. He was one of the most active members of the Newton Tariff Reform Club, and was for ten years secretary of the Massachusetts Reform Club.

He made a number of visits to the old world, and devoted much time to independent investigation. Last summer he was spending some weeks with a large family party at the sea side, and lost his life while bathing in the surf at Harwich.

JOHN SIMPSON EMERY, Esq., of Boston, a resident member of our Society since September 5, 1877, was born in Sullivan, Me., September 13, 1816, and died in his native place August 28, 1895. He was the eldest son of Hiram Eddy and Rachel (Simpson) Emery. His father was one of the leading citizens of Sullivan for more than fifty years. He was descended from Anthony Emery, who was born in Romsey, Hants, England, about the year 1600, and who sailed from Southampton, April 3, 1635, in the ship *James* of London, with his brother John and their families, and landed in Boston June 3 of the same year. He was in Newbury in 1638, but removed to Dover, N. H., and later to Kittery, Me. The family line is as follows : Anthony,[1] James,[2] Job,[3] Joseph,[4] William,[5] Hiram,[6] John Simpson.[7]

Mr. Emery in early life learned the trade of a blacksmith. Later he went to sea for a few years. In 1849 he came to Boston, and was in business as a ship broker forty-one years, being the principal in the well-known firm of John S. Emery & Co., 168 State street. At the time of his death he was a director in the China Mutual Insurance Company of Boston, and also in the Boston Marine Insurance Company, and president of the East Boston Dry Dock Company.

He was educated in the common schools of his native town. He was a man of broad sympathies, liberal in his opinions and with his means; a friend of the needy and distressed, of wide influence and acknowledged integrity. He was an intelligent friend of the shipping interests of his own country. The position which he occupied in Boston was indicated by the fact that almost all the older business houses in the city were represented by their partners at his funeral.

Although interested in public affairs, he never sought or held a public office. He had a strong attachment for his early friends and for his native town. He enlarged and kept up his father's old homestead, where he spent his summer vacations, and where he died. He contributed towards a town hall, for an improved schoolhouse, for the maintenance of the village cemetery, and for other interests connected with the old town. He was a member of the Pine Tree State Club, and an honorary member of the Boston Marine Society. He contributed a number of articles to the *Bangor Historical Magazine*, and to some other publications.

He had a leading part in the preparation of the genealogical records of the Emery family. He was a member of the executive committee of the family meeting of the Emerys for a number of years while the work was in preparation. He was also chairman of the genealogical committee. He aided this committee not only by his own researches among the ancient records of the family, but by his generous pecuniary aid. He left by will to this Society one hundred bound volumes of newspapers.

He married Prudence Simpson, December 1, 1850. They had no children.

GEORGE MORGAN BROWNE, A. B., of Washington, D. C., elected a resident member of this Society June 1, 1881, was born in Lisbon, formerly part of Norwich, Conn., May 7, 1811, and died at his home in Washington, April 25, 1895.

He was the son of Tyler[6] and Rhoda (Morgan) Browne, both of whom were natives of Preston, Conn., born the one in 1782, and the other two years later. His grandfather was William Browne,[5] who was the son of Samuel and Phebe (Wilbur) Browne. His grandmother, on the maternal side, was Joanna (Brewster) Morgan, a lineal descendant from Jonathan Brewster, who was a son of Elder William Brewster. His great-grandfather, Samuel Browne,[4] was the son of Daniel,[3] who was the son of Thomas[2] who came from Lynn to Stonington in 1684. He was the son of Thomas,[1] born in 1628, and Mary (Newhall) Browne.

Mr. Browne was prepared for college in Plainfield, Conn., and was graduated from Yale College in 1836. He studied law with Hon. Calvin Goddard of Norwich, and was admitted to the bar in 1839. He began the practice of his profession in Boston in 1841, and so long as he devoted himself to the law he was a successful lawyer. He was a member of the House of Representatives in 1857 and 1858, and took an active part in the discussions of that body. He was president of the Eastern Railroad Company from 1854 to 1871. Those were the years of the greatest prosperity of that corporation.

He visited Europe in 1872, remaining abroad more than a year. The visit was repeated in 1877.

He has published articles in the reviews, among which are : " Political Elements of the Constitution," and "Annexation," in the *American Review* of 1845. His argument on the trial of Rev. A. G. Prescott for heresy, before an ecclesiastical court in 1851, was published in the *Christian Witness.* He published an address as President of the Connecticut Association in 1857; a speech in the Legislature on the Kansas Resolves (1857); The Sinking Fund, a pamphlet, in 1874; Review of Müller's "Literature of Greece," and an article on Nice, in the *Literary World*, 1876.

His first wife was Caroline, daughter of John Linett. She died in 1847. He married Mary A., daughter of Henry Andrews. She died in 1858. He married Caroline, daughter of Edward Cabot of Boston. He left one son, George Morgan Browne.

EBEN DYER JORDAN, Esq., of the firm of Jordan, Marsh & Co., of Boston, a life member of this Society since 1869, was born in Danville, Me., October 13, 1822, and died in Boston November 15, 1895.

The life of Mr. Jordan was devoted to business and he has been said to rank next to A. T. Stewart as a successful man of business in lines that were quite similar. He was a poor boy, left an orphan and penniless at the age of four. As soon as he was old enough to work he was hired to labor on a farm in Roxbury, at four dollars a month. At sixteen he was employed in the store of William P. Tenney & Co. for two years. The third year he earned a salary of $275, a part of which he saved. When he was nineteen, a friend, Mr. Joshua Stetson, set him up in business in a small way, and his sales the first year amounted to $8000. At the end of four years his sales had amounted to $100,000. He sold his business at the age of twenty-five, and spent the next two years in the prosperous store of James M. Beebe, gaining a knowledge of the methods of a large business establishment. In 1851 the firm of Jordan, Marsh & Co. was formed, with a capital of $5000. By industry, enterprise and skill a large business was built up within the next few years. The crisis of 1857 taxed the firm severely, but it lived and prospered. In 1861 the firm added a retail department to its large wholesale trade. The growth of the retail store has been marvelous, and it now employs nearly three thousand persons in its various departments.

Mr. Jordan was a man of public spirit, though not an active politician. In the latter part of his life he made a tour around the world. Some years earlier he made a trip to Europe with twenty-five of the employees of the establishment. They were received by John Bright, by President Grévy, and by many other famous men in different countries as representatives of the enterprise and intelligence of American merchants.

Mr. Jordan leaves a widow and two sons and two daughters.

CHARLES JARVIS PICKFORD, Esq., of Lynn, was born in Kennebunk, Me., May 24, 1833, and died in Brookline, Mass., June 7, 1895. He was the son of John Kay Livermore and Elizabeth (Shepard) Pickford. He lived in Worcester from 1833 to 1864. In 1864 he engaged in the shoe business in Lynn. The firm was Winslow & Pickford. A few years later he engaged in the real estate and insurance business in that city. He retired some years ago from active business, on account of the failure of his health. He has been connected with religious and philanthropic movements, and has been a man of wide influence. He was for many years a leading deacon in the Washington Street Baptist Church. He was also superintendent of its Sunday School. He was a trustee of the Baptist Theological Seminary in Richmond, Virginia. He was also a trustee of the Tolman Temperance Fund.

He was elected a resident member of this Society in 1893. He was also a member of the Massachusetts Society of the Colonial Wars.

ARTHUR WELLAND BLAKE, Esq., of Brookline, a life member of this Society since 1885, was born in Boston, November 5, 1840, and died in Brookline February 28, 1893. His father was George Baty Blake, born in Brattleboro, Vt., May 19, 1808. His mother was Anna Hall. He was a lineal descendant, in the eighth generation, from William Blake, who was baptized in Pitminster, England, July 10, 1594, and who came to New England as early as 1636. He lived in Dorchester, and is spoken of in the old records as a useful and influential citizen. The line is as follows: William[1]; Edward[2], born about 1625, probably in England; Solomon[3], of Boston; Joseph[4], born August 10, 1709, also of Boston; Joseph[5], born February 5, 1739; John Welland[6], born 1759; George Baty[7].

His father was a banker and broker, who did business in Boston, under the firm name of Blake Brothers and Company. Arthur Welland Blake was prepared for college in the Boston schools, and entered Harvard College in 1857. He left during Freshman year to go into business. In 1861 he became a member of the firm, with his father, and continued in business up to the time of his death. He lived in New York about ten years, where the firm had a branch of their business. He returned to Boston about fifteen years ago.

He was a member of the Boston Stock Exchange, and of St. Botolph Club in Boston, the Union Club in New York, and a number of other organizations. He owned one of the most beautiful estates in Brookline, and was one of its wealthy citizens.

Mr. Blake always cherished an interest in Harvard. He gave $1000 toward the Class Memorial window, in Memorial Hall, and, more than any one else insured the success of the undertaking. He had been an invalid the past two or three years, during which time he did not take any active part in the business, which was cared for by the other partners—John P. Marquand, J. E. Brown, George R. Harris and Howland Davis.

He married April 25, 1878, Frances Greenough, daughter of Henry Greenough of Cambridge. His wife and two daughters survive him.

JAMES MONROE KEITH, A.B., of Boston, had been a resident member of this Society thirty-four years, having been elected September 5, 1860. He was the son of Bethuel and Mary (Pearson) Keith, and was born in Randolph, Vt., April 19, 1819. He died very suddenly at his home in Roxbury, Mass., April 12, 1894.

He was prepared for college partly at Randolph Academy and partly at the Academy in Royalton, Vermont. He was graduated at Brown University in 1845. He studied law with David A. Simmons of Roxbury, and was admitted to the Suffolk bar June 3, 1848. Later he opened an office in Boston. He was a member of the Legislature, from Roxbury, in 1851. Before Roxbury was annexed to Boston he was president of its Common Council. In 1855 he was appointed District Attorney for the district composed of Norfolk and Plymouth counties. The next year the office was made elective, and Mr. Keith was chosen for three years, but resigned in 1858.

During the war he was a prominent member of the Roxbury Relief Association. In 1868 and 1869 he was a member of the Boston Common Council, and the same years he was a trustee of the Boston Public Library. On several occasions he has been chairman of the Democratic State Convention, and on one of these he made one of the most noteworthy political speeches in the history of his party in this State. In 1868 he was a delegate to the national convention of the Democratic party. He was a member of the Boston Board of Health from 1877 to 1883.

Mr. Keith had long been recognized as one of the ablest lawyers in Boston. He was a man of integrity and of great practical wisdom. He filled every position well, and has left an honored name.

He was three times married. In 1849 he married Adeline Wetherbee of Boston. In 1856 he married Mary C. Richardson of Boston. His third wife, married in 1863, was Louisa J. Dyer of Providence.

CHARLES AUGUSTUS GREENE, M.D., of Arlington, Mass., was born in Batavia, New York, April 19, 1824, and died in Arlington, June 15, 1894. He was a descendant, in the seventh generation, from Thomas Green, who came from England before 1653, and settled in Malden. His father was Samuel Dana Greene, who was born in Leicester, Mass., February 9, 1788. Dr. Greene was educated in the schools of Batavia and in those of Boston. He also attended the academy at Monson, Mass., where he was prepared for college. He studied medicine in the medical school at Pittsfield, Mass., and was graduated in 1848. He was a practising physician for a number of years in Philadelphia. Later he resided in Harrisburg, from which city he removed to the vicinity of Boston. Dr. Greene was an independent student and practitioner. He adopted, in early life, original views in regard to medical practice. He was the author of a pamphlet entitled "Omnipathy," in which he set forth the principles of his method, to which he gave the name "Omnipathy." He followed this method through his whole career as a physician.

He was elected a resident member of this Society June 6, 1888.

He married Helen E. Hubbard, daughter of Willis H. Hubbard, April 18, 1855.

Hon. ALEXANDER HAMILTON RICE, LL.D., a resident member, elected February 3, 1858, was born in Newton Lower Falls, Mass., August 30, 1818, and died at the Langwood Hotel, Melrose, Mass., July 22, 1895. His father was Thomas Rice, who was the proprietor of a paper mill at Newton Lower Falls. The first part of his education was received in the public schools of his native town and in the neighboring academies of Needham and Newton, presided over respectively by Rev. Daniel Kimball and Mr. Seth Davis. After graduating from these schools he became a clerk in a dry goods store in Boston, where he performed his duties with such laboriousness and assiduity that his health gave way and he was obliged to stay at home for two years. Upon his return to Boston he was employed by the firm of Wilkins & Carter, who were wholesale dealers in paper, and publishers of music books and dictionaries. He remained here three years. During this time he united with the Mercantile Library Association and acquired such a taste for literature that he determined to go to college. In 1840 he entered Union College at Schenectady, N. Y., graduating in 1844. While in college he was a very careful student, his motto being that which is implied in the word "Thorough," and graduated with the highest honors of his class. He meant to become a lawyer, but was prevented by ill health, and instead became a member of the firm of his last employers. He continued in business during his life, associating with himself Charles S. Kendall, and establishing the well known firm of Rice, Kendall & Co., paper dealers and manufacturers; the firm name was changed, after about a half century's prosperity, to that of the Rice-Kendall Company, with Mr. Rice as president.

From the first of his engaging in an active business life, Mr. Rice took a large and serious interest in public affairs. In 1850 he was one of the Board of Visitors of the Lunatic Hospital. In 1853 he was elected to the Common Council of Boston, and was a councilman two years in succession, the second year being president. In 1854 he was president of the Boston School Committee. In 1856 and in 1857 he was mayor of the city of Boston. During his administration many important public improvements were made and several others begun. In 1858 he was elected to Congress and was a member of the thirty-sixth and the three succeeding Congresses, serving there in the troublous times of the late war, and for several years of his career there occupying the position of Chairman of the Committee on Naval Affairs. He was always an influential member of the House. In 1875 he was elected Governor of Massachusetts and was twice re-elected. As chief executive of the Commonwealth he acquitted himself well, and was a credit to the State.

Mr. Rice was president of the Keith Manufacturing Company of Turner's Falls, a director of the American Loan and Trust Company, and of the Massachusetts National Bank, and a trustee of the Mutual Life Insurance Company of New York.

He made many formal addresses; as, for example, at the opening of the Peace Jubilee in 1869; on the unveiling of the equestrian statue of Washington in the Public Gardens the same year; at the unveiling of the Sumner statue in the Public Gardens in 1878; as Chancellor of Union College in 1881; a Butterfield lecture at the same college in 1892; and at the setting up of the Farragut statue, Marine Park, South Boston, in 1893.

As instances of his many-sided interest in things, it may be mentioned that he was a member of the American Archæological Society; a fellow of the American Geographical Society of New York; a member of the American Historical Association; vice-president of the Webster Historical Association; a director of the Bunker Hill Monument Association and of the Commandery of the Loyal Legion; an honorary life member of the Farragut Naval Veteran Association; a trustee of the Massachusetts Institute of Technology, of the Boston Museum of Fine Arts, and of the Episcopal Theological School at Cambridge; president of the Sailors' National Home, and past honorary chancellor of Union College. He was also the first president of the old Central Club of Boston. He was a member of the St. Botolph, the Algonquin, the Commercial, and the Thursday Clubs.

Mr. Rice's first wife was Augusta E. McKim, a sister of Judge McKim of the Suffolk County Probate Court; his second wife was Angie Erickson Powell of Rochester, N. Y.

In 1847 he received the degree of A. M. from Union College, and in 1876 that of LL.D. from Harvard University.

Mr. Rice was about five feet eight inches high, and weighed about 165 pounds. He was erect and steady, and had prominent and expressive features. His manner and speech were always courtly. He walked to his office in a closely buttoned frock coat and a silk hat. His only relaxation was driving. He was careful and painstaking in the discharge of business, convincing and often eloquent in speech, a debater of large ability, and popular with the people. Ex-Governor Long has called him "A striking representative of Boston citizenship as merchant, scholar, magistrate. He was a man at once of great business sagacity, of ornate and attractive eloquence, and of high character. He has been an ornament to the city and the state."

By Rev. Bradford M. Fullerton, D.D., of Brockton, Mass.

JOHN SAMUEL HILL FOGG, A.M. Bowdoin, M.D. Harvard, was a native of Eliot, Maine, and bore the name of his grandfathers. The emigrant ancestor of the family was Samuel[1] Fogg, who settled at Hampton, N. H., in 1638, and remained a citizen there till his death in 1672. His farm, known as Bride hill, is still held in the family, possession passing by inheritance. No deed of conveyance has covered the property since the original grant. By his wife Anne, daughter of Roger and Anne Shaw, he had a family of four sons and one daughter, of whom, the youngest,

Daniel[2] Fogg, born at Hampton, 1660, became a blacksmith, and removed about 1680 to Black Point (Scarboro'), Maine, where he married Hannah, daughter of John Libby. The incursions of Indians forced removal, and he was at Portsmouth, N. H., for a period; but, in 1700, he purchased a farm on Sturgeon creek, in that part of Kittery now Eliot, Me. There he remained till his death in 1755. He was an original member of the Sturgeon creek (Congregational) church, organized in 1721. His family of nine children—five sons and four daughters—were severally born at Scarborough, Portsmouth and Kittery. The youngest of the family,

James[3] Fogg, born at Kittery, 1704, married Elizabeth, daughter of Dea. James and Mary (Woodman) Fernald, of Kittery, inherited the homestead and passed his life on it as a farmer. He died in 1787. His family of ten children consisted of four sons and six daughters, of whom the youngest surviving,

John[4] Fogg, born at Kittery, 1731, married Abigail, daughter of Dea. William and Katharine (Rogers) Leighton, continued the occupancy of the homestead and the ancestral occupation of husbandry, till his decease in 1827. He had a family of nine children, five daughters and four sons, of whom,

William[5] Fogg, born at Kittery, 1790, married Elizabeth Deed, only child of Samuel and Rebekah Hill of Eliot. He inherited a portion of the paternal homestead and cultivated it till his death. He was a prominent citizen, filling various public offices. Of his family of five children—four sons and one daughter—the only one who married was the subject of this notice,

John Samuel Hill[6] Fogg, born at Eliot, May 21, 1826. He was educated at the South Berwick Academy, Bowdoin College and Harvard Medical School. He married, 1850 (1), Sarah Frances, daughter of Capt. John[5] Stockbridge and Frances[5] Gordon of Exeter, N. H., who deceased in 1870. They had three sons born in Boston, viz.:

i. William John Gordon[7] Fogg, b. 7 August 1851, grad. Harv. A.B. 1873, M.D. 1876; m. 4 Nov., 1880, Ella Frances, dau. Henry E. and Louise Bradlee of Calais, Me. He d. *s.v.p.* 27 February, 1894.
ii. Charles Joseph Fogg, b. 29 October, 1853, d. 22 January, 1856.
iii. Francis Joseph Fogg, b. 4 August, 1857, d. 10 March, 1871, a pupil in the Boston Latin School.

Dr. Fogg married (2), 1872, Mary Griselda, daughter of Rev. Joseph Hart Clinch, D.D., rector of St. Matthew's church, South Boston, who survives him.

Dr. Fogg settled in the practice of his profession in South Boston, directly upon graduation in medicine, and practised his profession with conspicuous success till he was disabled by paraplegic paralysis. He represented the city of Boston in the Legislature of 1855. He served on the School Committee from 1869 continuously to 1873. He became a member of the New-England Historic Genealogical Society in 1858, and remained with us to the close of his life. On the retirement from his professional duties he entered with zeal upon genealogical and historical study and investigation and achieved a remarkable success. He inherited a strong love for history from his father, who was conspicuous as a local historian. Dr. Fogg, with indefatigable industry, collected valuable documents. He possessed the rare faculty of rightly estimating such values. He was seldom at fault in his judgment, and became a skilled expert in matters of Colonial history, and the personalities of the prominent men of those days. Bright in intellect, cheerful in spirit, patient in suffering, he never flinched from acceptance of the awful affliction which visited him.

Dr. Fogg increased the moderate patrimony which he inherited, and left, subject to the life interest of his widow, a considerable property to public uses in his native town, and to the Historical Society of Maine, his native state. He was a resident member, elected Feb. 3, 1858. He died at his residence in South Boston on Monday, October 16, 1893.

By Geo. A. Gordon, A. M., of Somerville, Mass.

ALEXANDER GREGG was born at Society Hill, Darlington District, South Carolina, 8 October, 1819, son of David and Athalinda (Brocky) Gregg, grandson of Capt. James and Mary (Wilson) Gregg, and great-grandson of John and Elinor Gregg of Williamsburg, S. C. He was graduated A.B. with the highest honors of the South Carolina college, at Columbia, in 1838, studied law, was admitted to the bar, and opened an office at Cheraw, S. C. A course of historical reading led to a change in his conception of duty, and he became a candidate for orders in the diocese of South Carolina, was ordered deacon in 1846, priest in 1847 and bishop in 1859. In 1847, he was called to the rectorship of St. David's church, Cheraw, S. C., and remained there till his election by the diocese of Texas, in 1859, as their first bishop. He was consecrated at Richmond, Va., in 1859, and straightway departed for his bishopric. He organized the new diocese and remained its bishop for thirty-three years. He died at Austin, Texas, on the 10th of July, 1893.

Bishop Gregg's ancestry was from the Scotch Presbyterians who were placed, by Oliver Cromwell, in possession of the northern section of Ireland after the battle of Drogheda. A century later, in 1752, John and Joseph Gregg obtained from the provincial authorities of South Carolina, grants of large tracts of land on the waters of the Pedee river, in that province. With their associates they constituted the colony of Williamsburg. John Gregg was the father of four sons and three daughters. As a family, they had no special loyalty for the house of Hanover. They entered heartily into measures for the defence of the rights of the people, resisted the Stamp act and other aggressions of the King's cabinet, and on the outbreak of hostilities rendered efficient service under Gen. Marion. Before the war was fairly afoot in South Carolina John Gregg died, near the close of the year 1775. He was the bishop's great-grandfather. His grandfather, Capt. James Gregg, lived on the west side of the Pedee river, and was an earnest and valuable officer in the American revolution.

Beside his work in his chosen profession, Bishop Gregg was the author of an historical work, the more gratifying that it was thoroughly local, and preserved from oblivion the character and deeds of men of a high order of nobility of character, dwellers in a locality removed from the scene of important military action, but unfaltering in their devotion to the spirit of liberty. This work was entitled "History of the Old Cheraws." He was author, also, of several papers in magazines and encyclopedias on various historical features of Texas and the church in the southwest. In 1859, he was honored with the degree of D.D., which was followed by that of LL.D. He was chancellor of the university of the South, at Sewanee, Tenn. In 1876, he became a corresponding member of the New-England Historic Genealogical Society. His popularity in his diocese extended far beyond the limits of the church. The length of his incumbency, the wisdom of his administration, his courtesy and kindliness of spirit towards all, warranted the epithet with which he was honored, "The best loved man in Texas."

LYMAN MASON, A.B. of Boston, Mass., elected a resident member November 3, 1852, was born in Cavendish, Vermont, April 2, 1815, and died at Boston, February 9, 1894.

He was the youngest of the eight children of Daniel and Betty (Spalding) Mason, and a direct descendant from Capt. Hugh Mason, the emigrant (who came from Ipswich, England, in 1634, and settled at Watertown with his wife

Esther) through John[2] and his wife Elizabeth (Hammond), Daniel[3] and his wife Experience (Newcomb), Samuel[4] and his wife Esther (Mirick) of Newton and Watertown, and Daniel[5] and his wife Betty, above mentioned. His mother, Betty (Spalding) Mason, was the eighth child of William and Esther (Dutton) Spalding of Westford, Mass., and a lineal descendant of Edward Spalding, of Braintree, the emigrant.

Daniel and Betty (Spalding) Mason were married at Cavendish, Vt., and settled there upon a large farm, some three miles from the village. There the large family was reared. The father died when Lyman was six years old, and he was then brought up by his mother, who was a woman of forceful character and spirit. Mr. Mason seems to have inherited from her his literary tastes and desire for an education. Among the hills, on the farm, he lived the life of a New England boy of his time, attending the district school in winter, working upon the farm the rest of the year. He attended the Duttonville Academy, in Cavendish, several terms, and there fitted for college. Mr. Mason entered Dartmouth College in 1835, and had the experience of many farmers' boys, whose ambition outran their financial means ; he had to teach school during a portion of his years, and work hard to "make up" his studies. During the last two years his vacations were spent in the study of the law, in the office of Mr. French, a neighboring lawyer. He graduated from Dartmouth College in 1839. In the autumn of 1839, Mr. Mason received an appointment at "Western Reserve College," Hudson, Ohio, as teacher of Mathematics and Latin. After a year of hard work he resigned this position, and entered the law office of G. N. Cumming of Zanesville, Ohio, a native of Windsor, Vt. In May, 1841, he was admitted to the bar, at Springfield, Ohio. Mr. Mason wrote to a classmate, at this time, that he did not consider his course of study sufficient preparation for the successful practice of the law, but that it seemed expedient in his case to take admission. Finding his health greatly impaired by confinement in the office and excessive study, he engaged in canvassing for a subscription agency, which gave him an opportunity to travel through parts of Ohio, Pennsylvania and Virginia. One year of this stirring out-door life restored his health so that he returned to Vermont in 1842, and was admitted to the bar in Woodstock, Vt., the same year. In the fall of 1842, he was appointed tutor in Dartmouth College, in which position he remained two years, and in this time entered his name, and pursued his law studies under the direction of Hon. Richard Fletcher, of Boston. In August, 1844, he came to Boston and opened an office, and began the practice of law, in the old "Tudor Building," where he remained until 1881, when the building was torn down. He then removed his office to 24 Congress Street, where he remained until his death.

Mr. Mason was an able and trusted counsellor and attorney, and besides his general practice held the care of several large estates for many years. He did not seek public office, but in 1874 was elected to the State Legislature; and he served on the Boston School Committee from 1868 to 1874. He was treasurer of the American Statistical Society for many years, and a member of the Natural History Society. During the late years of his life he attended the "Old South Church" in Boston.

Mr. Mason was of fine presence and impressive manners, carrying the conviction to all of the true gentleman. I have before me many testimonials, of those who knew him best, of his nobility of character and sweetness of disposition. Many men who are now successful have cause to remember a kindly hand of help in their time of struggle, and many outside his own home will remember his large sympathy and ready assistance.

Mr. Mason married at Cincinnati, Ohio, May 25, 1853, Mary Lucretia, daughter of Dr. Reuben D. Mussey. Mrs. Mason died March 19, 1889. Mr. Mason, though feeble in health for two years, continued his practice until a few days before his death. Three daughters survive him : Katie Mussey Mason, Mary Lyman Mason, and Elizabeth Spalding Mason.

By Rev. George Madison Bodge, A.M., Leominster, Mass.

Col. Roland Greene Usher was born at Medford, January 6, 1823, and died at Lynn, March 5, 1895. He was elected a resident member of this Society February 8, 1869, and became a life member in 1875.

Colonel Usher was descended in direct line from Robert Usher, the English emigrant of this branch, who came, with his brother Hezekiah, to Massachusetts, previous to 1638. He soon removed to Connecticut and settled at Stamford, where he lived, a man of wealth and influence, until his death in 1669. His son Robert[2] settled at Dunstable (now Nashua, N. H.) and had a son John,[3] born May 31, 1696, who had a son Robert,[4] born April 9, 1730, who lived at Merrimack and Medford, Mass., and whose youngest son was Eleazar,[5] born November 23, 1770. Eleazar[5] lived at Medford, married Fanny Bucknam, Oct. 6, 1799, and by her had eleven children, of whom the youngest was Roland Greene[6] Usher, the subject of this sketch.

At ten years of age young Usher removed, with his older brothers, James and Leonard, to Lynn, where they engaged in a bakery business in a small way, the younger brother assisting, and having some time to attend school. His health being very frail he was sent for two years to live with his sister Lydia at Londonderry, N. H., after which he returned to Lynn, and was apprenticed to Mr. John Lovejoy to learn the morocco-dresser's trade, which calling he followed for seven years. He married June 5, 1844, Caroline M., daughter of Daniel L. Mudge of Lynn, to whose loving care was due in large measure his restoration to health and the development of the qualities which made him so useful in many ways to his fellow men.

In 1847 Mr. Usher engaged in the business of ready-made clothing, a novel pursuit then, but with his care and devotion to it he achieved fair success. In 1861, at the breaking out of the war, his interest in military matters, and prominence in public affairs, withdrew him from a business career and held him, during his after life, in public office. As early as 1840 he had joined the "Lynn Light Infantry," and was afterwards elected first lieutenant of the company, and upon the organization of the Eighth Regiment was appointed lieutenant-colonel. When this regiment left for Washington, April 17, 1861, Colonel Usher was placed upon the staff as regimental paymaster. In July, 1861, he was commissioned by President Lincoln as a paymaster in the United States army, in which office he served until the close of the war, holding successively the appointments of paymaster-in-chief of the "Department of the Gulf," the "Department of Annapolis," and the "Department of Virginia and North Carolina," having supervision of some thirty subordinate paymasters. After the war, and upon the reorganization of the State militia, in 1866, Colonel Usher was appointed aide-de-camp to Major-General B. F. Butler, and held that office for ten years. In January, 1866, he was elected Mayor of Lynn, and served in that office three years, during which time great improvements were made in the reorganization of the police force, the new City Hall was erected and dedicated, and a complete system of sewerage was begun. He was elected and served as a member of the Massachusetts Council through three years, under Governors Bullock and Claflin. March 3, 1871, he was appointed by General Grant—then President—United States Marshal for the district of Massachusetts, and was reappointed in 1875. February 14, 1883, he was appointed by Governor Butler, warden of the State Prison, and held that position until 1886.

Colonel Usher was a member of the Masonic order, and received the Master's degree October 27, 1856, in Mount Carmel Lodge, in Lynn. He received the Knight Templar degree in Olivet Commandery February 3, 1875. In February, 1844, he was initiated a member of Siloam Lodge of Odd Fellows, in Boston, and afterwards joined the Bay State Lodge, of which he became Noble Grand in 1847.

He was a comrade of General Lander Post 5, G. A. R. He was a valued member St. Stephen's Episcopal Church, and took a warm interest in its prosperity.

Colonel Usher was public spirited and ever ready to give of his time, talent and means to whatever cause concerned the public welfare.

Two of the four children of Colonel Usher survive him: Edward Preston and Caroline Mudge, wife of Rev. Allen Harlow, an Episcopal minister in Trenton, New Jersey.

By Rev. George M. Bodge, Leominster, Mass.

HOWLAND HOLMES, A.M., M.D., of Lexington, a resident member, elected April 7, 1875, was born in Halifax, Plymouth County, Jan. 16, 1815, the son of Howland and Huldah (Copeland) Holmes. He traced his ancestry to John Holmes of Plymouth (1632) and, on his mother's side, to John Alden.

He attended school at Bridgewater and at Phillips Exeter Academy, and was graduated at Harvard in 1843, taking his medical degree in '48. He taught school at Belmont, Charlestown, and elsewhere in the intervals of study. He spent a year in Europe, attending medical lectures in Paris and visiting the hospitals of London.

Dr. Holmes began practice in West Cambridge (Arlington), where he found his wife, Sarah Maria Wellington, daughter of William Cotting. They were married August 28, 1849, at Albany, N. Y. In 1851 they moved to Lexington and made that their permanent home.

By his skill and sympathy Dr. Holmes acquired an extensive practice. He was always willing to respond to the calls of the poor. As a citizen he participated freely in municipal affairs, having plans and convictions of his own which he was always ready to advocate. Few subjects of importance came up in town meetings upon which he did not have something to say. He was a zealous promoter of several public measures which were of distinct advantage to the town. He originated a society for planting shade trees in 1853, and was an early member of the Farmers' Club. He served on many town committees and was an efficient member of the School Board. He was interested in the organization of the Cary Library in Lexington, and founded the Holmes Library in his native town. He enjoyed his membership in the Massachusetts Medical Society, the Middlesex East District Medical Society, and in the New-England Historic Genealogical Society, and attended the meetings with great regularity. Several of his papers on medical subjects were published.

Dr. Holmes inherited the sturdy qualities of his ancestors. Having been brought up on a farm he acquired that love of out-door work which was a characteristic of his whole life. His fruit and flower garden was one of the best in the village.

He was social, generous, hospitable, of medium stature, of a ruddy complexion and active temperament. His wife, a son and a daughter survive him.

He lived nearly four score years—more than a quarter of the entire period covered by our country's history. In his childhood he might have listened to some one who had known a man who had talked with the Pilgrim Fathers.

The manner of his departure was noteworthy. On the 16th of November, 1893, he drove down to Medford to take a basket of fruit of his own raising to some friends, and upon his return, as he crossed the Mystic River—how significant the name—at the same moment he passed over Jordan, and his spirit took its flight. The simple vehicle in which he had so often driven on his earthly ministrations bore him at last to his journey's end.

By Rev. Edward G. Porter, A.M., of Dorchester.

AUSTIN JACOBS COOLIDGE, A.M., LL.B., son of Dea. Josiah and Mary (Hastings) Coolidge, was born in Cambridge, Mass., April 18, 1824; married April 23, 1862, Susan Gibson, daughter of William and Susan (Spurr) Marshall; and died, without issue, in Watertown, Mass., March 20, 1895. His earliest ancestor in America was John Coolidge, who settled in Watertown about 1630, where are still standing the gravestones of himself and his wife Mary. The name is traceable to "de Coulinge" of the time of Edward the First, and is probably derived from the village of Couling in Cambridgeshire, Eng. The griffin and fleur-de-lis seem to have been connected with the family arms. Austin J. Coolidge traces his descent through fourteen generations in direct line to Thomas Colyng of Arrington, Eng., as follows: Austin Jacobs,[14] Josiah,[13] Joshua,[12] Joseph,[11] Simon,[10] Obadiah,[9] Simon,[8] John,[7] William,[6] Simeon,[5] John[4] (Colyng), Thomas,[3] John,[2] Thomas.[1]

Mr. Coolidge fitted for college at the Worcester Academy, graduated from Harvard College in 1847, from the Harvard Law School in 1850, and was admitted to the Suffolk bar in 1852. He engaged in teaching after graduating from college, but very soon turned to the law, which he practiced more or less through life, though his last twenty years were almost wholly devoted to commercial pursuits. He was at the head of the New England Machine Company in Boston, and for many years Secretary of the Mount Auburn Corporation.

He was an officer of the Watertown Historical Society, and a member of the New-England Historic Genealogical Society, and his training and tastes fitted him specially for historical work. In 1860 he published, as joint author with John B. Mansfield, the first volume of "A History and Description of New

England, General and Local," embracing Maine, New Hampshire and Vermont. The outbreak of the civil war unfortunately prevented the appearance of the remaining volume, which had been prepared for the press.

He was a public spirited citizen and a staunch republican from the beginning of the party. He was a member of several social organizations, and greatly interested in educational and religious work. He was for a time on the School Board of Cambridge, and for seventeen years the very efficient Clerk of the Old Cambridge Baptist Church of which he was an original member. He was always genial, kindly and unselfish, more mindful of the welfare and happiness of others than of his own personal interests.

By Rev. Sylvanus Hayward, A.M., Globe Village, Mass.

Franklin Leonard Pope, Esq., a resident member, elected March 2, 1887, was born in Great Barrington, Mass., Dec. 2, 1840. He was of the line of Thomas Pope, a resident of Plymouth in 1632, afterwards one of the founders of Dartmouth. He was a son of Ebenezer[7] (Capt. Ebenezer,[6] Seth,[5] Seth,[4] John,[3] Seth[2]) and Electa Leonard (Wainwright). He married, Aug. 8, 1873, Sarah Amelia, daughter of Captain M. Fayette and Hannah (Williams) Dickinson of Amherst, Mass. Three children of this union survive, viz.: Hannah Dickinson, Amy Margaretta, and Franklin Leonard Wainwright.

Mr. Pope began manly life early; was a telegraph operator in 1857 in his native town, and then in Springfield, Providence and New York. Here, during the draft riots of 1863, he personally joined the fragments of demolished wires to establish communication between New York and Boston. He was made assistant engineer of that party which undertook to establish a telegraph line between San Francisco and Russia by way of Behring's Straits; which made the first exploration of the country between the Skeena, Stickeen and Yukon rivers, 1865-67. He made important inventions in printing, telegraph and electric matters. Was a prominent patent solicitor in these subjects, and an expert consulting engineer in all electrical affairs, whose services were appreciated highly by Westinghouse and other strong operators. With Edison in 1870 he invented the one-wire printing telegraph or "ticker," and in 1872 he invented the rail circuit for automatically controlling block signals. He was president of the American Institute of Electrical Engineers in 1885-6; was editor of "The Electrical Engineer" several years. The re-construction of the Great Barrington electrical plant was one of his recent undertakings. He wrote many articles for the magazines, giving sometimes scientific theses, but oftener simple statements of the marvels of electricity. His published works were: Modern Practice of the Electric Telegraph, New York, Russell Bros., 1869, of which the 14th edition was issued in 1891, 234 pp., 8vo.; Life and Works of Joseph Henry, New York, Van Nostrand, 1879, 31 pp.; The Western Boundary of Massachusetts, a study of Indian and colonial life, Pittsfield, 1886, 61 pp., 8vo.; Evolution of the Incandescent Lamp, Elizabeth, N. J., H. Cook, 1889, 91 pp., 8vo., Capt. Ebenezer Pope of Great Barrington, privately printed; Genealogy of Thomas Pope (1608-1683) and some of his descendants, Boston, D. Clapp & Son, 1888, 22 pp., 8vo.

He resided many years at Elizabeth, N. J., having his office in New York city; the past year he spent at Great Barrington, in the house his ancestors had occupied, which he had re-modeled and converted into an elegant residence.

Death came to him in his cellar, where he had gone to adjust the electric light apparatus. The family heard him fall, his lamp explode, and found him lifeless under the power of 3,000 volts of electric current; a conspicuous victim of that force he had so deeply studied, so clearly explained, so extensively controlled, but against which even the wisest and wariest cannot be infallibly insured. Mr. Pope will be widely mourned; for in addition to his penetrating mind and admirable powers of investigation and expression, which promised to accomplish still more in various departments, he had remarkable personal qualities, which endeared him to very many relatives and friends.

By Rev. Charles H. Pope, A.M., of Cambridge.

Benjamin Pierce Cheney, A.M., a life member of this Society from 1870, born in Hillsborough, N.H., Aug. 12, 1815, was son of Jesse and Alice (Steele) Cheney. He was named for the village squire, ex-governor of the state, the father of one of the presidents of the United States. He received a present of three sheep in recognition of the naming. The sheep had to be killed because of a great drought, and the boy had no other dowry; but he entered life's tournament with the courage and sagacity of the Cheney family. Hard times made it impossible for his parents to furnish him any extended schooling or the least capital. But he found something to do and did it well. As a young man he handled the reins so skilfully and treated passengers so politely that he became a popular stage-driver on the route to Boston. His chief success was as travelling banker, conveyer of valuable parcels, particularly those containing money. Here he showed rare fidelity and ability; and won such fame that the united stage companies of the Montreal and Boston lines selected him to reside in Boston and manage their whole business of forwarding money and goods. Not rendered vain by such a position and a salary larger than any bank cashier in the metropolis was then receiving, he kept on systematizing and improving his methods and developing an industry. He profited by the example of W. F. Harnden, who created and gave the name to the "Express" business in its modern form, and of Alvin Adams who was engaged in it from 1840 onward; and while he stood by old employees and old principles he availed himself of every new mode of transportation and opening for business. He keenly perceived favorable prospects in real estate or railroad interests and discriminated sagaciously when new projects were suggested. Operating with various associates he at length rose to be treasurer of the great United States and Canada Express Company. He also possessed heavy shares in some of the most prosperous railways of the country.

He always recognized the rights of others, and took the greatest care of all that they entrusted to him. Many prospered because he protected their wealth: it was fair that he should become wealthy in such a course. He gave $12,000 to erect in Concord, N. H., a bronze statue of Daniel Webster, and $50,000 to the great college of his native state. These are shining samples of his beneficence. His charming gardens and grounds at Wellesley, so much enjoyed by multitudes, indicated his refined tastes. He well deserved the honorary degree of Master of Arts which Dartmouth conferred upon him, for his achievements in business were an *art*, and he patronized and grew in all true culture. It has been said of him that "he had no aspirations for public office; that in religion he never forgot the foundation, namely that of being a sober, energetic, industrious, honest, humble, God-fearing man."

He was in the eighth generation (Jesse,[7] Elias,[6] Tristram,[5] John,[4] John,[3] Peter[2],) from John[1] and Martha Cheney, who came in 1635 to Roxbury and removed in 1636 to Newbury, where they were valuable members of church and community. The intermarrying lines were among our worthiest New England people. His wife is a descendant of Rev. Samuel Whiting of Lynn and Elizabeth St. John, who traced her lineage back to ten European sovereigns. But he made no boast of family. He felt and proved the truth of that motto of the English Cheneys, "*Fato prudentia major,*" which may be paraphrased thus: Wise energy is mightier than circumstances.

He married June 6, 1865, a representative of one of the best Dorchester families, Elizabeth Stickney, daughter of Mr. Asahel and Elizabeth S. (Whiting) Clap, distantly related to him through the Clap line. They were blessed with five children: Benjamin Pierce junior, Alice, Charles P., Mary and Elizabeth, all of whom survive him. He has resided a portion of the time in his Marlborough street home in this city, and part at his lovely villa in Wellesley. He died July 23, 1895, having rounded out a long, useful, successful life.

By Rev. Charles H. Pope, A.M., of Cambridge.

Hon. WARREN LADD, a resident member, elected May 7, 1884, died at his home in New Bedford, Mass., on the 20th of February, 1895. New Bedford has lost one of her most highly esteemed citizens, and the New-England Genealogical Society a valued member and contributor. Mr. Ladd was specially interested in genealogical research, and, two years before his death, published a three-hundred page book on the Ladd family. The following sketch of his life is taken chiefly from the History of Bristol County. He was in the front ranks of progress and reform in all municipal, social and political movements. He was born in that part of Bradford, Mass., now Groveland, on the 21st of July, 1813. His line runs back to Daniel Ladd, who came to this country in the *Mary and John* in 1633, and who was one of the original settlers of Haverhill.

On his mother's side he was a descendant of Richard Ingersol, who came from Bedfordshire, England, in 1627, and settled at Salem. Mr. Ladd's mother was Sarah Ingersol, a daughter of Colonel Zebulon and Ruth (Moody) Ingersol. Her father was a soldier in the Revolution. Another ancestor was Rev. James Noyes, who came over in the *Mary and John* in 1633, "driven," wrote Cotton Mather, "out of the nation for his non-conformity to its unhappy ceremonies in the worship of God." His father was a prominent citizen of Groveland for many years, held many of the offices in the gift of the town, was postmaster and a leading member of the Congregational church.

Warren Ladd was educated at the public schools of Bradford and at the Merrimac academy. He went to New Bedford on the first of July, 1840, and entered the employ of the New Bedford & Taunton railroad company as clerk in its freight office. Soon he became freight agent, and then general agent. In 1862 he was appointed general superintendent of the road, a position which he held until 1877, when the consolidation with the Boston, Clinton & Fitchburg road resulted in an entire change of management. His connection with the road covered the entire period from its opening till its consolidation with the other road, an extent of about thirty-seven years. In April, 1877, he was elected president and superintendent of the New Bedford & Fairhaven street railway, and remained in that place till the company surrendered its charter, and entered into the combination with a competing road, ten years later. He has been connected with several corporations as a director, and was one of the trustees of the Five Cents Savings Bank of New Bedford.

Mr. Ladd always took a deep interest in public affairs, and was constant and faithful in the performance of his duties as a citizen. His spare time in his early life, and indeed so long as he lived, was earnestly devoted to reading on every subject which could store his mind with useful knowledge. He early became interested in municipal affairs, and for many years was prominent in their direction. Four years—1851, '52, '53 and '57—he was a member of the Common Council of New Bedford, and in one of them its president, and five years—1861, '62, '63, '64 and '65—he was a member of the Board of Aldermen. In November, 1868, he was elected a member of the School Committee, but he resigned before the expiration of his first year, saying that he had not the leisure to discharge its duties with satisfaction to himself or with that fulness and faithfulness which his constituents had a right to expect. For many years he was a trustee of the free public library. A high authority gives him the credit of being its father. When the corner stone of the present library building was laid, Mayor Howland used these words in his address: "On the 8th of the seventh month (July) of the same year (1851) Warren Ladd, a member of the Common Council from ward one, introduced an order into that branch of the City Government, for the raising of a committee to consider the expedience of establishing in this city a free public library. The order was adopted, but was non-concurred in by the board of aldermen. This is believed to be the first order ever introduced into any representative body for the establishment of such an institution, and to this gentleman must, and does, belong the honor of having taken the initiatory step toward the establishment of the library for the public by the people themselves." Only a few years later the library was established, and no doubt Mr. Ladd's order prepared the way for it.

Mr. Ladd was a determined advocate of the introduction of water into the city of New Bedford, when the idea was not popular. At that time the opposition was exceedingly powerful, including a large share of what were then known as "our leading citizens." He saw into the future better than they did, and his attitude is exhibited in this extract from a report made by him to the City Council, as a member of a committee to consider the subject: "Your committee are fully of the opinion that the introduction of an ample supply of pure water into the city is an imperative necessity, and one which should not be much longer delayed. It is the part of wise statesmanship to look at the future, to anticipate its wants, and guard against its casualties. Cities, like men, flourish and prosper only by their own exertions, and it becomes those whom the people have placed in power to be equal to the present emergency. We have the interest and the honor of the city in our hands. We know its wants and necessities, and can comprehend the crisis in our affairs. Shall we grasp and control the crisis, turn it with a steady hand to our interest and prosperity, or allow it silently and timidly to pass by and float beyond our reach?

Shall we legislate only for to-day, and shrink from looking the great future in the face, or shall we, knowing the necessity and perceiving the remedy, fearlessly perform our duty?" These were words which had a great influence in determining the course of the wavering City Council. Mr. Ladd was one of the three commissioners under whose direction the water works were built.

He was foremost in the improvement of the fire department, introducing into the Common Council the first order for the appointment of a committee to consider the expediency of procuring a steam fire engine. In this matter, more than that of the water works, he had to encounter a stubborn conservatism. There was a most persistent opposition to the New-England machine, which really never ceased until after a steamer had appeared in New Bedford and demonstrated beyond all cavil its superiority to a hand engine. Mr. Ladd's progressiveness was never more favorably shown than in his championship of the steam fire engine.

In politics Mr. Ladd was originally a Whig, but he became a Republican early in that party's history, and adhered to it till his death. For many years he was a member of the Republican city committee, and for a time its chairman. In 1876 he was presidential elector for the first congressional district. He contributed largely to the newspapers on political and other subjects. Much of his work in this direction was vigorous and forcible.

Mr. Ladd cherished a deep interest in historical and genealogical matters, and became a member of the New-England Historic Genealogical Society on the 7th of May, 1884, and here continued to the end of his life. He was also a member of the Webster Historical Society and the Old Colony Historical Society.

He was married Nov. 22, 1842, to Lucy Washburn Kingman, a daughter of Hon. Abel and Elizabeth (Manly) Kingman of North Bridgewater, and their golden wedding, celebrated in 1892, was one of the pleasantest occasions of its kind. They had five children. [One of them is Hon. Herbert Warren Ladd, for two years Governor of the State of Rhode Island, Chairman of the New State House Commission, and widely known as the head of one of the large dry goods establishments in the city of Providence.]

By Hon. Herbert W. Ladd, A.M., of Providence, R. I.

WILLIAM HENRY EMERY, Esq., of Boston, was born in Biddeford, Me., March 22, 1822, and died in Newton, Mass., November 28, 1893. He was elected a resident member of this Society January 7, 1877. He was descended from John Emery, one of the early settlers of New England. The family line is as follows:—

William Henry Emery[8], Isaac[7], Thomas[6], Thomas[5], James[4], James[3], Anthony[2], John[1]. Anthony[2] came to this country in 1635, in the "bark James" of London. Isaac Emery[7] was aid to Governor Paris of Maine, and a member of the Committee to receive Lafayette in 1824. He was also a member of Governor Boutwell's Council, and one of the founders of the John Hancock Life Insurance Company. His mother, Faith Bigelow, was a descendant of the noted Ann Hutchinson, also of Philip Savage, Chairman of the "Tea Party" meeting in the Old South Meeting House, December 16, 1773.

Mr. Emery was educated at Thornton Academy, Saco, Me. At the age of 18 he engaged in the coal trade, which afterwards became his life business, though he was for some years Entry Clerk in the Custom House. He was a man highly respected and sought for to fill positions of trust. He was a member of the Masonic Fraternity and a trustee of the Franklin Savings bank. He gave a good deal of time to genealogical researches. He had those traits of character which made him a great favorite, exceptionally popular in an extended social circle, "a man to be sadly missed," honorably known as a business man. His fellow tradesmen testify that "he earned and well maintained the title of a good citizen, an upright merchant, and an honest man, who could always be relied upon in the various duties and trusts in life."

He married first, October 5, 1847, Sarah R., daughter of Thomas Haviland of Boston. She died October 16, 1855, leaving two daughters, Mary Haviland and Helen Bigelow. He next married, October 22, 1856, Eliza Bishop, daughter of Nathaniel Holmes Bishop of Medford, Mass., by whom he had Eliza Kate, William Bishop, and Heber Bishop.

By Rev. Sylvanus Haywood, A.M., Globe Village, Mass.

JOHN BROOKS FENNO, Esq., a resident member, elected May 7, 1873, was a son of John and Temperance (Harding) Fenno, and was born in Charlestown, March 3, 1816. He was sixth in descent from John Fenno, one of the early settlers of Dorchester, who came there with his mother, Rebecca Fenno, she being a widow, his line being Rebecca,[1] John,[2] Ephraim,[3] John,[4] Samuel,[5] John,[6] John Brooks.[7]

He was named for Governor John Brooks, who was the family physician. He was educated in the public schools of Boston, graduating at the English High School in the class of 1832, and winning two Franklin medals during his school course. After his graduation he became connected with the importing house of Thomas and Edward Motley and remained till the dissolution of that firm. In 1841 he went into partnership with John Wetherell and George A. Whitney, under the firm name of Wetherell, Whitney and Company, which did a dry goods business at 59 Kilby street. In 1844 the firm was changed to Whitney & Fenno, subsequently to Fenno, Foster and Badger, and later to Fenno and Jones.

He went into the general commission business in 1864 with John L. Childs, forming the firm of Fenno and Childs, afterwards Fenno, Abbott & Co., and in 1874 Fenno, Son & Co. In 1879 he retired from business and remained out of active business life till his death, February 14, 1894.

In politics he was an ardent Whig, and later a stanch Republican, but declined to accept any public office. He was not a member of any club, but was a member of the Bostonian Society, Massachusetts Horticultural Society, and the Natural History Society. He had been a member of the New-England Historic Genealogical Society since 1873 and was a member of Trinity Church and a vestryman for several years.

He married in 1844 Sarah Elizabeth, daughter of Richard Smith of Smithtown, Long Island, N. Y., who inherited the lands purchased by his ancestors of the Indians, the previous owners, also granddaughter of General Nathaniel Woodhull, who was killed in the battle of Long Island in the war of the American Revolution.

They had four children — Edward Nicholl, Lawrence Carteret, John Brooks and Florence Harding. The two oldest sons succeeded to their father's business. The daughter married Walter Carey Tuckerman of New York.

By David H. Brown, Esq., of West Medford, Mass.

JOHN HEARD, Esq., a life member since May 4, 1870, was born in Ipswich, September 14, 1824; and died in Boston, February 19, 1894. He was the son of George W. and Elizabeth Ann (Farley) Heard. His mother was a granddaughter of General Michael Farley of the Revolutionary army. Mr. Heard descends from Luke Heard, an early settler of Ipswich. In his youth he received training at Greenleaf's school, Salem, from thence he went to the Andover Academy, and on the removal of his father to Boston he entered its public schools. His eyes were a source of trouble and he gave up school, making voyages to Cuba and Russia. He soon entered the employ of his uncle Augustine Heard, and accompanied him to Hong Kong in 1841. The opium war was then in progress. Mr. Heard soon became a partner and before he was twenty-one was the head of the Augustine Heard & Co. Tea House in China, his uncle returning in 1844. Mr. Heard remained in China until 1852, when he was absent four years, during which time he came to America and travelled in India and Europe. A year after the treaty had been made with Japan in 1859, Mr. Heard was invited to go with the Hon. Townsend Harris, the American Minister, to Yeddo. He was the first civilian to enter Japan, and his ship which came to take him back was the first merchant vessel that had ever passed the Straits of Uraga. He was also the first civilian to go up the Yangtse River. In 1861, the war culminated in a treaty by which China agreed to open three ports on the Yangtse River. Lord Elgin with a small squadron made an expedition to look at his new possessions, and Mr. Heard went soon after to Hankow, a distance of six hundred miles, in a steamboat belonging to his House. The river was entirely unknown and before then no foreigners had been admitted into the interior of China. In 1861 he was made the Portugese Consul, also the Russian Consul, and received honors from each of these governments. After 1862 Mr. Heard did not return to China excepting for a brief trip in 1876.

Mr. Heard married in 1867 Alice Leeds, daughter of the Rev. George Leeds,

D.D., Rector of St. Peter's Church, Philadelphia. A daughter and two sons were born to them, one of which sons died. Mr. Heard died at Boston, and his remains were interred in the family tomb, Ipswich, where he maintained a residence. Mr. Heard was member of the Board of Trustees of Public Library, Ipswich—which library was founded by his uncle. Though many years were spent in China, yet there was no spot so beautiful to him as his native town. He rejoiced in all her interests, and New England with its peculiar institutions was a source of pride.

By Rev. Anson Titus, of Somerville, Mass.

HENRY AUGUSTUS GOWING, Esq., son of John Hill and Sophia Viles (Bigelow) Gowing, was born in Weston, Mass., Aug. 2, 1834; married Sept. 8, 1859, Clara Elizabeth, only child of Dr. Franklin Fletcher and Mary Ann (Wentworth) Patch; and died in Boston, Dec. 14, 1894, leaving a widow and two children: Mrs. Mary Sophia Richardson and Franklin Patch Gowing. His earliest ancestor in America was Robert Gowing from Edinburgh, Scotland, who settled in Lynn, was made a Freeman at Dedham in 1639, and married Elizabeth Brock in 1644. The line of descent was Henry Augustus,[7] John Hill,[6] Samuel,[5] James,[4] Samuel,[3] John,[2] Robert.[1]

Mr. Gowing was educated in private schools at Waltham and Boston. In 1853 he obtained a position with J. W. Blodgett & Co., dry goods merchants of Boston, where he remained five years. He then accepted the position of bookkeeper with Dodge Bros. & Co., and became a member of the firm in 1868. He continued in the business under changing names of the same firm, which at the time of his death was "Gowing, Sawyer & Co. of Boston and New York." He held a high position in trade, as a man of business capacity and thorough integrity, whose "word was as good as his bond." His wide acquaintance, long experience, and well-earned popularity, contributed largely to the great success of the firm.

In politics, Mr. Gowing was always a republican, having cast his first vote for Fremont for president. Never desiring a public office, he was an earnest Christian citizen, and an enthusiastic promoter of whatever he believed to be for the best good of the country, state, city, or town in which he lived.

He belonged to the Sons of the Revolution, to the Boston Art Club, and to the New-England Historic Genealogical Society, having been elected a resident member December 7, 1870.

He was fond of Nature, delighting in the simple pleasures of gardening, and all out-door life, and had a wonderful love of flowers, especially when growing wild in field and forest. For many years he made his summer home in the old house where he was born, and here found his most restful and happy recreation.

He joined the Baptist Church in early life. His religious belief was "broad and settled," gladly accepting the best in all denominations. In his daily life he always trusted to a Higher Wisdom for guidance, and gave God the glory for all he received.

A boulder carried from his own farm to Forest Hills marks the place of his burial.

By Rev. Sylvanus Hayward, A.M., Globe Village, Mass.

DAVID PULSIFER, A.M., a resident member, elected June 2, 1847, died at Augusta, Me., August 9, 1894, in his 92d year, and was buried in Mount Pleasant Cemetery, in that city, by the side of his wife. He was the fourth son of Capt. David and Mrs. Sarah (Stanwood) Pulsifer of Ipswich, Mass., in which town he was born on Wednesday, September 22, 1802. He began going to school when he was four years old. The school was kept in the house where Rev. John Norton lived, who was settled, in 1636, as colleague of Rev. Nathaniel Ward, author of the Simple Cobler of Aggawam, which book Mr. Pulsifer edited and published nearly two centuries after the author's death.

"When I was about six years old," Mr. Pulsifer wrote to me, "I was sent to the Middle District School. While there, when I was about eleven years old, our master, Rev. Ebenezer Hubbard, called to me from his desk, 'David, don't you want a book to read?' I went to the desk and he handed me a volume of Mavor's Voyages, in which was an account of Sir Walter Raleigh's Voyages, which interested me in Sir Walter exceedingly. . . . When President James Monroe visited New England, I stood with my schoolmates in honor of the president while he rode slowly by us with his hat in his hand.

"When I was fifteen years of age I went to Salem to learn the art of book-binding of Mr. Isaac Cushing. While there, Benjamin R. Nichols, Esq., brought all the original records of Plymouth Colony, from 1620 to 1686, and had them interleaved and newly bound. He also brought the copies that he had made, and Hazard's Historical Collections, containing the Acts of the Commissioners of the United Colonies. I made copies of the Plymouth Charter, Myles Standish's Will and Inventory, and some Quaker 'Railing Papers.'

"Rev. William Bentley came to the bindery occasionally, and would bring a book and stay till it was done, saying, as he came, 'I have brought a book to be *stabadoed*,' meaning not to be taken apart. He was very much interested in the Plymouth records."

Before Mr. Pulsifer was twenty-one years old he entered the office of Ichabod Tucker, clerk of the Essex County Courts. There he remained about eight years. In February, 1841, he came to Boston, and was employed as a book-keeper by James Munroe & Co., publishers and booksellers. He was afterwards employed in the offices of the Clerk of the Courts and Registry of Deeds in the County of Middlesex, and transcribed several of the ancient books of record in each office. He had then become familiar with the handwriting of the seventeenth century, and gained a high reputation for his skill in deciphering it. He also copied the records of the old County of Norfolk, which comprised the portion of the present County of Essex north of the Merrimac and a part of the present State of New Hampshire. For the American Antiquarian Society he copied the first volume of the Massachusetts Colony Records, a part of which was published by that society in the third volume of its transactions. The printing of the records was discontinued when, in May, 1853, the Massachusetts General Court voted to print *its* early colony records. Hon. Nathaniel B. Shurtleff, M. D., was appointed editor of the work, and Mr. Pulsifer was employed as copyist. Mr. Pulsifer's copy of the first volume was purchased of the Antiquarian Society by the State, and was used in printing the work. After the issue of the Massachusetts Colony Records to 1688 was completed in five volumes, the State authorized the printing of the Plymouth Colony Records, and Dr. Shurtleff was appointed editor. Mr. Pulsifer copied a large portion of both works, though others assisted. In 1858, after the issue of six volumes (bound in four) of the Plymouth Records, Mr. Pulsifer succeeded Dr. Shurtleff as editor, and completed the work in twelve volumes. The tenth and eleventh volumes of these records comprise the Acts of the Commissioners of the United Colonies, and the editing of them is a model of thoroughness. Nearly the whole of two or more volumes, which do not bear his name as editor, were edited by him, the title-pages and a few pages of the text of each work having been stereotyped before his appointment. An account of the printing of these records and Mr. Pulsifer's connection with it may be found in the REGISTER for July 1885, pages 284-6. See also notices in the REGISTER for October 1858, page 85, by Hon. Timothy Farrar, LL.D., and the editor, Samuel G. Drake, A.M.

Mr. Pulsifer continued to be a clerk in the office of the Secretary of State till about a dozen years before his death. He married, in 1867, Mrs. Lucie Whaer, whose maiden name was Safford. She was a daughter of James and Mary Safford, and was born at China, Me. She died at Boston, October 28, 1887, aged 65, and was buried at Augusta, Me.

He published: 1. "Inscriptions from the Burying Grounds at Salem," 8vo, 1837; 2. "A Guide to Boston and Vicinity," 12mo, 1860. This was based on "Sights in Boston and Suburbs," by the late R. L. Midgley, whose copyright and plates he purchased. 3. "Account of the Battle of Bunker Hill, with General Burgoyne's account," 18mo, 1872. He also edited an edition of "The Simple Cobler of Aggawam," by Rev. Nathaniel Ward, 12mo, 1843; "A Poetical Epistle to George Washington," by Rev. Charles H. Wharton, 12mo, 1881; and "The Christian's A. B. C.," written by an unknown author in a previous century, 1883.

Mr. Pulsifer was librarian of this Society from 1849 to 1851, and recording secretary in 1857. He transcribed for the early volumes of the REGISTER, the records of Boston, and contributed other articles to this work.

He was an active member of the Masonic fraternity, being a member of the Winslow Lewis Lodge. He was a Fellow of the American Statistical Association, elected in 1848, and was its librarian 1863-5. He was a contributor of valuable articles to the early volumes of the REGISTER. In 1863 Amherst College conferred upon him the honorary degree of Master of Arts.

He was a resident of Boston till a few years before his death, when he removed to Everett, Mass., and subsequently to Augusta, Me.

A considerable portion of this sketch was contributed by me to the *Boston Evening Transcript*, Sept. 14, 1894.

By John Ward Dean, A.M.

WILLIAM JOHN POTTS, Esq., of Camden, N. J., was born in Philadelphia, October 14, 1842, and died in Camden, November 18, 1895. He was elected a corresponding member of this Society March 4, 1874.

He was the son of Robert Barnhill and Sarah Page [Grew] Potts. His father was a manufacturing chemist, having extensive works in Camden, to which place he removed in 1850. His mother was the daughter of John Grew of Boston. He was the sixth in descent from David Potts and Alice Croasdale. David Potts was born about the year 1671, in or near Llangurrig, North Wales. He was a Quaker, and was probably of Quaker parentage. He came to Pennsylvania about 1690, and died 1730. John Potts, who was his second son, died in Pennsylvania in 1766. Thomas, the second son of John, was several times a member of the Assembly of New Jersey, was an iron manufacturer, and died in 1777. William Sukens Potts, his son, was an iron merchant, and a Quaker, and died in Philadelphia in 1854.

William J. Potts was also the seventh in descent from Capt. John Hughes, a leading man in Pennsylvania in its early years. He was the eighth in descent from Peter Larson Cock, born in Sweden, 1611, died in Kipha, Pennsylvania, 1688.

John Grew, his mother's father, was born in Birmingham, England. He was educated in Bedfordshire, England, and was a man of great intelligence. His ancestors were people of intelligence and influence in the old country.

William John Potts attended school in Camden and in Philadelphia. He attended lectures on Chemistry at the University of Pennsylvania, and at the Polytechnic College of Philadelphia. For some years after completing his education he was an analytical chemist in Camden. He went abroad twice, spending several years in foreign countries. He visited England, Ireland, Scotland and Wales, France, Belgium, Germany, Switzerland, Italy, and Austria, Russia, Sweden and Norway, and Egypt.

He has devoted himself for several years to literary pursuits, and especially to historical investigations. He has written frequently for the New-England Historical and Genealogical REGISTER, and for Notes and Queries, the Pennsylvania Magazine of History, and for many other periodicals and newspapers. For the last thirty years he had been making researches concerning the Potts family, both here and abroad, and has collected a mass of valuable materials. He was preparing a dictionary of medical biography. He contributed valuable materials to Dr. Stephenson's History of Medicine in New Jersey. He furnished valuable materials for the Memoirs and Letters of Captain W. Granville Evelyn, of the 4th regiment of the "King's Own." Mr. Potts gained important information concerning the battle of Lexington, for this volume. The authors of several other books published in England give credit to Mr. Potts for securing very valuable materials for their use from America.

He was a member of the American Philosophical Society; the Historical Society of Pennsylvania; the Numismatic and Antiquarian Society of Philadelphia; Academy of Natural Sciences, Philadelphia; Sons of the Revolution, of Pennsylvania; New Jersey Historical Society; American Folk Lore Society; and the Wisconsin Historical Society.

In 1889 he published a brochure on Du Simitiere, artist, antiquary and naturalist. In 1895 he published a valuable paper on the late Hon. Thomas H. Dudley, United States Consul at Liverpool during and after the war of the Rebellion.

Mr. Potts was never married. He was a man of remarkable industry and skill in antiquarian research, and he has left many of his plans unfinished, on account of his too early death. He was a genial companion, agreeable in conversation, gentle and patient in enduring the long continued physical suffering of his last years. In his religious convictions he was an Episcopalian. "The death of such a man," says one of his old neighbors, "is a loss to the community which can only be properly estimated after the sad event has occurred."

Hon. WILLIAM CUSHING *(ante,* vol. 32, page 352).—Our attention is called to the fact that Benjamin Cushing, the grandfather of Mr. Cushing, is omitted in this pedigree. The line of descent (page 352, lines 5 and 6 from the bottom) should be Rev. Caleb[3] Cushing of Newburyport, by wife Elizabeth Cotton; Caleb[4] by wife Mary Newmarch; Benjamin[5], b. Jan. 1739, by wife Hannah Hazeltine of Haverhill; John Newmarch[6]; Hon. William[7].—EDITOR.

Hon. JOHN FORRESTER ANDREW, A.B., LL.B., a resident member of this Society, elected March 6, 1872, was born in Hingham, Mass., November 26, 1850, and died at his home, 32 Hereford street, Boston, May 30, 1895.

Mr. Andrew was a lineal descendant of Robert and Grace (———) Andrew, through their son Joseph and his second wife, Mrs. Abigail Walker (daughter of John Grafton), whose son, Nathaniel Andrew, married Mary Higginson and had a son John, who married Elizabeth Watson of Salem, and had Jonathan, who removed with his father's family to Windham, Me., there settled and married Nancy Green Pierce, and had John Albion, the illustrious war governor of Massachusetts, who was born in Windham, Me., May 31, 1818, and died October 30, 1867. Governor John A. Andrew married Eliza Jones Hersey of Hingham and had five children, of whom John Forrester, born in Hingham, as above noted, was the second. The boy received the rudiments of his education at the Phillips School, on the back side of Beacon Hill, and after passing the lower grades was fitted for college at a private school.

He graduated from Harvard in the class of 1872, and soon after went abroad with his mother, sisters, and younger brother, passing a year in travel, through England, Germany, Italy, Switzerland and France. Returning, he entered the Harvard Law School, and graduated in 1875. Immediately entering the law office of "Messrs. Brooks, Ball and Story," he was admitted to the Suffolk Bar the same year, 1875. He then began the practice of law in Boston, in the same office which his father had formerly occupied, 244 Washington street. In a few years Mr. Andrew had acquired quite an extensive practice, and was considered a wise counsellor, and a safe and able advocate. His public spirit led him inevitably to take an active interest in all questions of popular concern. His own personal qualities, as well as his name, soon drew him into political activity. In 1880 he was elected as representative to the General Court, by the Republicans of Ward 9, Boston, and served in that position until 1884, when he was elected to the State Senate by the largest majority ever received by any candidate in that district. During his first year in the Senate he was chosen a delegate to the Republican National Convention, but after the nomination of Blaine and Logan, he, with many other of the young Republicans of New England, became convinced that duty lay in the direction of the "Independent" movement, which he soon joined, thus sacrificing his renomination by the Republicans. He was chosen president of the "Young Men's Independent Club" of Boston, and took the stump for Cleveland. He received a nomination for the Senate on the ticket of the Independent Republicans, and being also endorsed by the Democrats, was elected by a large majority. The record of Mr. Andrew's five years in the Legislature is very honorable. During that time he served on many important committees with credit and fidelity. On the Judiciary Committee, especially, his personal independence and courage were shown by his position against the Metropolitan Police Bill, and his unyielding defence of the Civil Service Law. He declined the offer of a nomination to Congress, by the Democrats of his district in 1884, still considering himself a Republican. After the close of his term in the Senate he accepted the Democratic nomination for Governor, and came nearer an election than any candidate of that party had for years. In 1888 he was elected to Congress by the Democrats of the third Massachusetts district, and again in 1890; but in the exciting contest of 1892 he was defeated.

Mr. Andrew was an honest and earnest advocate of free trade, and it was upon the issue of "tariff reform" that he was elected to Congress. He stood consistently and firmly by his standards, advocating, particularly, "free raw material." In all his public career he was the unfailing champion of "Civil Service Reform," and an equally strong advocate of a sound "currency." He will long be remembered also as a faithful friend of the veterans of the war, and endeavored to secure legislation in their favor. As his father had been, so was he, always the true friend of the colored race. In all the relations of his public life he won the respect of both friends and opponents by his strict integrity and sincerity of purpose. He was especially known for his generous activity in many benevolent institutions. He was president of several of our benevolent associations, including that of the "Massachusetts Infant Asylum," that for the "Prevention of Cruelty to Children," and the "Home for Aged Colored Women," besides being active in various others. He was greatly interested in the improvement of Boston's public grounds, and rendered efficient service upon the "Park Commission." He was also an active member of the New-England Historic Genealogical Society, of which his father was an honored president. Mr. Andrew had a host of warm and sincere friends, who were greatly shocked and deeply pained at his sudden and altogether unexpected death. Apoplexy was undoubtedly the cause, but of this no one had any intimation of the danger. Flags at half-mast throughout the city, and the throngs which gathered at his funeral, testify to the high honor which the public paid to his memory, and to the real affection of his friends and associates. Governor Greenhalge and Mayor Matthews, with many other officials of the State, city and public institutions, joined in tributes of sorrow and sympathy with the stricken family. He will be greatly missed in all directions wherever his kindly and helpful influence has extended. Of his father's family, the mother, a brother and two sisters survive him; to these, and his young motherless daughters, his loss is irreparable.

Mr. Andrew was married, in Boston, October 11, 1883, to Harriet, daughter of Nathaniel and Cornelia (Van Rensselaer) Thayer. Mrs. Andrew died in 1891, leaving two daughters, Cornelia Thayer Andrew and Elizabeth Andrew.

The funeral of Mr. Andrew was at the First Church, in Boston, June 1, his pastor, Rev. Stopford W. Brooke, officiating. The burial was at Mount Auburn.

By Rev. George M. Bodge, A.M., of Leominster, Mass.

EDMUND BATCHELDER DEARBORN, Esq., a life member, elected a resident member September 3, 1845, and became a life member in 1858, was born at Hampton, N. H., November 28, 1806, and was the eldest son of Samuel and Ruth (Leavett) Dearborn. He died in Boston, Mass., January 22, 1886, in his 80th year. He was a descendant in the eighth generation from Godfrey Dearborn, an early settler of Exeter, N. H., who removed from that place to Hampton, where he died. His descent from Godfrey[1] Dearborn was through Henry,[2] Samuel,[3] Jeremiah,[4] Jeremiah,[5] Samuel[6] and Samuel[7] his father. His father lived at North Hampton on the Exeter road, and on the place previously occupied by Simon Page. Here the subject of this sketch was born and here he passed his boyhood.

Edmund B. Dearborn received the rudiments of his education in the public schools of Hampton, and later was a graduate of Hampton Academy. After leaving the Academy he spent many years in teaching in different parts of New England. He taught at Marblehead, where he went about 1830, near the time of the murder of Capt. Joseph White at Salem. He was also a teacher at Pierce Academy in Middleboro', Mass., and at Boston, Mass. At the latter place he was for a number of years a teacher at Chapman Hall School, of which Amos Baker was the principal. After giving up teaching, he held for several years a position in the United States Internal Revenue Service.

He was a frequent contributor to the literary newspapers in Boston and elsewhere, and wrote much on historical subjects. He contributed a number of articles to the REGISTER, two of which, on the descendants of Godfrey Dearborn, appeared in the second volume for 1850. He left at his death a very full genealogy of the Dearborn family, which is now in the possession of the New-England Historic Genealogical Society.

He was elected the librarian of this Society in January, 1846, and was its second librarian and the first after the society occupied a room of its own. He published in the REGISTER for October, 1879, an article on the Early History of the society, into which he introduced a description of the Society's room in the City Building, Court Square, and the furniture of the room. He held the office of librarian till 1849.

Mr. Dearborn had much musical taste and ability, and I believe was a teacher of singing at different times. He was an active member of the Handel and Haydn Society of Boston, to which he was admitted in 1841.

By John Ward Dean, A.M.

GENEALOGICAL GLEANINGS IN ENGLAND.

By HENRY F. WATERS, A.M.

[Continued from vol. xlix., page 516.]

WILLIAM WILLIAMS of Newport in the Co. of Monmouth gen[t], 28 March 1597. I have many poor nephews and nieces, sisters and a very unkind brother. My good cousins Valentine Prichard of the Inner Temple, London, Esq., Henry Williams of Matharine in the Co. of Monmouth Esq., William John Meredith of Abergavenny gen[t], Thomas Hopkins of the City of Bristowe, merchant. My brothers in law John Fownes of the City of Bristowe, grocer, and John Jones of Newporte gen[t]. My lands &c. in Rumpney. My sister Catherine and her son William. Lettice, eldest daughter to my sister Johane deceased, and Margaret, eldest daughter to my brother Richard (unmarried). Cicill and Lettice, two of the daughters of my sister Elizabeth. Roger and Thomas, my brother Richard's sons. Blanche and Anne, the daughters of my sister Joane. Andrew and William, the sons of my sister Elizabeth. Johanne, daughter to my brother Richard. Margaret, daughter to my sister Elizabeth. Johane, the youngest daughter of my sister Elizabeth. Mary and Hester, daughters to my sister Anne. Roger and John, the sons of my sister Johane. Margaret, the wife of my brother Richard Williams. The late lands of Roger Williams, my cousin deceased. My sister Lettice. My nephew John Evans. Roger Williams, my brother Richard's eldest son. Thomas, his youngest son. Margaret, eldest daughter to my brother Richard. My nephew William Jones, son of my sister Lettice. My cousin Thomas Scudamor, of Little Salisbury in the County, and my cousin Thomas Scudamor of York. If my nephew William Jones, whom I have constituted and made my executor, do happen to die before he shall have made probate of this my will then my nephew Andrew Jones, my sister Elizabeth's son, shall be my sole executor. I give to my nephew William Jones, my sister Elizabeth's son, the next avoidance, nomination and presentation unto the church of Newport and St. Wolloes and to the chapel of Bettus thereunto belonging and I do give unto him all my part of the Tythe, corn and hay in Bettus for so long time as he shall be Vicar in Newport and St. Wolloes and remain unmarried. To my aunt Mrs. Langley twenty pounds. John Fownes one of the witnesses.

Commission issued 27 June 1610 to Roger Williams, next akin &c. the executor named in the will having renounced.   Wingfield, 66.

HENRY ADDAMS of Bristol merchant, 12 October 1601, proved 10 November 1601. To my daughter Marie Addames one hundred pounds if my adventures by sea, made to France, do come safely home; otherwise only fifty pounds (at age of eighteen). The residue to wife Susanna, whom I make sole executrix. And I desire my father Thomas Addams and my brother in law John Phoens, now one of the sheriffs of the City of Bristol, to be my overseers. In the presence of my said father, brother in law, my brother Daniel Addams and William Robinson, Vicar of St. Nicholas.

The signature of the brother in law was Jo: Fownes.

Woodhall, 80.

John Fownes of Bristol, merchant, 28 March, signed 24 August, 1609 proved 23 October 1609.   If I die in Bristow my body to be buried in the parish church of St. Stevens within the city.   To wife Anne, for life, all my lands and tenements in the Co. of Monmouth, called by the name of Monioy, and my house in Newport and the five and twenty acres I bought of John Williams of All Souls Oxon ; and after her death the said lands and tenements shall remain to my son John Fownes.   To said wife my dwelling house in Bread Street so long as she shall remain a widow and unmarried; then to my son John, if living, and, if not, to my three daughters.   Son John at one and twenty.   Six hundred pounds apiece to daughters Mary Fownes, Hester Fownes and Sara Fownes at eighteen or days of marriage.   To daughter Hester my virginals, my best carpet of green cloth fringed with silk and my silver skynker.   Ten pounds apiece to my brother James Fownes' two daughters.   Ten pounds to my kinswoman Mary Longe.   My late servant Richard Longe.   Provision for two poor laboring men yearly to rake and keep clean the marsh of the City of Bristow and the walks round about the same.   To my brother Thomas Fownes my scarlet gown and tippet.   To Richard Longe and John Tomlynson thirty shillings apiece in gold to make each of them a signet with my coat armor engraven therein and to wear it in remembrance of me, sometime their master.   To wife Ann one half of all my plate and household stuff in my dwelling house in Bristowe and in my house at Catchcolde in the Co. of Gloucester.   The other half to my four children (equally).   Wife Anne to be executrix and my brother in law Mr William Williams, my brother Thomas Fownes, Mr Abel Kitchin and Mr John Guy to be my overseers.   To my good mistress Mrs Langley five pounds, to Philip Langley five pounds.   To my sister Susan five pounds.   To Philip Langley's wife and Philip Langley's sisters, vizt Mary Tomlynson and Anne Vawre, ten pounds, vizt to each of them three pounds six shillings eight pence, to buy them a ring to wear at their pleasure for my sake.   Mary Langley one of the witnesses.   Dorset, 94.

John Fownes, aged thirty six or thereabouts, 9 June 1624, proved 1 February 1624.   To wife Dorothy Fownes my two closes of land near adjoining to Lady well and my three quarter parts of the Dove of Plymouth, now at New Foundland, with my three quarters of her voyage which God shall bless them withal.   To my brother Warwick Fownes one hundred pounds, to be paid out of my five eighth parts of a ship called the Eagle of Plymouth, and her voyage from Virginia or New England if please God to send her and her proceeds safely to return.   To my mother in law Mrs Elizabeth Yarde thirty pounds.   To my nephew Francis Amadas fifty pounds.   To my two nieces Johane and Jane Amadas twenty pounds apiece.   To my servant Lawrence Beele fifty pounds.   To my two apprentices John Gay and Thomas Davies five pounds apiece.   To the new building behind the church steeple called the new Hospital one hundred pounds.   To the poor of Plymouth ten pounds.   To Mr. Mathias Nicholls, preacher of God's word at Plymouth, five pounds.   Wife to be executrix and Mr. Mathias Nicholls Mr Thomas Sherwell my brother in law Roger Beele and my brother in law Abraham Rowe to be supervisors.

Commission issued (as above) to Warwick Fownes, brother of the deceased &c., the executrix named in the will having died &c.

Clarke, 15.

ANNE FOWNES of the City of Bristol, widow, 11 February 1629, proved
10 November 1630. My body to be buried in the parish church of St.
Stephens. The six children of my son in law Mr. William Claxton.
Penelope Claxton one of them. My grandchildren Abell Rogers and
Mathewe Rogers. My grandchildren Andrewe Barker and Sara Barker.
My grandchildren Anne Fownes and William Fownes. My grandchild
John Fownes. My three daughters. William Evans the son of my kins-
man John Evans. My kinsman William Jones of Llansemfred in the Co.
of Monmouth. My sister Catherine Watkins. My cousin Elizabeth
Steevens. My cousin Mary Longe. My son John Fownes to be sole
executor and my good friends and kinsmen John Tomlinson and Richard
Long, merchants, to be overseers. My kinsman Mr. Roger Williams of
Newporte. Wit: Rich: Long: Willm̄ yeomans.   Scroope, 92.

[The will of Thomas Fownes of Plymouth, Devon., Esq. (1637–1638) which
should come in here, in chronological order, has already appeared among my
evidences concerning the Holworthy family (see REGISTER for 1891, vol. xlv.,
pp. 153–4). He refers to Mr. John Gayre, gives to the poor of Bristol, and names
Elizabeth, wife of William Stephens of Bristol, and Mary Longe daughter
of sister Mary Longe deceased. He calls Judith, wife of Francis Amadas,
kinswoman and Warwick Fownes of London, merchant, kinsman, and refers to
Humphrey Fownes as deceased. Richard Longe of Bristol he calls kinsman
and he also refers to an Aunt Yard as lately deceased. His daughter Mary, as
we know, was the wife of Richard Holworthy; another daughter, Prudence,
was the wife of John Waddon and he speaks of daughter Johan as wife of
Hugh Gayer deceased. He also names daughters Elizabeth Yard and Susan
Kellond. He names also John, Thomas and Susan Kellond, the children of John
Kellond. This will therefore binds together the Fownes family of Bristol and
those of Plymouth and of London.   H. F. WATERS.]

WARWICK FOWNES of London merchant and citizen and mercer of the
same City, 2 August 1638, proved 17 July 1640. My body I commit to
the earth from whence it came and to be decently interred as beseemeth
the body of a Christian in the parish church of St. Bartholomew the less
near the Royal Exchange in London, whereof I am a parishioner, without
any pomp or vain ostentation, only my corpse to be accompanied to church
with my kindred, household, neighbors and familiars, but mourning cloth for
my executors and household. After debts paid &c. the remainder of my
goods &c. shall be divided into three equal parts and portions, according to
the ancient and laudable custom of the City of London, one part whereof
I leave to my loving wife Julian for her customary and widow's part, one
other part I leave to my five children, Humphrey, Elizabeth, Mary, Martha
and Judith Fownes and such others as God shall send me hereafter. The
other third part remaining I reserve to myself, therewith to perform this
my last will and testament. Then follow bequests to wife and children
and others. My kinswoman Mary Fownes. My cousin Joane Large the
wife of ———— Large. My friend Charles Yeoman. Mr. Philip Androwe
the elder. Plymouth, Devon., mentioned. Certain servants named. My
brother James Yard and cousin Thomas Fownes to be executors. A brother
John Yard.   Coventry, 103.

[For assistance on the Kellond family I am indebted to Mr. Winslow Jones
who has a large knowledge of Devonshire families.   H. F. WATERS.]

WALTER KELLONDE of Tottones Devon, merchant, 15 May 34 Elizabeth, proved 11 November 1592. My body to be buried in the church of
Tottones. The poor of the Mawdelin house of Tottones. The poor of

South Tawton. To my son Christopher Kellonde the moiety and half of
all that tenement, houses, edifices, gardens, shops &c. in Totnes which were
demised to me by John and William Wotton, by their deed bearing date
4 October 18 Elizabeth. The other moiety I give to my son John Kelland; each to hold' for three score and nine years. [These two sons still
minors and unmarried.] To Christopher a tenement in Harberton. Other
bequests to John. To Mary my wife two chambers and gallery in the
house, with free ingress &c., and other bequests to her of household stuff
&c. Provision for the schooling of my children which I have by the said
Mary, they being now infants. To Richard, my eldest son, my messuage
and tenement in Tottones wherein I now dwell &c. and my messuage &c.
in Harpers Hill Street, with provision for entailing upon his lawful issue,
failing which to son Christopher, next to John, then to my son Walther,
then to son William, then to son Stephen. To my daughter Decous (or
Decons) Kellonde threescore pounds at twenty one. To daughter Mary
Kellonde fifty pounds at twenty one. The same to daughter Margaret Kellonde. To daughter Frideswell Kellonde forty pounds at twenty one. To
son Walther Kellonde fifty pounds at twenty one. The same to William and
Stephen. A bequest to a Thomas Kellonde, among others. To Agnes,
Walther, Thomas, Bartholomew and William Prideaux, children of Thomas
Prideaux. Henry and Thomas Bickforde sons of John Bickforde. The
child which my wife now goeth withal, yet unborn. Son Richard to be
executor and Bartholomew Laskie of Tottones, merchant, overseer.

Harrington, 83.

[The testator, Walter[1] Kellond of Totnes, Devon., merchant, whose will
heads an interesting group, died in 1592. By his first wife, Nichol ———, had:
John,[2] Christopher,[2] John,[2] Richard.[2] By his second wife, Mary, he had:
Fridswell,[2] William,[2] Stephen,[2] Walter.[2] His will is given and the other Walter
is probably his son mentioned in his father's will.

John[2] (1576-1623) married Mary .....and had: John[3] (1609-1679), Walter[3]
(died 1614), Samuel.[3]

John[3] married Susanna Fownes (1617-1649), daughter of Thomas Fownes of
Plymouth, England, and had: John[4] (1635-1692), married Bridget, Thomas,[4]
born 1636, Samuel,[4] Henry,[4] Samuel,[4] Richard,[4] James.[4]

Christopher,[2] son of Walter,[1] married Joan Brooking; she died 1624-5, and
the wills of husband and wife are given.

Thomas,[4] born 11 Dec. 1636, married Abigail, the widow of Samuel Moore
and daughter of Capt. Thomas Hawkin, and had: Susanna[5] b. 21 Oct. 1665;
John[5] b. 2 June, 1667, died young; John[5] b. 13 Feb. 1669, died young; Thomas[5]
b. 18 July, 1670, died young; Samuel[5] b. 11 Sept. 1671; Elizabeth[5] b. 14 Aug. 1673;
Thomas[5] b. 29 Aug. 1674; John[5] b. 15 June, 1678; Richard[5] b. 26 Sept. 1681.

In April, 1661, Thomas Kellond and Thomas Kirk, a relative of Sir David
Kirk, were commissioned to search for Cols. Edward Whalley and William
Goffe, two of the regicide judges then in New England. They started in pursuit of them from Boston, 1 May, 1661, and went to the colonies of Connecticut,
New Haven and New York; but unsuccessfully. In 1674 Kellond was appointed
a constable of Boston, but was excused on paying a forfeit. He died 12 July,
1686; his widow then married Hon. John Foster whom she outlived.

WALTER F. WATKINS.]

CHRISTOPHER KELLOND of Totnes, Devon., merchant, 22 September
1616, proved 10 April 1618. The poor of Totnes. My wife Johane.
My three sons. The moiety and halfendeale of a house joining to the
Mill Lane in Totnes, being the inheritance of William Wotton Esq. My
daughters. My wife to be sole executrix. I do desire my brother in law
Mr. Thomas Predeaux, my brother John Kelland and my brother in law
Christopher Broking to be my overseers. Richard Kellond a witness.

Meade, 26.

JOHN KELLOND of Tottones merchant, 26 August 21 James, proved 7 February 1623. The Maudlen House of Tottones. The poor of Tottones. My wife Mary. My son John. My son Samwell Kellond. at twenty one. To my daughter Dunes Kellond fifty pounds, but if she take a marriage by the consent and agreement of my overseers and executors in trust then she shall have five hundred and fifty pounds twelve months after her marriage, and for her maintenance I give her twenty pounds a year until she has her portion. My daughter Mary Kellond. My daughter Katherine Kellond. My daughter Agnes Kellond. My daughter Joan Kellond. My five daughters. To son John my house wherein I now dwell, with remainder to son Samuel, then to my daughter Dunes Kellond and the heirs male of her body. My cousin Henry Bickford of Rottery and each of his brothers and sisters. My cousin Agnes Kellond and Nell Kellond her sister, daughters to my deceased brother Richard Kellond. The children of my deceased brother Christopher Kellond and of my sister Dunes Ducke. Nicholas the son of William Squyer. My sister Agnes Prydiaux. My sister Jane Bickford. My sister Dunes Ducke. My sister Mary Kellond. My cousin Mr. Bartholomew Laskey of Tottones. My brother in law Mr. Nicholas Wyse. My friend Christopher Broockinge the son of the deceased Mr. William Broockinge. My cousin Philip Lea. Son John to be sole executor (he not yet twenty one). My brother Steeven Kellond. The mayor and burgesses of Tottones. To "dicayed" merchants. A new prison to be builded. Robert Shaplye one of the witnesses. A nuncupative codicil. Gifts in October and November 1623. William Squyer jun^r. now in Oxford at the University. My deceased brother Richard Kellond's daughter Joan Kellond. My sister Margaret Squyer, after the death of her husband.   Byrde, 16.

JOHANE KELLAND of Totnes, Devon., widow, 4 November 1624, proved 5 February 1624. The poor of Tottnes and the poor of the Mawdlyn of Tottnes. My son Walter Kelland. My son Christopher Kelland. My son John Kelland. My daughters Johane Kelland, Elizabeth Kelland, Jane Kelland, Margaret Kelland and Wethen Kelland. The last named to be sole executrix. My brother Christopher Broking and my brother in law Christopher Maynard.   Clarke, 17.

WALTER KELLAND of Stoke-canon, Devon., gent., 4 October 1671, with a codicil bearing date 14 October 1671. proved 29 June 1672. To wife Mary Kelland the tenement or living wherein she now liveth, commonly called Beere, within the parish of Broad-list, Devon. My daughter Hannah Kelland. My grandchild Audrey Kelland, daughter of my deceased son Richard Kelland. My four grandchildren the daughters of my said deceased son Richard Kelland, over and above the portions that their said father appointed and bequeathed unto them, vizt. to Elizabeth, Mary, Audrey and Dorothy. My estate of inheritance which I lately bought of Jonathan Wade of Topisham gen^t., situate, lying or being in Sowton, Devon, I give to my daughter Elizabeth Lee, the now wife of Edward Lee, for term of her natural life, then to their second son Walter Lee, next to their third son Edward Lee, then to John Lee, their fourth son, then to Richard Lee, their eldest son, then to their daughter or daughters. My grandson Walter Kelland, eldest son of my deceased son Richard. My grandson Richard Kelland, brother to the said Walter. My daughter Dorothy Vicary, widow, her daughter Mary Vicary and her son Walter Vicary. My grandson Walter Kelland, son of my son Walter, and his two sisters

Mary and Hannah. Mrs. Anne Robinson, widow. The Ward-house, wherein I now keep the Sheriff's ward or prison for the County of Devon, situate in the parish of Stoke-Canon. My son Walter Kelland and my son in law Edward Lee.   Eure, 76.

JOHN KELLOND of Paingsford, Devon, Esq., 22 September 1677, proved 16 July 1679. To Richard Bickford of Brent in Devon, yeoman, five pounds. Elizabeth Predham of Little Hempston, Devon, widow. Jane Barrie of Bridgetown in the parish of Berry Pomeroy, Devon, widow. The poor of Aishprington and those of other parishes that shall be at my funeral. The poor of Totnes, Devon. My servant Nicholas Francis. Item, I give and bequeath unto my son Thomas Kellond of Boston in New England, my second son, for his portion, two thousand pounds. To my daughter Joane Kellond one hundred pounds and no more because she hath departed from my house and married against my liking and consent. My grandson Francis Fullford, my godson, at one and twenty. My cousin Zachary Gould of Staverton. My grandson John Kellond, the son of my son John Kellond of Totnes. My farm and barton called Durleigh lying near Bridgewater, Somerset. My grandson Charles Kellond, the son of my son John Kellond of Totnes. My mansion house, barton, farm &c. called Tingrasse in the parish of Tingrasse, Devon. Other real estate. Son John. His daughter Susan Kellond, my grandchild, at day of marriage, and her sister Bridget Kellond. To every one of my son Thomas Kellond's children one hundred pounds, at day of marriage. My grandchild Elizabeth Sparke in Barbathos.   King, 174.

JOHN KELLOND of Painsford, Devon, Esq., 10 March 1690, proved 1 November 1692. Reference to a deed bearing date 16 October 36th Charles II, made between me, of the one part, and Francis Fulford Esq., Charles Kellond my son and Valentine Pomeroy gen[t] and John Rowe gen[t], of the other part, for the conveying and settling my manor and lordship of Slapton and the capital messuage &c. of Stancombe. My wife Bridget. My three daughters Susanna, Bridget and Katherine Kellond. My grand daughter Margaret Kellond, daughter of my son Charles. My brother in law Thomas Drewe Esq. and his now wife. My nephew Samuel Kellond, at the expiration of his apprenticeship. Certain servants. My kinsman George Yard of the City of Exon (Exeter) mercer. In a codicil he refers to kinsman M[r] George Yard of Stokegabriel.   Fane, 206.

LUCE SHORTE, widow, of Gillingham, 4 October 1603, proved 2 December 1603. To be buried in the churchyard of Gillingham. Brother Henry Shorte. My sister Alice Murgin. Alice Goodinge, Thomas Goodinge, Simon Gooding, Elizabeth Goodinge and Murgin Dauye which are my sisters children. James Arnolde and Richard Arnold at twenty one. My daughter Elizabeth Shorte. My son Thomas Shorte. My house in Maidestone to my son Thomas, and if he die without lawful heirs of body then to Thomas Goodinge and Simon Gooding, to be equally divided between them &c. Margaret Berry, Dorothy Kente, Joane Edwardes and Elizabeth Shorte my daughters. Marrian Astreates, Joane Astreates and Sara Astreates. Elizabeth, Richard and John Berry. Dorothy Kente's child. Joane Edwarde's child. Richard Kente of Stoke shall be guardian to my son Thomas Shorte till he comes to the age of fourteen. The residue to my son William Shorte whom I make sole executor. For overseers I appoint Richard Astreetes of Gillingham and Richard Kente of Stoke. Henry Short and James Thurston witnesses.   Bolein, 105.

WILLIAM SHORT of Gillingham, Kent, 16 November 1641, proved 21
December 1641. To be buried in Gillingham near the tomb of the Shorts,
my ancestors. My two grandchildren William Short and Elizabeth Man-
ser. My sister Johan Edwards and Mary Lofty her daughter. Richard
Arnold, William Berrye and Thomas Berrye, my sisters sons. Susan
Grauesden and John Wilson, my sisters daughters. Symon Gooddin my
kinsman. Mr. John Short, Mr. James Short, Henry Lawrance, Richard
Lawrance, William Lawrance, Thomas Lawrance, Sarah Baylie, Mary
Duck, widow, Elizabeth Smith, Mark Short and John Short, his brother.
Susan Gravesend again mentioned. My kinsman Richard Arnold to be
sole executor. My grandchild William Short, son of my son James.
Richard Baylye and Thomas Lofty. The capital messuage or tenement,
called the Brewhouse, in Week Street in Maidstone. Reference to will of
John Short deceased. John and Joseph, his sons. John Short the son of
Thomas Short. Johan Duke, the daughter of the aforenamed Mary Duke,
widow. The foresaid Joane Wilson. William Manser, my son in law.
Elizabeth Manser, his daughter.   Evelyn, 128.

[The testator of the above will is that William Short referred to in the will
of his nephew Richard Arnold, printed in the Gleanings for July, 1894 (pp. 374–
375).   H. F. W.]

JOHN LORDE of Redriff, Surrey, clothier, 14 September 1603, proved 8
December 1603. To wife Elizabeth, for life, my two houses in Sudbury,
Suffolk, one of them, with an orchard, being in the parish commonly called
Gregory parish, and the other in the parish commonly called Peter's parish.
After the decease of my wife I give them to my daughter Elizabeth. If
my wife die before my daughter shall have accomplished the full age of
nineteen years then the two houses aforesaid and the benefit of their rent
shall freely remain in the possession of Anthony Lord my father and . . . . .
my mother, or the survivor of them, until my daughter come to said age of
nineteen years. But if she die without issue then the said houses shall go
to the said Anthony Lord my father and . . . . . my mother and the survivor of them, and afterwards to my three sisters yet unmarried, Alice,
Jone and Prewe Lord (each one third) provided they pay to their other two
sisters ten pounds *i. e.* to Elizabeth . . . . . five pounds and to Anne
. . . . . five pounds. To my father Anthony Lorde ten pounds. To
Robert Lorde my brother forty shillings which he shall recover by a bond
due to me from William Johnson of Colchester, Essex. My wife Elizabeth to be executrix.   Bolein, 110.

JOHN LORD of Sudbury, Suffolk, 1 March 1640, proved 11 July 1655.
To the poor of all the three parishes in Sudbury forty shillings apiece.
To Mr Rogers minister of the parish wherein I now dwell, if he be living
and preach a sermon at my funeral, forty shillings, or otherwise unto such
godly minister as shall preach such sermon. I give to Bennett my loving
wife all that my messuage or tenement, with the yards, gardens, orchards
and appurtenances thereunto belonging, situate and being in the parish of
St. Gregory in Sudbury which I late purchased of Robert Lord my kinsman and Katherine his mother, or one of them, and now is in the tenure or
occupation of William Gunton the elder &c. My wife to hold this for
life, and after her decease I give and bequeath the said messuage &c. as
also the messuage &c. in the parish of All Hallows in Sudbury wherein I
now dwell and which my said wife holdeth for life, unto my daughter Elizabeth
wife of William Stacie the younger of Bocking, Essex, for life. And after

decease of said wife and daughter I give to Anne Stacy my grandchild the messuage in the occupation of William Gunton and to Elizabeth Stacie my grandchild the other messuage. If they die without issue &c. then to my grandchild Mary Stacy. Other gifts to grandchildren and to wife. To the children of Thomas Gunton the elder by my sister, vizt: to my cousin Thomas Gunton the younger and to William, his brother, twenty pounds each, for the benefit of their children, and to Anne and Elizabeth Gunton, sisters of the said Thomas the younger and William, ten pounds apiece.

Item, I give unto my cousin Robert Lord, if he comes again from beyond the seas to demand it, ten pounds.

William Stacie, the husband of my daughter Elizabeth, to be sole executor and my kinsman Thomas Gunton the younger to be supervisor. I will that my executor shall pay unto Susan Lord, my sister of the half blood, four pounds yearly during her life, to Oliver Dowdle (my servant that was) forty shillings, to my kinsman . . . . . son of Barwicke and Anne Lord my kinswoman, apprentice with one Bowser, a weaver of Sudbury, twenty nobles.   Aylett, 70.

BENNETT LORD of Sudbury, Suffolk, widow and aged, 26 September 1653, proved 26 July 1655. My son in law William Stacye of Bocking, Essex, and his children. Frances Gunton daughter of my cousin William Gunton. Oliver Dowdall and Martha Hugens my servants. My kinsman Richard Cooke of London for the use of his children. My kinsman William Wood of London in the behalf of his children. My sister Elizabeth Crewes of Tendring. Mihill Clarke of Much Bromly, Essex, to be my Executor.   Aylett, 76.

[We have now the English home of one of our distinguished Essex County families. Mr. Robert Lord was for years clerk of the courts for Ipswich, Mass. His son Robert filled the office of Marshal of the court for Ipswich, an office, the nearest equivalent of which now is that of High Sheriff. Mrs. Katherine Lord, widow, mother of the first Robert, received a grant of land in Ipswich (Mass) in 1641, within a few months, probably, after conveying to John Lord of Sudbury (England) her interest in the messuage, etc., in the parish of St. Gregory, referred to in the said John Lord's will.

I found at Finchingfield, when I went down to Essex in 1891, this entry on the register:

"1630, Nov. 11, Robert Lord and Mary Waite."

I do not find among my extracts any note of baptisms of any children of this couple. Mr. Lord probably took his wife back with him to Sudbury. Finchington Registers apparently began in 1617.—HENRY F. WATERS.

Mary Waite, who married Robert Lord, was a daughter of Samuel and Mary (Ward) Waite of Wethersfield in Essex. The will of her brother, Rev. Joseph Waite, M.A., Rector of Springton in Suffolk, is printed in vol. xlvi., p. 318. Other wills of Waites and Wards will be found in that volume, pages 313-320. —EDITOR.]

GEORGE MARVIN (parish not stated) 24 March 1648, proved 4 April 1649. I do acknowledge myself in debts—to Mr Colney four pounds five shillings, at the darke house a matter of eight shillings, Mr Haman, a seedsman, two or three shillings, one Edward three shillings, to the apothecary. I do will and bequeath fifteen pounds to my sister in Mislye, ten pounds to my uncle at Stutton, five pounds to my cousin William at Stutton, five pounds to my cousin John of Bentley, five pounds to my cousin John of Stepney, five pounds to my cousin Richard of Rushmore, ten pounds to Mrs Ward, widow of Mr Samuel Ward, five pounds to Mr Nath: Ward late of Walke-horne, three pounds to Mr Colney at whose house I

now am, two pounds to Barnabas Brag at Mr Colney's house, ten pounds
in Mr Nathaniel Ward's hands for the good of the child, to be paid
when he shall think best for its good, ten pounds Doctor Hubbard for his
pains and care, to John and Tobias Coachman ten shillings apiece, two
pounds to Mrs Thorneton, to the poor of Silver Street where I shall be
buried ten shillings, to the poor in Cobden twenty shillings, to the poor of
Bently ten shillings. The poor of . . . . . My cousin Knolls in Five
foot Lane. My cousin Bales; she lives at Coldharbor. Mr Thompson to
preach my funeral sermon. I do appoint and name for my executors Master Nathaniel Ward and Mr Joseph Ward. Due me in moneys upon a bill
a hundred and fifteen pounds in Mr Nathaniel Ward's hands. My books
in a square chest with a padlock, with linen &c., at Mr Colveye's. My bill
is in my desk. My friends Nathaniel and Joseph Ward, ministers, desiring
them to see my body to be decently interred.

Proved by Nathaniel Ward, power reserved for Joseph Ward.

Fairfax, 46.

[In the Probate Act Book he is described as late of the parish of St. Olave
in Silver Street, London.]

JOHN WARD of Stratford, Suffolk, clothier, 19 October 1629, proved 18
May 1631. 1 give and bequeath to Anne my beloved wife all that my
freehold tenement called Dawes, together with fifteen acres of land, more
or less, with the appurtenances, situate and lying in East Mersey, for term
of her natural life; and after her decease to John Ward my son and to his
heirs forever. I give to Anne, my wife, towards the proving and performing of this my last will, my fourth part of the ship called the Unity of
Maningtree, with all my part of the furniture and tackling thereof, with all
my stock, venture and profits therein, and also all my part in another ship
now begun to build in Ipswich, and all my cloth, wool and yarn, together
with all my debts owing and growing due to me by any person or persons
at London or elsewhere, and also all my cattle, household stuff, money,
goods, and chattels whatsoever. I give more to Anne my wife all my plate
for term of her natural life. I give to John Ward my eldest son one hundred and forty pounds of lawful money of England, to be paid by Anne my
wife (whom I make sole executrix of this my last will) when he shall
accomplish the age of three and twenty years. I give to Samewell Ward
my son one hundred pounds, at age of four and twenty years. I will that
Anne my wife shall bestow upon some of my former wives children (where
she sees most need) three pounds &c. To the poor of Stratford twenty
shillings. I make Mr. Samewell Linsell, minister of Stratford, my well
beloved friend, supervisor &c.

The witnesses were Lyonell Chewte, Nathaniel Backler.

St. John, 67.

[These two wills should interest some of our New Englanders. That of
George Marvin (which, by the way, had been entered on the margin of the
leaf as will of Roger Marvin) evidently refers to the family of Samuel Ward,
the famous town preacher of Ipswich, England. John Ward of Stratford,
whose will follows Marvin's, must have been the father of our John Ward, the
chirurgeon, of Ipswich, Mass. The will of his widow, Anne Ward, I have
already given (see REG. for 1892, pp. 317-8). To what family can these have
belonged? Our John Ward, the chirurgeon, spoke of a cousin Nathaniel, son
of an uncle Nathaniel Ward, and referred also to a cousin Ward's, of Wethersfield, two youngest sons.   H. F. WATERS.]

NICHOLAS CAREW of St. Martin's in the Fields, Middlesex, gentleman, 23 November 1657, proved 12 October 1670. I have had and received divers sums of money and sundry necessaries of and from my natural brother Swithen Carew of St. Giles in the Fields, Middlesex, grocer. I give to said Swithen all my goods &c. in or upon my now plantation in the island of Maryland, together with my whole interest and estate in the same plantation; and I make him sole executor.

Proved (at above date) by Swithin Carew. Penn, 132.

JOSEPH ADAMS of the Island of Antigua merchant but now residing in London, 1 April 1717, proved 13 October 1722. I give and bequeath all my estate, both real and personal &c., unto my brother in law Hopefor Bendall of Antegoa, merchant, and John Neale of London, dyer, in trust &c. To my beloved mother Elizabeth Adams thirty pounds a year, and twenty pounds also in one month after my decease. To the said Hopefor Bendall twenty pounds. To Daniel Davies of London, packer, twenty pounds in case he marries my sister Mary Adams. To the said John Neale twenty pounds. To my nephew Joseph Bendall, son of the said Hopefor Bendall, six hundred pounds in six months after the decease of my said mother. And after the payment of the said sum I give one hundred pounds unto my partner Edward Chester junior. The residue to and amongst the child or children of my loving sisters Elizabeth Bendall and the said Mary Adams, share and share alike, excluding thereout the said Joseph Bendall on account of the said legacy. The said Hopefor Bendall and John Neale to be executors. Marlboro, 188.

HOPEFOR BENDALL of the Island of Antigua Esq. —— day of June 1727. My late brother in law Joseph Adams, formerly of this Island of Antigua but late of London, merchant deceased, in and by his last will and testament bearing date 1 April 1717, did (among other legacies and bequests therein) give, devise and bequeath unto his nephew Joseph Bendall (son of me the said Hopefor Bendall) the sum of six hundred pounds, to be paid to him within six months next and immediately following the death or decease of Elizabeth Adams, mother of the said testator, and, after payment of that and all other legacies in the said recited will mentioned, did give, devise and bequeath all the rest and residue of his real and personal estate whatsoever unto and amongst the child or children of his sisters Elizabeth Bendall (late wife of me the said Hopefor Bendall) and Mary Adams late the wife of Daniel Davies of London, packer, share and share alike, excluding thereout the said Joseph Bendall on account of the said legacy &c., and thereof appointed me, the said Hopefor Bendall, and John Neale of London, dyer, sole executors, as in and by the said will, duly proved at London 13 October 1722 and remaining in the Prerogative Court of Canterbury &c. I give all my estate to the said John Neale of London my brother in law, Jonathan Perrie, late of London merchant but at present residing in the West Indies, Thomas Kerby and Francis Delap, both of this Island of Antigua, merchants &c., in trust (for the benefit of my children, so that they may all share alike) and I make them my executors.

Then follow certain depositions made in Antigua 1 November 1728, by which it appears that the above testator had been Collector of the Customs in Antigua, and that his death happened on Sunday the twenty-seaventh day of October last. Will allowed (in Antigua) 1 November 1728 and recorded in the Register's office. Proved in London (P. C. C.) 7 October 1729. Abbott, 263.

[Edward Bendall of Boston, an enterprising merchant, the father of Hopefor, the testator, probably came with Winthrop in 1630. His energy was strikingly shown in raising a vessel, the " Mary Rose," in 1642, which had been sunk in Boston harbor by a gunpowder explosion. He married, probably in England, Ann, and had Freegrace baptized July 5, 1635, who died; and he then had Freegrace, born Sept. 30, 1636, the mother dying Dec. 25, 1637. He then marries in about one year, Marah ——, and had Reform in 1639, Hopefor Oct. 7, 1641, Moremercy 1643. His wife Mary [sic] was buried May, 1644, and he then married Jane and had, in 1648, Ephraim, and, in 1649, Restore.

Mr. Savage gives the death of Edward Bendall as in 1682, probably misled by the fact of an administration being granted in that year on his estate, doubtless necessary in the settlement of the estate of his son Freegrace, and consequent on the action of the town of Boston, March 13, 1681-2. By deed, Jan. 26, 1660-1, Lib. iv., p. 88, of Suffolk Deeds, Jane Bendall, wife of Edward Bendall, deceased, authorizes Capt. Samuel Scarlett as her lawful attorney. In Suffolk Deeds, Lib. i., pp. 316, 317, under date of 1653, is given an execution on the estate of Edward Bendall.

Jane Bendall may be the " Jane Scarlett, now the wife of John Jacob," mentioned in the will of Samuel Scarlett in 1675; perhaps the daughter or sister of Samuel Scarlet, as the latter dying without children leaves property to Hopefor and Ephraim, and Freegrace. Mary, wife of Samuel Scarlett, may have been sister of Edw. Bendall. Freegrace Bendall married Mary, daughter of Francis and Alice Lyall, and had Bridget, Elizabeth, Ann, Alice, Richard, Pitford, Moremercy, Freegrace, Scarlett, and Marianna who married Dr. Daniel Allen of Boston. Freegrace and wife were drowned in the harbor coming from Noddle's Island, with two others, June 6, 1676. John Scarlet was appointed one of the administrators of his estate.

Hopefor Bendall, mariner, was of London March 14, 1708-9, at which time he disposed of certain lands at Merrimac, left him by Samuel Scarlet in 1675 (Suffolk Deeds, Lib. xxiv., p. 249).

He had also appeared at Boston as early as 1666, as commander of a vessel sailing between New England, New York and Old England.—WALTER K. WATKINS.]

JOHN PERRY late of Antigua but now of St. James Westminster, Middlesex, merchant, 24 June 1708, proved 4 April 1713. The parish of Youghall wherein I was born, in the Co. of Cork and Kingdom of Ireland. The parish of Christ Church in the City of Cork. The parish of St. John's in the Island of Antigua, one of the Leeward Islands. My sister in law Mary Perry, widow and relict of my deceased brother Samuel. My dear and well beloved sister Anne Osborne, widow, and her two daughters Mary Mills and Joyce Osbourne. Every of the grandchildren of my said sister Osborne (except Jo. Freeman the son of James Freeman to whom I have already given &c.). My nephew Samuel Perry at twenty one. My wife Anne. My daughter Anne Perry. A debt due to me from Major Long of said Antigua. Daughter Dorothy Perry. Debt due to me from Patrick Browne late of Antigua. Daughter Elizabeth Perry. My half of the plantation in St. Mary's, Antigua, lately rented to Patrick Browne deceased. To my daughter Mary all my right, title and interest of, in and to my plantation in the Province of South Carolina. My nephew Jonathan Perry, son of my brother Edward, at twenty one. My brother Edward Perry, my friend Archibald Hutchinson Esq. and my wife to be guardians of my children. My daughters Anne and Dorothy Perrey and my brother Edward to be joint executors.

Commission issued (at above date) to Jonathan Perry, lawful guardian of Anne and Dorothy Perry, to administer during their minority or until Edward Perry, the other executor, shall have accepted.

Proved 7 October 1713 by Edward Perry, power reserved for Anne and Dorothy.

Commission issued 23 May 1717 to Jonathan Perrie, guardian of Anne and Dorothy Perrie, to administer during their minority, Edward Perry the other executor having deceased.

Proved 5 August 1722 by Anne Rigby *als* Perrie (wife of Richard Rigby), power reserved for Dorothy. Leeds, 88.

EDWARD PERRIE of Antigua 24 February 1714, with a codicil dated 24 January 1716 proved 23 May 1717. My eldest daughter Mary Pullen of London widow. My only son Jonathan Perrie of London merchant. My well beloved friends Mr. Hopefor Bendall, Mr. Edward Chester jr. and Mr. Joseph Adams of Antigua merchants.

In the Codicil certain specific legacies. To son Jonathan all my plate with my coat of arms. To my sister Nisbitt my common prayer book and the seal that's hanging to my watch which did belong to my brother John Perrie. To Mr. Hopefor Bendall my sword, belt and gun. To Mr. Bendall's daughter (my godchild) the silver tankard I expect out of England. Other legacies. Whitfield, 101.

JOHN BARTON of Huntingdon in the County of Huntingdon, burgess and alderman of the same borough, 4 March 1642, proved 23 October 1647. My will and desire is that Mr. Pike the minister of All Saints in Huntingdon should preach at my burial for the edifying of the people; and I give him for his pains therein to be taken forty shillings. My lease of certain pasture grounds in Buckworth (Huntingdonshire) holden of the Duke of Richmond and Lenox and had by assignment from Robert Wapole of Woodwalton in said County I do give (the remainder of the term) unto the said Robert Wapole, and also my stock of cattle upon said pasture grounds, upon trust &c. Sixty pounds to be given to my sister Stumbles and her children, fifty pounds to my sister Allen's children, ten pounds to my servant Robert Berry. I give my messuage &c. in Huntingdon wherein I now dwell to my wife Elizabeth, for and during the term of her natural life, and after her decease to John Barton my uncle Thomas Barton's son and the heirs of his body &c., with remainder to all the children of my sisters Jane Stombles and Anne Allen. I give to my nephew John Gymber that part of my messuage or cottage in Godmanchester now in the occupation of Robert Litstar. The rest of said messuage, now in the occupation of John Tubbs I give to my sister Anne Allen. But my wife Elizabeth is to have the said messuage or cottage during her life. I give her also my four acres of meadow in Westmeadow in Godmanchester, for life and after her decease I give said meadow to my aforesaid kinsman John Barton. To my sister Lettice Kyte five pounds. To my aunt Vintner of Godmanchester forty shillings towards the buying of her a bullock. To the poor of Huntingdon forty shillings and thirty nine shillings more which is owing to me from the town. All the residue &c. to my wife Elizabeth and my aforesaid kinsman John Barton to be equally enjoyed and occupied between them in a joint partnership of trading together, which my desire is may continue between them during their joint lives. If not then an equal division to be made between them &c. They to be executors and Gervace Fullwood of Huntingdon, gen^t., and Thomas Pont of the same town, gen^t., to be overseers.

Wit: Richard Pike, clerk, Thomas Pont, Francis Bludwicke. Proved by John Barton. Fines, 199.

ELIZABETH BARTON of Hunt, widow, 10 July 1646, proved 23 October 1647. To my sister Lettice Kite twenty pounds and the bed on which I lie and the things which pertain thereto. To all the children of my brother Thomas Kite of Chatteis, by name Fortunatus Kite, Benjamin Kite, Rebecca Shepard, Elizabeth Blote, Mary Kite and Frances Neale, five pounds apiece. To Elizabeth Haines five pounds. To the poor of Huntingdon thirty shillings. To my servant Josiah Lambert one pair of sheets. To my servant Annis Web my old gown. All the rest of my worldly goods I give to John Barton whom I make sole executor.

Fines, 201.

[In the office of the Clerk of the Courts for Essex County, at Salem, Mass., are two volumes (I. and II.) of Notarial Records. In vol. i., fol. 56, begins a series of depositions and affidavits about the late John Barton of Salem, ancestor of many well known and important Salem people. The chief evidence is that of Lydia Barton, who calls herself relict widow of Doctor John Barton, formerly of Huntington, in the kingdom of England, more lately of Salem, aforesaid, deceased. She deposes that her late husband came to New England in 1672, that he was married to the deponent 7 June, 1675, that he was an apothecary by occupation at first and afterwards practised physic and chyrurgery, that he departed this life in the Island of Barbados in December, 1694, as she was certainly advised, and that she had often heard him say in his lifetime that he was the son of Mr. John Barton of Huntington, before mentioned, fellmonger, and that he had several brothers, the names of three of whom, the deponent well remembered, were Robert, Thomas and Furley, but that deponent's husband, John Barton, was the eldest brother. She further deposed that she had lawful issue by the said John Barton, five sons and one daughter, that the two eldest, both whose names were John, after their father and grandfather's names, died both in infancy, so that there were surviving, Thomas, Zacheus, Samuel and Elizabeth, of whom Thomas, the eldest surviving son of the said Dr. John Barton, deceased, was, at the time of the affidavit, bound on a voyage to Barbados and England.

The above affidavit was taken on the twenty-sixth or twenty-eighth day of February, 1705 (6). Let me add that Mrs. Barton had been Lydia Roberts and step-daughter of Mr. Moses Maverick of Marblehead.—HENRY F. WATERS.]

THOMAS COLES, citizen and clothworker of London, 23 August 1672, proved 7 September 1672. To be buried in the middle aisle of the parish church of St. Mary Islington, where I am now inhabitant. Wife Jane Coles. Her daughter Anne Delaune. Wife's sister Mary Chipchase. The five children of cousin Mr. Paul Pryaulx, William, Peter, Mary, Amee and Jane. Cousin Elizabeth Ellis living in the parish of Stepney, near Ratcliffe Cross, and cousin Anne Adams, her sister, living in or near Plumsted in Kent. Friend Thomas Reynolds of Byfield in the County of Northampton and my cousin Edeth Reynolds, widow, his mother, and Edith and Anne Reynolds, two of her daughters. Cousin Elizabeth Bellio, now servant with Mr. Skinner, merchant in Augustine Friers in London. Judith Chipchase, daughter of the aforenamed Mary Chipchase. The parish of Morton Pinckney (Northampton) where I was born.

Eure, 109.

[The will of Paul Mercer (see REG. for 1893, pp. 511–3) shows that Mary Chipchase was a daughter of Mercer's sister, Mrs. Judith Johnson. Jane, another daughter, was referred to in Mercer's will as then (1661) the relict of the late Gideon de Lawne. She must afterwards have become the wife of Thomas Coles, as above. The will of Mrs. Mary Coquell *alias* Le Mercier, widow of Martin Vander Bist, of which a large summary is given in the REGISTER for January, 1895 (pp. 137–140), should be studied in connection with all the other Mercer and Pryaulx wills. She was a sister of Paul Mercer, Judith Johnson, Hester Bachiler and others there named. In my note on page 140 (of REG. for Jan. 1895) I suggest that these Mercers, or perhaps more properly Le Merciers, may have migrated from France or the Channel Islands. I ought to have added that they may also have been of Flemish origin. There was evidently a large migration (of Protestants) from Flanders to England. The Registers of Wills show this. I believe the Houblon family (connected with the Mercers) was Flemish.—H. F. WATERS.]

JAMES CLARKE of East Farleigh, Kent, gen^t, 13 July 1614, proved 1 November 1614. Daughter Grace Clarke. I give to Abraham Preble, my servant, five pounds and to Anne Joye, my maid, forty shillings, to be paid to every of them within two years after my decease. I give to every of my servants which serve me without wages five shillings apiece. And to every one that serveth me for wages two shillings and six pence apiece, in token of remembrance. Payment made to Margery Baker. And she to have a dwelling in my house as before. The reparations of the church. The poor of the parish. Mr. Basden minister. Son Edward. Wife Mary. My two sisters (not named). I give unto Griffin Roches and Jane his wife my house and orchard lying at Court wood gate in the parish of Hynton, to have and to hold to them during the life of the said Jane. And after her death I give them to Weston Clarke and to his heirs for ever. I give unto Dolor Davis my servant my house and land lying in the parish of Marden, the which is in the occupation of one Terrye. And after the death of my wife Mary Clarke I give unto Weston Clarke all my lands, tenements and hereditaments lying in the parish of Hynton (he paying to his brethren to every one of them an hundred pounds according to my last will, for otherwise I know not how they shall be paid).   Lawe, 118.

ABRAHAM PREBLE of East Barming (Kent) husbandman, 12 April 1625, proved 28 April 1625. My body to be buried in the church yard of East Farleigh. To the poor of East Farleigh twelve shillings. To the poor of East Barming eight shillings. To Mr. Basden minister of East Farleigh fifteen shillings at the day of my burial. To the wife of Tobias Lowes, with whom I live, for her pains she hath taken with me, four pounds. To Annis Preble three pounds. To the three children of Mary Brodshew widow twenty shillings apiece. I do make Mr. George Carpenter of East Farleigh my executor. Mary Bradshawe a witness.   Clarke, 37.

[In the will of James Clarke we have a number of New England names, viz., Abraham Preble, Weston Clarke and Dolor Davis. See also Ped. of Clerk in Vis. of London (Harl. Soc. Pub., vol. xv., p. 172).—H. F. WATERS.

Eben Putnam, editor of Putnam's Monthly Historical Magazine, prints in the number for September, 1895, page 253, an abstract of the will of Robert Preble, who names among his children a son Abraham. The emigrant ancestor of the New England Prebles bore the christian name of Abraham. He came to this country with the "Men of Kent" and settled somewhere about the year 1636 at Scituate in Plymouth Colony. (See Rear Admiral Preble's Genealogy of the Preble Family, Boston, 1868.) These wills may assist in tracing the English ancestry of the New England family. The abstract of Robert Preble's will is as follows.—EDITOR.]

ROBERT PREBLE of Denton, the elder, carpenter. Will dated 2 March, 1634; proved 7 July, 1635. Son Robert Preble, £20. Son Abraham Preble, £20. Daughter Elenor Benjamin, £6. Daughter Frances Jacob, £8. Daughter Margaret Preble, £4. Brother Richard Preble and son Robert Preble to be executors and they are authorized to sell house and lands to meet the legacies.

Wit. by Mary Bushell, Lawrence Carington.   Arch. Kent., 69–85.

Rebecca Angell of London, widow, 15 April 1676, with a codicil added 9 May, proved 7 March 1676. My burial to be with as much privacy as well may be and without charge of mourning, only that rings of ten shillings apiece be given for a remembrance of me to every one of my own brothers and sisters and to such as are or have been their wives or husbands, and also to my sister Elizabeth Angell, widow to my cousin William Angell, and to my sister Mary Hocknell and to my cousin Michael Harvey and his wife and my cousin William Harvey. And concerning my estate I give the same wholly to my dear son William Angell &c., provided that if he die before his age of eighteen years then I give the sum of fifty pounds owing me by my brother Joshua Pordage to his son, my cousin George Pordage. I make and ordain my loving brother Henry Mellish the executor of this my will, in trust only for my said son William Angell, and do constitute my said brother the guardian of my said son, willing and desiring him nevertheless, in the education and disposing of my said son, to take the advice and direction of my loving cousins Mr. Michael Harvey and Mr. William Harvey and my brother Mr. Walter Hampton and my said brother Pordage.

In the Codicil Mrs. Angell desired that if her son William Angell should depart this life before the age of eighteen years that then what estate she hath left him, as in her will, shall be disposed of as followeth, vizt she gives to her sister Mary Steele wife to Sergeant William Steele one hundred pounds, to Mr. Michael Harvey twenty pounds, to his brother Mr. William Harvey twenty pounds, the rest to her brother Henry Mellish. Hale, 28.

[This will gives us a little more information about the English connections of George Pordage of Boston (Mass.), whose father, we have already learned, was Joshua Pordage.—H. F. Waters.]

George Alcock of the parish of St. Katherine Cree Church *alias* Christ Church in London gen^t, 27 February 1676, proved 9 March 1676. I give &c. all my lands, tenements &c. wherein I am now possessed or "interested" in, or whereof I shall be possessed or interested in, or which shall come to me by virtue of any Grant or Patent to be made to me, situate in New England in the parts beyond the seas, in manner and form following: one moiety, or half part, to my cousin Benjamin Walker, citizen and pewterer of London, to my brother John Alcock of New England, merchant, one fourth part, to my kinsman Joshua Lamb one eighth part, and the other eighth part to my brother Palsgrave Alcock and my five sisters, Ann Williams the wife of John Williams, Sarah Whitman the wife of Zachariah Whitman, Mary Lamb the wife of Joshua Lamb the father, Elizabeth Alcock and Joanna Alcock and their heirs, equally to be divided between them, to hold as tenants in common and not as joint tenants. Of my personal estate I give to my brother Zachariah Whitman ten pounds. Like sums to my uncle John Edwards the elder and Mr. Peter Thacher. To the church of Roxbury in New England five pounds. To the school there five pounds. The residue to be divided equally among my brothers and sisters. Benjamin Walker, Zachariah Whitman and Peter Thacher to be executors.

Proved by the oaths of Benjamin Walker and Peter Thacher, two of the executors named in the will, power reserved to grant similar commission to Zachariah Whitman, the other executor named in the will, when he should come to demand it.   Hale, 28.

[One has only to refer to Savage's Gen. Dict. to learn who this George Alcock was.—H. F. Waters.

George Alcock, grandfather of the testator, came in the fleet with Winthrop, and was connected with the Dorchester and Roxbury churches, as deacon. His will in 1640 (REGISTER vol. ii., p. 104) leaves his property for education of his children, among whom is specially mentioned his son John, whom he went to England for, and brought to New England, educating him at Harvard. John graduated in the class of 1646; married, about 1648, Sarah, daughter of Dr. Richard and Anne Palsgrave, and died in 1667. Among their children were George, the testator, born in 1655, and the brothers and sisters mentioned as legatees.

The testator was of the 1659 class of Harvard, and for a sketch of his life including an abstract of his will, see Sibley's Harvard Graduates, vol. ii., p. 420-422. The inventory of his estate is in the Suffolk County (Mass.) Probate Files, No. 938, and Records, vol. vi., p. 225.—WALTER K. WATKINS.]

EDWARD MOFFATT of St. Sidwell's in the city of Exon, linen draper, 3 March, 1726, proved 19 April 1727. To James Kennedy and to Anne, his daughter, twenty pounds apiece. To Edward Kennedy four hundred pounds. To my nephew William Kennedy fifteen hundred pounds. To my nephew John Johnson five hundred pounds. To my nephew James Johnson one hundred pounds. To my niece Sarah Johnson two hundred pounds. To my nephew William Johnson six thousand pounds. To my niece Mary Johnson two hundred pounds. To Jannet Paterson and Mary Paterson four hundred pounds apiece. To my kinsman Wm Moffatt fifteen pounds. To Adam Moffatt of Birmingham five pounds. To Margaret Moffatt five pounds. To Jannet Moffatt of Hook ten pounds. To Jannett Moffatt of Tundergarth five pounds. To William Tagert in London twenty pounds. To Thomas Armstrong two guineas. To Adam Smart a ring of fifteen shillings. A certain trust to be made for the use of four orthodox presbiterian ministers of the city of Exon. To my uncle Thomas Moffatt three pounds per annum for life. To the children of my kinsman John Moffatt two thousand pounds, they to have the income &c. for their maintenance and education, and I do appoint their father, William Johnson and John Kennedy trustees for the said children. To the parish of Corrie in the County of Annandale two hundred and eighty pounds the interest whereof is and shall be to maintain a schoolmaster for teaching the children there to read and write, and I give twenty pounds for building a schoolhouse. To the morning lecture at Bow meeting in Exon twenty shillings per annum and to the Charity School twenty shillings per annum. To James Scott of Shipton Mallet and his two sons two guineas each.

Item, I give unto Thomas Moffatt of Boston in New England a ring of sixteen shillings value. To John Kennedy all my household goods and one thousand pounds. All the residue to my kinsman John Moffatt and my nephew the said John Kennedy and I make them executors.

Wit: Roger Hopping, Robert Livingston, Jnº Conant.   Farrant, 95.

[Mr. Thomas Moffett, named by the testator, is first found in Boston, exercising the duties of a constable in the year 1715, and at about the date of the testator's bequest, held the then responsible office of scavenger, to be followed by the still higher honor of a town assessor. His further advancement was slow, but ten years later, in 1739, he was chosen as a collector of taxes, but unfortunately for the town Mr. Moffett begged to be excused, as he was soon to be bound for Great Britain, where he doubtless went, as we find no more trace of him in Boston. In 1757 there appears a John Moffett, probably a young man, as he was chosen to that position usually tendered the young and active, the office of hogreeve.

A Wm. Moffett was at Killingly, Conn., 1708-9, and later Dr. Thomas Moffatt of New London was of prominence.—WALTER K. WATKINS.]

THOMAS WILLSONNE of Bockinge, Essex, gen^t., 24 February 33^d Elizth, proved 31 March 1591. Thomas Willsonne my father, late of Bednall Green, Middlesex deceased, did make me by his last will &c. his sole executor. Leases of lands in Stepney, houses &c. in St. Martin's in the Fields by Charing Cross bequeathed by him. My daughters Susan, Elizabeth, Jane, Anne, Mary, Winifride, Frances and Dorothy at days of marriage or age of one and twenty years. My brother John Willsonn and his wife. My sister Bradburrie. My sister Pigott. My sister Barbara Lucas. My sister Anne Haines. My sister Joane. My sister Elizabeth. I give to Thomas Willsonn my eldest son a horn bordered about with silver parcel gilt. My son Philip Willsonn. John Robinson, my children's schoolmaster. My uncle Jeffrey Brooke's wife. To my mother Simons one ring of gold with a death's head. Henry Barr. Son Thomas at one and twenty. My wife to be executrix and beloved friends, Master Edward Thursbie and my uncle Master Jeffery Brooke to be overseers.

Among the witnesses were Lawncelott Browne, Doctor of Physic, and Humfrey Clarke.

Proved by William Creake, Notary Public, Attorney for Susan the relict of the deceased.   Sainberbe, 23.

SUSAN WILLSON of Bocking, Essex, widow, late wife of Thomas Wilson gen^t. deceased, her will dated 24 December 1615, published and declared 14 May 1616, proved 10 June 1616. To be buried in the church of Braintree. The poor of Braintree, Bocking and Stysted. My sons Philip and John Wilson. My son in law Thomas Trotter and my daughter Anne his wife. My son in law William Lyngwood and my daughter Mary his wife. My son in law Anthony Filioll. My daughter Winifride now wife of William Brocke. My grandchild Susan Spooner at one and twenty or day of marriage. Loving friends Christopher Thursbie Esq. and John Sorrell of Stebbing gen^t. My cousin and loving friend John Smyth late of Loughborough in Leicestershire. My loving friend Mrs. Thursbie the wife of Christopher Thursbie of Bocking Esq. and my godson Mr. John Thursbye, his son. My cousin Mary Meade of Stansted Monfitchet, widow, and my godchild Mary Palmer, her daughter. My godchild Susan daughter to Mr. John Sorrell of Stebbing. Henry Barre, sometimes my servant. Robert Byndes of Stisted, my good neighbor, and his daughter Susan now the wife of Matthew Francke of Bocking. Constance Bridge of Brayntree. Mary Sparhawke sometimes my servant. Margery Dixon sometimes my servant and now the wife of Robert Billing. My servant Susan Glascocke. My uncle Mr. Jeffrey Brocke and my aunt his wife. My loving cousin Mrs. Frances Iremonger daughter of my uncle Jeffrey Brocke. Edward Barre my servant. My daughter Dorothy Filioll. I give to my son Philip Willson my three little messuages &c. in Brayntree, in a place there called the Pounde End. I give to my son John Willson my messuage or tenement &c. in Braintree which I lately bought of one John Denman, now in the occupation of my son in law William Lyngwood, and two tenements &c. in Braintree now in the occupation of Richard Owltinge and Thomas Clarke. I give to William Lyngwood and my daughter Mary his wife my Inn &c. called the Horne in Braintree, which I purchased of Jervase Bradhawe and now in said Bradshawe's occupation. My eldest son Thomas Willson. My daughters Anne Trotter and Mary Lyngwood shall have that messuage &c. called Lulls in Bradwell by Coggeshall Essex which was given to them and others by my father in law Mr. Symons, notwithstanding any release they have heretofore made unto me. Son John Willson and two sons in law Thomas Trotter and William Lyngwood to be executors. Mary the wife of my son John. Mrs. Dorothy Glascock.   Cope, 62.

PHILIP WILSON of Bednall Greene, parish of Stepney, Middlesex, gen^t., 27 June 1620, proved 24 July 1620. Manor &c. of Bishop's Hall in Middlesex to my son Philip. My son Thomas and my two daughters Elizabeth and Margaret Wilson. My three messuages in Braintree, Essex, called the Pounde. My mother in law Elizabeth Weldinge. My uncle Thomas Hogge. My brother in law James Baynes. My sister in law Jane Weldinge.   Soame, 73.

JOHN WILSON of Wardon Abbey in the Co. of Bedford, gen^t., 16 April 1622, proved 31 July 1622. To be buried in the church of Wardon. My son Charles at one and twenty and daughters Mary and Elizabeth Wilson at eighteen or marriage. To my wife Bridget my messuages, lands &c. in Braintree, Essex, to hold till my son Charles comes to his full age of one and twenty years. My wife and my father in law Thomas Wynn, gent., to be executors and my brother Thomas Wilson and my brother in law William Lingwood to be overseers.   Savile, 64.

JOHN SMITH of London, gen^t., 7 December 1625, proved 8 November 1626. To my nephew Richard Morecrofte son of my sister Phillipp Morecrofte my house and messuage with land &c., being freehold land bought by me of his father Thomas Morecrofte, deceased some years past, situate in Loughborowe, Leicestershire; but the said Richard's mother, my sister, shall have her dwelling therein during her natural life. My niece Mary Newton wife of Miles Newton of London haberdasher. Thomas Newton, her son. My niece Margaret Allen, daughter of my sister Phillipp Morecrofte and wife to John Allen of Loughborowe. My niece Dorothy Lovet wife to William Lovet of Loughborowe, tanner. Niece Joane Morecrofte. To the late left wife of my nephew Lawrence Palmer, late of Stansteed Montfitched in the county of Herford and every one of said Lawrence Palmer's children born of this widow, his late wife. Matthew Palmer second son to my sister Mary Meade late of Stansted Montfitched, widow, and George Palmer her third son. Susan, her eldest daughter, Katherine, her second daughter, and Mary, her third daughter. Jane Ince *als.* ———, now living in the city of Dublin, Ireland, being the daughter of my niece Phillipp Turner *als.* Ince, late deceased, whilst she lived the wife of Richard Turnor. My cousin Richard Turnor and Anne Turnor, his daughter. My brother in law Thomas Howgh of Loughborowe dyer, sometime husband unto my sister Ann, and Thomas Howgh the younger, her son. My niece Elizabeth Fowler now dwelling in Loughborowe, daughter of my said sister Ann. My niece Patience Warde, wife to Michaell Warde of London, grocer, and each of her children. My niece Mary daughter of my said sister Ann. My niece Isabel Howgh, now in service in London, another daughter, and Ann Howgh the youngest daughter. My brother in law William Felgate and his daughter Ann, my god daughter, and every of his sons, being two in number, and each of his other daughters besides the said Ann and Blanch Felgate, his daughter (to whom a larger bequest). My cousin Mrs. Francis Iremonger and her daughter Katheren Iremonger and her other daughters. Every one of her sons. Their father Mr. Henry Iremonger, my cousin. My cousin Miles Newton.

I give to my cousin Mr. Thomas Trotter five pounds and to his wife, my cousin Ann Trotter, five pounds and to every one of their children twenty shillings apiece. I give to my cousin Mrs. Dorothy Filliall three pounds and to my cousin Mrs. Mary Lingwood three pounds and to my cousin Winifride Brocke three pounds. John Alleyn, my kinsman, one of the churchwardens of Loughborowe. My sister Morecrofte's two daughters Margaret Allen and Dorothy Lovett. My niece Mary Newton and her sister Joane. My cousin Edward Bagguley and his two sisters Elizabeth and Cassandra. My cousin Thomas Slywright of the Inner Temple Esq. Mrs. Bridget Wilson widow, late the wife of John Wilson gen^t. deceased. Mrs. Horsell widow, sister of my said cousin Mr. Henry Iremonger. Myles Newton and Henry Iremonger to be executors.   Hele, 116.

THOMAS WILSON of Bocking, Essex, gen^t., 16 October 1627, proved 9 November 1627. My body to be buried in the chancel of Braintree. The poor of Bocking, Stisted and Braintree. My messuage and farm in Great and Little Canfield to be sold by Humfry Mawditt, gen^t., and my brother in law William Lyngwood for payment of my debts and legacies. To my daughter Elizabeth my copyhold lands in Braintree, called Companes or otherwise, now in the occupation of the said William Lingwood, and the parcel of land in Braintree called the horsefair field and Windmill Hill in Braintree (and other lands), to enter upon the same at her age of one and twenty years, with remainder to daughter Mary, next to daughter Dorothy. Bequests to Mary and Dorothy. My eldest son, John, hath behaved himself very disobediently towards me and my wife, his mother, and I see little hope of amendment. My mill called Stisted mill, in Stisted. Although my son Thomas hath heretofore behaved himself undutifully to me and my wife, his mother, yet I hope better of him hereafter. My wife Elizabeth. My messuage and farm called Hatches in Braintree. My manor or messuage called Jenkins to my wife, for her life, and after her decease to my son Thomas. Sir William Maxey, knight, my worthy friend. My cousin James Heron Esq. My mother ln law Mrs. Mary Clarke. My sisters Mary Lingwood and Dorothy Filioll. My cousin and god daughter Susan Lingwood. Mrs. Catherine Mawditt. My wife to be sole executrix. I do earnestly entreat Sir William Maxey, knight, and my cousin Heron to be supervisors.

Among the witnesses were Fulke Wodhull and W. Lyngwood.
                                                    Skynner, 114.

THOMAS TROTTER of London, merchant, 30 November 1631, sealed and published 1 March 1631, proved 12 March 1631. Debts and funeral charges satisfied and paid my personal estate to be divided into two equal parts, one half being in my proper power, by the eminent and laudable custom of City of London, and the other half belonging to my children. I have already advanced and preferred in marriage my two eldest daughters, Anne and Elizabeth. My two youngest daughters unadvanced, Susanne and Thomasin Trotter. My eldest daughters (named) Anne Grove and Elizabeth Amos. My grandchildren Thomas and Anne Grove. My grandchild Isacke Amos. The Company of Salters of London whereof I am a member. I do forgive and release unto my uncle Nicholas Skynner and my cousin Martyn (Skynner) and to Thomas Skynner, his son, all such sum and sums of money as they owe unto me by specialty or otherwise. My cousin Daniel Skynner and my cousin Richard Wiseman. My sister Lyngwood, my cousin Susan Spooner and my cousin Laurence Arthure's

wife, my cousin Robert Whaple's wife and my cousin Myles Newton's wife.
To Nicholas Woodward of Bockinge. The pastor and curate of St. Dunstan in the East where I dwell. Mr. Nathaniel Shute to preach a sermon
for the instructing of the people that shall assemble at my funeral, which I
hope and desire the parson of St. Dunstan will give leave unto. My two
youngest daughters, Susan and Thomasine Trotter and my friend Joseph
Brand to be executors and my brother William Lyngwood, my son in law
Thomas Amos and my friends Myles Newton and Lawrence Arthur to be
supervisors. I have in my life time settled and assured, by several deeds,
certain lands and an annuity out of a house in Braintree and Bocking,
Essex, to the uses of the several poor in those parishes. Then follows a
note of such parishes as are to have fifty pounds distributed amongst their
poor. Eight parishes in Colchester, the three parishes in Sudbury (where
John Lord and Robert Whitinges were among those to oversee the distribution), Braintree (under the oversight of Mr. John Hawkins, Wm Lingwood, John Maryan, John Debnam, Adrian Mott), Bocking (John Keightlye,
Lawrence Arthur, John Ames (?), Isaack Ansell, Matthew Whipple),
Coxall (Coggeshall), Witham (Jeremy Garoad, William Skynner, ———
Nycholls), Halsted and certain parishes in London and four parishes in
Southwark.   Audley, 31.

MARY CLARKE of Bocking, Essex, widow, 4 September 1630, proved
1 June 1633. My body to be buried in the Chancel of Bradwell. The
poor of Bradwell, Bocking and Stisted. My loving brother Sir William
Maxey, knight, my son in law John Nodes, gen^t. My daughter Nodes.
My daughter Dorothy Wilsmore. I give to my son William Clarke four
pounds and to his two sons twenty shillings apiece. To my grandchild
Elizabeth Wilson twenty shillings. To my grandchild and god daughter
Mary Wilson twelve pounds, my silver spoon and my wedding ring. To
my grandchild Dorothy Wilson thirty shillings and my little ring. To my
grandchild John Wilson twenty shillings and I forgive him five pounds
which he oweth me. To my grandchild Thomas Wilson three pounds.
To my cousin Mr. Bryan Tuke forty shillings. To William Lingwood
gen^t. and Mary his wife, my god daughter, twenty shillings apiece. Mr.
Normington of Bradwell to preach at my burial. Four of Sir William
Maxey's men to carry my body to church to be buried. My grandchild
Mary Wilson to be executrix and William Lyngwood supervisor.
                                                           Russell, 58.

DOROTHY WILSON of Bocking, Essex, singlewoman (nuncupative), 6
October 1636. She gave all to her brother Thomas and his wife. Commission issued, 15 October 1636, to Thomas Wilson and Jane his wife, the
legataries, &c., to administer &c.   Pile, 105.

WILLIAM READ of Bocking, Essex, yeoman, 20 March 1646, proved
23 April 1649. To Daniel Read, one of my brother Francis Read's sons,
my tenement and freehold lands in Panfield, late purchased of the widow
Coggeshall, he to pay his brother Francis Read twenty pounds and twenty
pounds unto William Stoakes. To my brother Thomas Read, for life, my
two tenements called Levitt's, in Bocking, and after his decease to his son
William. To Elizabeth Wilson, my kinswoman, wife of John Wilson,
my tenement called Arnold's, for life, and next to her son William Wilson,
with remainder to the rest of her children. My godson William Stokes.
My godson James Freeman. The rest of the children of James Free-

man, vizt. Henry, John and Elizabeth Freeman. My godson William
Miller, son of William Miller of High Roding. Martha Princett daughter of John Princett. Agnes Clarke, the wife of Robert Clarke of Felsted, and Agnes Clarke her daughter. My brother Thomas Reade to be
sole executor and my kinsman Daniel Read to be overseer.

Fairfax, 45.

[A pedigree of this family of Wilson is given in the Visitations of Essex
(Harl. Soc. Pub., Vol. 13, p. 525).   These wills and a lot of other wills relating
to East Anglian families which I have been gathering for years I am getting
into print partly, perhaps chiefly, for my own convenience, since they are all
more or less connected with families who, I am sure, had each of them one or
more representatives in New England: when once in print they can be much
more easily referred to than if they were to remain, as hitherto, only in manuscript.   William Lyngwood who married into this family of Wilson was somehow
related or connected with numerous New Englanders, as appears from his letter
of 20 March 1651 to his " Cosen Clarke," to be found in Vol. 2 of Land Records
in the office of the Secretary of State, Hartford, Connecticut, and published in
full in The Goodwins of East Anglia, 1890.   No one acquainted with the records
of the early settlers of Massachusetts Bay and Connecticut will read these
East Anglian wills which I shall furnish without being struck, as I have been,
with their significance even where positive clews are not given.

HENRY F. WATERS.]

ELIZABETH CLOPTON late of Boxford, Suffolk, widow (nuncupative)
25 October 1603, proved 18 February 1603. The poor of Boxford.
Master Sandes the preacher. John Potter in whose house she lodged.
Mistress Brande her cousin. The widow Brag. The widow Brande. The
widow Clerke. All the residue (her debts being paid and legacies discharged) she willed should be divided between John Whiting, Henry Whiting, Elizabeth Tarver, her grandchildren, and Thomas Gates, her great
grandchild.

Wit: Anne Brande, John Potter and divers others.

Commission issued (at above date) to John and Henry Whiting as next
akin, to administer according to the tenor of the will.   Harte, 16.

SAMUEL ARMITAGE citizen and mercer of London, 23 September 1631,
proved 15 October 1631. Wife Joane Armitage to be executrix. My
brother in law John Seaman, my sister Sara, his wife, and every one of
their children. My brother in law Matthew Langley, my sister Mary, his
wife, and every one of their children. My brother in law James Boulton,
my sister Anne, his wife, and every one of their children. My brother
in law John Key, my sister Dorothy, his wife, and every one of their children. My sister Jane Armitage. My uncle Mr. Samuel Armitage. My
friend Mr. Arthur Lee. I do give unto my loving aunt Mrs. Hester Longley and Mrs. Susan Williamot ten shillings apiece. My cousin Elizabeth
Chambers. My cousin Mr. Samuel Slater, Mr. Dr. Burges and Mr. Shadrach Simpson, ministers of the word of God. Katherine and Ann Simpson daughters of the said Mr. Shadrach Simpson. My friend Mr. Edward
Taylor, citizen and girdler of London. Mr. John Basset, Mr. Edmond
Clerke and Mr. John Felton. My loving uncle Mr. Samuel Armitage and
my loving friend Mr. Arthur Lee to be overseers.   St. John, 105.

JOHN WHITING of Hadley, Suffolk, Mercer, 2 April 1637, proved 15
November 1637. To Rose my loving wife all those my lands and tene-
ments in Naughton (Newton?) and Neging, in the occupation of Robert
Marshall (and others) for and during her life, upon condition that she shall

seal a good perfect release unto my sons John and Henry of all her thirds
or dower of the rest of my lands and houses &c. And after the decease of
Rose my wife I give the said lands and tenements, both free and copy, in
Newton and Neging unto John Whiting my son. I give him my lands in
Layow with a mill thereunto belonging, called Coe mill. I give him my
house wherein I dwell in Hadly and the piece of ground near Tapsall
bridge. I give and bequeath unto Henry Whiteing my son my house and
land in Bramford, both free and copy, upon condition that he pay the rest
of the money which is behind and unpaid by John Beadswell out of the
land at Wenam which I purchased in his name for him and gave him at
Wenom, as by John Berde's will appeareth. I give unto Henry my son
seven hundred pounds of lawful money, *i.e.* five hundred at the age of five
and twenty years and the other two hundred within one year after his
apprenticeship come out. I give unto Rose my wife fifty pounds. To
Mary Coper my daughter forty pounds. To Henry my son my part of a
ship called the Roebucke. I give to Henry my copyhold house at Carsy.
I will that he shall pay unto his mother ten pounds a year during her widowhood. I give unto Robert Payne my son in law my house and land in
Newton, free and copy, called the Saracen's Head, with the appurtenances,
to him during his life and after his death to John Payne, my grandchild,
and his heirs forever; and for want of such heirs to return to my heirs
again; but upon condition the said Robert Paine do assure to his two sons
that he had by my daughter, John and Robert Payne, the sum of thirty
pounds apiece more as he stand bound to do upon marriage and that
he do seal a release to my son John Whiting of all former promises. I
give to Thomas Whiting my grandchild twenty pounds of current money to
be laid out in plate for him. I give to Hanna Proctor my grandchild
twenty nobles and to John Payne my grandchild forty pounds and to
Robert Payne my grandchild twenty nobles and to George Coper my
grandchild twenty nobles; and all these my grandchildren to be paid when
they shall come to the age of twenty one years. I give to Thomas Gattes
the younger, my godson, forty shillings at one and twenty. To my cousin
Thomas Gattes a black cloak. To Mary Bowes, Alles Upsher, my old
servant forty shillings. The poor of Hadley and of Boxford. My son
John to be residuary legatee and sole executor. And I do nominate and
entreat my two loving friends and cousins Mr. Robert Stansby, parson of
Westrop, and Mr. John Browing, parson of Semer, to be supervisors.
  Witnesses Richard Tilson, Thomas Gattes.   Goare, 150.

  JOHN WHITEING of Hadleigh, Suffolk, mercer, 16 January 1643, proved
30 January 1644. To wife Judith all my household stuff and fifty pounds
in money upon condition that she shall give a full release of the thirds of
my lands to my two supervisors to the use of my children. I give her my
house at Hadleigh wherein I dwell and all my lands and my mill in Langham and Raydon to have and enjoy only the time she shall continue my
widow. I have discharged my wife's former estate of those legacies which
it was engaged for. My desire is my two sons Thomas and John Whiteing
should be brought up with their mother so long as she remain my widow;
but if she happen to marry my mind is that my son Thomas should be
brought up by his grandmother Whiteing, or placed with one to bring up
by her appointment, and my son John, my desire is, that his grandmother
Harrison should bring up or place. I give to Thomas my son all those
lands and tenements, copy and free, in Nawten Nedging now in possession

of my mother Whiteing for term of her life (and after her decease bequeathed to myself by my father's last will). To Thomas my house at Hadleigh (all these at twenty two) and all my interest in the house called the Saruson's Head or else a hundred pounds which I lent my brother Payne of New England upon it, my son to have it at twenty two. To John my son all my lands and mill in Langham and Raydon (at twenty two). Eight hundred pounds to Thomas at four and twenty and five hundred pounds to John (at same age). To my loving mother Whiteing twenty pounds. To my mother ten pounds. Poor of Hadleigh. Wife Judeth to be sole executrix and my brother Henry Whiteing and my cousin Thomas Gates to be supervisors. Mr. Richardson and Richard Tilson of Hadleigh.

Wit. William Richardson and Nath. Gale.   Rivers, 31.

[Brother Payne is Robert Paine, a younger brother of William, one of the foremost business men in the Bay colony. Both were citizens of Ipswich, where Robert was ruling elder in the church, and feoffee of the Grammar school. They were sons of William Paine, of Nowton, in Suffolk. The late Henry W. Paine, LL.D., the eminent Boston lawyer, derived descent from this family.

Geo. A. Gordon.]

JOHN PROCKTER citizen and weaver of London, 11 November 1648, proved 5 March 1648. If Elizabeth, my dear and loving wife, shall within fourteen days next after my decease release and discharge to Henry Prockter citizen and weaver of London (father of me the said John Prockter) all that estate and jointure made unto my said wife by my said father, in and by a certain Indenture bearing date 20 December 1645, made between the said Henry Prockter on the one party and Edmund Staunton of Kingstone upon Thames, Surrey, Doctor in Divinity, on the other party, then I do give and bequeath to the said Elizabeth all my goods &c. in my house in Cheapeside, London, and the one half of all my goods &c. whatsoever. The other moiety to be divided into three parts, of which one third to my son John another third to my son Henry and the other third I give as followeth ; that is to say to my mother Jone Prockter three pounds (to buy her a ring) to my three sisters Sarah, Mary and Hannah Prockter each of them forty shillings (for rings) to my aunt Mary Pigeon five pounds, to my uncle Thomas Prockter five pounds and the residue of this third part of the moiety of my estate I give to my said son Henry. To wife Elizabeth the twenty pounds now in the hands of her uncle Robert Staunton Esq. and given to her by her late grandfather deceased.   Fairfax, 29.

HENRY PROCKTER, gen^t, of Kensington, Middlesex, 27 September 1650, proved 17 October 1650. My daughter in law Elizabeth the wife of my late son John Prockter. Four houses in Coleman Street, London. My wife Joane. My daughter Hannah Prockter. Seven houses in or near Coleman Street. The house I now live in, in Kensington. My daughter Sarah Prockter. My grandchild Henry Prockter. My sister Mary Pigeon. My lease of ground in Wapping, parish of Stepney. My sister's son Thomas Piggeon. Seven acres in Kensington I lately bought of George Harrison. My brother Thomas Prockter. Francis Prockter my present servant. My cousin Elizabeth Barnes and her four children. My grandchild John Prockter. My sister Frances Willson. Ten pounds to the parish of Kensington towards the building of a free school if begun within eighteen months after my decease. Capt. John Stone, Mr. William Mountague, Mr. John Upcher and William Viner to be overseers. Wife Joane executrix. Daughter Mary Backster.

John Stone one of the witnesses.   Pembroke, 158.

SARAH PROCTOR, daughter of Henry Proctor late of Kensington, Middlesex, gentleman, 17 January 1653, declared and published 14 August 1654, proved 25 October 1654. To my mother Johanna Proctor fifty pounds for a legacy and the ten pounds which I paid towards the building of two new chambers in the house at Kensington and five pounds for mourning. To my sister Hannah Tompson forty pounds and my chest of drawers and one gold ring and five pounds for mourning. John Proctor and Henry Proctor. My uncle Thomas Proctor and his nine children. My aunt Mary Pigeon. Thomas Pigeon. My cousin Elizabeth Barnes. My cousin Elizabeth Birdseye. My uncle Henry Whiting. My uncle Samuel Slator. John Upcher and his wife and two children John and Samuel Upcher. Thomas Hodges minister of Kensington. Patience Chapman and her two daughters Hannah and Grace. I give unto Margaret Cheevers widow ten pounds. To the poor of the church which my uncle Slator is pastor of ten pounds. My brother Fr. Tompson. My brother Jeremy Proctor to be executor and Francis Tompson and John Upcher overseers.

Wit. John Upcher, Peaceabl Power.   Alchin, 9.

JOHANNA PROCTOR of London, Widow, 23 April 1658, proved 3 April 1661. My grandchild Henry Procter at one and twenty. The children of my daughter in law Hannah Thompson. Samuel and Francis the two sons of my son in law Francis Thompson and of my said daughter in law Hannah Thompson, his wife, at their ages of one and twenty years. My sister Pigeon and my cousin Thomas Pigeon. My brother Thomas Procter and my cousin Frances his daughter. My sister Pigeon's daughter's five children which she now hath. My grandchild John Procter. The four daughters of Mrs. Patience Chapman widow, deceased. Mrs. Isabella Simpson, widow. Mrs. Martha Davis, widow, and her four daughters. Mr. Manning and his wife. My brother Slater minister at Katherine's near the Tower. Mr. Kentish also minister there. Mr. Philip Nye the elder and Mr. John Loder. I give unto Mrs. Chevers and her daughter Hannah twenty pounds. Mrs. Gabell. Mrs. Knight, widow. Mr. Richard Legate. The poor of Kensington, Middlesex, for the buying of coals to be distributed amongst the poor there. Mrs. Hodges wife of Mr. Hodges, minister of Kensington. Mrs. Steele the wife of Mr. Lawrance Steele of Kensington. My cousin Richardson. My brother Whitinge. My sister Lawrance. Mrs. Birdsey. Mrs. Sweet, late of Kensington, widow, and her daughter Hannah Sweet. Mr. Ragnor (Raynor?) minister of Egham. Surrey. The son of Mrs. Archer, widow. I give unto Captain John Stone forty pounds and to Mrs. Mary Stone his wife my best diamond ring and my bible with silver clasps. I give unto Mrs. Mary Stone the daughter of the said Captain Stone my ring with a great stone in it and my little cabinet. I give unto my son in law Mr. Jeremiah Backster forty pounds, vizt twenty pounds to be paid him by my son Francis Thompson and Mr. John Upcher out of the rents &c. of my houses in Wapping and twenty pounds out of my other estate. My grandchildren Charles and Elizabeth Zinzon. To Mrs. Slater living in Crutched Fryers, London, the wife of the brother of my said brother Slater, five pounds. To the poor of the church whereof the said Mr. Nye is teacher and the said Mr. Loder pastor, whereof I am a member, and not to the poor of the parish where they preach, twenty pounds. The poor of St. Ollave's Southwark. The poor of St. Katherine's near the Tower and the poor of the particular church or congregation whereof my said brother Slater is pastor. Mr. George Cooper a scholar of the University of Oxford. The poor of St. Stephen's Colman Street. My body to be buried in Bartholomew's near the Exchange, London, or at Kensington. I do make and ordain the said Captain John Stone sole executor and my said son in law Jeremiah Baxter, Mr. Francis Thompson and the said Mr. John Upcher overseers.

May, 60.

HENRY WHITING of Ipswich, Suffolk, gen^t, 22 March 1685, with a codicil bearing date 13 March 1686, proved 11 May 1687. To my daughter Mrs. Mary Blomfield three hundred pounds, to be secured for her sole and separate use and dispose. To my grandson Henry Blomfield one hundred pounds. To my son Peyton Ventris Esq. and to my daughter Margaret his wife my manors of Waylands and of Ipswich Atwards *als* St. Peters and all that messuage, with the garden, orchard and appurtenances, now in the occupation of the said Peyton Ventris, and all other manors, messuages, lands &c. that I lately purchased and were formerly the estate of Edward Mann Esq. deceased. I give to the said Peyton Ventris my messuage and lands in Wenham Parva, Suffolk, now in the occupation of John Gentry. Provision made for Henry Parsons and my daughter Christian his wife and the daughter of the said Henry which he now hath by the said Christian. My three daughters Mary, Margaret and Judith. I give to Judith my messuage, lands, &c., both freehold and copyhold, in Bromford, Suffolk. I give to my sister in law Mrs. Lawrence ten pounds. I give to Mrs. Thompson the wife of Francis Thompson, merchant, ten pounds. I give to George Cooper, clerk, ten pounds and to my cousin Robert Paine ten pounds and to the son of my nephew Thomas Whiting deceased ten pounds, to buy each of my aforesaid cousins pieces of plate in remembrance of me. I give to Mr. Raymer (or Raynier) minister of St. Lawrence Parish three pounds and to the poor of the parish five pounds. My cousin Lawrence Stisted. I give my house wherein I dwell at Ipswich and my shipping, plate, household stuff, moneys and the rest and residue of my estate to be equally divided among my three daughters (as above). I do require all my daughters and their respective husbands and their heirs to convey and release all their right in the houses and tenements in Coggeshall, Essex, to such persons as shall be interested in the same under a sale I formerly made of them. I make and appoint my son Peyton Vendris executor.

Among the witnesses were George Raymond and Mathew Harrison.

Foot, 70.

NICHOLAS STANTON of Ipswich, Suffolk, clerk, 9 November 1648, proved 14 February 1649. I will and bequeath to my executors all that land &c. which I lately purchased of Henry Stanton of Fritton, lying in the same town in the County of Norfolk, containing about thirty acres, to be by them sold for the payment of my debts and legacies, within one year after my decease, in the church porch of Stratton Mihills (Michaels) in the Co. of Norfolk, to such of those persons that live and have their abode in the said County, vizt to my kinsman William Sabbourne twenty pounds, part of it a debt due from my father to him and part of it promised by my father to him as a gift and legacy from him, to my sister Margaret Stanton fifty pounds, being that portion of money which my father intended for her if his estate would reach it, to Mary my wife twenty pounds which I had of her, which she intended for the use and behoof of George Cooper her son. I give to the poor of Margaret's parish, Ipswich, ten pounds, five pounds of it to be laid out in bibles for distribution and five pounds in money. The poor of Stratton Mihills. To the Library in Ipswich five pounds. To my mother in law Elizabeth Stanton, now living in Hempnall, Norfolk, ten pounds. To my mother in law Whiteing, to Mrs. Elizabeth Stebbing of Brandeston and to Mr. Thomas Waterhouse, living there also, forty shillings apiece. To my kinsman William Sabborne ten pounds. To my cousin Stanton's son of Fritton forty shillings. To Daniel Ray the son of Daniel Ray of Ipswich forty shillings. To my aunt Cooper, living in Hingham in Norfolk, forty shillings. To Joseph Moyse or his wife, living in New England, forty shillings. To my kinswoman Judith Smith the late wife of Henry Smith, living in New England, ten pounds. To her five children Judith, John, Elizabeth, Henry and Daniel, forty shillings apiece. To Mary my wife twenty pounds to be according to her discretion laid out or distributed for the good of the Plantation of New England in the general or to such particular persons living there as she think fit. To my brother Robert Stanton, living in Norwich, or the heir male of his body, forty pounds. To my brother Samuel Stanton ten pounds. To my brother Henry Stanton thirty pounds. These brothers to release all their title in the lands in Fritton bequeathed to my executors. Mr. Christopher Vyn of Stratton Michills. To Henry Stanton my youngest brother all my houses and tenements, with all my free and copyhold lands in Stratton Peters and Stratton Michaells, Norfolk, upon condition that he pay the following gifts and legacies; to my sister Elizabeth, to my sister Judith, to my brother Robert, to my brother Samuel, to my sister Frances (sundry specified gifts). And the said Henry shall pay to Nicholas Stanton, eldest son of my brother Robert, thirty pounds, at his age of one and twenty years, and to the other two children of the said Robert twenty pounds apiece, at their ages of one and twenty. The children of my sister Judith. To George Cooper, my wife's son, all my printed books, when he shall accomplish the age of one and twenty. In the mean time I commit them into the hands of Mary my wife.

Wit: Matthew Lawrence, Ben Wade.   Pembroke, 31.

An abstract of this will was printed in Emmerton & Waters's Gleanings, pages 117 and 118. We copy from that book the following annotation:

"The mention made by this testator of his mother-in-law Whiteing identifies him as the Nicholas Stanton who is shewn in the Candler Mss. to have married Mary, one of three daughters of John Whiting of Hadleigh, Co. Suffolk, and sister of Ann, who, with her husband, came to New England and settled in Ipswich. It also enables us to suggest a probable misreading on the part of that eminent antiquary, M͏r Joseph Hunter, or else a misprint in his article on Suffolk Emigrants in Mass. Hist. Coll., Third Series, Vol. X., p. 171; for it will be noticed that Mr. Stanton in his will mentions his wife Mary's son *George Cooper*, while according to M͏r Hunter's paper Mrs. Stanton's first husband was a *George Compe*. Her brother Henry Whiting is said to have been Portman of Ipswich. It will be recalled that John Sparhawke of Great Coggeshall in his will (*q. v.*) speaks of his cousin Whiting of Ipswich. According to Candler (N. E. Hist. Gen. Reg., IV., 180), Henry Whiting, Portman of Ipswich, married Mary daughter of Robert Crane of "Coxhall" by wife Mary daughter of Samuel Sparhawke of Dedham.

The M͏r Thomas Waterhouse, mentioned, had been educated at the Charter House, London, and afterwards at Emmanuel College, Cambridge, was a schoolmaster at Dorchester (Mass.), 1639: by wife Ann daughter of John Mayhew of Coddenham, Co. Suffolk, had a daughter Ann born here, bapt. 7 March, 1641, returned to England, became master of the Grammar School at Colchester, remaining there until the close of 1647. He must next, as the will shows, have been at Brandeston, Co. Suffolk, but ultimately settled at Ash Bocking, five or six miles from Brandeston and within a mile or two of Coddenham. He was ejected by the Act of Uniformity 1662 and died at Creting 1679 or 1680 at the age of almost eighty. The well-known Salem family of Rea or Ray are descended from a Daniel Ray who was of Plymouth 1631 and removed to Salem. His son Joshua married Sarah Waters (*not* a daughter of Richard, as Savage suggests). Bethia Ray a sister of Joshua became the wife of the famous Capt. Thomas Lothrop.

Joseph Moyse was of Salisbury, N. E., where his wife Hannah died 1655. Henry Smith was entered as a passenger for New England in the Diligent, 1638, with his wife, three sons and two daughters (without naming either wife or children). The will supplies the deficiency. Mr. Smith was a freeman 1639, representative 1641, removed to Rehoboth 1643 and died there 1649. His will dated 3 Nov., 1647 (Inventory taken 21–10mo –1649), mentions sons Henry and Daniel, daughter Judith and brother Thomas Cooper, and appointed his wife executrix. The witnesses were Stephen Paine, Thomas Cooper and Joseph Peck. The will of his widow, Mrs. Judith Smith, was dated 24 Oct., 1650, and named son Henry, daughter Judith, son and daughter Hunt, son John's three children, son Daniel and the three children of her son Hunt. The witnesses were John Pecke and Magdalen Smith. These two wills seem to account for all the five children named by their kinsman Stanton and brought over in the Diligent; for John Smith had married and got three children, and Elizabeth was probably the wife of a (Peter?) Hunt; Henry Smith, jr., also married and had issue; while Daniel became a very important citizen, filling the offices of repesentative 1672, Assistant 1679, and Councillor in the government of New England under Sir Edmund Andros, 1687. He married 20 Oct., 1659, Esther daughter of Francis Chickering. Thomas Cooper, of Rehoboth, witness to the will of Henry Smith and appraiser of the estate of the widow Smith, came over also in the Diligent 1638 from Old Hingham, and was doubtless a relative of Mrs. Stanton's former husband and of the ' aunt Cooper ' spoken of by Mr Stanton as living in Hingham."

[The names Nicholas and Henry do not appear in the nomenclature of the early New England Stantons. There was a Robert Stanton, from Dorchester, a soldier in the King Philip war. Another Robert Stanton is on record at Newport, R. I., as a Quaker, from whom descended Edwin M. Stanton, U. S. Secretary of War, 1863–8. Thomas Stanton, of Connecticut, the famous Indian interpreter, named his youngest sons, Robert and Samuel.
Joseph Moyse's name occurs among the 1639 settlers at Salisbury.
" Henry Smith, living in New England," is the well known Henry of Dedham, where he was Freeman 1639 and representative 1641. An abstract of his will and of his widow's, Judith, may be found in the REGISTER, vol. iv., pp. 318–20. His son, Henry jr., dwelt at Rehoboth, was representative 1662, '67 and '68, and died 1676. His son, Daniel was also of Rehoboth, where he was an influential citizen, representative 1672–8, Assistant 1672, and a member of the Council, 1687, under Gov. Andros. Dr. Nathan Smith, founder of the Medical department of Dartmouth College and professor at Yale and Bowdoin, was a descendant of this family.—GEO. A. GORDON.]

MATTHEW LAWRENCE of Ipswich, Suffolk, clerk, 19 February, 1651, proved 20 May, 1652. To my two daughters Elizabeth and Margaret Lawrence my house in Grantham &c. which my father-in-law Mr. William Wickliffe did purchase of Mrs. Peregrine Buck and did give and bequeath unto my late wife (his daughter) and to her heirs forever. To my said daughters two hundred and fifty pounds apiece, to be paid to my friend Mr. Francis Bacon of Ipswich for their benefit. To wife Judith my houses and lands in Westleton, Suffolk, which I lately purchased of Mr. John Barker of Ipswich, to enjoy for and during her natural life and then to my two daughters Judith and Mary Lawrence and to the heirs of their bodies lawfully begotten, failing which to my brother Charles Lawrence of Overstandon in Bedfordshire and to his heirs forever. Wife Judith to be sole executrix. Lawrence Sandon and his brother and sisters. My brother

Bedford. My two sisters. My cousins Maurice Berry and his wife. Six daughters of my sister Berry. John Whiting my wife's son. Robert How. Thomas Whitinge. To the Library of Ipswich two pounds. My cousin Stansby. Elizabeth Lawrence my brother's daughter. Robert Stansby one of the witnesses. A debt due from cousin Gates. Bowyer, 118.

[In Harleian MS. 6071, British Museum (the well-known Candler MS.), fo. 196 (fo. 383 originally), is a pedigree of Whiting which I give below, with such additions as I am warranted in making by the preceding wills and from the wills of Joseph and Margaret Waite given in my Gleanings for July, 1892 (Reg. Vol. 46, pp. 318–319).—HENRY F. WATERS.]

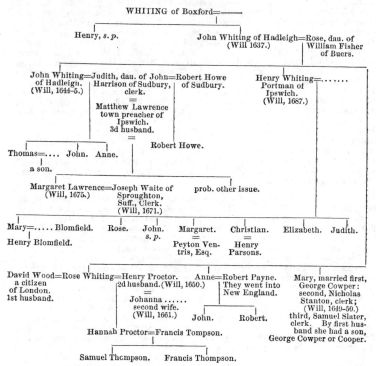

WILLIAM LITTLEBURY of Dedham, Essex, 20 July 1571, proved 26 January 1575. To be buried in the aisle within Dedham Church "whereas" I have used commonly to sit. To wife Bridget, for term of her life, my now dwelling house in Dedham and all other my messuages, lands &c. in Dedham aforesaid and in Stratford, Suffolk. Messuages and lands in Ardeley, Essex. A messuage in Much Bromley, Essex, called Morant's, now in the tenure and occupation of John Stone. To cousin Edward Littlebury (of Gray's Inn) son of Humfrey Littlebury of Hagwordingham in Lincolnshire lately deceased the manor of Netherhall in Bradfeild, Wrabnes, Misley and Maningtree, Essex; but if the said Edward die without issue of his body lawfully begotten I bequeath my manor of Nethershall in Bradfield, and my houses and lands before given to wife Bridget, unto

Thomas Appleton of Little Waldingfield, Suffolk, gentleman, and to the use of the said Thomas, my late wife's brother, and to the heirs of his body lawfully begotten forever. I give my messuage called Ragmershe &c. in Bradfield and Wrabnes, Essex, to Edward Waldegrave of Lawford, Essex, esq. and to Edward Waldgrave his son and heir and to Robert Gurdon of Asson, Suffolk, Esq. and to John Gurdon his son and to William Carnall of Much Bromley, Essex, Esq., to William Butter of Dedham clothier and Peirs Butter his son, to Rafe Starlinge, Robert Starlinge and Richard Starlinge his son, John Browne the elder and John Brown his son, Michael Upcher and Richard Upcher his son, Henry Shereman the elder and Henry Sherman the younger, with Edmond Sherman his brother, to Lewys Sparhawke and Nathaniel Sparhawke his son, to John Upcher, Robert Buskyn, John Wood and Richard Wood his son of Dedham, to them and their heirs for ever as ffeoffees in trust, as by a deed dated . . . . 1571 more at large may appear, to the use of this my last will. Whereas the Township of Dedham hath a fair school house builded, with a house joined to the same meet for a schoolmaster to dwell in, given by one Dame Jone Clarke to that use, and no living pertaining—(then follow certain provisions for the yearly stipend of the schoolmaster—for poor children of Dedham, Ardley, Much Bromley and Bradfield in Essex and Stratford in Suffolk). Provisions for poor in alms houses. Provision for poor young men to be brought up in the science of clothmaking to be assisted therein by loans. Ten pounds to be put into the church hutch of Dedham, called God's Chest, for the sustentation, relief and help of the blind, sick and lame of Dedham or of such strangers as by chance may happen to fall sick in the said town, going by the way and being poor. Reference to will of Robert Legate late of Ipswich, my late predecessor. Elizabeth Habberden my second wife's niece, at marriage or age of three and twenty. John Habberden her brother and my second wife's nephew. Jone Lufkyn sometime my maid now wife to William Lufkyn vicar of Boxsted in Essex. William Lufkyn my godson, son to Thomas Lufkyn of Boxford in Suffolk. His eldest brother Thomas Lufkyn who was brought up with me. Jone Lufkyn wife of Thomas Lufkyn of Boxford. The children of Humfrey Hill and Jone his wife late dwelling in Ardley, now deceased, viz. Thomas, Stephen, Frances, Anne, Margaret and Grace Hills. To Mary Appleton daughter to my brother Thomas Appleton of Little Waldingfield in Suffolk, gentleman, fifty pounds at day of marriage or age of eighteen. To Mrs. Margery Waldegrave the daughter of Edward Waldgrave of Lawford, Essex, fifty pounds at eighteen or day of marriage.		Pyckering, 52.

WILLIAM COLMAN of Thorington Essex, gen[t], 29 July 1586, proved 18 November 1586. The poor of Thorington and every poor widow there. To wife Anne one annuity or yearly rent of ten pounds to be taken out of my farm of Thorington Hall and lands belonging, for the term of twelve years if she so long live. To said wife one hundred pounds, accompting the twenty pounds I lent her in her widowhood parcel thereof. If wife be with child &c. My brother in law Richard Symnell shall have the custody &c. of my daughters Jane, Elizabeth, Martha and Joane untill they shall accomplish the full age of eighteen years. My brother Edward Colman. To daughter Jane her mother's marrying ring. My sister in law Jane Simnell. My cousin John Colman at twenty one. My brother in law Thomas Symnell. My servant Anne Lane. Nurse Lawrence. My servant Henry Cooke. My servant Rand. My sister in law Martha Saffold.

To my sister Taylecote thirteen shillings four pence to make her a ring and to her daughter Jane Lambert a French crown. To my sister Rachell, my wife's sister, ten shillings. Mr. Forbere. To Smithe (?) the "shepe milker" three loads of brush to be delivered at his house before the Feast of St. Michael next ensuing. My brother in law Lawrence Symnell. To John Cole four loads of brush. To Greeneleafe two loads of brush. William Day at age of twenty. The Master and Fellows of St. John's College, Cambridge, praying them to be good to my children, to grant Licence to my executor to let my farm to the most profit for my children. My brother in law Mr. Richard Symnell to be sole executor.   Windsor, 63.

WILLIAM HILLS of London pewterer, 7 October 1603, proved 18 October 1603. Son William. Daughters Anne, Sara and Judith Hills. Humfrey Lambert and his wife Hellen Lambert. Their children, William, Barbara and Sara Lambert. William Marshall and his wife. Robert Marshall and his wife. Thomas Marshall and his wife. Samuel Marshall. My brother James Hicks. John Tailcoate and Robert Tailcoat. Thomas Young. Thomas Skoophulme. John Hatche. Thomas Rowley. Alexander Waters. Katherine Hills. John Dickons. William Fells. Alice White the elder. To my son William Hills my seal ring. The Company of the Pewterers. My wife Parnell to be sole executrix. Anne Baylye the wife of Edward Bayllye.   Bolein, 78.

JOHN TAILECOT of Brainctrie, Essex, pewterer, A. D. 1604, proved 24 January 1604. The poor of Brainctrye. To wife Anne, for life, my messuage wherein I now dwell &c., in Branctry; and, after her decease I give the same to John Tailcot, my son, and the heirs of his body lawfully to be begotten, remainder to my right and next heir. I give to wife Anne my tenement in Braintrie now in the tenure or occupation of one Barnabie Boltell (Boutell?), taylor, to her and to her assigns for twenty years, and then to my daughter Rachel Tailcot &c., remainder to son John Taylcot, and lastly to my right heirs. To my son John Taylcot and to my daughters Anne, Mary, Grace and Sara Tailecot forty pounds apiece, at several ages of one and twenty. To son John (among other things) my book of Martyrs and my book intituled by the name of Mr. Rogers' book. My maid-servant Elizabeth Ingram. My apprentices William Mullinges and Thomas Clarke to serve with my wife after my decease. My wife Anne to be executrix and to enter her own bond in the sum of three hundred pounds to my father in law William Skynner and Robert Tailcot for the performance of my legacies &c.; and, if she marry again, to enter into sufficient bond, before such marriage, in four hundred pounds, with one sufficient surety, to my said father in law William Skynner and Robert Tailcot, my brother, truly to perform all the legacies, &c.

Wit: Marke Mott, Erasmus Sparhawke and James Sperhawke.

Proved (as above) by the oath of Moses Wall, husband of Anne, relict of the said deceased.   Hayes, 6.

[The above will of John Talcott, of Braintree, in Essex, is given in the Talcott Pedigree, Albany, 1876, page 15, and also the will of his father John Talcott, of Colchester, dated in 1606. The latter mentions his grandson John Talcott, son of his son John Talcott, late of Braintree, and also his sons Robert and Thomas.

This last John, a minor in 1606, came to New England in the "*Lion*," with others of Mr. Hooker's company, in 1632, settled in Cambridge, deputy to the

Massachusetts General Court, 1634, 1635, and March 1636; removed to Hartford in 1636, where he was one of the Committee who, for the first time, sat with the Court of Magistrates in 1637, afterwards Deputy and Magistrate, Treasurer of the Colony, 1654-1660, and Commissioner of the United Colonies; died in Hartford, March, 1660. He married Dorothy, daughter of Mark Mott, of Braintree. The chart appended may be found in the Harleian MSS., 1137, p. 148, containing the Herald's Visitation of Essex, 1634, with the Coat of Arms, granted in 1558, "Argent, on a pale sable, three roses of the field. *Crest.*— A demi-griffin, Argent wings, endorsed, collared sable." The family of John, of Braintree, has been added, and a few items from other sources, and this is the chart as it is printed in the Talcott Pedigree. But it will be seen that the wills confirm the chart. In the Talcott Papers, Vol. I, 276, 296, published by the Conn. Historical Society, Gov. Joseph Talcott makes mention of sending a letter to Mr. Thomas Talcott, in Warwick Lane, London, in 1732, very possibly a son or grandson of the Thomas Talcott who died in 1686.

M. K. Talcott.]

TALCOT OF WARWICKSHIRE.

1st wife
Daughter of=John Talcott=Marie, Daughter of
Wells. | died 1606. | Pullen.

2d wife

| Grace m. John Death. | Thomas Talcott= Rector of the Churches of St. Mary and Mile End in Colchester, and Chaplain to the Earl Marshal. | Margaret, dau. of Jeremy Bigg of Suffolk. | Joanna m. Knewstuble. | Marie m. Marshall. | Eme m. Thomas Adler. | John Talcott of Madrid in Spain, alive in 1625. |

Thomas.   George.   Jeremy, died single in Seville, Spain.   Mary.   Elizabeth.

John Talcott=Anne, dau.   Robert Talcott=Joanna, Daughter   Daughter
of Braintree. | of William   of Colchester, | of John Drane   m.
died 1604. | Skinner.   Alderman and | of Branford,   Barnard.
Justice of the | Co. Suffolk.
Peace.

John Talcott,   Rachel.   Anne.   Mary.   Grace.   Sarah.
a minor in 1604.
Hartford, 1636.

| Robert, John. both died without issue. | Thomas Talcott= of Horkesley in Essex, son and heir apparent, 1634; living in 1664. | Thamar, dau. of John Bull of Horkesley Priory. | Robert Talcott= m. in Arts. | Mary, dau. of Parkinson. | Sarah, m. Richard Dersley of Hockley on the Hill, Co. Essex. | Mary, m. John Langley of Colchester, Captain of the Trainband & Alderman. |

Robert Talcott.

Robert Talcott.   Thomas Talcott,   William   John.   Thamar,
Son and Heir, æt.   (twin with   b. after 1634,
31 years in 1654,   Thomas).   wife of Robert
Alderman, died   Wyles of
Feb. 22, 1685-6.   Colchester.
Buried in South aisle
of Holy Trinity Church, Colchester.

RICHARD SYMNELL of Colchester, Essex, gentleman and one of the aldermen of the same town, 9 December 1607, proved 22 July 1608. To be buried near first wife Jane. The poor of the several parishes of the town.

St John's College, Cambridge. The free or common Grammar School in Colchester to enjoy a scholarship there, my kindred to be preferred. To the Bailiffs and Commonalty of the town and their successors two bowls, double gilt, of the value of ten pounds, to be made of the best fashion, with my name to be set upon them, to be used at their feasts and meetings in the moot-hall. To my sister Emme Clarke, widow, my tenement &c. wherein she dwelleth, in the parish of All Saints, and twelve pounds yearly for life. My sister Johane Waford. My wife Elizabeth. I bound unto Eliazer Dunkon of Ipswich, Suffolk, Ph. D. for the payment of four hundred pounds to my said wife within six months after my decease. To my brother Thomas Symnell my messuage &c. wherein I dwell, in the parish of All Saints. My nephew Lawrence Symnell. Johan, Alice and Jane Symnell, the daughters of my late brother Lawrence Symnell, at twenty or days of marriage. The corner house in the parish of St. Nicholas, at the corner of Wyer Street, over against the church of St. Nicholas, now in the tenure of Francis Clayse. My niece Elizabeth Keltridge. My nephew Mr. Sydney. My cousin Mr. William Denman and my niece Thomazine his wife. My niece Mary Loue (or Lone). Her late husband John Lone (or Loue). My cousin Edward Lambard. My niece Jane Lambard, his wife. To my niece (s?) Jane Hindes, Elizabeth Fowler, Martha Cutler, Johan Cutbard and Jane Mathew, to every of them ten pounds, and to every of their husbands twenty shillings (for rings). Elizabeth Furlye the wife of Peter Furly. To my nephew Richard Clarke, my nephew John Clarke and my nephew William Taylecot ten pounds apiece. My brother Thomas Symnell's wife and son Richard. My cousin Robert Legg. My brother Thomas to be executor and my nephews Mr. Sydney Keltrich, Thomas Hyndes and Samuel Cutler to be overseers.

Admon. de bonis non granted 27 November 1620 to Thomas Pennington, a creditor, the executor, Thomas Symnell, having died &c.

Windebanck, 71.

JOHN MARSHALL of Chelmsford, Essex, woollen draper, 25 August 1604, proved 18 February 1608. The poor of Chelmsford and of Moulsham. My son Thomas. My house or Inn in Chelmsford, called the Dolphyn, wherein Edward Bigland my father in law dwelleth. Sons Thomas, John and Richard at twenty two. Daughters Ann, Elizabeth and Margaret Marshall at one and twenty. My mother Margaret Bigland and my sister Margaret Hamper. Every one of my brothers. My sister Joane. To wife Elizabeth my messuage in Much Baddowe, which I lately bought of the heirs of John Sturgeon, for term of her natural life; and after her decease I bequeath the same to my son John. To son Thomas my house in Chelmsford called the Dolphyn, to enter upon it after the decease of my mother Margaret Bigland. To him also my messuage in Cookesmill Green in Roxwell, Essex (and other land there), two crofts (of which) I purchased of Robert Ellyott. To son John my double stall in Chelmsford. To son Richard my messuage in Woodham Mortimer. The residue to wife Elizabeth whom I make executrix. If she refuse then I make my brother Mr. Edward Bigland and my brother in law John Hamper executors.

Dorset, 21.

CHARLES BIGLAND of Chelmsford Essex, 20 July 1624, proved 25 January 1624. Wife Grace to have all the rents &c. out of the copyhold lands in Chelmsford, which I lately purchased of the widow Browne of Moul-

sham, during the minority of my son Charles.   Lands lately purchased of
Mr. Theophilus Wiseman.   My daughters Margaret and Grace Bigland at
eighteen or days of marriage.   My messuage or tenement in Moulsham
which I lately purchased of my brother William Neale.   My daughter
Mary at eighteen or day of marriage.   My son Nathaniel at two and twenty.
Legacies to my children by the last will of Robert Robinson late of Springfield deceased.   To my father Mr. Edward Bigland and my brothers Edward and Ezekias Bigland.   My sisters Jane the wife of John Mortimer
and Margaret the wife of John Hamper.   My sister Mary Seaman, widow,
and John and Elizabeth Seaman, her children.   Rachell Clarke widow,
sometime the wife of my brother John Bigland deceased.   Good friend the
Lady Mildmay.   Mary the daughter of Alice Higham of Chelmsford.
Others.   Thomas Joslin.   Jane the wife of Ambrose Aylet.   Sara the
wife of my cousin John Marshall.   My cousin Robert Reynolds and the
wife of my cousin Samuel Clarke of Colchester.   Mr. Burre of Bromfield
clerk.   Henry and Edward Bigland sons of my brother Edward.   Grace
and William Sturton.   The wife of Samuel Thrasher.   Wife to be sole
executrix.   Clarke, 7.

JOHN MARSHALL of Chelmsford, Essex, woollen draper, 3 October 1625,
proved 5 January 1625.   The poor of Chelmsford and of Moulsham.   To
Mr. Hooker, by whose pains in the preaching of the Gospel I have received
much spiritual comfort, forty shillings, to be paid upon the day of my
funeral, whom also I desire to preach at my funeral.   My daughter Sara
Marshall at twenty.   If Sara my wife shall be with child &c.   My brother
Richard.   My brothers in law Samuel Clarke and Robert Reynolds.   My
father in law Thomas Dutchfield, my mother Elizabeth Dutchfield and my
mother in law Joan Coo.   My uncle William Neale.   My aunt Bigland.
My aunt Neale.   My sisters in law Joan Strutt, widow, Mary Higham,
Hanna Coo and Ede Coo.   My brothers in law Isaac Coo and George Coo
the younger.   Matthew Bridges and John Seely.   My servant Henry Bul-
locke.   My wife Sara to be sole executrix.   If she be with child &c.   My
father in law George Coo and my brother in law John Higham to be overseers.   My aunt Hamper of Bylliraykay, my aunt Joan Mortoner of London and my aunt Taylcote of Colchester.
Wit: Ma: Bridges, Thomas Ditchfield, John Seely.   Hele, 12.

ELIZABETH DUCHFEILD of Colchester, Essex, widow, 12 February 1638,
28 August 1651.   My grandchild Sara Marshall, daughter of my late son
John Marshall deceased.   My son Richard Marshall and his children John,
Mary, Elizabeth and Sara Marshall.   Samuel Clarke my son in law and
——— his wife my daughter.   My grandchildren Samuel Clarke, John Clarke,
Thomas Clarke.   Nathaniel Clarke, Benjamin Clarke and Francis Clarke.
John Marshall of Colchester, genᵗ, one of the aldermen of the said town,
and Mary his wife.   My daughter in law Anne Upcher, widow, and her
daughter Anne, now the wife of John Gale of Colchester, woollen-draper.
The poor, lame and impotent people of Chelmsford, Essex, and of Lexden,
within the liberties of Colchester.   The residue to my said son in law Samuel Clarke and to the children of my said son Richard Marshall, to be
equally parted and divided between the said Samuel and the said children.
The said Samuel Clarke to be sole executor.   Elizabeth Dichfeild (her
mark).   Grey, 158.

JOHN PARKINSON of Colne Engaine, Essex, clerk, 7 May 1628,•proved 2 December 1629.   To son John my "chare" which I use to ride to church, which I bought of Mr. Gurdon.   My son John's wife and his son John.   My daughter Agnes Wood *als* Davy and her daughters Anne Fisher, Elizabeth Fisher, Abigail Fisher and Margaret Fisher.   My grandchildren John Fisher and George Wood.   My daughter Joane Howe, and my grandchildren Matthew, John, Thomas, Anne and Mary Howe, her children, and Matthew Howe, her husband.   Agnes Rookes the daughter of my son Christopher Parkinson, and Richard Parkinson, his son, my grandchild. Henry Parkinson the son of my son Thomas.   My house in the town of Huntington, in the parish of St. Benett's, now called the "Checker." Dorothy, widow of my late son Thomas.

I give and bequeath unto Robert Tailecott, gentleman, twenty shillings. To Mary Taylecott my grandchild, the wife of Robert Tailecott, twenty shillings.   My son in law John Wood *alias* Davy.   My grandchild Daniel Fisher to be sole executor.

Sententia pro valore, in the case of the above will, was promulgated 2 December 1629, Mary Taylcott *als* Lumkin *als* Parkinson, a daughter of the testator, being one of the parties interested.   Ridley, 107.

WILLIAM TALCOTT of Colchester pewterer, 20 August 1638, proved 14 May 1639.   Eldest son Jeremy Talcott.   Wife Anabell.   Messuage &c. in All Saints Colchester.   Messuage &c. in Halsted, Essex, lately purchased of William Austen.   Son John.   Abigail Harris whom I have forbidden him to marry with.   Son William.   Daughter Elizabeth the wife of Thomas Jervis.   Elizabeth Jervys my grandchild.   Wife Annabell to be executrix.
Harvey, 71.

ROBERT TALCOTT of Colchester, Essex, the elder, gen[t], 11 August 1641, proved 1 October 1641.   To my son Robert all my lands, tenements and hereditaments, both freehold and copyhold, in Polden, Essex.   Other bequests to him.   My brother Thomas Talcott, clerk.   My eldest son Thomas to be executor.
Samuell Clerke one of the witnesses.   Evelyn, 128.

Sentence for the confirmation of the above was promulgated 14 May 1642, the parties in the case being Thomas Talcott, son and executor, of the one part, and Robert Talcott, also a son, and George Dearsley and Sarah Dearsley, nephew and niece (*nepotes*) on the brother's side, of the other part.   Cambell, 71.

JOAN COO of Great Maplested (Essex) 31 January 1641, proved 9 August 1647.   My son Isaac.   To my daughter Bridges twenty pounds. To my son Bridges twenty shillings.   Mrs. Hackett one of my grandchildren.   Mr. Hackett.   Matthew Bridges my grandchild.   My daughter Leigh and my son Leygh.   My god daughter Joane Leigh.   Anna Leigh and George Leigh.   My daughter Strutt and her sons John and Thomas Strutt.   My daughter Edith Coo.   My son George Coo.   I give to my sister Taylcott's son Thomas three pounds and to her other four children eight pounds to be equally divided between them.   My son Higham and his wife.   To my cousin Thomas Cooke twenty shillings.   The poor of Much Maplested and Mr. Shepherd.   My lands in Colne Byrt Hall.   Mrs. Blithe.   Mr. Dan Rogers.   Mr. Carr.   Mr. Brewer.   My cousin Lenton of Sudbury.   My cousin Greene of Hedingham widow.   My son Isaack Coo to be sole executor.   Fines, 180.

Moses Wall of Braintree, Essex, clothier, 16 September 1623, with a codicil dated 16 October 1623, proved 23 January 1623. To wife Anne my copyhold messuage in Little Bromley, Essex, for life. To son Moses all my lands, tenements &c. in Hatfield Broadoak in Essex. And I give him my copyhold tenement in Braintree provided that my wife shall have the benefit of all my tenements and lands &c. until Moses my son shall be thought fit to go to Cambridge. My two daughters Lydia and Mary Wall, at twenty one. My friends Mr. Collins of Braintree, Mr. Daniel Rogers of Wethersfield, Mr. Pumfritte of Bocking, Mr. Bucklye of Lyees, Mr. Wharton of Felsted and Mr. Blackerbye.

I give unto John Talkatt, my son in law, and to Rachel Taylcott and to Sara Taylcott, my daughters in law, five pounds apiece. My workmen John Longe, George Billingalle, Thomas Wilkinson, John Clarke and his wife, Robard Kellogg, William Ventris and John Springe. John Princett, Richard Claye and William Porter. John Jacob my apprentice. My brethren Nicholas and John Wall. My other brethren Bartholomew and Daniel Wall. John and Daniel Wall, sons of my brother Nicholas Wall. My customary lands &c. in Fingregoe, Essex. If Moses die and my daughters likewise, without issue &c. I give to John Taylcote my son in law my tenement in Braintree after my wife's decease. My friend Thomas Fitche of Bockinge. My loving sister Mary Peers, widow.

Wit: William Goodwin, George Steares.   Wit: to the Codicil, W. Lyngwood, George Stares, John Springe.   Byrde, 6.

[Those interested will see a very large abstract of the above will in The Goodwins of East Anglia, already referred to.]

Nicholas Wall of Langham, Essex, yeoman, 3 April 1647, proved 5 July 1648. I give unto every one of my "sonne in lawes," Mr. Thomas Gipps, Mr. Thomas Brandeston and Mr. William Allen, twenty shillings apiece to make each of them a gold ring. To my three daughters in law, my son John's wife, my son Daniel's wife and my son Bartholomew's wife (the same legacies). To the poor of Langham forty shillings. To my grandchildren, sons and daughters of my son John, vizt John, Daniel, Nicholas and Jane Wall, ten pounds apiece, the sons at one and twenty and the daughter at same age or day of marriage. To my grandchildren Daniel, John and Elizabeth Wall, children of my son Daniel (a similar bequest). To my daughter Mary wife of Mr. Thomas Gipps fifty pounds (with condition about their children). To daughter Elizabeth wife of William Allen (a similar bequest). A similar bequest to daughter Sarah wife of Mr. Thomas Brandston. To Elizabeth and Sarah Wall, the daughters of my son James, fifty pounds apiece at one and twenty or days of marriage. To my son Samuel Wall and Elizabeth his wife, after my wife's decease, my customary messuages, lands &c. in Kirkby and Thorpe in the "Sookne" in Essex. To wife Elizabeth, for life, fifteen pounds a year to be paid out of the profits of my lease of the demesnes of the Manor of Langham, provided she release to my son John and Jane his wife all her dower in that tenement &c. in Feering and Mark's Tey, Essex, called Dolmsey, in the occupation of —— Porter. My wife to release to my son Daniel and Mary his wife her dower in the messuage, lands &c. called Meere's Pightle, in Stratford, Suffolk, wherein the said Daniel now dwelleth. Other bequests and provisions. Bartholomew Wall my son to be my sole executor, or, in case of his death &c., my son in law William Allen.   Essex, 120.

BARTHOLOMEW WALL of Midleton, Essex, yeoman, 21 November 1651, proved 30 April 1655. To son Richard Wall of Dedham, Essex, clothier, the farm I now use and occupy called Midleton Hall, to hold for one year, he paying the year's rent &c. After that I give said farm to my wife Margaret for the rest of the term of the lease. My two daughters Sarah and Mary Wall. Household stuff I brought from Langford Hall. Messuage, lands, &c. in parish of St. Lawrence in Dengey Hundred, Essex (and other lands near by). To my son Bartholomew Wall an annuity of ten pounds per annum to be issuing out of the messuages, lands &c. given to my son Richard; also twenty pounds of lawful money, to be paid unto him within six months after my decease. My daughter Elizabeth Pennington and such child or children of hers as shall be living at the time of my decease. Every one of my brothers, living at my decease. Son Richard to be sole executor and cousin Daniel Wall of Stratford, Suffolk clothier, and my son's master Mr. Webb of Dedham, clothier, to be overseers.

Aylett, 349.

RICHARD WALL of Stratford, Suffolk, clothier, 12 November 1656, proved 23 February 1656. All my lands, tenements &c. to be sold for payment of debts and funeral charges. My sister Elizabeth, wife of Nathaniel Pennington, and her children. Edmund Cooke the younger of Stratford, clothier. Reference to will of father, Bartholomew Wall, deceased, dated 21 November 1651, and to the bequest therein made to Mary and Sarah Wall, his daughters (evidently still living). Elizabeth Pennington to be executrix.

Ruthen, 80.

MAYGARET SEBORNE of Dedham, widow, 17 August 1622, proved 18 September 1622. My son William Bentley. My son Edward Bentley. My son Bezaliall Bentley. My son John Bentley. My daughter Margaret Bentley. My son Thomas Seborne. My son in law Edmund Seborne. My five children, William, Edward, John, Bezaliall and Margaret Bentley. Son William sole executor.

Proved by William Bentley.

Savile, 83.

MARY BENTLY of Langham, Essex, widow, 27 December 1647, proved 3 January 1648. My son William Bently and his wife. To Mary Clark my grandchild the whole hundred pounds that is in my brother Howe's hand of Dedham, forty pounds whereof is the legacy that was given unto her by her grandfather at his decease, and the other three score pounds I give unto her with this proviso that she be subject to my executor and my loving brothers John Alfounder and Steven How, to be ruled and advised by them both now while she is in her single estate and also when she comes to enter into the married estate, and to contract matrimony with no man without their advice and consent. I give her a rug which I bought of my sister Salmon of Dedham. I give to my grandchildren Mary Clark, daughter to my daughter Clark deceased, and Anna, Elizabeth, Mary and Sara Wall, daughters to my daughter Wall, and John and Mary Rayner, the children of my daughter Rayner deceased, and John and Anthony Boggice, the sons of my daughter Boggice, all that my part in the ship called the Elizabeth of Maningtree. To my loving brothers and sisters, Henry Fenn and his wife, my brother Alderman and his wife, Steven How and his wife, Margaret Collings, my sister Salmon, Bezaliel Bently and John Bently, and to my sons and daughters Bartholomew Wall and his wife, Edward Rayner and his wife and Anthony Boggice and his wife, five shillings apiece, to buy them gloves with. My brother Thomas Sebborn. My brother Edward Bently. The poor of Langham. My brother Henry Fenn of Dedham to be sole executor.

Commission issued (at above date) to Bartholomew Wall and Anna his wife, Anthony Boggis and Susan his wife, daughters natural and lawful of the testatrix, to administer according to the tenor of the will for the reason that Henry Fenn expressly renounced the trust.   Fairfax, 16.

BOOK NOTICES.

[The Editor requests persons sending books for notice to state, for the information of readers, the price of each book, with the amount to be added for postage when sent by mail.]

London and the Kingdom. A History derived mainly from the Archives at Guild-hall in the Custody of the Corporation of the City of London. By Reginald R. Sharpe, D.C.L., Records Clerk in the Office of the Town Clerk of the City of London; Editor of "Calendar of Wills enrolled in the Court of Husting," etc. In three volumes. Printed by order of the Corporation, under the direction of the Library Committee. London: Longmans, Green & Co., and New York: 15 East 16th Street. All rights reserved. 1894 and 1895. Vol. I., pp. xv., 566. Vol. II., pp. xi., 650. Vol. III., pp. ix., 565.

The origin of London is lost in the mist of a remote, pre-historic past, and antiquaries by no means agree as to when and by whom its foundations were first laid. Its commercial fame, says Freeman, "dates from the early days of Roman dominion," and "amidst all changes within and without, it has always preserved more or less of its ancient character as a free city."

The first mayor of London was Henry Fitz-Alwin. He was elected in 1189, more than a century after the Norman conquest. In the year 1889, that being the 700th anniversary of the mayoralty, the corporation of London ordered this compilation to be made from the records in its archives, to show the influence of London upon the affairs of the kingdom. That influence, owing to the number and enterprise of its inhabitants, its geographical position and its wealth, was, as Dr. Sharpe shows, exceedingly great. The espousal by London of the cause of Parliament in the Civil War turned the tide against the king, and in more than one crisis in the history of England the decisive action of the citizens of London has shaped the course of the whole kingdom.

Each of these volumes has for a frontispiece a heliotype copy of an ancient document, the earliest being a fac-simile of the charter granted to the citizens of London by William the Conqueror.

There are two appendices, one comprising letters, early proclamations and other papers from the City's Record of Letters. It is a most interesting collection of documents, the value of which to historical students is much enhanced by their being printed in full.

These volumes and the Index to the Remembrancia* were presented by the corporation of London to the New-England Historic Genealogical Society, and are an important addition to the library of the Society. It is to be hoped that other English cities may be moved to follow the example here set them, and put in print their priceless records, in this way not only making them accessible to the historian, but preserving them from any possible risk of destruction; and it cannot be too strongly impressed upon the minds of the custodians of archives that in no surer way can they earn the gratitude of historical students than by printing all such records in full.

By John T. Hassam, A. M., of Boston.

* Analytical Index to the Series of Records known as the Remembrancia. Preserved among the Archives of the City of London. A. D. 1579–1664 [Arms of the City of London]. Prepared by the authority of the Corporation of London, under the Superintendence of the Library Committee. London: E. J. Francis & Co., Took's Court and Wine Office Court, E. C. 1878. pp. xv., 623.

The Stiles Family in America. Genealogies of the Connecticut Family. By HENRY
REED STILES, A.M., M.D., of New York City. Jersey City: Doan & Pilson,
Printers. 1895. Royal 8vo. pp. xii+782. Price, $5. Address H. R. Stiles,
M.D., P. O. Box 1810, New York City.

Dr. Stiles, the author of the work before us, has no superior as a writer of
local and family history. Over thirty years ago he published his History
of Ancient Windsor, Ct., in a goodly volume of over nine hundred pages.
The writer of this notice reviewed the work in the REGISTER for April,
1860, and thus characterized it: "This work," we said, "comes as near our
ideal of a good town history as any yet published." He has continued to do
good work in this line to the present time. His History of Brooklyn, N. Y.,
in three volumes, octavo, 1867–1870; his History of Kings County, N. Y., in
one thick quarto, 1884, and the second edition of Ancient Windsor, revised
and much enlarged, published in two thick volumes, noticed in the REGISTER for
July, 1893, may be mentioned as special instances of his work in this line. The
Stiles Genealogy, now before us, has been compiled in the same exhaustive manner as the author's previous works. It is full ten years since the first page
of this book was printed. It contains "descendants of John Stiles of Windsor, Conn., and of Mr. Francis Stiles of Windsor and Stratford, Conn.,
1635–1894; also the Connecticut New Jersey Families, 1720–1894; and the Southern (or Bermuda-Georgia) Family, 1635–1894; with Contributions to the Genealogies of some New York and Pennsylvania Families; and an Appendix containing Information concerning the English Families of the Name." The work
makes a handsome volume of nearly 800 pages, with ten portraits. It is well
arranged, well indexed and well printed. Only a limited edition is printed, and
those who want it should lose no time in securing it.

*The Fields of Sowerby near Halifax, England, and of Flushing, New York. With
Some Notices of the Families of Underhill, Bowne, Burling, Hazard and Osgood.* By OSGOOD FIELD, Fellow of the Society of Antiquaries, &c. London: Printed for Private Circulation Only. 1895. Folio pp. vii.+131.

Mr. Field, the author of the sumptuous book before us, has been interested
in the history of his ancestors for over a third of a century. In 1863 he contributed to the April number, then under the editorial charge of the writer of
this notice, a valuable "Sketch of the Family of Field," which was reprinted
in pamphlet form. Since then other valued articles from his pen have appeared
in the REGISTER.

"In the course of a life, which has extended beyond the usual term," says
Mr. Field, in his Preface, "the author has collected much information relating to
the family, and, in almost every case, from original sources. The facts which
he has gotten together are mostly contained in loose memoranda, which have
never been arranged systematically, and which will probably be scattered or destroyed after his death. Every year the task of compiling a family history becomes more difficult, owing to the loss or destruction of ancient documents.
For these reasons, he has thought it well to put the more important materials
he has gathered in such a shape, that those interested in these family matters
who survive, or come after him, may have the benefit of his researches."

A mere glance at the contents of this volume will show the richness of the
material collected by Mr. Field, and his mastery of his subject. He has shown
that the Fields of Flushing, Long Island, from which he himself is descended,
can trace to the Fields of Sowerby. He gives four tabular pedigrees showing his
descent and that of the other Flushing Fields from Richard del Feld of Sowerby,
son of Roger del Feld, born about 1240. Carefully prepared biographical notices of the members of the family are given, and records and documents illustrating its history. Though only one of the early settlers of the name in New
England, Robert Field, a patentee of Flushing, N. Y., has been traced in these
pages, it is possible that the descendants of other emigrants may find something about their ancestors in the records here preserved.

The book is from the Chiswick Press, and is elegantly printed. It is embellished by engravings in the best style of the art, among them views of churches
and other buildings with which the history of the family is connected.

American and English Sambornes. By V. C. SANBORN of LaGrange, Ills. Monitor Press, Concord, N. H. pp. 30.

The present tendency of genealogical research is towards establishing the Trans-Atlantic origin of our early New England families. This is the most difficult of all such investigations, since our ancestors rarely kept up any connection with their old world kindred. Year by year adds to the facilities for this research. Mr. Waters's publications, and those of the different English societies, render more available the mass of documentary evidence in existence. But thoroughly to trace out an ancestral line, one needs to consult the original records; parish registers, wills and inquisitions *post mortem* offer treasures to the genealogist who can avail himself of their contents.

Mr. Sanborn has interested himself in the Sanborn family for several years, and within the last six months has himself searched the records in England for the link which connects the English and American families.

The American family has been well tabulated, in a genealogy printed by Dr. Nathan Sanborn in 1856, and later by genealogies in the town histories of Hampton and Sanbornton, N. H.

The English pedigrees of the family have been full of errors, and Mr. Sanborn has, in the present volume, traced a consecutive and correct pedigree of the English Sambornes from 1350 to 1700. The line starts with one Nicholas Samborne of Wiltshire, born about 1350, whose son married the grand-daughter and heir of Sir Simon Lushill of Lushill, Steward to the Royal Household, and a connection of the Plantagenet Earls of Derby.

A branch of this Samborne family married into the Lisles of Hampshire, and we find in the sixteenth and seventeenth centuries a line of Sambornes, clergymen in Hants. One of these, Rev. James Samborne, was of Puritan tendencies, and an intimate friend of Sir Thomas Jervois of Herriard, a Puritan leader and a member of the "Rump" Parliament. This Rev. James Samborne, who died about 1628, was rector of the next parish to Wherwell, Hants., where Rev. Stephen Bachiler was rector from 1588 to 1605, and near which parish he lived until 1630, when he sold his land and moved to America. Mr. Sanborn deduces from those facts fair evidence of a connection between the English and American families. Some new discoveries have also been made by Mr. Sanborn in Holland and England as to Rev. Mr. Bachiler, whose interesting life has been told in the REGISTER by the late Judge Batchelder. Mr. Sanborn also describes and engraves English arms of Samborne, and proves the coat engraved in the Sanborn Genealogy of 1856 to be without any authority; it never belonged to any Samborne family. The volume is illustrated with charming engravings of churches and houses of the English Sambornes.

Rev. Mr. Bachiler, it will be remembered, was the grandfather of the first Sambornes in this country, and brought them over with him in 1632.

Copies of the genealogy (price $1 in paper, $1.50 in cloth) may be obtained of the author.   ***

The Rival Claimants for North America, 1497–1775. By JUSTIN WINSOR. Worcester, Mass.: Press of Charles Hamilton. 1895. 8vo. pp. 21.

In this pamphlet Mr. Winsor (an acknowledged authority in regard to our colonial history) has given, in a fair and impartial manner, the substance of the dispute between England and her colonies on the one hand and France and her colonies on the other. Let us examine briefly the points at issue between the two nations. France, in the time of Francis I. and later, claimed the new continent on account of Verrazzano's voyage along the Atlantic coast. But she did not permanently occupy any section of territory along the seaboard of what is now the United States; and, more than this, the Cabots in their voyage of discovery under Henry VIII. of England, had sailed along the coast at an earlier date—a seemingly conclusive settlement of the question, as far as priority of discovery (which appears to be the true test as between the two nations) could settle it. France laid special claim to the trans-Alleghany region because her subjects had first sailed down the Mississippi (although they were not the first to discover it) and had made a few settlements along the Illinois and the lower Mississippi, and still more because they had settled at the mouth of the great river. But, on the other hand, many of the British had penetrated into other parts of this region, And the English also claimed jurisdiction over this vast area because of an alleged deed of sale in 1701 from the powerful tribe of the Iroquois, who either owned or had acquired by conquest from the Hurons,

Eries, Shawnees and Illinois in the northern part, and the Cherokees, Chickasaws and Creeks in the southern part of the great valley lying east of the Mississippi, practically the whole territory in dispute. Moreover, France, by the treaty of Utrecht, in 1713, had acknowledged the sovereignty of the English over the Iroquois; so that, whether we consider the opposing claims of the two nations in the light of prior discovery and permanent occupation, or in regard to the cession to the English by the Iroquois (the then dominant aboriginal tribe), there can be no reasonable doubt that the English were right. And they proceeded to make this right good by permanent occupation, by opening up and settling (not by merely establishing a few trading posts and forts, as was the custom of the French) this immense territory they had acquired. The French never had the indispensable qualities of tenacity and steadfastness that go to the making of a colonizing nation—a ruling power. Their alertness, quickness, bravery even, were no match for the patient, persistent, determined spirit of our English forefathers. They may have been equally ready with the English to enter upon any given territory; but, unlike them, they did not come to stay. Excellent skirmishers in the onward march of the great western empire, they lacked the ability to hold and make fruitful even such settlements as they had established. Their purpose was in the main utilitarian. They came not, as did our New England forefathers, to establish and perpetuate a great republic on the basis of civil and religious liberty.

By Rev. Daniel Rollins, of Boston, Mass.

The Edward Jackson Family of Newton, Massachusetts, in the Line of Commodore Charles Hunter Jackson, United States Navy, Middletown, Connecticut. Compiled by FRANK FARNSWORTH STARR, for James J. Goodwin. Hartford, Conn. 1895. 8vo. pp. 85.

This book contains the results of an exhaustive search by Mr. Starr of Middletown, Ct., of one line of the descendants of Edward Jackson of Newton. The author has made a "thorough examination of the Massachusetts State Records, the records of Suffolk and Middlesex counties, of the cities of Cambridge and Newton, and family papers." He has made important corrections in the previously published genealogies of this family. He has made large extracts from the public records, and has prepared a large tabular pedigree of the descendants in this line of Christopher Jackson of Mile End and Bethnal Green, England. The book is handsomely printed and has a good index. Mr. Starr deserves much credit for the thorough manner in which he has done his work, and Mr. Goodwin is entitled to praise for the handsome way in which he has brought it out for his relatives and friends.

The Probate Records of Lincoln County, Maine, 1760 to 1800. Compiled and edited by WILLIAM D. PATTERSON, for the Maine Genealogical Society, Wiscasset, Me. Portland. 1895.

Within the last few years there has been a very commendable interest exhibited in the publication of early town records. Formerly the student who desired to ascertain authentic information respecting town history was obliged to spend a great deal of time in hunting up old records, many of which were inaccessible; but since the publication of so many town records, he is enabled to ascertain facts with a minimum expenditure of time. In England this work has been carried on by experts for a much longer period than it has been in this country, but it is encouraging to see with what facility we have adopted the example set us in this respect by the mother country. When the work of publishing ancient town records is completed, the re-writing of town histories will be necessary. The Genealogical Society is showing its great usefulness in publishing this book, and the compiler is to be congratulated for his share in it. Any one who desires to know something about Lincoln County will find this volume a mine of valuable and accurate information. Besides the items recorded in the records, there is a very interesting introduction, full of historical facts, written by that veteran Maine historiographer, Rufus K. Sewall, Esq., of Wiscasset, which in itself is well worth the cost of the book. What books of this nature require to make them accessible is a careful index of names, and from a cursory perusal of that at the end of this volume, the writer has no doubt of its accuracy. As a piece of book making the volume is a credit to the Society.

By Hon. James P. Baxter, A.M., of Portland, Me.

A Century of the Senate of the United States. Prepared by WILLIAM S. APPLE-
TON.

This list of the members of the United States senate for one hundred years
was "communicated to the Massachusetts Historical Society at its meeting 14
March, 1895," and is reprinted from the Proceedings of that society. "This
roll is believed," the author says, "to contain the names of all the men who sat
in the Senate of the United States during its first century, with the few who
never sat there, though having a perfect right to do." The list will be found
very useful. It must have cost the compiler much labor.

*Roll of Members of the Military Company of the Massachusetts now called the An-
cient and Honorable Artillery Company of Massachusetts, with a Roster of the
Officers and Preachers. 1638—1894.* Prepared by vote of the Company.
Boston, Massachusetts, U. S. A. 1895. 8vo. pp. xi.+148.

The title shows the contents of this book. A preface gives a brief history of
the company. The illustrations are a fac simile of the charter, a view of
Faneuil Hall, the head-quarters of the Ancients and of the Gorget, Espanton
and Halberd. It has an Index of Members.

*North Haven Annals. A History of the Town from the Settlement, 1680, to its
First Centennial, 1886.* By SHELDON B. THORPE. New Haven, Conn.: Press
of Price, Lee & Adkins Co. 1892. 8vo. pp. 422.

The work before us, the Annals of North Haven in Connecticut, is a history
of an important town of that state. The author has performed his work in a
manner that entitles him to much credit. The work is well printed and is embellished with a number of fine engravings, mostly portraits. President Stiles
of Yale College was a native of North Haven, and his portrait is here given.
Since the issue of this book the author has collected the early North Haven
families and their descendants in a manuscript volume, containing several thousand names, which we hope he will give to the public in print. Meantime he
will answer inquiries about those families.

History of the Town of Manchester, Essex County, Massachusetts, 1645–1895.
By Rev. D. F. LAMSON. Published by the Town. 1895. 8vo. pp. xii.+260.

On the 18th of July last the town of Manchester, Massachusetts, commemorated its quarter millenary. This was a noteworthy occasion. The present
volume was prepared in advance of that event and, we think, was ready for
subscribers on the day of the celebration. It is an excellent work and does
much credit to the author, Rev. Mr. Lamson, who has shown great care and
judgment in its preparation. An account of the celebration is printed in the
Appendix. The book makes an elegant volume, with engravings of historic
buildings and scenes, portraits, maps, &c.

*History of New London, Connecticut. From the First Survey of the Coast in
1612 to 1860.* By FRANCES MANWARING CAULKINS. With a Memoir of
the Author. New London: Published by H. D. Utley. 1895. 8vo. pp.
xviii.+696. Price $5 in cloth, or $5.50 in buckram.

Miss Caulkins's History of New London has long been a standard work, and
needs no praise from our pen. The work was first published in 1852, and only
a part of the edition was bound at that time. In 1860 the remaining sheets
were bound with additional matter bringing the history down to that date. The
edition was soon exhausted, and for thirty years only second-hand copies could
occasionally be procured. As high a price as $25, it is said, has been refused
for a copy. This edition contains a portrait and a memoir of the author, apparently that written by her half-brother, Hon. Henry P. Haven, and printed in the
REGISTER, vol. 23, pp. 396–407. The book is well printed and well indexed.

*The Battle of Brandywine. An Address delivered in Birmingham Meeting House
before the Pennsylvania Society of the Sons of the Revolution, June 18, 1895.*
By FREDERICK D. STONE. Philadelphia. 1895. 8vo. pp. 17.

Mr. Stone, the librarian of the Historical Society of Pennsylvania, has, in his
address here printed, done a good service to the cause of American history.
With great care he has gathered up the details of one of the most important
battles in the Revolution, and preserved the memory of those who participated
in the battle.

The Oxford Academy Centennial. A Record of the Proceedings and Exercises had in honor of the One Hundredth Anniversary of that Institution, with Notes by the Editor. Held at Oxford, Chenango County, N. Y., June 28, 29, 1894. Edited by Hon. O. H. CURTIS, Oxford, N. Y. Published by the General Committee. 1895. 8vo. pp. 145.

The addresses delivered upon this occasion by Hon. O. H. Curtis, Hon. A. C. Coxe, George Bundy Esq., Rev. W. B. Thorpe, Dr. L. Coville, Mr. De Shon, and Prof. E. R. Payson, all evince careful thought and preparation, but it seems to me that those delivered by Hon. A. C. Coxe and Hon. O. H. Curtis, and the poem read by Mr. E. C. Delevan (which contains some lines of rare beauty) call for special mention. Many and important are the far-reaching results that follow such a commemoration as this. Probably the greatest good that can be derived from such occasions is the stimulus, the impetus, which they give to the cause of education. Surely after careful and thorough moral and religious teaching, no other subject can be so important as that of careful mental training. Especially is this true in a great republic like ours, whose security and perpetuity depend in large measure upon properly guided public sentiment, for each individual is in a degree responsible for the welfare of the whole body politic. And as the state is made up of the aggregate of the individuals living under its protecting care, it behooves us as a people (if we would see our nation continue to be a power for good among the nations of the earth, a power for peace and righteousness) to see to it that education is widely diffused throughout our borders. Especially should the New England spirit, the counterpart or outgrowth of the sturdy English spirit (for no two nations in the world are so essentially one as our country and the mother country), be inculcated by means of the steady and persistent teaching of American history and institutions. It is not necessary that the State should give each citizen a college education; but it is highly necessary that it should see to it that every child born in this country (or coming to it from foreign lands) should be given the elements of a general education, supplemented by some knowledge of their privileges (and duties as well) as citizens of our republic, and as deriving therefrom liberty and protection to life and property. It is probably true that reliance may be placed to-day upon the great body of our people, but when we reflect that the average immigration to our shores is now over half a million of people annually (many of whom have no knowledge of our institutions) we cannot fail to see the necessity of persistent and systematic dissemination, through our schools and press, of a knowledge of what our country stands for, namely, civil and religious liberty under the law of the land. Only thus may we preserve and hand down to coming generations these rich blessings bequeathed to us by our forefathers.

By Rev. Daniel Rollins, of Boston, Mass.

Report of the State Librarian to the New Hampshire Legislature for the Period beginning October 1, 1894. Concord: Edward N. Pearson, Public Printer. 1894. 8vo. pp. 331.

The book before us is "The First Biennial Report, and the Twenty-fourth Report of the Librarian subsequent to the Act approved July 3, 1866." Mr. Kimball has done a good work in preparing this volume. Besides the biennial report proper, he has added an appendix of valuable matter, namely, 1, Official Publications of New Hampshire, 1892–94; 2, New Hampshire Regimental Histories; 3, Libraries of New Hampshire, 1894; 4, Library Laws of New Hampshire; 5, Biography of Dartmouth College; 6, Bibliography of Manchester, N. H.

A Grandfather's Legacy, containing a Sketch of His Life and Obituary Notices of Some Members of His Family; together with Letters from His Friends. Washington: Henry Polkinham, Printer. 1879. 8vo. pp. 251+ix.

The Grandfather whose story is here given is the late William Wilson Corcoran, the prominent Washington banker. He was the son of Thomas Corcoran, who was born in Limerick, Ireland, in 1754, and came to Baltimore in 1783. His son, whose life and correspondence are here given, was born Dec. 27, 1798. The history of the philanthropic banker is well, though briefly, told. Most of the letters are from men who were eminent in their day, and on subjects of interest that interest our people. The book is handsomely printed and bound, and is a worthy memorial of a worthy man.

Daughters of the Revolution and Their Times. 1769—1776. A Historical Romance. By CHARLES CARLETON COFFIN. Boston and New York: Houghton, Mifflin and Company. 1895. 12mo. pp. xi.+387. Price, $1.50.

Mr. Coffin has won a high reputation as a writer of history, biography and fiction. He has here given us a story of the Revolution; and yet this "romance" has more of fact than fiction in it. "The narrative of events," says the author in his Introduction, "takes the form of a story—a slight thread of romance being employed, rather than didactic narrative, to more vividly picture the scenery and the parts performed by actors in the great historic drama. It will not be difficult for the reader to discern between the facts of history and the imaginative parts of the story." The book is illustrated by portraits and views of real personages and buildings. A map of Boston which is here given will help the reader to follow the narrative. We commend the book especially to those interested in revolutionary history.

Publications of the Genealogical Society of Pennsylvania. January 1895. Vol. I., No. 1. Miscellany No. 1. Philadelphia: Printed for the Society. 8vo. pp. 40.

The Genealogical Society of Pennsylvania, recently organized at Philadelphia, has issued the first number of its Publications. It contains five articles, namely, The Sailing of the Ship Submission, 1682; Inscriptions on Ancient Tombstones; John Hart, Governor of Maryland; Data concerning the Taking of Wolves in 1676; and Notices of Justices of New Castle. The matter preserved is valuable, and the work does credit to those who have charge of the publication.

Corporations in the Days of the Colony. By ANDREW McFARLAND DAVIS. Cambridge: John Wilson & Son, University Press. 1894. 8vo. pp. 34.

The Law of Adultery and Ignominious Punishments. By ANDREW McFARLAND DAVIS. Worcester, Mass., U. S. A.: Press of Charles Hamilton. 1895. 8vo. pp. 32.

Provincial Banks: Land and Silver. By ANDREW McFARLAND DAVIS. Cambridge: John Wilson & Son, University Press. 1895. 8vo. pp. 40.

The three pamphlets, whose titles are here given, are recent contributions to our Colonial and Provincial history which Mr. Davis of Cambridge has given us. Like all his monographs, they are exhaustive in their treatment of the subjects. The first and last are reprints from the Publications of the Colonial Society, and the other is reprinted from the Proceedings of the American Antiquarian Society.

The Massachusetts settlers met with no little trouble in carrying on their government as a colony. One difficulty was in regard to corporations. They had no power under their charter to create corporations, while it was desirable that the several plantations should be corporations. In their dilemma they seem to have adopted this plan. They assigned to parties a particular territory, and allowed them to organize a town government for themselves. But the early town records are so defective that it would be rash to speak positively. When this was done the Court gave the plantation a name. I think no town in the Massachusetts Colony was incorporated under the first charter. Mr. Davis, in his paper on Massachusetts Corporations, read before the Colonial Society of Massachusetts, has taken a broad survey of the subject, and given us what he finds about them. Those who wish to know about them should study Mr. Davis's tract. The only corporation the Massachusetts Colony seems to have attempted to create was Harvard College. This was in 1650, when the government of the mother country was in the hands of the friends of New England.

Mr. Davis's next paper is on "The Law of Adultery and Ignominious Punishments, with Especial Reference to the Penalty of wearing a letter affixed to the Clothing." The author treats this in his usual thorough manner.

The last paper on Provincial Banks contains a summary of what can be learned on this important subject. Much has been written about "The Land Bank," "The Silver Scheme," and other financial expedients of the eighteenth century, but no full and exhaustive history has appeared before this.

Mr. Davis deserves the gratitude of historical students for these three tracts.

Tower Genealogy. An Account of the Descendants of John Tower of Hingham, Mass. Compiled under the direction of CHARLEMAGNE TOWER, late of Philadelphia, deceased. Cambridge: John Wilson & Son, University Press. 1891. 8vo. pp. xii.+887.

Whitney. The Descendants of John Whitney, who came from London, England, to Watertown, Massachusetts, in 1635. By FREDERICK CLIFTON PIERCE. Published by the Author. Press of W. B. Conkey Company, Chicago, Ill. 1895. Royal 8vo. pp. 692. Price, $10. Address R. C. Pierce, 161 Dearborn St., Chicago, Ill.

Genealogy of the Tucker Family. From Various Authentic Sources. By EPHRAIM TUCKER. Worcester, Mass., U. S. A. 1895. 8vo. pp. 414. Price, $5 bound in cloth, or $7.50 in turkey morocco. Address E. Tucker, 58 Laurel St., Worcester, Mass.

Sargent Genealogy. Hugh Sargent of Courteen Hall, Northamptonshire, and his Descendants in England. By JOHN S. SARGENT of Chicago, Ill. *William Sargent of Malden, New England, and his Descendants in America.* By AARON SARGENT of Somerville, Mass. Somerville, Mass.: Compiled and Published by Aaron Sargent. 1895. 8vo. pp. 218.

Our Family Ancestors. By THOMAS MAXWELL POTTS, Canonsburg, Pa.: Published by the Author. 1895. 8vo. pp. xiv.+428. Price, $3.50; postpaid, $3.70.

A Record of the Searight Family (also written Seawright) established in America by William Seawright. By JAMES A. SEARIGHT. Uniontown, Pa. 1893. 8vo. pp. 228.

Genealogy of the Crane Family. Vol. I. Descendants of Henry Crane of Wethersfield and Guilford, Conn., with Sketch of the Family in England. Worcester, Mass.: Press of Charles Hamilton. 1895. 8vo. pp. 201.

History and Genealogy of the Watson Family, descendants of Matthew Watson, who came to America in 1718. Compiled by Mrs. JULIA DRAPER (WATSON) BEMIS and ALONZO AMASA BEMIS, D.D.S. Spencer, Mass. 1894. 8vo. pp. 163.

Seth Reed, Lieut.-Col. Continental Army; Pioneer at Geneva, N. Y., 1781, and Erie, Penn., June 1795. His Ancestors and Descendants. By his Great Grand-Daughter, MARY HUNTER BUFORD. Boston: 1895. Sq. 8vo. pp. 166.

The Wyman Families of Great and Little Hormead, Herts County, Eng. By HORACE WYMAN. Worcester, Mass. 1893. Oblong 8vo. pp. 20.

A Chart of the Ancestors and Descendants of Rev. Robert Rose, who came to Virginia in 1725, and died 1751. Compiled by W. G. STANARD for Miss Annie Fitzhugh Rose Walker, Richmond, [Va.]: Wm. Ellis Jones, Printer. 1895.

Hersey Genealogy. Compiled by FRANCIS C. HERSEY, South Boston, Mass. 1895.

Family Record of John and Sally Hamlen of Plainfield, Mass. Arranged by FREEMAN (son of John and Sally) HAMLEN. Presented by Lavantia Ford Shaw, grand-daughter of John and Sally Hamlen, June, 1881. Boston: Frank Wood, Printer. 1881. Sq. 16mo. pp. 12.

Blanding of Upton on Severn, Worcester, England. Genealogical Chart. Compiled by H. W. ROBERTS, Boston, Mass., [and] WM. J. C. KENYON, St. Paul, Minn. 1895. 8vo. folded broadside, 16 in. by 13½ in.

We continue in this number our quarterly notices of works lately received relating to family history.

The Tower Genealogy was prepared under the direction of the late Charlemagne Tower, Esq., a wealthy and enterprising citizen of Philadelphia. His attention was called to his ancestry when he was a student at Harvard College, in 1830. He was a "man of cultivated tastes, a lover of books, particularly of those relating to the history of America. He was one of the first to recognize the importance of the comparative study of American colonial law." His unrivalled collection on this subject, begun when he was about forty years old, continued till his death, to receive rare and valuable accessions. The Tower genealogy is compiled in a very satisfactory manner. It is printed in the best style of the University press, and is well indexed.

The Whitney genealogy, by Col. F. C. Pierce, is a handsome volume of nearly seven hundred pages, and contains the records of nearly ten thousand persons. It is well arranged and is illustrated by numerous portraits. Several genealogies of the descendants of John Whitney of Watertown, Mass., have appeared before, but no attempt has been previously made to prepare a complete record of his descendants. The author has had much experience in compiling local and family histories. He is the author of the Histories of Grafton and Barre, Mass., besides the Peirce and other Genealogies. "It is a very remarkable history," says a writer, "not only in point of dimension, but in the prominent part many of the members have played in the unfolding drama of our national life."

The book on the Tucker family is another valuable addition to genealogical literature. It is an octavo of over four hundred pages, printed in clear type on fine white paper. The book deals principally with the descendants of Robert Tucker, who settled at Weymouth, Mass., as early as 1635, and removed in 1662 to Milton, where he was the first town clerk. It is well calculated to interest the various members of a widely scattered family in their common ancestry. It is well arranged on the Connecticut plan, and is filled with important and valuable matter. It is well indexed, and is illustrated with numerous portraits.

The Sargent Genealogy is published by the author of the small volume on that family, which appeared in 1858, thirty-seven years ago. Since then much new matter has been discovered. Mr. John S. Sargent of Chicago has discovered the English ancestry of William Sargent of Malden, to whose posterity both books are devoted, and Mr. Aaron Sargent has made large additions to his record of the descendants of William of Malden. The first edition of this book had become extremely rare before the new edition was undertaken, and large prices were paid for it. Only a small edition is now printed, and those who want copies should apply for them early.

The book entitled "Our Ancestors" consists of sketches of the families from which the children of the author, Hon. Thomas Maxwell Potts, are descended. The book is divided into two parts. Part I. gives the Paternal Ancestors, and Part II. the Maternal Ancestors. On page 381 is an ancestral chart, on which the work is based. The families are treated of in this order, commencing at the top of the chart and following down to the bottom. We can readily believe the author when he sayshe has devoted to the work much original research. Many prominent Pennsylvania and other families are to be found in these pages. The book has a good index.

The Record of the Searight Family is an elegant volume, printed in the highest style of the art, with numerous illustrations. The stirps of this family was William Seawright, "who came from near Londonderry in the north of Ireland to Lancaster county, Pennsylvania, about the year 1740." The book contains an account of his descendants as far as could be ascertained. It preserved much interesting family history.

The Crane Genealogy is by Mr. Crane of Worcester, Mass., who prepared and published several years ago an edition of the Rawson Genealogy. He has evidently devoted much research to the present work, which gives the descendants of Henry Crane of Wethersfield and Guilford, Conn. It is compiled with care, is well printed, and is embellished with numerous portraits. It has a good index.

The book on the Watson Family gives the descendants of Matthew Watson, who came to Boston, Mass., from Coleraine in Ireland, in the year 1718, "with his family consisting of his wife Mary Orr, to whom he was married in the year 1695, and their children." The first season he removed to Framingham. He seems later to have settled at Leicester. He was killed in 1720 by a tree falling on him. The book is well compiled. The record is well carried out and the book is well indexed.

Seth Reed: His Ancestors and Descendants, is the next book on our list. "This genealogy and the little sketch of the life of Seth Reed," the authors say, "were commenced several years ago as the result of interest roused by gathering data necessary for admission to the 'Society of Sons of the Revolution.'" The authors have produced a well written book full of interesting details.

The Wyman book contains the result of researches made in England by the author in 1889, stimulated by the discovery by Mr. Waters of the will of Francis Wyman of West Mill, Herts, the father of John and Francis Wyman, the Woburn immigrants, which will was printed in the REGISTER for April, 1889. The book is illustrated with views of buildings connected with the history of the Wyman family in England, and two maps, one of the locations of the Wymans in England, and the other of the location of the family in Woburn and Burlington, Mass. Besides the author of this book—Mr. Horace Wyman of Worcester—another descendant of the Woburn Wymans, Mr. Morrill Wyman, Jr., of Cambridge, has visited Hertfordshire and given the result of his researches in this number of the REGISTER (pp. 45-6).

The Chart of the Descendants of Rev. Robert Rose is a tabular pedigree, 27 by 32 inches, folded and enclosed in a cover. It shows much research.

The Hersey Genealogy is a broadside, 27 by 32 inches, folded into a cover. It gives a genealogical tree of the descendants of William Hersey, 1635, of Hingham, Mass. The lines seem to be fully carried out.

The Hamlen Family Record gives the record of the descendants of John and Sally (Town) Hamlen with praiseworthy fulness.

The Genealogical Chart of the Blandings gives in a tabular pedigree some of the descendants of William Blanding, who settled in Massachusetts in 1640, and also records of the Carpenter and Kenyon families.

RECENT PUBLICATIONS,

PRESENTED TO THE NEW-ENGLAND HISTORIC GENEALOGICAL SOCIETY FROM AUGUST 1, 1895, TO DECEMBER 1, 1895.

Prepared by the Assistant Librarian.

I. *Publications written or edited by Members of the Society.*

The Battle of Brandywine. An Address delivered in Birmingham Meeting-house before the Pennsylvania Society of Sons of the Revolution, June 18, 1895. By Frederick D. Stone. Philadelphia. 1895. 8vo. pp. 17.

Biographical Sketch of Hon. Thomas H. Dudley. By William John Potts. Camden, N. J. A paper read before the American Philosophical Society, April 19, 1895. Reprinted from the Proc. Amer. Philos. Soc., vol. xxxiv., June 4, 1895. Philadelphia. 1895. 8vo. pp. 36.

Charles Carroll, of Carrollton. Last Surviving Signer of the Declaration of Indepedence. [By] Rev. Horace Edwin Hayden, M.A. [Reprinted from the Library News-Letter.] Wilkes-Barré. 1894. 8vo. pp. 16.

Memoir of Gen. Edward Augustus Wild. H. U., 1844. By Bradford Kingman. Boston. Privately printed. 1895. 8vo. pp. 11. [Reprint, N.-E. H. G. REGISTER, 1895].

Inscribed Powder-Horns. By Hon. Samuel A. Green, M.D., of Boston. 8vo. pp. 3. [Reprint, N.-E. H. G. REGISTER, 1896].

A Sermon on the History and the Principles of St. Stephen's Parish, Portland, Maine. By Rev. Asa Dalton, D.D., Rector. Preached July 4, 1886, on the occasion of the Centennial Celebration of the City. Printed by request of the Vestry. Portland. 1886. 8vo. pp. 20.

Epochs of Church History. By Rev. A. Dalton, D.D., Rector of St. Stephen's Church, Portland, Me. Portland. 1894. 12mo. pp. 193.

The Geology of Vermont as Developed along the Western Border in the oldest Fossiliferous Rocks of the Continent. By A. N. Adams. Fair Haven, Vt. 8vo. pp. 12.

Daughters of the Revolution and Their Times. 1769-1776. A Historical Romance. By Charles Carleton Coffin. Boston. 1895. 12mo. pp. 387.

The Alleged "Toryism" of the Clergy of the United States at the Breaking out of the War of the Revolution. An Historical Examination by William Stevens Perry, Bishop of Iowa and Historiographer of the American Church. 16mo. pp. 26.

A Century of the Senate of the United States. Prepared by William S. Appleton, Communicated to the Massachusetts Historical Society at its meeting, 14 March, 1895. and reprinted from its Proceedings.

Stark's History and Guide to Barbadoes and the Caribbee Islands * * * Illustrated with Maps, Engravings and Photo-Prints. By James H. Stark. Boston. 1893. 12mo. pp. 221.

Supplement to the Revised Statutes of the United States, Vol. II., Nos. I.-V. Legislation of the Fifty-Second and Fifty-Third Congresses. 1892-1895. Prepared and edited by William A. Richardson, Chief Justice of the Court of Claims. Assistants: George A. King and William B. King of the Supreme Court Bar. By Authority of Congress. Washington. 1895. 4to. 437.+lxxx.

The Vermont Chronicle and the Earlier Religious Periodicals Published in Vermont. A Paper read at the Centennial of the General Convention of Congregational Ministers and Churches in Vermont, at Bennington, June 12, 1895. By Ezra H. Byington, D.D. Newton, Mass. Nar. 16mo. pp. 30.

II. *Other Publications.*

Memorial of Samuel Whitney Hale. Keene, N. H. Born April 2, 1822. Died October 16, 1891. By W. DeLoss Love, Jr. Privately printed. Hartford. 1895. 8vo. pp. 27.

Exercises commemorating the life and character of Hon. Eben Francis Stone. Held at the meeting house of the First Religious Society, Newburyport, Mass., April 21, 1895. Boston. 1895. 8vo. pp. 26.

The Life and Times of Hon. Humphrey Marshall. . . . . By A. C. Quisenberry. Winchester, Ky. 1892. 8vo. pp. 142.

Proceedings at the Banquet in honor of Torrey E. Wales and Eleazer Ray Hard at the close of fifty years at the bar. Tendered by their professional friends at the Van Ness House, Burlington, Vt., March 29, 1895. 8vo. pp. 32.

Biographical Sketch of Dr. Bennett F. Davenport. [Reprint from Physicians and Surgeons of America.] 1895. 8vo. pp. 4.

Fulton Paul. From the Biographical Review of Columbia County. New York. 1894. Boston. 1894. 4to. pp. 37.

Memorial Address delivered May 10, 1890, at Wilmington, N. C. By Hon. Charles M. Stedman. A Sketch of the Life and Character of General William MacRae. With an Account of the Battle of Ream's Station. Wilmington, N. C. 8vo. pp. 27.

Louisa Parsons Hopkins, Memorial Service in the Bellville Congregational Church, Newburyport, Mass., May 29, 1895. Address, Rev. Albert W. Hitchcock. Poem, Harriet Prescott Spofford. 1895. 12mo. pp. 15.

Historical Sketch of John Phillips. A Baccalaureate Discourse. By Rev. George E. Street, of Exeter. Before the Graduating Class of Phillips Academy, Andover, June 16, 1895. . . . . Exeter. 1895. 8vo. pp. 19.

The Seventy-Fifth Anniversary of the Consecration of Saint Paul's Church, Boston, Sunday, May 26, 1895. A Sermon by Rt. Rev. William Lawrence, D.D., Bishop of Massachusetts. Boston. Published by the Parish. 1895. 16mo. pp. 40.

The Boston Picture Book. Over one hundred Historic and Characteristic Views in and around Boston. Irving P. Fox, 8 Oliver street. Boston. 1895.

Dedication of the Ingalls Memorial Library at Rindge, N. H., Thursday, June 13, 1895. Concord, N. H. 1895. 8vo. pp. 51.

Wakefield Souvenir of the Celebration of the 250th Anniversary of Ancient Reading, May 28 and 29, 1894. Published by Chester W. and Will Everett Eaton, Wakefield. 1894. 4to.

A Brief History of the Town of Unity. Written and read by Edmund Murch, at a meeting of Harvest Moon Grange, Thorndike, 1892. Belfast. 1895. 16mo. pp. 16.

History of the Town of Lynnfield, Mass, 1635-1895. By Thomas B. Wellman. Boston. 1895. 12mo. pp. 268.

The Early Records of the Town of Providence. Vol. IX. Being part of the Book of Records of Town Meetings, No. 3, 1677 to 1750, and other papers. Printed under authority of the City Council of Providence, by Horatio Rogers, George Moulton Carpenter and Edward Field, *Record Commissioners.* Providence. 1895. Sm. 4to. pp. 234.

History of New London, Connecticut. From the first survey of the coast, in 1612, to 1860. By Frances Manwaring Caulkins. With memoirs of the author. New London. Published by H. D. Utley. 1895. 8vo. pp. xviii.+696.

(Document 147, 1895.) Message of the Mayor, transmitting a communication from the City Registrar, giving authority for adding the names of Lieutenant Benjamin West and Captain William Meacham to the List of Patriots who were killed at the battle of Bunker Hill. Boston. 1895. 8vo. pp. 12.

Acts and Laws relating to the Town of Brookline, together with the Town By-Laws, Building Laws, Regulations of Public Library, The Water Ordinances, and Police Regulations. Brookline. 1894. 8vo. pp. 198+vii.

Field Columbian Museum. Publication 2. Vol. I. No. 2. The Authentic Letters of Columbus. By William Eleroy Curtis, Honorary Curator, Department of Columbus Memorial. Chicago. 1895. 8vo. pp. 95-200.

Brookline Historical Publication Society. Publication No. 2, The Sharpe Papers in the Brookline Public Library. No. 3, Brookline in the Revolution. No. 4, Papers of the White Family of Brookline, 1650-1807.

Old Representatives' Hall. An address delivered before the Massachusetts House of Representatives, January 2, 1895, by Alfred Seelye Roe of Worcester. Boston. 1895. 8vo. pp. 22.

A History of the Emblem of the Codfish in the Hall of the House of Representatives. Compiled by a Committee of the House. Boston. 1895. 8vo. pp. 62.

First Annual Report of the Board of Registration in Medicine, January, 1895 Boston. 1895. 8vo. pp. 82.

Dedication of the State Library Building at Concord, N. H., Tuesday, Jan. 8, 1895. Published by Authority of the State. Concord. 1895. 8vo. pp. 180.

The Probate Records of Lincoln County, Maine. 1760 to 1800. Compiled and edited for the Maine Geneological Society, by William D. Patterson, Wiscasset, Me. Portland. 1895. 8vo. pp. 12+xxi.+368+53.

Revised Register of the Soldiers and Sailors of New Hampshire in the War of the Rebellion. 1861-1866. Prepared and published by Authority of the Legislature. Concord. 1895. Large 4to. pp. xii.+1347.

The War of the Rebellion. A compilation of the Official Records of the Union and Confederate Armies. Series I. Volume XLVI.—in three parts. Washington. 1895. 8vo. Part II. pp. 1493. Part III. pp. 1549.

New Brunswick. The Books and Writers of the Province. By W. G. MacFarlane, A.B. St. John, N. B. 1895. 8vo. pp. 98.

Proceedings and Transactions of the Royal Society of Canada, for the Year 1894. Volume XII. General Index i.—xii. Ottawa. 1895. 4to. Various pagings.

Leading Events of the American Revolution, Arranged by William H. Brearley. New York. [1895.] 32mo. pp. 32.

Requirements for Admission to the Society of Colonial Dames in the State of Rhode Island and Providence Plantations. *Instituted Anno Domini* 1892. Sq. 24mo. pp. 42.

Constitution and By-Laws. Society of Mayflower Descendants. New York. 1894. Sq. 32mo. pp. 20.

By-Laws of Elizabeth Wadsworth Chapter Daughters of the American Revolution. Chartered 1894. Portland. 1895. 16mo. pp. 23.

Ruth Wyllys Chapter Daughters of the American Revolution. Hartford. 1894. 8 vo. pp. 26.

Year Book of the Society of Sons of the Revolution.

Roll of Members of the Military Company of the Massachusetts now called The Ancient and Honorable Artillery Company of Massachusetts. With a Roster of the Commissioned Officers and Preachers, 1638-1894. Boston. 1895. 8vo. pp. 148.

Proceedings of the Worcester Society of Antiquity for the year 1894. Worcester. 1895. 8vo. pp. 86.

Proceedings of the Wyoming Commemorative Association on the Occasion of the 116th Anniversary of the Battle and Massacre of Wyoming, July 5, 1894. Wilkes-Barre. 1895. 8vo. pp. 48.

DEATHS.

DAVID GARDINER THOMPSON, Esq., a son of the late David Thompson and Sarah Diodate Gardiner, his wife, died at his residence in New York city from a stroke of apoplexy. Mr. Thompson was born in New York May 29, 1837, and died October 16, 1895. He was descended, on the paternal side, from the Thompsons of Sagtikos Manor, Long Island, and on the maternal side from the Gardiners of the Manor of Gardiner's Island. Mr. Thompson graduated, B.A., from Columbia College, 1856, and M.A., 1860, and devoted himself to literature and study; he also had travelled extensively in Europe and the Orient.

The funeral took place on Friday, October 18, Rev. Edward B. Coe officiating.

OMISSION.—The name of the author of the Necrology of Rt. Rev. Alexander Gregg, D.D., on page 91, was accidentally omitted. It was written by George A. Gordon, A.M., and his name should be appended to the article.

H.W. Smith Sc.

Alex. H. Bullock

NEW-ENGLAND
HISTORICAL AND GENEALOGICAL
REGISTER.

APRIL, 1896.

ALEXANDER HAMILTON BULLOCK.

MR. BULLOCK was a native of Royalston, Mass., where he was born March 2, 1816. His father, Hon. Rufus Bullock, a woollen manufacturer of that town, was a prominent citizen of that place, and was frequently honored with public trusts. The early education of the son was obtained in the public schools of his native town. From these he passed to the Leicester Academy, where he prepared for college. He entered Amherst College in 1832, and was graduated in 1836, delivering the Salutatory Address at the commencement exercises. After graduating he taught school a short time in his native town and elsewhere. He entered the Law School of Harvard University in 1838, and studied there two years, leaving the institution in 1840. Hon. Joseph Story, LL.D., had then been Dane Professor of Law at Harvard for nearly twenty years, and the Law School was then under the able management of Prof. Simon Greenleaf, LL.D., and himself. When he had completed his studies there he entered the office of Hon. Emory Washburn of Worcester, afterwards distinguished as a lawyer, a judge and a governor. Under so able an instructor he became familiar with the practice of his profession.

He was admitted to the bar of Worcester county in March, 1841, and immediately opened an office in the town of Worcester. In November, 1840, Hon. John Davis of Worcester, then a United States Senator, was chosen to the office of governor, a position which he had before held. He chose Mr. Bullock as one of his aids on his military staff with the rank of colonel. Gov. Davis was a whig in politics, and Mr. Bullock was of the same party, though on the dissolution of the Whig party he joined the Republicans.

The subject of this sketch soon after his admission to the bar took an active part in politics. He represented the town of Worcester in the Massachusetts House of Representatives in the years 1845 and 1847. In 1849 he was a member of the Massachusetts Senate. In 1859 he was chosen mayor of the city of Worcester, and served in that capacity very acceptably. In 1861 he was again a representative from Worcester in the General Court, and held the office till 1865. He was elected speaker of the house by a unanimous vote in 1862, 1864 and 1865, and in 1863 he had all the votes in the house but three. His discharge of the duties in this position won the approval of all the parties.

Hon. John A. Andrew, who had held the office of governor of Massachusetts during the whole of the civil war, decided after its close in 1865 to be no longer a candidate for the office, and in the fall of that year Mr. Bullock was chosen his successor. He served with ability in this office from 1866 to 1869. After a long and honorable service in public affairs, he now declined all further office. In 1879 he was offered by President Hayes the position of Minister to the Court of Great Britain, but even this tempting office could not not induce him to swerve from his resolution. Hon. Charles Devens says of this decision :

It was unfortunate for Gov. Bullock's own fame, certainly, that at the close of his gubernatorial career, he should apparently have formed the determination to end his active connection with public life. In the possession of an ample fortune, he could have made without difficulty those pecuniary sacrifices it so often entails, and from these he certainly would not have shrunk. In the discussions of Congress his words could not but have been of the highest value. A careful student, not of our own constitutional history only, but of the experience of other governments, he would have brought to the consideration of our then deeply interesting public affairs, the knowledge which such an education gives, while the graceful diction and elegant expression in which he was capable of clothing his thoughts would have imparted interest to all that he uttered. His moderation and fairness in stating the adverse position of others, while he enforced his own, would have always commanded respect even when it did not carry conviction. Gov. Bullock was never placed in any position where his powers as a debater were fully tested. He left the active practice of the profession of the law very early. As a member of the Massachusetts Legislature, both before and after the civil war, it was so strongly controlled by the party to which he belonged that there was not the same opportunity for discussion that a more evenly divided house would have presented. *

Mr. Bullock married August 29, 1844, Miss Elvira Hazard, daughter of Colonel Augustus George Hazard, of Enfield, Conn., founder of the extensive powder factories bearing his name. They had three children : one son, Col. A. G. Bullock, and two daughters, Mrs. Nelson S. Bartlett and Mrs. William H. Workman.

* Memoir of Alexander H. Bullock by Charles Devens. 1887. pp. 19-20.

On the 23d of August, 1865, he delivered the historical address at the celebration of the one hundredth anniversary of the incorporation of his native town, Royalston, Mass., which was published in that year with the other literary exercises on that occasion. He also delivered, before the City Council and citizens of Worcester, June 1, 1865, an address entitled "Abraham Lincoln: the Just Magistrate, the Representative Statesman, and Practical Philanthropist," which was printed for the city. Other public addresses by him were printed. In his early manhood he was a frequent contributor to the press, and edited *The Ægis*, a Worcester newspaper from 1848 to 1850.

He received the honorary degree of LL.D., from Amherst College, in 1865, and the same degree from Harvard University, in 1866. Of his *alma mater* he was a trustee for thirty years, from 1852 to 1882.

Besides the offices already named, he was Commissioner of Insolvency from 1853 to 1856, and Judge of the Court of Insolvency from 1856 to 1858.

We will close with another brief extract from Judge Devens's memoir:

In the daily concerns of the community in which he dwelt, Governor Bullock took, always, a strong interest. He was a good citizen, neighbor, and friend. He was ready to accept those offices of trust which the general public welfare requires to be discharged by men of judgement, and men of means who can have no ulterior object in the management of pecuniary affairs. It would be tedious to recount the number of those that were imposed upon him, the duties of which were faithfully and conscientiously discharged. While his lofty personal character inspired the profoundest respect, his gracious demeanor rendered him easily approachable by all. His politeness sprang from a good heart and a genuine, kindly feeling, and those in trouble found in him always a safe and consoling adviser. Of an affectionate nature, those widely separated from him in talent, ability, or worldly position could come to him, always sure of sweet and generous human sympathy.*

DIARY OF REV. WILLIAM HOMES OF CHILMARK, MARTHA'S VINEYARD, 1689-1746.

Contributed by Dr. CHARLES E. BANKS, U. S. Marine Hospital Service, Washington, D. C.

[Concluded from Volume xlix., page 416.]

May 18, 1718. * * * After sermon I baptized a child of Mr Experience Mayhew called Zachariah

June 8, 1718. * * * Mrs Abigail Smith departed this life last night about 9 of the clock. She was a peaceable, prudent, pious woman. * * * On Tuesday last in the afternoon she had a fever with a pain in

* Memoir of Bullock, pp. 21-2.

her head, Shortness of breath, with a great defluction yet though she had a small cough she raised nothing. I visited her Friday and Saturday. She seemed to have a good hope and well grounded of her future well being.

June 9, 1718. This day being Munday I attended the funeral of Mrs Abigail Smith, wife of Mr Shubael Smith of Chilmark.

June 15, 1718. Capt Zaccheus Mayhew and his wife were propounded to the church this day

June 29. 1718. * * * After sermon I baptized a child of Mr John Mayhew called Zilpha

July 6. 1718. * * * After sermon we received into the church of Christ Capt Zaccheus Mayhew and his wife.

July 13. 1718. * * * After sermon I baptized Capt Zacheus three children viz: Susanna Lucy and Elizabeth.

August 10. 1718. * * * Mrs Mary Allen was received into the church this day

August 15. 1718. * * * This day about two of the clock after noon several children particularly Ben: Ward and Thomas Allen having got a shot gun and some powder were diverting themselves near John Allen's barn, where were a considerable quantity of English grain and hay, some in the barn and some near it in stacks. Ben : Ward having a brand of fire in his hand, seeing his uncle Captn Mayhew riding by to sermon, threw the brand out of his hands, that his uncle might not see it. It chanced to fall near some English grain, which presently took fire, and consumed the barn and all the English grain to ashes in a very short time. All or most of the men in town presently came with an intent to extinguish the flames, but they did not effect anything.

7ber 7th 1718. * * * I heard some days ago that John McLelland son to James McLelland being engaged in a fishing designe, under took to wade over a creek at Sandy Point where the vessel wherein he was was riding at an anchor, and the day being foggy, he perished in the waters

8ber 19. 1718. On Monday last the house of Mr Zephaniah Mayhew was burnt to the ground by an accidental fire and much of his household stuff and wearing clothes were consumed in the flames. On Thursday James McLelland came here to look after his sons effects and went last week to Nantucket on that designe

9ber 9. 1718. * * * After sermon I baptized two children of Justice Allen, viz : Joseph and Benjamin. They were born on Monday morning at one o'clock

Dec. 16. 1718. This evening about 8 of the clock. Capt Zaccheus Mayhew his barn catched fire. How is not certainly known, and burned down to the ground, together with all his hay, except one load.

Febru. 15. 17$\frac{1}{1}\frac{8}{9}$. * * * After sermon Mrs Bethia Clarke was received into the church.

Feb. 22. 17$\frac{1}{1}\frac{8}{9}$. * * * Mrs Bethia Clarke was baptized after sermon.

March 1. 17$\frac{1}{1}\frac{8}{9}$. * * * Capt Zaccheus Mayhew had a child baptized this day called Sarah

March 15. 17$\frac{1}{1}\frac{8}{9}$. * * * Poor Mrs Skiffe is and hath been for several days past in a despairing condition.

March 22. 17$\frac{1}{1}\frac{8}{9}$. * * * Afternoon Mr Experience Mayhew preached from Cant. 1. 2. The sermon was well compressed but he was at some loss in reading of it.

Son John came home to see us yesternight

April 12. 17$\frac{18}{19}$. * * * After sermon I baptized a grandson called William Allen.

Apl. 19. 17$\frac{18}{19}$. * * * I baptized a child of Zeph^h Mayhew called Jedidah.

May 31. 1719. Deacon [James] Skiffe and his daughter were at sermon to day. I mean his daughter [Hannah] Daggett, [wife of Jacob], and another stranger.

June 21. 1719. Mr Experience Mayhew preached afternoon from Cant. 1. 3. The matter of the discourse was not despisable but his delivery was flat and dull.

July 5. 1719. * * * After sermon I baptized William Hunts first born child called Abia

Sept. 11. 1719. Mary Steel had a child baptized called Martha.

9ber. 29. 1719. I baptized a child this day to Simon Mayhew called Simon.

Jany. 10 17$\frac{19}{20}$. The week past hath been very cold especially Thursday last. Mr Bryce Blair by a fall yesterday in the evening broke his left arm above the elbow.

March 13. 17$\frac{19}{20}$. On Wed. last Sam : Barrett was wonderfully saved from drowning, for working upon a whale he was struck overboard by her and fell upon the whale, and his feet were entangled in the warp, so that she carryed him under water, and held him there for some time, but he got himself free from the warp. and some in the boat throwing him an oar he escaped the danger and received no considerable hurt.

April 10. 1720. Old Mrs Tilton was taken ill on Friday morning last with a convulsion of the nerves, and a dead pulse, and on Saturday evening she became speechless, and seems now to be near her end.

April 17. 1720. Mrs Tilton departed this life Munday last about one in the morning. * * * Old Mrs Allen is become very fraile. and is apprehendsive that the time of her departure out of this world draws near.

May 1. 1720. * * * Between Thursday and Friday last week died Matthew Mayhew of Edgartown eldest son of Matthew Mayhew Esqr of the same town deceased. A son also of Justice Norton died the same week.

May 8. 1720. * * * Mrs Hunt sen^r departed this life yesterday about five of the clock afternoon and was burryed this evening.

June 5. 1720. * * * Mrs Jane Hunt was received into the church this day.

July 10. 1720. * * * Mr Benjamin Smith of Edgartown died last week. He died suddenly July 4. 1720, being a Munday.

7ber 4. 1720. * * * Our house was raised on Tuesday of this week being the 6th day.

7ber 11. 1720. * * * I married Jethro Athearn and Mary Mayhew on Thursday last being ye 8th day.

9ber 13. 1720. Capt Mayhew's son Nathaniel died this morning.

Xber 25. 1720. * * * Our people here. some of them, brought a drift whale ashore at Squibnocket on friday and cut her up on Saturday.

July 23. 1721. * * * Justice Allen had a daughter born yesterday about half an hour afternoon and baptized today called Rebekah.

Xber 3. 1721. * * * The small pox I hear prevails at Sandwich.

Xber 10. 1721. Mr Clark had a child baptized today called Mary.

Jan. 26, 17$\frac{21}{22}$. Thomas Chase died friday the 22^d of December last.

Feby 25. 17$\frac{21}{22}$. On friday morning last died Samuel Tilton son to Will: Tilton, and this morning died Moses Allen, both of this town.

Mch 4. 17$\frac{21}{22}$. On friday last between five and six afternoon died Mrs Mayhew spouse to Mr Experience Mayhew.

March 18. 17$\frac{21}{22}$. * * * I understand that Shubael Cottle of [Cape pogue?] departed this life on thursday night last. He was a young man, son to James Cottle. He died of a distemper that has afflicted several people last winter and this spring, and hath carreed off several persons.

May 27. 1722. Mrs Mary Allen departed this life last Lords day about 7 of the clock afternoon and was buryed the evening of next day. She was a pious virtuous gentlewoman.

July 8. 1722. Poor Mrs Bassett is exceedingly tossed and harassed by grievous temptation, Satan taking advantage of the distemper of her body.

July 15. 1722. Poor Mrs Bassett continues still under great uneasiness by reason of the disquietment of her mind, occasioned by a melancholy which hath prevailed upon her gradually since the beginning of winter.

August 12. 1722. * * * Old Mrs Allen died Tuesday last being the 7th inst about 10 at night.

8ber 28. 1722. I had a letter from son John dated 7ber 29 wherein he writes that on the 20th day of said month James Steel fell overboard and was drowned.

March 31. 1723. * * * I had an account that Mr Newcomb died lately, he was taken suddenly while was in the cellar drawing molasses, either with an apoplectic fit or a lethargy.

April 7. 1723. Mr Little of Old town died lately

April 21. 1723. Mrs Mayhew of old town widow of Matthew Mayhew deceased died on Wednesday last

May 19. 1723. * * * I baptized a child of Captn Mayhew called Zaccheus, this day. I have been informed that this is a sickly mortal time in Newbury, Rowley and Marblehead.

May 26. 1723. I have heard that Mr Medcalfe minister of Sacconessett departed this life on Friday last. He sickened as I am told on Monday and died on friday. He was a young man. Left behind 8 children and perhaps no very plentiful estate to support them. He was a man, it is said of considerable worth.

August 18. 1723. * * * I baptized a child of William Hunts called Jane.

August 25. 1723. I was credibly informed that Andrew Stratton was drowned some time ago at Canso.

1723. 8ber 27. * * * This night about 10 of the clock Thomas Blair departed this life. He had gone some time ago to the Jarsies and came home with a fever and ague upon him.

8ber 8. 1723. * * * Mrs Bacon died on Thursday last and Mr Torrey on Saturday morning, her distemper was a consumption. Mr Torrey had been for some time under a bad habit of body. About a month agoe he was taken sick with the jaundice and voiding of blood from all the passages of his body, as I have been told, and then he was taken with a dropsie and flux. It was said that of late he had drunk too freely and too frequently of spirits. He was buryed on the evening of y^e Lords day. He was pastor of the church of Tisbury, had been a preacher about 20 years and died in y^e 43^d year of his age.

Feby 14. 17$\frac{23}{24}$ being friday about $\frac{1}{2}$ an hour after 2 afternoon, James Allen departed this life. His distemper was a putrid fever with cough.

He died the 26ᵗʰ day of his sickness. He was a pious sober man, and one of a publick spirit, well esteemed by his neighbours. He was buryed on Saturday about 5 afternoon.

June 7. 1724. * * * Mr James Skiffe died yesterday afternoon.

June 14. 1724. * * * I understand that Mr Worth departed this life this morning and that there was an Indian killed at Menamsha yesterday.

June 21. 1724. * * * Mrs Skiffe, spouse to Mr Nathan Skiffe departed this life on Friday last about noon.

July 12. 1724. * * * On friday last we raised our new meeting house. Gershom Cathcart, a young man belonging to New town fell from the third story, and was very much bruised. His recovery is uncertain [his] reason seems not to be impaired by his fall. Lord make the providence a wakening to others!

August 23. 1724. * * * I took occasion to reprove some young folk publickly for their irreverent and profane deportment in the time of Gods publick worship

August 30. 1724. * * * After sermon we received Jabez Athearn into the church and baptized him.

7ber 13. 1724. * * * Mr Clark had a child baptized today called Thankful.

7ber 20. 1724. My daughter Allen was delivered of a daughter Thursday last about one afternoon, being the 17ᵗʰ day of the month.

7ber 27. 1724. * * * This day my two daughters Agnes and Elizabeth were received into the church

8ber 4. 1724. I had an account today that John Manter's wife of New town departed this life yesterday

8ber 25. 1724. * * * I am informed that 7 Indians belonging to Gay Head coming from Rhod Island home in a whale boat were all lost, as is generally thought. It is said they were in drink when they went on board.

Jan: 10. 17$\frac{24}{25}$. * * * Last Monday son Allen carryed two men prisoners to Boston, viz: Capt Lane and Mr McGowan:

May 30. 1725. * * * Yesterday William Case of Tisbury, weaver, departed this life. He was a man between 30 and 40 years of age as I think.

June 27. 1725. * * * James Hamilton's wife of Old town died Thursday night last.

8ber 31. 1725. * * * I understand that Jonathan Hillmans child died suddenly last night.

Xber 5. 1725. * * * Last week a sloop came ashore on the south side of the island, the men and cargo were saved, the master having been long sick died Friday night last and was buryed this day. His name was Cash. the sloop belonged to Rhod Island.

Feb. 6. 17$\frac{25}{26}$. * * * Mrs Chipman departed this life last Saturday night, about midnight. She died in Dartmouth at Capt Popes. She was a pious good woman and died well, with a rational assurance of her future well being. She had long been in a languishing condition. She went in the fall to visit Captⁿ Pope and sickened there. She was buryed the Tuesday following in Dartmouth.

Feb. 13. 17$\frac{25}{26}$. On Wednesday morning last, being the 9ᵗʰ instant Mr Nathan Skiffe departed this life. He was, I hope, a good man and died well. He had been some months in a languishing condition and died in the 68ᵗʰ year of his age.

March 13. 172⅚. * * * The snow which has continued for most part since some time in November is now almost gone.

May 1. 1726. * * * Baptized a child of Mr Clarks this after noon called Jane.

May 8. 1726. On Monday last, in the evening, a child of widow Blairs of this town called Susanna dropt into a tanpit near her own house, but was taken out alive yet died about ten of the clock that night and was buryed next day.

June 8. 1726. * * * Baptized four children one to Jabez Athearn named Abigail, one to Hammet, named Abigail, one to John Cottle called Elizabeth, and one to Israel Butler named Nathaniel.

July 10. 1726. * * * I baptized two children to William Hunt, born some time ago, called Hanna and Sarah.

August 7. 1726. * * * I baptized a child belong to Mr Barnabas Taylor called Nathaniel.

August 14. 1726. * * * daughter Allen had a young child buryed on Saturday last.

August 28. 1726. * * * On Thursday last Capt Thomas Daggett of Old town departed this life. He had been ill several weeks. He was a peaceable man and well inclined and of good understanding.

Jany 8. 172⅚. Last night before sundown Old William Hunt departed this life, he was a man of good age, had been long fraile. He died suddenly, none of his family knowing when he died. [Aged about 73 years. grave stone]

Jany 15. 172⅚. * * * I heard that Mrs Ward mother to Capt Mayhews wife died lately, and a daughter of Captain Daggett.

March 19. 172⁶⁄₇. * * * Joseph Allen hath been for some time in a dangerous condition thro' vomiting etc

March 26. 1727. Mr Joseph Allen of Tisbury departed this life Munday night last. The distemper that carried him off seems to have been the iliac passion; he continued ill several days, was much out of his head at times, continued vomiting. He was a man of about 60 years of age, of good understanding, peaceable and industrious. I do not remember to have heard any evil report of him.

April 2. 1727. On Friday last one Thomas Lues of Tisbury helping to get off a vessel that had been forced on shore by a late storm, the pries not being well fixed, came down on his head, bruised his skull very much so that his recovery is despaired of by many. I am informed that the said Thomas Lewes departed this life Saturday night last. He was a poor man, and left a numerous family of small children behind him, and his wife a poor helpless woman.

May 7. 1727. * * * I understand that Hester Cottle departed this life lately.

June 11. 1727. * * * Samuel Hillman departed this life this morning, as I am informed. He was a church member, but became slack and negligent in his attending upon publick ordinances some time before his death.

June 18. 1727. Bethia and Mary Hillman departed this life June 21. 1727 in the afternoon. They died almost at one time and were burried together. Their distemper was a pleurisy fever.

July 23. 1727. * * * Mr Handcock is to be ordained pastor of the church in Tisbury on Wednesday next.

July 30 1727. Being Lords day Mr Handcock preached both before and afternoon from James 2. 23 And he was called the friend of God: the discourse was not very animate yet hope it may be useful. Lord follow thy word and ordinances with a blessing. The day was fair clear and hot. On Wednesday last, being the 26th instant, Mr. Handcock was ordained Pastor of the Church in Tisbury. I preached the ordination sermon and Mr Russell and I imposed hands on him, for there was none other minister there. Mr Russell made the first prayer and I gave the Charge and made the second prayer, and Mr Russell gave him the right hand of fellowship.

August 27. 1727. We had an account last week that King George died June 11th last past in Germany on his journey to Hanover, and that his son the prince of Wales was proclaimed King under the title of George 2.

7ber 10 1727. * * * Last friday morning Joseph Smith departed this life. He was a sober temporate Indian a young man about 26 years of age: he was so well as to be at meeting last Lords day.

Oct 15. 1727. Sam: Merry departed this life on Munday last was buried on Tuesday. Son John and Betty returned home Thursday last from Rhod Island.

October 22. 1727. * * * I heard the melancholy news of son Roberts death, but had no account of the circumstances of it.

9ber 5. 1727. Last Lords day, in the afternoon, about 11 of the clock we had a shock of an earthquake, that continued above a minute: it was considerably great, but seemed to be greater in some places than others, whether it hath been felt all the country over or not I have not yet heard.

9ber 12. 1727. I understand that the earthquake was much more severe easterly than in these parts.

9ber 19. 1727. This morning between eight and nine of the clock my daughter Jane was safely delivered of a daughter.

9ber 25, 1727. I baptized a grandchild of mine this day called Kathren daughter to Silvanus Allen.

Xber 31. 1727. We had a public fast on Wednesday last on account of y^e earthquake.

Jany 21. 17$\frac{27}{28}$. I heard today that Peter Rea died at Old town last week, he was formerly an inhabitant there, but had removed to Boston some time before he died.

Feb 25. 17$\frac{27}{28}$. I have heard that Thomas Weste died lately at Rhod Island. He had some time ago undertaken to pilot a vessel to Boston and was forced off the coast by a storm and driven to Martinico, and either by the fatigue of the voyage or by some distemper contracted in that island he was brought very low before he arrived at Rhod Island, and not long after he came on shore he died. His friends concluded he had been lost in the storm. I have also good intelligence that Dr Cotton Mather of Boston departed this life on Tuesday the 13th instant between 8 and 9 of the clock before noon, and was buried the 19th day. He was a man of superior parts and learning. He was when he died 65 years of age and some hours. The Lord prepare me for my great change.

March 10. 17$\frac{27}{28}$. On Wednesday last John Skiffe and Mr John Mills departed this life: the former about five after noon and the other about ten. John Skiffe was a young man about 23 years of age, son to Nathan Skiffe, late of this town: the other was born in England, but had lived in this town several years, and marryed above a year ago a daughter of Mr James Allen late of this town, but after marriage removed to Newtown and died there: he followed merchandizing

March 31. 1728. About three of the clock on Thursday morning, John Clifford a young man belonging to this town, departed this life, and it is said he died well. He died at Mr Cobbs of Newtown. I understand that John Campbell Esqr of Boston died the fourth of this month.

April 7. 1728. My daughter Margaret was safely delivered of a daughter Wednesday last, being the third day of the month, between 9 and 10 of the clock before noon.

April 21. 1728. John Hillman Junr died last Tuesday between nine and ten at night. His distemper was a malignant fever. He was often delirious. He died the eighth day of his sickness.

April 28. 1728. About one of the clock this morning Daniel Luke a young man, who was apprentice to Mr Bassett departed this life. He was out of his head most part of the time of his sickness: his distemper was a malignant fever.

May 19. 1728. On Munday last being ye 13th instant Jacob Robinson of Newtown departed this life.

June 2, 1728. I heard today that Isaac Robinson of Newton departed this life last evening. He was a man of an inoffensive conversation * * * * There were 18 days between the death of the two brothers, viz Jacob and Isaac Robinson.

July 7. 1728. We appointed Wednesday last to be observed as a publick fast, but we had a plentiful rain on Tuesday, which occasioned our changing the fast into a thanksgiving.

August 11. 1728. I heard that old Mr Newcome of Old town died lately.

8ber 17. 1728. I was informed that John Smith of Edgartown departed this life yesterday morning.

9ber 3 1728. I had a letter Saturday last from Mr Nathan Bassett informing that his brother Barachiah died lately in South Carolina.

Xber 29. 1728. I am informed that Justice Parker of Barnstable departed this life some day last week.

Jany 5. 17$\frac{28}{29}$. I was informed last week that Mrs Harlock and Joseph Norton's wife died lately, both of them belonged to the Old town and had been long indisposed.

Jany 26. 17$\frac{28}{29}$. Mr Draper of Boston died lately: he was a pious understanding man, and well stricken in years.

June 8. 1729. I baptized a negro of Captⁿ Mayhew called Ceasar this day.

July 6. 1729. I was informed this day that Rev^d Mr Cotton departed this life last week; he was minister of a church in Bristol: he was at the council in Sandwich that met the 18th of June last. On Saturday following as I was told, he was somewhat disordered in mind. On the Lords day his disorder increased upon him, yet he did attend the publick worship of God very composedly, and did preach to a considerable number of persons: in the evening on Munday his disorder increased so that all were sensible of it, and so it continued to do on Tuesday and Wednesday. He died July 3^d about 2 P. M.

July 13. 1729. Ichabod Allen's wife departed this life about midnight, between the 16th and 17th day of this month. She had been long in languishing circumstances, being a consumptive. She seemed to be pious and orderly in her conversation.

August 24, 1729. I understand that the poor in Ireland are in great distress thro' a famine of bread. Since, by a letter from daughter Betty we have the news of Abra Homes death confirmed. She died the third of this month. [She was daughter of William Homes of Boston, and granddaughter of the diarist].

August 31. 1729. I understand that it is a sickly time in Boston, but the sickness not very mortal.

October 5, 1729. Old Mrs Russell of Barnstable departed this life last Lords day after a short illness. She was a daughter of Rev^d Mr Moody, and widow to the Rev^d Mr Russell. She was a discreet pious gentlewoman. She died aged about 67 years.

8ber 26, 1729. I was informed today that Ben. Hillmans eldest son was lately dead, and that Sarah Hillman is dangerously ill.

9ber 23, 1729. I baptized today a child of Captn Mayhew's called Martha.

Xber 7, 1729. I baptized a child of Silvanus Allens named Mary

Xber 21. 1729. I understand that Mr Taylor is to be ordained pastor of a church in Bristol Wednesday night.

Jany 4, 17$\frac{2}{3}\frac{9}{0}$. I baptized a child of Mr Adams this day called Mayhew.

Jany 11, 17$\frac{2}{3}\frac{9}{0}$. I understand that Judge Sewall died lately in Boston, viz: on the 3^d day of the month in y^e 78th year of his age. On the eighth day of this month, about 3 in the morning Mrs Relyance Adams of this town departed this life. She was lately safely delivered of a child, but was soon after taken with a fever which carryed her off. She was a pious prudent woman of blameless conversation.

Jany 25, 17$\frac{2}{3}\frac{9}{0}$. I am informed that the Rev^d Mr Samuel Hunt pastor of a church in Dartmouth departed this life on Wednesday last which was the 21st instant and was buried on the Friday following.

Feby 8, 17$\frac{2}{3}\frac{9}{0}$. I am informed that Joseph Russells wife of Barnstable died lately in child-bed.

April 2. 1730. I have heard that the small pox prevails much in Boston. They have gone very much into the practice of communicating the distemper by inoculation, and many of those that take it, both in the natural way and by inoculation die.

May 17. 1730. I baptized this day a grandson called John Allen.

May 24. 1730. Mr Presbury of Old town died last Lords Day, and a child of William Hunts on Tuesday last.

June 14, 1730. I had an account by letters from good hands last week that my son in law Joshua Allen departed this life at Medfield the 30th day of May. His distemper was the small pox.

8ber 25, 1730. I have heard that it is a sickly time on the Mainland in several places.

July 12. 1731. Pam Mayhew Jr was drowned near the West Chop of Holmes Hole. He had been to Nantucket and was coming home and being steering the whale boat, the strap broke and he went overboard and was lost. It was in the evening. His corps came on Shore July 22 toward night at Gay Head, and he was buried the next day towards night in the burying place in Chilmark. My daughter Betty Hutchinson set out on her journey to Holmeshole with designe to take passage for Boston and from thence to Pennsylvania on Wednesday August 25, 1731.

7ber 6 1731. I am informed that the day abovesaid four men viz: Mr Taylor Mr Mood. Russell, John Sturges and the mentioned above called called also John Sturges [of Barnstable] took a whaleboat and went over to a point of land with a designe to kill some small birds, where they stayed so long that the tide left their boat dry, which they went about to carry to place where it might swim, but this Sturges complained that it was too heavy for him, so that he would not help to carry it any further and so left them, as they thought he intended to go to a place where they behooved to come after they got off the boat in their passage home, but he continued to move towards the sloop till he was drowned.

November 29, 1731. About midnight Mr. Samuel Tilton departed this life in the 94th year of his age: he was a man of good understanding, was an antipedobaptist in his judgment, but pious and regular in his conversation. He was against swearing and usery.

I was informed 9ber 9 1733 that John Cunningham of Edgar-Town died there yesterday somewhat suddenly and much out of his head.

Rachel Lumbert wife to Jonathan Lumbart the thirteenth day of February $17\frac{33}{34}$ about 8 at night, being in her ordinary health she went up stairs in her own house and dropt down in an apoplectic fit, and never spake. She continued till 2 of the clock afternoon of the next day, being the 14th day.

July 9 [1737] and the night after it, we had excessive rains which raised the rivers upon this island to such a degree that the dams of the water mills were carryed away by them, and the mowing ground near the rivers was very much damnified, to the great loss of several of the inhabitants.

August 11, 1737. The sky towards the N. and N.W. appeared with an unusual redness, which continued for some time extending itself more and more easterly. About 11 the red was mixed with white streaks that were very luminous, being broad below and gradual growing narrower till they ended in a point. About midnight there appeared a bow reaching from east to west in the form of a rainbow, only there was no diversity of colors, the whole bow was luminous so that the air was lighter than it is at full moon, tho' it was 2 or 3 days before the change [of] the moon. It did rather resemble day light before the sun rises than moonlight.

Xber 7, 1737. About 10 at night there was felt by several persons on the island, Martha's Vineyard, the shock of an earthquake.

Xber 13. 1737. About 5 weeks ago there came a vessel to the old town from Philadelphia that had the small pox on board and several persons there were infected with the distemper, of which I was informed that Doct Mathuz[?] died of it yesterday morning and Ezra Covel died last night. There have died of the same distemper five grown persons, in all seven grown persons, and several are sick of it there.

Xber 26. 1737. Some affirm that they felt the shock of an earth quake about 12 at night Xber 30. Last night David Dunham's wife died of small pox, as I am informed.

Jany 6. [$17\frac{37}{38}$]. I am informed that Samuel Smith of old town died Saturday night last of the small pox.

Jany 10. $173\frac{7}{8}$. I understand that Mrs Pease and a mulatto woman in the old town lately died of the small pox. A considerable shock of an earth quake was felt by some Jany 2. $173\frac{7}{8}$ about midnight.

I am informed Jany 13 that there have been 35 persons sick of the small pox this season in Edgartown, ont of which number 14 have died. By the best information I can get concerning the way and manner how the people in Edgartown were taken with the small pox the last fall, it was as followeth: Several persons belonging to the town were in Mr Hamiltons that kept a tavern the 18th of 9ber last; there was nobody sick of that distemper in that family: there was indeed a vessel in the harbour that had the small pox on board, but none of them that were sick lodged on shore:

those who took the distemper were all taken in one day. None of those that were in Hamiltons the day before nor afterward were infected.

November 21. 1738. There came a ship ashore on the South side of this island, belonging to New York. She came last from Jamaica: the lading and mens lives were saved, but it is supposed the ship cannot be got off again.

The 27th day of February 173$\frac{8}{9}$ I was informed that a flash of lightning we had the 25th day fell upon a house in Edgartown belonging to this island, where one Abram Ripley dwelt, and damaged it: yet none of the inhabitants were killed by it.

March 4. 17$\frac{38}{39}$. I was informed that Abigail Skiffe departed this life this morning. She had long languished under a consumption.

July 13. 1740. While I was at prayer in the morning I fainted away in the pulpit and fell down, so that I was rendered incapable of performing any further publick service that day, for which I desire to be deeply humbled. [This note conveys the premonitory sign of a failure in health from which he never entirely recovered, and accounts for the paucity of entries in his diary, of a public interest, from the date until his death, six years later.]

August 3, 1740. My grand daughter Kath: Smith hath been sick the most part of last week and continues so still.

1740 August 10. After sermon, Tim: Mayhew and wife were received into the church and she and the four children were baptized, viz: Reliance, Rachel, Hannah and Bathshebah. The first that was seized with that called the throat distemper in this town was Susan Allen; the next was Abigail Hillman, both these died. The next Katharine Smith, she also died. Next Mrs Little, she is in a fair way of recovery. Next Sam: Bassett's daughter, she also is in a hopeful way : next Bethia Clark and my grand daughter Mary Allen

August 17. 1740. After sermon received into communion of the church Josiah Crocker and Jonathan Mayhew.

August 24. 1740. After sermon Jane Hunt was received into the church as a member in full communion.

7ber 7. 1740. A child of Gunino Finla, of about 9 years of age died on Friday last of throat distemper, and three in my son Sylvanus Allen's family are under the distemper.

7ber 14. 1740. John Bassett and his wife were received into the church and their two children baptized, viz. Elizabeth and Ruth.

7ber 15. 1740. I had the uncomfortable news that my grandson William Daggett departed this life the day before.

7ber 17. 1740. Was observed through the island as a day of fasting and prayer to beg mercy of God that the distemper that has prevailed among us for some time might be removed and health restored*. . . . A child of Zach : Hatch died of the throat distemper this night.

7ber 28 1740. At 5 o'clock on Thursday morning in this week my grandson Eleazer Allen departed this life.

---

* This was an epidemic disease, known then as the "throat distemper," probably diphtheria, which broke out at Kingston, N. H., in the Spring of 1735 and gradually spread over New England during the next few years and later extended over all the colonies. The disease was very fatal and several thousand deaths of young people in New England are chargeable to its ravages. It lingered for several years, and the appearance of it on the Vineyard in 1740 may be traced to the general dissemination of the contagion over the New England colonies by that time.   C. E. B.

8ber 19. 1740. After sermon William Bassett and his wife, Abigail Allen and Hannah Clark were received into the church and Mrs Bassett and her six children were baptized, viz: Nathaniel, Barachiah, Nathan, Anna and Susanna.

9ber 2. 1740. Received into the church Ruth Mayhew and Susanna Hatch and baptized a child of the Rev. Mr. Taylor, called Eleazer and another of John Tiltons called Mary

9ber 16. 1740. After sermon Zephaniah Mayhew and his wife were received into the church and their two children viz Jehoiadah and Lucinda were baptized and a child of Ja⁸ Foster called Hanna was baptized also.

9ber 23. 1740. Received into the church Rebecca Allen in full communion.

Feby 22. 174⁴₋₁⁰. This day Mr. Sam¹ Allen and his daughter Mariah were received into the church as members in full communion.

March 15. 174⁰. Mary Mayhew was received into the church.

March 22 174⁰. Jedidah Allen was received into the church and was baptized.

April 5, 1741. This day Shubal Hawes was propounded to the church.

May 2. 1741. This day Mrs. Abigail Pees departed this life in the 80 year of her age. She was of a quiet inoffensive deportment. She died about 12 o'clock this day.

7ber 6, 1741. We had this summer a drought that hurt both the grass and the Indian corn very much. This was accompanied with an unusual number of grasshoppers that devoured both grass and corn.

9ber 12. 1741. We had a general Thanksgiving appointed by our Governour, William Shirley Esqr.

August 15. 1742. This morning Mrs Gold had withdrawn herself to some obscure place which put the family into disorder.

7ber 12. 1742. I baptized a child of Mr Taylors to-day called Elizabeth.

Oct. 19. 1742. About three afternoon the chimney in the room where I commonly stay catched fire, and being very foul, burned very fiercely, which put the whole house in no small danger. It continued to burn till within the night. It was a day time and the wind very high, yet through the mercy of God we received no great damage, only the mantle tree catched fire and is part damnified. Several of our neighbors came to our assistance seasonably. I desire to bless God for our preservation.

June 19. 1743. I went to the place of Gods public worship as usual, but was so faint that I fainted away in the time of the first prayer, and was carried home by my friends. I found myself very ill all morning and the most of the preceding week. About 3 years before I had such a fit in the pulpit and in the time of prayer too. Lord prepare me for my great change.

April 29. 1744. I received into the church Jonathan Hillman and his wife and baptized them and their children, and a child of John Cottles.

———

[The remainder of the diary, until June 22, 1746, when the last entry was made, is entirely composed of notes of the Sunday services; the name of the preacher who occupied his pulpit, for he was too feeble to continue work after the above entry was made, and the texts chosen by the preachers, usually followed by some pious ejaculation. As stated in the first installment the diarest died June 20, 1746.   C. E. B.]

THE FORT AT GREAT ISLAND,

(NEW CASTLE, NEW HAMPSHIRE.)

[Communicated by FRANK W. HACKETT, A.M., of New Castle, N.H.]

THE following depositions, with others in Walton's suit, are to be found in Provincial Court Records (1659-1672) page 341, Rockingham County Records. See Farmer's Belknap, page 62. "Dormon Doseagh" is sometimes Dormont Usher, and occasionally "Derment O'Shaw." It finally settles down into the name of "Derment Shaw." In laying out land on Great Island, as appears from the early town records of Portsmouth, a not infrequent reference is made to "Dorman's fence," as a division line. Shaw's Bridge and Shaw's Field are employed down to a late day to designate the locality of the land originally granted to "Dermont Usher." Town Records, 53 (1664). Rockingham Deeds, Lib. 325, fol. 145 (1839).

I think these depositions have never been printed. The first is particularly valuable as showing the size of the early fort, the site being included within the present limits of Fort Constitution, Portsmouth harbor.

The deposition of Thomas Roberts aged thirty three yeares or thereabouts testifieth that about eighteen or nineteen yeares or thereabout last past he then being serv^t to George Walton he helped to plant and cleare the fort poynt and likewise to plant and fence it which fence ran from An oke tree now standinge Right to ye sea hard by the wind mill : the point then was faer growne with wood which he likewise help to cutt Downe And cleere the fort then soe called was a kinde of rock Lyinge to the outt most poynt Toward Capt: Champernoons Island which fort was a kind of platforme made with Trees or the Like which contained about two or three Rod Square : Lykewise that my master Walton did quietly posses and Inioy the saied poynt a the Tyme he was his sev^t Theire which was About five yeares And further saith nott   This to the best of his knowledge.

Depo in Court of Associates ye 30 March : 69

Elias Stileman *cler.*

Dorman Doseagh aged sixtie or thereabouts testifieth that about fifteen yeares last past he then being servant to George Walton saith that ye said Walton had then And did quietly possess ye fort poynt and likewise did digg a seller and erect a house about eight yeares since upon ye said poynt with oute ye lett forbidence or denial of any person whatsoever. And never was for biden untill such tyme ye late forte began to be built : the above said land or part of ye poynte was fenced by the said Walton : from an oke tree with mortice holes which is now standinge which fence ran over the said poynt to the sea to ye South west side of the wind mill   This to the best of his knowledge

Depo : 30 March 1669 in Court of Assembly

Elias Stileman cler

ABSTRACT OF A DORCHESTER DEED.—1753.

By EDWARD S. HOLDEN, LL.D., Director of Lick Observatory.

THE following extracts from a deed in my possession have some interest to Dorchester people on account of the spelling of proper names, etc. It is otherwise interesting as showing that in 1753 *the* had not fully conquered the older form *ye* in the writing of educated men. Both forms occur in this deed, sometimes in the same handwriting.

To ALL CHRISTIAN PEOPLE . . . . John Holbrook of Dorchester, Gentleman, sends Greeting . . . . . KNOW YE that ye sd. John Holbrook in consideration of ye sum of Six Hundred Pounds . . . . to him in hand paid by William Holden of sd. Dorchester, Physician, ... Hath sold . . . unto ye sd. William Holden . . . . four parcels of Land . . . Butted and Bounded . . . . by land belonging to ye heirs of Capt. Thomas Wiswell* Dec^d . . . . by ye land of ye Honble James Allen Esqr . . . . by ye Ministerial Land, so called, belonging to ye Town of Dorchester . . . . . by ye land of John Maxfield . . . . . by ye Town's Pasture, so called . . . . by ye land of Edward Kilton† . . . . . by land belonging to ye heirs of Nathaniel Topliff, Dec^d . . . . by land belonging to ye heirs of Elijah Danforth Esqr Dec^d. . . . . by land of Mrs. Elizabeth Williams . . . . by ye saltmarsh of Thomas Bird . . . by ye marsh of Ebenezer Moseley . . . by ye land of John Wiswell‡ . . . . by land belonging to ye heirs of Joseph Weeks Dec^d . . . . . To HAVE AND TO HOLD . . . . IN WITNESS WHEREOF they ye sd. John Holbrook & Mary his wife have hereunto set their hands and Seals ye Ninth Day of June in the year of our Lord, one Thousand, Seven Hundred Fifty and Three And in ye Twenty Sixth Year of ye Reign of our Sovereign Lord George ye Second King of Great Britain &c.

JOHN HOLBROOK. [SEAL.]§

MARY HOLBROOK. [SEAL.]§

Signed . . . . in Presence of us

SAM^{ll} SEVER,   SAM^l TOPLIFF.

Suffolk ss. Boston May 14th 1756. Capt. John Holbrook personally appeared & acknowledged the . . . . . before me.

JONAS CLARKE, Justice Peace.

Boston May 14:1756. Received & Entred with the Records of Deeds for the County of Suffolk Lib^r. 88 folio 195 &c^{ra}

℘ EZEK^l GOLDTHWAIT, Reg^r.

* Wiswell, not yet Wiswall.
† Kilton, not yet Kelton.
‡ Wiswell (*sic.*)
§ The seal is the same for both husband and wife—a piece of square paper over a wafer impressed by a ring (?), bearing a device like a tower (light-honse?) from which rays proceed on the *dexter* side only.

EARLY STATEMENTS RELATIVE TO THE EARLY LIFE OF ROGER WILLIAMS.

Compiled by JOHN WARD DEAN.

HUBBARD, in his History of New England, written in 1680, says of Roger Williams, that he was "of good account in England for a godly and zealous preacher . . . . He had been some years employed in the ministry in England."

I find nothing in Mather's Magnalia (1702) relative to his life in England, nor in either edition (1720 and 1741) of Neal's History of New England.

In 1765, a series of articles on the history of Providence was published in the *Providence Gazette*, Jan. 12 to March 30, 1765. They are attributed to Gov. Stephen Hopkins and are reprinted in the Collection of the Massachusetts Historical Society, vol. xix, pages 160–203. In narrating the arrival of Williams in New England it is said "of whose life, before his coming to America we knew little more than that he had a liberal education and was sometime pupil of Sir Edward Coke, the famous English lawyer" (page 168).

Rev. Morgan Edwards, a Welsh clergyman of Philadelphia, prepared materials for a History of the Baptists of Rhode Island, which remained in manuscript till 1867, when the work was printed in the sixth volume of the Collections of the Rhode Island Historical Society. Benedict, in his History of the Baptists, vol. i., page 485, states that this manuscript History was prepared in 1771. Edwards says: "As to Mr. Williams he is said to have been a native of Wales, and to have had his education (which was liberal) under the patronage of the famous lawyer, Sir Edward Coke, under whom also he studied law, and by whose interest he got episcopal orders and a parish. The manner in which he obtained his patronage is said to have been this : ' Sir Edward one day observing a youth at church taking notes of the sermon, and the people crowding, beckoned to him to come to his pew ; and seeing how judiciously he minuted down the striking sentiments of the preacher, was so pleased that he entreated the parents to let him have the lad.' " (Page 316.)

In 1775, Rev. John Stanford, then preaching in Providence, prepared and entered on the church records a history of the First Baptist church in that town. This account was printed in 1813 by Rev. David Benedict, in the first volume of his History of the Baptists. Of Roger Williams he says : " Mr. Williams was a native of Wales, born in the year 1598, and had a liberal education under Sir Edward Coke. The occasion of Mr. Williams's receiving the favor of that distinguished lawyer was very singular. Sir Edward one day at church observing a youth taking notes from the sermon beckoned him into his pew. He obtained a sight of the lad's minutes, which were exceedingly judicious, being a collection of the most striking sentiments delivered by the preacher. This, with Mr. Williams's great modesty, so engaged Sir Edward in his favor as to induce him to solicit Mr. Williams's parents to let him have the care of their son, which was readily granted. Mr. Williams soon entered on the study of law and received all possible assistance from his generous patron ; but finding this employment not altogether agreeable to his taste, after pursuing it some time, he turned his attention to divinity, and made such proficiency therein as encouraged Sir Edward to obtain for him episcopal orders. His preaching was highly esteemed and his private character revered. By embracing the sentiments of the Puritans, he was greatly exposed to suffering and at last was thereby compelled to leave his native country." (Benedict's Baptists, i. 473–4.)

In 1777, Rev. Isaac Backus published the first volume of his History of New England, with particular reference to the Baptists. In regard to the early life of Roger Williams he repeats what Hubbard had said. In 1796 the third volume was issued. In this volume Mr. Backus says: "Mr. Roger Williams was born in Wales, in 1599, was educated at Oxford University, and was introduced into the ministry of the Church of England for some years before he came over to America and landed in Boston in February, 1631." (Backus, ed. of 1871, ii. 489.)

On reviewing these statements, I would remark that some of the assertions have been disproved and others rendered improbable. There is little likelihood that he was born in Wales. Mr. Waters's Gleanings show that his parents resided in London, and he was probably born there. The University at which he was educated is also wrongly given. It was not Oxford, but Cambridge. He was matriculated, a pensioner of Pembroke College, July 7, 1625, and took the degree of B.A. in January, 1626–7 (Greene's History of Rhode Island, vol. i. p. 49). Whether he commenced the study of the law before preparing for the ministry, I have as yet no means of determining. That he was patronized by Sir Edward Coke is proved by the statement of Mrs. Anne Sadlier, the daughter of Coke, whose correspondence with Roger Williams is printed in Elton's Life of Roger Williams, pages 106 to 110.

Mrs. Sadlier says: "This Roger Williams, when he was a youth, would in a short-hand take sermons and speeches in the Star Chamber, and present them to my dear father. He seeing so hopeful a youth, took such liking to him that he sent him in to Sutton's Hospital, and he was the second that was placed there." (Elton's Life of Williams, p. 108.) The records of Sutton's Hospital, now the Charter House, show that Williams was elected a scholar "June 25, 1621, and that he obtained an exhibition July 9, 1624" (*ibid,* p. 11).

The discoveries of Mr. Waters in 1889 (REGISTER, vol. xliii., pp. 291–303) ; the letters of Williams contributed to the REGISTER the same year by George Alan Lowndes, M.A. (*ibid*, pp. 315–320) ; and the article by that gentleman on " The Barrington Family," published in the Transactions of the Essex Archæological Society in 1878–9 (*ibid*, vol. l., pp. 65–8), throw new light on the history of Williams before his emigration, and lead us to hope for further discoveries.

From these we infer that Williams never held a living in England. He does not mention in his letter to Lady Barrington having held any, though two parishes had been offered to him which his conscientious scruples led him to reject. As early as 1629 he was chaplain to Sir William Masham, baronet, at Otes,* in High Laver, Essex, a position held either before or after by Rev. John Norton, who also came to New England and died the teacher of the First Church of Boston, Mass. Lady Masham was Winifred, daughter of Sir Francis Barrington, bart. She was a cousin of Oliver Cromwell. Here Williams was in a position to make the acquaintance of the leading patriots of that day. He refers to a " late New England call," presumably to Plymouth or Salem. His letters show that he sought unsuccessfully the hand of a relative of Lady Barrington. After his failure he probably accepted one of the " offers " he refers to, perhaps that put into his hand, " person and present portion worthy." At least he was married before he arrived in this country in February, 1630–1.

FAMILY OF GEORGE STOCKING.

Contributed by EDWARD E. CORNWALL, M.D., Brooklyn, N. Y.

1. GEORGE[1] STOCKING, born in England; married 1st, in England, Anna ———; married 2d, in Hartford, Ct., Agnes ———†. He came to Massachusetts about 1633. Had a house in Cambridge, situated on the southwest corner of the present Holyoke and Winthrop Streets, in 1635. Was admitted freeman in Massachusetts, May, 1635. Removed with the first settlers to Hartford, 1636, and had a lot of twenty acres there in the

---

* John Locke, the philosopher, spent the last years of his life at Otes, in the family of his friend, Sir Francis Masham, bart, whose wife was Damaris, daughter of Rev. Ralph Cudworth, D.D., and a niece of Gen. James Cudworth of Scituate, in Plymouth Colony, New England.
    † She may have been Agnes (Shatswell) Webster, widow of Gov. John Webster who died in 1661.

first distribution of land. Selectman in Hartford, 1647. Surveyor of highways, 1654 and 1662. Chimney viewer, 1659. Excused from military duty, 1660, probably on account of age. May, 1670, he with his second wife, Agnes, separated to the Second Church of Hartford. He died "at great age," May 25, 1683. He left no will and his estate,* which amounted to £257:09:00, was divided among his children: Samuel Stocking, Hannah Benton, the wife of John Richards, the wife of Samuel Olcott, and his grandson John Stocking. Family tradition says that he came from from the "West of England" and was derived from a good family there. In the older records the name is often written *Stocken* or *Stockin*. Children:

    2. i. Deacon SAMUEL,[2] b. in England.
       ii. HANNAH, m. Andrew Benton, of Hartford.
       iii. SARAH, m. Samuel Olcott, of Hartford.
       iv. LYDIA, m. John Richards, of Hartford.

2. Deacon SAMUEL[2] STOCKING (*George*[1]), married May 27, 1652, at Hartford, Bethia, daughter of John and Jane Hopkins. He came with his father to Massachusetts and removed with him to Hartford. About 1650 he removed with the first settlers to Middletown. Was one of the three signers of the Indian deed of Middletown. Was the first deacon in the Middletown Church, which was organized in 1668. Was representative from Middletown, 1658, 1659, 1665, 1669, 1674, 1677 and 1681. Served in King Philip's war, probably as sergeant. His house stood in Upper Middletown, now the town of Cromwell. In his will he mentions all his children, except Hannah, who was probably dead, and leaves all his land on the east side of the Connecticut river to his sons George and Ebenezer and gives £3 to his pastor, Rev. Nathaniel Collins. He died Dec. 3, 1683. The inventory of his estate amounted to £648:08:08. His widow married James Steele. Children:

    i. HANNAH,[3] b. Oct. 30, 1654; d. before 1683.
    ii. SAMUEL, b. Oct. 9, 1656; d. Dec. 2, 1697. Left his estate (£327) to his brothers John, George and Daniel, and his sisters Bethia Stow and Lydia Howell.
    iii. BETHIA, b. Oct. 10, 1658: m. Oct. 16, 1675, Thomas Stow, of Middletown.
    iv. JOHN, b. Sept. 24, 1660. Lived for some years with his grandfather in Hartford. Was later in Middletown, where in 1713 he was called "a distracted person." Was living 1718.
    v. LYDIA, b. Jan. 20, 1663; m. Joseph Howell, of Southampton, L. I.
    3. vi. GEORGE, b. Feb. 20, 1665.
    vii. EBENEZER, b. Feb. 23, 1669; d. before 1697.
    viii. STEVEN, b. March 23, 1673; d. before 1697.
    4. ix. DANIEL, b. April 14, 1677.

3. GEORGE[3] STOCKING (Deacon *Samuel,*[2] *George*[1]), married Elizabeth ———. Removed from Upper Middletown to East Middletown (later Chatham, now Portland) before 1710. His name appears for the single year, 1694, on the tax list of Southampton, L. I., but it is not probable that he lived there for any length of time. He died Feb. 17, 1714, and was buried in the old graveyard in Portland. His estate, which amounted to £359:09:01, was divided among his

---

* The inventory of his estate mentions "Bible, sermon book and spectacles."

six children, all of whom were living at the time of his death. His
widow married Deacon Samuel Hall, of East Middletown, and died
Nov. 16, 1737, aged about 63 years. Children:

    5. i. STEVEN,[4] b. Aug. 20, 1694.
      ii. ELIZABETH, b. March 6, 1697; m. Dec. 8, 1736, John Payne, of East
          Middletown.
    6. iii. SAMUEL, b. Oct. 16, 1700.
      iv. BETHIA, b. April 12, 1703; m. June 8, 1727, John Churchill, of East
          Middletown.
    7. v. Captain GEORGE, b. April 16, 1705.
    8. vi. NATHANIEL, b. June 28, 1709.

4. DANIEL[3] STOCKING (Deacon *Samuel*,[2] *George*,[1]), married Aug. 27,
1700, Jane, daughter of Hugh and Martha (Coit) Mould, of New
London. Lived in Upper Middletown. Died 1733. His widow
died April 1, 1758.

      i. DANIEL,[4] b. May 10, 1701; probably d. young.
    9. ii. Captain JOSEPH, b. Feb. 27, 1703.
      iii. EBENEZER, b. Nov. 23, 1704; d. Sept. 20, 1762. His estate was dis-
          tributed to Capt. Joseph Stocking, Elisha Stocking, Jane Ayrault,
          and the heirs of Jonathan Stocking.
      iv. Captain JOHN, b. July 14, 1707; m. Dec. 27, 1749, Mary Hall. He d.
          at Statia, Feb. 26, 1750, and his widow m. Jan. 10, 1751, Nathaniel
          Chauncy. He lived in Upper Middletown, but was, perhaps, for
          a few years, about 1738, in Haddam, or Middle Haddam.
    10. v. JONATHAN, b. Oct. 1, 1709.
      vi. JANE, b. Dec. 19, 1711; m. April 17, 1730, Nicholas Ayrault, of
          Wethersfield.
    11. vii. ELISHA, b. Mar. 25, 1714.

5. STEVEN[4] STOCKING (*George*,[3] Deacon *Samuel*,[2] *George*[1]), married 1st,
July 5, 1722, Elizabeth, daughter of Deacon Samuel and Sarah
(Hinsdale) Hall. She was born 1694 and died Aug. 1, 1756. He
married 2d, Feb. 24, 1757, Widow Sarah Andrews. Lived in Chatham. Was commissioned ensign of militia 1732. Died 1789. His
widow died July 29, 1790. Children:

      i. JOSEPH,[5] b. June 28, 1723; m. Nov. 1, 1753, widow Sarah (Shepherd)
          Cornwall. Children : 1. *Abraham*,[6] b. Sept. 26, 1754; 2. *Joseph*,[6]
          b. June 16, 1756; 3. *Lemuel*,[6] b. Aug. 10, 1758; 4. *Elizabeth*,[6] b.
          July 22, 1760; 5. *Amos*,[6] b. July 17, 1764; 6. *Sarah*,[6] bap. Sept. 1769.
          He lived in Chatham.
      ii. STEVEN, b. Aug. 15, 1724; d. May 2, 1775; m. July 14, 1752, Mary
          Andrews. She was b. Aug. 11, 1732, and d. Dec. 9, 1825. Chil-
          dren : 1. *Eber*,[6] b. Jan. 15, 1756; m., 1784, Olive Sage; served in
          the Revolutionary war. 2. *Steven*,[6] m. Jan. 31, 1782, Sarah Hill.
          3. *Jonathan*,[6] m. April 26, 1784, Polly Allen; removed to New
          York state. 4. *David*,[6] bap. Feb. 3, 1765; m. Phebe Cook. 5.
          Lois,[6] m. 1776, Benjamin Abby. He lived in Chatham.
      iii. ELIZABETH, b. June 1, 1726.
      iv. SARAH, b. Jan. 24, 1728; m. April 17, 1746, Dea. David Sage, of
          Chatham.
      v. DAVID, b. Sept. 20, 1730; d. March 3, 1807; m. July 14, 1753, Abigail
          Spencer. She was b. 1727, and d. July 25, 1810. Children : 1.
          Elizabeth,[6] b. Dec. 21, 1754; m. (?) June 3, 1776, Gabriel Ely. 2.
          Azubah,[6] b. Aug. 9, 1757. 3. *Abigail*,[6] b. March 25, 1760; m. Dec. 12,
          1788, Alexander Alvord. 4. *Huldah*,[6] b. Dec. 27, 1762. 5. *Rachel*,[6]
          b. Jan. 4, 1765. He lived in East Haddam.
      vi. LOIS, b. July 15, 1733; d. young.
      vii. AMOS, b. Aug. 7, 1736; d. Sept. 15, 1762.

6. SAMUEL⁴ STOCKING (*George,³* Deacon *Samuel,² George¹*), married July
    20, 1726, Abiah Boardman. Lived in Chatham. Died July 21,
    1772. His wife died Oct. 13, 1767. Children :

    i.   SAMUEL,⁵ b. June 17, 1727.
    ii. ELIJAH, b. Dec. 30, 1728 ; d. Jan. 19, 1807 ; m. Hannah ——. Chil-
         dren : 1. *Hannah.⁶* 2. *Samuel.⁶* 3. *John,⁶* b. May 5, 1763 ; m.
         Deborah Hurlbut ; served on a Revolutionary privateer ; removed
         to New York state. 4. *Abigail,⁶* b. 1766 ; m. Timothy Hurlbut.
         5. *Elijah,⁶* bap. March 19, 1769 ; m. Jan. 2, 1794, Mary Sage. 6.
         David,⁶ bap. 1770. 7. *Joel,⁶* bap. Aug. 21, 1774. 8. *Jared,⁶* bap.
         Nov. 2, 1777. He lived in Chatham.
    iii. MARSHAL, b. Aug. 15, 1730 ; m. 1st, Anne —— ; m. 2d, Sept. 3,
         1767, Esther Tryon. She d. Oct. 16, 1779. Children : 1. *Pru-
         dence,⁶* bap. Jan. 29, 1752 ; m. Dec. 29, 1773, Nathaniel Goodrich.
         2. *Jemima,⁶* bap. Dec. 28, 1754. 3. *Eunice,⁶* bap. Jan. 25, 1756 ;
         m. July 11, 1774, Ephraim Bowers. 4. *Marshal,⁶* m. Feb. 5,
         1783, Anna Bartlet ; served in the Revolutionary war. 5. *Anne.⁶*
         6. *Aseph,⁶* bap. July 10, 1768. 7. *Samuel,⁶* bap. Dec. 6, 1772. 8.
         Esther,⁶ bap. Sept. 11, 1774. 9. *Ruth,⁶* bap. Aug. 17, 1777. He
         lived in Chatham.
    iv. BENJAMIN, b. July 1, 1732 ; d. Dec. 4, 1808 ; m. 1st, Phebe ——.
         She d. Nov. 23, 1786, and he m. 2d, Jan. 7. 1789, widow Mary
         Stocking. Children : 1. *Benjamin,⁶* bap. Oct. 24, 1754. 2. *Phebe,⁶*
         bap. Oct. 28, 1756. 3. *Sarah,⁶* bap. 1757 ; m. Sept. 30, 1777,
         Gideon Hurlbut. 4. *Lucy,⁶* bap. Aug. 18, 1762. 5. *Grace,⁶* b.
         May 8, 1763 ; m. (?) Dec. 1, 1785, Joseph Willcox. 6. *Reuben,⁶*
         bap. March 9, 1777, and probably, also, (7) *Moses,⁶* m. Nov. 17,
         1785, Elizabeth Pelton ; removed to Sheffield, Mass. 8. *Joseph,⁶*
         bap. 1757. 9. *Lydia,⁶* bap. Oct. 1, 1764. He lived in Chatham.
    v.   ABIGAIL, bap. June 30, 1734 ; m. Benjamin Hale.
    vi. RUTH, bap. Oct. 3, 1736 ; m. John Penfield.
    vii. MOSES, bap. Jan. 5, 1739.
    viii. ABIAH, bap. June 15, 1741 ; m. Zaccheus Goodrich, of Middletown.
    ix. PRUDENCE, bap. Nov. 3, 1745.

7. Captain GEORGE⁴ STOCKING (*George,³* Deacon *Samuel,² George¹*), mar-
    ried March 1, 1727, Mercy Savage. Removed from East Middle-
    town to Middle Haddam (the Fourth Parish of old Middletown),
    where he had a grist mill, before 1740. Was commissioned captain
    of militia 1752. Died 1790. Children :

    i. GEORGE,⁵ b. May 11, 1728 ; m. Jan. 25, 1747, Eunice Cobb. Children :
        1. *George,⁶* b. May 15, 1750 ; d. 1777. 2. *Caleb,⁶* b. Aug. 31, 1752 ;
        m. Jan. 23, 1769, Alice Williams in East Haddam. 3. *Hezekiah,⁶*
        bap. July 25, 1756 ; d. 1777. 4. *Nathaniel,⁶* bap. Jan. 21, 1759 ; d.
        1777. 5. *Ansel,⁶* b. April 3, 1763 ; m. Jan. 31, 1786, Prudence
        Crosby. 6. *Eunice,⁶* b. April 20, 1765. 7. *Sabra,⁶* b. May 6, 1767.
        8. *Elisha,⁶* bap. April 8, 1770. He lived in Middle and East Had-
        dam till just before the Revolution, when he removed to East Glas-
        tonbury, where he was killed, with his sons George, Hezekiah and
        Nathaniel, by the explosion of a powder mill, Aug. 23, 1777.
    ii. Captain ABNER, b. April 1, 1730 ; m. Feb. 8, 1749, Ruth Higgins.
        Children : 1. *Abner,⁶* b. Jan. 2, 1753 ; m. Feb. 20, 1777, Lidea
        Bowers ; served in the Revolution. 2. *Ruth,³* b. Oct. 27, 1754 ; m.
        Dec. 7, 1775, Lieut. Shubal Brooks. 3. *Hannah,⁶* b. Sept. 11,
        1756 ; m. Oct. 25, 1774, Eleazer Bates. 4. *William,⁶* b. July 18,
        1758 ; served in the Revolution. 5. *James,⁶* b. Jan. 24, 1760 ;
        served in the Revolution. 6. *Amasa,⁶* b. Dec. 24, 1763 ; served
        in the Revolution. 7. Rev. *Jeremiah,⁶* b. Dec. 8, 1767 ; m. 1790,
        Mary Wood ; served on a Revolutionary privateer ; was a Meth-
        odist clergyman. 8. *Benjamin,⁶* bap. July 15, 1770. 9. *Alex-
        ander,⁶* bap. Jan. 10, 1773. He lived in Middle Haddam, was a
        sea captain, and is said to have commanded a privateer in the

Revolution that sailed out of New York, and was one of the leaders in the Point Judith Expedition. Was commissioned captain of the militia, 1780.

  iii. JOHN, b. Aug. 15, 1732; m. Jan. 28, 1753, Priscilla Mayo. Children: 1. *Mary,*[6] b. Sept. 6, 1754. 2. *Timothy,*[6] bap. June 13, 1756, and, perhaps, others. He lived in Middle Haddam.
  iv. MARY,[6] b. Jan. 12, 1735; m. Jan. 23, 1752, George Hubbard Jr.
  v. HEZEKIAH,[6] b. Feb. 1, 1737, probably d. young.
  vi. LUCY, b. Aug. 8, 1739; m. July 21, 1757, Sylvanus Higgins.
  vii. REUBEN, bap. Feb. 12, 1744; m, Sept. 19, 1765, Sarah Hurlbut. Children: 1. *Reuben,*[6] bap. Aug. 20, 1766. 2. *Samuel,*[6] bap. Dec. 17, 1767; m. April 7, 1789, Mary Ann Belden. 3. *Lucy,*[6] bap. Nov. 22, 1769. 4. *Steven,*[6] bap. March 24, 1771; m. Dec. 1, 1793, Mehitable Swift. 5. *Vinina,*[6] bap. June 9, 1776; m. Solon Ramsdell. 6. *Hezekiah,*[6] bap. Nov. 8, 1778. 7. *George,*[6] bap. Sept. 30, 1781; m. Fanny Hurd. 8. *Sarah,*[6] m. Sept. 21, 1791, Joel Bradford. He lived in Middle Haddam.
  viii. MARTHA, bap. Nov. 8, 1741; m. 1760, Jedidiah Hubbard.
  ix. MERCY, bap. May 1, 1746; d. Aug. 20, 1749.
  x. MERCY, bap. Nov. 26, 1752: m. Aug. 1, 1771, James Brainerd.

8. NATHANIEL[4] STOCKING (*George,*[3] Deacon *Samuel,*[2] *George*[1]), married Jan. 7, 1734, Abigail Cooper. Removed to Haddam Neck in the parish of Middle Haddam and town of Haddam, as early as 1735. Died "in a sudden manner" Jan. 24, 1781, intestate. Children:

  i. LYDIA,[5] b. Oct. 12, 1735; m. Lemuel Smith.
  ii. NATHANIEL, b. May 6, 1738; d. Oct. 7, 1751.
  iii. LAMBERTON, b. Feb. 9, 1739; m. 1st, Sarah ———. She d. July 3, 1778, and he m. 2d, April 21, 1779, Mehitable Young. Children: 1. *Timothy,*[6] b. June 24, 1764; 2. *Mary,*[6] b. Feb. 16, 1767; 3. *Sarah,*[6] b. June 18, 1770; 4. *Lamberton,*[6] b. June 23, 1775; 6. *Abigail,*[6] b. March 26, 1777; 7. *Elizabeth,*[6] b. March 26, 1777; 8. *Lucinda,*[6] b. April 23, 1778. He lived in Middle Haddam.
  iv. ELIZABETH, b. Dec. 12, 1741; m. May 1, 1769, Jonathan Brainerd.
  v. SAMUEL, b. Nov. 12, 1743; d. before 1781.
  vi. JEMIMA, b. Sept. 7, 1745; m. Oct. 22, 1765, Capt. David Brooks.
  vii. THOMAS, b. Sept. 20, 1747; m. Oct. 31, 1771, Elizabeth Hurd. Children: 1. *Joseph,*[6] bap. Jan. 16, 1775; removed to Buffalo, N. Y. 2. *Samuel,*[6] b. June 10, 1777; m. Phebe Sheldon; removed to Utica, N. Y. 3. *Jared,*[6] removed to Niagara Falls, Ont. 4. *Michael.*[6] 5. *Mary,*[6] m. ——— Root. He lived in Middle Haddam, Ct., and Pittsfield, Mass.
  viii. SARAH, b. Sept. 15, 1749; m. Elisha Day.
  ix. TIMOTHY, b. Aug. 18, 1751; d. Nov. 1753.
  x. RUTH, b. Feb. 2, 1756; was living 1781.

9. Captain JOSEPH[4] STOCKING (*Daniel,*[3] Deacon *Samuel,*[2] *George*[1]), married 1st, Dec. 20, 1726, Abigail Ranney; married 2d, Widow Hannah (Pitkin) Magill. Lived in Upper Middletown. Children:

  i. DANIEL,[5] b. Jan. 18, 1728; d. Dec. 23, 1800; m. 1st, Sarah, daughter of Rev. Hezekiah Gould, of Stratford. She d. Aug. 9, 1756, and he m. 2d, April 21, 1757, Bethia Kirby. Children: 1. *Mary Ann,*[6] bap. Nov. 5, 1752; m. David White. 2. *Jozeb,*[6] bap. Jan. 16, 1755. 3. *Daniel,*[6] bap. May 6, 1759. 4. *Sarah,*[6] bap. Sept. 21, 1760; m. Oct. 14, 1787, Nicholas Fox. 5. *Samuel,*[5] bap. Jan. 6, 1762. 6. *Seth,*[6] bap. Feb. 12, 1764. 7. *Abigail,*[6] bap. Oct. 27, 1767; m. Sept. 16, 1785, Thomas Clark. 8. *Clarissa,*[6] bap. Nov. 12, 1769. 9. *Huldah,*[6] bap. April 1772; m. March 29, 1795, Siras Willcox. 10. *John,* bap. Oct. 30, 1774. He lived in Upper Middletown. Graduated at Yale College, 1748. Was a schoolmaster.
  ii. ZEBULON, d. Oct. 6, 1741.
  iii. ABIGAIL, m. Oct. 28, 1757, Thomas Goodwin.

10. JONATHAN[4] STOCKING (*Daniel,[3]* Deacon *Samuel,[2] George[1]*), married
   1st, Patience ———. She died Oct. 23, 1746, and he married 2d,
   Oct. 8, 1747, Sarah Willcox. Lived in Upper Middletown. Died
   Oct. 17, 1761, by a fall from an apple tree near his house. His
   widow married, Oct. 25, 1765, Aaron Eels. Children:

   i. LYDIA,[5] bap. Oct. 19, 1746; m. April 2, 1765, Capt. Samuel Treat.
   ii. PATIENCE, bap. July 31, 1748; d. young.
   iii. JOSEPH, bap. Oct. 1, 1749.
   iv. LUTHER, bap. March 22, 1752; m. July 17, 1775, Sarah Goodrich, of
       New Britain. He removed to Kensington.
   v. JOHN, called 3d son in distribution of his father's estate. Probably
       served in the Revolution.

11. ELISHA[4] STOCKING (*Daniel,[3]* Deacon *Samuel,[2] George[1]*), married 1st,
   Jan. 26, 1737, Rachel Ranney. She died March 16, 1739, and he
   married 2d, Feb. 15, 1740, Margery Willcox. She died June 29,
   1757, and he married 3d, Feb. 4, 1758, Thankful Butler. Lived in
   Upper Middletown. Was quartermaster of troop of horse in militia.
   Died April 4, 1775. Children:

   i. LUCY,[5] b. June 10, 1737; m. Nov. 27, 1755, Thomas Kirby.
   ii. GRACE, b. Feb. 28, 1739; m. 1760, Nathaniel Savage.
   iii. Captain ZEBULON, bap. April 4, 1742; d. April 15, 1783; m. April
        10, 1765, Martha Edwards. Children: 1. *Lucy,[6]* b. May 5, 1765;
        m. April, 30, 1788, Hezekiah Warner. 2. *David,[6]* bap. March 1,
        1767. 3. *Lucretia,[6]* bap. Feb. 17, 1769; m. May 4, 1790, Hezekiah
        Kirby. 4. *Martha,[6]* bap. March 17, 1771; m. July 9, 1792, Israel
        Kelsey. 5. *Harriet,[6]* bap. Nov. 28, 1773. He lived in Upper
        Middletown.
   iv. THEODOSIA, bap. Feb. 23, 1745.
   v. SUBMIT, bap. Feb. 28, 1747; m. Oct. 20. 1770, Hezekiah Goodrich.
   vi. RACHEL, bap. June 29, 1749; m. Feb. 26, 1765, Capt. Eli Butler.
   vii. JOHN, bap. May 6, 1750.
   viii. ELISHA, bap. Aug. 17, 1751; d. Aug. 21, 1751.
   ix. ELISHA, bap. April 21, 1754; m. Dec. 15, 1793, Susannah Hamlin.
        Lived in Upper Middletown. Served in the Revolution.
   x. WILLIAM, bap. June 26, 1757; d. July 3, 1795; m. 1st, Elizabeth
        ———. She d. Nov. 8, 1787, and he m. 2d, Jan. 9, 1791, Anna
        Olcott. Children: 1. *Betsey,[6]* bap. July 22, 1782. 2. *Luther,[6]* bap.
        July 3, 1783. 3. *Nancy,[6]* bap. Nov. 28, 1784. 4. *Fanny,[6]* b. Nov. 1,
        1785. 5. *William,[6]* b. Nov. 2, 1792. 6. *George,[6]* b. Feb. 11, 1795.
        He lived in Upper Middletown.
   xi. MARGERY, bap. Jan. 7, 1759; m. Oct. 20, 1793, James Porter.

   The following of the name of Stocking, all descendants in the fifth and
sixth generation from George Stocking of Hartford, served in the Revolution: *Abner, Amasa, Ebenezer, Eber, Elisha, George, George Jr., Hezekiah,
Israel, James, John, John, Jonathan, Joseph, Marshall, Moses, Samuel* and
William. These are all mentioned in the adjutant general's list of "Connecticut Men in the Revolution," published by the State of Connecticut and
their specific services given. In addition to these the following probably
all served on Revolutionary privateers: Capt. *Abner,* who is said to have
commanded a privateer that sailed out of New York; Rev. *Jeremiah,* who
was put on board a privateer late in the war; *James* and *Nathaniel,* members of the captured crew of the "Sampson," who died in prison in New
York 1782; Capt. *John,* who spent six months in the prison-ship in New
York; and *Reuben.*

BAPTISMS IN THE SECOND CHURCH OF CHRIST IN
PEMBROKE, MASS., FROM 1748 TO 1803.

Communicated by MRS. ELROY M. AVERY of Cleveland, Ohio.

[Continued from vol. xlix., page 430.]

1774.

January	1774.	Zeheniah, son of Nathaniel Chamberlain.
March		Sarah, daughter of Samuel Howland.
"		Hannah, daughter of Hannah Cole.
"		Jacob, son of Jacob Bearse.
April		Christina, daughter of William Hayford.
"	24,	Hannah, daughter of Simeon Jones.
May	22,	Asia, son of Eleazer Hamlin.
"	22,	Calvin, son of John Thompson.
June	5,	Lurenna, daughter of John Hatch.
"		Eunice, daughter of Blaney Phillips, Jun'r.
"		John Allen, son of James Bourn.
July	3,	Chloe, daughter of Joseph Bonney.
August	14,	Elizabeth Josselyn, daughter of Seth Cocks.
"	20,	Abraham, son of Abraham Josselyn.
September		Elizabeth, daughter of Job House.
October	9,	William, son of William Cocks, Jun'r.
"		Joseph, son of Daniel Gardner, administered on account of his wife.
"	23,	Joshua, son of Joshua Barker.
"	23,	Mary, daughter of Joseph Nichols.
November		Samuel, son of John Pumpilly, baptised on account of his wife.
"	26,	Sarah Barstow, Lazarus, Alderson, children of Benjamin Ramsdell, Jun'r.

1775.

January	29, 1775.	Oliver Reed, son of Richard Smith, baptised on account of his wife Rhoda.
February	5,	Sarah, daughter of David Tilden.
"	19,	Betty, daughter of Nehemiah Ramsdell.
March	5,	Joseph, son of John Stetson, baptised on account of his wife.
"	25,	Luther, son of Ephraim Briggs.
"	26,	Hannah and Mary, twin daughters of Henry Monroe, Jun'r.
April	2,	John, son of Thomas Record.
"	9,	Levi, son of Nathaniel Chamberlain.
"	15,	Mary, daughter of Noah Perry.
May	7,	Betty, daughter of Captain Elijah Cushing.
"	7,	Job, son of Gideon Ramsdell.
"	14,	Benjamin, son of William Delano.

May	14, 1775.	Betsey, daughter of James Hatch.
"	14,	Seth, son of Howland Beals.
"	14,	Nathaniel, son of West Cole.
June	4,	Peggy, daughter of Joseph Howland, baptised on account of his wife.
July	31,	Increase, son of Deacon Increase Robinson.
August	13,	Anne Howland, daughter of Ephraim Lindsey.
"	13,	Rachel, daughter of Joseph Hanks, baptism administered on account of his wife.
"	27,	Ruth, daughter of John Thomas.
September	10,	Elizabeth, daughter of John Thompson.
November	19,	Warren, child of Samuel Howland.
December	10,	Joseph, son of (Jacob?) Gannett.

1776.

January	26, 1776.	Sarah, daughter of Eleazer Hamlin.
February	25,	Mary, daughter of Widow Hannah Phillips baptised on the Sabbath after the death of her husband.
"	25,	Gershom, son of Gershom Ramsdell.
March	24,	Ruben, son of Ruben Clark.
April	21,	Sophia, daughter of Gammelial Bisbee.
May	5,	Betty, daughter of Thomas Record.
"	26,	Gad, son of Lindes Tower, offered for baptism by Gersham Ramsdell and wife who have the care of the child.
June	2,	Mary, daughter of Matthew Whitten, Jun'r.
"	9,	Isaac and Harlow, sons of Samuel Harding, baptism administered on account of his wife.
"	16,	Sally, daughter of Richard Smith, baptism administered on account of his wife.
July	21,	Abner, son of Abraham Josselyn.
August	18,	Thirsa, Daughter of John Hatch.
"	25,	James, son of James White Cushing.
"	25,	Will, an Indian child baptised on account of Jackson's wife.
September	1,	Nathaniel, son of Nathaniel Thomas.
"	22,	Nathaniel, son of Joseph Bonney.
October	20,	Perez, son of Joseph Howland, on account of his wife.
"	27,	Anna Stockbridge, daughter of Thomas Josselyn, Jun'r.
"	27,	Polly, a child offered by William Cocks and wife as the care of it is committed to them.
November	3,	Samuel, son of Job House.
"	3,	Nathaniel, son of Major David Tilden.

1777.

January	25, 1777.	Ruth, daughter of Elisha Records.
April	6,	Joseph, son of Joshua Barker.
"	6,	Rachel, daughter of Zadoc Reed.
"	20,	Sarah, daughter of Gideon Ramsdell.
May	18,	Cloe, daughter of Nathaniel Chamberlain.

May	18, 1777.	Levi, son of William Hayford.
"	18,	Benjamin, son of Benjamin Monroe.
"	25,	Elijah Turner, son of Nathaniel Cushing.
June	2,	Rachel, daughter of Capt. Elijah Cushing.
"	2,	Gershum, son of Gershum Ramsdell.
"	8,	Nathaniel, son of William Delano.
"	14,	Christopher, son of Christopher Phillips.
"	22,	Sarah, daughter of John Thompson.
July	12,	Orphy, daughter of Lemuel Bonney.
"	27,	Lucy, daughter of Ephraim Briggs.
"	27,	Louise, daughter of Gamaliel Bisbee.
August	24,	John, son of Ephraim Lindsey.
"	24,	Anne, daughter of Howland Beals.
"	31,	Priscilla, daughter of Edward Hayford of Bridge-water.
September	14,	Enoch, son of Jacob Gannet.
"	28,	Cynthia, daughter of Thomas Record.
October	26,	Abigail, daughter of Benjamin Barnes.
November	9,	Nathaniel, son of Capt. James Hatch.
December	26,	Samuel, son of Samuel Ramsdell.

1778.

February	1, 1778.	Daniel, child of Doct. Daniel Childs.
March	29,	Eli, son of Alexander Soper, Jun'r.
April	26,	Rebecca, daughter of Noah Cole, baptised on account of his wife.
May	24,	Jonathan Bisbee, son of Joseph Nichols.
June	24,	Margaret, daughter of Matthew Whitten, Jun'r.
"	28,	Sylvina, daughter of Samuel Harding, administered on account of his wife.
July	5,	Jonathan, son of Samuel Howland.
"	26,	Nathaniel Twynge, son of Major David Tilden.
		Harvey, son of Lot Stetson.
August	26,	Mary, daughter of Job House.
September	27,	Henry, son of Henry Monroe, Jun'r.
October	18,	Elizabeth, daughter of Adam Perry.
"	30,	Barnabus, son of Barnabas Jackson.
November	8,	Betsey, daughter of Ruben Clarke.
"	29,	Betsey, daughter of Gersham Ramsdell.
December	20,	Betsey, daughter of Nathaniel Thomas.

1779.

February	7, 1779.	Edward, son of John Thomas.
"	21,	Dorothy, daughter of Doct. Gad Hitchcock.
"	21,	Joseph, son of Henry Monroe, Jun'r.
March	14,	Simeon, son of Zadoc Reed.
April	14,	Nancy, daughter of William Cocks, Jun'r.
"	11,	Sylvester, daughter of Joseph Bonney.
"	11,	Sarah, daughter of Nathaniel Chamberlain.
"	11,	Thomas, son of Elisha Records.
"	11,	John, son of Richard Smith, adminstered on his wife's account.

May	2, 1779.	Ruth, daughter of Doct. Daniel Childs.
"	2,	William, son of William White, baptism administered on account of his wife.
"	15,	Lydia, daughter of Ephraim Briggs.
"	15,	Ethelbert, daughter of Widow Anne Lindsey, born a few months after her husband's death.
"	23,	Elizabeth, daughter of Joshua Barker.
June	7,	Peddy, daughter of Joseph Howland, baptism administered on account of his wife.
"	13,	Rizpey, daughter of Gamaliel Bisbee.
"	13,	Ruth, daughter of Jos. Waterman.
"	20,	Olive, daughter of Adam Perey.
September	21,	Silvanus, son of Captain Joseph Smith.
October	31,	Richard, son of Samuel Hill.
December	5,	Tracey(?), son of Benjamin Barnes.

1780.

March	26, 1780.	Fanny, daughter of Doct. Gad Hitchcock.
April	16,	Ezra, son of Lot Phillips, baptism administered on his account only.
"	20,	Levi, son of Samuel Ramsdell, Jun'r.
May	7,	Isaac, son of Captain Elijah Cushing.
"	28,	Cyrus, son of Benjamin Monroe.
June	4,	Isaac, son of Richard Lowden.
July	2,	Cloe, daughter of Mathew Whitten.
"	2,	Nathan, son of Nathan Stephens.

[Leaves seem to be missing from the book and the next baptism recorded is Nov. 9, 1783.—Mrs. E. M. A.]

1783.

| November | 9, 1783. | Mary, daughter of John Barstow. |
| " | 23, | Daniel, son of Noah Perrey. |

1784.

May	30, 1784.	Lucy, daughter of Richard Smith, administered on account of his wife.
June	6,	Edward, son of Nathan Stevens, administered on account of his wife.
"	27,	Oliver, son of Nathaniel Chamberlain.
July	4,	Sylvia, daughter of Mathew Whitten, Jun'r.
August	1,	Clarissa, daughter of Joseph Bonney.
"	8,	Susannah, daughter of Abel Bourn.
"	8,	Lydia, daughter of Isaac Keen, die eod ' et anno.
September	5,	Lucy, daughter of Alexander Soper, Jun'r.
"	12,	Lowis, daughter of Leonard Hill.
"	26,	Anne, daughter of Capt. Elisha Cushing.
October	10,	Crowell, son of Noah Bonney.
"	24,	James, son of Job House.
November	7,	Lucy, daughter of Nathaniel Clark.
December	5,	Mary, daughter of Benjamin Barnes.

1785.

April	8, 1785.	Samuel, son of Samuel Howland.
"	24,	Susey, daughter of Capt. Isaah Stetson, on account of his wife.
May	1,	Lewis, son of Christopher Phillips.
"	15,	Lupira, daughter of Gamaliel Bisbee.
"	22,	Lettice, daughter of Joshua Barker.
June	5,	Francis, son of Francis Josselyn.
July	3,	James, son of Henry Monroe, Jun'r.
"	10,	Lucia, daughter of Capt. Joseph Smith.
		———(?) Hatch, daughter of Deborah Hatch.
August	14,	Joshua Pratt, Jun'r, an adult.
"	21,	Samuel, Matilda, Alpheus, John, Levi, Mercy, Joshua, children of Joshua Pratt, Jun'r.
"	21,	Abigail, daughter of Benjamin Mouroe.
"	21,	Lucinda, and Benjamin, children of ——— Stetson, baptised on account of Hannah Stetson, his wife.
September	11,	Anna, daughter of Zadoc Reed.
"	18,	Anna, daughter of Joseph Barstow.
October	2,	Mehitabel, daughter of Mathew Whiten, Jun'r.
"		Mary, daughter of Richard Smith, baptism administered on account of his wife.
November	27,	Lydia, danghter of Jeremiah Stetson, Jun'r.

1786.

March	26, 1786.	Mary, daughter of Nathaniel Thomas.
April	29,	Hannah, Charles, John, children of Calley and Margaret his wife, baptised on account of Margaret.
May	9,	Lydia, daughter of Lot Phillips, baptised on account of the father.
"	14,	Lydia, daughter of Eleazer Josselyn.
"	14,	Rebecca, daughter of Reuben Hardin, baptised on account of his wife.
June	4,	Betty, daughter of Doct. Gad Hitchcock.
"	11,	Priscilla, daughter of James Bourn, Jun'r.
July	2,	Nathan Turner, son of Nathan Sprague.
"	9,	Joseph, son of Joseph Thomas.
"	30,	Benjamin, son of Benjamin Pratt, Jun'r.
November	5,	Anne Cushing, daughter of Isaac Thomas.
"	26,	Hervey, child of Noah Bonney.
		Hannah, child of Nathan Hill.

1787.

April	16, 1787.	Mary, daughter of Zadoc Thomas.
May	27,	Nathaniel, son of Alexander Soper, Jun'r.
June	3,	Lucy, daughter of Samuel Briggs, baptised on account of his wife.
"	10,	Bathsheba, daughter of Capt. Joseph Smith.
"	10,	Eunice, daughter of Reuben Clarke.
July	1,	Oliver, son of Abel Bourn.

July	1, 1787.	Ruth Sprague, daughter of Isiah Keen, baptised on account of his wife.
"	8,	Chloe, daughter of Isiah Stetson, administered on account of his wife.
"	8,	Peter, son of Francis Josselyn.
August	25,	Salome Barstow, son of Samuel Harding, administered on account of his wife.
"	25,	John Hatch, son of Ichabod Howland.
September	9,	Nathaniel, son of William Collamore.
"	9,	Benjamin, son of Thomas Stetson.
"	16,	Phebe, daughter of Gamaliel Bisbee.
"	30,	Margaret, daughter of Henry Munroe.
October	7,	Beckey, daughter of Benjamin Beuker, administered on account of his wife.
"	14,	Sarah, daughter of George William Munroe.

1788.

March	8, 1788.	Abner, son of Benjamin Studley.
"	8,	Sylvester, daughter of Benjamin Studley.
May	2,	Gad, son of Doct. Gad Hitchcock.
"	18,	Benjamin, son of John Thomas.
"	18,	Eleazer, son of Eleazer Josselyn.
June	1,	Wealthy, daughter of Nathaniel Thomas.
"	1,	Samuel, son of Joseph Barstow.
"	15,	Jeremiah, son of Jeremiah Stetson, Jun'r.
"	15,	Seth, son of Seth Harding, administered on account of his wife.
"	22,	Betty, daughter of Capt. Elijah Cushing.
"	22,	Lucinda, daughter of Capt. William White, baptised on account of his wife.
		Joseph, son of Joseph Howland, administered on account of his wife.
		Isaac, son of James Bourn, Jun'r.
July	6,	Deborah, daughter of Isaah Keen, administered on account of his wife.
"	13,	Celia, daughter of Nathan Sprague.
August	23,	Sally, daughter of Lot Phillips.
"	23,	Patty, daughter of Richard Lowden, Jun'r.
		Harriott, daughter of Nathaniel Clarke.
"	31,	Martin, son of Leonard Hill.
"	31,	——— (?) Cushing, daughter of Christopher Phillips.
September	28,	Lydia Cushing, daughter of Isaac Thomas.
October	12,	Nathan, son of Isaac Beals.
November	9,	Melinda, daughter of Ezekial Bonney.

1789.

April	5, 1789.	Anne Thomas, daughter of Samuel Briggs, administered on account of his wife.
"	12,	Nancy, daughter of Barnabas Holmes, administered on account of his wife.
"	19,	Nancy, daughter of Noah Bonney.
May	24,	Nathaniel, son of Nathaniel Hill.

May	24, 1789.	Thomas Hill, son of Francis Josselyn.
"	24,	Benjamin, son of Benjamin Bowker, administered on account of his wife.
June	14,	Salome, child of Charles Ramsdell.
"	21,	Jubetta, daughter of Alexander Soper.
July	5,	Abigail, daughter of Isaac Josselyn.
"	26,	Judith Miller, daughter of Capt. Joseph Smith.
August	9,	Sarah, daughter of Abel Bourn.
"	30,	Deborah, wife of George Osborn.
"	30,	Elizabeth, Levi, Ebenezer, Deborah, Baruch, the children of George Osborn.
September	20,	Bartlett, son of John Ramsdell.
November	15,	Judith, daughter of Joshua Pratt.

1790.

January	3, 1790.	Ezekial, Dodge, son of Nathaniel Cushing, Jun'r.
March	28,	Daniel, son of Doct. Gad Hitchcock.
May	2,	Deliverence Crooker, an adult.
"	20,	Calvin, son of Nathaniel Thomas.
June	6,	Sarah Osbourn, an adult.
"	27,	Luther, son of Zadoc Reed.
July	4,	Ephraim Allen, son of Eleazer Josselyn.
"	4,	Nathaniel, son of Samuel Briggs, baptism administered on account of his wife.
"	11,	Lucy, daughter of Nathaniel Clarke.
"	14,	Lydia, daughter of Isaac Beals.
September	5,	Hetty, daughter of Seth Cocks, Jun'r.
"	5,	Betty, daughter of Isaac Keen, baptism administered on account of his wife.
October		Elizabeth, daughter of Henry Monroe, Jun'r.
"	17,	Tamer, daughter of James Bourn, Jun'r.
"	17,	Rudolphus, son of Nathan Sprague.
"	31,	Lydia, daughter of Samuel Hill, Jun'r.
November	7,	Avetus, son of Gameliel Bisbee.
"	7,	Judith, daughter of Barnabas Holmes of Plymouth, administered on account of his wife.

INSCRIPTIONS AT SANTA CRUZ, CALIFORNIA, 1891.

Copied by B. Frank Leeds, Esq.

[Continued from page 51.]

Lot 23.

Carrie S., dau^r. of W. H. and M. L. Bean, died July 1, 1882, aged 5 y. 10 m. 23 d.

Lot 24.

J. Chapin Willson, born at Canandaigua, New York, died at Santa Cruz, Cal., Dec. 30, 1869.

Fredrick E. Willson, born at Canandaigua, New York, died at San Jose Cal., June 19, 1865.

Norman J. Willson, born July 1, 1857, drowned May 28, 1882.

Chapin headstone. Harry—headstone. Perhaps children of J. Chapin Willson.

Lot 25.

Alfred son of John James and Mary Elizabeth Smith, drowned in San Francisco bay, May 7, 1856, ag^d. 4 yrs.

Two other graves in same brick enclosure unmarked.

Two children's graves and a recent grave in enclosure fronting above and apparently connected.

Lot 26.

Elizabeth Hihn, born Sep. 9, 1861, died Augt. 9, 1862.

Hugo Hihn, born June 26, 1869, died Feb. 10, 1871.

Lot 27.

Mrs. C. Dreher, born Nov. 12, 1828, mother.

Minnie Dreher, b. May 8, 1858, d. April 17, 1878.

Mary Dreher, b. Jan. 13, 1856, d. June 17, 1879.

John Dreher, a native of Germany, b. Sep. 23, 1814, d. Sep. 7, 1885, ag^d. 71, 11 m. 16 days.

Infant grave unmarked.

Lot 28.

Addison, Jr., son of Addison and Sarah Newell, died Sep. 10, 1862, ag^d. 19 y. 2 m. 20 d.

Sarah, wife of Addison Newell, d. Sep. 7, 1890, in the 74 year of her age. Native of Maine.

Lot. 29.

Sophia Elizabeth, wife of William White, born at Honolulu, S. I., July 4, 1836, died May 26, 1863.

Lot 30.

Henry Van Valkenburgh, died Jan. 13, 1862, aged 33 years.

Lot 31.

Mary Eli Day, wife of Joseph Perkins, d. Apr. 12, 1868, aged 61 years. Infant grave alongside unmarked.

Lot 32.

Henry Rice, aged 80 years.

Frances Minerva Thompson, b. Apr. 12, 1863, d. Dec. 25, 1865.

Franklin Wilson Rice, beloved son of H. and L. M. Rice, aged 19 years.

Walter H. Rice.

H. R.

Lot 33.

Helen Mary Williams, mother, d. Jan. 22, 1881, aged 83 years.

Alice, 1874.	
A. J. D., 1882.	
Helen, 1883.	Children perhaps of H. M. Williams.
John, 1887.	
Louis, 1889.	

Lot 34.

Margaret E., wife of James B. Harris, d. Jan. 2, 1870, aged 20 y. 8 m. 14 d.

William F. Jenkins, d. Mch. 22, 1870, ag^d. 59 y. 9 m. 5 d.

Lot 35.

Barbara Corbett, native of Scotland, aged 77.
Maryan Corbett.
Wood.

Lot 36.

P. W.
Wood.
A child's grave and another grave unmarked.

Lot 37.

Clara Belle, wife of H. W. Bassett, b. Sep. 30, 1864, d. Oct. 24, 1884.

Lot 38.

J. C. Marshall, aged 21 years, 7 months.

Lot 39.

Henry Pearce, died Feb. 8, 1887, aged 53 years.

Lot 40.

Otto N. Claussen, native of Germany, d. Mch. 24, 1878.

Lot 41.

Anna Marie, wife of J. F. Holtzman, born Sep. 5, 1845, died July 9, 1878, aged 52 (32) y. 10 m. 4 d.

Lot 42.

Helen Frances Twichell, b. Feb. 28, 1838, d. July 10, 1877, ag^d. 40 y. 4 m. 10 d.

Lot 43.

Alonz. Witham, of Embden, Maine, d. May 16, 1863, aged 27 y. 4 m. 9 d.

Lot 44.

John Spier, son of the late Robert Spier, builder, of Montreal, Canada, died at Santa Cruz, Cal., 1872.

Lot 45.

Charles Tinkham, d. Apr. 23, 1890, aged 74 years, a native of Massachusetts.

Lot 46.

John Keeney, son of Jerome Keeney, born in New London, Conn.

Lot 47.

Hugo Kuppe, d. Dec. 30, 1889, aged 32 years.

Lot 48.

Oscar Hader, died Oct. 14, 1888, aged 6 years.

Lot 49.

Maranda Moon, wife of Charles Carvalho, born Jan. 2, 1812, died Dec. 9, 1880.

Charles Carvalho, born Nov. 5, 1807, died May 17, 1888.

Lot 50.

Marie Christine Barbier, born at Valtin, Vosges, France, died at Loquel, Sta. Cruz Co. Oct. 9, 1879, aged 48 years.

Inscription in French.

Lot 51.

John P. Lykins, b. Oct. 9, 1854, d. Dec. 27, 1882, aged 28 y. 2m. 18 d.

Armenia Nancy Lykins, b. Dec. 30, 1881, d. Mch. 14, 1883, aged 14, 2 m. 14 d.

Lot 52.

Emily, beloved wife of H. D. Hollingsworth, daughter of W. B. Disbrow, died May 3, 1888, aged 29 years 8 days.

Clara P., wife of R. S. McGinty, dau^r. of W. B. Disbrow, died Dec. 16, 1878, aged 22 years.

Lot 53.

Our Baby, infant son of Mr. and Mrs. C. A. Reynolds.

Three other graves unmarked.

Lot 54.

Siddie.

Kittie.

Lot 55.

H. H. Gray, died Aug. 26, 1876, aged 50 years.

Lot 56.

Ellen Shaw, wife of Charles Storrar, d. Feb. 6, 1869, aged 66 years.

Charles Storrar, died June 2, 1873, aged 73 years.

Charles Hogquist, died April 10, 1877, aged 47 years.

Lot 57.

Louden Nelson, a native of Tennessee, b. May 5, 1800, d. May 12, 1866.

"He was a colored man and willed all his property to Santa Cruz School District No. 1."

Lot 58.

Luis La Pierre, son of Luis and Teresa La Pierre, died Dec. 6, 1874, aged 18 years.

A wooden cross.

Lot 59.

John Coveny, native of City of Cork, Ireland, died Sep. 13, 1875, aged 55 years.

Wood.

Lot 60.

J. R. B.

Wood.

Lot 61.

Isaiah Pitman, son of Thomas and Caroline Pitman Carleton, Yarmouth, Nova Scotia, born Feb. 13, 1847, died at Santa Cruz, Cal., Feb. 26, 1876, ag^d. 30 yrs.

Lot 62.

Charley, infant son of Joseph and Mary Reppata, died Apr. 12, 1877, aged 5½ mos.

Lot 63.

Ida May Schenk, born May 7, 1876, d. Apr. 19, 1877.

Lot 64.

Ruthie H. Kimball, died June 8, 1877 ag^d. 3 years 10 mos.

Lot 65.

Robbie R. Senate, only child of Harry L. and Jane E. Senate, died June 27, 1877, aged 5 y. 9 m, 27 d.

Lot 66.

Emma, wife of W. J. Dean, died May 25, 1877, aged 34 years.

[To be continued.]

ALPHABETICAL LIST OF PARTNERS IN THE LAND BANK OF 1740.

By ANDREW McFARLAND DAVIS, S.B., of Cambridge, Mass.

A RECENT examination of the papers connected with the Land Bank of 1740 has enabled me to construct a list of those who were interested in this unfortunate financial experiment. The names of the directors, given in Drake's Boston, have been referred to by subsequent writers as though they were all who were connected with the affair. So great a misconception of the magnitude of this extraordinary folly needs correction. For this purpose it might perhaps be enough to refer to the supplement to the News Letter issued January 2, 1745-46. The long list of names of subscribers to the Land Bank therein contained would be in itself an adequate correction of this error, and if this were all that was involved one might be content with this reference, especially since after the destruction of the papers of the commissioners of the Land Bank when the court house was burned in 1747, this very list was by Act of the Assembly in 1748 declared to contain a true and exact account of the partners in the late Land Bank scheme. Notwithstanding this declaration there were numerous subscribers whose names can be obtained from other sources, but do not appear in the columns of the News Letter. It may seem to be a matter of comparatively little interest who were directly interested in this attempt to issue a currency based upon real estate. Yet when we reflect that for several years their numbers were so great that they were able to control the House of Representatives, and their influence in many of the towns was so powerful that the towns voted to take Land Bank notes for town rates, we must admit that they carried with them the sympathies of the people in their efforts to furnish what they termed a medium of trade. If in these attempts to establish the Land Bank they had the good wishes of a majority of the voters of the Province, we cannot doubt that the same influences aroused popular indignation when the scheme was suppressed through the extension to the colonies of an Act of Parliament passed twenty years previously, which by its terms could never have been interpreted to apply to the Province of the Massachusetts Bay. Indeed, during the interval between the passage of the original act, which is generally called the Bubble Act of 1720, and the act through which it was declared to be in force and to have been in force all the time in the colonies, both the Board of Trade and the Attorney-General had placed themselves on record as being ignorant of any legislation through which proceedings like the organization of the Land Bank could be reached. It was essential, therefore, for Parliament to legislate that acts which were not in violation of any known statute were illegal and had been illegal from their inception. The means by which this was accomplished was to declare that the Bubble Act had from its passage applied to the colonies. This Parliamentary action brought to the attention of the subscribers to the Land Bank and their sympathizers, not only what Hutchinson terms the transcendent power of Parliament, but also the will of Parliament to use this power in a way that was unreasonable and even tyrannical. It must have led men to question whether they could abide the exercise of any such power. It prepared them for resistance when they deemed such exercise unreasonable, and fostered the spirit which found expression when the attempt was made to raise revenue through a stamp act and a tax on tea. When we reflect, therefore, upon what was involved in being a subscriber to the Land Bank, we can readily see that many of the men whose names are to be found there must have been ready to follow the lead of any strong mind which could point out to them the means of protecting themselves from tyranny of this sort. This may prove a compensation to those who shall find the name of some ancestor associated with this absurd folly.

The list which I submit is prepared from numerous papers in the Massachusetts Archives and the Suffolk County Files. The documents upon which I have especially relied may be subdivided into Lists of Subscribers furnished by the company, Lists of Subscribers made up by the commissioners, and Lists of Mortgagors furnished by the Registers of Deeds. In addition to these sources of information, proceedings instituted by the Attorney General, suits by possessors of bills and by the commissioners, warrants of distress issued by the commissioners, and fragments of the accounts of the commissioners, have been found to be of assistance. The names upon the list thus made up from manuscript sources have been checked with those to be found in the list in the supplement of the News Letter, which was made official by the Act of the Assembly after the burning of the court house.

The phonetic spelling in some of the papers would indicate that the names were called off by one person and inscribed by another. I have grouped together names of widely different orthography, where this seemed to me a plausible explanation of the eccentricities of the compilers of the lists, but in order that those who wish to make use of the list may be put upon their guard, I have indicated the various spellings under which the names have been found. The peculiarities of the chirography are in some instances also a source of doubt as to what the writer was actually trying to put down, but in the main I think the solution which I have adopted may be relied on.

In some instances the residence of the subscriber seems to have been in doubt. The subscribers from Woodstock are for instance sometimes put down as from Worcester. It will be remembered that in the days of the bank Woodstock was set off to Connecticut, and this will explain why the residence was changed in the return to Worcester, the place where the mortgage was recorded. In other instances the subscribers changed their residences. During these protracted proceedings there was plenty of opportunity for this, and it is rather a source of surprise to find so few with alternative residences than of wonder that we should find as many as we do. In a few instances I have found a name in one of the company's lists which was not repeated in the other, but in the second I have found a name of somewhat different spelling which I have thought was in all probability intended for the same person as the one described by the name in question in the other list. Where I have felt doubtful in such cases I have put both names down, giving a cross reference with the second entry.

In order that some knowledge might be gained of the participation of subscribers in this affair I have given references to the more important of the papers in which each name is to be found. From these it will be seen that there were quite a number of persons who were original subscribers, but who did not proceed beyond that point, while on the other hand there were many who did not come in at first, but who joined in the affair at a later date and suffered in consequence.

The total number of names on this list, throwing out those which are merely inserted as cross references, is twelve hundred and fifty-two. The list which is referred to as B in my references is undoubtedly the oldest of the two company lists. Throwing out duplicate entries there are three hundred and eighty names transferred from it to these pages. It is in all probability the list which was submitted to the General Court at the December session, 1739, when application was made for a charter, as was then stated, by John Colman and three hundred and ninety-five others. Felt arranged the papers in the archives according to the latest date that he could find upon them, and in pursuance of that plan he placed this document after the one which I refer to as A. The number of entries which I have obtained from A is nine hundred and twenty, which was about the number of subscribers just after their organization in the fall of 1740. Notwithstanding the fact that there is no date upon it to indicate that it should be placed in the archives in chronological sequence among the papers of that date, it cannot be doubted that it belongs there. Both of these lists were made up by the officers of the company. The list referred to as O was found among the papers of the commissioners. The names entered therein are arranged alphabetically and number eight hundred and nine. The supplement of the News Letter of January 1745–46 contains eight hundred and twenty-one names, which correspond very closely with those in list O.

Of the three hundred and eighty names which appear in B, sixteen are not to be found in any other list. One hundred and eighty-nine are to be found only in A, and twenty-seven are entered only in A and B. Altogether, then, we have the names of two hundred and thirty-two persons whose enthusiasm died out before they were called upon to take any of the notes of the Land Bank, and who although they were subscribers did not go beyond that step. Deducting this number from our total, we have one thousand and twenty as the number of those who can be demonstrated to have actually participated in the scheme. Of these, four names are furnished by a list of Partners who have paid their assessments, referred to as N; nineteen names are derived solely from the alphabetical list, referred to as O; eleven are gained from the lists of mortgages returned to the Governor by the Registers of Deeds; nineteen are found only in the files and records of Suffolk County, in some of the various legal proceedings against the Partners; and three names are only to be met with in the list published by the commissioners in the News Letter.

The length of the list would have been much extended if I had not in many instances consolidated, under one heading, names which if entered by careful clerks I should have been compelled to enter separately. Bridgham does not of necessity stand for Brigham. Fayerback would not ordinarily be interpreted Fairbank. Gutridge suggests Goodridge, but would not be refused a separate entry if one had full respect for the clerk who wrote the name. Naulton when written does not of itself bring before us Knowlton. Lece and Lee, Rist and Rice, Robertson, Roberson and Robinson are not respectively so much alike that they could not be awarded separate entries. Yet I have run them together, being governed in my conclusions somewhat by the different lists in which the names were found, the association with Christian names and with places of residence. In the case of Robertson and Robinson I have been unable to make any distinction, although it is possible that a person familiar with the family record might do so. If Muzzey is properly associated with Murray it must be due of course to chirography. The name certainly looks like Muzzey, and yet it only furnishes one link in the entries for Murray. There is, however, sufficient indication of my handiwork in making these consolidations to put the genealogist upon his guard.

It has been my intention to preserve every name which appears in A, B, O, in the mortgage returns, or in the official list in the News Letter. The Suffolk files have only been referred to where they contribute a new name or add information as to an old one.

Table of References.

The reference letters following each name in the subjoined list are intended to reveal the paper upon which the entry is founded. By examining the accompanying table the reader can ascertain the several sources of authorities designated by the respective letters.

A	Mass. Archives	102,	44.	List of Subscribers, Feb. 29, 1739-40—with amount of assessment in cash.				920 names
B	"	"	102,	46.	List of Subscribers.	March 1739-40	380	"
C	"	"	102,	103.	Suffolk Registry returns	Dec. 19 1740	122	"
D	"	"	102,	109.	Middlesex "	" Dec. 22 "	119	"
E	"	"	102,	117.	Essex "	" Dec. 30 "	115	"
F	"	"	102,	120.	Barnstable "	" " "	10	"
G	"	"	102,	122.	Worcester "	" Jan. 1 1741	165	"
H	"	"	102,	128.	" "	" 5 "	8	"
I	"	"	102,	129.	Plymouth "	" 5 "	42	"
J	"	"	102,	138.	Bristol "	" 27 "	50	"
K	"	"	102,	142.	Worcester "	" March 5 "	17	"
L	"	"	102,	143.	Hampshire "	" 9 "	7	"
M	"	"	102,	144.	Worcester "	" 13 "	19	"
N	"	"	136,	83-99.	List of some of the Partners who have paid their assessments.				580
O	"	"	136,	100-112.	Alphabetical List of Land Bank Subscribers.				823

P   Mass. Archives 270, 755–768.   List of Delinquents.
Q   "   "   104, 496.   Report of Commissioners.
R   "   "   Suffolk Court Files and Records.
S   "   "   News Letter, Nov. 15, 1744.   Jan˟ 2, 1745–46.

PARTNERS IN THE LAND BANK.

ABBOTT.
Jonathan, Andover. G.
ADAMS, ADDAMS, ADDAM.
Benjamin. A.
Joseph, Concord. A, B, D, N, O, S.
Josiah, Mendon. A, B, G, N, O, R, S.
Nathaniel, Dedham. A.
Samuel, Boston, A, B, N, O, P, S.
Thomas, Ipswich. E, N, O, S.
William, Rowley or Beverly. A, B, E,
   N, O, S.
ALDEN.
Daniel, Jr., Bridgewater. A, B, R.
ALDRICH, ALDRIDGE, ALLERIDGE.
Edward, Uxbridge. A, B, G, O, S.
Jacob, Uxbridge. A, B, G, N, O, Q, S.
Seth, Uxbridge. A, G, N, O, S.
ALLEN.
Daniel, Bridgewater. N, O, S.
Jacob, Bridgewater. A. N. O. S.
James, Chilmark. P. R. S.
Jeremiah, Rehoboth. A, J, N, O, S.
John, Jr., Braintree. A, C, O, P, R, S.
Jonathan. A, B.
Joseph, Chilmark. A, O.
Nehemiah. A.
Samuel, Manchester. A, E, N, O, S.
Thomas, Gloucester. E, N, O, R, S.
Thomas Allert. A.
AMADOWN, AMIDOWN.
Ichabod. A, B.
AMES.
Nathaniel, Dedham. A, C, N, O, R, S.
ANDREWS.
Nathaniel. A.
Samuel, Dighton. A, J, O, P, S.
ARNOLD.
Joseph, Stoneham. A, D, N, O, S.
ASHLEY.
Israel. A.
Noah. A, R.
ASPINWALL, ASPINALL, ASPINWELL,
   ASPINWAL.
Nathaniel, Woodstock. A, G, N, O, S.
Thomas, Brookline. A, B, C, N, O, S.
ATHERTON.
John. A.
Peter. A, B.
ATKIN.
Joseph. R.
ATWOOD, ATTWOOD.
John, Eastham. A, F, O, P, S.
AUCHMUTY.
Robert, Boston. A, B, N, O, S.

BADKOCK, BADCOCK.
Nathan. A, B.

BAILEY, BALEY, BAYLEY.
Israel. A, B.
Josiah, Lunenberg. A, B, G, N, Q, S.
Sarah, Lunenberg. O.
BAKER.
Isaac, Eastham. A, F, O, S.
John, Boxford. E, O, S.
Obadiah, Swanzey. N, O, R, S.
Thomas, Lynn. A, E, N, O, S.
Thomas, Topsfield. O, R, S.
BALCOM, BOLCOM.
Barrack or Beyrack. A, B.
BALDWIN, BALDEN.
Daniel. A.
David, Leicester. A, G, N, O, S.
Isaac. A, B.
John, Mendon. A.
Samuel, Leicester. G, N, O, S.
BALL, BALD.
Nathaniel, Concord. A, B, D, N, O, S.
BARBER.
Hezekiah, Dorchester. A, C, N, O, S.
Robert, Worcester. A, B, G, N, O, S.
BARKER.
Caleb, Hanover. N, O, R, S.
Daniel, Boston. A, N, O, S.
BARRETT, BARRET.
Isaiah, Boston. C, N, O, S.
Joseph, Chelmsford. A, B, N, O, S.
BATCHELER, BATCHELLER, BATCHEL-
   LOR, BATCHELOR, BATCHELTER.
David, Grafton. A, B, G, O, S.
Joseph, Wenham. A, N, O, S.
John, Lancaster. G, N, O, R, S.
Joseph, Dorchester. A, B, C, N, O, S.
BEAL, BEALE.
Benjamin, Braintree. A, B, C, N, O,
   R, S.
Lazarus. A.
BEAMAN.
Edmond. A.
BEDUNAH.
Benjamin. A, B.
BEIGHTON.
John, Dorchester. A, B, C, N, O, S.
BELCHER.
Clifford, Stoughton. A, B, C, N, O, S.
Jonathan, Chelsea. C, N, O, R, S.
Moses. A.
BELKNAP, BELNAP.
Samuel, Woburn. A, D, N, O, R, S.
BENNETT, BENNIT, BENNET.
Joseph. A.
Samuel, Middleborough. A, I, N, P, S.
BENSON.
Benoni, Mendon. A, G, N, O, S.

BENT.
Joseph, Milton. A, B, C, N, O, S.
Thomas, Sudbury. A, B, N, O, S.
BERRY.
Joseph, Framingham. A, D, N, O, S.
BIGELOW, BIGLO.
Daniel, Worcester. A, B, G, N, O, S.
Joshua, Weston. A, D, N, O, S.
BILLING.
Elkanah. A.
BIRT.
Daniel, Brimfield. A.
BISBEE, BISBE, BISBY.
Elisha, Pembroke. I, N, O, S.
John, Pembroke. I, N, O, S.
BLANCHARD, BLANCHER.
Hezekiah, Boston. A, O, R, S.
John, Weymouth. A, B, C, O, S.
Joseph, Dunstable. O, P, S.
Joseph, Littleton. A, D, N, O, R, S,
Nathaniel, Weymouth. A, B, C, N, P,S.
Samuel, Malden. D, O, S.
BLANEY, BLANY.
Benjamin, Malden. C, D, N, O, R, S.
BLOOD.
John, Concord. A, D, N, O, S.
Jonathan, Concord. A, B, D, O, S.
BLOWER, BLOWERS.
John, Boston. A, B, C, N, O, S.
BOARDMAN.
John, Ipswich. A, E, N, O, S.
BOLSTER, BOTSTER.
Isaac, Uxbridge. A, G, N, O, Q, S.
BOND.
Edward, Leicester. N, O, S.
BOSWORTH.
Henry, Mendon. A, B, G, O, P, R, S.
BOUND.
James. A, B.
BOWDITCH.
John. A, B.
BOWEN.
William. A, B.
BOYCE.
Benjamin, Jr., Mendon. G, P, R, S.
David, Mendon. G, O, P, R, S.
BOYDEN, BOYDON.
Benjamin, Jr., Mendon. O.
Daniel, Worcester. A, B, G, N, O, S.
John, Worcester, A, B, G, N, O, S.
Joseph. A, B.
BOYNTON.
Hilkiah. B.
BRACKETT.
Richard, Braintree. P, R.
BRECK.
Edward. A, B.
BREED.
Allen. A.
BREWER.
Daniel, Framingham. N, O, S.
BRIGHAM, BRIDGHAM.
Charles. A.
Samuel, Sudbury. A, B, O, S.

BRINTNALL, BRENTNALL, BRINTNAL,
BRENTNAL.
Benjamin, Chelsea. N, O, R, S.
John, Chelsea, C, O, S.
Paul, Sudbury. A, B, D, O, P, R, S.
Peneas or Phyneas. A, B.
BROWN, BROWNE.
Eleazer, Salem. A, E, N, O, S.
Ephraim, Stow. A, D, N, O, S.
John, Ipswich. A, D, N, R, S.
John, Leicester. A, G, N, O, S.
John, Newbury. A.
John, Watertown. A, D, N, O, R, S.
John, Jr., Ipswich. A, E.
Josiah, Cambridge. A, B, D, N, O, P,
R, S.
Luke, Worcester. A, G, N, O, S.
Samuel, Leicester or Stockbridge. A,
G, N, O, Q, R, S.
Timothy. A.
William, Leicester. A, G, O, S.
William, Newbury. A.
Zachariah, Leicester. A, G, O, S.
BRYANT.
Jonathan, Boston. O, P, R, S.
Samuel, Scituate. A, N, O, R.
BUCKLEY.
John. A, B.
BUCKMISTER.
Col. Joseph. A.
BUCKNAM, BUCKMAN.
Samuel, North Yarmouth. A, B, N,
O, S.
BUFFUM, BUFFAM.
Joshua, Salem. A, E, N, O, S.
BUGG.
Daniel. A.
BULLIN.
David. A.
BULLOCK.
Daniel, Rehoboth. N, O, R, S.
William, Rehoboth. N, O, S.
BURBANK.
Ebenezer, Suffield. O, P, R, S.
BURBEEN.
James, Boston. O, P, R, S.
BURGE.
Josiah, Westford, A, D, N, O, S.
Samuel, Wareham. A, O, P, S.
BURLEY, BURLEIGH.
Andrew, Ipswich. A, E, N, O, S.
BURNAP.
David, Hopkinton. A, D, N, O, S.
Jonathan, Hopkinton. A, D, N, O, R, S.
BURNET.
Samuel, Middleboro'. O.
BURR.
John, Bridgewater. A, I, N, O, S.
BUXTON.
John, Salem. E, N, O, S.
BYENTON.
Hilkiah. A. (See Boynton?)
BYLES, BOYLES.
Charles, Gloucester. E, N, O, S.

BYRAM, BYRUM, BYRAN.
Ebenezer, Bridgewater. I, O, S.
Josiah. A, B.

CALEF.
Joseph. R.
CALL.
Samuel, Oxford. G, O, P, R, S.
CANROE.
Samuel. A.
CAPEN, CAPAN, CAPON.
Edward, Dorchester. A, B, C, N, O, R, S.
John, Dorchester. A, O, R, S.
Samuel, Dorchester. O, R, S.
Samuel, Leicester. A, B, G, N, O, S.
CAPRON.
Banfield, Bellingham. O, P, R, S.
CARNEY.
John, Sudbury. R.
CARPENTER.
Eliphalet, Woodstock. A, N, O, P, R, S.
William, Attleborough. N, O, S.
CARR.
John. A.
CARRY.
Stephen. A.
CARTHOM.
John. A, B.
CARVER.
Eleazer, Bridgewater. A, I, N, O, S.
CARY.
Allen, Bristol. J, O, P, R, S.
Jonathan, Bridgewater. A, I, O, P, S.
Samuel, Littleton. O.
CASWELL, CASWALL.
Jedediah, Norton. A, N, O, P, S.
John, Norton. A, N, O, R, S.
CHAFFE.
Joel, Woodstock or Worcester. A, G, O, P, R, S.
Joseph, Woodstock. G, N, O, S.
Josiah. A.
CHAMBERLAIN.
John. Chelsea. A, C, N, O, R, S.
Joseph. A.
CHANDLER.
Josiah, Bradford. E, N, O, S.
CHAPIN.
Ebenezer, Mendon. B, G, N, O, S.
John, Mendon. B, G, N, O, S.
Jonathan, Kingsfield, Kingstown or Brimfield. L, N, O, R, S.
CHARDON.
Peter, Boston. A, B, N, O, S.
CHASE.
Philip, Sutton. A, G, H, N, O, S.
CHEEVER.
Nathan, Chelsea. A, C, N, O, S.
Thomas, Lynn. A, B, N, O, R, S.
Timothy. R.
William, Lynn. A.

CHENEY.
John, Sudbury. A, B, D, N, O, S.
CHILD, CHILDS.
Ebenezer, Woodstock. A, G, N, O, P, R, S.
Jonathan, Grafton. A, B, G, O. R, S.
Joshua, Worcester. A, B, O, P, R, S.
CHOATE, CHOAT.
Francis, Ipswich. A, E, N, O, S.
John, Ipswich. A, N, O.
Robert. A.
Thomas, Jr., Ipswich. A, E, N, O, S.
CHURCH.
Benjamin. A.
Nathaniel, Dartmouth. I, O, P, S.
Richard, Rochester. A, I, N, O, S.
CLAP, CLAPP.
Ebenezer, Rochester. A, I, N, O, S.
Ebenezer, Stoughton. A, C, N, O, S.
John, Scituate. N, O, S.
Peter. P.
CLARK.
Ebenezer, Wrentham. A, C, N, O, S.
Edward, Methuen. A, E, O, R, S.
Robert, Uxbridge. A, G, N, O, P, S.
William, Jr., Townsend. A, B, D, N, O, S.
CLEAVES, CLEEVES, CLEVES.
Benjamin, Beverly. A, E, O, S.
Ebenezer, Beverly. A, B, E, O, S.
CLOUGH.
Joseph, Salem. A, N, O, S.
COBB, COBBS.
Morgan, Taunton. A, O, P, R, S.
Thomas. P.
COBLEIGH.
John, Littleton. A, D, N, O, S.
COIT, COYT.
Job, Boston. A, B, C, O, P, S.
COKER.
———. P.
COLBURN, COLBRON, COLEBURN.
Abraham. A.
Jeremiah. A.
Samuel, Dracut. A, O, R, S.
COLE.
Jonathan, Beverly. A, B, E, N, S.
COLLINS.
Rebecca, Boston. A, C, N, O, S.
COLMAN.
John, Boston. A, B, O, P, S.
COMINS, COMINGS, CUMMINS.
Jacob, Oxford. A, G, N, O, S.
Josiah, Rehoboth. O, P, R, S.
CONANT, CONNANT.
Benjamin, Dudley. A, M, N, O, S.
Lot. A. B.
William, Acton. A, B, D, N, O, S.
COOK, COOKE.
Samuel. A. B.
William, Kingston. A, I, O, P, R, S.
COOMBS.
John, Rochester or Brunswick. N, O, R, S.

COPE.
Robert, Boston. R.
CORBETT, CORBIT, CORBITT.
John, Bellingham. A, O, P, Q, R, S.
CORBIN, CORBEN.
Ebenezer. A.
Eli, Woodstock. H.
Jabez, Woodstock or Worcester. A, H, O, P, R, S.
COREY, COORY.
Samuel, Littleton. A, N, S.
CORLIS, CORLES, CORLESS.
Jonathan, Methuen. A, B, E, O, S.
CORNEY.
Samuel. B. (Perhaps same as Samuel Canroe.)
CORNING.
David, Beverly. A, B, E, N, O, S.
CORNISH.
John, Boston. C, N, O, S.
COWDREY & MORSE, Boston. S.
CRAPO, CRAPOO.
Peter, Rochester. A, I, N, O, S.
CREESY.
Benjamin, Salem. A, E, N, O, S.
Joseph, Salem. A, E, N, O, S.
CROSBIE.
Thomas. A.
CURTIS, CURTICE.
Theophilus, Stoughton. A, C, N, O, S.
CUSHING.
James, Scituate. N, R, S.
Moses, Hingham. A, B, N, O, S.
Sam., Scituate. O.
CUTLER.
James, Cambridge. A, B, D, N, O, S.

DABY.
Joseph, Stow. D, N, O, S.
DAMON.
John, Uxbridge. O.
Joseph, Uxbridge. A, B, N, S.
DANIELS.
David. A, B.
DARBY.
Andrew, Acton. A, B, D, N, O, S.
DARLING, DARLIN.
David, Wrentham. A, C, N, O, P, S.
John, Mendon. A, B, G, N, O, S.
DAVIS.
Barnabas, Littleton. A, D, G, N, O, S.
Benjamin, Gloucester. A, B, N, O, S.
Ebenezer, Harvard. A, G, N, O, S.
Eleazer. A.
Joseph, Worcester. O, P, R, S.
Joshua, Woodstock. H, P, R, S.
DAVISON, DAVIDSON, DAVINSON, DAVESON.
John, Dudley. A, M, O, R, S.
DAVY.
Joseph. A.
DAY.
Joseph, Wenham. A, R.
Timothy. A.

DEAN.
Ichabod, Taunton. A, N, O, S.
Samuel, Dedham. A, I, N, O, S.
DEATH.
Oliver, Framingham. A, B, D, N, O, S.
DELINO, DELANO, DELANA.
Jonathan. A.
Nathaniel, Dartmouth. A, I, N, O, S.
DEMING.
Joseph, Jr., Woodstock. M.
DEMMON.
Ebenezer. A.
DEWEY, DEWY.
David. A.
Moses. A.
Zedekiah. A. B.
DEWING.
Andrew, Needham. A, B, C, N, S.
DEXTER.
Ephraim, Rochester or Plymouth. A, I, N, O, R, S.
Richard, Malden. A, B, N, O, S.
DICKERMAN.
John, Stoughton. A. C, N, R, S.
John, Jr., Stoughton. A, C, N, O, W, R, S.
DODGE.
John, Beverly. A, B, N, O, S.
John, Wenham. A, E, O, S.
Josiah, Wenham, Wrentham or Worcester. E, N, O, W, R, S.
Noah, Beverly. E, O, Q, S.
Parker, Ipswich. A, E, N, O, S.
William. A.
DOGGET, DAGGET, DOGGETT.
Ebenezer (Plymouth Co.) A, I.
Isaac, Braintree. A, B, C, N, O, R, S.
DOUGLAS, DUGLASS.
Asa. A.
Noa. B.
DREW.
Thomas, Grafton. A, N.
DRURY.
Thomas, Grafton. A, O, R, S.
Zedekiah, Bedford. D, O, Q, S.
DUDLEY.
Joseph, Concord. A. B, O, R, S.
Samuel, Sutton. A, H.
DUKERMAN.
John, Stoughton. O.
DUMBLETON.
Samuel, Kingsfield. A.
DUNTON, DUNTUN, DUNTEN.
Samuel, Wrentham. C, O, R, S.
DURANT.
Abraham. A.
DURFEY.
Thomas. P.
DUTCH.
Benjamin, Ipswich. A, E, O, S.
DYER, DYRE.
Benjamin. A, B.

EAGER.
Benjamin, Shrewsbury. A, G, N, O, R, S.
EAST.
Joseph, Dracut. O, S.
EASTABROOKE, EASTERBROOK, EASTERBROOKS, ESTABROOKS, ESTABROOK.
Benjamin, Sudbury. A,B,D,N,O,R,S.
Thomas, Concord. A, B, N, O, S.
EAYRES, EYERS, EAYERS.
Moses, Boston. C, O, R, S.
EDMONDS, EDMUNDS.
Ebenezer, Dudley or Worcester. A, G, N, O, R, S.
Joseph. A.
Robert, Lynn. A, E, N, O, S.
EDSON.
Josiah, Bridgewater. I, N, O, R, S.
ELLINGWOOD.
Jonathan, Woodstock. O, P, R, S.
ELLIS.
Benjamin, Dedham. C, N, O, S.
Eleazer, Dedham. C, O, P, R, S.
Joseph, Dedham. C, O, S.
William, Dedham, C, N, O, S.
EMERSON, EMMERSON.
Ephraim, Dighton. J, O, P, S.
Nathaniel, Mendon. A, B, M, O, P, S.
ENGS.
William, Boston. A, B, C, N, O, P, R, S.
ESTY, ESTI, EASTY.
Isaac, Sutton. A, G, O, S.
Joseph, Stoughton. A, B, C, N, O, R, S.
EVELETH, EVELITH.
Edward. A.
Isaac. A, B.
James. A.

FAIRBANK, FAIRBANKS, FAYERBACH.
Joshua, Wrentham. A, C, N, O, S.
Eleazer, Sherburn. A, B, D, O, R, S.
FAIRFIELD.
John, Arundel. A, O, R, S.
FARNUM, FARNAM.
John, Uxbridge. A, B, N, O, R, S.
FARNSWORTH.
Benjamin, Groton. A, N, O, S.
Isaac, Groton. A, O, S.
Jonathan, Harvard. A, B, G, N, O, R, S.
Jonathan, Jr., Harvard. A, B, G, N, O, R, S.
FARR.
Stephen, Stow. A, B, N, O, S.
FARRAN, FARRAH.
George, Jr. A, B.
FARWELL.
Isaac, Dunstable. O, P, S.
FAUNCE, FANCE.
Joseph, Middleborough. I, O, P, S.
FAY, FAYE.
Moses, Southborough or Hopkinton, A, G, N, O, Q, R, S.

FENTON.
Thomas, Braintree. A, C, N, O, S.
FERRING.
Israel. A.
FERRY.
Mark, Brimfield. A.
FIELD.
Daniel, Bridgewater. A, O, R, S.
Job. A.
FINNEY, FINEY.
John, Norton. A, B, J, O, P, S.
Pelatiah, Bridgewater. R.
FISH.
Daniel, Dighton. N, O, S.
Stephen, Uxbridge. A, G, N, O, S.
FISHER.
John, Needham. A, O.
FLAGG.
Benjamin. A.
Eleazer. A, B.
FLINT.
Edward. A.
FLOOD.
Hugh. A.
FLOYD.
Benjamin, Chelsea. A, C, O, R, S.
Hugh, Chelsea. C, N, O. S.
John, Chelsea. A, C, N, O, S.
Samuel, Chelsea. A, C, N, O, S.
FORD, FOORD.
Cadwallader, Wilmington. A, B, D. O, S.
Hezekiah, Abington or Weymouth. A, B, I, N, O, R.
FOSTER.
John, Jr., Attleborough. O, P, R, S.
Jonathan, Attleborough. J, O, P, Q, R, S.
Moses, Littleton, Lunenberg or Dorchester Canada. N, O, R, S.
FOWLER.
Joseph, Ipswich. A, E, N, O, S.
Samuel. A.
FOX.
John, Concord. A, D, O, S.
FREEMAN.
John, Norton. A, J, O, S.
Jonathan. A.
FRENCH.
William, Billerica. A, B, D, N, O, R, S.
FRISELL, FRIZZELL.
Andrew. A, B.
FROST.
Joseph, Brimfield or Kingsfield. L, O, R, S.
FULLER, FOOLER.
John, Barnstable. A.
Thomas, Lynn. A, B, E, N, O, S.
Timothy, Middleton. A, E, N, O, R, S.

GALE.
Arthur, Boston. N, O.

GARDNER.
Daniel, Salem. A, E, O, S.
John, Ipswich or Salem. A, E, N, O, R, S.
Thomas, Needham. A, C, N, O, S.
GARKER.
John. U.
GASKILL, GASKEL, GUSKILL.
Jonathan, Mendon or Worcester. A, B, G, O, P, R, S.
GIBBS.
Isaac, Sudbury. A, B, N, O, S.
John. A.
Joseph. B.
Robert. P.
GIBSON.
Timothy, Jr. A.
GIDDINGS.
William. A.
GILBERT.
Benjamin, Ipswich. A, E, N, O, S.
John. A, B.
Joseph, Ipswich. A, E, N, O, S.
GILMORE, GILLMORE.
David, Bridgewater. A, B, N, O, S.
James. A, B.
John, Bridgewater or Sudbury. D, N, O, R, S.
GLEASON, GLEESON, GLEZEN, GLESSEN.
Ebenezer, Framingham. N, O, S.
Isaac, Sudbury. A, D, O, S.
John. A, B.
Samuel, Framingham. N, O, S.
GLOVER.
John, Dorchester. B, M, O, S.
Thomas. A, B.
GOLDSMITH.
Richard, Wenham or Littleton. E, N, O, R, S.
Zaccheus, Wenham. E, N, O, S.
GOLDTHWAIT.
David, Salem or Danvers. A, E, N, O, R, S.
GOODALE, GOODELL, GOODEL.
Jacob, Salem or Danvers. E, O, W, R, S.
GOODENOW, GOODNOW.
Joseph, Sudbury. A, B, D, N, O, R, S.
Nathan or Nathaniel, Sudbury. A, B, N, O, S.
GOODHUE, GOODHEUGH.
Benjamin, Salem. A, N, O, S.
John, Jr. A.
GOODRIDGE, GUTRIDGE.
Benjamin, Lunenburg. A, B, G, N, O, S.
Joshua. A.
GOODSPEED.
Nathaniel. A.
GORHAM.
David, Barnstable. A.
Ebenezer, Barnstable. A.

GOULD.
Benjamin, Lunenburg. A, B, G, O, P, R, S.
David, Groton. A, B, D, N, O, R, S.
Jacob. A, B.
Samuel, Sudbury. A, B, D, N, O, S.
GOULDING, GOULDEN.
Palmer, Worcester. A, G, N, O, S.
GRANT.
John. B.
GRATON, GRAYTON.
John, Leicester. O, Q, R, S.
GREEN.
Ezra. A, B.
John, Concord. A, B, D, O, S.
Samuel. A.
GREENLEAF.
William, Boston. R.
GREENOUGH.
Thomas. B.
GREENWOOD.
Thomas. A. (Probably same person as preceding entry.)
GRIDLEY.
Richard. A, B.
GROUT.
Edward, Sudbury. A, B, D, O, R, S.
Edward, Jr., Sudbury. A, B, N, O, R, S.
John, Lunenburg. A, G, N, O, Q, S.
GUNN.
Aaron. A.

HAGAR, HAGER.
Ebenezer, Marlborough. A, D, N, Q, S.
HALE.
Jonathan, Newbury. A.
Robert, Beverly. A, N, O, R, S.
HALIBURTON, HALLIBURTON, HALYBURTON, HALLYBURTON.
Andrew, Boston. B, N, O, P, S.
HALL.
David, Sutton. A, B, G, N, O, R, S.
John, Medford. A, D, O, S.
Lechem. R.
Pelatiah, Dorchester. A, C, N, O, S.
Stephen, Stow. A, B, D, N, O, R, S.
Zaccheus, Sutton. A, B, G, N, O.
Zecharia, Sutton or New Braintree. B, R, S.
HALLOWAY, HALLIWAY.
William. A, B.
HALY, HALEY.
Samuel. A, B.
HAMDEN.
Benjamin, Wilmington. N, S.
HAMMOND.
John. A.
Joseph, Rochester. I, N, O, S.
Nathaniel. A.
HARBACK, HARBUCK.
Thomas, Sutton. A, B, O, P, R, S.

HARDY.
Aaron, Grafton. A, B, O, S.
Penias or Phyneas. A, B.
Timothy, Bradford. A, E, N, O, S.
HARNDON, HARNDEN, HARENDEN.
Benjamin, Wilmington. A, O, R.
HARPER.
Andrew, Harvard. A, G, N, O, S.
HARRENDEN, HARRANDIN.
Samuel. A, B.
HARRINGTON, HARRINTON.
Joseph, Weston. A, D, N, O, R, S.
HARTSHORN, HEARTSHORN.
Ebenezer, Charlestown. A, D, O, S.
Nathaniel, Marlborough. O.
HARWOOD.
Benjamin, Grafton or Shrewsbury.
  G, N, O, R, S.
John, Uxbridge. A, B, G, N, O, S.
HASEY.
Nathaniel, Sudbury. A, B, D, O, S.
William, Chelsea. A, C, N, O, S.
HASKELL, HASKEL, HASCALL, HAS-
  KALL.
James, Gloucester. A, E, O, S.
Joseph, Rochester. O, S.
Mark, Gloucester. A, E, O, S.
HATCH.
Colonel. A.
Estes. B. (Probably same person as
  preceding entry.)
HATHAWAY, HATHEWAY.
Ebenezer, Freetown. J, O, R, S.
Ephraim, Dighton. A, J, N, O, R, S.
HATHORN, HARTHORN, HEARTHAN,
  HATHOORN.
Nathaniel, Marlborough. A, D, N, S.
Samuel, Wilmington. A, D, N, O, R, S.
HAWS.
Stephen. B.
HAWKS, HAWKES.
Elkanah, Lynn. A, B, E, N, O, S.
John, Lynn. A, B, N, O, S.
John, Jr., Lynn. A, B, E, N, O, R, S.
John, 3d, Lynn. E.
Moses, Lynn. A, B, E, N, S.
HAYDEN.
John, Braintree. A, C, N, O, S.
Samuel, Braintree. A, C, O, P. S.
HAYNES, HAINES, HAINE, HAINS.
John, Jr., Sudbury. A, B, D, O, R, S.
Stephen. A.
HAYWOOD, HAYWARD, HAWARD,
  HEYWOOD.
Ebenezer, Bridgewater. A, I, O, R, S.
Ebenezer, Marlborough. O.
Eleazer, Brookfield. J, O, P, S.
Josiah, Concord. A, B, D, N, O, S.
HAZILTINE, HAZELTINE, HEAZELTINE,
  HAZELTON, HEZELTON, HASELTON.
Daniel, Mendon. A, B, G, N, O, S.
Ebenezer, Freetown. N.
John, Upton. A, B, G, N, O, S.

HEAD.
Edward, Swanzey. P, R.
HEALD.
Amos, Concord. A, B, N, O, S.
HEARSEY.
Israel, Boston. A, C, N, O, S.
Solomon, Boston. A, C, O, P, S.
HEDGE.
Elisha, Worcester. A, G, N, O, S.
HENDION.
Josiah. A.
HERBERT, HARBERT.
Joseph. A, B.
HERD, HEARD.
Zachariah, Sudbury. A, D, N, O, S.
HERRICK, HERRECK, HARRICK.
Robert, Manchester. A, B, E, N, O, S.
Rufus. A.
HEWES, HEWS.
George, Boston. O, P, R, S.
Robert. R.
Solomon, Wrentham. A, B, C, O, P,
  R, S.
HICKS, HICKE.
John, Westborough or Sutton. A, B,
  G, N, O, R, S.
Joshua. A.
HIGHLAND, HYLAND.
John. A. B.
HILL.
John. A, B.
Joseph, Jr. A.
HINES.
Hopestill. A.
HITCHCOCK.
David, Brimfield. A, L, N, O, S.
HITCHINGS, HITCHINS.
Daniel, Lynn. A, E, N, O, R, S.
HOARE, HOAR.
Daniel. A, B.
HOBBS, HOBS.
Josiah, Weston. A, B, D, N, O, S.
HODGES, HOGGES.
Benjamin, Norton. A, J, N, O. S.
Ebenezer, Norton. A, B, J, R, S.
Henry, Taunton. J, N, O, S.
HOLBROOK, HOLLBROOCK.
John, Eastham. A, B, F, N, O, P, R, S.
John, Grafton. A, G, N, O, R, S.
HOLDEN, HOLDIN.
James, Worcester. A, B, G, S.
Samuel, Worcester. O.
HOLLEY.
Gideon, Sandwich. A.
HOLMAN, HOLMON, HOLOMON, HOL-
  LOMAN, HOMAN.
Solomon, Sutton. A, B, G, N, O, R, S.
HOLMES, HOLMS.
Ebenezer, Roxbury. A, B, C, O, P, S.
Nathaniel, Dorchester. A, B, C, O, S.
HOOD.
Richard, Boston, A, B, C, O, P, R, S.

[To be continued.]

MISCELLANEOUS REVOLUTIONARY PAY ROLLS.

[Copied for the REGISTER by FRANCIS E. BLAKE, Esq., of Boston.]

I.

Camp Prospect Hill November the 8 1775.

We the Subscribers Commission^d officers Non Commission^d officers and Privates Recv^d of Wm Perkins Capt: Pay for the Month of September according to the abstract in full

Willm Perkins
David Allen
Samuel Treat
Joseph Loring
Zaccheus Dunnell
Ralph Bingham
Eliakim Caswell
Ephraim Titus
James moory
Henry Farington
Daniel Duncan
Job Littlefield
Penegrine White
Isaiah Audebert
Robert Cook
Samuel Trefry
Alexander Hutchinson
William McGilveray
ionathan farly

John Bancroft
Jacob Hardy
Benjamin Witham
John Noonan
Benjamin Burley
Simon Whetcomb
Joseph Nye
James Mecoy
William Coney
W^m. McCleary
Robert Savory
Thomas Herbert
his
Thomas x Matthews
mark
John Grant
John Rike
his
John x Howard
mark

Alexander Douglass
Connelius Baker
John Andrews
Joseph Mathews
Josiah Perkins
Joseph foster
his
Willm x croston
mark
Daniel Hodgdon
his
Ebz^r [Eliz^r ?] x Howard
mark
John x Willson
his mark
Samuel Rogers
John Presott bachelder

II.

June 29th, 1776.

We the subscribers Commission'd non Commission'd Officers & Matrosses have received of Capt Willm Perkins our Wages for the month April, Billitting & Blankett Money, with deduction of 10 shillings each man for Cloathing.

Saml Treat L^t
Hardy Peirce Lt
David Allen Esq.
Joseph Loring Lieut.
Isaiah Audebert
Jesse Fosdick
Thomas Wales
Jonathan Wharff
John Robinson
Christopher Stephenson
John williams
David Avery
William Thomas

David Forstor
Charles Ivory
William Wharff
Arthur Wharf
James Addams
Solomon morgan
Israel Herrick
Abraham Rand
Enoch Corey
Benjamin Witham
his
Richard x Simson
mark

James Mertho
his
Nathanal x Allen
mark
Josiah Perkins
Benjamin Ivory
Joseph Whitmore
Henry Farrington
William Deaniels
Joseph Spear
Joseph White
Zaccheus Dunnell

III.

New York, August 14, 1776.

We the Subscribers, Commission'd, non Commission'd Officers & Matrosses have received of Capt William Perkins our Wages for the Month of June, with a deduction of ten shillings from Each non-Commission'd officers & Matrosses for Cloathing.

Hardy Peirce Liu^t
Joseph White
William Wharff
Abraham Rand
Isa^h Audebert
Joseph Spear
Enoch Corey
    his
Nathanil x Allen
    mark
Joseph Whitmore
Henry Farrington
James Addams
Jesse Fosdick
Benjamin Ivory
William Deaniels
Zaccheus Dunnell
Charles Ivory

David Avery
Benjamin Witham
Joseph Loring Lieu^t
Saml Treat Lieu^t
David Allen Capt Lieu^t
    Rec^d of Capt William Perkins the full months pay for June for five men, Viz John Williams, Christopfer Stevenson, Sol^m morgan, Willm Thomas, Israel Herrick with stoppage 10 Shillings per month for Clothing at the store for the same Except Herrick   David Allen Capt L^t
    his
Richard x Simson
    mark
Jonathan Wharff
Arthur Wharf
Thomas Wales
Josiah Perkins

IV.

Harlem Hyths Oct. 2, 1776.

We the Subcribers Commission'd non Commission Officers and Mantrosses have Recd of Capt Willm Perkins our Wages for the month of July and Aurg^t with a deduction of ten Shillings from Each Non Commission Officer and Mantrosses

Isa^h Audebert
David Allen Capt L^t
Hardy Peirce

Fort Constitution Oct. 4th, 1776.

Rec^d of Capt. William Perkins Pay for the Months of July and August for the following Men, —Charles Ivory, Cristopher Stephenson, David Avery John Robinson, Israel Herrick, Solomon Morgan, Josiah Perkins, William Thomas, Jonathan Wharf, Arthur Wharf, Nathaniel Allen, John Williams, with a stoppage of ten Shillings per month for Cloathing at the Store, for the same, except Herrick.

David Allen Capt. L^t

Zaccheus Dunnell
Samuel Treat L^t
Jesse Fosdick

Joseph Louring, L^s
James Addams
Joseph Spear
Enoch Corey
Abraham Rand
Benjamin Ivory
Thomas Wales
Joseph Whitmore
William Deaniels
    his
Richard x Simson
    mark
Benjamin Witham
Henry Farington
Joseph White
William Wharff
David Forstor

V.

We, the subscribers, Field, Staff and Commissioned Officers of the 9th Mass. Regiment, have received of Robt. Williams, Paymaster, each of us the sum annexed to our names in full of our subsistance for the month of May, 1782.

Name.	Rank.	Amount of Subsistance.		Subscribers.
		Dolls.	100th.	
Henry Jackson . .	Col°	12	60	*
Lem¹ Trescott . .	Major	8	00	*
John Blanchard . .	Capt.	6	30	*
John Hastings . .	Capt.	6	30	*
Joseph Fox . . .	Capt.	6	30	*
Thos. Hunt	Capt.	6	30	*
Thos. Turner . . .	Capt.	6	30	
Robt. Walker . . .	Capt.	6	30	*
Wᵐ Watson . . .	Capt.	6	30	
Sam¹ Henley . . .	Capt.	6	30	Paid.
Oliver Rice	Lieut.	3	15	*
Sam¹ Cogswell . .	Lieut.	3	15	Paid.
Charles Selden . .	Lieut.	3	15	*
Jeremiah Hill . . .	Lieut.	3	15	*
Benjᵉ Parker . . .	Lieut.	3	15	*
Isaac Sturtevant . .	Lieut.	3	15	*
Caleb Clap	Cap. Lt	3	15	*
Thˢ H. Condy . . .	Lieut.	3	15	* Q. M.
Robᵗ Williams . .	Lieut.	3	15	
Ephᵐ Hunt	Lieut.	3	15	*
Edward Phelan . .	Lieut.	3	15	*
Patrick Phelan . .	Lieut.	3	15	*
Wᵐ Rickard . . .	Ensⁿ	3	15	* Lieut.
Dominie Trant† . .	Ensⁿ	3	15	
Ebenʳ Kent . . .	Ensⁿ	3	15	Paid.
John Hurd	Ensⁿ	3	15	*
James Thacher . .	Surgeon	4	60	*
Francis Goodwin . .	Mate	3	15	‡
		129	75	

* Those marked with an asterisk are autograph signatures.
† Possibly Trant.
‡ Signature F. L. B. Goodwin, S. M.

THOMAS WESTON AND HIS FAMILY.

EXTRACTS FROM THE RECORDS OF THE PROVINCIAL COURT OF MARY-
LAND. LIBER, W. R. C. No. 1, FOLIO 354–356.

Communicated by Dr. CHRISTOPHER JOHNSTON, of Baltimore, Md.

LAST summer, while at Annapolis, I found some matter relating to
the connection of the Conant family of New England with Thomas
Weston, which struck me as being worth noting.   I therefore copied
it out entire except portions (powers of attorney etc.) which contained merely the usual legal phraseology.   These I took in abstract.
It will be noticed that there is some discrepancy in dates, but it is
copied literally from the record book.   I send, for insertion in the
REGISTER, the matter which I collected.

Thomas Weston came to Maryland in 1640, bringing with him
five persons whose names are given below, and lived in S^t. George's
Hundred [Md. Archives, I. 144].   At the meeting of the Assembly,
September 5th, 1642, "Mr. Thomas Weston being called pleaded he
was no freeman because he had no land nor certain dwelling here
&c^a. but being put to the question it was voted that he was a Freeman and as such bound to his appearance by himse^{l}f or proxie
whereupon he took place in the house" [Ibid. p. 170].   In this
Assembly he was member of an important committee appointed
'for the drawing of a Bill touching a war to be made upon the
Indians and other matters pertaining to the Safety of the Colony'
[Ibid. p. 171].   The prominence of the other members of the
committee would make it appear that Mr. Weston was considered a
person of consequence.   Although at this time he possessed no
land, he obtained, January 10th following, a patent for 1200 acres,
which was erected into a manor under the name of Westbury Manor,
and he already had a house, since an order of Gov. Leonard Calvert,
dated August 28th, 1642, provided that the housekeepers of S^t.
George's Hundred were to convey their women and children to the
house of Mr. Weston in case of an Indian alarm [Md. Archives,
III. 108].   A writ, dated January 9th, 1644, is addressed to him
as "Tho: Weston of St George's Hundred mch^t" [Ibid. p. 163].
Numerous references to him are to be found in Maryland Archives,
Volumes I., III. and IV.   The latter volume, which embraces the
proceedings of the Provincial Court 1637–1650, contains (pp. 376-
377) a bond, dated July 20th 1641, from Thomas Weston Citizen
and Ironmonger of London to Thomas Stone, uncle of Gov. William Stone, and an interesting letter from Mr. Weston to Governor
(then Captain) Stone, dated "Mary-Land the 3^d January 1644."

Although John Hansford did not apply for administration on his estate until November 1647, Mr. Weston's death must have occurred some time before, as claims were filed against his estate as early as May 1647 [Md. Archives IV. 309].

It may be of interest to note that the Mr. Wilkinson mentioned in the deposition of Richard Moore was the Rev. William Wilkinson, a clergyman of the Anglican Church, who came from Virginia to Maryland with his family in 1650, and died in 1663—a man of considerable energy and force of character. He zealously ministered to the spiritual wants of his flock, and meanwhile supported his family by cultivating his land, there being, until 1692, no provision for the maintenance of ministers by the state. The Mr. Dent, mentioned in the same deposition, was his son-in-law, Thomas Dent, one of the Justices of St. Mary's County 1661–1668, High Sheriff 1664, and Burgess 1664, 1674–76. He died in 1676, and his widow Rebecca, daughter of the Rev. Mr. Wilkinson, re-married Col. John Addison. She left descendants by both marriages, who to the present day occupy a high social position in Maryland. Mr. Wilkinson had another daughter, Elizabeth, wife of William Hatton, a nephew of Secretary Thomas Hatton.

---

27 Sept[r]. 1684: " Elizabeth Connant relict widow of Richard (*sic*) Connant of Marble Head in New England decd, and only daughter and sole heire of Thomas Weston Citizen and Ironmonger of London," to her son John Connant of Marblehead, in New England aforesaid;—power of attorney to take possession and dispose of such plantations, lands, houses, tenements &c as lie in any part of Virginia and Maryland or elsewhere, which may belong to her as heir of her said father.

Witnesses. Stephen Sargent, Stephen Daniell,
Vincent Burton, John Allen.
John Hayward Not[rus] Pub[cus].

To all Christian people to whom these p[r].sents shall come. I Richard Norman of Marblehead in the county of Essex in the Collony of Massachusett in New Eng[d]. of the Age of ffifty yeares or there abouts doe testifie that John Connant now Resident in New England & bound for Virginia the said John Connant I knew him of a child & was a near neighbour to his ffather Roger Connant and his wife Elizabeth the daughter and the only daughter of Thomas Weston by comon repute and that the said John Connant was born of the said Elizabeth in lawfull wedlock with the said Roger Connant as can be shown by neighbours living neer and was bred up as her sonn & lived with her as her son untill said Roger and his wife Elizabeth went for Ireland and further saith y[t]. the said Elizabeth's ffather was that Thomas Weston that used formerly to trade in Virginia and soe to New England and afterwards went home for Bristoll and there dyed as by credible and comon report and further that I have been in Maryland in Virginia in West S[t]. Mary's and likewise in some part of York River in both which places there was Land comonly said to be and called by the name the said Thomas Weston his Land or Plantation & understood to be the same Thomas Weston aforesaid and further that I never heard of any other child the said Thomas Weston had but only the said Elizabeth but have often heard the said Elizabeth say her father had noe other child but her.

Richard Norman came before me 2 day of Decemb 1674 & made his psonal oath to what is above written before me   William Hathorn Assist in the Massachusetts.

Moses Maverick aged about 64 yeares saith
I Moses Maverick of Marblehead doe testifie to all [above] written saving only the latter part of haveing a personall knowledge of any plantations of the said Weston's but this I can testifie that the [within] said John Connant's mother (vizt.) Elizabeth the wife of the said Roger Connant & the daughter of the said Thomas Weston that she when a maiden lived with me and marryed to the said Roger Connant out of my house & that she had a Letter and orders from her mother after her father Thomas Weston's decease to look after her father's means in Virginia or Maryland and accordingly she sent and did receive some tobacco from Virginia in part or on the accompt of her father's estate there vizt. the said Thomas Weston.

Taken upon oath 23 of 10th mon : 1674   Moses Maverick before me W^m. Hathorn Assist.

Francis Johnson aged eighty yeares or thereabouts testifieth and saith that att my first coming to Marblehead in New England which was about ffourty yeares since I knew and was well acquainted with Elizabeth Weston the Reputed daughter of Mr. Thomas Weston of the Citty of London in the Kingdome of Engl^d. merch^t. who was then gone on a voyage from New England aforesaid to Virginia and that he left the said Elizabeth att the house of Mr. Moses Maverick of Marblehead aforesaid.

Jur cor me ⎱
27 Sep^t.   ⎰ S. Bradstreet Govr.

The Deposition of Richard Moore Senr. aged seaventy yeares or thereabouts. Sworn saith that being in London att the House of Mr. Thomas Weston Ironmonger in the year 1620 He was from thence transported to New Plymouth in New England and about two yeares and a half after the said depon^{ts}. arrivall at Plymoth. aforesaid the above mentioned Thomas Weston sent over a ship upon his p^{r}per accompt with passengers to settle in the Massachusetts Bay now called Braintree but soon after they deserted the same by reason of Indians & Sicknesse And within a short space of time after the above said Weston personally came over from London to Plymouth in New England and made his aboad there some time and traded from thence to Virginia and Maryland And att that time the said deponent knew that the said Thomas Weston had and was possessed of two plantations the one in Yorke River in Virginia att a place called Cheesecake, the other in Maryland att West S^t. Maryes by Storyes Island and heretofore were comonly known to be in the tenure & occupation of these persons here under exprest vizt. Mr. Wilkinson, Mr. Dent merch^t. &c. and they all acknowledged the said Weston to be the true proprietor and lawfull owner of the said plantations And further that the said deponent knew Elizabeth Weston now Elizabeth Connant of Marblehead to be the reputed and only child of the said Thomas Weston.   Jur cor me ⎱
27 Sep^t. 1684. ⎰ S: Bradstreet Govr.

Boston in New England

These are to certifie all whom it doth or anywayes may concern y[t]. Elizabeth Connant Relict widdow of Roger Connant late of Marblehead in New England aforesaid de&d. and the reputed daughter and only child of M[r]. Thomas Weston of the Citty of London in the Kingdome of England Ironmonger (according to the testimonys here unto affixed) appeared before me Simon Bradstreet Esq[r]. Governour of his Majestyes Collony of the Massachusetts Bay in New England on the day of the date of these p[r]sens in very good health & owned the Letter of Attorney hereunto annexed to be her act and deed Also these are to certifie that William Hawthorne who hath subscribed his name to some of the Testimonyes here unto affixed was on the day of the date thereof one of the Magistrates of the aforesaid Collony and had power to administer oathes in this and other like cases & therefore full faith and creditt is & ought to be given thereunto In testimony whereof att the request of the above named Elizabeth Connant I have hereunto sett my hand and caused the publique seal of the said Collony of the Massachusetts Bay to be hereunto affixed the 27[th]. day of Sep[t]. Anno Domini one thousand six hundred eighty & ffour   Annoq. RR[s] Caroli Secundi nunc Angliæ &c tricessimo sexto.   S: Bradstreet Gov[r]n[r].

Memorandum that I the [aforenamed] John Connant by vertue of the power to me [before granted] and for the acting and prosecuting the intent of the same Have ffeed nominated and appo[ted] Thomas Burford Attor: Gen[rll]. of y[e] Province of Maryland, Rob[t]. Carvile & Antho: Underwood Gent. two of the Attor: of the Provin[ll]. Court of the s[d] Province to plead manage and p[r]secute all matters and things relating to Law in order to y[e] recovering y[e] Right of y[e] [w[th].in] named Eliz[a]. Connant to any Lands Tenem[ts] & Hereditam[ts] in the Pro: of Maryland witnesse my hand this 27[th] of March 1685.

Witness   John Connant

  Tho Grunwin clk. Pro[ll] Co[rt].

  Recorded the 9th of Aprill 1686

                    p̄ Jam. Heath clk.

From Rec. Prov. Court of Md.   Lib. W R C.   No. 1, fol. 627.
13 March 1689–90. John Connant of New England now resident in Maryland, merchant, being now bound for New England, to his very loving friend Thomas Ebb of S[t]. Mary's County;—power of attorney to receive all monies &c due said John Connant, and also to let or dispose of his land Westbury manor for a term not exceeding two years &c.

29 August 1642. Thomas Weston demands 1200 acres due by conditions of plantation for transporting himself, and five able men into the province in the year 1640. Their names were Richard Haniford, William Marshall, William Palmer, John Kelly, and Jasper Collins.

10 Jan[y]. 1642. Thomas Weston further demands 100 acres for transporting William Hall in the year 1640, and 50 acres lately granted to George Pye and by him assigned to said Weston.

10 Jan[y]. 1642. Surveyor's certificate of 1200 acres laid out for Thomas Weston on the East side S[t]. George's Creek, bounding on the East with the lands of George Pye, John Edwards, Henry Lee, and Richard Nevitt.

10 Jan'y 1642. Patent for above land which is to be held of the Honor of West S[t]. Mary's, and is erected into a manor called Westbury Manor, with right of Court Leet, Court Baron, &c.

                    Maryland Land Records, Lib. A B H. fol. 58.

S[t]. George's Hundred
Acres. Rent
1200   £1. 5 " Westbury Manor.   Sur: 10 Jan[y]. 1642 for Tho Weston &
         50[a] Sur. 12: 9ber 1640 for Geo: Pye which was assign[d].
         to Weston & made part of Westbury Mannour. Poss[r].
         [circa 1707] John Conant of New England by Tho. Heb
         his attorney.
         [Transfers 1250 [a]. Rent £1. 5. 0. Josiah Conant from
         John Conant 14 May 1737].
                                   Rent Roll S[t]. Mary's County I. 16.

10 Nov[r]. 1647.   John Hanceford of Virginia Gent. maketh claim of the es-
                   tate of Thomas Weston of this Province mrch[t] deceed and
                   desired Letters of Administration ...... according to his
                   last will & testament."
                   Administration granted accordingly.
                                           Md. Land Records, Lib. 2, fol. 254.
1 June 1649.   Quietus est to John Hansford administrator of Thomas
               Weston.   Ibid 519.

NOTE BY THE EDITOR.

These extracts from the Maryland records, and the Introduction
to them by our correspondent, Dr. Johnston, furnish new particulars
concerning a prominent figure in early New England history, and
his relatives.   This person—Mr. Thomas Weston—rendered important assistance to the Pilgrims in their emigration from Holland
to New England, but afterwards lost their confidence by his conduct.   A full account of his dealings with the Plymouth people is
given by Gov. Bradford in his History of Plymouth Plantation.
His attempt to found a rival plantation at Wessagusset, now Weymouth, proved abortive.   But he was an enterprising man, and his
name often appears in the pages of our history.   The best sketch
of his life is a brief one by Charles Francis Adams, LL.D., in his
Historical Address in 1874, at the quarter millenary celebration of
the permanent settlement of Weymouth.*   Several letters from him
are printed in Gov. Bradford's History.

Mr. Weston's only daughter and heir, Elizabeth Weston, we
learn from these papers, married Roger Conant.   He was a son of
Roger Conant, the early settler of Salem.   F. O. Conant, in his
Conant Family (Portland, 1887), page 132, gives Elizabeth as the
christian name of the wife of Roger Conant, but he leaves her maiden
surname blank.   He quotes these extracts from the Salem church
records to show that her name was Elizabeth: "22 : 11 mo. 1661,
Y[e] church consented to the baptizing of Mrs. Elizabeth Conant's child
upon a letter from the church at Cork testifying to her membership

* Pages 5-22.   Other notices will be found in Gov. Bradford's History; Young's Chroni-
cles of the Pilgrims, page 78; Thomas Morton's New English Canaan, Prince Society's
edition, edited by C. F. Adams, pp. 245-6, 259-60; and Appleton's Cyclopædia of American Biography, vol. 6, pp. 443-4.

there," and "11th 1 : 1684, Mrs. Roger Conant was admitted to the first church by letter from the church in Ireland." Richard Norman, in his deposition, 1674, printed above, speaks of Roger Conant and his wife Elizabeth going to Ireland some time after the birth of their son John.

We derive from Dr. Johnston's communication a nearer approximation to the date of Weston's death. He must have died between January 3, 1644–5, and May, 1647. All that we had known before this was that he died at Bristol, England, of the plague, in the time of the wars.

We learn here also that he was a member of the Ironmongers' Company. This may aid in finding more about him.

ENSIGN WILLIAM HILTON OF YORK, ME.

[Communicated by JOHN T. HASSAM, A.M., of Boston.]

In the REGISTER for April, 1880 (xxxiv. 203), I published certain extracts from the Council Records and the Records of the Superior Court of Judicature in relation to a sloop taken out of York Harbor Nov. 8th, 1711, by a Frenchman and three Indians; their pursuit by Ensign William Hilton and his Company " consisting of six of the Standing forces there in the pay and six of the Inhabitants"; the killing of the Indians; the production of their scalps by Ensign Hilton before the Governor and Council in Boston; the reward of £105 to him and his company "for their good Service" in accordance with the "Act made for encouragement of the prosecution of the Indian Enemy and Rebels"; the subsequent order for the arrest of Ensign Hilton; his trial and acquittal.

At the time of that publication the Suffolk Court Files were practically inaccessible. The admirable re-arrangement of them now being made under the direction of Wm. P. Upham, Esq., has brought to light many documents the existence of which was hitherto unsuspected, and among them there are three papers [Suffolk Court Files lxxxv. 1–3] which throw more light on this affair. They are as follows :

York Novem[r] 8th. 1711

Wee who are your Excellencies moast humble Servants gives Our Duty to your Excellency and do hereby Assert that on the Eight day of Nouemb[r] wee Embarqut on Board a Small Sloop with Ensigne W[m] Hilton & made Saile into the Oacion in Chase of a Sloop taken out of York Harbour y[e] night before when wee came about Three Leauges without York Harbour Wee see a Saile in the Offing which Wee Expected to be the Said Sloop taken out of York Wee gave her Chase shee try'd uss upon a Wind

wee gain'd upon her apace shee went away a point or Two of the sheet
Wee gain'd upon her Still wch much Encouraged uss Wee Chast her upon
that Course about two hours Wee began then to Raise the man that Stood
at Helm very plain then shee bares away before the Wind it Seem'd to uss
as though Shee gain'd Ground on uss,   The next thing Wee put up our
Blankits to Starbord to make more Sail Wee came up with her apace Wee
Fires upon her Ten or Twelve Guns shee bringing too   Wee boarded her
Ensigne Wm Hilton Leaps On Board the Prize with Two other men he orders the Enemie to Jump into the Sloop he came Out of the Night coming
on and the Sea Runing so Extraordinarie Bigg Wee made the Best of our
way for the Harbour And Secured theese Rebells till Ensigne Wm Hilton
came in, As soon as he Arriu'd in the Harbour Capt Wm Heath & Capt
Abraham Preble sent Jobe Young a man belonging to York to Said Hilton to know what should be done with ye Rebels   He Immediately Went
on shore wth ye messenger Capt Heath & Capt Preble Invites him up in a
Chamber at Esqr Donniels what past between them We do not Know but
quickly said Hilton returns & goes to the place were said Rebels were &
they were put to Death & thrown into the Sea what Ever your Excellency
may have otherways this is the truth   FRANCES PEABODY

Wee whose names are Inserted Do testifie to the Withinmentioned as
specified

TIMOTHY DAY
SAM^ll CLARK

And wee do further Testifie
that Ensigne Wm Hilton who
was Command^r in that expedition took theese Indian Rebels
by the shoulders and delivered
them to be Executed and ordered
them to be thrown into the Sea
Wee as many of us as Could
get together haue here unto set
our hands

The Declaration of Edward Ball Job Avory Georg Jacobs & Thomas
More Inhabitants of the Town of Yorke Testifies that on ye Eighth day
of Novr Last Capt Abraham Preblee Ju Early in the morning missing his
ffishing Sloop who Emediatly Went in Serch thereof and about Seven or
Eight of the Clock Discouvred her about three Leagues distant from York
harbour Standing Seaward ye Wind at North North East ye Said Preble
desired our Assistance to fetch in his Sloop   Suposeing her to be in the
possession of the ffrench or Indian Enemie, Whereupon with ye Assistance
of more of our neighbours with a Sergent & Eight men und^r Comand of
Capt Heath, Imbarqued in two Small Sloops belonging to Job Avery &
Georg Jacobs of this place, Wee accounted our Selves Vnd^r Said Prebles
Comand as our officer. Wee Run in Chase of ye Said Sloop about nine
Leagues one of the Sloops being to Windward the other Sloop bore away
before the Wind. Wee in the Other Sloop had the advantage and haveing
Sayled before the Wind about four Leagues farther Said Avory Came up
with them first and found on board Said Prebles Sloop one french Man &
thre Indians took them on board our Sloop, and m^r Hilton & too other
men Kept on board s^d Prebles sloop & by this time the Other Sloop Came
up Were Cap_t Preble Was, ord^rs Was giuen for Killing the Indians butt the
Wind & Sea was So boistrous that nothing was done with them, night

coming on all three Sloops Stood Shoreward & Intended to haue Examined the Indians and dispach[d] them, butt in the night Lost Sight one of the other So that the Sloop the Indians were on board gott in first, the Indians Were Secured untill all y[e] Sloops Came in which was about Tenn of the Clock that night   Examination Was made by said Preble Wether any quarter Was giuen to the Indians   It Was Evident none was asked or giuen them by any of our Comany,   Said Preble there upon as the officer of the Inhabitants with Cap[t] Heath in Behalf of his party delivered up the Said Indians to death Death and Reserued the ffrenchman a Prissonar for his Exelencys pleasure.   this action was about half an hour after Ten of Clock at night the Eighth of Nov[r] aforesd after Which m[r] Hilton was Sent with the Scalps and the Letters Signed by Cap[t] Heath and Cap[t] Preble to his Exelency.   Wee being in the two Sloops thirty too men Equally Ingaged in Said action

EDWARD BEALE
JOB AVARALL
GORG JACOB
THOMAS MORE

York ss   The persons aboue named Personally appeared
                 before vs the Subscribers and made oath to the
                 within written this 2[d]. day of Aprill 1712

JOHN WHEELWRIGHT } of ye
ICHABOD PLAISTED } peace

Essex ss   At the Court of assize &c.
                                         May 1712

	£ :	s :	d :
The Queen's Charges for prosecuting Ensign William Hilton			
to M[r] Secretary Addington for copies orders and proclamation	00 =	12 =	00
to the Justices for taking affidavitts at York	00 =	6 =	00
attorney Generall	00 =	12 =	00
Jury	00 =	13 =	6
Clarks fees 3 ⁄ 6 Sheriff & his officers 7 ⁄ 6	00 =	11	
to the Justices at Salem for Recognisances or mittimus	0 =	4 =	0
Filing papers & Examing Bill	00 =	5 =	0
M[r] Harris Removing him from Salem	1.	–	
Taxing Costs	0.	1.	

Exam[d]. p ELISHA COOKE Cler   4 :   4.   6
          Allowed p Curiam
                    Attestr.   ELISHA COOKE Cler

Ensign William Hilton was son of William Hilton of York, and grandson of William Hilton who came from London to Plymouth in New England in the "Fortune," November 11, 1621.

For further information concerning him see the REGISTER for April, 1877 (xxxi. 179) and "The Hilton Family," privately printed, Boston, 1896.

MUSTER ROLL OF CAPT. THOMAS CARTWRIGHT'S COMPANY, 1777.

[Copied for the REGISTER by FRANCIS E. BLAKE, Esq., of Boston.]

Muster Roll of Capt Thomas Cartwright's Company of the Regt^t of Foot Commanded by Col. Henry Jackson in the Service of the United States.

Commissioned { Feb. 1, 1777 Capt. Thomas Cartwright
              { Feb. 1, 1777 Lieu^t John Hobby

Commissioned { May 12, 1777 Lieu^t John Child
              { Feb. 1, 1777 Ensign Nat. Thatcher, recruiting.

Nos.	Serjeants	appointed	remarks	Time
1	John Noonan	July 2		3 years
2	Richd Rolf	May 24		3 years
3	John Jones	June 2		3 years

Nos.	Corporals	appointed	remarks	Time
1	Tim^o Ralf	June 11		3 years

Nos.	Drum & fife	Time	appointed	remarks
1	Wm. Henly	3 years	July 7	
2	Nat. Disper	3 years	May 28	

Nos.	Privates	enlisted	remarks	Time
1	Joseph William	June 9		3 years
2	Nathl House	May 15		8 mo^s
3	Noah Barrett	May 15		8 mo^s
4	Richd Martin	May 24	Sick in Hospital	3 years
5	John McIntosh	June 2		3 years
6	James Martin	May 24		3 years
7	Philip Mosher	May 29		3 years
8	Amos Dwinels	May 24		3 years
9	And^w Nelson	June 21		3 years
10	Pat^k Brown	July 23		3 years
11	Wm. Norris	June 18		3 years
12	Joseph Souther	May 28		3 years
13	John Pattey	July 9	Furloughed	3 years
14	Peter Hewson	July 17	Furloughed	for ye war
15	Josh^a Austin	July 10		3 years

Dorchester 15th Augt. 1777 Mustered then Capt. Cartwright's Company as specified in the above Roll.

And^w. Brown Dy. Master Master

Proof of the Effectives

	Captain	Lieuts.	Ensign	Serjeants	Corporals	Drums	fifes	Privates
Present	1	2	0	3	1	1	1	12
Absent	0	0	1	0	0	0	0	3
Total	1	2	1	3	1	1	1	15

We swear that the within Muster Roll is a true state of Capt. Thos. Cartwright's Company without fraud to the United States or to any individual, according to the best of our knowledge.

Dorchester August 13, 1777.

Th. Cartwright, Capt.
John Child 2nd Lieut.

Sworn before me this 15th Day of Aug. 1777 W. Heath M.G.

COMEE–COMEY FAMILY.

By ALLEN H. BENT, member of the New-England Historic Genealogical Society.

1. DAVID[1] COMEE, who was in Woburn, Mass., in 1663, seems to be the first of the name in America. When or whence he came is not known with certainty, but the family tradition is that he was a Scotchman. His son John married the daughter of a Scotchman and this same John, in 1728, conveys a certain right in Concord "which belongs to the Tenement where my Hon^d father David Comey formerly dwelt in the Southerly part of Concord known by the name of Scotland." So it seems there was a part of Concord known as Scotland, perhaps because a Scotch colony had settled there. The name is generally spelled Comee until the nineteenth century, when there was a division, about half adopting the form of Comey. On the old records it is occasionally spelled, or misspelled Comy, Come, Comi, Comay and Coomy. The name seems not to be related to those of Coney (Cony), Comer, Comby (Combee) or Comley, that are occasionally met with in New England. Comrie and Comyn are old Scotch names.

About 1664 David Comee moved from Woburn to Concord (Mass.), where he lived until his death. He was killed, April 21, 1676, by King Philip's Indians in the adjoining town of Sudbury, in one of the bloodiest of Indian encounters. The following petition was presented by his widow:

"To the honored Court assembled at Cambridge ye 3 day of October 1676 The humble petition of Esther Comy of Concord humbly showeth y^t wheras ye said esther comy her husband Dauid Comy was slaine by ye jndians at Sudbury and lefte me a poor widow with six small children and foure of them bee by a former wife and non of them being com to Age or able to choose their own Gardens: I ye said Esther doe humbly entreat this honored Court to appoynt Gardens for them & to put y^m out to som good places: wherby ye boy may learne som trad y^t may bee for his futter beinfeet and dispoose of ye Girls as may bee for their weell fare also for ye settlment of y^t smal estate y^t my husband died seized of which doth amount to about eighty pounds which appears by An jnventory given in at court at Charlestown: and I doe humbly desir y^t Captaine Timothy Wheeler with on or tow mor may bee appointed for both ye ends aforesaid: whom ye honored court shall see causse to appoynt: hoping y^t ye honoured court will Consider me beeing poor and haueing serl children very small on of y^m not being Above six weeks old when my husband was slaine: so praying for your prosperity: your humble petitioner this 30 : 7 :: 76

ESTHER COMY."

The inventory accompanying the above is short and amounts to £87 –
14 – 0, of which £50 is for the house and land.

Children of David and his wife Elizabeth, ii. recorded in Woburn, iii. to
v. recorded in Concord:

 i. ELIZABETH, m. March 29, 1681, John Kendall (1646–1732) of
  Woburn, where she d. in December, 1701.
 ii. MARY, b. Jan. 30, 1663; m. May 24, 1688, Joshua Kibby, of
  Sherborn, and d. July 9, 1712, ae. 49. He d. in 1731.
2. iii. JOHN, b. Oct. 18, 1665.
 iv. DAVID, b. Nov. 14, 1666; d. before 1676.
 v. SARAH, b. Sept. 18, 1668.

David's wife Elizabeth died in Concord, March 4, 1671, and
he married, second, Esther ———, who married, Nov. 7, 1682,
Samuel Parry for her second husband.

Children of David and Esther born in Concord:

 i. Daughter, name unknown.
 ii. ESTHER, b. Feb. 14, 1676.

2. JOHN[2] COMEE (*David*[1]) was a farmer and moved from Concord to
 Cambridge Farms (Lexington) between 1689 and 1693. He
 died in Lexington, Dec. 6, 1729, ae. 64. Hudson is in error
 when he gives the date as 1723. He married June 21, 1688,
 Martha, born Nov. 2, 1667, eldest daughter of William Munroe,
 who came from Scotland in 1652.

  Children of John and Martha, i. recorded in Concord, iv. and v.
 in Cambridge. (The first four were baptised Feb. 26, 1699):

 i. JOHN, b. April 8, 1689; probably d. young.
 ii. HANNAH, d. unm. May 26, 1770.
 iii. MARTHA, m. July 9, 1713, Benjamin Smith, and d. Nov. 19, 1749.
3. iv. DAVID, b. Jan. 11, 1696.
 v. ELIZABETH, b. Jan. 29, 1701.
 vi. ABIGAIL, bap. Oct. 26, 1707; m. Jan. 4, 1728, Jonas Pierce, and
  d. in Westminster, Mass.

3. DAVID[3] COMEE (*John,*[2] *David*[1]) of Lexington, lived to be 104 years
 old, if family tradition is correct. This would bring the date of
 his death about the year 1800. In 1729 he is called a yeoman,
 in 1736 an innholder. He married first, Ruhama, born in Watertown July 15, 1701, daughter of Joseph and Ruhama Brown.
 She died June 3, 1730, and he married second, Sarah ———.

  David and Ruhama seem to have had five or six children, who
 died in infancy. Those that lived (born in Lexington) were:

4. i. JOHN, bap. Sept. 28, 1725.
5. ii. JOSEPH, bap. Aug. 4, 1728.

  Children of David and Sarah, all born in Lexington:

6. i. BENJAMIN, b. Nov. 15, 1733.
 ii. SARAH, b. Sept. 11, 1735; m. Dec. 4, 1755, Isaac Parkhurst (1731–
  ———) of Waltham, where they lived till 1786.
 iii. MARTHA, b. April 11, 1737; m. at Chelsea, April 2, 1761, William
  Williams.
7. iv. EZEKIEL, b. April 27, 1740.
 v. RUHAMA, b. April 15, 1742; m. Dec. 9, 1762, Isaac Corey (1740–
  1817) of Waltham, and d. at East Sudbury, March 2, 1819.
8. vi. DAVID, b. April 21, 1744.
9. vii. JONATHAN, b. April 4, 1746.

4. JOHN[4] COMEE (*David,[3] John,[2] David[1]*) a farmer, moved from Lexington to Milton in 1751, but soon after (1753 to 1755) removed to Stoughton, the part known as Stoughtonham (incorporated 1762 as Sharon). He seems to have been in the part of the latter, which in 1778 became Foxboro. His name is included in the unsuccessful petition of May 1773 for the incorporation of Foxboro. At the first town meeting June 29, 1778, he (or possibly it was his son John) was chosen constable. He died in Foxboro, Feb. 8, 1815, ae. 89. He was married at Milton in 1751 to Abigail, born Oct. 22, 1727, daughter of Roger Sumner and a descendant of William Sumner (1605–1688) of Dorchester, the ancestor of Charles Sumner. Mrs. Abigail Comee died at Foxboro, May 19, 1806, ae. 78.

Children of John and Abigail, i. recorded in Milton, ii. to v. in Stoughton, vi. in Sharon:

  10. i. JOHN, b. Jan. 14, 1753.
      ii. JERUSHA, b. Feb. 22, 1755.
  11. iii. OLIVER, b. June 11, 1757.
  12. iv. SPENCER, b. Jan. 24, 1760.
      v. ABIGAIL, b. Aug. 25, 1762; d. unm. Jan. 11, 1790.
      vi. EUNICE, b. July 15, 1766.

5. JOSEPH[4] COMEE (*David,[3] John,[2] David[1]*) moved previous to 1771 from Lexington to Wrentham, the part taken in 1778 to make Foxboro, where he was a cordwainer (shoemaker) and still living in 1809. He was one of the signers of the unsuccessful petition of 1773 for the incorporation of Foxboro. October 1771, Joseph Comee and wife Mary, of Wrentham, gave quitclaim to estate of their honorable father Benjamin Merriam, of Lexington. Hudson, however, in his History of Lexington makes it out that he was a member of Capt. John Parker's Company, April 19, 1775, and was wounded in the arm trying to get out of the meeting-house, whither he had been to replenish his powder-horn, but this was probably his son Joseph. He married, about 1750, Mary, born April 4, 1733, eldest daughter of Benjamin Merriam (1699–1773), of Lexington. Hannah, widow of Joseph Comee deceased, died in Foxboro, March 22, 1815. The death of a child of Joseph Comee is recorded in Lexington churchrecords in 1766.

Children of Joseph and Mary, all born in Lexington:

  13. i. EZRA, (twin) bap. Oct. 27, 1751.
      ii. MERCY, (twin) bap. Oct. 27, 1751.
      iii. JOSEPH, b. July 1, 1753; probably the Joseph who d. in Lexington, Oct. 12, 1776.
      iv. MARY, b. June 22, 1755.
      v. AARON, b. Aug. 15, 1757; nothing further known.
      vi. BETTY, b. March 23, 1760.
      vii. RUHAMA, bap. Nov. 14, 1762.
  14. viii. BENJAMIN, b. July 3, 1765; m. Ruth Trow.

6. BENJAMIN[4] COMEE (*David,[3] John,[2] David[1]*) was a cordwainer and at the time of his marriage (1762) was still living in Lexington, but moved soon after to Malden, where he died in 1774, ae. 40. He married first, March 25, 1762, Hannah Watts, of Chelsea, who died at Malden, Dec. 1, 1767. She was probably the Hannah Watts b. Chelsea, Feb. 17, 1743, dau. of Samuel and Hannah.

He married second, Oct. 17, 1768, Hannah Richardson, of Woburn, by whom however he had no children. She was probably the Hannah Coome, who married in 1783 Thomas Sargent, of Malden.

Children of Benjamin and Hannah, ii. and iii. recorded in Malden :

  i. HANNAH, d. in Boston, unm., in 1794.
 ii. SARAH, b. March 23, 1766.
15. iii. BENJAMIN, b. Nov. 21, 1767.

7. EZEKIEL[4] COMEE (*David,*[3] *John,*[2] *David*[1]) lived in Cambridge (Brighton) till 1783, when he probably went to Boston, where he appears in the directories of 1796 and 1800, but not in 1803, so he probably died before that. (No directories published between these dates). Feb. 12, 1806, Mary Ann Comee, singlewoman, and Charlotte Smith, wife of Ebenezer Smith, all of Boston, sell property in Cambridge, that descended to them from their father Ezekiel.

Children of Ezekiel and his wife :

  i. MARY ANN. Perhaps the Mary who d. in Boston, Aug. 12, 1824.
 ii. CHARLOTTE, b. about 1775; m. Ebenezer Smith, a painter and
       glazier in Boston, where he d. July 29, 1810, ae. 36. She d.
       in Boston, in June, 1809, ae. 34.

8. DAVID[4] COMEE (*David,*[3] *John,*[2] *David*[1]) was a farmer, but one of "the embattled farmers" that "fired the shot heard round the world." Though not a member of any militia company, as a citizen of Lexington he saw active service April 19, 1775, when his queue was shot off. At the battle of Bunker Hill a bullet from the enemy was shot into the barrel of his musket. He was out two days from March 4 to March 6, 1776, at Roxbury, in Capt. Stephen Dana's Company, while the forts were being erected on Dorchester Heights (Rev. Rolls, xviii. 239). Soon after he moved from Lexington to Westminster, the part that was incorporated in 1785 as Gardner (Mass.). His deed from Amos Gates was dated April 19, 1776. From Dec. 12, 1776 to March 1, 1777, he was out in Capt. Manasseh Sawyer's Company in Colonel Dike's Regiment (Rev. Rolls, xxvi. 419). Aug. 22, 1777, at the Bennington alarm, he marched to East Hoosick in Capt. Elisha Jackson's Company with Major Bridge (Rev. Rolls, xx. 108). From Sept. 7 to Nov. 29, 1777, he was in Capt. Nathaniel Carter's Company in Col. Job Cushing's Regiment (Rev. Rolls, xviii. 31). His house in Gardner, where he died March 8, 1826, aged nearly 82, was about one and one-half miles east of the Centre on the road to Ashburnham and before his day had been an inn. David married first, Christiana, daughter of James Maltman, who came from Scotland to Boston about the middle of the eighteenth century. She died in Gardner, May 17, 1789, ae. 33 years and 8 months, and he married second, her younger sister Hannah Maltman, who lived to be 88 years, 2 months and 18 days, dying in Gardner, Oct. 23, 1852. She was blind the last twenty years of her life.

Children of David and Christiana, i. born in Lexington, the others in Westminster (Gardner) :

16. i. DAVID, b. Sunday, March 26, 1775.
17. ii. JAMES MALTMAN, b. Friday, April 18, 1777.
   iii. BENJAMIN, b. May 28, 1779; d. Jan. 26, 1785.
   iv. CHRISTIANA, b. Oct. 30, 1781; m. March 29, 1804, Eliel Bacon, of
       Gardner, and about 1805 moved to Henderson, N. Y.
   v. MARY, b. Sept. 4, 1784; m. June 29, 1806, William Fletcher 2d, of
       Templeton, and d. Oct. 7, 1818, ae. 34.
   vi. BENJAMIN, b. Dec. 13, 1786; d. April 4, 1790.
   vii. JOHN, b. Jan. 24, 1789; d. May 25, 1803.

     Children of David and Hannah, all born in Gardner :

   i. HANNAH MORE, b. April 6, 1790; d. March 10, 1810.
   ii. SARAH, b. Feb. 12, 1793; m. Aug. 11, 1814, Elijah Breck (1792–
      1866), of Gardner, where she d. June 29, 1877, ae. 84, leav-
      ing several children, among them Sarah Breck, who m. A.
      Allen Bent; and has one son Allen H. Bent.
   iii. PATTY, b. Oct. 2, 1795; d. May 19, 1803.
   iv. RUHAMA, b. Feb. 20, 1798; m. June 28, 1835, Abram Jaquith
      (1802–1851), of Fitchburg, where she died Dec. 19, 1884, ae. 86,
      leaving one daughter, Abby Mead Jaquith, who m. David
      Damon.
18. v. BENJAMIN, b. Sept. 16, 1800.
19. vi. JOSEPH, b. Jan. 14, 1803.
   vii. MARTHA, b. June 20, 1805; m. Sept. 29, 1828, Ebenezer Fenno
      (1801–1846), of Gardner; and d. at Baldwinsville, Mass., Aug.
      4, 1880, ae. 75, leaving three daughters. Mr. Fenno was a
      son of Ephraim Fenno (1759-1820) of Westminster, Mass.,
      and a descendant of John Fenno, who was in Milton, Mass.,
      at its incorporation in 1662.
20. viii. GEORGE WASHINGTON, b. Aug. 22, 1809.

9.   JONATHAN[4] COMEY (*David,[3] John,[2] David[1]*) when a lad, followed
    his older brothers to what later became Foxboro, and while still
    young removed to Holliston, where he lived with a Mr. Samuel
    Messenger. After his marriage he went to the western part of
    Hopkinton to live on the west side of Whitehall Pond. At the
    time of the Lexington alarm he was out eleven days in Capt. John
    Homes' Company in Col. Samuel Bullard's Regiment. His name
    is spelled Jn° Commey on the muster roll. He married Eliza-
    beth Wells.

     Children of Jonathan and Elizabeth, all born in Hopkinton :

   i. PARMELIA, m. Nathaniel Chamberlain, of Hopkinton, and moved
      to Wardsboro, Vt.
21. ii. ROYAL, b. Jan. 29, 1772.
   iii. BETSEY, m. Joshua Mellen, and lived in Westboro; where they
      had one son, the late Judge Edw. Mellen, of Worcester, and
      four daughters.
   iv. POLLY, m. Jonathan Fairbanks, and lived in Holden, Mass.
   v. NELLIPEE, m. John Wheelock, of Hopkinton; where she died at
      the birth of her son John, who was brought up by a Mr. Adams.
   vi. HANNAH, m. Abner Prentiss, of Hopkinton.

10.   JOHN[5] COMEY (*John,[4] David,[3] John,[2] David[1]*) was a farmer and
    lived in Foxboro, where he died May 24, 1830, ae. 77. At the
    Lexington alarm he marched as corporal in Capt. Israel Smith's Com-
    pany and was out four days (Rev. Rolls, xiii. 103). From May to
    December, 1775, during the siege of Boston, he was in Capt.
    Samuel Payson's Company in Col. Joseph Read's Regiment. He
    was also out five and one-half days in Capt. Josiah Pratt's Com-
    pany in Colonel Gill's Regiment "that marched on y[e] alarme to

Roxbury the 5 day of March A.D. 1776 " (Rev. Rolls, xxi. 188).
He married Betsey Carpenter, daughter of Nehemiah. Betsey
died in Foxboro in February, 1823.
Children of John and Betsey, all born in Foxboro :

  i. CLARISSA, b. May 29, 1783; d. unm. Dec. 29, 1855, ae. 72.
 ii. BETSEY, b. Aug. 26, 1784; d. unm. Nov. 13, 1869, ae. 85.
iii. SPENCER, b. April 2, 1786; d. Foxboro, Dec. 14, 1859, ae. 73.
 iv. THATCHER, b. March 22, 1788; d. Foxboro, Dec. 23, 1867, ae. 79.
  v. NABBY, b. Aug. 9, 1790; d. July 13, 1796.
 vi. EUNICE, b. June 6, 1792; d. unm. Oct. 3, 1858, ae. 66.
vii. ESTHER, b. March 6, 1794; d. unm. May 25, 1831, ae. 37.
viii. NABBY, b. March 1, 1797; m. 1845, Amos Keith, of Norton;
        where she d. May 1, 1884.
 ix. JOHN, b. April 1, 1798; d. Foxboro, April 7, 1886, ae. 88.

11. OLIVER[5] COMEY (*John,*[4] *David,*[3] *John,*[2] *David*[1]) was a farmer and
     lived in Foxboro, where he died Jan. 4, 1842, ae. 84. He en-
     listed July 14, 1778, and served until Feb. 18, 1779, in Capt.
     John Ellis's Company in Col. Thomas Poor's Regiment, raised
     to fortify and secure the passes of the North River in New York
     (Rev. Rolls, xix. 3). In later years was called Captain Comey.
     He married, Dec. 21, 1786, Elizabeth, daughter of Eleazar Bel-
     cher. She died in Foxboro, May 12, 1851, aged 83 years, 3
     months and 26 days.
     Children of Oliver and Elizabeth, all born in Foxboro :

  i. OLIVER, b. Oct. 23, 1788; d. Foxboro, May 3, 1875, ae. 87.
 ii. AARON, b. July 5, 1789; d. Jan. 6, 1846, ae. 56.
iii. ELIZA, b. April 27, 1791; m. June 3, 1813, Abijah Fales. She d.
        Dec. 17, 1859, ae. 68. Children: Eliza M., Emily C., Abijah,
        Elizabeth and Abner.
 iv. LYMAN, b. Aug. 6, 1793; d. June 14, 1878, ae. 84.
  v. WILLARD, b. March 26, 1796; d. Foxboro, April 23, 1869, ae. 73.
 vi. PRUDENCE, b. July 7, 1798; d. Nov. 13, 1800.
vii. JASON, b. Oct. 4, 1800; d. Piinceton, Iowa, Sept. 15, 1853.
viii. MIRA, b. Dec. 8, 1802; m. Martin Copeland, of Easton. She d.
        March 19, 1878, leaving one son Ephraim M. Copeland, of
        Foxboro.
 ix. OTIS, b. Feb. 3, 1805; went to Pennsylvania about 1833; and is
        supposed to have been drowned.
  x. CHARLES, b. April 8, 1807; living in Kennebunk, Me.
 xi. OMAN, b. July 31, 1811; d. Foxboro, Nov. 12, 1895.

12. SPENCER[5] COMEY (*John,*[4] *David,*[3] *John,*[2] *David*[1]) of Foxboro,
     enlisted Aug. 14, 1777, (when only 17 years old), in Capt. John
     Bradley's Company in Col. Benjamin Gill's Regiment, marched
     to Manchester, Vt., to join the Northern Army and was out three
     months and twenty-eight days. He was in service again in Col.
     Thomas Nixon's Regiment from Sept. 1, 1779 to Feb. 3, 1780,
     when he was reported killed (Rev. Rolls, liii. 210).

13. EZRA[5] COMEE (*Joseph,*[4] *David,*[3] *John,*[2] *David*[1]) at the time of his
     marriage was of Cambridge, but seems to have lived on the south
     side of the river, that is, in the part set off in 1807 as Brighton.
     About 1782 he moved away. His later years were spent in Dana
     (Mass.), where he died Nov. 19, 1832, ae. 81. He married Feb.
     16, 1774, Anna Porter, of Newton. She died at Dana, Oct. 28,
     1838, ae. 81.

Children of Ezra and Anna:

   i. ELIZA, b. March 21, 1781; m. Dec. 29, 1802, Rev. Joshua Flagg.
   ii. SUSAN, b. July 19, 1791; m. Barney Flagg (1792–1857).
   iii. THOMAS WILSON, b. Jan 3, 1794; m. Lydia Towne, of Dana.

14. BENJAMIN³ COMEE (*Joseph,*⁴ *David,*³ *John,*² *David*¹) of Foxboro, is spoken of both as a cordwainer and a trader. He was a sergeant in the Foxboro militia in 1797. He died in Foxboro, Oct. 11, 1842, ae. 77. He married March 24, 1785, Ruth Trow. Children of Benjamin and Ruth, all born in Foxboro:

   i. AARON, b. Nov. 13, 1785; d. Nov. 13, 1785.
   ii. NANCY, b. April 8, 1787; d. July 20, 1811, ae. 24.
   iii. RUTH, b. March 17, 1790.
   iv. OTIS, b. Aug. 12, 1791; nothing further known.

15. BENJAMIN⁵ COMEY (*Benjamin,*⁴ *David,*³ *John,*² *David*¹) moved from Malden to Boston some time before 1793, and continued to live there until 1842, when he moved to Dorchester. In April 1848 he moved from Dorchester to Chelsea, where he died June 24, 1858, ae. 90. He was a mast-maker and built Comey's Wharf, which first appears in the Boston Directory of 1835. The wharf was taken in 1894 to become a part of the North End Park. Benjamin married first, Hannah Watts, who died in Boston, July 25, 1829, ae. 62. She was born in Boston, Dec. 11, 1767, dau. of Bellingham Watts (1732–1767), mariner, who was son of Samuel and Hannah. He married second, Nov. 29, 1830, Nancy, eldest daughter of Robert Howe, of Boston. She died in Reading, Kansas, in 1886. No children by the first wife. Children of Benjamin and Nancy, born in Boston:

   i. ISABELLA HARRIS, b. September, 1832; d. in Chelsea, Nov. 3, 1854, unm.
   ii. HANNAH WATTS, b. Sept. 22, 1834; taught school in Chelsea; m. in 1865, Joel Augustus Stratton, of Leominster, Mass., where they lived until February 1879, when they moved to Reading, Kansas. Mr. Stratton was a Capt. in 53d Mass. Vols.

16. DAVID⁵ COMEE (*David,*⁴ *David,*³ *John,*² *David*¹), of Gardner, married March 31, 1799, Esther, daughter of John and Betsey Baker, of Gardner, where she died Oct. 5, 1863, aged 88 years, 11 months and 5 days. He died Sept. 18, 1848, ae. 73. Children of David and Esther, all born in Gardner:

   i. DAVID, b. June 4, 1801; d. April 17, 1803.
   ii. BETSEY, b. Dec. 9, 1802; m. Dec. 28, 1826, Jesse Lovewell (1798–1838), of Hubbardston, Mass.
   iii. JOHN, b. Dec. 21, 1804; m. 1st, March 18, 1858, Mrs. Mary Ann Robbins, dau. of Robert Reed, of Dunstable, who d. Nov. 12, 1867, ae. 57. He m. 2d, March 10, 1870, Mrs. Harriet Stoddard, dau. of Luke Knight, of Winchendon. John d. in Gardner, March 5, 1885, ae. 80. No children.
   iv. LOUISA, b. Oct. 4, 1808; m. Dec. 2, 1829, Leonard Lovewell, of Hubbardston.

17. JAMES MALTMAN⁵ COMEE (*David,*⁴ *David,*³ *John,*² *David*¹) of Gardner, was the first in the town to engage in chair manufacturing, an industry for which the town has since become famous, some $2,000,000 worth being made there annually now. It

seems to have been in the year 1805 that he began the industry in a small way in one of the rooms in his own house. The chairs he teamed himself to Boston, Salem, Providence and Worcester. The very first were probably wood seats, but they were soon succeeded by the old flag seats. He and his older brother were Masons, probably members of the now extinct Lodge at Templeton. His house was on the Ashburnham road, a short distance from the centre of Gardner. He was the first Comee to indulge in the luxury of a middle name.

James M. married Jan. 26, 1802, Sally, daughter of John and Abigail Putnam, of Fitchburg. She died in Gardner, Dec. 23, 1863, aged 84 years, 6 months and 24 days. He died Aug. 27, 1832, ae. 55.

Children of James M. and Sally, all born in Gardner:

i. MARIA, b. Sept. 2, 1802; m. Nov. 22, 1821, Isaac Jaquith (1797–1861), of Gardner, where she d. Feb. 15, 1881, ae. 78.
ii. CHRISTIANA, b. April 1, 1805; m. June 23, 1825, William S. Lynde, of Gardner, where she d. May 7, 1842.
iii. SALLY, b. May 14, 1807; m. Oct. 27, 1824, Benjamin Franklin Heywood (1802–1843), a chair manufacturer, of Gardner. She d. at Fitchburg.
iv. JAMES MALTMAN, b. May 31, 1809; d. at Fitchburg, Nov. 11, 1893.
v. MARY, b. May 23, 1811; m. Aug. 25, 1829, Gen. Moses Wood (1803–1869), of Gardner, and afterward lived in Providence and Fitchburg. She is living in Brookline, Mass.
vi. WILLIAM WILLIAMS, b. Aug. 19, 1813; d. July 22, 1883; the father of Fred R. Comee, of Boston Music Hall.
vii. ABIGAIL, b. April 24, 1816; m. 1st, Nov. 3, 1836, Jonas Harwood (1812–1840), of North Brookfield; and 2d, Aug. 1, 1847, Rev. Sumner Lincoln (1799–1890), a Unitarian clergyman. She d. at Wilton, N. H., Jan. 24, 1895, ae. 78, leaving one dau. Mrs. Abbie L. Bridges, by her second husband.
viii. JOHN PORTER, b. Sept. 3, 1818; d. March 8, 1819.
ix. LEANDER PORTER, b. Dec. 26, 1819; d. Dec. 9, 1885.
x. ELIZA, b. April 28, 1822; d. March 10, 1836.
xi. DANIEL WEBSTER, b. Aug. 21, 1825; d. unm. in Sacramento, Cal.

18. BENJAMIN[5] COMEE (*David,*[4] *David,*[3] *John,*[2] *David*[1]) moved from Gardner, Mass., to Henderson, N. Y., about 1838, and thence in 1855 to Hebron, Wis., and later to Seymour, Wis., where he died Oct. 5, 1880, ae. 80. He married first, Sept. 30, 1823, Lovina Mead, born April 7, 1803, daughter of Thomas and Charlotte Mead, of Lunenburg, Mass. She died at Henderson, N. Y., July 11, 1842, ae. 39. He married second, Mrs. Eliza Ann Seger (born Dye), who died at Hebron, Wis., 1869, ae. 66. He was a cabinet-maker, painter, and decorator.

Children of Benjamin and Lovina:

i. CHARLOTTE EMELINE, b. Aug. 31, 1824; m. Feb. 20, 1841, Samuel Delos Ward; and lives (1895) with her only son, Benjamin Comee Ward, at Superior, Nuckolls Co., Neb.
ii. CAROLINE AUGUSTA, b. June 26, 1826; m. John Parsons, and lives in Wisconsin.
iii. MARTHA ANN, b. Aug. 28, 1828; m. 1st, —— Gates; and 2d, Nicholas Stokes. They live at Lacrosse, Wis.
iv. JAMES MUNROE, b. Aug. 8, 1830; m. Jennie Thornton; and d. at Lacrosse, Wis., 1862(?) ae. 32. No children.
v. SARAH MEAD, b. Oct. 12, 1832; m. 1st, Aug. 20, 1856, Orrin H. Emory, who d. during the War (Oct. 29, 1864). She m. 2d, Oct. 1, 1866, James H. Bower, and lives at Whitewater, Wis.

Children of Benjamin and Eliza, all born at Henderson, N. Y.:

    i. MARIA ROSETTE, b. Oct. 4, 1844; m. Jan. 1, 1860, Uriel Tibbets; and lives now at Franklin, Minn.

    ii. WILLIAM BENJAMIN, b. Nov. 11, 1846; m. 1867, Anna Eliza Francis, of Milwaukee, and lives at Seymour, Wis.

    iii. SQUIRE S., b. Aug. 9, 1848; unm.; lives at Lake Linden, Mich. A photographer.

    iv. HELEN, b. 1854; d. unm. March 15, 1890, at Seymour, Wis.

19.   JOSEPH[5] COMEE *David,[4] David,[3] John,[2] David[1]*), after the death of his father in 1826, took the old homestead in Gardner, but about 1837 moved to New York. He lived for a short time in Henderson and then in Belleville, but soon located in Ellisburg (N. Y.), where he died Jan. 10, 1856, ae. 53. He married, April 27, 1826, Miriam Stone, born Gardner, July 13, 1799, youngest daughter of Samuel Stone. She died in Ashburnham, Mass., Oct. 2, 1863, ae. 64.

Children all born in Gardner, except v., who was born in Henderson, N. Y.:

    i. CHRISTOPHER COLUMBUS, b. Jan. 28, 1827; was a captain in 94th Reg., N. Y. Vols., captured at Gettysburg and confined in Libby Prison. He is an artist and lives in Waseka, Minn.

    ii. SAMUEL STONE, b. June 17, 1830; m. Sarah W. Sawin.

    iii. JAMES, b. Sept. 12, 1832; d. May 26, 1839.

    iv. MARTHA STONE, b. Dec. 8, 1834; m. Aug. 19, 1858, Otis D. Sawin, and lives in Waseka, Minn. They have an adopted dau. Winnie.

    v. GEORGE WASHINGTON, b. June 9, 1838; m. Dec. 26, 1881, Elizabeth Kittredge, and has lived in Waseka, Minn., since about 1867. No children. He is a furniture mfr. with his brother-in-law, A. D. Sawin.

20.   GEORGE WASHINGTON[5] COMEE (*David,[4] David,[3] John,[2] Daivd[1]*) lived in Gardner, Templeton and Fitchburg, and about 1852 went to Worcester (Mass.), where he died May 28, 1878, ae. 68. He married first, May 2, 1833, Fanny Richardson Vining, born June 27, 1810, daughter of John Vining of Templeton. She became an invalid soon after her marriage and died at Templeton, Mass., Aug. 30, 1838, ae. 28. No children. George W. married second, Betsey Howard, of Brookfield.

Children of George W. and Betsey, all of whom died young:

    i. GEORGE M., b. May 1, 1842.

    ii. FRANCIS.

    iii. FANNIE.

    iv. FRANK.

21.   ROYAL[5] COMEE (*Jonathan,[4] David,[3] John,[2] David[1]*) was born in Hopkinton, Mass., Jan. 29, 1772; and died in Hopkinton, in October 1852, ae. 80. He was a well-to-do farmer and always lived in Hopkinton on the east side of Whitehall Pond. He owned a large tract on the west side of the pond and an island, now called Comey's Island. He married Polly Andrews, of Milford, who died Aug. 29, 1873, aged 88 years, 8 months and 8 days.

Children of Royal and Polly, all born in Hopkinton:

    i. HIRAM, b. July 18, 1806; m. 1832, Emily Gibbs.

    ii. ALBERT, b. Aug. 3, 1806; was twice m., and had seven children.

    iii. ELBRIDGE GERRY, b. Nov. 21, 1811; m. Abigail J. Pierce.

iv. DEXTER, b. Feb. 21, 1814; d. in Westboro, Mass., Nov. 8, 1892.
   v. MARTHA ANN, b. Aug. 19, 1817; m. William B. Wales, of Hop-
      kinton; and d. April 13, 1845, leaving one child, Mary Ann.
  vi. MARY, b. July 12, 1823; d. unm. July 18, 1844.

NOTES AND QUERIES.

NOTES.

SHAPLEIGH AND TREWORGIE.—In the REGISTER, July, 1851, p. 345, Mr.
Thornton gives the record of Alexander Shapleigh and his descendants; this
record in some cases is correct, but the conclusions that Mr. Thornton arrives
at are much in error; for example, in the foot note (3) referring to James
Treworgye he says: "Probably Mr. Treworgye left no male descendants, else
they would have claimed the estate, in company with the daughters, but there
was 'John Treworgy' at Saco, in 1728—Folsom's Saco and Bid., 207, 231, 5,
71. Who was he?" In speaking of Alex. Shapleigh, he supposes that he was
born about 1600. He says: "Mr. James Treworgye was born as early as 1614,
probably earlier, as in 1635," etc. In the deposition of Mr. Edward Johnson,
Mr. Thornton corrects his testimony by substituting the name of James where
that of John appears. He also corrects the testimony of Joan Atwell by substituting the name of James for John, and also the title of father-in-law for
grandfather, and at the end makes the following statement: "James, not John,
Treworgy, was employed by Alex. Shapleigh. The grandson, John, mentioned
by the witness Atwell, probably never existed except to be confused with the
father in the mind of the witness." In all these matters Mr. Thornton, as I
have previously stated, is in error. Mr. John Treworgye did exist, was the son
of James Treworgye and Catherine Shapleigh, and consequently was the grandson of Alexander Shapleigh. It is also now well known that he went as super-
cargo for his grandfather previous to 1642, and was of sufficient age to represent him and to manage his affairs, for he was born at Kingsweare on the Dart
River, directly opposite Dartmouth, in 1618, and was baptized in the Church of
St. Thomas a Becket at that place, the 30th Dec., 1618, so that the testimony
of these witnesses was correct and not to be corrected. The Western Antiquary or Note Book for Devon, Cornwall and Somerset, England, No. 10, March,
1886, vol. v., contains a record of the Shapleighs of Devonshire, by W. M. Sargent, A.M., in which also a number of errors occur, but he does not fall into
that of Mr. Thornton in ignoring John Treworgye, the grandson of Alex. Shapleigh, but takes Mr. Thornton to task for changing the testimony of the witnesses. Mr. Alex. Shapleigh is put down as being born in 1585, and as from
Totnes, Devonshire. Mr. James Treworgye is said to have died in Newfoundland some time before 1650, before he was 35 years of age. These two statements are somewhat upset by the following facts: Mr. James Treworgye and
Catherine Shapleigh were married in the Church at Kingsweare, March 16, 1616,
so that Mr. A. Shapleigh must have been born a considerable number of years
previous to 1585, and James Treworgye to have been much older than 35 when
he died, probably a short time previous to 1650. From the same Church Registry I obtained also the following: Nicholas, son of Alex^r Shapleigh, was bap^d
Jan. 1, 1617 or 18 (being at the close of the Registry for 1617.—John, son of
James Treworgye, bap^d 30 Dec., 1618. James Treworgye & Cath^n Shapleigh
were mar^d 16 March 1616 (James 14th.) Jos. Bereford & Eliz^h Shapley were
mar^d ye 4th of July Anne Dom 1626 (King Charles II.). In one of the numbers
of your magazine I noticed, in Notes and Queries, the question as to whether
anyone could tell how Kittery Point, Maine, founded by the Shapleighs and
Treworgyes, received its name. Alex. Shapleigh and his family lived in that
portion of Kingsweare called Kittery Point to this day, and which still contains
the Manor House, which was probably the residence of that family, and naturally when the family went to the new home in New England the old name was
perpetuated in that of the new town. There is not a trace of the name of
Alexander Shapleigh in any of the old papers relating to the history or records

of Totnes (which is a very old town about ten miles up the Dart River), but there are many other members of the family, some of whom were mayors of the same. Although not successful in my search at Totnes, I was somewhat so in looking over the records of Dartmouth, where I found five references to *Mr.* Alexander Shapleigh, merchant, of Kingsweare. He is so spoken of in an acknowledgement of a contribution of money in 1620. In the same and following year the following items appear:—

"In the ship ' Blessinge' of Kingsweare, from Lisbone, for Alexander Shapley, merchant (1620), £2 2. 0."

"1620. In the 'Gift of God' of Kingsweare, from Lichbone (Lisbon), for Alexander Shapley, merchant, £0 1. 9."

"1621. In the 'Gift of God' of Dartmouth, from Newfoundland, for Alexander Shapley, £0 2. 1."

"1621. In the 'William & John' of Dartmouth, from the Newfoundland, 20th Sept., for the said Mr. Alexander Shapleigh, merchant, £0 1. 3."

1720 Chestnut Street, Philadelphia, Pa.   Charles F. Haseltine.

The Number of one's Ancestors. —Having recently compiled an account in some detail of my American ancestors, it occurs to me that a few statistics from the record may have general interest:

The whole number of my male immigrant ancestors, so far as I have their names, is forty-six; of whom the first came to New England in 1630, thirty-seven before 1650, and all before 1687.

Judging by their names, one may have been French, one Irish, three Scottish, and thirty-six English, in origin.

Of my immigrant ancestors, so far as I know or can proximately estimate their ages, the average age of twenty-four men was 31 years, and of ten women 24 years, at the time of their arrival. The average age at death of twenty-eight men was 66 years, including two killed by Indians, and the average age at death of eighteen wives was 73. Nine men of the immigrants married twice and one three times. Five of their wives were married twice. The largest family of children was sixteen, by three wives.

The whole number of children of thirty-two immigrant ancestors was two hundred and forty-two (7.56 to a family) of whom two hundred and fifteen became adult; those who died in their minority being about one in ten of those born, and 52.7 per cent. of those born were sons.

I have records of twenty families of the second generation, showing the average of 7.75 children to each family, of whom 48.3 per cent. were sons.

Francis J. Parker.

Hamlin Families of Bridgewater and Pembroke.—Some where from 1742 to 1752 five persons of the name of Hamlin went to East Bridgewater, and settled near the town line, in that part of the town set off to Pembroke, June 5, 1754. I have not found the names of their parents, or the town from whence they came. Their names were:

1. *Mary Hamlin*, married in East Bridgewater, 1742, Joseph Richards. They moved to East Stoughton, now Avon, probably near the Randolph line. He died April, 1793, aged 81; the widow died Feb. 6, 1802. I have been unable to find her age.

2. *Isaac Hamlin*, m. Sarah, daughter of Nicholas and Lydia Shaw, of Abington, about 1747. He d. as of Bridgewater, 1763. The births of his children are recorded on Bridgewater records; and their baptisms, part in Bridgewater and part in Pembroke.

3. *Mary Hamlin*, m. in East Bridgewater, 1746, Thomas Moore. The births of his children are given on Bridgewater records; and their baptisms on Pembroke Church records.

4. *Elisabeth Hamlin*, m. in East Bridgewater, Nov. 5, 1750. I find the baptisms of two of their children on Pembroke Church records.

5. *Eleazer Hamlin*, m. in East Bridgewater, June 30, 1752, Lydia Bonney, by Rev. John Angier. The dates of birth of their two oldest children are on Bridgewater records, and the baptisms of their eleven children on Pembroke Church records. He is said to have moved from Bridgewater to Pembroke;

possibly he may have lived in that part of Bridgewater set off to Pembroke 1754. He moved to Harvard, 1780? And from there to Westford, 1789? where he d. Dec. 1, 1807, aged 75 years and 5 months. I think Eleazer and Isaac and Mary Richards and Elisabeth Holmes were brothers and sisters. This Eleazer was the grandfather of the late Vice-President Hannibal Hamlin, of Bangor. J. W. PORTER.

Bangor, Me.

QUERIES.

MANNING. — Information will gladly be received of the following persons: William Manning, a resident of Cambridge, Mass., as early as 1635, had wife Susannah, and, after her death, 16 Oct. 1650, he married Elizabeth ——. He died in Boston about 1666. His son William, a merchant of Cambridge, and, by virtue of his office as selectman, much associated with the affairs of Harvard College, married about 1640, Dorothy ——. Who were these three wives?

Abial (Wight) Manning, wife of Samuel of Billerica, was left a widow in 1711 at the age of 57. Her death has not been found. Did she marry a second time? Her daughter Abial, born 16 Dec. 1698, has not been traced. Benjamin Shedd, born 5 Aug. 1696, who was of Billerica at the same period of time, had a wife Abial. Who was she? Eliphalet Manning, son of the above Samuel, married about 1712, Rebecca ——. Can she have been daughter of Thomas Frost, of Billerica? He had a child Rebecca, and Rebecca Manning named her second son Thomas.

Captain John Manning was at Boston as early as 1640, where he was a merchant and member of the Artillery Company. His second wife was Ann, daughter of Richard Parker, and she married, second, Wm. Gerrish, then of Boston, and had a son Henry born in 1676. John was living in 1663. When, or about when, did he die?

Isaac Manning, born 15 April, 1685, at Billerica, married Margaret Eager and lived as late as 1723 at Cambridge, where he had eight children born. Did he continue to reside there, or remove? When and where did he and his wife die?

John Manning, born 29 Feb. 1695-6, at Billerica, lived at Cambridge as late as 1735; married, 1728, Rebecca Winship and had Sarah, baptized 20 April, 1729, John, 12 Dec. 1731, and Esther, 5 Jan. 1734-5. Were there other children? What became of the daughters? When and where did John, the father, die?

Joseph Manning, born at Cambridge about 1705, graduated at Harvard 1730; was a physician at Woburn when he made his will, 1744; probably practiced at Medford, 1739; died before 4 Nov., 1745. He left his property to Harvard, and to his father, brothers and sisters, evidently having neither children nor wife. Was he ever married? The REGISTER, vol. xxiv., mentions a John Manning who was surgeon in the Louisburg expedition of 1745. I know of no John of that period who was either a surgeon or physician. Was "John" an error of record for Joseph?

Edward Manning, born at Cambridge, 26 March, 1724, married 1745, Patience Day, of Boston, and had children, Margaret, born 27 Sept. 1747, at Cambridge; and, at Roxbury, Elizabeth, 28 Sept. 1750, Patience, 17 Dec. 1752, and Edward, baptized 14 July, 1754. Were there other children? When and where did the parents die? An intention of marriage at Boston, 6 May, 1759, is that of Casper Feiler [Fielder?] and Patience Manning, and she may have been widow of Edward, though there are some reasons for doubting it. Who married Mr. Fielder? Edward, father or son, was living in 1780. What became of the elder Edward's children? Was Edward, Jr., the Revolutionary soldier from Boston? and was he the Edward captured by the British, 1777, as one of the crew of the brigantine "Rising States," and confined in Forton Prison, England, as described in the REGISTER, vol. xxx., and after? Was he the Edward who probably married Patience Flagg, at Boston, 1779 (intention, Nov. 18), and who was she? Was Patience Day the same born at Dorchester, 11 July, 1729, daughter of John and Patience? What was her ancestry?

Caleb Manning, born 1746; lived at Charlestown, Medford and Salem; married Rachael Rand and had children Nathaniel, Caleb, Abigail, Mary and Elizabeth. Can additions be made to the imperfect Charlestown records? What was the history of the daughters? Caleb, Jr., married 16 April, 1801, Lois Graves, of Salem, where both died; she, in 1807; he, in 1810. What children did they have? Who was Lois?

Isaac Manning, Charlestown, married 8 Dec. 1763, Hannah Peirce, who died the next August. He then married Jane ——. I am anxious to learn the children of this marriage. What was Jane's maiden name? In the settlement of Isaac's estate, in 1787, the sureties for Jane, who was administratrix, were John Carter and Jabez Frothingham. Does this furnish a clew to her identity?

Willam Manning, born at Charlestown, married in 1798, Mehitable McIntire. When and where did he die? Their children were in part, and the list is believed to be correct, though possibly not full: Lydia and Samuel, said to have died unmarried; Eliza, married Abel B. King; Clarissa, (said to have married —— Penniman, and, second, —— Cannon), and William, who married Mary S. —— [Richardson?], and left children William, Edward, Augustus, Lenora, wife of Wm. Gove, and Catherine, wife of Wm. Blaisdell, some of whom are doubtless living. Their whereabouts, and suggestions as to where records may be found, are desired.

What children did the following members have? Mary, born 20 Feb. 1744, at Tewksbury; married Hezekiah Brown. Rebecca, born 24 May, 1751, at Tewksbury; married David Hardy. Hannah, of Tewksbury, married in 1800 Thomas Richardson, "of Dracut." Mary, born 26 May, 1720, at Cambridge; married Stephen Randall. Mercy, born 19 Nov. 1735, at Cambridge; married Samuel Woods and had a daughter Mercy born at Roxbury in 1756 (baptized Nov. 7). Rebecca, married Caleb Marsh at Boston, about 1787. Elizabeth, of Charlestown, married William Taylor in 1787.

Who were the contracting parties to the following marriages, and what families resulted therefrom? Dorothy Manning and Henry Wholman [Holman?] at Boston, 1732, intention Aug. 12. Sarah Manning and Edward Gray, at Boston, 1737, intention Dec. 15. Richard Manning and Eleanor Mitchell, at Boston, 1737–8, intention Feb. 27. Elizabeth Manning and William Thompson, at Boston, 1741, intention July 17. Nathaniel Manning and Elizabeth Larned, at Boston, 1795, intention Dec. 3. Robert Manning and Hannah Green, at Salem, 30 March, 1738. Jacob Manning and Mary Tyler, at Salem, 2 July, 1745. Mary Tyler's parentage I know; of the others I have learned nothing. Who were they?

What became of the following persons born at Cambridge? Sarah, born 27 March, 1708; Benjamin, 15 Oct. 1730; Thomas, 8 May, 1727. Born at Billerica: Mary, 21 Dec. 1705; Martha, 26 July, 1718. Born at Charlestown: Daniel, 4 March, 1740; Margaret, baptized 28 Jan. 1745. At Townsend: Martha, 4 Dec. 1755. In Connecticut: Samuel, Woodstock, 15 Aug. 1724; Jacob, Windham, 5 Oct. 1750; Samuel, Norwich, 15 Sep. 1749.

Wm. H. Manning,
Brooklyn, N. Y.

Care of Long Island Historical Society.

———

Kimball.—Solomon Farnham Kimball, born in or about 1774, married Anna Spalding, born same year, and settled in Sheldon, Franklin County, Vt., about 1794, where they had the following children, born between 1794 and 1808: Charles Spaulding, Eliza, Abigail, Heber Chase, b. 14 June, 1801; Melvina, Solomon F., Jr., b. 5 Feb. 1805, and Daniel. Heber C. was the famous associate of Brigham Young in the leadership of the Mormon people. In 1812 the family removed from Sheldon to Mendon, Monroe County, N. Y., where the parents both died in 1825, the age of each being given as 51 years. Information showing the parentage or birthplace of this Solomon Farnham Kimball will be paid for. Address B. F. Cummings, Jr., 15 Pemberton Square, Boston, Mass.

———

Booth.—Calvin Booth, or John Calvin Booth (full name uncertain), settled in Scipio, Cayuga County, N. Y., not far from 1800. Among his children were Lorenzo, b. there 13 Oct. 1807; Hiram, and, it is thought, Obadiah. Lorenzo married Parthenia Works, became a Mormon and went to Kirtland, Ohio, and later to Nauvoo, Ill. Gideon Booth had at Long Meadow, Mass., or near there, a large family, among whom was John Calvin, b. 6 June 1773. Is the latter the same person as the Scipio settler? Information that will determine this point, or lead to the ancestry of the Scipio settler, will be paid for. Address B. F. Cummings, Jr., 15 Pemberton Square, Boston, Mass.

WELD—KNIGHT—RICKARD.—

Weld.—Has the maiden name of Amy, wife of Edmund Weld of Sudbury, Eng. (whose will appeared in the October REGISTER) ever been ascertained? Who were the parents of Edmund Weld of Sudbury, and how connected with the " Welds of Eaton "? Information also desired concerning the family of Elizabeth, first wife of Capt. Joseph Weld of Roxbury, Mass.

Knight.—Who was the father of Richard Knight who married Lucy Short? He was of Cranston, R.I. The marriage took place not far from 1780. Wanted, the exact date.

Rickard.—Is it known in what ship Gyles Rickard arrived in America, and whether from England or Wales? He is first mentioned in Plymouth records in 1637.   A. S. W. RICKARD.

Woonsocket, R. I.

PALMER—MOORE.—Will some member of the N. E. Historic Genealogical Society inform me of the parentage of Mary Palmer, of Stonington, Conn., who married, 1729, at Stonington, William Moore, and about 1745 to '50, removed to Dutchess County, N. Y. Her children were : i. Allen, b. 1730 : ii. Andrew, b. 1735; iii. James, b. 1738; iv. Abilene; v. Elizabeth; vi. Content, b. 1743; vii. William; viii. Mary. The first three were born at Stonington, the sister at Westerly, L. I.   HELEN WILKINSON REYNOLDS.

Answer.—Mary Palmer, b. 1713, was a daughter of Moses and Abigail (Allen) Palmer, as will be seen by the following pedigree :

1. WALTER PALMER m. (2) at Charlestown, Mass., Rebecca Short.   Their sixth child,

2. MOSES, bapt. 6 April, 1640, settled at Stonington with his father.   His wife was Dorothy.   He died 6 July, 1701.   Their children were :

   3. i.   Moses, b. 20 October, 1673.
       ii. Dorothy, b. 11 August, 1675.
       iii. John, b. 1 September, 1677.
       iv. Annie, bapt. 25 April, 1680.
       v.   Rebecca, bapt. 30 April, 1682.

3. MOSES PALMER, b. 20 October, 1673 ; married 1 April, 1703, Abigail Allen. Their children were :

       i.   John, b. 19 June, 1705.
       ii. Anne, b. 3 December, 1706.
       iii. *Anonyma*, b. 28 August, 1708; d. 26 September, 1708.
       iv. Abigail, b. 10 September, 1709.
       v.   Dorothy, b. 20 November, 1711.
   4. vi. Mary, b. 28 June, 1713.
       vii. Moses, b. 18 July, 1715; d. 3 April, 1726.
       viii.Submit, b. 3 May, 1718.
       ix. Rebecca, b. 5 April, 1720.
       x.   Lois, b. 3 March, 1722.

4. MARY PALMER, b. 28 June, 1713; married at Stonington 4 June, 1729, William More.   Children :

       i.   Allen More, b. 17 Jan., 1730.
       ii. Andrew, b. 6 Jan., 1735.
       iii. James, b. 21 March, 1738; d. 14 Feb., 1739.

The remainder of the children of William and Mary (Palmer) More do not occur on the Stonington, Conn., record.   RICHARD A. WHEELER.

CORNWELL, ROBINSON, QUACKENBUSH. —

Cornwall.—Wanted the maiden name of Mary ———, wife of John Cornwell, married at East Middletown (now Portland), Conn., about 1743.

Robinson.—Wanted the ancestry of Susan Robinson and date and place of her birth and marriage to Ozias Cornwell, who was baptized April 3, 1763, at East Middletown (now Portland), Conn., and removed with his father, John Cornwell, to Granville, Mass., during or soon after the close of the Revolutionary War.

Quackenbush.—Wanted ancestry of Mary Quackenbush, b. March 8, 1753, married Gideon Marlett (variously spelled Merlet, Melat, Marlatt, &c.), and lived in Glen (then Charleston), Montgomery Co., N. Y.   R. S. TAFT.

Burlington, Vt.

NICHOLAS[1] CADY, of Watertown, Mass., 1645; of Groton, Mass., 1668; married about 1650, Judith, daughter of William Knapp, Sr., of Watertown, 1636. Desired, the dates and place of death of Nicholas and Judith (Knapp) Cady.

Joseph[2] Cady (Nicholas[1]), born in Watertown, Mass., May 28, 1666; of Groton, Mass., 1668; removed in 1703, to Killingly, Conn., and died there Dec. 29, 1742. He m. about 1689, Sarah ———. Desired, the place and date of her death, and her parentage.

David[3] Cady (Joseph[2], Nicholas[1]), born Sept. 1703, at Killingly, Conn., married Oct. 22, 1722, Hannah, daughter of Thomas and Mary (Waters) Whitmore. Wanted, date of death of David[3] Cady.

Daniel[3] Lawrence (Enoch[2], John[1]), born March 7, 1681, in Groton, Mass.; of Plainfield, Conn., about 1707; died May 8, 1777, in Canaan, Conn. He married 1st, about 1701, Sarah ———. She died Jan. 26, 1711-12, Plainfield, Conn. Desired, her parentage.

499 Jackson Boulevard, Chicago, Ills. SCOTT JORDAN.

BUZZELL.—I would like to have following queries answered.

1. Sarah, dau. of Francis Pitman, m. William Buzzell of Oyster River, N. H., Nov. 28, 1728. Should like to know something further about her.

2. Parents of Eunice Drew of Middleton, N. H., who m. William Buzzell about 1758.

3. Parents of Judith Horne, who m. Henry Buzzell before 1740.

4. Ancestry of Sarah Hill, who m. Silas Buzzell about 1765 and died June 5, 1782.

5. Parents of Sarah Wibird, who m. John Buzzell, Jr., Jan. 4, 1724-5.

6. One of the daughters of John and Sarah married a Gray. Can any one tell anything further?

7. Betsey, daughter of John and Phebe (Evans) Buzzell, married a Johnson. Molly, another daughter, married a Keneston; and Phebe, another daughter, married a Jiles or Giles. Can any one tell of the descendants of either of these?

8. About 1760 John Stevens lived in Barnstead, N. H., and had Sarah, who m. Andrew Willey, John, Olive who never m., one who m. Wiall Leavitt, Nancy, one who m. ——— Allen, another who m. John Dockum, and another who m. a Bunker. Can any one tell anything of the above John Stevens or of any of his children?

9. Ancestry of Patience Dogget, b. 1670, died 1760, m. 1695 Samuel Annable.

10. Ancestry of Ann Gorham of Barnstable, Mass., who m. Thomas Annable Aug. 7, 1740. H. L. BUZZELL.

Fairhaven, Mass.

LAYTON, LEACH AND HARWOOD.—*John Layton, or Lawton,* said to have been born 1630; in 1652 settled in Newtown, L. I., N. Y., removed to Suffield, Conn.; died September, 1690. He married twice: 1st, Joanna Williams, 1659; 2d, Benedicta, 1665. Wanted, fuller data and information of this family and its branches. A James Lawton m. 1st, November 1693, Abigail Lamb; m. 2d, Faith Newell. Who were her parents?

Bezer Leach,[5] (Zadoc,[4] Jesse,[3] John,[2] Giles[1]), a caster in an iron foundry, married 1793, in Middleboro', Betsey Shaw, and had: Ezra (a well-to-do citizen of New Bedford), Isaac and Anne. Wanted, the parents of Betsey Shaw, and her grandchildren.

George Harwood and Jane (REGISTER, vol. ii., page 189-90), had three children in 1639-1642 in Boston. Wanted, full name of wife, and further record of the family, male and female, B. A. LEONARD.

DePere, Wisconsin.

DEVOTION, HUNTINGTON.—Information is desired on the following points, viz. :—

1. The French ancestry of Edward Devotion [b. 1621] of Roxbury, Mass.

2. The lineage of Samuel Huntington, b. July 3, 1732, at Windham, Conn., d. Jan. 5, 1796, at Norwich, Conn., was one of the signers of the Declaration of Independence.

" *The Kingdom,*" *Xenia, O.* (Miss) EMMA C. KING.

CUSTOM HOUSE NOTES.—During the war of the Revolution, and up to the formation of the Federal Government in 1789, the custom houses, or ports of entry, in Massachusetts were controlled and managed by the State. Where are the records and papers of Boston, Salem, Marblehead, Newburyport, etc.?
Brookline, Mass.   A. A. FOLSOM.

MERCY AND MARY.—I have seen so often in old manuscripts the given names " Mary" and " Mercy " (or Marcy) used interchangeably that I am led to think that frequently in early times they were considered the same. The instances are so common that I cannot ascribe this interchangeble use of the words to clerical carelessness on the part of the writer. Have other persons noticed the same fact?   S. A. G.

GOLD OR GOULD.—Would like ancestry of Wm. Gold or Gould who married in Milford, Ct., about 1704–6, 1st Abigail Disborough, 2d Mary Adkins. He signs as of New Milford in 1724, and descendants easily traced.
Milford, Ct.   MRS. NATHAN G. POND.

REPLIES.

REV. WILLIAM STOUGHTON (*ante p.* 9).—On June 5, 1662, the town of Guilford (Conn.) voted to send George Hubbard as a messenger to invite Rev. Joseph Eliot to become pastor in the town. If he decline Hubbard is directed to ask the opinion of Messrs. Gookin, Mitchell and Mather with reference to calling " one Mr. Stoughton, who (as we hear) is coming out of England." Mr. Eliot, however, accepted the call. The life of Stoughton in the January number of the REGISTER reminded me of this, which has never been printed.
Enoch Pratt Free Library, Baltimore, Md.   BERNARD C. STEINER.

SETH INGERSOLL BROWNE.—REGISTER, vol. xliv. pages 281–286. Since writing the article on " Nicholas Browne of Reading and some of his Descendents," a few facts in connection with my grandfather, Seth Ingersoll Browne, have come to my notice, which may not make an uninteresting addition to that paper. In the first place, however, it may be said, that Inkburrow is not the right spelling of the name. In searching for some trace of my grandfather's English ancestry, I found in the Boston Public Library (where almost everything else can be found) " The Official Maps of the Imperial Gazetteer," in which the place was described as follows:—

" *Inkberrow*, a village and a parish in Worcestershire. The village stands near the boundary with Warwickshire, five and a half miles west of Alcester, on the M. R and G. W. R. . . . has a post and money order office under Redditch." The parish includes several others and the whole population is 1628. " The manor belongs to the Marquis of Abergavenny. . . The living is a vicarage in the diocese of Worcester. . . The church is large, chiefly perpendicular and contains Sedilia and an altar tomb of 1631, restored in 1888." I send these details hoping that some descendant, in visiting England, may be able to trace the ancestry of Edward and Jane Lide Browne, the parents of the first American of the name. Seth Ingersoll Browne's gun, which he carried at Bunker Hill, is now in the possession of his grandson, Eben O. Hawes of Roxbury. It was bequeathed by my grandfather to his daughter Mrs. Cynthia Browne Hawes, in about 1808. It is a King's arm with a flint lock, and weighs about ten pounds. It is over six feet long, and the ramrod is over three feet long. On the right side of the barrel is engraved or stamped " G. R." surmounted by a crown and the word " Tower"; on the left side there are two crowns under one of which there is something that looks like a " V " or an " A " upside down, and under the other an emblem not easy to describe.

Seth Ingersoll Browne was buried in the Granary Burying Ground in tomb No. 52, near Gov. Sullivan's, originally marked " Warren," and owned in part by a relative of my grandfather, Elisha Browne. But this tomb was sold after 1808, as were some others, by the selectmen of Boston, probably, and another name was substituted, and is now on the tomb. (See Records in the Office of the Board of Health in the City of Boston.)
Malden, Mass.   HARRIET H. ROBINSON.

KNOWLTON.—On pages 344-346 of this magazine for October, 1861, Volume 15, there is given a Genealogical Table of the Knowlton Family by Ashbel Woodward, M.D., in which several omissions and errors appear. The list of descendants of Lieutenant Daniel and Col. Thomas Knowlton given on page 346, should read as follows :

Lieut. Daniel[6] (21) and Elisabeth had :

(28)　i. Daniel,[7] born Dec. 7, 1765 : married Betsey Burchard.　He died February, 1834.　He had seven children, the fourth of whom, son Phineas,[8] died a soldier in the army.

(29)　ii. Elisabeth,[7] b. March 24, 1768 ; m. Frederick Chaffee, of Ashford.

(30)　iii. Nathaniel,[7] b. Dec. 24, 1770 ; m. Sarah Leach, and had children : Farnham,[8] Emily A.,[8] Hosea,[8] Myron,[8] William[8] and Nathaniel.[8]

(31)　iv. Manassah,[7] twin brother of Nathaniel,[7] b. Dec. 24, 1770 ; m. 1st, Lydia Burton and had children :　Oren,[8] Ephraim,[8] Isaac,[8] Orendia,[8] Almira,[8] Maria,[8] George W.,[8] and Permelia[8] ; m. 2d, Elisabeth Card ; m. 3d, Clarissa Cogswell.

(32)　v. Ephraim,[7] b. Oct. 3, 1773.

(33)　vi. Martha,[7] b. Feb. 24, 1777, m. Charles Brandon, of Ashford.

(34)　vii. Keziah,[7] b. Feb. 9, 1781 ; m. Jan. 3, 1805, Amasa Lyon, Esq., of Ashford.　Lineage of husband and children already given ; see page 351.

(35)　viii. Hannah,[7] b. April 19, 1783 ; m. Daniel Knowlton, Esq., and had sons : Miner,[8] Danford,[8] Edwin,[8] and daughters :　Amanda,[8] Miriam,[8] and Elvira[8].　Their eldest son, Miner, was educated at West Point ; was subsequently assistant professor in that institution, and now holds a commission in the Army of the United States. See page 225.

By wife Rebecca, had :

(36)　ix. Erastus Fenton,[7] b. Jan. 29, 1790 ; m. Waite Windsor, of Gloucester, R. I.

(37)　x. Marvin,[7] b. Sept. 3, 1794 ; m. Calista Leonard, of Stafford, Conn.

Col. Thomas[6] (22) and Anna, had :

(38)　i. Frederick,[7] b. Dec. 4, 1760 ; d. Oct. 9, 1841.　He served in the campaign of 1776, and was with his father at the battle at Harlem Heights.

(39)　ii. Sally,[7] b. Nov. 23, 1763.

(40)　iii. Thomas,[7] b. July 13, 1765.

(41)　iv. Dolly,[7] b. Jan. 11, 1767.

(42)　v. Abigail,[7] b. June 20, 1768.

(43)　vi. Samson,[7] b. Feb. 8, 1770 ; d. Sept. 10, 1777.

(44)　vii. Anna,[7] b. June 8, 1771 ; d. June 4, 1772.

(45)　viii. Anna,[7] b. March 19, 1773.

(46)　ix. Lucinda,[7] b. Nov. 10, 1776 ; d. Feb. 16, 1805.

All persons having in their possession copies of the New-England Historical and Genealogical REGISTER, Volume XV. (1861), and also copies of Ashbel Woodward's Life of Gen. Nathaniel Lyon, published by Case, Lockwood & Co., Hartford, 1862, are requested to send their names and addresses to Rev. Charles H. W. Stocking, D.D., No. 16 Prospect Terrace, East Orange, N. J., and will be furnished with a correct table of descendants, to insert at page 346 of the former volume, and page 356 of the latter.

EDWARD WHALLEY AND WILLIAM GOFFE.—The article in the January number of the REGISTER for 1896, recalls an item I copied several years ago, also bringing to mind the reason for my copying it. Nearly fifty years ago, when riding out with an uncle of mine, in passing an old forsaken house he said to me : "there's where the Whalleys used to live." In some way the remark he made concerning the house and the Whalleys was never forgotten. In the garret of the William Mudge house at Glen Cove, L. I., there was recently found an old account book in which " Moses Mudg," who was the early " store keeper " of Musceta Cove, had entered his charges against the inhabitants of " the plantation " for goods sold them. The entries commence with the year 1674,—and with 1676 there are many charges against persons who had sought refuge at Musceta Cove from Rhode Island, because of the King Philip war ; and among them was *Mr. Goff*,—the only " Mr." in the whole book. I have always thought since becoming interested in genealogical research that this " Mr. Goff" of Mudge's book was none other than the son-in-law of Edward Whalley—and that they both were in 1676 living in the house pointed out to me by my uncle, Charles Underhill, a descendant of " Capt. John," who had probably heard the tradition from the Underhill family—they having their plantation but a little way off from the Whalley house. The location of this house was in that part of the town called " Buckram," some three miles from Glen Cove, entirely isolated and well situated for the purpose of protecting the regicides from arrest. Again, after the Revolution, there were several families bearing the name of " Whalley" living in this immediate vicinity, and though their descendants know nothing of " Edward Whalley the Regicide," yet it appears to me that they must be in some way connected. In one churchyard there are four graves of Whalleys whose births date prior to the Revolution.

Maplewood, N. J. DANIEL H. CARPENTER.

HISTORICAL INTELLIGENCE.

THAYER.—Members of the Thayer family will be glad to learn that Mr. W. P. W. Phillimore has been induced to include in his forthcoming series of Gloucestershire (England) Marriage Registers the Marriage Registers of Thornbury, from whence came Thomas and Richard Tayer, or Thayer. The subscription price, 10s. 6d., for the Thornbury Marriage Registers when published, should be sent to Mr. Phillimore at 124 Chancery Lane, London, W. C., England.

H. E. W.

GENEALOGIES IN PREPARATION.—Persons of the several names are advised to furnish the compilers of these genealogies with records of their own families and other information which they think may be useful. We would suggest that all facts of interest illustrating family history or character be communicated, especially service under the U. S. Government, the holding of other offices, graduation from college or professional schools, occupation, with places and dates of birth, marriage, residence and death. When there are more than one christian name they should all be given in full if possible. No initials should be used when the full names are known.

Gifford.—Mr. H. E. Gifford, Wollaston, Mass., has in press a genealogy of the Gifford family, from 1630 to 1896, containing nearly 2000 names. Price $1.50. The edition will be limited to the number of copies subscribed for.

Lowell.—Rev. D. R. Lowell, Post Chaplain U. S. Army, Fort Douglas, Salt Lake City, Utah, has in preparation a genealogy of the Lowell family. He has been engaged in collecting data for eight years, and has travelled thousands of miles in the search. He has also obtained the MS. genealogical collections of the late Abner Lowell of Portland, Maine, who for years made a successful search for the Lowell genealogy. Circulars will be furnished by the compiler on application.

SOCIETIES AND THEIR PROCEEDINGS.

NEW-ENGLAND HISTORIC GENEALOGICAL SOCIETY.

Boston, Massachusetts, Wednesday, October 2, 1895.—A stated meeting was held this afternoon, at three o'clock, in Marshall P. Wilder Hall, in the Society's House, the president, Hon. William Claflin, LL.D., in the chair.

The president introduced the Rev. Lucius Robinson Paige, the oldest living member, and the first member elected after the formation of the Society, now in the 94th year of his age. Dr. Paige expressed his gratification at being once more present at a meeting of the society and the delight he experienced in visiting the Society's House and beholding the improvements in the library and building. When Dr. Paige withdrew the members rose and remained standing till he left.

Robert T. Swan, Esq., Commissioner on Records in this State, read a paper entitled "Some Observations of and upon the Town Records in Massachusetts."

Six resident members were elected.

A committee of three was appointed to report on the advisability of the creation of a Bureau of Public Records by the State.

Resolutions were passed on the death of Alexander H. Rice, LL.D., prepared by Hon. John D. Long; Hon. Henry Oscar Houghton, A.M., by Rev. Dr. Byington; and Rev. Alonzo Ames Miner, D.D., by Rev. Anson Titus. The reports of Rev. Ezra H. Byington, D.D., the historiographer, of Charles S. Ensign, LL.B., the corresponding secretary, and of John W. Dean, the librarian, were presented.

November 6.—A stated meeting was held in Marshall P. Wilder Hall, this afternoon, President Claflin in the chair.

The Rev. Egbert C. Smyth, D.D., President of Andover Theological Seminary, read a paper on "The Early Writings of Jonathan Edwards." Rev. Anson Titus followed with some remarks.

Rev. Dr. E. H. Byington, chairman of the committee on the Preservation of the Records of Massachusetts, made a report, the consideration of which was postponed till the next meeting.

The reports of the council, the corresponding secretary, the historiographer and the librarian were presented.

Fifteen resident members were elected.

December 4.—A stated meeting was held this afternoon. In the absence of the president, Charles S. Ensign, LL.B., was chosen president *pro tem.*

Rev. William Copley Winslow, D.D., LL.D., D.C.L., read a paper on "Governor Edward Winslow; his Part and Place in Plymouth Colony."

The report of the Committee on the Public Records was taken up and discussed. A committee of five was elected to appear at the several hearings of the committee in charge of the subject and urge such practical measures as they approve for the preservation of the Public Records.

The reports of the council, the corresponding secretary, the historiographer and the librarian were presented.

Nine resident members were elected.

A nominating committee, consisting of Rev. George M. Bodge and Messrs. Don Gleason Hill, George B. Knapp, William B. Trask and Hon. Charles Levi Woodbury, were elected by ballot; and Aaron Sargent, Esq., and Hon. Nathaniel J. Rust were appointed auditors.

January 1, 1896.—The fiftieth annual meeting was held at three o'clock this afternoon, at Marshall P. Wilder Hall, Society's House, 18 Somerset street, Boston, the president, Hon. William Claflin, LL.D., in the chair.

The monthly report of the council was presented.

Several resident members were elected.

The business of the annual meeting was then taken up, and the annual reports of the council, the treasurer, the corresponding secretary, the historiographer, the librarian and the trustees of the Kidder Fund were presented.

The Rev. George M. Bodge, A.M., chairman of the nominating committee, reported a list of candidates for officers for the ensuing year. Messrs. Albert A. Folsom and David G. Haskins, Jr., were appointed tellers. A ballot was taken and all the candidates nominated were elected.

President Claflin then delivered his annual address. The subject of his address was "The Life and Public Services of John Hancock."

Thanks were voted for their valuable services to the retiring officers and counsellors, namely, Charles S. Ensign, LL.B., Rev. E. H. Byington, D.D., Hon. Charles C. Coffin and Don Gleason Hill.

It was voted that the Address of the President, the Annual Reports this day accepted, the Special Report made to the Council at their June meeting, relating to the Towne Memorial Fund, the biographical notices of deceased members printed in the REGISTER for April, July and October, 1895, and January, 1896, together with the proceedings of this meeting, be printed in pamphlet form, and distributed to the members (including the families of members deceased during the year), donors and exchanging societies; the number of the copies to be determined by the committee on publication.

The following are the officers for 1896–7 :
President.—Hon. William Claflin, LL.D., of Newton, Mass.
Vice Presidents.—Hon. Charles Levi Woodbury, of Boston, Mass.; Hon. Joseph Williamson, A.M., of Belfast, Me.; Hon. Frederick Smyth, A.M., of Manchester, N. H.; Hon. James Barrett, LL.D., of Rutland, Vt.; Hon. Herbert Warren Ladd, A.M., of Providence, R. I.; Prof. Edward Elbridge Salisbury, LL.D., of New Haven, Conn.
Recording Secretary.—George Augustus Gordon, A.M., of Somerville, Mass.
Corresponding Secretary.—Albert Harrison Hoyt, A.M., of Boston, Mass.
Treasurer.—Benjamin Barstow Torrey, of Hanover, Mass.
Librarian.—John Ward Dean, A.M., of Medford, Mass.
The following are the members of the Council for 1896:
Ex-Officio.—Hon. William Claflin, LL.D.; George A. Gordon, A.M.; Benjamin B. Torrey; Hon. Charles Levi Woodbury; Albert Harrison Hoyt, A.M.; John Ward Dean, A.M.
For the Term Ending in 1897.—Francis Everett Blake, of Boston, Mass.; George Kuhn Clarke, LL.B., of Needham, Mass.; Albert Alonzo Folsom, of Brookline, Mass.
For the Term Ending in 1898.—William Tracy Eustis, of Boston, Mass.; David Greene Haskins, Jr., A.M., LL.B., of Cambridge, Mass.; Hon. Newton Talbot, of Boston, Mass.
For the Term Ending in 1899.—Charles Sidney Ensign, LL.B., of Watertown, Mass.; John Tyler Hassam, A.M., of Boston, Mass.; Henry Allen Hazen, D.D., of Auburndale, Mass.

February 5.—A stated meeting was held this afternoon, Hon. Charles Levi Woodbury, vice president, in the chair.

Rev. Carlton Albert Staples, of Lexington, Mass., read a paper on the " Hancock-Clarke House in Lexington."

Reports of the corresponding secretary, the librarian and the council were presented. Eight resident members were elected.

OLD COLONY HISTORICAL SOCIETY.

Taunton, Massachusetts, Thursday, October 24, 1895.—A quarterly meeting was held this afternoon at two o'clock, in Historical Hall, the president, Rev. Samuel Hopkins Emery, D.D., in the chair.

President Emery delivered a brief address.

Dea. E. W. Porter, the historiographer, made his report.

Joshua Eddy Crane read a memoir of William Allen of East Bridgewater.

Capt. John W. D. Hall, the librarian, made his report.

Monday, January 13, 1896.—The annual meeting was held this evening in Historical Hall.

President Emery delivered an address.

A report by Prof. John Ordronaux of New York, one of the early members of this society, was read, giving an account of the first annual meeting of the Mayflower Descendants, on the 22d of November, 1895, at Hotel Waldorf, in the city of New York, which he attended as the representative of this society.

The librarian made his quarterly report.

John F. Montgomery, the treasurer, made his annual report.

The nominating committee reported the names of the following candidates for officers for the ensuing year, who were unanimously elected :
President.—Rev. Samuel Hopkins Emery, D.D., of Taunton.
Vice-Presidents.—Hon. Edmund H. Bennett, LL.D., of Taunton, and Rev. William L. Chaffin of North Easton.
Recording Secretary and Librarian.—Capt. John W. D. Hall of Taunton.
Corresponding Secretary.—Hon. Charles A. Reed of Taunton.
Treasurer.—John F. Montgomery of Taunton.
Auditor.—Capt. George A. Washburn of Taunton.
Historiographer.—Joshua E. Crane of Taunton.
Directors.—Hon. William E. Fuller and Henry M. Lovering of Taunton; Hon. John E. Brayton of Fall River; Hon. William W. Crapo of New Bedford, and James M. Cushman and E. W. Porter of Taunton.

Hon. Charles A. Reed of Taunton read a paper on " The Early History of Bristol County."

RHODE ISLAND HISTORICAL SOCIETY.

Providence, Tuesday, October 1, 1895.—A quarterly meeting was held this evening, in the society's Cabinet in Waterman street.

The receipt of four thousand dollars, a bequest from Charles W. Parsons, M.D., was announced.

Twelve members, one life member and one corresponding member, were elected.

Oct. 15.—A stated meeting was held this evening, Hon. George M. Carpenter, vice-president, in the chair.

Hon. Horatio Rogers, the president of the society, read a paper on " The Bay State Puritans' Persecution of Mary Dyer."

Oct. 29.—A stated meeting was held this evening.

Miss Ellen D. Larned, author of the History of Windham County, Connecticut, read a paper on " The Relations of Providence and Windham County, Connecticut."

Nov. 12.—A stated meeting was held this evening.

The Rev. Ezra Hoyt Byington, D.D., read a paper on " The Early Puritan Ministers of New England."

Nov. 26.—A stated meeting was held this evening, President Rogers in the chair.

Miss Grace S. Kimball read a paper on " The East India Trade of Providence from 1787 to 1807."

Dec. 10.—A stated meeting was held this evening.

Robert T. Swan, the Massachusetts Commissioner of Public Records, read a paper entitled " Some Observations on Public Records and Papers."

Dec. 31.—A stated meeting was held.

Frank Greene Bates, a graduate and Fellow of Cornell University, read a paper entitled " Massachusetts and the Impost of 1781."

January 14, 1896.—The seventy-fourth annual meeting was held this evening at eight o'clock, in the Society's Cabinet, the president, Hon. Horatio Rogers, in the chair.

The annual reports were presented.

President Rogers delivered his annual address. He announced his decision not to be a candidate for re-election.

The election of officers was then taken up and resulted as follows :

President.—Hon. John H. Stiness.

Vice-Presidents.—George M. Carpenter, William B. Weeden.

Secretary and Librarian.—Amos Perry.

Treasurer.—Richmond P. Everett.

Nominating Committee.—Albert V. Jencks, James E. Cranston, Edward I. Nickerson.

Library Committee.—William D. Ely, Howard W. Preston, Amos Perry.

Lecture Committee.—Amos Perry, Reuben A. Guild, William B. Weeden.

Publication Committee.—James G. Vose, Wilfred H. Munro, Amos Perry, Amasa M. Eaton, John H. Stiness, Fred A. Arnold, J. Franklin Jameson.

Committee on Grounds and Buildings.—Isaac H. Southwick, Jr., Isaac C. Bates, Edwin Barrows.

Committee on Genealogical Researches.—Henry E. Turner, John O. Austin, George T. Hart.

Committee on Necrology.—Wilfred H. Munro, Samuel H. Webb, Amos Perry.

Finance Committee.—Robert H. I. Goddard, Charles H. Smith, Richmond P. Everett.

Audit Committee.—Lewis J. Chace, James Burdick, Ferdinand A. Lincoln.

Procurators.—For Newport, George Gordon King; Woonsocket, Latimer W. Ballou; Pawtucket, Samuel M. Conant; North Kingstown, David S. Baker; Hopkinton, George H. Olney; Chepachet, Dr. Potter.

February 10.—A stated meeting was held this evening.

John Eddy read a paper entitled " The Burning of the Steamer Martha Washington on the Mississippi River in February, 1852."

Feb. 25.—A stated meeting was held this evening.

William B. Weeden read a paper on " Minorities in Municipal Government."

March 11.—A stated meeting was held this evening.

Reuben A. Guild, LL.D., read a paper entitled "The Federal Adelphi of Brown University, Tristam Burgess and Francis Wayland.

MAINE GENEALOGICAL SOCIETY.

Portland, Wednesday, January 15, 1896.—The annual meeting of this society was held this evening, in its rooms in the public library building, the president, the Hon. M. F. King, in the chair.

The reports of the secretary, the treasurer and the librarian were presented. The following officers were elected:

President.—Marquis F. King.
Vice President.—Albion K. P. Meserve.
Secretary.—Fred O. Conant.
Treasurer.—Millard F. Hicks.
Librarian.—Joseph P. Thompson.

NECROLOGY OF THE NEW-ENGLAND HISTORIC GENEALOGICAL SOCIETY.

Prepared by the Historiographer, Rev. GEORGE M. ADAMS, D.D., of Auburndale, Mass.

THE sketches of deceased members prepared for the REGISTER are of necessity brief, because the space that can be appropriated is quite limited. All the materials for more extended memoirs which can be gathered are preserved in the archives of the Society, and they will be available for use in preparing the "Memorial Biographies," of which five volumes have been issued and a sixth volume is in preparation. The income from the Towne Memorial Fund is devoted to the publication of these volumes.

HENRY DELEVAN PAINE, M.D., of New York, a corresponding member of this Society since 1857, was born in Delhi, Delaware County, New York, June 19, 1816, and died in New York, June 11, 1893. His earliest ancestor in this country was Stephen Paine, who came to New England in 1638, and settled in Hingham. He removed to Rehoboth in 1641. The line of descent has been as follows: Stephen;[1] Stephen,[2] born in England, 1629, married Anne Chickering, and died 1679; Stephen,[3] born in Rehoboth, Sept. 29, 1654, married Mary Brintnall, died 1710; Stephen,[4] born in Rehoboth, 1707, married Deborah Skinner, and removed to Bolton; Ezra,[5] born in Bolton, 1749, married Abigail Ellsworth, died in 1803; Asahel,[6] Ellsworth, M.D., born July 30, 1770, married Anna Beers, died 1821; Henry[7] Delevan, M.D.

Dr. Henry Delevan Paine was the son of a reputable physician. He received an English and classical education at Delaware Academy, Delhi. At the age of sixteen he went to New York, and entered the office of Dr. Amos G. Hull, an eminent physician of that day. He was graduated from the College of Physicians and Surgeons of New York, in 1838. He began the practice of medicine in Newburgh, on the Hudson. In 1848 he removed to Albany, and in 1865 to the city of New York. During his residence of almost twenty years in Albany he acquired a large practice, and became a leader among physicians of the Homœopathic School. He was one of the founders of the American Institute of Homœopathy in 1844, and of the State Homœopathic Medical Society in 1850. He was a professor for a number of years in the New York Homœopathic Medical College. In 1880 he was appointed by the Regents of the University of the State of New York a member of the First State Board of Medical Examiners.

He was a frequent contributor to the journals of his school of medicine. He visited Europe, with his family, in 1884, and remained abroad two years. Dr. Paine gave much time to genealogical studies. He was concerned in the

publication of the Paine family Register in 1858 and 1859, and of the Paine family Records, 1878 to 1882. He was a devout member of the Protestant Episcopal Church. "His natural gentleness, and his deeply religious spirit," says one who knew him well, "made his last days like a beatitude. Yet the brightness of his wit and the genuineness of his humor never left him."
Dr. Paine was twice married. His first wife was Eliza Hale, daughter of Mr. Elisha Hale, of Newburgh. They had two children. His wife died in 1854, and in 1858 he married Lucy, daughter of Hon. Albert Gallup, of Albany, by whom he had a son, Henry G. Paine, now the managing editor of "Harper's Weekly."

By the Rev. E. H. Byington, D.D., of Newton, Mass.

BOOK NOTICES.

[The Editor requests persons sending books for notice to state, for the information of readers, the price of each book, with the amount to be added for postage when sent by mail.]

A Handbook to the Ancient Courts of Probate and Depositories of Wills. By George W. Marshall, LL.D., of the Middle Temple, Barrister at Law, and Rouge Croix Pursuivant of Arms. London: Horace Cox, Windsor House, Breams Buildings, E. C. 1895. Post 8vo. pp. vi.+75. Price 6s. 8d.

This invaluable little handbook, by one of the most conscientious and painstaking of English genealogists, marks an era in the popularization of the study of genealogy. The first edition, printed by subscription in 1889, at a guinea, was almost immediately exhausted, and the learned author has given us a new edition, compact and portable in form, and at a price that places it within reach of the most humble worker in the field, and it is a book that no one, interested in our trans-Atlantic genealogy, can afford to be without.

The English Government in 1828 printed a Report on the then condition of the Probate Records of the Kingdom, which was followed by others in the two following years, and in 1832; these reports, clumsy in arrangement, difficult to obtain, and not giving the slightest clue to the date of the earliest wills, were all that the working genealogist had for a guide until Dr. Marshall came to his rescue.

As in all the author's books, his preface is most interesting and instructive reading, and it should be attentively scrutinized before making use of the handbook.

If we might venture to offer a friendly criticism on so excellent a work, it would be to suggest that in certain cases the information should have been a little more detailed. For example: The Honour Court of Knaresborough, now at the Principal Registry in London, is given as dating from 1640. As a matter of fact, however, although this is the earliest date of wills in this Court at Somerset House, the Manor Court Rolls which remain at Knaresborough contain wills over a century earlier, but which, being entered, until 1640, on the rolls of the Manor in the midst of other business, could not be separated from them when the others were sent to London in 1858. The writer has abstracts of wills from these rolls as early as 1527 and believes that still earlier are to be found there.

In the Archdeaconry of Dorset at Blandford the date is given as 1568, and it is undoubtedly true that there are a few scattering wills, perhaps twenty in all, from that time to the period of the Commonwealth, but, for all practical purposes, this Court should be dated from 1660 or 1661, when the first connected series of wills begins, being of course too late to be of interest for our early New England emigrants.

The omission of the important Court of Hustings in London, the earliest extant register in England, dating from 1258, may also be noted as one of those slips that will occur in the most careful of work. But it is invidious to search for flaws in a book so conspicuous for their rarity, and the author's well known desire for accuracy will pardon the calling of attention to omissions which only emphasize the general perfection of the book.

The working genealogist, English or American, professional or amateur, is placed under renewed obligation to Dr. Marshall for this most useful tool of his trade which is a worthy companion on his shelf to the Genealogist's Guide so familiar and necessary to all.

By J. Henry Lea, of Fairhaven, Mass.

Transactions of the Royal Historical Society. New Series. Vol. IX. London: Longmans, Green & Co., and New York. 1895. 8vo. pp. 320.

All the papers contained in this volume bear marks of careful study and research and are replete with information concisely and clearly expressed. More than this, they furnish food for thought and are likely to lead to further research. While it is difficult to select from such a wealth of material, to the writer of this notice, the papers read at the Gibbon Centenary Commemoration, that entitled "Exploration under Elizabeth," and the translation of the "Journey through England and Scotland made by Lupold von Wedel 1584 and 1585," are especially interesting.

How fascinating is the study of history in all its labyrinthine branches, bringing us face to face with the study of the complex nature of man; it is one of the greatest teaching forces in the world; it registers (although imperfectly) the progress that has been made in the past; it stimulates the imagination; it arouses the better part of our nature, it fills us with a new purpose to follow where others have gone before. Out of the many rich truths which history teaches, may we not say that the greatest of all is the force of example? Some of the lesser facts of history, the accumulated data of the years, are of little importance, are but the back-ground of the great panorama of human life. But the living, moving, energizing moral and spiritual forces in human nature have ever been powerful factors in the upward trend of human life in the past as they will in the future. It is wonderfully interesting to trace the workings of these grand principles on the vast stage of human life. And the careful study of the noble results wrought in the past gives unfailing stimulus and momentum to action in the present and future. With all the noble advances which have been made, the great flood-tides of human progress, the world has not yet reached its meridian. But what has been is continual promise of what may be, nay what will be, as the golden hours laden with opportunity fly swiftly by. Do they not bring with them some faint reflection of the newer, fairer life in the New Jerusalem, the city of God? And so the examples of all those who have contributed in their measure to make history, the great men, the prophets and seers, all who have done something to shape thought or (better still) arouse emotion, direct action, to uplift human life, lead up (as far as mere human example may) to the spotless and adorable life of our Lord Jesus Christ, the Divine Exemplar of all humanity, the Savior of all who trust in Him.

By Rev. Daniel Rollins, of Boston, Mass.

Massachusetts in the Army and Navy During the War of 1861-65. Prepared under the authority of the State by THOMAS WENTWORTH HIGGINSON, State Military and Naval Historian. Vol. 11. Boston: Wright & Potter Printing Co., State Printers, 18 Post Office Square. 1894. 4to. pp. 805.

The first volume of this work has not been published. The first eleven sections of the volume just issued contain, besides a list and military history of Massachusetts general officers, lists and records of Massachusetts naval, field, line and medical officers, of Massachusetts officers in regular army and staff corps, of officers in regiments of other States, of officers in United States colored troops, together with lists of Massachusetts officers, soldiers and sailors receiving medals of honor, and of brevets given to Massachusetts officers.

Then follows a section of remarkable import, comprising extracts from the Annual Report of the Adjutant-General of Massachusetts for the year ending Dec. 31, 1865, relating to the behavior of the returned soldiers. A circular addressed to city and town officers, requesting information as to the conduct of the soldiers, some of whom had been released from military service for several years, elicited answers which to every American, responding as they do to his expectations, will afford the most irrefutable evidence of the moral effect of the social and political institutions by which they had been trained and for which they fought, since they returned from doing devils' work—which war in every respect most certainly is—to do the work of men as before, and, in many cases, of men of loftier manhood, of increased self-respect and fitness for citizenship.

The list of those who sent representative recruits records the names of those who, themselves exempt from any cause from military duty, yet accomplished by proxy their desire to share in the conflict, forwarding to the field recruits procured at their own expense, and thus personally representing them in the ranks. The names of 627 men are exemplars of this kind of practical patriotism of whose prevalence many, it is probable, are wholly unaware.

Mrs. Mary A. Livermore, herself one of the most effective assistants in the work of the Sanitary Commission—as Col. Higginson with justice reminds us in a note appended to her paper—has by the exact, however condensed, narration of the services of Massachusetts women in the Civil War, furnished the most absorbing portion of the book. To indicate its affecting details would require the reprint of the whole article, as her report from beginning to end discloses a series of benevolent and heroic enterprises, as also of names sacred to America—and some of them to the world—in recounting which one can allow the omission of not even the least.

Florence Wyman Jacques' "Bibliographical Index of the Periodical Literature bearing on Massachusetts Service During the Civil War," consisting of 124 pages, is the concluding section of the volume, and one of which the immediately recognizable utility will be to its author the reward for the laborious research necessary to its preparation.

By Frederick W. Parke, of Boston.

The Pilgrim Fathers of New England and Their Puritan Successors. By Rev. John Brown, A.B., D.D., author of "John Bunyan, His Life, Times and Work." *With Introduction* by Rev. A. E. Dunning, D.D., Editor "The Congregationalist." Fleming H. Rowell Company. New York, Chicago, Toronto. 1896. 8vo. pp. 368. Price $2.50.

This book by the pastor of the Bunyan meeting in Bedford, England, is one of the very best treatises which have ever been issued on this subject.

The book comes to our table from an American publishing house, and its title-page lacks any token of the residence of its author. This is all wrong; for any book's value is notably affected by the point of view. When we are mousing in English libraries, record offices and vestries, we find overwhelming evidence that the English people at large cared very little about the forthcoming of those who founded New England. It is peculiarly refreshing to receive from a native and resident of England a book which shows such a comprehension of that seventeenth century emigration, and honors so highly the Pilgrim *motif.*

The first hundred pages sagaciously trace the history of those congregations who met for worship in private dwellings, from the thirty Worcester weavers who were summoned before the council of Oxford in 1165 to the Wickliff preachers in 1382; to the "separated church in the time of Queen Mary, of which Mr. Rough was pastor and Cuthbert Symson a deacon;" and so down to the well-known band who met at Scrooby manor in 1605. The life of the exiles in Holland; the distinctive teachings of their leaders, and the belief and practice of the brethren; the circumstances of the sailing and the leading events of the early years in New Plymouth, Mr. Brown describes with the calm fidelity of a historian combined with the glow of one who loves the men he describes, and counts that piece of history one of the most significant pages of the annals of mankind. He has made admirable use of authorities (Bradford pre-eminently for what he describes), and does not distress us by gushing off the track or going out of his proper course to vent anger or spleen on any.

With much good sense he shows how *conforming Puritans* became *separatist Puritans,*—that is "Pilgrims,"—through the harsh measures which "harried them out of the kingdoms;" and the exigencies of a new country, which made Congregational "communion of churches" the policy of sanctified common sense. Then he traces the Pilgrimizing of Salem and Boston and Connecticut. He touches Richard Mather; but overlooks that very significant "church-colony," organized in 1629 at Plymouth, Eng., whose pastor and teacher, Wareham and Maverick, were there installed with a sermon from Rev. John White of old Dorchester; which came to this bay before Winthrop; did good service six years before Mather reached it; and gave half of its membership and one of its ministers for the nucleus of Connecticut Congregationalism. Dr. Brown's conclusion is eloquent; we quote one characteristic sentence: "There was in these makers of New England a grand, masterful sincerity, a noble courage of conviction, an overwhelming sense of the authority of righteousness in human life, and an everpresent consciousness of God's personal rule over the world, in spite of its confusions."

By Rev. Charles H. Pope, A.B., of North Cambridge, Mass.

History of the Military Company of the Massachusetts now called The Ancient and Honorable Artillery Company of Massachusetts. 1637-1888. By OLIVER AYER ROBERTS, Historian of the Company. Volume I.—1637-1738. Boston: Alfred Mudge & Son, Printers, 24 Franklin Street. 1895. 4to. pp. viii.+500.

The Ancient and Honorable Artillery Company, "designed in its Original, to be a sort of COLLEGE, to *train up* and *Educate* the *Sons* of *this People* in *Military Skill*, and make them *expert* and valiant Soldiers,"* was chartered by the General Court "the 13th of the First Month, @ 1638," and is the oldest military organization in America. It is a direct offspring of the Honourable Artillery Company of London—Captain Keayne, its chief founder and its first commander, having been long a member of that corporation.

The parent Company, chartered in 1537, was a century old when the Ancient was born. It is the oldest martial organization in Great Britain, and has rendered its country many distinguished services.

Since the publication of the second edition of Whitman's History of the Ancient and Honorable Artillery Company, several attempts have been made to write a more adequate history of this institution. From the material thus collected, supplemented by years of patient research, the Rev. Oliver Ayer Roberts has produced a work which gives great credit to him, and ought to be highly pleasing to the members of the Company. A †Committee of Publication, appointed in 1886, has had the work in charge, and the historian has had the hearty support and coöperation of this committee. They jointly are to be congratulated upon the success attending their labors.

This history will probably be comprised in four volumes. The present volume covers the first century of the Company's existence, and is a veritable mine of information for the antiquarian and the genealogist. The history of each year is complete in itself. An arbitrary system is followed, which gives the names of the officers for the year, historical facts relating to the Company, biographical sketches of the recruits, then the records of the Company, followed by a short sketch of the preacher for that year.

When one examines the roll of members whose biographies fill this volume, he does not wonder that this Company was "very much honoured by the magistrates of that day," and was "favoured and countenanced by the ministry."

The frontispiece is a fac-simile of Capt. Keayne's signature. Among the many other illustrations are a photograph of the Company's charter and a portrait of the diligent and faithful historian, Rev. Oliver A. Roberts.

Two things are worthy of a special mention—the volume has an excellent index, and references are made under each name to the sources of information.

One who becomes at all familiar with the history of this institution must feel like saying with the Rev. Samuel Stillman, "the continuance of this Ancient and Honorable Artillery Company is as expedient as its original institution. It was founded we know in the infancy of the province, when infested by cruel Indians, as a school to train up officers for the militia; some of whom have played the man for the people and the cities of their God, and though now numbered with the dead, they are remembered with affection. The appearances of this day convince us, that the spirit with which they were animated is not extinct; it lives in a degree in their posterity, who breathe in the same air, and have drank deep into the same principles."‡

By Wm. Prescott Greenlaw, of Cambridge, Mass.

---

* Rev. Oliver Peabody's Sermon, 1732, page 37.
† Edward Wyman, *Chairman*. Albert Alonzo Folsom. George Henry Allen. William Parker Jones. Henry Walker. William Lithgow Willey, *Secretary*.
‡ Rev. Samuel Stillman's Sermon, 1770, page 31.

Archives of the State of New Jersey. First Series. Vol. XI. *Documents relating to the Colonial History of New Jersey.* Edited by WILLIAM NELSON. Paterson, N. J. 1894. 8vo. pp. cxxvi. 1–623. Vol. XII. 1895. 8vo. pp. [8], cxxvi–cclxviii. 1–729.

No State in the Union has surpassed New Jersey in the intelligent interest and commendable liberality with which she has responded to the labors of the State Historical Society to secure a complete collection and publication of the documentary history of the State.

This—the First Series of volumes of the Archives of New Jersey—was begun in the year 1880, and now we have the two additional volumes whose general title is given above. These volumes are taken up with an extended and carefully prepared "Account of American Newspapers, particularly of the Eighteenth Century," giving the names of the libraries in which they may be found; and "Extracts from American Newspapers, relating to New Jersey."

This "Account of American Newspapers" is by far the most complete and authentic record of the newspaper press in America in the eighteenth century that has been published, and is invaluable for the general or the local historian. One of the most useful features of this record is the lists of files now extant, and the libraries where the files, more or less complete, are preserved. The extracts from newspapers of all matters of news, including many advertisements, letters, &c., illustrative of the history of New Jersey, constitute a rich mine of information.

After a careful examination of these volumes, one cannot fail to see how vast has been the research and labor expended upon them by the learned and indefatigable editor—Mr. William Nelson—who has for many years devoted a large part of his leisure from his profession, the law, to the interests of the New Jersey Historical Society, and so to the interests and honor of the State. It may give the reader some idea of Mr. Nelson's zeal and activity in the field of historical research to be told that the list of his separate historical publications relating to New Jersey, some of which are quite extended, exceeds fifty titles, and all are very useful as historical materials. To this list may properly be added Mr. Nelson's admirable memoir of Chief Justice Hornblower, which was published in the fifth volume of New-England Historic Genealogical Society's "Memorial Biographies," published in 1894.

It should be added that the editor's notes to these volumes now under notice give them increased value, and that each volume is furnished with a copious index.

By Albert H. Hoyt, A.M., of Boston.

The Salem Book: Records of the Past amd Glimpses of the Future. Prepared for publication by a group of Salem's sons and daughters. Salem, N. Y. The Salem Review Press. 1896. 8vo. pp. 250.

By the people of Salem, N. Y., this production of her enthusiastically filial children will be admiringly welcomed, and those to whom the history and the attractive features of the town are unfamiliar will receive from this volume the varied information expected from specially designated writers, to each of whom is entrusted a subject exhibiting some prominent characteristic of the place in its past or present.

The dedication to the "Gray Man"—a spirit, in fact—may be interpreted as a consecration of their labors by the Historical Committee to that impalpable essence constituted by the ideal aspirations of their townspeople, rather than to their embodiment in realizations that always appear crude in comparison with the formative purpose beneath them.

It is these realizations which are the subjects of the several sections, all of them topics of lively local interest, and some of them, such as the opening chapters on colonizations and genealogies, appealing to more general attention. The schools, the press, the literature, the music, the industries, societies, noted buildings, old time customs, historic trees, resting places, and even ghosts of the picturesque town, all obtain the treatment which a selected pen ensures.

The illustrations by T. A. Wright, New York, are extremely fine. The frontispiece is a portrait of Gen. John Williams, whose services, both to his country and to Salem, are commemorated in a chapter appropriated to "Salem's Distinguished Sons."

By Frederic W. Parke, of Boston.

The Old Houses of the Antient Town of Norwich, 1660—1800.   With Maps, Illustrations, Portraits and Genealogies. By MARY E. PERKINS. Norwich, Conn. 1895. Sq. 8vo. pp. xviii. 621. Price $10.

The perusal of this beautiful volume will excite in every reader the desire that as vividly pictorial a touch as that of Miss Perkins might be employed to revive the past of his own native place. It is a book in which the romance of local history finds like expression in the graphic text and in the strikingly artistic illustrations and portraits, these being half-tone prints and photogravures of exquisite finish.

It is romance, however, which is really documentary fact presented in an unusually attractive form. This volume is one of a proposed series containing accounts of the old houses of Norwich, from the settlement of the town until 1800, the present publication including the buildings on the main roads, from the corner of Mill Lane to the Bean Hill road. The work comprises two parts, the first, embracing 402 pages and entitled "The Old Houses of Norwich," being a compilation of details both of a public and domestic character whose variety well exhibits the author's literary tact as also her knowledge of her subject. Furniture, modes of heating, dress, entertainments, trades, occupations, class distinctions and business enterprises of the early days are elements of a picture enlivened by frequent strokes of humor supplied by journals, letters and songs. From each house selected for description is drawn as exhaustive and as dramatic a history as even its inmates or their descendants could desire.

The second part, devoted to genealogies, contains the first three generations of the earliest settlers, but after this period space is allotted only to descendants residing in the section of which this volume treats. This genealogical portion of the book is a feature imparting to it, as all will acknowledge, a species of superiority to other works relating to Norwich.

By Frederic W. Parke of Boston.

Vital Records of Rhode Island, 1636—1850. Vol. VIII.   Episcopal and Congregational Churches. Compiled by JAMES N. ARNOLD, Providence, R. I.: Narraganset Historical Publishing Company. 1896. 4to. pp. 48+632.   Price $7.50.

Another volume of Mr. Arnold's "Vital Records of Rhode Island" is on our table. It is the eighth volume of the series and the second of the church records. It is deserving of the same commendation given by us to the previous volumes. The town of Bristol, we notice particularly, has excellent records, kept by the Congregational Church, and by St. Michael's Episcopal Church. We are pleased to note how carefully Rev. John Bent, Rev. Henry Wight and Rev. Thomas Shepard kept their records. As Mr. Arnold says in his Introduction, if every church or minister had kept as full a record, his book would have been very much larger. He is doing a good service in preserving in print these records, even though those of some of the churches are scanty. As he expresses it: "I am saving all I can find, and am presenting it to the public just as I find it."   We congratulate Mr. Arnold on the successful publication of this new volume. We trust that he will realize, at no distant day, his long wish to complete this work on which he has so long labored.   *∗*

A Supplement to How to Write the History of a Family.   A Guide for the Genealogist. By W. P. W. PHILLIMORE, M. A., B. C. L., Member of Queen's College, Oxford.   London: Published by the Author, 124 Chancery Lane. 1896. 12mo. Price 3s. 6d. Hand-made paper edition, 50 copies only, 6 shillings.

Mr. Phillimore's former book, "How to Write the History of a Family," was published in 1888, and was noticed by us in our April number for that year. The first edition was sold within a few months of its publication, and the second has been long out of print. It was originally intended to incorporate this new matter in the third edition, but it was finally decided to bring it out in a separate volume. It contains new features as well as additional matter on topics treated in the former volume. The "Chapter for Beginners" is particularly commended to the reader's attention. The chapters on "Scottish and Irish Genealogies" are new, and furnish the only handbook to families of those nationalities. The chapters on "Surnames," "Antiquarian Societies," the "Table of Visitations," "Wills," and "Marriage Licenses," also add to the value of the book. A chapter on "Foreign Genealogies" is found here, and large additions are made to that on "American Genealogy."

The two works, "How to Write the History of a Family," and the "Supplement," will be found valuable helps to those who are compiling genealogical works, as well as to those of antiquarian tastes. We heartily commend them.

Cratfield: A Transcript of the Accounts of the Parish, from A.D. 1490 to A.D. 1642. With Notes. By the late Rev. WILLIAM HOLLAND, B.A, formerly of Lincoln College, Oxford; Rector of Huntingfleld-with-Cookley. With a brief Memoir of the author by his Widow. Edited with an Introduction by JOHN JAMES RAVEN, D.D., F.S.A., of Emmanuel College, Cambridge; Vicar of Fressingfleld-with-Witherdale; and Honorary Canon of Norwich Cathedral. London: Jarrold & Son. Royal 8vo. pp. 194. Published by subscription. Price fifteen shillings net. Sold by the publishers, Messrs. Jarrold & Son, 11 Warwick Lane, London, E. C.

This is the work announced by us, as in preparation, in the REGISTER for April, 1895, page 215. The late Rev. William Holland, B.A., rector of Huntingfield, Suffolk, left behind him a large collection of transcripts of ancient parochial accounts. Of these those of the parish of Cratfield have been selected for publication. They reach back to the days of Henry VII. They have been edited by Mr. Holland's friend and neighbor, Rev. Canon Raven, D.D., F.S.A., vicar of Fressingfield, who has performed his work in a highly satisfactory manner. Mr. Holland had appended to each year historical notes, so that the affairs of this remote village are a microcosm. The stirring events of the Tudor period find valuable and interesting illustrations. Many names occur of course, of old local families, some now extinct in East Anglia, but not unrepresented in New England and among the descendants of New England families in the great West. Canon Raven, the editor, says in his Introduction: "Few suspect the importance of those documents which are lying entombed in the parish chests of England. In too many cases clergy and laity alike have sold as waste paper, or committed to the flames, records of the past which can never be recovered, regarding them as useless lumber. Such, happily, was not the case with these." We trust that other selections from Mr. Holland's manuscripts will be made for publication, and that other parish chests will be searched for antiquarian treasures.

A brief memoir of the Rev. Mr. Holland by his widow, illustrated with a portrait, is prefixed to the volume. "As a small tribute to the memory of her dear husband and as the most fitting monument of the work he loved so well, she publishes these Archæological Notes on Cratfield, and she has presented to the Ipswich Museum his very valuable collection of Brasses which will be known as the Holland Collection."

The editor in his "Introduction" has given a sketch of the Cratfield parish incidents and an account of its parish papers exclusive of the register. Canon Raven's annotations greatly increase the interest and value of the work.

A History of the Town of Industry, Franklin County, Maine, from the Earliest Settlement in 1787 down to the Present Time, embracing the Sessions of New Sharon, New Vineyard, Anson and Stark. In Two Parts, including the History and Genealogy of the Leading Families of the Town. By WILLIAM COLLINS HATCH. Farmington, Maine: Press of Knowlton, McLeary & Co. 1893. 8vo. pp. 862. Price $5. Sold by the author, Dr. William C. Hatch, New Sharon, Me.

This volume of nearly nine hundred pages preserves the history of Industry, Maine, and the several towns taken from it, from the earliest settlement to the present time. The author has evidently bestowed much labor on the book and has collected very full particulars relating to Industry, its people, its schools, its churches, its military affairs, its mills and manufactures, its merchants, its physicians, its lawyers, etc. About half of the book is devoted to family history. A full record of the genealogy of the leading families in the town will be found here. The book is illustrated with numerous portraits. John F. Pratt, M.D., of Chelsea, Mass., who is familiar with the history of Maine, and who is a good judge of what a town history should be, writes to the author: "In my opinion the book does you great credit; its typographical appearance is excellent, the arrangement of your material is exceedingly commendable; in fact I prophesy that you will find the critics in such matters will compliment your work highly." Those interested should order the work early as the edition is nearly exhausted.

The Public Records of the State of Connecticut, from May, 1775, to April, 1780, inclusive. With the Journal of the Council of Safety, from May 18, 1778, to April 23, 1780, an and Appendix. Published in accordance with a Resolution of the General Assembly, by CHARLES J. HOADLY, LL.D., State Librarian. Hartford: Press of the Case, Lockwood & Brainard Company. 1895. Royal 8vo. pp. 607.

This is the second volume of the records of the State of Connecticut that has been printed. The records of the Colony have all been printed. They make fifteen volumes, besides two volumes of the records of the New Haven colony. There are nineteen volumes of records published in accordance with a resolution of the General Assembly of Connecticut,—that is, 15 Connecticut colony, 2 New Haven colony, and 2 Connecticut state. All of these except the first two volumes of Connecticut colony have been edited by the present editor, Dr. Hoadly. The other two were edited by Dr. J. Hammond Trumbull.

The volume before us is got up in the same excellent manner as the previous volumes, which have been noticed in the REGISTER, and the editorial work shows the same learning, care and accuracy. The people of Connecticut may well be proud of her printed records, and the moderate cost that the State has been put to is certainly remarkable.

Dunster Papers. By JOHN T. HASSAM. Cambridge: John Wilson & Son, University Press. 1895. 8vo. pp. 10.

The pamphlet before us is a paper read before the Massachusetts Historical Society in October last, and reprinted from the proceedings of that society. Mr. Hassam has lately discovered in the possession of a descendant of Rev. Henry Dunster, first president of Harvard College, two manuscripts that formerly belonged to Mr. Dunster. The first manuscript is a fragment of a letter written, probably to Dunster, from London, by Joseph Davyes, May 20, 1641, just before the outbreak of the Civil War. The second paper is a funeral sermon in manuscript, preached at Exton, March 31, 1614, at the funeral of John, Lord Harrington, Baron of Exton, by Richard Stocke, pastor of Allhallows, in Bread Street, London. These manuscripts are here printed, with Mr. Hassam's annotations. They furnish facts that will interest the students of Puritan history.

The Old Trunk, or Sketches of Colonial Days. By POWHATAN BOULDIN. Second Edition. Danville, Va.: Blair & Boatwright, Printers. 1896. 8vo. pp. 79. Price 50 cents, including postage. Address the editor and publisher, Powhatan Bouldin, Danville, Virginia.

We are glad to welcome these interesting sketches of colonial life in Virginia from the able pen of Mr. Bouldin, whose "Home Reminiscences of John Randolph of Roanoke" we had the pleasure of reading in 1878, and which we noticed in the October number of that year. We commend the book to our readers, and particularly to the members of the societies of Colonial Wars and Colonial Dames.

A Report of the Record Commissioners of the City of Boston, containing the Boston Town Records, 1778 to 1783. Boston: Rockwell & Churchill, City Printers. 1895. 8vo. pp. 354.

An Alphabetical Abstract of the Record of Marriages in the Town of Dedham, Massachusetts, 1844–1890. Compiled by DON GLEASON HILL, Town Clerk, Dedham, Mass.: Office of the Dedham Transcript. 1890. 8vo. pp. 165.

The first of the two books before us is the twenty-sixth volume issued by the Record Commission of Boston, to which series of volumes our readers have frequently had their attention called. The present book contains the proceedings of the town from 1778 to 1783. This completes a full record of the doings of the town to 1783. The previous issue (vol. 25) brought the selectmen's minutes down to 1786.

The next work is the seventh volume of the Dedham records, published by the town, under the editorship of the town clerk, Don Gleason Hill, Esq. The volume contains a record of the marriages in that town from 1844 to 1890, "arranged under the names of the grooms with an index of the names of brides." The two books are valuable additions to our printed genealogical matter.

The Hassam Family. By JOHN T. HASSAM, A.M. Privately printed. Boston. 1896. 8vo. pp. 11.

The Hilton Family. By JOHN T. HASSAM, A.M. Privately printed. 1896. 8vo. pp. 24.

The Cheever Family. By JOHN T. HASSAM, A.M. Privately printed. 1896. 8vo. pp. 54.

We give above the titles of three genealogies by Mr. Hassam of Boston. They are compiled with his usual care and accuracy.

The first pamphlet on the Hassam family is a genealogical account of the descendants of William Hassam, or Horsham, as the name was originally written. He came from England and settled in Manchester, Mass. It is illustrated with six fac-simile autographs.

The next pamphlet, on the Hilton Family, contains an account of the descendants of William Hilton, who came from London to Plymouth in New England, in the Fortune, 1621, and afterwards became a prominent citizen of Dover, N. H. The work is illustrated with seven fac-simile autographs and a heliotype copy of a letter written by Hilton to Gov. John Winthrop, July 14, 1637, never before reproduced.

The last of these genealogies contains a record of some of the descendants of Ezekiel Cheever. It is illustrated by four fac-simile autographs and one heliotype. Appendix A is devoted to a consideration of the question of the authorship of the manuscript volume of Latin poems now in the library of the Boston Athenæum, and the manuscript volume of Latin prose in the library of the Massachusetts Historical Society. Ezekiel Cheever, the famous master of the Boston Latin School, has hitherto been considered the author of these manuscripts, but this paper points out the real authors of many of these poems, several of which prove to be classics, and shows how slight is the possibility that Ezekiel Cheever could have written any of the few, the authorship of which is as yet unascertained. Neither of these manuscripts prove to be in his handwriting.

Appendix B contains two letters in Latin, never before published, by Ezekiel Cheever to his son, the Rev. Samuel Cheever, a graduate of Harvard College in the class of 1659. They are very interesting and relate to the steps taken to secure a wife for the latter, and the journey undertaken by the father from Boston to Cambridge to negotiate the marriage. It is satisfactory to learn that these efforts were crowned with success. There is a heliotype copy of one of the letters. Appendix C contains the Latin poems before referred to.

1637—1887. The Munson Record; a Genealogical and Biographical Account of Capt. Thomas Munson, a Pioneer of Hartford and New Haven, and his Descendants. By MYRON A. MUNSON. 2 vols. New Haven, Conn., U. S. A. Printed for the Munson Association. 1895. Royal 8vo. pp. 1235, in both volumes.

Boardman Genealogy. 1525—1895. The English Home and Ancestry of Samuel Boreman, Wethersfield, Conn. Thomas Boreman, Ipswich, Mass. With an Account of their Descendants (now called Boardman) in America. Complied by CHARLOTTE GOLDTHWAITE. Published by William F. J. Boardman. Hartford, Conn. 1895. 8vo. pp. 778. Price $10.00 a copy.

Genealogy of the Graves Family in America. Three volumes. Vol. I. *Sketch of the Family in England. Genealogy of the Family of Thomas Graves of Hatfield, Mass.* By JOHN CARD GRAVES, M.A. Published at Buffalo, N. Y., by Baker, Jones & Co. 1896. 8vo. pp. xxv.+521. Price for the three volumes $12.00. Each volume separately $5.00.

John Mallett, the Huguenot, and his Descendants. 1694—1894, Compiled by ANNA S. MALLETT. Harrisburg, Pa.: Harrisburg Publishing Company. 1895. Royal 8vo. pp. xx.+342. Price $5.00. Address the compiler, Miss A. S. Mallett, 1454 Rhode Island Avenue, Washington, D. C.

*Thomas Halsey of Hertfordshire, England, and Southampton, Long Island.
1591—1679. With his American Descendants to the Eighth Generations.* By
JACOB LAFAYETTE HALSEY and EDMUND DRAKE HALSEY. With an Introduction by FRANCIS WHITING HALSEY. Morristown, N. J. 1895. 8vo. pp. 550.

*The Tenney Family, or the Descendants of Thomas Tenney of Rowley, Mass. 1638
—1890.* By M. J. TENNEY. Boston, Mass. : American Printing and Engraving Company. 1891. 8vo. pp. 369. Price $3.00, or by mail $3.18. Address
the compiler, Miss Mary J. Tenney, P. O. Box 123, Haverhill, Mass.

*Davies Memoir ; a Genealogical and Biographical Monograph on the Family and
Descendants of John Davies of Litchfield, Connecticut.* By HENRY EUGENE
DAVIES. Privately Printed. 1895. 4to. pp. 138.

The Story of My Ancestors in America. By Rev. EDWIN SAWYER WALKER, A.M.
Chicago : David Oliphant, Printer. 1895. 8vo. pp. 72. 300 copies printed.

A Memorial Sketch of Roland Greene Usher. 1823—1893. By EDWARD
PRESTON USHER. To which is added a Genealogy of the Usher Family in
New England from 1638 to 1895. Privately Printed for the Family. 1895.
8vo. pp. 160.

The Severans Genealogical History. Compiled by Rev. JOHN F. SEVERANCE, of
Chicago, Ill. Chicago : R. R. Donnelly & Sons Company. 1893. 8vo.
pp. xix.+78.

The Seaverns Genealogical History. Compiled by Rev. JOHN F. SEVERANCE,
of Chicago, Ill. Huntington, Ind. Printed for the Author. 1893. 8vo. pp. 58.

Lewisiana or the Lewis Letter. A Monthly Inter-Family Paper. Elliott, Conn. :
Carll A. Lewis. From Vol. IV., No. 1, July, 1893, to Vol. VI., No. 9,
March, 1896. Price $1 a year.

The Elmwood Eatons. By ARTHUR WENTWORTH HAMILTON EATON, B.A. Privately Printed. 1895. Royal 4to. pp. 29

*The Thomas Spencer Family of Hartford, Connecticut, in the Line of Samuel
Spencer of Cromwell, Connecticut. 1744—1818.* Compiled by FRANK FARNS-
WORTH STARR for JAMES J. GOODWIN. Hartford, Conn. 1896. 8vo. pp. 44.

The Goodwins of East Anglia. 8vo. pp. 30. 1895. *The Lippincotts.* 8vo. pp. 3.
1895.

One Branch of the Descendants of Gov. William Bradford. New York. Printed
at the DeVinne Press. 1895. 12mo. pp. 29.

The Clevedon Family. By the late Sir JOHN MACLEAN, F.S.A. Edited by Rev.
F. W. WEAVER, M.A. 1895. 8vo. pp. 37.

Porter Family Record : A Few Twigs from a Branch of the Porter Family. By
CYRUS KINNE PORTER. Buffalo, N. Y. 4to. pp. 14.

Contribution to the Trumbull Genealogy, from Gleanings in English Fields. By
J. HENRY LEA. Boston : David Clapp & Son. 1895. 8vo. pp. 27. Price
$1. Address W. P. Greenlaw, 18 Somerset Street, Boston.

*Barnstable Gorhams. The Old House in which they lived, and their Services in
the Colonial Wars.* By FRANK WILLIAM SPRAGUE, Esq. Boston : Printed
for private distribution. 1896. 8vo. pp. 7.

A Brief Sketch of the Hutchinson Family of New Hampshire. Compiled by
FRANK ALLEN HUTCHINSON. Lowell, Mass. : Courier-Citizen Co., Printers.
1896. 8vo. pp. 23.

*The Descendants of James Skiff of London, England, and Sandwich, Mass., who
died April, 1688.* By FREDERICK LOCKWOOD PRESTON of Ellsworth, Conn.,
a descendant. Albany, N. Y. : Walsh & Griffin, Printers. 1895. 8vo. pp. 24.

*Genealogy and History of the Newbury Adams Family, formerly of Devonshire,
England, being the descendant of Robert Adams and wife Eleanor.* By I.
SMITH ADAMS. Calais, Maine. : Printed at the Calais Advertiser office.
1895. 8vo. pp. 64.

Our Folks. Second Preliminary Draft. 1895. 8vo. pp. 39. Address, George
M. Blake, Attorney-at-Law, Rockford, Ill.

*The Morse Record : A History of the Morse Family in Annual Meeting, Decem-
ber 4, 1895, and a Souvenir of the Dinner at the Windsor Hotel, New York
City, on the same evening.* 8vo. pp. 41.

Souvenir Programme of the Semi-Centennial Meeting of the Reed Family in the Reed Locust Grove, Wednesday, August 28, 1895, Taunton, Mass.
The De Lotbinieres: a Bit of Canadian Romance and History. By I. J. GREENWOOD. 8vo. pp. 8.

We continue in this number our quarterly notices of books relating to the genealogy which have been recently presented to the Society.

The first work on our list is the Munson Record, in two noble volumes, of more than six hundred pages each. The author, Rev. Myron A. Munson, of New Haven, Connecticut, deserves great praise for the admirable manner in which he has performed his work. A plan was adopted in publishing this work which is worthy of consideration in other families. Twenty-seven persons whose names are printed in the volume, became responsible to the extent of one hundred dollars each for the expense of publishing this work should the subscription be inadequate. The Richardson book published several years ago was issued on a plan somewhat resembling this. Several men of means of the Richardson name or blood, assumed the charge of obtaining the subscribers and paying the bills for printing and binding, so that the author, Rev. John A. Vinton, could give his time entirely to his genealogical labors, for which he received I think a certain number of copies of the work. We do not know whether there was a deficiency. But if there was, they probably shared the loss and divided the copies among themselves. The friends who guaranteed Rev. Mr. Munson from loss on the book before us have the satisfaction of aiding in a praiseworthy undertaking. The book is carefully compiled. Everything illustrating the history of the family or the individual members—portraits, fac-similes of documents and records, charts, maps, gravestones and autographs, have been gathered and preserved here. The book is handsomely printed, and the illustrations are numerous and of a high order of merit. The indexes are full. We would recommend it as a model for works of the kind.

The Boardman book of nearly eight hundred pages is another book to which we can give our hearty approval. By the fortunate fact that a sister of one of the Boreman emigrants wrote a letter to him from England which has been preserved and is reproduced in fac-simile here, the locality from which he came has been discovered, and the compiler of this book, Miss Charlotte Goldthwaite, who with her sister visited England a few years ago, made important genealogical discoveries in the home of the Boremans which she has preserved in this book. Some of the most interesting illustrations in the book are some English views. Miss Goldthwaite deserves high praise for the careful and thorough manner in which she has traced the numerous and scattered members of the Boardman family, and has preserved the individual records of the members. Mr. Boardman, of Hartford, the publisher of the book, in his circular " To the Subscribers," says : " In the preparation and publication of this work it was expected that the financial returns would not meet the outlay involved. About three hundred pages and many illustrations have been added. This expense, however, has been cheerfully assumed by the publisher, in the desire to present to the members of the Boardman Family scattered abroad a genealogy which would do honor to their worthy ancestors and receive the approval of their descendants."

The Graves genealogy, the next work on our list, is an undertaking of considerable magnitude. It is intended to give in three volumes, of which the first is before us, a record of the descendants of six emigrants to America, namely, Thomas, who settled in Hartford, Ct., in 1645, and subsequently in Hatfield, Mass. ; Thomas, who settled in Virginia in 1608 ; Samuel, who settled at Lynn, Mass., in 1630 ; John, who settled at Concord about 1644 ; Dea. John, who settled at Hartford about 1639 ; and Rear Admiral Thomas Graves, who settled at Charlestown, Mass., about 1637. Of these six great families the genealogy of only one has been completed, and that is now before us. The other five families are nearing completion. It is hoped that the issuing of this volume, devoted to the descendants of Thomas of Hatfield, will incite the members of the other families to furnish facts that will enable the editor to complete the entire work as soon as possible. Twenty years have already been spent on the work. If the editor does as satisfactory work on the succeeding volumes as he has done on this, the completed work will be a monument to his memory in coming years.

The next book, that on the Mallet family, is devoted to the descendants of

John Mallett, a Huguenot who, after the Revocation of the Edict of Nantes, came to America and settled in Connecticut. It is a handsome volume of over three hundred and fifty pages, printed on fine paper. It shows unwearied research in tracing the ancestry and kindred of the emigrant. After the Introduction and other historical matter a "Geneological Record," in tabulated form, is given, showing the name of each individual, date of birth, date of marriage, residence, date of death and place of burial. This record fills about three quarters of the volume. These tables give in compact form the records of the several individuals. An Appendix and a thorough index are given. This family history covers a period of two hundred years, and the descendants of John Mallett, the Huguenot, owe a debt of gratitude to Miss Millett, the author.

The Halsey family contains a record of the descendants, of Thomas Halsey, one of the founders of the town of Southampton, Long Island, who lived till after 1677. He was an Englishman, the main features of whose life are well known. The authors of this book have done their work in a very thorough manner. Mr. Jacob L. Halsey began the work and pursued it systematically for about ten years. He entered on an extensive correspondence. He and those assisting him obtained about 2300 names. "In the autumn of 1893, finding his business engagements would interfere with his plans for early publication, he prevailed upon Mr. Edmund D. Halsey of Rockaway, N. J., who had already been interested in the work for many years, and had collected a large mass of material, to undertake the final revision of the entire work and to see it safely through the press." Mr. Francis W. Halsey has furnished an Introduction, giving a history of the Halseys in England, and other interesting matters. The book is handsomely printed, with a good index. The illustrations are numerous, consisting of portraits, views of buildings, autographs, etc.

The Tenney genealogy is another well-compiled and handsomely printed book. Miss Tenney, the compiler, deserves much credit for the manner in which she has performed the labor on this volume, which is devoted to the descendants of Thomas Tenney, a member of the company of Rev. Ezekiel Rogers, who came from Yorkshire in 1638, and settled the town of Rowley the following spring. The descendants are quite numerous and scattered throughout the United States. Their record in this volume is full and precise, the portraits are numerous and fine, and the index is thorough and satisfactory.

The Davies Memoir is a fine specimen of what a family history can be made by the aid of typography. It is on heavy laid paper, each page being rubricated. The book is carefully compiled and gives the descendants of John Davies, who came to America in 1735, and settled at Litchfield, Connecticut, where he died, and where for nearly a century some of his descendants continued to reside. He had previously resided in the town of Kington, Herefordshire, England. The biographical sketches in the book are well written and interesting, and the genealogical records are full and precise.

The Story of My Ancestors in America is devoted to the ancestry of the author, the Rev. Edwin Sawyer Walker. He gives brief genealogies of the families of Walker, Sawyer, Gile and Gilkey, from which he is descended. An Introduction, a Bibliography and an Index add to the value. The book is handsomely printed.

The Usher book contains a memoir of Hon. Roland G. Usher by his son, to which is appended a Genealogy of the Usher Family, of about 80 pages, or one half of the volume. Mr. Usher was a resident of Lynn, Mass., and held many prominent offices under the state and general government. The book is a valuable addition to American biography and family history.

The two books by Rev. Mr. Severance of Chicago are bound together. They both are devoted to the descendants of John Severans, an early settler of Salisbury, Mass., some of whom now spell their surname Severance, while others spell it Seaverns. The compiler has been more than a quarter of a century collecting materials, and has produced a very satisfactory book.

Lewisiana is a monthly periodical devoted to the preservation of the genealogy of the Lewis family. It is edited and published by Carll A. Lewis of Elliott, Conn. This is a good form for collecting and preserving the history of a family, and is deserving of the patronage of those of the name or blood.

The Elmwood Eatons is a very able compilation concerning the descendants of William Eaton of Elmwood at Kentville in the county of Kings, Nova Scotia. Mr. Eaton was "for nearly fifty years a respected member of the community where he held many public positions, both local and provincial." Not only his descendants are recorded but genealogical records of some families with which they are connected are given, as Hamilton, Starr, De Wolf, Bliss, Layton and Thorn. Rev. Mr. Eaton of New York, the compiler, is well known as an author. The book is brought out in fine style.

Mr. Starr's book on the Spencer family, written for Mr. Goodwin of Hartford, Ct., throws new light on some of the early settlers of that name in New England. He shows that Michael, Gerrard, William and Thomas Spencer, who are found early at Cambridge, Massachusetts, were brothers, and he produces much documentary evidence about their relatives in England. He acknowledges indebtedness to Mr. Waters's Gleanings in the REGISTER, vol. 46, page 435, and vol. 45, page 231, where the wills of Francis Spencer and his wife Margaret and Richard Spencer, all of London, relatives of the above Cambridge immigrants, are found. Thomas Spencer removed from Cambridge to Hartford about 1639, and it is to his descendants through his great-great-grandson, Samuel of Cromwell, Ct., that the main portion of this book is devoted. The book is illustrated by a folding tabular pedigree.

The work entitled the Goodwins of East Anglia, is by Henry Barber, M.D., author of British Family Names. It is "designed to supply information somewhat anterior to what has been already published in the large and excellent work on the Goodwin family," noticed by us in April, 1891.

The Lippincott pamphlet is in the form of a letter from Dr. Barber, the author of the preceding work, to James J. Goodwin, Esq., of Hartford, relating to the Lippincotts of England and America, edited by Mr. Goodwin, and noticed in the REGISTER for April, 1893. It supplies some interesting facts relative to the name.

The neat little book on Gov. Bradford's descendants gives what the title shows one line of his posterity. That line is through his son William, deputy governor of Plymouth. The record is clear and precise.

The Clevedon family, by the late Sir John Maclean, F. S. A., "one who did much for archæology," is a work of much merit and its value is increased by the labors of the editor, Rev. Mr. Weaver, of Milton-Clevedon. It is reprinted from the Proceedings of the Somerset Archæological and Natural History Society. The family is traced to the time of William the Conqueror. A tabular pedigree for thirteen generations is given.

The Porter book contains a record of some of the descendants of Robert Porter, one of the early settlers of Farmington, Connecticut. The line is well traced, and the book is handsomely printed.

The Trumbull book gives much information about the Trumbulls in England from whom the New England family evidently sprung, as our readers who have perused the successive numbers as they appeared in the REGISTER, can testify. The book is very creditable to Mr. Lea's research.

The Barnstable Gorhams is a reprint of an article which appeared in the January REGISTER, with some additional matter and illustrations. The Barnstable people and particularly the descendants of the Gorhams will be pleased to possess it in a separate form.

The Hutchinson book is an interesting record of the Hutchinson Family of New Hampshire, descended from Timothy Hutchinson, found at Hampton Falls as early as 1710.

The Skiff book is a brief account of the decendants of James Skiff, who came to this country as early as 1637 and settled at Lynn, and thence removed to Sandwich, Mass., where he died.

The Adams book is devoted to the descendants of Robert Adams of Newbury, Mass., of which family a brief genealogy by the late Joshua Coffin was printed in the REGISTER for January, 1857. The present work is much fuller than Mr. Coffin's article.

The pamphlet entitled " Our Folks," relates to the descendants of John Blake, of Middletown, Conn., who came to this country, probably with his parents, about 1660. It is sent out to obtain help on a larger work on which the author, George M. Blake, of Rockport, Ill., is engaged.

The Morse Record contains the proceedings of the Morse Society at its annual meeting Dec. 4, 1893, in New York city. The Morse Society, of which Jerome E. Morse, of New York city, is president, is formed for revising and publishing the late Rev. Abner Morse's " Memorial of the Morses." The new work is to be published in quarterly parts.

The proceedings at its half century meeting of the Reed Family, as printed in the pamphlet before us, are quite interesting. The association, we think, has held annual meetings at Taunton, Mass., during the fifty years of its existence. The pamphlet of the De Lotbinieres is a reprint of one of Mr. Greenwood's contributions to the REGISTER for January, and our readers know its value.

RECENT PUBLICATIONS,

PRESENTED TO THE NEW-ENGLAND HISTORIC GENEALOGICAL SOCIETY FROM DECEMBER 1, 1895, TO MARCH 1, 1896.

Prepared by the Assistant Librarian.

I. *Publications written or edited by Members of the Society.*

Documents relating to the Colonial History of the State of New Jersey. Edited by William Nelson. Paterson, N. J. Volume XI. 1894. 8vo. pp. cxxvi.+623. Volume XII. 1895. 8vo. pp. cclxviii.+729.

An Alphabetical Abstract of the Record of Marriages in the Town of Dedham, Mass. 1844-1890. Compiled by Don Gleason Hill. Dedham. 1896. 8vo. pp. iv.+165.

The Cabells and their Kin. A Memorial Volume of History, Biography and Genealogy. By Alexander Brown, D.C.L. Boston. 1895. 8vo. pp. xvii.+641.

A Report of the Record Commissioners of the City of Boston, containing the Boston Town Records, 1778 to 1783. Boston: Rockwell & Churchill, City Printers. 1895. 8vo. pp. 354.

Manual of the Union Congregational Church, East Bridgewater, Mass. June. 1894. [By James Sidney Allen.] Wm. L. Puffer, Printer, Brockton. 16mo. pp. 51. [Price 50 cents.]

Official Report of the Tenth Annual Meeting of the New England Association of Colleges and Preparatory Schools, held at Providence, R. I., Oct. 11 and 12, 1895. Hamilton, N. Y. 1895. 8vo. pp. 91.

Meadville Theological School Catalogue. 1894-1895. Meadville, Pa. 1895. 12mo. pp. 26.

The Capture of Louisbourg. By Rev. George Leon Walker, D.D. Address delivered May 1, 1895. 8vo. pp. 16.

Bulletin of the Harvard Medical School Association. Boston. 1892. 8vo. pp. 70.

Bibliography of the Historical Publications issued by the New England States. By Appleton Prentiss Clark Griffin. Reprinted from the Publications of the Colonial Society of Massachusetts. Volume III. Cambridge. 1895. 8vo. pp. 47.

Dunster Papers. By John T. Hassam, A.M. Reprinted from the Proceedings of the Massachusetts Historical Society for October, 1895. Cambridge. 1895. 8vo. pp. 10.

The Indians of New Jersey: Their Origin and Development; Manners and Customs; Language, Religion and Government. By William Nelson. Paterson, N. J. 1894. 8vo. pp. 168.

Records of the Township of Paterson, New Jersey, 1831—1851: With the Laws relating to the Township; Extracts from Contemporary Newspapers, and Notes. Compiled and edited by William Nelson. Paterson, N. J. 1895. 8vo. pp. 233.

The Fate of the Bath Monks. By F. W. Weaver. Reprinted from the Downside Review. 12mo. pp. 5.

Contributions to a Trumbull Genealogy, from Gleanings in English Fields. By J. Henry Lea. Boston. 1895. 8vo. pp. 27.

The Clevedon Family. By the late Sir John Maclean, F.S.A. Edited by Rev. F. W. Weaver, M.A. [Reprinted from the Proceedings of the Somerset Archæological and Natural History Society. Vol. XLI. 1895.] 12mo. pp. 37.

The American and English Sambornes, with a notice of Rev. Stephen Bachiler. By Victor Channing Sanborn. [Reprinted from the Granite Monthly.] 8vo. pp. 25.

Biographical Sketch of David Pulsifer, A.M. By John Ward Dean. [Reprinted from the Necrology of the New-England Historic Genealogical Society, in the Register for January, 1896.] 8vo. pp. 2.

Howland Holmes, M.D. [Reprinted from the New-England Historical and Genealogical Register for January, 1896.] 8vo. pp. 1.

Eighth Report on the Custody and Condition of the Public Records of Parishes, Towns and Counties. By Robert T. Swan, Commissioner. Boston. 1896. 8vo. pp. 42.

The De Lotbinieres. A bit of Canadian Romance and History. By I. J. Greenwood. 8vo. pp. 8.

Barnstable Gorhams. The old house in which they lived, and their services in the Colonial Wars. By Frank William Sprague, Esq. Boston. 1896. 8vo. pp. 7.

Remarks on the names of Townsend Harbor, Massachusetts, and of Mason Harbor and Dunstable Harbor, New Hampshire. By Dr. Samuel A. Green. 8vo. pp. 3.

The Thomas Spencer Family of Hartford, Connecticut, in the line of Samuel Spencer of Cromwell, Connecticut, 1744-1818. Compiled by Frank Farnsworth Starr for James J. Goodwin. Hartford, Conn. 1896. 8vo. pp. 44.

Grave Stone Records. From the ancient cemeteries in the town of Claremont, New Hampshire. With historical and biographical notes. Compiled by Charles B. Spofford. Claremont. 1896. 8vo. pp. 86.

The Story of My Ancestors in America. By Rev. Edwin Sawyer Walker, A.M. Chicago. 1895. 8vo. pp. 72.

II. *Other Publications.*

Searches into the History of the Gillman or Gilman Family, including the various Branches in England, Ireland, America and Belgium. By Alexander W. Gillman. Illustrated with Engravings of Coats of Arms, Portraits, Copies of Ancient Pedigrees, Monuments, Inscriptions, &c., &c. London. Elliot Stock. 1895. 2 vols. Crown 4to. pp. xxii.+334 in the two volumes.

[We hoped to be able to print in this number of the REGISTER a notice of this work by a gentleman familiar with the history of the Gilmans in Europe and America. The notice will however have to be deferred to the next number.]

State of New Hampshire. Town Charters granted within the present limits of New Hampshire. By Albert Stillman Batchellor, Editor of State Papers. Vol. XXV. Concord, N. H. 1895. 8vo. pp. xi.+835.

The New England Indians: A Bibliographical Survey, 1630-1700. By Justin Winsor. Reprinted from the Proceedings of the Massachusetts Historical Society, November, 1895. Cambridge. 1895. 8vo. pp. 35.

The New Hampshire Grants, being Transcripts of the Charters of Townships and minor grants of land made by the Provincial Government of New Hampshire, within the present boundaries of the State of Vermont, from 1749 to 1764. By Albert Stillman Batchellor, Editor of State Papers. Volume XXVI. Concord, N. H. 1895. 8vo. pp. xvi.+792.

Collections of the Massachusetts Historical Society. Sixth Series. Vol. VIII. Boston. 1896. 8vo. pp. xix.+580.

Historical Collections. Collections and Researches made by the Michigan Pioneer and Historical Society. Lansing. 1895. Vol. XXIII. 8vo. pp. 718. Vol. XXIV. 8vo. pp. 706.

Proceedings in Masonry. St. John's Grand Lodge, 1733-1792. Massachusetts Grand Lodge, 1769-1792. Boston. 1895. 8vo. pp. x.+521.

Massachusetts in the Army and Navy during the War of 1861-65. Prepared under the authority of the State by Thomas Wentworth Higginson, State Military and Naval Historian. Vol. II. Boston. 1895. 8vo. pp. 805.

Bulletin of the Bureau of Rolls and Library of the Department of State. No. 3. January, 1894. Washington. 1894. 8vo. pp. 382.

Smithsonian Contributions to Knowledge. The Composition of Expired Air and Its Effects upon Animal Life. By J. S. Billings, M.D., S. Weir Mitchell, M.D., and D. H. Bergey, M.D. Washington. 1895. Fo. pp. 80.

Catalogue of Alumni and Past Cadets of Norwich University. May, 1895. Northfield, Vt. 8vo. pp. 39.

Chicago Historical Society. Report of Annual Meeting, Nov. 19, 1895. 12mo. pp. 5.

Index of Archæological Papers, published in 1894 [being the fourth issue of the series and completing the index for the period 1891-94]. 1895. 8vo. pp. 51.

Report of the Sub-Committee on a Photographic Survey of England and Wales. 1895. 8vo. pp. 6.

Twenty-fifth Anniversary Celebration, New England Society of Orange, 1870-1895. Orange, N. J. 1895. 8vo. pp. 49.

Annual Reports of the Historical and Philosophical Society of Ohio for 1895. Cincinnati. 1895. 8vo. pp. 18.

Smithsonian Institution. Bulletin of the United States National Museum. No. 48. By John B. Smith, Sc. D. Washington. 1895. 8vo. pp. 129.

Catalogue of the University of Pennsylvania. 1895-6. Philadelphia. 1895. 12mo. pp. 428.

Catalogue of the University of Vermont and State Agricultural College. Burlington, Vt., 1895-96. Burlington. 1895. 12mo. pp. 124.

Annual Reports of the President and Treasurer of Harvard College, 1894-95. Cambridge. 1896. 8vo. pp. 278+72.

Catalogue of Tufts College, 1895-96. Boston. 1895. 12mo. pp. 189.

Catalogue of Amherst College for the year 1895-96. Amherst. 1895. 8vo. pp. 72.

Catalogue of the Officers and Students of Brown University, 1895-96. Providence, R. I. 1895. 12mo. pp. 250.

The Harvard University Catalogue, 1895-96. Cambridge. 1895. 12mo. pp. 656.

Catalogue of Yale University, CXCVI. year, 1895-96. New Haven. 1895. 12mo. pp. 426.

Catalogue of the Centre College of Kentucky, 1894-1895. Danville, Ky. 1895. 8vo. pp. 52.

Thirty-first Report of the Trustees of the Boston City Hospital; with reports of the Superintendent, for the year, February 1, 1894, to January 31, 1895, inclusive. Boston. 1895. 8vo. pp. 162.

Sixty-fourth Annual Report of the Trustees of the Perkins Institution and Massachusetts School for the Blind, for the year ending August 31, 1895. Boston. 1896. 8vo. pp. 275.

Ninth Annual Report of the Kindergarten for the Blind. August 31, 1895. Boston. 1896. 8vo. pp. 153.

Thirtieth Annual Report of the Board of Managers of the Winchester Home Corporation for Aged Women. January, 1896. Boston. 1896. 8vo. pp. 30.

Twenty-seventh Annual Report of the Children's Hospital, from December, 1894, to December 28, 1895. Boston. 1896. 8vo. pp. 49.

Reports of the Town Officers of the Town of Lexington for the year 1895. Boston. 1896. 8vo. pp. 208.

260th Report of the Payments of the Town of Dedham for the year ending January 31, 1896, * * * and Abstract of Marriages, 1844-1890. Dedham. 1896. 8vo. pp. 165.

List of Taxable Polls and Estates in the Town of Dedham, 1895. Dedham. 1896. 8vo. pp. 193.

Report of the Committee on the Purchase of the Plant of the Dedham Water Company. Dedham. 1896. 8vo. pp. 48.

Manual of the Congregational Church, Durham, N. H. Dover, N. H. 1895. 8vo. pp. 48.

Minutes of the General Conference of the Congregational Churches in Maine. Sixty-ninth Anniversary, Portland, Me. 1895. 8vo. pp. 153.

Seventh Report of the Trustees of the Salem Public Library, Salem, Mass. December, 1895. Salem. 1896. 8vo. pp. 22.

United States Army Directory. January, 1896. 8vo. pp. 38.

Congress Hall. An Address by Hon. Samuel W. Pennypacker, LL.D., at the Last Session of the Court of Common Pleas, No. 2, in Congress Hall, Philadelphia. September sixteenth, 1895. 8vo. pp. 34.

Manor Hall Number. Yonkers Historical and Library Association Bulletin. 8vo. pp. 45.

Brookline Historical Publication Society Publications, No. 5. Roxbury Church Records relating to Brookline. January, 1896. 8vo. pp. 3.

Ninetieth Anniversary Celebration of the New England Society in the city of New York, at Sherry's, 402 Fifth Avenue, Monday, December 23, 1895. 8vo. pp. 124.

Pedigree Building. Meeting of the Wyoming Historical and Geological Society. [Wilkes-Barre Record, June 11, 1896.] 8vo. pp. 4.

Schedule of Prizes offered by the Massachusetts Horticultural Society for the year 1896. Boston. 1895. 8vo. pp. 45.

Nicholas Perrot. A Study in Wisconsin History. By Gardner B. Stickney. Milwaukee, Wis. 1895. 8vo. pp. 15.

The Morse Record. A History of the Proceedings of the Morse Society in Annual Meeting, December 4, 1895. 8vo. pp. 44.

Martha, daughter of Mehitable Chandler Coit. 1706-1784. 12 mo. pp. 33.

Rev. Jacob Bailey. His Character and Works. By Charles E. Allen. Read before the Lincoln County Historical Society, November 13, 1895. 8vo. pp. 16.

A Memoir of Edmund B. Willson, Fifth President of the Essex Institute. By Robert S. Rantoul. Salem. 1895. 8vo. pp. 39.

Some Letters of Elbridge Gerry of Massachusetts. 1784—1804. Edited by Worthington Chauncey Ford. Brooklyn, N. Y. 1896. 8vo. pp. 28.

Address at the funeral of Mrs. Eleanor J. W. Baker, of Dorchester. By Rev. Theodore T. Munger, D.D. January 17, 1891. Boston. 1895. 16mo. pp. 19.

In Memoriam. Lavinia Farnham. Cambridge. 1894. 12vo. pp. 91.

Commemorative Exercises of the Middlesex Bar Association, in memory of George M. Brooks, held in the Supreme Judicial Court, at Cambridge, April 23d, 1894. So. Framingham. 1895. 8vo. pp. 23.

Memorial and Historical Discourse, Trinitarian Congregational Church, North Andover, October 20, 1895. By the Pastor, Rev. Henry E. Barnes, D.D. 8vo.

Military Order of the Loyal Legion of the United States Commandery of the State of Massachusetts. In Memoriam. Companion Alexander Hamilton Rice.

DEATHS.

Capt. JOHN WILLIAMS DEAN HALL, Secretary of the Old Colony Historical Society, died at his home in Taunton, January 18, in the 89th year of his age.

Capt. Hall had suffered from infirmities for several weeks, but was able to be present at the annual meeting of the Society in January, and with a resonant voice to read his official report. But this brief interval of service which gave promise of speedy restoration to his customary condition of vigorous health, was but a dramatic scene of farewell to the duties of his office, and was succeeded by a period of rapid decline, but with no suspension of his faculties to the very hour of his death.

John Williams Dean Hall was a son of John Williams and Anna (Dean) Hall of Raynham, and a lineal descendant of George and Mary Hall, of Taunton. In early life he was an apprentice in the printing office of Barnum Field, of Providence, and became the publisher of the "Literary Subaltern" of that city; but in 1835 he removed to Taunton, and in the course of a few years became the editor and publisher of the "Taunton Whig," which was afterwards known as the "American Republican." He was also associated in the editorial charge of the "Taunton Daily and Weekly Gazette," and for several years was its publisher; and was engaged in active journalistic life for more than forty years.

Capt. Hall was early interested in the welfare of the local militia, especially of the Providence Cadets and of the Taunton Cohannet Rifle Corps, and resigned from the command of the latter in 1841; at the outbreak of the Civil War he was indefatigable in his efforts as a drillmaster of recruits, and held the office of United States Provost Marshal of the Second Massachusetts District until the close of the conflict: he was a member of the State Legislature in 1863.

As secretary and librarian of the Old Colony Historical Society for the past nine years, Capt. Hall pursued his antiquarian tastes with much enthusiasm, and contributed in great measure to the development of the resources and to the accumulation of treasures of the organization. He was a compiler of a work entitled "The Taunton and Raynham descendants of George and Mary Hall," and was a voluminous contributor to the History of Bristol County. Capt. Hall m. Nov. 13, 1831, Abby Southworth Jackson, dau. of John T. and Elizabeth (Southworth) Jackson, of Providence.

By Joshua Eddy Crane, Esq., of Taunton, Mass.

Hon. DANIEL R. HASTINGS, a distinguished member of the Oxford County Bar, and widely known throughout the State, died at his residence in Fryeburg, Maine, January 13, 1896, aged 72 years, 4 months and 19 days. He was the son of John and Abigail Straw Hastings of Bethel, and was a graduate of Bowdoin College, of the famous class of 1844, having among his classmates Judge William Wirt Virgin, Judge Charles W. Goddard and General Samuel J. Anderson of Portland, the Hon. Horatio G. Herrick of Lawrence, Mass., the Hon.Josiah L. Pickard, LL.D., of Iowa, and the Rev. George M. Adams, D.D., of Auburndale, Mass. N. J. H.

GENEALOGICAL GLEANINGS IN ENGLAND.

By HENRY F. WATERS, A.M.

[Continued from page 141.]

THOMAS GIPPES of Langham, Essex, gentleman, 1 January 1652, proved 12 May 1653. All my houses, lands and tenements in Thirston, Bayton and Tostocke, Suffolk, to wife Mary (for life) and after her decease to John Wall of Broomeley, Essex, clerk, Daniel Wall of Stratford, Suffolk, clothier, and Thomas Brandeston of Langham aforesaid, gentleman, my brothers, and to Daniel Wall of Stratford, son of the said Daniel Wall my brother, to be sold by them or any two of them within one year after the death of Mary my said wife and the moneys thereof arising to be divided among my children Thomas, Henry, Nicholas and Elizabeth Gippes, Thomas to have a double portion. My messuage or tenement, with garden, &c. in Cook Row, Bury St. Edmunds, in occupation of Nicholas Batteley apothecary, my messuage in Southgate street in Bury St. Edmunds, in occupation of one Edward Taylor, and my other houses, lands &c. in Bury St. Edmunds to wife Mary to be sold for payment of my debts, only ten pounds thereof to be first paid to my son in law Robert Manning, he first sealing and delivering to her a release of all actions, legacies, debts and demands. The overplus to said wife Mary whom I make &c. sole executrix.

Brent, 23.

ROBERT WORTHAM of Braintree, Essex, grocer, 16 June 1656, proved 23 February 1657. I desire Mr. Samuel Collyns, minister of Braintree, to preach at my funeral. To my loving wife Judith. My cousin John Sparhawke and James, Mary and John, his three children. To John Clarke, the son of my kinsman John Clarke, at one and twenty. Joseph Taylor the son of my kinsman John Taylor. My sister in law Martha Mann shall have the interest of the forty pounds which Rice Thursby of Braintree, gen^t., doth owe unto me. To my kinsman Richard Wortham of Braintree the house wherein I now dwell, called the Swan, and a butcher's stall in the market place, to the said Richard and his lawfully begotten heirs, with remainder to James Sparhawke, the son of my kinsman John Sparhawke, and to John Clarke, the son of my kinsman James Clarke, and to their heirs forever. I give to James Wall the son of my kinswoman Elizabeth Wall the sum of ten pounds to be paid when he shall accomplish his age of one and twenty years. I give unto my brother in law Daniel Wall forty shillings. To Elizabeth Johnson, the daughter of my kinsman Henry Johnson, ten pounds at one and twenty. My nephew Richard Wortham to be sole executor. And I do also resign to my executor my executorship of the last will and testament of James Sparhawke late of Braintree gen^t. deceased.

Wootten, 182.

BARTHOLOMEW WALL of Blakenam upon the Waters, Suffolk, yeoman, 11 March 1672, proved 23 April 1673. To my dear and loving wife Susan one hundred and fifty pounds, according to an agreement before marriage, also a silver tankard as a further token of my love. To my two daughters

Mary and Martha Wall all my lands and tenements in Bradfield, Essex, these to be sold and the money arising therefrom divided, but Mary to have one hundred pounds more than Martha. To my daughter Susan Wall all my land in Dedham or Langham, Essex. I give unto my daughter Anna Jacob, living in New England the sum of ten pounds, to be paid within eighteen months. My daughter Mary Wall to be sole executor. John Wall one of the witnesses.　　　　　　　　　　　　Pye, 51.

Susan Bantoft of Ipswich, 5 July 1676, proved 7 November 1676. To George and Edmond Boggas, two of the sons of John Boggas deceased, brother to my former husband Anthony Boggas, ten pounds each. To Sarah and Elizabeth the two daughters of Mary Sparrow deceased, my former husband's sister, five pounds each. To Mary Crouch wife of Samuel Crouch of Colchester five pounds. To the four children of Samuel Salter of Dedham which he had by Abigail Salter five pounds apiece at eighteen. To William Bentley son of my brother William Bentley ten pounds at twenty-four. To the four daughters of my said brother, Sarah Arnall ten pounds, Mary Bentley twenty pounds, Anne Bentley twenty pounds and Margaret Bentley ten pounds.

To Mary Wall one of the daughters of Ann Wall, my sister deceased, fifty pounds, to Martha Wall her sister thirty pounds and to another daughter of my sister Anne Wall, in New England, late Anne Jacob, ten pounds. To Susanna Wall, another daughter, fifty pounds.

Elizabeth Bantoft, my husband's daughter. John Bentley son of Edmond Bentley of Langham deceased. Samuel Bantoft son of Jonathan Bantoft. Samuel Bantoft, my husband's son. Thomas Bantoft, my husband's son, his wife and four children. Cousin John Rayner and Mary Chaplyn, children of Margaret Rayner, my sister deceased. The poor of St. Margaret's parish, Ipswich. To Mr. Owen Stockton five pounds. The residue to my husband Thomas Bantoft and he to be executor.

　　　　　　　　　　　　　　　Book Fauconberge, Leaf 259.
　　　　　　　　　　　　　　　　Suffolk Wills (at Ipswich).

[I was first indebted to Dr. J. J. Muskett for reference to this will and its mention of the Wall family. Later, when in Ipswich myself examining the wills there, I came upon it once more and added to my former notes received from Dr Muskett.　　　　　　　　　　　　　　H. F. Waters.]

John Wall of Stratford, Suffolk, clothier, 26 March 1678, proved 3 June 1678. To dear and loving wife Debora all those lands and tenements settled upon her according to agreements upon marriage. To my son Nicholas, after my wife's decease, those lands and tenements, now in the tenure of William Cooper, in Stratford, and also three hundred pounds at the age of two and twenty. To my eldest son Daniel Wall my lands and tenements in Dengy Hundred. I give him also my " Coﬁonteere plonkets " to be delivered him by my executors immediately after my decease if he goes not beyond sea in my life-time and receive them by my order. To him also four hundred pounds when he shall have served out his apprenticeship, provided that his master, and my loving brother, Mr. Edmund Shearman give in to my executors my bond I gave to him for his truth. To son John my mansion house that I dwell in, my woad-house, with fatts and coppers &c. (and other real estate and money). To daughter Deborah three hundred pounds at day of marriage or age of one and twenty. A similar bequest to daughter Elizabeth. To son Bartholomew the house and lands which I lately bought of Richard Havens, called Thorpe's, in Stratford (and other real estate and money). To son Samuel my lands &c. in Awdly Essex (and other gifts). To wife my lands &c. in Fingerego which were surrendered to me by one Samuel Makeing (Makin). Son John shall have sole management of my concerns in Brantham. To Samuel Backler (and others). My sister Fenne. Wife Deborah and son John to be executors and Mr. John Maxey and my brother in law Mr. Nathaniel Shearman to be supervisors.   Reeve, 71.

DEBORAH WALL of Brantham, Suffolk, widow, 31 August 1684, proved 9 July 1685. Son John Wall to be sole executor. My sons Nicholas and Bartholomew and my two daughters shall be paid their portions given them by their father's will. To my grand daughter Anna Wall five pounds. To my sister Fenn ten shillings. Wit: Nathaniel Sherman, John Hobert, Ester Fenn.   Cann, 94.

WILLIAM GRIGLE *als.* GRIGGES of Branktree, Essex, yeoman, 18 October 1575, proved 10 June 1577. To be buried in the church or churchyard there. Lands and tenements in Bocking. Wife Alice to have lands, tenements &c. in Braintree except certain lands and tenements called Boram's and Marshall's and one orchard called the Cheker Orchard whereupon one barn and other edifices are now newly builded by John Mott my wife's eldest son. To Adrian Smart all my lands and tenements in Stysted, Essex, called Gull's. Servant John Bragge. Friend Jeffery Caldwell of London. Wife Alice to be executrix and Robert Clerke, gen^t., steward to the Right Hon. Sir Robert Rich, knight, Lord Rich, and John Goodaye the elder to be overseers.   Daughtry, 22.

ALICE GRIGLE otherwise GRIGGES of Branktree, Essex, widow, 22 February 1577, proved 16 February 1584. My body to be buried in the parish church or churchyard or Branktree. I give and bequeath unto John Motte my son one field or croft of land lying in Bocking, by the high way side leading from Branktree towards Coggeshall, containing by estimation three acres and a half, late purchased of ———— Dryland, as the same is now in the manurance* or occupation of the said John Motte, to have and to hold the said field or croft during the term of his natural life; and after his decease the said field or croft shall remain unto John Smarte, son of Adrian Smarte, and to his heirs and assigns forever. I give, devise and bequeath unto Mark Motte my son all those my messuage, lands, tenements &c. &c. in Bocking and Branktree, or elsewhere in Essex, which sometime were of Raphe Rocheford, citizen and grocer of London, or of Jane Rocheford his daughter deceased, and which were late purchased of Stephen Craske, citizen and vintner of London, to have and to hold forever. I give to the said Mark Mott my son that my messuage wherein I now dwell, called the White Greyhound, and two tenements adjoining on either side of the said messuage, one of which is a new house and the other was late in the occupation of Philip Ingram *als.* Wylson (and other estate including ten acres of land) in Branktree, and a parcel of pasture, sometime Dorwardes, in Bocking, near unto Bocking End, by the highway side leading from Bock, ing to Reyne. To John Motte my son one other croft containing by estimation three acres, sometime Dorwarde's, and another parcel called the Harp-

---

* This word was used in its original and proper signification of cultivation, or tillage. Manure is simply the English form of manoeuvre.—H. F. W.

with a "Chaceway" adjoining, lying in Bocking, to hold during his life, and after his decease the said croft or chaceway shall wholly remain and come unto Adryane Smarte, son of Adryane Smarte. I give and bequeath unto Mary, Alice and Katherine, daughters of the said Adryan Smarte (certain household stuff). I give and bequeath unto John, son of the said Marke Motte my son, twenty pounds to be paid unto him at his age of twenty four years. Also I give unto every other child which the said Marke my son shall have born and living at the time of my decease twenty pounds, at their several ages of twenty four years. And I give &c. unto Peter, John and Adrian, sons of the said Adrian Smarte, twenty pounds apiece, at their several ages of twenty four years. The residue to my son Mark whom I make sole executor &c.

Rob^te Stanton one of the witnesses.

File 1584, Com. of London (Essex and Herts).

ADREAN SMART of Brainktree, Essex, yeoman, 23 December 1583, proved 2 April 1584. Wife Margery. The tenement wherein I now dwell and that in the occupation of Alexander Browne. My tenement called the Swan. My son Peter Smart. My son John. My son Adrian. My brother Thomas Smart. My three daughters, Mary, Alice and Katherine Smart. My stall place which I have usually occupied on market days. Money received to the use of my three daughters from Alice Grigges, widow, my wife's mother. I will that John Sperhawke shall hold my shop belonging to the Swan according to a former grant made to him by James Wedon. I make and ordain Margery my wife my only executrix. And I will that she shall find Thomas Smart my brother sufficient meat, drink, lodging and apparel &c. And I ordain my brothers in law John Mott and Mark Mott my supervisors.   Butts, 35.

ROBERT MOTT, one of the aldermen of the town of Colchester, 31 May 1603, proved 27 April 1604. Wife Anne shall have her dwelling in the house that I do now inhabit and dwell in, during the time of her widowhood (*i. e.* certain portions of it set forth and described). Son William shall occupy certain portions in common with her. The next house, called the Crown, wherein Robert Hayward now dwelleth. To wife such household stuff &c. as were hers before I married her. My executor shall pay unto her twenty pounds for Thomas Walker.

Item, as I have always heretofore wished well to the good estate of the Corporation of Colchester and now being much grieved for some unkind dissension lately risen there, so, as a fellow feeling member of that body, I do heartily desire their peace and unity, and to that end and as a token of my well meaning to them all do give and bequeath to the Bailiffs and Commonalty of the said town a piece of plate to be delivered unto them by the discretion of the said William Mot, my executor, so as before the delivery and receipt thereof thereby by some good means a charitable reconciliation made among them, which plate, my meaning is, shall be used in their great chamber at their Moot hall where they are appointed to have their diet at their Assemblies, and so to continue there to that use forever. To my son Thomas the house that my son William now dwelleth in, called the Bull &c. and the house and ground at Barfolde (Bergholt?), which I bought of M^r. Shirlock, and the wood, called Poor's wood, in Barfold, which I bought of my father in law Mr. Robert Mydleton the elder, and the moor now in the occupation of George Sutton, and two tenements in East Street which I

bought of my father in law Mr. Midleton and now in the occupation of
Michael Arnould. Other bequests to him (among other things "my birde
carpet"). I give to my brother Hilles and my sister and Giles Marsh and
Mary Marsh twenty pounds amongst them to be divided as my brother
Hilles thinketh best. Thomas Winiffe to whom I forgive the ten pounds
lent him to buy his house at Lanham withall. To Doctor Harris, Mr.
Lewis, Mr. Newcombe and my brother Clay, either of them forty shillings
apiece. To my brother Cuttle if he be living. To my sister Mydleton, my
aunt Raynoldes, my sister Stevens, my brother and sister Steele and my
son Harmonson and his wife, either of them, a gold ring, price twenty shillings. Residue to son William, whom I do ordain and make my sole executor. And I do appoint and desire my loving friends Robert Mydleton the
younger, gen^t., and Richard Symnell gent. to be overseers.   Harte, 35.

JOHN SMARTE of Branktrye, Essex, yeoman, 7 June 1604, proved 14
July 1604. Wife Thomazine. Free lands and tenements in Bocking.
Adrian, my second son. I do devise my messuage or tenement wherein I
now dwell to my uncle Mott for seven years, towards the performance of
this my will. I do devise all and every my customary lands and tenements
in Branktrye unto my said uncle Mark Mott for seven years &c. &c. I do
give unto the child that my wife now goeth withal (if she be with child) one
hundred marks in manner following; forty pounds thereof remaining in the
hands of my wife's father John Curd of Sudbury, being part of my wife's
portion which he promised me with her in marriage, to be paid to her from
him within one year after my decease to the use of her child, if she be
with child &c., and twenty six pounds thirteen shillings and four pence,
residue of the said sum of one hundred marks &c. Provision for the
wardship of eldest son, John Smarte. My uncle Marke Motte to be sole
executor. My four children named John, Adrian, Mary and Ellinor
Smarte.
    Wit: Peter Smartt, Richard Owtinge and Erasmus Sparhawk.
                                                              Harte, 70.

JOHN GALE of St. Leonard within the liberty of Colchester, Essex,
mariner, 23 May 1606, proved 2 July 1606. John Mott the son of my
brother John Mott of Much Wigburrowe Essex. Bridget Adams *als.* Mott
the daughter of my said brother Mott. Marcy and Mary Mott two other
of his daughters. George and Bridget Adams the children of the said
Bridget. Johan Samon *als.* Miller of Much Wigborowe my sister. My
tenement &c. in Peldon Essex. William Samon her son and Robert and
Anne Samon her children. My wife Katherine. George Adams the elder
of Aberton Essex yeoman. Matthew Pickors my wife's grandchild. Susan
Lambert another of my wife's grandchildren. Elizabeth Godsalle my
wife's daughter.   Stafford, 58.

CATHERINE GALE of St. Leonard's (as above), widow, 28 November
1606, proved 19 December 1606. My two daughters Mary Dinbye and
Elizabeth Godsall. My grandchild Matthew Pickas. My grandchild Susan
Lambert. My ketch or ship called the Elizabeth of Colchester. My cousin
Susan Bragge wife of John Foorde of Brightlingsea Essex. My cousin
Unitye Kinge (female). My cousin Jasper Randall of St. Leonard's.
John Dinby and my said daughter Mary his wife. Her two children.
                                                        Stafford, 91.

SAMUEL HILLES of Christ Church London, merchant taylor, 17 June 1609, proved 20 July 1609. To be buried in the parish church of Christ Church where my late wife lieth buried. The poor of Much Taye in Essex where I was born. The children of my cousin Thomas Hilles, citizen and merchant taylor of London. Four of the youngest of my brother Thomas Hill's children. The children of my cousin William Mott of Colchester, Essex, gen^t. I give to my cousin Thomas Mott all such household stuff as the aforesaid William Mott hath of mine in his hands, amounting to the sum of seventeen pounds fourteen shillings or thereabouts. My cousin Thomazine Greene wife of Richard Greene joiner. My tenement at Stoke Newington, Middlesex. My grandchild Mary Marsh at twenty one or day of marriage. My tenement called the Blue Anchor in Mark Lane, London. Giles Marsh, my grandchild, at one and twenty. My two tenements in Aldersgate Street, London, which I hold of Mr. William Gregory of Coventry, gen^t., and his wife. Thomas Sparke citizen and merchant taylor of London. My cousin William Mott and my cousin Thomas Hills to be my executors.   Dorset, 75.

MARK MOTT of Braintree, Essex, gen^t., 1 March 1636, proved 7 May 1638. The poor of Bocking and of Braintree. Eldest son John Mott to ratify and confirm a jointure of the manor of Shimpling Hall, Norfolk, and the land thereunto belonging unto Alice Mott, wife of the said John Mott. Daughter Sara Wolrich. My cousin Collyns, minister of Braintree. My cousin Wharton, minister of Felsted. Every one of my children. Mark Draper, son of Alice Draper, my grandchild. My son Adrian Mott to be sole executor.

Wit: Thomas Jekyll, Richard Outing and Nicholas Jekyll.

Lee, 60.

[I have already given in the REGISTER for July 1892 (Vol. 46, pp. 320-323) a large abstract of the will of Mark Mott, D.D., rector of Rayne Parva in the County of Essex, who was a son of the above testator and who named a lot of relatives, among others Dorothy the wife of John Taylecott. Samuel Collins the Vicar of Braintree, whom both father and son called cousin, was directly connected with New England through Mr. Edward Collins of Cambridge and Charlestown. Morant's Essex (especially vol. ii., p. 376) furnishes some account of this family of Mott. I have other wills referring to the Motts of East Mersea and of Bradwell which I have not thought it worth the while to send at present.   HENRY F. WATERS.]

In the name of God amen. I, JOHN ROGERS of Moulsham ioyner &c. My body to be buried in the churchyard of the parish of Chelmsford. I give to my wife Annys my house wherein I dwell, so long as she liveth here in this world, and after her decease I will that my oldest son John Rogers shall have it, on this condition that within one year after his mother's decease he pay to my son Richard Rogers twenty nobles and to my daughter Mary Rogers likewise twenty nobles of lawful money of England if the said John refuse so to do, or do it not, then I will that the goodman Graveley, the goodman Manne and the goodman Reade, or their assigns, shall sell the aforesaid house to the most advantage, and the money thereof to be equally divided amongst my children, John, Richard and Mary, and either of them to be the others' heirs. I give to my son John a featherbed with all things belonging thereto. I give to my son Richard a featherbed likewise with all things belonging thereto. I give to my daughter Mary also a featherbed with all things belonging thereto; which featherbeds with all things belonging to them I will to be delivered to my forenamed children and either of them at the day of their marriage. I appoint my neighbor John Graveley and my neighbor Nicholas Manne my assignees for the sale of the house of one Thomas Ashbey deceased to the use of the four children which he left behind him, as it appeareth in the last will and testament of the said Thomas Ashbey. I will that my wife Annys shall receive and pay all my debts, and therefore I give unto her all the rest of my goods whatsoever they be, and I do make and appoint the said Annys my only executrix of this my last will and testament. Finis.

No. 17, 9th File, 1575, Com. of London (Essex and Herts) Wills.

[John Rogers, of Moulsham, the testator, is, I believe, the father of Rev. Richard of Wethersfield and grandfather of Rev. John of Dedham. Turning to my Gleanings for April, 1887 (REGISTER, vol. 41, page 158 and onward) the reader will note that on page 170, extracts from the Parish Register of Chelmsford are printed. If I am now right, then John of Moulsham, father of Rev. John of Dedham, was born in 1548, instead of in 1538, as I have given,in the pedigree on page 158. I had already suggested such a thing on page 170 (after giving the baptisms). If I am now right, too, we now know who the mother was of Richard of Wethersfield, and grandmother of John of Dedham. She was Agnes (or Annys) Carter, married in 1541) as I say on page 170). Now this marriage becomes important, so I give it from my note-book:

"John Rogers, wedowr was maryed to Agnes Carter, wedowe on sonday the viij daye of Maye 1541."

We have yet to learn her maiden name. I shall have to bear the Carters in mind, and see if I can get the will of her former husband.

Since the Rogers pedigree, in April, 1887, was printed, I have obtained the record of the marriage of Rev. Nathaniel Rogers to Margaret Crane, as follows:

"1625 January 23. Nathaniel Rogers minister of Bocking and Margaret Crane of Cockshall [Coggeshall] were married by license Jan. 23."
Parish Register of Messing.

I owe the above to the thoughtful kindness of Mr. William Brigg, editor of the Herts Genealogist and Antiquary. When I went down into Essex with Mr. Starr to examine parish registers in the neighborhood of Bocking for Mr. Goodwin, I did not see the Messing registers, having learned from Mr. Starr that he had culled the Goodwin entries there. Otherwise I should probably have noted the above important entry. Mr. Brigg took other Rogers entries, but I see nothing among them especially relating to our New England family.

H. F. WATERS.

In 1868, I stated in print that there are in the Bodleian Library two volumes of Candler's, MSS. Tanner 180 and 257, of which the former bears to the well-known Harleian 6071 of the British Museum, the relation of finished work to rough notes. They ought to be carefully studied. In 1888, I copied from 180 a part of the Rogers pedigree, which explains one of the puzzles in it, and corrects the chart printed in the REGISTER, Vol. 41, page 158-9.

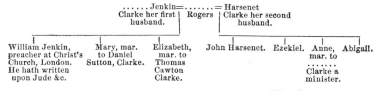

WM. S. APPLETON.]

EDWARD HASTELER of Maldon, Essex, merchant, 11 June 1622, proved 4 October 1622. Messuages, lands, leases, shipping, goods, merchandizes, &c. By the will and testament of that reverend man Mr. Richard Rogers of Weathersfield deceased, my late father in law, I had a sum of money the which by said father in law was meant and intended for the purchase of lands and tenements to be estated upon me and Rebecca my now wife, his daughter, for our lives and after our deaths to remain and come to the equal benefits of Richard, Joseph, Nathaniel, Hester and Mary Hasteler, five children which I then had by the said Rebecca my now wife. I bequeath my capital messuage wherein I do now dwell and the tenement wherein Thomas Betts cordwainer dwelleth, which was anciently also part of my said messuage, with lands &c., being in Maldon, unto the said Rebecca my wife for the term of her life and after her decease to the five children before named. Other portions to these children and to John the youngest son by wife Rebecca. My ten other children which I had by my former wife, viz[t] Benjamin, Edward, John, Philip, Andrew, Thomas, Stephen, Susan wife of William Squire, Sara Hasteler and Mary Hasteler. Provision for the education of the six children had by wife Rebecca. My brother in law Sheppard and my sister his wife. The poor of the parish of St. Mary's in Maldon and of St. Peter's in Maldon and of All Saints in Maldon. Judith the wife of John Saffould of Maldon. Rebecca and Martha Wrighte my daughters in law. I have put my son Thomas into the University of Cambridge. I have sent my son Benjamin unto the Islands with an adventure. Son Edward to be sole executor. My loving and trusty friends John Wrighte Esq. and John Soane to hear and end any questions about my will.

Wit: Ezechiell Rogers, John Soane, Frauncis Long.   Saville, 92.

JOHN MARKAUNT of S[t]. Gyles within the town of Colchester, Essex, gen[t]., 14 September 1583, proved 12 November 1585. The poor, impotent and aged poor of the township of Stooke in the County of Suffolk. Edmond Markaunt, commonly called eldest son of me the said John Markaunt the father. John Markaunt, commonly called the second son &c. &c. William Markaunt, commonly called the third son &c. &c. Elizabeth Markaunt, commonly called one of the daughters &c. &c., at day of marriage or full age of one and twenty years. The aforesaid William Markaunt, my youngest son, at his full age of one and twenty. Margaret Markaunt, now the wife of me the said John Markaunt the elder. To the aforesaid William, third son &c., all those my copyhold lands and tenements in Myldenhall, Suffolk, now in the tenure of William Place &c., and also my messuage in Colchester wherein one —— Smythe, butcher, lately did dwell, the messuage in the parish of St. Mary Magdalen, Colchester, wherein one William Beriffe now dwelleth and those three rentaries or tenements, with one little garden plat adjoining lying in Beare Lane, Colchester, now or late in the several tenures and occupations of Robert Middleton, gentleman, the widow Vincente, the widow Helgrave and the widow Rushbrooke. To son John two messuages in Bury St. Edmond's, Suffolk, after the death of Elizabeth Markaunt my sister, and rents arising out of my copyhold lands &c. in Kyrby and Thorpe or elsewhere in Essex (and other lands in Suffolk and Essex) and all my lands and tenements in the parish of S[t]. Martin in the Vintry, London. Wife Margaret shall cause the said John and William my sons to be taught and instructed in good literature and learning, according to their several capacities, shall place and maintain them in the Universities or Inns of Chancery and Court to study the Law or some such art as their minds shall be most inclined unto &c.; and if the capacity of either of them shall be adjudged by their learned tutor or tutors and by my supervisor unable and unapt to receive learning then I will that he which so shall be deemed not capable of learning shall be placed by the said Margaret, with the consent of my supervisor, with some discreet and godly person to be trained up in some good honest trade or science during his nonage. Wife Margaret to be sole executrix and my cousin Joseph Scotte to be supervisor. Brudenell, 49.

EDMOND CLARE of Old Newton, Suffolk, gen[t]., 20 April 1630, proved 12 May 1631. Wife Marey. Son in law Richard Sidaye. Son in law Rapfe Sidaye and his daughters Marey Sidaye and Margrett Sidaye. Lands at Mount Buers, Essex. My kinsman Raynould Rous. Mr. Penn, minister of Newton. My sons in law Edmund Markant and William Markant. My nephew Rous. Philip Garrard. Wife Marey executrix. John Penne a witness. Proved by Mary Clare the widow. S[t]. John, 65.

WILLIAM MARKANT of Kelvedon, Essex, clothier, 8 January 1643, proved 18 December 1644. The poor of Kelvedon and of Great Coggeshall. To wife Mary my messuage or tenement, with the yards and garden to the same belonging, situate in or near Church Street, in Great Coggeshall, now or late in the occupation of William Lowe, she to hold for life ; the reversion to my daughter Goulding and her heirs. To my undutiful son John Markant fifty pounds, but the same to be paid into the hands of my brother in law Mr. Robert Crane and my cousin Mr. Thomas Guyon the elder, both of Great Coggeshall, desiring them to dispose and order the money whereby it may become a yearly maintenance for my said son, his wife and children, knowing that he is not of himself able to govern himself or order an estate for the good of himself nor them that depend upon him, having misspent what I have formerly bestowed upon him. Two hundred pounds to such child or children as he hath or shall have &c. To my said brother Crane and cousin Guyon my messuage called the Checquer (with land &c.) in Gouldanger, Essex, upon trust to bestow the yearly maintenance of him, his wife and children ; and after his death to the heirs of the body of my said son John forever. The residue of my goods &c. to my wife and my daughter Crane, whom I make executors.

Proved by Mary Markant the relict and —— Crane the natural and lawful daughter of the deceased. Rivers, 19.

THOMAS CRANE of Kelvedon Essex, gen[t]., 11 November 1654, proved 6 March 1654. The poor of Kelvedon. Mr. Channdler, my minister. My loving wife. My daughter Mary. Certain messuages in Colchester which I purchased of Christopher Yeoman and John Yeoman his son. And I do give undo her, more, seven hundred pounds which I will and desire shall be laid out in lands for her use, and what other money she shall have by this my will, by my father Mr. Robert Crane and my brother Mr. Henry Whiteing. To son Robert all the residue of my freehold, copyhold and lease lands and tenements. I make my said son and daughter executors. And I nominate and entreat my said father and brother Whiting to be their guardians. If they die without issue within the age of one and twenty all their estate shall be to the use of the children of my sister Margaret the wife of Nathaniel Rogers now in New England and to the children of my sister Whiting, part and part alike. Aylett, 159.

[This is the will referred to by me in a foot-note on page 177 of Vol. 41 of the REGISTER, on which page a pedigree of Crane is printed. As to the other foot-note on that page (will of Samuel Crane, 1609), I have already entered in my note-book that this date must be an error in Morant for 1669, which was the actual date of the will of Samuel, brother of the above Thomas Crane, and of Margaret wife of Rev. Nathaniel Rogers, of Ipswich, Mass.—H. F. WATERS.]

[The following four wills, those of Joseph Collyer, Philip Watton, Christopher Cary, and Dame Mary Sergeant, break the group of East Anglian wills; but this could not well be prevented.]

Joseph Collyer the elder, citizen and grocer of London, 21 August 1648, proved 28 September 1649. To the poor of the parish of St. Saviour's in Southwalk, where I dwell, ten pounds. Twenty pounds to be distributed to ten or twenty poor godly christians. My brother Abel Collyer. My niece Elizabeth Bourne the daughter of my sister Elizabeth Bourne. My sister Judith Warner. My sister Rhoda Dorton. I give to my sister Mary Browninge in New England the sum of ten pounds. My sister Dorcas Slingsby and her youngest child. I give the sum of fifty pounds to be distributed amongst the children of my brother Abel and my sisters. My sister Rachael now the wife of Richard Parnell of Epsham. I purchased a house and certain lands in Epsham wherein my said sister and her husband have dwelt and enjoyed about ten or twelve years and have not paid any rent for the same (the said house and land being worth ten pounds per annum). I do hereby remit all the rent that is past, and they to hold the same during the life of said sister, paying only forty shillings per annum for the rent thereof unto my son Joseph. Reference to an Indenture of bargain and sale, bearing date 19 May 1647, from Marlyon Rithe of Chipstead, Surrey, gen^t., of a messuage and farm called Storrocks in said parish, and other lands about there (evidently a mortgage). Bequests to son Samuel (at one and twenty) and to sons Joseph and Benjamin (partners in trade). To sons Joseph, Abel and Samuel all my household stuff and plate which I was possessed of before I was last married to Elizabeth my now wife. My daughter in law Anna Harris at one and twenty. Susan Warner daughter of my sister Judith. The two daughters of my daughter Savage, namely Hannah and Elizabeth Savage.

Fairfax, 136.

Philip Wotton of East Budleigh, Devon, yeoman, 26 October 1657, proved 10 February 1662. My lands at Salterton within this parish. A messuage or tenement called Haymill in East Budleigh to John Channon the younger, Roger Bagwill and Richar Curtis of this parish to and for the only use, best benefit and behoof of my brother Matthew Wotton (reserving to my wife Jane two days' cut of "turfes" yearly out of the moors of the said tenement during my said wife's life). Philip Wotton son of my brother Matthew. Richard Courtis the son of Richard Courtis aforesaid and Susanna Courtis the daughter. I do give and bequeath unto my daughter in law Jane Bennett in New England five pounds to be paid unto her and her children within one year and half after my decease, my wife, if please God to enable her in estate, to make up the same thirty pounds. My kinswoman Sarah Wotton. My houses in Peter Street in the City of Westminster. Philip, Sarah and James Wotton children of my brother Matthew. Mary, Susanna and Anne Veryard children of my sister Mary Veryard deceased. John and Susanna Gary children of my sister Thomasine Gary deceased. Susanna, Mary and Elizabeth Wotton children of my brother Matthew. Thomasine Vergard daughter of my said sister Mary Veryard. Mary and Philip Gary children of my said sister Thomasine Gary. The said houses &c. being the grant of Sir Robert Pye knight. Michael Arnold the son of Michael Arnold the elder of Westminster brewer. Rebecca, my master Michael Arnold the elder's sister. Mr. John Thornell's widow, being my said master's brother in law. Amye

Hynes the wife of George Hynes of this parish.   Mary Follett my now servant.   Matthew Wotton the son of my brother Matthew.   I do give and bequeath unto my brother in law Richard Gary all the right and interest that I have in and to that plot of ground called the Pound lot adjoining to his now dwelling house.   To my master Michael Arundell (*sic*) the elder's wife my book of Martyrs.   Juxon, 26.

CHRISTOPHER CARY, of Bristol, merchant, 10 September 1672, proved 28 October 1672.   Contract made 19 January 14th of his Majesty's reign that now is, between myself and wife Margaret, of the one part, and Jeremy Hollwey of Bristol, merchant, and Thomas Sterne, of the same city gen^t, of the other part, to levy a fine &c. of the messuage on the Back at Bristol, the church yard of St. Nicholas on the South side thereof, a little lane lying between said house and churchyard.   Messuage in St. Stephen's, in a place or street commonly called the Key.   I dwelling on Stony Hill, St. Michael's, Bristol.   My two sons Richard and John.   My son in law Henry Daniel and his wife.   Eure, 118.

Dame MARY SERGEANT, late Phips, relict of Sir William Phipps, late of Boston in New England, knight, deceased.   Reference to marriage contract with present husband, Peter Sergeant Esq., bearing date 24 September 1701.   My honored mother in law Mrs. Mary Howard, widow; her son Philip White oweing and indebted to me a considerable sum of money, for securing the payment whereof this houseing and lands lying in Beverly stand engaged and made over by way of mortgage and are become forfeit, the time for payment being long since elapsed.   My sister Mrs. Rebecca Bennett.   The Rev^d Mr. Increase Mather, the Rev^d Mr. Cotton Mather and my friend Mr. John White.   Margaret, wife of Matthew Armstrong, and her daughter Mary Armstrong.   To Dorcas Salter, wife of Eneas Salter jun^r, that silver tankard which my son Spencer used at the college &c.   My adopted son Spencer Phipps als Bennet to be my heir.   Margaret Armstrong and Dorcas Salter two of my said husband's (Sir William Phipps') nieces.   My houseing, land and wharf at the North End of Boston, called the Salutation, I give to my two nephews David and William Bennet.   My house at the North end, in the present tenure &c. of Samuel Avis, I give to Mary Armstrong.   Gift to a free school in the North end.   Bequests to Benjamin White, Elizabeth Holland, Margaret Armstrong and William Bennet.   My two sisters in law Mary Bridger and Margaret Andrews.   Spencer Phipps als Bennet to be executor and, during his minority, my friends John Foster and Andrew Belcher esquires to be executors.   Signed 19 February 1704 and proved 29 January 1706.
                                                               Poley, 16.

[Dame Mary Sergeant was a daughter of Roger Spencer.   She married 1st, John Hull of Boston, not the mint-master; 2d, Sir William Phips, the first governor of Massachusetts, under the second charter; 3d and lastly, Peter Sergeant, whose house was afterwards purchased by the province and known as the Province House.   He survived his wife.—EDITOR.]

[We now continue the abstracts of East Anglian wills].

MATHEWE STEPHENS of Colchester, Essex, gen^t.   2 March 1597, proved 13 May 1599.   Dwelling in the parish of All Saints.   Wife Priscilla to have all my houses, lands &c. for life if she continue unmarried.   House called the walnut tree house.   A copyhold in Grinstead.   Priscilla my daughter. William Stephens my brother. My house and lands at Wyvenhoe. Lands and tenements called Stephens in Ardeley and Langham. My daughter Elizabeth. Lands and tenements in Much Horcksley. Lands in Lexden. My daughter Martha. My daughter Anne. Lands and tenements in Much Holland. My very good uncle John Stephens of Ardeley. My tenement called Cole's in Ardeley. My uncle Robert Stephens. My said five daughters. I, being one of the executors of the last will of Thomas Laurence, lately alderman of Colchester, with Martin Bessell, alderman, and William Laurence, make my good friend Sir Thomas Lucas my executor for those matters only, he to be bound in such manner as my brother Robert Myddleton gen't. shall think meet. Lands and tenements called Hunters in Wigborowe and Pelldon. My brother Bessell and his wife. My brother John Stephens. My loving friends and kinsfolk Mr. Thomas Reynoldes my father in law Mr Myddleton, Mr. Northey, Mr. Lobell and my uncles John and Nicholas Stephens.

Thomas Reynolds, Roberte Middleton and Raphe Northey were among the witnesses. Proved for Priscilla Stephens the relict &c., Sir Thomas Lucas renouncing &c.

Proved 13 December 1626 for Elizabeth Gilberd *als* Stephens a daughter of the deceased, Priscilla Stephens, the relict being dead.

Kidd, 41.

PRISCILLA STEPHENS of Colchester, Essex, widow, 5 June 1626, proved 17 March 1626. To be buried in the church of All Saints, Colchester, near my husband. My son in law George Gilberd and Elizabeth my daughter, his wife. My grandchild Elizabeth Gilbert, his daughter, and her son, my great grandchild, George Gilberd the younger. My daughter Buxtone. My son and daughter Norfolke. My grandchild Priscilla Cosen at four and twenty. John Cosen at one and twenty. William and Thomas Cosen at four and twenty. My grandchild and god daughter Anne Buxtone. My grandchildren Thomas and Robert Buxton at four and twenty. My grandchild Mary Peeters at one and twenty. My godson Robert Middleton at four and twenty. My cousin Samuel Motte's wife and his son William Mott my godson. My cousin Robert Mott and his wife. My cousin Shirley and his wife and Elizabeth Mott the wife of John Langy. Mr. Thomas Tatem and his wife. My old cousin Holmes his wife. My son and daughter Norfolke to permit and suffer my other children to enjoy all the goods and chattells of my late husband deceased without making any claim to the same. Legacies to their children. The said George Norfolke. My daughter Anne Buxton. I make my cousin William Mott and my cousin Samuel Mott executors and my cousin Thomas Mott and my cousin Thomas Holmes overseers. If my cousin Mott and and his son Samuel shall refuse to be executors then I appoint my daughters Gilberd and Buxtone. Proved by William and Samuel Mott. Skynner, 26.

Sententia was promulgated 19 June 1630 in a cause between Edmund Peirce Not. Pub. curator ad lites of Mary Peter a minor, grand daughter of the deceased, on the daughter's side, and William Mott and Samuel Mott, executors of the above will. Scroope, 59.

EDMOND SYBORNE of Dedham, Essex, clothier, 15 December 1617, proved 2 March 1617. To wife Margaret all my houses and lands that I bought of Simon Fenn and Roger Barat during her life; then to son Edmund, with remainder to son Thomas. To wife all the household stuff that was hers before our marriage. Bequests to the said two sons and they to be apprenticed to some clothier or some other honest trade. My wife's children Margaret Bentley, Hanna Bentley, Beazadle (Bezalliel), John and Edward Bentley. Edmund Syborne my brother's son. Cousin Mary Wrighte of Colchester. To Edward Newman of Colchester such sums as he doth owe me. To Edmond Spynke the five pounds that he oweth me upon this condition that he do give an acquittance for five pounds that was given him by my brother Thomas. The poor of Dedham and of St. James Parish, Colchester. To Mr Rogers as much of my best cloth as shall make him a gown. Mr. Cotsford. My brother William Syborne. Wife Margaret to be executrix and Robert Alfounder and William Bentley supervisors. Loving friend William Cole. Meade, 25.

ROBERT WARD of Lexdon within the liberties of Colchester, 8 January 1616, proved 9 May 1617. To wife Parnell two hundred pounds, partly in money & partly in goods, household stuff &c., and the benefit of my lease of Lexden Lodge and the grounds therewith demised, until the Feast of St. Michael "Tharkengell" which shall be in A.D. 1620, and the rent of Shalford Mill until the said Feast (1620). And if she remain a widow until the said Feast &c. and so be unprovided of a convenient habitation then I will that she shall relinquish the said lease of Lexden Lodge and grounds there and the said mill &c. and at the said Feast &c (1620) shall enter upon my messuage in Wethersfield, called Ward's to have, hold, occupy and enjoy the said messuage &c. for and during the term of her natural life, if she shall happen to continue sole and unmarried (except my hopgrounds there &c). But if she shall change her estate by marriage then she shall only hold my said messuage, called Ward's, until the Feast of St. Michael &c. next after her marriage and no longer. My wife shall pay yearly unto my mother in law, the late wife of my father Lancelot Ward, thirteen pounds six shillings eight pence out of the said lands according to a grant thereof made by me in satisfaction of her dower out of said lands and tenements. Provision for sixteen loads of firewood, from trees which have been usually lopped and topped within twenty years past, to be used at the said house only. If wife marry again then she to have and hold the said mill and lands from the Feast of St. Michael &c. next after her said marriage for term of her natural life. My wife to bring up my three youngest children, my son Samuel (one of the said three) to be fitted for the University and there by her placed. I give to said Samuel, for his maintenance at the University, eighteen pounds by the year for six years after he shall be there settled and one hundred pounds six months after the last payment thereof. To son John my free tenements in Blakemer End in Wethersfield, called Chappell Howse, late in the tenure of one Collins, and those closes of copyhold which I lately purchased of the sons of John Clarke of Shinborowes, or of one of them. To said John one hundred pounds, to be paid unto him by Robert my son within nine months after the said Robert shall lawfully enter upon my said messuage called Ward's. But if John is not then of the age of twenty one then the said money shall be paid by Robert to such person or persons as the greater part of their brothers and sisters then living shall nominate and appoint, to be employed in some honest use and benefit for the said John till he shall be fit to use it himself, he being entered into some profession or trade of living. I give to Robert my son my capital messuage called Ward's &c. which I late had of Lancelot Ward my father deceased (with certain

exceptions) to hold &c. for ever at and from his age of twenty three (if my
said wife's estate therein shall happen to be then determined); but if Robert die before that age then to son John and his heirs forever, upon condition he pay Samuel twenty pounds yearly during Samuel's life. Other
estate to Robert. To my said two younger sons, Samuel and John, each
of them an annuity of six pounds thirteen shillings four pence out of my
mill called Shalford mill, after Robert enters upon and enjoys the said
mill. To said Robert, my eldest son, the said mill &c. Bequests of money
to daughters Mary, Martha and Sarah. My said five younger children.
To my reverend and well beloved friend Mr. Richard Rogers of Wethersfield forty and eight shillings by the year to be paid unto him yearly during his life. My servants Robert Middleton, Phillip Clarke, Thomas
Scott and Robert Smyth. The poor of Wethersfield and of Lexden. I
constitute and ordain my well beloved brother John Ward, my loving uncle
Robert Spring of Wethersfield, my brother in law John Upcher of Dedham and my brother in law George Sewell of Halsted executors and my
cousin Thomas Cole and my cousin Samuel Springe supervisors. (Sarah
one of the three youngest children). Wit: Isacke Ford, Tho: Cole,
Phellep Shearman.

Com. of London for Essex and Herts
Bundle for 1616 (not numbered).

Robert Alefounder, husband of ANNE ALEFOUNDER of Dedham deceased,
appeared and sought administration of her goods.
Colchester die Saturni vizt. primo die mens Junii Anno Dñi 1622

Com. of London for Essex and Herts.
Act Book for 1622–1623.

[Robert Ward, the testator, may have been a relative of John Ward, chirurgeon, of Ipswich, Mass., whose will dated Dec. 18, 1652, and proved March 25,
1656, is printed in the REGISTER, vol. xxii., pp. 31–2; and the will of whose
mother, Anne Ward, is abstracted and annotated in these Gleanings (REGISTER,
vol. xlvi., page 318). The testator had property in Wethersfield, and John of
New England had relatives there. Other Ward wills are found in that volume,
pp. 314-19. There is some probability that John Ward of Ipswich, N. E., was
a relative of Rev. John Ward of Haverhill, Eng., and Bury St. Edmunds, whose
three sons, Samuel, Nathaniel and John, were distinguished Puritan ministers
and authors (see Dean's Memoir of Rev. Nathaniel Ward, author of The Simple
Cobler of Aggawam, Albany, 1868).—EDITOR.]

MARY ALEFOUNDER, wife of Robert Alefounder of Dedham, Essex,
clothier, 27 June 1627, with the good will and consent of said husband.
To grandchild Elizabeth Wodward my house and lands in Thorpe. To
grandchild Mary Wodward my house and land in Beamont. To my son
John Wodward five pounds. My kinswoman and godchild Mary Large.
My daughter in law Sarah Brunninge. My daughter in law Susan Alefounder. My daughter in law Anne Fenne. To my [daughter Rachael
Sherman my best peticoat. To my son in law Robert Alefounder a nut-
shell footed with silver. To my son in law Matthew Alefounder one silver
spoon. To my son in law John Alefounder one silver spoon. To my
brother in law John Alefounder one silver spoon. All the rest of my silver spoons I give to my grandchildren Mary and Elizabeth Wodward,
equally to be divided betwixt them. To my daughter in law Mary Wodward my cloak and safeguard that were mine when I was a widow and a
piece of new cloth to make her a cloak. To my loving husband Robert
Alefounder my biggest gold ring and a piece of gold of thirty three shil-

lings. To my daughter Anne Fenne a little gold ring. To my daughter in law Susan wife of Matthew Alefounder another gold ring. My maid Anne Deane. To Mr. John Rogers forty shillings and to Mr. Cottesford thirty shillings. Mr. Witham of Misley. The poor of Dedham. I make Ezekiell Sherman my son in law sole executor.

Wit: Lyonell Chewte, Symon Fenne and George Spinke.
Proved 5 September 1627.

Com. of London for Essex and Herts.
File for 1627–1628. No. 126.

JOHN ALEFOUNDER of East Bergholt, Suffolk, clothier, 3 July 1627, proved 9 November 1627. My sisters Emme White, Mary Howard and Audrey Moore, My son Benjamin Alefounder. My cousin Robert Alefounder. My wife Mary.   Skynner, 108.

MATTHEW ALEFOUNDER of Dedham Essex, clothier, 20 December 1628, proved at Colchester 5 June 1629. To wife Susan, for life, my house wherein I lately dwelt, called Sturgeon's, with all my lands and meadow ground now in the tenure &c. of Steven Howe and his assigns. I give her also my house and lands called Knappe's, now in the tenure &c. of Henry Renolds (with other lands). After my wife's death I give these houses and lands to my brother John Alefounder. To my brother Robert Alefounder and his heirs forever all that my free land in Walton, Essex, called Grovehouse land, with a barn thereupon built, now in the occupation of John Cole, after my father's decease. I give to my sister Susan Salmon, for life, my tenement or cottage wherein Joseph Tompson dwelleth, called Sturgeon's (with other land). I give and bequeath unto my sister Rachel Sherman, during her natural life, all my lands lying in Lawford, called Foxash. And after the death of the said Susan Salmon and Rachel Sherman I give and bequeath to my brother John Alefounder and to his heirs forever all those lands, meadow and tenement before given to the said Susan and Rachel. I give to my father Alefounder five pounds to buy a piece of plate and to my mother Alefounder forty shillings to buy her a ring. To Mr. John Rogers, preacher of God's word in Dedham, five pounds, to Mr. Cottesford, minister of Dedham, three pounds and to Mr. Witham, minister of Mislie, three pounds. To my father in law Upcher and to my mother in law Upcher five pounds apiece. Item, I give to my father in law Goodwyn and to my mother Elizabeth Goodwyn forty shillings apiece to buy them, each of them, a ring. To my brother Quarles, minister of Raydon, and to my sister his wife forty shillings. To my brother Hayward and Anne his wife forty shillings apiece. To my sister Alefounder (wife of my brother Robert) forty shillings. To my brother William Hubard, to my brother John Goodwin and to my sister Mary Holloway, to either of them forty shillings apiece. To my brother Richard Bruning forty shillings. To my brother in law Ezekiell Sherman forty shillings. To my brother in law Henry Fenn forty shillings. To my brother in law Edmund Seaburne and Anne his wife forty shillings apiece. To my sister Mary Bentlie forty shillings. To my aunt Emme White, widow, three pounds. To my aunt Mary Howard three pounds. To my aunt Audrie More, widow, forty shillings. To my cousin George White five pounds. To my cousin Sarah Fintz, widow, three pounds. To my cousin Richard Alefounder forty shillings. My two servants John Starke and Elizabeth Rogers. My workmen Thomas Darbie, Gilbert Hilles and Miles Robertson. The widow Pakyn of Much Broomlie. To my niece Anne Fenne and to my nephew Mathew Sherman five pounds apiece, to be paid to their fathers for them. To my brother Steven Howe twenty pounds. To my sister Anne Fenne twenty pounds. To my sister Sarah Bruning and to my sister Susan Alefounder ten pounds apiece. To the poor of Dedham five pounds. The lands bequeathed to Susan my wife shall be in full lieu of the thirds of my free lands. All the rest of my goods &c. I give to my wife. Provision in case she be with child. Wife Susan to be sole executrix and my father Robert Alefounder supervisor.

Wit: Lyonell Chewte, Robart Makin and Joseph Tomsone.

(Signed) MATHEW ALFOUNDER.
Com. of London for Essex and Herts.
File for 1628–1629. N°. 98.

ROBERT ALEFOUNDER of Dedham, Essex, clothier, 16 March 1629, proved 6 May 1630. Wife. To son Robert Alefounder my lands and tenements in Kirkeby, Essex, and house and lands in Walton, Essex. To son John Alefounder houses, lands and meadows in Dedham, which I bought of Mary Bentley, Hanna Neavard and Susan Salmon. To John other houses and lands in Dedham (including lands in occupation of Thomas Wilson). To my daughters Sara Browninge, Rachell Sherman and Anne Fenne one hundred pounds apiece. To my daughter Susan Alderman three hundred pounds in discharge of her portion which I agreed to give her upon marriage. To my daughter Browning's ten children, being my grandchildren, ten pounds apiece at several ages of eighteen. To every of son Robert Alefounder's children excepting his son Robert, ten pounds apiece at eighteen. To my daughter Sherman's children, being my grand-children, vizt to my godson Robert Sherman twenty pounds and to her three other children ten pounds apiece, to be paid in like manner. To my grandchild John Wilkinson ten pounds and to my grandchild Anne Wil-kinson thirty pounds (to be paid as above). To my daughter Fenne's three children ten pounds apiece (in same manner). To Stephen Howe twenty pounds, he to make a general release of all demands. To my daughter in law Susan Salmon ten pounds, to be paid unto her at such time or times as Mr. Rogers shall think fit. To the children of my wife's daughter Mary Bently that were born before my wife's death ten shillings apiece at ages of eighteen. To the children of wife's daughter Hanna Payte that were born before wife's death twenty shillings apiece at eighteen. To the child-ren of my wife's daughter Susan Salmon ten shillings apiece at eighteen. To my sister Emma White five pounds. And my sons Robert and John shall give thirty shillings apiece yearly to my said sister. Gifts to sisters Mary Howard and Awdrie Moore. My sister Groome's children. My kinsman Richard Alefounder. To my kinsman George White forty shil-lings. The poor of East Bergholt and of Dedham. Mr. Rogers. Thomas Darbie. My brother John Upcher and his wife. My brother Thomas Woodgate and his wife. Thomas Branston of East Bergholt. My son Thomas Glover. My son Richard Browninge. To my son Ezekiell Sher-man three pounds to buy him a ring. My son Henry Fenne. My son John Wilkinson. My sister Cole. A silver bowl each to daughters Sarah Browninge, Rachel Sherman and Anne Fenne. Wine cups to daughter Susan Alderman. My daughter in law the widow Alefounder. My six children. My two sons to be executors and loving friends Mr. John Rogers, George Cole the elder and William Cole to be supervisors.

Wit: Andrewe Bacon, Edmund Sherman and Edward Cardinall.
Scroope, 49.

Sentence for confirmation of the above was promulgated 19 June 1630 following litigation between Robert and John Alefounder, sons and executors, of the one part, and Elizabeth Alefounder, the relict, and Anne Fenne, Rachel Sherman, Sara Browninge and Susan Alderman, daughters of the deceased, of the other part.
Scroope, 58.

ROBERT ALEFOUNDER the elder of East Bargholt, Suffolk, clothier, 10 February 1635, proved 18 June 1639. To wife Elizabeth three score pounds a year out of lands in occupation John Cole in Wolton (Walton) in Essex. Other provision for her. The above lands (and others) to my son Robert. Lands in occupation of Thomas Whiting. To Robert my capital messuage in Kirbye. To Robert, my eldest son, my copyhold house and land &c. where I now dwell in East Bergholt. Lands in occupation of George White. Other lands in occupation of James Barker, Thomas Greene and myself in East Bergholt. To youngest son John Alefounder my farm in Winson, Suffolk, for life (he evidently unmarried). To my eldest daughter Elizabeth Trenham one hundred pounds to be paid unto her within one year after John Trenham have made her a jointure which he promised upon marriage and when he received her former portion. To daughter Anne Alefounder four hundred pounds, at age of twenty or six months after marriage. To my daughter in law Mary, Robert's wife, ten pounds to buy her a piece of plate, for a token of my love to her, and to George White and Robert White, her sons, five pounds apiece, George to be paid within a year after my decease, and Robert to be paid at his age of two and twenty. My son in law John Trenham. My sister Sara Brauning and my brother Brauning. My brother John Alefounder and Martha his wife. To brother in law Ezekiell Sharman and my sister Rachell five pounds apiece. My brother Henry Fenn and my sister his wife. My brother in law John Alderman. My brother Thomas Wood and his wife. Mr. Cornelius Fisher. Mr. Thomas Barker of Sipton and his wife. My loving friend Mr Samuel Ward of Ipswich. Eldest son Robert to be executor. Then follows sententia pro valore of same date as probate, the parties being Robert and John the two sons.
Harvey, 98.

THOMAS BRAUSTON of Flowton, Suffolk, clothier, 3 September 1638, proved 29 July 1641. Wife Mary to give a sufficient release in law to my son John of the thirds of all my lands &c. To son Thomas messuages, lands &c. in Curby (Kirby) and Walton in the Soken, Essex. John my eldest son. My sister Judeth Clearke the wife of Joseph Clearke of East Bergholt, Suffolk. John Clarke, Judeth Clarke and Nahomy Clarke, the children of the said Judeth Clarke. William Maxcie (Maxey) and Thomas Briminge(?) my grandchildren. I give to my brother in law Mr. Robert Alefounder and my sister his wife thirty shillings apiece. To my cousin Robert Alefounder, my said brother's son, twenty shillings. To my cousin Elizabeth Trenham, the wife of John Trenham of East Bergholt, twenty shillings. To the town of Bargholt fifteen pounds towards the purchasing of a workhouse for the poor to work in. Five pounds to the poor of East Bargholt. Steven Brauston the son of John Brauston. Steven Brauston the son of Edmund Brauston of East Bargholt. Rose Braberton, the wife of William Braberton of Bergholt, and all her children, at ages of one and twenty. Richard Alefounder the elder of Berg-

holt and Richard his son and Susan his daughter. To my brother in law
Mr. John Alefounder of Dedham, Essex, my sister Briminge (Brunninge?),
my sister Sherman, my sister Fenn and my sister Alderman twenty shillings apiece to buy each of them a ring. To son John all the rest of
my messuages, lands &c. in Suffolk and Essex or elsewhere which is not
heretofore bequeathed, and the rest of my goods &c. I give to my son in
law Maxey and my son in law Bruninge ten pounds apiece. To William
Boggas my son in law forty shillings.   Evelyn, 92.

JOHN ALEFOUNDER of Finchingfield, Essex, yeoman, 5 February 1642,
proved 2 August 1647. Wife Anne. Son John at one and twenty. Son
Henry at one and twenty. Wife with child. Wife executrix. The widow
died before taking out probate.   Fines, 182.

ROBERT LYNKON of East Bergeholte, Suffolk, clothier, 15 August 1559,
proved 23 October 1559. To be buried in the church or churchyard of
East Bergholt. Wife Marion. Son Stephen at twenty one. Son Robert
at twenty one. Son William at twenty one. Daughters Edith, Joane and
Elizabeth at twenty or days of marriage. Wife Marion to have my tenements and all my lands in East Bergholt till my son Robert comes to age
&c.; then he to have them. To son Stephen lands in Stratford. I have
a state in my brother Thomas' house for certain money which I stand bound
to one Henry Wallys for him. Sons Stephen and Robert to be executors
and Stephen Cardynall and William Amys supervisors. To this witnesseth
Ric. Cole, John Borrowe and others.
    Commission issued, at the date given above, to the supervisors to admin-
ister during the minority of the executors.   Chaynay, 45.

ROBERT LINCON *alias* Skynner of East Bergholt, Suffolk, clothier, 20
March 1590. To eldest son Stephen Lyncolne *als* Skynner my messuage,
lands &c. which I bought of my brother Stephen, now in the tenure of my
said brother, situate in Dedham, Essex. To son Robert the messuage
wherein I now dwell, in East Bergholt, and the tenement and lands I lately
bought of Thomas Bacon of Bramford, situate in East Bergholt. To said
eldest son Stephen two hundred pounds at age of one and twenty, together
with the profits of his said houses and lands, which my brother in law Stephen Woodgate shall take and receive until his said age of one and twenty.
To son Robert two hundred pounds (at same age). To Samuel two hundred pounds (at same age). To daughter Elizabeth two hundred pounds
at eighteen, or at marriage if with consent of my brother in law Stephen
Woodgate and my brother Stephen Lyncolne *als* Skynner. The same to
daughter Mary who is to obtain the consent of my brothers in law Stephen
and John Woodgate and my said brother Stephen to her marriage. My
said children Stephen, Robert, Samuel, Elizabeth and Mary. My uncle
Thomas Skinner. My good friend Christopher Burrowe of East Bergholt.
My kinsman John Goodwin to have the custody of the two hundred pounds
given to my son Robert. John Brauston of East Bergholt to have Samuel's
portion. Others named. Commission issued 4 September 1591 to John
Goodwin to administer during minority of sons Stephen and Robert, the
executors.
    Commission issued 27 August 1601 to Elizabeth Hollaway *als* Lincoln
als Skynner, daughter of the deceased, to administer the goods &c. left unadministered by John Goodwin, for the reason that Stephen and Robert
Lincoln *als* Skinner, executors, and sons of the deceased, had died before
taking upon themselves the burden of the execution of the will.
                                                      Sainberbe, 69.

STEVEN WOODGATE of East Bergholt, Suffolk, clothier, 10 May 1598, proved 23 November 1598. To Steven, my son by Mary my late wife, the messuage &c. wherein I now dwell and all my lands and tenements whatsoever which came to me by the gift of Steven Woodgate my late father deceased and all my lands and tenements which I lately purchased of Edward Cole and copyhold lands lately bought of Edward Forthe gentleman (and other lands), with remainder to my son Thomas Woodgate, then to my son Benjamin and lastly to my son John and his heirs forever. A tenement (described) to son Thomas. To son Benjamin the house I lately bought of my brother John Woodgate. To son Daniel Woodgate three tenements in East Bergholt (described). Houses and lands to son John. Gifts of money to sons Benjamin, John and Daniel at one and twenty years of age. To daughter Hanna two hundred pounds at eighteen. My son in law John Goodwin shall have the education and bringing up of my son John and the care of his money until he is of age, being bound therefor by an obligation which shall be delivered unto my brother John Woodgate to be safely kept to the use of my said son. My kinsman Robert Deraughe of Gray's Inn, gent, shall receive my son Daniel's portion. His obligation shall be committed and delivered unto my son in law John Goodwin to be safely kept to the use of my son Daniel. Brother John Woodgate shall receive Hanna's portion and if he refuse to become bound to my said daughter Anna then my kinsman Edmond Barker of Sipton, gentleman, shall receive my daughter Anna's portion, his obligation to be committed and delivered unto my son in law John Goodwyn &c. My son in law John Howe. My cousin Robert Deraugh. My kinswoman Elizabeth Houburd. My kinsman Samuel Skynner. My kinswoman Mary Skynner. Every of my grandchildren. Anna Borrowe the wife of Christopher Borrowe. My sister in law —— wife of my brother John Woodgate. Habygall Borrowe her daughter. Elizabeth Borrowe also the daughter of the said Anne Borrowe. My godson Steven Thorpe. My kinswoman Elizabeth Woodgate. Edmond Woodgate. John Woodgate my kinsman. Anne Woodwarde. Others named. Son Stephen Woodgate and son in law John Goodwin to be executors and Robert Deraugh and Christopher Borrowe supervisors. Christopher Borroughe one of the witnesses. Robert Wyles the writer another.   Lewyn, 80.

GEORGE HEWBURD of East Bergholt, Suffolk, 2 March 1598, proved 16 June 1599. To wife Elzabeth tenement at Puttocke's end in East Bergholt wherein Michael Tranam now dwelleth, to hold and enjoy during her life; and after her decease I give said tenement to my son William. Other tenements described, one of which occupied by Richard Hedge. Certain household effects to wife and to son William. The latter's mother to have the custody of his part till he come to the age of one and twenty. My sister Margaret Hewburd. My brother William Hewburd and his son William. My aunt Margaret Robertes. Tenement at Puttocke's End wherein William Hutchenson now dwelleth. My brother William Hewburd's wife. My cousin Nathaniel Clayse of Colchester. My brother Philip Barwicke. My aunt Rose of Clafton (Clackton?). Robert Buttler my aunt Rose's son. My aunt John Woodgate's wife. William Hedge the elder. Wife Elizabeth shall have the education and bringing up of my son William during his minority. Christopher Burrowe of East Bergholt clothier and my cousin John Goodwin to be executors. Proved, at above date, by Thomas Lovell Not. Pub., acting for John Goodwen, power reserved for Christopher Burrough.

Commission issued 25 October 1600 to William Hewburd, brother of the deceased, to administer the goods &c. left unadministered by John Goodwyn the executor, during the minority of William Hewburd the son, for the reason that Christopher Burroughe, the other executor named in the will, had, in the person of Mr. John Burroughe, Not. Pub., expressly renounced &c. The foregoing Grant of Admon. was recalled and annulled and a new grant issued 13 May (or March?) 1606 to Elizabeth Holloway *als* Hewburd, relict of the deceased, to administer according to the tenor of the will during the minority of the son.   Kidd, 54.

STEPHEN LINCOLNE *als* Skynner of East Bergholt, Suffolk, clothier, 27 January 1598, proved 13 June 1600. My four children, that is to say, Steven Lincolne my eldest son, Robert, Elizabeth and Mary Lyncolne. Money which was given to me by a certain gift of my uncle Richard Clarke late of Dedham deceased, now being in the hands of Thomas Sharpe of Dedham, to deliver and pay according unto the gift of my said uncle. John Mannynge son of John Mannynge late of Stratford, Suffolk, deceased, to have a part of it. Wife Alice. Youngest daughter Anna Lincolne at eighteen. Youngest son Steven Lyncolne at one and twenty. My faithful friend Christopher Borrough of East Bergholt. Money in the hands of John Goodwyn of East Bergholt given me in the last will and testament of Robert Lyncolne my brother, late of East Bergholt deceased. Wife Alice to be sole executrix.   Wallopp, 52.

JOHN GOODWIN of East Bergholt, Suffolk, clothier, 10 May 1600, proved 16 June 1600. Sundry bequests to the poor of that town. To son John my messuage there which I lately purchased of my cousin Philip Berwicke, in the occupation of William Hallaway or his assigns. Another parcel of land in the occupation of Richard Hedge. Other lands there (one parcel being in the occupation of George Hayward). Lands bought of John Branson in the tenure of John Branson. Lands in the tenure of John Clarke. Lands bought of William Hubert of East Bergholt. To son Daniel messuage and lands bought of Robert Wiles of Bergholt (and other real estate). To daughter Mary Goodwin messuage in Thorpe, Essex, lately purchased of Adam Barwicke and lands in occupation of Philip Barwicke &c. and also five hundred pounds to be paid her at age of eighteen. To son Daniel my manor of Boyton's in Capell and East Bergholt lately purchased of Stephen and Thomas Woollward. My kinsman William Goodwin to have the use of one hundred pounds out of my son Daniel's portion, during said Daniel's nonage, provided the said William, together with William Goodwin his father, shall enter a bond for the sure payment of said sum when my son Daniel attains the age of one and twenty. The said William Goodwin, my servant, to have the use of a part of my daughter Mary's portion provided he and his father William Goodwin enter a similar bond. Sundry servants named. Edmond Woodgate late my servant to have the use of a part of my daughter Mary's portion provided the said Edmond, with John Woodgate his father, shall enter into a bond for sure payment &c., this bond to be left in the hands of Francis Cole of Holtonne, Suffolk, to her use. A gift to Edmond Chapman of Dedham, Essex, Doctor of Divinity. My cousin Reginald Catlin. My cousin Francis Cole. Master Burges of Ipswich. To William Huberd the younger son of George Huberd twenty pounds to be delivered into the hands of William Hallaway for the use of said William Huberd, in consideration of one long cloth left out of the inventory of the goods of George Huberd his father deceased.

Isaacke Mitchell to have the custody of my son John's portion and to have him brought up to the trade or mystery of a clothier until his age of one and twenty and to enter into a good bond for payment &c., which bond is to be left in the hands of Robert Alefounder to the use of my son. William Halloway and Elizabeth his wife to bring up my son Daniel. Halloway's bond to be left in the hands of John Arblaster of Hadleighe, Suffolk, to the use of said Daniel. Robert Alefounder to bring up my daughter Mary Goodwin, his bond to be left with Mr. Robert Snellinge of Ipswich. I give and bequeath the bringing up of William Huberd, the only son of George Huberd deceased, clothier, into the hands of William Halloway and Elizabeth his wife, mother to the said William Huberd. I the executor of George Huberd. I give and bequeath the bringing up of John Woodgate, one of the sons of Stephen Woodgate deceased, into the custody of John Woodgate his uncle, and with him the sum of three hundred pounds bequeathed unto the said John in the last will and testament of his father Stephen Woodgate. Mary the now wife of Philip Barwicke. Isaac Mitchell and Robert Alefounder to be executors and the right worshipfull Robert Barker councillor and my brother William Goodwin to be supervisors.   Wallopp, 39.

Sentence for the confirmation of the Will of John Goodwyn of East Bergholt, Suffolk, was promulgated 16 June 1601 after litigation between Isaac Mitchell an executor (*alterum executorum*) of the one part and John Goodwyn, Daniel Goodwyn and Mary Goodwyn, natural and lawful children of the deceased, also William Goodwyn, Richard Goodwyn, Margaret Keppinge *als* Goodwyn, —— Clarke *als* Goodwyn, John Woodgate, Anna Alefounder and Stephen Woodgate, next akin to the said deceased, and all others interested &c. of the other part.   Woodhall, 45.

[John Goodwin, the testator in the above will, was a party to chancery suit of which, my friend Dr. Joseph James Muskett, author of the Suffolk Manorial Family, has furnished me with the following record.   H. F. W.]

In most humble wise complayning sheweth yor Orator Stephen Woodgate of Estbergholt co Suff. clothier, that Stephen Woodgate late of Estbergholt clothier ffather of yor Orator was seased of one Messuage and lande in Estbergholte and did mary one Kattryn Whiter widow and for a ioynture made a ffeoffament of said messuage to the vse of the sayd Stephen Woodgate the ffather and Kateryn his wife and to the heyres of the sayd Stephen for ever. Sayd Stephen and Kateryn had issue Elizabeth Kateryn and Ane, wch Elizabeth afterwards maryed John Goodwyn. Kateryn maryed Edward Clarke and Ane maried John How. Stephen the ffather gave good sumes of money in advancement of said maryages. Kateryn his wyfe dyed. And afterwarde sayd Stephen Woodgate the ffather dyd mary one Mary Derehaw and for her ioynture made a ffeoffment of sayd messuage and land to vse of sayd Stephen the ffather and the sayd Mary and the heyers males of the body of sayd Mary, and for wante of such issue male to the right heyres of sayd Stephen for ever and sithens Elizabeth Goodwyn and Kateryn Clarke are both dead havyng seu^rall issues of theare bodies begotten. And Stephen Woodgate the ffather and Mary his second wyfe had issues male Stephen, Thomas, Beniamyn, Daniell and John and afterwardes Mary the second wyfe likewise died, and Stephen lived many yeres vnmaryed and died abowte the space of one yere and halfe last past. By his will he did devise the messuage and land abovesayd to Stephen Woodgate his suñ yor Orator and made yor Orator and abovenamed

John Goodwyn his executors. He did also devise to John Woodgate one
of his yonger suñes thre hundred powndes at his age of xxi yeres, an obligacõn to pay the money to be given, aud kept by John Woodgate of
Estbergholt, yoman brother of the testator: Yoʳ Orator being but yonge
and vnexperyenced in the world did seale an obligacõn in the latyn tunge to
save Goodwyn harmles for the execucõn of sayd will. Now so it is that
John Goodwyn Edward Clarke and Añe How widow having gotten the
evidences concernyng sayd messuage and lande have combyned together
and contryved (as is supposed) secret conveyancs of sayd messuage.
The Answere of John Goodwin. Steven Woodegate ffather of the Complaynnt was greatlie advanced by Katherine Whiter widdowe his wife having by her fifty poundes by yeare in lande and one thowsand poundes in
goods and did in consideracõn of saide marriage enfeoffe said Katherine
in said messuage and lande. Elizabeth eldest daughter of saide Stephen and Katherine was married to this Defendᵗ. Stephen her ffather
made great promises for her advancement as eldest daughter. In regard
that Defendᵗ had no benefit nor pʳferment it was the purpose of said
Stephen that Defendᵗ shoulde take suche benefite by said will, havinge a care
to see the same duelie pformed. Not longe before his deathe Stephen
Woodgate the ffather dyverse tymes tolde this defendᵗ that he reposed his
wholle trust and confidence in him about the execution of his will. He
saide " Sonne Goodwine I woulde have the to take vppon the my wholle estate bothe of reconinges wᵗʰ my debtors and to see my children paide there
legacies, alledgeinge further that he greatlie feared that if his estate shoulde
come into complaynnts handes his other children shoulde verie slenderlie be
paid there porcons." Defendᵗ was vnwillinge to entermeddle wᵗʰ the execucõn of said will because Complaynnt kept all the goodes from this de-
fendt. Defendᵗ hathe hearde that Complaynnt made a very vntrue Inventarie
of the said goodes. As sone as Complᵗ shall satisfie said legacie of three
hundred pounds vnto his said brother John Woodegate this Defendᵗ is
readie to become bounden for the repaymᵗ of the same. Defendᵗ is verylie
pswaded that Complᵗ can reade the condicõn . . . . vpp in learn-
inge both at the Englishe and grammer schoole. Defendᵗ hath no wrytinge
and evidencs concerninge said messuage and lands. Defendᵗ saythe that
if Steven Woodgate, Complaynnts brother, sonne to Steven Woodgate deceased by the sayde Katherine his ffirste wife, since gone beyond the seas,
shoulde come home againe, he should be compelled to buye said messuage
of his saide brother, &c.

Chancery Proceedings. Woodgate c̃ Goodwin. 1599.
Eliz. B. & A. W W. 21.55.

BENJAMIN WOODGATE of East Bergholt, clothier, 23 July 1603, proved
the last day of February 1603 (at Ipswich). Wife Susan (if with child).
Son Benjamin at one and twenty. Father (?) in law Robert Alefender.
Sister Alefender. Brother Stephen Woodgate and sister his wife. Sister
Mary Bright's children. Brother in law Henry Bright. Cousin William
Hollawaye.   Archdeaconry of Suffolk, B. 39, L. 341.

WILLIAM HOLLAWAY of East Bergholt, Suffolk, clothier, A.D. 1608,
proved 24 March 1608. To our Reverend Pastor Doctor Jones eleven
pounds upon condition that he shall make a funeral sermon at my death.
Five pounds to the poor of East Bergholt. To loving wife one hoop ring
of gold with this engraven within it—Memento Mori and W H. A ring
to every one of my children at age of twenty, to my good lady and mis-

tress my Lady Greselley and to Sir John Drury her son, to my very good friends Mr John Brewster, Mr William Judson and John Goodwyn, to Danyell Goodwyn, at age of nineteen, and to my very good neighbors and friends Stephen Woodgate, Edward Clarke, Mr William Cardinall, Francis Coole (Cole), Isaac Mychell, John Blackeshaw, Thomas Branston (or Brauston) and my uncle Richard Woodgate. And to my cousin Mary Goodwyn. Tenement in little Bentley. My daughter Sara Hollaway. Lands &c. in Thorpe. My daughter Sara at one and twenty to convey and release to the use and behoof of my son William lands &c. in Tendring, Essex, and to release to my daughter Mary Hollaway tenement &c. in Kyrby. Daughter Mary to release to son William the lands &c. (Casnell's) in Tendring. My wife shall have the letting of my daughters' lands until their several ages of twenty or days of marriage. Her bond therefor shall remain in the hands and custody of my cousin John Goodwyn to their use. Son William in his nonage. My cousin Stephen Woodgate. My very good friend Mr Rogers of Dedham. My cousin Neflocke's wife and my cousin Gladwyn's wife. My cousin Philip Cock. My very good friend Mr John Hollaway. My work folks Gladwyn, Hedge, Wesson and Barker. Robert Alfounder and my uncles Thomas Wyles and Robert Wyles. John Goffe's wife and Anne Hollaway and Jane Hollaway. Stephen Skynner and Robert Skynner. Others named. Wife Elizabeth to be sole executrix, desiring her that she will have a motherly regard of my four youngest daughters for their virtuous bringing up of them in the fear of God until their several ages of twenty years.

Wit : Edward Clarke, Richard Woodgate, J. B. and Richard Alefounder.
Dorset, 24.

SAMUEL SKYNNER of East Bergholt, Suffolk, clothier, 6 December 1608, proved 30 March 1609. My cousin Stephen Skynner which I have brought up, at one and twenty. Stephen Skynner of the same town. Robert Skynner of the same town. My cousins Mary and Elizabeth Skinner. My loving wife Clemence Skynner. My son Samuel at one and twenty. My houses and lands in East Bergholt. My daughter Clemence Skynner at eighteen. My brother William Hollaway and my sister Elizabeth his wife. Mr William Cardinall of East Bergholt. Stephen Woodgate. William Huberd my sister's son. My sister's four children and that she is withall. Old Stephen Skynner and his two children. Robert Skynner and his three children. Stephen Skynner that dwelleth with me. John Buckle. My brother William Hollaway and my said sister shall have the letting of my lands and tenements given to my said children, they entering into sufficient bonds unto Mr William Cardinall &c. My said brother William Hollowey and Stephen Woodgate for to be mine executors and William Cardinall and Robert Lynche overseers.

Proved by Stephen Woodgate, William Hollaway the other executor being dead.
Dorset, 26.

EDWARD CLARKE the younger of East Bergholt, Suffolk, clothier, 8 June 1625, proved 30 November 1625. Son Edward at one and twenty. Daughter Elizabeth Clarke at one and twenty or day of marriage. Wife Mary to be sole executrix. My customary capital messuage or tenement, with one house called a " woade howse," and divers tenements and certain lands to the same belonging lying on the back side of the said messuage (and other lands described) to wife Mary for life and then to son Edward, with remainder to my daughter Elizabeth and next to my brother Robert

Clarke. And it shall be lawful for my loving uncle Thomas Woodgate of London, merchant, and Stephen Woodgate of East Bergholt, clothier, and either of them, with laborers and workmen, from time to time during the life of the said Mary, to come into all and every of the houses and buildings to view and see in what reparations the same shall be. Provisions made in case of waste, decay or spoil. Stephen Brauston (or Branston) one of the witnesses.　　　　　　　　　　　　　　　　　　Clarke, 127.

STEPHEN WOODGATE senior of East Bergholt, Suffolk, clothier, 1 October 1625, provod 12 December 1625. To son John (a lot of lands and tenements). A parcel abutting upon the common way that goeth from Stratford towards Ipswich. A meadow near Stratford mill. To son Thomas land late in the occupation of Henry Munninges, being near Richardson's, and land bought of Mr. Foorth of Hadley (and other real estate). To son Steven the messuage where I now dwell and a parcel of land called the " Woade howse feild wth woad house " and all the things used in it (and other lands). To wife all my lands in Packnam (Packenham) or the towns adjoining. Thomas shall not enjoy his lands until he shall attain the full age of twenty four. My brother Thomas Woodgate shall have the bringing up of my said son Thomas until he come to that age and shall receive the rents &c. and shall put in sufficient bond unto my brother Daniel Woodgate &c. Brother John Woodgate to have my son John's portion until his full age of twenty two and to give bond to my brother Daniel. One hundred pounds to my daughter Martha, to be paid her at eighteen, which portion shall be put in the hands and remain with Margaret my wife in full satisfaction of her education and bringing up fitting for one of her fashion, my wife putting in good bond unto my brother Daniel. To daughter Anne one beer bowl of silver. I was executor of will of Samuel Skinner of East Bergholt deceased. Wife to be executrix and brother Thomas executor and brother Edward Clarke and brother John Woodgate supervisors. Wit: Edw: Clarke, Steven Clarke and Joseph Weston.

　　　　　　　　　　　　　　　　　　　　　　　　Clarke, 146.

DANIEL WOODGATE of East Bergholt, Suffolk, clothier, 24 October 1625, proved 13 December 1625. To wife Sara, for life, my tenement and lands, both free and copy, and all the appurtenances, with the woad house thereunto belonging, the which I purchased of Isaac Mitchell, lying in Baker's End in East Bergholt. After her decease I give it son William at age of twenty four. Lands in Thorpe, Essex. Daughters Mary Woodgate, Anne Woodgate, Susan Woodgate, Elizabeth Woodgate and Sara, each at eighteen. My brother John Woodgate. Flatford mill in East Bergholt. Brothers Thomas and John Woodgate. Wife Sara to be executrix and brother Thomas supervisor.　　　　　　　　　Clarke, 146.

Sentence for the confirmation of the will of Daniel Woodgate, lately of East Bergholt in the county of Suffolk, Diocese of Norwich and Province of Canterbury deceased, was promulgated 20 June 1627 after litigation between Sara Woodgate *als* Chaplin, relict and executrix named in the will &c., of the one part, and Mary, William, Anna, Elizabeth and Sara Woodgate, his natural and lawful children, Thomas and John Woodgate, his natural and lawful brothers, and Mary Cole *als* Woodgate and Hannah Wragge *als* Woodgate, his natural and lawful sisters, of the other part.

　　　　　　　　　　　　　　　　　　　　　　　　Skynner, 72.

DANIEL GOODWYN of Yoxford, Suffolk, gentleman, 29 October 1625, proved 16 February 1625. To wife Dorothy all such goods and chattels that are now in my possession which were hers before her marriage with me. To my eldest son Edmond Goodwin all my lands and tenements (except my copyhold lands and tenements in East Bargholt, Suffolk, holden of Sir John Brewse), with remainder to my son Daniel, then to son Stephen. To son Stephen I give the said lands &c. in East Bargholt. Said Edmond at age of two and twenty. To son Daniel threescore pounds at age of twenty two. My father in law Edmond Barker, gen^t., and my brother John Goodwyn to be executors. Wit: Wm. Buckenham and Tho: Barker,

Proved by John Goodwyn, power reserved for Edmond Baker.

Hele, 32.

Mary Hollaway of East Bergholt (Suffolk), 3 June 1631, proved 5 July 1631. To Father Mr. John Goodwyn five pounds within one year after my decease. To brother John Goodwin of Emanuel College, Cambridge, ten pounds at one and twenty. Brother William Hubbert of East Bergholt. Sisters Sara Chapleyne and Mary Woodgate. Stephen Skinner the elder and Stephen Skinner the younger of East Bergholt. To Mary Skinner, daughter of Stephen Skinner the elder, a bible. To Mary Tranham, daughter of Robert Tranam, when she can read perfectly in the bible, a bible. Robert Skinner, son of Robert Skinner late of East Bergholt (at one and twenty) and Mary Aldham, daughter of Robert Skinner late of East Bergholt. Elizabeth Tassell of East Bergholt and William Clarke her son. The poor of East Bergholt. The rest to my three sisters Susan Bacon, Elizabeth Quarles and Ann Heyward, except one silver salt and a spoon which I give to my nephew Thomas Quarles. Brother Mr. Francis Quarles of Newton juxta Sudbury, clerk, to be sole executor.

Arch. Suffolk (Ipswich) 1631. B. 60.

John Goodwyn of East Bergholt, Suffolk, clothier, 19 July 1638, proved 12 September 1638. The poor of the parish. Mr. Nathaniel Bacon, Mr. Francis Quarles, Roades Hayward, my "sonne in lawes." Susanna the wife of the said Mr. Nathaniel Bacon and Nathaniel his son. Thomas Barker, gen^t., my brother in law and Mary my sister his wife and every one of their children. Elizabeth, one of my wife's daughters, the wife of Mr. Francis Quarles, and Anne, one of my wife's daughters, the wife of Roades Hayward. Francis Quarles the son of the aforesaid Francis. My nephews Edmund and Daniel Goodwyn. Mr. William Jones preacher of East Bergholt and Mr. John Long his curate and Mr. Cornelius Fisher schoolmaster here. To every one of the children of Mr. John Rogers deceased, late preacher of Dedham, to every of them forty shillings apiece. Mr. Wittam preacher at Misley in Essex.

Item, I give the sum of fifty pounds to be paid within one year after my death into the hands of Mr. Mathew Cradock, merchant of London, to be by him paid over to the governor of New England, there to be employed for the best benefit of the plantation there as shall be by the said governor for the time being and the assistants thought fit. My menservants and maidservants. Robert Riges my workman. Tobias Ballard and John Pod and Elizabeth the wife of Robert Backler sometime my servants. John Goodwyn my grandchild at one and twenty. All my lands and tenements whatsoever, with all my whole personal estate unbequeathed, I give and bequeath to John Goodwyn my only child, whom I make my sole executor of this my last will and testament. Twenty pounds more to my daughter Hayward. To Goodman Cannan of Dedham forty shillings. Proved by John Goodwyn the only son and executor. Lee, 111.

EDMUND GOODWYN of Neyland, Suffolk, 10 June 1645, proved 11 February 1645. Wife Margaret. Son Edmund at one and twenty. Daughter Mary at one and twenty. Son Daniel at one and twenty. Wife executrix. I desire that my worthy friends Nathaniel Bacon Esq. and Col. Brampton Gurdon Esq. would be pleased to see this my will performed.

Twisse, 13.

JOHN CHAPMAN alias Barker of Sibton, Suffolk, 16 February 25th Elizabeth, proved 31 October 1583. Wife Julian. Houses in Bedfilde. Son Edmund. My capital messuage with all my lands in Sibton and Yoxford to Edmund, with remainder to son John, then to son Anthony, lastly to the next heir male at the common law. To Edmund after decease of my brother Thomas Barker, my houses and lands in Pesenhall. To John lands in Farnam and Blaxall and meadow in Benhall. To Anthony, at twenty one, houses and lands in Alborough, Haslewood, Saxmundham and Standfild. Daughters Elizabeth and Dorothy. To my brother Thomas Chapman alias Barker my house in Pesenhall called New Inn. To Anne Barker of Colchester the whole sum of ten pounds and no more, to be paid by my son Edmund. Sons Edmund, John and Anthony to be executors.

Butts, 9.

THOMAS BARKER of Colchester, Essex, clothier, 27 February 1584, proved 5 May 1585. Lands and tenements in Nayland and Stoke by Nayland, Suffolk, to wife Anne for life. Son John at one and twenty. Sons Richard and Thomas at one and twenty. The child wherewith my wife is now pregnant. Servant Robert Cocke. Edmund Seborne and Thomas Foster. Kinswoman Elizabeth Coppin. Sister Elizabeth Preston. Her husband. Kinsman George Preston. Richard Coppinge dwelling with Hawkins. Cousin Thomas Coppinge. The widow Briant. Cousin Dorothy Preston. Wife Anne executrix and friends Mr. John Pye and Richard Symnell supervisors.

Brudenell, 19.

JOHN BARKER of Nayland, Suffolk, clothier, 24 June 1587, proved 10 December 1588. To wife Margaret my house which I now dwell in and my house where William Harvye now dwells and my house where Robert Webbe now dwells &c. for life and afterwards to my son Richard and his heirs forever. To her my house which I bought of Mr. Horne of London and my house and ground where John Knope now dwells &c. for one year and then to my son John. Other houses and lands disposed of. My son Thomas. My son William. Daughters Dorothy and Alice Barker. Daughters Anne and Joice Barker. Daughter Katherine Beriffe. Son Legate. Cousin John Leache. Margaret Fenner. Cousin William Killmache. Cousin Thomas Koppine at one and twenty. Dorothy Prestone. Provision made for good bringing up of Richard, Thomas and William Barker, my three younger sons, and of Dorothy, Alice, Anne and Joice Barker, my four younger daughters. Wife Margaret to be executrix and John Beriffe my son in law and John Barker my son to be my faithful supervisors.

Among the witnesses were William Fisher senior and William Fisher junior.

Leicester, 14.

[These Barkers of Nayland I am watching as well as the Chapmans *alias* Barkers of Sibton.—H. F. W.]

MARGARET BARKER of Nayland, Suffolk, 24 December 1589, proved 7 February 1589. To be buried in the churchyard of the village of Nayland. My brother James Mawle of Nayland. My children. Their late father John Barker my husband. John Barker of Nayland my son. Messuage, croft and garden sometimes William Hornes and Thomas Hornes grocers of London, situate in the village of Nayland. My son Richard Barker. A legacy bequeathed unto him by his father. Messuage &c. and lands lying in Wethermounteford *als.* Wormingeford and Mount Bures, Essex. My son Thomas Barker. A legacy from his father. A deed of Christian Turnour of Colchester, Essex, widow. Messuage &c. in Lammarshe and Much Henny, Essex. My daughter Alice Barker. The rest of my daughters. To John Gent. yeoman, of Walton on the Naues (Naze) in the Sooke, Essex, messuage and land in Much Horskley, Essex, (upon certain conditions). My daughter Margaret Legatt. Thomas Legat of Sutton in Hornchurch, Essex, gen*t*. A messuage &c. there. My grandchild Jane Legate. My grandchild Margaret Barker. Margaret Fenner. My grandchild John Berriffe. The three children of my brother James Mawle, James and Anne (*sic*). The two children of my brother John Mawle, John and Robert. The two children of my brother George Mawle, John and Margaret. The children of my brother Richard Barker at marriage or age of one and twenty. To my sons Richard, Thomas and William three pounds each, which was their grandmother Mawle's gift. My brother James Mawle's wife. John Bowes and Margaret his wife. My cousin Kynwellmarshe his wife. The wife of William Fisher of Buers. My cousin Leache. For executors I appoint Mr. Thomas Waldgrave of Buers in Essex Esq. and John Berriffe of Brightelingsey, my son in law, and for supervisors Mr. Wynterflood of Ason (Assington) and William Fisher of Buers. Thomas Winterflood one of the witnesses.   Drury, 10.

ANTHONY CHAPMAN *als* Barker of Aldbrugh, Suffolk, gentleman, 29 August 1594, proved 26 June 1595. Every one of my brother Edmond's children at one and twenty. The children of my sister Smithe at one and twenty. Their father. John Barker and Richard Barker his brother, children of my sister Anne deceased, at their ages of one and twenty. My sister Dorothy at her day of marriage. My kinsman Edmond Barker son of John Barker my uncle. My kinsman John Lane of Baddingham, Suffolk. My brother John Chapman *alias* Barker. Messuages, lands, &c. in Aldburgh, Haselwood and Sternefield, Suffolk.   Scott, 43.

ROBERT BARKER Sen*r* of Nayland, Suffolk, oadsetter, 7 March 1617. To be buried in the parish church of Nayland. Son Robert. Daughter Margaret. Two grandchildren Robert and Richard Albone. Daughter Mary Barker. Tenements in Nayland. Wife Elizabeth. Godson Robert Fisher, son of John Fisher of Assington, Suffolk.——Stickle, son of Edward Stickle of Hintlesonne. Robert Warren, son of Samuel Warren, begotten of the body of Abigail my daughter. Susan Stickle the wife of the aforesaid Edward Stickle. John Leggate's two children begotten of the body of Bridget my late daughter deceased. Ann Barker wife of the aforesaid Robert my son. Benjamin Cooper citizen and fishmonger of London. My daughter Mary to be sole executrix and my brother George Clarke supervisor.

Commission issued 4 March 1632 to Susan Stickle and Abigail Warren, natural and lawful daughters of the deceased, to administer &c. on account of the death of Mary Barker, daughter and executrix named in the will.
                                                             Russell, 10.

ELIZABETH BARKER of Nayland Suffolk, widow, 16 January 1627, proved 22 June 1632. Grandchild Edmond Ward. Grandchild Richard Albone. Daughter Elizabeth wife of John Wendlock. Grandchildren James and Robert Albone. The said Elizabeth mother of the said Richard Albone. Robert his brother. To grandchild Thomas Ward my copyhold tenement in Hadleigh, Suffolk, now in the occupation of the widow Sparrow. My daughter Margaret mother of the said Thomas. Charles Ward his brother. His sisters. Two grandchildren Henry and Bridget Webb children of Henry Webb and of the said Elizabeth my daughter. Margaret, Mary, Elizabeth, Sara and Martha Ward, the five daughters of my son in law Thomas Ward. William the son of John Wendlocke my son in law. The said John Wendlocke and Edmond Ward I make executors and Edmond Glandfeild my brother supravisor.

In the Probate Ac Mr. Ward's name is written Edward.

Audley, 62.

MARRION BARKER of Yoxford, Suffolk, widow of Edmond Barker late of Sibton, gen[t], deceased, her will dated 2 September 1635, proved 15 October 1635. To be buried in Chancel of Sibton church near late husband. Grandchild Mary Barker daughter of my son William Barker. William Barker brother of the said Mary. Mary Barker wife of son William and mother of said Mary. Grandchild Mary Hodierne. Grandchild Mary Yeardley daughter of Edward Yeardley. Her next sister. The third son of my son in law Edward Yeardley. My grandchild Daniel Goodwyn at four and twenty. Stephen Goodwyn his brother (at same age). Katheryn Ritchman daughter of John Ritchman of Heddenham, Norfolk, gen[t]. Thomas Bridges son of Walter Bridges, clerk. Grandchild Thomas Barker son of my son Thomas. Grandchild Edmond Barker son of the said Thomas. Grandchild Mary Alefounder sister to the said Edmond and daughter of the said Thomas Barker my son. Daughter Thomasyn Harman. Daughter Dorothy Yeardly. Mary Crispe daughter of Thomas Crispe late of Dunwich. Mary Barker daughter of my son George. Elizaboth Barker daughter of my son Thomas. Thomas, John and William sons of the said Thomas Barker my son. Agnes Vesey wife of Nicholas Vesey my kinsman. The widow Thorne of Yoxford. God daughter Mary Thorne. Richard Searles son of Robert Searles. The eldest daughter of my son George Barker. Mary Barker daughter of son Edmond, and Anthony Barker, his son. Edmond Barker their brother. Mary Barker wife of son Thomas. Grandchild Edmond Goodwyn called a son of Daniel Goodwyn. Reynold Vesey, Francis Vesey, George Vesey, Edmond Vesey and Robert Vesey and Margaret Fella the wife of William Fella of Bramfield, my cousins. My god daughter Mary Browne wife of William Browne of Bramfield. Henry Searles son of Anthony Searles of Yoxford. Reference to will of late husband. His manor of Peasenhall. Friends Henry Coke of Thorington, Suffolk, Esq. and Nicholas Vesey of Yoxford my kinsman.   Sadler, 106.

THOMAS BARKER of Sibton, Suffolk, Esq., 28 July 1643, proved 11 April 1645. Wife Elizabeth. Lands and tenements in Holbrooke, Suffolk, which I lately purchased of William Barker my brother. Daughter Elizabeth wife of Thomas Woodgate. Son in law Robert Alefounder gen[t]. Son William Barker. Son Edmond Barker. Kinsman Samuel Hustler of Bury St. Edmonds gen[t] and Elizabeth his wife. Reference made to

deed of gift to said wife bearing date 20 June 1642.   Brother in law Henry
Maxey Esq.   Friend Mr. Thomas Manwood.   Sir William Maxey (whose
mansion house is called Bradwell Hall in Essex).

Rivers, 59.

Sir EDMUND BARKER of Sibton, Suffolk, knight, 10 February 1671,
proved 3 February 1676.   To be buried in the chancel of Sibton church
towards the North window.   Reference to a Fine and Recovery suffered
by my father and myself for the cutting off the entail of my lands made by
my grandfather, and a new settlement made.   Three brothers living when
the settlement was made.   The two elder since dead without issue.   The
third brother, William, now living.   Manor of Peasenhall &c.   My cousin
Francis Barker senior of Stogussey (Stoke Courcy?) in Somerset.   My
cousin Francis Barker senior, of Fairfield in Somersetshire, and Francis
his son.   Nicholas Barker eldest son of Edmund my cousin german.   Edmund Barker his second son.   Francis Barker *junior* of Stoake gursey in
Somersetshire.   My house in Hornsey lane in Islington.   My sister Alefounder.   My sister Woodgate.   My nephew Thomas Woodgate.   My
niece Woodgate.   John Alefounder and Matthew Alefounder* and their
youngest sister.   My cousin Edward Yerdley.   My cousin Yerdley's wife.
My godson Edward Yerdley.   My cousin Edmund Alefounder.   Fifty
pounds of my cousin Jane Hodyern's money in my hands to be paid her.
Wife executrix and brother William Barker executor.   Proved by Dame
Mary Barker the relict, the other executor renouncing.   Hale, 12.

WILLIAM BARKER of Dedham, Essex, clothier, 23 December 1676,
proved 10 October 1678.   To wife Hannah my messuage and twenty
acres of land called Cheeringer, in Langham, Essex, now in the occupation
of Enoch Ham, and my messuage in Stratford street Suffolk, now in the
occupation of John Haward, and my tenement in North Street, Dedham,
now in the occupation of George Barker; all for life, and, after her decease,
to be equally divided between Hannah and Dorcas Barker, my two daughters born to me by my said wife Hannah.   To my two daughters Sarah
and Mary Barker my copyhold lands in Boxsted, Essex, to which I was
admitted by the surrender of John Barker, my father, to enjoy after his
decease (and other land) upon condition they pay to my brother Samuel
Barker or his heirs &c. one hundred pounds within six months after the
decease of my father John Barker and twenty pounds more to those to
whom it is given in the last will &c. of my said father.   To said two daughters one hundred pounds apiece at ages of twenty one or days of marriage,
the money to be paid into the hands of my father in law Edmund Gibson
whom I earnestly entreat to take care of those my two motherless daughters.   Reference made to "my other two daughters" Hannah and Dorcas
Barker.   To the poor of Dedham forty shillings to be distributed by my
executrix with the advice of my two fathers in law Edmond Gibson and
Bezal. Angier.   To my brother Mr. John Saunder and to Mr. Samuel
Brinsley twenty shillings each.   I have undertaken to bring up Thomas Pemberton until he be fit to shift for himself.   Wife Hannah to be sole executrix (and to give bond to my brother Samuel Barker) and loving brothers
Samuel Barker and John Blumfield junʳ to be supervisors.

Reeve, 107.

* The words "and Matthew Alefounder" scratched through and "Dead" written above
the line.

THOMAS CLERE of the parish of St. Peter in Colchester, clothmaker, 23 September A.D. 1520 and 12ᵗʰ year of Henry VIII, proved 25 January 1520. My body to be buried within the Chapel of Jesus in the parish Church of St. Peter. To the Vicary of the same church for tithes and offerings negligently forgotten and not paid. To the parson of St. James for like cause. " I bequeth to Powlys pardon iiijᵈ." To wife Emme the messuage &c. in St. Peters, which I bought of Thomas Browne brasier. My son Thomas at twenty one shall have my tenement &c. in Wire Street. I will that my mother keep and enjoy the tenement and garden in East Street which was sometime Mundies and which I late had of the gift of my father, she to hold for life, and that after her decease that John my son at the age of twenty one years shall have the same tenement. If my wife be with child &c. My daughters Elizabeth and Joone at eighteen. The sons of my brother John Clere. The executors to be my wife Emme and Philip Heyward, clothmaker, and the supervisor to be my brother John Clere.

Wit: John Clere, John Cole and John Gyllys.

Maynwaryng, 4.

JOHN CLERE of the town of Colchester, clothier and " oon of the Aldremen," 26 December 1538 proved 1 February 1538. To be buried in the churchyard of St. James in Colchester at the West end of the said churchyard. Five sermons to be made in that church by the " moost discretist wisist and best lerued men that can be gotten, within the space of oon hole yere next after my deceas." To the high altar &c., to the amending of the highway " where as I haue begonne all redy," to " fyve poure maydens marriages " &c. &c. I will that Jane my wife shall have the custody and keeping of my son Nicholas Clere till he come to the age of seven years and after that my executors shall have the custody, tuition and keeping of the said Nicholas in bringing him up in learning and " vertue " till he come to the age of twenty and one years. Certain provisions for wife Jane. A conditional bequest to John Best and his children and the children of my daughter in law Katheryn Bradok and also to my nephew Nicolas Clere, with reversion (in case of their deaths) to the children of my son in law William Bonham, and lastly " to be doon in dedes of charitie." To John my son &c. The messuage that Benjamin my son now dwelleth in, with five " Rentaryes " to the same belonging. My wood lying on Wyvenho heath. I give and bequeath my copy lands in Brokford and Medillsham, Suffolk, to John Clere my eldest son, for life, the remainder thereof to Benjamin Clere my son. Provision for minor son Nicholas. I will that all my plate be divided among my three children, saving that I will that my son Nicholas shall have the better part by five pounds sterling. My son Benjamin Clere and William Bonham, my son in law, to be executors.

Dyngeley, 25.

JOHN FOWLE of the parish of Sᵗ Leonard of the New Hithe of the town of Colchester, Essex, merchant and one of the aldermen, 13 April 1572, proved 4 June 1572. To be buried in the parish church of Sᵗ Leonard. To son Robert my capital messuage &c., with remainder to son John. To John the tenement or Inn called the White Lion in Colchester (and other property) with remainder to Robert. All my shipping, both small and great, shall be sold and the money thereof coming equally divided between Robert and John at age of twenty two. To Robert Lambart my father in law my scarlet gown and to my mother in law my best ring and to every of the sons and daughters of the said Robert Lambart now alive ten shillings. To my sister Alice Lambart a "selfe-growe" cassock with a gard of velvet which was my wife's. To Roger Carter my kinsman ten pounds and to Avice Carter his sister five pounds. To Strynger's wife of Burneham ten pounds. Thomas Upcher, clerk, and Mrs. Upcher. To mine uncle Nicholas Clere twenty shillings and to his wife twenty shillings and to every of his children now alive ten shillings. Forty shillings each to my cousin John Fowle of Leigh and to his son in law John Beane. I do give and forgive to my cousin John Fowle of Milton the forty shillings which he borrowed of me and for the which he hath delivered unto me the deeds of his house. My friend William Cocke of Wyvenhoo. Thomas Fowle of Burneham. Others named. The five children of mine uncle Lambart now alive at twenty one. The residue to my two sons Robert and John, to be equally divided between them and to be paid to each at age of twenty two. If both die without lawful issue before they shall accomplish such age then I give to and amongst my kinsfolk, Roger Carter, Avice Carter, Stringer's wife and Crippe's daughter and their children, two hundred pounds and to the poor of Colchester one hundred pounds, to the hospital newly begun to be erected one hundred pounds, to the relief of poor scholars at Cambridge and Oxford fifty pounds and to the repairing and amending of the high ways, the chancel and other decayed places fifty pounds. All the rest to be divided into three parts, one of which I give to my brother in law John Lambart, the second to my brother in law Richard Lambart and the third to my brother in law Thomas Lambart. My said three brothers in law to be executors and father in law Robert Lambart, Thomas Upcher, William Cocke and uncle Nicholas Clere supervisors.

Daper, 17.

The will nuncupative of JOHN SHARMAN of Dedham. He "geve" unto his brother in law William Pettfylld twenty pounds, unto his brother in law Nycollas Fynce forty shillings, unto his brother Robart Sharman twenty shillings, unto Mr. Edmond Chapman, preacher, twenty shillings, unto my mother my mare, unto William Ballden's son and to Hassele's "sonn" my "coult" to be "sould" and parted "betwene" them. "I geve unto my father a lytell bollocke." To my brother Robart my apparell and a chest.

Witness, Rychard Clarke and Henry Sharman the "yonger."

Com. of London for Essex and Herts.
File for 1576, N° 49.

JOHN WOOD of Dedham, Essex, clothier, 8 March 19th Elizabeth, proved 2 April 1577. To eldest son Richard my tenement and grounds called Stevens in Dedham and twenty acres called Dawes and Bromeleye in Lawford, Essex. My houses and lands in Carsey and Lynseye, Suffolk, both free and copy, to be sold within four years and the money divided between my two sons Henry and George Woodd, part and part alike, to be paid at their several ages of twenty and five years. To wife Mary my tenement called Pidgewells, with all the grounds, being about ten acres, in Dedham, and all my lands called Foxes Pightells in Lawford, an acre of free hold meadow in Stratford, holden of Sir John Syllyard, and one free meadow in Stratford holden of the Earl of Oxenford and three Roodes of free meadow holden of Stratford Hall and one acre of copyhold meadow in Stratford holden of the said Sir John Sylliard, to have and to hold the above-said premisses during the time of her natural life; and after that to my son Robert, provided that if my said son Robert at the death of his mother be not then of the full age of twenty and five years, the above premises to be let and the rent &c. to be equally divided betwixt all the rest of my children then living until the said Robert do accomplish his said age. And if Robert die before that then these lands &c. shall be and remain unto my son John. If both die then to my two daughters Frances Woodd and Mary Woodd. To my son John my farm house &c. with lands &c. in Starthford in the Co. of Hertford, he to enter at twenty-five. If Richard (*sic*) die before that my son Henry shall have all the said lands &c., next my son George. To wife Mary my little meadow called Crab tree meadow in Stratford, Suffolk, for life, paying to the churchwardens of Dedham for the poor there twenty shillings at two several terms in the year. After her decease the Governors of the Free Grammar School of Queen Elizabeth in Dedham shall have the meadow for ever, paying yearly the said twenty shillings &c. To daughter Mary my warehouse or salt house in Harwich (at twenty one), remainder to daughter Frances. To the latter ten pounds at twenty one. If my said son Richard shall go about to trouble or otherwise deal with Mary my wife and Henry Sherman, my only executors, to the intent that this my last will and testament cannot nor may not take effect then I will that the said Richard shall take no benefit of any of my lands &c. unto him bequeathed. And the said Richard shall suffer my wife to carry away all such goods &c. as I have given unto her. To my brother Thomas Wood ten shillings. My wife Mary and my cousin Henry Sharman the younger of Dedham, clothier, to be my executors, and to my said cousin Henry Sherman, over and besides his ordinary charges about this my last will &c., I give three pounds. I make John Lucas of Manyngtree my supervisor, bequeathing him twenty shillings. Among the witnesses was Henry Sherman the elder (by mark).   Daughtry, 12.

Nicholas Clere of the parish of St. James, Colchester, Essex, clothier and one of the alderman of the same town, 24 February 1578, proved 9 June 1579. I do will and require mine cousin Mr. Challenor to preach in the said parish church of St. James four sermons for me. To the poor of the town. To wife Anne Clere my head tenement in St. James wherein I now do dwell (and other property) to hold for life, and then to my son Nicholas. A certain lease of land back of my head tenement, called Mary Land, by lease from the late Abbot of St. John's, confirmed by the Queen's Highness, I give to my wife for life, then to my son Nicholas. Certain property to son Thomas at age of twenty one. Property in Ballingdon, Essex, near adjoining to the town of Sudbury, Suffolk, to son William at age of twenty one. Lands in Haberton and groves of wood in Grynsted and Wivenho to wife to enjoy the rents for her own use &c. and for and towards the education and bringing up of my children. To said wife the tenement in St. James, Colchester, which I late bought of my brother Benjamin Clere and wherein one Joice, a stranger, now inhabiteth, to hold for life and then to son Nicholas. To my said son Nicholas forty pounds of good and lawful money, my best silver salt, one goblet of silver and twelve silver spoons marked in the tops with the letters N. and C., to be paid and delivered when he shall accomplish his age of twenty one years. To William forty pounds &c. The same to Thomas. To my daughter Mary Clere forty pounds at twenty one or day of marriage. To my daugh-

ter Anne Clere forty pounds at twenty one or day or marriage. The same
to daughter Jane Clere. To my son in law Thomas Hasilwood my best
gelding. To my daughter in law Anne Read one bullock of the age of
two years. My daughter in law Margaret Hasilwood and my daughter in
law Elizabeth Hasilwood. My cousin John Clere and my cousin Benjamin
Clere. Wife Anne to be sole executrix and brother Benjamin Clere the
elder supervisor.

Nicholas Challoner and Thomas Crosse two of the witnesses.

Bakon, 25.

HENRY REIGNOLDES of Little Belsteade, Suffolk, Esq. 9 August 27
Elizabeth, with a codicil bearing date 22 September 1585, proved 13 October 1587. To be buried on the North side of the chauncel of the parish
church of Little Belstead. Gravestones to be laid over bodies of Anne my
late wife and Christopher Goldingham her former husband. Another over
body of my father Robert Reignoldes in chancel of South side of church of
East Bergholt. Another over body of my first wife in church of Much
Ocle (Oakley). The poor of Ipswich and of East Bergholt. To wife Elizabeth. Son Henry at one and twenty. My cousin Francis Reignolde of
—— in Norfolk. His son Thomas Reignolde. William Goldingham, Doctor of Law. Henry Reignolde, one of the sons of my brother Edward, and
Robert, Christopher and Francis, his brothers. Henry Goldingham. Jonas
Goldingham. Conditional bequest for endowment of almshouses in Ipswich.
Niece Anne Reignoldes and her brothers and sisters of the whole blood.
The children of my late sister —— Browne deceased. Niece Anne Reignolde referred to as one of the daughters of brother Edward. I give to
Rose and Mary Browne thirty pounds each and to William Warner their
brother forty pounds and to Thomas Warner their brother ten pounds,
and to Francis Browne five pounds and also to my cousin Sherman of
Colchester five pounds. My brother Philip Reignolde. William Goldingham, Doctor of Law, and Henry and Jonas his brethren and Hansarde
Aldeham their sister. Each of the children of my cousin Francis Reignolde. My cousin Richard Kempe and his wife. My brother Edward Withipoll, Peter Withipoll and Benjamin Withipoll. My loving friends Mr. Edward Grimstone the elder and Mr. Edward Grimstone the younger, my
cousin Thomas Kempe, Mr. Humphrey Sackforde, my cousin Walker, my
brother Paul Withipoll his wife, my brother Wolverstone, my nephew
Veasie of Burstall and Mr. Richard Newman (rings). My sister Frances
Withipoll. John Warner of Ipswich. William Goldingham Doctor of Law
to be sole executor and friends William Plumbe Esq., cousin —— Davison
and Edward Grimston the younger, esquires, and Ralphe Scrivenour gent[t]
supervisors. Robert Sherman one of the witnesses both to will and codicil. In the codicil reference to bequest made in above will to niece Rose
Browne and her sister Mary the wife of Heriche of Chelmsford. These
legacies already paid.   Spencer, 61.

HENRY SHEARMAN the elder of Colchester Essex, (by mark) 20 January 1589, with a codicil, proved 25 July 1590. To be buried in the parish
church of Dedham. To Doctor Chapman the preacher of Dedham six
pounds. To Mr. Parker forty shillings. To the poor of Dedham twenty
pounds, to be a continual stock for the poor to the world's end, and
it shall be ordered at the discretion of the Governors of the Free School
of Dedham. To Henry Shearman my son my shearman's craft to him and

his heirs forever and all the household (stuff) in his house. To my son Henry's children, that is to say, Henry, Samuel, Daniel, John, Ezechiell, Phebe, Nathaniel and Anne Shearman, to each of them five pounds apiece, to the sons at two and twenty and the daughters at one and twenty. To my son Edmonde Shearman ten pounds. To Edmonde Shearman, the son of my son Edmonde, thirteen pounds, thirteen shillings and four pence at two and twenty, and if he die before then to be divided between Richard, Bezaliell and Anne Shearman, the children of my son Edmonde. I will and bequeath to Richard, Bezaliell, Anne and Sara Shearman, the children of my son Edmonde, forty shillings apiece, to the sons at two and twenty the daughters at one and twenty. To my son in law William Petfield twenty pounds and to his three children, Richard, Susan and Elizabeth Petfield, six pounds thirteen shillings four pence each (at ages as above). Margerye my wife shall have all my broom wood and logs which I have at my departure and twenty shillings of money and that twelve pounds due unto me from Tendring if my executors can recover it of him. She shall have her dwelling for two years in that part of the house wherein we do now dwell, that is in the lower parlour and the two chambers next Mr. Rudd's and part of the backhouse if my son Robert do enjoy the house. But if it be redeemed and he do not enjoy it then I will that my son Robert shall pay unto Margery my wife four pounds for two years' dwelling. To my wife my tipped pot, term of her life, and then to my daughter Judith. To my son Robert three score pounds, the which I gave for the state of the house wherein I now dwell, which was lately Richard King's, beer brewer, of Colchester. Other real estate to Robert. To Jane and Anne Shearman, daughters of Robert, five pounds apiece (at one and twenty). To Robert all the household stuff which I had before I married Margery, my wife. To him also my silver and gilt goblet, a sword and bill &c. To my daughter Judith Petfield the chest and linen upon the " soller." To my son in law Nicholas Fynce forty shillings. To my son Henry Sherman twelve silver spoons. The poor of All Hallows. To Henry my son all my armour except that which I gave to my son Robert. Other bequests to children. To Christopher Stone a cloth doublet. To each of my sons, Edmond, Henry and Robert, twenty shillings in gold and to each of their wives twenty shillings in gold, and to daughter Judith the same. My sons Henry and Edmond to be executors.

Drury, 51.

THOMAS CLERE of Colchester, Essex, clothier, 11 January 1594 (probate not given). The house I now dwell in, lying in the parish of St. James, Colchester, shall be sold to the most advantage and the money that shall arise thereof shall be given as followeth. To my loving mother Ann Clere ten pounds. To my brother Haselwood ten pounds. To my brother Lewis ten pounds. I give unto my mother ten pounds to be employed to the best advantage and benefit for my sister Elizabeth Westones maintenance. To my brother Nicholas Clere twenty pounds. To my brother Woodes seven sons forty shillings to either of them, that is to say, Richard Wood, Nicolas Woode, John Wood, Samuel Wood, Daniel Wood, Griffyne Woode and Joseph Wood, and every of them to be paid when he shall accomplish his age of one and twenty years.

Item, I do give and bequeath unto my brother Sherman's four children which he had by my sister Anne the like sum of forty shillings to either of them, that is to say to Sara Shermane forty shillings, to Ane Shermane forty shillings, to Susane Shermane forty shillings and to Samuel Shermane forty shillings, to be paid by my executor, or by his executors or administrators, when they and every of them shall accomplish their several ages of one and twenty years, or at the day of marriage, which of them shall first happen.

To my brother Thurstone's three sons the like sum, *i. e.* to Thomas, John and Edmund Thurstone forty shillings apiece, at their several ages of one and twenty, and to Mary Thurstone, his daughter, the like sum at one and twenty or day of marriage. Lands in Ballingdon, Essex, near adjoining to the town of Sudbury, Suffolk, given unto me by my father, Nicholas Clere, to be sold to the most advantage and the money arising thence to be equally divided among my four sisters' children, *i. e.* my sister Reade's children, Elizabeth, Anne and Nicholas Reade, my sister Elizabeth Weston's children, Theophilus, Jone, Elizabeth, Anne and Nathaniel Weston, my sister Anne Shereman's children (name as above) and my sister Jane Thurstone's children (name as above). Brother Nicholas Clere to be my sole executor.

Thomas Thurston and Thomas Cross among the witnesses.

Original will Nº. 40 in Bundle Lawrance,
Arch. Colchester.

EDMOND SHERMAN of Dedham, Essex, clothier, signed 1 August 1599, with a codicil made 20 December 1600, proved the last day of April 1601. To wife Anne my house and tenement and all the meadow and lands which I do now occupy and dwell in, for her natural life. I give her my woodhouse and hopyard annexed which I lately bought of John Upcher, for term of her natural life, and five acres, parcel of the land which I bought of John Webb (and plate and household stuff and cows and horses and grain &c). To son Edmond, after decease of my wife all the houses and lands before given to said wife and a house and seven acres called Ryes, where he now dwells, and my sherman's occupation. To son Richard fifty pounds at four and twenty. Similar bequests to sons Bezaliell, Samuel, John and Benjamin. To my eldest daughter Anne Sherman fifty pounds at one and twenty. A similar bequest to daughter Sarah. I give to Hanna my daughter which I had by Anne my second wife fifty pounds at one and twenty. The same sum each to daughters Susan and Mary at similar ages. To sister Judith Pettfield the tenement wherein Edmond Browne the taylor now dwelleth, term of her life. My house at the church gate, my house that Robert Finch now dwelleth in (and other lands &c.) shall be sold within six months of my decease by my brother Henry Sherman and my kinsman Symon Fenne, clothier, of Dedham. Certain other houses and lands to be let until my youngest daughter Mary come unto the age of twenty years, or the term of twenty years after the date of this my will shall be expired. I do then give to John my son (certain portions) and to sons Benjamin and Samuel (certain other portions). After my wife's death I give to Bezaliell my son my tenement called Ryes, now in occupation of son Edmond, on condition he pay to my son Richard, within one year of his entry and possession of the same, the sum of fifty pounds. If Bezaliell die &c. then to Richard. After my sister's death I give the field and tenement, before given unto her during life, unto the Governors of the Public Grammar School in Dedham, to be improved for a dwelling house for a schoolmaster that shall teach children to read and writing, which said schoolmaster shall freely teach one poor child which shall be from time to time appointed unto him by my son Edmond and after him by his heirs forever. To wife Anne all my malt. To Sarah, Hanna the daughter of Anne my second wife, Susan,

Samuel and John, my children, twenty shillings apiece which was bestowed upon them by their grandmother Cleere. To John Elmes my kinsman ten shillings. Others (servants &c.) Wife Anne to be executrix and Mr. D[r]. Chapman and my brother in law Robert Lewys to be supervisors.

Wit: Robert Lewis, Henry Sherman and William Cole.

(Codicil) To eldest daughter Anne Sherman and son Bezaliell and daughter Sarah, each forty shillings which their grandfather Sherman gave them, to be paid them at the ages mentioned in his will.

Woodhall, 24

ROBERT SHERMAN of London, "Doctor in Phissick," 10 January.— All my goods, debts and else whatsoever I in this life enjoy (my lands excepted) I will shall be duely and rightly valued and apprized and sold and the same to be equally divided into three equal parts, one part whereof I will shall remain to the discharge of my debts and funeral charges, another I freely give unto my well beloved wife Bridget Sherman, the third I will and give shall remain to be divided by my executors amongst four of my children, Jane, Mary, Anne and Robert. And if there shall any surplus remain of my third left to my executors I will it shall be equally divided to my said four children. More I will my freehold land shall remain wholly to my loving wife during her natural life, not doing any manner of waste upon the house and lands, and that my son Richard shall have and enjoy all the said lands, copy and free, to him and his heirs forever (with remainder to son Robert and lastly to my three daughters, Jane having 6[lb] more in value than the other two. My executors to be my loving brother Henry Sherman and loving friend Roger Gwynn.

Proved 20 January 1602 (Stilo Angliae) by Roger Gwynn, one of the executors, power reserved for granting similar commission to Henry Sherman, the other.

Commissary C[t] of London vol. 19, fol. 318.

In the Act Book testator is described as lately of the parish of St. Stephen Coleman Street.

ANNE SHERMAN of Dedham, Essex, widow, 3 August 1609, proved 12 January 1609. To John, my son, at twenty one, my house and land that the widow Fence hath now in occupation. The rents &c. of the said house and land, until then, shall be equally divided between Samuel Sherman, my son, and the aforesaid John Sherman. All my goods, plate, household stuff &c. shall be to the payment of my debts and my late husband's legacies. The remainder (my funeral expenses discharged) I will shall be equally divided amongst my seven children, viz[t] Samuel, John and Benjamin Sherman, Sara Warner, Anna Sherman, Susan Sherman and Mary Sherman at the several ages of twenty one years. I will that mine executors shall see my six children which are yet under age well and faithfully brought up until they shall accomplish their several ages aforesaid. I do make, ordain and appoint my loving brother Nicholas Clarr of Colchester and my son in law Thomas Warner my executors and I give to either of them forty shillings. And I do intreat my loving brother Mr. Thomas Haslewood and my brother Mr. Robert Lewes to be overseers. I give either of them ten shillings.

Wit: John Rogers, Thomas Thurston, William Cole.

Wingfield, 9.

SIMON FENN of Dedham, Essex, clothier, 16 January 1609, with a codicil, proved 11 May 1610.   To wife Phebe my messuage &c. commonly
called Sowthowse, wherein I dwell, lying in Dedham, to hold for life.
After her decease I give the said messuage &c. to my son Henry Fenn.
To wife my meadow called Mill Fenn in Stratford, Suffolk, for life and
afterwards to son Henry, he paying five pounds yearly to my son John
Fenn.   To said Henry my part of the wood in Langham, Essex, which
George Cole and I bought of William Thedham.   To son Clement all my
right, title, &c. in a tenement and twelve acres of ground called Randes in
Dedham (and other lands and tenements) he to enter at four and twenty.
To son Samuel my tenement wherein Henry Cartwright now dwelleth, in
Dedham (and other lands &c.) at four and twenty.   I give him also my
free lands in Bramford, Suffolk.   My cousin Samuel Salmon shall surrender eight acres in Bramford &c.   To son John my tenement in Little Clackton &c. at twenty-four.   Provision made for wife.   My daughter Susan
Salmon.   My daughters Phebe, Anne, Mary and Martha Fenn at one and
twenty.   My executors shall upon good security lend unto Daniel Sherman fifty pounds and to Nathaniel, Ezechiell, John and Edmond Sherman,
my brethren in law, to each of them of like security ten pounds.   To Mr.
John Rogers preacher of the Word of God in Dedham ten pounds, to his
son Daniel Rogers, my godson, forty shillings at one and twenty, and if he
happen to die before that to the rest of his brothers and sisters.   To Mr.
Henry Sage vicar of Dedham.   The Free Grammar School &c.   Mr.
Bedell minister of Wolverston.   Mrs. Dowe of Stratford.   Francis, wife
of Candishe, my sister.   My brother Clement Fenn late of Clacton deceased, his children, Clement, Symon, John, Helen and Susan Fenn, at
twenty one.   My brother George.   John Fenn, son of my brother Thomas
deceased (late of Stratford), and his sister Margery.   Thomas Revell my
sister's son, and Rose his sister.   My sister White.   I give to John Stanton of Dedham the third part of the occupation which I bought of Pexall
remaining in his hands.   Sundry servants and others.   The residue to wife
Phebe to pay my debts and legacies and fulfill this will, whom, together
with my brother Henry Sherman and my son Robert Salmon, I make my
executors.   I give the said Henry and Robert three pounds apiece.   And
I nominate the aforesaid Mr. Rogers, Henry Sherman my father in law
and Samuel Sherman my brother the overseers of this will.

Anthony Whitinge one of the witnesses.   Wingfield, 43.

HENRY SHERMAN the elder of Dedham, Essex, clothier, 21 August 1610,
proved 8 September 1610.   To Susan my wife my house wherein I now
dwell and the lands, with the " Oadehouse " &c. belonging, holden of the
manor of Dedham Hall, by estimation twelve acres, which I had of the
surrender of my father.   The above to her for life and then to my son
Henry.   Other bequests to wife and son Henry, including a bed and bedstead in the parlor, a cubboard in the parlor and two chests in the same
place, the one a Danske chest and the other a joined chest.   To son Nathaniel Sherman the house wherein William King now dwelleth, with lands
belonging, called Scott's, by estimation five acres, he to pay to my son
Daniel Sherman ten pounds in two years.   I give Nathaniel my broad
loom, now in occupation of John Orris of Lawford, with the furniture belonging.   To John and Ezeckiell Sherman my sons all those my lands
which were late Doctor Sherman's, called the Heckell and golding acre, to

be equally divided betwixt them. Other lands to these two (severally). To son Edmund garlick field and Ardley lands and Boreman's acre. Reference to cousin Edmund Gallaway. To Henry Fenn son of Simon Fenn five pounds. To Mr. Rogers, preacher of Dedham, eight pounds. The poor of Dedham. Phebe Fenne my daughter. My son in law Symon Fenne deceased. My daughters in law, each of them. Anna Petfield daughter of William Petfield. To Anne Sherman, my brother Dr. Sherman's daughter, five pounds which was the gift of her grandfather at her full age of two and twenty years; it was once before paid into her father's hands, yet fearing that she should be voyd of it for want of provision on his part I will that it be paid as aforesaid. Gilbert Hills my brother in law. My brother Lawrence of Esthorpe. Others named. I will that George Cole the elder, William Cole, Edmund Sherman and John Pye shall indifferently divide my goods unbequeathed betwixt my children. I make Susan my wife sole executrix and I give her my part of the lease of the Rayes. I appoint my cousin Edmund Gallaway, clerk, the supervisor of this my will and for his pains he shall have twenty shillings.

Proved, as above, by George Cole, notary public, on behalf of Susan the relict of the deceased.

Admon. de bonis non was granted 12 September 1610 to Henry Sherman the younger, natural and lawful and eldest son of the deceased and executor also of Susan Sherman deceased &c.

Consistory C^t of London.
Book Hamer (N° 7) leaves 33–36.

SUSAN SHERMAN of Dedham, Essex, widow, 31 August 1610, proved 12 September 1610. I give unto Harry Sherman my son my silver and gilt salt and my best tapestry covering. To Samuel Sherman my son my six silver spoons which my husband gave me, marked E and S (and certain bedding). To Daniel Sherman my son twenty pounds in money and four of my eight beasts which my husband gave me and are marked out for my use. To Nathaniel Sherman my son twenty pounds. To John Sherman my son my cubbord standing in the parlour. To Ezekiel Sherman my son ten pounds and my new silver cup. To Edmund Shearman my son ten pounds (and bed &c. in the parlor). To Phebe Fenne my daughter my least silver cup (and other articles). To Anne Whighting my daughter my Danske chest in the parlor (and other articles). Son Daniel's wife. Son Nathaniel's wife. Robert Salmon's son, my great grandchild. Mary Sherman, my son Samuel's daughter. To Susan Sherman, my son Daniel's daughter, my leaved table in the parlor. My brother Gilber Hilles. To Mr. Rogers my black mare. Susan Galloway daughter of my cousin Edmund Galloway. My son Henry to be sole executor and for his pains I give him the lease of the Rayes given me by my husband.

Wit: Edmunde Gallowaye, John Pye.

Consistory C^t. of London
Book Hamer (N° 7) Leaf 13.

TOBIAS MAKIN of Fingringhoe Essex yeoman, 14 May 1610, proved 10 September 1610. Wife Katherine to have my lands &c. (described) for life, she to bring up my children and also to pay unto Grace Sherman, my daughter, ten pounds and to John Makin the elder, my son, ten pounds.

After the decease of my wife my son John Makin the younger to have the lands &c. and to pay Joane and Rebecca, my daughters, five pounds apiece and to John Makin, my eldest son, twenty pounds and to Grace Sherman, my daughter, ten pounds &c. If said son John die before entering to be seized of the land it shall remain &c. to Thomas, my youngest son, upon same conditions. If he die &c. then to Samuel my son. Certain house and land to wife for life, then to son Westbroome Makin, who shall pay to my son Thomas thirty pounds. If Westbroome die then it shall remain to son Robert and if he die then to Thomas. Other bequests to his children (including a son Tobias). Reference to " my three daughters naturall." To Elizabeth Potter, my grandchild, at twenty one years of age, five pounds of lawful English money. The same to Richard Sherman, the son of Edmund Sherman, at twenty one. To Richard Weald, the son of Richard Weald of Kyrbie, my kinsman, five pounds at twenty one. To Thomas Weald, the son of Thomas Weald deceased, six shillings eight pence in one year. To John Wealde, son of John Weald the younger, six shillings eight pence at twenty one. To Mary Payne a bullock. To Bridget Bury a lamb. Residue to wife Katherine whom I make executrix. And I ordain Thomas Whiting the supervisor.

Thomas Whiteing one of the witnesses.

Book Hamer (as above) Leaves 45–48.

NICHOLAS CLEERE (by mark) one of the aldermen of the town of Colchester, 15 March 1611. Wife Susan. Daughter Susan Cleere. Younger daughter Anna Cleere. My well beloved brethren Master Thomas Haslewood, and Master Thomas Thurston to be my executors.

Proved 25 May 1612 by Thomas Thurston and 28 May 1612 by Thomas Haslewood.   Fenner, 46.

NATHANIEL SHERMAN of Dedham, Essex, clothier, 13 January 1615 (date of probate not given). To son Nathaniel forty pounds to remain in the hands of my brother in law John Ainger till my son Nathaniel shall accomplish the age of two and twenty years; he to give bonds to my brothers Henry and Samuel Sherman for the payment of the said sum of forty pounds. To my two children Joseph and Elizabeth twenty pounds each. The residue to my wife Priscilla.

Com. of London for Essex and Herts.

File for 1615 &c.

ROBERT LEWIS, minister of the Word of God and parson of Rashbrooke Suffolk, 9 January 1615, proved 23 April 1618. The poor of the parish of St. Mary's in Bury St. Edmund and the inhabitants of the same parish, I having " binne" sometimes a preacher of the Word of God unto them. My body to be buried (there) as near unto the body of my dear and faithful brother Mr. George Estey as conveniently may be. My loving brother Mr. James Wallis, minister &c. at Stowe Lanthorne, Suffolk. My loving brother Mr. Ward, parson of Lyvermeere. My loving brother Mr. Bedell, preacher &c. at Bury. My loving brother Mr. Helye, preacher likewise at Bury. My loving brother Mr. Wolfenden, parson of little Wheltam. My true and faithful wife Mary Lewis the daughter of Mr. Nicholas Cleere, alderman of Colchester deceased. My loving brethren in the law Mr. Thomas Haselwoode and Mr. Thomas Thurstone, aldermen of Colchester.

Meade, 28.

BEAZALIELL SHERMAN of Ipswich, Suffolk, grocer, 7 October 16th James, proved 3 December 1618. To Joane Sherman, daughter of my brother Edmond Sherman, forty pounds at the age of four and twenty years. To John Sherman, son of my said brother, twenty pounds at same age. Mary Colman now my servant. George Bloldroe now my servant. Erasmus Bushells now my servant. Mr. Chapline father of my servant Henry Chapline. To my loving wife all my plate and household stuff. To her the house wherein I dwell, for life, and after her decease I give it to my son John and his heirs. One half of my goods shall remain and be unto my said wife and the other half be equally divided betwixt my children, and if my wife be with child such child to have a portion with the other two, at the age of two and twenty years, that is to say, to my son at his age of twenty four and to my daughter at her age of twenty one. To the poor of the town of Dedham five marks and the same to the poor of Ipswich. To the library of this town a book called Speede's chronicle. Thomas Cooke my servant. I make my loving wife and her father, Doctor Burges, executors.

Wit : El. Dunkon, Edmund Sherman, Henry Buckenham, Joseph Parckhurst, Richard Naser.

Proved (as above) by Priscilla Sherman, the relict of the deceased and John Burges S. T. P., executors named in the will.   Meade, 125.

Mary Sherman, wlfe of Bezaleel Sherman, was buried 11 February 1613. Ursula, daughter of Bezaleel Sherman, baptized 30 April 1615. John Sherman, son of Bezalleel Sherman, baptized 4 May 1617. Bezaleel Sherman was buried 9 October 1618.

Register of St. Lawrence Parish, Ipswich.

THOMAS HASLEWOOD of Colchester, Essex, merchant, 7 May 1619, with a codicil added 9 May 1619, proved 7 June 1619. The poor of St. James, Colchester, of All Saints, Sudbury, and of the Hamlet of Ballington near Sudbury. Mr. Samuel Cricke. Mr. Saundes preacher &c. in Boxford. The children of John Haslewood late of Sudbury deceased. My kinsman Nicholas Reade and his children. To my sister Mary Lewis part of my messuage in All Saints, Colchester, for life, providing that she dwell in the same. To my kinswoman Anna Weston another part of the said messuage, for life. The remainder to my kinsman Thomas Haslewood. The children of my brother Thurston which he had by my sister Jane Cleere. My two kinsmen Daniel and Samuel Wood. Susan and Anna Cleere the daughters of my brother Nicholas Cleere. To my kinsman Theophilus Weston all that my third part of the ship called the Hopewell, now riding in the River of Colne. My kinsman Nathaniel Weston. My kinswoman Elizabeth Weston. My kinsman Richard Wood. Ten pounds apiece to my kinsman Samuel Sherman, to the wife of my kinsman Thomas Warner, to the wife of my kinsman Richard Bacler, to my kinsman Benjamin Sherman, my kinsman John Sherman and my kinswoman Mary Sherman. Mary Mathewe the daughter of Benjamin Mathewe. The town of Colchester and the Company of Bay makers there. My loving friend Nathaniel Northie. My messuages, lands &c. in Boxford. My messuage in St. Buttolph's, Colchester. Lands &c. in Copford and Stanaway, Essex. Kinsmen Thomas Warner and Theophilus Weston executors. My son in law Nathaniel Claise (and Clayse). Tenement late my brother Nicholas Cleere's in St. James, Colchester.   Parker, 61.

Record of sentence in the case of the above will may be found Parker, 103.

Charles Carleton Coffin

NEW-ENGLAND
HISTORICAL AND GENEALOGICAL
REGISTER.

JULY, 1896.

HON. CHARLES CARLETON COFFIN.

By the Rev. GEORGE M. ADAMS, D.D., of Auburndale, Mass.

CHARLES CARLETON COFFIN, A.M., was descended, as are most of the Coffins of this country, from Tristram Coffin, who came from Brixton, near Plymouth, England, to Massachusetts, in 1642, with his widowed mother, Joanna Thember Coffin, and his sisters Mary and Eunice. He settled at Newbury, where he built a house and remained till 1660, when he removed to Nantucket and died there in 1681, leaving five sons.

Captain Peter Coffin, a descendant of Tristram, and the grandfather of Charles Carleton, removed in 1769 from Newbury to Boscawen, New Hampshire, where he was prominent in public affairs, especially in energetic resistance to the oppression of the mother country. He fought at the battle of Bennington. His wife, Rebecca (Hasseltine) Coffin, shared his patriotic spirit. In July, 1777, all the able-bodied men of Boscawen hastened with General Stark to defeat Burgoyne. There were two soldiers who had no shirts to wear. Mrs. Coffin cut an unfinished web from the loom and sat up all night to make the shirts. Then, when the wheat was ready for the sickle, mounting the mare she rode six miles through the forest, with her babe in her arms, to find a boy of fourteen to reap the wheat, while she laid the child in the shade of a tree and bound the sheaves. If the idea of heredity is of value, it is not surprising that she had a grandson who was, in a marked degree, both energetic and patriotic. The babe under the tree was Thomas Coffin, born ten days after the making of the soldiers' shirts.

Thomas Coffin married Hannah Kilborn, daughter of Deacon Eliphalet Kilborn of Boscawen. The youngest of their nine children —Charles Carleton Coffin—was born in Boscawen, N. H., July 26,

1823. His boyhood was passed on the farm, with early rising and hard labor. His education was in the district school, with a few terms at Boscawen Academy and Pembroke Academy. But a decided taste for reading was doubtless of more value to him than the schools. He read Milton's "Paradise Lost" before he was eleven years old, and the essays of the "Federalist" before he was fourteen. The account of Lewis and Clark's Expedition beyond the Rocky Mountains was one of his favorites, which he read repeatedly. All that the little circulating library of the town had to offer in the way of Indian wars, Pilgrim History and stories of the Revolution, he perused again and again. When he was thirteen years old the boys of Boscawen formed a military company and chose him captain. He drilled them so thoroughly as to win the admiration of their elders. He had a great longing for a college education, but the partial failure of his health made it unwise to attempt it. Then he turned to surveying, obtained a surveyor's compass and made himself familiar with the elements of the business. A year or two later the Northern Railroad was chartered, and he found employment as chainman, and three days after was promoted to the charge of the surveying party. He says of it : "My smattering of land surveying was bringing forth fruit." This was in August, 1845. In the autumn of the same year, while at the head of a party making surveys for the Concord and Portsmouth Railroad, he received a wound from a glancing axe, which produced a slight permanent lameness and disqualified him for military service.

Feb. 18, 1846, he married Sallie Russell Farmer, daughter of Colonel John Farmer of Boscawen. The day and night work of the leader of a surveying party at length told upon his health, and he resigned the position and engaged in the lumber trade. This proved somewhat profitable, and, wishing for a home, he purchased a farm in West Boscawen and began housekeeping in November, 1846. In 1851 he constructed the telegraph line from Cambridge Observatory to Boston, by which uniform time was given to the Massachusetts railroads. During the following winter and spring he set up the Telegraphic Fire Alarm in Boston, under the direction of his brother-in-law, Professor Moses G. Farmer. In connection with Professor Farmer he had taken out a patent for a contrivance connected with the electrical battery, which proved to be valuable and was sold, Mr. Coffin receiving for his share two thousand dollars. The possession of such a sum of money encouraged him to strike out for a new home in the vicinity of Boston, and he rented a house in Malden for one hundred dollars a year.

He had been, for a few years, writing for the newspapers occasional articles, both in prose and in poetry. The favor with which those were received drew him more and more toward literary and editorial work. His first engagement in Boston was as assistant editor of the *Practical Farmer*, a weekly agricultural paper. He became an intimate friend of James A. Dix, editor of the *Boston Journal*, and spent many odd hours in the office, writing short editorials and reporting meetings without pay, to educate himself. He analyzed the speeches of Webster, Erskine, Brougham and Burke, for the cultivation of a concise and forcible style. It was the period of white heat in the anti-slavery struggle. He listened to the leading speakers of New England on this question, and may well have caught from their impassioned words vigor and keenness of utterance. In 1856 and 1857 he was connected with the editorial work of the *Daily Atlas*, the organ of the anti-slavery wing of the Whig party, and of the *Atlas and Bee*. In 1858 he came into a connection with the *Boston Journal*, which was to continue, in one form or another, for many years. His first duties were those of reporter and correspondent. He was sent to Canada in connection with the visit of the Prince of Wales, and wrote daily letters to the *Journal*. He attended the festivities at the opening of more than one of the great western railroads, meeting many public men. In 1860 he was present at the convention in Baltimore which named Bell and Everett as candidates for President and Vice-President, and at the Chicago convention which nominated Lincoln. He went to Springfield with the committee which bore to Mr. Lincoln the official notice of his nomination, and made the acquaintance of the coming President. The following winter he became night editor of the *Journal*. Those were the last months of President Buchanan's administration. It was an exciting period in public affairs. The Southern States were, one after another, seceding from the Union. The North was slowly waking up to the seriousness of the issue.

Upon the breaking out of the war in 1861, Mr. Coffin was sent to the front as correspondent of the *Journal*. He saw the engagement at Blackford's Ford, and at the first battle of Bull Run narrowly escaped capture by the Confederate cavalry. His commission as correspondent left him free to govern his own movements, and he hastened from point to point, seeking to be promptly wherever the most active operations were to be expected. In December, as all seemed likely to be "quiet on the Potomac," he obtained letters of introduction from the Secretary of War to General Grant and General Buell, and hastened west. At Louisville he presented his letter to General Buell, only to have it tossed aside with a contemptuous remark and a refusal. Then he made his way to Cairo, seeking General Grant. In the second story of a dilapidated building he found a man in a blue blouse, sitting on a nail keg, at a rough desk, and smoking a cigar. Presenting his letter from the Secretary of War, he requested the man to hand it to General Grant. Instead of turning to the inner office, the supposed orderly read the note and, rising, extended his hand and said, "I am right glad to see you. Please take a nail keg." Mr. Coffin was at once on the best of terms with the General, who gave him all needful facilities for obtaining information.

As a correspondent, Mr. Coffin made it his rule to describe, but never to criticise. He was careful, too, to publish nothing that could be used in any way to the disadvantage of the army or of the country. His judicious methods were soon recognized, and he enjoyed in an unusual degree the confidence of the generals in command. Commodore Foote's gunboats were at Cairo, preparing for the successful expedition up the Tennessee river, and Mr. Coffin formed a pleasant acquaintance with the Commodore and his officers, which was of special value to him later. After the capture of Fort Henry he met the fleet at the mouth of the Tennessee, and receiving from the Commodore the particulars of the engagement, took the cars bound east, wrote his account on the train, and so gave the first published report of the important capture. Returning west, he made his way to Fort Donelson and witnessed the surrender of the fort, with fifteen thousand Confederate soldiers, to General Grant. Then he hastened to Cairo and again secured an early report for his paper by writing his account on an east-bound train, leaving the cars when his letter was completed.

He was with the fleet during the operations at Island No. 10, and later at the capture of Memphis. Then he came east and made report of the seven days' battles before Richmond. His account of the battle of Antietam was very highly commended. An immense edition of it was disposed of in the army. Another of his reports which became somewhat famous was that describing the three days' struggle at Gettysburg.

" He witnessed the repulse of Pickett's magnificent charge, standing near Howard's batteries on Cemetery Hill and timing the discharge of one of the pieces, watch in hand. As soon as that desperate charge was repelled, he mounted his horse and started at top speed for the nearest railroad station to take train for Baltimore. His practiced eye told him that Pickett's repulse ended the battle, and he waited for nothing more. He bore the first assured news of the great victory to anxious and expectant congressmen at Baltimore, and next morning before light he was in the *Journal* office at Boston, with a wood engraver taking down his diagrams to accompany one of the clearest and best reports of the decisive battle of the war, printed in any journal."

This report was reprinted far and wide in America, and translated and republished in France and Germany.

He continued his service as correspondent to the end of the war, witnessing and making record of all the principal engagements of the army of the Potomac under General Grant. He was with the fleet of General Gillmore, which took possession of Charleston, when General Sherman with his flying army from Atlanta and Savannah approached the rear of the city. He was so prompt and energetic in sending his despatch to Boston that it was published in the *Journal*, telegraphed to Washington, and read in the House of Representatives as the first account received there. In his enthusiasm he begins :—

"Off Charleston, February 18, 2 P.M. The old flag waves over Sumter and Moultrie and the city of Charleston. I can see its crimson stripes and fadeless stars waving in the warm sunlight of this glorious day. Thanks be to God, who giveth us the victory."

After the close of the war Mr. Coffin went to Europe as correspondent of the *Boston Journal*. Mrs. Coffin accompanied him on this journey, which finally became a tour around the world. He spent a year and a half in Europe, writing with reference to public affairs and describing the life of the common people. The passage of the Reform Bill in England, the evacuation of Northern Italy by the Austrians and the enthusiastic reception of Victor Emanuel at Venice, the coronation of the Emperor of Austria as King of Hungary, furnished material for interesting communications from his pen. Bearing letters of introduction from General Grant, Chief Justice Chase, Charles Sumner and other public men, he had the opportunity of meeting almost all the noted men of that day in Europe. At the banquet given to Charles Dickens, before the departure of that author for the United States, he saw the chief literary men of England. At the Social Science Congress at Belfast, Ireland, he gave an address on Common Schools in the United States, which was warmly commended.

Leaving Europe, he visited Turkey, Syria, Egypt, India, China, Japan and California, reaching Boston in December, 1868, after an absence of two years and five months. His travelling experiences furnished interesting material for public lectures, and for some years after his return he was one of the popular lyceum speakers. He delivered a course of lectures before the Lowell Institute. He is said to have given, first and last, two thousand public addresses. In 1870 Amherst College conferred upon him the honorary degree of Master of Arts.

His later years were largely devoted to authorship. His published works number nineteen volumes, besides eight or ten pamphlets. The volumes are as follows :—

"My Days and Nights on the Battlefield," published in 1864 ; "Following the Flag," 1865 ; "The Boys of '61," first published as "Four Years of Fighting," 1866 ; "Winning his Way," 1866 ; "Our New Way Round the World," 1869 ; "The Seat of Empire," 1870 ; "The Boys of '76," 1877 ; "History of Boscawen and Webster, New Hampshire," 1878 ; "The Story of Liberty," 1878 ; "Dan of Millbrook," first published as "Caleb Krinkle," 1879 ; "Life of James A. Garfield," 1880 ; "Old Times in the Colonies," 1881 ; "Building the Nation," 1883 ; "Drum Beat of the Nation," 1888 ; "Marching to Victory," 1889 ; "Redeeming the Republic," 1890 ; "Freedom Triumphant," 1891 ; "Life of Lincoln," 1893 ; "Daughters of the Revolution," 1895.

Many of these books were written specially for the young. Mr. Coffin had a hearty sympathy with young people, and his. books touch them as with the voice of a friend. It was said a few years since, that there were fifty copies of "The Boys of '76" in the Boston Public Library, and all in constant use.

Mr. Coffin was repeatedly invited to return to his old home in Boscawen to assist in celebrating occasions of public interest. July 4, 1876, he was the orator at the observance there of the centennial of American Independence, and he rendered the same honorable service at the one hundred and fiftieth anniversary of the settlement of the town, Aug. 16, 1883.

He was a member of the Legislature of Massachusetts in 1884 and 1885. In the former year he served in the committees on the liquor law, on education, and on civil service. He was the author of the bill, which became a law, closing the saloons at eleven o'clock P.M. and on election days. He reported the draft of the law which makes text books free to pupils in the public schools. In the Legislature of 1885 he was chairman of the special committee which considered the bill establishing a police commission for the city of Boston. He was earnestly in favor of the measure, as one calculated to remove the police system from political influence. Though outvoted in the committee he carried the contest into the open House, and after a prolonged struggle the friends of the measure were successful.

In 1890 he was a member of the Senate of Massachusetts, and did good service on the railroad committee. He introduced a bill which became a law, making the Commonwealth a party to aid in abolishing the crossing of the highways at grade by the railroads.

Mr. Coffin was an honorary member of the New Hampshire Historical Society and a member of the American Geographical Society, of the American Association for the Advancement of Science, of the Massachusetts Club, of the Boston Congregational Club, and of the New-England Historic Genealogical Society. The last named society celebrated its semi-centennial anniversary April 19, 1895, and Mr. Coffin was the orator of the occasion.

On the eighteenth of February, 1896, a distinguished company assembled at the house of Mr. and Mrs. Coffin in Brookline to celebrate their golden wedding. The esteem in which the venerable author was held had large and joyous expression. Hundreds of friends from far and near brought their congratulations. Mr. Coffin was apparently in the fulness of health and vigor. Two weeks later, on the second of March, he suddenly and peacefully passed away.

Mr. Coffin was an admirable example of what New England ancestry, and New England training, and New England courage and energy can bring to pass for a poor boy, under narrow conditions and opportunities. His life is a word of cheer to every young person who proposes to make the most of himself and to accomplish something for which the world shall bless his memory.   From his boyhood Mr. Coffin was possessed with a kind of ambition of which there is never too much in the world,—an ambition to do his best in the duty just before him, and to make that a stepping-stone to something higher.   He was hopeful, alert, enthusiastic.   His frankness, honesty, faithfulness, were proverbial.   "It was not uncommon," says an old associate, "when a knot of correspondents were discussing some doubtful question, for one of them to look up, and, seeing Mr. Coffin approaching, say, 'Well, here comes Old Reliable, he will settle it for us.'"   He was never ashamed of his early struggles.   In all the success and honor of his riper years he remained simple, unostentatious, transparent, pure—a whole-souled Christian gentleman.   The sentences with which he closed his oration before the Historic Genealogical Society on its fiftieth anniversary show something of the bright, cheerful tone of the man :—

" Notwithstanding the iniquity of the age, the world is vastly better at this moment than it was when Charles Ewer and Wingate Thornton and their associates founded this society.   The historic evolution of the past indicates that it will be better to-morrow than it is to-day. . . . . The voices of nature, of prophecy and history, are in accordance with the longings of the world for the coming of a time when there shall be a consummate flowering of the human race.   Grant, if you please, that this is optimistic; but it is the optimism of history.   During the eighteen hundred years that have passed since the Man of Nazareth, in this month of April, rose victor from the grave, triumphant over death, the banner of progress has borne this inscription :—

THE BROTHERHOOD OF MAN; THE REDEMPTION OF THE WORLD !"

THE HUSSEY ANCESTRY OF THE POET WHITTIER.

By Rev. ALONZO H. QUINT, D.D., of Dover, N. H.

I DESIRE to put into the pages of the REGISTER, as the proper and permanent place, a statement regarding the "Hussey" ancestry of John G. Whittier.

In the *Arena*, February, 1896, page 381, it is said :   "I had been to the site of the house of Christopher Hussey, from whom, notwithstanding some late genealogical confusion, he traced his lineage, his mother being a Hussey."   The phrase "genealogical confusion," without the slightest presentation of facts, is not a sufficient answer to those who have, after careful investigation, asserted that Whittier's mother was not of the lineage mentioned.   I venture without hesitation to make the following assertions :

1. The poet never "traced" his lineage from Christopher Hussey, although he doubtless took it for granted that he was of that descent.

2. The records are ample, and without a flaw or need of inference, which show that Whittier's mother, a Hussey, was descended in a direct line, not from Christopher Hussey, of Hampton, but from Robert Hussey, who was of Dover as early as 1659.

3. Between Christopher Hussey and Robert Hussey, no wills, deeds, or any other papers, and no similarity of Christian names, have ever suggested any connection in the slightest degree.

Some years ago, in my work upon Dover history, and also from my warm love toward the poet (much of whose poetry I can repeat), I made a thorough investigation of the mother's ancestry. She was born in old Dover, and I have studied the trout-brook, the spring, and all the scenery of the spot where she was a child. I found her father's will, and traced back the pedigree in its every step by public and Friends' records. To my surprise I found that the family ancestor was Robert Hussey.

Two or three years ago, I found in the Boston *Transcript* a complete and elaborate statement of the pedigree, with full names and dates, made by a gentleman of the Whittier name and blood. He had gone over the same ground which I had traversed, although entirely ignorant of my own labor ; and our results, equally elaborate and complete, were exactly alike. My own papers I have preserved ; his went into print.

Some time ago, I made in the *Congregationalist* a brief assertion of the frequent mistake as to Christopher Hussey, which was extensively quoted but never answered. Now, before any further assertion of "genealogical confusion" as being a sufficient answer to authentic evidence, it is proper to demand the production of the pedigree, which is supposed to connect Whittier's mother with Christopher Hussey.

BARTHOLOMEW DAY.—On the twenty-fourth of August 1862, two centuries were completed since the ejection of the nonconformist ministers under the Bartholomew Act, with which Charles the Second and his obsequious Parliament rewarded the Presbyterian clergy, who then filled the greater portion of the livings in England, for their constant prayers during his exile that he might be permitted to return to his native land and be restored to the throne of his ancestors. Nor did they rest satisfied with this. Besides praying for his restoration, they were active in placing him upon his throne ; and, it is almost certain, that without their aid, or at least if they had been as persistent in opposing as they were in supporting him, he would never have been restored. The characteristic return which their profligate sovereign made to them for their loyalty, was the Act of Uniformity, which drove multitudes of their most conscientious ministers from their livings. This act is one that the friends of toleration must always condemn. But, though the individual suffering and the temporary check to religion and morality produced by this and the supplementary laws, are to be deplored, yet it may well be doubted whether liberty of conscience would have been advanced by allowing the ejected ministers, most of whom were the avowed enemies to toleration, to retain their livings. The English Presbyterians afterwards became bold advocates for religious freedom.—HISTORICAL MAGAZINE.

A PIECE OF FAMILY SILVER, AND A BOSTON SILVERSMITH OF 1712.

By Edward S. Holden, LL.D., Director of the Lick Observatory.

The accompanying cut is made from a photograph of a silver tankard in my possession. The tankard is about $7\frac{1}{4}$ inches in extreme height and $4\frac{5}{8}$ inches in extreme diameter. The cut should be examined with an ordinary hand-glass.

Through the great kindness of Henry E. Woods, Esq., Chairman of the Society's Committee on Heraldry, I have lately been able to obtain a pedigree for this piece of silver, proved in every part; and, incidentally, it has been the means of discovering two hitherto unknown Boston silversmiths, namely, William Cowell, father and son.

The tankard came to me through my father, Edward,[6] and my grandfather, Edward.[5] As a boy I was told that it formerly belonged to Phineas[3] Holden of Norwich, Connecticut (Justinian,[1] Samuel,[2]), born 1715, May 12, died 1763, married Hannah[4] Bushnell (Benajah,[3] Richard,[2] Richard[1]). Phineas[3] Holden left no children, and from his estate the tankard came to Justinian[5] Holden (Samuel,[4] William,[3] Samuel,[2] Justinian[1]), who gave it to his brother Edward,[5] my grandfather. Phineas of Norwich was uncle to Dr. Phineas of Dorchester.

On the handle of the tankard is engraved

B
B . Z

which stands for Bushnell, Benajah and Zerviah, as is shown by the following from the Hyde Genealogy, by R. H. Walworth, p. 186, which Mr. Woods has extracted:—

"Benajah Bushnell, born 11 March, 1715, at Norwich, eldest son of Benajah Bushnell and Zerviah Leffingwell, and grandson of Capt. Richard Bushnell and Elizabeth Adgate." Mr. Woods gives the following also: "Benajah Bushnell, Sr., was born in 1681;[*] Zerviah Leffingwell was born 17 Oct., 1686, and was the daughter of Thomas Leffingwell (of Saybrook and Norwich) and Mary Bushnell (sister of Capt. Richard Bushnell of Norwich), and consequently Benajah and Zerviah were cousins, as well as husband and wife."

The base and the cover of the tankard are stamped (with the

[*] Born May 4, 1681,—E. S. H.

same stamp) *W. Cowell.* Near the handle is a small private mark which can best be described heraldically as follows : Argent, in fess the letters W C, in chief a mullet between two pellets, in base a pellet. The extreme height of this stamp is about $\frac{3}{32}$ of an inch.

Cowell has hitherto been unknown as a silversmith, but the following excerpt from a letter of Mr. Woods (dated March 12, 1896) entirely clears up his history :—

"From the very complete account of your piece of plate, I too was convinced that it was made in America, and so set upon a systematic search for the obscure W. Cowell, with the following success : In the ' Annals of King's Chapel, Boston,' I found : ' 1728, May 7, To Cash pd. Wm Cowell for Mr. Wats's plate £25. 05. 10,'" and that in a legacy of a Mrs. Ireland to the Old South Church, Boston, was a silver tankard bearing the single mark " W. Cowell," and inscribed :

The legacy
of Mrs. Mary Ireland
to the Old South
Church Sept. 25
1763

Those first clues led to what now comes :

Suff. Deeds, vol. 27, p. 161. "——— said Mary, Hannah and Mehetable being the three daughters of John Cowell* late of Boston, Blacksmith, deceased . . . . . .   Whereas William Cowell of Boston aforesaid, Goldsmith, only son of said deceased," etc.

(Dated, 12 Aug. 1712.)

Extracts from *Boston Records :*

Births.—1669 Nov. 20—Mary of John & Hannah Cowell
          1674 Jan. 12—John   do.   [died ?]
          1677 Mch. 9—Hannah   do.
          1680 Oct. 3—Mehetable   do.
          1682 Jan. 25—William   do.
Deaths.—1693, Dec. ?, John Cowell
Births.—1707 July 1—John of William & Elizabeth Cowell
          1709 May 13—Hannah   do.
          1713 July 19—William   do.
          1715 Dec. 27—Elizabeth   do.
          1717 Jan. 6—Mary   do.
          1720 June 1—Richard   do.
          1727 May 18—Rebekah   do.
Suff. Probate Records :—

(6882) 1736—William[1] Cowell of Boston, Innholder, decd.—admtn. to widow Elizabeth.

(6882)[2] 1745—William[1] Cowell of Boston, Innholder, decd.—admtn. to William[2] Cowell, Goldsmith, upon the decease of widow Elizabeth with the estate not yet administered.

(12763) 1761—William[2] Cowell of Boston, Goldsmith, decd. admtn. to sisters Hannah Simpson, widow, & Rebecca Cowell, spinster.

---

* John Cowell was son of Capt. Edward Cowell who figured in King Philip's War.

"From all the foregoing it will be seen that the William Cowell who in 1712 was a goldsmith, and who undoubtedly made 'Mr. Wats's plate' in 1728, afterwards turned innholder and was succeeded in his former trade by his son William Cowell. I find there was no other William Cowell on record at that particular time. Which William made the Old South Church tankard it is difficult to determine."

It thus appears that the researches of Mr. Woods have resulted in the discovery of two Boston silversmiths, previously unnoticed.

Justinian[1] Houlding came to America with his brother Richard[1] on the *Frances*, sailing from Ipswich "the last of April, 1634" (REGISTER, vol. xiv. p. 331), and settled in Watertown. On the same ship was William Houlton, aged 23, who was an original proprietor of Hartford, and the first Deacon at Northampton (1663). Paige's Cambridge (pp. 585–6) gives a correct account of the two brothers named above. The home of Justinian was where the Fresh Pond hotel stood in my boyhood. His grandson Dr. William Holden moved to Bridgewater, and from thence to Dorchester (about 1740).

The arms on the tankard are those granted to Robert Holden of Hockeridge (Oak-ridge), Cranbrook, Kent, May 20, 1663 (Mss. Herald's Office D. 18, fol. 177 *b*, and British Museum Ms. Add. 5507, 291 *b*).

Robert Holden has no descendants in America who are entitled to bear these arms. Indeed his descendants left Cranbrook about 1762, and I have not been able to meet with any of this family in England. Mss. in the possession of the descendants of Justinian[1] (in Massachusetts), and of Richard[1] (in Vermont), and of Capt. Levi[4] Holden* (in Pennsylvania), all agree in placing the English home of the two emigrants in Cranbrook. The arms were undoubtedly engraved on the tankard during the lifetime of Phineas Holden (1715–1763).

It is Mr. Woods's opinion that the arms might have been engraved by one of the Hurds, goldsmiths of Boston (Jacob Hurd, died 1758; Nathaniel Hurd, died 1777), judging from the style of the engraving. If so, the tankard must have been carried from Norwich to Boston and back again.

The crest is undoubtedly assumed, like so many "doves and olive branches" of the period. I am of the opinion that the *Oliver* crest is responsible for the popularity of that particular device in and around Boston. When it was assumed by Phineas Holden, he had no idea that a subsequent marriage (Anne Payson, b. Oct. 2, 1772, with Edward Holden) would make his act, in some sense, a family affair.

---

* Levi,[4] Jonas[3], John,[2] Justinian[1]; member of the Society of the Cincinnati, and one of the innumerable "Commanders of Washington's Life-Guard."

NOTE.—In J. H. Buck's "Old Plate," page 116, there is an illustration of the "Ely tankard," in the possession of Mr. R. S. Ely, which bears the mark: "W. C., a mullet between two pellets above, a pellet below," on a shield, and the general form of the tankard is similar to Dr. Holden's. It is there described as "brought from England about 1660," but Dr. Holden's article now identifies the maker.—EDITOR.

A MANUSCRIPT GENEALOGY MADE BY THE REV. SAMUEL WOODWARD,

WHO DIED IN WESTON, OCT. 5, 1782.

[Copied for the REGISTER by MARY FRANCES PEIRCE of Weston.]

Ebenezer Woodward Son of John & Rebecca Woodward
born at Newton . . . . March 12 : 1690–1
Mindwell Stone Daugh of Ebenez: (Esqr) & Margaret
Stone born at Newton . . . . . . June 26 : 1696
The above s^d. Ebenezer & Mindwell Marry,d Jan^{ry}. 25 1716 p J Cotton.

1. C: { Mindwell Woodward born . . . . Feb: 26 : 1716–7
{ Marry,d to Nathanael Shepard . . . Nov : 30 : 1736
2. C: Eleanor* Woodward born . . . . June 20 : 1720
3. C: { John Woodward born . . . . . Feb. 4 : 1724–5
{ Marry,d to Hannah Greenwood . . . May 21 : 1747
4. C: { Samuel Woodward born . . . . Feb : 1 : 1726–7
{ Ordain,d at Weston . . . . . Sept : 25 : 1751
{ Marry,d to M^{rs}. Abigail Williams . . . Jan^{ry} : 11 : 1753
5. C: { Mary Woodward born . . . . . Feb : 28, 1732–3
{ Marry,d to Jonathan Richardson . . . Oct : 31 : 1751
The aboves^d Eleanor Woodward was married to Nathan-
ael Jones of Charlton . . . . . . June 22, 1758
Eli Son of Nathanael & Eleanor Jones born . . June 5, 1759
Hannah Daugh^r. of Nathl & Eleanor Jones born . Sept. 28, 1760
Phinehas Son of Nathanael & Eleanor Jones born . Febr : 17, 1763
Eleanor

Abigail Daugh^r of Sam^{ll}. & Abigail Woodward born . Decem : 8 : 1753
Abigail Daugh^r. of Samuel & Abigail Woodward dy,d Feb : 10 : 1756
Sam^{ll}. Son of Sam^{ll} Woodward & Abigail born . . 11 July : 1756
Abigail Daugh^r. of Sam^{ll} & Abigail Woodward born . Sept. 25 : 1759
Sylvester Son of Samuel & Abigail Woodward born May 11, and dyed
   Jun. 11, 1761 Sm. Pox
Nov 22, 1762 Miranda Daugh^r of Sam^{ll}. and Abigail Woodward born, 25m.
   after 3. A.M
May 12, 1764 Cyrus Son of Rev^d. Saml. & Abigail Woodward born 30m :
   after 11

[A full list of the children of Samuel and Abigail Woodward is given later.—M. F. P.]

*Bond's Watertown has Ebenezer instead of Eleanor, an evident error.—M. F. P.

Some acc^t. of the Estate* at Waltham :

Buildings and Land in Waltham prized at . .	500– 8–0
Lands in Deerfield prized at	152–19–4
Lands in Stockbridge & adjacent prized at . .	158–10–0

The Sum Total of all the apprized Estate . . .	811–17–4
Thirds Taken out of the whole	270–12–5–1

Remains to be divided among the children . .	541–4–10–3
A Single Share of which is	90–4– 2
A Sixth part of Thirds is	45–2– 1

Therefore agreed that the D^r. [Leonard Williams] have the
thirds quitted to him upon his obligation to pay us respectively
at Mothers decease 45– 2–0

Instruments to be given.

The Doctors 4 Bonds to his Brother and Sisters
Our acquittance of what is in Waltham to him
His acquittance of the Country Lands ; and also Mr^s. Williams Security
to us of what is overplus in Waltham; in all, 49–7–3–1.
NB   The Dr to have part of Country Lands unprized.
57–6 –8   What Mrs. Woodward rec^d. when She married.
33–18–5–2 A Single Share in the Moveable Estate.

23–8–2–2

The Ages of my Sister Shepard,s Children.

Jonathan Shepard born	Sept. 24, 1737
Nathanael Shepard born	Feb. 25, 1739
Elener Shepard born	Oct. 7, 1740
Ebenezer Shepard born	Jan^ry 13, 1742
Mindwell Shepard born	Nov. 14, 1743
Isaac Shepard born	Sept. 15, 1745
Elizabeth Shepard born	Jan^ry. 20, 1747
Jacob Shepard born	Decemb. 13, 1748
Hannah Shepard born	Sept. 1, 1750
Samuel Shepard born	June 24, 1752

These	⎱ Sam^ll. and Hannah Twins . . .	Nov: 16, 1755
are	⎰ Penuel	Sept. 3, 1758
Everitts†	Levi	Sept. 23, 1760

The Ages of my Sister Richardsons Children.

Mary born	Sept. 27, 1752
Jonathan born	Decemb: 30, 1753
Susanna born	Decemb: 12, 1755
Abigail born	Oct: 28, 1757
Nehemiah born	June 29, 1759
John born	April 22, 1761
Mehetabel born	July 21, 1762

Mehetabel died at about a Fortnight old.

* Estate of the Rev. Warham Williams.—M. F. P.
† Everett was probably her second husband.—M. F. P.

My own and Family's Ages.

Samuel Woodward born	Feb: 1, 1727
Took my Degree at Harvard College	1748
Ordained at Weston	Sept. 25, 1751
Married to Mrs Abigail Williams	Jan^{ry} 11, 1753
X Abigail our first Daughter born	Decemb: 8, 1753
X Samuel born	July 11, 1756
Abigail born	Sept. 25, 1759
X Sylvester born	May. 11, 1761
Miranda born	Nov: 22, 1762
X Cyrus born	May 12, 1764
Warham born	Sept. 22, 1765
Sarah born	Sept: 29, 1767
X Nelly born	Oct: 2, 1769
X Martha born	March 5, 1772
X Eunice born	Sept. 14, 1779
X John born	Jan^{ry} 27, 1776
My honr'd Father Mr Eben^r. Woodward died	Jan^{ry} 1, 1770
My honr^d Mother Mindwell Woodward died	Feb: 1774
NB. Our first Nabby died	Feb: 10, 1756
Sylvester died	June 11, 1761
Eunice died in half an hour after Birth.	

[The crosses against the names of Cyrus, Nelly, Martha and John are in another hand.—M. F. P.]

An Account taken from Records in Watertown of our Family.

Richard Woodward & Rose his Wife } probably came over from England
George Woodward & Mary his Wife } and settled in Watertown.

George and Mary,s Children were

Rebeckah, born 39 Day of 10 Month	1647
John born 20 Day of March	1649
Susanna born 30 Day of Sept.	1651
Daniel born 2 Day of April	1653
Mary born 3 Day of June	1656

April 17 1659 } Married George Woodward to Elizabeth Hammond. } This George is the Son of the aboves^d George Woodward. [An error.]*

George & Elizabeths Children.

George born the 11 Day, of the 7 Month	1660
Thomas born the 15 Day of ye 7 Month	1662 Died Sept. 3, 1666
Elizabeth born the 8 Day of May	1664
Nathanael	Dyed 28 Day 3^d Month 1668
Sarah born the 3^d Day of October	1675

The aboves^d Richard Woodward Died 16 Day of 12 Month . 1664
The aboves^d Rose his wife Died 6 Day of 8 Month . . . 1662

---

* Bond is probably correct when he says that George was the son of Richard; that he came from England at the age of 15; that he married, first Mary, second Elizabeth. The names of his three oldest children, found in the Middlesex Court Records, are not here given.—M. F. P.

Some account of yᵉ Family of yᵉ Stones.

Simon Stone married in England to a ―――― Clark and after came over
to New England.

Simon their Son was four years old when he came from England,—he
married Mary Whipple of Ipswich.

Ebenezer his Son, married first a Trowbridge, then yᵉ widow Wilson,
then yᵉ widow Livermore, who was a Neverson.

INSCRIPTIONS AT SANTA CRUZ, CALIFORNIA, 1891.

Copied by B. FRANK LEEDS, Esq.

[Continued from page 187.]

Lot 67.

Mary Schwan, our only child, died Nov. 5, 1863, aged 5 years 9 mos.
26 days.

Henry, son of H. and C. Johans, died Nov. 5, 1881, aged 17 years, 5 mos.

Anne Johans, died May 13, 1864, aged 37 years.

Inscription in German.

Henriette Adaline Wey (or Mey) born Aug. 2, 1863, died Jan. 27, 1865.

Inscription in German.

Lot 68.

Allan G. Wright, born 1816, d. June 17, 1885.

Rosaline Strong, wife of A. G. Wright, born in 1818, died May 22, 1859.
Native of Williamstown, Vermont.

Lot 69.

Joseph Coats, d. Jan. 18, 1887, aged 71 years.

Louisa Coats, d. June 22, 1889, aged 66 years.

Lot 70.

Seth Blanchard, died Dec. 13, 1889, agᵈ 67 y. 7 mos.   A member of
Santa Cruz Pioneers.

Lot 71.

Martha M. Button, wife of Ruben Button, born Feb. 21, 1833, died Apr.
28, 1864.

Wood.

Martha Jane Button, daughter of Ruben and Martha, born Sep. 29, 1861,
died Apr. 16, 1863.

Lot 72.

Eunice Dodge, died Nov. 21, 1871, aged 71 yrs. 1 mo. 3 d.

Lot 73.

J. B. Arcan, born Apr. 14, 1813, died Sep. 15, 1869.

Julia S. dauʳ of J. B. and A. H. Arcan, died July 19, 1850, aged 19 yrs.

Unmarked grave between the above and one other with 18 inch high stone column resting on earth. No inscription.

Lot 74.

John Shearer, died Jan. 2, 1866, aged 65 years.
Sophia Robinson Clark, died Aug. 17, 1866, aged 31 yrs. 8 mos. 17 days.

Lot 75.

Alida Ostrum, died Oct. 27, 1869.

Lot 76.

Mary, wife of Richard Anderson, d. Mch. 26, 1887, aged 30 yrs. 10 mos. 3 days.
Baby Ray, son of the above, d. July 14, 1885, ag^d 11 mos. 3 days.
Eliza, wife of William McElroy, d. May 20, 1887, ag^d 67 y. 8 mos.

Lot 77.

Fanny Meyrick, dearly beloved daughter of Henry and Mary Meyrick, died Aug. 26, 1877, aged 15½ years.

Lot 78.

Stephen Hunt, born 1826, died 1890.
Henry H. Hunt, born 1874, died 1877.
H. S. H. (grown person.)

Lot 79.

Lizzie Ruthrauff Brown, 1878.
Wooden cross.

Lot 80.

Carolina Severn, wife of Gilbert M. Cole, died Aug. 19, 1862.

Lot 81.

Carl Sabish, born in Germany, Aug. 30, 1804, died Aug. 19, 1881.
Augusta Sabish, wife of Carl Sabish, born in Germany, June 11, 1807, died Sep. 27, 1859.

Lot 82.

Minott S. Isbell, born in Milford, Conn., Aug. 1, 1815, died Mch. 23, 1861.

An unmarked grave alongside the above decorated with flag.

Lot 83.

An above-ground tomb stuccoed and painted a pinkish color; iron door; no inscription.

Lot 84.

John Curtis, born in Biddeford, State of Maine, Jan. 11, 1825, died Nov. 29, 1861, ag^d 36 y. 10 m. 10 d.
Phebe L. Goodwin, wife of D. C. Feeley, born Dec. 24, 1824, died Apr. 23, 1870.
C. H. C.

[To be continued.]

LETTER OF REV. THOMAS WELD.

DUNSTABLE LAND.

Communicated by SAMUEL B. DOGGETT, Esq., of Boston.

A PETITION " To his Excellency Jonathan Belcher Esqr Govr,   To the honble His Majesty's Council and House of Representatives in General Court assembled at Boston November 1738 " was granted by the House Dec. 12, 1738, concurred in by Council and consented to by the Governor on the following day.   This petition was made by the heirs of Hon. Samuel Sewall for right to sell sundry small pieces of land in Dunstable and Wilmington at a place commonly called the land of Nodd.*

Hon. Samuel Sewall was one of the non-resident proprietors of Dunstable and regarding his land I hold the following paper in his handwriting :—

A Copy of a Letter from Mr Thom^s Weld Minister of Dunstable 30th of the 11 Month 168$\frac{3}{4}$.

Kind Sir,

Having about a Month since when I was last in the Bay laid myself under Obligation by promise to give you an acc^t of that Tract of Land, which sometimes Mr. John Turner Dec'd was posses'd of, which falls within our Township : I could not without manifest imputation of unfaithfullness to myself for Kindnesses in many respects to me expressed   Omit by this opportunity as thoroughly as I am able & as I think is needful ever since My return home.   I have entertained discourse with diverss persons conserning it.   But not being myself satisfied with some uncertain conjectures which I had from Vulgar Informers concerning its position quantity &

* The land of Nodd was within the original territorial limits of Woburn, but was never the property of the town.
The General Court, in 1642, at its adjourned meeting, on 27th September, ordered :
" Charlestoune village is called Wooborne." v. Colony Records, vol. ii : 28.
In the division of territory between the parent town and the village, it was provided :
" That Charlestown shall have three thousand acres of land within the boundaries of Woburn, to begin ' at the uttermost corner northerly, next Reading line and so to run southerly along two miles deep on the east side of Shawshine line.' "—(Frothingham's History of Charlestown, p. 111.)
This tract was called, on the Charlestown records, " the land of Nod."   Frothingham, in his history of Charlestown, thinks the name was suggested by the spiritual condition of this distant territory, as compared with that of Charlestown, recalling the wandering of Cain. Gen. iv.   In Woburn, however, the tract was known as Goshen, significant of higher appreciation than the *nomen joculare* of the proprietors.   In 1730, with a westerly portion of Reading, it was incorporated by the General Court, 25th September, as " a township by the name of Wilmington." v. Province Laws, vol. ii : 556.   Here the term " land of Nod, so called," is used to establish the beginning of the town's limits.   In common acceptation, today, the term is confined to the land lying between Lubber's brook and the Andover line.
The original grantees did not regard the 3000 acres as of high value.   Some of them refused it and resigned their titles to Charlestown.   By others it was held, as modern " wild cat" property is, of convenient value for trading.   Francis Willoughby, a principal merchant of Charlestown, and lieutenant governor, thus became possessed of more than a third of it.   His widow married Lawrence Hammond, the town clerk, who conveyed the property to John Hull, the mint master.   Judge Sewall acquired this large portion of the " land of Nod " by his marriage with Hannah, the only child and heiress of Hull.

GEO. A. GORDON.

quality I judged such a slender report which I must upon such Intelligence have made would not have been satisfactory to you. I have therefore thus long delayed to give any acct thereof. The last week I happened to meet with a draught of the whole as delineated by Mr Jonathan Danforth the surveyor: Which I have extracted & endeavoured so far to imitate as to render it intelligable which is contained in this inclosed Paper. I shall for your more plenary satisfaction comment a little upon it. The whole Tract contains 600 Acres which was laid out at three different times and the several parcels are distinguished by the points. The marked Trees are signified by this figure [☉]. The 250 Acres Mr Turner purchased of Mr Edward Cowel. The 150 Acres adjoining was granted him by the Gen[l] Court. The 200 Acres on the south west side of the Plott is part of his proportion to the Right of a 30 Acre Home Lott which Land he hath taken up of the Town.

Unto which 300 Acres more belong which is not laid out. The upland I understand is very good well wooded & bearing both Oakes & Pines in diverse parts of it. There is also as I am informed a considerable quantity of Meadow which lies partly & chiefly on both sides of the Head of Salmon Brook: & partly by Mashapaog pond side. The Farm is distant near four miles from our Meeting House, almost in the midway between Dunstable & Groton.

If you should be the Possessor of this Land & be desirous to build. I can supply you with what Boards you may want from a Saw mill that is but about half a mile from some part of this Farm.

If you desire fuller information in any respect conserning it you may I suppose obtain your desire by consulting Mr Jonathan Tynge who is now at Boston.

But I have already exceeded the Bounds of an Ordinary Epistle & my Pen wearys me in writing. I shall not therefore now enlarge but with humble service tendred to yourself & Mrs Sewall desireing your patience with me & Prayers for me I shall rest subscribing myself your quondam sodalis & friendly Lover.　　　　　　　　　　　　　　Thom[s] Weld.

At the end of the letter Mr. Sewall writes as follows :—

Inclosed the Original of the above copied Letter to Capt Henry Farwell with a Letter of Attorney to him desireing he would strenuously exert himself in asserting & defending my Interest as for himself Carefully return the Letter of Mr Weld. I have inclosed your Plott which lay hid in my till I accidentally lit upon it. Gave his son 3s. 6d. towards bearing his expences.

Boston Feb'y 25th 1725-6　　　　　　　　　　　　　　　　　　S. Sewall.

Rev. Thomas Weld, the writer of the original letter, was a native of Roxbury, grad. H. C. 1671, went to Dunstable 1678-9, and died June 9, 1702. "He was much beloved by his people, esteemed in his day as a man of great piety, supposed to be author of verses in Mather's Magnolia on death of his uncle Rev. Samuel Danforth."*

Judge Sewall died Jan. 1, 1729-30, and his son Samuel makes memo. regarding the land at Dunstable :

Boston Feby 13th 1735-6. Taken out of a long Pocket Book viz. May 23[d] 1685.

* History Dunstable by Fox, 1846.

Dunstable Land. Dr.

Cash paid Marshall Green for Fees . . .	2	0	0
Apprezers & Charges in sending S. Clark . .	2	0	0
To George Monck the overplus	2	5	6

	£6	5	6
Execution being for	66	4	6
And the Land vallued at £72 10 0			

Memorandum out of Hon^d Fathers Almanack viz : Meet the Proprietors of Dunstable at Woburn July 17th 1694

Memorandum Taken out of Hon^d Fathers acct Book Nov^{br} 1st 1733 p̨ me Samuel Sewall

Non Resident Proprietors of Dunstable.

Timothy Clark Esqr	Marg^t Woodmansy
Samuel Sewall Esqr	John Legg
John Vial	William Brown
Widow Monk	Thaddeus Maccarty
John Edwards	Sampson Sheaf
Col Hutcheson Esqr	David Edwards
John Hubbard	Joseph Dowding
Thomas Clark	John Colman
Jonathan Wardwell	Giles Dyer

Dunstable 250 Acres.   Sold to John Sawyer of Lancaster for 200^{lb} one to be paid down, & to give Bond for one Hund^d pounds to pay within 12 months or 2 years at farthest   Sept 29th 1726 S Sewall with Rights & Priviledges if any be

Notea Bene   If the Tract of Land hold out above Three hund^d acres the sd Sawyer is to have the refusal of it be it more or less

Samuel Sewall

Page 174 Acc^t Book
1727–8   To Thom^s Cummins for Mr Nathl Prentice 5s
Nov^{br} 19th To Capt Henry Farwell for Assisting Capt Danforth in surveying Lands at Dunstable 15s   Danforth 2s

An acc^t of what I lay out as to Dunstable Lands

Capt Blanchard at Orange Tree	0	1	0
To Mr. Foxcroft for Coppy		1	6
April To Journey to Dunstable spent with Mr. J. Tyng	1	14	7
July 17th Looking Records			
Mr. Phypps Charlstown	1	1	6
Col Balantine Ditto	0	1	6

	2	0	1
Marked " 1734 Dunstable charges "	£2	0	1

Rev. Elias Nason, in his History of Dunstable, 1877, page 108, says, " In 1772 Nathaniel Balston* of Boston sold 350 acres bounded Easterly by Brattles farm, south by Tyngs farm, north by land formerly owned by Edward Cowell."

---

* The wife of Nathaniel Balston was granddaughter of Judge Sewall, and this land may have been a portion of his estate.

ALPHABETICAL LIST OF PARTNERS IN THE LAND BANK OF 1740.

By ANDREW MCFARLAND DAVIS, S.B., of Cambridge, Mass.

[Concluded from page 197.]

HOOPER.
James, Bridgewater. A, I, N, O, S.
Nathaniel, Bridgewater. A, O, P, S.
HOSMER.
Manassah. A.
HOW, HOWE.
James, Worcester. A, G, N, S.
Moses, Rutland. A, G, N, O, S.
Perley, Dudley. O, R, S.
Samuel, Worcester. O.
Timothy, Marlborough. A, D, N, O, S.
HOWARD.
David, Bridgewater. A, B, O, S.
Ephraim. A, R.
Jonathan. A.
Thomas. A.
HOWELL.
Henry. A, B.
HUNT.
Daniel, Norton. A, J, O, P, S.
Ebenezer. A, B.
Samuel, Weymouth. O, R, S.
Thomas, Weymouth. A, B, O, R, S.
William, Boston or Braintree. A, B, C, O, P, S.
HUNTER.
Samuel. A.
HUTSON.
James. B.

INGERSOLE.
Jonathan. A.
IVES.
Benjamin, Salem. A, E, N, O, R, S.

JACKSON.
James, Leicester. A, G, O, P, S.
Jonathan, Framingham, Framington. A, D, O, P, R, S.
JACOB, JACOBS.
Benjamin, Scituate or Plymouth. I, N, O, R, S.
John, Hingham. A, B, C, N, O, P, S.
JAMES.
Benjamin, Scituate. A, B, I, N, O, S.
JARVIS.
James. A, B.
JEFFERSON, JEPPHERSON, JEPERSON, JEPHERSON.
Thomas, New Sherborn. A, G, M, N, O, R, S.
JENKS.
John, Lynn. A, E, N, O, S.
Nathan, Lynn. A, E, N, O, S.
Samuel, Lynn. A, E, N.

JENNINGS, JINNINGS.
Edward, Boston. O, P, R, S.
JEWELL, JEWILL, JUELL.
John, Stow. A, D, N, O, S.
William, Plymouth Co. I.
JOHNSON.
Benjamin, Leicester. A, G, O, P, R, S.
John, Bridgewater. A, B, N, O, S.
Joseph, Marlborough. A, D, N, O, Q, S.
William, Worcester. G, N, O, S.
JONES.
Cornelius, Sandwich. A.
Elisha, Weston. A, D, O, S.
Elyas. B. (probably same person as preceding entry.)
Ephraim. A, B.
James, Jr., Weston. A, B, R, S.
Nathaniel, Falmouth. A, B, N, O, R, S.
Samuel, Boston. A, B, C, O, P, R, S.
Samuel, Lynn. O, S.
Samuel, Jr., Weston. O.
Thomas. A.
William, Lunenberg. A, B, N, O, S.
JORDAN, JORDEN, JORDIN, JOURDEN, JOURDIN.
Baruck, Braintree. A, O, P, S.
Joseph, Stoughton. A, C, N, O, R, S.
Thomas, Stoughton. A, N, O, R, S.
JOSSELYN, JOSELYN, JOSELINE, JOSLIN, JOSLING, JOSSLYN.
Ebenezer, Abington. A, B, I, O, P, R, S.
Thomas, Hanover. A (twice), B (twice), I, N, O, R, S.
JOY.
Prince. A, B.
JUSTICE.
John, Halifax. A, I, O, P, R, S.

KEITH.
Ephraim, Bridgewater. A, O, S.
George, Mendon. A, G, N, O, S.
Gershom, Uxbridge. A, B, G, N, O, S.
Isaac, Uxbridge. O.
Israel, Uxbridge. A, B, M, R, S.
Job, Mendon. A, B, G, O, P, R, S.
Josiah, Easton. C, J, O, P, R, S.
Simeon or Simon, Mendon. A, B, G, O, P, R, S.
William. A.
KELLY, KELLEY.
Abiel, Methuen. E, O, S.
Abiel, Jr., Methuen. A, R.
Richard, Methuen. A, E, O, S.

KENDELL.
Samuel. A.
KENNEY, KENNY.
Daniel. A, B.
KEYES, KEYS.
Solomon, Brookfield. G, O, S.
KIDDER.
Nathaniel, Cambridge or Charlestown.
A, B, D, O, R, S.
KILBOURNE, KILBORNE, KILBEN.
Samuel, Brimfield. L, O, R, S.
KIMBALL, KIMBAL, KYMBAL, KEM-
BALL.
Abner, Haverhill. B, E, N, O, S.
Ebenezer, Beverly or Haverhill. D,
N, R, S.
Ebenezer, Hopkinton. O, W, S.
John, Wenham. A, N, O, S.
KINDSMAN.
John. A.
KING.
David. A.
John, Kingsfield. A.
John, Norton. A, J, N, O, S.
KINGMAN.
Eben, Beverly. O.
John, Bridgewater. A, B, O, P, R, S.
John, Weymouth. A, N, O, R, S.
Sam. Jr., Bridgewater. A, O, P, R, S.
KINNEY.
Daniel, New Sherborn. G.
KINSLEY.
Harris. A.
KNIGHT, KNIGHTS, NIGHTS.
John, Manchester. E.
Joseph, Manchester. A, B, E, O, S.
KNOWLTON, KNOULTON, NAULTON.
Abraham, Ipswich. A, O, W, R, S.
Ebenezer, Ipswich. A, B, E, N, O, S.
H., Ipswich. N.
John, Manchester. A, B, E, O, S.
Samuel. A, B.
KNOX.
William, Boston. O, R, S.

LANE.
Benjamin, Norton. A, N, O, S.
Ephraim, Norton. A, J, N, O, R, S.
Job, 3d. A, B.
LAWRENCE, LAWRANCE.
Jonathan, Norton. A, J, O.
Thomas. A.
William. A, B.
LAWTON, LAUTON.
Jacob. A.
Thomas, Bristol. J, N, O, S.
LEACH.
David, Bridgewater. I, N, O, R, S.
LEARNED, LARNED.
David, Watertown. A, D, Q, R, S.
Edward, Sherburn. N, O, S.
Isaac, Oxford. G, O, R, S.
LEAVITT, LEAVIT.
Solomon, Pembroke. I, N, S.

LEE, LECE.
Henry, Worcester. A, G, O, R, S.
John, Boston. A, D, O, N, S.
Joseph, Concord. A, D, O, S.
Samuel. A.
William, Boston. A, B, N, O, S.
[The names of four of the Lees will
be found in the alphabetical list of the
Commissioners under Lece.]
LELAND, LALEND, LEALAND, LEE-
LAND, LEYLAND.
Benjamin, Grafton. A, B, G, N, O, S.
James, Grafton. A, B, G, N, S.
Samuel, Grafton. O.
LEONARD.
David, Watertown. O.
Eliphalet, Easton. A, J, N, O, S.
Elkanah, Middleborough. J, N, O.
R, S.
Ephraim. A.
George, Norton. A, N, O, S.
Isaac, Oxford. O.
LEWIS, LEWES.
Isaac, Chelsea. A, N, O, R, S.
LITTLE.
Isaac, Pembroke. A.
John. A.
Otis. P.
LITTLEFIELD.
Nathaniel, Braintree. A, B, C, O, S.
LITTLEHALE.
John, Dracut. A. D, N, O, S.
LOCHMAN.
Leonard. A, B.
LOCK.
Daniel, Woburn. A, B, D, N, O, S.
LONEY.
Anthony. A.
LOOMIS.
Samuel. A.
LORD.
Nathaniel, Berwick. A, O, R, S.
LORING, LORRING.
James, Hull. A, C, N, S.
John, Hull. A, C, N, O, S.
Samuel, Hull. O.
LOVEL.
Solomon, Pembroke. O.
LOVET, LOVETT.
Woodward, Attleborough. A, J, O,
P, S.
LUTWICK, LUTCHWICK, LUTWICH,
LUTWYCH, LUTWYCHE.
Edward, Hopkinton. A, B, D, N, O, S.
LYNES.
Joseph. A.
LYON.
Elkanah, Stoughton or Braintree. A,
B, C, O, P, S.

MAGEE.
Uriah. A.
MAKEPEACE, MAKEPEICE.
Gershom, Brookfield. A, H, O, S.

MALCOM, MALLCOMB.
Michael, Georgetown. ⚓N, W, S.
MAN.
Ebenezer. A.
Insign. A.
Pelatiah, Wrentham. A, C, O, Q, S.
MANNING.
Samuel, Salem. A, E, N, S.
MARBLE.
David, Scituate. O, R, S.
MARION.
Joseph. A.
MARSH, MARSCH.
Benjamin, Sutton. A, B, G, H, N, O, S.
Joseph, New Sherburne. A, M, N, O, R, S.
MARSHALL.
John, Billerica. A, B, D, O, S.
MARVELL.
David. A.
MATHEWS, MATHER.
John, Southborough. A, K, N, O, S.
MAUDSLEY, MAUDLEY.
David. A.
Ebenezer. A.
MAY.
Benjamin. A, B.
Ephraim, Rehoboth. N, O, P, R, S.
Samuel, Stoughton or Weymouth. A, N, O, R, S.
MCCLURE.
Samuel, Newbury. O, R, S.
MCCOMB, MCCOMBS, MCCOOMB, MAC-COME, MACOMB.
John, Brookfield. A, G, N, O, R, S.
MCHARD, MCCHORD, MACKHARD, MCHERD.
James, Haverhill. A, B, E, N, O, S.
MELLETT.
John. A.
Nathaniel. A.
MELVIN.
David, Concord. A, B, D, N, O, S.
Eleazer. A, B.
Robert. A, B.
MERRICK, MERICK.
Ebenezer, Kingsfield. A.
Ezra, Bradford. S.
Timothy, Methuen. E, N.
MERRITT, MERRET.
Ichabod, Leicester. A, G, O, Q, R, S.
MERRY.
George. A.
METCALF.
John, Dedham. J.
MIGHILL, MEGHILL.
Nathaniel, Rowley. A, E, N, O, S.
MILLER.
Francis, Middleborough. A, I, N, O, R, S.
John, Middleborough. N, O, P, S.
Samuel. A.
MILLET, MILLETT.
John, Gloucester. B, E, N, O, S.
Nathaniel. B.

MIRICK, MYRICK, MIRECK, MYRECK.
Ebenezer, Kingsfield. J, O, P, R, S.
Ezra, Bradford. A, B, O, R.
Samuel, Berkley. N, O, R, S.
Timothy, Methuen. A, B, O, R, S.
MOFFAT, MOFFATT, MOFFET, MOO-FET, MUFFATT.
Joseph, Lunenberg. A, G, N, O, R, S,
William, Lunenberg. G.
MONROE, MUNROE, MUNRO.
Thomas, Concord. A, B, D, N, O, R, S.
MOORE, MORE, MOWER, MOOR.
Collins. A.
Daniel, Sudbury. D. N, O, S.
Elias, Sudbury. A, B, N, O, R, S.
James, Worcester. G, N, O, S.
Richard, Lynn. A, E, N, O, R, S.
Uriah, Sudbury. A, B, N, O, S.
William, Sudbury. A, B, D, N, R, S.
MOREY, MORY.
Daniel. A.
George, Norton. J, N, O, S.
John. A.
Thomas, Norton. A, J, O, S.
MORGAN, MORGAIN.
Ralph, Dorchester. C, N, S.
———, Stoughton. N.
Samuel, Manchester. A, B, E, O, R, S.
MORGRIDGE.
Samuel. A.
MOSEY.
George. B. [Morey?]
MORSE, MORSS, MORRSE, MOSS.
Benjamin, Sutton. A. G. N, O, S.
Edmund, Mendon. G, N, O, Q.
Edward, Mendon. A, S.
Samuel, Mendon. A, B, G, O, R, S.
William, Sudbury. O.
MORSE, COWDREY &.
See Cowdrey & Morse.
MUDGE, MUGG.
John, Malden. A, D, N, O, S.
MURREY, MUZZY, MUZZEY.
Joseph, Sudbury. A, B, N, O, S.

NASH.
John, Weymouth. B, C, O, R, S.
NAZRO.
Stephen. B.
NELSON.
James, Boston. S.
Jonathan, Upton, A, B, N, O, S.
Nathaniel, Mendon. A, B, G, N, O, S.
NEWELL, NEWALL, NEWILL.
Eleazer. A.
Ebenezer. A. B.
Josiah, Needham. C, N, O, S.
NEWTON.
Aaron, Eastown. R.
Aaron, Shrewsbury. A, G, N, O, S.
Hibbert, Boston. A, B, C, O, P, R, S.
Isaac, Southborough. A, G, N, O, Q, S.
Uriah, Marlborough. A, D, O, Q, S.

NICHOLLS, NICKELS, NICOLS.
Ebenezer, Reading. A, B, D, N, O, S.
James, Jr.,Reading. A,B,D,N,O,R.S.
John, Reading. N, O, S.
Jonathan, Sutton. A, B, G, N, O, S.
Joshua, Brookfield. R.
Joshua, Leicester. A, G, O, S.
William. A, B.
NORCROSS.
Jeremiah, Lunenburg. A, B, G, N, O.
Q, S.
NORISH.
John, Sen. A.
NORTON.
John. A.
NORTHEY.
David, Salem. N, O, R, S.
NORWOOD.
Francis, Lynn. A, B, E, O, S.
Stephen, Attleborough. A, O, P, S.
NOWELL.
Zachariah. A.
NUTTING.
James. A.
NUZURAN.
Stephen. A. Probably same as Nazro.

ORCUTT, ORCUT, ORCUTE.
Benjamin, Weymouth and Dedham.
A, B. C, N, O, S.
ORDWAY.
Stephen, Newbury. N, O, S.
OSGOOD.
Peter, Salem. A, E, N, O, S.
William, Boston. N, O, R, S.
OTIS.
Job, Scituate. I, N, O, S.
OWEN.
Daniel, Easton. J, N, O, S.
William. A, B.

PACKARD.
Samuel, Bridgewater. A, N, O, R, S.
PAGE.
Christopher, Hardwick. G, O, S.
David, Lunenburg. A, B, G, N, O, Q, S.
PAIN, PAINE, PAYN, PAYNE.
Ebenezer, Woodstock. A, G, O, P, S.
Robert, Boston. O.
Samuel, Braintree. A, B, C, N, O,
P, S.
PARK, PARKS.
Edward, Newton. A, N, R.
Edward, Jr., Newton. B, D, O, R, S.
John, Newton. A, D, N, O, S.
Nathan, Uxbridge. A, B, G, O, P, Q,
R, S.
PARKER.
Henry, Dunstable. O, P, R, S.
Isaac, Groton. A, B, D, N, S.
Jacob, Boston. A, B, C, N, O, R, S.
Jacob, Watertown. A, C, O, P, R, S.
James, Jr. A.
PARKINS.
Solomon. A.

PARKMAN.
Ebenezer. A.
PARMENTER, PARMETER, PARMITTER,
PARMITER.
Amos, Framingham. A, D, N, O, S.
Joseph or John, Sudbury. A, B, D, N,
O, R, S.
PARSONS.
Bartholomew, Newbury. R.
Eleazer, Gloucester. A, B, E, N, O,
R, S.
John, Gloucester. A, E, N, O, R, S.
PATCH.
John, Ipswich. A, N, O, S.
PATTEN, PATTIN.
Thomas, Billerica. N, O, R, S.
Thomas, Jr., Middlesex. A, B, D.
PATTESHALL, PATTERSHALL.
Robert, Boston. C, N, O, S.
PAYSON.
Jonathan, Boston. N, O, S.
Henry. A, B.
PEABODY.
Francis, Middleton. A, E, O, S.
Francis, Jr., Middleton. A, E, O, S.
Nathaniel, Middleton. E, N, O, R, S.
PEAR.
Nathaniel. A.
PEARSON, PEIRSON.
Bartholomew, Newbury. A, B, E, N,
O, S.
Jonathan, Newbury. A, B, E, N, R, S.
PEASLEY, PEASLY, PEASLEE.
Nathaniel, Haverhill. A, E, N, O, S.
Robert, Haverhill. E, N, O, S.
PECK.
William, Middlesex. A, B, D.
PECKER.
John, Haverhill. A, E, N, O, S.
PEEK.
Nathaniel. A.
PEIRCE, PERCE.
Elisha, Scituate. A, B, N, O, S.
Jeremiah. B.
John, Rehoboth. A, J, N, O, R, S.
Thomas, Scituate. A, N, O, S.
PENGELLY.
John, Suffield. A.
PERKINS.
Jacob, Ipswich. A.
John, Bridgewater. O.
John, Ipswich. A, E, N, O, R, S.
Solomon, Bridgewater. O, P, S.
Thomas, Arundel. N, O, S.
Timothy, Bridgewater. A, R, S.
PERRY.
Benjamin Jr., Stoughton. A, C, N,
O, S.
John, Grafton. G.
Josiah, Stoughton. A, C, N, O, R.
Nathaniel, Easton or Stoughton. A,
C, N, O, R.
PHILLIPS.
Thomas. A, B.

PIECKLER.
Benjamin. B.
PILSBURY, PILSBERY.
Amos, Rowley. A, B, E, N, O, S.
PLATTS, PLATIS.
Abel, Lunenberg. A, B, G, N, O, S.
PLUMMER, PLUMER.
David, Gloucester. A, B, N, O, R, S.
Daniel, Rowley. O, S.
POND.
Eliphalet, Dedham. C, N, O, S.
POOL.
Thomas, Dighton. A, I, O, P, S.
POOR.
David, Sudbury. A, B, D, N, O, S.
POPE.
David, Lunenburg. R.
Ralph, Dorchester. C, N (twice), O, S.
Ralph, Stoughton. A, C, N, O, S.
Robert, Boston. A, N, S.
PORTER.
Israel, Salem or Danvers. B, N, O, R, S.
Israel, Jr., Salem. A, E.
John, Salem. N, O, S.
Joseph or Josiah, Salem or Danvers. E, N, O, R, S.
POTTER.
John, Leicester. N, O, R, S.
Nathaniel, Leicester. O, R, S.
PRATT, PRAT.
Phineas, Sudbury. A, B, D, O, R, S.
Phineas, Worcester. M, O, P, R, S.
Samuel, Chelsea. A, C, N, O, S.
Thomas, Chelsea. A, C, N, O, S.
PRENTICE.
Solomon, Grafton, A, B, G, N, O, R, S.
PRESCOTT, PRESCOT, PRESCUT, PRESCUTT.
Charles, Concord. A, B, D, N, O, R, S.
Jonathan, Concord or Littleton. A, B, D, O, P, R, S.
Peter, Boston. A, B, C, D, O, S.
PRESTON, PRESSON, PRESON.
Randall or Randolph, Beverly. A, B, C, N, O, S.
PRICE.
Henry. A, B.
PRIEST.
Jonah or Jonas, Charlestown. A, D, N, O, R, S.
Joseph, Middlesex. A, D.
PROCTOR, PROCTER.
Benjamin, Boston. A, C, N, O, S.
Gershom, Chelmsford. A, B, N, O, S.
John, Salem. N, O, S.
John 3d, Salem. A, E.
Jonathan, Harvard. A, B, G, N, O, S.
Thorndike, Jr., Salem. A, O, S.
PUFFER.
Joseph, Sudbury. A, B, N, O, S.
William, Needham or Wrentham. A, B, D, O, P, S.
William, Jr., Needham or Wrentham. C, L, O, P, S.

PUTNAM.
Elisha, Sutton. A, G, N, O, S.
Henry, Charlestown. A, R.
Henry, Salem. A, E, N, O, S.
Isaac, Sutton. A, G, N, O, R, S.
RANDALL, RANDAL.
Robert, Easton. A, J, O, S.
RAYMOND, RAMOND.
Benjamin, Beverly. A, E, N, O, S.
Daniel, Concord. A, B. D, O, P, R, S.
REA, RAY.
Bartholomew, Salem. E, N, O, R, S.
READ, REED.
Ebenezer, Uxbridge. A, B, G, N, O, R, S.
Isaac. A, B.
John, Uxbridge. A, B, M, N, O, S.
Joseph, Westford. A, D, N, O, S.
Samuel, Lunenberg. A, B, G, N, O, Q, R, S.
Samuel, Uxbridge. A, B, G, N, O, S.
Thomas, Sudbury. A, B (twice), N, O, R, S.
REDWAY, REDAWAY.
James, Rehoboth. N, O, R, S.
RICE, RISE, RIST.
Eliakim, Worcester or Sudbury. A, B, G, N, O, R, S.
Gershom, Worcester. A, N, R.
Gershom, Jr., Worcester. G, B, O, S.
Jotham, Worcester. A, B, G, O, P, S.
Mathew. A.
Mathias, Worcester. B, G, O, S.
Moses, Rutland. A, B, G, O, P, R, S.
Perez, Sutton. A, G, N, O, S.
Peter. B.
Phineas, Stow. A, B, G, N, O, S.
Thomas, Uxbridge. A, G (twice), O, S.
William, Sudbury. A, B, D, N, O, R, S.
RICH.
Thomas, Brookfield. A, G. O, S.
RICHARDS,
John, Dedham. C, N, O, R, S.
Samuel, Dedham. C, N, O, S.
RICHARDSON.
William, Lancaster. A, G, N, O, P, S.
RICKS, RIX.
Joseph, Boston. C, N, O, P, S.
RIDER.
Daniel, Sherburn. D, O, P, R, S.
Samuel, Plymouth Co. I.
ROBINS, ROBBINS.
Eleazer, Harvard. A, G, O, S.
Joseph. A.
Robert, Littleton. A, N, O, R, S.
ROBINSON, ROBERSON, ROBERTSON.
John, Jr., Dorchester. A, B, O, R, S.
Josiah, Leicester. A (twice), B, M, O, R, S.
Samuel, Hardwick. A, G, N, O, S.
William, Newton. A, D, N (twice), O, R, S.

ROGERS.
Samuel, Ipswich. A.
RUDDOCK.
John, Boston. A, C, N, O, R, S.
RUGGLES, RUGGELS, RUGGLS.
Edward, Roxbury. A, B, D, N, O, S.
Capt. Joseph, Roxbury. A, C, N, O, S.
Samuel. A.
RUSSELL.
Joseph, Charlestown. A, D, N, O, S.

SABIN, SABINE.
David, Hardwick. A, B, G, O, S.
SALTER.
Thomas, Boston. A, B, C, N, O, R, S.
SAMPSON, SAMSON.
Isaac, Middleton or Middleborough.
    A, I, O, R, S.
SANDERS, SAUNDERS.
Philip, Salem. N, O, S.
SAWYER.
John, Harvard or Nichaway (Nashua)
    or Lancaster. N, O, P, S.
Jonathan, Harvard. A, M, N, R.
SAYWARD, SAYARD.
Joseph. A. B.
SCOTT, SCOT.
Samuel, Oxford. A, G, O, R, S.
Samuel, Wrentham. A, N, O, R, S.
SEAVER, SEAVOR, SEVER,
John, Brookline. A, B, N, O, S.
Nathaniel, Brookline. A, B, N, O, S.
Robert, Framingham. A, B, D, N, O,
    P, S.
SEAVERY, SEVERY.
Joseph, Sutton. A, N, O, S.
SELEW, SILEW.
Philip, Harwich. A (twice), B, F, O,
    S.
SERGEANT, SARGENT, SERJENT.
John, Gloucester. A, O, S.
SEYCOMB.
John. A, B.
SHATTUCK, SHATUCK.
Benjamin, Jr. A.
Stephen. A.
SHAW.
Ichabod, Norton. A, B, J, O, P, R, S.
James, Plimpton. A, O, P, R, S.
John, Harvard. O.
Jonathan, Plimpton. O, P. R. S.
Joseph, Leicester. A, N, O, R, S.
SHEAFE.
Jacob, Boston. A, B, C, O, S.
SHELDEN.
Jonathan. A (twice).
SHEPPERD, SHEPPARD, SHEPARD.
John, Stoughton. C, J, O, P, R, S.
Thomas, Stoughton. A, C, N, O, S.
SHERMAN.
Daniel, Brimfield. A.
George, Boston. O.
SHILLEBAR, SHELEBAR.
William. A.

SHOVE.
Edward, Dighton. O, P, R, S.
SIMMONS, SYMONS, SIMONS, SYM-
    MONS.
Constant, Dighton. A, O, R, S.
SKINNER.
George, Boston. A, B, C, N, S.
SMITH.
Ebenezer, Suffield or Woodstock. A,
    N, O, P, R, S.
Ebenezer, Woodstock. A, G, O, P. S.
Elkanah. A.
Israel, Weymouth or Dedham. C, N,
    O, S.
John, Hingham. A (twice), C, N, O,
    R, S.
Nathaniel, Rehoboth. A, J, N, O
    (twice), P, S.
Samuel, Eastham. A, F, N, R, S.
Samuel, Suffield. A.
Solomon, Attleborough. A, J, O, P, S.
Stephen, Dighton. J, N, O, S.
SNELL.
Amos, Jr., Bridgewater. A, N, O, R,
    S,
Daniel or David, Bridgewater. A, O,
    R, S.
SNOW, SNOE.
Ebenezer, Bridgewater. A, N, R, S.
James, Bridgewater. A, R, S.
Jonathan, Nottingham. A, O, P, R, S.
Samuel, Bridgewater. O.
Tobin, Bridgewater. O.
SOAPER, SOPER, SOOPER.
Samuel, Bridgewater. O, P, R, S.
SOUTHWORTH.
John. A.
SPAFFORD.
John, Rowley. E, O, S.
SPOONER.
Daniel, Dartmouth. J, N, O, S.
SPRAGUE, SPRAIG, SPRAGE.
Ezeh. ? A.
Timothy, Malden. A (twice), D, N,
    O, R, S.
SPRING.
John. A, B.
SPURR, SPUR.
Thomas, Stoughton. A, C, N, R, S.
STACKPOLE.
John, Biddeford. O, P, R, S.
STANWOOD, STANNERD.
David, Gloucester. A, O, S.
James, Gloucester. A, E, N, O, R, S.
STEAD, SLEAD.
Edward, Swanzey. O, S.
STEARNS, STERNS, STERNES.
Ebenezer. A.
John, Worcester. A, B, G, S.
Josiah, Watertown. A, D, N, O, S.
Samuel, Littleton. A, N, O, S.
Thomas, Worcester. A (twice), B.
STEARRY.
John, Worcester. O.

STEBBINS, STEBINS.
Thomas, Brimfield. A, J, N, O, S.
STEPHENS, STEVENS.
Israel, Grafton. A. G, N, O, S.
John, Townsend. A, B, D, N, O, S.
Nicholas. A.
Phinehas, Rutland. A, G, O, S.
Roger, Brookfield. N, O, R, S.
Samuel, Roxbury. A, B, C, O, P, R, S.
Timothy, Boston. N, O, P, R, S.
STETSON, STUTSON.
Amos, Braintree. A, C, O, S.
James. A.
Joseph, Jr., Pembroke. I, O, P, R, S.
Nehemiah, Pembroke. I, O. R, S.
STEWARD.
Joseph. A.
STOCKBRIDGE.
Benjamin, Scituate. A, B, I, N, O, S.
Joseph. A, B.
STOCKWELL, STUCKWELL.
David, Sutton. A, G, O, P, S.
John, Sutton. A, G, N, O. S.
STODDARD.
William, Boston. A, B, N, O, S.
STONE.
Daniel. A, B.
David, Beverly or Tewksbury. A, B,
   E, N, O, S.
James, Framingham. A, B, D, O, S.
Jonathan. A.
Robert, Salem. A, E, N, O, S.
Simon or Simeon, Harvard. A, B, G.
   N, O, S.
Thomas, Framingham. A, D, O, S.
Uriah,|Leicester or Oxford.A,G,N,O,S.
William, Norton. A (twice), B, J, N,
STORY.   [O,R,S.
William. A.
STOUGHTON.
Jonathan. A.
STOWELL.
John, Watertown. A, D, N, O, R, S.
STOWERS.
John, Malden. A.
Samuel, Malden. A,
SUMNER.
Benjamin, Milton. A, N, O, S.
Josiah, Milton. A, C, N, O, S.
SWIFT.
Giles. A.
Josiah, Sandwich. A, F, N, O, R, S.
Josiah, Wareham. F, N, O, P, S.
Thomas, Plymouth. A, F, N, O, S.

TAFT.
Benjamin, Uxbridge. A (twice), B,
   G, N, O (twice), S.
Israel. A, B.
John, Uxbridge, A, G, N, S.
Jonathan, Charlestown. O.
Josiah, Uxbridge. A, B, N, O. S,
Mijamin, Uxbridge. A, B, G, R, S.
Robert, Mendon. G, N, O, S.
Samuel, Uxbridge. A,B,G,O(twice),S.
Stephen, Uxbridge. A, B, O.

TALBOT, TALBOTT, TALBUTT, TAL-
   BUT.
Benjamin, Dighton. A, J, N, O, P, R,
   S.
Josiah, Dighton. A (twice), J, N, O,
   S.
Samuel, Dighton. A (twice), N, O, P,
   S.
TAYLOR.
Abraham, Jr., Dunstable. A, B, D,
   O, R, S.
Daniel, Townshend. A, B, D, N, O, S.
Eldred. A.
Ephraim. A, B.
Jacob, Westford or Westfield. A, N,
   O, S.
Jonathan, Littleton. A, N (twice),
   O, S.
William. A.
TERRELL, TEREL, TERREL, TIRRELL.
William, Abington. A, B, N, O, R, S.
TERRY.
John, Grafton or Sutton. N, O, S.
Josiah. A.
THACHER.
Peter, Middleton or Middleborough.
   A, I, N, R, S.
Samuel. A.
THAYER, THARE.
Benjamin, Mendon. A (twice), G, N,
   O, R, S.
Daniel, Braintree. A, B, C, O, P, S.
David, Mendon. A, R.
David, Jr., Mendon. A, B, N, O, R, S.
John, Mendon. A, B, G, N, O, S.
Jonathan, Bellingham. A, B, C, N,
   O, S.
Richard, Bridgewater. B, R, S.
Uriah, Mendon. B, G, N, O, S.
THOMAS.
John, Barrington. N, O, S.
THOMSON.
Joshua, Jr. A.
THORNTON.
Joshua, Boston. A, B, C, D, N, O, P,
   R, S.
TILDEN.
David, Stoughton. A, B, C, N, O, S.
Jonathan, Boston. A, I, N, O, S.
TILTON.
Daniel. A.
TISDALE.
Barnabus, Freetown. O, P, R, S.
TOOY.
John. A.
Josiah. B.
TORREY.
William. A.
TOWN, TOWNS.
Richard, Topsfield. A, E, N, O, S.
TOWNSEND, TOUNSHEND.
David, Lynn. A, B, E, N, O, S.
TOWSLEY, TOUSLEY.
Micah, Brimfield. A, L, N, O, S.

TRESCOTT.
John. A.
TROW.
William, Beverly. E, N, O, S.
TRUMBULL.
John, Wenham. E.
TUCKER.
Ephraim, Milton. A, C, N, O, R, S.
TUFTS.
Jonathan, Charlestown. N, R, S.
TURNER.
Abner, Hanover. A, I, O, P, S.
Ezekiel, Hanover or Plymouth. A, N, O, R, S.
John, Scituate. I, O, P, R, S.
John, Jr. A, R.
Seth, Scituate. A, B, I, N, S.
TUTTLE.
Edward, Chelsea. A, C, N, O, S.
Elisha, Chelsea. A.
Samuel. A. B.
TYLER.
Joseph. A.
Nathaniel. A, B.

UNDERWOOD.
Joseph. A.
UPHAM.
Ebenezer, Malden. A, B, D, N, O, S.
Jabez, Brookfield. A, N, O, S.
James. A.
Phinehas, Malden. A, B, D, N, O, S.

VINAL, VINALL, VINELL, VINEL.
Elijah, Boston. A, B, N, O, P, S.
Israel. A, B.
John. A, B.
VINCENT.
Samuel. A, B.
VOSE, VOCE.
David. A, B.
Elisha, Milton. A, N, O, S.
Nathaniel, Milton. A, N, R, S.

WADE.
Timothy. A.
WAIT, WAYT, WAITE.
John. A.
Jonathan, Lynn. A, E, N, O, R, S.
Joseph. A.
Nathaniel, Leicester. M, N, O, S.
William. A.
WALCUT, WALKUTT, WALCOT, WAL-
COTT, WOOLCUT, WOOLCOT.
Benjamin, Boston. A, C, N, O, P, S.
Ebenezer, Andover. E, N, O, S.
Nathaniel, Brookfield. O, S.
WALES, WHALES.
Elkanah, Braintree. A, B, O, R, S.
WALKER.
Seth. A, B.
WALLIS.
William, Lunenberg. A, B, G, N, O, P, R, S.

WARD.
Abraham, Sudbury. R.
Daniel, Marlborough. A, D, N, O, R, S.
Daniel, Worcester. A, G, Q, N, O, R, S.
Jabez, Marlborough. A, D, O, Q, S.
William. A.
WARE, WEARE.
William, Norton. A (twice), B, J, N, O, S.
WARNER.
Joshua. A, B.
WARREN.
John, Marlborough. A, D, N, O, Q, S.
WATSON, WETSON, WATTSON, WHAT-
SON.
James, Leicester. A.
Isaac, Cambridge. A, B, D, O, R, S.
Oliver, Leicester. G, N, O, S.
Patrick. A.
William, Leicester. A, G, N, O, S.
WATTS.
Daniel, Chelsea. A, C, N, O, S.
Samuel, Chelsea. A, N, O, S.
WEBB.
Joseph, Boston. A, C, N, O, S.
Nathan, Uxbridge. A, B, G, N, O, S.
WEBSTER.
Israel, Salisbury. A, E, O, R, S.
Stephen, Salisbury. A, E, O, Q, S.
WELD, WEILD.
Joseph, Roxbury. A, B, C, O, R, S.
Thomas, Upton. A, B, N, O, R, S.
WELLOCK.
Daniel. A.
WELLS.
Moses. A.
Nathaniel. A.
Thomas (see Weld.)
WESBROOCK.
John. B.
WESSON.
John. A, B.
WEST.
Samuel, Salem. N, O, S.
WETHERBEE, WITHERBEE, WITHER-
BY, WYTHERBY, WETHERBY, WE-
THERBE, WHETHERBEE, WETHERS-
BY.
Daniel, Stow. A, D, N, O, S.
Ephraim, Lunenberg or Taunton. A, B, G, N, O, R, S.
John, Harvard. A, G, N, O, S.
Josiah, Stow. A, D, N, O, S.
WETHERELL, WITHERELL, WEATHER-
ELL, WITHREL, WITHERALL, WHI-
THERALL.
Jeremiah, Taunton. J, O, R, S.
John, Eastham. A, F, O, P, R, S.
WETHRIDGE.
Livermore. A.
WHEATON, WHEATEN.
Caleb, Needham. A, B, C, N, O, P, S.

WHEELER, WEELER.
Abijah. A, B.
Benjamin. A.
Philip, Rehoboth. A, J, N, O, P, S.
Thomas. B.
Timothy, Concord. A, B, D, N, O, Q, S.
William, Boston. C, R.
William, Jr., Boston. A, O, S.
WHEELOCK, WILLOCK.
Daniel or David, Uxbridge. A, B, G, N, O, S.
WHETELS.
Thomas. A.
WHIPPLE, WIPPLE.
Jacob, Grafton. A, B, G, N (twice), O, R, S.
John, Jr., Ipswich. A, E, N, O, R, S.
Joseph, Grafton. A, B, G, N, O, R, S.
Joseph, Jr., Ipswich. A, B, O.
WHITAKER.
Richard, Rehoboth. J, P, R, S.
WHITCOMB, WITCOMB, WHETCOME, WHITCOMBE, WHITTCOMB.
Benjamin, Leominster. A, B, G, O, Q, S.
James, Rochester or Weston. I, N, O, R, S.
Jonathan, Bolton. A (twice), N, O, R, S.
Joseph, Lancaster. A, G, N, O, Q, S.
Hezekiah, Lancaster. G, O, S.
WHITE,
Aaron, Uxbridge or Mendon. A, M, O, R, S.
Benjamin, Middleborough or Middleton. A (twice), O, P, R, S.
James, Wenham. O.
John, Gloucester. A, E, O, R, S.
John, Uxbridge. A, G, N, S.
John, Wenham. A, E, O, R, S.
Joseph, Sutton. A, N, Q.
Joseph, Uxbridge. G, O, S.
Josiah, Sutton. A, B, M, N (twice), O, S.
Josiah, Wenham. A, E, R, S.
Mark, Acton. A, B, D, N, O, S.
Philip. A.
Thomas, Uxbridge. A, G, O, S.
William, Mendon. G, O, S.
WHITNEY, WHITTNEY, WITNEY.
Jonathan, Lunenberg. A (twice), B (twice), G, N, O, S.
WHITRIDGE, WHITTERIDGE, WHITTEREDGE,
Livermore, Beverly. B, E, N, O, S.
WHITTEMORE, WITTIMORE.
John, Leicester. A, G, N, O, S.
Pelatiah, Malden. N, O, S.
Samuel. A, B.
WHITTIER.
Richard, Rehoboth. O.
WILDE, WILD.
Jonathan, Braintree. A, B, C, N, O, S.

WILDER.
Thomas, Jr. A, B.
WILEY, WILLEY.
Benjamin, Lynn. A, E, N, O, R, S.
Benjamin, Jr., Lynn. E,
WILKINS.
Acquilla, Middleton. E, O, S.
David, Middleton. E, O, R, S.
Isaac, Middleton. A (twice), E, N, O, S.
WILLIAMS.
Benjamin, Easton. A, J, N, O, R, S.
Isaac. A. [entered Williams or Wilson.]
John. A, B.
Joseph. A.
Nathaniel, Roxbury. A, C, O, S.
Obadiah, Boston. A, N, O, R, S.
Seth. B.
WILLIS.
Joshua, Bridgewater. A, N, O, S.
Samuel. A.
WILSON.
Isaac. (See Williams.)
James, Leicester or Stockbridge. A, H, N, R, S.
Joseph, Malden. A, D, N, O, S.
Sam ? Leicester. O.
Samuel, Woodstock. G, O, P, R, S.
WINSLOW.
Edward, Jr. A.
John. A.
Samuel, Rochester. A, I, N, O, S.
WISE.
Ami R., Ipswich. E, O, S.
Daniel, Ipswich. E, O, S.
WITCHER.
Richard. A.
WITHINGTON, WITHINTON.
Ebenezer, Dorchester. A, B, C, N (twice), O, S.
WOOD, WOODS.
Abraham, Sudbury. A, B, N, O, R, S.
Abram, Jr., Middlesex. D.
Ezekiel, Uxbridge. A, B, G, O, S.
James, Uxbridge. A, G, N, O, S.
John, Concord. A, D, O, S.
Joseph. A, B.
Josiah. A.
Obadiah, Uxbridge. A, N, O, S.
Solomon, Uxbridge. A (twice), B, G, N, R, S.
Solomon, Jr., Uxbridge. A, B, G, O, P, R, S.
WOODBURY, WOODBERY, WOODBERRY.
Benjamin, Sutton. A, G, N, O, S.
Humphrey, Gloucester. A, E, N, O, S.
WOODCOCK.
Jeremiah, Needham. A, B, C, N, O, R, S.
Michael, Needham. A, N, O, R, S.
Nathaniel, Attleborough. A, J, O, P, S.

WOODWARD, WOODARD.
Abraham, Brookline. A, B, C, N, O, S.
Benjamin, Scituate. O, S.
Ezekiel, Gloucester. N, O, R, S.
Ezekiel, Jun. Gloucester. A, N, S.
John, Sudbury. A (twice), D, O, P, R, S.
WOODWORTH.
Benjamin, Scituate. N. (Probably same as Woodward, Benjamin.)
WOOLEY, WOOLLEY, WOLEY.
Jonathan, Bradford or Bedford. A, B, O, R, S.
Thomas, Bedford. A, B, N, O, R, S.

WOSTER, WORSTER, WOOSTER.
Francis, Sandwich. A, F, N, O, R, S.
WRIGHT, RIGHT.
James, Rutland. A, B, G, R, S.
Samuel, Rutland. O.
Thomas. A, B.
William. A.
WYMAN.
Samuel. A, B.
YORK.
Thomas, Gloucester. A, E, N, O, S.
YOUNG.
William. A, B.

BAPTISMS IN THE SECOND CHURCH OF CHRIST IN PEMBROKE, MASS., FROM 1748 TO 1803.

Communicated by MRS. ELROY M. AVERY of Cleveland, Ohio.

[Concluded from page 183.]

1791.

February	27, 1791.	Nathaniel, son of Henry Perry, Jun'r.
March	5,	Clarissa, daughter of John Ramsdell.
"	31,	Josiah Cushing, son of Isaac Thomas.
April	17,	Debby Allen, daughter of Richard Lowden, Jun'r.
May	7,	Benjamin, son of Thomas Stetson.
"	23,	William, son of Gersham Ramsdell.
"	22,	Chloe, daughter of Reuben Harding, administered on account of his wife.
"	29,	Gideon Thomas, son of Elijah Damon, Jun'r.
June	5,	Sarah, daughter of Snow Baker.
"	5,	Fanny, daughter of Reuben Clark.
"	5,	Rachel, daughter of Ebenezer Bonney.
"	5,	Dianna, daughter of Lot Phillips.
July	10,	Joseph, son of Capt. Joseph Smith.
"	15,	Sarah Lindsey, daughter of Nathaniel Hill.
"	15,	Christiana, daughter of Isaac Josselyn.
"	17,	Richard, son of Benjamin Beuker, administered on account of his wife.
August	14,	Ezra, son of Noah Bonney.
September	5,	Warren, son of Abel Bourn.
"	5,	Gad, son of Alexander Soper, Jun'r.
October	2,	Calvin, son of Nathaniel Thomas.
"	30,	Ebenezer Standish, son of Isaac Thomas, Jun'r.
"	30,	Roland, son of Ezekial Bonney.

1792.

March	11, 1792.	Mehetabel, daughter of Nathaniel Cushing.
"	25,	Sagey, daughter of Doct. Gad Hitchcock.

May	13, 1792.	Lurania, daughter of Ichabod Howland.
June	3,	Jemima Lindsey, daughter of Francis Josselyn.
"	10,	Priscilla, daughter of Isaac Josselyn.
"	17,	Sally, daughter of Isaah Keen, administered on account of his wife.
"	17,	Charles William, son of Charles William Soul.
July	1,	Betty, daughter of Charles Ramsdell.
"	15,	Elijah, son of Samuel Ramsdell, Jun'r.
"	15,	Isaac, son of Isaac Beals.
"	29,	Lyman, son of Eleazer Josselyn.
August	5,	Jotham, son of Joshua Pratt, Jun'r.
"	26,	Earl, son of Joseph Josselyn, Jun'r.
"	26,	Betty, daughter of John Beals.
"	26,	Nabby, daughter of Nathan Sprague.
October	2,	Nancey, daughter of Snow Baker.
September	8,	Nabby, daughter of Samuel Holmes, administered on account of his wife.

1793.

March	7, 1793.	Bethiah Barker, daughter of Barnabas Perry.
May	4,	Zavan, infant Christopher Phillips.
"	26,	Lettuce, daughter of Samuel Hill, Jun'r.
June	9,	William Peaks, son of Elijah Damon, Jun'r.
July	7,	Elizabeth Paris, daughter of Ebenezer Bonney.
"	7,	Joe, daughter of Reuben Harding.
"		Lucy, daughter of Zadoc Reed.
"	25,	Roxanna, daughter of Ezekial Bonney.
"		Isaac, son of Seth Cocks.
August	11,	Bethiah, daughter of James Bourn, Jun'r.
"	18,	Orphey, daughter of Gamaliel Bisbee.
September	15,	Elizabeth, daughter of Bowen Baker.
"	22,	Martin, son of John Ramsdell.
"	29,	Joshua, son of Capt. Joseph Smith.
October	27,	Isaac Smith, son of Isaac Thomas, Jun'r.
November	24,	Chrissey Wadsworth, daughter of Lot Phillips.

1794.

March	23, 1794.	Nathaniel, son of Nathaniel Cushing.
"	23,	Judith, daughter of Jeremiah Stetson, Jun'r.
"	23,	Harriott, daughter of George William Munroe.
"	30,	Luther, son of Nathaniel Thomas.
April	20,	Lydia West, daughter of Barnabas Holmes, administered on account of his wife.
May	4,	Sophia, daughter of Isaac Josselyn.
June	1,	Turner, son of Nathaniel Clarke and Sally, daughter of Nathaniel Clark.
"	1,	Mary, daughter of Francis Josselyn.
"	8,	Judah, son of Noah Bonney,
"	15,	Alexander, son of Alexander Soper, Jun'r.
"	15,	Avice, daughter of Abel Bourn.
"	22,	Lydia, wife of Gersham Ramsdell.

June	22, 1794.	Edna, daughter of Isaih Keen, administered on account of his wife.
"	29,	Mary, daughter of Gersham Ramsdell.
July	5,	Katey, daughter of Henry Perry, Jun'r.
September	14,	Charles, son of Doct. Gad Hitchcock.
October	12,	Cushing, son of Snow Baker.
"	12,	Nathan, son of Eleazer Josselyn.
November	16,	Nahum, son of Richard Lowden, Jun'r.
"	30,	Polly Turner, daughter of Bowen Barker.
December	28,	Betsey, daughter of Nathan Dwelling (Dwelley?).

1795.

March	29, 1795.	Debby Hatch, daughter of Joseph Josselyn.
May	10,	Luther, son of Isaac Beals.
"	17,	Seneca, son of Samuel Briggs, administered on account of his wife.
June	14,	Betty, daughter of Elijah Damon, Jun'r.
"	14,	Zavon, son of Christopher Phillips.
"	28,	Mercy, daughter of Henry Munroe.
"	28,	Ebenezer, son of Ebenezer Bonney.
"		Richard, son of Nathaniel Hill.
July	5,	Sally, daughter of Isaac Soper.
August	30,	Charles, son of Nathan Sprague.
September	6,	Briggs, son of Leonard Hill.
October	4,	Avenic Standish, daughter of Isaac Thomas, Jr.
"	25,	David, son of Samuel Ramsdell, Jun'r.
"	25,	Joshua, son of Gersham Ramsdell.
November	15,	Thomas, son of Capt. Joseph Smith.
December	6,	Rhoda, daughter of John Perry.

1796.

January	17, 1796.	Roland, son of Ezekial Bonney.
March	27,	Lucy, daughter of Nathaniel Cushing.
April	17,	Polly, daughter of Zadoc Reed.
May	22,	Isaac Bourn, son of Isaac Josselyn.
June	19,	Sibyll Angier, daughter of Dr. Gad Hitchcock.
July	3,	Betty, daughter of Alexander Soper, Jr.
"	3,	Reuben, son of Reuben Harding, administered on account of his wife.
August	7,	Isaac, son of Isaac Soper.
"	14,	Bethiah, daughter of Eleazer Josselyn.
"	28,	Nabby Colemore, an adult. [wife.
September	11,	Thirsa, daughter of Isaiah Keen, on account of his
"	18,	Hannah Josselyn, daughter of George William Monroe.
October	16,	Polly, daughter of Nathan Sprague.
"	30,	Ruth, daughter of Isaac Bowen Barker.
"	30,	Lucy, daughter of Oliver Whitten.
November	6,	Sarah, daughter of Gersham Ramsdell.
"	13,	Deborah, daughter of Abel Bourn.
"	13,	Roland, son of Nathaniel Hill.
December	15,	Eli, son of Thomas Stetson.

1797.

February	12, 1797.	Benjamin, son of Isaac Beals.
"	19,	Polly, daughter of John Beals.
April	23,	Lurania, daughter of Nathaniel Jones.
May	7,	Nabby Barker, daughter of Henry Perry, Jun'r.
"	7,	John, son of Jeremiah Stetson, Jun'r.
"	7,	Nathan, son of Nathan Dwelley.
June	4,	Thomas, son of Samuel Hill, Jun'r.
"		Blaney, son of Lot Phillips.
"	18,	Lucy, daughter of Bennet Munroe.
"	25,	Lucia, daughter of Noah Bonney.
July	23,	Betsey, daughter of Simeon Jones.
August	27,	John, son of John Perrey.
September	3,	Elizabeth Paris, daughter of Ebenezer Bonney.
"	3,	Elijah, son of Elijah Damon.
"	5,	The Widow Honor Prat, an aged person.
"	17,	Stetson, son of Gamaliel Bisbee.
November	12,	Charles, son of Charles Cushing.

1798.

January	21, 1798.	Deborah Thomas, daughter of John Briggs, now resident at Salem.
March	18,	Priscilla, daughter of Eleazer Josselyn.
April	1,	Ezekial, son of Ezekial Bonney.
"	5,	Thankful, daughter of Captain Joseph Smith.
"	12,	Emala, daughter of Elisha Josselyn.
May	20,	Branch, son of Joseph Josselyn.
June	10,	Osen, son of Charles Josselyn, Jun'r.
"	10,	Sarah Hill, daughter of Frank Josselyn.
"	23,	Isaac, son of Samuel Briggs, baptised on account of his wife.
September	9,	Luther, son of Gersham Ramsdell.
"	16,	Maria, daughter of Isaac Bowen Barker.
"	23,	Nathaniel, son of Nathaniel Cushing.
October	28,	Deborah, daughter of Nathaniel Thomas.
"	28,	Priscilla Bourn, daughter of Isaiah Keen, administered on account of his wife.
"	28,	Charles, son of Isaac Thomas 2d.
November	11,	Heman, son of Isaac Soper.
"	25,	Lucy, daughter of Lemuel Bonney, Jun'r.

1799.

May	17, 1799.	Lydia, daughter of Snow Baker.
"	17,	Eunice Buck, daughter of Nathan Sprague.
"	17,	Eleanor, daughter of Isaac Josselyn.
June	9,	Luther, son of Zadoc Reed.
July	23,	Abel, son of Abel Bourn.
"	23,	Perez, son of Isaac Beal.
October	6,	Mary Sheldon, daughter of Dr. Gad Hitchcock.
"	6,	Lewis, son of John Perry.
"	6,	George, son of Nathaniel Cushing.

October	6, 1799.	Dolly, daughter of Nathaniel Jones.
"	6,	Nathaniel, son of Elijah Damon, Jun'r.
"	6,	Hannah, daughter of Samuel Hill.
"	6,	Lucy, daughter of Alverson Ramsdell.
November	17,	Lydia, daughter of Enos Cocks.
"		Samuel Williams, son of Samuel Josselyn.

1800.

April	13, 1800.	Bennet, son of Bennet Monroe.
June	8,	Bowen, son of Isaac Bowen Barker.
"	8,	Rufus, son of Gersham Ramsdell.
"	8,	Joseph, son of Joseph Monroe.
"	8,	Mary, daughter of Jacob Bearse, Jun'r.
"	8,	Charles Josselyn, son of William Monroe.
"	8,	Thirza Hatch, daughter of Seth Beal.
"	8,	Samuel, son of Samuel Briggs.

Here the record stops abruptly, but his son Dr. Gad Hitchcock records: "My honored father died Aug. 8, 1803, after an indisposition and confinement of four years."

THOMAS JEFFERSON AND JAMES THOMSON CALLENDER.

Contributed by WORTHINGTON CHAUNCEY FORD, Esq., of Washington, D. C.

OF all the foreigners who were connected with journalism in the United States at the beginning of the century, James Thomson Callender was easily first in the worst qualities of mind and character. It cannot be said that the ideals of journalism were high in those days, and the intensity of party struggle made the lowest instruments acceptable. Personalities were freely exchanged, and the character of no man was safe from the assaults of anonymous scribblers, who as easily changed their allegiance as their coat, and gained a precarious support from sensational paragraphs containing the least amount of truth expressed in the most outrageous language. Neither the journalist nor his half-brother, the pamphleteer of the day, was choice in his object or manner of attack. One of the ablest, Cobbett, wrote in the *Political Censor* for September, 1796 : "That lump of walking tallow, streaked with lamp-black, that calls itself Samuel F. Bradford, has the impudence to say that my wardrobe consisted of my old regimentals." This is only a sample.

The biographical details of Callender are very few. He was born in 1758, and wrote in Scotland in such a way that he was obliged to leave the country to avoid a prosecution for a political pamphlet. He was in Edinburgh in January, 1793, but must have come to the United States soon after. He became connected with the Philadelphia press, reporting the proceedings of Congress for the *Philadelphia Gazette.* In his third session, he said, circumstances "which I could neither foresee nor prevent made my situation there extremely unenviable." These circumstances are probably those retailed in his "History" for 1796.

"A person had, for almost two preceding sessions, attended the house to take minutes of its proceedings for the *Philadelphia Gazette.* In this wilderness of scribbling, many particulars transpired, which members were ashamed to confess and afraid to deny. Four gentlemen were especially irritated, viz. Theodore Sedgwick, Dr. William Smith, Samuel Dexter, and Robert Goodloe Harper. Messrs. Dexter and Sedgwick were not able to forgive the figure that they had made in the nobility debates, as well as on some other occasions. Harper had disputed with Col. James White, delegate from Tennessee, on the defence of the South-Western frontier; and the particulars, which were not to his advantage, had been related with unfailing accuracy. But Dr. Smith was by far more rancorous than the other gentlemen collectively. During the debate on Madison's resolutions, Mr. Abraham Clarke of New Jersey said, turning round to his right hand, and *looking at Mr. William Smith,* that a stranger in the gallery might suppose there was a British agent in the house. The name of *British agent* became general. Mr. Smith was burnt in effigy at Charleston. On the rising of the session he found it convenient to shun a meeting with his constituents by a tour for the ensuing summer into the Eastern States. The blame of this whole scandal was imputed to the pen of the guilty taker of minutes for the *Philadelphia Gazette.* Influence was employed, but in vain, to procure his dismission. This occurred in January, 1794.*

In March, 1795, the complaints against the *Gazette* reports were renewed, and a resolution was adopted for appointing a committee to examine a stenographer. In January, 1796, Andrew Robertson, a Scotsman, from Petersburg, was favored; but payment for his services, at four thousand dollars a year, was to be divided between Congress, who contributed $2900, and Andrew Brown, publisher of the *Gazette,* on condition that the debates were to be printed first in his paper. Such an arrangement was not acceptable to the House, and in February the committee was released from further consideration of the question. It was without doubt about this time that Callender ceased to report the debates, for in May he appeals to Madison for the position of a schoolmaster, and mentions an unprofitable connection in Baltimore, where he then was.†

* "History of the United States for 1796," p. 279. There must have been some strong provocation on Callender's part, as William B. Giles, who generally acted with the extreme republicans, was one of those who spoke in favor of his dismissal, an act not forgotten by the intended victim.

† At some time he was engaged by Mathew Carey to prepare additions to Guthrie's Geography, for which he was paid two dollars a printed page. "a rate of payment for literary composition not usual in America." The connection ended, as was usual, in a difference.

"About two hundred pages of the American edition of Guthrie's Geographical Grammar were written by me; besides the correction of some thousands of errors in Guthrie's original text. In July, 1798, when I left Philadelphia, I parted with Mr. Carey in terms of con-

He then turned up in Philadelphia in 1797, engaged in printing his History of 1796, and receiving financial assistance from Thomas Leiper and Alexander J. Dallas, and calling upon Jefferson to advance some pecuniary assistance which had been promised. At this time the History of 1796 had so far advanced as to have published the charges of dishonesty against Hamilton, and to have called out a reply entitled "Certain Observations," in which Hamilton proved his honesty at the expense of his private morality.

In a letter to Jefferson, Callender gloats over this episode : "If you have not seen it, no anticipation can equal the infamy of this piece. It is worth all that fifty of the best pens in America could have said against him" (28 Septem. 1797) ; and Jefferson seems to have given the aid to this wretched scribbler.* Madison was also involved, not only as a subscriber to his libels, but more directly as willing to supply material for his productions.†

It must be admitted that his first formal publication—"The American Annual Register ; or, Historical Memoirs of the United States, for the year 1796," is a sorry piece of work. From his reports of the proceedings of Congress he hastily patched a few chapters together, with much desultory writing on Edmund Randolph, John Adams and Hamilton, the state of the press in America, a defence of Jefferson, and many other topics at home and abroad. It never rises above mediocrity, and the form is such as to make the reading a painful effort and an unprofitable expenditure of time. He has not yet acquired the knowledge which could give compact and consecutive narration, nor is he so devoted a partisan as to see the true bearing on party success of the questions he handles so clumsily. The "Gazette of the United States" was not far from wrong when it described the "Annual Register" as the veriest catch-penny that ever was published, the mere tittle-tattle of jacobinism. This first work of his, better as it was than his later writings, produced a feeling of disappointment in Jefferson, who had in some way imbibed an opinion favorable to his ability.

Of Jefferson, Callender fails for words to express his admiration. The Notes on Virginia "unites the sweetness of Xenophon with the force of Polybius, information without parade, and eloquence without effort." With Jefferson's retirement from the Cabinet of Washington began the downward career of the administration, a career so utterly condemnable that he cannot restrain his wrath when an occasion for noticing it arises. Monroe was a greatly injured man, sacrificed because he "loved" France, and had given expression to his love. Paine was quotable, as he had attacked savagely "Mr."

Washington. Madison was not of much account in Callender's collection of notables; but, at all events, he did not censure him.

When a leader of the opposite party is mentioned, Callender seems to froth at the mouth. His rage seeks out the strongest words of contempt and defamation, and in that direction alone he shows strength. Of humor he has not a trace. The highest expression of his wit is to speak of Mr. Guelph (George III.), Mr. Washington, Dr. Ames, the six per centers, and the infamous editor of the *Minerva*, Noah Webster. Against these his hatred knows no bounds; no act of theirs or their sympathizers can find favor in his eyes; no effort to expose their misdeeds, vilify their characters, public or private, and smear them with his pitch of libel and slander, is ungrateful to him. The excise duties on spirits, sugar and snuff excite him to uncontrollable outbursts of anger. For Jay's treaty, and the men who were responsible for it, he has nothing but adjectives which would not and will not be tolerated at the present day. Hamilton's error is again and again dwelt upon, the prominent details exposed, and with such evident gusto as to leave no doubt of the true quality of Callender's mind. Having hinted that the ex-secretary of the treasury was dishonest in one direction, he does not hesitate to hint further commission of bribery. "When we see an American envoy [Jay] who, without any apparent motive, breaks his orders and clandestinely signs a British treaty, and when we see a thread-bare lawyer [Hamilton] forgetting to earn daily subsistence for his family, that he may write two hundred newspaper columns for nothing, one cannot help recurring to the query of Peter Pindar, ' *Pray what might his majesty give you for it?* '"

It would be unprofitable to follow Callender through his books, as they become poorer in quality as his fortunes sink. The main point of interest is his connection with Jefferson, and the incidents of this connection are told in the following letters, in the very words of the leading actors in the comedy. The surprising thing is that Jefferson did not recognize the danger of countenancing such a man. Having befriended and used him, he thought the poor journalist would not turn upon him; but he learned that Callender was as ready to libel him as any member of the Federalist party.

His libels are dead and forgotten, but no one can read of Jefferson without a feeling of surprise that he could have had any connection, direct or remote, with so good an example of the adventurers who controlled the journalism of a century ago. From the note books of Jefferson, my brother, Paul Leicester Ford, has supplied me with the following items of interest in explaining the progress of the connection with Callender:—

1797	June 19	pd Callender for Hist of U. S. 15.14
	Dec 14	Callender for pamphlets 4.33
	23	Callender for books & pamphlets 5 D
1798	Jan 9	pd T. Leiper for Callender for 5 copies of his sketches for 1797. 5 D

Mar 23   gave Leiper order on Barnes for 16 D for Callender
May 23   pd Callender for books 3 D
May 29   pd Callender for books 5 D
June 25   paid Callender for his next book.   5 D
1799 Sept 6   Wrote to G. Jefferson & Co. to pay Callender 50 D.
1800 Oct 22   directed G. Jefferson to pay Callender 50 D

One more incident in this connection may be mentioned, one that is very creditable to both parties. In 1804 Mrs. Adams wrote to Jefferson on the death of his daughter, and gave him an opportunity to express his respect for John Adams, while regretting that a single act of Adams' life, "and one only, ever gave me a moment's personal displeasure." This act was the appointment of Federalists, made in the last hours of Adams' service, appointment which would have seriously embarrassed Jefferson, as they were opposed to him in party beliefs, and in a few instances had shown bitter personal enmity.* Mrs. Adams was by no means backward in replying to Jefferson's complaint, and in her first letter brought forward the case of Callender. This led to an interchange of opinion which is included in this series, as rounding out the story of Jefferson's connection with this scandal-monger and partisan scribbler.

LETTERS.

Callender to Madison.

Baltimore, 28 May, 1796.

Sir

    Among the unexpected incidents of my life, it is one of the most singular, and partly one of the most painful, that I am now intruding upon your time with a letter. You shall not be detained with any idle parade of words. I shall tell as shortly as possible what I wish to say.

    In the third session of my attendance on Congress, circumstances which I could neither foresee nor prevent made my situation there extremely unenviable. I came to this place, on an offer made in the most liberal terms, and with the most solemn assurances that it would be punctually fulfilled. My efforts have been attended with as much success as I could reasonably expect; and the gentleman with whom I engaged, who is a sober honest character, gives me full confidence. But he has not that regularity in conducting business which I wish to see, and I have reason to fear that he is incapable of fulfilling his engagements, though a farther trial might prove me to be mistaken.

    My wishes in life are of the humblest kind. It is very long since I envied the independance of a journeyman carpenter. But I am now in my thirty-ninth year, with a wife and four young children; and is too late to think of anything of that sort by at least a dozen years.

    I think myself capable of teaching what is commonly expected from a country schoolmaster, vizt. English grammer, writing, arithmetic, and if required Latin; none of them with eminent skill but not I think below

* Jefferson to Mrs. Adams, 13 June, 1804.

mediocrity; for I know persons whom I hardly think my superiors, who have earned a subsistence in that way, and whose peaceful situation I have invariably regarded as much better than mine, while they in turn wondered how rich I was growing on seven or eight hundred dollars a year. I mention this to shew that my present inclination to try that plan, which you will anticipate is not any new thought, but a settled habit of mind, arising from my fondness for living in the country, and my experience that of the little moral worth to be found, youth possesses the greater part, and is therefore the least offensive society. The *jocunda oblivia vitæ* are the only things for which I consider life as worth a wish.

If, from the little that you know of me, you think me capable of such a task, and that in your part of the country, you could find me any vacancy of this kind, and that it is worth your while to take the trouble of doing so, I premise that I ask for nothing but a decent subsistence for myself and my family, who are at present entirely incapable of aiding themselves.

Were you disposed to befriend me, it would be impossible to give me a final answer for a considerable time. But you may very probably and very justifiably, be, at the first blush, altogether averse to the business. For this reason, I solicit at your convenience a mere acknowledgment of the letter, and I shall be far from thinking myself authorized to complain, if you at the same time hint that my application was unsuitable. Mr. Venable once this session, spoke to me of a vacancy as a Latin teacher, somewhere in Virginia; but having at that time engaged to come here, I was not at liberty, in justice to myself, to enter into terms.

I would not wish the most intimate friend whom I have in the world, to be acquainted with the contents of this letter, unless the affair had come to maturity, on any account.* I am, sir, &c.

Callender to Jefferson.

Philadelphia, Septr. 28, 1797.

Sir

I expect that your remaining numbers of the History of 1796 have come duly to hand. The other copy will be ready for you on your return to town.

I would not have intruded on you at this time about that; but am to request your indulgence for a few moments. I have begun another volume on American history; and it will be ready for the press in about a month. Having been in bad health, for a time, now better, having by the desertion of the town been reduced to some inconvenience, & having a small family, I laid my plan before Mr. Leiper & Mr. Dallas, who handsomely gave me most effectual assistance till the time of printing & selling the book.

In this dilema, I recollected something that dropt from you, when I had the honor of seeing you at Francis's hotel. It related to some assistance in a pecuniary way, that you intended to make me on finishing my next volume. Now, Sir, my design at present is to hint that, in the present dreadful situation of the town, if the matter in reserve could be made in *advance*, it would really treble the greatness of the favor. If it was a draft or check for 5 or 10 dollars, say, it might be made in favor of a third per-

---

*"I see Hamilton has put a short piece into the papers in answer to Callender's publication, and promises shortly something more elaborate."—*Jefferson to Madison,* 24 July, 1797.

son, my name not being very proper to appear; vizt. "Mr. James Ronaldson," a particular friend of mine.

I hope in a few months to be (if I escape the fever) much less dependent than I have been upon my pen. Bookselling is at present in an entirely ruined state, otherwise my last two volumes would have put me far beyond the need of asking help. Your answer to me, *to be left at the Post office till called for*, will much oblige Sir, Your &c.

P. S. Since the printing of Mr. Hamilton's *Observations*, Bishop White has, in a public company, declined to drink his health, assigning the pamphlet as reason. If you have not seen it, no anticipation can equal the infamy of this piece. It is worth all that fifty of the best pens in America could have said against him, and the most pitiful part of the whole is his mention of you.

Callender to Jefferson.

Philadelphia, March 21st, 1798.

Sir

Your interference with respect to my getting payment in a certain quarter has not had even the smallest effect. Before, or at the time of going there I had a claim on a gentleman for 34 dolls. and 5 ⁄ s. I have got, at length 19. dols. So want 15 & 5 ⁄ s. besides my gratuitous attendance now in the 4th &, as I believe, in the last week. For I will, if I can only get the balance *due*, to answer some cogent demands, (I am asking no advances, nor pecuniary favors, but my own) proceed immediately to print my proposals for the next volume; and the money I should raise by that would serve to protract the burden of existence for a few months longer.

My sale has been rapid beyond all hope. In less than 5 weeks, 700 have gone off, and some commissions and subscribers are yet unanswered. A gentleman came lately six miles to Albany to buy a copy, and told our correspondent that in his country neighborhood, he believed that he could sell 500.

The next is to be a book of only 1 ⁄ 2 a dollar, good paper and print, and will I fancy all sell fully faster than the other, as being on a more *comeatable* size & price, the type close, to contain much matter. The six per cents, in *quite a new light*, the Indian wars, the power of making treaties, a Review of Fenno's Gazette, are among the chief articles. I could have sold this week, for the country, 150 of 1796, but they are all, or as good as all gone.

If your good offices could get the bals. due, I think I shall not run scores with the society again. With a little help, and Mr. Bache's and other correspondence I could soon come to dispose of an edition of 2,000. I will bring you a sample sheet of the print, paper and if it is agreeable, next week. One gentleman has promised to pay down at least 30 dollars for the new volume, as soon as printed. If I could afford to lye out of my money like other people, I could sell many more, but this I cannot do, which increases the wonder at my sale of 700, of which only 190 are on credit. But after all I am in danger of sticking for want of that help necessary to set up the smallest hucksters store. If I could find any 4th person to do what Mr. D[alla]s, or 1 ⁄ 2 of what L[eiper] or Mr. Jefferson have already done, I would make myself heard very distinctly for a considerable distance.

I hope I need not add, that I have not ment'd one word of the society to any human being but you. If they would only keep the agreement for 3 months, till I get the piece out I would do. I am &c.*

Callender to Jefferson.

Raspberry Plain, 22d Septr. 1798.

Sir

I request your indulgence for a few lines. I shall be as concise as possible.

A few days after I had the honor of seeing you last, a very particular reason made it proper for me to quit the city next day I consulted on this emergency Mr. Leiper & General Mason. The former offered to take charge of my children, the latter to give me, or find me lodgings, if I came to Virginia. Accordingly, I walked down to this place. The General, in a few days, came after me, and has in every way behaved with the utmost kindness. He proposes that I should stay here till winter, and go back with him to town, to try my fortune. There is, however, no more security in returning than there would have been in staying. It was Mr. Leiper's parting injunction not to come back, because there is no more safety in philadelphia than in Constantinople. Besides I am entirely sick even of the Republicans, for some of them have used me so dishonestly, in a word I have been so severely cheated, and so often, that I have the strongest inclination, as well as the best reason, for wishing to shift the scene.

Since I came here, the Aristocracy in this neighborhood, which is one of the vilest in America, has never ceased to abuse General Mason and myself. They have found means to make me very uneasy at being the cause of so much noise. Horace brags of being pointed at. My ambition does not run in that way. I engaged in American controversies not from choice, but necessity; for I dislike to make enemies, and in this country the stile of writing is commonly so gross, that I do not think the majority of such a public worth addressing. I hope another couple of years will put it in my power to go home again, but I must, if possible provide for myself in the mean time. It is needless, even were it safe, to write any more. The party are doing their own business as fast as can be.

If I were in any part of the country, where I could be permitted to live in peace, which here I cannot, I think I could win my bread, I mean my own individually, either by keeping a school, or assisting to keep a store, or in some other way, (as I have not the happiness of being able to go through country work,) till matters clear up on the other side of the Atlantick. You will easily see that I am aiming at some assistance in the matter from you, and if you can think of any one way in which I can be worth my

---

* In April a motion was made in the House to modify the citizen law, and in the Senate, to give power to send out of the country suspected aliens. The first measure was thought to be directed against Gallatin, and the second against Volney and Collot. Further, to control the press, a sedition bill was proposed, and Bache's and Carey's were in the view of the framers. These two journals "totter for want of subscriptions. We should really exert ourselves to procure them, for if these papers fall, republicanism will be entirely brow-beaten." *Jefferson to Madison,* 26 April, 1798. While the citizen bill, after passing the House, was in a committee of the Senate, Callender, "a principal object of it," eluded it, by "getting himself made a citizen." He was not entirely successful, as he tells us in the "Prospect before us" that "In consequence of this act (alien), I have been menaced with prosecution and imprisonment, by David Call, that sorry understrapper of Federal usurpation."

room, I care very little what it is, provided that I am in a Republican part of the country, for I find by wretched experience in other instances as well as at present, that I can go to no place where my name is unknown. This has hindered me from going to Winchester, as I designed, and from writing to Richmond and some other places, till I hear (if I am worthy of an answer) from you. I am, Sir, &c.

P. S. The scenes of printing, and swearing, and flat perjury that we have had here, if acted in Elysium would make any man sick of it. The General took my cause with more keenness than I wished (but perhaps because your name also was brought in). He is on his own ground, but as Ossian says "I am alone in the land of strangers."

I request the inclosed to be put in the fire, as soon as read. Since writing the above, I have reason to hope we shall make no more Replies, though *they* have had one out, some days ago.*

Callender to Jefferson.

Raspberry Plain, 26 October, 1798.

Sir

I am sensible that this freedom needs an apology. I wrote you a letter in last month and if nothing can be done, or ought to be done, in one quarter, *it is time* that I should be making application, in another, if I can say that I can have another; for I have not only motives of one kind, but others quite different, for not wishing to revisit that sink of destruction Philadelphia; for whose inhabitants I at present sympathize as much as, and not more than, I would do for those of Grand Cairo, in the same situation. If anybody can believe in *judgments*, I think that the two newspapers printed in that porch of perdition were sufficient for bringing on a yellow fever, if all their other enormities were extinguished. I hope that this pestilence, so justly deserved by all the male adults, will prove a happy check to a much worse one, the black cockade fever,† I mean the fever that, under the pretence of defending us from a *foreign* war, aims at promoting a *civil* one.

In Europe it is understood, and I mean, if I ever get into the press again, to tell the people of this country, for the sake of giving them information, in Europe it is understood, that if a political party does not support their assistant writer, they at least do not crush him, whereas I have been crushed by the very Gentry whom I was defending. I have actually vindicated the political character of a man, after I knew that he was in his private capacity, doing his utmost to injure me, and of course a dying woman and 4 innocent children, and I did so, because though I knew him to be in private a rascal, yet I knew him to be an useful public character, and in that light an injured man. This shews that I was superior to personal revenge.

I am sure that you will be shocked to hear the treatment I have met with even from men, whom I really consider as good men. For instance, Mr. Giles, in Congress, made a splendid reference to the esteem in which

---

* "I received lately a letter from Mr. Callender to which the inclosed is an answer. After perusing it, be so good as to stick a wafer in it and (after it is dry) deliver it. You will perceive that I propose to you the trouble of drawing for 50. D. for Mr. Callender on my correspondent in Richmond, George Jefferson, merchant. This is to keep his name out of sight."—*Jefferson to Mason*, 11 October, 1798.

† The badge adopted by the sympathizers with England in her contest with France.

Muir and Palmer were held in America; vid: debate on Democratic Societies. I was their intimate friend, and quite as deep in the unlucky business as they were. This same Mr. Giles, I had taken some pains in praising, and the defect of performance might have been palliated by the kindness of intention. A man has no merit in telling the truth, but he may claim the privilege of not being the object of persecution, from the hero of his encomium. This I was; for Mr. Giles, (the printed debates attest it) joined as a leader in conspiracy with Doctor Phocion* for getting me out of Congress & the man offered afterwards to speak to me in the street! He was aided in this affair, by an old and intimate friend of yours, a real and worthy man, whom I respect and love at this moment, and who, 14 days before, had told me with the tear half in his eye, that my minutes of Congress were of essential service to the country, and who yet, without pretending provocation did this. The latter was not a member, but I suppress his name as he has since obliged me. Now I would be glad to hear how Mr. Giles made his encomium on Mr. Palmer square with his attack on me, an attack so scouted, that he and his 6 per cent ally durst not risk a division on it. If such was my treatment from men who were very good men, what was I to have from those who were constitutionally, and systematically rascals. I am sure that, at least I hope that, if Giles had known the distress he was to bring upon my family, he would rather have bit his tongue than have said what he did on that day.

Bache is buried, and I wish I could *bury* the consequences of his behaviour to me. I know he had many useful and many pleasing qualities; but I was never the better for the one, or the other, he would not extract from my publications, a matter most essential, he would not let me advertise my last in his name, (none of the booksellers durst do so, excepting honest James Carey)† although he was to be defended in it. But he knew very well how to get books, without the least concern as to paying for them. In July last, just after I came away, Mr. Fenno printed an attack on me, which, callous as I am, hurt me sensibly. I instantly sent up an answer which this worthy Republican refused to print, but which I must take some notice of, with an explanation, that Bache would not print it, as a reason why I did not answer it sooner. This was my thanks for the multitudinous columns I have wrote for him, and the blame which I have incurrred as author of pieces in his paper I had nothing to do with, such as Dr. Jones's profound observations on Mr. Adams wanting his teeth, and being bald; while this reprintative himself was attacking, or at least snubbing me, on account of my stile, as if a man in rags were to upbraid another for wearing an unfashionable coat. This Sir (I ask pardon for the length of the detail) is a part of my obligations to the democrats; and though I have not the egotistical effrontery of Dr. Priestley, I shall contrive to give a general and genuine character of democrats, which will hit *my* friends the harder, because it is known, though not always confessed that I write truth, and am not a commonplace railer. Last summer, when Giles, whom I admire, and would scorn to speak to, was vilely abused by Brookes, I wrote a defence which Bache (Oh such Republicans!) would not print, because Brookes was " a fighting man," and so had to print it in my last volume, a stranger in the

---

* Jefferson speaks of " Phocion Smith," meaning Dr. William Smith of South Carolina.
† James Carey was a brother of Mathew Carey, well known as a writer and publisher in Philadelphia. James had served as stenographer to Congress succeeding Lloyd, but returned to England, and issued the " Official Letters of Washington," in two volumes. See my " Spurious Letters attributed to Washington," 123 and following.

country, without 6 people in it, who care a farthing, if I were gibbetted, while the mighty Republican with half of Philadelphia at his back, durst not defend one of the most meritorious members that ever sat in a legislative assembly, a man whose eloquence has often made every fibre in my composition thrill with pleasure, as I yet hope to make *him* thrill with shame. If they really have almost any tolerable writers except James Carey I would think less of their treatment of me. I am with much respect.

Callender to Jefferson.

Raspberry Plain, 19 Novr. 1798.

Sir

I never write a letter, when I can avoid it. I much less desire to trouble my superiors. But I received, some days ago, your favor of October 11th. The nature of its contents supercedes the necessity of saying that it was welcome. I have only to add that some parts of it seem to me an explanation on my part of what brought me here. When you are quite at leisure what follows will explain that circumstance. I did understand, in a way which admitted of no doubt, that I was very early in the same situation as that in which I found myself at Edinburgh, on January 2d, 1793. *Out of sight, out of mind,* says the proverb. My immediate disappearance was likely to make the proposal, for it was but a proposal to be dropped; and, if it should be concluded on I would be beyond its reach. I went very late to Genl. M[ason] who was in bed, told him the particulars, and by his permission, set out early next morning, on foot, for this place. He was to overtake me at Lancaster with the stage coach. I had hardly got there, when people who knew me, *met* and I was well assured that I should not be sure of safety. This was the natural consequence of the ballot-box criticisms, as to October, 1796; so bidding adieu to Messrs. Barton & Hamilton (printer, vid. Ann : Register) I set out for York town, having just got a letter from the General that he could not come up, and that I must not halt at Yorktown, so I walked straight forward. When he came here, he presented me with an account of my *Journey,* which has, I suppose been printed in ten newspapers by this time. I instantly wrote an answer, for very luckily every word of the story was false, and Mr. Leiper writes me that with his own hand he delivered this answer to Bache. The publisher of the *second* edition of the forged letters in the name of General Washington,* (and which the General, forgetting the respect due to his character, condescended to deny) the publisher of the second part of the Age of reason, after the *first part* had produced so much scandal, the publisher of the libel agt Mr. Adams for being bald and toothless, and of the ballad praying that the Queen of England's head might be passed in a basket, and, what is hardly better, the heads of *all* the sovereigns in Europe, this publisher, who by his indiscretion, has done such infinite mischief to the cause of liberty, refused to print my defence.

I cannot conceive that things are to go on, as they have done of late, for any considerable time. The 800,000 dollars of July 1797, are not yet borrowed. The 5 millions that are to be borrowed at any interest, must, like Jupiter, descend in a shower, for they are not to be found upon earth. the 2 millions of a direct tax will not chink for eighteen months. I guess

* See my edition of those Letters, printed in 1889.

another loan and tax will be adopted this winter, but the impost must, I think, be contracting, while expences are enormously augmenting, and loans cannot be raised, nor taxes realized in any effective time. In the meanwhile, direct taxation will force the people to think, and the prosecutions will provoke them to clamor. The system seems to be to waste money, and break the constitution as fast as can be. All this has had effect in England, where the throne rested on the shoulders of an enormous hierarchy and aristocracy. But even there it is like sleeping sound after swallowing 100 drops of Laudanum. It is an expedient that involves the approach of death. Accordingly, England is now expending for 1798 6 or 7 millions sterling more than either loans or taxes can produce. I have a complete statement of the particulars ready for the press from accompts laid before parliament. Indeed their own newspapers own 3 millions of *deficit* annually, but I have proved that it is not one farthing less than 6. For 99, it will be 8 millions, in spite of gifts, assessed taxes, and the very auspicious sale of the land tax. Of this last measure I do not know the particulars, but the very endurance of such an idea announces the consciousness of impending ruin. I do not recite this under the impertinence of pretending to inform, but merely to *remind.*

Now, if England has come to this plight, she can lend nothing to America, and where we are to find money even to carry out the peace, it seems hard to say. As for war, I do not see even a shadow of finance. My inference is that the system cannot last any time, and must land its apostles in the mire. Already, the X. Y. Z. mania is greatly cooled. It was amusing to see how Mr. Pickering tried to conjure up this phantom in his answer to the Edward county. I felt it like "a tale of the days of old, and of the heroes that are no more." The Virginia Assembly, if they act like men, may knock this usurpation on the head by a protest to Congress. Many foolish things will be said and done in next session at Philadelphia, and by next March, the public mind will be much riper than it is at present for the admission of truth. If I knew how to spend the intermediate time, I would then go down to *Richmond* and there publish a small volume. I think no judge in this state, will, by that time, dare to raise a process of sedition. The people will be apter to take a good impression than in Philadelphia, and I would in the end of the book advertise all my former books. This could hardly fail to produce a demand for new editions, for the books have only been limited in their circulation by the ruined state of printing, the dread of the banks at Phila: and their being all published only in *one* state nor ever taken properly by the hand of any bookseller, for *fair play* would have made them bring me a handsome income. After all I have sold above three thousand volumes in less than 2 years, of which time one-half almost has been taken up with yellow fevers. A Richmond publication would make many know the former books that never heard of them, and though they are poor enough, yet they at least are better than the common rubbish of newspapers. If the Assembly had any good measures, I would like to go before March, indeed before they rise. But at any rate, in spring, I would like to print something there, for the various reasons of safety, and impression, and the prospect of reprinting what is at present out of *print.* I am sorry for having wandered into details so uninteresting to anybody, but myself, but I cannot think I should be safe in Philadelphia, so soon as I shall be in Richmond. Either however at the latter place, or Norfolk, or anywhere that I know, can I not be safe to live at peace, I mean in *a town,* till the tide turns. Among other things, I would print

Barlow's letter, of which I would now send a copy but that I am satisfied you have seen it.   If you have not seen Lyon's *Scourge*, I would send a printed copy of that, if you choose as it has some articles irresistibly ludicrous, but that also I presume you have got by post.   Nothing like the Colonel's Indictment was ever heard of.   Barlow agrees so exactly with all I had said on the Paris embassy that I should have a threefold pleasure in reprinting him.   I would go round the country myself with the book, for when there is a proper object in view I can promise on taking any reasonable degree of pains.

Since I came here, I have got much information that I had not before, have made large notes on various points entirely untouched, and would very gladly stay here, with the advantage of a good library, till I have completed and extended an Address to the Citizens of Virginia on the present state of public affairs.   The "whale caught in a net."   The "*dust* and *ashes*" answer to Bath county &c. afford overwhelming materials for ridicule.   I can speak more frankly from the internal consciousness of never having wrote an unfair thing to serve any party, if I could have been indeed capable of service.   I cannot break to the General [Mason] this wish of staying past the sitting down of Congress, though it would take at least 2 months to arrange my present materials.   I would then be ready to give our readers such a Tornado as no Govt ever got before, for there is in American history a species of ignorance, absurdity, and imbecility unknown to the annals of any other nation.   Before the rising of Congress I could be completly ready.   My board at 15 dols per quarter is not the object, but I could not take away with me, a whole load of books, &c. that I have marked for reference.   The General is indeed all goodness.   Without parade or effort, his benevolence like a natural fountain flows from the sweetness and rectitude of his primitive composition.*   I would like very well to be in the situation of a lawyer's clerk, such as the general had before he gave up business.   But if I could weather out 3 months or so, till the weather clears up as it will do, I would like printing much better.   It would at least pay for itself.   I have got much better since I came here of a terrible complaint that I had got in Philadelphia ; and for any word, the General would bid me stay, but *that one word I cannot get myself to pronounce.*   You will see that the Aurora has got into most excellent hands.   In the first number, Liston's man looks like a bull frog in the fist of Hercules.   I have got more sound sleep since I came here than I have enjoyed for some years before.   I am now master of my own time and rid of the burden of too much society, so that I can write at leisure, and not scrawl myself into headaches.

Sir, my anxiety to communicate some ideas has branched out into a length of which I had no design.   If the letter is read at all, of which I have humiliating doubts, my last and hopeless request is your pardon for this prolixity.   I am, Sir,

* " With an happy temper, an invulnerable character, an independent fortune, and an amiable family, with every physical and moral circumstance about him, which can provoke the envy, or challenge the esteem of mankind, General Mason has presented an object of calumny for a set of miscreants, whom his good sense obliges him to despise, but whom his good nature will hardly suffer him to detest.   Without parade, or effort, his patriotism flows, like a natural fountain, from the sweetness and rectitude of the primitive elements of his mind."—*The Prospect before us*, I, 147.

[To be continued.]

INSCRIPTIONS IN THE OLD PROTESTANT GRAVEYARD AT ST. AUGUSTINE, FLORIDA.

Communicated by B. FRANK LEEDS, Esq.

[Concluded from vol. xlviii., page 464.]

Row 16 (continued).

Helen Porter, daughter of Moses H. Baldwin, depart[d] this life March 16, 1859, in the 16th year of her age.

A vertical headstone. A fine white marble box, seven feet high, with considerable carving on it.

Lot enclosed with a fence of nine granite posts with lines of wrought iron bars uniting them.

Joseph Hunter, Esq[r]., a native of Ballymore, County Antrim, Ireland. For a long time a respectable planter of Mosquito. Died May 14, 1836, æt. 30 years. This memorial is erected by his only child, M. A. H.

A marble horizontal slab on raised marble faced foundation. Lot enclosed with iron fence.

Mrs. ———, 1841.

A bit of stone with this inscription. In a lot with cement (over coquina) curbing level with the ground without it.

Harry Wilbur, son of James and Carrie Goss, who died Sep. 3, 1874, aged 10 years.

A marble head and footstone.

James Goss, died Nov. 20 (or 26), 1877, aged 37.

A wooden head and footboard. Each of these two lots enclosed in a paling fence now in weak condition.

L. B.

A narrow headboard a foot high. The footboard between the graves of Harry W. and James Goss.

Rachel T. Goodrich, Feb. 19, 1842; Apr. 27, 1869.

A low, broad granite stone. The grave directly adjoining, northwardly, that of James Goss.

M. R. Castle, son of Martin Castle, of Connecticut, died Nov. 28, 1878, aged 4 mos. 16 days.

A marble vertical headstone.

Lizzie McDonald, who died May 7, 1875, aged 36 years.

This grave is west of the preceding; has a high marble headstone; and is enclosed with four posts single uniting rails.

Row 17.

John Drysdale, who died 24th May, 1845, aged 62 years.

Ann Drysdale, dau^r of John and Lois H. Drysdale, born on the 22nd of June, 1823; died at S^t. Augustine, 14th January, 1844.

Forty lines of inscription, the last words of which are "beloved friend and pastor, Rev. Joseph H. Rutledge, of Trinity Church, of St. Augustine."

Thomas W. Drysdale, who depart^d this life at S^t. Augustine, 11th day of October, 1841, in the 17th year of his age.

Thirteen lines of inscription follow.

The above, each covered with horizontal marble slab on raised cement foundation, differ only in length. The middle slab is quite a foot longer than the other two. A low coquina curb around the three.

Elizabeth Mary Hanson, wife of J. M. Hanson, obit May 14, 1838, aged 82 years.

Eleven lines of inscription follow.

A horizontal marble slab on a brick raised foundation. Space for another grave. The lot cement curbed.

Henry V. S. Frey, son of Henry and Elizabeth Frey. He was born at Palatine, in the State of New York, 27th day of Dec. 1807, and died at S. Augustine, 8th day Jan. 1830, aged 22 years, 12 days.

A high, vertical headstone.

Erected to the memory of Lieu^t. Stephen Tuttle of the United States Corps of Engineers, a native of the State of New Jersey, who depart^d this life Jan. 21, 1835, aged 36 years.

This stone, perhaps once erect, now lies horizontally, partly covering the raised cement grave.

Lucy, wife of F. E. Mitchell, died Feb. 18, 1884, aged 42 years.

A low marble headstone and footstone.

Rev. Parker Adams of New Hartford, Oneida Co., New York, who died in St. Augustine, 10th day of June, 1835, aged 56 years.

A vertical marble head and footstone.

Marian Anita and John Cobb, infant children of George and Louisa H. Washington. (No dates.) (On the footstone there are 3 initials, M. A. W., J. C. W., J. A. W.)

Low marble head and footstones within a fence of posts and light square rails.

Jonathan Olivar Whaley, born Oct. 18, 1879; died June 11, 1880, aged 8 months.

A wooden headboard and wooden curb to grave.

Edward McGraw, born May 18, 1863; died Nov. 16, 1877.
A low wooden headboard.
A low wooden headboard two feet away from above with inscription destroyed; perhaps a relative of E. McG.

Venice Johnson, born 1859; died Nov. 23, 1874.
The inscription just decipherable. The head and footboard painted black; perhaps grave of colored man or woman.

Lewis Drysdale, died Dec. 2, 1857, æt. 27.
Perhaps other persons buried in western part of lot.
A horizontal slab considerably moved. This grave is in the western part of the Drysdale lot, the wall of which is in a ruinous condition.

Row 18.

A sacred Dedication by an affectionate mother to the memory of her son, Alfred Robinson, born at Richmond, Virginia, Oct. 26, 1815; died 1st of Decem. 1834, aged 19 years, 1 mo. 5 d.
A vertical slab and footstone.

Mrs. Mary, wife of Rev. Aaron Warner, of Medford, Mass., who died June 12, 1834, aged 45 years.
A vertical head and footstone.

Andrew J. Peck, son of G. D. Peck, M.D., and Mrs. S. F. Peck, of Milford, Mass., drowned near Saint Augustine, Apr. 19, 1835, aged 20.
An upright head and footstone.

Erastus Nye, of Onondaga Co., New York, who died January 12, 1835, aged 35 yrs. 6 mos.
An upright headstone.

John Lyman, of Southampton, Mass., died January 20, 1835, æt. 26 years.
An upright headstone.

John Gifford Hull, of Dutchess Co., New York, born May, 1808; died January, 1835.
An upright headstone.

David Merriman, of Watertown, Conn.
The vertical headstone buried so that balance of inscription cannot be copied.

Nellie Van Dorn, died Oct. 10, 1875, aged 8 years, 10 mos. 11 days.
Wooden headboard with paling fence around lot in frail condition.

Row 19.

Col. Lucius D. Mower, of Granville, Ohio, who departed this life whilst on a visit to this city for the benefit of his health on the 19 day of Feb. 1834, aged 41 years.
An upright head and footstone.

———

Hardinia M. Burnley, daughter of Hardin and Mary Burnley, of Hanover Co., Virginia, died 6th of March, 1834, of consumption, aged 24 years, 7 mos.
An upright headstone.

———

(A grave with heavy wooden curbing, but no inscription adjoining the above.)

———

Matthew Peck, a native of Berlin, Conn., who died after a lingering illness June 5, 1834, in the 39th year of his age.
A square column with capital and base, and obelisk above, of coarse grained marble.

———

Ella Bond Reynolds, born Dec. 10, 1862; taken home Nov. 28, 1877.
A vertical marble headstone.

———

A grave enclosed with iron railing adjoining above, but no tombstone.

———

Row 20.

Eliza C. Whitehouse, who died in this city (St. Augustine) 3rd June, 1838, aged 52 years.
A flat slab on the marble faced raised foundation.

———

Charles Downing, who depart'd this life Nov. 24, 1841, in the 45th year of his age. A native of Virginia, he removed to Florida and early became identified with the prosperity of the Territory. He frequently served in the Territorial Legislature, and was twice elected to the Congress of the United States. Ardent, bold, and generous to a fault, he was beloved in life, and died universally regretted.
A marble slab on a raised coquina foundation.

———

Eliza Archer, died Nov. 20, 18(73) or 78, aged 45 years.
A wooden headboard.

———

Joseph L. Smith, died May 25, 1846, æt. 69.
A colonel in the army of the United States in the war of 1812, and sometime judge of the Superior Court in the Territory of Florida.
To great assiduity in the performance of his duties he united a dignity and learning which adorned his office, and to a commanding presence were added the higher attributes of distinguished ability.
Marble upright head and footstones within iron railing.

Dr. Samuel Robinson, a native of Attleboro', Mass., and during 18 years a celebrated physician of Indiantown, N. C. From early life he was a sincere and consistent Christian, and a number of his last years were much devoted to the Bible cause chiefly in the southern States. In 1824 he removed to Providence, R. I., where he became eminent as a mineralogist. He died in this place Feb. 17, 1826, in the 44th year of his age.

Marble vertical head and footstones. A large cedar tree close to the footstone.

A lot with two graves marked with cement headstones, but no inscriptions thereon.

A smaller lot to north of above without stones.

Both these are fenced.

LISTS OF SOLDIERS OF NEWBURY, AMESBURY, BRADFORD AND VICINITY,

AND OTHER MILITARY DOCUMENTS, 1686–1746.

[Copied for the REGISTER by FRANCIS E. BLAKE, Esq., of Boston.]*

A

The names [   ] Soldiars under ye command of Capt Tho Noyes

Left trustrum Cofen	Abil Huse	Ephrim Davis
Ins Jecob taping	Abiall Somarby	Edward poure
Sarg^t Browne	Androw Stickney	†Elisha tredwell
Sarg^t Jno Emary	Abraham Annis	Edmong Grenlef
Sarg^t Jno Webstar	Aquilah Ches	Edward wodman Ju^r
Sarg^t Joseph Litlel	†Aquilah Annis	gedeon Lowle
Drumars	†[ ] Miller	†Mr Hugh March
Joshuah Morce	†[ ] [ ]opping	Hananiah Ordway
Jno Stickney	Benj poure	†Henry Bradley
Benj Morce(?)	Benj Morce Sn^r	Ha[ ] Adams
Couprall Wodman	Benj Morce ju^r	Hugh March Ju^r
Benj Lowle	Benj Sanborne	Harcules wodman
Daniell Merell	Charls Annis	Hucker osgood
Jno. Ba[ ]t	Cornelious Davis	Mr Jno Sewall
Abraham Merell Ju	Calu[ ] richardson	Jno Michell
†Abil Merell Su	Cyprian whiple	Jno davis
Abil Merell	†Ephrim davis	†Hercules Adams
Abiall Long	Elisha tredwell	†Jno Sawyer
Abill plisbury	Edmond Grenleaf	Jno worth
Augustan Stedman	Daniell Ma[ ]way	James ordway Sn^r
Andrew Godfery	Daniell Chase	James [ ] Ju^r
Abrahan Merell Ju^r	Daniell Merell	Jno ord[ ]
	Edward Wodman	[ ]

* Copied from the Robert Adams Manuscripts in the possession of the New-England Historic Genealogical Society, presented to the Society by Robert Adams of Newbury, who died there August 2, 1855. A memoir of the donor is printed in the Memorial Biographies, vol. 2, pp. 398-400. Another list, dated 1704, is published in the REGISTER, Vol. XIX., page 312.

† These names were probably intended to be erased.

[Upon the back of the original is the following endorsement:]

                    training Day ye 26 day of F[   ] 1688

    Abraham [   ]
    Corp^l Lowle Sen
    Corp^l Woodman Sen

Se[   ] men att Jno Brownes hous

B

Delinq [ ] s   the 20 day of June ye 168(9 ?]
Left trustrum Cofen
Nathel^l Cofen
peter Cofen   [this name is erased]
m^r William Nesbit
    William pilsbory
      A true Acoump^t p^r me HENRY LUNT
                          Clarke

C

To Clarke John Swett
      you are to Inspect the two west
      Block Houses and se that the men
      posted there do their duety
                 T. N.
                 L. Col

D

              philip fland [   ]
              Thomas Williams wanted some powder
[   ] escified   Samuell Swett wanted a sword
[   ] aining day   Daniell Pettengaill wanted a sword
              Amos pilsbury wanted a sword
Was on the [   ] October 1700
  JOSHUA MOODY Clark   the above written acount I receved of those
                      that vieved them as atts
                          JOSHUA MOODY Clr^k

E

[   ] *men that went to Amsbry*

Sar Aqvila Chase	John devis	dannil osilou
peter Cofen	Jemes ordway	Benjamin Chese
timothy mirrick	thomas wales	nathan merril
nathannil noyes	John aiers	Benjamin long
Aberaham tappen	John worth	Zackarie devis
Samuel bartlit	bat molten	

F

A List of the names [   ] *that are* [   ] *apointed to keep*
Snow Shoos & Moggensons for [   ] *ties Service.*

Richard Brown Senr	Corp^{ll} Smith	James Coffin
William Salmon	Joshua Moody	Edward Richardson
Anthony Somerby	Nathaniell Coffin	John Woodbridg

Benjamen Woodbridg
Abraham Lunt
John Weed
Henry halle
Thomas Moody
Edward Sergant
William no[   ]

Banajah [   ]
Archelaus Woodman
Robert Rogers
Samuell Sawyer
Enoch Litle
Corp^{ll} Brown
Nathan Merrill

Daniell Merrill
Corp^{rll} Chess
Daniell pilsbury
Caleb pilsbury
John Sewell
Abraham Toppan
A [   ]ams
[   ]

G

S^r   By His Excellencies direction & Comand I requir you, on sight hereof to call together, & have forthwith a strict muster of all your Snow-shoe men, appointed by Law; to know how they are fitted, and capable if called for, which I must have a speedy account of, and shall wait for; That I may know what return to make to His Excellency, as I am enjoyned to do; I am your Servant   N. Saltonstall

Haverhill Jan: 9 1705–6.

To L^t. Col^o. Tho. Noyes

H

A list of the naimes of the Soulders posted at the Block house In Bradford: Begining: Jun: 9: 1707

	Entred	Dismised
Samuel Gage		
Samuel Burbank	Jun: 9:	Jun: 22
Jonathan kimbel: Son to Thos kimbel		
Samuel Gage		
Samuel Burbank	Jun: 23	July: 6
Isaac hardy: Son to Thom^s hardy		
Robert Haseltine Sen		
Edward wood: Son to John wood	July: 7	July: 20
Thomas hardy: Son to John hardy		
Ebenezer kimbel		
Richerd kimbel: Son to richerd kimbel	July: 21	augu: 3
Edward hasen Sarvint to francis wostir		
Gershum haseltine		
Samuel Gage	augu: 4	augu: 17
Edward Carlton: Son to Edward Carlton		
Samuel Gage		
Thomas Green	augu: 18	augu: 31
Samuel west		
[ ]bert haseltine Sen		
[ ]l west	Septm: 1	Septm: 14
[ ] Boynton: Son to John Boynton		
[ ]	Sept: 15	Septm: 28
[ ]		
[ ] wood	Septm: 29	octob: 12
[ ] hardy		
[ ] hardy	octob: 13	octob: 26

I

A list of the Names of the men put under the Comand of Ser James Jackman ye 15th of July 1707 Thomas Noyes L Coll

Ser James Jackman	nathaniell Rolfe	John Haskins
William Salmon	Hilkiah Boynton	John Smith
Richard Pettingale	Moses Coacker	Joseph Ilesley Junr
Jonathan moores	Anthony Somerby	Samuell Hasletine
Cuttin Pettingale	John Noyes 3^d	John Sewall
Jonathan Ilesley	John kingsbury	Abraham Toppan
Tho Pettingale	Amos Pilsbury	James Wi[ ]
		[ ]

[   ] cified served Her
[   ] dayes and owne night
[   ] 1707 : under the Comand

JAMES JACKMS (*sic*) Ser

J

These are in Her majesties Name to requier you to impress theses men under specified to appear compleat in arms and Amunition and all firniture as the law directs fit for a march, at my House on wensday next at eight of the clock in the fore noone which will be ye 14th of this Instant Aprill 1708 : of this faile not and make return to me of your doings herein, given under my hand this 8th day of Aprill 1708 :

THOMAS NOYES Capt

To Ser William Titcomb,

Stephen greenleafe tirsius
James Ordway the Son of
Jams ordway
John Haskins

[Endorsed]

Aprill ye 12th 1708

p^rSuant to the within warrant I have imprest Stephen Greenleaf Senr John Haskins & James Ordway the third according to the tenner of the within warrant

p^r   WILLIAM TITCOMB

K

Almsburey desember ye 23! 1708!

To :
Colanall Thomas noyes Sir in obedance to your warant baring dat ye 6! of this enstant desembere we have taken a vew of our armes amonison and snow hose [shoes] magsons and find them genralye well fixed sir I am your honars most humbl sarvt.

THO : HARVEY Capt :

Ye snoshoe men of Almsbury

Joseph davese	Robart hoyt	Samuell huntenton
william fowler	John hunt	Samuell Clough
Thos Sargnt	gorg watken	Samuell goodwing

John martone	frances gorge	John Colbey
John Challes	Samuell Colbey	Richard Currier
william Currier	Ephram blasdell	nathaniel weed
John bagley	John nickels	Thomas weed—2
Ephram weed	henerey Rusell	Joseph Kimball
John Kimball	Joseph Sargnt	Thomas Chales
Tho. Colbey ; iun^r	henerey blasdell	Jeremiah fowler
[ ]ey tucker	william harvey	Jacob Rowell
[ ] Stevens	william presey	Thomas hoyt
[ ]am barnard	Tho: Colbey : senr	Samuell Silver—3
[ ]ll gold	Isaac Colbey: iun^r	Samuell hadley—4
Samuell barnard	Richard goodwing—1	Joseph prechet
Samuell Stevens	Joseph busall	John foot
Charls Sargnt	Ebenezerr blasdell	Tho : harvey

[Endorsed]   To
ye honorabell Colanall
Thomas noyes at nubury

L

Essex Ss

To the Sherrif of the County of Essex his under Sherriff or Cunstables of the Townes of Newbury or Salsbury or Almsbury or to any or eather of greeting

Complaint being made to me this morning by James wise of Newbury in the county of Essex in the behalfe of her majesty, that last night bein the thurteenth of october one thousand seven hundred & nine there wase taken out of a canno which was in his posession one barrell of sider contrary to the peace of our souvrain lady the queene and prayes for a warrant and He hath given five pound bond to prosecute the above complaint

Theses are therfore in Her majesties Name to Requier you to make surch after the abovsaid barrell of sider taken away from James wise the thurteenth of october at night, and to make diligent surch after said sider in such plase or plases according to the direction of James wise of Newbury in the county of Essex and In in cause you meet with any oposition you are to open any dores or lockes or bolts to surch for the same, and in Cause you finde the barrell of sider you are to secure it, and to sease the man in whose possession it tis found with and bring him before me or one of Her majesties Justis of the pease to answer for the same, of this faile not and make return of your doings heerin under my hand this forteenth day of october onethousand sevenhundared and nine in the eighth yeare of her majesties Rain Annoque Domini

THOMAS NOYES
[Endorsed]   Justice of the peace

Essex Ss.

[Seal]   By warantie of this with In Ritt I have made search after the with In named Barel of sider and found same In Left Benaga Titcomb Warhouse and sesed s^d sider and sackuested said sider and sesed Left titcomb and brought him Before Justs noyes Esq this 14 Day of october 1709 By me BENJ^a COKER Constable for Newbury

M

Andover: October y^e : 17 : 1709
A muster Roll of the men that sarvd her majesty in the block houses in Andover in the yeare: 1709: Viz—

Danel Baxby for himself was posted the : 7 of June and was Releast the : 4 of October

Sam^ll phelps for himself was posted the : 7 : of June and was release the : 4 : of October

John Dane Son to Francis Dane was posted the : 7 : of June and was release the : 4 : of October

David blanchard for himself was posted the : 7 : of June and was releast the : 4 : of October

Stephen barnard for himself was posted the : 7 : of June and was release the : 4 : of October

pasco Chub sarvant to georg Abbott was posted the : 7 : of June and was release the 4 : of October

william Barker [   ]fe was posted the : 7 : of June and was release [   ]

Timothy [   ] was posted the [   ] and was re[   ]

John parker for [   ] was posted the : 7 : of [   ] and was releast the : [   ]

Henery Boodwell for himself was posted the : 7 : of June and was release the : 4 : of october

Daniel Grainger son to John Grainger was posted the : 7 : of June and was release the : 4 : of October

Benjamin Stevens for himself was posted the : 7 : of June and was release the : 4 : of October

Nathan Barker son to Ebenezer barker was posted : the : 7 : of June and was release : the : 4 : of october :

John stevens : son to John Stevens was posted : the : 7 : of June and was release the : 4 : of october

These men found themselves armes and subsistance

BENJAMIN STEVENS Capt
JOHN CHANDLER Capt

N

In obedience to Comand from His Excelency:
These are In Her majesties Name to Requier you to Impress these men under specified to appear compleat in Armes & amunition and all firniture as the law directs with two dayes provition [   ] order them to appear at the House of Capt Edw[   ] sargent His House in Newbury on Monday by twelve of the Clocke at noon which will be ye 28th of this Instant of this faile not & make return to me of your doings heer in given under my hand this 25 of november 1709 from your servant

THOMAS NOYES Capt

Stephen poore
Stephen greenleafe
John Sawyer
Zachary Davis
To Benjamin more Ju
To Stephen webster
or John Stickny

Tristram x Coffin
malachi Edwards
Josiah x pilsbury
John [   ]ns

[   ] greenleafe
Thom[   ] Browne
Timothy putnam

[Endorsed]
    25 1709
    november : A Cording to the Whithin riten wornt I have impresst thies
men under named
    Thomas Brown
    John Scoder
    malachi Edwards
    Danill Grienleafe
    Stephen Grenleafe   JOHN STICNY
                                                     STEPHEN WEBSTER

                                    O

    To the Honourable Colonoll Thomas Noyes Esquire Sir these lines may
Sarue to Informe your hono[ ] that by all we know and Can understand
Captain Dauid Haseltine is both [ ]xous as well as willing to lay downe
his Captainship over the foot Soldiears and wold very gladly be freed from
Sarving any longer in the place as he hath informed many of us and Sir as
a Leading proper Steep in the mater in order that the head & public good
may Cheifly loocked at a[ ]ll as the Seurting weel as wee do think or
know we Can a mongs [ ] this towne in genorall but more Espeshauly
uss ye Subscribers are [ ]rous that m^r Philip Atwood may be the man
that may s[ ] that place if his Excellency may aprove of the same
which with [ ] houners motion to his Excellency in this Case may be
very Lickly to [ ]ine the end Considring how well thes gentelmen is
aquired & generaly the minds of the people being for him that he may
serve her majesti in the place of a Captain which we the subscribers do
ofer ouer Earnest deziar unto your honour that your honour wold do for us
in this mater when you are before the gouernour what you shall think proper so that we may be hea[ ] so fare obliged we the subscribers take
leave & rest your honours Humble Seruants in what we may or Can bring
the foot Soldgers of Bradford
    Bradford Janauery the 25th day 1710–11

Nathanill Geag	John(?) gage	Joseph Hardy Saner
James Tiler	Daniell Jones	Joseph Hardy Juner
James Fry	Onis [ ]prus Mash	Ebenezer Burbank
William West	Abr[ ] parker Sener	Thomas Hardy
Samuel gage	Ja[ ]nly	Benjamin Hardy
James Buswell .	Jaco[ ]ardy	Jacob Hardy Saner
timothy haggt	Jose[ ] Hardy	Samuell hardy
James head	John Pembarton	daniel Tenny
Zakriah Simons	Eleazar Burbank	John Tenny Ju
Joseph Hall	Isaac [ ]ardy	Daniel Hardy
Joseph willson	thomas bayley	J[ ] Hall
Eleazer Lurn	John Green	G[ ]om heslton
Samuell Runels	Dainil Clev[?]	A[ ]aham parker
daniel Gage	nathan webster	

                                    P

    Newbury Sept ye 22^d 1712 A List of the names of the New Raisd
forcis to be put under Capt. Joseph Eaton
    Henry Dresser Servant to Decen Nathanil Coffin
    Tristram Coffin Son to m^r James Coffin

Elias Titcomb Son to William Titcomb
Samuel Wood Servant to Joshua Moodey
Thomas Adkinson Son to John Adkinson
Benjamin Mors Ju^r
Thomas Chase Ju^r
James Brickit
Ebenezer Barton
Mosis Richardson
Israel Adams
James Jackman
John Pettinggall
Richard Hale
Daniel Roberson Servant to John Noyes Ju^r
Lawrance Hart Servant to m^r John Calef
Ebenezer Burbank
William Herdy
Jacob Herdy
Joseph Moulton Servant to Cutting Noyes Ju^r [this name is erased].

THOMAS NOYES Coll

To Capt Joseph Eaton

Q

[   ]
In obedeince to his majesty by your warrant to me directed accordingly
I have Mustered ye foot Company of Soulders of ye west part of ye Town
of Almsbury on y^e : 30th : day of July Currant and have notifyed and ap-
poynted one quarter part of s^d Company to be Ready to March into his
Majesties Sarvice at an houres warning
[   ] Almsbury July y^e : 30th : 1722

ROG^r STEVENS lieut

[Endorsed]
for his Majesties
Sarvice to Collon^l
Noyce   D D

R

Capt Gerrish Compny	Sam^{ll} Duty Jr	aprill 18 1746
Amos Pearson	Enoch Boynton	Sam^{ll} Kelly
thomas tenny	Stephen Pearson	June 11 1746
william tenny		Joseph Russell
June 1745	*in Capt Hobson Rowly*	July 18 1746
Natham adams	James Hidden	John Yell
John Woodman	Stephen Dresser	Christopher Hodgskins
July 27 1745	Joh^a Hobkison	John Dreser
Ebenezer Clark	mark Platt	
April 28 1746	John Chaplain	*Major Greenleaf 1744*
John Jackman	June 1745	Joseph Woodbrige
May 29 1746	Jona Elsworth	martin Jose
Edmund Cheeny	July 27 1745	John Bosell
July 18 1746	Isaac Burpe	Eliphalet Brown

Peter ingrewel ?	July 18—1746	Cap[t] *mighill 1745 Jun*
John Bean	Humphery Richards	Daniel Todd
Daniel fling	Sam[ll] Lunt	Nathan Lombard
July 27—1745	Benj[m] Pike	Stephen Dole
Sam[ll] Lunt	Stephen morgan	July 18—1746
aprill 28—1746	oliver titcomb	Thomas Eaton
Benj[m] Long	James Woodbury	Thomas Dickerson
Thomas Bartlet		Jerediah Killbourn

ALLEN CONVERSE, OF WOBURN, MASS., AND DESCENDANTS.

By WILLIAM R. CUTTER, Esq., Librarian of the Public Library, Woburn, Mass.

PREVIOUS writers, notably Sewall* and Vinton,† differ vastly from the conclusions of the present writer in relation to the genealogy of this person and that of Josiah[3] of this list. The hint that the latter was descended differently from what previously accepted authorities supposed him to be, was received from the statements purporting to be from a family bible of date 1761, mentioned by Seymour Morris, of Chicago, in his *Morris Genealogy*, p. 45.

1. ALLEN[1] CONVERSE, ancestor of one line of the Converse family in Woburn, Mass., was a kinsman of Edward Converse, well known as the ancestor of another line of the Woburn Converse family. Previous authorities have confounded the lines of these first settlers of the ancient town, and the following is an attempt to correct the line of Allen. The name of his wife has also been wrongly given as *Sarah*—the name of his daughter —and the date of death of the daughter has also been given as that of the wife.

The family of Allen Converse is notable for the large number of deaths in it at one period (1679), covering the space of a few months; in the following order : —

> Hannah, wife of Zachariah (son), January 1, 1679.
> Zachariah (the son himself)   "   22, "
> Hannah Pierce (daughter)   March 23, "
> Allen (the father)   .   .   April 19, "
> Sarah (daughter)   .   .   "   22, "

All these died apparently of the small pox, which was rife in Woburn at the time.

Allen Converse needs no especially lengthy mention here. His name is found in the first volume of the Woburn town records many times, from 1645 and onwards, as the holder of minor town offices, as taxed in the rates, the recipient of grants of town land near his house and at longer distances; facts of peculiar interest, as showing the locality of his residence, and the

* Sewall's *Hist. Woburn.*

† A. C. Vinton, app. to *Woburn Marriages*, compiled by Judge Edward F. Johnson, who contributed the abstracts from the official records of the Middlesex County Registry found in this article.

estimation in which he was held by his fellow-townsmen.* Both he and his wife were school-teachers, and both taught school in Woburn and were compensated for their services by the town. I have mentioned the manner of his death by the small pox. This dread disease afflicted the family in a melancholy way by destroying five members, as I have shown above, in the course of a few months. At the close of the year 1678, a number of persons in Woburn were ill of it. The disease continued to prevail until May, 1679, when twenty-seven persons, at least, were suffering with it, and were publicly made mention of in the town records.†

The will of Allen Converse, of Woburn, was dated April 14, 1679, five days before his death. By it he gives ten pounds to his grandson, the son of his daughter Hannah Pierce—the daughter having died just a short time before—using, as expressed in the will, the strange spelling and statement: "my sonn Peirces child, borne of my daughter Hannah;" the legacy to be paid when he, the said grandson, came of age. In the will Allen speaks of his deceased son Zechariah (who had died January 22, previous), of his own wife Elizabeth, his son Samuel, and of his own two daughters—Sarah and Mary.

Allen Converse died April 19, 1679, and Elizabeth Converse, widow— evidently his widow—died August 9, 1691.

To illustrate localities, an important feature in the determination of this lineage, the following inventory of Allen Converse is presented:—

Inventory of estate of " Alen Converse, taken 4th of yᵉ 4th [mo.] (1679)."

	£ sh. d.
Imprims, one hous, barn, orchard, with about 20 acurs of land ajassent to yᵉ same	100 00 00
Itm. for about 40 acurs of land at a place caled boggy meddow feild,	050 00 00
Itm. for 5 acurs of land neer goodman bakers	010 00 00
Itm. for about 10 acurs of land att maple meddow plain . . .	010 00 00
Itm. for about 10 acurs of land one yᵉ north side of maple meddow river	005 00 00
Itm. for about 54 acurs of upland and meddow att a place caled Lubers [Lubber's] brooke	015 00 00
Itm. for woodland and herbidg	030 00 00
Itm. for about 7 acurs of meddow att maple meadow, att 5ˡᵇ pʳ acur,	035 00 00
Itm. for 4 acurs of meddow att lows [Loose] meddow att .	008 00 00
Itm. for one acur & ½ of meddow att boggy meddow . .	006 00 00
Itm. for about one acur of meddow att Steprock	002 00 00
Itm. for qarter part of a sawmill.‡	005 00 00
The totall [including personal]	370 12 00

Aprised by Josyah Convers, James Conuars, Sᵉⁿ., James Convars, Junʳ.

Item first is thus disposed of:—

Joseph Whittemore conveys to Caleb Blodgett, a mansion house, barn, and 20 ac., being part of the homestead formerly Allen Converse's—N., Col. Jonathan Tyng; E., Daniel Baldwin; S., partly by James Burbeen, at both ends of said southerly line; elsewhere by Daniel Baldwin; W., by Wright St., or High St.,§ which leadeth from Colonel Tyng's to Joshua Sawyer's, June 15, 1714. [18 : 257.] Thirty acres at Humble Bee Hole—[near the present village of North Woburn] —was " formerly Allen Converse's," per a deed [13 : 521].

Some of the items of land named in Allen Converse's inventory are mentioned in that of his son Samuel in a somewhat modified form, and the similarity of names of localities is extended to that of the grandson Josiah.

* Compare *Woburn Records*, vol. 1 (printed edition, with index); Cutter's *Woburn Historic Sites*, p. 23.

† Compare Sewall's *Woburn*, pp. 122-23, 606.

‡ John Walker, to proprietors of sawmill at Boggy-Meadow Field, viz., Francis Wyman, Allen Converse, Henry Summers, and Joseph Winn, deed, April 8, 1678; original in Woburn Public Library, *Wyman Coll.* 11:1.

§ Now Middle Street, Woburn.

Children of Allen Converse, per Woburn Records:

2. i. ZACHARIAH, b. Oct. 11, 1642; d. Jan. 22, 1679. Mentioned as deceased, in father's will, April 14, 1679.
   ii. ELIZABETH, b. March 7, 1645; d. (dau. of Allen) Aug. 2, 1661.
   iii. SARAH, b. July 11, 1647; d. April 22, 1679. She is named in father's will, April 14, 1679, being one of his three children then living. The Sarah Converse who was interested in the estate of Allen Converse, in 1703, was evidently Sarah, his granddaughter, daughter of Samuel (3).
   iv. JOSEPH, b. May 31, 1649; not living at time when his father's will was made; evidently died young, as the mortality of children dying young in the family is marked.
   v. MARY, b. Sept. 26, 1651, d. (dau. of Allen) Nov. 10, 1651.
   vi. THEOPHILUS, b. Sept. 21, 1652; d. (son of Allen) Sept. 28, 1652.
3. vii. SAMUEL, b. Sept. 20, 1653; d. Oct. 25, 1699. Named in his father's will, as one of his three children then living.
   viii. MARY, b. Nov. 26, 1655, apparently unmarried when her father's will was made, April 14, 1679, and named therein as one of his three children then living. She married apparently, Sergt. Jacob French, at Billerica, June 30, 1685; d. 1686, *Hazen*.
   ix. HANNAH, b. March 13, 1660; m. Nathaniel Pierce. Dec. 27, 1677. She d. (wife of Nathaniel Pierce) March 23, 1679. This was before the date of her father's will, April 14, 1679, in which her son and only child is mentioned in her stead, to whom the grandfather gave £10, to be paid when he became of age. The child was *Nathaniel*, b. Feb. 2, 1679.

2. ZACHARIAH[2] CONVERSE (*Allen*[1]), born Oct. 11, 1642; died Jan. 22, 1679, evidently of the small pox, then generally prevailing. He is called deceased son Zachariah, in father's will, April 14, 1679. Hannah, his wife, died Jan. 1, 1679, evidently of the prevailing small pox. She was Hannah Bateman, married June 12, 1667. She is evidently the Goodwife Converse referred to in Volume II. of the Woburn town records as one of those sick of the small pox, and who died of the disease at that period. In the list were Zachariah Converse's wife and child. This is, therefore, a reference to her, and not to Allen Converse's wife, as others have supposed. Zachariah had:

   i. ZACHARIAH, b. Nov. 4, 1670. He was one of the volunteers from Woburn in Phips's 1690 expedition to Canada.—Mass. Archives, v. 36, pp. 246-7.—*Zachariah Converse*, 1690; order of name (in document) 2d; 1738: personally present; attest by Joseph Reed. He was one of the few surviving soldiers from Woburn, of the campaign of 1690, who were living in the year 1738. His uncle, Samuel Converse, served in 1690, in the same expedition. Zachariah d. Dec. 30, 1747. There is no evidence of marriage of Zachariah on the Woburn Records, either of the ceremony or the births of any children.
   ii. ELIZABETH, b. Oct. 29, 1672; living single, 1747-48; d. Jan. 27, 1755.
   iii. RUTH, b. Oct. 3, 1674; dr. of Zachariah, d. Jan. 8, 1675.

[Judge Edward F. Johnson contributes the following from the Middlesex County Registry regarding these two Zachariah Converses:

ZECHARIAH[2] CONVERSE. Will of Zachariah Converse, being weak in body by reason of the distemper of the small pox. I make my *honoured* father, *Allin* Converse, sole executor * * I bequeath my 2 children to my father, my son and my daughter, Zachariah and Elizabeth, to bring them up in the *feare of god*. * * If they die in minority, I bequeath my estate to my brother Samuel and my sisters equally, Jan. 22, 1678[-79]. Inventory, which he died seized of, Jan.

22, 1678[-79],—house, barn, and land adjacent thereto, and his meadow at Willow Meadow, with upland at Settle Meadow and Wood Hill.   Josiah Converse and James Converse Senr., appraisers.

ZACHARIAH[3] CONVERSE.   Feb. 1, 1747, Josiah Converse, Samuel Kendall, and William Tay, administrators of estate of Zachariah Converse.   Ebenezer Richardson appears afterwards as one, appointed July 25, 1748.   The inventory discloses homestead of about 60 ac., and about 3 ac. of meadow at Willow Meadow, lying on the west side of road to Andover, near said homestead.   Feb. 15, 1747, Samuel Kendall and Josiah Converse represent that "we have *bin* to the house of Mr. Zachariah Converse, late of Woburn, and requested of *Ms.* Elizabeth Converse, sister to said Converse, the goods of said Converse, and she altogether refused to us the possession."   [The dates are more correctly, February, 1747-48.   Josiah Converse, above, died June 17, 1748 (his successor in this administration being appointed July 25, 1748).   The circumstance of his connection in this matter is an additional proof of his family relationship, he being a cousin of the Zachariah, here mentioned, who, from the facts here presented, evidently died single, as did also his sister Elizabeth,—see following paragraph.   There are interesting facts regarding the location of the house of the last named Zachariah in deeds, but enough has been given to locate him genealogically.]

What follows relates to Elizabeth Converse, who died January 27, 1755.

In corroboration of this date, and the identification of the individual, the following facts are adduced: Feb. 1, 1747, the selectmen of Woburn represent "*Mis* Eliz^a Converse of this our town" *non compos.* (Mem.: On margin of account, containing expenses of funeral, etc.,—"deceased Jany 27, 1755.") In a petition signed by many citizens, dated Jan. 18, 1749, it is represented that Elizabeth Converse, single woman, needs a guardian. Inventory taken April 9, 1751, shows homestead of about 60 ac., and meadow of 3 ac. at Willow Meadow, on west side of road leading to Andover, near said homestead. (Josiah Johnson had been appointed guardian, Feb. 12, 1749.) Benjamin Johnson was appointed administrator, Feb. 17, 1755. Receipt of Susanna Wright for 2 yrs., 5 mos. board of Elizabeth Converse, deceased, dated Feb. 20, 1755. Inventory of *Mr'ss* Elizabeth Converse, single woman, taken April 9, 1755, includes mention of 59 ac., part in Woburn and part in Wilmington.—E. F. J. [Her estate, it will be observed, is identical with that of her father and brother,—see preceding paragraph.]

The fact, too, that no one of the name of Converse is mentioned in the disposition of her affairs, after the death of Josiah Converse in 1748, is further proof that he was her kinsman, and evidently the nearest of kin.

In further proof that the right Elizabeth is here given, and that Mr. Vinton is in error in date ascribed— *Woburn Marriages,* part 3 of series, p. 328, No. 63— to Elizabeth, b. 1699, daughter of Robert and Mary, of Edward line, a deed, apparently unrecorded, from Mary Converse, and Ann, and others, to Ebenezer, dated Nov. 2, 1737—Wyman Coll., Woburn Public Library, 11 : 10—is cited. In this deed of release Mary Converse, widow, Ebenezer Thompson and Hannah Thompson, Josiah Simonds and Elizabeth Simonds, Isaac Snow, and Ann Converse, maiden, all of Woburn; Daniel Reed and Mary Reed, of Charlestown; and Samuel Smith, of Leicester, and Sarah Smith, his wife, quit claim to Ebenezer Converse, of Woburn, their interest to the estate which James Converse [their brother], late of Woburn, deceased, died seized of . . . . . Nov. 2, 1737. Signed by all the foregoing, except Isaac Snow, and also signed by Ruth Snow, Jonathan Reed and Keziah Reed, Benjamin Converse, and Lois Carr, other members of the family, but not named in the body of the document.   The Elizabeth—63, *Vinton*—thus married Josiah Simonds.   The marriages of nearly all these persons are noted in the printed records, to which the reader is referred for dates.]

3. SAMUEL[2] CONVERSE (*Allen[1]*), b. Sept. 20, 1653 ; d. —— 1699, per Woburn Records. He was a volunteer from Woburn in Phips's 1690 expedition to Canada.—*Mass. Archives,* 36:246-7. The expedition was to Quebec—compare work entitled " 1690 : Sir William Phips devant Québec : histoire d'un siège ; par Ernest Myrand," Quebec, 1893, 8°, 429 pp. *Samuel Converse,* 1690 ; order of name (in

document) 28th; 1738 : Samuel Converse, in right of his " father," Samuel Converse, Woburn. " The first Samuel was son of Allen Converse and b. 1653. Samuel, son of Samuel, was b. 1686. The first Samuel d. in 1699, and the death of the second Samuel is not a matter of Woburn record. There are no entries in the Woburn record of marriages referring to either of these two men. The first Samuel (1653-1699) was an uncle of the Zachariah Converse, who was in the same expedition."—*Note by Cutter.* His daughter Sarah, appears to be a party in interest in his father's (Allen Converse's) estate, in 1703.

Samuel and Sarah had :—

i. SARAH, b. Jan. 10, 1684, d. (?) of small pox, Nov. 25, 1721.
ii. SAMUEL, b. Nov. 22, 1686; living 1738, see mention under father.
iii. MARY, b. Sept. 26, 1688; m. Gregory Stone, of Lexington.
iv. JOSEPH (of Samuel, Sen.) b. May 4, 1691; m. Isabell Furbush, both of Woburn. at Medford, by Thomas Tufts, Esq., July 14, 1719. Had *Abigail,* b. Jan. 17, 1719-20.
v. HANNAH, b. Dec. 28, 1693; bedridden, in 1714; prob. dead before 1720.
4. vi. JOSIAH, b. May 10, 1699; d. June 17, 1748.

I venture the suggestion that Sarah Converse, of Woburn, who married Thomas Dutton, Jr., of Billerica, at Billerica, Nov. —, 1721, is identical with Sarah, the widow of this Samuel Converse. Sarah Dutton, widow, died in Woburn, Dec. 18, 1738. Examination of the official records of deeds and probate fails to discover anything concerning the settlement of her affairs. Her son Josiah Converse appears in the tax lists in 1721, and immediately disappears, going apparently with her to Billerica, and returning to Woburn after 1732, where he was married. In the Reading record of his marriage, he is called of Malden, which would apparently be one of the places where he had lived before returning to Woburn.

Inventory of Samuel Converse, Sr., of Woburn, died Oct. 25, 1699, as it was apprized Nov. 7, 1699, by James Fowle, Joseph Pierce, and John Walker, Sr. :—Homestead and woodland adjoining, £100; 1¼ ac. of meadow at Boggy Meadow, £3 15s.; woodland near Step Rock Meadow, 10s.; woodland at Forest Field Hill, £1 5s.; 1½ ac. at Loose (?) Meadow, £3; woodland near Butters' Saw Mill, £2 10s,; woodlot near James Thompson's, £5; total, including personal property, £143 5s.

January 8, 1699 [1700] Sarah Converse, relict widow of Samuel Converse, late of Woburn, husbandman, dec'd intestate, admitted administratrix, made oath to above;—bond in £280—Joseph Pierce and Zachariah Converse, sureties.

Articles of agreement made Dec. 16, 1714, between Sarah Converse, relict widow of Samuel, late of Woburn, and the children and heirs of said deceased, whose names are underwritten. It is agreed for the settlement of said deceased's estate, which was valued at £130, that our honored mother, Sarah Converse, aforesaid, shall have for her use £50, during her life, to wit, that she shall have the use of half the house and cellar; that Joseph Converse (shall provide her certain things, etc.) . . that Joseph shall have £11 18s., besides what he hath purchased of his eldest brother Samuel; it is agreed that Josiah, who being under age, shall have £11 18s.. etc.; lastly, it is agreed that Hannah Converse, who lies bedrid, shall have £11 18s.; and it is agreed that Joseph shall have the whole of the estate of the deceased, he to pay the rest of their several parts and portions, as above. Signed Sarah Converse, Joseph Converse, Mary Converse, Hannah Converse (the foregoing made their marks) and David Roberts, Jr., guardian to Josiah Converse,

Jan. 5, 1714, David Roberts appointed guardian of Josiah Converse, a minor, in his sixteenth year of age, son of the late Samuel Converse.

Joseph Converse conveys to Eleazer Flagg, 10 ac., near a certain mill of Samuel Eames, called Boggy Mill. Dower of Sarah [the mother of Joseph] released, Jan. 28, 1715. [20:353.] The same Joseph conveys to Samuel Damon, of Reading, 12 ac., lying between Boggy Field and Step Rock. Release of Sarah Converse, mother of Joseph, Feb. 25, 1715. [21:314]. He conveys to Philip Alexander, a homestead and 55 ac.; E., road to Eames sawmill, etc., and N., county road; 14 ac. at Cold Spring; 5 ac. at Wood Hill; 1½ ac., Boggy Meadow; and 2 ac. at Loose Meadow, Dec. 22, 1719. [This is evidently the homestead of his father Samuel.] Connected with this is the following genealogically important release: We, Gregory Stone and Mary Stone, of Lexington, Sarah Converse, and Josiah Converse, Jr., of Woburn, quitclaim to Philip Alexander all interest in estate of our father Samuel Converse, late of Woburn, dec'd, which estate said Alexander hath lately purchased of our elder brother Joseph Converse, March, 31, 1720. [23:164].—E. F. J. [The daughter Hannah, who was mentioned in the agreement of 1714, did not join in the release of 1720, and died apparently before that date.]

In relation to Josiah being called Jr., in 1720—see paragraph above. In 1708 Robert Converse conveys real estate by deed to his brother Josiah Converse, Jr. (34, *Vinton*): Josiah, Sr., in that year, was Josiah (d. 1717)—(*Vinton*, 6). In 1720, Josiah (*Vinton*, 34) was Senior, called Ensign Josiah Converse, in tax lists, 1721, whence his name disappears before 1727—he having removed from the town—*Morris*, p. 43, where his descendants are traced. Josiah, Jr., in 1720, was, therefore, the Josiah of the text.

4. JOSIAH[3] CONVERSE (*Samuel*,[2] *Allen*[1]), b. May 10, 1699, d. June 17, 1748; m. Sarah Evans, of Reading, Dec. 27, 1732,* who survived until after the Revolutionary period, as widow being taxed in the East List, 1777, and marrying Capt. Timothy Brooks, of Woburn, March 30, 1781, died his widow, Feb. 22, 1789, aged 81 y., dying of cancer, and being buried at Woburn, Feb. 24, 1789—*per Thompson's Diary*—see also N. E. HIST. GEN. REG. 29:154. The estate of Capt. Timothy Brooks was insolvent in 1789, and the court ordered the administrator to pay a certain per cent. of the creditors' claims, which was all they could receive until his widow's death.

Sept. 1, 1748, administration on Josiah Converse granted to widow Sarah, who gives bonds, £300, with Pierson Richardson, Jr., and Benjamin Richardson, sureties.

Inventory of real and personal estate of Josiah Converse, of Woburn, dec'd June 17, 1748: homestead and buildings, £3,200; 3 ac., adjoining, £210; 12 ac., called Reed Field, £480; 5 ac., called Upper Orchard, £180; 19 ac., Wood Hill, £300; 2 ac., Boggy Meadow, £150; 10 ac., Loose Meadow, £200. Benjamin Richardson, Pierson Richardson, Jr., and David Fisk, appraisers. (The widow adds the provisions and a right in a School House.) April 3, 1749, Mrs. Sarah Converse, the administratrix, exhibited this inventory on oath.

Agreement of heirs of Josiah Converse [d. 1748] sets forth full inventory, including homestead of 100 acres, 120 perch, and bounded N. and E., Road; W., by road, by Mary Tidd and John Fowle's lands; S., Joshua Thornton, Joshua Richardson, and John Leathe, etc., etc.; and Sarah Converse, deceased's widow, Josiah Converse (eldest son), Samuel Converse, and Sarah Converse, the deceased's daughter, all of age, mutually agree to divide, etc.,—Nov. 30, 1759.

Sarah Converse, widow, consideration £100, mortgages to Samuel Nevers, 25 ac., bounded S., town way; W., Ezekiel Reed; N., Abijah Smith; and E., James Fowle, Jr.; also, 4 ac. woodland, bounded W. and N., Timothy Reed; S., Abijah Smith; E., Edward Walker and Francis Kendall; also 11 ac. woodland, bounded W. and N. by land late Doctor Jonathan Hayward's; S. and E. by Nathan Kendall. Provided if said Sarah and her heirs shall from Feb. 4, 1761, take care of said Samuel Nevers and wife Deborah in a manner suitable to their old age,—then to be void. Witness, Mary Nevers, Josiah Johnson. Rec. Feb. 20, 1761.—E. F. J. [The Nevers property, here mentioned, was located in the westerly part of Woburn.]

* March 9, 1732, per Reading Records.—A. S. WOOD.

Josiah and Sarah had:—

i. JOSIAH, b. Jan. 27, 1734; m. Hephzibah Brooks, March 28, 1758; and d. Feb. 2, 1810; she d., his widow, March 11, 1813, æ. 74. He was furnished with a bayonet according to law as a member of the East company of Woburn Militia, in 1758. He was a member of the same company during the Revolutionary War, the captain then being Jesse Wyman. His son *Josiah*,[5] b. March 14, 1759, d. Sept. 8, 1840 (epit. 282, 2d Burying Ground) went personally into the service for the Northward Army, against Burgoyne, in August, 1777. His son, *Jesse*,[5] b. Feb. 9, 1765, d. July 17, 1864, æ. 99 y. His son, *Joshua*,[5] b. Jan. 20, 1767, d. Feb. 5, 1868, æ. 101 y. His son, *Luther*,[5] was the father of Parker L.[6] Converse, judge, writer, etc.; and *Joshua*,[5] the centenarian, was the father of Sherman[6] Converse, b. March 5, 1810, d. April 16, 1896.

ii. SAMUEL, b. Nov. 23, 1735; m. Mary Tyler, Oct. 9, 1760; and d. Nov. 30, or Dec. 1, 1775—*Thompson's Diary*—funeral, in Old Parish, Dec. 2, P. M., attended by Rev. John Marrett, of the Second Parish; Samuel being 40 years of age. His widow Mary d. June 27, 1814, æ. 75. He died intestate and an inventory of his estate was taken Sept. 23, 1784. In the division his widow Mary, and eldest surviving son Jeremiah, and children Joseph, Jacob, Mary, Abigail and Lydia were mentioned. *Jeremiah*,[5] the son, was the grandfather of Alva S. Wood of Woburn, antiquary.

iii. SARAH, b. Aug. 26, 1736; m. Bartholomew Richardson, April 10, 1760, who was b. in Woburn, March 25, 1730, and d. June 14, 1812. She d. Feb. 1, 1825. They were ancestors, through *Sarah*,[5] m. Josiah Walker, and Hannah,[6] m. Benjamin F. Thompson, of Abijah Thompson, officer of the Winchester Historical Genealogical Society.

iv. ZACHARIAH, b. Dec. 28, 1741.

v. JOHN, b. Oct. 23, 1748, after his father's death.

BILLETING ROLL OF CAPT. LAWRENCE'S COMPANY, 1758.

Copied for the REGISTER by FRANCIS E. BLAKE, Esq., of Boston.

A Billiting Roolle of Capt Thomas Laurance Company in Cor^{ll}: Nichols Rigment 1758.

Mens Names	when Commenced	Time Ends	Number of Days	what p^r day sterling	Total	old tenor
Moses Sawtell	march 29	may 25	58	6:d	1:9:0	14:10:0
David Shattuck	Dt^o		58		1:9:0	14:10:0
Eleazer Parker	Dt^o		58		1:9:0	14:10:0
John Boydon	Dt^o		58		1:9:0	14:10:0
Simeon Foster	Dt^o		58		1:9:0	14:10:0
Henery Woods	Dt^o		58		1:9:0	14:10:0
Ephraim Severance	Dt^o		58		1:9:0	14:10:0
Abel Sawtell	Dt^o		58		1:9:0	14:10:0
Jonathan Shipley	Dt^o		58		1:9:0	14:10:0
Eleazer Ames	Dt^o		58		1:9:0	14:10:0
Joseph Kemp	Dt^o		58		1:9:0	14:10:0
oliver Laken	Dt^o		58		1:9:0	14:10:0
Joseph Page Ju^r	march ye 30		57		1:8:6	14: 5:0
William Parker	Dt^o		57		1:8:6	14: 5:0

James Fisk Ju^r	Dt^o		57	1:8:6	14: 5:0
Lemuel Sheple	Dt^o		57	1:8:6	14: 5:0
obediah Perry	Dt^o		57	1:8:6	14: 5:0
Joseph Sawtell	April 1.		55	1:7:6	13: 5:0
John Erven	Dt^o 4.		52	1:6:0	13: 0:0
Daniel Douglass	Dt^o		52	1:6:0	13: 0:0
Nathaniel Lakin	Dt^o 5.		51	1:5:6	12:15:0
oliver Farnsworth	Dt^o 7.		49	1:4:6	12: 5:0
Stephen Peirce	Dt^o		49	1:4:6	12: 5:0
David Shattuck Ju^r	Dt^o		49	1:4:6	12: 5:0
Daniel Gilson	Dt^o 10		46	1:3:0	11:10:0
Simeon Nutting	Dt^o		46	1:3:0	11:10:0
Simon Lakin	march 30.		57	1:8:6	14: 5:0
Silas Kemp	Dt^o		57	1:8:6	14: 5:0
Isaac Nutting Ju^r	Dt^o		57	1:8:6	14: 5:0
Jonathan Phelps	Dt^o		57	1:8:6	14: 5:0
Nathan Wesson	Dt^o		57	1:8:6	14: 5:0
Thomas Shattuck	Dt^o 31		56	1:8:0	14: 0:0
Nathaniel Parker	April 3		53	1:6:6	13: 5:0
Eleazer Spalden	Dt^o		53	1:6:6	13: 5:0
Stephen Foster	Dt^o 4		52	1:6:0	13: 0:0
Robert Blood	Dt^o 5		51	1:5:6	12:15:0
William Farnsworth	Dt^o		51	1:5:6	12:15:0
oliver Shattuck	Dt^o		51	1:5:6	12:15:0
Thomas Scott	Dt^o		51	1:5:6	12:15:0
Stephen Kemp	Dt^o		51	1:5:6	13:15:0
John Chamberlain	Dt^o 10		46	1:3:0	11:10:0
Aarron Blood	march 31		56	1:8:0	14: 0:0
Benjamin Nutting	April 3		53	1:6:6	13: 5:0
Benjamin Richardson	Dt^o 5		51	1:5:6	12:15:0
Oliver Wright	Dt^o 7		49	1:4:6	12: 5:0
Zachariah Willis	Dt^o 10		46	1:3:0	11:10:0
Josiah Butterfield	Dt^o 13		43	1:1:6	10:15:0
Joel Crosbey	Dt^o 14		42	1:1:0	10:10:0
Archeles Addams	Dt^o 10		46	1:3:0	11:10:0
John Nutting	Dt^o 13		43	1:1:6	10:15:0
Simon Gilson	Dt^o		43	1:1:6	10:15:0
Eleazer Fisk	Dt^o		43	1:1:6	10:15:0
Leonard Parker	Dt^o 14		42	1:1:0	10:10:0
John Gragg	Dt^o 26		30	0:15:0	7:15:0
Benjamin Shattuck	Dt^o 25		31	0:15:6	7:15:0
Josiah Shipley	Dt^o		31	0:15:6	7:15:0
Benjn Woods	may ye 2		24	0:12:0	6: 0:0
Oliver Parker	Dt^o		24	0:12:0	6: 0:0
Joseph Hartwell	Dt^o		24	0:12:0	6: 0:0
Simon Wheler	Dt^o		24	0:12:0	6: 0:0
Benjn Farmer	Dt^o		24	0:12:0	6: 0:0
Moses Blood	Dt^o		24	0:12:0	6: 0:0
Ephraim Hall	Dt^o		24	0:12:0	6: 0:0
Nehemiah Gould	Dt^o		24	0:12:0	6: 0:0

76:15:6

EPHRAIM WESSON Capt

THE READ FAMILIES OF WESTERN (WARREN) AND SUDBURY, MASS.

Communicated by Hon. JOSEPH WILLIAMSON, A.M., of Belfast, Me.

THE following record is extracted from the papers of the late Hon. Nathan Read, of Belfast, Maine.

Capt. Nathaniel Read, born Sept. 28, 1702, Died June 9th, 1785.
Phebe Read, wife of Capt. N. Read, born March 14th, 1706, Died Sept. 16th, 1788.

Children of the above.

Joshua Read, born Dec. 25th, 1732. Died March, 1743.
Phebe Read, born Feb. 8th, 1735.
Lidia Read, born March 24th, 1737. Died August 10th, 1769.
Mary Read, born Feb. 10th, 1738.
Nathan Read, born March 19th, 1741. Died Oct. 1st, 1758.
Martha Read, born Sept. 13th, 1743.
Abigail Read, born March 28th, 1746.
Ruth Read, born Feb. 10th, 1748.
Nathaniel Read, born March 26th, 1750. Died aged 4 days.
Eunice Read, born August 15th, 1751.
Reuben Read, Sen. born Nov. 13, N. S. 1730.

Children of the above Reuben Read, Sen.

Reuben Read, Jun. born Jan. 20th, 1756.
Elizabeth Read,* born Oct. 26th, 1757.
Nathan Read, born July 2nd, 1759.
Nathaniel Read, born April 4, 1862.
Joshua Read, born Jan. 20th, 1764. Died in Jan'y, 1826.
Sarah Read, born April 29, 1768. Died Oct. 24th, 1768.
Tamsin Read, born Dec. 25th, 1769.
Levi Read, born July 17, 1773. Died in Vernon, Ind., Oct. 19, 1819.
N. B. The above account was put down in New Stile.

WILL OF CAPT. ROBERT SLYE OF MARYLAND, 1670.

Communicated by Dr. CHRISTOPHER JOHNSTON, of Baltimore, Md.

ROBERT SLYE of Bushwood, on St. Clement's manor, St. Mary's County, merchant, dated 18 Jan'y, proved 13 March, 1670 (Wills, Lib. 1, fol. 422). To my little daughters Elizabeth and Frances, Rich Neck, 500 acres, between Mattapany and Bushwood; to my said daughters 30,000 lb. tobacco apiece, to be shipped to England the first next years after my death, by 10,000 lb. each year, consigned to Col. Henry Meese and my kinsman Mr. Strangewayes Mudd of London, for the use of said children. To my youngest son

---

* My sister, Elizabeth Sexton, whose first husband was Rev. Daniel Foster of New Braintree, and her second Squire Goodale of Munson, Mass., died at Munson, Oct. 20, 1830 (her birthday), aged 73.

Robert (under ⅒8) my plantation called Lapworth, together with three adjoining tracts called Norwood, Lapworth Lodge, and Clear Doubt; also all my negroes at Lapworth, stock &c. To my dearly beloved wife Susanna Slye, in lieu of dower, one half my stock of cattle, swine, horses, sheep &c. (excepting stock at Lapworth given my son Robert), one half all my negroes belonging to Bushwood, half the white servants belonging thereto, and half my household and other goods, together with the dwelling house and half the housing at Bushwood during her life, and after her death the land and houses to descend to my son Gerard. To my eldest son Gerard Slye (under 18) all the rest of my estate real and personal, and I constitute him sole executor. I request my loving friends Mr. Thomas Notley, my brother Mr. Justinian Gerard, my brother Mr. Nehemiah Blackstone, and my loving friend Mr. Benj. Folly *(sic!)* to act as overseers and feoffees in trust of this my last will and testament. My wife to have the guardianship of my children during their minority, and to take care that they be brought up in the true fear of God, and instructed in such literature as may tend to their improvement, both for their present and future good. But if my dear wife should die, then my brother Mr. Neh. Blackiston and my loving friend Mr. Benj. Solly *(sic!)* to have the guardianship of such of my children as may be under 16 years of age. Should all my children die under age, and without issue, then I give Bushwood (1000 acres) to my brothers-in-law Thomas and John Gerard, and my sister-in-law Mary Gerard, survivors or survivor, after the decease of my beloved wife; Rich Neck, on St. Clement's manor, to the eldest son of my dear sister Mrs. Elizabeth Russell of London; my plantation called Lapworth to my nephew Timothy Cooper, and Norwood, Lapworth Lodge, and Clear Doubt to my nephew Thomas Cooper, both of Springfield in New England.

Witnesses. John Blackiston, Ebenezer Blackiston, John (signum) Bullock, Mary Gerard.

NOTES.

Captain Robert Slye was a man of some prominence, a captain of militia, councillor in 1655 under the Parliamentary administration, and subsequently for a number of years Burgess for St. Mary's county. His wife Susanna was the eldest daughter of Thomas Gerard of St. Clement's manor, and her sister Elizabeth Gerard married Nehemiah Blackiston whom Capt. Slye mentions as his "brother" (*i. e.* brother-in-law). Capt. Slye had other relatives not mentioned in his will. A certain Samuel Smith of Charles county died 5 or 6 March 1661, and the inquisition held a number of years later (I have unfortunately lost the date) states that Mr. Robert Slye, Senr., was called cousin by said Smith and was commonly considered his next heir. Job Chandler, in his will (24 Augt.- 7 March 1659) appointed his "loving friend and brother Mr. Robert Slye" one of his overseers. I do not know anything about Capt. Slye's nephews Timothy and Thomas Cooper "both of Springfield in New England," but I notice that a Timothy Cooper is mentioned in Mr. Waters's "Gleanings," Part II., p. 142. REGISTER, vol. xxxix., p. 335.

I have a brief account of Job Chandler, with an abstract of his will, in the Va. Mag. of Hist. and Biog., Jan. 1896, pp. 321–324.—C. JOHNSTON.]

Savage, i : 455, says Thomas Cooper, Boston, "came perhaps in the Christian, 1635, aged 18, was prob. early at Windsor, rem. 1641 to Springfield, freem. 1649, a lieut. killed by the Indians 5 Oct. 1675. His d. Rebecca m. 12 July 1677 John Clark of Northampton." Rev. George M. Bodge, in "Soldiers in King Philip's Indian War" (REGISTER, 1884, p. 432), says of his death : "Two men and one woman were killed, viz. : Lieut. Thomas Cooper, who before the assault [on Springfield] rode out towards the fort to treat with the Indians, having two or three men with him, and was shot by an enemy concealed in the bushes a short distance from the town, but managed to ride to the nearest garrison-house, where he died." The substance of the account of which the above is a portion is from letters written by Major Pynchon and Rev. John Russell to the governor and council.

Mr. Mason A. Green, in his History of Springfield, p. 168, after frequently mentioning him in connection with the settlement of Springfield, speaks of his death as follows: "The loss of Lieutenant Cooper was severely felt. For many years he had been a wheel-horse in the town affairs. He was auditor of the selectmen's accounts at the time of his death. His various accomplishments showed how wide were the demands upon the early dwellers. He was a practising attorney before the County Court; he was a practical carpenter and farmer; he was a bonesetter, and a surveyor; he had been a deputy at the General Court, and townsman, and had been an invaluable agent in dealing with the Indians. His descendants may well place him beside the good and noble Deacon Samuel Chapin as a pillar of the town. His deeds fully warrant it."

Mr. Green also says: "Thomas Cooper was a useful man, a good fighter, and was held in great esteem in this valley. His personal influence with the natives was great, and it was his over-confidence in their fidelity to Springfield which eventually cost him his life."

Thomas Cooper was a member of the first board of selectmen elected in 1644, the town having previously been governed in open town meeting. In February, 1645, it was voted to erect a meeting-house and Thomas Cooper superintended its construction.

Mr. George Sheldon, in his History of Deerfield, ii: 124, says that Sarah, the widow of Lieut. Thomas Cooper, married second, Nov. 5, 1676, Lieut. William Clark of Northampton, and that she died May 8, 1688. Mr. Sheldon says with Savage that Rebecca Cooper, probably daughter of Lieut. Thomas, became the wife of John Clark, son of foregoing William Clark, and that she died in 1678. The late Rev. Dorus Clarke, D.D., for many years interested in the REGISTER, was a descendant of the immigrant Lieut. Wiillam Clarke.

The account of Job Chandler which Dr. Johnston contributes to the Virginia Historical Magazine, January, 1896, not only contains information upon the Chandler family, but also upon the Allerton and Willoughby families. It seems that Isaac Allerton married Elizabeth, daughter of Captain Thomas and sister of Colonel Thomas Willoughby, which accounts for the naming of one of their sons. See REGISTER, 1890, p. 290. Elizabeth may have been the first and only wife of Isaac Allerton.　　　　　　　　　　　　　　ANSON TITUS.

NOTES AND QUERIES.

NOTES.

ROBERT PEIRCE of Woburn had son Nathaniel, who by second wife, Elizabeth, had son Robert. This was first recorded in Woburn Records, born May 14, 1689. The word *born* was changed to *Dyed*. It is probable that the birth and death occurred the same day. A second Robert was born, and is mentioned in his father's will, May 2, 1691. He was never taxed in Woburn. In the History of Reading, pp. 131-2, we find "In this year [1711] and in the preceding, expeditions were formed against the French and Indians at Nova Scotia and Canada." In a list of men who went from Reading are the names of Jonathan Eaton, "who died at Annapolis Royal 1711," Robert Pierce and ―― Parker. This Robert Peirce could not have been born in Reading; for in a list of families previous to 1700, no Peirce is given. In the Parker Genealogy, p. 40, is a letter from a soldier, Hananiah Parker, born in Reading, written from Annapolis Royal, dated March ye 8th 1710 [11]. He says that there is a great deal of sickness in the company. "Jonathan Eaton is verry sick." "One man Dyed out of our company. He belonged to Wobone, his name was Robert Pierce." This letter shows that the Robert Pierce in the Reading list in the same company with Jonathan Eaton was from Woburn, and in all probability the son of Nathaniel. The Parker of the same list, whose first name is omitted, is doubtless Hananiah.　　　　　　　　　　MARY F. PEIRCE.

　Weston, Mass.

WHITNEY GENEALOGY.—I send for the REGISTER corrections to the " Whitney Genealogy " by Col. F. C. Pierce.
No. 193, pp. 59-60. " Squire" Joshua Whitney's wife was *Amy* Blodgett, daughter of Dr. William and Sarah (Spalding *née* Hall) Blodgett. She was born 16 February, 1723-4, in Plainfield, Conn., and died 24 December, 1819, in Canaan, Conn. Their daughter ABIGAIL WHITNEY was born 10 January, 1744, in Plainfield, married 2 June, 1768, in Plainfield, Capt. Asa Bacon of Canterbury, Conn., and died 21 September, 1821, in Woodstock, Conn. Captain Bacon was a son of " Leftenant " John and Ruth (Spalding) Bacon, was born 21 November, 1734, in Canterbury, and died there 15 October, 1819. He was active and prominent in town affairs, and was an officer in the Revolution.

New Haven, Conn.   FRANCIS BACON TROWBRIDGE.

DIARY KEPT IN THE REVOLUTIONARY WAR.—The following is a letter from Prof. Samuel C. Derby, No. 93 Fifteenth Avenue, Columbus, Ohio, to Hon. Samuel A. Green, LL.D., July 23, 1894. :

" During a visit at Dublin, N. H., I have seen a small fragment of a diary purporting to have been kept by Joseph Adams of Holliston, Mass. The portion which I saw contains 8 leaves (16 pp.) and is in the possession of Mr. A. L. Ball of Dublin. Another fragment of nearly the same number of pages is owned by Mr. E. G. Snow of Fitchburg, Mass., and comprised the beginning and a later portion. The part found by Mr. Ball begins Nov. 9, 1775, and ends Feb. 26, 1776; both portions—which by no means make up the whole of the original diary—consist of a brief account of the weather from day to day, the movements of the writer, who I think was a non-commissioned officer in the Massachusetts troops, and occasionally a very short description of military operations. Its chief value will be, I suspect, the light it may throw upon the military history of Holliston, Mass., in 1775-76.

" In it mention is made of Capt. James Mellen, Abner Perry, Sam. Pike, Ensign Proctor, Lt.-Col. Holden, Samuel Grant, Capt. Miller (?), John Gould, Obed Thurston, Oliver Works (Weeks?), Timothy Twitchell, John Harding, Seth Holbrook, Sergt. Freeland. Other persons are named in Mr. Snow's portion.

" The portion of the diary which came to Dublin was apparently brought there by some member of the family of Sergt. Josiah Wait, a brother-in-law of Joseph Adams the writer of the diary.

" Josiah Weit was killed, I think, in the battles about Long Island and New York in 1776."

RE-RECORDED BARNSTABLE COUNTY DEEDS.—It is a well-known fact that the Barnstable County Records and Deeds were burned in 1827. While in Barnstable recently, I was informed that after the fire of 1827 many citizens of all the towns in the county brought in their old deeds and had them " *re-recorded*," and there are today over thirty volumes of these re-recorded deeds. One volume only remains of the records saved from the fire. This volume was saved by Josiah Hinckley, Esq., father of Gustavus A. Hinckley, Esq. In looking over these re-recorded deeds I found important ones in which I was interested. Would it not be well to make some note of this fact in the REGISTER, that it may be generally known?   FRANK W. SPRAGUE.
Norfolk House, Roxbury.

HESSIAN UNIFORMS.—I had lately the opportunity to examine the journal kept by Lieut. Wm. Heth, of Morgan's Riflemen, on the expedition under Arnold to Quebec in 1775-6; and among the entries made during his imprisonment he notes the visits made to the prisoners by the Hessian and Hanoverian troops, early in May, 1776, just arrived in Canada for the relief of that province. He gives the following description of the uniforms worn by these troops :—

" Their uniform is Blue wth L[t] Yellow facings (wth only 4 Buttons on Lapels), white Vest & Breeches, narrow Lac'd Hats, all their Coats short waisted & long skirts, Hats of large size. They all wore silver gorgets wth the white Horse painted on a red ground in the center, the Hannoverean Horse w[ch] His Majesty has quarter'd in his Coat of Arms."

" Several of the German officers visited us again today—all Booted to a Man, even a Boy of 7 or 8 years of age strutted in Boots."

Washington, D. C.   CHARLES E. BANKS, M.D.

QUERIES.

GILBERT.—I want to know to what family of Gilberts Samuel Gilbert belonged. He married in Litchfield County, Conn., Deborah Sanford, moved to Tully, New York, then to Le Roy, New York, early in 1800, dying in Le Roy April 21st, 1843, aged 71. He had sisters Chloe and Dimmis, brothers Francis and Chauncey, may be others. Chauncey was named after Nathaniel Chauncey of Middletown, Conn., who married Susannah Gilbert, his uncle's widow.
464 La Salle Ave., Chicago, Ill. ISABELLA A. GILBERT.

WOODALL.—Who was Frances Woodhall, who on Jan. 17th, 1654, married Samuel, son of Thomas Kent of Gloucester, Mass.? What was the name of Thomas Kent's wife, and was he the first of his family in this country? How was Elisha Kent Kane, the Arctic explorer, connected with these Kents? He was the son of Judge John Kent Kane of Philadelphia.
352 Genesee St., Utica, N. Y. Mrs. JOHN FREDERICK MAYNARD.

STEWART.—Wanted, information as to names of parents of William Stewart of Red Lion Hundred, St. George's Co., Del. In 1775 he married Jane, daughter of David and Elizabeth Barr of Elkton, Cecil Co., Md. She died 1776, leaving a daughter Jane Barr Stewart. In 1809 William Stewart died, leaving a widow Deborah and five children; 1st, Jane Barr Stewart (m. William Newton of Alexandria, Va.); 2d, Wilhelmina (m. W. J. Hurlock of St. George's, Del.); 3d, Julia Ann (m. Dr. James Sutton of Del.); 4th, Mary (m. Benjamin Ricketts of Alexandria, Va.); 5th, Andrew M. Stewart.
352 Genesee St., Utica, N. Y. Mrs. JOHN FREDERICK MAYNARD.

MARGARET ADAMS.—Can any one inform me if Margaret Adams, daughter of John[1] Adams (Fortune, 1621), James[2] Adams and Frances Vassall, his wife, baptized Scituate, March 18, 1654, was the same Margaret who married John Pease 11th mo 30th 1676-7 as per Salem Records? (References. *N. E. H. G. Reg.*, Vol. xxxiii., p. 410; *Hist. Coll. Essex Inst.*, Vol. iii., p. 15.)
FRANCIS OLCOTT ALLEN.
Historical Society, 1300 Locust St., Philadelphia, Pa.

SWETLAND, SWEETLAND, ROAPER.—"Sarah yᵉ wife of John Swetland who was yᵉ widow Treadway Deceased February 28th 1773, Old Style." [REGISTER, Vol. xliii., p. 256.] Wanted, her maiden name. "Feb. 13, 1704-5. Joseph Sweetland, was Maried to Mercy Badcock, both of Milton." [REGISTER, Vol. xxxvi., p. 304.] Wanted, their children. Did Rev. Sylvester Dana (born at Ashford, Ct., Oct. 14, 1769) publish his history of Wyoming, and is there in it a list of persons saved from the "Massacre"?
Did Jane Zullesh, sister or daughter of David Zullesh, who was made freeman May 18, 1642 [Colonial Records, Vol. ii., p. 18] marry John Roaper, or what was his wife's name? B. A. LEONARD.
De Pere, Wisconsin.

SNOW.—Leonard Snow had children born in Chicopee, Mass., viz.: Benjamin, in 1800; Sarah, who married Belcher of Belchertown, and David who lived in Keene, N. H. Information is desired concerning the origin and parentage of this Leonard Snow. JAMES D. BUTLER.
Madison, Wis.

BUTLER.—Notices are solicited of the following Boston Butlers or their descendants: Robert, born 1729; William, 1733, and Christopher, born 1740—all brothers, and sons of William (born 1704) and Susanna: also concerning Bennet, born 4 January, 1711, son of Stephen and Joanna (Bennet) Butler.
Madison, Wis. JAMES D. BUTLER.

NEWELL, PITT AND JOHNSTON.—On a gravestone in Charlestown, Mass., is seen this record: "Mary Pitt, who died Sept. 26, 1684, in 78th year, relict of Andrew Newell of the city of Bristol, merchant, daughter of William Pitt, sheriff of the City of Bristol."

I would like the lineage of Andrew Newell, merchant of the city of Bristol, and also the lineage of William Pitt, sheriff of the city of Bristol.

Andrew[4] Newell, born Feb. 28, 1701-2, great grandson of Andrew Newell (of Charlestown, Mass.) and wife Mary Pitt, married Eunice Coffin, great granddaughter of Tristram Coffin. The will of Andrew[4] Newell is dated at Rotherhithe, co. Surrey, England, Nov. 19, 1741.

Andrew[1] Newell came to Charlestown, Mass., near the year 1630.

Wanted, the lineage of Thomas Johnston, or Johnstone, who was the builder of the organ, erected in its present position in 1759, in the " Old North Church " on Salem street, Boston, Mass. Tradition has said that he was of German origin. His grave is in King's Chapel Burial Ground; " departed this life, in 1776." Mrs. MARY D. NEWELL.

South Yarmouth, Mass.

FANNING.—I am searching for information of the Fannings. Edmund Fanning settled in New London, Conn., in 1652, and had many descendants scattered throughout the State of Connecticut and on Long Island. Bond's Watertown speaks of a Thomas Fanning of Watertown, who married Elizabeth Daniell. There was also a William Fanning who appeared early in Newbury, Mass., 1668. I have tried in vain to connect these Fannings. They would appear to have been all of the same family. Can any one give me any information of the descendants of this Thomas or William, or connect them with the Connecticut Edmund? There would certainly seem to be a connection between the Watertown and Connecticut settlers, as the name Daniell appeared in New London as early as 1663. I should be very glad to hear from any descendant of these settlers, or to receive any information concerning them, or any suggestion as to how to proceed to connect these three early settlers.

Worcester, Mass. WALTER F. BROOKS.

SHELDON.—Through a descendant of the Francis named below, we learn that there was early in London one Sheldon who was Archdeacon in St. Paul's Cathedral, and who had three sons — Francis, Ralph and Gilbert.

1. *Francis* went to Sweden. A coat of arms comes down in his family.
2. *Ralph*, b. 1595. Settled in London, had : Gilbert, b. May 28, 1627. Joseph, b. Sept. 28, 1628; Lord Mayor of London 1676; knighted; had children who went to America. Daniel, b. Sept. 13, 1632; had daughters Judith and Maria.
3. *Gilbert*, b. 1598. Was the distinguished Archbishop of Canterbury, and author of the " Sheldonian Compact," in the reign of Charles II.; was founder of Sheldonian Theatre at Oxford. His portrait, presented by his nieces Judith and Maria, is still to be seen there.

Tradition connects the Connecticut Valley Sheldons with Archbishop Gilbert. Isaac, of Windsor, about 1629-30, was the head of this tribe. Could he have been the son of Ralph 2, between Joseph and Daniel, and so nephew of the Archbishop?

Wanted, any connection between the London family and the American family.

Deerfield, Mass. GEORGE SHELDON.

WANTED.—The ancestry of the following persons :—

1. Sarah Hart, who married Geo. Norton of Ipswich, Oct. 7, 1669.
2. Mary Bartlett, who married Nathaniel Norton of Suffield, Conn., July 8, 1729.
3. Joseph Cook, b. about 1760, married Abigail Wright of Winchester or Colebrook, Conn.
4. Lieut. John Wright, served in French and Indian War, b. about 1710, probably at Wethersfield, Conn.
5. John Hancock, who married Anna Webb of Springfield, Mass., Nov. 19, 1713.
6. Lydia Wilmot, who married Daniel Candee of Oxford, Conn., May 7, 1784.
7. John Warner, married Margaret Loomis of E. Windsor, Conn., Dec. 1754.
8. Elizabeth Strickland, married Wm. Stoughton, of E. Windsor, Conn., July 6, 1710.

Waterville, N. Y. L. C. HAWKINS.

SNOW.—Benjamin, b. 1800, near Springfield, Mass., m. Lavina Warner—said to have been of South Hadley,—was a gunsmith, removed to Pulaski, N. Y. The names and dates of his parents are desired.
Madison, Wis. JAMES D. BUTLER.

MASSACHUSETTS PROCLAMATIONS.—The New-England Historic Genealogical Society would be glad to receive copies of any Massachusetts Fast and Thanksgiving proclamations, and especially the following:
Thanksgiving, 1852, 1853, 1860, 1878.
Fast, 1854, 1861 (April), 1881 (September).
The society has some duplicates for exchange.
Address JOHN WARD DEAN, Librarian, 18 Somerset St., Boston, Mass.

REPLIES.

GEORGE M. BROWNE'S BREWSTER ANCESTRY (*ante*, p. 86).—In the necrology of Mr. George Morgan Browne in the January number of the REGISTER I feel sure the assertion that he was descended from *Jonathan* Brewster, Elder William's son, is a mistake.

Joanna (Brewster) Morgan was my great-grandmother. She married Daniel Morgan 23 January, 1777, and her last child was born 14 January, 1795. It is she who was Mr. Browne's grandmother.

Now there was a Joanna Brewster who was descended from Elder William's son *Jonathan*. Her great-grandfather was Benjamin[3] Brewster of Norwich, Ct., who married—Feb., 1659, Anna Dart, and whose son Jonathan[4] (b. — Nov., 1664) m. 18 Dec., 1690, Judith Stephens of Norwich. Joanna's father, Jonathan[5] Brewster of Norwich (b. 2 April, 1694) m. 25 Feb., 1718–19, Ruth Morgan, and again m. 29 April, 1736, Lucy Andrus. The birth of Joanna, "eldest daughter," and of Simon, "eldest son," of Jonathan Brewster of Norwich (see Norwich Probate Records, 4 May, 1754), is not on record; they are not Lucy Andrus' children, all of whom are then mentioned: the two sons of Ruth Morgan (whose births are recorded in Norwich) are not then alive, though two of her children were living in 1744 (see New London Probate, 16 March, 1747); Joanna was born prior to 1736, and so could not have been Daniel Morgan's wife.

Another Joanna Brewster, as you will see, was the grandmother of Mr. George Morgan Browne—viz.: the daughter of Benjamin Brewster of Preston, Ct. This Joanna's father I believe to be the son of William[3] Brewster, the son of Love[2], Elder William's son; for he manifestly was not Benjamin Jr. (b. 28 Nov. 1673), Anna Dart's son, who lived in Lebanon, Ct. (Norwich Deeds, 10 Jan., 1732–3).

Thomas Sluman sells 8 Dec., 1699, land in Preston to William Brewster "of Duxborough," Mass., which same land William Brewster gives, 6 March, 1710–11, "in consideration of ye goodwill love and affection," etc., to his son, Benjamin Brewster "of Duxborough"; thereafter a Benjamin Brewster appears in Preston. William's son Benjamin, we know by Plymouth County Records, was in Connecticut in 1714.

Benjamin Brewster of Preston m. 16 Oct., 1713, Elizabeth Witter (who d. there 21 Feb., 1740–1, leaving several children), and again m. 10 June, 1741, Sarah Caulkins (whose only child recorded was Jonas, b. there 16 June, 1742). The births of his daughters Lois and Joanna (Norwich Probate, 20 Nov., 1753) are not on record; but 20 Sept., 1764, Joanna[5] "being of lawful age to choose a guardian," chose Jonas. Jonas Brewster is recorded, 3 May, 1777, as having been "guardian to Joanna, wife of Daniel Morgan."

I suppose there is no doubt as to William Brewster of Duxbury, Mass., that he was the son of *Love* Brewster, and the grandson of Elder William Brewster.
Norwich, Conn. FRANK PALMER.

MARSHALL'S COURTS OF PROBATE (*Correction*).—In the review of Dr. Marshall's Ancient Courts of Probate in the April number of the REGISTER (page 232), the writer stated that the Court of Husting had been omitted. This is an error; it *is* in the book, but, being indexed under Husting it escaped his notice in a very hurried review, though it is cross-referenced under London.
J. HENRY LEA.

PROCTOR.—(*ante* vol. 49, page 462.)—In the notice of Thomas Emerson Proctor in the REGISTER for October, 1895, vol. 49, p. 462, it is stated that the Proctor family in this country is descended from John Proctor who came from London in 1635 in the ship "Susan and Anne" at the age of forty. This statement I think is too broad, for many of the name in this country are descendants of Robert Protor, who was admitted freeman May 10, 1643, and who resided at Concord and later at Chelmsford. This Robert could not have been a son of John Proctor above named. FRANCIS JEWITT PARKER.

HISTORICAL INTELLIGENCE.

LIST OF GENEALOGIES IN PREPARATION.—Mr. Seymour Morris, of 142 La Salle street, Chicago, Ill., has nearly ready for publication a list of family histories now in preparation, with the names and addresses of the compilers. He proposes to add to this a list of manuscript genealogies which have been deposited with historical societies or in public libraries. Any aid that genealogists or librarians may render will be appreciated by Mr. Morris.

GENEALOGIES IN PREPARATION.—Persons of the several names are advised to furnish the compilers of these genealogies with records of their own families and other information which they think may be useful. We would suggest that all facts of interest illustrating family history or character be communicated, especially service under the U. S. Government, the holding of other offices, graduation from college or professional schools, occupation, with places and dates of birth, marriage, residence, and death. When there are more than one christian name they should all be given in full if possible. No initials should be used when the full names are known.

Adams.—Andrew N. Adams, of Fairhaven, Vt., has in preparation and will soon publish a genealogical history of the family of Henry Adams, of Braintree, Mass., and will include in his work the family of John Adams, of Cambridge, Mass. The book will make a volume of 800 octavo pages, or more, and will record over 2,000 families and 12,000 persons. Subscriptions are solicited. Price $5.50 in cloth, or $7 in full morocco. Circulars furnished by the author on application. Mr. Adams is also collecting materials relating to other large families of Adams, such as the descendants of John of Plymouth, William of Ipswich, Robert of Newbury, George of Watertown, and others, but they are too voluminous to be included in this volume.

Brewster.—Lucy Hall Greenlaw, of Gordon Place, Cambridgeport, is preparing a genealogy of the Brewster family. The early generations will probably be printed in the REGISTER, and all the material collected will be deposited in the library of this Society.

Carpenter.—Daniel H. Carpenter, of Maplewood, N. J., is nearly ready to publish a work, entitled The Carpenter Family in America, being an historical and genealogical account of William Carpenter, of Providence, R. I., and his descendants. It will embrace eight or nine generations. Nearly 2000 persons, representing 500 families will be given. There will be maps, photo-engravings, autographs, etc. No pains will be spared to make the book acceptable in style, paper and binding. A list of subscribers will be printed in the book. Circulars furnished on application.

Cheney.—Rev. Charles H. Pope, of Cambridge, Mass., has a history of this family well advanced, and is to spend some time in England this summer to complete investigations which were begun several years since by Rev. W. F. Cheney, of Dedham, Mass.

Choate.—"The Choates in America" is now in the hands of the printer. It will be ready for delivery to subscribers in the Fall. Price $5. As soon as published the price will be advanced. Orders returned before the book comes from the publishers will be filled at the price named. Information, additional data and orders may be sent to Rev. E. O. JAMESON, No. 49 Hancock Street, Boston, Mass.

Claflin.—Mr. Charles H. Wight, of 415 Broadway, New York City, has a genealogy of the Claflin family in preparation. As the work is nearly completed, persons interested should send in the records of their families at once.

Fanning.—Walter F. Brooks, 54 Queen Street, Worcester, Mass., has in preparation an historical and genealogical record of the Fanning family from the 12th century to the present time. Previous to publishing the work, which is now near completion, the author requests persons of the name to send sketches of their families.

Goldthwaite.—Miss Charlotte Goldthwaite, Hartford, Conn., has now near completion a history of this family for which she began collecting data nearly thirteen years ago. She has a full account of those of the name in America, with valuable information obtained in England, where in 1890 she discovered and visited the original home of the family, and made extended and successful research in public records. Circulars will be sent on application.

Kellogg.—Timothy Hopkins, Mills Building, San Francisco, Cal., is preparing a genealogy of all branches of the Kellogg family and is particularly desirous of ascertaining the relationship, if any, between the several emigrants of the name in this country, and their connection with English families.

Manning.—William H. Manning, of Brooklyn, N. Y., is preparing a genealogy of the Manning families of New England. Address, care of the Long Island Historical Society, Brooklyn, N. Y.

Ripley.—Willis J. Ripley, 120 Fifth Avenue, Chicago, Ills., is engaged in compiling the genealogy of the Ripley family in America, from William Ripley, who came from Wymondham, Norfolk County, England, in 1638, and settled with his family in Hingham, Mass., and incidentally is collecting data of the families of William Ripley, who settled in West Bridgewater, Mass., about 1695, and of James Ripley, who came from Ireland and settled in Virginia about 1750. Some material has been found relating to the family in England prior to 1638. He will be pleased to hear from anyone interested in the above families.

SOCIETIES AND THEIR PROCEEDINGS.

NEW-ENGLAND HISTORIC GENEALOGICAL SOCIETY.

Boston, Massachusetts, Wednesday, March 4, 1896.—A stated meeting was held this afternoon at three o'clock in Marshall P. Wilder Hall, 18 Somerset Street, the Hon. Charles Levi Woodbury in the chair.

Sixteen resident members were elected.

On motion of Henry E. Woods, resolutions were passed to join other societies in petitioning Congress to make an appropriation to enable the Secretary of State to prepare and publish the records and papers of the Continental Congress.

Charles Sidney Ensign, LL.B., of Watertown, Mass., read a paper entitled "Watertown's Eldest Daughter," giving a sketch of the history of Wethersfield, Connecticut, which was settled by Watertown people.

A committee was appointed to prepare resolutions on the death of Hon. Charles Carleton Coffin, to report at the next meeting.

The monthly reports of the corresponding secretary, the council and the librarian were presented.

Resolutions were passed congratulating the Rev. Lucius Robinson Paige, D.D., the oldest and first elected member of the society, who will be 94 years old on the 8th of this month, on the near approach of his birthday, and testifying our sentiments of respect, love and affection for him.

Wednesday, April 1.—A stated meeting was held in Marshall P. Wilder Hall, Vice-President Woodbury in the chair.

Nine resident members were elected.

Rev. Sanford H. Cobb, D.D., of Albany, N. Y., read a paper entitled "The Story of the Palatines: an Episode in Colonial History."

Resolutions of respect to the memory of Hon. Charles Carleton Coffin, A.M., were reported by the committee appointed in March. They were supported by Rev. Ezra H. Byington, D.D., George K. Clarke, Charles S. Ensign and Oliver B. Stebbins, and unanimously adopted by a rising vote.

The reports of the corresponding secretary, the librarian, the council and the historiographer were severally presented.

The committee appointed to attend the hearing of a committee of the General Court in regard to the preservation of the public records reported that they had attended to this duty.

May 6.—A stated meeting was held this afternoon. In the absence of the president and vice-presidents, the Hon. Joseph B. Walker, of Concord, N. H., was chosen president *pro tem.*

Resolutions were passed protesting against the demolition of the Bulfinch front of the State House, and against any more alteration of it than is indispensable to its permanent preservation.

William Carver Bates of Boston read a paper entitled " Websteriana," with selections from unpublished letters of Hon. Daniel Webster.

Seven resident members were elected.

The monthly reports of the corresponding secretary, the librarian, the council and the historiographer were presented.

Asa Warren Brown of Kensington, N. H., addressed the meeting on various phases of genealogical research that had come under his observation.

RHODE ISLAND HISTORICAL SOCIETY.

Providence, Tuesday, March 24, 1896.—A stated meeting was held this evening.

Norman M. Isham, A.M., Instructor in Architecture in Brown University, read a paper on " The Old Houses of Colonial Rhode Island."

April 7.—A quarterly meeting was held this evening. A committee, of which Hon. Thomas Durfee was chairman, was appointed to act with a similar committee of the Sons of the American Revolution, in laying before the commissioners of the New State House the names of distinguished Rhode Island citizens deemed worthy of being enrolled on the walls of the new state capitol.

The president was requested to appoint a committee of five to make arrangements for the observance of the seventy-fifth anniversary of the formation of the society, which, according to the records, was on the 19th of April, 1822.

April 21.—A stated meeting was held this evening.

Dr. Lewis G. Janes, president of the Brooklyn Ethical Association, read a paper on " The Life, Works and Political and Religious Opinions of Samuel Gorton, one of the Founders of the Town of Warwick." A report of this paper is printed in the *Providence News* for April 22, 1896.

MAINE HISTORICAL SOCIETY.

Portland, Thursday, March 26, 1896.—Two sessions were held this afternoon and evening at the Society's rooms in Baxter Building. In the absence of the president, Hon. James P. Baxter, Hon. George F. Emery presided.

Mr. Hubbard W. Bryant, the librarian, made a report showing large additions to the library and cabinet during the last year.

Mr. Samuel T. Dole of Windham read a paper on the " History of Little Falls Village."

Mr. L. B. Chapman of Deering read a paper on the " Early History and Settlement of Sacarappa."

Mrs. Sarah Fairfield Hamilton of Saco presented her "Personal Reminiscences" of her father, the late Governor John Fairfield.

Rev. Henry O. Thayer read a paper on a pioneer minister of the Kennebec.

At the evening session, President Baxter in the chair, Rev. Henry S. Burrage, D.D., read a paper by Hon. James W. Bradbury, D.D., of Augusta, entitled " Some Railroad Reminiscences."

Hon. James P. Baxter read a paper on " Municipal Government."

Friday, April 24, 1896.—A meeting was held this day in the Society's rooms in Baxter Building. In the absence of President Baxter, Rev. Henry S. Burrage, D.D., presided.

Mr. L. B. Chapman of Deering read a paper on " The Mast Industry of Old Falmouth."

Mr. Nathan Gould followed with a paper on " Col. Edmund Phinney's Eighteenth Continental Regiment."

Chairman Burrage next read a paper written by Mr. John F. Sprague of Monson, Me., entitled "Hon. Thomas Daves, one of the Founders of Piscataquis County."

Mr. Hubbard W. Bryant then announced that he had received from London a pamphlet entitled "Description of Portland in the United States, from an English Gentleman in America to his Friend in Shropshire." The author was James Gay, who sojourned in Portland, Me., in 1817.

NECROLOGY OF THE NEW-ENGLAND HISTORIC GENEALOGICAL SOCIETY.

Prepared by the Historiographer, Rev. GEORGE M. ADAMS, D.D., of Auburndale, Mass.

THE sketches of deceased members prepared for the REGISTER are of necessity brief, because the space that can be appropriated is quite limited. All the materials for more extended memoirs which can be gathered are preserved in the archives of the Society, and they will be available for use in preparing the "Memorial Biographies," of which five volumes have been issued and a sixth volume is in preparation. The income from the Towne Memorial Fund is devoted to the publication of these volumes.

THOMAS HUGHES, Q. C., F. S. A., was born at Uffington, Berkshire, England, October 20, 1823. He was the son of John and Margaret Elizabeth (Wilkinson) Hughes. He was educated at Rugby under Dr. Arnold, and at Oriel College, Oxford, where he took his B. A. degree in 1845. He was called to the Bar in 1848, and was made a Queen's Counsel 1869. In 1882, he was appointed Judge of the County Court. From 1865 to 1874, he was in Parliament, where he was classed as an advanced Liberal, and gave his chief attention to what he called "social political questions." He was known as an energetic friend of the working classes, seeking their social and educational improvement. In 1870 he made a tour of the United States. He had stood up boldly for the Union in the darkest days of our civil war, and when he came to visit us he received a most enthusiastic welcome. One of the results of this visit appeared some years later in the "New Rugby" colony in Tennessee. Mr. Hughes was deeply interested in the plan, as one offering a home under favorable conditions to young English people, for whom the outlook in England had less of encouragement. A large tract of land was purchased on the Cumberland plateau, and English families numbering about two hundred persons came over. Mr. Hughes came to this country a second time in 1883, chiefly on business connected with the colony.

He will probably be longest remembered as the author of "Tom Brown's School Days," which was published in 1856 and ran through several editions. It has been called the most successful book of the century for boys. A French version was published in Paris in 1875. He was also the author of "The Scouring of the White Horse," 1858; "Tom Brown at Oxford," 1861; "Religio Laici" (afterwards printed as "A Layman's Faith"), 1861; "The Cause of Freedom: Which is its Champion in America, the North or the South?" 1863; "Alfred the Great," 1869; "Memoir of a Brother" (George C. Hughes) 1873.

He married in 1847, Anne Frances, eldest daughter of Rev. James Ford, Prebendary of Exeter. She, with three sons and three daughters, survives him. Mr. Hughes was elected a corresponding member of the New-England Historic Genealogical Society in 1861. He died at Brighton, England, March 22, 1896.

HENRY CHANDLER BOWEN, Corresponding Member since February 3, 1858, died at his home, 90 Willow street, Brooklyn, N. Y., February 24, 1896. He was born in Woodstock, Connecticut, September 11, 1813, and was descended from Griffith[1] Bowen, the immigrant (see REGISTER, 47, p. 453), through Henry,[2] Isaac,[3] Henry,[4] Matthew,[5] William[6] and George,[7] who married Lydia Wolcott Eaton, a daughter of Dr. John Eliot Eaton. His ancestors have for most part resided in Roxbury, Pomfret and Woodstock. At the age of twenty he went to New York city, finding employment in the silk-house of Arthur Tappan & Co. In 1839 began the firm of Bowen & McNamee later Bowen, Holmes & Co., which conducted the dry-goods business until the Civil War, when they were obliged to suspend. The firm several years before, in a historic card, gave notice to the trade at large that "our goods and not our principles are on the market." In young manhood he began an active religious life, and was foremost in promoting the enterprises of the Congregational Church. In 1848 with others he began the *Independent*, becoming full proprietor in 1861. With retirement from trade he gave himself to its business management. In 1862 he was appointed Collector of Internal Revenue by President Lincoln, continuing five years. During the history of the *Independent* its influence has been in behalf of the best causes. In anti-slavery days, the trying times of the Civil War, the period of reconstruction, and all the larger interests of peace, education, reforms and Christian missions, the *Independent* has been a leading force. Mr. Bowen was its soul and life. He attracted able writers, and by wise management secured a patronage making the *Independent* probably the ablest and widest read religious periodical in America. Among the editors whom he employed, of world-wide reputation, were Reverend Doctors R. S. Storrs, J. P. Thompson, Joshua Leavitt : Henry Ward Beecher, Theodore Tilton and Rev. Dr. William Hayes Ward. In recent years it has been his delight to gather at Roseland Park, his gift to Woodstock, on each successive Independence Day, a company, illustrious in every department of the world's better ways. These famous celebrations have been highly productive of the historic and patriotic spirit of our day. Mr. Bowen married first June 6, 1844, Lucy Maria, a daughter of Lewis Tappan, by whom he had ten children, eight of whom are living. He married second, December 25, 1864, Ellen, a daughter of Dr. Hiram Holt, Pomfret.

By the Rev. Anson Titus, Somerville.

FREDERICK LOTHROP AMES, A.B., of North Easton, Mass., a life member, elected January 5, 1881, was born at North Easton, June 8, 1835, and died while passing over Long Island Sound, Sept. 13, 1895, aged 60 years. For a memoir, with portrait, see REGISTER, vol. 49, pp. 273–275.

Hon. CHARLES HENRY BELL, A.M., LL.D., of Exeter, N. H., a life member, elected June 3, 1868, born at Chester, N. H., Nov. 18, 1823, and died at Exeter, Nov. 11, 1893. For a memoir, with portrait, see REGISTER, vol. 49, pp. 9–25.

Hon. ALEXANDER HAMILTON BULLOCK, A.B., LL.D., of Worcester, Mass., a life member, elected Sept. 6, 1865, was born at Royalston, Mass., March 2, 1816, and died at Worcester, Jan. 17, 1882, aged 65 years. For a memoir, with portrait, see REGISTER, vol. 50, pp. 153–155. See also REGISTER, vol. 36, pp. 413–414.

DAVID CLAPP, Esq., of South Boston, Mass., a resident member, elected March 7, 1866, was born at Dorchester, February 6, 1806, and died at Boston, May 10, 1893, aged 87 years. For a memoir, with portrait, see REGISTER, vol. 48, pp. 145–156.

Hon. CHARLES CARLETON COFFIN, A.M., of Brookline, Mass., a resident member, elected July 5, 1865, was born at Boscawen, N. H., July 26, 1823, and died at Brookline, March 2, 1896, aged 72 years. For a memoir, with portrait, see REGISTER, vol. 50, pp. 289–295.

DANIEL RAVENEL, Esq., of Charleston, S. C., a corresponding member, elected June 2, 1875, was born at Charleston, S. C., Sept. 5, 1834, and died in that city Sept. 4, 1894, aged 60 years. For a memoir see REGISTER, vol. 49, pp. 297–299.

GEORGE CHEYNE SHATTUCK, A.M., M.D., a resident member, elected Feb. 7, 1883, was born in Boston, Mass., July 22, 1813, and died in Boston, March 22, 1893, aged 79 years. For a memoir, with portrait, see REGISTER, vol. 48, pp. 277–280.

CHARLES TURELL, Esq., of New York city, a corresponding member, elected January 6, 1847, was born at Salem, Mass., August 7, 1786, and died at Red Bank, N. J., May 26, 1863 (not June 5, 1863, as given in the Rolls of Membership), aged 76. For a memoir see " Memorial Biographies," vol. v, pp. 221–229.

BOOK NOTICES.

[THE Editor requests persons sending books for notice to state, for the information of readers, the price of each book, with the amount to be added for postage when sent by mail.]

Searches into the History of the Gillman or Gilman Family, including the Various Branches in England, Ireland, America and Belgium. By ALEXANDER W. GILL-MAN. Illustrated with Engravings of Coats of Arms, Portraits, Copies of Ancient Pedigrees, Monumental Inscriptions, &c., &c. London: Elliott Stock. 1895. In two volumes crown 4to. pp. 334 in the two volumes. Price $7 for sending by book post to America. The book is also issued in one volume, but in this form it is too heavy to send by mail.

A genealogy of the Family of Gilman in America was published in 1869, which contained extended references to the family in England. The investigator visited England and obtained many documents that had been preserved by Gilmans there. He made no pretensions, however, of writing a genealogy of the English family. This has not yet been done, but a noble contribution to the subject has been made by Mr. Alexander W. Gillman, grandson of that distinguished surgeon who for so many years befriended the poet Coleridge. When Mr. Gillman began to investigate is not known to us, but after he had had his interest aroused he discovered that another member of the family then living in Ireland had already made extensive researches among ancient records, and he discovered also the American book. These discoveries, Mr. Gillman says, stimulated him to carry on his investigations as thoroughly as possible. The result is an elegant small quarto, luxuriously printed and amply illustrated, and inscribed to President Daniel Coit Gilman, of Johns Hopkins University.

Mr. Gillman properly calls his work "Searches" into the history of the family of Gillman or Gilman. He has not prepared a consecutive genealogical record, but rather a series of chapters which treat the subject in many different phases. The opening chapter is upon the spelling of the name. It constitutes an interesting historical study of orthography. The second chapter is on the Welsh origin of the family, taking as text a statement made by Mr. Arthur Gilman, in his American genealogy, and proving its truth. Mr. Gillman carries the Welsh pedigree very far back into remote antiquity by taking advantage of the work done by order of Henry VII., in tracing his descent through Owen Tudor, Coel Godeboc, and the mother of the Emperor Constantine the Great, to Brutus of Troy through a hundred generations, sixty-eight of which are acknowledged to be "mythical." However, as the historical record runs as far as the year 300 A.D., the antiquity of the family may be considered established.

In his third chapter, Mr. Gillman takes up the family in the vicinity of London in the reign of Henry VIII., and his daughters Mary and Elizabeth. This chapter, like others, is well illustrated with fac-similes of coats of arms and monumental inscriptions. The author has been indefatigable in following up clews and in copying records, thus accumulating a storehouse of facts which will doubtless lead to further discoveries. Succeeding chapters show the family in Surrey, in Ireland, in Hertfordshire and Essex, in Bristol, Gloucestershire, and Kent. Here is a chapter on the Gilmans in Norfolk, who are the ancestors of the Americans, or of most of them, who are more fully represented in another chapter, made up of copious extracts from Mr. Arthur Gilman's book, of 1869.

Chapter ten is devoted to "The Gillmans of Highgate," the writer's own line, and, as might have been anticipated, it gives many particulars in regard to the life of Coleridge when under the hospitable roof of Dr. Gillman, a term of residence covering nineteen years, and ending only with the poet's death. This chapter is also separately printed, and has already been extensively commented upon as giving new light on the sometimes distorted record. Dr. Gillman is set before us as a most disinterested as well as hospitable man, and the account of these years will possess great interest to all readers of Coleridge. The chapter is illustrated with views of the house and portraits of the poet as well as of Dr. and Mrs. Gillman and other members of the family.

The Gilmans of China and of Belgium have separate chapters assigned to them, and it sounds strange to read of "Baron de Gilman" in the latter land.

The volume contains an ample table of contents and full indexes. The list of illustrations covers two pages and more, and it must be said that the portraits and views are real additions to the interest of the book. The members of the family on both sides of the ocean are to be congratulated that filial piety and a good bank account have been found in the same person, for without either of these qualifications the searches into the past of the house of Gillman and Gilman could not have been successfully conducted upon such a liberal scale, nor with such long-continued interest.

* *

The Bibliography of the State of Maine, from the Earliest Period to 1891. By JOSEPH WILLIAMSON. In Two Volumes. Portland: The Thurston Print. 1896. 8vo. Vol. I. pp. viii.+738. Vol. II. pp. 669. Price $7.00 for the two volumes. Address, The Maine Historical Society, Portland, Maine.

This work has been compiled under the auspices of the Maine Historical Society, and is published by that society. It is well known that Judge Williamson has been engaged many years in preparing the work, and has been unsparing in the time and labor which he has bestowed on it. Each book has, when practicable, been examined by the compiler and the titles copied and other memoranda taken by him. There are probably omissions, for it would be strange if there were not, but it has not been for lack of persistent effort to make the bibliography complete under his plan.

" With certain exceptions," Judge Williamson states in his Preface, " its purpose is to give the full title of every book, pamphlet and reputable magazine article at any time printed in or having reference to Maine, and also all of which the authors were at the time of writing or publishing residents within the State. The exceptions are chiefly public, municipal and legal reports, and pamphlets which relate to organizations not of an historical, literary, charitable or religious character. Although many of the best literary productions of the State are to be found only in its newspapers, no attempt to enumerate them has been made with the exception of such as have been preserved in other form. The plan also excludes the writings of native authors printed or published after they had ceased to be residents, unless these have some special relation to Maine."

The work, as we stated in July, 1894 (REGISTER, Vol. 48, p. 248), when we announced that the work was drawing near its completion, embraces " about ten thousand titles and the names of over 2500 authors, with brief notices. It contains numerous notes and cross references; the whole constituting a complete key to the biography, history and literature of the State." A glance through the pages of this work shows that Maine has a goodly host of authors, past and present, among whom are many who have won a high place in the literature of the country. The people of that state owe a debt of gratitude to Judge Williamson for collecting the titles of the works of her writers and for the admirable manner in which he has performed his task.

Only a few State Bibliographies have been undertaken, and none have approached this in completeness. The labor of such an undertaking would appal most men. But to Judge Williamson it was a labor of love, and he has persevered and brought his work to a successful conclusion. May he live many years to enjoy his labors and to do other historical work. His History of Belfast, Maine, published nearly twenty years ago, and noticed in the REGISTER for October, 1877, is a model for a local history.

Contributions to the History of Christ Church, Hartford. I. Commemorative Sermon. By Rt. Rev. THOMAS M. CLARK, D.D., LL.D. *II. Annals of the Parish.* By CHARLES J. HOADLY, LL.D. *III. Reports on the Funds of the Parish. IV. Abstract of principal Votes, with comments and additions.* By GURDON W. RUSSELL, M.D. *V. List of Baptisms, Marriages and Burials, from 1801 to 1895.* Hartford: Belknap & Warfield. 1895. 8vo., pp. 787. Illustrated. Price, $4.00.

The parish of Christ Church, Hartford, is fortunate in having two such parishioners as Dr. Charles J. Hoadly, the learned Librarian of the State of Connecticut, and Dr. Gurdon W. Russell, the " beloved physician " of Hartford, both experts in local civil and ecclesiastical annals; and another parishioner such as " the gentleman by whose generosity and interest " the publication of the sumptuous volume before us has been made possible. Dr. Hoadly's "Annals of the Episcopal Church in Hartford to the year 1829," the date of the consecration of the present church building, were prepared for the semi-centennial anniversary in 1879; they include most valuable information as to persons and events connected with the first attempts to organize an Episcopal society and build a church in Hartford in 1762, and the organization of the present parish in 1786, and its history for forty-three years. Dr. Russell's "Abstract of principal Votes" covers over three hundred and twenty pages, and is in the literal sense the annals of the parish from its organization, the important acts of parish and vestry meetings being given under each year, with many papers in full and, what is of especial value, antiquarian, historical, and genealogical notices in abundance. No event of any importance passes without full consideration, and no prominent member of the parish or the congregation is mentioned without some account of his family, his position in the community, and his character. Thus we have not only notices of the rectors, and they include such men as Bishops Philander Chase, J. M. Wainwright, T. C. Brownell, George Burgess, T. M. Clark and W. F. Nichols, but also sketches of such men as Charles Sigourney, James Ward, William H. Imlay, Nathan Morgan, Cyprian Nichols, George Beach, Samuel Tudor, Isaac Toucey, James Goodwin, Ebenezer Flower, Charles H. Northam and Junius S. Morgan, and the famous organist Henry Wilson. The volume is thus made a mine of information for future investigators, as well as a model for future annalists; while it may be added that this proof of the value of full records may be an encouragement to some weary clerks of parishes and vestries. The "Report on the Funds of the Parish," due to Dr. Russell's painstaking labors, is of general interest chiefly (one regrets to say) as a warning to administrators of trusts.

To genealogists the most valuable part of the volume is the full transcript, covering nearly two hundred pages, of the register of baptisms, marriages and burials; that of the baptisms and marriages beginning in 1801, and that of the burials in 1812. Fortunately they have been carefully kept and entered; yet additions and corrections of some importance have been made in the burials register. The number of names included is very large, and any one looking into the pedigree of families which have belonged in Hartford during the present century can hardly fail to find here something that he needs.

It may be added that, besides fac-similes and views, the volume contains beautifully executed reproductions of portraits of the fifteen rectors, pains having been taken to represent them as they were at the time of their rectorships, and also of Dr. Russell and Mr. Wilson.

By Prof. Samuel Hart, D.D., of Hartford, Conn.

Suffolk Manorial Families, being the County Visitations and other Pedigrees. Edited with Extensive Additions by JOSEPH JAMES MUSKETT, Corresponding Member of the Historic Genealogical Society of New England. Privately Printed. Exeter: William Pollard & Co., Printers. 1896. Royal 4to. Vol. I. Part 6. Price 5 shillings. The edition is restricted to 250 copies. Communications should be addressed to the editor, care of J. Muskett Yetts, Esq., 50 Lincoln's Inn Fields, London, England.

Another Part of the Suffolk Manorial Families is before us. The editor expresses his desire "to make this work an exhaustive *resumé* of the Genealogy of the Shire," and the numbers that have thus far been issued show that his desire has a prospect of being fulfilled.

The Part before us contains the Suffolk Goodwins. Sections are devoted 1st to Goodwin of Blaxhall; 2d, Goodwin of Bocking; 3d, Goodwin of Bull's Hall; 4th, Goodwin of East Bergholt; 5th, Goodwin of Framlingham; 6th, Goodwin of Hartford, Connecticut; 7th, Goodwin of Marlesford; 8th, Goodwin of Stonham Parva; 9th, Goodwin of Torrington, and 10th, Goodwin of Yoxford.

The plan of the work is to give under each section abstracts of wills of persons of the family to which the section is devoted and close with one or more tabular pedigrees. The portion devoted to the Goodwins of Hartford, Connecticut, will particularly interest our New England people, though other portions have a value to them. Six years ago James Junius Goodwin, Esq., of Hartford, published a bulky volume (see REGISTER, vol. xlv., p. 171) devoted to the descendants of William and Ozias Goodwin, to which was prefixed "The

Goodwins of East Anglia," by Rev. Augustus Jessopp, D.D., and a " Report on English Investigations," by Henry F. Waters, A.M.   The latter article contained the result of his researches concerning the Goodwins of England up to that date. The readers of the REGISTER are aware that he is still adding to his Gleanings on that family.

Mr. Muskett says: "The paternity of William Goodwin, the New England emigrant of 1632, has not as yet been definitely ascertained; but it is probable that he came from Braintree or Bocking, which together form one long street in the county of Essex.   He was one of the so-called 'Braintree Company' which Mr. Hooker followed to the western world.   Men from Braintree were amongst his fellow voyagers.   His brother Ozias Goodwin had married a Braintree woman.   A William Goodwin of Bocking, who may well have been himself, was son-in-law to Robert White of Messing."

We trust that Mr. Muskett will receive many additions to his subscription list.

Popular County Histories.   The History of Suffolk.   By Rev. JOHN JAMES RAVEN, D.D., F.S.A.   London: Elliott Stock.   1895. 8vo. pp. viii.+287.   Price 5s. 8d.

Many of the settlers of New England came from the County of Suffolk in the mother country.   Their descendants naturally take a particular interest in the history of this county.   The book before us, by Canon Raven, gives a good synopsis of this.   The matter is arranged chronologically rather than topically. " The changes in the social condition of the inhabitants of Suffolk have not been over-looked, and much light has been thrown upon the subject by extracts from diaries and letters which could not be gained by any other means."

The county of Suffolk has been the scene of many important events in the history of England.   It has been also the home of many great men who are an honor to the nation—statesmen, warriors, authors and others.   Dr. Raven has done justice to his subject.   He has compressed into a volume of moderate size a comprehensive survey of the centuries through which his history runs.

The author begins with a chapter on the physiography of Suffolk, and what is known of its prehistoric events.   Then follow chapters on the Roman occupation, the Saxon times, the conquest and occupation by the Norman, the Plantaganet times, and the reigns of Edward III. and Richard II.   We have next a chapter on Colleges, Lollards, Pilgrimages, etc., followed by one on Perpendicular Architecture, Domestic Life, etc.   Then we have chapters on the various periods and reigns to the present time.   The last chapter is on Ethnology, Surnames, Dialect and Folk Lore.

Dr. Raven has given us an impartial summary of the important events that have happened in Suffolk.   His book, as will be seen, is not a mere chronology, but is enlivened by interesting details giving us a picture of the men and times of other days.

Beneath Old Roof Trees.   By ABRAM ENGLISH BROWN.   Boston: Lee & Shepard.   1896.   12mo. pp. xiii.+343.   Price $1.50.

The towns from which flowed the currents of energy that, concentrating at Lexington and Concord, culminated in the Fight of the first day of the Revolution,—it is these towns whose heart-fading memories of their heroic period Mr. Brown has so industriously gleaned, and on the pages of his very entertaining book has reproduced in the form of story, picture and verse.   He makes those actions which, as apprehended in our school-days, seemed half-mythical, appear as events of yesterday, while the actors who, haloed by our reverence, were to our imaginations a race unallied to common flesh and blood, become as the friends with whom we have talked by the fireside, and whom we have accompanied to their daily labor.

The impression left by the perusal of the enticing chapters,—which no one lacking leisure should glance at, as he would never cease to regret his inability to finish them,—is one that can best be described by saying that, upon closing the volume, one is henceforth undoubtingly aware that the authors of the Revolution were the very men whom he has known from infancy.   Thomas Ditson, whose tar-and-feathers burst into a flame that overran New England; Capt. John Parker,who, enfeebled with disease that in a few months was to bring him to his death-bed, was at the head of the minute-men of Lexington; John Tidd, who was wounded by a British cutlass, but who nevertheless lived many years afterward; Ebenezer Monroe, who was the first to discover, by his wounded arm, that the enemy were using something deadlier than powder; Joshua Simonds, whom the "Right about, march!" of a red-coat officer alone deterred, as he stood with his gun placed on an open cask of powder, from blowing to atoms the regulars, his comrade, and himself, together with the church which was the arsenal of the town; Capt. Isaac Davis, whose owl foreboded the death which he met at Concord bridge; these and all the others into whose faces we seem to gaze as we read, are personalities whom we have all beheld reclothed with flesh, and with whom we have been intimate for many a year.

The book is, in brief, a recapitulation of the actions performed April 19, 1775, on what the author felicitously calls " the battlefield of Middlesex." The quotas furnished by the several towns of the county, the dramatic incidents which each town now regards as the richest embellishments of its history, homesteads and inns, features of landscape, sketches of the annals of prominent patriotic families,—such details as these, together with an introductory chapter on " Some of the General Facts of the opening Revolution," and one devoted to Gen. Artemas Ward, constitute the principal contents of the work.

The illustrations, both from the subjects selected and the style of execution, are exceptionally fine, completing the attractions of a production which, as one of a prospective series, will surely prepare a welcome for those that are to follow.

By Frederick W. Parke, of Boston.

Memorial Sketches and History of the Class of 1853, Dartmouth College. By MOSES T. RUNNELS, Class Secretary. Newport, N. H.: Barton & Wheeler. 1895. 8vo. pp. 320.

Literature of this kind is of great intrinsic value, for the life-work of every college class forms an important part of the history of the country. The Dartmouth class of '53 is no exception to this rule. Numbering only 50, of whom 29 survive, its influence has been felt in all lines of public life. Ten served in defence of their country. Two have been college presidents, and Prof. Young, now of Princeton, has achieved a world-wide reputation in the field of astronomical research. This class is specially fortunate in having for its secretary one who is admirably fitted, by his historical and literary tastes and experience, for the work which he has here accomplished. This book is among the best, if not *the* best of its kind. In completeness, impartiality, and literary finish, it leaves nothing to be desired. Its nineteen portraits with other illustrations add greatly to its value. Every Dartmouth man, not to say every college graduate, should deem his library incomplete without it.

By Rev. Silvanus Hayward, of Globe Village, Mass.

Centenary of Columbian Lodge A. F. and A. M., Boston, Mass., 1795—June, 1895. Boston: Published by order of the Lodge. 1895. 8vo., pp. 254.

Beside the orations, poems, toasts and speeches, appropriate to the event, this beautiful volume is replete with historical matter. Not only the masonic happenings of the century, but also many public occasions, are herein noted with a fidelity and accuracy obtainable only by careful research. The book is a handsome specimen of the printer's art of to-day, and is embellished with cuts of a portrait of Paul Revere, who, as Grand Master, signed the charter of the Lodge; of many of the officers and prominent brothers; of views of various halls, wherein the lodge has held meetings for a hundred years—Concert Hall 1796, Masons' Hall 1806, Exchange Coffee House 1817, Old State House 1821, First Masonic Temple 1832, Winthrop House 1859, Thorndike Hall 1864, Second Masonic Temple 1867-95, and interior views of the lodge room, Sutton hall, and the members' room, in the last mentioned edifice. Other illustrations are of the Green Dragon Tavern, the Centennial medal, the Banner Emblem, and the Seal of Columbian Lodge. Appropriate foot notes give admirable sketches of the personal careers of many deceased members, and thus add a large value to the book, which concludes with a list of the officers and members on the day of the Centenary. Copious indices are provided.

The contentment and pride, with which such an elegant book must be regarded by the members of this ancient fraternity, will be matched in the gratification with which every good citizen will recognize the abundant evidence of the harmony with which this lodge was instituted, which it has cherished throughout its history, and which it maintains and exhibits as it enters upon the second century of an honorable career. " *Semper Ubique.*"

By Geo. A. Gordon, A.M., of Somerville, Mass.

Life and Speeches of Thomas Corwin, Orator, Lawyer and Statesman. Edited by JOSIAH MORROW. Cincinnati: W. H. Anderson & Co. 1896. 8vo. pp. 477+10.

In this work the editor, Mr. Josiah Morrow, has given an appreciative and yet critical estimate of the life and speeches of Thomas Corwin, one of our greatest American statesmen. His early struggles and privations (like those of Lincoln and many others of his time) served to develope and strengthen his sturdy qualities of American manhood. He had not the advantage of an early education, but he had good native ability, and was a keen student of human nature, a more important study than that of books merely; he however supplemented his lack of early training by a wide range of reading in English history and in the English classics, both prose and poetry. Like Webster, he was a great student of the Bible, and drew his inspiration largely from this the greatest source of learning. In one of his speeches he pays the following glowing tribute to the descendants of the Puritans: "They are an industrious, thriving, pains-taking race of men. The frailties of these men grow out of their very virtues, those stern virtues which founded liberty in England, and baptized it in their own blood upon Bunker Hill, in America. They will do so again if there is a necessity for it. It is a hard matter to deal with men who do verily believe that God Almighty and His angels encamp round about them. * * * In the hour of battle they seem to themselves to stand, like the great Hebrew leader, in the cleft of the rock; the glory of the most high God passes by them, and they catch a gleam of its brightness. If you come in conflict with the purposes of such men, they will regard duty as everything, life as nothing." But his remarkable speech against the unjust Mexican War is (of all his speeches which have been preserved) the greatest effort of his genius, the crowning work of his life. It is from the beginning to the end a terrible arraignment of the administration. The righteous indignation of the orator is thoroughly aroused, and he displays a power of invective, hardly equalled by John Randolph himself. Yet even this triumph of oratory is said to have been surpassed by an unreported speech delivered at his home in Lebanon, Ohio, in defence of his course in the United States senate during the Mexican War. Taken altogether, his speeches form a lucid and powerful commentary on many vital questions of constitutional law. Perhaps Corwin stood next to Webster and Marshall in their marvellous grasp and interpretation of this great branch of our law. It is interesting to observe, in these days of wild and absurd financial and free trade theories, that Corwin was an uncompromising advocate for a currency with a gold basis, and for a protective tariff. He never forgot that he was an American, and he never forgot the duty he owed as a citizen to the great American commonwealth. A copy of his splendid speech in which he lays much stress not only on the duty of each citizen to vote intelligently but also to take an active interest in politics, ought to be in the hands of every voter in the land. Perhaps the most striking features of his speeches are the notes of patriotism and religion which ring clear and true through them all. He firmly believed in and asserted our inalienable American heritage of freedom of thought and speech, of civil and religious liberty under the law of the land.
By Rev. Daniel Rollins, of Boston.

County Records of the Surnames of Francus, Franceis, French. By A. D. WELD FRENCH, author of "Index Armorial," "Frenches of Scotland;" Fellow of the Society of Antiquaries of Scotland, Member of the Scottish History Society, and of the Committee on Heraldry of the New-England Historic Genealogical Society.

This volume is an illustration of what a person of erudition can find among the ancient English archives, in looking up the records of surnames. It is introduced by a scholarly preface on the cognomens mentioned on the title, to which is added the first great charter of liberties of the Anglo-Norman period of English history. The body of the volume is arranged alphabetically under the headings of the different counties. The first records in each county are general, to which succeed the sub-divisions of the hundreds, all of which are in chronological order. Besides the continuous documentary evidences of the surnames of Francus, Franceis, and French, there are many records of other surnames, and even in some cases their pedigrees, while the historical value of some of the translations cannot help being recognized as interesting additions to what is known as the ancient English laws, as well as its feudal customs. The index is arranged in such a way as to be particularly pleasing to the antiquary and genealogist.

As copies of the previous privately printed works of this author were presented to the leading libraries, we naturally infer he will pursue the same course with this volume.

By Charles E. Hurd, of Boston.

The Literature of Witchcraft in New England. By JUSTIN WINSOR. Worcester, Mass.: Printed by Charles Hamilton, 311 Main Street. 1896. 8vo. pp. 25.
The New England Indians: A Bibliographical Survey, 1630-1700. By JUSTIN WINSOR. Cambridge: John Wilson & Son, University Press. 1895. 8vo. pp. 35.

Dr. Justin Winsor, Librarian of Harvard University, renders valuable service by two papers upon literature relative to Witchcraft and the Indians of New England. These two monographs—both reprints, the first from the Proceedings of the American Antiquarian Society, and the other from the Proceedings of the Massachusetts Historical Society—probe the subjects, and he who would pursue them will be aided by having them at hand. The paper upon Witchcraft concerns its leading literature, while the bibliography upon the Indians is limited to 1630-1700.

By Rev. Anson Titus, of Somerville, Mass.

Genealogical Queries and Memoranda. A Quarterly Magazine devoted to Genealogy, Family History, Heraldry and Topography. Edited by GEORGE F. TUDOR SHERWOOD. Vol. I. No. 1. London, May, 1896. 8vo. pp. 8. Price one shilling per number, three shillings and six pence per annum. Address all communications to the editor at 99 Angell Road, Brixton, London, S. W. Postal Orders payable at 304 Brixton Road.

The greater part of this magazine is made up of genealogical queries, notes and references, arranged in alphabetical order. A query occupies usually but two or three lines, and the information wanted is indicated by italics. By this arrangement the editor is able to get a great many wants into a few pages.

If this periodical receives the support that it deserves, it cannot fail to be very useful to American genealogists who are searching for English ancestry.

By Wm. Prescott Greenlaw, of Cambridge, Mass.

History of the Town of Springfield, Vermont, with a Genealogical Record. By C. HORACE HUBBARD and JUSTUS DARTT. 1752-1895. Boston: Geo. H. Walker & Co., 160 Tremont St. 1895. O. pp. xi+618. Price $2.50; by mail, $2.80.

A long delayed and increasingly arduous task reaches its accomplishment in the publication of this comely volume. It is the record of a sturdy, independent, enterprising and most remarkably inventive people,—a record which, although regarded by its authors as irreparably defective in consequence of a procrastination that forfeited the contributions of memory and tradition from those personally acquainted with the early days of the town, is nevertheless so variedly copious as to embrace in its contents such articles as Mrs. Louisa Griswold Field's "North Springfield,"—a delightful reminiscential talk such as every person with mind similarly stored ought to be induced to indulge in—and the Genealogical Record of three hundred and nineteen pages, with its biographical details, portraits and autographs.

The history of the town from 1752 to the present time is distributed throughout the chapters on the settlements, churches, societies, manufactures, departments of business, and on Springfield's share in the War of the Rebellion.

Hardly any other place of its population has produced so many inventors of essentially Yankee ability as the town at the head of whose list of mechanical geniuses stands the name of John Davidson, the maker of a vibrating machine for shearing cloth, the superiority of which over any similar contrivance of his day was immediately recognized. The catalogue of inventions,—circumventions, as they might be called, of labor and time,—which three or four pages only are required to exhibit, is indubitably the weightiest portion of the book, presenting Springfield as a benefactor of the peculiarly American stamp, that is to say, as the originator of benefits which, while of incalculably wide operation, concentrate also very agreeably calculable results on their author. To trace the spring clothes-pin to Springfield and to David M. Smith is like discovering a home and friends where one had expected to find only closed doors and strangers. The interminable procession of toy carts, and doll carriages,—with jointed dolls capable of adjusting themselves to a seat,—first issued from the streets of the same centre of inventive power.

The typographical aspect of the book is attractive. The portraits, if as excellent as likenesses as the greater part of them are as illustrations, must be very gratifying to the originals and their friends.

The appendix, consisting of documents relating to the earliest years of the town, is the section of the greatest historical importance incorporated in the work, the records of town meetings abounding in items of engrossing interest.
By Frederick W. Parke, of Boston, Mass.

" *Pennsylvania Dutch" and other Essays.* By PHEBE EARLE GIBBONS, author of "French and Belgians." Third Edition, revised and enlarged. Philadelphia: J. B. Lippincott & Co. 1882. 12mo. pp. 427.

In this volume, intended to afford a description of the majority of the Pennsylvania Germans, although not of all, and in the publication of which Miss Gibbons has had the assistance of ministers, lawyers, physicians, editors, bankers, merchants and teachers of Pennsylvania German stock, are found chapters of unusual interest on such topics as the Schwenkfelders, Ephrata and the Swiss Exiles, while the other subjects, if producing a less immediate impression on the reader, because popularized by frequent treatment, are nevertheless very ably handled.

The article which gives the title to the book, and which appeared in the *Atlantic Monthly* of October, 1869, contains the observations of a twenty-years' residence among the people described, and supplies therefore reliable exact details respecting their religion, language, politics, festivals, and manners and customs. Its piquantly curious particulars relating to the dialect of the Pennsylvania German region are continued in an appendix of forty-six varied pages, a section of the book which to the lover of the humerous is, perhaps, the most attractive of all.

The " miners of Scranton" is a chapter which, owing to its sympathetic and intelligent account of the Irish and Welsh miners,—these constituting the majority of the laborers,—may be considered a most valuable contribution to the literature of our age,—the age of labor problems,—which the author has included in her collection.

The chapters entitled " Irish Farmers " and " English " are of allied import to the above, forming the concluding portion of a work which one would not properly designate as entertaining in a specially applicable sense, being of too serious a design to invite such an epithet, but which nevertheless offers, in its very readibly presented facts, the entertainment which many a lighter production fails to impart.
By Frederick W. Parke, of Boston.

Bibliography of the Historical Publications issued by the New England States. By APPLETON PRENTISS CLARK GRIFFIN. Reprinted from the Publications of the Colonial Society of Massachusetts. Vol. III. Cambridge: John Wilson & Son, University Press. 1895. 8vo. pp. 47. Price $1.00.

The first eleven pages of this work contain an excellent historical account of the printed archives of the thirteen original States and Canada. Following this sketch there is a minute analysis of the published records of the several New England States.

Mr. Griffin's explanation of the duplicate records found in volume three of Shurtleff's Massachusetts Records is interesting.

The pamphlet will be useful to the students of early American history, and is worthy of a place in every historical library.
By Wm. Prescott Greenlaw, of Cambridge.

Early Long Island. A Colonial Story. By MARTHA BOCKEE FLINT. G. P. Putnam's Sons. New York. 1896. 12mo. ix.+549 pp. 8vo. Price $3.50.

The quickened interest in local history, of which marked signs have been observed in the last few years, has hardly borne better fruit than the attractive volume before us. The writer has forborn to advance any theories, but has allowed the records to tell their own story. The manuscript and printed sources have apparently been examined with industry and faithfulness. The work has much to enlist the interest of the New Englander, particularly in the accounts of the "Stamford emigration"; Sir Lyon Gardiner; Lady Deborah Moody, who found a refuge at Gravesend, after her unhappy experience at Salem with the ecclesiastics; and of the Connecticut towns. The bibliographical references might have been fuller,with advantage. The "Journal of a Voyage to New York, in 1679-80, by Joseph Dankers," and forming Vol. I. of the Memoirs of the Long Island Historical Society, is too briefly mentioned in the "List of Books consulted," as Dankers and Sluyter's Visit to New York, 1679–1680. It would have been worth while to state that the "Commodities of the island called Manati" was printed by Dr. J. G. Shea in 1865; and not only accessible in "Earl Strafford's Letters and Despatches"; and in the extracts printed in the present work. Furthermore the edition of Strafford before us does not appear to contain the pamphlet. The chapter on "names" is a serviceable contribution to a study of geographical terminology.

By Appleton P. C. Griffin, of Boston.

History, Charter and By-Laws of the Society of Colonial Wars of the State of Illinois. List of Officers and Members. Together with a Record of the Service performed by their Ancestors in the Wars of the Colonies. Publication No. 2. Chicago. 1896. 8vo. pp. 170.

The elegant year book of the Illinois branch of the Society of Colonial Wars is the second volume issued by that society. It was compiled by the secretary, Seymour Morris, Esq., of Chicago, a member of the New-England Historic Genealogical Society. He has shown ability and taste in bringing out the volume. The charter of the society is printed first. Then follow the members with their ancestors, whose colonial service entitles them to membership, the line of their descent from them being carefully given, also a portrait of each member. The arrangement of the members is alphabetical. Other illustrations of a superior character are given. An appendix is devoted to the ancestors of members, with their military record. The members of the society whose right to membership is derived from each colonial ancestor is given under the several ancestors' names.

This society and the other patriotic societies are doing praiseworthy work in gathering and preserving in print a record of our colonial worthies.

Society of Mayflower Descendants. First Year Book. New York. 1896. Fcp. 4to. pp. 127.

The Society of Mayflower Descendants in the city of New York was incorporated December 5, 1895. The volume before us has a list of the passengers in the Mayflower; the compact signed November 11, O. S., 21 N. S., 1620, with the names of the signers; the Certificate of Incorporation, the constitution and the by-laws of the society; the addresses of Henry E. Howland, governor of this society; Frederick De Peyster, governor general of the Society of Colonial Wars; Frederic H. Betts; Charles C. Beaman, vice-president of the New England Society; William H. McElroy; and Arthur Lord, president of the Pilgrim Society, at the first annual meeting of the society in November, 1895. The volume closes with a list of the members of the society and another of their ancestors. The book is handsomely printed and rubricated. It is embellished with the flag of the Society in colors, and many other fine illustrations.

Sixth Report on the Custody and Condition of Public Records of the Parishes, Towns and Counties. By ROBERT T. SWAN, Commissioner. Boston: Wright & Potter Printing Co., State Printers. 1894. 8vo. pp. 67. *Seventh Report, &c.* 1895. 8vo. pp. 39. *Eighth Report, &c.* 1896. 8vo. pp. 42.

The first Report on the Custody and Condition of the Town Records of Massachusetts was issued by the State of Massachusetts in 1889, and was fully noticed in the REGISTER for July, 1889. Our readers are referred to that number for the plan and scope of the inquiries made by the commission. Later Reports have been noticed by us as they appeared.

We have now before us the Sixth, Seventh and Eighth Reports of Mr. Swan, the commissioner. These reports contain much information about the condition of the Massachusetts town and parish records and valuable suggestions for the improvement and preservation of the records. Among Mr. Swan's suggestions is a Public Record Office for the State. If such an office is not established, he recommends, "where records are in a bad condition, to bring them up to the condition required by the statutes at the expense of the State. * * * Should the State bear the expense of putting the records in proper condition and of providing safe receptacles for them, the towns would feel that they could afford to pay more for their care than they do now." Other valuable suggestions are made by the commissioner.

The Lower Norfolk County Virginia Antiquary. Edited by EDWARD W. JAMES. Richmond, Va. Parts 2 and 3. Price 50 cts. a part. No more than 350 copies will be printed of any number. For sale by George M. West, 909 E. Main street, and J. W. Randolph Co., 1304 E. Main street, Richmond, Va.

In our number for October, 1895, we noticed the first part of this periodical. The work is published at irregular intervals, and each part contains about forty pages. We have now before us two more parts. The second part was issued in October, 1895, and the third in May of this year. Like the first part of this work, these two numbers contain a large amount of documentary and other matter illustrating the history of the Lower Norfolk County, Virginia. It promises to be a valuable repository of historic material, and we hope it will have a liberal patronage.

An Historical Sketch of Bradford in the Revolution (including East Bradford, now Groveland). By LOUIS A. WOODBURY, M.D.   Groveland, Mass., 1895. Sq. 16mo., pp. viii. + 113.

Dr. Woodbury has done a good service for his townsmen by collecting and preserving in print a record of the part taken by citizens of Bradford and Groveland in the revolutionary struggle. The sketch was begun as a serial in the *Valley Visitor*, a monthly paper published in Groveland, but as that paper was discontinued before the series was completed, the work, revised and continued, has been published in this neat little volume. It will be of great use to those who wish to join the Sons and Daughters of the Revolution, and whose revolutionary ancestors resided within the limits of Ancient Bradford. The volume is illustrated with fine engravings.

Gravestone Records from the Ancient Cemeteries in the town of Claremont, New Hampshire. With Historical and Biographical Notes. Compiled by CHARLES B. SPOFFORD. Claremont: George J. Putnam. 1896. 8vo. pp. 88. Edition 300 copies. Price $1. Address the compiler, Claremont, N. H.

The elements are fast effacing the inscriptions from the stones in the two old burial grounds in Claremont, and in 1892 Mr. Spofford carefully copied them and has printed them in this book. The total number of names is said to be nearly 1600.

Mr. Spofford has performed a meritorious work in rescuing these inscriptions from oblivion. His notes add much to the value of his book.

Pedigree Building.—[Wilkes-Barre. 1896.]   12mo. pp. 4.

This pamphlet is reprinted from the *Wilkes-Barre Record* of January 11, 1896. It is a paper read before the Wyoming Historical and Geological Society by Dr. William H. Egle, librarian of the State of Pennsylvania. In it Dr. Egle shows the benefits, the difficulties and the perils of pedigree building. We extract from the paper the following paragraphs:

"There may be some who sneer at pedigree building ; but there is a wide difference between the laudable work of gathering up and preserving the record of your family and the hunting for fortunes or the snobbish efforts of establishing one's self as an American of royal descent. You see there are two classes of pedigree hunters which disgust, one hunting for fortunes, the other for blood royal. It is wonderful to what lengths these people go. It is their dream by night and their theme by day. True blood is better than to be a descendant of a royal house through a morganatic alliance. 'Tafelfaehig' is the pride of the German, and purity of lineage outranks the titles which a sovereign may confer.

"That class of people who are worthy of emulation, deserving of unstinted praise, are those who, with the pious motive of preserving the record of their ancestors, gather up the precious threads of genealogical woof they may find scattered here and there and without inordinate vanity weave them into a continuous story of family history, honorable in the beginning, in the patriotism of a long line of God-fearing and estimable men and women. They seek not descent from a debauched monarch or an inheritance to a mythical fortune. They are to be honored for what they have done and to be admired for their loving and patriotic work which will live long among family annals, free from the self-aggrandisement of royal descent and the taint of cupidity, when these shall have been discarded and ignored by their former devotees."

The Parish Registers of Wellow in the County of Nottingham. Edited by GEORGE W. MARSHALL, LL.D. Privately printed. Exeter: William Pollard & Co. 1896. 8vo, pp.iv+41.

The work before us adds another to the many Registers of English Parishes that are now in print. The editors of these works are doing a great service, particularly to genealogists, by preserving and making accessible these important records which are so liable to destruction. The present work, the Registers of the parish of Wellow in Nottinghamshire, which Dr. Marshall, of the Heralds College, has edited and has had privately printed in so handsome a manner, shows a laudable desire to help his brethren in their genealogical researches. The Registers extend from 1704 to 1812. The work has a good index.

The Ancestry of John Whitney who, with his wife Elinor, and sons John, Richard, Nathaniel, Thomas and Jonathan, emigrated from London, England, in the Year 1635 and settled in Watertown, Massachusetts; the first of the Name in America, and the one from whom a great majority of the Whitneys now living in the United States are descended. By HENRY MELVILLE, A.M., LL.B., of the City of New York. New York: Printed at the De Vinne Press. 1896. Super royal 8vo. pp. xviii.+295. Bound in vellum. Price $20.00 net. Address the author, 120 Broadway, New York city. Sold also by William B. Clarke & Co., 340 Washington St., Boston, Mass.

The Follett–Dewey Fassett–Safford Ancestry of Capt. Marshall Dewey Follett and his wife Persis Fassett. By HARRY PARKER WARD. Anno Domini 1896. Royal 8vo. pp. 281. Price $4, or by mail $4.25. Address Major Harry Parker Ward, Columbus, Ohio.

Genealogy of the Jaquett Family. By EDWIN JAQUETT SELLERS. Philadelphia. 1896. Royal 8vo. pp. 190. Address the Author, 229 South 6th Street, Philadelphia, Pa.

The Williamson and Cobb Families in the Lines of Caleb and Mary (Cobb) Williamson of Barnstable, Mass., and Hartford, Conn., 1896. Compiled by FRANK FARNSWORTH STARR for JAMES J. GOODWIN. Hartford, Conn. 1896. Super royal 8vo. pp. 66.

Genealogical and Historical Sketches of the Allen Family of Dedham and Medfield, Mass. Compiled by FRANK ALLEN HUTCHINSON. Privately Printed. Lowell, Mass. 1896. 8vo. pp. 80. Edition 100 copies. Price $1.

Family Register of Richard Paul, born in England and emigrated to America during the early part of 1635; also his descendants as far as ascertained. Traced by Dea. LUTHER PAUL, of Newton, Mass., FULTON PAUL of Hudson, N. Y., and MARTHA C. CRANE, of Dedham, Mass. Oblong 4to, 10 by 13 inches.

Statue of Col. Thomas Knowlton. Ceremonies at the Unveiling. Hartford, Conn.: Press of the Case, Lockwood & Brainard Company, 1895. 8vo. pp. 53.

Descendants of Daniel Cooper and Grace Runyon, Long Hill, Morris County, New Jersey. Collated by ARTHUR E. COOPER, Cooper's Plains, N. Y. Genealogical Tree, 22 by 28 inches. Folded and bound in cloth.

Genealogy of the Mills Family. 1896. 18mo. pp. 36.

The Butler Ancestry of Gen. Benjamin Franklin Butler in America. Lowell, Mass. 1895. 8vo. pp. 26.

Notes upon the Ancestry of John Platt, born in Burlington County, N. J., August 13, 1749, died near Wilmington, Del., December, 1823; and also a List of his Descendants. Printed for David Pepper for Private Distribution. 1896. Royal 8vo. pp. 29.

Descendants of Henry Hutchinson. Compiled by EDMUND D. BARBER of Boston, January 19, 1888. Tabular Pedigree. Broadside 14½ by 24 inches. Folded and bound in cloth.

The Blyenbeck and Afferden Branch of the Family of Schenck and Nydeck. From *the Family of Schenck van Nydeggen ; Cologne, 1860.* Hampton, Va. : 1885. Normal School Press Print. 1885. 8vo. pp. 26.

A Brief Sketch of Thomas Fuller and his Descendants, with Historical Notes. Appleton, Wis. Crescent Printing House. Pot 4to. pp. 47. By J. F. FULLER, of Appleton, Wisconsin.

The Descendants of Aaron and Patience Sweetland of Hebron, Conn. 1890. Sq. 16mo. pp. 30. By LUCY W. S. JEROME, of Denver, Colorado.

Glances at the Ancestry of John Parker (born 1807, died 1891). 8vo. pp. 18. By HARRY PARKER WARD, of Columbus, Ohio.

The Family of George Stocking. By EDWARD E. CORNWELL, M.D. Boston : David Clapp & Son, Printers. 1896. 8vo. pp. 8.

Historical Journal of the More Family. 1895–6. Issued annually. DAVID F. MORE, Editor. Bangor, Pa. : W. R. Grubb, Publisher. Royal 8vo. pp. 12.

Bagg Ancestry and Atwater Ancestry. Printed for Private Circulation by Karl Kran, Publisher, 107 Waverley Place, New York city, Nov. 1895. Edition 400. Royal 8vo. pp. 4.

Pedigree of Lawrence. Compiled from *Herald's Visitations, Inquisitions post mortem, Deeds, Charters, Wills, Parish Registers and other Original Manuscripts.* Tabular broadside pedigree. 17 by 18 inches.

Cornell Genealogy. By H. H. H. CRAPO SMITH, Detroit, Mich. Broadside, 7½ by 14 inches.

Circular Letter No. 5. Ancestry of Ezra Green and Extracts from *Various Letters and MSS.* showing evidences of Connection with Gen. Nathaniel Greene. Offered by CHARLES R. GREEN, Secretary of the Ezra Green Family Association. Lyndon, Kansas. Folio. pp. 6.

We continue in this number our quarterly notices of works recently published relating to family history.

The Ancestry of John Whitney, the first title on our list, is a superb volume. Its elegant paper and print, its stamped vellum cover, and the number and excellence of its illustrations, commend it to the most fastidious taste. " At the beginning of the work, the results of which appear in these pages," says Mr. Melville, " Mr. Joseph C. Whitney, of Boston, with great courtesy placed freely at my disposal a mass of memoranda accumulated in the course of several years of investigation by his late father, Henry Austin Whitney." With the clews found in Mr. Whitney's manuscripts Mr. Melville pushed his investigations into English genealogy with enthusiasm, and the result is the volume before us. The surname Whitney is traced in this volume to Sir Robert de Whitney of Whitney, &c., Knight, living in 1242 and mentioned in " Testa de Neville." Abundant details of later generations of the Whitneys to the beginning of the seventeenth century, when John Whitney came to New England and settled in Watertown, are here preserved. There are nearly fifty appropriate illustrations, such as views of castles and their ruins, monuments, coats-of-arms, maps and plans, fac-similes of ancient documents, etc. Several large folding tabular pedigrees are also given. The Whitneys of America owe a debt of gratitude to Mr. Melville for the thorough manner in which he has pursued his researches into the history of the English Whitneys and their honorable record.

The next book, the Follett-Dewey and other families, is devoted to the ancestry of Capt. Martin Dewey Follett who died at St. Albans, Vt., February 4, 1831, and of his wife Persis, daughter of Capt. John Fassett, Jr. It gives more or less extended genealogies of the Follett, Dewey, Fassett, Safford, Hopkins, Robinson and Fay families, from which the author, who is a state officer of two patriotic hereditary societies, is descended. In this capacity he had the privilege of examining many historical and genealogical records, and has been stimulated to trace and preserve the records of his own ancestors of various names. Besides the genealogical matter in the book we have a diary of Lieut. John Fassett in the expedition against Quebec under Gen. Montgomery in 1775, and other historical matter. Mr. Ward is the editor of the Year Book of the Ohio Sons of the American Revolution for 1896. The book before us makes a handsome volume printed on fine heavy paper, strongly bound in cloth with gilt top and uncut edges. There are fifty-six family portraits and fifteen other fine illustrations. The author has printed a small edition of the work on thinner paper without the illustrations, which he will sell for $2, or by mail $2.15.

The Jaquett book is devoted to the descendants of Jean Paul Jaquett of Huguenot descent, who emigrated from Holland to the New Netherlands in 1654, and was appointed in November, 1655, Vice-Director on the Delaware. The book shows much antiquarian research. Over one hundred pages are devoted to the emigrant. Much documentary matter illustrating his history is given. The book is well written and carefully compiled. It makes a handsome volume.

The next work contains the records of the Williamson family descended from Caleb Williamson of Barnstable and of the Cobb family descended from Henry Cobb of Plymouth, Mass. Caleb Williamson was a son of Timothy and Mary (Howland) Williamson of Marshfield. The book is carefully compiled and well arranged. Many wills and other documentary evidence are given. A large folding tabular pedigree of the Williamson family makes the frontispiece and a similar pedigree of the Cobb family is given. The book, which is from the University Press at Cambridge, is handsomely printed on superior paper. It has a good index.

The book on the Allen family is devoted to the descendants of James Allin of Dedham and Medfield, a nephew of Rev. John Allin, the first minister of Dedham. A good account of the latter by the late Prof. William F. Allen of Madison, Wisconsin, was printed in the REGISTER for July, 1888, pp. 267-9. The book is carefully compiled and handsomely printed with good indexes. An appendix contains a sketch of Rev. John Allin of Dedham and other valuable matter.

The preliminary sheets, seven in number, of the Paul family are before us. They are compiled with care. A manuscript history now in preparation, we are informed, is in a good state of forwardness and will soon be printed and published.

The book on the Statue of Col. Thomas Knowlton, besides an account of the unveiling of his statue, and the organization of the Knowlton Association, contains several pages of family history.

The work on the Cooper family is very useful. In the form of a genealogical tree, it gives the outlines of much genealogical research, the descendants here preserved being very numerous.

The Mills book contains one branch of the Mills Family gathered from some old records and from stories told the author, Miss Susan L. Mills, by her parents and grandparents, and " copied solely for her nephews and nieces." It is a very interesting book and appears in a very neat dress.

The Butler Ancestry shows that the emigrant ancestor of Maj. Gen. Benjamin F. Butler was Nicholas Butler, who came to this country in 1637 and settled in Dorchester, Mass., and thence removed to Martha's Vineyard, where he died. The book, which was compiled by Gen. Butler's daughter, Mrs. Blanche Butler Ames, contains much interesting genealogical matter relative to the Butler and allied families. It is handsomely printed.

The pamphlet on the Platt family is by Franklin Platt, of Philadelphia, Pa. It is devoted to the descendants of Thomas Platt, who as early as 1712 was living in Burlington County, New Jersey, who had three sons, Thomas, John and Joseph, and one daughter Elizabeth. The pamphlet is well compiled and handsomely printed.

The Hutchinson tabular pedigree contains four generations of the descendants of Henry Hutchinson of Boston, born in that town, October 31, 1763, and died there July 17, 1833. It is well printed.

The Schenck pamphlet is by Capt. Alexander Du Bois Schenck, U. S. Artillery, and is intended to take the place of pages 20 to 23 of the author's book on the Schenck family published in 1883. The data are taken from the History of the Schenck van Nydeggen (Nydeck) (Cologne, 1860). It is an interesting addition to the Dutch genealogy of New York.

The Fuller pamphlet is by J. F. Fuller of Appleton, Wisconsin, and is devoted to the descendants of Thomas Fuller, who died in Salem (the part now Middleton), in June, 1698, aged 80. An article on this family, by Rev. Arthur B. Fuller, afterward chaplain of the U. S. Volunteers, was printed in the REGISTER for October, 1859, pp. 351-363. Rev. Mr. Fuller was a brother of the author Sarah Margaret Fuller, Marchioness d' Ossoli. The work before us is a well compiled history of one branch of the family and makes a neat pamphlet.

The Sweetland pamphlet gives the descendants of Aaron and Patience (Clark) Sweetland of Hebron, Ct.   The descendants are fully traced and the pamphlet is neatly printed.

The Parker pamphlet is by Major Harry Parker Ward, a grandson of John Parker.   Besides the descendants of John Parker an appendix is devoted to the "First Jewetts of America."   The pamphlet is well prepared.

The pamphlet on the family of George Stocking is a reprint from the REGISTER for April, 1896.

The Historical Journal of the More Family gives an account of the second reunion of the More family at Roxbury, N. Y., in September, 1895, with other interesting matter relating to the Mores.

The pamphlet on the Bagg and Atwater families was compiled by Lyman Hotchkiss Bagg of New York city, who contributed to the REGISTER in 1876, and later a transcript of the records of West Springfield, Mass.

The Lawrence tabular pedigree, which begins with Sir Robert Lawrence, 1191, was printed at Boston in May, 1896, for John Lawrence of Groton.   The edition was only 100 copies.   It gives much information in tabular form.

The Cornell Genealogy consists of one line of the descendants of Thomas Cornell, who came from England and settled first in Boston, Mass., and next in Portsmouth, R. I.

The Circular Letter on the Ancestry of Ezra Green contains genealogical matter upon the Green and other families.   Besides the Circular Letter No. 5 we have before us Circular Letters No. 6, July 22, 1895, and No. 7, January, 1896 (both broadsides) ; Family of Ezra and Amy Church Green, 4 broadsides; Genealogical Pamphlet No. C (10 pages), and other broadsides issued by the "Ezra Green Family Association."

RECENT PUBLICATIONS,[*]

PRESENTED TO THE NEW-ENGLAND HISTORIC GENEALOGICAL SOCIETY FROM MARCH 1, 1896, TO JUNE 1, 1896.

Prepared by the Assistant Librarian.

I. *Publications written or edited by Members of the Society.*

Genealogy.
The Williamson and Cobb Families in the Lines of Caleb and Mary (Cobb) Williamson, of Barnstable, Mass., and Hartford, Conn. 1896. Compiled by Frank Farnsworth Starr for James J. Goodwin. Hartford, Conn. 1896. 8vo. pp. 66.

Descendants of Henry Hutchinson. Compiled by Edward D. Barbour, of Boston, January 19, 1888. Tabular Pedigree. 48 × 15 inches.

History.
Beneath Old Roof Trees. By Abram English Brown. Boston. 1896. 12mo. pp. xiii.+343.

Revolutionary Fragments, Morris County, N. J. By Rev. Joseph F. Tuttle. Morristown, N. J. 1896. 8vo. pp. 38.

Local History.
An Historical Sketch of Bradford, Mass., in the Revolution. (Including East Bradford, now Groveland.) By Louis A. Woodbury. Groveland, Mass. 1895. 16mo. pp. 112.

An Historical Address delivered in St. John's Church, Dubuque, Iowa, at the Semi-centennial Celebration of the Organization of the Parish, by Rt. Rev. William Stevens Perry, D.D., Bishop of Iowa. Davenport. 1896. 16mo. pp. 36.

Biography.
Hugh Sugar *alias* Norris, LL.D., Treasurer of Wells (1460–89). By Rev. F. W. Weaver. (Re-printed from the Downside Review.) Yeovil : Printed by the Western Chronicle Co., Ltd. 8vo. pp. 7.

---

[*] This list does not include publications which are elsewhere noticed, unless written by a member.

Colleges and Schools.

Harvard College. Secretary's Report. Class of 1882. IV. Jan. 1, 1890 to Dec. 31, 1895. Boston. 8vo. pp. 101.

The Class of 1844, Harvard College, Fifty Years after Graduation. Prepared by the Class Secretary, Edward Wheelwright. Cambridge. 1896. 8vo. pp. xi.+353.

Societies and Institutions.

History, Charter and By-Laws of the Society of Colonial Wars in the State of Illinois. List of Officers and Members. Together with a record of the service performed by their Ancestors in the Wars of the Colonies. Publication No. 2. Chicago. 1896. 8vo. pp. 170.

The Archives of Canada. The Presidential Address for 1895, by J. McPherson Lemoine, President of the Royal Society of Canada for 1894–5. (From the Transactions of the Royal Society of Canada; Second Series,—1895–96.) 1895. 8vo. pp. 24.

Southern Historical Society Papers. Vol. XXIII. Edited by R. A. Brock, Secretary of the Southern Historical Society. Richmond, Va. 1895. 8vo. pp. vii.+387.

U. S. Government, State and Municipal Publications.

History, Jurisdiction, and Practice of the Court of Claims (United States). By William A. Richardson, Chief Justice of the Court. Washington. 1885. 8vo. pp. 38.

Rules of the Court of Claims (United States), adopted Jan. 7, 1895, and of the Supreme Court relating to Appeals. Washington. 1895.

The Acts and Resolves, Public and Private, of the Province of the Massachusetts Bay; to which are prefixed the Charters of the Province. With historical and explanatory notes and an Appendix. Vol. viii., being vol. III. of the App.; containing Resolves, etc., 1703–1707. Boston. 1895. 8vo. pp. 931.

A Memorial of the American Patriots who fell at the Battle of Bunker Hill, with an account of the Dedication of the Memorial Tablets on Winthrop Square, Charlestown, June 17, 1889, and an Appendix. Fourth edition. Boston. 1896. 4to. pp. 274. Edited by William H. Whitmore.

Miscellaneous.

A Bibliography of the State of Maine, from the earliest period to 1891. By Joseph Williamson. Portland. 1896. 2 vols. 8vo. pp. 738; 669.

Remarks on an early Book-Catalogue printed in Boston; with other bibliographical matter. By Dr. Samuel A. Green.

Rev. John Higginson, of Salem, Mass.—Rev. Mather Byles, Jr., of Boston. Remarks at meetings of the Massachusetts Historical Society by Dr. Samuel A. Green.

II.   *Other Publications.*

History.

History of Colonel Edmund Phinney's Thirty-First Regiment of Foot, eight months' service men of 1775. With biographical sketches of the Commissioned Officers and Rolls of the Companies. By Nathan Goold, Historian of the Maine Sons of the American Revolution. Portland. 1896. 8vo. pp. 54. Price $1.00.

Local History.

A Historical Sermon preached April 15, 1896, in the Congregational Church, Central Village, Conn., in recognition of the 50th Anniversary of its Organization, together with a brief Report of the Services of the Day. By Rev. Orlando M. Lord, Pastor. Central Village. 1896. 16mo. pp. 21.

The Story of New Sweden, as told at the Quarter Centennial Celebration, June 25, 1895. Portland, Maine. 1896. 8vo. pp. 134.

Staten Island Names. Ye Olde Names and Nicknames. By William T. Davis, with map by Chas. W. Leng. Published by the Natural Science Association, New Brighton, Staten Island, N. Y. 1896. 8vo. pp. 76.

An Historical Sketch of the First Church in Roxbury. 1896. 12mo. pp. 18.

Centennial Celebration of the Building of the First Parish Meeting-House at Westford, Mass. Lowell, Mass. 1894. 8vo. pp. 35.

Historical Address delivered at the One Hundred and Fiftieth Anniversary of the Congregational Church at Windham Hill, Dec. 14, 1893, by Samuel T. Dole. Portland. 8vo. pp. 10.

Biography.

Extracts from the Journal of the Reverend John Graham, Chaplain of the First Connecticut Regiment, Colonel Lyman, from September 25 to October 19, 1762, at the Siege of Havana. Printed by order of the Fourth General Court of the Society of Colonial Wars in the State of New York, Office of the Society, 37 Liberty Street. New York. 1896. 8vo. pp. 17.

Memorial. Dr. Joshua Bartlett Rich. 8vo. pp. 6.

Biographical Sketch of Gen. Charles W. Darling, from Encyclopædia of Contemporary Biography of New York, Vol. VI. Atlantic Publishing and Engraving Company, New York. 1890. 4to. pp. 6.

Colleges and Schools.

Catalogue of Andover Theological Seminary, lxxxviii. year, 1895–'96. Andover, Mass. 1896. 12mo. pp. 28.

The College Ideal and American Life; an Address delivered at the Seventy-Fifth Anniversary of Colby University, by Nathan Butler, Director of the University Extension of the University of Chicago, July 3, 1895. Portland, Maine. 1896. 8vo. pp. 23.

The Seventy-Sixth Annual Catalogue of the Officers and Students of Colby University, for the Academic Year 1895–96. Waterville, Me. 1896. 8vo. pp. 84.

Dartmouth College Catalogue, 1895–96. 8vo. pp. 160.

Forty Years' Record of the Class of 1855 of Dartmouth College. By the Secretary. Boston. 1895. 8vo. pp. 54.

Description and Dedication of the High School Building, Fitchburg, Mass. 1895. 8vo. pp. 47.

Harvard College. Class of 1876. Report of the Secretary. Number Six. Oct., 1894–May, 1896. Printed for the use of the Class. Boston. 1896. 8vo. pp. 26.

A Brief Account of the Lick Observatory of the University of California; prepared by Edward S. Holden, Director of the Observatory. Second Edition. Sacramento. 1895. 8vo. pp. 29.

Meadville Theological School. Catalogue. 1895–96. Meadville, Pa. 1896. 8vo. pp. 19.

Seventy-Seventh Annual Announcement of the Medical College of Ohio, Cincinnati. For the Session of 1895–'96. Cincinnati. 1895. 12mo. pp. 31.

Directory of the Officers and Alumni of the University of Rochester. 1850–1895. Rochester, N. Y. 1895. 8vo. pp. 78.

Annual Report of the President of Tufts College. 1894–95. Boston. 1896. 12mo. pp. 54.

Catalogue of Washington and Lee University, Lexington, Virginia, for the year ending June, 1896, and Announcements for 1896–'97. Press of Geo. H. Buchanan & Co., Philadelphia. 8vo. pp. 85.

Catalogue of the Officers and Students of Westford Academy, Westford, Mass., for the academical year 1892–93. Lowell, Mass. 1893. 8vo. pp. 16.

Report of the President of Yale University for the year ending Dec. 31, 1895. 1896. 8vo. pp. 118.

Societies and Institutions.

Proceedings of the Bostonian Society at the Annual Meeting, Jan. 14, 1896. Boston. 1896. 4to. pp. 70.

Worcester Births, Marriages and Deaths. Compiled by Franklin P. Rice. Part II. —Marriages. The Worcester Society of Antiquity. (Pt. 2 of Vol. XII.) No. XLIII. Worcester, Mass. 1894. 4to. pp. 291–450.

Brookline Historical Publication Society. Publication No. 6. Early Notices of Local Events. No. 7. Letter from Brigadier-General Edward A. Wild to the Brookline War Committee.

Transactions of the Oneida Historical Society, at Utica, 1892–1894. Resident and Honorary Members. No. 6. Utica, N. Y. 1894. 8vo. pp. 207.

Annual Report of the Board of Managers of the Buffalo Historical Society for the year 1895, and the Society Proceedings at the Annual Meeting, January, 1896. Buffalo. 1896. pp. 64.

Publications of the American Jewish Historical Society. No. 4. Papers presented at the Third Annual Meeting, held at Washington, Dec. 26 and 27, 1894. Published by the Society. 1896. 8vo. pp. 243.

American Historical Association. Officers, Act of Corporation, Constitution, List of Members, Historical Societies in the United States. 1896. 12mo. pp. 55.

Annual Report of the American Historical Association for the year 1894. Washington. 1895. 8vo. pp. xii.+602.

Parkman Club Publications. No. 2. Exploration of Lake Superior: The Voyages of Radisson and Groseillers. Henry Colin Campbell. No. 4. The Aborigines of the Northwest: A Glance into the remote Past. Frank Taylor Terry. No. 5. Jonathan Carver, his Travels in the Northwest in 1766-8. John Goadby Gregory. Documentary Material relating to the History of Iowa, edited by Benjamin F. Shambaugh. Nos. 3, 4. Published by the State Historical Society of Iowa. Iowa City. 1896. 8vo. pp. 46-99.

Transactions of the Boston Society of Architects. 1891. 8vo. pp. 83.

Journal of the Forty-Third Annual Convention of the Church in the Diocese of Iowa, held in the Cathedral, Davenport, Dec. 3 and 4, 1895. 1895. 8vo. pp. 80.

Minutes of Richfield Reunion Association, held at Viall's Hotel, May 24, 1893. Akron, Ohio. 1893. 16mo. pp. 11.

Minutes of Richfield Reunion Association, held at Kirby's Grove, June 13, 1894. Akron. 1894. 16mo. pp. 11.

Annals of the Third Annual Meeting of the Richfield Reunion Association, held at Kirby's Grove, Richfield, Ohio, June 26, 1895. [1895.] 16mo. pp. 13.

Addresses delivered at the Fourteenth Annual Banquet of the Boston Merchants Association, Jan. 3, 1895, on the Currency and Banking System of the United States. Boston. 1896. 8vo. pp. 76.

Thirteenth Annual Report of the Trustees of the Soldiers' Home in Massachusetts at Chelsea, for the year ending June 30, 1895. Boston. 1895. 8vo. pp. 76.

First Annual Report of the Trustees of the Forbes Library, Northampton, Mass., for the term ending Nov. 30, 1895. Northampton, Mass. 1896. 8vo. pp. 71.

Addresses delivered at the Fifteenth Annual Banquet of the Boston Merchants Association, Nov. 15, 1895, on the Improvement of Boston Harbor. Boston. 1896. 8vo. pp. 64.

Trustees of the Museum of Fine Arts. Twentieth Annual Report, for the year ending Dec 31, 1895. Boston. 1896. 8vo. pp. 68.

Eighteenth Annual Report of the Providence Public Library, Providence, R. I., comprising reports of the Treasurer and Librarian, for the year ending Dec. 31, 1895. Providence. 1896. 8vo. pp. 53.

Eighth Annual Meeting of the Board of Trade, Hartford, Jan. 14, 1896. Report of the Secretary and Treasurer, P. H. Woodward. Hartford, Conn. 1896. 8vo. pp. 33.

Eighty-Second Annual Report of the Trustees of the Massachusetts General Hospital. Including the General Hospital in Boston, the McLean Hospital and the Convalescent Home at Waverly. 1895. Boston. 1896. 8vo. pp. 87.

Report of the Boston Young Men's Christian Union, for the year ending April 10, 1895. 12mo. pp. 144.

Annual of the University Club. Thirty-Second Year, 1896-7. April 15, 1896. 8vo. pp. 117.

The Constitution of the Aztec Club of 1847, and List of Members. 1896. 8vo. pp. 50.

Proceedings at the Sixteenth Annual Meeting and Sixteenth Annual Festival of the New England Society in the City of Brooklyn. Officers, Directors, Council, Members, Standing Committees, and By-Laws of the Society. Brooklyn. 1896. 8vo. pp. 108.

The Massachusetts Medical Society. A Catalog of its Officers and Fellows, honorary, active and retired, borne upon the Rolls, 1 Jan., 1896. Boston. 1896. 8vo. pp. 125.

The Two Hundred and Fifty-Seventh Annual Record of the Ancient and Honorable Artillery Co., Massachusetts. 1894-95. Sermon. By Rev. Percy Browne. Boston. 1895. 8vo. pp. 105.

Proceedings of the Most Worshipful Grand Lodge of Ancient Free and Accepted Masons of the Commonwealth of Massachusetts. Special Communications: June 6, 8, 13, 17, 1895. Quarterly Communication: June 12, 1895. 8vo. pp. iv.+80-199.

Proceedings of the Grand Lodge of Masons of Massachusetts. Special Communications: Aug. 27; Oct. 16, 25; Nov. 7, 30, 1895. Quarterly Communication: Sept. 11, 1895. 8vo. pp. iv.+201-208.

Proceedings of the Grand Lodge of Masons of Massachusetts. Quarterly Communication: Dec. 11, 1895. Stated Communication: Dec. 27, 1895. 8vo. pp. iv. +260-283+xci.

Report of the Triennial Committee of the Grand Commandery of Knights Templars of Massachusetts and Rhode Island, for the 26th Triennial Conclave of the Grand Encampment of Knights Templar of the United States, held in Boston, Mass., Aug. 27-30, 1895. Boston. 1895. 8vo. pp. viii.+236.

Consecration of the Burial Lot at Mount Auburn by Columbian Lodge, F. & A. M., of Boston. St. John Baptist's Day, Friday, June 24, 1892. Boston. 1892. 8vo. pp. 35.

Proceedings of the Grafton and Coös Bar Association, at its Annual Meeting held at Littleton, Feb. 14, 1895. Published by the Association. 1895.

U. S. Government, State, and Municipal Publications.

The War of the Rebellion: A Compilation of the Official Records of the Union and Confederate Armies. Published under the direction of the Hon. Daniel S. Lamont, Secretary of War. Series I.—Vol. XLVII. Part 1. Reports. Parts 2 and 3. Correspondence, etc. Washington. 1895. 3 vols. 8vo.

Documents of the City of Boston, for the year 1895. Published by order of the City Council. Boston. 1896. 4 vols. 8vo. Various pagings.

Thirty-Second Annual Report of the Board of Overseers of the Poor of the City of Boston. Feb. 1, 1895 to Jan. 31, 1896. Boston. 1896. 8vo. pp. 33.

City of Boston Voting Precincts. 1895. Boston. March, 1896. sq. fo. pp. 61.

Annual Report of the Chelsea City Government for 1895, including the Mayor's Address, and List of elective and appointed Officers for 1896. Chelsea, Mass. 1896. 8vo. pp. 380.

City of Cambridge. The Mayor's Address at the organization of the City Government, Jan. 6, 1896, and the Annual Reports made to the City Council for 1895. 8vo. pp. 650.

Annual Report of the Town of Framingham for the year ending Feb. 29, 1896. Compiled by William A. Brown. South Framingham, Mass. 1896. 8vo. pp. 248.

Municipal Register, City of Medford, Mass. 24to. pp. 43.

Town of Needham. Copy of Town Clerk's Record of Town Meetings, March 5 and 14, and April 2, 6 and 7, 1894. Needham. 1894. 8vo. pp. 37.—Record of Town Meeting, March 4, 1895. Needham. 1895. 8vo. pp. 18.

Annual Reports of the Town Officers of the Town of Millbury, for the year ending March 1, 1896. [With] Annual Report of the School Committee for the same year. Millbury, Mass. 8vo. pp. 84.

Annual Reports of the Selectmen, Assessors, and Town Clerk, of the Town of Swansey, together with a Tax List for the year ending Jan. 31, 1896. Fall River, Mass. 1896. 8vo. pp. 55.

Annual Reports of Town Officers of the Town of Ware, for the year ending March 1, 1896. Ware, Mass. 1896. 8vo. pp. 89.

Annual Reports of the School Committee, Superintendent of Schools and Special Teachers of the Town of Ware, for the year ending Feb. 1, 1896. Ware, Mass. 1896. 8vo. pp. 51.

Miscellaneous.

Handbook of the New Public Library in Boston. Compiled by Herbert Small. With contributions by C. Howard Walker and Lindsay Swift. Boston. 8vo. pp. xxxii.+77.

A Review of Bryce's American Commonwealth, a Study in American Constitutional Law. By Edmund J. James. A Paper submitted to the American Academy of Political and Social Science. Philadelphia. 8vo. pp. 34.

Early Connecticut Marriages as found on Ancient Church Records, prior to 1800. Edited by Frederic W. Bailey. New Haven. [1896]. 8vo. pp. 116.

Statement of the Financial Condition of the County of York [Me.], for the year 1895. Plans of Additions to the Court House at Alfred, and Lists of County Officers from 1820 to date. Press of Biddeford Journal. 1896. 8vo. pp. 22.

RICHARD SIMS, Esq.—Our readers will be glad to learn, as we are, that the recently reported death of this gentleman—so long and widely known through his connection with the British Museum, and by his many publications relating to the antiquities of England and the genealogies of its people—is untrue. Mr. Sims is alive and in good health.

See his advertisement in this number of the REGISTER.

DEATHS.

Miss SARAH ELIZABETH TITCOMB died at Boston, Mass., April 15, 1895, aged 54. She was a daughter of Louis Frederick and Sarah Bradley (Dow) Titcomb of Lowell, Mass., where she was born. She was a well-educated and talented lady, with strong antiquarian tastes and acquirements. She was the author of a volume published in 1882, entitled "Early New England People. Some Account of the Ellis, Pemberton, Willard, Prescott, Titcomb, Sewell, Longfellow and allied Families." In this book, pp. 144 to 158, will be found her Titcomb ancestry, and pages 238 to 243 is her Dow ancestry. The genealogies of some other families from which she was descended are also printed here. She was the author of another volume, published in 1885, entitled " Mind-Cure on a Material Basis."

EDWARD JACOB FORSTER, M.D., a physician of Boston and surgeon general on the staff of the governor of Massachusetts, died suddenly on the steamboat Puritan lying at her pier in New York. He was a son of Jacob and Louisa (Webb) Forster, and was born at Charlestown, July 9, 1846. He was descended from Reginald Foster of Ipswich, of whom he furnished an account with a genealogy of some of his descendants, to the REGISTER for January, 1876, pp. 83 to 102. Dr. Forster was of the 8th generation from Reginald[1] through Reginald,[2] Isaac,[3] Jacob,[4] Jacob,[5] Jacob,[6] Jacob[7], his father. He was graduated at the Medical Department of Harvard University, July 15, 1868, soon after which he went to Europe, studying his profession in Paris and Dublin. At the latter place he became a licentiate in midwivery of the Kings' and Queens' College of Physicians in Ireland. On his return to Massachusetts in 1868 he became a member of the Massachusetts Medical Society, and commenced the practice of his profession in Charlestown, Mass. " As a physician he at one time held an official position in Charlestown. Four years ago he removed to Boston, having become a visiting physician to the Boston City Hospital and also secretary of the medical staff at that institution. For many years he was the treasurer of the Massachusetts Medical Society. About a year ago he was appointed surgeon general of Massachusetts. Upon his appointment he resigned the office he then held of secretary of the Board of Registration in Medicine. He was much interested in military affairs and had served on the medical staff of various military organizations of Boston. Besides this he was the first vice-president of the Society of Military Surgeons. He married Miss Anna Lyon, sister of Commander Henry E. Lyon now stationed at the Charlestown Navy Yard. He was the father of three daughters, aged respectively seventeen, twenty and twenty-three years, who with their mother survive him. Dr. Forster was a member of the Union and the University clubs of Boston."–(*Boston Transcript, May* 16, 1896.) He was a frequent contributor to the REGISTER. Besides the article on Reginald Foster above referred to, he furnished one on the Family of Foster of Charlestown, Mass., to the number for January, 1871. Both articles were reprinted as pamphlets. He was also the author of " The Pedigree and Descendants of Jacob Forster, Sen., of Charlestown, Mass.," privately printed in 1870.

ERRATA AND ADDENDA.—Vol. 49, p. 223, line 14, *for* Tarbell, *read* Tarbel. Page 299, line 8 from bottom, *after* Harriet Parker, *insert* daughter of Dr. H. W. Parker. Page 352, lines 25 and 26, *for* was made Master of the Rolls, *read* was appointed by the Master of the Rolls. Page 354, line 4, *for* Hagarstown *read* Hagerstown. Page 473, line 43, *for* James H. Heywood *read* John H. Heywood.

Vol. 50, page 102, line 20, *for* Sukens *read* Lukens ; line 22, *for* seventh in descent *read* fifth in descent ; lines 43 and 44, *dele the sentence beginning* He contributed, *and read* He contributed valuable materials to the History of Medical Men in the History of Medicine in New Jersey by Dr. Stephen Wickes of Orange, N. J. Page 163, line 1, *for* Abra *read* Abia; line 13 from bottom, *for* Paw *read* Pain. Page 165, line 13 from bottom, *for* Gunino *read* Ganino. Page 170, line 15 from bottom, *for* Greene's History *read* Arnold's History.

GENEALOGICAL GLEANINGS IN ENGLAND.

By HENRY F. WATERS, A.M.

[Continued from page 288.]

MARY LEWES of Colchester, Essex, widow, 12 October 18th. James, A.D. 1620, proved 21 November 1620. The poor of St. James in Colchester and of All Saints in Colchester. To the Master or Seniors of St. John's College, Cambridge, one hundred pounds, to be employed and put to the best use for the said College that the said Master and Seniors and Mr. Beadle, preacher &c. in Horninghearthe, Suffolk, and my executor, hereunder named, shall devise and think fit of. Susan Cleere, one of the daughters of my brother Nicholas Cleere, deceased, and Anna Cleere the other daughter of my said brother.

Item, I do give and bequeath unto Samuel Sherman, the son of my sister Anna Sherman deceased, ten pounds &c. To John Sherman, Beniamyn Shearman, Sara Sherman, Anna Sherman and Mary Sherman, the other children of my said sister Anna Sherman deceased, five pounds apiece. To the said Samuel Sherman one of my silver bowles. Mary Heckford, one of the children of my sister Jane Thurston deceased. Stephen Thurston, one of the sons of my said sister. Edmond, Joseph, Thomas and Jane Thurston, the children of my said sister Jane Thurston deceased. Anna Thurston, another of her daughters. To Nicholas Read, the son of my sister Read deceased, five pounds. Elizabeth Kyng, the wife of William Kyng (a similar bequest). Anna Weston, the daughter of my sister Elizabeth Weston deceased. Mary Mathewe, the daughter of my kinswoman Johane Mathewe.

Item, I do give unto Anne Anger, one of the daughters of my brother Shearman deceased, one pair of sheets and one pair of pillowberes, to be delivered within one month next after my decease. I do give and bequeath unto Edmond Shearman, Richard Shearman and Anne Shearman, and to every of them, a piece of gold of two and twenty shillings apiece. To Anne Butler (Qu. Backler?) my said sister Shearman's daughter, the other of my silver beer bowls. Sundry gifts to the Thurstons. My good friend Mr John Inman of St. Edmondsbury. To my sister Thurstone my best gold ring. To Mrs Mary Marshall, wife of Mr. John Marshall, my other gold ring. John Brattle of Ardleigh and his eldest son.

Item, I do give and bequeath unto the child of my cousin John Anger to which I was surety eleven shillings &c. To Mr Taylecott, minister of the Word of God in the parish of All Saint's aforesaid, a piece of gold of twenty two shillings. To the widow Starke twenty shillings. My late maidservant Mary Kyng. Thomasine Waford my now maidservant. The child of my late maidservant Alice Kyng. My late manservant George Wymple. The children of Robert Osborne and Henry Osborne, every one of them. Sara Fuller the daughter of Henry Osborne. Mary Calthrope the daughter of Philip Calthrope deceased. I do give and bequeath unto my said kinsman John Shearman my silver high standing wine cup. To my kinswoman Mary Shearman half a dozen of my best silver spoons and the other half dozen thereof I do give and bequeath unto Beniamyn Sherman my kinsman. Anne Hadley the daughter of William Kynge. Wil-

liam Kyng the son of William Kyng. Sarah Wood the daughter of
Nicholas Wood deceased. My very good friend Mr William Beadle of
Horningesherthe aforesaid. My kinsman Nathaniel Northie.

Item, I do give and bequeath unto my kinswoman Anne Searles and to
my kinswoman Mary Bacon, and to either of them, a piece of gold of twenty two shillings apiece. I make my loving brother Thomas Thurston executor. All the rest of my goods &c. unbequeathed (my debts paid and
funeral charges discharged) I will and my mind is shall be equally divided
by my executor between Samuel Shearman, John Sherman, Beniamyn
Sherman, Anne Sherman and Mary Sherman, the children of my sister
Sherman, and Edmond Thurston, Stephen Thurston, Joseph Thurston,
Thomas Thurston, Mary Heckford, Anne Thurston and John Thurston,
the children of my late sister Jane Thurston, part and part alike, within
twelve months next after my decease.

William Kynge a witness.   Soame, 109.

SUSAN CHAPMAN of Dedham, Essex, widow, 30 June A.D. (——),
proved 4 September 1624. To John Chapman my son my silver pot called
the College pot and one silver spoon. To son Paul Chapman the silver pot
with the cover which hath the letters of his name upon it, and a silver spoon. I give to my daughter Susan Tofte the wife of Thomas Tofte
of Norwich my new gown cloth of serge which lieth by me unmade and
one of my silver spoons. I give to Susan Sherman, my daughter
Christian's daughter, the posted bedstead where I use to lye &c. To
Christian Sherman my grand child five pounds at twenty or day of marriage. Sundry plate and furniture to these two. The poor of Dedham.
I give to Edmond, John, Daniel and Henry Sheareman, my grandchildren,
ten shillings apiece. To my cousin Rounces wife of Norwich my book of
Mr Calvin upon the 119th Psalm. To Christian Shearman my grandchild
my book of Mr. Calvin upon Job. To my two sons John and Paul Chapman each of them a piece of gold of twenty shillings. The residue equally
to my two grandchildren Susan Sherman and Christian Sherman. My two
sons to be executors. To Mr Rogers, preacher of Dedham, a piece of gold
of twenty shillings and a piece of ten shillings to Mr Cotsford minister of
Dedham. The poor of Dedham.

Wit: John Pye and Francis Bridges.

Commission issued (at above date) to Daniel Sherman.

                                Consistory Ct of London.
                                Book Allen (No 9) Leaf 59.

JOHN PYE of Dedham, Essex, clothier, 8 November 1624, proved 24
February 1624. Wife Rachell. To her my great bible and a book called
Mr Rogers 7 treatises &c. John Neale, my sister's son, and his children.
My kinsman Thomas Lawe and his sister Elizabeth Lawe. The said
Thomas Lawe's wife and Rachell Lawe his daughter. My kinswoman Elizabeth Lawe. I give to Mr Rogers, preacher of God's Word at Dedham,
six pounds and to Mr Cotsford, minister of Dedham, four pounds. To the
poor of Dedham six pounds, to be distributed to the most honestest poor
and those that are most painful in their callings, at the discretion of my
executors and my two loving friends Edmund Sherman, senr, and John
Crosse. Gifts to Joseph Morse of Dedham, senr, Isaac Ham, John Peri-
man and Robert Ham. Abraham Ham, Miles Robinson, Samuel Holborne,
John Ham, Abraham Watson, Richard Ellinot, John Singlewood, Robert

Lingwood, George French the weaver, Peter Boston and Clement Cotton both of London. Symon Cooper of Dedham and Goodman Chute, the widow Cartwright, John Canum, —— Spinke, Nicholas Prigg and Jeremie Morse. John Wood. Symon Fenn whom I have brought up. I give and bequeath the sum of twenty pounds to be put into the hands of Mr John Rogers, preacher of Dedham and Mr Samuel Warde, preacher of Ipswich, within a year after my decease, to be given to poor scholars in the University of Cambridge, at their discretions. Five pounds to be put into the hands of Mr Wittam, minister of Misley, and John Peagrome of Maningtree towards the repairing of Maningtre chapel. The free Grammar School in Dedham. The house of correction or workhouse for the poor, lately authorized to be set up. Money to be lent to a young clothier. First to John Weed of Dedham. Mr. Harrison preacher of Layerdley. Mr Edes minister of Lawford. Mr Liddall preacher of Colchester. Mr Hopkins preacher of Great Venham. Mr Hudson preacher of Capell. Mr Collins of Boxsted. Mr Beadle the scholar, which was the son of Mr Beadle sometimes minister of Wolverston. Mr Aldridge. Margaret Ruggle the wife of Jeffry Rugle of Sudbury. Mary Hudson the wife of Christopher Hudson. To Elizabeth Rogers daughter of Mr Rogers of Dedham forty shillings, to be put into her father's hands, to be paid her at her age of twenty years. Elizabeth Toughe, my wife's sister. Rachel Toughe wife of Raphe Toughe of Colchester. Robert Makin.

Item, I give to Nathaniel Sherman, committed to me by his uncle Ainger to bring up, forty shillings, to be paid him when he shall accomplish his age of twenty one years. Martha Salmon. The widow Hand. Whereas Nathaniel Sherman was committed to me, with his stock of forty pounds given him by his father and the sum of five pounds given him by his uncle John Ainge (*sic*) to be brought up till he should come of age I would intreat my loving friend Christopher Hudson take him and his stock to bring him up and learn him an occupation as I should have done if I had lived. I give to goodman Richard Backle (Backler?) my best cloak which goodman Ainger gave me. To Mr Samuel Warde preacher of Ipswich forty shillings. To the widow of Whiting of Fingrego forty shillings. The residue to my kinsman John Neale if living, or if dead to his children. If he be known to be dead leaving no children then of the overplus &c. to Edmund Spinke of Dedham one half and the other half to be put into the hands of Mr Rogers and Mr Cottesford of Dedham to be bestowed upon the English school house, if there be need to use any of it that way, or otherwise their discretions &c. I do make and ordain my loving friends Richard Backler of Dedham, clothier, and Christopher Hudson of Dedham, likewise clothier, my two executors &c. and do request and intreat my reverend friends Mr Rogers preacher of Dedham and Mr Cottesford vicar of Dedham to be supervisors.

Wit: Robert Seaman, John Burr, Bezaliell Anger.   Clarke, 13.

ANTHONY WHITING of Dedham, Essex, clothier, 1 September 1628, proved 14 July 1629. To wife Anne my messuage and lands now in the tenure and occupation of Benjamin Thorpe or his assigns, for term of life, and after her decease to Symon Whiting my son upon condition he pay out of the same to my son Anthony Whiting thirty pounds within one year after my wife's decease and forty pounds to my daughter Phebe. To wife Anne my tenement and yard now in the occupation of Gilbert Hills, for term of her life, and after that to my son John. To my son Anthony and to Mary his wife my two fields bought of the widow Shereman and after their decease to the said Anthony's heirs. To son Symon fourteen pounds. To daughter Susan Whiting three score pounds and to daughter Phebe forty pounds. My two brothers Henry and Ezechiell Shereman shall sell my house and lands in Langham to best advantage, the money arising thence to be paid to my executor for the performance of this my will. To my son John six score pounds at age of twenty three. To my daughter Anne Loveran five pounds. To Mr Rogers forty shillings and to Mr Cottesford twenty shillings. To the poor of Dedham forty shillings and of Stanaway thirty shillings. My wife shall pay unto Mr Lawrence How one hundred pounds for a lease of lands bought of him. She to be executrix.

Wit: Lyonell Chewte and Henry Shereman.

Consistory of London,
Book Bellamy, Leaf 326.

THOMAS WILSON of Dedham, Essex, butcher, 30 January 1630, proved 24 May 1631. Wife Anne. Brother John Wilson and his son Thomas. Brother Henry Wilson and his now wife and his son Thomas and his two daughters Elizabeth and Mary. The children of Lewes Elmes my brother in law, late deceased. To my sister Mary Emery the rents of my house wherein Richard Crowe now dwelleth during her life and after her decease to Mary Parker and Susan Smith, two of the daughters of the said Mary Emery. The other two children of my said sister, viz. Henry Smith and Judith Thornton. My sister Straunge and her children (except her son Robert). My nephew Robert Straunge. Mary Mun the younger, at one and twenty. Every one of the daughters of my brother John Wilson. Robert Alderton and his son Robert. My sister Syday's children. Mr John Rogers, preacher of God's word, and Mr Thomas Cottesford. Elizabeth and Joyce Elmes. Judith Gosline and her children. Mr Anthony Whiting, Phebe Whiting and the rest of my wife's children. Margaret Morse. William Wood. Thomas Makin's son. John Garrad's child. I make my brother in law Henry Sherman senior and Thomas Wood of Dedham executors. St John, 54.

JOHN BURGES parson of Sutton Coldfield, Warwick, 12 September 1634, proved 26 October 1635. My body I commit unto the earth to be honestly buried in the chancel of Sutton church in the same vault where the body of Dorothy my late wife was laid. To the poor of Sutton ten pounds. To the poor of the town of Ipswich six pounds six shillings eight pence. To Dorothy Burges daughter of my dear son John Burges ten pounds. To John Thurlbie, Robert Thurlbie, Elizabeth Thurlbie, the relict (*sic*) and children of my late daughter Ursula Thurlbie, twenty pounds each at age of one and twenty. As for Mary Thurlbie and Ursula Thurlbie I have already provided for them and given them their portions and undertaken by bond to pay it. To Thomas Breedon, John Breedon and Elizabeth Breedon my grandchildren ten pounds apiece at twenty one.

Item, I give to John Sherman and Ursula Sherman and to their mother, my dear daughter Painter, to each of them, to be paid within eighteen months after my death, ten pounds apiece. To all my servants which shall be in my service at the time of my death one quarter's wages. To my dear brother John White of Dorchester I bequeath Stephanus his Latin Concordance, which he gave to me, and to my dear sister Anne his wife, for a token, five pounds. Finally to my dear son John Burges I give the silver cup or can which was given me by the Honorable House of Parliament and my greatest standing bowl of silver and gilt, with the cover thereof, and all the books which I lent unto him and be at this present in his hands. And my will is that if he will undertake to pay one hundred and fifty pounds within one year after my death unto mine executors for the discharge of debts and legacies he shall have all other my books, which otherwise I leave to mine executors pleasure to sell for the payment of my debts and legacies. To all the children of my dear patron Mr Robert Shilton of Birmingham living at my death I give and bequeath five pounds apiece and to himself and his beloved now wife Mary each a ring of gold with a death's head of twenty shillings price as a token of love. The like to my beloved cousin Thomas Willoughbie and Elizabeth his wife. Provision for maintenance of beloved wife Lettice.

On the margin is written T. Johannis Dĕoris Burges
in Medicinis Rectoris de Sutton Coldfeilde.   Sadler, 105.

JOHN WILKINSON of Dedham, Essex, clothier, 17 October 12th Charles, proved 1 December 1636. To Judith Wilkinson my daughter, wife of Edward Sherman, and to her heirs forever my copyhold lands and tenements in Thorpe in the Soaken, Essex, known by the name of Risbridge lands, now in the tenure of Henry Andrewes or his assigns. To daughter Anne Wilkinson all other my copyhold lands &c. in Thorpe. To my daughter Anne Cole the wife of George Cole two hundred and fifty pounds and to Judith Sherman (the same). To daughter Anne Wilkinson five hundred pounds. To Margaret Horneby, widow, ten pounds. To my loving friend Mr. John Rogers of Dedham five pounds and to his son Samuel three pounds. To Mr. Cottesford, vicar of Dedham, three pounds. Thomas Witham of Musley and Mr. Edes of Lauford. The poor of Dedham. My sister Mary Wellocke, widow. My brother Edward Wilkinson. My sister Person. Richard Cocke my sherman. Samuel Person, sherman. Mary Hills widow. Old Boone, weaver. Purdy, my weaver. Edward Rampton, weaver. Daniel Sherman, my servant. Troth Stympson, my servant. The residue to be divided into three parts, one part whereof I give to my daughter Anne Wilkinson and the other two parts shall be equally divided amongst my other children. My two sons in law, George Cole and Edward Sherman to be executors. Daniel Sherman one of the witnesses. Proved by George Cole, power reserved for the other executor.   Pile, 122.

SYMON WHITING of Dedham, clothier, 17 April 1637, proved 15 June 1637. To Jane my beloved wife all my houses and lands in Dedham for term of life. To son Symon my house and lands which I now dwell in after wife's death. I give and bequeath my house and one acre and half of land, now in occupation of Roger Cole my brother in law, unto that child which my wife is now withall, after her decease; but if it die before my wife I give it to my son Simon. If all my children happen to die before their mother all those houses and lands shall be heired by Anthony Whiting, son of Anthony Whiting my brother, with remainder to Thomas Whiting brother of my nephew Anthony Whiting. To son Symon fifty pounds at two and twenty. To daughter Jane Whiting one hundred and fifty pounds at nineteen. To brother John Whiting twenty shillings. To brother Roger Cole forty shillings and to Martha his daughter, my god daughter, ten shillings, to be laid out for two lambs. To Edmond Sherman of Colchester, my kinsman, ten shillings. To Thomas Whiting of Colchester, my cousin, ten shillings. Item, I give unto "ould" Richard Sherman of New England ten shillings. Mr. Thomas Cottsford our pastor and Mr. Matthew Newcom our preacher. John ――――― the Bohemian scholar. The poor of Dedham. Miles Roberson. Elizabeth Raynold the wife of John Reynold. The widow Burredge, late wife of Hugh Burridge. The widow Hassett. If all my children die before the age of one and twenty then my mind and will is that one hundred pounds of their legacies be equally divided amongst so many of my brother in law Cole's children which he shall have by Susan my sister as shall be then alive. My wife to be executrix together with my cousin Clement Fenne of Jupe's Hill.

Proved by the widow, Clement Fenne renouncing.   Goare, 99.

Anne Wilson of Dedham, Essex, widow, 15 September 1638, proved 13 December 1638. I give and bequeath unto my son Anthony Whiting of Bentlie, clerk, a long table cloth, half a dozen napkins and a needle work cushion. I give to John Whiting my son and to Susan Cole my daughter all the rest of my household stuff &c. To my said daughter Susan Cole ten pounds. To my daughter Phebe Barnard of New England ten pounds, and to her two children born here before she went over, vizt John and Samuel, to each of them twenty shillings apiece. To all my daughter Cole's children, being four, to each of them twenty shillings apiece. To my son John Whiting eleven pounds and to Anne, his daughter, twenty shillings. To my nephew Symon Whiting, the son of my son Symon Whiting, deceased, a little silver wine cup at his age of one and twenty years, if he live so long; but if he die before his said full age then I will that my son John Whiting have the same cup. I give unto Jane Whiting, daughter of my said son Symon, two silver spoons if she lives to her full age of one and twenty years, otherwise to my son John. To my two nephews Anthony and Thomas, the sons of my son Anthony Whiting, to each of them five pounds apiece, at one and twenty. Mr. Thomas Cottesford, vicar of Dedham, Mr. Newcomy, of Dedham, clerk, and Mr. John Edes of Lawford, clerk. The widow Bacon, the widow Horne, the widow Chase dwelling near the heath, the widow Goffe, the widow Howchen. The poor of Dedham. I give unto my brother Edmund Sherman of Colchester twenty shillings. My neighbor William Wood. All the rest I give unto my loving brother Ezekiel Sherman, to discharge my debts, legacies and funeral charges, and I make and ordain my said brother Ezekiel Sherman sole executor, &c. I give to my son John Whiting my bible that was his father's.

Wit: Lyonell Chewte, William Wode.

Com. of London for Essex and Herts.

Original will in File for 1638–9.

Number, 152.

Richard Backler of Dedham, Essex, clothier, 25 June 1639, proved 25 July 1639. To wife Anne the house my son Nathaniel now dwells in &c., for life, and one hundred pounds (and household stuff &c.). To son Richard the said house &c., after my wife's decease, and four hundred pounds at two and twenty (he under seventeen). I do entreat my cousin Bezaliell Anger to take him for an apprentice. To my daughter Anne Smith one hundred pounds. The same to daughter Joane Crosse. Daugh-

ters Mary, Sarah (at 18) and Elizabeth (at 18). My cousin Elizabeth
Backler to be kept and maintained by Anne my wife and after her decease
by my executor. If God shall take away my wife before my two youngest
daughters accomplish their said ages they shall be at the disposing of my
brother Samuel Sherman. To son Nathaniel my moiety and part in the
mill and the meadow therewith occupied, now in the occupation of John
Marsh. John Sherman referred to. Son Nathaniel to be sole executor.
Peter Fisher one of the witnesses.   Harvey, 125.

SAMUEL SHERMAN of Dedham, Essex, clothier, 14 June 1643, proved
12 December 1644. To wife Ester the house I now dwell in, with lands
&c. thereunto belonging, in Dedham, for life, and six acres now in occupation of John Crosse jun^r; the house wherein the said John Crosse dwelt is
hers already for term of life. To her also my house and lands in Suffolk,
in Crettinge or elsewhere, all which I lately bought of Samuel Salmon,
now in occupation of William Richardson; all these for life. Other provision made for her. After her decease son Samuel to have the house I
now dwell in, with remainder to son Edmond, then to son Bezaliel. To
Samuel my piece of land in Ardleigh holden of the Pigot's Hall. To him
my oadhouse and oadhouse yard, fats and lead, with all those implements
belonging to the said oadhouse, the rent and profit thereof to be taken by
my cousin Edmond Sherman and reserved in his hands until my son Samuel
be twenty-two, and then paid over to the said Samuel. Other bequests to
Samuel. To daughter Ester five hundred pounds at twenty or day of marriage. And the same to daughter Anna. To my son John the rents that
shall arise of my farm at Empsted called Stevenses, now in occupation of
John Barker or his assigns, to maintain him, my said son John, at Cambridge or Oxford, for I would have him brought up to learning that he
might be fit to honor God in his church, that is if God inclines his mind
thereunto and if my loving brother Dr. Burges and my loving friend Mr.
Newcomen, they being consulted with, shall think him fit. Loving kinsman Bezaliel Anger, or, if he be dead, loving friend Robert Webb to
receive the rents and reserve them in their hands and then pay to my son
John, or rather to his tutor at Cambridge, every quarter six pounds ten
shillings a quarter. Other provisions for John. He to have my house and
lands and meadows in Cretinge and Barking in Suffolk, called great Ravenses and little Ravenses &c., after my wife's decease, all which I bought
of Samuel Salmon late of Ireland. To son John also two hundred pounds,
which is to be paid into the hands of my brother John Sherman and laid
out in lands to be estated upon my said son, the profits to be kept by my
friend John Webb and then paid to my son John to buy him books with at
his age of twenty-two. Son Edmond to have Stevenses farm at Empsted
after wife's death. To son Bezaliel three hundred pounds at twenty-three,
and six hundred pounds more to be laid out in lands, with the advice of my
brother John Sherman, John Crosse sen^r, Robert Webb, Bezaliel Angier
and Edmond Sherman. To daughter Deborah five hundred pounds to be
laid out in lands (she under nineteen). To son Nathaniel, after wife's
decease, my house and lands wherein John Crosse now dwells, my wood in
Langham &c. (he under the age of twenty-two). Seven acres of wood
called Catt's rent, given to Nathaniel, shall be by my cousin Richard Sherman once felled and my wife shall have ten load of the underwood. To
Samuel, my brother John Sherman's son, twenty pounds, and to Mary
Sherman, my brother John's daughter, ten pounds. My cousin John An-

gier. To my brother Benjamin's children twenty pounds. To my sister
Warner's son Samuel Warner twenty pounds, and to Mary Abbott ten
pounds and to Henry Warner ten pounds, all to be paid into my brother
Warner's hands. To my sister Backler twenty shillings.

Item, I give unto my sister Bacon in New England ten pounds, to be
sent her or her husband in linen cloth and shoes by my cousin Edmond
Sherman. To my loving sister Sherman, Edmond's widow, twenty shillings, and to her son Samuel ten pounds, to her son John Sherman twenty
shillings and to her daughters, Grace and Ester Ward and her youngest
daughter, to either of them twenty shillings. All these legacies given to
sister Edmond's (*sic*) and her children shall be paid into Edmond Sherman's hands. I give to my brother Richard Sherman five pounds and to
his son Samuel five pounds and to his daughter Alice Sherman twenty shillings, these legacies to be paid into cousin Edmond's hands &c. I give to
Anne Sherman forty shillings and to Priske Sherman forty shillings. To
my loving cousin Mr. Smith, now vicar of Dedham, ten pounds. To my
loving friend Mr. Nathaniel Rogers forty shillings. Others. To my loving brother Dr. Burges twenty shillings and to his son Samuel twenty shillings and to his son Nathaniel twenty shillings and to his son Daniel twenty
shillings, all to be paid into my brother Burge's hands. To my loving sister Nash twenty shillings and to her son twenty shillings and to her daughter, now at London, twenty shillings; all to be paid to my brother Nash.
I give forty shillings to be paid into the hands of my brother John or
James Burges, they to procure four godly sermons to be preached at the
town of Stanton Drew every quarter and they to give the preacher ten
shillings for every sermon. Gifts to Thomas Younge, old Carter, George
Barker sen[r], William Cooper, Robert Woodward, widow Carver, Ed.
Grome, my old friend Thomas Boylson, Robert Jennings, Joseph Mose,
Mr. Norcrosse, Mr. Knowles and others. The Free Grammar School in
Dedham a gift to enlarge the English schoolhouse. I would have my son
Samuel, when the Lord hath taken away to himself his dear loving father
and mother, to be a father to all his brothers and sisters that they may
come thither at times convenient and find brotherly entertainment and welcome; God having made him the elder brother I would gladly have him
to be a father to my children. Reference to Daniel Rogers, Henry Wright,
Thomas Ingoldsby and Nathaniel Page. Wife Ester and son Samuel to be
executors and John Crosse sen[r], John Sherman, Bezaliel Angier and Edmond Sherman supervisors.   Rivers, 14.

ROBERT BURGES of Stanton Drew, Somerset, yeoman, 17 November
1626, proved 14 December 1626. Son James Burges. Son in law James
Nash. Wife Alice Burges. Son John Burges. My sister Anne Hinton.
My two daughters. To the two children of my daughter Hester Sherman
five pounds, viz[t] to each of them fifty shillings, which I will my said son
James shall pay unto them. The children of my son in law James Nash.
My brother in law Thomas Benbrick. Wife and son James to be execu-
tors.

Proved, at above date, by James Burges and probate granted 22 December 1626 to the widow Alice Burges.   Hele, 145.

[This will was again registered in Quire 149 of same book.]

ESTER SHERMAN of Dedham, widow, 14 August 1646, proved 3 September 1646. To my son John that forty pounds that was added to the two

hundred which was lent my brother John Sherman upon his land, and my will is that my son John shall receive the benefit of that forty pounds for and towards his maintenance at Cambridge. I give to my brother Cornelius Burges five pounds. To my brother John Burges five pounds. To my brother James twenty shillings. To my brothers John Sherman and Benjamin Sherman ten pounds each. To Mr. Nucomen and Mr. Smith, the ministers of Dedhâm, five pounds each. To my cousin Ruth Marsh two pounds ten shillings. To my Aunt Bembory of Pencford and to my uncle Samuel Lush of Stanton Drew ten shillings each. To my cousins Henry Warner and Mary Abbott ten shillings each. Goody Robertes of Langham and Goody John Garrood my neighbor. To my cousin Samuel Cole's wife and my cousin Henry Wright's wife five shillings each to buy a pair of gloves. Old Carter and Elizabeth Howard. My daughters Hester, Hannah and Deborah. My sons Edmond, Beza and Nathanael. All my eight children. My cousin Beza Angier's wife. To John Crosse senior and Edmund Sherman, either of them, twenty shillings. Item, I give to Richard Sherman of New England three yards of broadcloth. The poor of Dedham. Goodwife Bowtell. Reference to husband's will. My two youngest children Deborah and Nathanael to be brought up to school according as my husband did appoint. My cousin Bezaliel Angier to be sole executor and John Crosse senior and John Sherman supervisors.

Twisse, 125.

HENRY SHERMAN of Dedham, Essex, clothier, 3 February 1642, proved 12 April 1645. To my son Edward a parcel of land called the Hikel now in the occupation of Marten Garrad; he to pay Thomas Wattes fifty pounds; with the use. To son Henry the Waye (?) lands and a parcel called "goalden aker" now in the occupation of Marten Garrood. To Edward the furniture of my painted parlor &c. The rest to son Henry Sherman.

Witness, Henry Fenn and Ezechiell Sherman.

Com. of London for Essex and Herts.

File for 1644–5, No. 85.

CLEMENT FENN of Dedham, Essex, clothier, 4 November 1651, proved 17 December 1651. To wife Marcy my house and land (described) during her natural life and after her decease to be sold and equally divided amongst my children. All the rents &c. of lands in Lawford to wife towards the education of all my children until my daughter Mary shall accomplish her age of one and twenty, and then to be sold by my wife and brother Henry Cussens of Ipswich and my kinsman Edmond Sherman and my brother Henry Fenn and the money arising to be equally divided amongst my five daughters. Daughters Martha, Mary, Sarah, Anna and Lydia Fenn. To John Cole my son in law five pounds and to Thomas Cole my son in law the best feather bed his mother brought. The rest to my wife whom I ordain sole executrix.

Edmund Sherman a witness.   Proved by Mercie Fenn the relict.

Grey, 239.

EZECHIELL SHERMAN of Dedham, senior, clothier, 26 August 1653, proved 14 August 1654. Wife Anne. Youngest son John. My daughter Mary Sherman. To her one wainscot chair, one pumell chair, a wicker chair, a green chair, two wrought stools &c. My brother Alfoveer (?).

My brother Stephens. My daughter Salmon. My son Ezeckiell. A codicil made 1 September 1653.   Alchin, 199.

[The will of Ezekiel Sherman, eldest son of the above testator, proved 12 May 1657, has already been printed in these Gleanings (Part I., p. 4).]

HENRY SHERMAN of Bentley, Essex, 9 August 1654, proved 22 May 1655. Loving friends Edward and Daniel Sherman of Dedham. My five children. Sons Andrew, James, Zebius and Nathaniel. Wife Loere Sherman.   Aylett, 365.

JOHN SHERMAN of Dedham, Essex, clothier, 5 August 1654, proved 10 November 1655. To son John twenty pounds. To son Samuel twenty pounds within six months, so be it he doth not demand the twenty pounds my brother Samuel gave him by will, which hath " bin " in my hands ever since. To son Nathaniel thirty pounds, at age of twenty three. To my daughter Anne thirty pounds at twenty one. The same to daughter Elizabeth. These three of my last wife's children, vizt, Anne, Nathaniel and Elizabeth, to be heirs to one another. Forty pounds to loving wife and she to be executrix. To my daughter Peachey forty shillings. I do intreat my loving neighbours Capt. Webb and my loving cousin Samuel Sherman and my loving cousin Bezaleel Angier and my loving cousin Edmund Sherman to be supervisors.

Proved by Anne Sherman the relict &c.   Aylett, 440.

REBECCA COLE of Dedham, Essex, widow, 29 November 1655, proved 20 February 1655. Loving friend Mr. Lyonell Bacon of Hyem in Suffolk. Mr. Matthew Nucomen and Mr. George Smith, ministers in Dedham. John and Artor Cole the two sons of John Cole deceased. Samuel Cob the son of Thomas Cob of Dedham, at one and twenty. The remaining children of the said Thomas Cob. Rebecca Cricke at one and twenty. If she die before then her legacy shall be divided between her two uncles John Cob and Artor Cob,* before named, and her two aunts Elizabeth Raymont and Alice Munt. Rebecca Tanner the daughter of my brother William Tanner. The children of my cousin William Tanner. My cousins Mary Cox, Sarah Cox and Elizabeth Tanner the three daughters of my brother William Tanner. My copyhold lands and messuages in Clafton Parva, Essex. My cousin William Cox of Coggshall. My cousin Samuel Sherman of Dedham. Priscilla Tanner, my kinswoman whom I have brought up, and her two brothers Henry and William Tanner. Daniel Cob, son of Thomas Cob* deceased. Andrew Cole of Brumley, son also of Thomas Cole, forenamed. The wife of Thomas Cropley of Colchester. Brother William Tanner of Coggshall to be executor.   Berkley, 57.

SAMUEL SHERMAN, clerk, late rector of Alderton Suffolk, declared his nuncupative will 30 December 1658, proved 28 February 1658. He made and appointed Mr. John Sherman, Fellow of Jesus College in Cambridge, and Mr. Edmond Sherman, minister in Ipswich, to be his executors. He gave his notes to Mr. Edmond Sherman of Ipswich. He gave to Mr. Martin Carter of Shufford in Essex five pounds, desiring him to take his horse again which he bought of him. He gave to his eldest brother John thirty pounds, to his sister Hannah ten pounds, to his sister Elizabeth eight pounds, to his brother Nathaniel twenty pounds, to Mr. Samuel Jacombe ten pounds, to his cousin Sherman of Bradwell five pounds and to his brother Peachie's boy Sam: ten pounds.   Pell, 38.

* I suspect that for Cob, in the above will, we should always read Cole.

JOHN SHERMAN of Norwich in the County of Norfolk, clerk, 6 July 1658, proved 20 July 1661. To the Free School of Dedham where I was born five pounds, to be disposed of for books by the present schoolmaster, the present ministers and two of the chief men in the town; and my will is that those books be chained as my uncle's are. To ten of the oldest and poorest people in the town of Dedham ten shillings apiece. To the free school in the Charter House, where I was bred, five pounds to be disposed of for books; and my order is that these books be chained. To the Library of Norwich five pounds. To the oldest poor in my close of Christ Church, Norwich, ten shillings apiece. To my half sister Christian Sherman twenty pounds. To my half sister Martha Darie twenty pounds. To my brother Bur who married my sister Susan Sherman twenty pounds. To my nephew by my sister, John Bur, Bachelor in Arts, the little bed which was my uncle's Court and College bed &c. and all my books and MSS. To my niece Christian Swuriburn (?) ten pounds. Niece Susan Bur. To nephew Henry Bur ten pounds at age. My sister Sherman, my brother Daniel's widow, being executrix, oweth upon a bond to my uncle one hundred pounds. I give her a half year to pay fifty pounds. The other fifty pounds I order her to pay upon the day of her marriage. To my nephew Daniel Sherman, son of my brother Daniel, ten pounds at age. The same each to Elizabeth Sherman his eldest daughter and Susan Sherman his second daughter. Fifteen pounds to Christian Sherman, my brother Daniel's youngest daughter. Forty pounds to be equally divided among the children of my half sister Mary Alexander. Five pounds apiece to the nine children of my aunt Toft. To my uncle Toft five pounds. To my aunt Toft my best ring. Forty shillings each to cousin Robert Chapman, cousin Longthorn the widow who dwells in Beast Street, Norwich, to uncle Toft's sister the widow Rownse, to cousin Elizabeth Answorth now married and in the Barbados, if she comes into England, and to cousin Robert Gooch of Norwich (for rings). Rings to others. Mr. Coleman student of Physick in Norwich. Five pounds apiece to the two children of my uncle Edmond Sherman.* To my brother Henry my house and lands in Ubbeston, Suffolk, he to pay to my aunt the annuity (forty pounds a year) charged upon it by my uncle. If brother Henry die without heirs male then I give this to my nephew Daniel Sherman and to his heirs. Brother Henry Sherman to be executor. I give him the household stuff in the house of goodman Stor at Ipswich. Thomas Crane one of the witnesses.

Consistory Court of Norwich (1660–61) Fo. 451.

JOHN SHERMAN, D.D., Rector of Bradwell juxta mare, Essex, 31 October 1666, proved 24 May 1667. Wife Rebecca. Lands and tenements which are the inheritance of my said wife and which I enjoy in right of her. My son John and my daughter Elizabeth Sherman. My daughter Jane Sherman at nineteen. My children Charles, Susan and Sarah, which I have by my said wife. My copyhold messuage &c. in Bradwell. My copyhold messuages &c. in Lachingdon cum Lawling.   Carr, 70.

SAMUEL SHERMAN of Dedham, Essex, clothier, 6 September 1670. Wife Mary. My children, vizt, Mary Cole wife of George Cole jun^r, Judith Sherman, Samuel, Mark and John Sherman. The messuage &c. which I bought of William Boggas and Priscilla his wife. To son John

* This "uncle Edmond" must have been the Edmond Sherman (of Colchester) who married Judith Anger.   H. F. W.

the mansion house which I now live in, eighteen acres and a woad house. If wife be now with child &c. My friend Bezaliel Angier of Dedham to be executor.

Commission issued 22 January 1672 to Mary Sherman the relict &c. Bezaliel Angier refusing.   Pye, 11.

JOHN SHERMAN S. T. P. (nuncupative). To my Bro: and sisters married forty marks apiece. To my Bro: Bezaliell I remit his interest now due to sister Fen, twenty pounds more. My library to Mr. Mawd and Mr. Roe the better part to Mr. North my robes and all my lands I give to my Bro: Edmund Sherman and his heirs forever together with all my goods and moneys not disposed and I make my said Bro: Edmund the sole executor.

John Mawhood and others testified that Doctor John Sherman did declare his last will &c. 16 March 1670. Proved 29 March 1671.

Duke, 43.

Sententia pro valore Testamenti JOHANNIS SHERMAN sacrae Theologiæ Professoris nuper Universitatis Cantabrigiensis sed intra parochiam Sancti Sepulchri London defuncti &c. was declared 13 June 1672; the parties in the case being Edmund Sherman, brother and executor, on the one part, and Nathaniel Sherman, also a brother, together with the Master, Fellows and Scholars of Jesus College in Cambridge &c.   Eure, 39.

EDMUND SHERMAN of Dedham, clothier, 11 April 1673, proved 28 May 1673. Wife Grace. Son Edmund. My three children, John, Martha and Edmund. To John, my son, two hundred pounds at twenty two; and if he shall be judged fit to go to the University then he shall have yearly so much allowed him as is fit and necessary for his maintenance out of that two hundred. To Martha at twenty. To Edmund at twenty two. Wife Grace to be executrix. Wit: Bezal: Angier Senr, William Barker.

Pye, 64.

EDMUND SHERMAN of Dedham, Essex, clerk, 20 November 1674, proved 3 February 1674. To wife Sarah all the right, title, interest and claim in certain freehold land situated in St. Margaret's Ipswich or in Tudnam Suffolk, containing forty acres, more or less, which title &c. accrued unto me by virtue of a deed from William Stockton gent., bearing date 25 August 1665. Daughter Priscilla Sherman. Daughter Margaret. Daughter Mary, at nineteen or day of marriage. Wife Sarah to be executrix.

Dycer, 19.

BEZALIEL SHERMAN of Mitcham, Surrey, merchant, 10 May 1687, proved 15 September 1687. Reference to an indenture made 16 December 1685 between the said Bezaleel, by the name of Bezaleel Sherman of London, merchant and citizen and mercer of London, and Anne my wife, of the one part, and Richard Norton of Mitcham Surrey Esq., Richard Niccoll of London, merchant, John Knapp, citizen and wax chandler of London, Francis More of London, gen^t, and Richard Bowater, citizen and mercer of London, of the other part, and certain Articles of Agreement, dated 19 January 1677, concerning my marriage with the said Anne, one of the daughters of the said Richard Norton. The manor of Thorington, Suffolk, and the capital messuage or farm in Wherstead, called Thorington Hall, and the manor of Chatford *alias* Churchford *alias* Chestford Hall,

Suffolk, and several other messuages, lands &c. in Wherstead, Belstead, Ipswich, Capell, Great Wenham, Little Wenham, Boyden, Baddingham, Cransford, Stoake next Nayland, Polsted and Wiston, in Suffolk. My son Norton Sherman. My three daughters Anne, Elizabeth and Hester Sherman. The patronage and advowson of the church of Capell. My nephew Bezaleel, son of my brother Nathaniel Sherman, late of Dedham, clothier, deceased. My brother in law Mr. Edward Fisher. My kinsman Mr. John Wall of Stratford, Suffolk, clothier. My three nieces, the daughters of my said late brother Nathaniel. Wife Anne to be executrix.

Foot, 121.

EZEKIEL SHERMAN of Colchester, Essex, linen draper, 20 August 1715, with a Codicil annexed 31 August 1716, proved 6 November 1716. Reference to marriage of eldest son Ezekiel, to whom silver tankard marked E. ^{S,} H. To son Stebbing Sherman my copyhold lands &c. called the Hall lands *als* Hallfield lands (about sixteen acres) in Dedham, holden of the manor of Overhall and Netherhall in Dedham, with remainder to my two sons William and John Sherman, in common. Other lands. Daughters Martha Sherman, Mary Sherman and Hannah Jones, the now wife of Edward Jones. Sundry articles of silver &c. given. To son William my eight day clock and my silver caudle cup with the cover marked S. ^{B,} G. To my daughter Martha my silver server marked M. P. to M. S. To my daughter Hannah Jones my large silver salt marked W. S. ad H. S. To my son Stebbing Sherman my small silver spoon marked H. S. and my small silver salt marked R. ^{S,} G., and also my little silver cup with two ears marked M. P. My daughter Martha Sherman to be executrix. My brother in law Daniel Day to be guardian of my son Stebbing until he shall attain his full age of one and twenty. My brother in law Daniel Day of Colchester, Baymaker, to be executor if my daughter Martha shall happen to die. Proved by Martha Sherman, the daughter &c.   Fox, 214.

ANN SHERMAN of Kensington, Middlesex, widow, 26 November 1720, proved 2 November 1722. My body I commit to the earth to be buried as privately as possible in the vault in the churchyard of Mitcham in Surrey, wherein Mr. Bezaleel Sherman lies interred. To my daughter Ann Fielding a diamond ring made of part of my diamond pendants. My father's picture and the picture of my said daughter Ann. To my daughter Elizabeth Vincent all the rest and residue &c. and I do nominate &c. my said daughter full and sole executrix.

Proved by Elizabeth Vincent wife of Henry Vincent Esquire.

Marlboro, 222.

[I have note of Marriage Allegation of Bezaleel Sherman of London, merchant, bachelor, about 40, and Mrs. Anne Norton of Mitcham, Surrey, spinster, about 19, with consent of her father, Richard Norton, Esq.; at St. Mary, Aldermary, London, 19 January, 1677-8.—H. F. W.]

THOMAS FONES citizen and apothecary of London, 14 April 1629, proved 29 April 1629. Have disposed, by Acts executed in my life time, the greater part of my personal estate to and among my children and to the use and benefit of my wife. I commit the tuition &c. of my son Samuel, during his minority, unto his uncle John Wynthropp of Groton, Suffolk, Esq., John White of the Middle Temple, London, Esq., and James Thurlby citizen and grocer of London. The tuition of my daughter Elizabeth and Martha I do commit unto my said loving brother John Wynthropp until they shall be married or attain their full age of one and twenty years. The tuition of my youngest daughter Mary Fones I commit unto my loving wife her mother. And I do make my said wife Priscilla Fones and my said brother John Wynthropp the executors.   Ridley, 28.

[The above testator married Priscilla widow of Bezaleel Sherman of Ipswich and daughter of John Burgess S. T. P. She afterwards became the wife of the Revd Henry Painter. This family will be found referred to in the Life and Letters of John Winthrop. See also N. E. H. and G. Reg. for 1856. Mr. Fones died the day after making his will.

The following three wills relate to the family of the wife of our Revd John Sherman. My friend Lt Col. Vivian gives us, in his Visitations of Cornwall, a pedigree of the Launce family, to which Mrs. Sherman belonged, and shows the connection of that family with the Darcy family of Dartford, Kent, not of Essex Co. as has been thought.   H. F. W.]

PHILIP HAYNE, widow, of the parish of St. Petrock in the city of Exeter, 18 January 1639, proved 18 May 1640. I give towards the maintenance of poor boys in the hospital of this city ten pounds. To Mr. Richard Harris, my brother in law, twenty pounds. To the two children, the son and daughter, of my sister the deceased wife of the said Richard Harris, one hundred pounds, *i.e.* to each of them fifty pounds. To my brother in law Mr. Simpson twenty pounds. To Francis Lance, the eldest daughter of my sister Simpson, one hundred pounds. To my nephews David and John Lance and the two other daughters of my said sister Simpson, to each of her said several children fifty pounds, to be employed and disposed of by my executors, hereafter named, to the only use and benefit of the said five children, for the augmenting of every of their said legacies so far as they lawfully and safely may till they and every of them be married or attain to the age of one and twenty years, and then to be respectively paid unto them, with the increase and benefit thereof. And if my said sister Simpson be now with child and shall be delivered of the same then I give fifty pounds unto the said child, son or daughter. Provision in case of death of any of them. To the two daughters of my deceased sister Caldecott twenty pounds each. To John Pattison the son of my former husband Dr Pattison, thirty pounds and to his sister Mary the like sum. To Henry Painter, clerk, minister of St. Petrock's in Exeter, fifty pounds. To Mr. Fardinando Nicholls, minister of St. Mary Arches in Exeter, three pounds and to Mr. Mark Downe, curate of St. Petrock's, forty shillings. To Mr. Timothy Shute, preacher in Exeter twenty shillings and the same to Mr. Allen, preacher, and likewise to Mr. Bartlett, minister of St. Thomas parish. To Mary, wife of Francis Fryer, five pounds. To my sister Prouze my best diamond ring. To Priscilla Paynter, the wife of the aforesaid Henry Painter, my other diamond ring. To Mrs. Joane Collamore my wedding ring which I wear, having this poesy on it, Loue is the bond of peace. To Mrs. Mosyer, the wife of Mr. Stephen Mosyer, my two silver salts. To Mrs. Mules, widow, my best beaver hat and my mourning gown. To Mrs. Manton, widow, five pounds. To my nephew James Lance one silver can. To Mr. John Gill. merchant, my little bible with silver clasps. To his three children, each, two silver spoons with gilt knobs or tops. To my servant Mary twenty shillings. To the two children of my son John Hayne, each, two silver spoons of them that have their grandfather's mark upon them. To Mrs. Martha Spicer, wife of Nicholas Spicer, for a remembrance of my love unto her, my silver sugar box. To my foresaid sister Isabella, the wife of Mr. Sidrack Simpson, before named, all my wearing apparell, linen

and other, not before given.   To the three daughters of her my said sister
Simpson, namely, Francis, Mary and Isabella, all the residue of my plate,
jewels, linen and household stuff and utensils, to be equally divided between them after the decease of my said sister Simpson, into whose hands,
my will is, it shall be delivered and that she shall have the use thereof
during her life.   All the rest of my goods &c., my debts, legacies and funeral
expences discharged, I give and bequeath unto my well beloved brother
and trusty friends Mr. Richard Harris of St. Clement's in the Co. of Cornwall gen^t, and Henry Paynter, aforesaid, clerk, whom I make &c. my
executors.   And I give unto my two brothers in law, Mr. Richard Prouze
and Mr. Richard Harris, each of them, a mourning cloak of good cloth and
to the aforesaid Henry Painter, clerk, a mourning gown of the same and to
my dear sister Prouze and to Priscilla Paynter, wife of the said Henry, to
each of them a mourning gown of silk, "Tabey or Calaminco" and to my
niece Mary Lance a mourning gown of Turkey "tammey."

In a Codicil she gives to Mr. Painter her large bible with purple velvet
covering and silver clasps.   Coventry, 61.

SYDRACH SYMPSON of London, clerk, Master of Pembroke Hall in the
University of Cambridge, 2 April 1655, proved 15 April 1655.   I will that
fifty pounds be paid unto my dear and loving wife Isabella Simpson within
one month next after my decease and that my executors shall lend unto my
said wife fifty pounds more during her life, she giving bond for the repayment thereof within one month after her decease.   I give her one such of
my feather beds &c. as she shall make choice of and one little case of silver
cups, now in my trunk at Cambridge.   To my son Sidrach all my lands
and tenements in Bocking, Essex, which I purchased of Alderman Thomas
Andrewes.   To the poor of Black Notley in Essex, where I was sometimes
preacher, forty shillings.   To the poor scholars of Pembroke Hall twenty
pounds.   To the children of my brother Joshua Simpson of Boston in the
Co. of Lincoln twenty pounds, to be equally divided amongst them.   To
my brother Robert Sympson of Bristol ten pounds.   To Mistress Symonds
my late servant five pounds.   To my daughter Katherine Denham two
hundred pounds.   To my daughter Priscilla Sympson three hundred pounds.
To my said son Sydrach twenty pounds to pay his debts which he owes at
Oxford and I desire my son in law Master Joseph Denham to take care of
paying the same, so far as the said sum will extend.   To my son in law
Master James Lane my new black cloak faced with velvet.   To my man
servant Thomas my black horse that is at grass and twenty shillings.   To
old Mrs. Chapman widow ten pounds.   All the rest and residue to my said
daughter Katherine Denham, the wife of Joseph Denham, and to my said
daughter Priscilla Simson, to be equally divided between them.   And I do
make and ordain Captain John Stone and my said son in law Joseph Denham executors &c. and entreat Master Richard Fludd, Master Samuel Warner, Capt. Mark Coe and George Peryer to be overseers.   Elizabeth
Symons one of the witnesses.

Proved by both executors.   Aylett, 346.

ISABELLA SIMPSON of London, widow, 29 May 1668, proved 4 August
1669.   To my son James Launce one hundred pounds of that which he
hath in his hands.   The other fifty pounds which he hath I give to my son's
daughter Isabella Launce.   My trunk, with all the things in it, which is in
Exeter at Mr. Pamor's, I give to my son James Launce; also a box, with

the things in it. There is a paper upon it written it is for my son James. Other things to James (including a striking clock). To my son's wife Rebecka Launce one drinking silver cup with two handles. To my son Darcy Launce five pounds.

Item, my will is that my daughter Mary Sherman have " thartine 30 " pounds, and I give her my cawdle silver cup with a silver porringer that covers it, a ring with three diamonds in it and one silver spoon. I give her my clothes and household goods &c. and my watch. What money is left when all things is discharged I would have my son Launce's children, those that are not married, and daughter Mary Sherman's children, those that are not married, to have it equally divided between them. To old Mr. Nye and Mr. Loader five pounds each. To ministers and prisoners twenty pounds. Item, I give to my son Sherman five pounds and the half of my books, with the great bible I read, his name is writ in it for him. To my son Powell twenty shillings to buy him a ring. To Dr. Gorden three pounds. To Mrs. Nye ten shillings to buy her a ring. To Mrs. Loader a similar bequest. To cousin Kifen ten shillings (for a ring) and the same to Mrs. Turner and Mrs. Perie. Others. My friend Mr. Methuselah Turner of London, merchant, to be executor.

Methuselah Turner, the executor, and James Launce, a son, renouncing, as by Acts of the Court appears, commission issued, as above, to Darcy Launce, a son, to administer according to the tenor of the will.

Coke, 99.

WILLIAM ANGER of Dedham, Essex, clothier, 24 October 1620. To son John my " Oadehouse" (woad house) &c. and sufficient ground about it to lay both fuel for the use of the same and " Bever." To wife Josan the occupation of my house and grounds where I now dwell during her natural life; and after her decease to my son John, he paying to my son Edmond forty pounds. Other bequests to Edmond. To son William thirty pounds. To my daughters Elizabeth and Bridget forty pounds each, at age of twenty or day of marriage. The rest of my daughters. My executrix shall pay to Mr Rogers, preacher of Dedham, three pounds within one year next after my decease. To Mr Cottesford, minister of Dedham, twenty shillings. To every one of my grandchildren twenty shillings apiece. To the poor of Dedham forty shillings. To son John forty pounds. My wife Josan to be executrix and son John supervisor.

Wit: Lyonell Chewte, Edmund Sherman, Richard Backler.
Proved at Colchester 2 August 1622.

Com. of London for Essex and Herts.
File for 1622-1623 No. 186.

JOHN ANGER of Dedham, Essex, clothier, 19 January 1623, proved 18 February 1623. I give the house and ground now in the occupation of Samuel Deacon, or his assigns, which I had of Mr Godscall and John Cole, to Anna, my beloved wife for term of her natural life, then to my son John and his heirs forever. I will that my executors, with my two loving friends George Cole the elder and my cousin John Ward, shall, within a year &c., buy as much land in the country as shall cost three hundred and forty pounds, my executors to pay it out of my goods, the assurance to be made to my son John. But until he arrive at the age of three and twenty my executors shall employ the rents and profits to maintain my son at Cambridge in the study of learning. If he die before that age I give said lands

&c. to my sons Bezaleell and Samuel Anger, equally to be divided &c. To wife Ann one hundred and fourscore pounds, either in money or goods, wooll or cloth, which she think best. To John my son three score and ten pounds, twenty pounds whereof shall be added to the three hundred and forty pounds before given to buy land and the other fifty to be paid him at three and twenty. I give him my silver and gilt salt after my wife's decease. I give the house that Groome dwells in and the two fields thereto belonging, called Woodcockes, which I had of the surrender of William Ainger my brother, to wife Ann for life, then to son Bezaleell. I give the house that my mother Ainger dwells in, with the field and meadow &c. with my wood (woad?) house to son Bezaleell, but what profit is made of the wodd (woad) house till he come to his age of xxiii my wife shall have, if living, and Bezaleell take the profit thereof after her death. My executors shall, within a year after the decease of my mother in law Ainger, pay to my brother Edmund Ainger forty pounds which my father did bind me to pay by a conditional surrender made to me of the aforesaid house and I give to my son Bezalell; for if the money be not paid my brother is heir at common law. To son Bezalleell two hundred pounds at three and twenty. To son Samuel four hundred pounds at three and twenty, and my will and meaning is that my executors shall, within twelve months after my decease, pay into the hands of my loving friend Mr Hugh Perry, merchant, now dwelling in Soper Lane, London, three hundred pounds of the said portion (given to son Samuel), whom I do intreat to take the care of the bringing up of the said Samuel my son till his age of three and twenty; and my mind is he shall keep him to school till he be perfect in the Latin tongue and then take him apprentice and make him free of London and of those companies of merchants whereof he is free, and to learn him the trade of merchandize; Mr Perry to put in a bond to pay the three hundred to my son at his aforesaid age. The other hundred pounds, part of the portion bequeathed to Samuel, my executors shall pay to my son Bezaleel at his age of three and twenty and take his bond to pay it to Samuel at his said age. To wife Ann the field I bought of John Garrard, now in occupation of Robert Baker, for life, then to my son Edmund. I give my part of Frost's grove in Langham (twelve acres) to Edmund at three and twenty, and during the mean time mine executors shall take what profit shall be made of the underwood and timber felled, by the consent of my friend Mr. Doctor Duke who hath two parts of said grove to my one, and allow my wife every year four load of two band wood and four load of one band wood, and what profit more shall be paid to Edmund at his said age. To Edmund also three hundred and fifty pounds, my executors to get a good place in London for him, to place him with a woollendraper, and my mind is that they would intreat my good friends Mr Richard Turner, at the Key, Mr Daniel Eliot, at the Lion, and Mr Thomas Bridges, at the three half-moons, woollen drapers in Watling street, if they be not in want of one, to help place him with some honest man, and my executors shall lend to the draper that shall take Edmund to apprentice two hundred and fifty pounds, out of the said portion (to be repaid Edmund at his said age) and the other hundred to be lent to son Samuel (at his said age) he to give bond to pay it to Edmund at his said age.

Item : I give my daughter Mary Sparhauke the hundred pounds that I did lend her husband Nathaniel Sparhacke and twenty pounds more, and my posted bed &c. in the entry chamber and also my silver wine cup after my wife's decease. To my daughter Ann two hundred and twenty pounds at age of twenty. And my executors shall pay into the hands of my son in law Nathaniel Sparhauk three score and ten pounds out of Ann's portion, he giving bond to pay it to her at her said age. To my brother William Ainger of Colchester forty pounds. To his daughter that I was witness to twenty shillings, to be paid into her father's hands. I give to Judith Sherman the daughter of Edmund Sherman of Colchester, my god daughter, and to John Gillson, my brother Gilson's son, my godson, twenty shillings apiece &c. To Ann Sherman, daughter of Edmund Sherman of Colchester, five pounds. To my sister Smith the use of thirty pounds for life, and if she happen to have a child or children alive at her death it shall be then divided among them at ages of one and twenty, if only one it shall have the whole. To my brother Edmund Ainger and my sisters Elizabeth and Bridget Ainger forty shillings apiece, at ages of twenty years. To my Rev^d friend Mr Rogers, preacher of Dedham, five pounds. To Mr Cotsford, minister of Dedham, forty shillings. Mr Harison, of Layer, Mr Wittam, of Misley, Mr Collins, of Boxsted, Mr John Edes, of Lawford, and Mr Gullson, schoolmaster of Dedham. To my goddaughter Abigayll Rogers five pounds, to be paid into her father Mr John Rogers hands within three years &c. and he to pay it her at her age of twenty. To the poor of Dedham six pounds to be bestowed at my burial by the discretion of my executors and my brother Edmund Sherman and my cousin John Wardes and that they respect the honestest and painfullest in their callings most. To my sister Judith Sherman, the wife of Edmund Sherman of Colchester, ten pounds, which I lent her husband in April last, and thirty pounds more on condition he free my executors of all bonds wherein I stand bound with him and on condition that the brethren and friends of my brother Sherman proportionably do for him to clear him of his debts and to set up his estate. My sister Anna Smith. Mr Lyddall, preacher of Colchester. To Joseph Morse the elder, Samuel Holborne, Andrew Taylor, Robert Risbye, Thomas Yonge the elder, Bezaleell Ravens, Edmund Ravens and Robert Webb twenty shillings apiece. My godchildren John Backler, Robert Sherman, Joan Backler, Dorothy Garrard, Rachel Crosse and Elizabeth Robinson. Susan Crosse my goddaughter. Her father Benjamin Crosse. John Deacon my godson. His father Samuel Deacon. Matthew Shuckford. Whereas my brother Nathaniel Sherman, on his death, did intreat me to take the charge of Nathaniel, his son, and to bring him up and did give him a portion of forty pounds, which he willed I should have in hand and to put in bond for the same to my cousin Henry Sherman and my cousin John Ward for the payment of said portion when he come to age, now, therefore, I entreat my friend John Pye to take the charge &c. After wife's decease my silver beaker to son Bezaleell, my great silver bowl to Samuel, three silver spoons to Edmund and three silver spoons to Ann. My cousin old Cartwright, widow, and my cousin John Shinglewood's wife. The widow Browne, and her son Samuel Browne. Elizabeth Rickes of Ardley, widow. My brother Richard Sherman. My sister Sarah Gillson. To Annah Sparhawke my grandchild five pounds (into her father's hands). Mary Hayes daughter of Mr Thomas Hayes. Wife Ann, friend John Pye and brother in law Richard Backler my executors and reverend friends Mr Rogers and Mr Cotsford supravisors. Samuel Cole a witness. Byrde, 19.

Ann Anger, 2 September 1625. I give and bequeath to John Anger my son, to Bezaliell Auger my son and to Mary Sparhake my daughter all my moveable goods &c., to be equally divided betwixt them, and I would desire my loving brothers Richard Sherman, Richard Backler and Samuel Sherman to divide it betwixt them. To my daughter Sparhake all my wearing linen and woollen and the sum of twenty pounds. To my son John Anger fifteen pounds, at age of one and twenty years. The same to son Bezaliell at three and twenty. To son Samuel Anger five and twenty pounds at three and twenty. The same to son Edmund Anger. To daughter Ann Anger forty pounds at age of twenty. To Mr. Rogers preacher of Dedham three pounds and to Mr. Cotsford, minister &c., forty shillings. To the poor of Dedham three pounds, to be distributed by my brother Richard Sherman and Samuel Sherman with the assistance of mine executors. To Mr. Carter, preacher of Bellsted and to Mr. Beadel the scholar, son of Mr. Beadell, sometime preacher of Woverston (Wolverston), to Mr. Alldridge and to Mr. Edward Sparhake twenty shillings apiece. Mr. Witham preacher of Mislye, Mr. Culverwell of London, Mr. Edes of Lawford and Mr. Liddall of Colchester. To my two brothers Edmund and Richard Sherman ten pounds apiece. To Samuel Sherman, John Sherman, Sarah Warner, Anna Backler, Mary Bacon, my brothers and sisters, to every of them twenty shillings. To my brother Benjamin Sherman three pounds. To William Anger, Judith Sherman, Anna Smith, my husband's brother and sisters, thirty shillings apiece. To Ann Sherman and Jone Sherman, daughters of my brother Edmund, twenty shillings apiece. To Judith Cartwright and Alice Mase, widow, and to Ann Sherman daughter of my uncle Sherman, doctor departed, twenty shillings apiece. To William Petfild, son of Richard Petfild, twenty shillings at age of one and twenty. To Anna Shinglewod, daughter of my cousin John Shinglewood, and Elizabeth Smith, daughter of my cousin Robert Smith, and to Anna Sherman, daughter of my brother Richard Sherman, twenty shillings apiece, at ages of twenty. Katherine wife of John Garrad, Margery wife of Isaac Hame, Nicholas Prig's wife, Susan, Robert Ham's wife, William Skot's wife, the widow Hame, Elizabeth, Edmund Robinson's wife, Margaret Thorpe and Joseph Thorpe her son. I give to the two children of the wife of Thomas Rogers, John Sherman and Richard Sherman, my kinsmen, ten shillings apiece at their ages of one and twenty. To Edmund Anger, my husband's brother, and to Sarah Gillson, Susan Cross, Elizabeth Gellson and Brigit Anger ten shillings apiece. To Anna Sparhak my grandchild five pounds to be put into her father's hands. To my brother Bezaliell's two children, John Sherman and Usalye (Ursula) Sherman, ten shillings apiece at their ages of one and twenty. Ann Taylor daughter of Andrew Taylor, Katherine the wife of Robert Freman and Amie which was my servant and the widow Blake. To my two executors forty shillings apiece. To Brigit the wife of Edmund Anger twenty shillings. Bezaliell Ravens, Edmund Ravens and Robert Webe. Elizabeth Bluit of Groten, Rosse Pirson of Ardlye and Elizabeth wife of William Cartwright. Joseph Morse. I do make and ordain for my executors my loving son Nathaniel Sparhauck and my brother Edmund Sherman. I stand bound as being an executor with Richard Backler and John Pye to the paying of all legacies given by my late husband John Anger in his last will and testament and to all his debts I never being possessed with any of my said husband's goods nor never meddled with any of them to any use but only took of the other executors my portion which was given me &c., &c. To goodman John Cañum ten shillings.

Wit.: Thomas Makin and Jerimiah Morse (by mark).   Proved at Colchester 16 December 1625.   Com. of London for Essex and Herts.

JOYSEN ANGER of Dedham, widow, 27 August 1627, proved at Colchester 23 May 1628. Eighteen pounds each to son Edmond Anger, daughter Sara Gilson, daughter Susan Crosse, daughter Elizabeth Gleeson and daughter Bridget Anger, the latter at twenty or day of marriage. To my son in law William Anger ten shillings. To Mr. Rogers preacher at Dedham twenty shillings and to Mr. Cotsforde minister of Dedham ten shillings. Son Edmond Anger to be sole executor. To the poor of Dedham twenty shillings.   Com. of London for Essex and Herts.

File for 1627–1628 N° 18.

BENJAMIN CROSS being very sick &c., 19 December 1638, proved 4 April 1639. To wife Susan two hundred pounds &c. To daughter Susan one hundred pounds. To son Benjamin one hundred and fifty pounds at age of twenty two. My executrix shall pay into the hands of my loving brother Edmund Angier three score and fifteen pounds to be improved by him for the bringing up of my son, and the other part of my son's portion which is three score and fifteen pounds, shall be paid into the hands of my loving cousin Bezaleel Angier (for the same purpose). My will is that my son shall be educated at the Grammar School "while"* he is fifteen years of age. And my executrix (with the help of my friends Edmund and Bezaleel Angier) shall provide a good master for my son and bind him "while"* he is two and twenty years of age where he may learn the trade of clothing and clothworking. My friends, on receipt of these sums, to give bonds to pay according to my will. To my three daughters Sarah, Bridget and Anna fifty pounds apiece at age of twenty. To my loving mother thirty shillings. To my sister Margaret Burrowes three pounds. To my sister Ann Branch twenty shillings. To my brother William Angier my best coat. The poor of Dedham. Mr. Thomas Cottford and Mr. Matthew Nucumen. Others. Wife Susan to be executrix provided that within one week after my decease she put in Bond of eight hundred pounds unto my loving brother John Cross and my cousin Bezaleel Angier to perform this my last will and testament. They two to be supervisors.

Thomas Lufkin jun. one of the witnesses.

Com. of London for Essex and Herts.

File for 1638–1639 N° 252.

SAMUEL FENN of Dedham, Essex, clothier, 9 February 1654, proved 13 April 1655. Wife Lydian. Cousin Bezaleel Angier. My sons Joseph, Simon and John, at their several ages of two and twenty. My five daughters Lydia, Deborah, Priscilla, Abigail and Phebe, at twenty. Wife Lydian to be sole executrix. Daniel Sherman one of the witnesses.

Aylett, 355.

SAMUEL ANGIER, merchant adventurer dwelling in Dordrecht in Holand, 1 April 1667, stilo novo, proved 22 May 1667. To Mr. Thomas Marshall the minister of God's Word to the Merchants Adventurers' Church in Dordrecht. To John and Samuel Ford the sons of Sir Richard Ford, kn*t*. and alderman of London. To my three brothers, John Angier, preacher of God's Word, Bezaliell Angier, clothier, in Essex, England, and Edmund Angier, at present at Cambridge, in New England, twenty pounds sterling. My cousin Mary Smith the daughter of the late George Smith, preacher of Dedham in Essex. My wife Barbara Angier, formerly Barbara Colemore, to be executrix.   Carr, 57.

---

* The word "*while*" in these two cases evidently means *until.*—H. F. W.

JOHN ANGIER, pastor of the Church of God at Denton in the parish of Manchester and County of Lancaster, 27 August 1677, proved 8 November 1677. To be buried in Denton Chapel where are buried my late dear wife Margaret and others. To daughter Mary Angier my silver bowl marked J. M. A. &c. The daughters of my son John. My seven grandchildren. My silver bowl marked J. F. A. My son's son John Angier. My grandson Eliezer Heywood. Houses and free lands in Ardleigh, Essex. Grandson Samuel to be brought up in learning. My son Angier's present wife. My cousin Samuel Angier, son of my beloved brother Bezaliell. The three daughters of my son John. To son John my signet ring. Mary Ashton. I give out of my library to Denton Chapel Mr. Hildersham's Lectures upon the One and Fiftieth Psalm and Bishop Jewell's Works against Harding, as a remaining testimony of my love, to be chained up in a convenient place at the charge of the Chapelry, hoping that others will make additions. Other books to grandsons John Angier and his brother Samuel. My manuscripts &c. to my four grandsons, John and Samuel Angier and John and Eliezer Heywood. To my brother Bezaleel my ring with the Moseley's arms and to his son Samuel after his death. To his sons Nathaniel and Mathew twenty shillings apiece. Sister Angier. Brother Edmund Angier. My daughters in law Angier and Heywood. Cousin Samuel's wife Anne. My sister Russell and her two daughters. To Nicodemus Monks and two children. To the child or children and grandchildren of my sister Tongue. My son Heywood. Aunt Bourdman. Loving friend Mr. Nathaniel Hulton and his wife. The poor of Dedham in Essex. My cousin Mary Snelling and her children. To my cousin Samuel Angier, if he live with me at my decease, and to his children Bezaleel and Margaret. Cousin Samuel to be sole executor. Cousin Oswald Moseley of Ancoats, Esquire.   Hale, 112.

EDMUND ANGIER of Wiston, Suffolk, 16 March 1677, proved 12 June 1678. To my wife Bridget my land in Dedham. Sons Samuel, Edmund, John and Nathaniel. Nathaniel to be executor.   Reeve, 60.

[Bridget, daughter of John Rogers, the famous preacher of Dedham, married Edmond Anger. See REGISTER, vol. 41, p. 159.]

BEZAL: ANGIER Sen[r] of Dedham, Essex, clothier, 25 October 1678, proved 11 November 1678. Wife Anne. All my children. Son Matthew Angier. Son Samuel. Son in law Samuel Barker. To son Samuel the tenement wherein the widow Hichcock liveth. Son Bezal:. Son Nathaniel. My three daughters, Mary Barker, Hannah Barker and Sarah Blomfield. My grandchildren. I give unto my brother Edmund Angier of New England twenty shillings, to buy him a ring, and to my cousin Deborah Wall, widow, twenty shillings &c. The same to Elizabeth Astye, Mary Snelling, wife of John Snelling, Priscilla Garrod, wife of Martin Garrod and my uncle Samuel Smith. Others. Wife Anne to be executrix and brother John Blomfield to be assistant to her.   Reeve, 120.

SAMUEL AUNGIER of London, merchant, outwards bound in a voyage to Barbadoes, 1 November 1692, proved 4 May 1693. Everything to wife Sarah, whom I appoint executrix.   Coker, 73.

SAMUEL ANGIER of Duckinfield, Co. of Chester, Minister of the Gospel, 4 July 1712, proved 24 December 1713. To be buried in the yard of the new Chapel in Duckingfield, over against the South door, in the middle between the said door and the wall. Eldest son Bezaliell. Son John Angier of Bristol. Son in law Mr. Ralph Lathropp. My daughter Margaret, his wife. My daughter Anne and her children. Son John Angier. I give my small tenement in Dedham to my son Bezaliell, desiring him to give ten shillings apiece to such children to whom I am an uncle, *i. e.* the children of my brethren and sisters &c. My brother Nathaniel. My two sisters Hannah and Sarah. My brother in law Edmund Sherman. To the poor of Dedham five pounds, to be distributed by my two sisters Hannah and Sarah. All my four children.   Leeds, 267.

JOHN GOODWIN *(ante* p. 288):

[To Mr. Goodwin's will, printed in the April REGISTER, Mr. Waters appended a record of a chancery suit, Woodgate *c* Goodwin, furnished him by Dr. Joseph James Muskett, author of Suffolk Manorial Families. Dr. Muskett has furnished him with the following additional matter relating to the suit.—EDITOR.]

CHANCERY PROCEEDINGS. WOODGATE *c* GOODWIN.

James I. B. & A. W. 30. 1.

JOHN WOODGATE of Estbergholt in y⁶ countye of Suff., clothier, sheweth that Wiłłm Holloway late of Estbergholt was seised of divers lands & tenemᵗˢ cald Casnells in Essex, y⁶ reverc͠on therof to Sara now y⁶ wife of Danyell Woodgate & yo : Orˣ Mary expectant. He was also possessed of goods, ready money plate &c. to a great value and did about nyne yeeres last past make his will & did geue y⁶ sᵈ lands vnto Wᵐ Holloway his sonn by Elizabeth his second wife & to the heires of the same for ever & did give vnto yo: Orˣ Marye [Her name is omitted at the head of this Bill] y⁶ some of 120ˡⁱ at her age of 20 yeers or at y⁶ daye of her marriage vppon condic͠on yᵗ she should convey her right to said lands to y⁶ vse of sᵈ Wᵐ Holloway y⁶ sonne. He did make Elizabeth his wife, now wife of John Goodwin his sole executrix & shortly after died. In a short time she tooke to husband y⁶ sᵈ Jo: Goodwyn of Estbergholt, clothier, who possessed himself of testators psonall estate. Goodwyn refused to pay y⁶ sᵈ 120ˡⁱ to yo: Or: as a legacy vntill sᵈ Mary should accomplish her full age of 21 yeeres vnless yo: Orˢ: should give obligac͠on of 240ˡⁱ for the setlinge of their right vppon Wᵐ Holloway y⁶ sonne, but he before any assignment was made died without issue, Elizabett, Ann, Susan & Mary daughters of Wᵐ Holloway the father by y⁶ sᵈ Elizabeth his last wife being his sisters and coheirs, since whose deatt yo: Orˢ. together with Daniel Woodgate & Sara his wife conveyed all their right to sᵈ p'miss͠ called Casnells to y⁶ sᵈ Elizabett, An, Susan & Mary & their heirs. But soe it is Goodwyn doth refuse to deliver up to yo: Orˢ sᵈ bond or to allow sᵈ 120ˡⁱ bequeathed to yo: Orˣ Mary.

Woodgate *c* Goodwin. Jaˢ I. B. & A. W. 29. 43.

Answere of John Goodwyn & Elizabett his wief. William Hollowaye did by his last will bequeathe vnto Marye his daughter wief to said John Woodgate the Complaynnte the som͠e of six skore pounds to be paide vnto her at her day of marriadge yf it were wᵗᵗ the consent of his wiefe now the defendᵗ Elizabett, sᵈ Mary to assure her right vnto Casnells to the said William Hollowaye her sone Woodgate did become bounde by obligac͠on of twoe hundred & fortye pownds dated 15ᵗᵗ Marche in the nienthe yere of his Maⁱᵉˢ reigne, about three yeres before the full age of the saide Marye, for the payment of sixe score pownds lent him by this defendant. Wiłłm Hollowaye the sone being this Elizabeths sone being of the age of fower yeres or thereabouts at the tyme of the deatt of his father. After the deatt of

William Hollowaye the sone, Elizabett, Anne, Susan & Marye this defend^t
Elizabeths daughters were of their then severall ages of sixtene, fowertene,
tenne & eight yeres.   After the deatt of Wiłłm the sone aboute one yere
past Complaynant did make Clayme vppon Casnells.   Complaynñt & Marye
his wife & Daniell Woodgate & Sara his wife have not assured by sufficient wayes their right to Casnalls to Elizabett Anne Susan & Marye sisters
& coe-heyres of the saide Wiłłm the sone deceased.   Capt. 6 Jun. 16 Iac.
apud Eastbergholt.

JOHN PERRIE, late of Antigua, now of St. James, Westminster, Middlesex.   Will June 24, 1708 (*ante* pp. 115–116).

[John Perrie, Esqr, was a member of the Council and Secretary of the Island
of Antigua and Provost Marshal General of the Islands of St. Christopher,
Nevis, Mont Serrat and Antigua.
His daughter and coheiress Anne married Richard Rigby of Mistley Hall in the
Co. of Essex, Esqr, a member of the Council of the Island of Jamaica.   Dor-
othy married George Baker of London, merchant.   Elizabeth died young and
unmarried.   Mary married the Honble John Cleland, member and President of
H. M. Council for S. Carolina and H. M. Collector of Customs at Charles Town.
Mr. Perrie's " S. Carolina plantations " stretched four miles along Peedee River
from Weehaw creek to and including George Town and " Richmond," " Rose
Mont," " Kensington " and " Weehaw " plantations.   The latter (the old settlement) has ever since remained in the possession of his descendants.—LANGDON
CHEVES, of Charleston, S. C.]

RICHARD DOWNING of Donington (Suffolk) yeoman, 22 December 1594,
proved (at Ipswich) 2 October 1595.   To eldest son Robert land bought of
Thomas Colbye of Beccles Esq. and one close bought and purchased of
Lewes Sparhauke of Dedham, Essex.   Sons Edward and John, daugh-
ters Rose and Jane Downing and daughter Alice Grosse.   Son Robert
Downing and George Grosse of Midleton to be executors.
Arch. Suffolk (Ipswich) B. 35 L. 434.

LEWES SPERHAWKE of Dedham, Essex, mercer, 4 November 1597,
proved 9 March 1597.   Nuncupative will.   To wife Margaret ten pounds
a year, to be paid by son Nathaniel.   To Nathaniel Thorne the house
wherein William Elmes now dwelleth.   Son Daniel Sperhauke to be sole
executor.   Nathaniel Sperhauke one of the witnesses.   Proved by Thomas
Iles, notary public, for Daniel Sparhawke.   Lewyn, 23.

ARTHUR SPARHAWKE of Wytham (Essex) yeoman, 15 June 1605,
proved 4 July 1605.   The poor of Witham.   Dorothy Barre the daughter
of Henry Barre.   The child of Richard Newman my brother in law.   Symon Rychold and Mary Richold, my wife's children.   My wife Johane to
be executrix.   Ja: Sphawke and Nicholas Sphake witnesses.
Arch. Colchester, Bundle Adam No. 36.

JOHN SPARHAWKE, Commissary of Musters for the King, 25 October^r
1605, proved 25 June 1608.   I have ever "bynne" from my cradle a tru^e
protestant in heart and soul, detesting from the very inward parts of my
heart the Pope with all his shavelings and all their papistical trumperies
and most ungodly and execrable courses in religion.   My old good friend
Sir William Browne, knight, "Liefetenñte" Governor of Vlishing (Flushing) whom I have heretofore with an entire affection dearly loved.   Captain Flem̃ynge, Lieut. Johnson, Capt. Throgmorton, Sergeant Major of
Vlishinge, Capt. Younge, Mr. Daniell and Mr. Abraham, preachers of

God's word in Vlishinge.   Sir William Waade, knight.   My cousin Edward Hodierne.   My cousin Reynolde Rabbatt.   My brother Erasmus
Sparhawke.   My mother in law and every one of her children, except
Erasmus and James Sparhawke.   Brother in law James Sparhawke to be
sole executor.   All my goods &c. remaining in Vlishinge.   Signed and
sealed 9 November 1603.   The Lord's most blessed name be praised for
ever and ever, Amen, Amen.   There is an inventory of all my money here
in Vlishinge.

Then follows a Memorandum made by Sir William Browne and witnessed (among others) by Richard Johnson and John Throckmorton.

Windebanck, 56.

RICHARD BOGGAS of Brantham, Suffolk, gen^t., 22 October 1610, proved
28 November 1610.   Wife Susan.   Godson Richard Boggas, son of brother
William.   Robert Boggas, my brother William's other son.   Brother
Robert's four children, Robert, Mary, Anne and Jane Boggas.   Brother John.
The poor of Brantham and of Dedham.   Mr. Rogers.   Brother Robert
and his wife.   Aunt Watson.   I give to my cousin Samuel Sperhawke and
to his wife, to buy them two rings, four pounds.   Sister Anne Moptide.   My
god daughter Anne Clercke at marriage.   Aunt Clerk and Aunt Cotton.
Sister Ellete's children, Joseph and Anne, at his age of one and twenty and
at her day of marriage.   The mother of the said Joseph and Anne.   Thomas
Ufford.   House at Shotlie.   The widow Wythe of Dedham.   My three
brethren, Robert, William and John.   If it happen my wife to be with
child &c.   Brother William executor.   Samuel Sperhawke a witness.

Wingfield, 97.

ERASMUS SPARHAWKE of Branktrie, Essex, Innholder, 26 January 1611.
Wife Elizabeth.   Son John and my three daughters, Alice Sparhawke, Rachael Sparhawke and Johan Sparhawke.   Friend John Lawrence and brother
James Sparhawke.   I do give unto the said John my son and to Alice, Rachael and Johane my three daughters all such goods and moveables as are
now in my possession which were my brother John Sparhawke's the elder
deceased.   I give all my lands, tenements and hereditaments in Branktrie
and Böcking to wife Elizabeth for life, with authority, in her widowhood
being uncontracted, to sell for payment of debts.   I have purchased of William Webbe, gen^t., and Mary Motte, then spinster, three crofts in Bocking upon which I have erected a windmill and other new buildings.   These
conveyed in trust to Robert Walford and Thomas Wood gen^t.   Wife Elizabeth and son John to be executors and she to be his guardian during his minority.   John Lawrence and James Sparhawke to be overseers.   To son
John and daughter Alice my wine license for town of Branktrie.

Commission issued 23 March 1611 to Alice Barr *als* Sparhawke, a sister of the deceased, to administer &c. during the minority of John Sparhawke one of the executors &c., Elizabeth Sparhawke the relict and other
executor renouncing.   Fenner, 23.

ELIZABETH YOUNGE wife of Thomas Younge of Braintree, Essex, brasier, 14 September 1625, proved 15 November 1625.   Reference to Contract of Marriage dated 1 August 16 James.   Testatrix a daughter of John
Daye of Braintree deceased.   Son Henry Wilkinson deceased.   His children Elizabeth, Sara, Joane, Mary and Frances Wilkinson.   Son William
Wilkinson.   His children William, Susanne, James, John and Mary Wilkinson.   Daughter Alice.   Daughter Rachel.   Daughter Joane Sparhawke.

Son John Wilkinson deceased. His children James, Joane and Elizabeth Wilkinson. Mary Wilkinson wife of son William. Son John Sparhawke. Son Thomas Wilkinson. His son James. Daughter Rose Camper. Son in law John Camper. Mr. Buckley of Stisted, clerk. Mr. Samuel Collyns, clerk. Thomas Perry son of John Perry and Bridget his wife, my daughter. Among the witnesses were Daniel Collins, James Sparhawke, Adrian Mott and Thomas Younge.

Com. of London, Essex and Herts, No. 218.

ELIAS WORTHAM of Branktrye, Essex, yeoman, 20 January 1624, proved 2 August 1627. The poor of Brancktrye, Bocking and White Notley. Samuel Collin, clerk, minister &c. in Brancktrye. To son Richard my copyhold lands and tenements in White Notley. To daughter Elizabeth now the wife of James Sparhawke of Branktrye messuages &c. in Bocking. To Susan Sparhawke, Martha Sparhawke, Elizabeth Sparhawke, John Sparhawke and Hanna Sparhawke, James Sparhawke's five children, thirty pounds apiece at one and twenty or days of marriage. Similar bequest to Elizabeth. Francis and Richard Wortham, the three children of the said Richard Wortham. Richard Wortham's wife and Robert Wortham's wife. To my son Robert my messuage &c. known as the Swan (and other houses) and a copyhold stall in Butcher Row, all in Branktrye. I make him sole executor and Richard Wortham overseer.

James Sparhawke one of witnesses. Skynner, 85.

[The will of Robert Wortham the son and executor, named in the above will, has been already given among my wills relating to the Wall family (see REGISTER *ante* p. 249).—H. F. W.]

HUGH SHERIFFE of Rochford, Essex, yeoman, 23 December 1640, proved 8 July 1641. One hundred pounds each to eldest daughter Sara and to daughter Martha at twenty one or days of marriage. Kinsman Richard Pitches et uxor of Stebbing, yeoman, to have the disposing and governing of daughter Sara during her minority and kinsman John Sparhawke and Easter his wife of Cogshall to have the disposing &c. of daughter Martha. To my grandchild Thomas Maule of Eastwood twenty shillings. The residue to my two sons Elihu and Nathaniel. Loving kinsman Simon Bowtell of Prittlewell shall have the ordering and bringing up of my youngest son Nathaniel during the time of his minority or else my kinsman Matthew Butcher of Castle Heningham. Son Elihu to be sole executor and my kinsman Symon Bowtell aforesaid and Thomas Harrison of Leighe in said county to be overseers. Christ : Sheriffe a witness.

Commission issued (at above date) to Simon Bowtell, supervisor &c., to administer during minority of Nathaniel, Sara and Martha Sheriffe, children of the deceased, Elihu Sheriffe, son and executor named in the will, having died before taking upon himself the burden of execution, &c.

Arch. Essex, Book Whitehead, L. 103.

JAMES SPARHAWKE of Brayntree, Essex, gen[t]., 1 January 1644, signed and sealed 29 May 1645, with a codicil dated 10 September 1646, proved 24 October 1648. Mr. Samuel Collins Vicar of Braintree. The poor of Braintree, of Bocking and of Stisted. My cousin John Sparhawke son of my brother Erasmus. My cousin Joane daughter of my brother Erasmus. Mr. Lyngwood the elder, Mr. William Lawrence, John Kent the elder and Henry Browne. My brother Robert Wortham. Mr. Adryan Mott and John Marryon. My cousin Nicholl's wife, William Elders, John Barnard,

Elizabeth now the wife of Johnson &c. My sister Wortham. My son in law John Kent. My son John. The house wherein I dwell in Braintree. My three daughters Martha, Elizabeth and Hannah. James Wall my grandchild, son of my daughter Elizabeth. My godson James Sparhawke, son of my said cousin John. My cousin James Barker, son of my sister Joane. My grandchild Elizabeth Johnson. Essex, 143.

JOHN WESTLEY of Stanaway, Essex, clerk, 18 October 1652, proved 30 January 1653. Eldest daughter at seventeen or day of marriage. Daughters Mary and Jane at ages of sixteen. The poor of Hempsted, Samford Magna and Stanaway. To son Samuel messuages and lands which I purchased in Barnestones, otherwise called Barnardistones, Suffolk, now or late in occupation of Thomas Deekes and William Chinery, and lands and tenements in Hempsted, Essex, which John Westley his grandfather purchased of Thomas Cotton sometime of Panfield Esq. and now or late in the occupation of John Heard. Wife Mary to be guardian of son (now under the age of fifteen). Certain lands &c. in Hempsted to honored friend John Gurdon of Assingdon, Suffolk, Esq. and loving cousin John Sparhawke of Great Coggeshall, clothier, to be sold for children's portions. Residue to son Thomas whom I make executor. Alchin, 373.

JOHN SARHAWKE the elder of Great Coggeshall, Essex, clothier, 29 March 1653, proved 30 September 1653. To the honest poor people of Great Coggeshall five pounds. To wife Hester for life an annuity of five and forty pounds yearly issuing out of my two messuages and all the freehold lands &c. belonging, in Braintree, Bocking and Stisted, now or late in the occupation of George Palmer and William Woodley, and out of my messuage near Church pond in Great Coggeshall wherein I now dwell and my two cottages in Church Lane (and other real estate there). To my son John the aforesaid houses and lands in Braintree, Bocking and Stisted, charged with said annuity. To son Samuel my messuage or inn called the George in Witham and messuage in Great Coggeshall had of Nicholas Northy deceased (and other lands) and five hundred pounds, to be paid into the hands of my brother Christopher Sheriffe whom I desire to be my son Samuel's guardian. To my daughter Hester five hundred pounds, to be paid into hands of my cousin —— Whitinge of Ipswich and he to pay her at age of twenty or day of marriage. And I will that the four hundred pounds now in the hands of my cousin Stuckey of London and one hundred pounds in the hands of my brother Mr. Robert Crane shall be for her portion. To my daughters Sara, Susan and Elizabeth five hundred pounds apiece at twenty or days of marriage, to be paid to my said brother Sheriffe and my neighbor William Coxe. To the children of my brother Sparhawke in New England all the money which their father was indebted to me, with the debt which their father did assign to me to receive of their uncle Samuel Anger, which still rests in their uncle's hands. To my cousin Pechy and her children ten pounds; and the money which her brother John owes me I will shall be divided between him and his brother Samuel. Loving friend Mr. John Owyn, dean of Christ Church, Oxford, and my late minister. Lands in Much Baddow assured to me upon condition. Mr. John Sames my minister. The executors of my cousin Westly late of Stanaway, clerk, deceased. To the children of my brother Edward Sparhawke fifty pounds, to be paid to their father. To my cousin Samuel Crane ten pounds. My servants William Courtman and Samuel Bridgwood. Daniel

Larke sometime my apprentice. George Ireland's wife for their children. Richard Trewe sometime my apprentice. All my workmen which at present work with me and those that have wrought with me a year now last past. The children of Thomas Hawes and of Benjamin Hawes. I give to Samuel Sherman my kinsman, the son of John Sherman, five pounds. To Edward Bridgwood five pounds. I do appoint my said brother Christopher Sheriffe and William Coxe guardians to my said son John and his estate until he attain the age of one and twenty years. Provision made in case the personal estate (legacies first paid) shall surmount one thousand pounds. Son John and brother Sheriffe to be executors.   Brent, 30.

[In the gleanings concerning the Sparhawke family in Emmerton and Waters's "Gleanings from English Records about New England Families," pp. 113–115, this will and that of Lewis Sparhawke, 1597, are printed, with a long note. See also REGISTER, vol. xix, pp. 125–127, and vol. xxi, pp. 172–3, for articles on the Sparhawke family by William S. Appleton, A.M.—EDITOR.]

ESTER SPARHAUKE of Great Coggeshall in the county of Essex, widow, 15 April 1668, proved 1 July 1668 by Matthew (?) Burrell, son and executor. To son John Sparhauke of Marsden twenty shillings. To son Nath (*sic*) Burrell one hundred and fifty pounds now in the hands of Mr. Josh. Draper of Braintree, and due from him to myself upon bond, which money did belong to his wife. To my daughter Esther, wife of the said Nathaniel, twenty pounds, to be divided between the two children of my said daughter, Nath and Esther, to each an equal share &c. My son Samuel Sperhawke. My three youngest daughters, Sara, Susanna and Elizabeth. The widow Hawes. Son Nath Burrell to be sole executor and my friend William Cox to be supervisor. The witnesses were Richard Pemberton, Elizabeth Bufton (by mark) and Elizabeth Tanner.   Hene, 97.

JOHN SPARHAWKE of Bocking, Essex, grocer, 29 April 1667, proved 25 November 1670. Son James. John Sparhawke my other son and Mary Sparhawke my daughter. Messuages and lands in Braintree, Shalford and Saling. Martin Kelloge (by mark) one of the witnesses.
                                                                Penn, 170.

JAMES SPARHAWKE of Bocking, Essex, citizen and leatherseller of London, 13 April 1679, proved 27 May 1679. Kinsman Thomas Swift son of my brother in law James Swift of Braintree, Essex, clothier. Mary Swift daughter of said James. Said brother in law James Swift and Mary his wife. Brother John Sparhawke and Mary his wife. Kinsman John Deadman citizen and mercer of London. Sister Mary Swift. Her son James Swift. Kinsman John Clarke of Gray's Inn. Kinsman Elizabeth Walford. Brother John executor.   King, 64.

[The foregoing wills clearly relate to our well known family of Sparhawke, and the will of Richard Downing (1594–1595) which begins the series seems to point to N.E. Suffolk as the original home of Lewis Sparhawke of Dedham. When examining the wills at Ipswich and Norwich, England, years ago, I often came across the name and took sundry brief notes like the extract of Richard Downing's will referred to. I found them, usually as Sparhawkes (with varied spellings of the name) but sometimes as Ive *als* Sparhawke (once as Sparrocke *als* Ive). They were to be found perhaps chiefly in and around Easton Bavent, South Cove, Walpole and Bramfield. I could see no Lewis Sparhawke among them however. It was reserved for my researches at London to discover that. I give the following very brief note of my discovery and I suggest that it may possibly indicate the family from which our New England family has sprung. Accompanying it will be found some of my notes gathered at Norwich and Ipswich.—
                                                                H. F. W.]

HARRY EVE *als* SPARHAUKE of Southcowe (South Cove) Suffolk, yeoman, 12 May 1565, proved 21 May 1568. Wife Margaret. The poor of Eston Bavent. Lands in Wapull (Walpole) and Bramfelde. My wood at Frosondon (Frostenden). My wood at Stoven. Son Harry at 21. My children. Sister Cicely and her children. My brother Lewes Eve *als* Sparhawk and Anthony Reve of Walpoll to be executors. Proved by Rafe King as attorney for the executors.   Babington, 11.

ROBERT SPARHAWKE of Eston Bavent (1456) proved 21 February 1456. Son Robert. Nephew Robert Birt. Niece Isabella Birt. Wife Margaret.
Norwich Consistory Court, Book Neve, Leaf 54.

ALICE SPARHAWK of Northalys (North Hales or Covehithe) widow, 8 November 1532, proved 12 December 1532. To Simond South a sparling net &c. Elizabeth and Alice Brush. John Brush and Elene Brush. Richard Brush. William Walshe. To John Sparhawke a ix score nette. William Sparhawk. Sister Anyce (Agnes) Buntyng of Halesworth. Sister Johan Cook. Alice Burde, William Burde. Others.
Norwich Consistory Court, B. Punting, L. 15.

AGNES BARSHAM of Beccles 20 September 1474, proved 24 November (1474). To be buried in the church yard at St. Michael Archangel in Beccles. To daughter Johanne forty shillings. To said Johanne all my household utensils. To said Johanne Sparhawk my principal messuage. She to sell one acre of land and (expend) the money thence arising for celebrating one Trentall of St. Gregory. John Sparhawke to have one cow and twenty shillings in money at age of twelve years. To Thomas son of said Johanne, one "vitulum" of one year of age and three shillings four pence, at same age. The messuage &c. which I have sold and given ly in Beccles and Barsham &c. Daughter Johanne to be executrix and John Frank supervisor.   Arch. Suff. (Ipswich) B. 2, L. 267.

JOHN WALPOLL 2 December 1494, proved 11 December (1494?). To be buried in the churchyard of Walpole. To William Lane forty shillings. To John Bruar twenty shillings. To Edmund Sparhawk the son of John Sparhawke six shillings eight pence. To John Sparhawke three shillings four pence. To Robert Sparhauke three shillings four pence. The same to Harry Moor. Executors John Baldwyn and Thomas Cownter.
Arch. Suff. B. 3, L. 168.

EDMUND SPARHAWKE of Laxfeld 8 October 1505, proved 20 October 1505. To be buried in the churchyard there. A priest to sing for my soul, my wife's soul &c. To the parish church of Laxfield. To the parish church of Walpole. To the parish church of Cokeley. Katherine Warde, Christian Warde. Elianore Dowe of Rekynghale (Rickinghall). Edmund Sparhawke. Each of my godchildren. Each of my wife's godchildren. The residue to son Nicholas and he to be executor.
Arch. Suff. B. 4, L. 213.

JOHN IVE *als* SPARHAWKE of Bramfeld—February 1510, proved 28 September 1510. Son John Ive. Son Robert Ive at twenty two. Daughter Anne Ive. Son Edmund Ive. Brother Edmund Ive. Wife Margaret. Reference to "my" dairy at Walpole.   Arch. Suff. B. 5, L. 140.

[Note that testator has sons John, Robert and Edmund, and compare will of John Walpoll (1494) where similar names are to be found, though without the alias of Ive.—H. F. W.]

ALICE PEERS widow, 12 March 1514, proved 22 April 1515. To be buried in the churchyard of St. Andrew of Nothalys. Margaret Jekkes. Isabel Jekkes. Helen Sparhawke. Johane Wryght my god daughter. Nicholas Jekkes. Emme Sparhawke. Henry Crosse. Alice Prowdefoote. Robert Edmundes. Thomas Crosse. Agnes Edmundes. William Holme and Alice Brushe. Executors William Sparhawke and Thomas Harding.   Arch. Suff. B. 7, L. 75.

JOHN IVE *als* SPARHAWKE of Walpole, 4 May 1525, proved 26 October 1525. Son Henry. Reference to father's last will and testament. Son Thomas Ive. Wife Alice. Every one of my sons. Every daughter. The last will and testament of my mother in law Margery Smyth late departed. Wife and John Bryan of Bramfelde to be executors. Cousin Robert Melle to be supervisor.   Arch. Suff. B. 9, L. 107.

ALICE SPARHAWKE of Northalys widow, 13 November 1532, proved 12 December 1532. To be buried in the churchyard of said town. Simond South. Elizabeth Brush, Alice Brush, John Brush. William Walsle (?). Elene Brush. John Sparhawk. Sister Anyce Buntyng of Hallysworth. Sister Johan Cook of Yermouth. Alice Byrde. Margaret Byrde. Alice Barwyke. Richard Brush. William Sparhawke.   Arch. Suff. B. 11, L. 69.

JOHAN WALPOLE of Huntyngfeld widow, 2 July 1539, proved 3 October 1539. To Johañ Sparhawke daughter of Edmunde Sparhawke six shillings eight pence. To said Edmund Sparhawke the bargain and sale of my land, all my moveables &c. He to be executor. Robert Smyth of Huntyngfeld to be supervisor.   Arch. Suff. B. 13, L. 140.

HENRY SPARHAWKE of Cockley (Cookley) yeoman, 20 September, with a codicil dated 16 October, 1584, proved 4 October 1591. Tenements, lands &c. in Walpole, Bramfeild and Sipton. Wife Alice. Son John at twenty three. Son Henry. Daughter Margaret. Brother Timothy. Uncle John's second son and third son &c.   Arch. Suff. B. 33, L. 485.

LEONARD SPARROCKE *alias* IVE of Laxfield yeoman, proved 7 April 1597. To John Taller of Laxfield late son of Hugh Taller my kinsman all my messuages &c. in Laxfield, being copyhold. Wife Johañe. Sister Elizabeth Sparrocke *als* Ive. Elias Fyske of Laxfield to be supervisor.   Arch. Suff. B. 36, L. 605.

[I found also at Ipswich that License was granted to Daniel Sparrowhawke of Bentley in Essex and Elizabeth Hall of Clopton to be married in Clopton. Unfortunately I have lost the date. Some of Mr. Appleton's notes on this family may be found in the REGISTER of 1865 and of 1867 (p. 172). Other notes will be found in Gleanings from English Records by Emmerton and Waters (Essex Institute 1880) pp. 113-116. Whether Lewis Sparhawke of Dedham was an uncle of our Nathaniel Sparhawke, as I find suggested by me in 1880, I cannot say. I feel rather doubtful. He might have been the grandfather for aught I can now see.—H. F. W.]

JOHN COWLFAX of Willingham Suffolk 20 May 1569, proved 6 October 1569. Wife Margaret late wife of Martin Frens of Dickleborowe. Daughter in law Prudens Frens. Reignold and Alice Gybbon. My five children. Brother Arthur Cheute gen^t. and Robert Payn to be executors. Lyonell Chewte a witness.   Cons. Court Norwich, Ponder, 232.

LIONELL CHEWTE of Brampton clerk 24 July 1592, proved 1 August 1592. To be buried in the chancel there. He did gyve to Lionell Chewte his son his graye nagge wch he did ride on to Ippisw^ch. Item he did gyve to Grace, Sara and Judith Chewte his dawters to everye of them a cowe ; Item he did gyve and bequethe to Susan his wief all the residue of his goodes and cattalls whatsoever desiringe her to have care of the bringinge upp of his children and willed that she shoulde have the execucon of his goodes and named her his executrix. Theise beinge witnesses Arthure Chewte gen^t. Thomas Jollye and others.

Cons. Court Norwich, Apleyard, 128.

WILLIAM BEADLE of Beccles gen^t. 5 January 1620, proved 10 February 1629. To be buried by my wife in the chancel of Beccles church. Sister Sherman. Cousin (female) Daies. Cousin Lionell Chowte of Dedham. Cousin Cuddon's wife of Chaddingfield. Cousin Wade's wife. Cousin Hammond's wife. Goddaughter Dorothy Hammond at one and twenty. Cousin William Harvy and his now children. Cousin Barnebie's wife. Cousin Pring's wife. Cousin William Wade my godson at twenty one. Cousin John Cuddon my godson at twenty one. Cousin William Greene my godson. Cousin Francis Greene. Cousin Richard Carter's son. Cousin Glemham Wade of Ditchingham to be executor.

Arch. Suff. (Ipswich) B. 53, L. 215.

[Some years ago, through the kindness of our constant friend George W. Marshall, LL.D., I had the chance to take a few notes from Col. Chester's book containing his extracts from the parish Registers of Dedham. I noted the following. I hope my readers will not place too implicit trust upon its accuracy. My work was done hurriedly.]

Marriages (in Dedham).

1566   Oct. 27   Willm. Pettfyld and Judith Shareman.
1570   Ap^l 25   Edmund Sharman and Ann Pellatte.
1575–6   Feb. 26   Mr. Phillip Hart and Susan Sparhawk.
1576   May 8   Martin Garrard and Eliz. Webb.
1582   June 1   Henry Sherman wid^r. and Maryan Wilson widow.
1583   Dec. 9   Mr. Robert Sherman and Barbara Browne.
1584   Sep. 11   Edmund Sherman and Ann Cleare.
1594–5   Jan. 8   Anthony Whiting and Ann Sherman.
1601   May 15   John Anger and Ann Sherman.
1601   Aug. 18   Daniel Sherman and Christian Chapman.
1605   Ap^l —   Thomas Branson and Susan Woodgate.
1610   May 13   Richard Backler and Ann Sherman.
1611   May 15   Edmund Sherman and Judith Anger.
        [Hiatus of about 30 years.]
1642   May 9   Walter Alexander wid^r. and Mary Sherman.
1645   Aug. 21   Ezekiel Sherman and Martha Stevens, both single.
1656   June 24   John Wall of Stratford and Debora Sherman mar. at Colchester.
1656   Dec. 8   Edmond Sherman of Dedham wid^r. and Grace Steevens of Stratford.
1658   March 25   Martin Garwood wid^r. and Priscilla Sherman.
1661   Oct. 17   Mr. John Whiting and Mrs. Mary Raney mar. at Langham.
1681   May 5   John Cooke wid. and Martha Petfield.

1683   Sep. 11 Will[m]. Smith wid[r]. and Priscilla Garwood wid.
1684   July 7 Jos. Nichols of St. Peters Colchester and Christian
   Sherman.
1693   May 18 Edmund Sherman single and Sarah Bloomfield widow.
1693-4   Jan. 18 Nath[l]. Sherman and Susan Sharpe.
1694   June 5 Will[m]. Sherman and Sarah Sharpe.

Baptisms.

1560-1   Feb. 6 Robert son of ——— Sherman.
1564   July 2 Nathaniel son of Lewis Sparhawk.
1567   May 25 Ann dau. of John Rogers.
1570   May 1 Phebe dau. of Henry Sherman jr.
1570   Sept. 4 (?) Henry son of Edmund Sherman.
1571   Aug. 26 Henry son of Henry Sherman jr.
1572-3   Jan. 11 Samuel son of Henry Sherman.
1575   Aug. 7 Susan dau of Henry Sherman.
1575   Oct. 9 Ann dau. of Edmund Sherman.
1576   Ap[l] 2 John son of Will[m]. and Anne Anger.
1576   Sep. 22 John and Edward sons of John Rogers.
1576-7   M[ch] 3 Richard son of Edmund and Ann Sherman.
1578   May 22 Susan dau. of John Rogers.
1580   June 19 Nath[l] son of Henry and Susan Sherman.
1580-1   M[ch] 7 Anna dau. of Edmund and Anne Sherman.
1582   July 11 Nath[l] son of Henry Sherman jr.
1585   Aug. 17 John son of Henry Sherman jr.
1587   Nov. 14 Daniel son of Samuel Sparhawke.
   [Hiatus from Jan. 1587-8 to 29 Sept. 1590.]
1590-1   Feb. 17 Susan dau. of Edmund and Ann Sherman.
1592   July 27 Mary dau. of Henry Sherman.
1595   Ap[l] 13 Thomas dau. of Thomas Sparhawk.
1596   May 31 John son of Anthony Whiting.
1597   M[ch] 27 Benjamin son of Edmund Sherman.
1597-8   Feb. 16 Nath[l] son of Sam[l] Sparhawk.
1598-9   M[ch] 20 Mary dau. of Edmund and Ann Sherman.
1599   Ap[l] 20 Christian son of Thomas and Susan Chapman.
1599   Oct. 2 Mary dau. of Sam[l] Sherman.
1599   Oct. 23 Edmund son of Edmund Sherman jr.
[(In another hand) Edmund the son of Edmund Sherman was bap. the
23 day of June 1599.]
1600   Feb. 1 Mary dau. of Samuel Sparhawk.
1601   Sept. 15 Ann dau. of Edmund Sherman.
? { 1601   Oct. 20 a son of Samuel Sherman.
 { 1601   Nov. 20 Henry son of Samuel Sherman.
1602   May 22 Edward son of Samuel Sparhawk.
1602-3   Jan. 25 Henry son of Henry Sherman.
1603   Aug. 21 Mary dau. of John Anger.
1603   Dec. 13 Joan dau. of Edmund Sherman.
1603-4   Jan. 24 Martha dau. of Sam[l] Sherman.
1603-4   M[ch] 6 Benj. son of Sam[l] Sparhawke.
1604   Dec. 16 Edmund son of Dan[l] and Christian Sherman.
1605   Oct. 8 John son of John Anger.
1605-6   Feb. 11 Seara dau. of Samuel Sherman.
1606   Ap[l] 1 Hester dau. of Edmund Sherman.

1607 May 27 Henry son of Daniel Sherman.
1607 July 24 Samuel son of John Anger.
1608 Oct. 16 Richard son of Edmund and Jone Sherman.
1608–9 Jan. 1 Nathaniel son of Nathaniel Sherman.
1610 March 31 Edmund son of John Anger.
1610–11 Jan. 10 Elizabeth dau. of Mr. Rogers.
1610–11 Feb. 15 Philip son of Samuel Sherman.
1611 April 14 John son of John Bacon.
1611 June 25 Edward son of Henry Sherman.
1611 Sep. 17 Bezaleel son of Edmund Sherman.
1612 June 21 Daniel son of Daniel Sherman.
1612 Sep. 1 Abigail dau. of Mr. John Rogers.
1613 Oct. 23 Elizabeth dau. of Nathaniel Sherman.
1613 Nov. 21 Anna dau. of Richard Sherman.
1613–14 Feb. 2 James son of Lionell Chute.
1614 April 30 Martha dau. of John Rogers.
1616 June 18 a child of Edmund Sherman.
1616 Oct. 22 William son of Richard Sherman.
1617 March 30 Mary dau. of John Bacon.
1618 July 12 Samuel son of Edmund Sherman.
1618 Aug. 18 Robert son of John Firmin.
1618 Sep. 27 Priscilla dau. of Richard Sherman.
1619 Nov. 23 Mary dau. of Lionell Chewte.
1619–20 Feb. 27 Robert son of Ezekiel Sherman.
1620 April 25 Thomas son of John Anger.
      [Hiatus of about eighteen years after Oct. 29, 1620.]
1638 Oct. 21 Mary dau. of Richard and Mary Sherman.
1638 Dec. 9 John son of Daniel and Frances Rogers.
1638–9 Feb. 28 Nathaniel son of Samuel and Hester Sherman.
1639 May 3 Alexander son of Henry and Lore Sherman.
1639 May 5 Edmund son of John and Anne Sherman.
1639 Sep. 8 Samuel son of Bezal: and Anne Anger.
1641 May 30 Bezal: son of Bezal: and Ann Anger.
1641 Dec. 5 Elizabeth dau. of John and Ann Sherman.
1641–2 Feb. 1 Andrew son of Henry and Lore Sherman.
1641–2 Feb. 20 Elizabeth dau. of Daniel and Eliz: Sherman.
1642 Oct. 30 Simon son of John and Alce Whiting.
1642 Dec. 2 Elizabeth dau. of Daniel and Frances Rogers.
1643 May 14 Martha dau. of Edward and Martha Sherman.
1643 June 23 Anne dau. of Bezal: and Ann Anger.
1643 Aug. 31 Sarah dau. of Richard and Mary Sherman.
1643 Nov. 3 John son of Daniel and Elizabeth Sherman.
1643–4 Feb. 8 Bezal: son of John and Ann Sherman.
1644 Aug. 18 James son of Henry and Lore Sherman.
1645 April 13 Daniel son of Daniel and Elizabeth Sherman.
1645 Oct. 26 Mary dau. of Edward and Martha Sherman.
1646 May 3 Sara dau. of Bezal: and Ann Anger.
1646 June 27 Martha dau. of Ezekiel and Martha Sherman.
1646 Oct. 18 John son of Daniel and Elizabeth Sherman.
1647 Sep. 5 Grace dau. of Ezekiel and Martha Sherman.
1647–8 Feb. 3 Edward son of Edward and Martha Sherman.
1648 May 16 Lebbeus son of Henry and Lore Sherman.
1648 July 23 Nathaniel son of Bezal: and Ann Anger.

1648   Oct. 29 Mary dau. of Samuel and Mary Sherman.
1648   Nov. 26 Anna dau. of John and Anna Rogers.
1648   Dec. 31 Susan dau. of Daniel and Elizabeth Sherman.
1649   Sep. 19 Sarah dau. of Bezal : and Anne Anger.
1649-50 Feb. 17 Hanna dau. of Ezekiel and Martha Sherman.
1650   Sep. 8 Samuel son of Samuel and Mary Sherman.

Burials.

1562   April 30 Eliz : ux^r. Lewis Sparhawk.
1563-4 March 16 Thomas Sharman.
1571   June 25 Wife of John Rogers.
1571-2 Jan. 4 Agnes Rogers widow.
1576   Oct. 16 John son of Henry Sharman the elder.
1580   June 21 Nathaniel son of Henry and Susan Sharman.
1580   Oct. 14 Agnes ux^r. Henry Sharman the elder.
1584   June 8 Anne ux^r. Edmund Sharman.
1587   June 1 Ezekiel son of Dr. Chapman.
1600   Dec. 22 Edmund Sherman the elder.
1602   Dec. 30 Dr. Chapman.
1604-5 Feb. — Man child of Henry Sherman unbapt.
1610   Aug. 28 Henry Sherman the elder.
1610   Sep. 13 Wife of Henry Sherman the elder.
1611   April 23 Phebe ux^r. Nathaniel Sherman.
1612   Dec. 5 Sara dau. of Samuel Sherman.
              [Hiatus of about twenty-eight years.]
1641   May 13 Widow Greenlef.
1641   July 14 Elizabeth dau. of Daniel Rogers.
1642   Aug. 30 Mary ux^r. Henry Sherman.
1642-3 March 3 Robert son of Ezekiel Sherman.
1643   April 4 Frances ux^r. Daniel Rogers.
1644   April 28 John son of Daniel Sherman.
1644   Sep. 4 Ezekiel son of John Sherman.
1647   Sep. 5 Sarah dau. of Bezal : Anger.
1647   Oct. 26 Benjamin Sherman.
1647   Oct. 27 Richard Sherman.
1647   Dec. 7 Mary dau. of John Rogers.
1648   Dec. 15 Martha dau. of Ezekiel Sherman.
1653-4 Jan. 21 Ezekiel Sherman.
1656   Oct. 24 John Sherman.
1657   March 31 Daniel Sherman.
1678   Nov. 1 Bezal : Angier.

[I found that a John Sherman was buried at St. Nicholas, Colchester, 16 October, 1544, and that a Daniel Sherman and Sara Mitchell were married there 23 April, 1622.

In Chelmsford John Sherman and Agnes Jobson, widow, were married 20 October, 1561 and Ezekiel Sherman and Elizabeth Samfford were married 7 December, 1582. Who they were I know not. I found the baptisms of Ezekiel's children recorded there from 1588 to 1596 inclusive. I noted also a number of entries of burials of persons of the name of Sherman there from 1580 to 1608 inclusive. John Sherman, householder, was buried 1 March, 1586, Anne, wife of John, 23 April, 1587, Ezekiel, 19 February, 1603, Elizabeth Sherman, widow, 18 October, 1608.

In Feet of Fines for Essex County, Paschal Term, 40th Eliz : I found Henry Sherman and Edmund Sherman *quer.* Robert Sherman, Dr. in Medicine, and Bridget his wife *deforc.* concerning two messuages, one curtilage, two gardens, eight acres of land, with the appurtenances in Dedham. Consideration eighty pounds sterling.   H. F. W.]

EDMOND CHAPMAN of Dedham, Essex, D.D., 12 May 1601. To wife Susan all my houses, lands, tenements &c. in Dedham and Ardleighe, Essex, for life; and then to my son Paul. To son John all my books (other than those bequeathed to my wife) for his better encouragement in the course of his study. To my daughter Susan Chapman two hundred pounds at marriage or age of twenty. A messuage &c. in Bread Street, London. Brother Nicholas Chapman and his sons Thomas and Edmond. My nephew Dannocke. Master John Hare of London Esq. Master —— Osborne of Hawkestead, Suffolk, Esq. and Simon Fenn of Dedham, clothier, to be the executors.

In a codicil (of same date) testator ordains that daughter Christian (although not named in the will) should have as good part &c. as if expressly named.

Commission issued 10 February 1602, the executors having renounced.

Bolein, 16.

[The above, I suppose, was the father of Christian wife of Daniel Sherman.—H. F. W.]

WILLIAM SKINNER of Braintree (Essex) yeoman, 14 August 1616, proved 26–7–1616. The poor of Braintree twenty six shillings eight pence. To wife Margery my freehold lands, messuages, tenements, shops &c. in Braintree for life; afterwards to second son John. To John copyhold lands &c. in Braintree, he to secure his mother the rent it now goeth for &c. To John twenty pounds and to his son John, my grandson (silver). To eldest son William one hundred and sixty pounds. To his daughters Rebecca and Francis Skinner (silver) and thirty pounds apiece at eighteen years of age, and to his son Richard forty pounds. To my youngest son Richard (inter alia) my book of my brother Allyn's works. To John and Mary Skinner children of said son Richard (household stuff). To son Richard ten pounds for use and benefit of Mary, Ellyn and Richard, his children, at ages of eighteen. To eldest daughter An, wife of Moyses Wall, forty pounds. To John Taylcoate, Sara Taylcoate and Rachell Taylcoate, Moyses Wall, Lidia Wall and Mary Wall, the children of my said daughter An, five marks apiece, to be paid to the said Moyses Wall my son in law to their use &c. To my son in law Moyses Wall ten pounds to be employed about a building which he did intend to do within the house wherein he now dwelleth. To Sara Taylcoate my bible. To John Gill my son in law twenty pounds to the use of Mary Gill and An Gill, children of my daughter Margery. To my said daughter Margery Gill two silver spoons. To my son in law Edmund Allstonne ten pounds. To Rachell Skinner my daughter, the wife of Edmund Allstonne (household stuff). To my brother Allin "my new hatt turf^t wth velvett." To Mr. Collen ten pounds for a sermon to be preached at my burial. To Edmund, Rachel and Mary Allstone children of my said daughter Rachel five marks apiece. To said my daughter Rachel my book of Mr. Perkin's works after wife's decease. Susan wife of Joseph Man and her daughter Susan. Godson William Skinner son of William Skinner of Bocking. Godson William Winterflood. Godson William Skinner son of Martin Skinner. Cousin Martin Skinner. To Mr. Daniel Rogers ten shillings. To Cousin Richard Barnard ten shillings. Wife Margery to be executrix and friends Martin Skynner, sons in law Moyses Wall and Edmund Alstone, and Richard Barnard to be supervisors.   Com. Court of London for Essex and Herts,

Unnumbered will, File for 1616.

MARGERIE SKYNNER of Brainctree, Essex, widow, 2 March 1617, proved at Brainctree 16 December 1620. To my daughter Margerie five pounds (and other goods) and to her son John Gill a bullock. To my son William Skynner five pounds. To my son John Skynner twenty pounds. To my daughter Rachell five pounds. I do give and bequeath further to my daughter Rachell three pewter platters of the greater sort and three of the best cushions in the great chamber and my warming pan. To Sara Taylcoat a flock bed and a flock bolster, a coverlet and a pair of blankets (and other effects). To Rachell Taylcoate a little kettle of a gallon, a brass pot, a posnet (&c.). And I will that the pewter which I had of my son in law John Taylecoat I will the same to Sara and Rachell to be equally parted and divided between them ; and I give more to Sara my kneading trough. If my son John Skynner's son do die before he be of age to receive his gift which my husband gave him, which is a silver bowl and two silver spoons ; then I give the same to my son John. To my son John Skynner's wife two silver spoons. The residue of my pewter I will shall be equally parted and divided between my daughter Ann her two daughters she had by my son in law Moses Wall, my son Richard's wife and my son John his wife, by even portions, and I give more to my son John his wife a kettle next the biggest. And I give to my son Richard twenty pounds and the residue of my household stuff unbequeathed. I give more to my daughter Anne a two and twenty shillings piece in gold and to her husband Moyses Wall a two and twenty shillings piece in gold. I make my son Richard sole executor. I give to Mr. Collen ten shillings to preach at my funeral. To the poor of Brainctree six shillings eight pence. I nominate and appoint my son John Skynner overseer. Christopher Taylor, scr. a witness.

Com. of London for Essex and Herts.

File for 1620–1621, Nº. 121.

[See wills of John Tailecot and Moses Wall in last January Gleanings (pp. 134 and 139) and pedigree of Talcot (p. 135) in the same Gleanings.—H. F. W.]

ROBERT COLE of Stratford, Suffolk, clothmaker, 29 January 1527, proved 5 March 1527. To be buried within the parish church of our blessed Mary of Stratford next my wife. A gravestone to be laid over me and my wife. To the church for breaking of the ground. To the high altar there. To the poor people being inhabitants and dwellers within the parish of East Bargholt sixty shillings sterling. To the poor people dwelling in Dedham twenty shillings. To the poor people dwelling in Manytre twenty shillings. To the poor dwelling in Lawford five shillings. To the poor in Ardeleigh five shillings. To the poor in Langham five shillings. To the poor in Boxstede five shillings. To the poor in Horkesley five shillings. To the poor in Stoke ten shillings. To the poor in Colchester twenty shillings. To the poor in Hadley thirteen shillings four pence. Other parishes named. To Margaret Darnell my daughter sixty six pounds thirteen shillings four pence. The same to daughter Agnes Mannok. To my daughter Elizabeth, to be delivered to her at such time as she shall come to the full age of twenty years or at such time as she shall be married, one hundred pounds sterling. Every child of the said Margaret Darnell and of the said Agnes Mannok. My godson James Benet. I will that my executors, after my departure at times convenient, do deliver or cause to be delivered to the use and building of the church of East Bargholt as much freestone as shall make up the work there, that is to say the body of the same church with the North Aisle, according to such promise as

I have made. Thirteen pounds six shillings eight pence to be employed and bestowed upon a vestment and cope to be delivered to the said
Church of our Lady of Stratford. My godson Robert Patche. Others
named. To my son Richard at twenty one all that moiety or half part of
the lordship of Newhall in East Bargholt and my head house with the appurtenances in the "Valye" in Bargholt which I purchased of the executors
of Robert Florett, also the half part of the mill called Flatford mill. To
son Edward at twenty one my house or mansion place the which I now
dwell in and all my lands, tenements &c., as well freehold as copyhold,
in the town of Stratford and my lands and tenements in Bargholt called
Tyntes in Gassondes end and the other half part of the foresaid mill called
Flatfordes mill. To son Robert at twenty one my land in Bargholt called
Hedgehouse (and other lands there) and the lands and tenements I bought
of Gregory Dey in Bergholt and my house and land which sometime was
my father's in Bergholt (and other lands). To sons William and Anthony
at twenty one all my other lands and tenements, except my lands in Alderton, Rameswolde and Bawdesey, evenly to be divided betwixt the said
William and Anthony. The lands excepted shall be sold and the money
thereof coming shall be equally divided and delivered to them as they shall
come to the full age of twenty one years. If any of my said five sons die
before coming to the said age his part shall be equally divided among the
residue of all my other sons then living and to be delivered at said age.
My executors to be Jakes Darnell, Richard my son and Robert Bogas and
the supervisor to be William Smythe of Stratford, clerk.   One of the witnesses was Adam Barwyk.   Porch, 29.

EDWARD COLE of Stratford 7 May 1542, proved 22 November 1542.
My body to be buried where is shall please God. John Chese my servant
at age of twenty one. The poor of Stratford. To Elizabeth Fene my sister five pounds. To Agnes Mañok my sister five pounds. To my brothers
Richard, Robert, William and Anthony Cole all the the residue of my
goods &c. equally to be divided between them.   Brother Richard to be executor.   Spert, 13.

RICHARD COLE of East Bergholt, Suffolk, 1 September 1559, proved 14
September 1559. To be buried in the church there. To wife Jone all my
house and lands and tenements &c. which I now have in mine own occupying so long as she do remain a widow (certain lands excepted). When
she shall marry or depart this world Robert my son shall have them.
Among real estate described is house, land &c. purchased of Jakys Darnyll,
also the moiety of mill called Flatford mill. To Robert houses and tenements in Ipswich to hold so long as Jone my wife shall hold my mansion
house in East Bergholt and no longer. To son Christofer other lands
and tenements if he live to the age of twenty one years. To my daughter
Agnes Hedge a hundred marks. One hundred pounds to each of two sons
Robert and Christofer. One hundred marks each to daughters Elizabeth,
Bridget, Jane and Jone at marriage or at age of twenty. Gifts to John,
James and George Fenne. To brother Anthony Cole twenty pounds of the
debt he oweth me if he pay the rest in two years. If brother William pay
my executors five pounds within a month next after my decease then I will
that my executors shall deliver him an obligation that Robert Cole stood
bounden to me in. Son Robert to be executor.   Among the witnesses
were Robert, William and Anthony Cole.   Chaynay, 41.

ROBERT COLE of East Bergholt, Suffolk, the younger, clothier, 19 December 19 Eliz:, proved 6 February 1576. The poor of that parish. I have entered into the administration of the goods &c. of Robert Moyse late of Holbroke, Suffolk, deceased, for the true performance of whose will and testament I have entered into a bond by recognizance to the supervisors of the testament and last will of John Warren, executor of the said will &c. of the said Robert Moyse. I desire my uncle William Cole and my brother Christofer Cole to enter into the administration and ordering of the said Robert Moyse's will and my uncle William to have the bringing up of John Moyse and my brother Christofer the bringing up of Robert Moyse. My wife Edythe to be executrix. Alice the former wife of Robert Moyse. My brother Hedge's children, begotten of my sister his late wife, at their ages of twenty one. My part of the mill called Flatford Mill. My son Richard at twenty one. My three daughters. My kinsmen Francis and Anthony Cole. Catherine my late wife was seized of certain lands and tenements in Thorpe and Kyrbye, Essex, which after her decease did descend unto Richard my said son, of her body begotten. My daughter Catharine at twenty and my two other daughters at twenty. My cousin Elizabeth Cole dwelling with me and Priscilla Blosse and Anne Cocke. Four gold rings to be given to Francis Cole, Anthony Cole, Priscilla Cole and Nicholas Fryer's wife to the end they remember me.

Daughtry, 4.

EDWARD COLE of East Bergholt, Suffolk, yeoman, 1 April 1606, proved 4 February 1606. I give to Robert Cole my son all my copyhold lands called Tintes. To my grandchild Simond Rosier twenty pounds at age of one and twenty years. To my brother in law Richard Ravens, minister of Wattesfield, four pounds. The residue of my goods &c. to my son Edward Cole whom I make sole executor. Memorandum, that Edward Cole the elder did give and surrender into the hands of the Lord of his tenements, messuages and lands holden of the manor of Old Hall in East Bergholt to the use and according to his last will &c., Edward Cole the younger being instead of bayliff &c. 2 May 1606.

Hudleston, 16.

FRANCIS COLE of East Bergholt, Suffolk, yeoman, 12 September 1616 proved 28 November 1616. My prentice Robert Snelling. Others. My daughter Mary Edwards. My daughter Edith Clarke. My grandchildren Richard Edwardes, John Edwardes and Mary Edwardes. My daughter Margaret. My daughter Francis at one and twenty. My daughter Elizabeth at one and twenty. To wife Margaret for life the rents and profits of the Mayors house which I purchased of Mr. John Clarke and his wife &c., and of the tenement wherein Francis Richardson now dwelleth and of my messuages or tenements at Gassons end wherein Richard Aylefounder, ———— Hale and Christofer Goodwyn do now dwell, also with these my lands called Tyntes, both free and copy, in the occupation of John Woodgate, upon condition that my said wife shall, upon reasonable demand, release all her right and claim to any dower or thirds unto Francis my son of all my lands which I shall hereafter give unto him. To son William, after death of my wife and at his age of four and twenty, my messuage called the Mayors house (and other lands). To son Robert, after my wife's death and at said age, my messuage or tenement at Gasson's End &c. and my lands called Tyntes &c. A tenement to daughter Francis. My said three daughters at one and twenty. Son Francis to be sole executor.

Cope, 106.

CHRISTOPHER COLE of East Bargholt, Suffolk, yeoman, 3 December 1622, proved 27 January 1622. Thomas Gillmore of East Bargholt, yeoman, husband of Susan daughter of Susan my loving sister deceased, to be my executor. During all the time of my sickness I have been tenderly regarded and tended by the said Thomas Gillmore and Susan his wife by the space of many years in which it hath pleased God to visit me with lameness and have not been regarded by others of my kindred who have sought always to hinder and disturb me.   Swann, 3.

Sentence to confirm the above will was promulgated 24 May 1623 following upon litigation between Thomas Gilmore the executor of the one part and Benjamin Catlin, William Crosse and Christopher Aldham, calling themselves next akin to the said Christopher Cole.   Swann, 43.

BRIDGET BRAND of Bilston, Suffolk, widow, aged, 24 February, 1632, proved 19 September 1633. To my grandchild Abigail Firman, wife of Edward Firman of Dedham, twenty pounds, or to her son Robert Firman, to be paid him by his father Edward Firman. The said Edward Firman shall become bound unto Edward Cole of East Bergholt, my son in law, to pay back again the said twenty pounds to be equally divided amongst all the children of the said Edward Cole and Abigail Cole my daughter after the death of the said Abigail Firman and the death of the said Robert Firman, her son, if he happen to depart this life before he come to age of one and twenty years. To my grandchild Edward Cole twenty pounds to be paid unto him within one month next after my decease. To six of the other children of my daughter Abigail Cole and Edward Cole of East Bergholt ten pounds apiece, vizt. to Peter Cole, John Cole, Grace Cole, Sarah Cole, Mary Cole and Abigail Cole, to be paid unto them at their several ages of one and twenty years. To the youngest daughter of Sarah Welde, my daughter late of Dublin in the kingdom of Ireland, twenty pounds at one and twenty or day of marriage. To Thomas Andras my grandchild forty shillings at one and twenty. To Mary Andruas my grandchild ten pounds at one and twenty or within two months after my decease. To my son in law Thomas Andruas of Bilston twelve pence and to my son in law Daniel Weld twelve pence. To the inhabitants of Bilston twenty shillings. The remainder of my household stuff &c. to be divided equally amongst seven of the children of my daughter Abigail Cole and Edward Cole. The residue to son in law Edward Cole whom I constitute sole executor. Edward Cole junior a witness. John Layman another.   Russell, 79.

[It is to this family of Cole that Edward Cole of East Bergholt must have belonged, whose will I gave more than a dozen years ago (see Gleanings, Part I, p. 31). He mentioned wife Abigail, sons Edward and Peter, daughters Sarah and Mary, and grandchildren in New England. Cannot some of the New England genealogists tell us who those grandchildren were? The will of Mrs. Brand shows us who his wife was, and gives the names of other children. Benjamin Brand (or Brond) went over to New England (with Winthrop I think). Perhaps the Life and Letters of John Winthrop may throw some light on the question.   H. F. W.]

JAMES HAMPSTED (Holmsted) of Much Leighes Essex, yeoman, 20 May 1592. To eldest son Thomas, according to the custom of the manor, a parcel of land in Braintree (and other lands described) which lands are customary lands and holden of the manor of Braintree. To my second son Richard, according to the custom of the said manor, a tenement known as Forde's and Marshalls (and lands &c.) in the tenure or occupation of me the said James, and of John Allen, joiner, all in the same parish. To third son James, according to the custom of the said manor (certain lands described). To fourth son Nicholas (lands in the same manor) and a free tenement in Braintree. To fifth son John a messuage or tenement in Fairsted, in the tenure &c. of one William Steele or his assigns, and a house and three acres of land in Hatfield known as Sparrowes Arbor. If any of my said five sons die before day of marriage or age of one and twenty then the part or portion of him or them so dying shall be equally divided between and amongst the rest of my said sons then living. To my daughter Mabell forty pounds at age of one and twenty or day of marriage. A similar bequest to daughter Elizabeth. If either of them die before receiving the portion then such portion shall be equally divided between my two sons James and John. All my lands to my wife Jane, during nonage of sons, for the education and bringing up of said sons. All goods and chattels &c. to her and she to be sole executrix.

Proved at Chelmsford 8 January 1595. From a copy of the original will. Com. of London for Essex and Herts.

Bundle for 1610 (unnumbered).

JOHN HOOD of Halsted, Essex, weaver, 6 November 1622, proved at Halsted 20 November 1622. To daughter Anne forty shillings to be paid by my son John out of my house within the first year after the death of Anne my wife. To my daughter Jane the like sum of forty shillings to be paid (as before) the second year &c. To Avese my daughter the like sum &c. (payable the third year), to Cattronn (Catherine) my daughter the like sum &c. (payable the fourth year), to Grace my daughter the like sum &c. (the fifth year), to Mary my daughter the like sum &c. (the sixth year) and to Rose my daughter the like sum &c. (the seventh year). Wife Ann to be executrix. Com. of London for Essex and Herts.

File for 1622-1623 N°. 134.

[The above testator must have been the father of our John Hood of Cambridge, afterwards of Lynn, ancestor of a large and well-known family in Lynn and elsewhere. In Lechford's Note-Book (pub. by the American Antiquarian Society, A.D. 1885), on pages 10 to 15 inclusive (I ignore the wretched Index appended to that book), will be found the confirmation of my assertion made above. John Hood, late of Halsted, Essex, weaver and now (20th and 22d of 8th month 1638) of Cambridge in New England, weaver, makes conveyance of houses, lands &c. in Halsted now or late in the tenure of Thomas (or John) Beard and Anne his wife, mother of the said John Hood. Confirmation of all this is supplied by the following extract from Registry of Deeds for Essex County, Mass., which I made at home many years ago. HENRY F. WATERS.]

14th of the 6th moneth 1654.

JOHN HOOD of Lyn in the county of Essex in New England yeoman for thirty pounds in hand paid hath sold vnto Wiłłm Crofts of the same yeoman three dwelling houses or tenements wᵗʰ all thereto belonging in Halsted in the county of Essex in old England, wᵗʰ a covenant for further assurance, And the said Wiłłm is to pay 40ˢ a peice to the sisters of the said John according to his fathers will, the wᶜʰ apeth in the bargaine and sale by deed dated the 10th day of December 1652.

ANNE GRAVE of St. Buttolph without Algate, London, widow, 10 February 1675, with a codicil dated 1 March 1675-6, proved 20 March 1676. To my grandson Joseph Hardey my messuage or tenement wherein I do now inhabit and dwell, situate &c. in the Great Minories street in the said parish. I give the messuage adjoining to my said dwelling house, now in the tenure or occupation of Andrew Furgland, chirurgeon, to my grandson Jonathan Hardey. Both these houses I hold by lease from the city of London. To my said grandson Joseph Hardey five hundred pounds, to be paid into the Chamber of the City of London and the same, with interest, paid him at his age of one and twenty. To my grandson Jonathan Hardey six hundred pounds (in the same way). To my said grandson Jonathan my messuage heretofore called Hunwicke and now or late by the name of Hewes house, with the orchard belonging called Graye's yard, in Aldersford street in Hedingham Sible, Essex, and other lands &c. in Maplested and Hedingham Sible, now in the occupation of Gregory Glascock, to the said Jonathan and the lawful heirs of his body, with remainder to my grandson Joseph Hardey. Failing issue to him then to George Grave the elder of Hartford in Connecticot in New England and John Grave of Guilford in the County of New Haven in New England and to their own natural sister living also in New England an annuity of six pounds issuing out of said premises and the residue of the rents &c. shall be employed in putting forth poor children to prentice. Reference to the Company of Leathersellers. My cousins Charles and John Ellis at one and twenty. To the said George Grave the elder, John Grave and their own natural sister ten pounds and twenty pounds to be distributed amongst the children. My kinsman Thomas Williams now resident at Barbados, and Anne Butler his sister. His children and her children. Godfrey Watkinson, son of ——— Watkinson of Chesterfield, Derby, husbandman. To my said grandchild Joseph Hardey one silver tankard marked D L A and one gilt bowle marked W T A. To Jonathan one large silver tankard marked A: G, one large silver salt marked R W M, one small silver salt marked also R: W M, three small silver wine cups marked A: G and seven silver spoons marked J: P:. My cousin Francis Smith grocer. William Kiffin Esq. and Hannah his wife. My cousin Bennett, late wife of James Bennett deceased. Anne Butler's three children. To my grandson Jonathan Hardey my messuage lately erected in Watling street, in the parish of St. Mary Aldermary, on the North side of the said street, now in the occupation of Jacob Diston, now known by the sign of the Fox, which I hold by lease from the Goldsmiths. Provision for the maintenance of eight poor, aged, decayed ministers, whereof Mr. Hanserd Knowles, Mr. ——— Cox, Mr. ——— Forty, during their natural lives, to be three. William Kiffen and James Orbell executors in trust with and for the said Joseph and Jonathan Hardey. Proved by William Kiffin, power reserved for James Orbell.

A new grant of Probate made 11 October 1688 to Joseph and Jonathan Hardey, the former grant having expired by reason of the full age of said Joseph and Jonathan.   Hale, 31.

[I have no doubt the Connecticut genealogists can give some account of the Connecticut families referred to in the above will. Perhaps too my friend Eben Putnam can throw some light on the family of Grave.   H. F. W.]

HENRY REIGNOLDES, will 1585 (*ante*, p. 281).

[IN the April number of the REGISTER, among these Gleanings, is the will of Henry Reignoldes of Little Belsteade, Suffolk. From the striking similarity of Christian names, it seems to furnish a clew to the English origin of the numerous family of the name in Rhode Island.

HELEN W. REYNOLDS, *of Poughkeepsie, N. Y.*]

Peifer Bros, Phila

Clifford Stanley Sims

NEW-ENGLAND
HISTORICAL AND GENEALOGICAL
REGISTER.

OCTOBER, 1896.

CLIFFORD STANLEY SIMS.

By William Nelson, A.M.

That fair Border land, lying along the peaceful Tweed, gives little token to-day of the olden time when

> Briton's breach of faith
> Wrought Scotland mickle wae:

but traces are still plain of the mighty wall erected by the Roman soldiery to stay the tide of Scottish invasion that ever and anon poured down from the rocky fastnesses of the present Roxburgh-shire into the fertile Lowlands of Cumberland and Northumberland. Here and there a ruined pile gives token of some ancient "strength" —whether peel, or tower, or castle—whereby the freebooters of those stormy times made firm their footing in the wild hills, for sally or retreat. Truly

> Much of wild and wonderful,
> In these rude "hills," might fancy cull;
> For thither came, in times afar,
> Stern Lochlin's sons of roving war,
> The Norsemen, trained to spoil and blood,
> Skilled to prepare the raven's food;
> Kings of the main, their leaders brave,
> Their barks the dragons of the wave.

Fairer spoil than mere plunder oft rewarded the daring raids over the Border, and it is not unlikely that there was a relic of the primitive custom of marriage by capture—of which we have traces in Bible story, and in the Rape of the Sabines—in that union between Sym of Yetheram Tower, in Roxburghshire, Scotland, and Ada, granddaughter of Oswulfe, Earl of Northumberland. Another of these Lowlanders who had been given the Apostolic name, contracted from Symon into Sym or Sime, was Bueth Sym (grandson of him of Yetheram Tower), who had established himself firmly on

English soil, being Thane of Gilles Land, in Cumberland. In common with his Saxon compatriots he sallied forth to resist the invasion of his distant kinsmen, the Normans, and fell in the Conquest, in 1066. The family was too strongly rooted in the soil to be extirpated, and so we find in the obscure annals of the Border a constant succession of Syms, Simes or Sims, of most of whom it can be only said with certainty that they were born, married and were gathered unto their fathers, sometimes in battle, sometimes in wild forays, and more seldom in peaceful homes. With infinite patience, to be appreciated only by those who have attempted such a task, Judge Sims, the subject of this sketch, had traced his ancestry back for twenty-seven generations to Sym of Yetheram Tower.

In this line was the Rev. John Sim, of Aspatua, Cumberland, who married Anne Osmotherly, and had a son, Launcelot Sims, born in 1687, and who died July 26, 1712. Launcelot's great-grandson, John Simm, born Oct. 24, 1769, came to America in 1793, and married Mary Neale, of Burlington, N. J., July 18, 1797; he died July 9, 1826, at Uniontown, Penn. She was born June 29, 1774, and died July 10, 1867. Mr. Simm, the immigrant, changed the final letter of his name into an s, so that his name became Sims, which orthography has been followed by his descendants. One of his sons was John Clarke Sims, born at Burlington, N. J., Feb. 11, 1807; he removed to Philadelphia, and there married Emeline Marion Clark, Dec. 8, 1830; she was born at Philadelphia, Penn., Oct. 8, 1807, a daughter of John Lardner Clark, of Philadelphia (born March 20, 1770), and Sophia Marion Ross, who were married Aug. 1, 1797. Miss Ross was born Nov. 18, 1779, daughter of John Ross, M.D., of Mount Holly, N. J. Dr. Ross was born March 2, 1752, at Mount Holly, being a son of Dr. Alexander Ross, born in Scotland in 1713, who married Elizabeth Becket, niece of Dr. De Normandie, of Bristol, Penn., and settled at Mount Holly prior to 1752. He served some time as a surgeon in the Revolutionary war, and was one of the original members of the New Jersey Society of the Cincinnati. Dr. John Ross, son of Dr. Alexander Ross, was commissioned a captain in the Third New Jersey Regiment, Feb. 9, 1776, and major of the Second New Jersey Regiment, April 7, 1779. Subsequently, he was commissioned brigade-major, and inspector of the Jersey Brigade, and on Dec. 18, 1782, lieutenant-colonel of the Second New Jersey Regiment. In these various positions he rendered excellent service during the war. Major Ross married, July 8, 1778, Mary, only daughter of the Rev. John Brainerd, who succeeded his sainted brother, David Brainerd, as missionary to the Indians of New Jersey, and was the originator of the idea of an Indian Reservation, which he was largely instrumental in having established, near Crosswicks, and not far from Mount Holly, in New Jersey. This, the first reservation of the kind in America, was significantly called "Brotherton."

How readily may we fill in this bare outline with fancies of deeds
of derring-do wrought in those eight centuries by him of Yetheram
Tower, by the victim of the Conquest, and all their long line of
descendants ! With the fascination of the olden days upon us we
are fain to say with the passing Arthur :

> I think that we
> Shall nevermore, at any future time,
> Delight our souls with talk of knightly deeds,
> . . . . . . as in the days that were.

But, indeed, as the dying king saw, with the clearer vision often
vouchsafed to those from whom the things of earth are dropping
away,

> The old order changeth, yielding place to new,
> And God fulfils himself in many ways.

Such was the ancestry of Clifford Stanley Sims. He was born
Feb. 17, 1839, at Emeline Furnace, near Dauphin, Dauphin
County, Pennsylvania, son of John Clarke Sims and Emeline
Marion Clark. He was educated at the Episcopal Academy, in
Philadelphia. He began to study law when only seventeen years
old, and was admitted to the Pennsylvania bar, May 6, 1860. His
father was interested at the time in Philadelphia journalism, and
his son's attention was quite naturally inclined toward literature, his
particular bent even thus early being in the direction of history
and genealogy. In recognition of this taste, and of some work he
had already accomplished, he was elected a Corresponding Member
of the New-England Historic Genealogical Society, July 3, 1861,
when but twenty-two years of age. Few so young have ever been
named upon its rolls. Still earlier, March 9, 1857, he had become
a member of the Historical Society of Pennsylvania. On July 4,
1861, he was admitted to the New Jersey Society of the Cincinnati,
by virtue of his descent from Major John Ross. In 1862 he published his first book :

> The Origin and Signification of Scottish Surnames. With
> a Vocabulary of Christian Names. Albany, J. Mun-
> sell, 1862. 8°. Pp. 125.

This work evinces a degree of scholarship quite remarkable in a
young man of twenty-three. In the meantime he had been delving
among the archives of the New Jersey Cincinnati, with the result
that on July 4, 1862, he submitted an historical account of the
foundation of the Society, with a list of its original members, their
successors, and other valuable historical data. It was intended to
publish this work, but the young author caught the war fever, and
enlisted as a private in the Twenty-fifth Pennsylvania Infantry,
Sept. 15, 1862, the regiment having volunteered to repel Lee's
invasion of Pennsylvania ; Lee having been repulsed at Antietam,

the regiment was mustered out of service Oct. 1, 1862. Young Sims, however, had already entered the navy, having been appointed captain's clerk, on the steam frigate *Colorado*, Sept. 28, 1862. On Feb. 11, 1863, he resigned, to accept the higher rank of acting assistant paymaster of the U. S. Navy, to which he was commissioned March 10, 1863. He did service in this position for nearly a year, most of the time west of the Mississippi, where he took part in a number of scouting expeditions, capturing prisoners and intercepting the communications of the enemy. On Jan. 27, 1864, he was in a skirmish at Carson's Landing, Miss., where he had charge of a twelve-pound field howitzer on the hurricane deck of the U. S. gunboat *Queen City*, while exposed to the fire of a body of Confederate infantry at short range. He handled the gun with great coolness, and so effectively as to disperse the enemy, for which service he was thanked by the commanding officer of the vessel. He was commissioned lieutenant-colonel of the Fourth Arkansas Infantry, U. S. Volunteers, June 22, 1864, but only two days later had the misfortune to sustain a slight wound in an engagement at Clarendon, Ark., where he was taken prisoner, and consequently was never mustered into service. He remained a prisoner for some time, and was then released on parole, but was not exchanged until the close of the war, when he resigned, June 10, 1865. During the period of his enforced non-combatancy he was by no means idle, but turned his attention to a study of the laws of Arkansas. On Sept. 13, 1864, he was appointed judge advocate general of that state, with the rank of colonel, by Gov. Isaac Murphy.

At the close of the war he removed to Tennessee, where he married Mary Josephine Abercrombie, daughter of Charles Steadman Abercrombie, M.D., of Roseland, Tenn. (and granddaughter of the Rev. James Abercrombie, of Philadelphia), at Memphis, Tenn., Aug. 2, 1865.* He was licensed to practise law in Tennessee shortly thereafter. Various causes induced him to return to Arkansas, where he had made many friends during the military occupancy of that state. He accordingly settled in Desha County, Arkansas, and engaged in cotton planting. In 1866 he was commissioned United States Deputy Marshal for Eastern Arkansas; Major General Ord appointed him a justice of the peace in 1867, and he was an active magistrate until the completion of the reconstruction of the state. On May 18, 1867, he was offered the presidency of the board of registrars of Desha County, but declined the office. Taking a deep interest in the work of reconstruction, he was elected a delegate to the constitutional convention of Arkansas, Nov. 5, 1867, and in that body his abilities as a lawyer, a scholar and a man of affairs were recognized by his assignment to a dozen of the most important

---

* Issue: 1, Charles Abercrombie; 2, Clifford Stanley; 3, Launcelot Falcon; 4, Ralph Abercrombie (dec.); 5, John Clarke; 6, Thomson Neale; 7, James Ross (dec.); 8, Ross Brainerd.

committees, of several of which he was chairman. As a natural corollary of his service in that body he was appointed, Feb. 12, 1868, a commissioner to prepare a digest of the laws of the state. Three days later he was named as a commissioner of elections. In seemed but fitting that one who had had so large a share in framing the new organic law should have a part in the passing of the new body of statutes requisite to carry its provisions into effect. Accordingly, on March 13, 1868, Col. Sims was elected a member of the House of Representatives, and in the new legislature was chairman of the committee on ways and means, and a member of the committee on banks. Gov. Powell Clayton appointed him judge advocate general of the State, with the rank of brigadier-general, July 14, 1868. Through the personal friendship of Senator Simon Cameron and Senator Roscoe Conkling, President Grant appointed him United States Cousul for the district of Prescott, Canada, embracing Ottawa, the capital of the Dominion, April 21, 1869. Besides attending to the purely commercial duties pertaining to that position, he conducted a correspondence with the Department of State relative to the action of the Dominion Parliament regarding the Treaty of Washington. He discharged the duties of this important office with characteristic ability and fidelity, until 1878, when he resigned, to accept the more lucrative position of secretary of the Pennsylvania Company, and of the Pittsburg, Cincinnati & St. Louis Railway Company—both connceted with the Pennsylvania Railroad system. In 1881 he was appointed general assistant in the service of the Pennsylvania Railroad Company. In this latter capacity he prepared a series of volumes of several thousand pages, containing the legislation in Pennsylvania, New York, New Jersey, Delaware, Maryland and Virginia, relative to the Pennsylvania Railroad and its several subsidiary companies. He also spent several years in studying and perfecting the legal titles of the New Jersey lines of that great corporation, and having a more accurate knowledge of their charters, leases and grants than any one else, his advice was continually sought in their management. In 1887 he relinquished this connection, and became president of the Delaware Company, a construction company, which built a number of water works in Pennsylvania and Ohio, several of which it practically owned and operated.

Upon retiring from his Canadian consulship, Col. Sims took up his residence at Mount Holly, N. J., which was associated in his mind with the memories of his maternal ancestors, John Brainerd, Dr. Alexander Ross and Major John Ross, and there he spent the remainder of his life. On July 4, 1883, he was elected President of the New Jersey Society of the Cincinnati, over whose deliberations he presided with grace and dignity, even so late as Washington's birthday, 1896, when the Society met at Lakewood, although he was somewhat of an invalid at the time. The report prepared by him relative to the Society, in 1862, was published at Albany in 1866, under the title:

> The Institution of the Society of the Cincinnati, together with the roll of the original, hereditary, and honorary members of the Order, in the State of New Jersey, From 1783 to 1866.

This is a handsomely-printed octavo volume of seventy-nine pages, with rubricated title page. Under his presidency the New Jersey Society became one of the most successful, numerically, financially and socially, in the country, a result largely attributable to his earnest and capable supervision of its affairs. He had acquired an important body of literature and unpublished material bearing on the history of the General Society, which it is to be hoped will be published some day.

An outcome of his legal studies was the publication at Albany, in 1870, of a new edition of Noy's "Grounds and Maxims; and also an Analysis of the English Laws," with a biographical sketch of the author. This edition is accepted as a standard work in law libraries and schools.

His extensive investigations into land titles in the southern or western section of New Jersey, led to his becoming a member of the Council of Proprietors of West Jersey, a body whose existence dates back to the Colonial period of New Jersey, more than two centuries ago.

The Court of Errors and Appeals of New Jersey is composed of the nine justices of the supreme court, and six other judges specially appointed. Or, as a clever satirist has epigrammatically put it, "It consists of six laymen and the Court below." Occasionally a governor has seen fit to select as one one of the "lay" judges a person particularly fitted, by reason of his legal attainments, for the place, and it was with this in view that Col. Sims was appointed judge March 28, 1894. He brought to the bench a mind thoroughly trained for the exercise of the judicial function, and in every respect he fulfilled the highest anticipations of his friends in that position. In the same year he was licensed to practise law in New Jersey, and thus had the peculiar distinction of having been admitted to the bar of four different States. In 1895 he received the degree of D.C.L. from St. Stephen's College, N. Y. He was a deputy from the Diocese of New Jersey to the General Convention of the Protestant Episcopal Church, in 1889, 1892 and 1895.

In addition to his membership in the historical societies already mentioned, he was elected a resident member of the New Jersey Historical Society, January 15, 1885, and a corresponding member of the New York Historical Society, October 6, 1888. His investigations into his Scottish ancestry, in which he always felt a pardonable pride, had caused him to acquire a very extensive and minute knowledge of the history of families of the Lowlands of Scotland, and with the characteristic generosity of the true historical student he was ever ready to place his material at the service of other investigators. As an aid to his genealogical researches he had made himself also proficient in the kindred arts of heraldry and numismatics.

In politics he was a democrat, and in 1895 was somewhat prominently mentioned in Western New Jersey for the nomination for governor, his own County of Burlington sending a strong delegation in his favor to the State Convention; but seeing that the Hon. Alexander T. McGill, the able, upright and scholarly chancellor of the State, was preferred by some other sections, Judge Sims gladly threw his strength to aid in the nomination of the chancellor, who was a man after his own heart.

In person, Clifford Stanley Sims was of medium height, somewhat large of frame, yet spare of body, giving the impression of rugged virility, which was intensified by his square-cut visage; this aspect, however, was softened by an indefinable gentleness of expression that was very winning to those who knew him. There was about him a masterfulness, a strength of will, a superior mentality, all modified yet strengthened by his thorough training and scholarship, that caused him to be recognized as a man among men. His inflexible integrity, his high-mindedness, were the natural outcome of an instinctive purity that was childlike in its transparency. These qualities won for him a host of friends among his numerous personal, business, social and political associates in New Jersey, Philadelphia and New York, and to these the intelligence of his sudden death, at Trenton, on March 3, 1896, while on his way to sit in the Court of Errors and Appeals, came with the sense of shock of a personal bereavement. But

> To live in hearts we leave behind
> Is not to die.

GEN. THOMAS LINCOLN CASEY.

By Rev. SILVANUS HAYWARD, A.M., of Globe Village, Mass.

THOMAS LINCOLN CASEY was born at Madison Barracks, Sackett's Harbor, N. Y., May 10, 1831, and died at Washington, D. C., March 25, 1896. His earliest known ancestor, Thomas Casey, was at Newport, R. I., probably as early as 1658. The line of descent was Thomas[1] and Sarah———, Adam[2] and Mary (Greenman), Thomas[3] and Comfort (Langford), Silas[4] and Abigail (Coggeshall), Wanton[5] and Elizabeth (Goodale), Silas[6] and Abby Perry (Pearce), Thomas Lincoln[7] Casey. His father, Gen. Silas[6] Casey, was graduated at West Point in 1826; served with distinction in the

Seminole and Mexican wars and the war of 1861–65, being several times brevetted for gallantry in battle, and was retired in 1868 as Major General in the regular army.

Thomas Lincoln Casey was appointed, by President Polk, a cadet at large at West Point, where he was graduated in 1852 at the head of his class, among whom were many who became distinguished in the service. On his graduation, he was appointed second Lieutenant of Engineers, and soon after superintended the construction of Fort Delaware. From 1854 to 1859 he was Assistant Professor of Engineering at West Point. For the next two years he was engaged on the Pacific coast; but on the outbreak of the Rebellion he was first stationed at Fortress Monroe, serving on the staff of Gen. Butler, and was afterward in charge of the permanent coast defences of Maine. In March, 1865, he was brevetted Colonel for faithful and meritorious service during the war. After March, 1867, he was on duty at Washington, where he developed a remarkable talent for accurate supervision of large enterprises, and a positive genius for reliable estimates. His promise to perform a piece of work within a given estimate of time and money was regarded as absolutely trustworthy; and Congress paid him the compliment of appropriating all the money for which he asked. His great work was finishing the Washington Monument, of which he took charge in 1878, and placed the capstone in December, 1884. The monument had been started in 1848, and left without a stroke for twenty-two years. The general opinion was, that it would have to be torn down and a new foundation laid, or the height of five hundred and fifty-five feet abandoned. When Gen. Casey reported that the old foundation might be strengthened and the monument raised to its full height without tearing down any of the shaft, he was only laughed at. But by the influence of President Grant, who had great confidence in Gen. Casey, he was permitted to carry out his plans. The old foundation was too small and too shallow, entirely inadequate to support the immense weight of the gigantic shaft of the original design. Gen. Casey decided to dig beneath the foundation, underlying it with another, covering one and a half times as much area, and deeper than the old one. On this excavation and filling he labored for two years amid the sneers and derision of high officers and expert engineers. He then rapidly completed the obelisk. No one now doubts his wisdom, or fears for the ridiculed foundation on which rests many thousand tons of masonry. The engineers of the world regard it " as one of the most remarkable pieces of work ever accomplished, one of the engineering marvels of the century." While completing the monument, he was also superintending the construction of the building occupied by the War and Navy departments, one of the finest edifices in Washington. The care and anxiety incident to the completion of the monument brought on nervous prostration, from which he never fully recovered.

In 1888 he was appointed Brigadier General and Chief of Engineers, giving him charge not only of the purely military engineering, but of the river and harbor works throughout the country.   In 1890 he secured an appropriation, by which he was enabled to initiate an important and elaborate system of permanent defence to the principal seaport cities.   At the time of his death he was in charge of building the Congressional Library, which he had estimated could be built for six millions of dollars and be finished in the spring of 1897, and there was every prospect that he would have accomplished it accordingly.

In announcing his death, Secretary Lamont said : "His absolute honesty, thorough devotion to public duty, and rugged force of character, won for General Casey the supreme confidence of the country, and contributed in a marked degree to the high reputation of the corps of which he was long a distinguished member."

The following well-deserved tribute to his character is from the Washington Post :

> In the death of Gen. Thomas Lincoln Casey, the army loses a most efficient officer, and the country a faithful servant.   Endowed with engineering abilities of a high order, Gen. Casey's name is indentified with many public improvements in every section of the United States.   But especially in Washington will his name be ever held in grateful remembrance.   In face of difficulties which would have been insurmountable to men of less capacity, he reared the Washington Monument to its imposing height, while the magnificent monument on Capitol Hill known as the National Library must ever be a memorial of his splendid career.   Upon all the public works with which his name is associated, he left the impress of his genius, and best of all the record of unimpeachable integrity and sturdy honesty.   He was an industrious but quiet worker, jealous of the interests of the government in the broadest and most patriotic sense, and earnest always in the discharge of his duty.   Great as are the monuments which he has left in marble and granite, he has bequeathed a still more glorious heritage in his eminent career and unspotted name.

Gen. Casey was a man of fine literary tastes and acquirements. He wrote many articles of great value and interest on engineering subjects, and his reports are in constant use as works of reference. Generosity, a high sense of honor and integrity, and an ardent love of justice were prominent traits of his character.   He was a member of the Society of the Cincinnati of Massachusetts, of the Loyal Legion of the United States, of the National Academy of Sciences, and in 1890 was created an officer of the Legion of Honor by President Carnot of France.   In religion, Gen. Casey was an Episcopalian, and generous in support of the church.   In politics, he was strictly independent.

Gen. Casey married May 8, 1856, Emma, daughter of Prof. Robert Weir, of West Point, who was born June 2, 1834, and survives her husband.   They had four sons, of whom the oldest and youngest are still living :— Thomas Lincoln, now Captain of Engineers at Norfolk, Va.; and Edward Pearce, an Architect of New York, who was associated with his father in the construction of the Library Building. At the graduation of the former from the Military Academy, his father and grandfather, both graduates of the institution, were present. As a member of the New-England Historic Genealogical Society, to which he was elected Sept. 6, 1882, Gen. Casey was highly esteemed. He conducted genealogical investigation with the careful attention to detail characteristic of his professional work. With untiring, patient industry, he unravelled intricacies, traced obscurities, and verified names and dates by examination of unquestioned records. To accomplish this, he spared neither time nor expense. His death was announced at the April stated meeting and was deplored by all.

AUTOBIOGRAPHY OF HON. NATHAN READ,

WHO DIED AT BELFAST, MAINE, JAN. 20, 1849.

Communicated by the Hon. JOSEPH WILLIAMSON, Lit. D., of Belfast, Me.

I WAS born at Western (now Warren) in the County of Worcester, Massachusetts, July 2, 1759, and lived with my father, Reuben Read, till I was about fifteen years old, and worked with him at farming, and occasionally with my grandfather, Capt. Nathaniel Read, who owned a large farm adjoining my father's, which, being good land and easily cultivated, he made quite productive. Having learned in early life the carpenter's trade, he had a good set of tools, which enabled him to make his own farming utensils, and even his own buildings, which was a great advantage to him. My grandmother's maiden name was Pheby Lamb, a very benevolent, pious, kind hearted woman. My mother's maiden name was Tamsin Meacham, of Enfield, Connecticut, and was cousin to General Green of Rhode Island, who, in the Revolutionary war, was next in command to General Washington. My father was a major in a regiment of minute men in the Revolutionary war, and was under the command of General Ward of Shrewsbury, and being appointed by him to take charge of the Hessians and British troops captured with Burgoyne, and then prisoners of war at Cambridge, he removed them to Rutland in the County of Worcester, and superintended them to the close of the war. In the autumn of 1776, having had very little schooling, I was permitted to attend Rev. Samuel Willard's school at Stafford about three months, and was taught arithmetic, English grammar, and Burr's Latin grammar; and then returned to Western and attended the town school, kept about two months by Dwight Foster, an undergraduate of Providence College. I was then inoculated for the small-pox, and in the spring went to Mr. Nathan Goddard's private school at Shrewsbury; and in April, soon after I began to study Greek, I was taken sick with the measles, which injured my eye sight, and disqualified me for several weeks for reading Greek. Mr. Goddard being called away to preach for several months as a candidate for the ministry, I was necessitated to go to school to a clergyman in a neighboring town to study Greek and qualify myself as well as I could to enter college. At the close of the summer vacation in 1777, I was examined by Mr. Caleb Gannett and Mr. Benjamin Guild, and admitted to Cambridge College. As my parents were desirous that I should be qualified for a preacher, I attended Professor Sewall's lectures on the Hebrew language, and acquired so much knowledge of it as to be appointed to deliver a Hebrew oration at a public exhibition. During the interval between the death of Professor Sewall and the appointment of Professor Parsons, I was requested to instruct such students as wished to learn the Hebrew language, which I did, and was handsomely rewarded for my services. Previous to Commencement in 1781, I was selected by my class-mates to deliver a valedictory address on a fixed day previous to Commencement in compliance with a long established custom; but in consequence of hard times the students were dismissed from college much sooner than usual; and, of course, the address was not delivered. After Commencement I went to Beverly and taught the town school about a year and a half, and boarded at the house of Hon. Nathan Dane, the founder of the Law School at Harvard University. He was then a student of law with Mr. Pynchion of Salem, a distinguished and highly respectable member of the bar. After leaving Beverly I taught a private school for young ladies in Salem, which I kept till I was elected tutor of Harvard College in October, 1783.

I resigned my office of tutor immediately after Commencement in 1787, and studied physic with Dr. Edward Augustus Holyoke of Salem till October, 1788; and then opened an apothecary's in Main Street, Salem. In February, 1790, went to New York. Had letters of introduction to President Washington and several of the most respectable and influential members of Congress. On the 8th of that month (February) presented a petition to Congress praying for an exclusive privilege of constructing and using several machines and engines which I had invented for promoting the purposes of navigation and land carriage. After spending considerable time in New York without effecting the object I had in view, I returned to Salem, and in October, 1790, was married to Miss Elizabeth Jeffrey, daughter of the late Elizabeth Jeffrey and William Jeffrey, Esq., clerk of the courts in the County of Essex, and granddaughter of Joseph Bowditch, Esq., for many years clerk of said courts. August 24, 1791, was elected a member of the American Academy of Arts and Sciences.

April 4, 1795, moved to my farm in Danvers, and in eight months built a permanent bridge over Water's River which cost $4,355.00, exclusive of $400.00 extra expense as a dam.

1796 the Salem Iron Factory was built and put in operation by Capt. Osgood at $50.00 per month, and I was afterwards appointed agent.

1797, constructed and put in operation at the Salem Iron Factory my patent nail machine, which cut and headed nails at one operation.

October, 1800, was elected a member of Congress for the County of Essex, South District, to fill the place of the late Judge Sewall, who died at Wiscasset; November 5, 1800, was elected again for the next two years.

February 10, 1802, while a resident of Danvers, I was appointed by Governor Strong a special Justice of the Court of Common Pleas for the County of Essex.

November, 1807, removed my family from Salem to Belfast. Was appointed Chief Justice of the Court of Common Pleas for the County of Hancock.

At a meeting of the Linnean Society of New England, May 21, 1815, I was elected an honorary member.

[The writer of this autobiography, Hon. Nathan Read, of Belfast, Me., left a record of the children of his grandfather Nathaniel Read, and his father Reuben Read, which was printed in the REGISTER for July, page 354. A memoir of him was published in 1872 by Hurd & Houghton of New York, in a volume entitled "Nathan Read; his Invention of the Multi-Tubular Boiler and Portable High-pressure Engine, and discovery of the true mode of applying steam-power to Navigation and Railways. A Contribution to the Early History of the Steamboat and Locomotive Engine. By his friend and nephew, David Read." The author of this book resided at that time at Burlington, Vt.—EDITOR.]

RECORD OF THE BOWDITCH FAMILY.

Communicated by Hon. JOSEPH WILLIAMSON, Lit. D., of Belfast, Me.

THE following record is copied from the papers of the late Hon. Nathan Read of Belfast, Maine.

A copy of the Minutes of my marriage and the birth and death of my children and the death of my wife. J. B. (III.)

Joseph Bowdich and Elizabeth Hunt were married the 25th day of July, 1725. He was 24 years and 11 months old. She was 21 years and seven months old.

First Child, a Son, William, was born February ye 4th, 1726, and died June 27th, 1769.

Second Child, was a son and born dead February 10, 1728-9.

Third Child, a son, Joseph, was born November 27th, 1730, and Died at Sea. (after he was taken Coming from Surrinam) May 27, 1758, his son Joseph Born Nov. 1757.

Fourth Child, a daughter, Mary, was born Dec. 11th, 1732, married to J. O. August, 1760. 1st child born and Died March, 1766. 2nd Child Eunice, Born June 26, 1769, she Died Jan. ye 1st, 1774.

Fifth Child, a daughter Elizabeth, Feb. 8, 1734–5. married W. J. (II.) Sept. 21st, 1766, child Elizabeth, Born Feb. 10th, 1772, she Died July 1772.

Sixth Child, a daughter, Sarah, was born January 17, 1736–7. Died October 2, 1764.

Seventh Child, a daughter, Eunice, was born May 20th, 1739. Died June 11th, 1765.

Eighth Child, a son, Daniel, was born April 26th, Monday Morn 1742, and Died May 14th, 1743.

Friday, May 7th, 1743, Elizabeth Bowditch died about 12 o'clock in ye 39th year of her age.

Taken Jan. 7, 1744.

1764, August 12th, Sarah was at Meeting Sept. ye 16th, kept Chamber and died ye 2nd October.

1765, May 25th, Eunice rode to Lynn Spring to Meeting, 26th rode out, 28th Headache, Sick at Stomach, 29th; June 3rd confined to her Bed and Dyed ye 11th.

II.   1772.   June 19th, Mr. Jeffrey was taken with Excessive Pain in his Bowels, 21st kept his bed and Died ye 8th July in ye 35th year of his age.

III.   1780.   October 1st, Father was taken with a Violent Pain across his Breast which abated the next day : he grew better until the 6th, when the Pain returned and he Died in a minute after 9 years 3 months confinement with the Palsey, aged 80 years.

(This was Joseph Bowditch, the head of the family whose record is here given.)

Children of Jos. Pratt.

Margaret,	born	March 1, 1694.
Abigail,	"	May 17, 1696.
Mary,	"	Aug. 22, 1698.
Eliza,	"	Aug. 24, 1700.
Elias,	"	Aug. 23, 1702.
Ruth,	"	Aug. 25, 1704.
Hannah,	"	Jan. 25, 1706–7.
Elias,	"	Nov. 17, 1707.
Susanna,	"	April 25, 1709.
Lydia,	"	May 27, 1711.
Mavench,	"	July 20, 1713.

ADDITIONS BY HARRISON ELLERY, Esq., of Brookline, Mass.

WILLIAM[1] BOWDITCH was admitted an inhabitant of Salem on the 20th 9 mo. 1639, and on 23d 11 mo. 1642, he had a grant of ten acres of land. He had another grant of thirty acres on the 13th 8 mo. 1649. His wife, Sarah Bowditch, joined the Salem church 10th 3 mo. 1640, and on the 4th 6 mo. 1646, was presented at the quarterly court " for offensive withdrawing from ye ordinance of Baptizing of Infants," for which she was excommunicated. Their children were William[2] Bowditch and Nathaniel Bowditch. The latter was baptized 15th 8 mo., 1643.

WILLIAM[2] BOWDITCH (*William*), born about 1640, was a merchant at Salem and collector of the customs at the port of Salem. His death in 1681 is spoken of on the colonial records as sudden and untimely. He had a wife Sarah. His son, Capt. William³ Bowditch, who was born in September, 1663, became an eminent merchant and useful citizen. He was frequently a selectman and moderator of the town meeting, a representative of Salem in the General Court, and in 1721 was one of three prominent citizens appointed as trustees to manage £5000 of the town's money, but he refused to serve. He died May 28, 1728. His gravestone is still standing in the Charter Street Burying Ground, as is also one to his wife. He married, Aug. 30, 1688, Mary Gardner, who was born Feb. 14, 1669–70, and died in 1724. She was a daughter of Lt. Thomas and Mary (Porter) Gardner of Salem. By her he had the following children :

i. MARY³ BOWDITCH, b. Aug. 2, 1689; d. Oct. 2, 1689.
ii. WILLIAM BOWDITCH, b. Oct. 31, 1690; d. Oct. 12, 1706.
iii. MARY BOWDITCH, b. Dec. 18, 1693. She m. 1st, Sept. 8, 1715, James Butler, of Boston, and 2d, Dec. 26, 1723, Samuel Barton, of Salem. She had no children by either husband.
iv. SARAH BOWDITCH, b. Jan. 10, 1696; d. in March, 1761. She m. June 30, 1715, Joseph Hathorne, of Salem. He d. June 3, 1760. Among their numerous descendants was Nathaniel Hawthorne the author.
v. THOMAS BOWDITCH, b. June 5, 1698; d. Nov. 30, 1702.
vi. JOSEPH BOWDITCH, b. Aug. 21, 1700, and is the subject of the record in the Read papers. He was a man of wonderful humour and there are many pleasant anecdotes related of him. He was clerk of the Court for a great number of years, justice of the peace, etc. It may safely be affirmed that there was not in the town of Salem a gentleman of more respectability than "Squire Bowditch," as he was universally called. He once failed and received a discharge from his creditors upon paying them a certain dividend. He was afterwards successful and paid each of them the whole amount that he owed them.
vii. EBENEZER BOWDITCH, b. April 26, 1703; d. Feb. 2, 1768. He was a shipmaster and merchant of Salem. His wife to whom he was m. Aug. 15, 1728, was Mary Turner, b. Nov. 1, 1706; d. May 1, 1785. Her general appearance was very dignified and commanding. She was a daughter of the Hon. Col. John Turner, an eminent merchant and citizen of Salem, by his wife Mary, daughter of Lieut. Robert Kitchen, of Salem. Ebenezer and Mary Bowditch were the ancestors of the distinguished Nathaniel Bowditch, LL.D.
viii. EUNICE BOWDITCH, b. June 8, 1705; d. July 2, 1705.
ix. EUNICE BOWDITCH, b. March 22, 1707; m. Dec. 12, 1728, William Hunt, of Salem.
x. DANIEL BOWDITCH, b. June 19, 1709; died at the age of 19 or 20 years.
xi. WILLIAM BOWDITCH, b. Feb. 1, 1713; d. Nov. 1, 1715.

INSCRIPTIONS AT SANTA CRUZ, CALIFORNIA, 1891.

Copied by B. FRANK LEEDS, Esq.

[Concluded from page 304.]

Lot 85.

Sarah, wife of Asa Anthony, died May 25, 1854, aged 64 y. 7 mos. 9 days.

Asa Anthony, born May 25, 1793, died July 14, 1869, aged 76 y. 1 mo. 19 days.

Asa, son of George and Hannah Anthony, died Jan. 1, 1861, aged 18 years, 7 mos. 9 days.
Mary, Elihu and Nellie, children of George and Hannah Anthony.

Lot 86.

Samuel Morgan, son of J. and M. A. Morgan, b. July 29, 1849, d. Jan. 18, 1873.
Joseph W. Morgan, d. Oct. 20, 1863, aged 32 years.
James A. Morgan, son of J. and M. A. Morgan, b. May 18, 1838, d. Jan. 6, 1859.

Lot 87.

Margaret Bell. Jan. 1791, April 1857.
Charlotte McQuesten, Lanesboro, Mass., July 27, 1839, May 31, 1872.
William Blackburn, Harper's Ferry, Va., Feb. 14, 1814, Mch. 25, 1867.
Freddie (Blackburn), July 7, 1862, Oct. 19, 1864.

Lot 88.

Rev. William Foreman, died Dec. 19, 1861, ag^d 61 y. 10 m.
Susanna Foreman, d. Jan. 27, 1874, ag^d 61 y. 4 m. 11 d.
Josephus Foreman, aged 29 years.
Samuel B. Foreman, d. May 12, 1875, ag^d 22 y. 1 m. 19 d.
Stephen Foreman, d. June 6, 1861, aged 7 mos.
William A. Cloud, d. Sept. 29, 1859, aged 2 mos.
Infant daughter of A. J. & S. Cloud, d. June 29, 1863, aged 3 m. 29 d.
J. C.   D. C.   J. A. C.
Lotta C. Cloud, died Oct. 14, 1877, ag^d 1 year, 9 m. 20 d.

Lot 89.

Robert Bennett, d. Jan. 21, 1878, aged 55 years.
Gordon G., son of E. and M. E. Bennett, d. June 26, 1867, aged 10 mos.
E. Bennett.

Lot 90.

J. C. Shelby, died Dec. 30, 1869, aged 44 yrs. 2 mos. 27 d.   A native of Tennessee.
Sarah L., dau'r of G. C. and M. A. Shelby, d. Apr. 16, 1855, aged 2 yrs. 9 mos.

Lot 91.

Clarissa Olive, dau^r of J. F. and M. P. Simpson, died Oct. 19, 1860, aged 1 year 6 mos. 8 d.
Mary P., wife of J. F. Simpson, d. Mch. 10, 1870, aged 28 yrs. 5 m. 24 d.

Lot 92.

James Monroe, son of James and Ida Hecox, born Sep. 24, 1835, died in the service of his country July 24, 1864.
Mrs. Hattie T. Hecox, born 1840, died Sep. 1, 1885.

Lot 93.

Little Josa A., dau^r of J. and M. King, d. July 26, 1862, aged 4 yrs. 1 m. 7 d.

Lot 94.

Daniel Scott, d. Aug. 21, 1867, ag^d 73 yrs. 6 m.
Henry Archer Scott, b. Feb. 25, 1853, d. Nov. 24, 1870.
George E. Scott, born Mch. 12, 1828, d. Sep. 3, 1881.
Emma F. Barker, born Oct. 24, 1794, d. Oct. 6, 1855.

Lot 95.

Henry Harris, born Aug. 19, 1821, d. Mch. 9, 1868.
J. H. Guild, born Jan. 25, 1863, d. June 10, 1865.
Alamo Guild, born Mch. 23, 1858, d. Nov. 5, 1865.
Jonathan H. Guild, born Apr. 4, 1814, d. Dec. 23, 1870.
Little Joney, dau^r of H. and S. Harris, d. Dec. 17, 1858, ag^d 8 mo. 22 d.

Lot 96.

Eliza Sloan, born July 23, 1792, d. Nov. 20, 1863.
A. J. Sloan, born Sep. 22, 1826, d. Feb. 11, 1865.

Lot 97.

Mary Archer, died June 30, 1887, aged 78 years.
Another headstone, directly back of above, fallen, inscription side down.

Lot 98.

Lillie, dau^r of Jacob and Emma Hartman, d. Mch. 10, 1887, aged 3 years, 22 days.
Georgie, son of Jacob and Emma Hartman, died Oct. 19, 1886, aged 1 mo. 27 d.
Philip Hartman, died Aug. 2, 1877, aged 26 yrs. 2 mos.

Lot 99.

Sarah Jane, wife of W. C. Greenleaf, b. Nov. 22, 1818, d. Nov. 10, 1866, native of Ossipee, N. Hampshire.
Robert Simpson, born May 1, 1838, died Apr. 18, 1866.

Lot 100.

Little Pearl, dau^r of J. C. and E. T. Horr, born Jan. 4, 1871, died Sep. 24, 1871.

Lot 101.

Alice Maria Paxon, wife of John L. Cooper, born Sep. 24, 1838, died July 12, 1866.
Mary Lavinia Cooper, born July 11, 1863, d. Oct. 24, 1864.
Walter Cooper, a native of Gettysburg, Pa., died April 25, 1870, aged 32 years.
Two other graves without inscriptions.

Lot 102.

Harriet C. Richards, died Sep. 9, 1857, aged 37 yrs.

Lot 103.

Sarah P. Hutchins, d. Sep. 19, 1864, aged 67 yrs.

Lot 104.

Abba W., wife of Walter M. Jordan, born at Westbrook, Maine, Feb. 11, 1834, died Dec. 25, 1864.
Ralph W., son of Walter and Abba W. Jordan.

Lot 105.

Kate E. Farrand or Farraud.
An obelisk of wood with square base, panelled.
Another grave behind this, unmarked.

Lot 106.

Henry A., born May 24, 1862, d. Feb. 10, 1865.
John W., born Sep. 18, 1864, d. Jan. 31, 1865.
Sons of H. A. and C. Trust.

Lot 107.

Elizabeth C., beloved wife of Lawrence Pollard, died Dec. 12, 1876, aged 64 years.

Lot 108.

Clarence J., son of U. and Eliza Sloan, d. Jan. 22, 1877, aged 2 years.
Charles W., son of U. and Eliza Sloan, d. Jan. 21, 1877, aged 6 yrs. 9 mos.
Georgie B. Griffith, born Nov. 15, 1864, d. Dec. 17, 1870.
Rosa Keeton, born July 29, 1869, died Dec. 13, 1870.

Lot 109.

Eliza Imus, died July 15, 1879, aged 74 years. A pioneer of 1849.
Hiram A. Imus, Jr., died Oct. 4, 1876, aged 74 years. A pioneer of 1849.
James R.
Nettie, dau^r of W. and S. A. Imus, died Dec. 6, 1872, aged 11 yrs.
Charles C. Imus, son of Hiram A. Imus, died May, 1856, aged 54 years. A pioneer of 1846.
Ruth Palmer, wife of Hiram A. Imus, died June 24, 1860, aged 84 yrs.
Hiram A. Imus, died July 22, 1864, aged 94 yrs. A pioneer of 1849.
Several other graves in this lot with stakes, but without inscriptions.

H. L. Wallace, Post No. 32, G. A. R.
Four graves with stakes; no inscriptions.
Large lot adjoining old cemetery.
Masonic cemetery adjoining above; the lot larger than the G. A. R. lot.
1. William Foster, d. Oct. 7, 1866, aged 59 yrs.
2. Daniel Monteath, d. Oct. 16, 1882, aged 50 yrs.
3. Daniel W. Scoville, born Sep. 5, 1823, died Dec. 21, 1867.
Henry W. Peck, born Wayne Co., New York, Apr. 16, 1818, died Sep. 14, 1873.
Dr. A. G. F.
A wooden board.
J. H.
Wood.
P. T.
Wood.
Another of wood; inscription worn off.
Five or six other graves with and without stakes.

BERMUDA DURING THE AMERICAN REVOLUTION.

By Isaac J. Greenwood, A.M., of New York City.

Saturday, July 15, 1775, the Continental Congress at Philadelphia, having considered Dr. Benjamin Franklin's motion, passed a resolution to the effect that, " whereas, the Government of Great Britain had prohibited the exportation of arms and ammunition to any of the Plantations, and had endeavoured to prevent other Nations from supplying us with the same "; now " for the better furnishing these colonies with the necessary means of defending their rights, every vessel importing Gunpowder, Sulphur and Saltpetre, * * * Brass Field Pieces, or good Muskets fitted with Bayonets, within nine months from the date of this resolution, shall be permitted to load and export the produce of these Colonies, to the value of such powder and stores aforesaid, the Non Exportation Agreement notwithstanding."

The following Monday an address was read from the Deputies of the several parishes of Bermuda, the people of which island, apprehensive of being reduced to a state of starvation, as a consequence of the existing situation of public affairs, had requested the Congress to take their case into serious consideration. The President was now ordered to return a favorable reply, desiring an account of such provisions as had been imported for their use, for some years past, and to enclose a copy of the foregoing resolution.

Some three weeks later (August 4), Gen. Washington addressed a letter from the camp at Cambridge, to Gov. Cook of Rhode Island, telling him, in strictest confidence, that so great were his necessities in the articles of powder and lead, as to require an immediate supply; that he had "listened to every proposition, which could give the smallest hope," and had learned through a gentleman lately from Bermuda, that "there is a very considerable magazine of powder in a remote part of that island; the inhabitants being well disposed not only to our cause in general, but to assist in this enterprise in particular." He then suggests that one of the two Rhode Island armed vessels be sent out to secure the essential article.

This proposition meeting with the Governor's approval, Capt. Abraham Whipple, with a crew of 61 men, was despatched in the larger of the armed sloops, and sailing from Providence, September 12th, carried with him a letter (of the 6th) from the Commander in Chief to the Bermudians, concluding as follows: "If your favor and friendship to North America and its liberties have not been misrepresented, I persuade myself you may, consistently with your own safety, promote and further this scheme, so as to give it the fairest prospect of success." In which case he promises them his influence with the Continental Congress for supplying them with provisions, and keeping up a friendly relationship.

But a few days had elapsed since the vessel's sailing when it was announced publicly that one hundred barrels of powder had arrived from Bermuda by two vessels, the one from Philadelphia,* the other from South Carolina. The second provincial vessel was now sent after Capt. Whipple, who was supposed to be cruising for a few days off New York, but who, it turned out, had proceeded direct to Bermuda. Here he put in at the west end of the island, much to the alarm of the inhabitants, who at first took his armed sloop for another British vessel of war; for Gen. Gage, hearing through the Governor of the loss of the powder, had immediately despatched an armed sloop from Boston, with a 600 ton transport, and both were, at the time, lying in Georgetown harbor with a view of intercepting all future supply of provisions to the inhabitants, who were treated as rebels. Capt. Whipple returned to Providence, October 20th, after an absence of 38 days; he had been received with great cordiality and friendship; had entertained five members of the Council on board of his sloop, and "all had assured him that the people were hearty friends to the American cause, and heartily disposed to serve it."

November 22, the Committee of the Whole House in Congress, to whom

---

*A report from the Penn. Com. of Safety, September 20th, mentions the receipt August 26, of sundry casks, containing 1800 lbs. of powder, 700 of which were not fit for use, imported in the Lady, Capt. Ord, from Bermuda.

had been referred the several petitions from the Island of Bermuda for relief, made a report in favor of supplying that people with what might be necessary for their subsistence and home consumption, as the inhabitants " appear friendly to the cause of America." This supply was to be paid for in salt, though this resolution was not to exclude them the privilege of receiving American produce, to any amount, in exchange for arms, ammunition, sulphur, &c., agreeable to the previous resolution of July 15th. The Committee of Safety for North and South Carolina, Virginia, Maryland, Pennsylvania and New York were to superintend any exportation to Bermuda, and no vessel could be loaded without their permission. " These resolutions were to be kept as private as the execution of them would permit," and Edward Stiles, under direction of the Pennsylvania Committee of Safety, was to send the brig Sea Nymph, Saml. Stobel, master, to the Island forthwith, with corn, flour, bread, pork, beef, apples, &c., as part of the annual allowance. Just about this time we read of eight half barrels of powder, belonging to Capt. John Cooper of North Carolina, and intended for the use of the inhabitants of that province, being sent from Bermuda by Henry Tucker, Chairman of the Deputies of the several parishes of the Island, and which were then in the keeping of the Pennsylvania Commissioner, Robert Towers.

In April, 1776, Silas Deane, our secret agent to France, stopped on his way, at Bermuda, and in a letter of advice to Philadelphia, a portion of which was afterwards published anonymously, he fully describes the peculiar situation of the island, its approach and intricate channel, and the resources and condition of the people, whose whole trade, in cedar and shipbuilding, " depended on their intercourse between the American colonies on the Continent, and foreign ports. This ceasing throws them instantly into distress, without stock of provision, and without the means of paying for it, could it be procured ; and on a soil incapable of supplying them, were they to cultivate every inch of it." The Governor, he states, was obnoxious and had threatened the inhabitants with troops and cruisers stationed at either end of the island, and " in such case instant famine is inevitable, unless they can subsist on fish alone ; and if they cannot by some means procure speedy supplies from the Continent, they will be in the same unhappy situation." He advises, therefore, that they be taken immediately under the protection of the united colonies ; that either end of the island be fortified ; a safe harbor made for cruisers ; and that then, with " a small fleet of swift sailing frigates and sloops," all the West India trade of Great Britain be intercepted. At the island, he concludes, a number of vessels, suitable for privateers, and guns for the same, 4 to 9 pounders, could be readily procured.

In pursuance of this letter, Congress resolved, June 6, " that the Secret Committee be instructed to fit out two fast sailing vessels loaded with provisions, for the immediate supply of the inhabitants of the Islands of Bermudas ; and that the Com. of Secret Correspondence be directed to take such measures as they may think proper by those vessels to discover the state of those islands, and the disposition of the inhabitants ; and that the Marine Committee be instructed to take such measures, as they may think proper for purchasing, arming and fitting, at the said Island, two sloops of war for the service of the United Colonies."

Deane, writing from Paris, August 18, to the Committee of Secret Correspondence, says : " I wrote you from Bermuda on the subject of seizing and fortifying the Island. I am well informed the British Ministry have had it in contemplation, and propose doing it next spring;" and again he writes, October 1, "you are desired by no means to forget Bermuda. If you should, Gt. Britain will seize it this winter; or France on the first rupture. * * * An agent from Barbadoes is arrived in London, to represent their distresses. Another from Bermuda, with a declaration to the Ministry of the necessity of their being supplied with provisions from the Colonies, and saying if not permitted they must ask the protection of Congress."

It was towards the end of this month (October 21, 1776) that the schooner Sally, arriving at Philadelphia with salt, &c., reported the " Galatea," of 20 guns, and the "Dreadnaught," of 18 guns, at Bermuda, where they had carried in several prizes, and that the " Galatea " was to sail in a short time, to cruise off the Virginia capes; accordingly a few days later, the American Commodore, Esek Hopkins, was ordered by the Marine Committee to look out both for this vessel and the " Nautilus," which was in company.

About June, 1777, two American armed brigs from South Carolina, said to have been commanded by Bermudian captains, arrived at the west end of the island, where they remained, keeping up friendly intercourse for a week. The Governor complained bitterly of this fact to the Assembly, and that body, in retort stated that H. M's 14 gun sloop-of-war " Nautilus," Capt. John Collins,* was lying at the time in Castle Harbour, but had done nothing to drive them off; the Executive, indignantly replying, said that the vessel was foul, having been off the careen for two years or more, and could not be brought up in time; besides, she could not have overtaken the enemy, as they were twenty miles ahead.

By this time it appears that the islanders were in receipt of some provisions from the home government, though one vessel might still be licensed from each parish, to go in quest of the same, if necessary, and without which license or protection they were liable to capture; this trade, however, by 1779, was confined to Savannah and New York, the only colonial ports then held by Great Britain.

Meanwhile on January 10, 1778, a commission had been granted by the Governor for cruising against the commerce " of the American Colonies in Rebellion," and this, apparently their first armed vessel, was the " Hammond " of 100 tons, 8 carriage-guns (no swivels), and 20 men, owned by Robert Shedden and Wm. Goodrich, merchants of the island, and commanded by Capt. Bridger Goodrich.† Several other vessels were fitted out during this and the two following years, "to cruize against the French, Spaniards and Americans"; among them the " Miraculous Pitcher," Capt. H. Middleton; the sloop " Whalebone," Capt. John Bryce; the " Spitfire"; the " Jolly Bacchus," &c.; and other vessels served as cartels to convey prisoners, colonial or foreign, to various ports for exchange. These commissions were all signed by Gov. George James Bruere,‡ who after administering the affairs of the island for sixteen years, died September 10, 1780, and the reins of government passed temporarily to the eldest councillor, the Hon. President, Thomas Jones, a native, by whom a meeting of the Assembly was called on the 18th. The next month Lt. Gov. George Bruere was in office and remained so till December, 1781. In a speech of November 23, 1780, he expressed a hope " that all trade and correspondence

---

* Knighted 1783 for bravery.

† The Hon. Bridger Goodrich, Esq., died June 12, 1795, æ. 38, and was buried under an armorial tablet in St. Peter's church, St. George's, Bermuda.

‡ A MS. book in the Secretary's Office, Hamilton, lettered " Commissions, V, Pt. I," contains no naval commissions later than 1780, and unfortunately " Pt. II " is missing.

with Rebels & the Enemies of Gt. Britain, will forthwith cease, &c., &c., and encouragement be given towards fitting out private Ships of War to distress all the Enemies of our Most Gracious Sovereign, which it is so much in the power of these happy situated Isles to effect, so much for the true Interest of the people instead of assisting Rebells & their Confederates, the French and Spanish."

Again in a speech to the House, of June 19, 1781, the Lt. Gov. accuses the people of favoring and trading with the Rebels. " To what a state," he says, " have wicked & designing men brought these islands; instead of fitting out Armed Vessels, enriching themselves, and perhaps even being Instruments in shortening a cruel bloody civil war, they have caused a misguided & deluded people to do all they could to serve the Americans." On September 20th, however, he says: " At length a family is fitting out a Noble ship (spight of the great obstacles in their way; spight of the many discouragements thrown out by the restless few, who have long had too much influence for the good harmony and happiness of the country). I flatter myself her success, as well as the good fortune the other Armed Vessels constantly meet with, will convince the reasonable and dispassionate that Interest as well as duty lay on the side of Equipments against our Confederate Enemies, not an illicit trade with them, which I forsee aright will, however artfully covered, be in the end brought to light, to the shame, confusion and utmost danger of the Traiterous delinquents that now carry it on under false Oaths, Papers and Colours."

The fiery Governor, however, stepped down from his rostrum when, on January 4, 1782, Col. Wm. Brown, a loyalist from Salem, Mass., succeeded him. Whether by this time the islanders were becoming less dependent upon their rebellious fellow colonists; or whether Gov. Brown was trying to make the best of things when writing to the home government; whatever the cause, we find him in one of his letters, among the Lansdowne MSS. (vol. 78) expressing his opinion that " the spirit of privateering will draw the resentment of the enemy." Happily a cessation of hostilities was near at hand, and Peace, floating westward o'er the deep, soon followed, dropping palms and lilies on this nursling of the sea.

THOMAS JEFFERSON AND JAMES THOMSON CALLENDER.

Contributed by WORTHINGTON CHAUNCEY FORD, Esq., of Washington, D.C.

[Continued from page 333.]

Callender to Jefferson.

Richmond, August 10th, 1799

Sir

I hope you will excuse my freedom in writing this letter. You have no doubt seen our Examiner. It has by no means been conducted as I could exactly wish it to be, since I came down, for though Mr. Jones is a good writer and a good man, yet as he is not himself a printer, and is only beginning his office, matters do not go on with all the rapidity that one could sometimes wish. We are daily expecting new types, new paper and ink ; and I hope it will then cut a more brilliant figure.

I expected that Duane would copy from us more than he has done. I think some of our columns would have been more to the purpose than his endless trash about Arthur McConnor and Hindustan, of which I, for one, have never read a single line. He began to copy from us, and sickened I believe at hearing that the things were good. Thus the interest, or what I considered as the interest of the cause was betrayed from the meanest personal jealousy of me. I thank heaven that I feel none at him. I neither envy his abilities nor his situation. We have got 79 new subscribers since I came here; and I have no doubt that if I got anything like encouragement to stay at it, I would soon help Mr. Jones, who is himself really a good writer, to make the subscription much more numerous. We exceed 800. The Genius of liberty copies not a word for fear of advertising our paper. All this I look upon as pique and jealousy.

You will no doubt hear, by this post, of the disturbance in this town. Since I began to write the present letter some time has elapsed; and the matter has grown to a magnitude I had not thought of. While I am in danger of being murthered without doors, I do not find within them any very particular encouragement to proceed. I shall therefore probably cease from writing until Mr. [James] Lyon comes down. This will be soon. I shall then begin with him in the magazine, a work I like much better than newspapers, and he is also to publish my proposals for a volume, and undertake the mechanical part of that work. I have got very large offers of subscription, and I doubt not of having 1,000 copies bespoke. One gentleman has promised to take 100, at 1 dollar each, and to get his brother to take as many, I mean to be responsible for being able to sell them. I write in this paper merely for victuals, at least I have never heard of anything more, except having borrowed some trifles. This will never do.

I believe that by this time we have as many as an hundred and fifty new subscribers since I came here. Large recruits have been made in the country by the late hubble, which has made me a gazing stock to everybody. What you see of mine in future will probably be most of it in *Pleasant's paper.*

That no circumstance might be wanting to make me uneasy, I had a very blunt letter concerning one of my boys. I had sent up all the money of which I was master, and which I did believe to be fully sufficient to pay for him. I understood that more was expected, and I promised some time ago to send it; for I counted upon it that I would have been offered some, and that has not happened.

Now, as you are to be a subscriber to my next volume, and as it is the fashion on Virginia to pay such things in advance, my present suit is that whatever little matter of that sort may be designed, it would be particularly acceptable if your relation here were ordered to pay it to me in course of post. The conspiracy hindered the proposals from being printed some weeks ago; and the people say they are ready to pay in advance.

I learn from Mr. Lyon that he has got the utmost encouragement. He is to cast off 1500 of his second number. I think him an excellent young man. And I dare say that we shall do very agreeably together. Sir, excuse this long scrawl. I have the honor to be.

Jefferson to Callender.

Monticello, Sept. 6, '99.

Sir,—By a want of arrangement in a neighboring post-office during the absence of the postmaster, my letters and papers for two posts back were detained. I suppose it was owing to this that your letter tho' dated Aug. 10, did not get to my hand till the last day of the month, since which this is the first day I can through the post office acknowledge the receipt of it. Mr. [George] Jefferson happens to be here and directs his agent to call on you with this and pay you 50 dollars, on account of the book you are about to publish. When it shall be out be so good as to send me 2. or 3. copies, and the rest only when I shall ask for them.

The violence which was meditated against you lately has excited a very general indignation in this part of the country. Our state from it's first plantation has been remarkable for it's order and submission to the laws. But three instances are recollected in it's history of an organized opposition to the laws. The first was Bacon's Rebellion; the 2d. our revolution; the 3d. the Richmond association who, by their committee, have in the public papers avowed their purpose of taking out of the hands of the law the function of declaring who may or may not have free residence among us. But these gentlemen miscalculate the temper and force of this country extremely if they supposed there would have been a want of either to support the authority of the laws: and equally mistake their own interests in setting the example of club-law. Whether their self-organized election of a committee, and publication of their manifesto, be such overt acts as bring them within the pale of law; the law I presume is to decide: and there it is our duty to leave it. The delivery of Robbins to the British excites much feeling and enquiry here. With every wish for your welfare I am with great regard sir Your most obedient servt.

Callender to Jefferson.

Richmond, Sept. 26, 1799

Sir

Along with this letter you will receive another, which has lain by me a fortnight, the contents being so unimportant, (some printed papers) that I had a doubt of sending them at all.

In the Examiner which comes with this post, you will see a specimen of our troops here, and an abominable defence of all the worst measures of government. The latter piece was foisted in without my knowledge; I am very much ashamed at seeing it where it is; and then people pretend to call me the *Editor.*

Mr. Lyon has not yet returned. After selling all his magazines, and he could have sold 150 more, if he had had them; instead of coming home to print his second number, he set out for Vermont in order to fetch Mrs. Lyon here. "We once were young ourselves" says an old man, in a Scots pastoral, "as the only apology that could be made for the follies of youth. I cannot tell how much vexation his absence has caused his friends. I inclose 16 pages of the new matter, as a specimen of the Prospect.* I hope you will excuse this freedom. I had not an intermediate 8 pages between what I send. It is not yet worked off. People in the country are willing to accept of amusement that would be not worth having in town. I will send all I print by the first opportunities, to Charlottesville.

I am in hopes of probably getting as many of my own books bespoke. The Virginians promise with prodigious fluency. But I am in trembling hesitation about the execution of their promises. If I could dispose of as

---

* " The Prospect before us "—Callender's most scurrilous volume.

many copies of 3 successive volumes in the course of 18 months, I should save some money, and then come up James River, (which, by the healthy looks of the people who *come down*, I take to be one of the paradises of nature,) and try to find 50 acres of clear land, and a hearty Virginian female, that knows how to fatten pigs, and boil hommony, and hold her tongue; and then adieu to the rascally society of mankind for whom I feel an indifference which increases *per diem.* I had your letter, and its important contents.

Sir, there are two points on which, if convenient, I solicit your help. 1. What was the sum which Vergennes told you was necessary to make *a Turkish treaty?* You know you have the memorandum somewhere. 2. What was the mode adopted by the several states in chusing the electors at the last presidential election. I am master of the latter, except in 2 or 3 instances, but as it is very material, and I have not been able to obtain exact information, I could wish a few sentences upon the whole subject; under cover to Mr. George Jefferson, who could let me copy it off. Your attention, Sir, to these two points would be an important favor to sir your most obedient servant.

P. S. If there was ever anything at once the most perfectly distressing, and ridiculous, it is surely our present situation with France and England. The amicable assurances of Talleyrand are now like last year's almanack. We would not strike the iron when hot. O vanity, treachery, ignorance, & madness.

Jefferson to Callender.

Monticello, Oct. 6, '99.

Sir,—On receiving your favor of Sept. 29, I did believe it would be in my power to answer you satisfactorily on both the points on which you asked information: I knew indeed that I had not made any particular memorandum of the sum which the Ct. de Vergennes supposed a treaty with the porte would cost; but I expect that I had mentioned it either in my letter on the subject to Mr. Jay, or in that to Mr. Adams my colleague in the Barbary negociations. After a very long search yesterday I found both letters but in neither have I stated any particular sum. They are of May 1786, and only say generally that in a conversation with the Ct. de Vergennes on the subject, he said that a treaty with the porte would cost us a *great deal* of money, as great presents are expected at that court, and a great many claim them; and that we should not buy a peace one penny the cheaper at Algiers; that the Algerines did indeed acknowledge a certain dependence on the Porte, and availed themselves of it whenever anything was to be gained by it, but disregarded it when it subjected them to any demand: and that at Algiers there were but too (sic) agents, money and fear. This is the statement in those letters, and my memory does not enable me to fix any particular sum having been named by him; but only generally that it was very far beyond any thing then at our command.—All who were members of Congress in 1786, may be supposed to remember this information, and if it could be understood to come to you through some such channel, it would save the public from reading all the blackguardism which would be vented on me, were I quoted; not that this would weigh an atom with me on any occcasion where my avowal of either facts or opinions would be of public use; but whenever it will not, I then think it useful to keep myself out of the way of calumny.

On the other point I can be more certain. Georgia, N. Carolina, Tennessee, Kentucky, Virginia, Maryland and Pennsylvania choose their electors by the people directly. In Massachusetts the choice is, first by the people in districts: But if a candidate had not a majority of all the qualified voters of the district; it devolves on the legislature to appoint the elector for that district, besides as they have but 14. districts (laid off for some state purpose) and are entitled to 16. electors, the legislature name the two extra ones in the first instance. Again, if any of those elected either by the people or legislature die, or decline to act, the residue of the electors fill up the vacancies themselves. In this way the people of Massachus. chose 7. electors on the last occasion, and the legislature 9. In New Hamp. Rho. Isld. Connec. Vermont, New-York, Jersey, Delaware and South Carolina, the legislature name electors. My information is good as to all these particulars except N. Hampshire and Connecticut: and as to them I think I am right; but speaking only from memory it should be further ascertained before asserted. I thank you for the proof sheets you inclosed me. Such papers cannot fail to produce the best effect. They inform the thinking part of the nation; and these again supported by the tax-gatherers as their vouchers, set the people to rights. You will know from whom this comes without a signature; the omission of which has rendered almost habitual with me by the curiosity of the post offices. Indeed a period is now approaching during which I shall discontinue writing letters as much as possible, knowing that every snare will be used to get hold of what may be perverted in the eyes of the public.

Callender to Jefferson.

Richmond, Oct. 7th, 1799

Sir

   With reference to mine of last week, I now with submission, inclose 8 additional pages. I had 8 intermediate ones laid by for you, but they have been somehow picked up, and it is too late at night to get others. Mr. Lyon has at last come, and the magazine will be sent out in two days. Hoping your pardon for this freedom, I am sir, &c.

Callender to Jefferson.

Richmond, Nov. 16, 1799

Sir:

   I gave Mr. Jefferson, some days ago, from p. 9 to p 48 inclusive of the Prospect, to be sent to you. Having the opportunity of a private hand, I now send forward 16 additional pages. There is much bad print in it.

   I inclose the copy of a plan which has occurred here to Mr. James Lyon,* and which if conducted with taste and perseverence, bids fairer than any other which I have yet seen, to shed the necessary rays of light over our political atmosphere at a trifling expense.

                              I am Sir &c.

Callender to Jefferson.

Richmond, Decr. 18th, 1799

Sir

   I understood by Colonel Quarrier that you were on Sunday to set out for philadelphia.

---

* Probably the " Scourge of Aristocracy " noticed later.

I therefore venture to inclose the yesterday's Examiner, lest it should be sent on to Monticello, as it contains some articles of mine, that I wish you to see.

On Friday I shall take the freedom of sending to you 50 or 60 additional pages of the Prospect.

Sir, I hope that you will pardon this freedom, (I do not edit the Examiner at all, though I sometimes write in it.) From, sir, your very obliged and humble servant.

Callender to Jefferson.

Richmond, Feb. 15, 1800.

Sir

I did not until this day, know that your Examiner has not been forwarded to Philadelphia. It shall be done in future. The Prospect goes off very well to many parts of the country. About 500 are sent off and many more bespoke, but not yet sent. A parcel will come to Philadelphia, as soon as the river opens. Chancellor Wythe is the law officer referred to in the inclosed, as speaking of the prospect. Colonel Quarrier went to fight a duel with Major William Preston at Manchester, and let his pistol go off through his own foot; so the duel ended for that time. I have begun extending a clean copy of vol. 2d of the prospect, for the Staunton *Scourge of Aristocracy,* set up by Lyon; as all depends on haste, and the momentous month of October. It will be there first printed in separate pieces, or at least a part of it. They wanted to burn the office of the Scourge. vid next Examiner. I am, Sir, &c.

P.S. Some weeks ago, Mr. George Jefferson sent you a complete copy of the Prospect per post.

Callender to Jefferson.

Richmond, March 10, 1800.

Sir

I now inclose for you a number of the Republican, along with the last number of the Examiner, containing a copy of the letter from you. Some *errata!*

The second part of *the prospect* will be continued in the *Republican,* and reprinted at Staunton, and all, or part of it, in the national magazine.

I had once entertained the romantic hope of being able to overtake the Federal Government in its career of iniquity; but I am now satisfied that they can *act* much faster than I can *write* after them.

I will send you the continuation of the second part of the Prospect, and I am sir &c.

P.S. Every engine has been set at work to do me all kinds of mischief since I came here; the satisfaction of knowing that they are exceedingly provoked is to me a partial compensation for the inconvenience of being belied and stared at, as if I was a Rhinoceros. They are chop fallen, and many turn round that were very bitter against me at first. Will you have the goodness to let General Mason know that I send him two franks by this post?

Callender to Jefferson.

Richmond, March 14, 1800.

Sir.

I hope you will excuse the freedom I took last week of sending you some Examiners, and a number of the *Republican.* I now inclose a continuation. *Some errata!* This is to be printed again in *Staunton*, and perhaps in the *national magazine* and the *friend of the people*, which will soon go on again, having been only interrupted by that idle thing *the press.* And so I am firing through five port holes, at once, which is enough for one hand; besides what is reprinted from me in Connecticut, &c. They cannot blame me, if the most enlightened people in the world are as ignorant as dirt.

The Examiner augments in circulation, and the Prospect is already more than half sold. We are in a small canvass here about who is to be Attorney General. If merit has anything to say George Hay will get it. Of the other candidates, one is only not a boy, the second is incessantly drunk; the third is a Tory of the dirtiest kind, and the 4th is G. K. Taylor. I understand that some of the above named candidates have given up.

I wish the inclosed to be forwarded, (as I cannot get a spare one) to Mr. Leiper, because he has understood I am *idle.* I am sir &c.

Callender to Jefferson.

Richmond, April 21, 1800.

Sir

I inclose two newspapers. I mean to go to Petersburg in 8 or 10 days to begin printing Part 2d of Prospect.

We shall have a long article in the Republican on Thursday next. I hope you will excuse this freedom, and I am, sir &c.

P.S. I thought it but justice to send Mr. Adams, under a blank cover, a copy of my address to the public.

Callender to Duane.

Richmond, April 27, 1800.

Dear Sir,

Since my last, the elections for next assembly have begun, and the people are almost every where turning out the tories. Mecklenburg, which sent two of the *dust and ashes* kidney, has replaced them by two republicans. Tho's Griffin, of York, a gentleman of great influence, has in the same manner, obtained leave of absence. Rich'd Bland Lee, ditto. In short, the next assembly will undoubtedly be more democratical than the last one; and we shall, as formerly, do just what we please. This State is understood to contain more than a million of people, including above an hundred thousand white families. When despotism advances her profane footsteps towards the verge of Virginia, she will do well to remember, like the Jewish shepherd, that T h i s g r o u n d i s h o l y ; for, as I lately remarked in an address to the public, we are too numerous to be bullied, and too intelligent to be cheated. Nothwithstanding, therefore, a few Scots pedlers, and place-hunting grumblers, an immense majority of citizens will be arranged around the banners of constitutional freedom. This division of the American empire forms the foundation stone of the southern

states; and, like the thunder of Omnipotence, the voice of u n i t e d a n d
i n d i g n a n t V i r g i n i a will be heard with awe from one end of the
continent to the other. John Marshall used sometimes to brag that he
would one day be chosen Vice President. Believe me, sir, that at this day
he could not keep his seat in the event of a new election for Congress.
The last election cost him five or six thousand dollars for barbacues ; and
this was the man who complained of French bribery! Was there ever
such another farce?

The states south of the Potowmac choose fifty-two electors for President;
and I am satisfied that Jefferson will have at least fifty of them. These,
with five in Maryland, and your fifteen in Pennsylvania, will make seventy,
and carry off a majority of the whole votes, even upon the supposition that
Newyork and Jersey were unanimous against us. But farther, we count
upon a majority both in Newyork and Jersey; and if these states should
not vote at all, even then our victory will be still certain and complete. At
the last election, North Carolina gave Jefferson eleven votes, and Adams
one. The gentleman who gave that odd vote has pledged himself, if chosen
again, as he expects to be, that he will vote for Jefferson. This is an absolute and important fact; I give it from the highest and best authority.
The six per cent. people built much upon their intrigues in N. Carolina;
but I can assure you that the clouds of aristocracy have been rapidly dis-
sipated; and the decisive example of Virginia will be as powerful to the
southward as that of your great state will be to the eastward; I mean in
Newyork and Jersey.

Print the above, that it may fly as far as the four winds can carry it ; and
fan the flame of patriotism that glows in every republican breast. *Let us,
by one grand effort, snatch our country from that bottomless vortex of corruption and perdition which yawn before us.* The more violence, the more
prosecutions from the treaty, so much the better. Those of yourself and
Cooper will be of service. You know the old ecclesiastical observation,
that *the blood of the martyrs was the seed of the church.*

J. T. C.

P.S.—I had almost forgot your grand committee of t h i r t e e n, who
are to choose the next President. Various pieces, exposing this trade of
usurpation, have appeared in the Examiner; and yet, although we have
two federal newspapers in Richmond, and abundance of government writers, *such as they are,* no answer has hitherto come out. Indeed, I believe
there is only one serious opinion upon the subject, to wit: that the Grand
Seignior has an equal title to send thirteen of his Janizaries to investigate
the nomination. If the law passes, I am satisfied that our assembly, whenever they sit down, will give notice to Congress that Virginia cannot submit
to degrade herself by crouching under this imposture. We are all confident
here that Pennsylvania will not endure to be trampled upon by such an
atrocious usurpation.

Callender to Jefferson.

Richmond, April 28th, 1800

Sir

Inclosed I send a list of the new elections for the assembly, so far
as they have come to hand. Mr. Jones assures me that not less than twenty
of the Aristocracy have been turned out in this list. It is but moderate to
guess at least twenty more will be dismissed, so that in the whole they will

be reduced to 40 less, and the Republicans will be augmented by an equal number. This amounts almost to the annihilation of their power; 140—20, or so.

If General Mason has not left the city, you will perhaps do him a pleasure by saying that I have just now seen R. Williams here in good health. I am, sir.*

Callender's Trial, June, 1800.

[From the "Virginia Gazette."]

The Trial of J a m e s T h o m p s o n C a l l e n d e r, for sedition, took place the 6th instant, in the Circuit Court of the U. States. This being the first instance of this kind in this state, it excited great curiosity. The room was thronged with spectators from every quarter. The trial was opened at 10 o'clock, and continued till 6, when the jury retired; and, after some deliberation, bro't in a verdict of GUILTY.

The succeeding day, at 10 o'clock, the traverser appeared at the bar to receive his sentence. Judge C H A S E, after making some observations upon the dangerous consequences that must result from a disobedience to the laws, and recommending most seriously the constitutional mode of redress whereby a law might be deemed a grievance, addressed himself to the prisoner, to inform him of the determination of the Court; which was, that he be fined in the sum of 200 dollars, imprisoned nine months, and to be bound over, in the penalty of 1200 dollars, during the term of two years, for his good behaviour, himself in the sum of 600 dollars, and two securities for 300 each.

We hope and trust that this prosecution may have the desired effect, in deterring others from any attempts to violate the laws of our country—under which banners rests all that is dear to us.

Judge Chase, when about to pass sentence on Mr. Callender, observed that his offence against the laws was great, and that it was aggravated by its having been wilfully committed. He told Mr. Callender that he seemed to be a man of some information, and by no means destitute of good understanding; that, with these, he must have known that Mr. Adams was far from deserving the character which he had given him; that it was a fact generally known, and of which Mr. Callender could not plead ignorance, that the American people had repeatedly confided their most important concerns and dearest interests to Mr. Adams: that he was one of the principal characters in the revolution, and had acted a most conspicuous part in carrying it on: that Congress knew his virtue, abilities and patriotism, after having successfully employed him in other very important business, appointed him as a minister, in conjunction with two others, to make the treaty which terminated the war and established our independence; and that the best parts of that treaty of peace were to be ascribed to Mr. Adams, whose conduct was so greatly misrepresented, and to Mr. Jay whose character in this part of the Union has been so shamefully vilified—

---

* "The G[rand] Jury of which McClurg was foreman presented Callender under the sedition law, and Chase drew the warrant and despatched the marshall instantly in search of him. This was yesterday at 12, since which we have not heard of either. If taken, I hope the people will behave with dignity on the occasion and give no pretext for comments to their discredit. If I could suppose the contrary I would take proper steps to aid in bringing him forth; I mean to prevent any popular meeting to the contrary. Will it be proper for the Executive to employ counsel to defend him, and supporting the law, give an éclat to a vindication of the principles of the State?" *Governor Monroe to Jefferson*, Sunday, 25 May, 1800.

that these were facts which he would mention, because he supposed they were not generally known in Virginia: that Congress highly approved of the conduct of Mr. Adams in that negotiation: that the people of America, having increased confidence in him, elected him Vice President when the present constitution was adopted, and re-elected him thereto; and at last chose him to the eminent station he now occupies. He asked if it was possible for any rational mind to believe such a man guilty of the atrocious crimes laid to his charge by the traverser? To believe such an accusation was, he said, an attack upon the people themselves; for that it was self evident that an intelligent stranger, who could read these severe charges and believe them, must unavoidably think that the people who had elected to so dignified a station so abandoned and infamous a character, must be depraved and wicked themselves; that no people could be virtuous who are capable of promoting so base and profligate a person—But, that the truth was, that Mr. Adams had been long deserving well of his country: that in various important situations he had been thirty years in its service which never would have been the case if the abandoned character ascribed to him by Mr. Callender had been merited. That Callender could not have been personally acquainted with him, and that, as he had ample means of information, he must have defamed him wilfully.

Judge Chase then drew the true distinction between the licentiousness and the liberty of the press; and expatiated largely on the utility of the latter: it was true that despotism could not exist where the liberty of the press was enjoyed—that there was a very great difference between the liberty and abuse or licentiousness of the press; that the licentiousness of the press would most certainly destroy any government, and particularly a a republican form of government—that it would corrupt the public opinion, and destroy the morals of the people; and that on public opinion and the principles of morality and virtue, a republican government was founded— that undoubtedly the liberty of the press might be enjoyed in the fullest extent, to every rational and valuable purpose, without its licentiousness: If calumny, defamation and falsehood were to be indiscriminately tolerated and encouraged, it would reduce virtue to the level of vice, and no man, however upright in his conduct, could be secure from slander—there would be no encouragement to integrity: that the liberty of the press consisted in the unrestrained but fair discussion of principles and conduct, and would never be said to consist in securing impunity to wilful and malicious slanderers. It was to be lamented, that this doctrine was not sufficiently understood by printers—that some of the best of them seemed to mistake the licentiousness for the liberty of the press. That Callender, avowedly for an electioneering purpose had ascribed to Mr. Adams a worse character than the worst minister of the worst of tyrants had—that he represented him in blacker colors than Sejanus himself. He then reminded him that as a foreigner he found an asylum in this country—that he had been treated with hospitality and kindness, and ought not in return to have defamed some of the best characters in the country, and sow dissensions, discontent and discord among the people: that his conduct would be much more severely punished in any other civilized country than this: that the sentence which the court was about to pronounce would shew the moderation of the government, and how much more mild and temperate in principles, than those of other governments. He recommended to the traverser to pursue a different course of conduct for the future, and told him that the government of the United States did not wish to punish or oppress, but to enforce obedience to just laws, made by the representatives, chosen by the people themselves —that there were but two ways of remedying the evils of bad laws, to petition those who made them to repeal them, or to remove those representatives, and choose better men in their stead—that bad Senators, members of the House of Representatives or a corrupt Judge, could be constitutionally removed. He lamented that there was a propensity in the human mind to approve of defamation. Many high characters would permit the circulation of the vilest slander, without contradiction—they would not command or direct the propagation of the slander, but they would listen to it without contradicting it. Men might have their motives for such conduct, but it was improper.

Callender to Jefferson.

Richmond Jail, August 14th, 1800

Sir

This letter will inclose a few pages of the second part of the Prospect. They contain nothing but what I fancy that you have seen already, as I sent you regularly the Petersburg paper, wherein they were printed. But next week, I shall send some sheets, that you have not seen before. A half volume will be ready, price half a dollar, in about a fortnight. I have by me as much manuscript as would fill two volumes, and materials, for twice as much more, so that, like the ass between the two bundles of hay, I am at a loss where to begin, or stop. I have been in very bad health, owing to the stink of this place, but I have got some better.

Mr. Rose, my worthy landlord, desires you to accept of his compliments. I have the honor to be Sir, &c.

Callender to Jefferson.

Richmond Jail, Sept. 8th, 1800

Sir

I had expected to have the honour this day of inclosing for your perusal 24 additional pages; but upon looking among my papers, I find only 8; and cannot get any more before the post goes off. The farther that I go the more am I lost in amazement at the precipitation and absurdity which marked the acceptance of the federal constitution. I had more manuscript before I came here, than would fill a large volume, but as my amusement I continue to write, and wonder at what I have written; such a mass of deformity!

I have warned my readers that the present band did more mischief in 6 weeks than can be repaired in 4 years; and that they must not blame the next administration for the continuance of the assessed tax. " Like the incendiary of the temple of Ephesus, Mr. ——— has taken full care that he shall be remembered by posterity."

One of my printers has fallen sick, which greatly retards the publication. If I ever live to see better days, I shall set up a printing office of my own here. The expense will be great; but you may be [   ] one half the certainty of getting the work done will be the greatest thing of all. I wish to dedicate the remainder of my life to the Federal faction.

I hope you will excuse this long letter, I am Sir, &c.

Callender to Jefferson.

Richmond Jail, Sept. 13, 1800

Sir

Nothing is talked of here but the recent conspiracy of the negroes. One Thomas Prosser, a young man, who had fallen heir, some time ago, to a plantation within six miles of the city, had behaved with great barbarity to his slaves. One of them named Gabriel, a fellow of courage and intellect above his rank in life, laid a plan of revenge. Immense numbers immediately entered into it, and it has been kept with incredible secrecy for several months. A number of swords were made in a clumsy enough manner out of rough iron; others by breaking the blade of a scythe in the middle which thus made two swords of a most formidable kind. They were well fastened in proper handles, and would have cut off a man's limb at a single blow. The conspirators were to have met in a wood near Prosser's house, upon Saturday before last, after it was dark. Upon that day, or some very short time before it, notice was received from a fellow, who being invited, somewhat unguardedly to go to the rendez-vous, refused, and immediately informed his master's overseer. No ostensible preparations were, however, made until the afternoon preceding the night of the rendez-vous. And as the militia are in a state of the most contemptible disorganization, as the blacks are numerous, robust and desperate, there must have been bloody work. But upon that very evening, just about sunset, there came on the most terrible thunderstorm, accompanied with an enormous rain, that I ever witnessed in this state. Between Prosser's and Richmond, there is a place called Brock Swamp, which runs across the high road, and over which there was a bridge. By this, the africans were of necessity to pass, and the rain had made the passage impracticable. Besides, they were deprived of the junction and assistance of their good friends in this city, who could not go out to join them. They were to have attacked the Capitol and the penitentiary. they could hardly have failed of success; for after all we only could muster four or five hundred men, of whom not more than thirty had muskets. This was our style of preparation, while several thousands stands of arms were piled up in the Capitol and Penitentiary. I do not pretend to blame the executive Council, for I really am not sufficiently master of the circumstances to form an opinion. Five fellows were hung this day; and many more men will share the same fate. The plan was to massacre all the whites, of all ages and sexes; and all the blacks who would not join them; and then march off to the mountains, with the plunder of the City. Those wives who should refuse to accompany their husbands were to have been butchered along with the rest, an idea truly worthy of an african heart. It consists with my knowledge that many of these wretches, who were, or would have been partners to the plot, had been treated with the utmost tenderness by their owners, and more like children than slaves.

I hope, Sir, that you will excuse me for the freedom of sending you the above details. I have been, for some days past, incommoded with so great a dimness of my sight, that I was obliged to employ an assistant in writing the last page. A great part of the above details I had from your old acquaintance and Protege, Mr. Rose. To a man of liberal feelings, there are few situations that can be more painful than his; and I heartily wish that it were in my power to smooth the protuberances of his descent along the down hill of life.

The news from Italy, from France, and from New Hampshire, is all capital. I learn also by more ways than one (what you undoubtedly know much better than I do) that there has been a very great revolution in the sentiments of Connecticut. I can hardly go on for the bellowing of the banditti down stairs, who were not carried directly, as they should have been, from the bar to the gallows.

I find much difficulty in getting the Prospect printed, from the sickness of one hand, the laxness of another, and the difficulty of getting a third. If I live to see a republican president in the chair, I shall have a press of my own in Richmond; and give the aristocrats a cut and thrust volume per annum for some years to come. This may be of use; for it is not only proper to knock an adversary down, but to *keep* him down; the best government will afford an ample verge for damnatory criticism; and the federal viper will undoubtedly continue to hiss; but I make no doubt of living to trample him in the mire of universal detestation.

I hope, Sir, that you will pardon the tediousness of this letter. The naval Remarks, of which I sent you a copy last summer, will not get into the first part of this volume. I have the honor to be sir, &c.

P. S.   By naval Remarks, I mean the essays that were printed in the Republican, and which I sent you. The boy has not come this evening to take my letter to the Post office, so it stands till next week.

(On a separate sheet.)

The tryal of the conspirators is going on. Fifteen have been hanged. Three others were in the cart, and had got about half way to the gallows, when they were intercepted by an order from the executive council. this was in consequence of a petition that had been presented a few minutes before, by some ladies of Richmond who lived not far distant from the place of execution. perhaps you will suppose that the prayer of their petition was to save the lives of these wretches, but it was only that they might be hung *in some other place* because the exhibition was offensive. I do not design to make the slightest insinuation at the expense of female sensibility, for the application for mercy would have been very ill-timed, and I trust it would have been refused. These men have not yet been hung. Several others are since condemned, and it is expected that there will be a general clearance upon the third of next month. Much blame has been cast, but I can not say with what justice, and it is probable with very little, upon the baptists, for having put impracticable notions of liberty into the heads of these fellows. But this I can say with certainty that one of the baptist ministers who chanced to be upon the bench, acted in a very unaccountable manner. The circumstances are worth relating. You must observe that, by a very humane Law, no negroe can be condemned in Virginia to capital punishment unless the judges are unanimous in their opinion. This gives the prisoner the greatest possible chance of safety. A baptist minister acted as one of the five judges, in the case of the negro GEORGE, who was himself a *baptist preacher*, and the property of a Billy Burton. It was proved, by such evidence as had been thought sufficient for the execution of other blacks, that this minister of the Gospel of *peace* made the following declaration, to wit: That he would wade up to his hands and his knees in the blood of the white people rather than desist from the completion of his purpose. There could not be a stronger proof of guilt than such an expression. The four other judges voted for hanging him. But his neck was saved by the negative of the fifth one. This fact, every syllable of which is incontestably true, was stated in civil, but in plain terms, in the Examiner.

A prodigious racket was raised against the Editor, as if he had designed to insult the whole sect of Baptists. Thus you see that illiberal superstition and the most rancourous prejudice, are not excluded from this state. On the tryal a very curious circumstance occurred. It had been sworn that GEORGE, the prisoner, was at a meeting of the conspirators upon a certain day. His master, Burton, swore that, upon that day and at the hour specified the man was in his service. This proof of an *alibi* was said to be the cause of his acquittal. Burton soon after the tryal was over began to recollect himself, and acknowledged that his *alibi* was founded upon a mistake. Reports have been circulated that in King William, in Gloucester, and in some other counties, numbers of negroes have refused to work, but I believe that the story has been without foundation.

Callender to Jefferson.

Richmond Jail, Sept. 29, 1800

Sir
  I have not been able to get any more of the Prospect; but next week I shall be able to send either the whole, or nearly so. I beg leave to inclose the copy of a letter to Mr. Duane on the negro business. It contains some trifles, which may amuse. Governor Monroe has, last night, lost his only son. It has come out that the fire in Richmond, within these two years was the work of negroes. I have the honor to be, &c.

[To be continued.]

RECORDS OF NEW CASTLE, N. H.

Communicated by Hon. Ezra S. Stearns, A.M., of Concord, N. H.

THE first book of records of the ancient town of New Castle, New Hampshire, is worn by usage and dilapidated by age. The book should be copied before continued waste effaces the margins of the decaying leaves. The volume of 174 pages contains the records of the town meetings from 1693 to 1726. In the first 90 pages the records originally were transcribed on every other page. Subsequently the blank pages were partly filled from time to time by records of highways, miscellaneous entries and family registers. The following is an exact transcript of all the records of births, marriages and deaths found in the first volume of the records of New Castle :

Sam^{ll} Brackett and Lydea his wife were maried Jany 23^d 1713.
Jno Brackett Born Feby 8th 1714.
Mary Brackett Born May 27th 1716.
Pheeby Brackett Born Decemb^r 7th 1718.
Sam^{ll} Brackett ye son of Sam^{ll} Brackett and Lidia his wife born 13th Novem^r 1721.
Ann Brackett ye daughter of Samuel & Lydia Brackett Born Jany 31 1725.

Love Brackett the Daughter of Sam^ll Brackett & Lydia Brackett his wife was born in the town of New Castle the eighteenth day of Aprill 1727
Francis Crunch was Born May 2^d 1715.
Mark Fernald and Mary Simpson were married to each other by the Revd Mr Stephen Chase on the 3^d day of May 1752.
Gilbert Fernald the son of Mark Fernald and Mary his wife was born on ye 27th day of June 1753.
Jno. Frost and Mary Pepperrell both of Kettery Maryed Septemb^r 4th 1702 by Joseph Hammond Esq.
Margery Frost Born on Munday feb^r the first Day 1703 / 4.
Margery Frost Dyed at Boston Septemb^r 9th 1704 it being Saturday 9 o'clock Evening.
William Frost Born Aug: 20th 1705 on Tuseday at 2 o Clock in ye morning.
Jno. Frost Born May ye 12th 1709 on Thurdsday 9 o Clock in ye morning.
Charles Frost Born ye 27th 1710 on Sabath Day 9 o Clock at night.
[By a subsequent entry August is interlined to supply the missing month.]
Mary Frost Born Aug: 19th 1711 being Sabath Day at 2 o Clock in ye morning.
Sarah Frost Born Wednesday July 1st 1713, at 5 o Clock in ye morning.
Mary Frost Dyed June 12th 1714 being Saturday 42 mint's past 2 in ye morning.
Mary Frost Born Saturday ye 26th Day of february at 9 o Clock in ye morning. Anno 1714 / 5.
And^r Pepperrell ffrost born Thursday ye 12th Aprill 1716 at 6½ o Clock in ye Evening.
Mary ffrost ye 2nd Dyed fryday ye 15th day March 1716 / 7 at three o Clock in ye afternoon.
Joseph ffrost born Sept. 29: 1717 at 40 ^m past one o Clock the day being Sunday.
Abagaill ffrost born May 26: 1719 being Tuesday 20 minutes after 4 o Clock at night.
Daniel Greenough & Abigail Elliott were Marryed Decemb^r 16th 1708.
Sarah Greenough was Born June 31st 1710.
Robert Greenough was Born Sept 1st 1712.
Daniel Greenough was Born Aug: 13th 1714.
Abigail Greenough wife of Dan^ll Greenough Dyed ye 5th of June 1719.
Nathanael Greenough Son of Dan^ll & Abigail Greenough was born at New Castle 11th Day of Feby 1718 / 9.
Dan^ll Greenough & Eliz Hatch were maryed 25th Jany 1721.
Symonds Greenough, son of Dan^ll and Elizabeth Greenough was Born att New Castle ye ninth Day of Novem^r 1722.
William Greenough son of Dan^ll and Elizabeth Greenough was Born at New Castle ye 2^d Day of May 1724.
John Greenough Son of Dan^ll & Elizabeth Greenough was born at New Castle the 17th Day of March 1726.
Margerett Hickson was Born 8th May 1714.
Tobias Leer son of Tobias & Hannah Leer was born March 29th 1706.
Nathan^ll Leer was born July 25th, 1712.
Tobias Leer was married to his wife Elizabeth Aprill 14, 1714.

Elizabeth Leer was Born May y[e] 10th 1716.
Mary Leer was Born Novem[br] 24th 1717.
Walker Leer was Born Aug 25th 1719.

William Mardon, the son of W[m] & Dorcas Mardon was borne at New Castle the 14th day of June 1705.

Sam[ll] Mardon, the son of W[m] & Dorcas Mardon was borne at New Castle the 15th day of June 1707.

Jonathan Mardon y[e] son of W[m] & Dorcas Mardon was borne in this Town y[e] 7th day of Septemb[r] 1709.

Mary Mardon ye Daughter of W[m] and Dorcas Mardon was borne in this town y[e] 22[d] day of Aprill 1712.

Dorcas Mardon ye Daughter of W[m] and Dorcas Mardon was borne in this town ye 15th day of february 1714.

Jno. Marshall Was Born June 14th 1697.
Hawly Marshall was Born Ap: 13 1699.
Henry Marshall Was Born Novemr 14 1701.
Joseph Marshall was Born Aug 3[d] 1703.
Mary Marshall was Born Novem[r] 17th 1705.
Joanna Marshall was Born Sept. 6th 1708.
Martha Marshall was Born Sep[t] 12, 1712.

Ann Muttleberry the Daughter of Enoch Muttleberry & Mary his wife was born at New Castle, this town, the fifth day of Septemb[r] Anno Dom[i] 1726.

Benjamin Parker & Eliz[a] Gilman were married in this town by the Reuerend Mr. Sam[ll] Moody Decemb[r] the seventh 1702.

Thomas Parker the son of Benj[a] Parker & Eliz[a] his Wife was born at N. Castle Sep[t] ye Twenty fifth, 25, 1703.

Eliz[a] Parker the Daughter of Benj[a] Parker & Eliz[a] his Wife Was born at N Castle September ye twenty fourth 1709.

Benj[a] Parker the son of Benj[a] Parker & Eliz[a] his Wife was born at N. Castle the Twenty ninth day of July An[o] 1713.

Hannah Parker the Daughter of Benj[a] Parker & Eliz[a] his Wife was born at N Castle the Thirteenth day of August An[o] 1718.

Eliz[a] Parker the wife of Benj[a] Parker Dyed at New Castle the fifth day May An[o] 1721. Buried behind the Church at N Castle ye 7th day following.

Thomas Parker and Anna Jenness was married Decemb[r] the 12th 1734.

Benj[a] Parker, the son of Thomas Parker and Anna his wife was born Aprill 10th 1736.

Thomas Parker the son of Thomas Parker and Anna his wife was born March 10 1737/8.

Eliz[th] Parker the Daughter of Thomas Parker and Anna his wife was born Feby 10th 1739/40.

William Parker the son of Thomas Parker and Ann his wife was born June 12 1743.

Christian Perry was Born Aug. 3[d] 1690.
Rich[d] Perry was Born Feb. 18th 1695.

Sampson Sheafe, the son of Sampson Sheafe & Mehetabel his wife and Sarah Walton the Daughter of Shadrack Walton & Mary his wife, were married by the Rev. Mr. Jn[o] Emerson the 27th of November Anno one thousand seven hundred and eleven. 1711.

Jacob Sheafe, the son of Sampson Sheafe & Sarah his wife was born at N Castle ye first day of Octob^r 1712.   Died ye 19th day of May following Buried ye 21st following.

Sampson Sheafe, the son of Sampson Sheafe & Sarah his wife, was born at N. Castle ye third day of Decemb^r An° 1713.

Jacob Sheafe, the son of Sampson Sheafe and Sarah his wife was born at New Castle the twenty first day of Octob^r Ano 1715.

Matthew Sheafe, the son of Sampson Sheafe and Sarah his wife Was born at New Castle the eighth day of October anno 1717.

Mary Sheafe the daughter of Sampson Sheafe and Sarah his wife was born at New Castle the Eighteenth day of Aprill An° 1720.

Sam^ll Sheafe, the son of Sampson Sheafe and Sarah his wife was born at N. Castle the twenty fifth day of June An° 1722.

Henry Sheafe, the son of Sampson Sheafe and Sarah his wife was born at New Castle the twenty third day of May An° 1724.

Sarah Sheafe the Daughter of Sampson Sheafe & Sarah his wife was born at New Castle the fifth day of Jany Anno 1726.

Mehetabel Sheafe the Daughter of Sampson Sheafe & Sarah his wife was born at New Castle Tuesday ab^t nine of ye Clock—Evening, the twelfth day of Aug^st 1729.

Elisabeth Sheafe, the daughter of Sampson Sheafe and Sarah his wife, was born at New Castle in New Hampshire in New England abovesaid Wednesday the third day of December Anno Domini One thousand seven hundred and thirty five, December 3 1735.

John Simpson married to Sarah Sheafe Sept. ye 4th 1748 by the Revd Mr Samuel Parsons minister of Rhy.

Mehetable Sheafe the daughter of John Simpson & Sarah his wife born the 23^d day of July 1751 being Tuesday.

Joseph Simpson & Hanah Lewis the Daughter of John Lewis were married by the Rev. Mr Sam^ll Moody on May the 11th 1702.

Hanah Simpson the Wife of Joseph Simpson Dyed the 26th of June 1712.

Joseph Simpson & Miriam Easman were married March the 17th Day 1713.   .

Joseph Simpson the son of Joseph Simpson and Miriam Simpson his Wife was Born in the town of New Castle the Sixteenth Day of January 1714 / 15.

Abagail Simpson the Daughter of Joseph & Miriam Simpson was Born October the fourteenth 1716.

John Simpson the son of Joseph and Miriam Simpson his Wife was Born the fourteenth of ffebruary 1722 / 3.

Mary Simpson the Daughter of Joseph & Miriam Simpson was Born Aug^st the Nineteenth Day 1724.

Mary Simpson the daughter of Joseph & Miriam Simpson Dyed the twelfth Day of September 1724.

Theodore Simpson, the son of Joseph and Miriam Simpson was Born ffebuary the fourteenth 1726 / 7.

Miriam Simpson the daughter of Joseph & Miriam Simpson was Born the twenty ninth day of March 1728.

Mary Simpson the daughter of Joseph Simpson & Miriam his wife was Born at New Castle Sept ye 7th 1732.

Benjn Slade & Mary Perry was Married in this town by the Rev^d M^r. John Blunt January ye 8th 1736.

Nath[ll] Sargent and Ruth Jukson ware married the 24 Day of Feby 1736 ∕ 7.

Edward Sargent, the son of Nath[ll] Sargent & Ruth his wife was Born y[e] 15th Day of Decemb[r] 1737.

Joseph Sargent the son of Nath[ll] Sargent & Ruth his wife was Born the 3d Day of Decemb[r] 1739.

Nath[ll] Sargent the son of Nath[ll] Sargent and Ruth his Wife was Born April 29 1741.

Benjamin Underwood & Abigail Simpson ware married by the Rev. Mr. John Blunt Decem[r] the fifth 1737.

Temprance Underwood the daughter of Benj[a] Underwood and Abigail his wife was born Septem[r] 21th 1738.

Benj[a] Underwood the son of Benj[a] Underwood and Abagail his wife was Born February 27 1740 ∕ 1.

Joseph Underwood, the son of Benja Underwood and Abigail his wife was Born April 6th 1743.

Joseph Underwood died April 20 1745.

John Watkins married to M[rs] Dorothy Pepperrell Thursday March 26th 1719 about 12 o Clock forenoon.

John Watkins son of John Watkins & Dorothy his wife born Jan[y] 19th 1719 ∕ 20 about 9 o Clock in y[e] Morning being Tuesday.

Will[m] Watkins son of John Watkins and Dorothy his wife born June 4th 1721 Sunday about 4 o Clock afternoon.

And[w] Watkins son of John Watkins and Dorothy his wife born Wednesday June 13th 1722 about 11 o Clock at night.

Josiah Webster & Elizabeth Leer ware married in this town by the Rev[d] M[r]. John Blunt July ye 11th 1734.

Sarah Webster the Daughter of Josiah & Elizabeth Webster was born Aug[t] ye 6th 1735.

Sarah Webster the Daughter of Josiah & Elizabeth Webster Dyed Aug[t] 15th 1735.

Elizabeth Webster the wife of Josiah Webster Dyed Aug[t] 17th 1735.

Solomon White of New Castle and Mary Lock of Rye were married to each the other on y[e] 25th day of June 1745.

Joseph White the son of Solomon and Mary White was born the 11th of July 1746.

Nathan White the son of Solomon and Mary White was born on the 16th day of Aug[st] 1749.

DOROTHY MAY AND HER RELATIONS.

Communicated by Capt. CHARLES HERVEY TOWNSHEND, of "Raynham," New Haven, Conn.

RICHARD CLOPTON, of the knightly family of Clopton of Melford and Groton, County Suffolk, England (the latter manor and patronage of the church for some years previous to the settlement of New England was in Governor Winthrop's family), had, with other issue, a son and heir William Clopton (of whom hereafter) of Groton, and daughter Frances Clopton, married to Martyn Bowes, second son of Sir Martyn Bowes, knight, goldsmith, Lord Mayor of London, son and heir of Thomas Bowes, "an inhabitant of Ye City of York." This Martyn Bowes, son of the Lord Mayor, 1645, had a daughter Cordelia, who married John May of Shouldham Abbey, County Norfolk, who was son of John Mey or May, Bishop of Carslile.*

In the Harleian Manuscripts, B. M., Visitations of Essex, 1634, 1083, fol. 4, I find this note : "This John Mey or May was Doctor of Divinity and Master of Catherine's Hall, Cambridge, and was consecrated Bishop of Carslile by John Elmer, Bishop of London, deputed thereunto by the Archbishop of York, September ——, Anno 1577. He died in the month of April, A.D. 1598." In this visitation his son, John May, is called of Kings Lynn, County Norfolk, Esq., who had a daughter, Elizabeth, wife of John Sedgwick of Wisbach in the Isle of Ely, County Camb. and of Lynn Regis, County Norfolk, who had male issue, viz. : Edward, John and William Sedgwick, all living in 1619, and some of whom may have settled in New England and connect with the noted General Sedgwick of colonial times. This John May or Mey of Shouldham Abbey and Kings Lynn, Norfolk, in the visitation of Norfolk, 1555–1613, Harleian Manuscript, 1552, fol. 94, is recorded as having by wife Cordelia Bowes the following issue, viz. : *Margaret May*, married to Richard Faucet, *Francis May, o. b., Farnneru (Jacomye?) May, Francis May, Henry May*, 1st son, *John May*, 2d son, *Stephen May*, 3d son, and *Dorothy May* who was probably first wife of William Bradford (the Pilgrim Governor of Plymouth Colony) who was drowned Dec. 7th, 1620, from the "Mayflower" in Provincetown, Cape Cod Harbor, while her husband was absent on an exploring expedition, and whose banns, according to the Lyden Holland Records, 15th Nov., 1613, to William Bretfoot (Bradford) fustian worker from Oosterfeldt in England, affianced to Dorothy May from Witesbuts (Wisbach Co. Camb⁴ near Lynn, Co. Norfolk) ; these banns are again recorded November 23d and 30th, and we find from his marriage registered in the Pulboeken at Amsterdam, he was a fustian worker. The full entry is as follows : "1613 Nov. 9th, William Bradford of Austerfield, fustian worker, 23 years, living at Lyden, where the banns of marriage were laid, it was declared that he had no elders (*i. e.* parents) and Dorothy May, 16 years, of Wisbech. The attesting witness is Henry May.† We may mention that four years earlier Dorothy May's sister *Jacomye May*, also of Wisbach in Cambridge, was married to Jean de l'Ecluse, a book printer from Rouen, who was an elder of the Ancient Church of Amster-

* See Biographical Sketch of Bishop May. Willis's Survey of Cathedrals, Vol. I., pp. 298-9.
† The Dutch spelling is very difficult to decipher, but a glance at the original is sufficient to satisfy one of the meaning thereof.

dam, having come over from the French Church of know evils existing among them."*

Among the English residents of Holland during the early part of the 17th century was a certain John May and wife; of the latter, Ephraim Paget, minister of St. Edmond's, Lombard Street, London, in his "Heresiography,† or a Description of the Hereticks and Sectarie, mentions 'Mistress May, who used to in her house sing (psalms) being more fit for a common brawl,'" as he termed the singing of psalms. Again he says : "By reason of such uncouth and strange translations and the meeter used in them the Congregation was made a laughing stock unto strangers."

In a letter to Governor Bradford from Roger White, a brother-in-law of the Rev. John Robinson, written from Holland in December, 1625, mention is made of John May, your (Governor Bradford's) "father in law."

In Mary E. Perkin's "Old Houses," Norwich, Connecticut, I find a Bradford Pedigree giving John Bradford, son of Governor Bradford and Dorothy May. This son John by wife Dorothy May married Martha Bourne, daughter of Deacon Thomas Bourne and Martha . . . ? of Marshfield, Mass. She died in 1678 without issue, and Martha, his wife, married before 1679, Lieutenant Thomas Tracy — no issue.

Returning to the before-mentioned William Clopton, of Groton, County Suffolk, to show his family relationship with others interested in New England settlement, he had issue : Anne Clopton, bapt. 29 of January, 1580, and married John Mateson‡ of Boxted, Suffolk, and Walter Clopton, a grocer of London, bapt. June, 1585, who married Margaret Mateson, a sister of aforesaid John Mateson, and she secondly Robert Crane. This Walter Clopton came to New England with his relation, Governor Winthrop, in 1630 and returned home soon after. His elder brother, William Clopton, was baptized 9th of April, 1584, and married at Whatfield, Suffolk, 3d August, 1615, Alice, daughter of Edmund D'Oyley, of Shottisham, Norfolk, esquire, and Pond Hall, Hadleigh, County Suffolk, whose cousin, Elizabeth D'Oyley of the Chislehampton, married Edward Goddard, Esquire, of Englisham, County Wilts, whose family, about 1630, emigrated with Governor Winthrop to New England. This Edmund D'Oyley and Thomas Goodwin, of Stoneham, County Suffolk, were trustees for Henry Townshend,§ of Breakon Ash, whose second wife, Anne Calthrone, was sister to Mary, wife of Edward D'Oyley, brother of Edmund

---

* See Pilgrim Fathers of New England, by John Brown, p. 126. Also H. C. Murphy's History, 1859, p. 261.

† The first edition was printed in London, 1645, and the sixth edition, from which the above is abstracted, was printed in 1661 by William Lee and sold at his shop the Turk's Head in Fleet Street.—C. H. T.

‡ This name, in deeds and inquisitions, is spelt *Maydston, Maistone.*

§ Henry Townshend's first wife was Margaret Forth, daughter of Robert Forth, LL.D., by whom he had two sons, Robert and Thomas.

D'Oyley, uncle of Alice D'Oyley, wife of William Clopton, a brother of Thomasine* Clopton, second wife of Governor Winthrop. Another daughter of William Clopton was Bridget, bapt. 29 January, 1581, and married 27 June, 1598, John Sampson of Sampson Hall, Kersey, County Suffolk, whose son, Robert Sampson, came with Governor Winthrop to Boston, and were relations of Henry Sampson and Humility Cooper, cousins of John Tilly, the Mayflower pilgrim, and as the surnames, Tilly, Cooper, Carver and Sampson are all found in the same neighborhood in County Suffolk, the tradition seems sustained that these families were all connected with the Forth family, from which Governor Winthrop married his first wife.

SIR NATHANIEL BACON, KT., SIR ROGER TOWNS-HEND, KT., BART., AND THEIR CHAPLAIN REV. SAMUEL WHITING AFTER-WARDS OF LYNN, MASS.

Communicated by Capt. CHAS. HERVEY TOWNSHEND, of " Raynham," New Haven, Conn.

COTTON MATHER, in his Magnalia, writes of the Rev. Samuel Whiting, of Lynn, Mass. :

" Having proceeded Master of Arts, he removed from Cambridge [Emanuel College] and became chaplain to Sir Nathaniel Bacon [Kt.], and Sir Roger Townshend [Bart.], where he did for three years ... serve the interest of religion in a family which had no less than two Knights and five Ladies in it."

The Ladies were The Right Honorable, the Lady Berkely, who was mother of Sir John Townshend, Kt., and widow of Sir Roger Townshend of Armada fame, 1588; Lady Bacon, Lady Ann Townshend, eldest daughter of Sir Nathaniel Bacon, mother of Sir Roger Townshend, Knight and Baronet, who was then *unmarried;* Lady Elizabeth Knevetts and Lady Winifred Gaudy, daughters of Sir Nathaniel Bacon.

Sir Nathaniel Bacon was second son by the first wife of the Lord Keeper, Sir Nicholas Bacon, an elder brother of the half blood of the famous Lord Bacon, Baron Verulam. He died November 7th, 1622.† His will, dated May 10th, 1614, proved P. C. C. Swan, Fol. 2, Jan. 24th, 1622, which is very lengthy and has several codicils, and is printed—abridged—in The English State Papers Domestic Addenda, 1580–1625, pp. 541-4, No. 61, and also contains

---

* Mary Clopton, sister of Thomasine, the second wife of Governor Winthrop, married Thomas Dogget or Daggett, of Boxted, County Suffolk, who settled in New England, and was connection of the Dagget family of Martha's Vineyard.
† Monument in Stifkey Church.

a large amount of family history; but not the probate of his will
(in Latin) which surely connects our Samuel Whiting with these
families, as given us by Mather; and is one of the connecting
links which strongly sustains the traditions of the Whiting and
Townsend families of Lynn, Mass.

The Latin Translation of the probate of Sir Nathaniel Bacon's
will, as made by Mr. E. O. Impey of the Record office, London,
is as follows :

"The above written will was proved at London before the venerable
father—Sir William Bird, Knight, Doctor of Laws of the Prerogative
Court of Canterbury, Master Keeper, was committed and not constituted
on the twenty fourth day of the month of January, Anno Domini, according to the course and computation of the Church of England, 1622, by the
oath of Lady Elizabeth Knevit and Lady Winifred Gaudy, daughters and
executrixes in the said will named. To whom was committed the administration of the goods, rights and credits of the said desseased to well and
faithfully administer on the Holy Gospel of God by virtue of a commission
in another place in the presence of William Armestead* and Samuel Whiting,† clerks. Dame Ann Townshend, a daughter, and the other executrix
being dead.

Appended.

As the will of Lady Ann Townshend of Heyden, Co. Norf.
widow. P. C. C. Swan, No. 15. Proved 4th Feb. 1622. Mentions several names that afterwards appear in New England. An
abstract may interest :

"To Sir Nathaniel Bacon Knt my father my best Diamond ring and 50
of my best weather sheep. To Lady Bacon my mother in Law a Silver
Tankard. To sisters Ladies Gaudy and Knevetts each a bowle of Silver
Gilt. To loving cousin Sir Edward Bacon. To cousin Corbet the late
wife of Thomas Corbet‡ Esquire deceased, a pendant of four Diamonds.
To Wm Biggin £50 on conditions that within five months after my decease,
he deliver to my son Sir Roger Townshend Kt Bart all evidence as his late
father had concerning lands &c &c which I bought of him. To the Lady
my son Sir Roger Townshend§ marryeth my muff of purple velvet with
pearls, and lined with sable &c. &c. To my daughter Anne, wife of John
Spelman‖ Esq my house in London also 42 buttons of Gold—One gown of
Black Satin—one silver basin given me by the Rt Hon The Lady Bercke-
ley my *late mother* in law. To s^d daughter Anne £100. To son Sir Roger
T. a farm also my chief messuage in Hayden forever provided he bestow
£500 to the purchase of lands in Norfolk and Suffolk, the rents to be paid
for the education of poor children of Heydon, Stifkey, Salle Little Ribough
& Stanhow Co Norf &c. &c., buinding them apprentices in such course as
the children of the Hospital lately erected in Berkshire by my good aunt
the Lady Peryam &c. &c. To Mr Partington minister of Heydon 20 s,

---

* Minister of Stifkey, Norfolk, England.
† Minister of Raynham, Norfolk, England.
‡ Rev. Thomas Cobbett of Lynn perhaps of this family.
§ Unmarried, but after his mother's death married Mary, daughter of Horatio Ld Vere
    of Tilbury.
‖ John, son of Sir Henry Spelman.

also five Gold rings value 20s each with this posy " Remember the End "—
One to Mr Gardiner* minister of East Raynham—One to Mrs Mitchell of
Salle—One to Mr. Partingen.   One to Mrs Symonds wife of my steward
Mr Edward Symonds and one to Mr Martyn Mann servant to my father Sir
Nathaniel Bacon Kt To Edward Symonds one cup of silver value £5
with my arms and name thereon.—To Thomas Jeffers £30—To Anne Jeffers my servant £30—To Robt Raby of East Raynham £10—To my apprentices & servants 40s each.   To my son Sir Roger Townshend all remaining property whatsoever and I make him sole executor.

Witnesses   Thomas Partington   Signed Anne Townshend.
             Edward Hampton
             Edward Symonds
             Edward Symonds Jr.
             Martyn Dewyen.

Will of Sir Roger Townshend, Knt & Barronett.   P. C. C.
Goare.   Page 104.   Proved June 10th, 1637.

To the poor of East Raynham Norfolk—Furniture Plate & Jewells to
wife Lady Mary—My family one month after my death to continue in
charge of my executors—To William Palphry† £20 – To Walter Vaugham
£10—To William Marshall £10—To house hould servants one month wages
—To Mr Ramsey‡ having paid to Mr Stanhow for Rectory of East Raynham £40 to be repaid—To Mary Spilman daughter of John Spilman Esq§
£100 to be paid at such time and sort as Mrs Anne Townshend be paid her
portion—Land bought of Sir Roger Townshend in Stifkey of James Cal-
thorpe Esq to be convey to Dame Mary Townshend for life—To eldest son
Roger Townshend.‖ To servants Jack £20 Ed Symonds¶ £100—Erasmus
Earl £40—John Yates** clerk £80.   John Spelman Esq £5000 which sum
he has secured by law to Sir Ralph Whitfield.†† To Mr Roger Townshend
£2000—To Mr Wyndam £2000—To Mr Thomas Townsends‡‡ children
£400—To Richard Mason £1000—To Mr Sydney £300   To Mr Beck-
erston £300—To Mr Mason—To the children of Nicholas Beaming £100.
To John Thorold £140.

Appointed Sir Thomas Ashley—Phillip Woodhouse Esq—Edward Symonds Court Executors   Signed   Roger Townshend§§

---

* He was succeeded by the Rev. John Goodwin, who was followed about 1630 by the Rev.
John Yates. Goodwin then went to St. Nicholas Kings Linn, where he succeeded the Revs.
Nicholas Price and Samuel Whiting afterwards of Lynn, Mass. Goodwin, Dec. 18, 1633,
succeeded John Davenport at St. Stephen's, Coleman St., London.
    † There came to New England a William Palphrey.
    ‡ Mr. Ramsen was minister of Rudham and a noted Presbyterian, mar. the widow of
Gile Fletcher.
    § John Spelman, a son of Sir Henry Spelman, Sec. for the New England Co.
    ‖ Sir Roger Townshend 2d, Bart., died 1648 at House of Rev. John Diodati at Geneva,
Switzerland.
    ¶ Edward Symonds may have emigrated to New England 1640.
    ** Minister of Stefkey and Raynham.   John Yates was a correspondent of Rev. John
Robinson in Holland.
    †† Sir Ralph Whitfield of the Barbecan, London, and cousin of Rev. Henry Whitfield
of Guilford, Conn.
    ‡‡ Thomas Townshend may have been the Lynn settler 1638-9.
    §§ Sir Roger Townshend died at Raynham Jan. 1st, 1637, N.S.

JAMES BARRETT'S RETURNS OF MEN MUSTERED INTO SERVICE, 1777–1778.

Copied for the REGISTER from papers in the possession of the NEW-ENGLAND HISTORIC GENEALOGICAL SOCIETY by FRANCIS E. BLAKE, Esq., of Boston.

NOTE.—All of these returns are superscribed "To John Avery, Esq. Dep^ty Secretary at Boston."

[Continued from page 15.]

No. 1.

To the Honor^bl Council of the State of the massachusetts Bay — in Compliance to an ordor of Council of the 2: Instant to me directed this may sartify that I have mustered & paid the Bounty to Seventeen men Enlisted under Lie^u Wareham Wheeler of Concord in Capt Thomases Company & Co^l marshals Battalion as he Saith also two in Capt Allens Company and Co^l Aldens Battalion and two in Capt Jacob Steils Company & Co^l Francis Battalion

Concord January ye 20 : 1777

17 : men Col marshal
2 in Co^l Aldns
2 in Co^l Francies Battalions

in Co^l Francis Bat^l
Nathan Chapman
John Burridg

in Co^l Aldens Bat^ln
James McCaffrey
Joseph mors

N. B. the above namd Nathan Chapman & John Burridg Inlisted at New York and have Returned their Six pounds Bounty according to proclimation.

JAMES BARRETT } muster master

the mens names in Co^l marshels Battalion
Abraham Pribble
Robort Ritchardson
David Evans
Samuel Harden
John Darling
Amos Brown
William Tomson
Simeon Burridge
William Burridge
Francis Legros
Edmund Horton
Elisha mores
Pelham Wood
John Blatch
John Tingle
William Wheeler
William Pribble

No. 2.

Concord February ye 3 : 1777

To the Hono^l Councel for the State of the massachusetts Bay I have musterd & paid the Bounty to the men Whose names are hereafter menshond Sence my Last Return Viz —

in Co^l Wigelsworths Battallion & Capt Haynes Company
Peter marshal
Benj Darling
Aaron Haynes J^r
Job Wathrel

in Co^l Gratons Battallion & Capt Childs Company
John Lande

in Co^l Franseis Battallion & Capt Stels Company
John Jones

in Co^l marshals Battallion & Capt Thomases Company
Oliver Emerson
James Ritchardson

JAMES BARRETT } muster master

No. 3.

Febuary y[e] 12 1777
To the Honor[y] Councel for the State of the Massachusetts Bay I have musterd & paid the Bounty to the men Whose names are Hereafter menshand Sence my Last Returen that is

in Capt Stiles Compn
Col Frances Battallin
Robart Anger
Peter Calle
Brayty Gray
Daniel thomas walker
Jacob Coray
Nathaniel Ladd
John Starns

In Capt Allen Compeney
Col Alden Battallen
Barron Brown

in Capt Haynes Comp
Col Wiggelsworth
Battallin
Benjamin Smith

in Capt Childs Com
Col Gratten Battallen
John Lande

in Capt Watson
Compeney
Amos Taylor

JAMES BARRETT muster master

No. 4.

Febuary y[e] 26 : 1777   To the Honor[b] Council for the State of the Massachusetts Bay I have musterd & paid the Bounty to the men Whose names are Hereafter menshand Sence my Last Returne Viz

Col Wiggilsworth Battallion
Capt Hanes Company
Ephiram Goodmon
William Gardner
Abner Biuines

in Capt Blaisdell Company
Zechariah Willes
John Davidson

Col Gratons Battallion
Capt Childs Company
Artemas Reed
Zoath Handason
Stephen Lufkin
John Bortor

in Capt Worthel Company
Eli Stiles

in Capt Watson Company
Jotham Staple
David Farwell

Col Aldens Battallion
Capt Parker Compiny
William Hardwick
Enoch Cleveland
Benjamin osgood
Joshua fassett

Col Kise Battallion
Capt Cory Company
Jeremiah Temple
Isaac Russell
Silas Cory
Isaac Ramsdell
Stephen Cory

Col Mershals Battallion
Capt Brooks Company
Aaron mason
Charles millor
Sipio obid

JAMES BARRETT muster master

No. 5.

March y[e] 4 : 1777
To the Honor[b] Councel for the State of the Massachusett Bay I have musterd & paid the Bounty to the men Whose names are Hereafter menshond Sence my Last Returne Viz*

* Endorsed " James Barret Muster Master's Acc. of Men enlisted in the Continental Army."

Col Jackson Bat^ln
Capt Benjamin Brown
Company
James mc Conno
Jonas Green
Ebenezer Shattuck
Abraham Shattuck
Daniel Shattuck
Benjamin Green
Samson Woods
Stephen Shattnck
William Scott
John Willit
John Gilson
Thomas Lawrance
Willow Lakin

in Col mershal Battallen
Capt Thomas Company
Charles Prescott
John Whittemore
Charles Hoyd
Job Spauildind
oliver Barrett

Col Alden Battalen
Capt Allen Company
Arthur Ellet
John moozay
John Walker

Col^o Wiggelworth Battal
Capt Blaisdel Company
willim Duggins
Benjamin Chamberlin

in Capt Farefeeld
Company
Willim Suttleff
Poly Rodmun
Benjamin Ballurd

Col Frances Battal
Capt Stiles Company
Thomas Gary
Joseph Gilson
Thomas Plates
Elias mackintire
Amos Nutten
Joshua whiting
James Carter
Clark Bancroft
John Jones
Samuel Danforth
Benjamin Gary
Thomas Ditson
Nathaniel Hunt

in Capt Wheeler
Company
Sambeo Hankins
thomas Woods
mather Jamerson
Josiah Blood Jun.

Col Kise Battallen
Capt Cory Company
Cornelius Baker
Isaac Whitcomb
Aroon wood
John Parker

Joshua Proughty
Joshua White
Samuel Rogers
David Fleem

Col^o Biggelos Battallen
Capt Smiths Company
John Sloon
David Sloon
John Davis
Joseph Chaplin
Seth Harrington
Willim Kemp
John Jupp
George Ross

Co^l Baley Battallen
Capt Maxwell Company
Peter Davis
Benjamin Patting
Abner Mitchell
Josiah Blood
Ebeneser Richardson

in Capt Baker Company
Elisher Procter
Peter Baker
Jonathan Phelps
Samuel Phillips
Epherim Procter
Peter Cummings Gilbert
John oakes
Joseph Lewis
obediah Howord
Samuel woods junr

JAMES BARRETT muster master

No. 6.

March ye 24 : 1777

To the Honori^b Counciel for the State of the Massachusetts Bay I have mustered & paid the Bounty to the men Whose names are Hereafter men-shond Sence my Last Returne Viz

Col Wesson Battalo
Capt Ward Company
John Gaild
Joseph Gay
Isaac Baley
Edmand Gould
Joseph Tombs
William Tombes
Silas Haven
oliver Rise

Capt Woods Company
Joseph Starkwether
William Putnam
Benjamin Hadley
Stephen Stearns

Capt Fearfeeld Companey
John Dallison
Ruben moore
Zubel Stone
John Brown

Col Wigglesworth Battal
Capt Hanes Compa
Moses Gooch
Eleaser Lawrance
oliver Sonderson
Jonas Beains
Joseph mitter

Capt Farefeeld Company
Samuel Ballard

Col Bigglow Battallen
Capt Barrans Company
Samuel Gates
Stephens Phelps
James Luzen
William Henry woods
Stephen Hale
Daniel Gales
Jonathan Gates
Philmon Allen
Thomas Cheney Ridgway

Capt Smith Companey
Asa Jones
Elijah Putnam
Jonathan Barrett
Daniel Cole
Seth wyman
Ebenezer scarf
Samuel Hutchson
Solomon Russell
Edmond Farnsworth

Col Nixson Battallon
Capt Wheler Comp
William Wilson
David Jenners
Partrick Neef
Abraham davis

in Capt Cory Comp
Dan¹ Darling

Colo Jackson Battaln
Capt Cleavand Compan
Charlee Procter
david Chamblin

Colo Brewer Batta
Capt witkens Com
John whiting

Col Frances Batt
Capt Stiles Company
John Hoggman

Col Pattison Battal
Capt Hils Compan
Gese Gustin

Col Bigglow Battal
Capt munro Company
Levi Mead
Pomp Blakman
Titas Haywood
Joseph Cox

Col Baley Battallen
Capt Markswell Compa
Nathan Russell
John Stevens
William Blasdell
Samuel Stevens

Capt Smith Comp
John moors
John Davis Junr
Cornelos Davis
David Tarbell
William Snow
John Searle
David Laugton
Jabez Steven

Col marshal Battall
Capt Broaks Co
Nathan Dowe
Philip Alaxander

Col marshall Battal
Capt warren Compan
John Cily

Col Pattison Battal
Capt Ashby Comp
Gorge Brown
Jack Farret

Col Aldens Batta
Capt Parker Comp
Ebenezer Hilddreth (?)

Col Jackson Batta
Capt Brown Com
Levi Reed

JAMES BARRETT muster master

No. 7.

Apriel yᵉ 9: 1777

To the Honorb Councel for the State of the Massachusett Bay I have musterd & paid the Bounty to the men Whose names are Hereafter menshond Sence my Last Returen

Col Biggelo Battallon
Capt munroe Company
John Barker Junr
Theodore Barker
James Lawe
Daniel Simonds
Ebenezer Hadley
David Fisk Jr
Nehemiah Esterbroaks
Peter oliver
Richard Antony
Thaddeus munroe
George Wheeler
Jupeter Free

Capt Barrens Company
Rubin Wyman
Elisher Austin
Zerubbabel Eager
John Dexter
Benjamin Brullo
Timothy Johnson

Cap Cory Company
Jacob Kilburn
Samuel White
Able Bigelow
Ephraim Gates
John Wheeler

Capt Broaks Compny
Thomas orgin
William Antony
James osborn
Silas Evens
Isaac wyman
Jack Ran
Thomas Newman
Edward Admes[?]
Alrobing Stuard
James Bennet
John Edwards
Edward Smith

Col Bigglow Battllon
Capt Smith Company
Dudley Keep
Jonathan Stevens
Primpes Negorman
John Blood
Emsomen parker
Caleb Blood
David Wilson
Samuel Farley
Morres Caley
Jonathan Longley

Col Gratten Battallno
Capt Childs Company
Abijah Childs Jr
Jonthan Gales

Col Baley Battal
Capt markswell
Solomon Pires
Abiathar Eton

Col Wiggelworth Battalen
Capt Hanes
Joseph maynard
Joseph Russel

Col Wesson Battal
Capt Dix Compy
John oaks
Pareit Caley
Richard Condin
Jonathan Hushan
James Twrrsey [*sic.*]
Thomas Field

Col Nixon Batl
Capt wheeler
Amos Wheele
Jeremiah Green
Charles Peirce
Silas Cuttin
Lemuel wheeler
Nathaniel Draper

Capt Bancroft Company
James Bancroft
John Brayant
Samson London
Joshua Eaton
Ruben Geary
Joel Holdden

Col Aldens Battall
Capt Parker Company
James Butterfield
Parker Emerson
Noah Foster
Pelatiah Adams
Peter Wright
Jonathan Johnson
Cato Abbot
oliver Cory
Ezra Cory
Stephen Sheppard
Francies Smith
Ephraim Cummings
Amos Hardy
Isaac Glenne
Zach^{ah} Longly
James Emery

Capt Reed Company
James Berten
Nathan malad

Col Putman Battalen
Capt Stiles Company
Jams mill
Jonas Carter
Henry ^{mc} Noil
Benjamin Brazen
Aaron Taylor
John Cogor

Col Jackson Battalen
Capt Brown Company
Daniel Brown
Robet Blood Junr
Joel Jenkius

Capt Noah Allen
Company
Abishah Beard
David Tweed
Timothy Richardson
Samuel Penny

Col Nixon Battallen
Capt Holden Company
Joseph Cutter
John Buck
Benjamin Clark
Joseph Filling
Jessa mosman
Joshua manard

Co^l Wigelsworth Battalen
Capt Danforth Company
Jonathan Gleason
Jonathan Hemingway

Capt Spur Company
John Hood

Capt Dannels Compny
Ruben Pike

Col Biglow Battallen
Capt Smith Company
Benjamin Peirce
Solomon Peirce
Abisha wetheby
John Schott
Benjamin Steven
William Lord
William wyman

Col Pattason Battallen
Capt Hunt Company
Benjamin Goat

Col Nixon Battaln
Capt Barrens Compan
Peter Calem
John Tayler

Capt Danforth Company
Jessa Danforth
Benjamin Baldwin
Phinis osgood
David osgood Ju
Joseph Rugels

Coll Sheppard Batt
Capt Slayton Comp
Thomas Shorp
James Antony

Col marshel Battal
Capt warner Company
Joseph wetherby junr

JAMES BARRETT muster master

No. 8.

Concord April 25: 1777
To the Honor[b] Council for the State of the massachusetts Bay I have musterd & paid the Bounty to the men Whouse names are Heareafter menshond Sence my Last Returne Viz

Col Bigglow Battalen
Cap[t] Smith Company
John Blood
Warfe Rane
Zachriah Langley
Asa Longley
James magares
John Haskell
Samuell Hearts
Nathaniell Gilson
Jonathan Bancraft
William Holt

Cap[t] munroe Company
Peter Bowes
Luke Fletcher
Amos Russell
Jonathan Porte
Jenone Allbrones

Cap[t] Brown Compan
Jonathan Robbens
Daniel Barker
Benjamin Gates
James Barker

Col Bradford Battalle
Cap[t] Reddings Company
oliver mosman
James Snow
John Elestings
Abner moor
Joseph Platt
Isaac Buck

Col Aldin Battallen
Cap[t] Parker Company
Ephraim Warren
Willam Dutton
Jonathan Stratten
Willam Davis
Gethro wilkens
John Parker
Epharim Dutton

oliver Barnes
oliver Heald
Samuel Ross
Jeramiah Robbens

Cap[t] Allen Compny
Cato Hearts

Col marshal Battallen
Cap[t] Thomas Company
John mc grah
James Allen
Samuel Cutrly

Cap[t] Warnors Company
Levi Pagel
Joseph Robbins
Silas Sarron
Pomp Cuffreer
Thomas Pratt
Ephraim Tempel

Col Wesson Battallen
Cap[t] Ward Company
Aaron Jackson
John Burridg
Nathan Jackson

Cap[t] Dix Company
William Tarbox

Cap[t] Cory Company
Luke Wilson
Joshua Johnson
James Battles

Col Baley Battallen
Cap[t] Maxwill Com
Willim moors [Mears?]
John Teneoy

Col Gratton Battale
Cap[t] Sumner Comp
Joseph Barrett

Cap[t] Williams Comp
John Stedman
Amos Stedman

Col Jackson Battallen
Cap[t] Brown Company
Able Blood
Edmond Parker
Lemul Blood
Frances Lee

Col Nixon Battallen
Cap[t] Towgood Compn
Samuel Emery
Phineas Butlar
william Dutton

Cap[t] Barnes Compny
Solomon Smith
Zipron Newton

Capt Wheeler Compn
Nathan Wheeler Junr

Cap[t] Holdens Compney
Nathanial Cutter

Col Biglow Battall
Cap[t] Barnes Company
James Crosmun jr
John Barnard Jr
Stephen Hudson
Eli How
Charles Hudson
Solomon Jones
John Rice
Abraham Brigham

Col Wigelworth Batta
Cap[t] Danforth Company
Henery Wariner

JAMES BARRETT, Muster Master.

No. 9.

To Col¹ James Barrett Concord May 12th 1777
Sir it is the unanimous opinion of the Selectmen and Commᵗᵉᵉ of this Town that Thos. B. Ball is a person that will answer for the Continental Service and we expect to pay him the Town Bounty By order of the Selectmen and Committee.

NATHAN STOW

No. 10.

May yᵉ 16 : 1797
To the Honorᵇ Council for the State of the Massachusetts Bay I have musterd and paid the Bounty to the men Whose names are Hearafter menshond Sence my Last Returne Viz

Col Bigelow Battalen
Capt munroe Company
Jeremiah Tyler
Benjamin Ston
Ebenezer Lock
Richard Wesson
oliver Wheeler
James Fletcher
Thomas Ball
Prince Sutten
Jonathan munro
Isaac Berbudas

Capt Brown Company
Willam Procter
Thomas Law
William Gates
Benjamin Willard
Zadarck Burning
Eblathan Daroy
Samuel Farnworth
Levi Farnworth
Titus Colbarn
Corsuter Turner

Capt Smith Company
Jonathan Cummings
Ebenezer Harrington

Capt Danforth Company
Forten Conant
Thomas Richardson
Solomon Pollord
William Currier
John Wyman
John Needham
micah Baldwin
Joel Crosby
John Foster Jun
Aaron Kingsbury

Ruben Shed
medford Calewell
John Edes
Roger Tuthaker
David Shed
Jonathan Frost Jun
Amariah Wyman
Justus Blanchard
Asa Richardson
Stephen Barrett
Jonathan Starns
Nathanel Blanchard
Nathaniel Starns

Col Jackson Battallen
Capt Vernam Company
Nathan Farrer
Willard Peirce
Peter Fulsom
Isack Clement
Joel Fox
oliver Hall
Samuel Whiting
Daniel Abbot
George Kalley
Silas Chamerlam
John Fox
Joshua Jones
Josiah Richardson
Samuel Mears
David Linsday
James Lafferty
Asa Coburn
Samuel Pirkens
Joshua Atwood
moses Estterbrooks
William Dunnes
John Glood
Benjamin Pirce

Col Aldin Battallen
Capt Parker Compa
Richard michel
Daniel Dudley
Jacob Robbens
Ebenezer Foster

Capt Allen Company
Cesar Boston

Col Biglow Batta
Capt Barnes Company
Jonathan Cory
Prentice Russell
Francies Somes
Jonah Newton

Col Jackson Battallen
Capt Vernam Company
Sherebi Fletcher
Solomon Adams
Benjamin Barron
Timothy Halle
Samuel mears
Thomas Thissell
moses Richarson

Col Bradford Battal
Capt Reddin Compny
Joseph Houtchon

Col Bayley Battallen
Capt maxwill Comp
William Stacey
Benjamin Taylor

Col Wigelsworth Batta
Capt Allen Company
Benjamin Gloyd
John Trask

Capt Porter Company
Daniel North

Col Bruer Battallen
Capt Bruer Company
Thomas Winch

Col Nixon Battallen
Capt Holden Company
Isaac Rice
Thomas Nixon Ju
Joseph Veal [Neal?)
Nathaniel Cuttor

Capt Towgod Company
John Emery
micah Davis
Samson Ayner

Col Putnam Battalen
Capt moos Company
Daniel Gillson
Daniel Gillson

Col Wesson Battallen
Capt Pattison Compan
Robert Fisk

Capt Ward Company
Samuel Pike

Capt Ashby Company
Prince Collins

Col Grattons Battallen
Capt Childs Company
Joseph Burkmer

Capt Brooks Company
Cesear wyman
Nathan Beard
James Fowlor
Peter Hassey
John Collel
Jonathan Snow

JAMES BARRETT muster master

No. 11.

June : 6 : 1777
To the Honorb Council for the State of the massachusetts Bay I have musterd & paid the Bounty to the men Whose names are Heareafter menshond Sence my Last Returne Viz

Col Biglow Battallen
Capt munroe Company
Elisha Herghton
Job Priest
Samuel worster
Thomas Greant
James Fowl
Frances Chaffin

Capt Brown Company
Elezer Parker
Jonas Davis
manass Farnsworth
John Buram

Capt. Cory Comp
Jacob Davis
Jonathan Russell
Wm Bigelow
Benj^m Goold
Lemuel Burman

Col Jackson Batt
Capt Benj^m Brown
Company
Joseph Chamberln
Henry Woods
Phinas Douglass
Joseph Tarbell
Benjamin Chamberln
Jabes Keep

Jabes Keep Junr
William Harvas[Harris?]
Phiness Whitney
Samuel Atherton
Isral Hale
Ezekiel Cox
Jonathan Huthins
Thomas Burges
Jonathan Farnsworth
Abraham munroe
William Stone
Daniel Burt
Frances Sansusee

Col Bayley Battallen
Capt Darby Company
oliver Sawyer
Zachariah Robbens
Jona Tuttle
Benjamin Durant
Timothy Baker
Henry Durant
Paul Robbens
Benjamin Hoar

Capt maxwell Company
Joseph Rumrill
Noah Farrer
Joseph Baldwin Jun
William Clarke
Daniel Conant

Ephraim warren
Asa merrel
Daniel Champbell
John Gassett
Daniel Holt Jr
Henry Blasdell
Joseph Warren
Asa Heald

Col Putnam Battal
Capt Wintchip Compan
Joseph Hoar
Timothy Johnson
Joshua Holden
Jacob Lock
Thomas Ross
E. Bennit Davis
John witer
Adam Rodiman

Col Aldin Battal
Capt Parker Campany
Amos Russell
Samuel Kyes
Elezer Read
Jacob Wendell
Jonas Kemp
Thomas Nutten
Elnathan Read
Jesee Dudley

Col Biglow Battal
Capt Smith Compa
Ezra Smith
william Bartlat
Amos Dale junr
John moors
Joseph Longley
Jonathan Davis
Charles [phy?]
William Bancroft
Aaron Bigelow
Timothy Eatton
Stephen Fuller
Robert Hill

Capt Barnes Compa
William Carrath
Gideon Bowker
Sippeo Adams
Elishar Foster Jr
Silas Sawir
moses Willams
Wm Rice

Capt Brooks Company
Lenard Richardson
Gideon Richardson
Nathan Hales

Col Wigelsworth Battal
Capt Davis Company
John Dresor Davis

Col Jackson Battalle
Capt Clevland Com
Enoch Jenkins
Israel Jonson

Col Marshall Battallen
Capt Warners Comp
David Clark

Capt Danforth Company
Charls Homs
David Lenestone

Col Putnam Battallen
Capt Moos Company
Solomon Waupam
Jonas Procter
Jonas mills

Col Bradford Battallen
Capt Reddings Company
John Caycoze Jr
William Hildreth Jr
Joseph Bosset
Josiah Woods
Hinksman Rardson[?]

Col Pattison Battallen
Capt Ashly Company
John Robets
York Rugels

Col Nixon Battallen
Capt Towgod Company
Pomp Edes

No. 12.

Concord June y[e] 23 : 1777

To the Honor[b] Council for the State of the Nassachusetts Bay I have musterd & paid the Bounty to the men Whose names are Hearafter menshond Sence my Last Retune Viz*

Col Nixon Battallo
Capt Towgod Compa
Jonathan Wright
Daniel Starnes

Col Jackson Battallon
Capt Bancroft Comp
John Boyd

Capt James Keith Company
Obediah Perry

Capt Cleavland Compa
Dors freeman
Henry Hawks
John Rebosquet
Henry Lobsquet

Capt Brooks Compa
Jabez Carter

Col Wiggleworth Battallen
Capt Hanes Company
John Haman

Col Aldon Battal
Capt Warren Com
Antono Lewis
Prince Redwood

Col Nixon Battallen
Capt Holden Compa
Joel Brigham

Capt Cory Compa
Nicholars Durham
Asa Wesson
Shadrach Newton
George Stone
Abel Peirce
James Bowers
Joseph Carvender

John Ball
William Prentice
Pelatiah Everett
Butler Whetney
Richard Pattin
Abel Whitcomb

Col Baley Battallen
Capt mackwell Com
Abel Foster

Col Biglow Battallen
Capt munroe Company
Jam Barrett
Joel Dodge
william wheeler
william Bordman
David Fisk
Job Spauldin

Capt Smith Company
Willaim Conn

---

* Endorsed " James Barret Esq[r] Muster Master's return of Men enlisted during three years & the war."

Capt Barnes Compa	Capt Danforth Company	Jonathan Hildrich
Lionard Eagr	Isaac Baldwin	Joseph Underwood
		Samuel Darley
Col putnam Battallen	Col Aldin Battalle	Smith Foster
Capt wintchip Company	Capt Parker Compa	John Nutting
Benja Stuart	John Patch	Abijah Reed
	Isaac Proctor	Stephen Temple

Concord June ye 28: 1777
the Nuams of the men Inlested Into the Continental army till the Tenth
Day of Jeneary

Col Biglow Battallen	Nehemiah Earker	John Starnes
Capt munroe Company	[Parker?]	Samuel Gould
Robet Parker		Aaron Bennett
obidiah Jenkins	Capt warners Company	Jonathan Boyden
David Fish	Rober Houghton	Ebenezer Farnsworth
Samuel Craft		Ephraim warren
William Thomas	Col Biglow Battallen	Ep^m Smith
	Capt Smith Company	John Wesson
Capt Hanes Comapny	Amos Dal [Doll?]	Abel Procter
Timothy Bellows	John Reed	John Keley
Charls Bellows	John wheeler	Abel Holden
Wil^m Winchester Junr	Caleb Nurse	Timothy Boston
	Isaac Gregory	John Woodbeay

JAMES BARRETT } muster
master

No. 13.

Concord August ye 5 :1777
To the Honor^b Council for the State of massachusetts Bay I have mus-
terd & paid the Bounty to the men Whouse names are Heareafter menshond
Sence my Last Return Viz :—*

Col Biglow Battallen
Capt Barnes Company
Ebenezer Hudson
Elisha Rice
James Gamwell
Thomas Keyes
John Tenney
Robet Balies
David Fay

Capt Brown Com
John Whitney

Capt munroe Company
matthew Farrington
Samuel Craft

Capt Smith Comp
Benjamin Bailey
Isaac Phillips

Col Aldin Battallen
Capt Allen Company
Cesear Thompson
Nathan Champney

Capt Parker Company
Ebenezer Cory
Joseph Kidder

Col Nixon Battal
Capt Twogod Com
Isaac Davis

Capt Lane Campa
Isarel Davenport

Capt Holden Compa
Francis Green

Col Wigglesworth Battallen
Capt Hanes Company
Have Inlested Into the
Continantal army till
the Tenth Day of
Jeneary next to come.
Lemuel Newton
David Fay

Col Shepard Batt
Capt Slayton
Christopher Vickery

Col Jackson Batta
Capt Wiley Company
Thomas Jackson
michael Jackson
Amasa Jackson
Charles Jackson

* Endorsement " James Barret Esqr Muster Master's return of Men musterd during
three years & until Jany next—Aug. 1777."

Capt Browen Company Col Wigelsworth Battallen Caley mers [mors?]
Joseph Frie   *Capt Noah Allen Company* William onthank
Samuel Procter   John Ralford   Edmand moore

Capt Hayns Company   Joseph Day
John Hamon   Jesse Amsden

JAMES BARRETT } muster
              } master

Col Roberson Battallen   Ebenezer Chandler   Samuel Lovejoy
Capt Brown Company   Simeon Kemp   Abner Lovejoy
John Edwards   Daniel Whitney   Thomas Capin
Bezeleh Herdeen   John Spauldin   Phillip Lovejoy
Nathanel Davis   Isaac Parker   Isaac Williams
Simon Wheler   Josiah Fletcher   Daniel Wetherby
Ephraim Farrer   Samuel Chamberling   James Darlin
Amos Haggot   Joseph Richardson   Aaron Farmer
Samuel Melven   Daniel Twiss   Jona Jonson
Purchis Brown   Benjamin Farmer   Peter Gibson
Joseph Davis   Isaac Kent   John Parham
Silas Wood   Jonathan Roff   James Cummins
Nathan Dudley   John Crosbe
Josiah Melven   Nathaniel French   *Col Roberson Battallen*
Jonathan Couck   Jesse Heywood   *Capt Brown Company*
Amos Stow   Sisrah Sweet   Thad Blood
Jonathan Heald   Joseph Spalddind Jr Jonathan Barnes
Jesse Davis   Elias Barnes
Nathan Wheeler   *Col Roberson Battallen* Stephen Law
Joel Wheeler   *Capt Lacin Company* Ebenezer Heald
Isaac Melven   David Jenkins   Amos Parling
                           Thomas Nichols   Isaac Brown
Col Roberson Battallen   Daniel Willard   James Faulkner
Capt Parker Company   William Kemp   Amasa Piper
Paas Holden   Oliver Farnsworth   Josiah Abbot
John Packer   Ambros Lakin   Silas Parling
Isaac Chandler   Amos Ames Ju   John Shed
Nathan Chamberlen   Henry Swan   Solomon Willson
Thomas Robbins   moses Ames   Abraham Tempel
James Bennet   Moses Chase
oliver Reed   Thomas Tarbel   *Capt Reed Company*
David Cowdin   John Trowbridge   Isaac Green
Philip Procter   Uriele Whitney   Jeremiah Robinson
                                                John Diseo

No. 14.

December ye 27 : 1777
  To the Honor^b Council for the State of massachusetts Bay I have mus-
terd & paid the Bounty to the men Whose names are Hearafter menshond
Sence my Last Returne Viz

Col Aldin Battallen   James Nahor   *Col Jackson Battallen*
Capt Allen Company   Pall Canoonaugh   *Capt Cleavland Company*
Renzy Simpson   Frances Lines
                                            Hugh hinds

JAMES BARRETT } Muster
              } master

No. 15.

December ye 27: 1777
To the Honor[b] Council for the State of the massachusetts Bay I have musterd & paid the Bounty to the men Whose names are Hearafter menshond Sence my Last Returne, Viz:—

Colo Jackson Battallen
Capt Burnam Company
James Hindes
Robert Wheeler
Bryant mochinil
William Greeoch
Dennis Whealan
Labrick Dannosan

Colo Handly Battallen
Capt Fox Company
William pedly
John Hill
Aaron trick
John Hopkens
John Duxon
Samuel Cummings
Abraham Wilson
Rich[d] Bourk

John Williams
Edward Bedford
John Salter
William money
John Cannon
William Isason
the three above
Naimed are in
Capt Scott Company

, *Colo Alden Battallen*
Capt Allen Company
Michael Lyons
Joseph Goldig
Thomas Swindle
Thomas Stepenes
Mich[l] Menley
Cornel Lee
James Michell

Thomas Brant
William Brown
John Smith
James Davis
Matthew Falsom
William Davis
William Richardson
Matthew Kennedy

Colo Lee Battallen
Capt Suel Company
Abrm: Seney
John Britton

Capt Peter Hasten Comp
Samuel Woods
Joseph Dixon
James Geozzop [?]
John White

No. 16.

Concord January ye 29: 1778
To the Honor[b] Council for the State of the massachusetts Bay I have musterd & paid the Bounty to the men Whouse nams are Hereafter menshond Sence my Last Returne Viz

Colo Bigglow Battallen
Capt Smith Company
Richard Holden
Thomas Burnim
Samuel Thomson
Peter Youngnam

Capt Monroe Company
David Parker

Capt Barnes Company
Levi Flitcher
Willard Hall

Colo Jackson Battallen
Capt Benjamin Brown
James Pieart

Colo marshall Battallen
Capt Warners Company
Ahimaaz Sherwin

JAMES BARRETT } muster master

No. 17.

March ye 6: 1778
To the Honor[b] Council for the State of massachusetts Bay I have mustered & paid the Bounty to the men Whose names are Hereafter menshond Sence my Last Return Viz

Colo Hanly Battallen
Capt Scot Company
Lawrence Johnston
John Beardsworth
James Cult
Steven McLouchlin

Thomas Chatmon
John McGregre

Capt Fox Company
Jonathan French
Joseph Henderson

Colo Biglow Battallen
Capt Smith Company
Michael Keenir
Amos Atherton
Amos Dole
Joseph Jones

Colo Nixon Battallen *Colo Wiggleworths Bat-* *Colo Jackson Battallen*
Capt Toogood Company   *tallen*   *Capt Brown Company*
William Neef   *Capt Danforth Company* Abner Lovjoy
                              [?] Sweet

Colo Aldin Battallen
Capt Allen Company
John Moruson

JAMES BARRETT } muster
            } master

No. 18.

May ye 23: 1778
To the Honor^b Council for the State of the massachusetts Bay I have musterd & paid the bounty to the men whose names are Hereafter menshend Sence my Last Returne Viz

Colo Bruer Battallen   *Colo Graton Battallen*   John Fenderson
Capt Paxton Company   *Capt Child Company*   Ruben Cambell
James Jones   John Bryant   George hut
John Stearns   Jonathan Libby
                           Colo Lee Battallen   Henery Small
Colol Nixon Battallen   *Capt North Company*   Peltih Fenderson
Capt Holden Company   William Braydon
William Crafford   James milliken   *Capt Scott Company*
Joseph Nixon   James mars [mors?]   John Brooks
Calven Emes   Ruben Severs   Samuel Speer

JAMES BARRETT } muster
            } master

No. 19.

may ye 23: 1778
To the Honor^b Council for the State of the massachusetts bay I have musterd and paid the twelve pounds bounty to the men whouse names are Hereafter menshond

Colo Jacobs Battallen   Joseph Dudley   Jesse Hopkins
Capt Smith Company   John Holdin   Thomas Gleson
Simeon Fisk   Abel Holdin   John Bennett
William Clott   Abraham Holdin   John Nickols
Isaac Williams   Solomon Sawtell   Roburt Hollon
John Parcker   Daniel Smith   Abel Lad
John Reed   Calvin keny   Jesse Fletcher
Simeon Fisk   Abel Brown   Isaac Peetten
oliver Darlings   Daniel Brown   Simeon Kemp
Ebenezer Gording Juner   Edmond Rise Jr   Philip Procter
Amos Atherton Junr   Cheaver Kendall   Jesse Colburn
Jonathan messer   mechel ones
Jonathan messer   *Capt Curtis Company*   James Forbush
James Colman Harper   James Allen   Aaron Wright
Lemuel Holden   Peter Jones   Newhall Reed
mel Parker   Aaron mason
William Williams Jun   *Colo Jacobs Battallen*   Cesar Hollon
Ephraim Warren   *Capt Andrews Company*   Bristol Cumings
Ephraim Warren Jun   Solomon Twiss   John Rose

Colo Waid Battallen	Amos Blood	Jonas Kemp
Capt Boyanton Company	Jonathan Barreon	Jacob Wetherbee
James Lake J[r]	Nathaniel Sartell	Samuel Parker
Josiah Robens	Isaac Blood	Isaac Wetherbee
Josiah Adems	Samuel Seward	Thomas Fillute
Ase Kemp	John Scott	David Gunkins
Lemuel Jenkens	Joseph Kemp	Calvin Parker

JAMES BARRETT } muster master

No. 20.

June y[e] 11 : 1778

To the Honor[b] Council for the State of the massachusetts bay I have musterd & paid the Bounty to the men Whose names are Hearafter menshond Sence my Last Returne viz

Colo Lee Battallen
Capt North Company
James Whitney
James Small

JAMES BARRETT } muster master

No. 21.

Concord August y[e] 8 : 1778

To the Honor[b] Council for the State of the massachusetts Bay I have musterd & paid the Bounty to the men whose names are Hereafter menshond Sence my Last Returne Viz

Colo Nixon Battallen	Thomas Robberson	*Colo Lee Battallen*
Capt Towgod Company	James Larry	*Capt North Company*
John Cannda	James Parkson	James Small
	James Boyes	James Whitney
Capt George marsdin Comp	Thomas Jones	Jonas Childs
John King	Nichlas Brown	Humfrey Alden

JAMES BARRETT } muster master

No. 22.

Concord August y[e] 8 : 1778

To the Honor[b] Council for the State of the nassachusetts bay I have musterd & paid the twelve pounds bounty to the men in Colo Jacobs & Colo Wade Battallen Sence my Last Returne Viz

Colo Jacobs Battallen	*Capt Smith Company*	*Colo Wade Battallen*
Capt Andrews Company	Benjamin Jefts	*Capt Parker Company*
John Cole		Nathel Chamberlin
Joseph Fowle	*Capt Curtis Company*	
Jonathan Eimes	John Prescott	*Capt Byanton Company*
Samuel Brek		John Chamberlin
		Joseph Boynton

JAMES BARRETT } muster master

No. 23.

September y[e] 19 : 1778

To the Honor[b] Council for the State of the massachusetts bay I have musterd & paid the bounty to the men Whose names are Hereafter menshond Sence my Last Return Viz

Colo Nixon Battallen	moses Sewers	Peter Rankins
Capt Gorge marsdin	William Broyan	Genderson Christopher
Company	John Brown	William Edwards

JAMES BARRETT } muster master

The three following lists (Nos. 24, 25 and 26) are without date or signature, but are in the same file as the foregoing returns.

No. 24.

Col marshels Battallen	John warner	Levi Priest
Capt Warner Company	Ezra Temple	Levi Carter
Silas Carter	Abel Wilder	Edom Lomrs
Nathaniel Evenes	Samuel mason	micah Nichals
william Parker	Thomas Robbins	Levi Dodge
Luke Aldrich	Asa Priest	Pyam Cushing
Thomas Rugg	Levi Blood	George Sardoars
Francies Pollord	John Joslin	Ammi Harrington
Adonijah Raly	John Bass	Joseph Batsla

This memorandum is not signed or endorsed.

No. 25.

Col Gratens Battallen	*Col Patterson Battallen*
Capt Childs Company	*Capt Hils Company*
John Barbarick	Thomas Fitch
Joseph Foster	

This memorandum is not signed or endorsed.

No. 26.　(A Pre-revolutionary Roll.)

Groton first Comp[a]
under y[e] Command of
Joseph Sheple
John Sawtell first L[t]
Ephraim Sawtell
　　Second L[t]
Phinehas Wait Ens[n]

Littleton first Company
Jonathan Read Cap
Aquilla Jewett L[t]
Joseph Dole Ens[n]

Second Company in Littleton
Elias Taylor Cap
Jonathan Patch Lt
Eleazer Fletcher Ens[n]

First Company in Westford
Amos Fletcher Cap
Jonas Prescott Jur L[t]
Nath[l] Boynton Ens[n]

Second Company in Westford
Jonathan Minott Cap
Moses Parker L[t]
Benj[n] Carver Ens[n]

The town of Ashby
　　　　Cap[t]
　　　　Liet
　　　　Ensign

Second Company in Groton
Nath[l] Parker Cap
Benj[n] Lawrence L[t]
John Woods Jur Ens[n]

first Company in Stow
William Whitcomb Cap
Joseph Taylor L[t]
Sam[l] Wetherbee Ens[n]

Second Company in Stow
Jonathan Hapgood Cap
David Jewell L[t]
Jacob Hale Ens[n]

Townshend Company
Isaac Farrow Cap
Benj[n] Brooks Ju Lt
Oliver Heldreth Ens[n]

District of Shirley
Sam[ll] Walker Cap
Asa Holden Lt
Obediah Sawtell Ens[n]

District of Pepperril
William Prescott Cap
Isaac Woods L[t]
John Nutting Ens[n]

Endorsed "Col[o] Prescott's Reg[t]."

WAS JOHN KETTELL KILLED BY THE INDIANS?

By Rev. GEORGE F. CLARK, of West Acton, Mass.

AT the bi-centennial of Stow, May, 1883, a stone was erected near the spot where it is believed that John Kettell, supposed to have been one of the first settlers of the town, built his log cabin. It bears this inscription: " John Kettell, one of the first two settlers of Stow, lived here. He was killed by the Indians Feb. 10, 1676." We think this statement is wholly erroneous, as we shall attempt to show. It is true that tradition, a very unreliable authority, as will appear by what follows, says that John Kettell and his two sons were slain at the above date, when the Indians destroyed Lancaster, and Mrs. Rowlandson, Mrs. Kettell, two daughters and others were taken prisoners. In fact, Hon. Henry S. Nourse of South Lancaster, in Lewis & Co.'s History of Worcester County, states that John Kettell, æ. 36, John Kettell, Jr., Joseph Kettell, æ. 10, were among the killed. Rev. Mr. Harrington of Lancaster, in his century sermon of 1753, says John Kettell and two sons were killed. We have recently given the matter a pretty thorough examination and find there is documentary evidence that seems to disprove the statement. Indeed there is very serious doubt whether John Kettell ever lived upon the place in the westerly part of Stow, near the original line of Lancaster. Rev. Jonathan Newell, of Stow, in his century sermon, in 1783, says: " About one hundred and thirty years ago two adventurers from Charlestown, Messrs. Kettell and Boon, with their families, settled upon lands they had purchased of the Indians, which land is known by their names to this day." He further states that Boon was "murdered by the Indians" in King Philip's war, but says nothing relative to the death of Kettell, which is a very significant fact.

John Kettell, according to T. B. Wyman, the compiler of the Genealogies and Estates of Charlestown, was the son of Richard Kettell of that place, and was born December 6, 1639. He had an older sister Hannah, and younger brothers, Joseph, Samuel, Nathaniel and Jonathan. He was sometimes at Lancaster, and was at Portsmouth, N. H., in 1663. From the will of Abraham Joslin, of Lancaster, probated in 1671, it appears that Goodman Kettell lived on one of his (Joslin's) farms; and he probably never owned land at or near Lancaster. He was a cooper by trade, and Portsmouth seems to have been a favorable place for his business. He married Sarah, the daughter of Mr. Edmund Goodnow, of Sudbury, who was born March 17, 1641-2. His second wife was Elizabeth Ward, of Ipswich. His children, so far as known, were: John, born 1661; Sarah, born March 8, 1662, at Sudbury; Joseph and Jonathan, born at Lancaster, November 24, 1670.* He and wife Sarah made a deed of land, in 1671, as per Exeter records. In March, 1675-6, just after the Lancaster raid, he was a culler of fish at Great Island, now New Castle, N. H. He made a deposition in 1678, on file at Exeter, wherein he gives his age as "about 38 years." This same man, then of Portsmouth, July 6, 1680, deeded land to Thomas Boylston of Muddy Brook, now Brookline.† At the request of his brother

---

* Probably there was another daughter, as it is stated that July 11, 1676, goodwife Kettell's elder daughter got away from the Indians to Marlborough, bringing her little sister upon her back.

† Middlesex Deeds, Vol. x., page 129.

Nathaniel, a commission was issued by the court in 1720-21 to appraise the estate of John Kettell, "sometime of Charlestown," "who died at sea about 30 years ago." James and Richard Kettell were appointed administrators, Feb. 22, 1720-21. The heirs appear to have been Richard, James and Benjamin Kettell. Wyman says the direct heirs of John had died. The estate comprised a lot of marsh land, described as the same piece of marsh which Richard Kettell gave in his will to his son John.

Now it seems pretty evident from these facts that Kettell was not killed by the Indians.

Again, just before the release of Mrs. Rowlandson, in May, 1676, an Indian sent word to John Kettell: " Your wife and all your child is well, and all them prisoners taken at Nashaway* is all well." Furthermore, James the printer wrote to Governor Leverett, in answer to a letter from the governor, dated March 31, 1676, saying: " We desire you to send Mr. Rolandson and Goodman Kettell (for their wives) and these Indians Tom and Peter to redeem their wives * * We ask Mrs. Rolandson how much your husband willing to give for you. She gave answer 20 pound in goods, but John Kettel's wife could not tel." Some of the Indians were acquainted with Lancaster people, and probably knew who were killed, and they certainly considered Mr. Kettell alive.

John Kettell, jr., reported as slain, married Abigail Austin, and died, of small pox, in March, 1691, æ. 30 years. In his will, dated March 11, 1690-91, he gave his wife one third of a farm his grandfather Goodnow gave him at Sudbury, and his widow subsequently joined with heirs of Edmund Goodnow in a deed of land. Thus John Kettell, jr., was alive some years after 1676. Joseph Kettell, son of John, sen., was one of the two grandsons of Edmund Goodnow mentioned in his will, in 1680, four years after the Lancaster raid. Samuel Kettell, the uncle of Joseph, " was appointed his guardian," who, as guardian, in connection with John Goodnow and Abigail Kettell, the widow of John, jr., whom Joseph calls his sister, deeded land to Noah Clap, March 8, 1692.† Dec. 27, 1693, Joseph Kettell ratifies this sale of land.‡ Does this mean that he was not of lawful age until 1693? If so, he surely could not have been ten years old in 1676. This evidence confirms us in the belief that the three Kettells were not killed by the Indians at Lancaster in 1676.

There was, however, another John Kettell, of Gloucester, but afterwards of Salem, whom some suppose to have been the one killed at Lancaster. He was about 18 years older than John of Charlestown, and his history is well known, and he died at Salem, Oct. 12, 1685. The inventory of his property was taken Nov. 10, 1685, about a month after his death. One item of the property was "a farm near Nashaway of 300 acres." This farm was undoubtedly the one called " Kettell's place " in Stow near the old Lancaster line. The selectmen of Stow, March 29, 1704, at the request of James Kettell, of Salem, surveyed this land, which he said was "formerly purchased" by his father. James Kettell, of Salem, sold the farm March 27, 1706, to Israel Held (Heald?) and it was bounded partly on " Elsabeth plain " and formerly a Court's grant to Samuel Symonds.‖ In the Massachusetts Colony Records, Vol. 4, Part 2, p. 139, is found a record of this grant to Mr. Symonds, in May, 1660, of three hundred acres " at Assibath

---

* Lancaster was originally called Nashaway.
† Middlesex Deeds, Vol. x., page 244.
‡ Middlesex Deeds, Vol. x., page 245.
‖ Middlesex Deeds, Vol. xiv., page 373.

Plain,"* on both sides of the road from Lancaster to Concord, bounded entirely by the wilderness. This Samuel Symonds belonged to Ipswich, and was for some years one of the magistrates of Massachusetts, and afterwards deputy governor, who died in office October, 1678. The bounds of the land, as given by the Court's grant and by the survey of the selectmen of Stow, are substantially the same. William Raymond, jr., quit-claims to James and Elizabeth Kettell his right to this land, which he says was "formerly in possession" of his honored grandfather John Kettell, who was the Salem man. Though this farm was "formerly purchased" and "formerly in possession" of John Kettell, of Salem, there is no evidence that he, or any other person, ever lived on it by the name of Kettell. Perhaps after the death of Mr. Symonds, Kettell "purchased" this tract of 300 acres, and thus came into the "possession" of it. However this may have been, we have already shown that *he* was not killed by the Indians, and it could not have been his wife and children who were taken prisoners at Lancaster. Mr. Wyman, already quoted, Mr. Frothingham, the historian of Charlestown and connected by marriage with the Kettell family, and Hon. James Savage, all agree that Mrs. Kettell, the prisoner, was the wife of John of Charlestown, and they were undoubtedly correct. How it happened that John Kettell, jr., and his brother Joseph were not slain in the Indian raid we do not know. They might have been at their grandfather's in Sudbury at the time. But conjecture is useless.

From the foregoing statement we submit to the candid critic whether the memorial stone erected by the town of Stow in 1883 states an historical truth.

MARRIAGES PERFORMED BY DANIEL WETHERELL IN NEW LONDON COUNTY, CONN.

Communicated by FRANK FARNSWORTH STARR, Esq., of Middletown, Conn.

RECENTLY, while examining the records of the New London County Court, at Norwich, I found the following marriages which were performed by Daniel Wetherell, commissioner : —

1667   November 28.   Gershome Palmer and Ann Denison
1668   July 2.   Charles Hill and Ruth Pickett widow to Jo^n Pickett Deceased.
1668   August 6.   Thomas Stedman and Hannah Nicholls
1668   October 1.   Daniel Lester and Hanah Foxes.
1668   November 11.   Eliezer Isbell and Elizabeth French
1668   December 24.   John Allen and Mary Gager.
1669   February 18.   James Avery Junior and Deborah Stullion.
1669   March 4.   Richard Smith and Bathsheba Rogers.
1669–70   "   18.   John Willye and Miriam Moore
1670   September 22.   Thomas Diman and Elizabeth Bradley.
1670   September 22.   Abell Moore and Hannah Hempstead.

---

* What is now called "Assabet brook" runs near and perhaps through a part of this plain, from which it probably took its name. It is variously spelled on old records as Assibath, Elsabeth, Assabet, &c.

NOTES AND QUERIES.

NOTES.

HERMON CAMP GOODWIN.—He was born October 13, 1813, in the town of Ulysses, Tompkins County, New York. His father, Joseph Goodwin, was a native of Pennsylvania, and his mother, Ruth Stout, was born in New Jersey(?). He was first married September 3, 1839, to Miss Jane Babcock, who died September 17, 1849. He was next married August 8, 1851, to Miss Lucy Wilson, who died July 4, 1886. He had two children, both still living, a son from his first marriage, named Benjamin Franklin Goodwin (P. O. address, Alfred Station, N. Y.), born May 24, 1841, married December 24, 1867, to Miss Cyrena A. Call; and a daughter from his second marriage, named Luella Andrea Goodwin (P. O. address, Cortland, N. Y.), born October 3, 1853, married (1) December 25, 1878, to Otis B. Woodward, and (2) October 28, 1893, to John P. Hamilton.

He died December 31, 1891, at Alfred, Alleghany County, New York.

His vocation was that of a writer of books and for the newspapers and periodicals. His principal work was the well-known History of Cortland County, so frequently referred to on account of its information in regard to the pioneers of central and southern New York. It is now quite rare and commands a high price in the second-hand sales. He also wrote a history of Ithaca, N. Y.; the Life of John Jacob Astor; Legends of Poland; Edgar Wentworth, a novel; and several other works that had quite a large circulation a quarter of a century ago. He also wrote poetry that was appreciated in their youth by men who are now old or dead. He was the editor of several country newspapers and a constant writer for others during a period of over forty years. He held no public office, so far as I am informed, except that of census enumerator for the county of Cortland during the Federal census of 1870.

Although he wrote to earn his living and hence wrote hastily, he had literary ability of a high order, but was oppressed throughout his life almost by that spectre of authors, *res angusta domi.*

For the parentage of Joseph Goodwin, father of Hermon C., see "The Goodwins of Hartford," by James Junius Goodwin, published by Brown & Yoass, Hartford, 1891.

The full title of Mr. Goodwin's History of Cortland County is "The Pioneer History of Cortland County and the Border Wars of New York," published by A. B. Burdick, New York, 1859.

By Hon. Irving G. Vance, of Syracuse, N. Y.

THE ST.-MEMIN COLLECTION OF PORTRAITS.—In 1862 a folio volume with this title was published by the late Elias Dexter of New York. It contained photographic copies of several hundred engraved profiles of American people executed by Charles Balthazar Julien Fevre de Saint-Memin, while residing in the United States, between the years 1793 and 1814, with 104 pages of letter press, consisting of an introduction, a memoir of St.-Memin and biographical notices of the persons whose portraits are in the collection. The artist was born at Dijon in France, March 12, 1770, and died there June 23, 1852. At his death he had proof impressions of all or nearly all of the portraits he engraved in this country, which are said to have been over 800 in number. He formed two sets of the profiles and wrote upon each impression the name of the subject. In 1859 one set was purchased at Dijon by Mr. James B. Robertson of New York and brought to this country. From this set the portraits in Mr. Dexter's volume were photographed. A set, either this or another, is said in Appleton's Cyclopædia of American Biography, vol. v, page 373, to be in the Corcoran gallery at Washington, D. C.

It would be a good thing, now that photo-engraving has been perfected to such an extent, if some one could make an arrangement by which a new edition of this volume, or a new work containing the portraits, could be brought out. More biographical details could be obtained now and more portraits identified. A third of a century has passed since Mr. Dexter's volume was issued.

J. W. D.

QUERIES.

NEW ENGLAND VESSELS CAPTURED BY PIRATES.—Is there anywhere on record an account, full or otherwise, of, or any illusions to, the loss of vessels, with names, experienced by the early merchants or shipowners of Boston, or other New England seaports, at the hands of the pirates that used to sweep the Spanish main? I ask, having come across the following old letter, amongst my family papers, written by one Captain Alexander Cupples, relating to his being taken and carried into St. Jago de Cuba, December 8, 1729 :—

Kingston, 8th Dec. 1729.

Sir,

Being acquainted with your desire I should give under my hand the particulars of my being taken and carried into St Jago de Cuba by the Spaniards, and their behaviour while I was among them, with what particulars I know relating to the Mulatoe Pyrate, I shall do in the manner following.

On the 28th Sept. I sailed from Jamaica in company with a ship called the Tryal, on the 5th Oct. I was taken about two leagues off Cape Donamaria Bay, by a Portorico Privateer commanded by Capt. Francesco Purdomo, who without asking any questions, commanded me on board, and robbed my ship of all moveables, on the 8th they carried me into St. Jago de Cuba; on my arrival there, the Governor immediately came on board with a Guard of Soldiers, after staying some time, he ordered my self and all my people on shore, except my Mate and Doctor; on the 9th they discharged some part of my cargo, but finding nothing prohibited, they loaded my ship up again, and the next day put her in my possession, and I should have gone away, had it not happened, that a Packet boat from Spain was taken in sight of their harbour by a ship which the Governor took to be one of your English Men of War, immediately they fitted out a sloop with a Flag of Truce for Jamaica to demand the Packet, telling me I must stay till the return of the Sloop from Jamaica, promising to make good all damages I should sustain thereby; it happened the Governor went to Porto Prince four days before the arrival of the Sloop, on her arrival the Alcaldes of the Town told me, I might take the ship, and be gone, but they could not make good any damages, unless the Governor was present; I drew out a Manifest of what Damages I had received, which amounted to on the Ship's account £250, and on my own £164, besides my people being stript, and very barbarously beat and abused.

I heard of the Mulatoe Pyrate every week, and very often saw her Lieutenant in that Port, also have seen and heard of 180 men that travelled to Bareyco to him, who continually cruizes from that Place and Crooked Island, he has joined Company with another Sloop and Periauger, who keeps in the Passage; they have brought into some Harbour about six leagues to the windward of Bareyco, two French ships, one Rhode Island Sloop and sent into St. Jago de Cuba two Boston built Sloops, taken in their passage from Jamaica, to whom or where they belong no person knew; they took a Sloop bound from Cape Francois to Boston, in some few hours after they killed eleven men out of thirteen, one of the two left I have now on board. The above are the particulars as far as I know.

I am, etc.

To the Hon'ble Charles Stewart Esqr   ALEXANDER CUPPLES.
Commander in Chief of His Majts Ships
in the West Indies.

The above Hon. Charles Stewart, 1681–1740, succeeded Admiral St. Loe, coming to the West India waters in the " Lion," Dec. 7, 1729, the latter dying that month. He was the son of Sir W. Stewart who became the celebrated Lord Mountjoy; returned to England in 1731, and died unmarried in 1740. This letter seems to me to be worthy of being printed in the REGISTER, especially if its appearance should be the means of bringing out facts, throwing light on a subject which, I think, has not been touched upon by any of our New England writers versed in the art of historiology.

Longwood, Mass.   JOSEPH GEORGE CUPPLES.

QUERIES:—
Colerain Presbyterian Church.—The first church in Colerain, Franklin County, Mass., was Scotch Presbyterian. Can any one give information of the whereabouts of the early records of this church?

Peter Shaw.—On the 14th October, 1705, the intention of marriage of Peter Shaw and Bethia Lovett was published in Beverly, Mass. Can any one give me the names of the parents of this Peter Shaw, or the date or place of his birth?

Joseph Anderson.—The intention of marriage of Joseph Anderson and Charity Nichols was published in Hingham, Mass., 3d December, 1724 (subsequently married in Boston). Can any one give me the names of the parents of this Joseph Anderson, or the time and place of his birth, or the time and place of death of Joseph Anderson or Charity Anderson, his wife?

Any one who can answer either of the above, will please write to R. K. SHAW, Marietta, Ohio.

WOODS AND WINTHROP.—Wanted the ancestry of the following persons:
1st. William Woods, born in Dorchester, Mass., died January 30th, 1779, in Dorchester, Mass.
2d. Capt. Winthrop, Boston, born in York, Maine, and died June 25th, 1817, in North Yarmouth, Me. EDWARD A. WOODS.
Pittsburg, Pa.

HOOPER.—Boston records state that Nathaniel Adams married Elizabeth Pormort 24 November, 1652; his children's birth notices and his wife's gravestone show that she was named Mary; probably the sister of Elizabeth born at Alford, England, 24th November 1633.

Elizabeth Pormort married Samuel Norden in August, 1656, and their daughter Mary, born 22 March, 1669, married (perhaps as Mary White in Boston, 16th February, 1693, by Cotton Mather) Samuel Hooper of Marblehead, who died before 1724, leaving children Samuel and Mary; and his widow then remarried a Perkins.

What was the ancestry of this Samuel Hooper? J. R. K.
47 West 9th St., New York City.

CALEB HILL.—Who was Caleb Hill of Rhode Island, who had a daughter Elizabeth (Betsy) born 20 July, 1776? Elizabeth's mother died when she was ten months old, and her father married again and lived in Massachusetts. By second marriage he had Polly (Mary), and sons, one being named Rufus. Was he one of the Hills of Prudence Islands and that vicinity—in which family the name Caleb Hill is used in three generations? Where did he live in Massachusetts, and who was Elizabeth's mother? R. S. TAFT.
Burlington, Vermont.

SIMONDS, MONTAGUE, ASPINWALL, &c.—Mary Simonds of Pawlet, Vt., (born April 23, 1754; died August 16, 1831), married Adonijah Montague, November 28, 1778. Wanted, the ancestry of Mary Simonds.

Zerviah Hawkins, of Coventry, Ct., married about 1793 or 1794, John S. Porter of that place. Wanted, her ancestry.

Sarah Collins married, October 20, 1732, Aaron Aspinwall of Farmington, Conn. Wanted, her ancestry. ALGERNON A. ASPINWALL.
1305 Riggs Street, Washington, D. C.

REPLIES.

KIMBALL.—A query in volume 18 of the REGISTER, page 244, quotes from an old account book thus: "Mothere Adams wente to live at brother John Kimbals the fifteene day of decembere 1680." Recently discovered data enable us to answer Mr. Appleton's query thus: Hannah Adams of Ipswich, born before 1641, daughter of William the ancestor, married Francis Muncy in December, 1659; she married secondly John Kimball. There were but three Johns then old enough. Which of them was it? ‡
47 West 9th St., New York City. J. R. K.

HISTORICAL INTELLIGENCE.

INDEX TO AMERICAN GENEALOGIES.—Joel Munsell's Sons, Albany, N. Y., have in preparation a supplement to the fourth edition of the Genealogical Index. The publishers desire to make this work accurate and complete. To do this they ask the coöperation of interested persons in correcting errors in the last edition and supplying things omitted.

THE WOODBURY GENEALOGICAL SOCIETY.—A society has been incorporated under the laws of Massachusetts with the above name, having for its object the collection of a history and genealogy of the Woodbury family. Hon. Charles Levi Woodbury of Boston is president, John Woodbury of Lynn treasurer, and Mrs. Lora A. (Woodbury) Underhill clerk of the society. Any descendant of John or of William Woodbury (the first settlers of Beverly) may become a member. Annual membership fee, $1.00; life membership, $10.00; honorary membership, $100.00. The society held a meeting at the rooms of the Essex Institute, Salem, June 13, 1896. Much valuable historical material has already been collected. Communications may be sent to the clerk, 127 St. Botolph street, Boston.

GENEALOGIES IN PREPARATION.—Persons of the several names are advised to furnish the compilers of these genealogies with records of their own families and other information which they think may be useful. We would suggest that all facts of interest illustrating family history or character be communicated, especially service under the U. S. Government, the holding of other offices, graduation from college or professional schools, occupation, with places and dates of birth, marriage, residence and death. When there are more than one christian name they should all be given in full if possible. No initials should be used when the full names are known.

Aspinwall.—Algernon A. Aspinwall, 1305 Riggs street, Washington, D. C., has been engaged for five years upon a genealogy of the Aspinwall family.

Blood.—John Balch Blood, Salem, Mass., has been engaged for a considerable time in gathering what facts and genealogical information he could of the Blood Family in America. The first settlers of the name came to Concord, Mass. The matter has assumed such proportions that he is unable to give the time to the work that he would like to, and he has placed the work of compilation in the hands of Eben Putnam of Salem, who has had much experience in such work. Subscriptions are solicited. Price, $7.50 to $10, according to binding. Address, Eben Putnam, P. O. Box 301, Salem, Mass.

Dickinson.—Frederick Dickinson, 226 La Salle street, Chicago, Ill., is compiling a genealogy of the family and descendants of Thomas Dickinson, son of Nathaniel Dickinson of Wethersfield, Conn., 1637.

Higginson.—Eben Putnam of Salem is engaged upon a genealogy of the Higginson family.

SOCIETIES AND THEIR PROCEEDINGS.

NEW-ENGLAND HISTORIC GENEALOGICAL SOCIETY.

Boston, Massachusetts, Wednesday, June 3, 1896.—A stated meeting was held this afternoon at three o'clock, in Marshall P. Wilder Hall in the Society's House, 18 Somerset street, Hon. Charles Levi Woodbury, vice-president, in the chair.

Charles Edwin Hurd, Esq., literary editor of the *Boston Evening Transcript*, read a paper on "The Boston Rebellion of 1689."

MAINE HISTORICAL SOCIETY.

Brunswick, Wednesday, June 24, 1896.—The annual meeting was held this afternoon, the president, Hon. James Phinney Baxter, in the chair. The following officers were chosen:

President.—James P. Baxter, Portland.
Vice-President.—Rufus K. Sewall, Wiscasset.
Corresponding Secretary.—Joseph Williamson, Belfast.
Biographer.—Joseph Williamson, Belfast.
Treasurer.—Fritz H. Jordan, Portland.
Recording Secretary, Librarian and Curator.—H. W. Bryant, Portland.
Standing Committee.—Henry S. Burrage, Portland; Henry L. Chapman, Brunswick; John Marshall Brown, Falmouth; Edward P. Burnham, Saco; Samuel C. Belcher, Farmington; Henry Ingalls, Wiscasset; Charles E. Nash, Augusta.

Three resident and five corresponding members were chosen.

RHODE ISLAND HISTORICAL SOCIETY.

Providence, July 7, 1896.—A quarterly meeting was held this afternoon at three o'clock.

Numerous additions to the library were reported. The committee on revolutionary records reported that the Rhode Island secretary of state had succeeded in obtaining the original military rolls that had long been in the Massachusetts state house.

NECROLOGY OF THE NEW-ENGLAND HISTORIC GENEALOGICAL SOCIETY.

Prepared by the Historiographer, Rev. GEORGE M. ADAMS, D.D., of Auburndale, Mass.

THE sketches of deceased members prepared for the REGISTER are of necessity brief, because the space that can be appropriated is quite limited. All the materials for more extended memoirs which can be gathered are preserved in the archives of the Society, and they will be available for use in preparing the "Memorial Biographies," of which five volumes have been issued and a sixth volume is in preparation. The income from the Towne Memorial Fund is devoted to the publication of these volumes.

WILLIAM GOODWIN RUSSELL, LL.D., elected a member of this society in 1891, was born on November 18, 1821, in Plymouth, Massachusetts, and died in Boston, February 6, 1896. He was the son of Thomas and Mary Ann (Goodwin) Russell, and came of Pilgrim stock, tracing his ancestry back to Miles Standish, John Alden and Richard Warren, of the passengers in the Mayflower. His earliest ancestor of the name of Russell in this country was John Russell, a merchant who came from Greenock, Scotland, and settled in Plymouth about 1745.

Mr. Russell received his early education in the schools of Plymouth, and for a few months before entering Harvard College came under the tuition of John Angier Shaw of Bridgewater. He entered Harvard College at the age of fourteen, and graduated in the class of 1840, assisting in paying the expenses of his college course by teaching school during the long vacations.

After graduating he taught a girls' school in Plymouth for a time, and was for a year master of the Academy of Dracut, where he succeeded the late Benjamin F. Butler.

He studied law in the office of his brother-in-law, William Whiting, and at the Harvard Law School, from which he graduated in 1845, and was admitted to the bar of Suffolk County in July of that same year. He at once entered into partnership with Mr. Whiting, and formed the firm of Whiting & Russell, which continued until the death of Mr. Whiting in 1873, when Mr. Russell took into partnership with him George Putnam, constituting the firm of Russell & Putnam, which continued until Mr. Russell's death.

At the time of Mr. Whiting's death Mr. Russell was already recognized as one of the leading men at the bar, and on the death of Mr. Sidney Bartlett he became the undisputed leader, a position which he filled to the day of his death. This position caused him to be consulted by men of all ranks and positions in the profession, who sought him as a friend and adviser in the many questions occurring in the practice of the legal profession that lie outside the province of courts and juries to decide. They always found him busy, but with time to listen and take an earnest interest in their difficulties and give his best thought to the solution thereof.

Mr. Russell, though taking a lively interest in public matters, had no desire for public office, and confined himself to the regular practice of his profession, refusing on several occasions judicial office; the last occasion being in 1881, when he was tendered the chief justiceship of Massachusetts by Governor Long.

He served as Overseer of Harvard College from 1869 to 1881, and from 1882 to 1894, and was at different times President of the Association of Alumni of Harvard College, President of the Bar Association of Harvard College, and of the Social Law Library, and trustee of the Boston Art Museum, and held other similar offices. He received the degree of LL.D. from Harvard College in 1878.

Mr. Russell's legal residence was in Boston from the time he began the practice of law until his death. His summer home he made in Plymouth, returning each year to the old house belonging to his wife's parents, which was always to him a second home.

An earnest, absorbed worker, devoting his whole energy to his profession, he yet had a great love for nature and for out-of-door life, and especially for the sport of fishing, and every summer holiday would see him either in the bay off Plymouth after mackerel or codfish; or off the rocks of Manomet fishing for tautog; or, with his light boat, which could be carried on wheels from pond to pond, trying every lurking place of the trout in Forge Pond, which he knew, from a boyhood passed in its vicinity, almost as well as its finny denizens, or fishing for bass or perch in the many ponds of the Plymouth woods, returning at evening sometimes with a good string of fish and sometimes without, but nearly always with a bunch of whatever wild flowers might be in season in the special locality which he visited.

His enjoyment of the beautiful in nature and art was keen, and his eye was as quick to detect a new flower or shrub while driving through strange or familiar country, as it was to pick out a good picture in a gallery or a choice piece of glass or pottery in a collection.

He was a reader of the best literature of the day, and while not a great *raconteur* or brilliant conversationalist, his talk was always interesting and commanded attention from the wide scope of his information and the soundness of his views and the simple clearness of his statements.

On October 6th, 1847, Mr. Russell was married to Mary Ellen, daughter of Thomas and Lydia Coffin Hedge, who died on September 13th, 1886. They had three children, two daughters and a son, who survive them.   T. R.

JOHN STANWOOD PULSIFER, a corresponding member, elected July 6, 1859, was the eldest of nine children of Bickford and Sarah (Stanwood) Pulsifer, of Ipswich, Massachusetts. He was born in that town, Tuesday, September 18, 1798. He learned the trade of a silversmith. On the 28th of February, 1817, he entered Phillips Andover Academy. After studying there a year, he left in 1818 and pursued his studies elsewhere, probably in New York city, with the intention of fitting himself for a clergyman. His brother David has this entry in his diary under 1825 : " In the first part of the spring my brother John came home from New York. I had not seen him since August, 1818." Mr. Pulsifer himself once told Mr. Samuel H. Madden, of Orwigsburg, that " he was away at school seven years and when he came back he could preach." The seven years may have included the one year which he spent at Andover Academy. I have no evidence that he was ever ordained. Rev. Charles C. Carpenter thinks it "much more probable that he was licensed to preach as teachers often were." He does not find his name as a licentiate of the Essex North Association. It is more likely that he was licensed before his return to Ipswich. I find no evidence that he was ever settled as a minister. He probably preached occasionally and supported himself by teaching, as we know that he afterwards did. A manuscript address by him is preserved, delivered before the Sunday School of the First Parish in Ipswich, October 28, 1827. He left New England in the summer of 1833 and went to Morris County, New Jersey, where he resided about four years and a half, engaged in teaching in various places. He taught school at Dover and German Valley, and had charge of the Academy at Parsippany. A manuscript address is preserved, which he delivered before the Parsippany Temperance Society, on the 4th of July, 1835. In 1837 he went to Pennsylvania and taught school in Easton and Upper Mount Bethel, in Northampton County. In the spring of 1838, he returned to Ipswich, Mass., going by the way of Kingston and Albany, N. Y. He spent a year or more in Ipswich, Boston and Salem. He left New England again, in 1839, and settled in Schuylkill County, Pennsylvania. His principal residence was Orwigsburg. Here and in towns in the vicinity, he taught school and exercised his profession of land surveyor. From several letters written in 1890 to Rev. Mr. Carpenter, of Andover, Mass., by Mr. Madden, of Orwigsburg, Mr. Pulsifer's administrator, I glean the following facts:

"My first acquaintance with him was in 1846. For a number of years prior to his death, we were intimate acquaintances. I visited him two or three times a week. His principal profession was that of a surveyor of lands. He served one term as county surveyor. He was educated for a Congregational minister. During my acquaintance with him he preached occasionally; I heard him once or twice, both in English and German. He was a man well informed, of sound judgment, and had a mechanical genius.

"While he lived here he invented a new alphabet of the English language, consisting of forty-four characters—representing the sounds of our language. To this alphabet he gave the name of Aubaot. He made the type for printing works in these characters, much of which was of wood. He printed some of his compositions in this type, but not for general distribution.

"He was much interested in Sunday Schools, and for a long time was superintendent of a Sunday School here. He also taught the public school in this borough. He was a staunch republican, and was a strong Union man during the war.

"In 1849 or 1850 he was sub-editor of the *Stimme des Volks* (Voice of the People), a German newspaper, published in this place.

"The year that President Pierce was elected he made a visit to his relatives in Massachusetts, and during his absence he corresponded with me."

He was made a Royal Arch Mason, August 27, 1844, by Schuylkill Royal Arch Chapter, No. 159, being then a Master Mason of Schuylkill Lodge, No. 138. In his application for the degree, he represents that he is a minister of the gospel, and "prays that in accordance with the established custom in such cases, he may receive the said degree without charge."

James Safford Norton, M.D., of Everett, Mass., has some numbers of *The Phonal Depot*, a newspaper printed in the type invented by Mr. Pulsifer. The size of the paper is 8 by 10½ inches. Many of the articles are printed in our common type. One, entitled *The New Alphabet called the Aubaot*, explains this new alphabet. From another number of the paper we glean these facts: "On the 3d day of June, A.D. 1848, the copyright of *The Writing Aubaot* was secured. On the 10th of July, A.D. 1848, the first number of the *Phonal Depot* was published. On the 20th of the same month, the *Writing Aubaot* was published. On the 19th day of October, A.D. 1848, the copyright for a book entitled ' *The English Alphabet* as formed by using and variously combining the letters of the Roman alphabet, illustrated and explained by *The New Alphabet* of the English language' was secured. The first edition of this work was on the 9th of November published in *The Depot*."

Dr. Norton, who is a nephew of David Pulsifer, has also several manuscript addresses and sermons by John S. Pulsifer. Some of the sermons are in the German language.

Mr. Pulsifer died at Orwigsburg, Sept. 6, 1866, and is buried in that town. A stone was erected over his remains by his brothers, with an inscription written by his brother David.

By John Ward Dean, A.M.

WILLIAM HOLCOMB WEBSTER, A.M., LL.B., elected a resident member April 6, 1870, admitted a life member in 1874, was born in Burlington, Hartford Co., Conn., Jan. 24, 1839. He was a son of Wm. Burnham Webster, born in Harwinton, Conn., in 1808, and Sarah Adelia Hull, born in North Haven, Conn., in

1817, and was eighth in descent from Gov. John Webster of Hartford, one of the founders of the Connecticut Colony.

In 1857 he was admitted to Trinity College at Hartford, and was graduated in 1861. He entered the military service at once, and was commissioned second lieutenant of company I, fifth regiment of Conn. Volunteers, Col. O. S. Ferry, July 10th, 1861. August 9th, 1862, he was promoted to the rank of first lieutenant, but on account of disability resigned April 6, 1863. His health having improved, he was appointed first lieutenant in the Veteran Reserve Corps in January, 1864, and was assigned to the Freedman's Bureau and abandoned lands, serving four years in Louisiana, during the reconstruction period. In June, 1869, Lieut. Webster was appointed a clerk in the Pension Office at Washington, and in 1875 was appointed chief of the Widows' Division of the Pension Office. Two years later he was placed at the head of the Old War and Navy and Bounty Division, where he remained till 1886, when he was appointed by President Cleveland Chief Examiner of the Civil Service Commission, to succeed Mr. Lyman, who had been appointed Commissioner. He was not a candidate for the place, but his experience on the departmental board of examiners, and his recognized ability, preëminently fitted him for the position, and he was chosen, though the place was eagerly sought by many others. He performed the duties of the new position with great success, till his sudden death of heart disease, March 23d, 1896. In addition to his work at the Pension Office he studied law and graduated at the Columbian Law School in 1871. He had prepared a History and Genealogy of his ancestor, Gov. John Webster, and descendants, but did not live to publish it. He aided the Adjutant General of Connecticut in recovering some of the army rolls giving the names of Revolutionary soldiers of Connecticut, and was greatly interested in genealogy.

He was married in Washington in 1871, and his wife and a daughter survive him. He was a member of the Loyal Legion, Grand Army, Sons of the American Revolution, Society of Colonial Wars, and N. E. Historic Genealogical Society. A memorial service was held in Washington, March 25th, by the Civil Service Commissioners, Board of Examiners, and others connected with this part of the government service, in memory of Mr. Webster, and in recognition of his high character, marked ability and great services during the thirty-five years of his public career.

By David H. Brown, A.B., of West Medford, Mass.

Prof. BENJAMIN FRANKLIN TWEED, A.M., elected a resident member, June 2, 1875, was born at Reading (South Parish), Mass., 17 January, 1811, and died at Cambridge, 2 April, 1896, aged 85 : 2 : 16. He was third of the four sons of Joshua and Elizabeth (Pratt) Tweed. Beginning as a shoemaker, while seated at his work the South Reading Academy was but a short distance away, and with teachers and pupils passing was in full view. There the inspiration was received for an education which was subsequently obtained at that institution. He taught winter terms of school in Lynnfield, Hyannis and Cotuit, and yearly terms at Medford, Cambridge and Charlestown; was resident of South Reading for many years, and during 1851, 1854 and 1856 served the town upon its school committee, as his father did in 1818 and 1823. He was professor of rhetoric, logic and English literature in Tufts College, 1855 to 1864, and of English literature in Washington University, St. Louis, Mo., 1864 to 1870; superintendent of schools, Charlestown, 1870 to 1876, and a supervisor of schools, Boston, 1876 to 1880. In 1853 he received the honorary degree of A.M. from Harvard University.

He was the author of Tweed's Grammar, and a partner in Tower & Tweed's (private) school, existing nearly half a century ago under Park Street Church.

He was twice married, first to Clara Foster of Danvers, who bore him one child, now the wife of Judge John W. Hammond of the Superior Court of Massachusetts, a former preceptor in South Reading Academy. His second wife, Miss Mary J. Herrick, also of Danvers, was a niece of the first Mrs. Tweed.

In personal appearance Prof. Tweed bore strong resemblance to the late Horace Mann, and to him may be considered a fitting successor.

Of his brothers, Joshua prepared for the ministry, but early deceased; Harrison was for many years the well-known head of one of the largest iron foundries, and Austin was a judge in California. All excellent vocalists, the older people of Wakefield yet recall with pride the rich harmony of their united voices.

By I. Gilbert Robbins, of Melrose, Mass.

AMOS[9] STONE, a resident member, elected January 7, 1874, was born August 16, 1816, in Weare, N. H., and died at his home in Everett, Mass., February 13, 1896. His parents were Phineas[8] and Hannah [Jones] Stone. On his paternal side he descends from Samuel[1] Stone through Gregory[2], John[3], Nathaniel[4], Ebenezer[5], Silas[6] and Silas[7]. His father was born in Harvard, Mass., removed to Weare in 1803, and in 1824 removed to Charlestown, Mass. Mr. Stone was educated in the schools of Charlestown, and assisted his father in the grocery trade. In comparative young manhood he began dealing in real estate, and became an authority on the titles of land in his city. When Charlestown became a city in 1847 he was elected its treasurer and collector, which offices he held seven years, when he was elected treasurer of Middlesex County, and until 1886, without a clerk or assistant, filled this important trust. He was treasurer of the Charlestown Five Cents Savings Bank, of which his brother Jonathan was president from 1854 onward; president of the Bunker Hill National Bank, and was actively connected with the Mutual Protection Fire Insurance Company, and also of the Mystic River Land Company. His brother Jonathan Stone was the last mayor of Charlestown, previous to its annexation to Boston. Mr. Stone was a public spirited man, with keen foresight, and regarded the permanent well-being of the community. In 1861, with twenty-one citizens, he equipped the first three military companies from Charlestown, and hastened them to the defence of the Union. He was also active in Masonic circles. In 1872 he removed to Everett, and entered at once into the improvement of this growing suburban city. He married, in 1866, Miss Sarah E. Mills. He left no children. For further literature upon his ancestry and career *vide* Histories of Weare, N. H., and of Harvard, Mass.

By Rev. Anson Titus, of Somerville, Mass.

Brig.-Gen. THOMAS LINCOLN CASEY, U.S.A., of Washington, D. C., a resident member, elected Sept, 6, 1882, was born at Madison Barracks, Sackett's Harbor, N. Y., May 10, 1831, and died at Washington, D. C., March 25, 1896, aged 64. For a memoir see REGISTER, vol. 50, pp. 431–434.

Hon. CLIFFORD STANLEY SIMS, D.C.L., a corresponding member, elected July 3, 1861, was born at Emeline Furnace, near Dauphin, Dauphin County, Pennsylvania, February 17, 1839, and died at Trenton, New Jersey, March 3, 1896. For a memoir with portrait, see REGISTER, vol. 50, pp. 425-431.

BOOK NOTICES.

[THE Editor requests persons sending books for notice to state, for the information of readers, the price of each book, with the amount to be added for postage when sent by mail.]

History of Danbury, Conn. 1684-1896. From Notes and Manuscript left by JAMES MONTGOMERY BAILEY. Compiled with Additions by SUSAN BENEDICT HILL. New York: Burr Printing House. 1896. Royal 8vo. pp. xxii.+583. Sold by A. N. Wildman, Danbury, Conn. Price in cloth $3, not including postage. Better bindings at higher prices. Send for circular.

Danbury, Connecticut, has been settled over two hundred years, eight persons from Norwalk with their families having in the summer of 1684 begun here some improvements in building, sowing grain, etc. The book before us gives the history of this town for the two hundred and twelve years of its existence. This is the first history of the town printed, though the Rev. Thomas Robbins, D.D., then a young man, in his Century Sermon at Danbury, January 1, 1801, commemorating the beginning of the Nineteenth Century, gave in his sermon a sketch of the history of the town, which is reprinted in this book.

The late James Montgomery Bailey, the popular author, and editor of the *Danbury News,* several years before his death began the preparation of a history of the home of his adoption. He died March 4, 1894, leaving his history unfinished. The Danbury Relief Society, of which Mr. Bailey was president at the time of his death, undertook, in accordance with his wishes, the completion and publication of the book. The society had the good fortune to secure the services of Mrs. Susan Benedict Hill, a lady whose tastes and literary ability in every way fitted her for the work she undertook. Mrs. Hill in her Preface says : "The broken threads that fell from lifeless fingers have been reverently gathered up and woven into the web of this history in the hope that the sons and daughters of Danbury, wherever they are scattered, may find some pleasing words of the old home, its early settlers and its citizens of today."

The goodly volume before us contains a comprehensive record of the events that have transpired in this ancient town. We have here the lives of those who have been prominent in local affairs and in the annals of our country ; accounts of the development of its various industries ; an account of the patriotic services which its citizens rendered in the several wars ; and its progressive movements in the cause of education with its schools, newspapers and other evidences of intelligence. The whole is told in an attractive manner, giving a lively picture of what has happened in Danbury for two centuries. Among its celebrities may be named Enoch Crosby, who is generally believed to have been the original of "Harvey Birch," the hero of Cooper's famous novel "The Spy." A good account of Crosby and his services is here preserved.

The book makes a handsome volume with its clear print, generous margins and elegant illustrations. There are about seventy pages of engravings, principally portraits of old residents and views of their residences, showing us the faces and homes of people "whose names and histories are allied with the beginning and growth of the town." Other views are given, as are also facsimiles of old documents, &c., &c.

The book does great credit to Mr. Bailey and to the compiler, Mrs. Hill, who has done her work in a very thorough manner. We trust that the Relief Society, in whose interest the book is published, will derive a handsome sum from its sale.

The New Education in the Old Dominion. Address before the Society of Alumni of the University of Virginia. By Rev. JOHN S. LINDSAY, of Boston. June 17, 1896. Sm. folio. pp. 8.

The Rev. Dr. Lindsay, rector of St. Paul's Church, Boston, a graduate of the University of Virginia, was honored by his *alma mater* with an invitation to address the Society of the Alumni at the last commencement. Dr. Lindsay accepted the invitation, and chose as the subject of his address "The New Education in the Old Dominion." He treats his subject in an impartial manner, and eloquently enforces his views. While giving due credit to the old Education in Virginia, he calmly considers the new ideas, the new conditions and the new needs which call for a new education. Dr. Lindsay is in full sympathy with the recent methods of instruction. As a specimen, both of his style and his views, we quote the closing paragraph of the address :

"In the future, when the patriotic pilgrim shall visit this shrine of learning, and see these hills crowned with stately buildings and these halls crowded with students eagerly seeking knowledge under wise leadership and with all modern facilities of study, or gathering up the results of observation and intellectual work for the benefit of mankind, he will recognize in this University one of the foremost forces of American civilization and appreciate the prophetic foresight of Jefferson, who, in writing the epitaph that should commemorate his highest achievements that claim for him chiefly the gratitude of generations to come, added to the sentence 'Author of the Declaration of American Independence and of the Statute of Virginia for Religious Liberty,' the pregnant words, ' *and Father of the University of Virginia.*'"

Rev. Jacob Bailey, his Character and Works. By CHARLES E. ALLEN. Read before the Lincoln County Historical Society, November 13, 1895. Printed for the Society. 1895. 8vo.

The Rev. Jacob Bailey was a "Missionary of the Church of England on Kennebec River," from 1760 to 1779. A memoir of him by the late Rev. William S. Bartlet, of Chelsea, Mass., was published in 1853, under the title of "The Frontier Missionary." Rev. Mr. Bailey left a valuable collection of historical documents which were placed in the hands of Mr. Bartlet, and which, we understand, have been used by Mr. Allen. The paper before us gives a vivid sketch of the trials of the loyalist missionary on the Kennebec river.

Celebration of the One Hundred Twenty-fifth Anniversary of the Massachusetts Lodge, 1770, May 17, 1895, with Historical Notes, By-Laws and a List of Members [coat of arms of Mass.]. Boston. Printed by order of the Lodge, 1896. 1 vol. 8vo. pp. 144. Press of T. R. Marvin & Co.

This venerable lodge is one of the only two who enjoy the honor of possessing a charter signed by Joseph Warren, the patriot of 1775. The difficulties and opposition attendant upon its formation are fully and comprehensively told in the Historical Notes, found in this volume, which comprise a resumé of prominent events in the history of the lodge, description of the halls in which its communications have been held, of their ornament, furniture and garniture, and presenting well executed cuts, viz.: portrait of Gen. Joseph Warren, Grand Master, 1770; of the dwelling on Warren street, Roxbury, in which he was born; of the various halls in Boston occupied by the Massachusetts Lodge; the Green Dragon Tavern, the Exchange Coffee House, the First and the Second Masonic Temples, with an interior of Sutton Hall. The full text of the historical address at the celebration of the 125th anniversary of the foundation of the lodge, 17 May, 1895, is given with an engraving of the portrait of the orator, S. W. Creech, Jr., a past master of the lodge. An interesting and valuable feature rests in the biographical sketches of gentlemen distinguished in the history of Boston, who have been members of the lodge. The code of by-laws and the list of members and officers conclude the volume, which is plentifully illustrated with half-tone cuts of the officers of the lodge at the date of the celebration, of the Grand Master of the Grand Lodge, of many of the Past Masters of Massachusetts Lodge, and of the Centenary Gavel of its members, and an engraving of the seal of the Grand Lodge. Comprehensive indices accompany the text.

The still, though deep current of usefulness and duty well performed, which has characterized the career of this lodge and of its members, is appropriately set forth in the pages of this well printed volume, constituting a cherished and convenient treasure and keepsake.

By Geo. A. Gordon, A.M., of Somerville, Mass.

Officers and Graduates of Columbia College: General Catalogue, 1754-1894. By JOHN H. VAN AMRINGE, Ph.D., and JOHN B. PINE, A.B., Committee. Printed for the College. 1894. 8vo. pp. 620.

Twelve general catalogues of the institution known successively as King's College and Columbia College have been published since its establishment in 1754. The improvement in the system of compilation of such works is well illustrated in a comparison of this work with the first general catalogue of King's College, published in 1774, and prefixed to this work in fac-simile. The first catalogue was a barren list of names in Latin, printed as a broadside. The present is a good-sized volume, comprising a brief historical sketch, followed by exhaustive classified lists of all officers of government and instruction, and graduates of the several departments, and recipients of honorary degrees. In the case of each graduate the occupation is given, together with university degrees received, offices held, etc., and in the case of living graduates the present address.

A useful part of the work, not yet common in general catalogues of colleges, is a locality index. This fills 100 pages, and in it are given the names of all living graduates grouped by states and cities. To each name is added the year of graduation and department of the college, and the street address. The number of graduates presumed to be living is 9082, and of these the addresses of about 4300 living in New York city are given, and more than 500 living in Brooklyn. The holders of degrees living in New England number 518, the professional schools being naturally most largely represented.

Where residences are given with the names of graduates, whether a locality index is added or not, the value of the work is greatly increased, for the graduates as well as for others who may have occasion to consult it. In the general catalogues of the two largest New England colleges the residences of alumni are not given. The compiler of one of them, in assigning the reason, said that the catalogue might be employed by advertisers to the annoyance of those whose addresses were given. It would hardly seem that the annoyance would counterbalance the advantages to be derived from publishing the places of residence.

The compilers of this work, and the printers as well, are deserving of much credit. The painstaking effort of the compilers is indicated by the fact that they issued nearly 10,000 return postal cards in order to secure accuracy. *By Samuel Merrill, LL.B., of Cambridge, Mass.*

Papers relating to Capt. Lawrence's Company raised in Groton, Massachusetts, during the French and Indian War, 1758. Remarks made before the Massachusetts Historical Society, May 8, 1890. By SAMUEL ABBOTT GREEN, M.D. 8vo. pp. 10.

On the 8th of May, 1890, Dr. Green presented to the Massachusetts Historical Society, some manuscripts relating to a military company raised in Groton during the French and Indian War. Dr. Green's remarks on the occasion and extracts from the manuscripts themselves are printed in the pamphlet before us. It is an interesting addition to the local military history of the time.

In the last number of the REGISTER, pp. 352 and 353, is printed from the Shattuck Manuscripts in the possession of this society a Billeting Roll of Capt. Lawrence's company March 28 to May 25, 1758. It gives some new items about this company.

Annual Register of Officers and Members of the Society of Colonial Wars. Constitution of the General Society. Published by authority of the General Assembly. New York. January, 1860. pp. 422+lxi.

Year Book of the Illinois Society of the Sons of the American Revolution. Organized January 14, 1890. Chicago. Wm. Johnston Printing Co. 1896. 8vo. pp. 319.

Eighth Annual Report of the Pennsylvania Society of the Sons of the Revolution, with Sermons and Addresses delivered before the Society, 1895-96. Philadelphia. 1896. Sm. 4to. pp. 319.

Order of the Founders and Patriots of America. Constitution, By-Laws and Charter Associates. Officers of the New York Society of the Founders and Patriots of America. April, 1896. New York. 12mo. pp. 47.

The brilliant exterior of the first three of the above list of publications will not be found to belie the worth of their contents. The first-named, besides presenting the roll of the General Officers and Delegates, and the Constitution of the General Society, contains the names of the officers and members of seventeen State Societies in the order of their establishment. An appendix of fifty-seven pages comprises the Report of the Committee on the Louisburg Memorial. Among the contents of the second of the list—which, as all similar works, supplies a catalogue of the Officers and Members, the Constitution, By-Laws, History and Necrology of the Society that issues it,—in addition is furnished a sketch of the services of Illinois in the Revolution, preceded by a notice of the National Society, explaining its origin, plan of organization and objects. An account of the Chicago Continental Guard is also included in the work. The third volume is more distinctively literary, with addresses whose noticeably religious earnestness and sermons whose flaming patriotism are exemplifications of the spirit of those ancestors whose memory the Patriotic Societies are designed to perpetuate. The title-page of the fourth describes the book.

Such publications as these must surely assist in promoting those objects for which the societies were founded, and multiply results of the nature defined in the Illinois Year Book in the closing paragraphs on the National Society, recapitulating "What the Society has done." *By Frederick W. Parke, of Boston.*

The Frontier Forts within the Wyoming Valley, Pennsylvania. A Report of the State Commission appointed to mark the Forts erected against the Indians prior to 1783. By SHELDON REYNOLDS, a Member of the Commission, and President of the Wyoming Historical and Geological Society. *With a Brief Memoir of the Author.* By ANDREW H. McCLINTOCK, M.A. Wilkes-Barré, Penn. 1896. Royal 8vo. pp. 48+4.

This admirable paper was read before the Wyoming Historical and Geological Society, December, 1894, and was first published by the State of Pennsylvania in one of two volumes, entitled "Frontier Forts." The writer of the paper was the president of the society, Sheldon Reynolds, M.A., who died at Saranac Lake, N. Y., February 8, 1895. The pamphlet is illustrated by views of some of the forts and other engravings. It is a valuable contribution to local history.

History of Tufts College. 1854-1856. Published by the Class of 1897. Editor in Chief : ALARIC BERTRAND START. Associate Editors : LEM G. BLANCHARD, FRANKLIN B. WILLIAMS, J. B. W. DAY, ROLLA E. HEALEY, STEPHEN C. M. MITCHELL, EDITH L. HODGE, GEORGIA L. HODGDON, FLINT M. BISSELL and R. WALDO PLACE. Business Manager : Warren S. Parks. Assistant Business Manager ; E. J. Hewett. Tufts College, Massachusetts. 1896. 8vo, pp. 382.

The class of 1897, Tufts College, rendered conspicuous service to its *alma mater* by the publication of its history. The College was founded in 1854, and during its forty years has made for itself a worthy place among the leading colleges of the country. Its presidents have been Hosea Ballou, D.D., 1854-1861, Alonzo A. Miner, D.D., 1861-1875, and Elmer Hewitt Capen, D.D., 1875 to the present time. This volume tells the story of its founding and marvellous growth and concerning its generous benefactors, its faithful instructors and alumni. The institution takes its name from Charles Tufts, a benefactor on whose homestead farm the College is situated. The site is historic ground. From its eminence a bird's-eye view of the scenes of the most exciting incidents of the Colonial and Provincial period is gained. The buildings for most part are in Medford, in which city is its corporate title; while much of its splendid campus is in Somerville (formerly a portion of Charlestown). During the past year there has been almost five hundred students in its various departments. The work of its College of Letters, Engineering, Divinity and Medical departments remind the reader that the institution is fast becoming a fully equipped University. This volume is graced by towards fifty views of its buildings and portraits of its faculty. Its index is excellent. It is the custom in this College for each class during its Junior year to publish a volume of some character. The class of '97 has abundant reason for gratulation upon its undertaking and superb accomplishment in the publication of this history. It easily takes a front rank, and serves as a worthy model to students in other colleges.

By Rev. Anson Titus, of Somerville, Mass.

George Huntington Williams. A Memorial by Friends for Friends. 1856-1894. Privately Printed. 1896. 1 vol. 8vo. pp. 150.

This series of monographs from most competent pens on the career of one of the most brilliant young Americans, terminated too soon by the chance accident of indulgence in a draught of water from an infected well, has been beautifully printed at the De Vinne Press. Mr. Williams was gifted with intellectual endowments of the highest order, and furnished with all the aids that wealth can bestow. His intense zeal and activity were restrained by the inheritance of a descent unsurpassed and tempered by the culture of family and social ties rare and unusual. To such an one life meant a great deal; and to his friends and admirers much more.

Mr. Williams was a contributor to the REGISTER before he was twenty-five, and it is with a large measure of regret that we place this beautiful volume among our biographies.

By Geo. A. Gordon, A.M., of Somerville, Mass.

A List of Genealogies Being Compiled. Collected by SEYMOUR MORRIS, Member of the N. E. H. G. Society. Chicago. 1896. 8vo. pp. 19. [For sale by the the compiler, at 142 La Salle street, Chicago. Price 50 cents.]

In July, 1895, a genealogical department, similar to that in the Notes and Queries of the *Boston Saturday Transcript,* was begun in the Saturday issues of the *Chicago Evening Journal,* with Seymour Morris as editor. Mr. Morris published in that column, from time to time, lists of genealogies in preparation. This department was suspended in the early winter, not for lack of success but on account of a change in the management of the paper. Mr. Morris, however, continued to gather the names of family historians, and has given in this pamphlet the result of his labors.

This work contains about four hundred family names, arranged in alphabetical order. Following each name is the address of the compiler of the family history, making a convenient directory. This directory fills fifteen octavo pages, and gives a very good idea of the present amount of interest in genealogical matters. The pamphlet also contains lists of manuscript genealogies in possession of various societies, of town histories in preparation and of genealogical periodicals.

Excepting Durrie's Index there is probably no single publication which will be of more service to the genealogist and searcher for ancestry than this little pamphlet.
By Wm. Prescott Greenlaw, of Cambridge, Mass.

Publications of the Library of Leland Stanford Junior University. I. *Catalogue of the Hopkins Railway Library.* By FREDERICK J. TEGGART, B.A., Assistant Librarian. Palo Alto, California. 1895. Sq. 8vo. pp. x.+231. Price $1.50 bound, $1.25 paper.

The Hopkins Railway Library is a collection of nearly ten thousand books and pamphlets relating to railroads and railroad subjects. The first two thousand volumes were gathered by Timothy Hopkins, while he was treasurer of the Southern Pacific Company, and presented to the Stanford University, in April, 1892, together with ample means for the increase and care of the collection. It is by far the largest mass of railway matter yet brought together.

This catalogue, the first publication of the library of the University, is a creditable piece of work. It is well classified for convenience. There is an author index, which also includes names mentioned in the notes. There are two columns to the page, printed from plain type on good paper. The Stanford University seems to have not only the lead in railway literature, but the men and the means to retain this advanced position.
By Wm. Prescott Greenlaw, of Cambridge.

The Equipment of the Sanctum. Address before the Maine Press Association, at its Annual Meeting, January 9, 1896. By SAMUEL LANE BOARDMAN. Portland : Printed for the Author. 8vo. pp. 18.

Mr. Boardman's address contains some valuable advice and suggestions as to the proper equipment of the editorial room of a newspaper, and particularly that of one of the great daily papers. He has had much experience in editorial work, and his remarks will well repay their perusal and study.

The Hazard Family of Rhode Island, 1635-1894; Being a Genealogy and History of the Descendants of Thomas Hazard, with Sketches of the Worthies of this Family, and Anecdotes Illustrative of their Traits and also of the Times in which they Lived. Embellished with Portraits and Fac-Similes, and with Map and Index. By CAROLINE E. ROBINSON. Boston : Printed for the Author. 1895. 4to. pp. vii.+293.

Genealogical Record of the Hodges Family of New England, ending December 31, 1894. Third Edition. Compiled by ALMON D. HODGES, Jr., and other Members of the Family. Boston : Printed for the Family by Frank H. Hodges. 1896. 8vo. pp. 566. Edition limited to 300 copies.

History and Genealogy of the Bangs Family in America, with Genealogical Tables and Notes. By DEAN DUDLEY. Tracing the Descendants, Male and Female, from the Pilgrim Ancestor, Edward Bangs of Plymouth and Eastham. Illustrated with Numerous Fine Engravings and Portraits. Published by the Author, Montrose, Mass. 1896. Royal 8vo. pp. 360. Price $5.

The Third Annual Meeting of the Governor Thomas Dudley Family Association, and Fourth Reunion of the Descendants of Governor Thomas Dudley, held in Boston, Oct. 15, 1895. 8vo. pp. 53.

The Comey-Comee Family in America, Descendants of David Comey of Concord, Mass., Killed in King Philip's War, 1676. With Notes on the Maltman Family. By ALLEN H. BENT. Boston : David Clapp & Son, Printers. 1896. 8vo. pp. 50.

American Ancestors of the Children of Joseph and Daniella Wheeler of whom we have records. Compiled by JOSEPH AND DANIELLA WHEELER, Alabama. 8vo. pp. 24.

Hills Family Genealogical and Historical Association. Incorporated July 6, 1894. Second Annual Report of the Directors, Boston, June 2, 1896. 8vo. pp. 10.

Short Notes on the Baker Family and also the related families of Clark, Comstock, Baxter, Chaffee, Brown and Mason. Compiled by GEO: COMSTOCK BAKER, LL.M. Comstock, N. Y. Privately Printed. 1896. Broad 8vo. pp. 11.

The Genealogy of the Atwell Family of New London, Conn. Prepared by CHARLES BEACH ATWELL, Evanston, Illinois. 1896. 8vo. pp. 10.

We continue, in this number, our quarterly notices of works recently published on family history.

The book on the Hazard Family of Rhode Island fills a long felt want. The Hazards have long held a prominent place in New England history, and particularly in that of Rhode Island. Thomas Hazard, the progenitor of the families recorded in this book, was born about 1610, and came to New England about 1635, his name being found at Boston in that year. On the 25th of March, 1638, he was admitted freeman of Massachusetts. In 1639, he with William Coddington and others removed to the island of Aquidneck, now Newport, R. I., where they founded a colony. Mr. Hazard was chosen one of the first officers in the colony. Mrs. Robinson, of Wakefield, R. I., the compiler of the volume before us, is a descendant of this family. She tells us in her prospectus that she "has not endeavored to make a scientific, formal, or final historical work, but a collection of materials which shall serve the future historian not alone of this family, but of the period covered by its life. . . . The data for the work has been for some years past patiently gathered from all kinds of sources, not the least interesting part of the book being the stories of old Narragansett life, often taken from the mouths of the inhabitants of the country side, who in their isolated surroundings preserve with singular vividness the traditions of an older day." Mrs. Robinson has succeeded in gathering in this book a full and precise record of nearly three thousand descendants, including some of the tenth generation. The book is carefully arranged, well printed in antique style, and has a thorough index. It is illustrated with a number of portraits, among them one of William Coddington, and numerous fac-similes.

The book on the Hodges family is the third book giving the genealogy of that family which has been printed in New England. Mr. Hodges, the compiler of this volume, prefers to call it a "third edition"; that is, he considers it the third edition of the book published in 1837 by Rufus Hodges of Cincinnati (12mo. pp. 22), which was enlarged by the late Col. Almon Danforth Hodges, and published in 1853 (8vo. pp. 71). The compiler of the present volume, who is a son of the compiler of the edition of 1853, has very much enlarged the work. Instead of seventy-one octavo pages we have now five hundred pages besides the index; and each page contains much more matter. Mr. Hodges has devoted much time to compiling this work and has succeeded in making it a remarkably full and accurate genealogy. Indeed we know of no work on which so much time has been expended in verifying the statements and freeing the work from error. The book is arranged on the REGISTER PLAN, and makes a handsome volume. The index is a remarkably full one. Each person mentioned is indexed, and in cases where the person's name was changed the new name is also indexed. We understand that all, or nearly all, of the copies printed were subscribed for, so that it will be difficult to obtain the book.

The volume on the Bangs family is by Dean Dudley of Montrose, Mass., who commenced his labor on the work in 1849, nearly half a century ago. He is the author of the Dudley Genealogy, of which the first edition, an octavo of 144 pages, was published in 1848, and the second of twelve hundred pages was issued in 1894. Mr. Dudley is the author of a number of other works that have found favor with the public. The present volume is compiled with great care, and is clearly arranged. The book makes a handsome volume, is well printed, with numerous illustrations, principally portraits. It is thoroughly indexed. The emigrant ancestor of this family was Edward Bangs, born about 1592, who came to New England in the Anne, which arrived here July, 1623. He settled at Plymouth, but afterwards removed to Eastham, where he died. His descendants are numerous and scattered over the country. Mr. Dudley has done a good service to his kinsmen in collecting the records of a widely scattered race.

The pamphlet report of the third Annual Meeting of the Governor Thomas Dudley Family Association is edited by Messrs. L. Edwin Dudley, Albion M. Dudley and Dudley R. Child. The proceedings on that occasion are well calculated to interest the descendants of Gov. Dudley in their ancestry, which is a very honorable one. The pamphlet is well printed, and is illustrated with portraits of Paul Dudley and Lucy Wainwright Dudley and a view of the Parting Stone at Roxbury.

The Comey-Comee pamphlet is a reprint from the REGISTER for April, 1896, with the addition of an article on the Maltman Family, some other historical matter and a good index.

The American Ancestors of Joseph and Daniella Wheeler contains brief records of several families, from which Hon. Joseph Wheeler of Alabama and his wife are descended.

The pamphlet on the Hills Family Association contains an account of the encouraging work done in collecting material for a history of Joseph Hills of Malden, his ancestors and descendants. A report of the proceedings at the second annual meeting of the association, June 2, 1896, has also been printed and is before us.

The Baker pamphlet gives genealogical records of the descendants of John Baker, a soldier in King Philip's War, and notes on the other families named in the title page.

The Atwell pamphlet is devoted to the descendants of Benjamin Atwell of New London, whose name appears in 1663. It is well compiled.

RECENT PUBLICATIONS,*

PRESENTED TO THE NEW-ENGLAND HISTORIC GENEALOGICAL SOCIETY FROM JUNE 1 TO JULY 15, 1896.

Prepared by the Assistant Librarian.

I. *Publications written or edited by Members of the Society.*

Genealogy.

Genealogical Record of the Hodges Family of New England, ending December 31, 1894. Third edition. Compiled by Almon D. Hodges, Jr., and other members of the family. Boston. Printed for the family by Frank H. Hodges. 1896. 8vo. pp. 566.

County Records of the Surnames of Francus, Franceis, French, in England, A.D. 1100–1350. By A. D. Weld French, *Author of the " Index Armorial," " Frenches in Scotland," Fellow of the Society of Antiquaries of Scotland, Member of the Scottish Historical Society and of the Committee on Heraldry of the New-England Historic Genealogical Society.* Boston. Privately printed. 1896. 8vo. pp. 594+8.

Genealogical and Historical Sketches of the Allen Family of Dedham and Medfield, Mass., 1637–1890. Compiled by Frank Allen Hutchinson, *member of the New-England Historic Genealogical Society, and corresponding member of the Dedham Historical Society.* Privately printed. Lowell, Mass. 1896. 8vo. pp. 80. [100 copies printed. Price $3.00 and not $1.00 as given in the July Register.]

The Comey-Comee Family in America. Descendants of David Comey, of Concord, Mass., killed in King Philip's War, 1676. With notes on the Maltman Family. By Allen H. Bent, of Boston, *member of the New-England Historic Genealogical Society.* Boston: David Clapp & Son, Printers. 1896: 8vo. pp. 50.

Biography.

Rev. William Blackstone, the Pioneer of Boston. By John C. Crane, *member of the New-England Historic Genealogical Society.* Worcester, Mass. Charles R. Stobbs, printer. 1896. 8vo. pp. 14.

Andrew P. Peabody, D.D., LL.D. A Memoir. By Edward J. Young. Prepared for the Massachusetts Historical Society. Cambridge: John Wilson and Son, University Press. 1896. 8vo. pp. 28.

II. *Other Publications.*

History.

The Frontier Forts within the Wyoming Valley, Pennsylvania. A report of the State Commission appointed to mark the forts erected against the Indians prior to 1783. By Sheldon Reynolds, M. A., a member of the Commission, and president of the Wyoming Historical and Geological Society. With a brief Memoir of the author. By Andrew H. McClintock, M. A. Read before the Wyoming Historical and Geological Society, December, 1894, and reprinted from the State Report, 1896. Wilkes-Barre, Penn'a. 1896. 8vo. pp. 48.

------

* This list does not include publications which are elsewhere noticed, unless written by a member.

Biography.

Memorial Tributes to Eben D. Jordan. Born Oct. 13, 1822—Died Nov. 15, 1895. Boston. Press of George H. Ellis, 141 Franklin street. 1896. 8vo. pp. 98.

In Memoriam. Deacon Joshua Hale. Biografhical Sketch and Funeral Sermon. [Sermon preached in the Bellevue Church, Newburyport, Massachusetts, by Rev. Albert W. Hitchcock, May 6, 1894.] 12mo. pp. 28.

Memorial Sermon on the Rev. David Greene Haskins, D. D., Rector of St. Bartholomew's Church, Cambridge, Mass., by The Rev. Horatio Gray, A. M. Delivered in St. Bartholomew's Church, Cambridge, May 31, 1896. Repeated by request in Grace Church, Medford, Mass., June 14, 1896. Published by request. Boston: Damrell and Upham, the Old Corner Bookstore, 283 Washington street. 1896. 8vo. pp. 20. Arthur Clark Sisson. 12mo. pp. 17.

Colleges and Schools.

Thirtieth Annual Catalogue of the Massachusetts College of Pharmacy. 1896–97. College Building, corner St. Botolph and Garrison streets, Boston. [1896.] 12mo. pp. 58+xiv.

Addresses of the Living Graduates of Dartmouth College, the Medical College and the Thayer School of Civil Engineering. March, 1894. [Rochester, N. H., 1894.] 8vo. pp. 70.

Report of the President of Bowdoin College for the Academic Year 1895-96, to which are appended the reports of the Librarian and the Special Committee on Library. Brunswick, Maine. 1896. 8vo. pp. 30.

Obituary Record of the Graduates of Dartmouth College and the Associated Institutions, whose decease was reported during the year ending at Commencement, 1896. By John M. Comstock, statistical secretary of the Association of Alumni of Dartmouth College. Hanover, N. H. Dartmouth Press. 1896. 8vo. pp. 20.

Catalogue of the Trustees, Instructors and Students of Lawrence Academy, Groton, Mass., for the year ending June 25, 1896. One Hundred and Third Year. Ayer, Mass. Wm. M. Sargent, printer. 1896. 12mo pp. 17.

Obituary Record of the Graduates of Bowdoin College and the Medical School of Maine for the year ending, June, 1896. No. 7, Second Series. [1896.] 8vo. pp. 299 to 342.

Societies and Institutions.

Proceedings of the Massachusetts Historical Society. Second Series,—Vol X. 1895, 1896. Boston. Published by the Society. 1896. 8vo. pp. xx.+616.

Collections of the Connecticut Historical Society. Vol. V. Hartford. Published by the Society. 1896. 8vo. pp. xviii.+517.

Methuen Historical Society Publications. Publication No. 1. [1896.] 12mo. pp. 19.

Publications of the Ipswich Historical Society. I. The Oration by Rev. Washington Choate, and Poem by Rev. Edgar F. Davis, on the 200th Anniversary of the Resistance to the Andros Tax. At Ipswich, July 4, 1887. Salem: Salem Observer Book and Job Print. 1894. 8vo. pp. 30.

Publications of the Ipswich Historical Society. II. The President's Address and other Proceedings at the Dedication of their New Room, Friday, Feb. 3, 1896. Ipswich: Independent Book and Job Print. 1896. 8vo. pp. 8.

The Proceedings and Transactions of the Nova Scotian Institute of Science, Halifax, Nova Scotia. Session of 1894–95. Vol. IX. (Being volume II. of the Second Series). Part I. With six plates, Halifax, N. S. Printed for the Institute by the Nova Scotia Printing Company. 1896. 8vo. pp. xxii.+100+3.

Transactions of the Massachusetts Horticultural Society for the year 1895. Part I. Boston. Printed for the Society. 1896. 8vo. pp. 175+2.

Forty-Third Annual Report of the Directors of the American Congregational Association. Presented May 25, 1896. Boston. American Congregational Association. Congregational House. 1896. 8vo. pp. 18.

U. S. Government, State and Municipal Publications.

Report of the Superintendent of the U. S. Coast and Geodetic Survey, showing the progress of the work during the fiscal year ending with June, 1894. In two parts. Part II. Appendices relating to the methods, discussions, and results of the Coast and Geodetic Survey. Washington: Government Printing Office. 1895. 4to. pp. 615.

Thirteenth Annual Report of the Bureau of Ethnology to the Secretary of the Smithsonian Institution, 1891–'92. By J. W. Powell, Director. Washington: Government Printing Office. 1896. 4to. pp. lix+462.

The War of the Rebellion: A Compilation of the Official Records of the Union and Confederate Armies * * * * Series I.—Volume XLVIII. In two parts. Part I.—Reports, Correspondence, etc. Washington: Government Printing Office. 1896. 8vo. pp. 1657.

Copy of that portion of the Proprietors' Records of Tyng's Township relating to the present Town of Jaffrey. Compiled and presented to the Town of Jaffrey by the City of Manchester in recognition of the gift of the original records to the City by the Town. 1896. 8vo. pp. 14.

Report of the City Auditor of the Receipts and Expenditures of the City of Boston and County of Suffolk, Commonwealth of Massachusetts. For the Financial Year 1895-96. February 1, 1895, to January 31, 1896 (both included). City Document, No. 3. Boston: Rockwell and Churchill, City Printers. 1896. 8vo. pp. 294.

Annual Report of the Trustees of the Public Library of the City of Boston. 1895. Boston: Rockwell and Churchill, City Printers. 1896. 8vo. pp. 158.

Rules and Regulations of the Public Library of the City of Boston. Revised to March, 1896. 16 mo. pp. 16.

Miscellaneous.

A Review of a So-called Supplement to the Acts and Resolves of Massachusetts, 1780-1784. [By James J. Tracy, Chief of Archives Division, Office of the Secretary of the Commonwealth. June 3, 1896.] Boston. 8vo. pp. 8.

Catalogue of Loan Collection at Punchard Hall. The Two Hundred and Fiftieth Anniversary Celebration, Town of Andover, Massachusetts. 1896. 12mo. pp. 42.

DEATHS.

Mrs. MARY BUCKLIN CLAFLIN, wife of Hon. William Claflin, LL.D., president of the New-England Historic Genealogical Society, died at Whitinsville, Mass., Saturday, June 13, 1896. She was a daughter of Hon. Samuel Daniels and Mrs. Mary C. (Bucklin) Davenport, of Hopkinton, Mass., and was born July 31, 1825. On the 12th of February, 1845, she married Mr. Claflin, who was then in business in St. Louis, Missouri. She was a woman of great resources, benevolent and public spirited. Soon after they were married, Mr. Claflin built a handsome house in Newtonville, where Mrs. Claflin exercised a generous and warmhearted hospitality. Particularly was this the case during the three years from 1869 to 1872, when her husband was governor of the Commonwealth of Massachusetts. Among her guests were Harriet Beecher Stowe, the poet Whittier, Charles Sumner and Henry Wilson. She was chosen a trustee of the Boston University in January, 1878. "At the date of her election," says Rev. Dr. William F. Warren, president of that institution, "no woman had ever served in like capacity in any university in Europe or in the eastern portion of our wide republic.

The original statutes of the University had purposely been so drawn that women should be eligible equally with men, and to her and her friend, Mrs. Mary Hemenway, fell the honor of being the first to illustrate in this part of the world the fitness of able and cultured women to bear a hand in shaping and conducting the highest agencies of liberal and professional education. Both abundantly justified the confidence reposed in them; particularly must this be said of Mrs. Claflin, who was permitted to give more years than her friend to this absorbing work." She was also a trustee of Wellesley College. She was the author of "Brampton Sketches," "Personal Recollections of John G. Whittier," "Real Happenings," and "Under the Elms." The last title has reference to her residence in Newtonville, which was known as "The Old Elms." It is "a book of reminiscences of the many distinguished friends entertained by the family." Her funeral took place at their Boston residence, 63 Mount Vernon street, on the 16th of June, at two o'clock in the afternoon. Her husband and two sons survive her. A daughter Agnes died at Rome, Italy, in 1869.

IRVING WHITALL LYON, M.D., of Hartford, Conn., died suddenly at his home in that city, March 3, 1896. He graduated at the Medical School of the University of Vermont, in 1862, and at that of Columbia College in 1863. In 1866, on the formation of the Hartford Life and Annuity Company he was chosen Medical Examiner, and held the office till his death. He had been also president of the Hartford County Medical Society. Hon. Charles J. Hoadly, LL.D., president of the Connecticut Historical Society, in his annual address before that society, May 26, 1896, says of Dr. Lyon, who had been a member since April 6, 1866: "As a man and friend he was honored and respected by all who knew him. In his profession he stood high..... In the midst of his busy professional life he found time to gratify his antiquarian tastes, and in 1891 he published as the result of years of research his "Colonial Furniture in New England," a volume which at once became the recognized authority upon its subject, and made its author known throughout this country and Europe. As soon as this work was published he began upon another, which would have added still further to his renown, and which his sudden death left uncompleted. This last was a study of the architecture of the early houses of New England."

He left two sons and one daughter, besides a widow. The elder son, a graduate of Yale, is now a student at Johns Hopkins University, Baltimore.

GENEALOGICAL GLEANINGS IN ENGLAND.

By HENRY F. WATERS, A.M.

[Continued from page 424.]

JAMES ALLYNE of Swimbridge (Devon), 26 June 18ᵗʰ James (1621), proved 4 January 1621. The poor of Swimbridge and of Launkey. To my daughter Mary one hundred pounds at seven years of age. To my brother George ten pounds to be paid 25 March 1624. To my brother Matthew ten pounds to be paid 25 March 1623. John Badcocke, George Cruse, Em Gull and Hugh Meare. My "godchiller." My wife Joane to be sole executrix and John Leuse and Matthew Allyne to see the will performed. Matthew Allyne a witness. Savile, 5.

BARTHOLOMEW CHICHESTER of Braunton Devon, gentleman, 10 October 1632, proved 17 February 1635. The poor of Braunton. To wife Katherine all my messuages, lands &c. in Georgeham Devon (except a close called the new close). I give and bequeath unto Margaret Allyn my kinswoman the wife of Matthew Allyn ten pounds. To Philip Wyott my kinsman all my messuages &c. in Newknoll in said parish of Braunton, after the decease of my wife Katherine until 10 December 1699 and my new close in Georgeham, late purchased of Robert Baker. To my cousin John Chichester of Arlington Esq. a silver bowl worth five pounds sterling. My cousin George Beare. My cousin Dr Peter Muden. My cousins Johane Wyott and Agnes Wyott. John Wyot of Horridge. My servant Thomas Jones and Marrian his wife. Other servants. Wife Katherine and cousin Philip Wyot to be executors and residuary legatees. Pile, 16.

RICHARD ALLEN the elder of Branton in Devon 29 November 1647, proved 10 May 1652. To my son Thomas Allinge five pounds. To my son Mathew Allinge five pounds. To Mary Allinge daughter of son Thomas twenty shillings. I give and bequeath unto my son Mathew's three children, to John the sum of twenty shillings, to Thomas, his son, twenty shillings and to Mary, his daughter, twenty shillings.   To my grandchild Mary Tamling five pounds, to my grandchild Elianor Tamling four pounds, to my grandchild Obedience Garland twenty shillings and to my grandchild Elizabeth Tamling twenty shillings.   To my daughter in law Elizabeth, wife of my son Richard, twenty shillings in gold to buy her a ring.   To my grandchild John Alling, son of my son Richard three pounds.   To my grandchild Margaret, daughter of my son Richard, three pounds.   To John Rice of Barnstaple twenty shillings.   To the poor of Branton three pounds, to be distributed to their houses within ten days after my decease.   To Walter Cutt five shillings.   To every servant in my house at the time of my death two shillings sixpence apiece.   Son Richard Alling to be executor and residuary legatee.   Bowyer, 108.

[On page 496 of REGISTER for October, 1894 (Vol. 48), I gave the will of William Thorne of Estdowne Devon and in the note appended to that will furnished my reasons for supposing the Mr. Mathew Allyn mentioned in Mr. Thorne's will was our Matthew Allyn of Cambridge, Mass., and afterwards of Hartford and Windsor, Conn. I made it clear too that our Thomas Allen of Barnstable, Mass., was of the same family and that the latter had a brother Richard living in Braunton Devonshire. Now the foregoing will of Richard Allen the elder of Braunton names sons Thomas, Matthew and Richard and also Mary the daughter of Thomas, and John, Thomas and Mary the children of Matthew, while the will of Bartholomew Chichester of Braunton calls Margaret* the wife of Matthew Allyn " kinswoman." I have not the Visitation of Devon at hand to examine the Chichester pedigrees, but I doubt not we have here a promising clew to help some of our Connecticut and Massachusetts friends in tracing their English ancestry.—H. F. W.]   .

RICHARD ALLYN of Branton in the County of Devon, yeoman, 12 May 1662, proved 17 June 1662. To my son John tenement in Bushton in the Parish of West Buckland. Daughter Margaret. To my wife my messuages, lands &c. in Bowde within the said parish of Branton. Son Richard to have my part of grounds in Frithelstock at age of twenty one. To said Richard the tenement in Branton town within the manor of Branton Deane. To son Thomas messuages &c. in Barnstaple. To son Matthew messuages &c. in Northam. My daughter Elizabeth. Daughter Mary, at twenty one. Wife Elizabeth to be sole executrix and good friends and kinsmen Philip Dennys of Ilfarcombe (Ilfracombe), Thomas Denys of Barnstaple, John Symons the elder of Branton and Richard Tamlyn of Marwood to be aiding and assisting unto my said executrix, whom I make overseers.   Laud, 78.

CHRISTOPHER CADE of Northam, Devon, mariner, 8 February 1622, proved 25 June 1623. To the reparations of the church and the poor of the parish. Whereas I have an estate &c. of messuages, lands and tenements wherein I now inhabit and dwell for certain years determinable upon lives, as in and by the deed indented thereof shall or may appear, the same messuages &c. I give to Mary my wife during her life, and after her decease to my son William during all my estate therein &c. if the said William die not before he be married. If he so die &c. then it is to come to my son James, next to my son John. One annuity or yearly rent of five pounds issuing out of certain messuages, lands &c. called Knap *als* Lower Knapp, in Northam to wife Mary and sons James, William and John (as above). A certain estate in Hartland to sons John, William and James (as above),

* See Lechford's Note-Book, page 86 (as printed).

they to pay to my sister Ellinor Bante every year during the life of Clase Middleton three pounds &c. To son William all my fishing nets and all my salt and caske in Ireland, all my wearing apparel and implements for the sea and twenty pounds &c. To son James twenty pounds. To my daughter Phillipp Cade fifty pounds, and forty pounds more to her at day of marriage if she marry with consent of my overseers. To my daughter Thomzin Cade ten shillings. The residue to wife Mary whom I make sole executrix.

James Cade the elder one of the witnesses.   Swann, 58.

HENRY CADE of Northam Devon, shipwright, 6 April 1645, proved 25 September 1646. Daughter Mary Cade. Dwelling house standing on Mr Lee's lands. Son Henry and daughter Elizabeth. My barque called the Elizabeth. To wife Christian Cade my now dwelling house for life and next to son Henry and my two daughters Margaret and Joane. I give my two third parts of the barque called the Phillipp to my son Phillipp Cade and my daughter Margaret Cade. To daughter Joane one eighth part of the barque James of Appledore. Wife to be executrix.

                                              Twisse, 131.

[The foregoing couple of wills relate to a family which was represented in New England by James Cade of Boston, Mass., shipwright, who, with wife Margaret, conveyed 4 December, 1638, to George Strange, gentleman, a dwelling house (lately erected) and fourteen acres of land in the parish of Northam Devon, and also an interest and right unto one rent charge or annuity of five pounds per annum going or coming out of three messuages and tenements and four acres of land in Northam, lately purchased by William Lee, of Northam, Esq., of Christopher Cade, father of the said James, or to be paid by the said William Lee, after the death of Mary Hopper, the mother of James Cade, for and during the lives of said James, John Cade, his brother, and Thomazin Roe, wife of John Roe of Abbotsham in the county of Devon, mariner, and the longest liver of them. (See Thomas Lechford's Note Book, pp. 42-44 (as printed) as also for a reference to a tenement in Biddeford Devon, held by the said James and Margaret during the life of the said Margaret). It will be seen therefore that the Christopher Cade, whose will I have given, was the father of our James Cade, and that the mother of James afterwards became the wife of —— Hopper, and his sister Thomazin was married to John Roe.—H. F. W.]

WILLIAM MIRRIAM of Hadlowe, Kent, clothier, 8 September 1635, proved 27 November 1635. To the poor of Hadlowe ten shillings. To my daughter Susan, already preferred, fifty shillings. The like sum to daughter Margaret, likewise preferred. To daughter Joane, already preferred, one shilling. To my daughter Sara forty pounds within three months next after my decease. To wife Sara all the household stuff of mine which is in my now dwelling house situate at Barnestreet in Hadlowe and the five pounds per annum which is to be paid out of my lands in Goodherst, Kent, during her natural life. I give her also three pounds per annum to be paid to her during her natural life out of my tenements and lands in Yalding, Kent. And she shall have her dwelling and abiding in my dwelling house aforesaid after my decease during the whole term of her natural life, with free access, ingress, egress and recourse to and from the same and into and from the gardens and orchards for herbs, water and for her brewing, baking, washing, drying and the like needful occasions. To my son Joseph Myrriam all such household stuff as I shall have at the time of my decease remaining and being in the house wherein he now dwelleth situate in Tewdly, or elsewhere where he shall then dwell, being in his custody or possession. To George Mirriam my son five pounds and to his daughter Mary, my god daughter, five shillings.   To William Howe, my grandchild, ten shillings and to every child of his father Thomas Howe which he had by my daughter, his late deceased wife, I will five shillings.   To William Mirriam my grandchild, son of the said Joseph my son, five shillings.

As touching my lands and tenements I will to Joseph Mirriam my son &c. all my lands and tenements in Yalding charged with the before mentioned annuity of three pounds.   To Robert my son the messuage wherein I now dwell, in Hadlowe with the barns, outhouses, yards, gardens, orchards and all my lands thereto belonging, and all other my lands, tenements &c. in Hadlowe.   And I give him all my goods and chattels not formerly bequeathed.   And I make him sole executor.

Proved by Christopher Crispe, Notary Public, attorney for Robert Mirriam, son and executor.

Rochester Wills, Vol. xxii. (1631–1644), fol. 165.

[This will, which Mr. W. S. Appleton published long ago, I give now in order to show the significance of the following wills.—H. F. W.]

Robert Goldston of Tonbridge, Kent, 10 April 1637, proved 16 May 1637.   The poor of Tunbridge, Tewdly and Capell.   Loving friend Mr. Joel Callys.   To Elizabeth the wife of William Howe twenty shillings or a ring of that value for a testimony of my thankfulness for her great pains taken with me.   William Dyker.   Thomas and Francis the sons of Sara the daughter of Waller Thompson.   William Howard and Robert Rootes the apprentices of Thomas Diker.   Elizabeth Goldstone, the late wife of William Goldstone of Brenchley deceased, and Elizabeth, Frances and Anne Goldstone his three daughters.   Frances my loving mother, now the wife of Thomas Dyker of Tonbridge, taylor.   My sister in law Elizabeth the daughter of the said Thomas Diker.   Francys, Anne and William Diker the three children of the said Thomas Diker.

Item, I give and bequeath unto Jane the wife of Thomas Howe of Tonbridge, clothier, and to Sara the wife of Joseph Merryam of Tewdly, clothier, my sisters, ten shillings apiece, to be paid them within one month next after my decease.   I will and give to Hanna Mirriam, my god daughter, the daughter of the said Joseph, one pair of fine sheets which are in the house of Richard Kipping of Tewdly, tanner.   Anne Tanner the wife of James Tanner.   My god daughter ———— the daughter of Stephen Bennett late of Tewdly deceased.   The four children of Roger Thomsett of Brenchley my uncle.   William Howe, Sara the wife of Nathaniel Weller, Elizabeth the wife of Josias Johnson, Mary, Susan and Thomas How the children of the said Thomas How.   John, William, Jane, Martha and Susan the five children of William Jeffrey of London.   Simon, John and Thomas Jeffrey the three sons of Thomas Jeffrey of Tonbridge and the two children of Nicholas Jeffrey.   John Baldock, Jane the wife of Christopher Constable and Martha Harborough.   To Francys, John and Mary Johnson, the three children of the said Jane my sister by Benjamin Johnson her late deceased husband, and to Alice and Francys, the two other children of the said Jane by the said Thomas How her now husband, six pounds apiece.   Item, I give and bequeath unto William, Sara, Joseph, Thomas, Elizabeth and Hanna, the six children of the said Joseph Mirriam by the said Sara his now wife, to either of them the like sum of six pounds apiece, to be paid them within five years next after my decease.   Thomas Dan the son of Thomas Dan by Elizabeth my sister deceased.   My brother Roger Goldston certain household stuff &c. in the now dwelling house of Richard Kipping. The residue I wholly give to the said Thomas How and Joseph Merriam whom I make and ordain full and sole executors.

Then follows the disposition of the lands and tenements in Brenchley, which are to go to brother Roger Goldston at the end of five years (the executors receiving the rents &c. during that period). If Roger die before the end of the said term then all these lands and tenements to go to sisters Jane the wife of Thomas How and Sara the wife of Joseph Mirriam &c., provided the said Roger leave no issue. And the said Francys my mother, if then living, shall have the use and occupation of that part of the said lands &c. which is now in the occupation of one William Turner, containing by estimation fourteen acres more or less.

Rochester Wills, Vol. xxii. (1631-44), fol. 248.

[The above will evidently throws light on the connections of Sarah, the wife of our Joseph Meriam of Concord, who, as we have learned from his father's will, was living at Tewdly in 1635. This makes the following will worth saving, since the testatrix may have been the grandmother of Mrs. Meriam.

H. F. W.]

Jane Jefferie of Pepingburie *als* Pemburie, Kent, widow, 28 April, 21 James, proved 11 March 1623. The poor of Pemburie. To my daughter Francis the now wife of John Gouldstone my gold ring and my best suit of apparel, that is to say, gown, petticoat, kirtle, hat and band of cambric or holland. To Susan the now wife of my son Roger Thompson my second suit of apparel &c. To Susan the now wife of my son William Jefferie my third suit of apparel. The rest of my apparel I give to Jane and Martha Baldocke daughters of my daughter Margaret. To Jane Gouldstone my god daughter, the daughter of my daughter Francis, five shillings and one pair of sheets. My god daughter Elizabeth Wood the daughter of my sister Wood. All the children of my daughter Francis. All my other godchildren. John Jeffrey the son of my son John Jefferie. John Jefferie the son of my son William Jefferie. Ten shillings each to my son John Jefferie and to my son Roger Thompson. All the children of my two sons Waller Tompson and Roger Tompson. John Baldocke and the said Jane and Martha Baldocke, the three children of my daughter Margaret deceased, to have thirty pounds divided equally between them in full payment and satisfaction of all such duties and demands which they or any of them shall or may claim or demand by and after the death of Roger Tompson their deceased grandfather or by and after me the said Jane as administratrix after the death of the said Roger Tompson or by gift, promise or otherwise of me or of John Jefferie my late husband deceased, the same to be paid unto them by my executors hereafter named at the age of twenty and two years of them the said John, Jane and Martha Baldocke or at their day of their several marriage if they or any of them shall marry before their said age &c. with the advise and consent of my sister Elizabeth Wood and of my daughter Francis Gouldstone. My son Thomas Jefferie. Edward and Nicholas Jefferie my sons. Every of my servants. To my said son Thomas Jefferie my silver cup and to William Jefferie my son my silver salt. Other gifts. I make Thomas Jeffrey and Edward Jeffrey my sons executors &c. Then follows the disposition of landed property. Land in Capell. House or cottage and lands in Pepingburie *als* Pemburie. To son Thomas Jeffrey the house wherein I now inhabit called Crowherst.

I appoint my well beloved friends Stephan Jefferie of Grays Inn, gent., and Edward Jefferie of Tunbridge, yeoman, my brothers in law, Thomas

Wood of Capell my brother in law and John Gouldstone of Tudely my son in law to be my faithful overseers.

Rochester Wills, Vol. xxi. (1606-81), fol. 20.

["Stephen Jeffrey of Staple Inn, gent.," admitted to Gray's Inn, November 25, 1602. See Foster's Gray's Inn Admissions, page 105.—EDITOR.]

EDWARD JEFFREY of Pepingburie *als* Pemburie, Kent, yeoman, 3 November 1623, proved 12 March 1623. To the poor of Pembury and of Speldherst in the said county twenty shillings (each parish) to be paid by my brothers William Jeffrey, Thomas Jeffrey and Nicholas Jeffrey within one year next after the decease of Jane Jeffrey my mother. To brother Nicholas Jeffrey a piece of land in Speldherst in payment and full recompence and satisfaction of the sum of thirty pounds which was given unto him, the said Nicholas, by John Jeffrey our late deceased father in and by his last will and testament. All other my messuage &c. and all other my lands, meadow, pasture and woodland containing by estimation fifty acres, in the parishes of Speldherst and Aishurst in the said county, all which came unto me by the will and testament of John Jeffrey my deceased father, to have and to hold unto me and mine heirs after the decease of Jane Jeffrey my mother, I give to William, Thomas and Nicholas Jeffrey my brothers, they to pay out of these lands to my brother John Jeffrey the sum of twenty pounds within one year next after the decease of Jane Jeffrey my mother, which is the full part and portion which I mean unto him the said John Jeffrey. I give to my mother Jane Jeffrey one annuity or yearly rent charge of three pounds out of certain lands in the county of Kent granted by William Jeffrey unto John Jeffrey my father and his heirs.

Rochester Wills, Vol. xxi. (1606-31), fol. 25.

JOHN JEOFFREY of Ligh, Kent, yeoman, 9 September 1624, proved 23 October 1624. To be buried in the churchyard of Pembury near the foot of my father's tombstone. Lands and tenements in Stapleherst. Wife Jane. Son John. Father in law John Newington. If wife be with child &c.

Rochester Wills, Vol. xxi. (1606-31), fol. 95.

WILLIAM PIPER of Tewdly, Kent, bachelor and by trade a clothier, 24 July 1632, sworn to 6 March 1632. The poor of the parish. My eldest sister Elizabeth Tary, her (children) John Statkey and Thomas Tary. Michael Hartridge the eldest son of my second sister Ann Hartridge. My younger sister Mary Piper. My aunt Morris. Elizabeth Benet the daughter of Steven Benet unto which I was witness in baptism. I give unto Elizabeth Mirriam daughter of Joseph Miriam, unto which I was witness in baptism, the sum of twenty shillings. The servants of my father in law's house (one of them Henry Swan). I will that my younger sister Mary Piper be at the charge for my burial and also for the proving of my will and for a sermon at my burial, to give twenty shillings if it be to him that I appoint. And also I will and appoint and give power and authority unto my father in law Richard Dan and Joseph Miriam for to sell and make sale of the lands (called Mill fields, containing about ten acres) and for to take in the twenty pounds which is in my brother Michael Hartridge's hands and also to pay these legacies &c., and if the lands be sold for more than a hundred pounds then I will that the overseers of this my will &c. have it for their pains. Mary Piper to be executrix. Wit: Thomas Tarry and Richard Dann.

In the probate act the name of the executrix is given as Mary Peper.

Rochester Wills, Vol. xxii. (1631-44), fol. 1.

GEORGE DANN of Tewdly, Kent, tanner, 9 August 1633, proved 26 September 1634. The poor of Tewdly. To wife Frances all my goods, cattle, chattels, stock and debts, towards the payment of my debts and legacies, the which Frances I do make executrix &c. Tenements and lands in Brenchley purchased of Thomas Dann to my brother Thomas after decease of my wife, he paying to Dorothy, Elizabeth, Jane and Margery, my sisters, ten pounds apiece and to Ann and Sara Wooddy, children of Dennyes my late deceased sister, ten pounds apiece, and also to Ann and Mercy Rootes, children of my said sister Dorothy, ten pounds apiece. Joseph Meriam one of the witnesses.

Commission issued, at date given above, to Robert Goldstone natural and lawful brother of Frances Dann, relict of the said deceased and executrix named in his will, because the said Frances died before accepting the trust.

Rochester Wills, Vol. xxii. (1631-44), fol. 94.

FRANCES DANN the relict of George Dann late of Tewdly, tanner, deceased, and the executrix named in his testament and last will did make her testament and last will by word of mouth 18 September 1634, proved 26 September 1634. Her brother Robert Goldstone to be her executor and pay such debts as ought to be paid by her. Her debts and funeral charges being paid and such charges as should happen by reason of her death and about her will being discharged, her said executor should have twenty pounds of her personal estate and the rest should be and remain to him to pay legacies. To the poor of Tewdly the twenty shillings which her husband had willed them and ten shillings more which she gave them (saving that her desire was that her kinsman John Baldcocke or his wife should have the greatest share with them thereof) and also to pay two shillings six pence to Harborowe, her husband's godson, and six shillings eight pence to Thomas Mirriam, likewise her husband's godson, and to Joane Peerse forty shillings and ten pounds apiece to every one of her brothers and sisters, which she willed unto them in this manner, vizt. to her brother Roger ten pounds, to her sister Howe ten pounds, to her sister Mirriam ten pounds and to her sister Dann ten pounds if her personal estate should extend to so much, otherwise they should have equal shares in the remainder. And if her estate should amount to more she willed the overplus to her executor.

Wit: Frances Dyker, Agnes Cowchman and Joane Peirse.

Rochester Wills, Vol. xxii. (1631-44), fol. 95.

[Of course I have gathered other Meriam wills, but I take it for granted that Mr. Appleton has seen them and furnished notes from them. I may possibly have two wills which he has not noticed. One is the will of Mildred Hatche (nuncupative) proved 29 November 1599, which refers to father Hatche's will, to brothers Richard, James and Thomas Hatche, father Merriham and her mother and her mother's three youngest children. Her mother to be executrix. Proved by Henry Meriham husband of Susan the executrix. The will of James Hatche of Yalding, proved 30 November 1600, mentions brothers Richard Hatche, Thomas Hatche, Edward Mower and John Merriam, and sister Elizabeth Mower, father Merriam and mother Susan Merriam.—H. F. W.]

THOMAS SHOTTON of Cropson in the County of Leicester yeoman, 21 October 1631, proved 8 February 1631. The poor of Crapson, of Anstie and of Thurcaston. The old hospital in Leicester. The new hospital of the same. To my son William Shotton thirty pounds. To my daughter Martha Shotton fourescore and ten pounds, one half upon the day of her marriage and the other half that day twelve month. To all my daughter's children that now are ten shillings apiece. To my son Sampson Shotten that house where Tho: Sauidg dwelleth in Crapson, with all the lands, leas, meadow, with all common and pasture thereunto belonging, with all other profits and commodities thereunto appertaining, to the said Sampson and his heirs forever, except my son Anthony Shotton do give him for the same fourescore and ten pounds within one six years after my decease. To Mary my well beloved wife half my dwelling house with half the farm and profits &c. during her natural life, and after her decease to my son Anthony Shotton and his heirs forever. And in the mean time Anthony shall have the other half to him and his heirs forever. Wife Mary and son Anthony to be full executors.   Audley, 15.

[In Lechford's Note-Book, p. 16 (as printed) can be found a formal acknowledgment, made 22 October 1638, by Samson Shotton of Mount Woollaston in New England, planter, that he had received of his brother Anthony Shotton of Cropston in the County of Leicester (England) yeoman the sum of fourscore and ten pounds (the very sum fixed in above will) and, in consideration thereof, he gave to his said brother Anthony a general quit-claim.

I had saved a note of the will years ago on account of the baptismal name Sampson which I knew to be the name of our New England settler. This evidence from Lechford establishes the identity.—H. F. Waters.]

Richard Clarke of Bulmer, Essex, yeoman, 31 August 1556, proved 5 September 1558. To the Vicar of Bulmer, in recompence of my tithes and "dewties" negligently forgotten and not paid, six shillings eight pence. To Augnes Rande now the wife of ――― Rande all that my garden with the appurtenances lying and being within the hamlet of Balidon next to Sudbury, within the County of Essex, and all that my croft of arable land called Tilles Croft, in Bulmer, to hold for her natural life, and after her decease I will that Richarde Rande, the son of Thomas Rande and of the said Agnes, shall have and enjoy my said garden and croft to him and his heirs forever. I give the said Richarde Rande my capital messuage wherein I now dwell &c. To Robert Briggestocke my servant my tenement called Shakespeares which I late purchased of George Claypole, lying in Bulmer. Other gifts to him. A tenement to William Clovier my servant. Certain copyhold lands to Richard Rande. And where John Coole (Cole) of Sudberry "marchauntma" standeth bound by his deed indented unto me for the payment of one hundred six pounds thirteen shillings and four pence &c. a certain amount (out of it) to be paid to the said Agnes wife of Thomas Rande, a certain amount to Jane Ingeham wife of John Ingeham, a payment to Richard Rande. To the said John Cole twenty shillings and to Elizabeth now his wife twenty shillings; and more I give to Marten Cole and to Willm Cole, to every of them twenty shillings and to Robert Cole, Richard Cole, Mary Cole, Thomas Cole, Giles Cole, John Cole and Edward Cole, children of the said John Cole and Elizabeth, to every of them six shillings eight pence. To Elizabeth and Joane Clarke, being two sisters, to every of them six pounds thirteen shillings four pence, and to their natural mother twenty shillings. My late servant Alice Andrewe and Richard Andrewe. Mary Rookes, the daughter of Nicholas Rookes of Newport, and her brothers and sisters. "I the saide Richarde Clarke wolde be right glade and desireous to joyne in lawfull marriege the saide Richarde Rande and one Anne Rookes nowe one of the daughteres of the saide Nycholas Rookes." In case of such marriage they to have all the residue &c. The said Nicholas Rookes and Richard Rande to be executors and Thomas Rande of Sudbury to be supervisor.

Noodes, 41.

THOMAS RUSSHAM of Sudbury, Suffolk, gen^t. and one of the aldermen of the same town, 31 May 1578, proved 23 October 1578. To be buried in the churchyard of St. Gregory "whereas" my father and mother were buried. To wife Thomasine my house which I now dwell in, situate in the parish of St. Peter in Sudbury and purchased hy me of John Cole the elder and also a shop and a chamber over the same, which I purchased of George Alliston the elder. I give her my four butcher stalls right over against my said house wherein I dwell, sometimes Tanner's stalls. I give her my orchard and garden commonly called the Pound garden, sometime belonging to the College and walled about with a middle wall, situate in the parish of St. Gregory. Also my three tenements right against Mr. Eden's place, called sometimes the Friars. Also my house a little from the Gull. She to hold all these tenements &c. for life; and after her decease I give them to my son Jefferey Russham. I give my wife my house in the parish of St. Peter now in the tenure of William Gardyner, with a barn and stable and an orchard thereunto belonging, in a street leading towards Much Waldingfield. To son Jefferey sundry furniture &c., among which a joined chair, a wicker chair, a chest with bars of iron &c. Also to him my best bowl of silver, parcel gilt, and six silver spoons. To Elizabeth Cole my daughter and wife unto William Cole my other bowl of silver and three silver spoons and ten pounds in money. To William Cole her husband my black gown faced with budge. To my daughter Frances Prentyse, wife unto John Prentyse of Cowlne, ten pounds and three silver spoons. Elizabeth Russham daughter unto my son John late departed. Anne Ellys, my wife's daughter and wife unto Peter Ellis now dwelling at the Swan. Samuel Russham son to Ellin Russham my daughter late deceased. Ten shillings each to John Cole the son of my daughter Cole, to Martyn Cole, her next son, to William Cole, her youngest son, to Ellyn Cole, her daughter, and to Parnell Cole, her next daughter, John Prentyse, son of my daughter Frances, William Prentise, her next son, Robert Prentyse, her third son, and Johan Prentyse, her daughter. Wife Thomasyn to be executrix and son Jefferey supervisor.

Langley, 37.

MARTYN COLE of Sudbury, Suffolk, mercer, 9 August 1588, proved 29 October 1588. To be buried in the churchyard of St. Gregory by the chancel door there. The poor of Sudbury, vizt. the halt, lame, blind, sick and such other as be comfortless. I will that upon the day of my funeral, when the people are gathered together, some learned man shall make a sermon unto them and I do give unto him, for his pains in that good exercise taken, six shillings and eight pence. To wife Hellen my capital messuage &c. in Sudbury, near unto the Bars in Boramgate end (and other land) to hold for life. After her decease I give it to my son Thomas Cole, with remainder to my son Cesar Cole. Gifts to son Martyn Cole and my daughter Cole his wife. I give and bequeath unto my well beloved father Mr. John Cole my best felt hat, one of my dublets and one shirt. Gifts to brothers Robert and Richard Cole. To my brother William Cole my Spanish leather bag. I give unto my brother Edward Cole my gold ring, desiring him after his decease to give it unto his son, my godson, Martyn Cole. My brother John Cole. My sister Gibbones of Ipswich. Agnes Hilles the wife of Robert Hilles. Loving friend Robert Gale of Edwardston. To son Cesar Cole my messuage wherein I now dwell and lease of land lying by the Windmill hill, and, after wife's decease, land lying at Gallow hill. Mary and Susan Browne, my daughter's daughters, at one and twenty. John and Thomas Browne their brothers. My daughter Mary Browne the wife of John Browne of Dedham, Suffolk (*sic*). Wife Hellen and son Cesar executors. Leicester, 3.

WILLIAM COLE of Sudbury, Suffolk, 17 October 1588, with a codicil dated 18 October 1588, proved 9 January 1588. To wife Elizabeth my house wherein I now dwell during her natural life, also my house and orchard which I lately purchased of William Curde the younger. To daughter Ellen Cole twenty pounds at day of marriage (and certain household stuff). To son Martyn Cole twenty pounds at twenty one or day of marriage (and other property). The same to son William at twenty one &c. Similar gifts to sons Edward and Geffrey Cole, each at twenty one. Daughters Parnell and Mary Cole at marriage or twenty one. To son Roger Cole twenty pounds within two years next after my decease. To son John twenty pounds in one year. To son Robert twenty pounds in one year. Brother John Cole. Wife Elizabeth executrix and brother in law Jeffery Rusham to be executor with her, if he will. Leicester, 17.

JEFFERYE RUSHAM of London gen[t]. 22 July 1587, proved 12 June 1589. To wife Mary my messuage &c. in Cornard Magna, Suffolk, called Parkers, lately purchased by me of Roger Warren Esq., to hold for her natural life and after her decease I devise and give the said messuage to John Cole, eldest son of Elizabeth Cole my sister, to hold for ten years after my wife's decease, then to Martin Cole his brother, then to William Cole another brother, next to Edward Cole another brother, then to Jeffery Cole another brother, afterwards to my right heirs forever. To the children of my sister Elizabeth now wife of William Cole of Sudbury a hundred and three score pounds, viz[t]. twenty pounds apiece. To the children of my sister Frances Prentise now living ten pounds apiece. To Elizabeth Rusham daughter of my elder brother John twenty pounds. The portions severally due to the foresaid children to be delivered unto my brother William Cole for his children and my brother Prentise for his children and to my brother Hunwick for Elizabeth Russham. To the children of my sister Anne Ellis now widow five pounds apiece. Margaret —— mother of the said Elizabeth Rusham. To my brother John Hunwick of Colchester twenty pounds to buy him a gilt salt. To sister Ellis, sister Cole and sister Frances Prentice fifty shillings each to buy them rings. Mr. Garnett my wife's father. Mr. Donatte. Mr. Albery. The poor of Sudbury. Wife Mary to be executrix and her father and my brother Hunwick overseers. In a codicil added 9 June 31 Eliz: he refers to John Hunwick of Stebbinge, to Parnell Cole daughter of William Cole lately deceased, to Robert Garthe, to brother Jasper Garnett, to cousin John Curde of Sudbury and others.
Leicester, 51.

JOHN HUNWICK of Colchester, Essex, merchant, 24 November 1593, proved 8 June 1594. Wife Anne. Capital tenement in Fryers Street near East Gate. Christopher Curde, son of John Curde of Sudbury the only son of Anne Ellis my sister deceased, my only sister. John Curde his elder brother. My servant John Hunwicke son of Thomas Hunwicke of Bromefield. Gyles Hunwicke brother of said John. Hugh another brother. Thomas Hunwicke their brother by their father and by another vent. Lands &c. in Bradwell, in Middleton and in Little Birche &c. Two tenements in the parishes of St. Giles and St. Mary's Colchester, now or late in the tenure and occupation of John Morrice and Marcillus Goodwyn. Other real estate. John Hassard son of Thomasine daughter to Anne Ellis deceased my only sister. Thomas Rande. William Saunders son of Valentine Sanders of London gen^t. Melford and Acton Suffolk. My good sister Mrs. Mary Daniell. Sister Elizabeth Palmer of Sudbury and her husband ———— Palmer. My sister Frances Isaack and her husband Isaack. My sister in law the mother of Elizabeth Rusham and her son by her second husband. I forgive John Cole my godson that my debt of one hundred marks by specialty, which bond I will, if he return again into England to be delivered him, if not to be delivered to his brother Roger Cole as a debt to him. Frances Slaterforde, daughter of my sister Anne Ellis deceased, and her sisters Thomazine Hassarde, Margaret Ellis and Parnell Ellis, Richard Ellis being bound to leave it her children. Her sister Elizabeth Maior of Melford and Maior to do the like. My godson John Wiles of Dedham. His father Robert Wiles. Elizabeth Rusham and John Eldred her husband. Wife's sister the wife of one Phillippes of Oxford. Judith Phillippes her daughter that dwelleth with John Warner. Parnell Ellis daughter of John Ellis of Middleton. Wife's brother John Warner. Thomas Furnace of Malden and Harry Freeman his wife's brother. My cousin William Haynes of London goldsmith. John Cotwyn and Mary his wife. Frances the wife of ———— Slaterforthe and Thomas Harrison her son. Mr. John Bird, now fellow bailiff with me, and his wife. Mr. Glover, parson of St. Laurence,' and his wife and their son John Glover. Others mentioned. Large charities to the poor of various parishes and towns, the free school in Colchester &c. The executors to be wife Anne, cousin Mr. Valentine Saunders of London, Esq., William Beriff of Lincolns Inn gen^t. and ————. For overseers I nominate and appoint Thomas Taylour of Colchester, Bachelor of Law, and my loving cousin Roger Cole of London gen^t.

Confirmed by Sentence Diffinitive, Trinity Term 1599.   Dixy, 45.

Magdalen Maister of St. Saviour's Southwark, Surrey, widow, 9 December 1609, with a codicil dated 12 November 1614 and another (nuncupative) made in the time of her last sickness and about two months before her death, proved 18 January 1614. To my son Olave Maister, one of his Majesty's yeoman warders of the Tower of London, one hundred and threescore pounds and my best salt of silver all gilt, one tankard of silver all gilt, one bowl of silver parcel gilt and six of my best silver spoons parcel gilt and one French chest of walnut tree standing in the now dwelling house of my son Roger Cole, also one Turkey carpet belonging to my square table, hereafter given him, one Irish rug chequered and one loomworks carpet wrought with flowers (and a lot of linen and other household stuff). Among the latter were Spanish leather "quishous" gilt and Spanish stone platters and dishes. I give to said Olave twenty pounds which I will that he shall give unto Mary Master, his daughter, at her day of marriage or age of one and twenty years. A similar gift for his daughter Margaret. A similar gift for his daughter Magdalen Darby.

I give and bequeath unto my loving daughter Anne Cole wife of Roger Cole of London gentleman one hundred and threescore pounds. Also I give and bequeath unto Saraa Stokes *als* Cole, daughter of the said Anne my daughter, twenty pounds, to be paid unto her on the day of her marriage or at her full age of twenty and one years. To Elizabeth Cole, daughter of the said Roger Cole and of my said daughter Aune, twenty pounds (at marriage or age of twenty one). The same to Susan Cole and Catelina Cole, daughters of the said Roger and Anne. These legacies to be delivered to Roger Cole for the use of the said children. Twenty shillings to the poor sisters of the Trinity House in Deptford. Loving friend John Partridge, scrivener. The poor in the Clink liberty in St. Saviour's. Every poor widow in Reddrith. The residue of goods &c. to my said son in law Roger Cole and my said daughter Anne his wife. The residue of debts and ready money to be equally divided between my said son Olave Maister and my said son and daughter Roger Cole and Anne. The said Roger and Anne to be executors and the said John Partridge overseer. (The mark of Magdalen Master). Oleffe Master, Roger Cole and Anne Cole among the witnesses. In the first codicil she desires her son Olave to live quietly and peaceably with Roger and Anne Cole. Thomas Stockes one of the witnesses to this.   Rudd, 2.

JOHN COLE of St. Olave, Hart Street, London, gent., 25 July 1620, with a codicil dated 10 August 1620, proved 11 October 1620. To the poor people of the town of Sudbury, Suffolk, three pounds sterling, to be distributed amongst them by the Mayor of the town there and the head churchwarden of St. Peter's church for that year being. The poor of St. Olave where I am now a parishioner. To my wife Temperaunce Cole all my lands and tenements in and near Milton next Sittingborne, Kent, and after her decease I give and bequeath all the said houses and lands unto my brother Edward Cole for life, then to Anthony Thomas the younger, the eldest son of my sister Mary, and unto his heirs forever. I give and bequeath unto my brother Roger Cole and to my cousins William Oland and William Locke the sum of three score and six pounds of lawful money for the use and behoof of my sister Parnell Fettiplace, to be put out and disposed by them to the best advantage that may be. If she die before it shall be paid unto her I give it amongst the children of my brother in law Anthony Thomas, excepting twenty pounds which I do then give unto the said Roger Cole, William Oland and William Locke. My cousin Elizabeth Wraye. The four children of my said sister Mary Thomas. To my said brother Edward Cole fifty pounds sterling in three months next after my decease; and if he shall happen to decease before that time then I do give the said fifty pounds unto Mary Thomas the eldest daughter of my said sister Mary. I give and bequeath unto my said brother Roger Cole and unto his three daughters twenty pounds sterling, *i. e.* five pounds apiece, to be paid within one year next after my decease, hoping that they being in so good case to live in, in this age, and the blessing of Riches being upon them more than upon the others of my kin they will take in good part this poor gift and legacy given them by me. My kind friend Mr. Thomas Jones, skinner. My countryman John Florey. Reference to a grant made 6 August 5th James by Richard Cole late of Buckesh Esq. unto Thomas Lea of East Putford, Devon, gen[t]. &c., which the said Thomas Ley assigned and set over unto testator. I give it unto my brother Edward Cole, my brother in law Anthony Thomas and my son in law Francis Wall. Wife Temperance to be sole executrix. To my father Heywood my seal gold ring of arms.   Soame, 88.

Sententia pro Valore Inventarii et Compoti bonorum Johannis Cole &c. was promulgated 16 February 1621 after litigation between Parnell Fettiplace of the one part and Temperance Cole, relict and executrix, also Roger

Cole, William Oland, William Locke, Elizabeth Raye, Anthony Thomas and Mary his wife and Anthony, Mary, Temperance and Robert Thomas their children, Edward Cole, Elizabeth Oland, Susanna Locke and Catherine Cole.

Savile, 16.

MARTIN COLE of Sudbury, Suffolk, draper, 28 September 1620, proved 19 December 1620. To be buried in the churchyard of St. Gregory's in Sudbury by the chancel door beside the body of late deceased father Mr. Martin Cole. The parish of St. Peters. A yearly sermon there on Ascension day. Another sermon at St. Gregorys. Wife Anne Cole. Martin Cole son of brother Cesar Cole. Thomas Cole another son. Rose Andrewe daughter of my late brother Francis Andrewe of Hadleigh. Margaret the wife of my brother Cesar Cole. Elizabeth Smith late my servant now the widow Starke of Needham. Elizabeth Andrewe daughter of my brother Francis Andrewe. John Cole son of my brother Cesar. Anne Andrewe daughter of my brother Francis Andrewe. Lands in Layham now in the occupation of my said brother Francis Andrewe. Jane Andrewe his daughter. Elizabeth Cole daughter of brother Cesar. Lands &c. in Hadleigh purchased of Mr. Adam Winthropp. Lands purchased of Mr. Appleton. Francis Andrew son of my said brother Francis Andrewe. Ellen, John, Mary, Martin and Elizabeth, children of my cousin Mary Garford now wife of George Goldinge of Sudbury. The four children of my cousin Susan Brown now wife of William Sermon of Creatinge. Rose Fuller daughter of John Fuller of Nayland my wife's brother. Edward Andrewe son of my said brother Francis Andrewe. Rose Richards of Langham. Rose Walker late the wife of Robert Walker of Stratford. Robert Hawkins son of my cousin Robert Hawkins late of Ardleigh. Sara Andrewe daughter of my said brother Francis Andrewe. Land in Great Cornard, Suffolk, purchased of Joseph Weld. Mary and Rose Andrewe daughters of my brother William Andrewe of Hadleigh. I give and bequeath to my cousin Mr. Roger Cole five marks if he overlive me, to make him a gold ring. The same to my cousin Mr. John Cole. My brothers William and Edward Andrewe. My sister Barbara Andrewe. My cousin George Golding of Sudbury. My said cousin Susan Brown wife to the said William Seamans. John Bond the elder of Ipswich, chapman. Wife Anne executrix and brothers Edward and Francis Andrewe supervisors.

Soame, 104.

[The family of Cole of Sudbury and of Southwark is of interest to us on account of Gov. Willoughby's connection with it (through the Locks). In my Gleanings for January, 1895 (Vol. 49, p. 129), I gave the will of Roger Cole, the maternal grandfather of Mrs. Margaret Willoughby. The Visitations of Surrey (1623) give a pedigree of this family probably furnished by this Roger Cole or constructed for him. See Harl. MSS. 1046 (fo. 46), 1147 (fo. 72b), 1397 (fo. 84), 1433 (fo. 78b), 1561 (fo. 136) and Add. MS. 4963 (fo. 94b).

Mundy, in his copy of this Visitation (Harl. MS. 1561, fo. 136), calls William Oland Proctor of the Civil Law, and says that his widow Elizabeth was married secondly to William Ayscough Register of the Court of Audience to the (Arch) bishop of Canterbury. The wills show that William Cole of Sudbury, father of Roger, had another wife not given in the Surrey pedigree. She was Elizabeth the daughter of Thomas Russham and sister of Jeffery Rusham. She was probably the mother of all William Cole's children, named in his will, except Robert and Roger.—H. F. W.]

[See Notes on the Families of Locke and Cole, in Family Histories and Genealogies, by Prof. and Mrs. E. E. Salisbury, Vol. I., Part 2, pp. 605–625. See also REGISTER, Vol. 35, pp. 59–65; and for Locke, see Book of the Lockes, pp. 347–359.—EDITOR.]

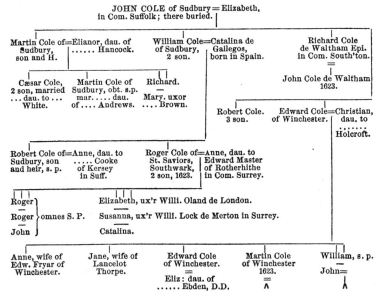

JOHN LOCKE, citizen and mercer of London 13 November 1510 (2 H. viii.), with a codicil bearing date 20 April 1518, proved 16 December 1519. If it please God that I decease within the city of London or within twenty miles nigh unto the same city then I will that my body shall be honestly conveyed and brought from the place where it shall happen me to decease unto the church of St. Thomas of Acres in West Cheape of London. My goods &c. to be divided into two equal parts if I die without issue, the one half for myself for the performance of this my will &c. and the other half to remain unto Mary my wife. But if I die leaving issue &c. then three parts, whereof one part to myself one to my wife and the third to such issue as God shall send between her and me. The church of St. Antonyne, London, where as I am a parishioner. The church of Aldermary. The church of St. Mary Bothawe next London stone. Other churches &c. A marble stone of the value of ten marks to be laid upon me, to be graven with such convenient pictures and sculpture as shall be thought requisite. Gowns of black cloth of the price of five shillings the yard for my wife, my mother, Thomas Foster and his wife, John Bodman grocer, William Burwelles and his wife, William Locke and his wife and other persons, to the number of twenty persons. The poor. An honest priest of good name and fame to sing for my soul and my father's soul and all my kinsfolkes' souls in the foresaid church of St. Thomas of Acres, in the chapel there called the Mercers' Chapel, at seven or eight of the clock in the morning to begin his mass and at the Lavatory of mass to turn him to the people to say de profundis for my soul and the souls abovesaid by the space of ten years next ensuing after my decease. Other services. To Elizabeth Bulstrode my mother, if living at day of my decease, ten pounds. To Edith Underhill, late dwelling in St. Bartilmewe Spitell, if she be alive the time of my decease, twenty pounds sterling. Thomas Foster, "Browderer" of

London, and Effie his wife. Jane my "sustre" in law. Alice Heron late
servant with Edith Underhill. Dorothy my sister in law. Margaret Burwell. To twenty poor maidens' marriages thirteen pounds six shillings eight
pence. Wife Mary to be executrix. Lands in Bedfordshire. William Burwell mercer of London.   Ayloffe, 24.

OTWELL HYLL citizen and mercer of London, 11 November 1543,
proved 21 November 1543. Goods &c. to be divided into three equal
parts, whereof Dorothy my wife shall have one, according to the laudable
custom of the City of London. The second part I give to the child now
being in my wife's womb (if she be with child), to be paid at age of twenty
one or marriage. If said child die before that time I give said part to my
wife Dorothy. My brother Thomas Lok of London, mercer, shall have
the governance, keeping and bringing up of my said child. The third part
of my goods I reserve to myself to perform my legacies and bequests. My
late master Mr. William Gresham of London, mercer. Anthony Gresham
of London, mercer, deceased. The last will and testament of my uncle
Aleyn Hill deceased. My mother and my natural brethren and "sustern,"
being in the County of Lancaster. My uncle Randolfe Smyth. The
parish of Rachdale in the County of Lancaster. My mother and my
brother Thomas Hill (evidently living there). My brother Randolfe Hill.
My brother Richard Hill. My brother Aleyn Hill. I give and bequeath
to every of Thomas Lok, James Broun, Edmunde Lok, Matthew Lok and
Thomas Stacye a black gown and a ring of gold of the value of forty
shillings a piece. To either of my father in law Mr. William Lok of
London, mercer, and my mother in law his wife a ring of gold of the value
of forty shillings and a black gown. To every other my said father in
law's children a black gown. My wife Dorothy to be sole executrix and
Thomas Lok and James Broun overseers.   Spert, 27.

MY last will 1549 in March. WILLIAM LOK mercer and alderman of
London (indexed on margin " T. Willi Lock militis") proved 11 September 1550. Written 15 March. To be buried in the mercers church at the
great Conduit in Cheape, in the middle of the body of the church there
where lieth buried my father and mother and my first wife. Money to be
given to the four prisons, Newgate, Ludgate, the Marshalsey and Kings
Bench. Money to be given in alms at Martyn, Wymbilton, the two
Totings and Totnam. The poor of the Vintry Ward. Other poor. I
give to Thomas, Mathew, John, Henry and Myghell Lok, my five sons,
my dwelling house in Bow Lane and my house at the Lock in Cheape and
my house at the Bell in Cheape, with all the shops and appurtenances
belonging to them to that intent that they, or some of them, may dwell in
them and keep the retailing shop still in my name to continue there. I
give to John Loke my house that Parris now dwelleth in. To Henry Lok
my house that John Edwardes dwelleth in. Three houses to Mighell Lok.
Another house to Henry. Two houses to Matthew Lok. To John, Harry
and Mighell Lok all my houses in the Poultry and Bucklersbury and in
St. Johns Street. To Mathew Loke all my houses at Dowgate and in the
Vintry. To Thomas Lok all my houses in Cheape being in St. Peters
parish there. I give more to Thomas Lok my land at Martyn and Wymbilton that I may give him except one farm which I give to Henry and
Mighell Loke my young sons. I give the lease of my garden betwixt my
five sons to be kept in their hands for all their recreations in Grub Street.

Other property divided among them. They to pay to my well beloved wife Elizabeth, for dower, forty pounds every year during her natural life out of all my lands and houses, as appeareth by a certain Indenture of Covenants &c. She to have a certain sum of money for her part of all my goods &c. by the custom of this noble City. My daughter Elizabeth to have to her marriage as much as any of my daughters that be ready married have had of my goods. My executors to be Thomas, Mathew and Henry Lok and my overseers John and Myghell Lok, and because some of my sons be young I shall desire my trusty and well beloved friend Sir Rowland Hyll, knight and alderman, to be my chief overseer. Per me Sir William Lok knight and alderman.

Commission issued 6 April 1571 to Michael Lok natural and lawful son &c. to administer the goods left unadministered by Thomas, Mathew and Henry Lok executors; now deceased.   Coode, 20.

ELIZABETH LOCKE, widow, of the city of London ("Domina" in Act Book) 8 September 1551, proved 27 February 1551. Many legacies to individuals named. Margaret the maid that dwelleth with my daughter Anne Lock. Thomas Typkyne, brewer, for that he lost certain money by my husband Hutton. William, Mary, Elizabeth and Ellen Meredyth the children of my late husband Robert Meredithe. My house hold stuff at Newington. Newington Green. I give and bequeath to these persons following, each of them, a gold ring of the value of forty shillings apiece to Thomas Locke and his wife, to Mathew Loke and his wife, to Henry Lock and his wife, to Anthony Hickman and his wife, to Thomas Stassye and his wife, John Cowswarth and his wife, Mighell Locke, John Locke, Richard Hills and Elizabeth Locke. My sister Elizabeth Farthinge. My sister Myston and her husband. Mr. Blundell and his wife. David Apowell and his wife. Mathew Fylde and Elizabeth Meredithe. William Meredith and Ellen Meredith. My mother Meredith. Others. To Elizabeth Locke one gilt cup with a cover, weighing twenty five ounces, with her arms on the cover. Richard Spryngham and his wife. Elizabeth Springham my son's daughter, to her marriage. Elizabeth and Robert Nicolles my godchildren. My son Richard Springham. Thomas Stacy mercer. John Cowswarthe mercer. I make my son Richard Springham and Thomas Nicolles the elder my executors.

Memorandum that the last day of November Auno 1551 this testament was presented as the last will and testament of this testator by the hands of Ellen Meredithe, this present day the day of the departure of the same in presence of &c.   Powell, 7.

MATHEW LOCKE citizen and mercer of London, 23 February 1551, proved 27 May 1552. Goods &c. to be divided into three equal parts whereof wife Johan to have one, after the laudable custom of the city of London, the second to my daughter Elizabeth at age of twenty one or marriage, the third I reserve to myself and to mine executors. If daughter die before age or marriage then a part of her portion to the mercers' company and part to be divided among the children of my brother Thomas Locke and my brother Anthony Hickman, one half to each. Twelve sermons to be preached in St. Stephens Walbrooke. My cousin Makebray. Poor householders in Merton, Surrey, and at Tottenham. To my father Rigges and my mother his wife a standing cup, gilt, that my father Sir William Lock gave me at the day of my marriage. To wife Johan the lease of my house in which I dwell in London and my part of a lease in Tottenham. A ring of gold of forty shillings each to my father Rigges and his wife, my father Jermayn and his wife, my brother Thomas Locke and his wife, my brother Henry Locke and his wife, my brother John Lock, my brother Mighell Loke, my brother in law Anthony Hickman and his wife, my brother Thomas Stacy and his wife, my brother John Cosowarth and his wife, my brother Richard Hill and his wife, my brother Marshe and his wife, my cousin Richard Springham and his wife, my cousin Feilde and his wife, Mr. Robert Rose and his wife, my sister in law Elizabeth Baker and my friends Edward Castlen, William Dale and William Pierson. The residue to wife and daughter equally. Wife Johan and the said Thomas Lock and Anthony Hikman to be executors. Thomas Rigges and Edward Castolyn among the witnesses. The widow renounced execution.

Powell, 16.

THOMAS LOK citizen and mercer of London, 21 March 1553, with a codicil, proved 11 December 1556. To be buried in the Mercers Church in West Cheape, London, commonly called St. Thomas of Acorū church, as nigh to the place there where my late father lieth buried as conveniently may be. My loving brethren and friends John Cosowarth, Thomas Stacy and Anthony Hykman citizens and mercers of London. My younger sons Rowland, Thomas and Mathewe Lok. Houses, lands, &c. in the city of London and the Suburbs and in the Counties of Middlesex and Surrey. Wife Mary to have (among other property) my best ring of gold set with a diamond that was my father's. My daughter Mary at lawful age or marriage. My four sons, William, Rowland, Thomas and Mathew Lok at twenty one. William, my eldest son, and Anthony Hikman, my brother, to be executors, my said brother to administer by himself alone until my said eldest son shall accomplish the age of eighteen years.

In the codicil he speaks of his brother Thomas as having deceased. And God hath given me one other son whose name is John and one daughter called Anne and besides my said wife is with child, at this present uncertain whether it be a man child or a woman child. Mary mine eldest daughter.

Ketchyn, 26.

RICHARD HYLL citizen and mercer of London, 2 June 1564, proved 13 November 1568. Goods &c. to be divided into three portions according to the custom of the city, whereof one part to wife, the second to my children and the third I reserve to myself and mine executors to perform my legacies. My bastard daughter Mary at marriage if with consent of my overseers. My maid Alice Dewerden at her marriage. To Dick my "fole" three pounds six shillings eight pence, to be given as he shall have need by the discretion of mine overseers. I forgive Richard Hyll all that he owes me and I give to my brother Cowsewarthe and my sister his wife and to my cousin Feilde and his wife, every of them a ring of gold of forty shillings apiece. My wife shall have of my portion so much as will make her portion five hundred pounds and the rest to go to my children (equally). My wife to enjoy my house at Newington Green so long as she lives. My executors to be my children Otwill and Katherine and Elizabeth. The overseers to be my cousin Matthew Feilde, my brother Cowswarthe and my friend Thomas Aldersey, cousins Edward Best and Thomas Boldnes. Memorandum that this will was found 16 September, sealed up with his seals and opened in our presence: Anthonye Hickman, Henrye Lock, Edwarde Best, Thomas Boldnes.

Commission issued at above date to Elizabeth the relict and Michael Lock, citizen and mercer, to administrate during the minority of the three executors. Babington, 21.

JOHN COSOWARTH of Cosowarth, Cornwall, Esq., 3 August 17 Eliz: proved 5 March 1575. To be buried in the parish church of Colan if I die within the said County of Cornwall. The poorest people of Colan and the poor of nine other parishes near adjoining to the parish of Colan. To Dorothy my wife two chambers over the buttry in Cosowarthe for life. Other bequests to her (including one thousand pounds in money). Tin work in the parish of St. Agnes. My five sons Thomas, John, Edward, Michell and William. Son Thomas to be sole executor and residuary legatee. Carew, 3.

[The above testator was probably the one referred to in the following will, of which I give a brief abstract. For a pedigree of this family see Vis. of London of 1568, published by the Harl. Soc., vol. 1, p. 16.—H. F. W.]

JOHN COSOWARTHE of St. Colan (Cornwall) 10 January 1567 (10 Eliz:) proved 17 March 1568. Wife Elizabeth. Uncle John Cosowarthe mercer of London to be executor. Sheffelde, 8.

JANE LOCKE, wife of Michael Locke of London mercer, 9 February 1570, proved 6 April 1571. All my worldly goods are my husband's by whose love I have hitherto enjoyed them; and now with his consent I bequeath part of them. To my son Zacharia a goblet of serpentine stone garnished with silver. Rings, jewells, goblets &c. to sons Eleazar, Gersom and Benjamin. To son William a ring of gold with a lock graven. Daughters Anne, Joane and Elizabeth. My sister Anne Locke. My cousin Kateryne Segar. My cousin Joane Argall. My Lady Cromwell wife of Sir Henry Cromwell, knight. My cousin Richard Spryngham, mercer. My cousin Raphe Hethington. My good friend Mrs. Anne Warcuppe. My kinsman Raphe Warcupp, now my servant. Margaret Yale. My husband to be executor. Holney, 14.

HENRYE LOK, mercer, 28 January 1570, proved 31 October 1571. As touching my worldly goods whatsoever they be I give and bequeath them to my wife Anne Loke; and I do make my only executor unto this my last will my good and well beloved brother Michael Lok.

Holney, 39.

MATHEW LOCKE of Marton in Surrey, Esq., 14 May 1599, proved 13 June 1599. My body to be buried in the Mercers Chapel, called St. Thomas of Acon, London, as near to my mother as possible. To my eldest daughter Mary Locke, if she shall marry with her mother's good liking and consent, a thousand marks, to be paid her at the day of her marriage or the age of one and twenty years. If she marry without the consent of her mother she shall have but five hundred marks. If she die before the day of her marriage the said portion shall be divided equally between my other two daughters. To my second daughter Elizabeth Locke (under similar conditions) three hundred pounds. A similar bequest to third daughter Anne Locke. To my son Robert, after the death of his mother, Hares Marsh in Stepney, provided that if my son Thomas pay my said son Robert three hundred pounds then Thomas shall have it; and in the meantime Robert to have sufficient maintenance from my executor. It

Robert die before this bequest shall take place the same gift shall be and remain to my son Francis in all things as aforesaid. To Francis, after his mother's death, all my land at Dowgate and in the Vintry in London, Thomas to have similar power of redemption at three hundred pounds; in the mean time to have sufficient maintenance. If Francis die &c. then to my son Robert. To my son William my free land at shore ditch, now in the tenure of Humfrey Bigges. Five pounds to the poor. Forty shillings to the repairing of the church way from my house to the Rushe. Mr. Gally my curate. To my good friend Serg^t. Muschampe ten pounds to buy a gelding. Residue to wife Margaret. She to be executrix.

Kidd, 54.

ZACHARY LOK, 29 January 1602, proved 4 April 1603. I desire that my body might be buried in Mercers Chapel in London near to the place where my great grandfather Thomas Lok and my grandfather Sir William Lok were buried, if it please God I die near London, or otherwise in the parish church of that place where it shall please God to call me. The poor of Bow parish. To my father Mr. Michael Lok my seal of arms &c. To my brother Eleazer Lok my hoop ring with a diamond which I wear and the "Armyng swoorde" and dagger which my Lord Willoughby gave me. My brother Benjamin Lok. My brother Jenny and his wife. My brother Sansom and my sister Jone his wife. My sister Sansom's children. My brother Bleuett in Cornwall and each of his children by my sister Anne Lok. I give to Sir Edward Norris knight mine armor complete, with the trunk wherein it is, which I pray him to accept, which I do in consideration of a wrong which I was privy unto that was done to his brother Sir John Norris in the low countries. And I know not where else to make any satisfaction for the clearing of my conscience. The residue I give and bequeath to my dearly beloved mistress Ursula Johnson whom I intend, by God's grace, to make my wife; and her I do nominate, constitute and appoint to be the sole executrix of this my will.

Bolein, 27.

Sentence to confirm the above will was promulgated 11 July 1606 after litigation between Michael Locke of the one part and Ursula Johnson executrix &c. of the other. Stafford, 53.

ELEAZER LOKE, 25 March 1605, proved 2 May 1605. To be buried in the church of All Hollowes in Huntington. Six pounds thirteen shillings four pence to be bestowed at the George in Huntington for my funeral amongst my kindred, friends and fellows. The poor of Huntington and of Brampton. I give unto my master, whose favor I crave towards my poor father and my "travailinge" brother, my great black mare and her colt and my parcel gilt cup. To his four other brothers each a ring of gold of twenty shillings price. To my father twenty six pounds a year, payable quarterly. And after his departure out of this world I give to my brother Benjamin two hundred pounds, to my brother Sansome (besides twenty pounds by promise I owe unto him) the sum of twenty pounds, to my brother Jenney and my sister thirty pounds and my silver tun. My father shall have my gown and best black cloak and my seal ring. My brother in law William Sansom of London and Mr. John Hearne of Godmanchester to be executors. A codicil added 10 April 1605.

Hayes, 34.

BENIAMYN LOCKE of London, merchant, 6 January 1606, proved 29 August 1611. My will and desire is that if it shall please God to suffer me to die in England that then my body shall be interred in the Mercers Chapel in London in the place where my grandfather Sir William Locke knight lieth buried &c. Reference to a joint bond wth Mr. Henry Garway to one Abraham Cartwright and to another debt owing to Mr. Thomas Cordell and Mr. William Garway upon the foot of an Accompt. I give and bequeath to my father Michael Locke thirty pounds and do further release and discharge him of and for all such debts and sums of money as he oweth me by specialty bill bond or otherwise. The poor prisoners of Ludgate, Fleet and Newgate. The fellowship of the Mercers. Johan Martin maid servant to my brother Sansom. The poor children harboured in Christ's Hospital. St. Bartholomew's Hospital. To Mr. Henry Garway my sealing ring of gold. To my cousin Michael Locke my velvet hose and jerkin and a satin dublet. My brother Jenny, my brother Sansom and my cousin Edward Phillippes. Mr. Doctor Moydon. To my said brother Sansom my Turky carpet which lieth in the hall of his dwelling house in London. My sister Jenny and her four children. My cousin Henry Locke. My brother Sansome's two children. Friends Mr. Henry Garway and John Munnes to be executors.

These executors renounced and commission issued, at above date, to Michael Locke the father to administer according to the tenor of the will.

Wood, 72.

RICHARD CANDLER, citizen and mercer of London, 12 December 1614, proved 20 March 1614. Goods to be divided into three equal parts, one part whereof to my wife, another to my son Ferdinando and the third reserved to myself for legacies &c. My loving aunt Mrs. Elizabeth Candler. My loving kinswoman the Lady Anne Heyborne. Brother in law Richard Rygdale. Brother in law Richard Pulford. Wife's mother Mrs. Anne Smythe. To my mother in law that was my father's wife twenty pounds. My half sister Margaret Candler. My other half sister Sara Candler. The poor of Little Walsingham, Norfolk, where I was born. My worshipful good friend Sir Ferdinando Heyborne of Tottenham knight. If my son die before coming to the age of one and twenty then his portion to be divided into four equal parts whereof one part to my wife, another to my Lady Heyborne, another to my brother in law Richard Rydgedale and Susan his wife and another to my brother in law Richard Pulforde and Anne his wife.

Rudd, 24.

ELIZABETH CANDELER of Tottenham, Middlesex, widow, 8 December 1622, with a codicil without date, proved 14 January 1622. To be buried in the parish church of Tottenham under the tomb where Sir Ferdinando Heyborne knight, my late loving son in law, and my loving daughter Dame Anne his wife lie buried, which tomb I did erect at mine own charge. Gifts to sundry servants and others. My kinswoman Mrs. Preston and my servant Anne Locke her sister. My cousin Baker's wife. My cousin Travis his wife. My cousin Anne Baker, daughter of Robert Baker deceased, now wife of Mr. Tyroo apothecary. My cousin Robert Baker her brother, at his age of twenty. My cousin Fardinando Baker at one and twenty. Every of the other younger children of the said Robert Baker deceased (sons and daughters). Fardinando Heyborne, son and heir to Sir Fardinando Heyburne knight my loving son in law deceased, at his age of one and twenty. The seven younger children of my said cousin Robert Baker deceased. To my Lady Heyburne my diamond ring, of the value of twenty pounds or thereabouts. And also I give unto her my silver warming pan weighing fifty ounces and odd, the which my mind is and I do desire her, besides the natural affection of her to her son, that it shall be given to the said Fardinando Heyburne her son, at her death, if he shall be then living, or some other thing of the like value. To the said Fardinando Heyborne the picture fastened over the chimney of the chamber where I now lie.

Item, I give and bequeath to my kinsman William Locke son to Matthew Locke the sum of one hundred pounds of lawful money of England and my " bedsteed " wherein I usually lie with fine taffata silk curtains of crimson color. To my cousin Robert Locke five pounds. To Elizabeth Pulforde daughter of Richard Pulforde citizen and iremonger of London thirty shillings to make her a ring of gold. The same to cousin Susanna Crewe wife of Mr. Anthony Crewe. To my cousin Barbara Preston the wife of George Preston of London merchant one hundred and fifty pounds. To Susan Traves daughter of Mr. Edmund Traves of Tottenham thirty shillings to make her a ring of gold. To my kinswoman Anne Locke, if she shall dwell in house with me at my decease and be unmarried, one hundred and twenty pounds. To Elizabeth Preston the daughter of the said George Preston five pounds. Goodwife Wilder. Edward Beecher son of Mr. Henry Beecher deceased. Richard Avery stationer in London. Mrs. Chamberlaine. Mrs. Traves wife of the said Edmund Traves. My cousin Mrs. Jenings. My kinswoman Mrs. Threele. To the parish of Newington towards the better maintenance of the new foot cawsey made by me five pounds and to the parish of Hackney for the maintenance of the like cawsey within that parish five pounds. To every of the children of the said Thomas Locke that shall be living at the time of my decease twenty pounds apiece except unto Elizabeth Locke unto whom I do give my chain of pearl which cost me fourscore pounds. To my loving cousin Mr. Thomas Locke of Martin Abbey four hundred pounds in money and five pieces of tapestry and two pieces of bordering under the windows and five curtains of purple and yellow taffata and vallance to them. To my loving friend Sir Thomas Fowler the elder knight five pounds to buy him a piece of plate withall. I make my trusty and loving friend Arthur Robinson Esq. full and sole executor &c. and for his pains herein to be taken I give unto him one hundred pounds. And overseers I do make and nominate my said loving cousin William Locke and Richard Pulforde. My said cousin Thomas Locke of Marten Abbey aforesaid and his heirs after my decease shall have and enjoy my copyhold and customary lands, tenements &c. in Tottenham &c. To Christopher Heyborne of Tottenham gen‌‍t. forty shillings to buy him a ring. The same to my cousin Fardinando Candler, and to Mrs. Siñes and to my cousin Charles Locke. To the said Richard Pulford my " Scrittory " with drawing boxes. To Barbara Locke the elder forty shillings and to Elizabeth Killam twenty shillings. To my cousin Robert Locke five pounds more than formerly given him and to Benjamin Jeninges forty shillings towards his schooling. The residue to my cousins Thomas and William Locke equally to be parted and divided between them.

The codicil notes a bequest to every of the children of her kinsman Thomas Locke except her god daughter (meaning and naming Margaret Locke, daughter to the said Thomas, unto whom she did give and bequeath her chain of pearl which cost her fourscore pounds, which legacy, by error of the writer of her said will, is not therein set down according to her direction and meaning aforesaid). Swann, 4.

Sentence to confirm the above will and codicil was promulgated 24 May 1623 following upon litigation between Arthur Robinson, executor, of the one part, and Thomas Lock, Robert Lock, William Lock and Elizabeth Genny, kinsfolk of the deceased. Swann, 43.

ANN LOCK of Newington Surrey, one of the daughters of Matthew Locke late of Marten in the County of Surrey Esq. deceased, her will made 13 April 1623 and proved 23 May 1623. To be buried in the Chapel belonging to the Right Worshipful the Company of Mercers in London so near the place where my said loving father was buried as conveniently may be. To my loving mother Dame Margaret Muschampe, widow, twenty pounds to buy her a ring in remembrance of my love and duty unto her. To my brother Thomas Locke Esq. twelve pence to buy him a pair of gloves. To my brother Robert Lock fifty shillings to buy him a piece of plate. To my brother William Locke (the same). To my aunt Allin fifty shillings to buy her a ring. The same each to Thomas Boughe and his wife. To my god daughter Mary Locke, daughter of my said brother Robert, fifty shillings to be paid unto her at her age of fifteen years. To my god daughter Mary Locke, daughter of my said brother William (the like sum at the same age). To my loving brother in law Edward Thrille fifty shillings to buy him a ring. To my well beloved friend Lyonell Ashenhurst gen^t. four hundred pounds of lawful money of England to be paid unto him as soon as my executor, after named, can or may receive and get in so much of my estate as will satisfy and pay the same. Fifty pounds to be bestowed by my executor out of my estate upon my funeral. The residue and all sums accruing to me by reason of the decease of my late sister Elizabeth Lock, or otherwise, I give to my sister Mary Thrille wife of the said Edward Thrille. And I do nominate and appoint the said Edward Thrille the full and sole executor &c. And if any person or persons before in this my last will and testament particularly named shall by any manner of ways or means whatsoever directly or indirectly endeavor or go about to question or avoid this my last will and testament and not hold themselves fully satisfied with such legacy, gift and bequest as I have given, willed and bequeathed then such legacy as I have given unto any such person or persons as shall so endeavor or go about to question or avoid this my present last will &c. shall be utterly void unto them and the legacy hereby given to such person and persons I do give and bequeath unto the said Lyonell Ashenhurst.

Then follows Sentence to confirm the above will which was promulgated 24 May 1623 following upon litigation between Lionel Ashenhurst, principal legatary named in the will, of the one part, and Edward Thrill, executor &c., and Mary his wife and Thomas Locke, William Locke and Robert Locke, natural and lawful brothers of the deceased, and all others interested. Swann, 36.

DAME MARGARET MUSCHAMPE of Newington, Surrey, widow, 2 May 1621, proved 15 September 1624. My body to be buried in Mercers Chapel, London, as near unto my husband Matthew Lock as may be convenient. I give and bequeath to the poor of the parish of Newington ten pounds of lawful money of England. To my two daughters Mary Lock and Ann Lock all my goods, chattels, leases, household stuff, ready money and money owing unto me, debts whatsoever and movables, my debts being paid, to be equally divided between them, and to make my loving daughter Mary Locke my full and whole executrix of this my last will and testament and I do appoint my son William Lock to be my overseer.   Byrde, 75.

MARY THREELE of Newington, Surrey, widow, late the wife of Edward Threele Esq., 21 February 1637, with codicil dated 6 March 1637, proved 12 March 1637. To be decently buried in the Chancel of the parish Church of Greene, Sussex, as near unto my late loving husband as conveniently may be. To the poor of the parish of Newington, where I now live, five pounds, to be paid unto such of the said poor as shall inhabit or dwell near my dwelling house and not to be given unto any of the said parish dwelling in Kent Street or Blackman Street. To the poor of the parish of Greene in Sussex five pounds. To my brother Thomas Lock Esq. three pounds to buy him a gold ring. My god daughter Mary Justice the wife of Mr. Hugh Justice. My niece Elizabeth Lock the daughter of my late brother Robert Lock and my sister Elizabeth Lock the late wife of my said brother. I give and bequeath unto my sister Susanna Lock the wife of my brother William Lock my satin gown and my crimson velvet petticoat. I give unto my niece Hanna Lock daughter of my said brother William my Turkey tammett petticoat and waistcoat and my orange colored satin damask petticoat. To my sister Mary Threele the silver and gilt bowl which was her aunt Ward's and ten silver spoons which were her father's. My good friend Mary Brockwell widow for her pains she hath taken with me in my sickness. My ancient servant Thomas Treape and Anne Treape his wife. My god daughter Susan Threele the daughter of Mr. William Threele. The widow Wood and the widow Payne. Whereas I am indebted unto my loving brother Mr. William Lock in certain sums of money my will is that he should be paid and satisfied, and likewise all other my debts and legacies, out of my personal estate; and I do make and ordain the said Mr. William Lock, my loving brother, full and sole executor. More, I do give unto my brother in law Mr. William Threele the gold ring with the seal at arms which was his father's. To the rest of the children of my brother Thomas Lock I do give twenty shillings apiece to buy them rings. To the other of my brother William's children not named in this my will twenty shillings apiece to buy them rings. The same to the two sons of my late brother Lock.

Elizabeth Lock the elder, Elizabeth Lock the younger and Mary Brockholl witnesses. George Brockholl and Daniel Cooper also witnesses.
                                                                    Lee, 28.

[My friend R. Garraway Rice, Esq., F.S.A., has given me the following extracts from the parish registers of Merton and Mitcham, Surrey.

Merton Co. Surrey—Burials.

1610 Apl 12 Mrs Elizabeth Lock, gent.
1613 Sep. 23 Edmunde son of Thomas Lock, esquyre
1620 Nov. 30 Francis Locke, gent.
1625 Aug. 29 Susã the dau. of Mr Tho: Locke, Esqr
1633 Dec. 26 Thomas son of Thomas Locke, Esqr
1648-9 Feb. 6 Mr Thomas Locke, Esquire.

Hiatus in Register 1656 to 1694.

N. B. Lock was one of the names in which I was interested, and I had it in my mind when searching the register; so presume I could not find any baps. or marriages of the name.

Mitcham Co. Surrey—Burials.

1625 "John lock ye Sonne of Mr Thomas Lock was buryed (of the sicknes) ye 22 day of August."

N. B. Could not find Will or Admon. for Thos. Lock, Esqr. 1649 in P. C. C. or Surrey Courts. A Thos. Lock of Christ Ch. See Probate Act Book 1 July 1623.

[In Harl. MS. 1096 (fol. 20), is given a pedigree of this family of Lock or Lok. On fol. 33^b of the same MS. I note that Mathew Loke, born 23 February 1521, of London, merchant, the 9th child and last of Sir William Locke by his first wife, had a daughter and sole heir Elizabeth, the wife of Richard Candeler of London, mercer. Their daughter Elizabeth was married to Ferdinando Richardson *als* Heborne, who is called groom of the Privy Chamber to Queen Mary; but in Harl. MS. 1541 (fol. 168), he is called Sir Ferdinando Hayborne, Knight, Groom Porter of the Privy Chamber to Queen Elizabeth, and his wife Elizabeth is called the daughter of Ric: Candler of Lond. mercer by the dau. of Bromley.—H. F. W.]

ALEXANDER EMERSON of Sereby in the County of Lincoln, yeoman, 10 April 1604, proved 10 February 1605. To be buried in the church of Serebye. To my wife all my lands and tenements in Serebye during her life if she do not marry after my decease. And whensoever she shall happen to marry or to die then my will is that Michaell Emerson my son shall have all my said lands and tenements to him and to his heirs male of his body lawfully begotten for ever, with remainder to my son Robert and the heirs male of his body &c., then to my son Thomas &c., then to my son John and lastly to the right heirs of Michaell Emerson my son for ever. To my son Thomas all my lands, tenements &c. in Howsam and Cadney, with remainder to John, then to Robert, then to Michaell and lastly to the right heirs of my son Thomas. To my wife all my houses, lands and tenements &c. in Glamford Brigges for life and then to my son Robert. To Margery and Margaret Emerson, the daughters of my son George deceased, twenty shillings each. All my goods &c. shall be equally divided amongst these five, vizt. my wife and John, Michaell, Robert and Thomas Emerson my sons. I make my son Michaell full and sole executor. A Michaell Emerson and a Thomas Emerson among the witnesses.

Stafford, 8.

[I have ventured to insert the above will for the reason that the names of Michael, John, Robert and Thomas were to be found among our earliest Emersons in Essex County, Massachusetts Bay.—H. F. W.

The parties, named above, may have been kinsfolks of the Haverhill, Mass., Emersons; but the families at Haverhill were certainly of a later generation.

Michael Emerson appeared in Haverhill in 1656, and married, the next spring, Hannah, a daughter of John Webster of Newbury. Their eldest child, Hannah, married Thomas Dustin and was the heroine of the massacre of Indians, 1697.

Robert Emerson, who married Ann Grant, was a householder at Haverhill in 1660.

Thomas Emerson, wife and two children were killed by Indians, 1697. He had brothers, Joseph and Stephen.

These, with Samuel, who married Judith Davis, were residents at Haverhill, where descendants are yet numerous.

Thomas Emerson at Ipswich, 1635, brought with him children born in England. He was the ancestor of a long line of distinguished New England ministers, the most noted of whom was the poet, Ralph Waldo Emerson. No connection between the Haverhill and Ipswich families has been discovered.

GEO. A. GORDON.]

EDMOND BURTON, citizen and cloth worker of London, 10 April 1577, proved 23 April 1577. To be buried in the church of St. Martin's where I now dwell. My debts paid all my goods &c. to be praised according to the order of this worthy city, to say into three parts, one part for my beloved wife, one other part for my children, the third for my self which I have to bequeath; and out of my own part I will that my funerals and my legacies shall be paid and out of my own part I do give to my wife three hundred pounds, and the rest of my goods, my legacies being paid, I do give to my children to be divided equally amongst them by even portions. Bequests to the hospital of the Grey Friars, for poor children, to twelve poor men, to the poor at my burial, to the Company of Clothworkers, of which company I am one, &c. I do forgive my brother Deves all such sums of money as he doth owe me and I give Anne Deves my cousin ten pounds and to my cousin William Burton six pounds thirteen shillings and four pence and to my cousin John Burton forty shillings. Gifts to Lucy Hoocker, if she continue with me, and to Richard Southwick. To "my maister and to my maistres." My well beloved father and mother, to wit, my father in law Mr. John Knighton and his wife. I give to my son Symes and his wife and to John Le, each of them, a black gown at fifteen shillings a yard. My god daughter Martha Golston. My sister Maryett. My well beloved wife and my eldest son Humfrey Burton to be executors and my brother George Knighton and my son Symes overseers. My cousin Bridget Hinde. My two tenements in Shoreditch. Written with my own hand. Reference to "my small children." Mary Syfmes my daughter's daughter. One of the witnesses was Randall Syfmes. Proved by Dionis Burton, the relict, and Humfrey Burton, the executors.   Daughtry, 13.

[See the will of John Scrogges of Patmer in REG. for 1894 (vol. xlviii., p. 123), who mentions mother in law Dyonice Burton and brother in law Mr. Randolfe Symmes. See also REG. for 1895 (vol. xlix. pp. 485-6) for other notes about the family of Randall Symmes. For pedigree of this Burton family see Vis. of London, 1568 (Harl. Soc. Pub., vol. 1, p. 31).—H. F. W.]

EDMOND BURTON of St. Martin's Orgar in the city of London, draper, 7 January 1605, proved 7 February 1605. To be buried in this parish church. To my well beloved wife, who, as at all other times so in this time especially of my long lingering sickness, hath been a most loving and careful wife unto me, so much out of my third part as shall make her third part due unto her by the custom of this city a full thousand pounds. I give her my dwelling house here in London so long as she shall continue unmarried if the lease so long continue. I give her also the lease of the house and land at Hadham, Herts. And I make her executrix. The residue I give unto my son Edmunde, to be paid unto him at his full age of one and twenty years. Twenty nobles to be bestowed upon a dinner for the Company of Drapers. Reference to the lease of the moiety of my dwelling house made unto me by my brother Mr. Doctor Aylmet (Aylmer?). Among the witnesses were Theoph: Ailmer and Randall Symes.
Proved by Cicely the relict &c. of the deceased.   Stafford, 10.

WILLIAM MORE of Groton, Suffolk, gentleman, 6 October 1566, proved 8 March 1566. Wife Alice. To son in law Thomas Lappage my capital messuage in Boxford &c. Lands in Boxford and Edwardeston. Raffe Lappage. William Lappage. Robert Lappage. Mary and Alice Lappage, daughters of the said Robert. Alice Edgar my wife's daughter. Margare

Pigott of Ippiswiche my sister. Paskynge Nedeham, my sister's daughter, and her daughter Anne Newton. My kinsman Henry Fox and his children. My kinsman Robert More. John More. Thomas Cowper the elder of Ipswich and his children at their ages of one and twenty. Tenements &c. in Stoke next Nayland. Thomas More the son of Richard More. Alice Starlinge sister of the said Thomas. The eldest son of the said Thomas. Mr. John Holte of Bury. William, Thomas and Margery More the children of John More of Hengham in Norfolk. The children of Symon More my brother (John and Robert evidently two of them). I give and bequeath unto John Wyntroppe gent., John Spencer, William Coo and John Gale and to their heirs forever, after the decease of my wife, my messuage and lands &c. thereunto belonging or with the same occupied or "letten to ferme" in Boxford and Hadleigh (for three pounds twelve shillings yearly above all charges) to the use and intent that they the said John Wyntroppe &c. shall suffer the churchwardens of the towns of Boxford and Groton to receive and take the whole rent &c. of the said lands, tenements &c. for the poor of those towns. The poor of Edwardeston. Mary and Bridget Starlinge the daughters of Raffe Starlinge. My sister Elizabeth Spencer. To Margaret —— a blind maid now dwelling with mother Plome. Henry Browne and Agnes his wife. Elizabeth More the daughter of my brother Richard More at her age of twenty two. Richard Cowper of Ipswich. The residue to my said wife and Thomas Lappage her son whom I make executors. And I appoint my well beloved friend Master Robert Thorpe overseer. Reference to the last will of brother John Cogate to whom I was only executor.   Stonarde, 9.

ELIZABETH LEE, of Hambledon, co. Southton. My now husband Richard Lee; to Ann King, wife of Thomas King of New England of Westweltringe or Westreitringe Parish ten pounds. To Henry Fleshmonger Senior fower pounds. To John Courtnell fower pounds. To Elinor Collens, dau. of Thomas Collens fower pounds. To Thomas Courtnells three children Elizabeth, Margaret and Anne Courtnell 20 / apiece in gold. To Richard Lee, son of Richard Lee my wedding ring which he gave me. To my brother Thomas Collens the use of 20£. Kinsman Thomas Courtnell executor.   Elizabeth Lee.
                                                                                  her ✕ mark.

   Pec. Ct. of Bishop Waltham, Winchester Reg'y. 22 Mar 1660. 19 Apl 1661.

WEST. A note from Will.—Margaret West of Petersfield, co. Southton, widow—" to my beloved Son Edmunde West now in Pensylvania the sum of Five Pounds to be paid him by my Executrix hereafter named if he ever come to England again and not otherwise." 30 April 1737. Proved 5 Oct. 1737 by Margaret Horrod wife of William Horrod natural and lawful daughter and executrix.
   Consistory Ct. of Chichester. Volume 36, p. 226.
                                                        R. GARRAWAY RICE, F.S.A.

FRANCIS ARCHER of Bocking Essex, clothier, 25 November 1578, proved 24 October 1579. To wife Amye my messuage or tenement where I now dwell and those two tenements now in the occupation of John Fuller and my six tenements which I lately purchased of Thomas Brokeman, gentleman, now in the occupation of Daniel Dobson, John Andrewe, Charles

Hunt, Harry Coper, John Buntinge and Thomas Hardinge, and my two tenements which are now in the occupation of George Clarke my son in law and of Agnes Wickham widow. The said Amye to hold these from the day and hour of my death forwards during her natural life, paying and discharging the quitrents &c. and suffering and appointing sufficient rooms for John Goodwin and Jacob Huet to occupy in according to the order of this my last will. I give to my said wife my two tenements in Bocking End now in the several occupations of Thomas Miller and Edie Goodwin, widow. After my wife's decease all my said messuages &c. to be demised and let to farm by George Clarke my said son in law for the term of eleven years (for certain uses). Frances Archer, my son Robert's daughter. Robert Archer her brother. Thomas another brother. Johan Archer her sister. Margaret Archer another sister. Richard Archer another brother. Mary Archer another sister. Edmond Clarke one of the sons of the said George Clarke and Prissille my daughter. Amie Clarke a sister of Edmond. Francis, his brother. Mary Clarke another sister. The said eleven children being the children of Robert Archer and Prissille Clearcke my said children. I give to said George Clearke and Prissilla his wife, my daughter, the two messuages now in the several occupations of the said George and of one Agnes Wickham, widow. The reversion of the other tenements &c. after my wife's death I give to my son Robert. I give to Robert my messuage called the Grayhound in Bocking, for his life and then to his next heirs. To son Timothy lands &c. in Hawlsted, Essex (aud other bequests to him). I give and bequeath to John Goodwin and Jacob Hartt (*sic*) my two faithful servants sufficient house rooms within my tenement wherein I now dwell only to use and occupy the art of cloth making to have and to hold for the term of fourteen years &c. and twenty pounds to be delivered to them to remain in their custody the whole term of twelve years. Three pounds to the children of John Causton of Loñysse beside Maldon. John Sparhawke a witness.   Bakon, 41.

JOHN BLEWITT of Hadley Suffolk, clothier, 28 December 1621, proved 8 February 1621. Wife Phillis. My daughter Margery and John Orsbye and her daughters Mary, Margery and Elizabeth. To Philip Crane my kinsman five pounds to be paid to him at the end of his now apprenticehood. The wife of John Chambers. The two eldest children of Samuel Bird by my kinswoman. John Blewitt my kinsman. The wife of James Blewitt. Susan Greenwood my servant.

I give unto the son of ——— Goodin my weaver, towards his maintenance at Cambridge, twenty shillings. I give unto ——— Boram and Richardson my weavers six shillings eight pence apiece. To the churchwardens of Hadley twenty pounds to be employed and lent out to young men clothiers of the said town or otherwise for the good of the poor of the town. To my son John my mansion house and my house in Duck Lane in Hadley. My sister the late wife of Paule of Bongey (Bongay). To Eliazar Moody of Ipswich my kinsman ten shillings. Mr. Butler minister of Hadley. Son John to be executor. If he refuse then son in law John Orsbye to be executor. Good friends Mr. Robert Hanbye and John Alabaster to be overseers. To Edward Greene of Hadley my kinsman twenty shillings. Proved by John Blewett.   Savile, 21.

WILLIAM SMITH of Hadleigh, Suffolk, beerbrewer, 13 January 1624, proved 3 February 1626. Wife Alice to have my capital messuage &

houses, buildings, mills, mill houses, mill yards &c. for life or so long as she keep herself unmarried. She shall not suffer any clothiers or diers trade to be used in them and shall not suffer any clothier, dyar or worker of any dyed wool, yarn or cloth to dwell in said houses, but shall either maintain my said capital messuage for a brewhouse herself or let the same to a brewer to use brewing there and no other trade. Thomas Smith son of my brother Thomas deceased. My godson William Scrivener. John and Henry Scrivener children of Matthew Scrivener deceased. Edmond and James Scrivener children of the said Matthew. Grace Smith daughter of brother John. The children of my said brother Thomas. I give and bequeath unto the children of John Goodinge of Hadleigh, brewer, which shall be living at the time of my decease, eight pounds to be paid equally amongst them as they shall come to full age. Friend Mr. Francis Andrewe. To Elizabeth the wife of James Howes the younger of Hadleigh nine pounds, in no ways to come to the hands of the said James, but the use thereof to be paid to her as she shall need and the principal to be paid to her if she survive the said James, otherwise to the children of the said Elizabeth. Signed 30 December 1625. John Goodwyn one of the witnesses.

                                                           Skynner, 19.

HENRY BUCKENHAM of Hadleigh, Suffolk, draper, 3 February 1649, proved 10 July 1650. Wife Sarah. Freehold and copyhold lands in Debenham, Suffolk. Eldest son Isaac. Lands, tenements, &c. in Redgrave, Suffolk. Sister Anne Catchpole of Withersfield, Suffolk. Son Henry. Freehold and copyhold lands in Langham, Essex. My mother Anne Carver now the wife of John Carver. Son John to have all those closes or fields of land and pasture, with the appurtenances, which I lately purchased of my brother Robert Goodwyn, clerk, situate and being in Hadleigh and Layham or both or one of them in the said County of Suffolk, both freehold and copihold. To wife Sarah the tenement wherein I now dwell. She to be executrix and my brothers in law John, Isaac and George Jaquis to be supravisors.   Pembroke, 106.

CHARLES HENRY LORD WOTTON of Wotton in the County of Kent and Earl of Bellomont within the Realm of Ireland, 6 October 1682, proved 14 July 1688. To be buried in the Cathedral Church of Canterbury and a monument to be erected for me to the value of five hundred pounds. My dear wife that now is. My manor of Belsise in Hampstead, Middlesex. Plate, linen and household goods bought from Swakeston House in the County of Derby unto my house of Belsise. Forty pounds a year to Mr. Tobias Eden during his natural life. My manor or reputed manor of Wroxham, Norfolk. My Barony and Seigniory of Kirkhoven in the Province of Flanders. The reversion in fee of certain enclosed grounds and lands called St. Johns Wood in Hampstead and Marybone. My dear and loving nephew Charles Stanhope younger son of the truly noble and my honored good brother Philip, Earl of Chesterfield. My dear and loving nephew Philip, Lord Stanhope, eldest son and heir apparent of my said dear brother. My dear and loving nephew Edward, Lord Noell, Baron of Titchfield. My dear and loving kinsman Edward Hales, son and heir apparent of Sir Edward Hales of the County of Kent, Baronet. The right heirs of Thomas late Lord Wotton my grandfather. My will and mind is that out of the rents &c. of my manor of Belsise, every year, a dinner shall be provided at my mansion house of Belsise, by the present owner or possessor thereof,

the dinner not exceeding five pounds, for the Dean and Chapter of Westminster (of whom the manor is held) and my executors, or so many of
them as can conveniently come to view the said house, gardens, orchards
and outbuildings belonging to the said house, to the end the same may be
preserved and kept in good repair and order. The poor of Swakestone in
the County of Derby and the poor of Hampstead. Several great debts
due to me from His Majesty. Exton, 101.

[Charles Henry Kirkhoven, Baron Wotten, was by patent 9 Dec. 1680, created
" Earl of Bellomont." He died *s.p.* 5 Jan. 1682-3, when all his honors became ex-
tinct. Six years after his death, Richard Coote, Lord Coote and Baron of
Coloony, was created Earl of Bellomont. (See Complete Peerage, by G. E. C.,
vol. 1, p. 313). The latter Earl of Bellomont is known to the readers of New
England history as the second governor of Massachusetts under the charter of
William and Mary. He was born about 1636, and died in New York, March 5,
1701.—EDITOR.]

KATHERINE NEEDHAM of Chipping Barnett in the County of Hertford,
spinster, 1 February 1691, proved 12 March 1691. To be buried in the vault
of the parish church of St. Martins Ludgate in the County of Middlesex and
laid as near my father and mother as possibly may be. Fifty pounds to be
laid out for the defraying of my funeral charges. To brother John Needham ten pounds a year for life. To his four sons Edward, Daniel, Samuel
and Benjamin ten pounds apiece. To brother John Needham's daughter
Abigail Towers, widow, ten pounds. To sister Briant's daughter Elizabeth
East ten pounds. To brother Benjamin Needham one hundred pounds and
to his wife a piece of old gold, value five pounds. To Benjamin's daughter
Susan one hundred and twenty pounds and to his daughter Sarah one hundred pounds. To the poor of St. Martin's Ludgate four pounds. Five
pounds each for mourning to brother John, brother Benjamin and his wife,
cousin Samuel Needham and his wife, cousin Benjamin and his wife, cousin
Abigail Towers, cousin Elizabeth East and her husband, cousins Susan
and Sarah, daughters of brother Benjamin, cousin Edward Needham and
his wife, cousin Daniel Needham and his wife and cousin John Needham
and his wife. Certain articles of silver to cousins Susan and Sarah Needham. To cousin Joseph Needham, son of brother Benjamin, my copyhold
field or close of meadow or pasture ground (eleven acres) called Upper
Bartrom's in Hampstead and in the manor of Hampstead, Middlesex, now
in the tenure of Thomas Marsh or his assigns, and my two houses in South-
mims, Middlesex. The residue to my loving cousin Joseph Needham whom
I make sole executor. Fane, 43.

[I look on the above as a very valuable will. Testatrix must have been the
sister of our Edmond Needham of Lynn, from whom very many Essex County
families are descended. This will shows where the father and mother of our
Lynn man were buried. I suspect they had lived in Ave Mary Lane in a house
which fell to Benjamin, brother of our immigrant, under their mother's will (*q.
v.* REG., xlv. pp. 294-5). Note that the name Brent in the mother's will is given
as Briant in the daughter's will.—H. F. W.]

ANDREW NEWELL, of Charlestown in the Province of the Massachusetts
Bay in New England but now in Rotherhith in the County of Surrey in
old England, mariner, 19 November 1744, (*sic*) proved 4 December 1741.
To wife Eunice all my estate during her widowhood in order to enable her
to bring up my children; but in case she marries then I bequeath it all to
my children, Joseph, Andrew, Eunice and Mary Newell, my said wife
reserving out of my said estate, for her own proper use and benefit, one-

third part thereof according to the custom in such cases. To eldest son Joseph all my interest in the New Wharf at Nantucket (at twenty one). Wife Eunice executrix and friends Henton Brown and John Owen, merchants, trustees or executors in old England. Spurway, 356.

[Andrew Newell, the testator, was a son of Joseph and Elizabeth (Tuck) Newell of Charlestown. He was born Feb. 28, 1701–2. His daughter Eunice married Henry Quincy, and his daughter Mary married Israel Loring (Wyman's Charlestown, vol. 2, pp. 703–4).—EDITOR.]

EDWARD FULLER of Olney Bucks, yeoman, 22 August 1656, proved 20 September 1656. To my eldest son John Fuller my house, cottage or tenement in Olney, with the arable land &c. belonging, wherein I now dwell, next the cottage or tenement there now or late of Robert Martin on the one side. To my second son Ignacious Fuller my freehold lands, houses &c. in Olney and Sherrington Bucks. To my third son Thomas Fuller two hundred pounds, to be paid him a year after my decease. To my daughter Abigail ten pounds, to be paid in a year &c. More to my eldest son John five pounds within a year. The residue to son Ignacious whom I make full and whole executor. Berkley, 334.

[John Fuller, the eldest son of the above testator, was that John Fuller of Boston in the Colony of Massachusetts Bay from whom the well known family of Fuller of Lynn are descended. In Lechford's Note-Book (pp. 152-153 as printed) we find that Francis Godsome of Lynn in New England granted (apparently in August A.D. 1639) to John Fuller of Boston in N. E. joiner his house and home lot, containing five acres, and three acres of meadow and thirty acres of wood and upland thereto belonging and all privileges and accommodations thereto belonging by the Townsmen's grant or promise,—if Edward Fuller of Olney in the County of Bucks yeoman shall pay unto the said Fuller sixty pounds on or before the second day of February next. By an Article in the Agreement John Fuller had the right to refuse the bargain and require his money "at returne." In that case if Allen Brade (now Breed) Edward (Edmond?) Farrington and William Knight should deem the premises worth sixty pounds then he was to pay five pounds for damages to Francis Godsome. Later there is reference of a conditional return of the money "to his father." It seems that Edward Weeden, carpenter, was engaged to work upon the house. The Editor of the Note-Book does not seem to be aware that Brade (Breed), Farrington and Knight were all of Lynn.—H. F. W.]

EDWARD BARNEY of Braddenham, Bucks, yeoman, 13 April 1643, with a codicil bearing date 9 October 1643, proved 25 October 1645. I give and bequeath unto my daughter Agnes Loveday, now wife of Francis Loveday, one silver bowl and six silver spoons, to have the use of them during her life, and after her decease to her daughter Hanna Loveday. Other household stuff to daughter Agnes. To son Francis Loveday a piece of gold of twenty shillings, and to his six children, Robert, Hanna, Mary, Joane, William and Thomas Loveday, my grandchildren, ten pounds each, to be paid into the hands of my overseers for their benefit until they attain to their several ages of one and twenty years or days of marriage. To my daughter Katherine Dorvall, now wife to John Dorvall, a silver bowl, a silver salt and six silver spoons, to have the use of them during her natural life, and after her decease to remain to her daughter Sarah Dorvall. To my grandchildren, the six children of my said son John Dorvall, vizt. John, Edward, Symon, Sara, Mary, and Christian Dorvall, ten pounds each (as above). Other bequests to two daughters Agnes Loveday and Katherine Dorvall.

Item, I give and bequeath unto my son Jacob Barney the sum of ten pounds of lawful money of England (if he be living at the time of my death and do come over into England and personally demand the same). To the poor people of Braddenham five pounds. The residue to my said son in law John Dorvall whom I make full and sole executor and I do entreat my loving friends John Penny of Little Marlowe, gentleman, Thomas Chandler of Hugenden, gen^t., and William Davenport of Chepping Wicombe, yeoman, to be overseers of this my last will and I do give unto each of them five shillings as a pledge of my love to them, desiring their best assistance to see my will herein performed.

Arch. Bucks, 1645, § 36.

[I have no doubt that the Jacob Barney above referred to as out of England was our Jacob Barney the elder of Salem from whom are descended the well known family long settled in Swansey, the Barneys of Rhode Island and of New York. I have a few references to other wills showing that the name was to be found in the South Western portion of Bucks, at Turvile and Medmenham, neither of which parishes is far from Bradenham. The following notes therefore seem worth preserving.—H. F. W.]

JOHN ROOLES of Turfile, yeoman, 13 December 1586. To be buried in Turfile. Son John and his two children, son Richard and his son William and son Jeffery and his daughter Agnes. Daughter Joane Keene and her son William Keene. Daughter Isbell Barney. Daughter Syms and her son Thomas Syms. Daughters Sisselie, Ann and Alice (unmarried). Wife Sibell. Son Henry. Brother in law John Pytcher. Date of probate not noted.   Arch. Bucks, Original Wills, Bundle for 1587.

HENRY BISHOPP of Medmenham Bucks 23 February 1626, proved 4 May 1648. Brother John Bishopp and his eldest son and the rest of his children. I make Jeffery Barney my executor and I give to him forty shillings. Elizabeth Reddinge. Wit: Anne Barney and Elizabeth Reddinge (her mark).   Arch. Bucks 1648, § 115.

JEFFERY BARNEY of Medmenham Bucks bricklayer, 12 December 1653, proved 15 May 1655. My brother in law John Bray of the parish of Bray in Berkes and his four children. John Bray of Maydenhead. Edward Turrey of Maydenhead. Thomas Bray of Great Marlow. Samuel Barney of Turville. John Barney of Turville. William Barney of Hambleden and his son Jefferie. Henry Barney of Fawley. Richard Barney of Hambleden and John Barney of Hambleden. Joane Barney of Cromish in the County of Oxford. Anne Ware in the City of London. Others named. My wife Anne Barney to be whole and sole executrix.

Aylett, 115.

MARY MORE, wife to Steven More, citizen and clothworker of London (by virtue of an agreement before marriage &c. and a bond bearing date 14 January 1666 &c.) 22 August 1670, proved 19 October 1678. A conditional bequest (of three hundred and fifty pounds) to said husband. Otherwise fifty pounds of it to my son Samuel Hardie in New England, fifty to his son Robert Hardy of New England, one hundred to my daughter Sarah Duke, one hundred to my grandchildren Adam Jordain, fifty of it to his sister Sarah Jordaine; the other fifty to be divided amongst the children of my deceased brother of New England. Only I will that my aged mother, if she should survive, may have the improvement of that hundred pounds to Samuel and Robert Hardie during her life. Also I will unto my said mother, Margaret Chalpont, the profit of my lease in Fore Street near Criplegate (ten pounds a year) during her life. After her decease I will said lease to my daughter Sarah Duke. To my son Samuel Hardy, out of other estate, fifty pounds and to his son Robert twenty pounds and to his wife Mary Hardy my diamond ring, my silver tankard. To my daughter Sarah Due (*sic*) the several sums due upon bonds put out by her in her Aunt Norise's name or otherwise (and other bequests to her). The two children of my said daughter. Bequest to abovesaid grandchildren Adam and Sarah Jordine at age of one and twenty. If the said Sarah Duke should have any other child or children then &c. My sister Sarah Norise. My daughter in law Ane Auey (*sic*) and each of her children. My cousin Prisilow Harwood. Mary Strett, widow. Mary Marshall, widow. The widow Harrington. Matthew Davise. Ann Westbe nurse to Adam Jordaine. Loving friends Edward Palmer, wine cooper, and Isaac Gildersleve, pewterer, to be executors. My husband's son Steven More. My husband's grandchildren. Each of my deceased brother's children in New England. The three children of Anne Avery (see Auey above). Mary Jordan one of the witnesses.

Reeve, 112.

MARGARET CHALFONT of the city of London, widow, 12 August, 1678, proved 9 October 1678. To my daughter Sarah, widow and relict of Timothy Norris deceased, twenty pounds, to be paid out of the money now in the hands of Mr. George Hocknell, and all my plate and goods in my chamber. To my daughter Mary More, the wife of Stephen More, thirty pounds. To my grandchild Samuel Hardye five pounds. To my grandchild Sarah the widow and relict of Adam Jordan, five pounds and to Adam and Sarah Jordan, her children, six pounds between them. To my sister Susanna Harris of New England five pounds if living after my decease. To Mr. Edmund Callamy, minister, ten shillings. To my son in law Stephen More ten shillings. Ten pounds to be expended at my funeral. The residue to my said two daughters Mary More and Sarah Norriss whom I make joint executrixes &c. Proved by Sarah Norris.

Reeve, 108.

[In the Probate Act Book for 1678 (fo. 113) the above testatrix is described as of the parish of Sepulchre's, London. Her daughter, Mrs. Mary More, is in the same Probate Act Book (fo. 118) described as of Kennington, Surrey. The will of Robert Hardie who married Mrs. Chalfont's daughter and was the father of Samuel Hardie the town clerk of Beverly in Massachusetts, is here given.]

ROBERT HARDIE citizen and haberdasher of London, 28 May 1661, proved 18 December 1662. Personal estate, according to the laudable custom of the city of London, to be divided into three equal parts, one part whereof I give to dear and loving wife Mary, as due to her by custom of London, another third to my children, vizt. Mary, Elizabeth, Sarah and Samuel, to be equally parted and divided between them, vizt. to Samuel at one and twenty and to Mary, Elizabeth and Sarah at one and twenty or days of marriage. The other third reserved to myself at my own disposal. To wife twenty pounds. To son Samuel twenty pounds and also my seal ring with a cornelian stone and my arms engraven thereon. To my brother John Hardy and to my mother Margaret Chalfont, widow, twenty shillings apiece. To John, Edward, Mary and Martha Hardy, children of my said brother John, ten shillings apiece. To my sister Gillian Taylor, widow, twenty shillings and to her son Joseph and her daughter ———— ten shillings apiece. The residue to wife and children. Wife to be executrix and brother John and mother Margaret Chalfont overseers.

Laud, 155.

ANN HALE of Bristol, widow, 20 June 1763, with a nuncupative codicil dated 11 September 1764, proved 20 January 1768. To be buried in Christ Church, Bristol, in the grave there where my late dear and loving husband was interred. The poor of Christ Church and St. Michael's. I give the sum of one hundred pounds for and towards the education and support of the poor charity boys chiefly supported and educated at the expence of the parish of St. Michael, at a school now kept in Horse Street in the said city of Bristol. One hundred pounds to the Treasurer of the Bristol Infirmary, to be laid out in old South Sea Annuities or any other good security.

Also I give to my cousin Thomas Jackson of Boston or elsewhere in New England, merchant, if he shall be living at the time of my decease, the sum of three hundred and fifty pounds &c. but if he shall happen to die in my life time then and in such case I give the said three hundred and fifty pounds to and amongst all and every his children that shall be living at the time of my decease, to be equally divided between them, or to his grandchild or grandchildren &c. Also I give to my cousin Mrs. Mary Potwine wife of John Potwine now or late of Hartford in New England, goldsmith, the sum of four hundred pounds (or to her children &c.) and if it shall happen that there shall be no such child or children of my said cousin Potwine's living at the time of my decease then and in such case I give the said last mentioned sum of four hundred pounds to her two grandchildren Joseph Church and Elizabeth Church equally between them. Also I give to the said Joseph and Elizabeth Church fifty pounds each. My respected friend the Rev^d. Mr. John Culliford of Bristol. Edward Colston Grevile son of my respected friend Giles Grevile of the same city, apothecary. Mr. Peter Goodwyn son of Austin Goodwyn late of Bristol Esquire deceased. Other friends named. My niece Sarah Hale eldest daughter of my brother in law Edward Hale deceased. Ann Hale youngest daughter of said Edward Hale. To Sarah my messuage or tenement wherein I now live, on St. Michael's Hill. To Ann my two messuages &c. in Earl Street in the parish of St. James. To both my moiety or half of the messuage in Broad Street in the parish of St. Ewen. Friend John Skynner of Bristol gentleman to assist in the making of the remittance to New England.

Secker, 18.

[See Report of the Record Commissioners of Boston, Vols. 9 and 24, for Jackson and Potwine. See also Wight Genealogy, 1890, page 225, and Stiles's History of Windsor, Vol. ii,, page 625. Further information about the Jacksons will be given in the January number.—WILLIAM P. GREENLAW *of Cambridge.*]

ROBERT LUCAS of the city of Bristol, hooper, 28 January 1774, proved 13 February 1776. I am seized in fee of three several messuages or tenements and of a piece of ground now used as a garden on King's down in the parish of St. James in the city of Bristol, in one of which messuages I do now reside and dwell, one other is now in the possession of Samuel Berry, custom-house officer and the other in the possession of my son in law James Lockyer or of Charles Kemeys as his under tenant, and am also possessed of two cellars and two lofts in St. Nicholas Street and am also possessed of two cellars and two lofts in St. Nicholas Street and am possessed and interested in one share of and in a certain Glass Bottle Manufactory, Glass House and buildings near the Limekiln Dock in the parish of St. Augustine, Bristol, which I hold in partnership with other persons therein concerned, and am also concerned in partnership in the Hooper and Brewing business with my nephew William Lucas, now carried on in Nicholas street where I formerly resided and carried on the same. I give unto my son in law James Lockier of Bristol, upholder, and my nephew William Lucas, my partner, the annual sum of forty pounds upon trust that they pay the said annual sum of forty pounds unto my daughter Frances, the present wife of Jonathan Nash who now resides in America, separate and apart from her said husband, such annual sum not to be subject to or liable for any or either of the debts or engagements of the said Jonathan Nash but to be for the separate and entire maintenance of my said daughter Frances independent of her said husband, who shall have nothing to do therewith. To the same trustees a thousand pounds, the interest whereof is to be paid to my said daughter (separately as above) and after her death to her children. Other provision for daughter Frances. Daughter Elizabeth wife of the said James Lockier. Daughter Ann Manley, widow. Her house in Brunswick square referred to. Daughter Mary Lucas at day of marriage. My wife her mother. Daughter Sarah Lucas at marriage. My only son John Robert Lucas at age of twenty two years. The share in the Glass Bottle Manufactory divided into six parts, one for each child. To my grand daughter Elizabeth Nash two hundred pounds at age of twenty one or day of marriage. The children of daughter Elizabeth Lockier. The residue to wife Elizabeth and she to be executrix.   Bellas, 80.

JOHN ERVING, of Boston in the County of Suffolk and Commonwealth of Massachusetts in New England, 20 August 1784. To each of my children, besides what I may hereafter give them, five pounds in lawful money. My real estate to be sold and the proceeds given to my children. To my son John two seventh parts. To son William one seventh part. Another part to son George. Another to daughter Elizabeth Bowdoin. Another to daughter Sarah Waldo. Another to daughter Ann Steward. It is my will that my pew in the Meeting House of the late Dr. Cooper shall be the property of my son William. To the poor. My executors to lend four hundred pounds to each of my two grandsons John and Shirley, to help to set them forward in their business, to be accounted as so much out of the estate given to their father which they are to pay him as soon as they are in a capacity to do it. Legacies to the Honble Oliver Wendall Esq. (he to be an executor), to my book-keeper John Southack, to my housekeeper Experience Bridge, to the Marine Society in Boston for the benefit of poor widows and children of distressed seamen, to Sarah McCauley, a servant maid in my house, and to my negro man Cæsar. My three sons John, William and George, my son in law the Honble James Bowdoin Esq. and the Honble Oliver Wendall Esq. to be executors. Wit: Sol: Davis, James Lloyd, James Carter, John Southack.

Then follows a letter signed by James Bowdoin, Oliver Wendell and Wm. Erving, dated at Boston Oct. 6, 1786 and addressed to George Erving Esq., in which he is informed that his honored father died the 20th of August last and suggesting to him to appoint some one (other than an executor) as his attorney to receive his portion and give legal discharges &c.

Next follows a deposition, bearing date March 15, 1787, made by George Erving of Froyle in the county of Southampton Esq.

Proved 20 March 1787 by John Erving and George Erving Esquires, two of the sons of the deceased and two of the executors named in the said will. Major, 118.

[The testator was a prominent merchant of Boston. He was born about 1690 at Kirkwell in the Orkneys; married in 1720, Abigail Phillips; and died Aug. 20, 1786. His eldest son John (Harvard College, 1747) married Maria, daughter of Gov. William Shirley, and was father of John and Shirley Erving, named as grandson in the will. His daughter Elizabeth married Hon. James Bowdoin, governor of Massachusetts 1785 and 1786. (See The Bowdoin Family, by Temple Prime, pp. 41-52).—EDITOR.]

MARY MACINTOSH ERVING, late of the town of Boston in the Province of the Massachusetts Bay in New England in America but now resident in the parish of Froyle in the county of Southampton in the Kingdom of Great Britain, the wife of George Erving, late of the town of Boston aforesaid but now of the aforesaid parish of Froyle, Esquire, 30 October 1780, proved 10 March 1787. Reference to the last will and testament of Elizabeth Royall late of Nedford (Medford) in the county of Middlesex and Province of Massachusetts Bay in New England, my late mother deceased. I give my part, being one full, equal, undivided quarter or fourth part or share of and in all that plantation commonly called or known by the name of Fairfield, near Commeririe(?) River in the parish of ——— Surinam in America, which were given, devised and bequeathed to me in and by the last will and testament of my said late mother Elizabeth Royall, bearing date on or about 13 July 1754, unto my loving husband the said George Erving for term of life and after his decease to my cousin Thomas Palmer of the Province of Surinam in America aforesaid Esquire and my worthy friend Thomas Fraser of Nicholas Lane, London, merchant, to sell the same and lay out the moneys arising therefrom (and the interest accruing) in an accumulating fund for the benefit of my nephew and three nieces, William, Elizabeth, Mary and Harriet Pepperell, son and daughters of my late sister Elizabeth Pepperell deceased wife of Sir William Pepperell, Baronet, until they shall respectively attain the age of twenty one years. Then this property to be transferred to them in equal proportions or shares. If they die before attaining such age I give it to my son in law George Erving (son of my said husband) at his age of twenty one years. Other small bequests to said nephew and nieces. My said husband George Erving and my said cousin Thomas Palmer to be joint executors.

Proved by George Erving Esq., power reserved of making the like grant to Thomas Palmer Esq., the other executor named in the will when he shall apply for the same. Major, 118.

[Mrs. Mary MacIntosh Erving, the testatrix, was the oldest surviving daughter of Isaac and Elizabeth (MacIntosh) Royall, and was born Jan. 10, 1744-5 (REGISTER, vol. 39, p. 356). She married in 1775, George Erving (Harvard College, 1757) the second son of John Erving, whose will is given above. She died in 1786.—EDITOR.]

WILL OF ALEXANDER SELKIRK, 1720.

Communicated by HENRY F. WATERS, A.M.

THE following will does not relate to us genealogically. But it seems a pity to lose it. It really looks as if I had found the Alexander Selkirk who resided on the island of Juan Fernandez,—the real Robinson Crusoe. My friend, Mr. William Dean, who was present when I found it, was interested enough to look up the history of Alexander Selkirk a little. I send Mr. Dean's minutes, which can be appended to the will. It is a pity that the will is just like nine sailors' wills out of ten, and gives no information about his family to enable us to identify him. We can only *guess* that he was the real Alexander Selkirk.

ALEXANDER SELKIRK of Oarston within the parish of Plymstock in the County of Devon, mate of His Majesty's Ship Weymouth, considering the perils and dangers of the seas and other uncertainties of this transitory life. Every thing to wife Frances whom I make sole executrix. 12 December 1720. Proved 5 December 1723 by Frances Selkirk, *als* Candis *als* Hall, now the wife of Francis Hall, widow relict and executrix named in the said will.   Richmond, 268.

MR. WILLIAM DEAN'S MINUTES.

From *Stephen's Dictionary of National Biography*, under DEFOE, page 288 (now publishing, 1896).—On the 25th April 1719 he published the first volume of Robinson Crusoe, founded on the four years residence of Alexander Selkirk in the island of Juan Fernandez. Captain Rogers, who released Selkirk, had told the story which was also told by Steele in the *Englishman* from Selkirk's own account. Defoe sold his book to William Taylor, a publisher. Gibbon attacked it in 1719 and said every old woman bought it and left it as a legacy with Pilgrim's Progress.

From *Chalmers's Biographical Dictionary, 1813*, under DEFOE.—As to the story that DeFoe had obtained the papers of Alexander Selkirk, a Scotch mariner, who having suffered shipwreck lived on the island of Juan Fernandez for four or five years, it is scarcely worthy of serious refutation. Selkirk in truth had no papers.

From *Chalmers's Dictionary, 1813*, under SELKIRK.—Alexander Selkirk, whose adventures have given rise to the romance of Robinson Crusoe, was born at Largo in Fifeshire about 1676 and was bred a seaman. He left England 1703 as sailing master to a small vessel the Cinque Ports Galley, Charles Pickering captain. In September he sailed from Cork in company with the St. George, 26 guns, 130 men, Captain Dampier, to cruise against the Spaniards. On the coast of Brazil Captain Pickering died and was succeeded by Lieut[t]. Stradling. The vessels rounded Cape Horn to the island of Juan Fernandez, whence they were driven by two French ships of 36 guns each and left five of Stradling's men on shore who were taken off by the French. Hence they sailed to the coast of America, where Dampier and Stradling quarrelled and separated. This was in May, 1704. In September they came to the island of Juan Fernandez, where Selkirk and his captain having quarrelled he determined to remain there alone. But when the ship was ready for sea his resolution failed him and he desired to be taken on board; but the captain refused and he was left with his clothes, bedding, a gun, a small quantity of powder and ball, some trifling implements, a few books, some mathematical and nautical instruments.

Thus left sole monarch of the island, he found himself at first in a position scarcely supportable. It was fully 18 months, according to his own account, before he could reconcile himself. At length he employed his time in building and in decorating his huts, in chasing goats, in taming kids and other animals to be his companions. He made garments from the skins of goats, the flesh having furnished food. His only liquor was water. He computed he caught altogether about 1000 goats, half of which he suffered to go free after marking each with a slit on the ear. Commodore Anson thirty years after found a goat so marked.

Though he constantly read aloud, yet when taken off his language was scarcely intelligible. He remained alone 4 years 4 months, during which only two incidents occurred worthy of record: the first, in chasing a goat he caught the edge of a precipice and fell over, becoming senseless for a long time. When he recovered he found the goat under him dead. The other incident was the arrival of a ship, at first supposed to be French, but he found it to be Spanish, of whom he had great dread. They noticed him and he found it difficult to escape.

He remained until 2 Feb'y 1709, when he saw two English ships come to the bay. He lighted a fire as a signal and he found they were two privateers commanded by Captains Rogers and Courtney. After a fortnight's stay they embarked, taking Selkirk with them, and returned by way of East Indies to England, arriving 1 Oct. 1711, Selkirk having been absent eight years.

Public curiosity having been much excited, he after his return drew up some account of what had occurred during his exile, which he put into the hands of Defoe, who made it the foundation of Robinson Crusoe.

The time and place of Selkirk's death are not on record. It is said that as late as 1798 the chest and musket which Selkirk had with him were in possession of a great nephew, John Selkirk, a weaver in Largo, North Britain.

Such are the particulars as recorded in the *Englishman* and elsewhere, but what credit is due to it we do not pretend to say.*

[Mr. Waters has evidently found the will of the famous Alexander Selkirk. Appleton's Cyclopædia of American Biography says that Selkirk "joined the navy and rose to the rank of lieutenant," and that he "died at sea in 1723." John Howell's Life of Alexander Selkirk, Edinburgh, 1829, p. 135, refers to Selkirk's will, dated Dec. 12, 1720, and states that his widow, Frances Candis, came to Largo, and proved her marriage and the death of her husband, Lieut. Alexander Selkirk, on board of his Majesty's ship Weymouth, in 1723. Her claim was adjusted, and in a few days she left Largo.—EDITOR.]

THE BRUNSWICK STANWOODS.

By Mrs. ELLEN DUNLAP HOPKINS, Member of the New York Genealogical Society.

1. PHILIP[1] STANWOOD, or STAINWOOD, according to Babson's History of Gloucester, Mass., page 163, appeared in Gloucester in 1653; married in 1654. He bought a house and land of Robert Tucker, and in the same year had a grant from the town of six acres on the east side of Lobster Cove. He was a selectman in 1667, and died August 7, 1672, leaving an estate of £87 10s. His widow, Jane, became the second wife of John Pearce, September 12, 1673, and died August 18, 1706. From Philip 1st, and Jane of Gloucester, sprang the Stanwoods of Gloucester, Ipswich, Falmouth, Brunswick and Mount Desert. Their issue were:

2.　i. PHILIP, m. 1st, Mary Blackwell, 1677; 2d, Esther Bray, 1683.
　　ii. JOHN, b. 1653; m. 1680, Lydia Butler; had John, Jonathan, James, and six others; two sons settled in Falmouth.
　　iii. JANE, b. 1655.
3.　iv. SAMUEL, b. March 5, 1658: m. Hannah Pressey at Amesbury, Nov. 16, 1686. From him sprung the *Brunswick Stanwoods.*

---

* Sinclair's Statistical Reports of Scotland. Chalmers's Life of Defoe.

v. JONATHAN, b. 1661; m. Mary Nichols in 1688; Ipswich settlers.
vi. NAOMI, b. 1664; m. William Sargent 1681.
vii. RUTH, b. 1667.
viii. HANNAH, b. 1670.
ix. LAWRENCE.

2. PHILIP[2] STANWOOD (*Philip[1]*) lived in Gloucester; married Mary Blackwell, November 22, 1677. She died January 3, 1679, and he next married Esther Bray, October 30, 1683. He died September 24, 1728. Issue, with perhaps others:

4. i. JOB, m. in 1749 Hannah Byles; m. 2d, Martha Bradstreet. Mt. Desert settlers.
ii. JOHN, whose descendants settled in Falmouth.
iii. SAMUEL.

3. SAMUEL[2] STANWOOD (*Philip[1]*) lived in Gloucester; removing about 1695 to Amesbury. He married Hannah Pressey, November 16, 1686, and had five children, born in Gloucester before 1695, Ebenezer being the only one whose name is known. Later they had five children born at Amesbury.

From Notes and Additions to "History of Gloucester":—Philip Stanwood had Samuel, b. March 5th, 1658, who m. Hannah Percy or Pressey, at Amesbury, Nov. 16, 1686; they had Ebenezer, b. July 10, 1695, m. Jane, whose issue was Samuel,[4] David,[4] William[4] and Susan,[4] born at Brunswick.

Samuel Stanwood was a soldier in King Philip's war, under Capt. Jonathan Poole, in 1675, at Hadley, Mass., and received grant of soldier's lot at Kittle Cove in 1679, for military services (Philip and John also received the same honor). He had a son Ebenezer,[3] the same, perhaps, who has two children recorded in Gloucester records as born in Brunswick, besides others born in Gloucester. From N. E. Collins, town clerk of Amesbury, in a letter dated January, 1896, I have the following information: "I find the marriage of Samuel Stanwood of Gloucester and Hannah Pressey of Amesbury (in a note he adds: the marriage of Samuel Stanwood and Hannah Pressey of Amesbury is the first marriage upon our records), Nov. 16, 1686." Issue:

5. i. EBENEZER, b. July 10, 1695; m. Jane ———.
ii. JOHN, b. Aug. 22, 1700.
iii. JUDA, b. Dec. 11, 1702; m. ——— Brown.
iv. HANNAH, b. Dec. 29, 1704; m. Jacob Bagley, Jan. 21, 1722.
v. PHILIP, b. July 15, 1707.
vi. RACHEL, b. May 22, 1711; m. ——— Anderton.
vii. JOSEPH.
viii. MARY, m. John Barnard, April 16, 1724.

He adds, "there were probably other children born previous to 1700, but I do not find them on our records."

This material, added to the will of John Stanwood, of Pemaquid, printed in "Maine Wills," edited by W. M. Sargent, p. 584, connects the Gloucester and Brunswick families. He names his brothers Joseph and Philip, sister Hannah Bagley, sister Judey Brown, sister Mary Barnet, sister Rachel Anderton; and his brother Ebenezer Stanwood, etc., which fixes the fact of the connection of the Brunswick Stanwoods with those of Gloucester, and that Ebenezer, of Brunswick, who settled in Brunswick, in 1719, was the grandson of the original Philip of Gloucester, and if he came at all, from Ireland, which I see no evidence whatever for supposing, as Gloucester was settled principally by Devonshire people, he came there via Gloucester and Amesbury.*

With the aid of Maine records I find Benjamin Stanwood was a son of Job Stanwood of Gloucester, who was a son of Philip² and Mary Blackwell.

Traditions are enchanting things in the study of genealogy. But facts, not traditions, are the only material the genealogist recognizes, leaving the tradition to wear itself into firelight romance.

4. JOB³ STANWOOD (*Philip,² Philip¹*) married 1st, Hannah Byles, in 1749; married 2d, Martha Bradstreet. After his second marriage, he is said to have gone to Mount Desert, and settled at Duck Brook. Their issue were (children probably not in order):

   i. ZEBULON (by 1st wife), b. 1751; m. Mary Rust; never went to Mount Desert.

   ii. HANNAH BYLES, b. Nov. 25, 1755.

   iii. BENJAMIN BRADSTREET (by 2d wife) was in Mount Desert in 1768; a petitioner to the general court. He was undoubtedly the Benjamin mentioned in Mrs. Blaine's letter, who owned so much land in Mt. Desert. He m. 1st, Margareta —— dau. of Thomas Wasgatt; 2d, Miss Zilpah L. Hotchkiss of New York.

   iv. HUMPHREY, b. 1767; m. 1st, Reliance Higgins; 2d, Mrs. Hannah Higgins Leland, she d. April 27, 1851, aged 73. He d. Oct. 22, 1847, aged 80.

   v. DAVID, m. Eunice Wasgatt, probably in 1792.

   vi. ENOCH, m. and resided in Nova Scotia.

   vii. ESTHER, m. 1st, Andrew Tarr, Jr., of Fernald's Point; 2d, David Bunker of Otto Creek, probably in 1794.

   viii. SALLY, b. 1776; m. David Roderick. She d. Feb. 19, 1853, aged 77. He d. 1856, aged 80.

Note.—Olive Stanwood, widow, bought of Jonathan Rich, late of Marblehead, now of Cranberry Island, in 1792, property for £200. All his property in Mount Desert.

SURVEY OF LOTS AT BAR HARBOR, MOUNT DESERT, BY JOHN PETERS, 1789-1791.

Benjamin Stanwoods Lot. Begin at Stakes & Stones the bounds between him and Robert Young, run first So. 45 W. 340 rods to a tree then So. 45 E. 58 rods to a spruce tree, thence No. 45 E. to the shore then follow the shore to first bounds; this finishes said Stanwoods lot of 100 acres, exclusive of roads.

---

* In connection with the origin of the family, comes the question of the right to a coat of arms in this branch of the Stanwood family. There seem to be two Stanwood coat of arms. I can find no authority for the New England family using arms save by tradition; back of that claimed by descendants of Col. William Stanwood of Brunswick, grandson of Ebenezer 1st, a man who won great distinction in the battle of Monmouth or White Plains.

Mrs. James G. Blaine, a descendant of Philip's son, Jonathan, who removed to Ipswich, in a letter to me, dated Augusta, Jan. 31, 1896, writes: " All my early lifetime an illuminated Coat of Arms of the Stanwood family hung in the dining room. I am sorry to say it has been destroyed, at least cannot be found; for many years it has been hunted for in vain." And in another, of later date, mentions a fact of historical value: " My father thought that all those in this country by the name of Stanwood must be of close kin, and yet, when the title deeds of our property at Bar Harbor came over from the law office of Hale & Emory, at Ellsworth, it was a complete surprise to Mr. Blaine to find that the land he had purchased belonged originally to the lot of a Benj. Stanwood. This lot, and a very large one it was, was held by him in 1797, when Mme. Terisa di Gugoin came to Mount Desert, to take possession of one half of the Island, deeded by the U. S. Government to her (for services of her father during the Revolution), subject to any lien there might be on it. We called our place 'Stanwood,' in memory of this unknown Benjamin; and many, many of the beautiful places at Bar Harbor belonged to Benjamin Stanwood."

These accumulated facts may, with the addition of a word about Ebenezer of Brunswick and his children, and others, by those interested in this family, complete the history of the Stanwoods of Maine, and possibly in time their English connection may appear in Hull, England. It seems to be the place family tradition points to at present, as the original home of the Stanwoods.

5. EBENEZER³ STAINWOOD, (*Samuel,²* *Philip¹*), or STANDWOOD, as he himself spelled the surname, born July 10, 1695, was, as the records of Gloucester and Amesbury tell us, the grandson of Philip 1st of Gloucester. He married Jane ———. He settled in Brunswick, Me., in 1719, where he was deacon of the church in 1770. He was a soldier in the Indian wars in 1723, and a lieutenant in 1757 in Capt. John Getchell's company. He was the father of :

i. SAMUEL, b. 1720; my great grandfather; m. 1st, Jean Lithgow, widow of James McFarland, had dau. Susannah, b. 1742, who m. 1769, Deacon Samuel Dunlap, son of Rev. Robert Dunlap of Brunswick, and Jane Allison; 2d, Mary Woodside. He was one of the petitioners for the incorporation of the town of Brunswick, 1735. (Others were, Ebenezer Stanwood, Samuel Stanwood and Rev. Robert Dunlap.) He was a very distinguished man, holding offices of trust, to the honor of his country. He was made captain in the Indian war, 1735-49; received from Lord Loudon, at the seige of Louisburg, 1750, commission as chaplain, and was representative to the Provincial Legislature from Harpswell in 1770; representative to legislature from Brunswick in 1776; selectman, 1752, '54, '56, '57, '58, '59, '61, '62, '63, '64, '65, '66, '67, '72, '73, '74, '76, '77 and '82; original proprietor of Harpswell, 1740; commissioner to present petition to the general court, May, 1776; delegate to the general court, June, 1776. Member of the Committee of Safety, 1776, for Brunswick. This able and distinguished gentleman died in 1790.

ii. DAVID, b. Aug. 3, 1721. He lost an arm at the seige of Louisburg. Married, 1741, Mary Reed of Topsham. She was b. Dec. 25, 1723, and d. Dec. 22, 1798, leaving a son, William, Colonel, b. 1752, who m. three times : 1st, Mary Orr (dau. of John Orr, son of Daniel Orr of Orr's Island; had 11 children; 2d, Hannah Thompson; 3d, Ruth Thompson. David d. 1777, "on the sea."

iii. WILLIAM, b. 1726; m. Elizabeth Reed of Topsham. He owned land in Brunswick, 1752; was in King Philip's war, between 1735-49. Sergeant in Capt. William Lithgow's company in 1776. He d. in 1797.

iv. SUSAN, m. John Reed of Topsham, in 1747.

INDEX OF PERSONS.

NAMES UNCERTAIN.

INDEX OF PLACES.